Fodor's 06

FRANCE

**Where to Stay and Eat
for All Budgets**

**Must-See Sights
and Local Secrets**

Ratings You Can Trust

Fodor's Travel Publications   New York, Toronto, London, Sydney, Auckland
www.fodors.com

FODOR'S FRANCE 2006
Editor: Robert I. C. Fisher

Editorial Production: David C. N. Downing
Editorial Contributors: Nancy Coons, Thomas Cussans, Jennifer Ditsler-Ladonne, Sarah Fraser, Simon Hewitt, Rosa Jackson, Christopher Mooney, Mathew Schwartz, George Semler, Heather Stimmler-Hall
Maps: David Lindroth *cartographer;* Rebecca Baer and Robert Blake, *map editors*
Design: Fabrizio La Rocca, *creative director;* Guido Caroti, *art director;* Moon Sun Kim, *cover designer;* Melanie Marin, *senior picture editor*
Production/Manufacturing: Angela L. McLean
Cover Photo (Grape harvesting on the Côte d'Or, Burgundy): Owen Franken

SPECIAL SALES
This book is available for special discounts for bulk purchases for sales promotions or premiums. Special editions, including personalized covers, excerpts of existing books, and corporate imprints, can be created in large quantities for special needs. For more information, write to Special Markets/Premium Sales, 1745 Broadway, MD 6-2, New York, New York 10019, or e-mail specialmarkets@randomhouse.com.

AN IMPORTANT TIP & AN INVITATION
Although all prices, opening times, and other details in this book are based on information supplied to us at press time, changes occur all the time in the travel world, and Fodor's cannot accept responsibility for facts that become outdated or for inadvertent errors or omissions. So **always confirm information when it matters,** especially if you're making a detour to visit a specific place. Your experiences—positive and negative—matter to us. If we have missed or misstated something, **please write to us.** We follow up on all suggestions. Contact the France editor at editors@fodors.com or c/o Fodor's at 1745 Broadway, New York, NY 10019.

PRINTED IN THE UNITED STATES OF AMERICA

10 9 8 7 6 5 4 3 2 1

Be a Fodor's Correspondent

Your opinion matters. It matters to us. It matters to your fellow Fodor's travelers, too. And we'd like to hear it. In fact, we *need* to hear it.

When you share your experiences and opinions, you become an active member of the Fodor's community. That means we'll not only use your feedback to make our books better, but we'll publish your names and comments whenever possible. Throughout our guides, look for "Word of Mouth," excerpts of your unvarnished feedback.

Here's how you can help improve Fodor's for all of us.

Tell us when we're right. We rely on local writers to give you an insider's perspective. But our writers and staff editors—who are the best in the business—depend on you. Your positive feedback is a vote to renew our recommendations for the next edition.

Tell us when we're wrong. We're proud that we update most of our guides every year. But we're not perfect. Things change. Hotels cut services. Museums change hours. Charming cafés lose charm. If our writer didn't quite capture the essence of a place, tell us how you'd do it differently. If any of our descriptions are inaccurate or inadequate, we'll incorporate your changes in the next edition and will correct factual errors at fodors.com *immediately.*

Tell us what to include. You probably have had fantastic travel experiences that aren't yet in Fodor's. Why not share them with a community of like-minded travelers? Maybe you chanced upon a beach or bistro that you don't want to keep to yourself. Tell us why we should include it. And share your discoveries and experiences with everyone directly at fodors.com. Your input may lead us to add a new listing or highlight a place we cover with a "Highly Recommended" star or with our highest rating, "Fodor's Choice."

Give us your opinion instantly at our feedback center at www.fodors.com/feedback. You may also e-mail editors@fodors.com with the subject line "France Editor." Or send your nominations, comments, and complaints by mail to France Editor, Fodor's, 1745 Broadway, New York, NY 10019.

You and travelers like you are the heart of the Fodor's community. Make our community richer by sharing your experiences. Be a Fodor's correspondent.

Bon Voyage!

Tim Jarrell, Publisher

CONTENTS

16 BORDEAUX, DORDOGNE &
  POITOU-CHARENTES 753
  Including St-Émilion, Rocamadour,
  Lascaux, Cognac, and Poitiers

UNDERSTANDING FRANCE

MAPS

CLOSEUPS

ABOUT THIS BOOK

Our Ratings

Sometimes you find terrific travel experiences and sometimes they just find you. But usually the burden is on you to select the right combination of experiences. That's where our ratings come in.

As travelers we've all discovered a place so wonderful that its worthiness is obvious. And sometimes that place is so experiential that superlatives don't do it justice: you just have to be there to know. These sights, properties, and experiences get our highest rating, Fodor's Choice, indicated by orange stars throughout this book.

Black stars highlight sights and properties we deem Highly Recommended, places that our writers, editors, and readers praise again and again for consistency and excellence.

By default, there's another category: any place we include in this book is by definition worth your time, unless we say otherwise. And we will.

Disagree with any of our choices? Care to nominate a place or suggest that we rate one more highly? Visit our feedback center at www.fodors.com/feedback.

Budget Well

Hotel and restaurant price categories from ¢ to $$$$ are defined in the opening pages of each chapter. For attractions, we always give standard adult admission fees; reductions are usually available for children, students, and senior citizens. Want to pay with plastic? AE, D, DC, MC, V following restaurant and hotel listings indicate if American Express, Discover, Diner's Club, MasterCard, and Visa are accepted.

Restaurants

Unless we state otherwise, restaurants are open for lunch and dinner daily. We mention dress only when there's a specific requirement and reservations only when they're essential or not accepted—it's always best to book ahead.

Hotels

Hotels have private bath, phone, TV, and air-conditioning and operate on the European Plan (a.k.a. EP, meaning without meals), unless we specify that they use the Continental Plan (CP, with a Continental breakfast), Breakfast Plan (BP, with a full breakfast), or Modified American Plan (MAP, with breakfast and dinner) or are all-inclusive (including all meals and most activities). We always list facilities but not whether you'll be charged an extra fee to use them, so when pricing accommodations, find out what's included.

Many Listings

★	Fodor's Choice
★	Highly recommended
✉	Physical address
✛	Directions
⌂	Mailing address
☎	Telephone
🖷	Fax
⊕	On the Web
✍	E-mail
💷	Admission fee
☺	Open/closed times
▶	Start of walk/itinerary
Ⓜ	Metro stations
☰	Credit cards

Hotels & Restaurants

⌂	Hotel
➟	Number of rooms
⚇	Facilities
❙⊘❙	Meal plans
✕	Restaurant
⚇	Reservations
⋔	Dress code
⚘	Smoking
⛟	BYOB
✕⌂	Hotel with restaurant that warrants a visit

Outdoors

⛳	Golf
⚑	Camping

Other

⊙	Family-friendly
♫	Contact information
⇨	See also
✉	Branch address
☞	Take note

WHAT'S
WHERE

PARIS

Paris is one of the most written about, raved about, and spat upon cities in the entire world. Droves of people have come for hundreds of years looking to inject their lives with beauty, glamour, culture, scandal, and romance. They have sung about Paris, painted her, found themselves, lost their religion, and learned how to eat well and smoke too much. Gargoyles leering down from medieval walls, the smell of freshly baked croissants, the pulse of jazz through overcrowded streets, and that first sip of wine to start off the evening are all part of the Parisian obsession with the physical world. Fashionable 85-year-old matrons parade their freshly coiffed Pekingese pooches past boutique windows, spruced-up facades of medieval buildings, and artfully arranged *pâtisserie* (pastry shop) displays. All the while, tourists sweep through town, trying to see in a week what locals haven't seen in a lifetime. The **Eiffel Tower,** needless to say, gives you an overview; the **Louvre,** a good look at the art of the past (with a peek, too, at architecture's present and future). Light a candle at **Notre-Dame,** buy a dress you'll love forever, and eat an unforgettable meal anywhere at all. Open your eyes—there's something beautiful or amusing at every step. Dawdle around the **Latin Quarter,** climb up to **Montmartre** for a peek at **Sacré-Coeur,** spend a morning at the *marché aux puces* (flea market), discover elegant mansion-museums, explore time-machine streets like the **Cour du Commerce St-André,** and sail down the Seine on the **Bateaux Mouches.** Does Paris have a downside? Only one—it is too beautiful, and, consequently, too popular. A visit to the Tour Eiffel is the ultimate experience in crowd tolerance. But you'll find that even the presence of millions of tourists can't break the mood of Paris's most glorious sights, such as that stained-glass time capsule of the Middle Ages, the **Sainte-Chapelle.**

ILE-DE-FRANCE

Kings, clerics, paupers, and ordinary Parisians have long taken refuge from urban life in Ile-de-France, the green surround of Paris. Most have been content to spend a day in the country, which is lushly forested and islanded by meandering rivers, while others have left behind spectacular secular and religious monuments. Biggest and most ostentatious of the Ile's palaces, the **Château de Versailles** is pompous proof that French monarchs lost their heads long before Louis XVI and Marie-Antoinette, the last occupants, walked to the guillotine. Other palatial piles

include **Fontainebleau, Vaux-le-Vicomte,** and Napoléon's **Malmaison**. All this worldly froth fades in the stained-glass luster of **Chartres Cathedral,** so sublime its soft limestone hulk has brought the faithful to their knees for centuries. Then skip over the centuries to discover Monet's **Giverny** and Van Gogh's **Auvers.** Today, many Parisians follow in the footsteps of the kings and queens (but wearing Reeboks instead of square-toed heels) and make the Ile's other dazzling sites their weekend retreats. These delights include the ancient régime grace of the park and château de **Rambouillet**—an 18th-century Neoclassical landmark; the gigantic château and park at **St-Germain-en-Laye,** which includes famed gardener Andre Le Nôtre's spectacular Grande Terrasse; the regal elegance of the château de **Maisons-Laffitte,** a masterpiece by architect François Mansart; the lovely medieval town of **Senlis;** and the picturesque forest of **Barbizon,** immortalized by dozens of 19th-century plein-air painters. Overrated? Uncle Walt's **Disneyland Paris** is quite the vogue these days—especially if you've ever wondered what Donald Duck sounds like speaking French. But others gripe about the Americanization of Europe, heavy crowds, bad food, bratty kids, and prices that, in the summer, rise turret-high. Ticket prices not only fluctuate with the temperature but with the week (school vacations, ski season, etc.), so check on ticket prices beforehand, as going a day later could make a big difference.

THE LOIRE VALLEY

Sometimes owned by England, and fought over for centuries, this stretch of the Loire southwest of Paris resounds today with the noise of contented tourists, music festivals, and son-et-lumière spectacles at its extraordinary châteaux. This is *la belle France* at its purest and most elegant—just wait until you hear the diamond-sheen of the French spoken hereabouts. Super-stylish château-hotels and lovely country auberges tempt the traveler at nearly every bend in the river. Staying in a château-hotel is a must (surprise!—a goodly number of them are very affordable). The roll-call of châteaux that are open to the public is legendary. At the **Château de Chenonceau,** Catherine de' Medici built a white pleasure palace to hover over the river Cher. At the **Château de Chambord** it's easy to imagine the days when King François I arrived with a retinue so large it took 12,000 horses to transport them. At magical **Château de Ussé,** Charles Perrault was inspired to write the fairy tale we know as "Sleeping Beauty." The most celebrated gardens are those

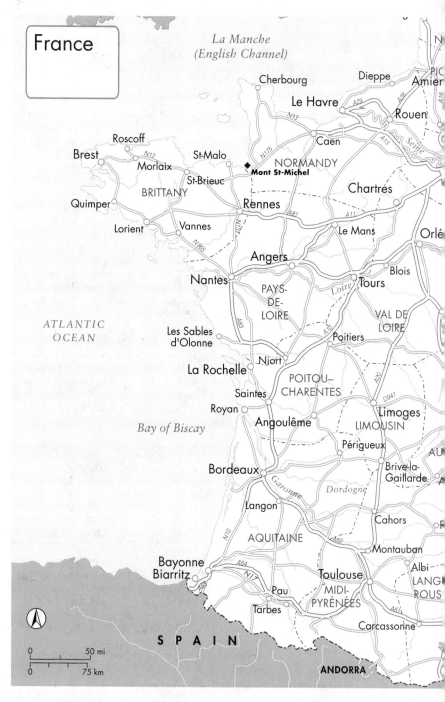

France

La Manche
(English Channel)

NORMANDY

BRITTANY

ATLANTIC
OCEAN

PAYS-
DE-
LOIRE

VAL DE
LOIRE

POITOU–
CHARENTES

LIMOUSIN

Bay of Biscay

AQUITAINE

MIDI-
PYRÉNÉES

SPAIN

ANDORRA

Cherbourg
Dieppe
Amier
Le Havre
Rouen
Caen
Roscoff
St-Malo
Brest
Morlaix
St-Brieuc
Mont St-Michel
Quimper
Rennes
Chartres
Lorient
Vannes
Le Mans
Orlé
Angers
Blois
Nantes
Tours
Loire
Les Sables
d'Olonne
Poitiers
Niort
La Rochelle
Saintes
Royan
Angoulême
Limoges
Périgueux
Bordeaux
Brive-la-
Gaillarde
AU
Garonne
Dordogne
Langon
Cahors
Montauban
Bayonne
Biarritz
Albi
LANG
ROUS
Pau
Toulouse
Tarbes
Carcassonne

PIC
N13
N175
N12
A29
A28
A16
A13
Seine
A81
A11
N137
A10
N165
A83
A20
A62
D941
N10
A64
N117
A63
A61
A6

0   50 mi
0   75 km

Corsica

Bastia
Calvi
Corte
N198
Ajaccio
Bonifacio

NORTH
Lille
BELGIUM
Arras
PICARDY
Cambrai
miens
St. Quentin
LUXEMBOURG
en
Beauvais
CHAMPAGNE
ARDENNES
ILE-DE-
FRANCE
Reims
Metz
LORRAINE
Paris
Châlons-en-
Champagne
Nancy
Sens
Strasbourg
Troyes
Orléans
Colmar
ALSACE
Mulhouse
Auxerre
Belfort
Bourges
Nevers
Beaune
Dijon
Besançon
BURGUNDY
FRANCHE-
COMTÉ
Mâcon
Bourg-en-
Bresse
Vichy
Clermont-
Ferrand
Lyon
Rhône
ALPES
AUVERGNE
Chambéry
Le Puy
Aurillac
RHÔNE
VALLEY
Grenoble
Rodez
Montélimar
Gap
Millau
PROVENCE
Sisteron
Albi
Avignon
Nîmes
CÔTE D'AZUR
LANGUEDOC
ROUSSILLON
Montpellier
Aix-en-Provence
Nice
MONACO
Monte Carlo
Cannes
Narbonne
Marseille
Toulon
Perpignan
Mediterranean Sea
Corsica

GERMANY

SWITZERLAND

ITALY

Rhône
Rhône
Saône

at the **Château de Villandry,** whose vast Renaissance-style parterres and water terraces are best seen in early July during its Festival of 1,000 Lights. But the Val de Loire is far more than just châteaux. Gorgeous villages like **Saché** (Balzac's favorite) await. Historic manors, such as Leonardo da Vinci's own Clos-Luce in **Amboise,** intrigue. **Fontevraud** allures as the largest medieval abbey in France, while storybook **Chinon** has block after block of houses built during the days of Joan of Arc, and hyperelegant **Saumur** has an historic center and Gothic castle that can't be beat (although we can do without the *haut snobbisme* of the locals). The glamour level falls off precipitously in the region's three big cities. In the center, hub-city **Tours** has the half-timbered Place Plumereau but also plenty of dreary suburban homes. Modern **Angers,** to the west, has some nice museums but it also has skyscrapers and industrial complexes. To the east, big-city **Orléans** makes much of Joan's visit, but you'll be hard-pressed to find any charm among the ugly modern buildings. No matter—you'll find that the poppy-covered hillsides and gentle climate throughout the entire Val de Loire do wonders for your temperament. No wonder so many harried Parisians vacation at least one week a year here.

BRITTANY

"Finistère," or "land's end," is what a part of Brittany is called, and the name suits the entire region. A long arm of rocky land stretching into the Atlantic, Brittany lives to the rhythm of tides and winds, with its own language and legends. The people are Bretons first, rather than French, Celtic rather than Latin, and proud of their difference. They are also proud of their land—with reason. Here you'll find time-defying monuments and customs in awe-inspiring landscapes, such as those at **Pont-Aven,** which once inspired Gauguin (sigh—this charming town now has more art galleries than France has little yapping dogs). Although some people leave the prehistoric megaliths of **Carnac** in disappointment—some say they just look like a bunch of standing stones surrounded by an equal number of tourists—they remain the gateway attraction to the sandy peninsula of the **Côte Sauvage,** where birds and flowers abound. The craftspeople in **Quimper** carry on a centuries-old practice of hand-painting delicate-looking faïence wares. Tides bathe the foot of **St-Malo**'s impressive fortifications, still haunted by phantom pirates. A trip across the waters to the aptly named **Belle-Ile,** or "beautiful island," will take you to heaths of yel-

low broom, fine beaches, and quaint towns. Today **Nantes,** the working-class heart of the province, pumps the economy of the region and provides a daily swig of Breton life, while **Rennes,** the student-fueled mind, gives way to poets and painters, bringing a refreshing breeze to the region. Other sites include the elegant Belle Époque resort of **Dinard** and the granite splendors of the Corniche Bretonne, replete with those famous pink-granite boulders. The closer you get to the sea, the more authentic Brittany seems to become. And the more xenophobic—*S'il te mordent, mords-les* ("If they bite, bite them back") goes one of the local sayings. And some of those waterside hotels, come July and August, believe in those let's-milk-tourists-for-all-they're-worth prices. Still and all, Brittany remains a rare gift from the sea.

NORMANDY

Normandy is a land of fashionable resorts and austere abbeys, warriors and prolific painters, saints and sinners. At **Bayeux,** the town's famous tapestry provides a scene-by-scene look at the Norman invasion of England in 1066 and stars William the Conqueror. Not far away, **Mont-St-Michel** may be the sublimest sight in France, perching dramatically atop its rocky shoreline roost. In **Rouen,** famed for its cathedral immortalized by Monet in paint, medieval rue du Gros-Horloge leads to the spot where Joan of Arc was burned at the stake in 1431. German bombs and Allied raids ruined much of the historic center, but enough half-timbered houses remain (along with kitschy cafés, souvenir shops, and miniature sightseeing trains). Off to the west at **Omaha Beach,** vast expanses of windswept dunes pay quiet homage to the 10,000 Allied soldiers who lost their lives during 1944's D-Day. Norman people are friendly, but a bit reluctant to speak openly about World War II, so don't be surprised if their typical response to a question is *Peut-être que oui, peut-être que non* ("Maybe yes, maybe no"). Elsewhere lovely seascapes and lush fields allure. Pretty **Honfleur** made Impressionists long to paint the sea and sky. **Étretat** invites a day of ambling along limestone **falaises** (cliffs). Proust and Monet may have been inspired by this scenery but they probably didn't spend too much time sunbathing in their Speedos: this coast is known for its *galets*—large pebbles that cover the beaches. Chic **Deauville** and **Trouville** beckon you to stroll along their seafront boardwalks, eyeball elegant hotel lobbys, and gape at Rothschilds. Of course, indulge in the region's cuisine,

	ruled and inspired by local cream, butter, eggs, and apples, along with fine lamb sweetened by the salty grasses on which the animals graze. Heady apple brandy, or calvados, is often downed with a meal to make a *trou normand* (Norman hole)—room for more rich food.
THE NORTH & CHAMPAGNE	"Brother, come quickly, I'm drinking stars," exclaimed Dom Pérignon upon first sipping the bubbling beverage that he invented through luck and alchemy. The blind 17th-century monk put **Hautvillers** and an entire region on the world map; he also ensured that vineyards around **Épernay** and elsewhere in the vicinity produce some of the world's finest wine grapes. Many of the great champagne producers offer tours, ranging from hilarious to desparingly tedious (though the glass of bubbly at the end makes even the mediocre ones worth it). Two—Taittinger and Piper-Heidsieck—are based in big-city **Reims,** once important enough to host the coronation of French kings, with many an amiable monument and its spectacular cathedral as proof of its stature. Too bad World War II left only 16 historic buildings intact. Besides fine food and drink, there's plenty in the north to capture your attention—the lively city of **Lille** (just an hour from Paris by TGV) is still redolent of its 17th-century Flemish heyday, while the long stretches of empty sand along the Channel coast and the haunting cemeteries that evoke crucial battles of World War I provide meditative, if not uplifting, experiences. The Channel Tunnel, like the traditional ferries, arrives at **Calais** (beware the city's rough weather and shopping-mall ambience); head inland to admire the palace of **Compiègne,** the picture-perfect storybook castle of **Pierrefonds,** and some of the most awesome cathedrals in France: **Soissons, Amiens, Noyon, Laon,** and **Beauvais,** the tallest of them all.
ALSACE - LORRAINE	"Let them speak German," said Napoléon of the Alsatians, "as long as they think in French." The emperor would be pleased to know that after centuries of conquest and liberation Alsace and its neighbor Lorraine are now resolutely and proudly French. Yet there are enough imports from beyond the Rhine to make the region fascinating, attracting lots of Germans with pulled-up socks and plenty of cash. **Strasbourg,** capital of Alsace and the cosmopolitan home of the European Parliament,

has sophisticated restaurants and fine museums as well as a lacy-spired cathedral, an old quarter known as La Petite France, beer gardens, and *winstubs* (wine pubs). **Nancy,** capital of Lorraine, adds another element to the region's cultural mix: much of the elegant, easygoing city was laid out with pomp and grandeur by Stanislas Leszczynski, dethroned king of Poland; it was also a center of Art Nouveau architecture in the late 19th century. **Metz** has a grand cathedral, **Domrémy-la-Pucelle** claims the birthplace house of Joan of Arc, and **Ribeauvillé** is famous for its half-timber Renaissance houses. For many, the high point hereabouts will be found in **Colmar,** home to Grünewald's incomparable 16th-century *Issenheim Altarpiece.* The **Route du Vin,** running through the green foothills of the **Vosges mountains,** leads to half-timber, impossibly picturesque wine villages such as **Riquewihr.** Along the way, enjoy feasting on that regional specialty *choucroute garni alsacienne,* but remember that the locals only eat it in the winter.

BURGUNDY

Farms, pastures, and fall foliage make Burgundy enticingly, romantically rural. But it's also evident that whether building, ruling, worshiping, dining, or drinking, Burgundians have never embraced life on anything less than a grand scale. From magnificent palaces like the one in the city of **Dijon** and châteaux like the one at **Tanlay,** dukes more powerful than kings once ruled vast tracts of Western Europe. They left behind mighty medieval cathedrals in **Sens** and **Auxerre,** and religious orders built the other Burgundian architectural masterpieces—the Romanesque basilica at **Vézelay** and even more impressive abbeys, such as the Abbaye de **Cluny,** the largest church in the world until the construction of St. Peter's in Rome. Unfortunately, Cluny has been ransacked over the centuries, so a few travelers leave grumbling, " Is this all that's left?" but what remains is impressive, to say the least. **Fontenay** has the best preserved of the famous Cistercian abbeys, while **Autun** has some of the greatest Romanesque sculptures in the world in its church. Most likely to evoke a reverential hush, though, is a first sip of one of Burgundy's treasured wines. Follow the **Côte d'Or,** perhaps the world's most famous wine route, out of Dijon, a gastronomic hub and cultural center, and then visit the Marché aux Vins in the wine capital of **Beaune** (with its great Rogier van der Weyden altarpiece), often packed with upscale Eurosnobs ordering cases of wine in English. As you sample the bounty of the highly anticipated annual

vendange (harvest) in such towns as **Clos de Vougeot** and **Nuits-St-Georges**, you'll be introduced to wines so fine that, as the novelist, playwright, and observer of French life Alexandre Dumas once counseled, they should only be drunk on bended knee. Before leaving Burgundy, don't forget to buy a pot of Dijon mustard (although you might wind up paying a hefty price for a small ceramic pot—*without* the mustard.)

LYON & THE ALPS

If the very mention of **Lyon** teases the taste buds, give credit to this sophisticated city's chefs—masters like Paul Bocuse who can render even a plate of fruit ethereal. Savor their creations, then enjoy the city's visual delights—Lyon's covered passageways, known as *traboules,* lead to treasure-filled museums and a first-class opera house. Near at hand, seek out more *sportif* amusements: a sail from canal-lined, bridge-bedecked **Annecy** across its breezy and gorgeous lake, perhaps, or a gambol through meadows near **Chamonix,** a resort with a reputation for winter pleasures overshadowed only by its Alpine peaks. Great dining can also be had elsewhere, such as at Pic in **Valence** and Marc Veyrat's Ferme de Mon Père in chic **Megève,** nestled in the shadow of Mont Blanc. Discover the **wine villages of the Beaujolais** and the **Dombes lakes,** then venture down the Rhône to **Vienne** for Roman ruins and Renaissance facades. Pass through **Grenoble** with its fine museums. The 19th-century writer and music critic Stendhal remains the town's most celebrated citizen, although people seem generally surprised if you know who he is. Enjoy the town's "Stendhal Itinerary" en route to the Alps. Squished between mountains and river, Grenoble's layout is maddening: your only hope lies in the big, illuminated maps posted throughout town.

THE MASSIF CENTRAL

"Early to bed, early to rise" is the rule of thumb in this craggy, rural heartland at the center of France. You'll want to rise early to venture into the spectacular gorges or tackle the slopes of the highest of the region's 80 dormant volcanoes and *puys* (peaks), the **Puy-de-Dôme**—one heck of a climb (just ask the Tour de France racers). Early risers in **Bourges,** a medieval city gloriously bypassed by time, have a special reward in store—the sight of the stained-glass windows of the 13th-century Cathédrale St-Étienne achieving their fullest luster in the morning light. This is also the gateway city to the Loire Valley ap-

proached from the south. In the real heart of central France is the famous **Parc des Volcans,** here even the churches are constructed from polychrome lava. Other top sights in the Massif include the museums and cathedral in **Clermont-Ferrand** (a great hub for the Auvergne and volcanoes region, although one disfigured by stark 1960s architecture) and evocatively medieval towns and villages like **Salers, Ste-Foy,** and dramatic **Rocamadour,** hanging on a cliff 1,700 ft above the Alzou River gorge. If you ever get weary of climbing up to churches behind panting tourists, you can always hike up into the neighboring hills.

PROVENCE

Even the cattle and flamingos wallowing in the salty coastal marshes of the **Camargue** enjoy the sun-drenched good life that Provence provides so generously. In this smiling landscape and in soft-hue, elegant cities, where life still proceeds at an old-fashioned pace, you'll find no end of pleasures. Favored hangout of the French café-squatting, people-watching, and boutique-shopping yuppie, elegant **Aix-en-Provence** has museums, fountains, and the gracious Cours Mirabeau boulevard. Charming and laid-back **Arles** and crowded **Avignon** (get off the main streets to see *Avignonnais* leading their daily lives) have bewitched Roman legionnaires, popes, and Vincent van Gogh. The tarnished, exotic, and newly chic port of **Marseille** continues to intrigue sailors and travelers with its hint of mystery (note: you should have some big-city smarts to cope with its colorful, almost defiant spirit). And dusty **Nîmes** headlines the ancient Roman splendors of the Pont du Gard aqueduct and the Maison Carrée temple. But the region works its charms most potently in rural places, aided in no small part by cypress trees, vineyards, and a cooling glass of pastis. And let's not forget the heavenly lavender fields at the foot of Mont Ventoux or Provence's ocher-color villages, few more enticing than pretty **St-Rémy-de-Provence,** birthplace of Nostradamus and retreat of Van Gogh, where sunlight really does dapple lanes of plane trees. Other delights include the magnificent Romanesque abbey of **Montmajour,** the craggy towns of **Les-Baux-de-Provence** (home to the famed L'Oustau de la Baumanière hotel) and **Le Barroux,** and the scenic hill-town splendors of **Roussillon** and **Gordes.** Another treat is getting to know the refreshingly friendly *Provençaux.* You'll get to know them hiking the white-cliffed calanques or exploring the rich landscape of the Route des Vignobles (Vineyard Route) through the region.

THE CÔTE D'AZUR	
	Invisible celebrities, pebbly beaches, backed-up traffic, hordes of sunburned bathers—why do people come? Because the medieval hilltop villages (**Mougins and Èze,** to name two), the fields of fragrant flowers that supply the Grasse perfume factories, the wonderful museums, and the lovely, limpid light are still as magnetic as ever. Stylish boutiques, splendid food, exciting nightlife, and spectacular views of crystal bays and cliff-side villas don't hurt either. Great art is also to be had—in the Musée Renoir in **Cagnes-sur-Mer,** the collection at the Musée National Picasso in **Vallauris, St-Paul-de-Vence**'s extraordinary Fondation Maeght—filled with Calders and Mirós—or Matisse's sublime Chapelle du Rosaire in **Vence.** For other sorts of aesthetic splendor, explore the lively, cobbled streets of **Nice**'s Vieille Ville (Old Town), the pretty, pastel colors of **St-Tropez**—once again a celeb mecca—or the millionaire mansions of **Villefrance-sur-Mer** or **St-Jean-Cap-Ferrat,** where you can experience more than a true flutter of glamour. If only once in your lifetime you want to sip champagne from a slipper or slink up to a roulette table and go for broke, **Monte Carlo** and **Antibes** are the places to do so. Or you may simply want to enjoy the sun here, yours for the basking on the beach at stylish **Cannes** or in such enchanted seaside retreats as **Beaulieu.** All these pluses outweight the minuses: sand beaches are rare, the movie stars have fled to more secluded regions, and those crowds can cause you to flee up the trails leading into the hills.
CORSICA	
	For centuries great powers have fought over this strategically placed piece of Mediterranean real estate, leaving behind both architectural and cultural relics that set this stunning island (about 160 km [100 mi] southeast of Monaco) apart from the rest of France. In **Piana** and other ancient stone villages, news from across the sea still seems far removed—delightfully so. Corsica's capital, **Ajaccio,** hometown of the greatest empire builder of them all, Napoléon Bonaparte, is now a port for launching pleasure craft, not naval fleets. Today's spoils are granite peaks, pine forests, and crystalline waters—those around **Bonifacio,** where Ulysses was besieged, are especially inviting. Explore the mountains along the **Scala di Santa Regina;** see **Corte**'s citadel; hear folk songs in **Pigna;** and splurge at the Grand Hôtel de Cala Rossa in the walled town of **Porto-Vecchio.**

THE MIDI-PYRÉNÉES & THE LANGUEDOC-ROUSSILLON	
	In the vast stretches of southwest France the strong sun makes fields of flowers glow and renders the brick buildings of Toulouse-Lautrec's native **Albi** and lively, cosmopolitan, Spanish-flavored **Toulouse** a rosy pink. It reflects upon walled, storybook **Carcassonne** and hilltop **Cordes,** medieval towns with long histories of defending the region. It brightens the cloisters at **Moissac** and **St-Guilhem-le-Désert,** and beckons you to climb the Pyrénées' peaks. Along the scenic way, you'll be sure to build up your appetite for the trout, foie gras, and cassoulet, three of the region's many culinary specialties. Forging onward, you'll discover relaxing spa towns and wonderful views enliven the Pyrénées' twisting roads on the way from the rolling plain known as the Roussillon to **Céret,** heart of the gorgeous "open-air museum" known as the Côte Vermeille (or Vermilion Coast). And when you see **Collioure**'s enchanting Mediterranean setting you'll know why artists like Matisse and Derain were so inspired. But remember: near the mountains a few passing clouds can rapidly turn into a full-blown storm, Toulouse holds the French record of the hottest summer temperature, and Collioure swells from 3,000 to 15,000 people during August.
THE BASQUE COUNTRY, GASCONY & HAUTES-PYRÉNÉES	
	At its southwesternmost corner, France eases with grace and dignity toward Spain, separated from it in many ways only by the Pyrénées. Basque country, south from **Bayonne** to the border with Spain, along the coast and in the Pyrénées, is a world of its own. Come here to discover the ancient and mysterious Basque culture, and dine on the unique cuisine—father of *cuisine minceur,* superchef Michel Guérard holds down the stove at his posheries in **Eugénie-les-Bains.** Napoléon III and his Spanish wife, Empress Eugénie, put the resort town of **Biarritz** on the map, and today it lures both surfers and supermodels. **Ainhoa, Ste-Engrâce,** and many other towns and villages have a distinctly Basque look and temperament. To the east are Béarn and its capital, the elegant city of **Pau.** The Hautes Pyrénées, the most central and the highest part of the range, hold, among other treasures, two of the region's most famous natural phe-

BORDEAUX, DORDOGNE & POITOU-CHARENTES

nomena, the **Cirque de Gavarnie** and the **Brèche de Roland**. The peaks of the Pyrénées are just made for hiking—when you come back down, the incomparable local cuisine and wine taste all the better.

Since prehistoric times this hinterland near the Atlantic coast has had its appeal, as is apparent when you see the cave paintings at the **Grotte de Lascaux** or the storybook villages of the **Dordogne** region, now one of the hottest destinations in all Europe. Its villages seem ripped from the pages of a child's fairy-tale book—notably **Sarlat-la-Canéda, St-Cirq-Lapopie,** and **La Roque Gageac**. In the Middle Ages the French and British fought over the area, leaving behind many castles and cathedrals. The continued allure of the rural landscape lies in the opportunity for pleasurable idleness. Float along the waters of Green Venice, as the **Marais Poitevin** near Coulon is known, or explore the fabled vineyards around **Cognac** and **Bordeaux,** perhaps ambling through an estate that rolls right up to the walls of **St-Émilion,** the loveliest of many villages producing wines that are sure to add a memorable note to any day. Come in May to Bordeaux, the regional capital, for the music festival, or any time to sip splendid wines while you indulge in oysters, truffles, foie gras, and caviar. Life is beautiful, *non?*

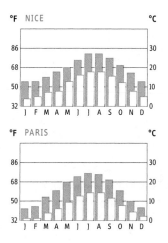

Like many of its European neighbors, France is swamped with travelers in summer, especially after June 29th, when all the European schools get out. French school children actually have five holidays a year: in addition to all of July and August, one week at the end of October, two weeks at Christmas, two weeks in February, and two weeks in April. During these times travel in France is truly at its peak season, which means that prices are higher, highways are busier, the queues for museums are long, and transportation is at its most expensive. Your best bet for quality and calm is to travel off-season—June and September. If you're heading to Paris, remember that Parisians take vacations, too, especially during the final two weeks of August, when the city becomes really stuffy and uncomfortable. During this time, all Paris used to close up like a clam, with lots of shuttered theaters, restaurants, and stores but these days enough stay open to make a low-key, unhurried visit a pleasure. As for southern France, July and August can be stifling and, back in the old days, no one ever vacationed here during those months. In the 1930s, however, the great couturier Chanel decreed that suntans (once the giveaway for fieldhands) and sunglasses were chic, and ever since, more athletic generations, which spend much of their time in the water, have made summer in Provence and the Côte d'Azur hyper-popular, with Riviera beaches as crowded as Paris is deserted. But anytime between between March and November will offer you a good chance to soak up the sun in these southern regions. If Paris and the Loire are among your priorities, remember that the weather is unappealing before Easter. If you're dreaming of Paris in the springtime, May is your best bet, not rainy April. But the capital remains a joy during midwinter, with plenty of things to see and do. As our On the Calendar section reveals, France is a fête all year-round.

Climate

The graphs above show the average daily maximum and minimum temperatures for Paris and Nice.

📱 Forecasts Weather Channel Connection 🌐 www.weather.com.

QUINTESSENTIAL
FRANCE

Café Society

Along with air, water, and wine, the café remains one of the basic necessities of life in France. You may prefer a posh perch at a renowned Paris spot such as the Deux Magots on boulevard St-Germain or opt for a tiny *café du coin* (corner café) in Lyon or Marseilles, where you can have a quick cup of coffee at the counter. Those on Paris's major boulevards (such as boulevard St-Michel and the Champs-Élysées) will almost always be the most expensive and the least interesting. In effect, the more modest establishments (look for nonchalant locals) are the places to really get a feeling for French café culture. And we do mean culture—not only the practical rituals of the experience (perusing the posted menu, choosing a table, unwrapping your sugar cube) but an intellectual spur as well. You'll see businessmen, students, and pensive types pulling out notebooks for intent

scribblings. In fact, some Paris landmarks like the Café de Flore host readings, while several years ago a trend for *cafés philos* (philosophy cafés) took off. And there's always the frisson of history available at places like La Closerie des Lilas, where an expensive drink allows you to rest your derrière on the spots once favored by Baudelaire and Apollinaire. Finally, there's people-watching, which goes hand in glove with the café lifestyle—what better excuse to linger over your *café crème* or Lillet? So get ready to settle in, sip your *pastis,* and pretend your travel notebook is a Hemingway story in the making.

Street Markets

Browsing through the *marché couvert* (covered food markets) of France are enough to make you regret all the tempting restaurants around. But even though their seafood, free-range poultry, olives, and produce cry

If you want to get a sense of contemporary French culture, and indulge in some of its pleasures, start by familiarizing yourself with the rituals of daily life. These are a few highlights—things you can take part in with relative ease.

out to be gathered in a basket and cooked in their purest form, you can even enjoy them as a simple visual feast. At other markets, food plays second fiddle. You can spend a morning "flea-ing" at the Marché aux Puces—Paris's funky Clignancourt antiques market—or the day trawling for treasures at Provence's *brocante* (collectibles) fair in L'Isle-sur-la-Sorgue. With any luck, you'll find that little 18th-century engraving that makes your heart go *trottinant*.

Bistros & Brasseries

The choice of restaurants in France is a feast in itself. Of course, at least once during your trip you'll want to indulge in a luxurious meal at a great haute cuisine restaurant—but there's no need to get knee-deep in white truffles at Paris's Alain Ducasse to savor the France the French

eat. For you can discover the most delicious *French-Women-Don't-Get-Fat* food with a quick visit to a city neighborhood bistro. History tells us that bistros served the world's first fast food—after the fall of Napoléon, the Russian soldiers who occupied Paris were know to cry bistro ("quickly" in Russian) when ordering. Here, at zinc-topped tables, you'll find the great delights of *cuisine traditionelle* like *grand-mère*'s lamb with white beans. Today, the bistro boom has meant that many are designer-decorated and packed with the trendoisie. If you're lucky, the food will be as witty and colorful as the clientele. Brasseries, with few exceptions, remain unchanged—great bustling places with white-apron waiters and hearty, mainly Alsatian, food, such as pork-based dishes, *choucroute* (sauerkraut), and beer (brasserie also means brewery). *Bon appétit!*

IF YOU LIKE. . .

Great Food

Forget the Louvre or the Château de Chenonceau—the real reason for a visit to France is to dine at its famous temples of gastronomy. Once you dive into Taillevent's lobster soufflé, you'll quickly realize that food in France is far more than fuel. The French regard gastronomy as essential to the art of living, the art of transforming the gross and humdrum aspects of existence into something witty, charming, and gracious. So don't feel guilty if your meal at Paris's Le Grand Véfour takes as long as your visit to the Musée d'Orsay: two hours for a three-course menu is par, and you may, after relaxing into the routine, feel presured at less than three. Gastronomads—those who travel to eat—won't want to miss a pilgrimage out to Megéve to witness the culinary acrobatics of superchef Marc Veyrat, half mad scientist, half inspired artist. These days, la haute cuisine in the States and England is nearly as rare as Tibetan food, so plan on treating dining as religiously as the French do—at least once.

- **La Ferme de Mon Pére, Megéve.** Billionaires and foodies fight for seats at Marc Veyrat's Alpine aerie, France's newest culinary shrine.
- **Le Grand Véfour, Paris.** Guy Martin's Savoyard creations are extraordinaire, but the 18th-century décors are almost more delicious.
- **L'Auberge de L'Ill, near Ribeauville.** Master chef Paul Haeberlin marries grand and Alsatian cuisine, with the emphasis on proper marriage, not passionate love.
- **Le Louis XV, Monaco.** If you're going to feast like a king, this Alain Ducasse outpost is the place to do it.

La Vie de Château

From the humblest feudal ruin to the most delicate Loire Valley spires to the grandest of Sun King spreads, the châteaux of France evoke the history of Europe as no museum can. Standing on their castellated ramparts, it is easy to slip into the role of a feudal lord scrambling to protect his patchwork of holdings from kings and dukes. The lovely landscape takes on a strategic air and you find yourself role-playing thus, whether swanning aristocratically over Chenonceau's bridge-like *galerie de bal* spanning the River Cher or curling a revolutionary lip at the splendid excesses of Versailles. These are, after all, the castles that inspired Charles Perrault's "Sleeping Beauty" and "Beauty and the Beast," and their fairy-tale magic—rich with history and Disney-free—still holds true. Better yet, enjoy a "queen-for-a-stay" night at one of France's many châteaux-hotels. Many are surprisingly affordable—even though some bathrooms look like they should be on postcards.

- **Château de la Bourdaisiére, Loire Valley.** Not one but *two* princes de Broglie welcome you to this unforgettably idyllic and elegant neo-Renaissance hotel.
- **Vaux-le-Vicomte, Ile de France.** Louis XIV was so jealous when he saw this 17th-century xanadu, he comissioned Versailles.
- **Chambord, Loire Valley.** This French Renaissance extravaganza—all 440 rooms, 365 chimneys, and 5,000 acres—will take your breath away. Be sure to go up the down staircase designed by Da Vinci.
- **Château d'Ussé, Loire Valley.** Step into a fairy tale at "Sleeping Beauty"'s legendary home.

Beautiful Villages

Nearly everyone has a mind's-eye view of the perfect French village. Oozing half-timbered houses and roses, picturesquely set with potager gardens and swans posing for your cameras, these once-upon-a-time-fied villages have a sense of tranquillity not even tour buses can ruin. The Loire Valley's prettiest village, Saché is so small it seems your own personal property—an eyebrow of cottages, a Romanesque church, a 17th-century auberge inn, and a modest château. It is sublimely lovely—little wonder Honoré de Balzac came here to write some of his greatest novels. Auvers-sur-Oise, the pretty riverside village in the Ile de France, inspired some of Vincent van Gogh's finest landscapes. South in the Dordogne region, hamlets have a Walt Disney–like quality, right down to Rapunzel windows, flocks of geese, and storks'-nest towers. Along the Côte d'Azur you'll find the sky-kissing, hilltop *villages perchés*, like Èze. All in all, France has an *embarras de richesses* of nestled-away treasures—so just throw away the map. After all, no penciled itinerary is half as fun as stumbling upon some half-hidden Brigadoon.

- **Riquewihr, Alsace.** Full of storybook buildings, cul-de-sac courtyards, and stone gargoyles, this is the showpiece of the Alsatian Wine Route.
- **Peillon, Côte d'Azur.** This perfect example of the eagle's nest village above the coast has been voted boutique-free by its citizens, and remains marvelously ancient in atmosphere.
- **La Roque-Gageac, Dordogne.** Lorded over by its immense rock cliff, this centuries-old, riverside village is the perfect backcloth for a beautiful pique-nique.

Monet, Manet, and Matisse

It is through the eyes of its artists that many first get to know France. No wonder people from across the globe come to search for Gauguin's bobbing boats at Pont-Aven, Monet's bridge at Giverny, and the gaslit Moulin Rouge of Toulouse-Lautrec—not hung in a museum but alive in all their three-dimensional glory. In Arles you can stand on the spot where van Gogh painted and compare his perspective to a placard with his finished work; in Paris you can climb into the garret-atelier where Delacroix created his epic canvases, or wander the redolent streets of Montmartre, once haunted by Renoir, Utrillo, and Modigliani. Of course, an actual trip to France is not necessary to savor this country: a short visit to any major museum will probably just as effectively transport the viewer—by way of the paintings of Pisarro, Millet, Poussin, Sisley, and Matisse—to its legendary landscapes. But go beyond museums and discover the actual towns that once harbored these famed artists.

- **St-Paul-de-Vence, Côte d'Azur.** Pose oh-so-casually under the Picassos at the famed Colombe d'Or inn, once favored by Signac, Modigliani, and Bonnard.
- **Céret, Languedoc-Roussillon.** Pack your crayons for a trip to Matisse Country, for this is where the artist fell in love with the fauve ("savage") hues found only in Mother Nature.
- **Giverny, Ile de France.** Replacing paint and water with earth and water, Monet transformed his 5-acre garden into a veritable live-in Impressionist painting.
- **St-Remy, Provence.** Tiptoe through the sunflowers in this shady hillside market town, where even Van Gogh was happy.

Le Shopping

Although it's somewhat disconcerting to see Gap stores gracing almost every major street corner in Paris and other urban areas in France, if you take the time to peruse smaller specialty shops, you can find rare original gifts—be it an antique brooch from the 1930s or a modern vase crafted from Parisian rooftop-tile zinc. It's true that the traditional gifts of silk scarves, perfume, and wine can often be purchased for less in the shopping mall back home, but you can make an interesting twist by purchasing a vintage Hermés scarf, or a unique perfume from an artisan perfumer. Bargaining is traditional in outdoor and flea markets, antiques stores, small jewelry shops, and craft galleries, for example. If you're thinking of buying several items, or if you're simply in love with something a little bit too expensive, you've nothing to lose by cheerfully suggesting to the proprietor, "Vous me faites un prix?" ("How about a discount?"). The small-business man will immediately size you up, and you'll have some good-natured fun.

- **Colette, Paris.** Wiggle into the ultimate little black dress at this fashionista shrine.
- **L'Isle-sur-la-Sorgue, Provence.** This canal-laced town becomes a Marrakech of marketeers on Sunday, when dazzling antiques and brocante dealers set up shop.
- **Grain de Vanille, Cancale.** These sublime tastes of Brittany—salted butter caramels, rare honeys, and malouine cookies—make great gifts, *non?*

Gothic Churches and Cathedrals

Their extraordinary permanence, their everlasting relevance even in a secular world, and their transcending beauty make the Gothic churches and cathedrals of France a lightning rod if you are in search of the essence of French culture. The product of a peculiarly Gallic mix of mysticism, exquisite taste, and high technology, France's 13th- and 14th-century "heavenly mansions" provide a thorough grounding in the history of architecture (some say there was nothing new in the art of building between France's Gothic arch and Frank Lloyd Wright's cantilevered slab). Each cathedral imparts its own monumental experience—knee-weakening grandeur, a mighty resonance that touches a chord of awe, and humility in the unbeliever. Even cynics will find satisfaction in these edifices' social history—the anonymity of the architects, the solidarity of the artisans, and the astonishing bravery of experiments in suspended stone.

- **Notre Dame, Paris.** Make a face back at the gargoyles high atop Quasimodo's home.
- **Reims, Champagne.** Tally up the 34 V.I.P.s crowned at this magnficent edifice, age-old setting for the coronations of French kings.
- **Chartres, the Ile de France.** Get enlightened with France's most beautiful stained-glass windows.
- **Mont-St-Michel, Normandy.** From its silhouette against the horizon to the abbey and gardens at the peak of the rock, you'll never forget this awe-inspiring sight.

L'Esprit Sportif

Though the physically inclined would consider walking across Scotland or bicycling across Holland, they often misconstrue France as a sedentary site where one plods from museum to château to restaurant. But it's possible to take a more active approach: imagine pedaling past barges on the Saône River or along slender poplars on a route départementale (provincial road); hiking through the dramatic gorges in the Massif Central or over Alpine meadows in the Savoie; or sailing the historic ports of Honfleur or Cap d'Antibes. Experiencing this side of France will take you off the beaten path and into the countryside. As you bike along French country roads or along the extensive network of Grands Randonnées (Lengthy Trails) crisscrossing the country, you will have time to tune into the landscape—to study crumbling garden walls, smell the honeysuckle, and chat with a farmer in his potager vegetable garden.

- **The VBT Loire Biking Tour.** Stunning châteaux-hotels, Pissarro-worthy riverside trails, and twenty new best friends make this a fantastique way to go "around the whirl."
- **The GR 20 Hike, Corsica.** Tackle a part of this 100-mile path from Calenzana to Conca and you'll understand how this island kingdom fashioned and tempered Napoléon.
- **Kayaking the Gorges du Tarn, Massif Central.** France's "Grand Canyon" has never looked so spectacular than from its swirling waters.

Clos Encounters

Bordeaux or Burgundy, Sauternes or Sancerre, Romanée-Conti or Côte du Rhône—wherever you turn in France, you'll find famous Gallic wine regions and vineyards, born of the country's curvaceous landscape. Speckled unevenly with hills, canals, forest, vineyards, châteaux, and the occasional cow clinging to 30-degree inclines, the great wine regions of France attract hoards of travelers more interested in shoving their noses deep into wine glasses than staring high into the stratosphere of French cathedral naves. Fact is, you can buy the bottles of the fabled regions—the Côte d'Or of Burgundy, or the Rhône Valley, or that oenophile's nirvana, Bordeaux—anywhere, so why not taste the lesser-known local crus, such as the lovely vineyards in the Loire Valley. Explore the various *clos* (enclosures) and *côtes* (hillsides) that grow golden by October, study the *vendangeur* grape-pickers, then drive along the wine routes looking for those "Dégustation" signs, promising free sips and soundbites from the local vintner. Pretty soon you'll be expert on judging any wine's aroma, body, velvet, and backwash.

- **Mouton-Rothschild, Route de Médoc.** Baron Philippe perfected one of the great five premiere crus here—and there's a great visitor's center.
- **Clos de Vougeot, Burgundy.** An historic wine-making barn, 13th-century grape-presses, and its verdant vineyard make this a must-do.
- **The Alsace Route de Vin.** Between Mulhouse and Strasbourg, many picture-book villages entice with top vintners of Riesling and Gewürztraminer.

GREAT ITINERARIES

THE GOOD LIFE

8 to 11 Days. Great châteaux, fine porcelain, superb wine, brandy, truffles, and foie gras sum up France for many. Beginning in château country, head south and west, through Cognac country into wine country around Bordeaux. Then lose yourself in the Dordogne, a landscape of rolling hills peppered with medieval villages, fortresses, and prehistoric caves.

Loire Valley Châteaux

3 or 4 days. Base yourself at the crossroads of Blois, starting with its multi-era château. Then head for the huge château in Chambord. Amboise's château echoes with history, and the neighboring manor, Clos Lucé, was Leonardo da Vinci's final home—or instead of this "town" château, head west to the tiny village of Rigny-Ussé for the "Sleeping Beauty" castle of Ussé. Heading southeast, finish up at Chenonceau—the most magical one of all—then return to the transportation hub city of Tours. ⇨ *The Loire Valley* in *Chapter 3*

Cognac Country

1 to 2 days. Cognac's very air is saturated with evaporations of its heady product, enough to grow mushrooms on its black stone walls. Hennessy and Martell give tasting tours. In neighboring Jarnac you can visit Hine and Courvoisier—and François Mitterrand's grave. ⇨ *Charentes* in *Chapter 16*

Bordeaux Wine Country

2 days. Pay homage to the great names of Médoc, north of the city of Bordeaux, though the hallowed villages of Margaux, St-Julien, Pauillac, and St-Estèphe aren't much to look at. East of Bordeaux, via the prettier Pomerol vineyards, the village of St-Émilion is everything you'd want a wine town to be, with ramparts and medieval streets. ⇨ *Bordeaux* in *Chapter 16*

Dordogne & Périgord

2 or 3 days. Follow the famous Dordogne River east to the half-timber market town of Bergerac. Wind through the green, wooded countryside into the region where humans' earliest ancestors left their mark, in the caves in Les Eyzies-de-Tayac and the famous Grotte de Lascaux. Be sure to sample the region's culinary specialties: truffles, foie gras, and preserved duck. Then travel south to the stunning and sky-high village of Rocamadour. ⇨ *Dordogne and Poitou-Charentes* in *Chapter 16*

By Public Transportation

It's easy to get to Blois and Chenonceaux by rail, but you'll need to take a bus to visit other Loire châteaux. Forays farther into Bordeaux country and the Dordogne are difficult by train, involving complex and frequent changes (Limoges is a big railway hub). Further exploration requires a rental car or sometimes sketchy bus routes.

FRANCE FROM NORTH TO SOUTH

6 or 9 Days. So, you want to taste France, gaze at its beauty, and inhale its special joie de vivre—all in a one-week to 10-day trip. Let's assume at least that you've seen Paris, and you're ready to venture into the countryside. Here are some itineraries to help you plan your trip. Or create your own route

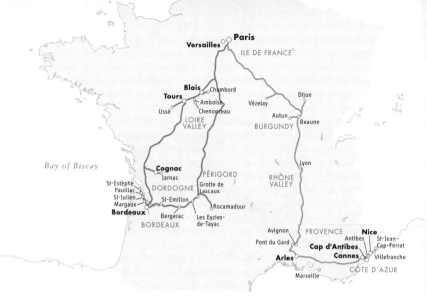

using the suggested itineraries in each chapter. First, zoom from Paris to the heart of historic Burgundy, its rolling green hills traced with hedgerows and etched with vineyards. From here, plunge into the arid beauty of Provence and toward the spectacular coastline of the Côte d'Azur.

Burgundy Wine Country

2 to 3 days. Base yourself in the market town of Beaune and visit its famous Hospices and surrounding vineyards. Make a day trip to the ancient hill town of Vézelay, with its incomparable basilica, stopping in Autun to explore Roman ruins and its celebrated Romanesque cathedral. For more vineyards, follow the Côte d'Or from Beaune to Dijon. Or make a beeline to Dijon, with its charming Vieille Ville and fine museums. From here it's a two-hour drive to Lyon, where you can feast on this city's famous earthy cuisine. Another three hours' push takes you deep into the heart of Provence. ⇨ *Northwest Burgundy and Wine Country* in *Chapter 8* and *Lyon* in *Chapter 9*

Arles & Provence

2 to 3 days. Arles is the atmospheric, sun-drenched southern town that inspired Van Gogh and Gauguin. Make a day trip into grand old Avignon, home to the 14th-century rebel popes, to view their imposing palace. And make a pilgrimage to the Pont du Gard, the famous triple-tiered Roman aqueduct west of Avignon. From here two hours' drive will bring you to the glittering Côte d'Azur. ⇨ *Arles, Avignon, and Pont du Gard* in *Chapter 11*

Antibes & the Côte d'Azur

2 to 3 days. This historic and atmospheric port town is well positioned for day trips. First head west to glamorous Cannes. The next day head east into Nice, with its exotic Vieille Ville and its bounty of modern art. There are ports to explore in Villefranche and St-Jean-Cap-Ferrat, east of Nice. Allow time for a walk out onto the tropical paradise peninsula of Cap d'Antibes, or for an hour or two lolling on the coast's famous pebble beaches. ⇨ *Cannes, Nice, Villefranche-sur-Mer, St-Jean-Cap-Ferrat,* and *Cap d'Antibes* in *Chapter 12*

By Public Transportation

The high-speed TGV travels from Paris through Burgundy and Lyon, then zips through the south to Marseille. Train connections to Beaune from the TGV are easy; getting to Autun from Beaune takes up to two hours, with a change at Chagny. Vézelay can be reached by bus excursion from

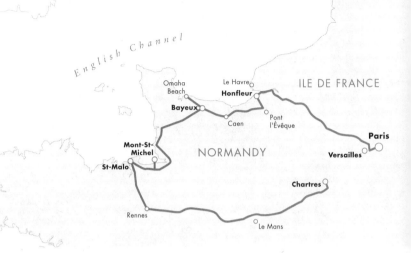

Dijon or Beaune. Rail connections are easy between Arles and Avignon; you'll need a bus to get to the Pont du Gard from Avignon. Antibes, Cannes, and Nice are easily reached by the scenic rail line, as are most of the resorts and ports along the coast. To squeeze the most daytime out of your trip, take a night train or a plane from Nice back to Paris.

A CHILD'S-EYE VIEW

7 Days. Lead your children (and yourself) wide-eyed through the wonders of Europe, instilling some sense of France's cultural legacy. Make your way through Normandy and Brittany, with enough wonders and evocative topics, from William the Conqueror to D-Day, to inspire any child to put down his computer game and gawk. Short daily drives forestall mutiny, and you'll be in crêperie country, satisfying for casual meals.

Versailles

1 day. Here's an opportunity for a history lesson: With its amazing Baroque extravagance, no other monument so succinctly illustrates what inspired the rage of the French Revolution. Louis XIV's eye-popping château of Versailles pleases the secret monarch in most of us. ⇨ *Southwest from Versailles to Chartres* in *Chapter 2*

Honfleur

1 day. From this picture-book seaport lined with skinny half-timber row houses and salt-dampened cobblestones, the first French explorers set sail for Canada in the 15th century. ⇨ *Upper Normandy* in *Chapter 5*

Bayeux

2 days. William the Conqueror's extraordinary invasion of England in 1066 was launched from the shores of Normandy. The famous Bayeux tapestry, showcased in a state-of-the-art museum, spins the tale of the Battle of Hastings. From this home base you can introduce the family to the modern saga of 1944's Allied landings with a visit to the Museum of the Battle of Normandy, then make a pilgrimage to Omaha Beach. ⇨ *Lower Normandy* in *Chapter 5*

Mont-St-Michel

1 day. Rising majestically in a shroud of sea mist over vacillating tidal flats, this mystical peninsula is Gothic in every sense of the word. Though its tiny, steep streets are crammed with visitors and tourist traps, no other sight gives you a stronger sense of the worldly power of medieval monasticism than Mont-St-Michel. ⇨ *Lower Normandy* in *Chapter 5*

St-Malo

1 day. Even in winter you'll want to brave the Channel winds to beachcomb the shores of this onetime pirate base. In summer, of course, it's mobbed with sun-seekers who stroll the old streets, restored to quaintness after World War II. ⇨ *Northeast Brittany and the Channel Coast* in *Chapter 4*

Chartres

1 day. Making a beeline on the autoroute back to Paris, stop in Chartres to view the loveliest of all of France's cathedrals. ⇨ *Southwest from Versailles to Chartres* in *Chapter 2*

By Public Transportation

Coordinating a sightseeing tour like this with a limited local train schedule isn't easy, and connections to Mont-St-Michel are especially complicated. Versailles, Chartres, and St-Malo are easy to reach, and Bayeux and Honfleur are doable, if inconvenient. But you'll spend a lot of vacation time waiting along train tracks.

VINTAGE SAMPLER

6 to 9 Days. Tasting wines in a cool, mossy cave redolent of cork gives vintages new dimensions, and you'll meet vintners of every stripe, from gnarled-fingered grandpas in blue aprons to ascoted gentry in cashmere. Along the way, taste the widely varied wines of eastern France, from Champagne to Alsace to the little-known whites of the Jura, then on to Burgundy, Beaujolais, and the Côtes du Rhône. Take it easy on the *dégustations* (tastings) if you're driving.

Reims

2 days. At the heart of the green panorama of Champagne country lies Reims, with its magnificent cathedral. There's no shortage of downtown sources of bubbly, but you'll probably also want to venture south down the *Route du Vin* (Wine Road) to Épernay, home to Moët et Chandon. Just northwest is the old-fashioned village of Hautvillers, which claims Dom Pérignon as its native son. ⇨ *Champagne and the Ardennes* in *Chapter 6*

Ribeauvillé

2 days. Head east to Franco-Germanic Strasbourg and south down Alsace's Route du Vin. At the foot of forested Vosges foothills, the tiny wine village of Ribeauvillé sums up the spirit of Alsace. Here you'll taste sharp, fruity Rieslings and late-harvest Gewürztraminers as sweet as sauternes. Picture-perfect Riquewihr and Colmar are a stone's throw away. ⇨ *Alsace* in *Chapter 7*

Arbois

1 day. South of Alsace, follow the Doubs River through the citadel town of Besançon to Arbois. This is the center for the production of the Jura region's obscure and eccentric *vin jaune*: sharp, dry, and sherrylike. Venture to the other-worldly hilltop village of Château-Chalon for some of the finest of the genre. ⇨ *Franche-Comté* in *Chapter 7*

Beaune

2 days. Press westward to Beaune, Burgundy's wine-market town (⇨ France from North to South itinerary, *above*). Wine shops abound in the center, but you'll want to cruise along the famous Côte d'Or. ⇨ *Wine Country* in *Chapter 8*

Villefranche-sur-Saône

1 day. Head south along the west bank of the Saône. South of Mâcon, home of the last and lightest of the Burgundies, veer westward and follow the winding southbound Route du Vin through Beaujolais country. Cruise through the famous villages that produce this fruity, Gamay-based red. If you're traveling in autumn, look for the sharp young Beaujolais nouveau: the market-town of Villefranche-sur-Saône celebrates annually with carnival-like festivities. ⇨ *Wine Country* in *Chapter 8* and *Beaujolais and La Dombes* and *The Rhône Valley* in *Chapter 9*

Châteauneuf-du-Pape

2 days. At Lyon you'll merge into the Rhône Valley. Just north of Valence cross the river at Tournon and pay homage to the vineyards at Tain-l'Hermitage. Press on south past Orange to the famous wine region and village of Châteauneuf-du-Pape, named for the Avignon popes who weekended here. You could continue from here into the region of the "sun wines" of the Côtes de Provence and Languedoc, but you might never get home. ⇨ *Lyon and the Rhône Valley* in *Chapter 9* and *Avignon and the Vaucluse* in *Chapter 11*

By Public Transportation

An abbreviated version of this journey can be worked out via train, leaving out the inaccessible vineyards and villages (which serve as lovely scenery through the train window). Start in Reims, move directly on to Colmar (substituting the atmospheric wine-market center for Ribeauvillé); take the train onward to Beaune. From Beaune the train makes stops along the northbound Côte d'Or route, but the best vineyards are hard to reach on foot. To get closer to the sources, look into package excursions or rent a car.

France is a festival year-round, with special events taking place throughout the country. In Paris check the listings in *Pariscope* (which includes *Time Out,* a section with reviews in English of the week's main events), *L'Officiel des Spectacles,* or *Figaroscope* to find out what's going on around town. The *International Herald Tribune* also lists special events in its weekend edition but not in great detail. The most complete listing of festivals comes in a small pamphlet published by the French Government Tourist Office, or you can consult the official Web site of the *Maison de la France,* which has a list (more than 3,000 strong) of current festivals, seminars, antique fairs, concerts, and temporary exhibits at ⊕ www.franceguide.com.

WINTER

December

On the 24th, a Christmas celebration known as the **Shepherds' Festival,** featuring midnight Mass and picturesque "living crèches," occurs in Les Baux, Provence. From the end of November through the New Year, Strasbourg mounts its famous **Christmas Market,** with echoes of German Gemütlichkeit. **Christmas in Paris** spells celebrations, especially for children, from late December to early January. A giant crèche and a full-size ice-skating rink are set up on the square in front of the Hôtel de Ville.

January

The **International Circus Festival,** featuring top acts from around the world, and the **Monte Carlo Motor Rally,** one of the motoring world's most venerable races, take place in Monaco. Wine-producing villages throughout France celebrate **St. Vincent's Day** with festivities on January 22 in honor of their patron saint. The **Tournament St-Vincent,** a colorful Burgundy wine festival, takes place on the third weekend in Meursault in 2004; more than 200,000 wine lovers are expected to attend. Angoulême hosts the world's biggest and most popular comic-book festival, the **Fête de la Bande Dessinée,** from January 24 to January 27.

February

The **Carnival de Nice** ⊕ www.nicecarnival.com is a period of parades and revelry in the weeks leading up to Lent. Other cities and villages also have their own smaller versions. **The Carnival de Dunkerque,** on the weekend before Shrove Tuesday, is the most rambunctious street carnival in northern France. The **Festival de Film Fantastique** is the international horror film festival, which takes place in Gerardmer. The **Fête du Citron** ⊕ www.feteducitron.com is held in the Riviera town of Menton, replete with fruit-filled floats and gardens.

SPRING	
March	The **Salon de Mars**, an art and antiques fair, and the **Salon du Livre**, France's biggest book festival, take place in Paris. **La Foire à la Brocante et au Jambon** is an important, high-quality antiques fair held every year in Chatou, a beautiful village outside Paris. **Grenoble Jazz Festival** ⊕ www.jazzgrenoble.com has been going strong for more than 30 years. In late March the **Open House at the Médoc Vineyards** ⊕ www.bordeaux-vineyards.com is a rare chance to see some great château-vineyards not usually open to the general public.
April	The **Monte Carlo Open Tennis Championships** get under way at the Monte Carlo Country Club. At the end of April **Les Fêtes Musicales** ⊕ www.biarritz.tm.fr are held in Biarritz for the pleasure of all classical-music lovers.
May	Complete with cathedral illuminations and religious processions, **Les Fêtes Johanniques** ⊕ www.ville-orleans.fr, on the first weekend in May, offers a commemoration of the liberation of Orléans from the English by the French troops led by Joan of Arc. The **Cannes Film Festival** ⊕ www.festival-cannes.fr sees two weeks of star-studded events. Classical-music festivals get under way throughout the country. The **Foire de Paris** is a giant fair with food and agricultural products from all over France; it takes place at the Porte de Versailles in Paris. The prestige event of the Formula 1 car circuit is the **Monaco Grand Prix** ⊕ www.acm.mc, usually held around May 20th. At the end of the month are the **French Open Tennis Championships** ⊕ www.frenchopen.org at Roland Garros Stadium, in Paris. Kicking off at the end of May is the extraordinary summer-long **Festival des Jardins** ⊕ www.chaumont-jardins.com, held in the gardens of the Loire Valley château of Chaumont-sur-Loire.
SUMMER	
June	From now until September you will find **son-et-lumière** (sound-and-light) shows—historical pageants featuring special lighting effects—at several châteaux (notably Amboise) and churches in the Loire Valley. Throughout France there's dancing in the streets during the **Fête de la Musique**, a free live-music festival on June 21 that lasts all night. From mid-June through the end of August, Paris's Tuileries Gardens host a **Fête des Tuileries** ⊕ www.paris-touristoffice.com in the shadow of the giant Ferris wheel. In mid-June look for the explosive fireworks festival, the **Nuits de Feu** ⊕ www.chantilly-tourisme.com, in the gardens of the great château at Chantilly. Strasbourg's **Fête de la Musique** features concerts in the Cathédrale Notre-Dame and various halls.

	This is a popular time for horse races: the **Prix du Président de la République** is run at the Hippodrome de Vincennes, the **Grand Steeplechase de Paris** is at the Auteuil Racecourse, and the **Grand Prix de Paris** is at Longchamp Racecourse. The **24 Heures du Mans** ⊕ www.lemans.org, the famous 24-hour car race, is held in Le Mans. The **Paris Air Show** is a display of planes at Le Bourget Airport, near Paris. On the last weekend in June the **Fête du Cinéma** allows you to take in as many movies as you can for the price of a single ticket. In northern France, Joan of Arc is feted at Reims's **Fêtes Johanniques** ⊕ www.tourisme.fr/reims, complete with pageants, processions, and a medieval market, all usually held at the end of June.
July	The **summer arts festival season** gets into full swing, particularly in Provence. **Avignon** ⊕ www.festival-avignon.com is one of the biggest celebrations with top-notch theater and avant-garde art, while Aix-en-Provence specializes in opera, Carpentras in religious music, Nice holds a big jazz festival, and Arles mounts a major photography festival. Northern France's spectacular **Fête de Gayant** (Festival of the Giant, in local patois) is held in Douai on the first Sunday after July 5. The wine hub of France, Bordeaux, hosts its **Bordeaux Fête le Vin** ⊕ www.bordeaux-tourisme.com in early July, replete with expositions, tastings, parades, and fireworks. The **Tour de France** ⊕ www.letour.fr, the world's most famous bicycle race, dominates national attention for three weeks before crossing the finish line on the Champs-Élysées on the last Sunday of the month. **Jazz à Juan** ⊕ www.antibes-juanlespins.com has topped the 40-year mark and this jazz festival is usually held in mid-July. The **Festival de l'Art Lyrique** brings more than 1 million music lovers to Aix-en-Province to hear music spanning several centuries. On **Bastille Day** (July 14) all of France commemorates the storming of the Bastille in 1789—the start of the French Revolution. Look out for fireworks, free concerts, and street festivities beginning the evening of July 13, with the **Bal des Pompiers** (Firemen's Ball) organized by local firemen. Head to the Place de la Bastille for the Grand Paris Ball. On July 14th a military parade goes down the Champs-Élysées, with fireworks after sundown. From July 14th on through summer, **Paris Quartiers d'Eté** ⊕ www.quartierdete hosts theater, dance, and concerts in many scenic neighborhood locales throughout Paris. Music aficionados head to Prades in southern France in late July for the famous **Pablo Casals Festival** ⊕ www.festival-piano.com, held through August at many medieval sites.
August	On **Assumption** (August 15) many towns, notably Chartres and Lisieux, hold religious festivals and processions dedicated to the

Virgin Mary. On the first Sunday following August 15, the **Festival de la Force Basque,** in St-Palais, brings together participants from eight villages to compete in contests of strength. The most famous annual religious festival in Brittany is the *pardon* in Ste-Anne-la-Palud, near Quimper, on the last Sunday of August. If you want to drive yourself insane, you can always visit the **International Mime Festival,** held in early August, when the city of Perigueux, in Dordogne, is overtaken by those white-face Marcel Marceau wannabes. The **Festival Interceltique** ⊕ www.festival-interceltique.com takes place in Lorient, Brittany, from August 2 to August 11, with a street fair commemorating contemporary expressions of Celtic art, music, and dance. In mid-August, Colmar hosts a big wine fair, the **Foire aux Vins** ⊕ www.colmar-expo.fr that attracts hundreds of thousands of wine tasters.

FALL	
September	The **vendanges** (grape harvests) begin, and festivals take place in the country's wine regions. The **Grande Braderie** turns Lille into one giant street fair on the month's first weekend. The **Fête de Musique de Besançon et Franche-Comté** consists of a series of chamber-music concerts in and around Besançon during the month. The **Fête d'Automne,** a major arts and film festival, opens in Paris and continues until December. France's biggest dance festival—the **Biennale de la Danse** ⊕ www.biennale-de-lyon.org—kicks off in mid-September (to early October) in Lyon. The **Rencontres Polyphoniques,** in Calvi, is an excellent chance to hear authentic Corsican music. The **Journée du Patrimoine,** on the Sunday nearest September 21, opens the doors of many official and private buildings usually closed to the public. The **American Film Festival,** in Deauville, is one of the most important international events (second to Cannes) for American film. The **Biennale des Antiquaires** is held in the Carrousel du Louvre in Paris this month with more than 120 antiques dealers from Europe and the United States. The **International Car Salon** takes place in the Porte de Versailles from September 28 to October 13 with one of the most impressive car selections in the world (second only to Tokyo).
October	The **Prix de l'Arc de Triomphe,** horse racing's most prestigious flat race, is held at the Longchamp Racecourse, in Paris, on the first Sunday of the month. A giant contemporary art exhibition called **FIAC** ⊕ www.fiac.reed-oip.fr takes place in Paris early in the month. The weeklong **Paris Indoor Open** attracts the world's top tennis players at the end of the month.
November	**Les Trois Glorieuses,** Burgundy's biggest wine festival, includes the year's most important wine auction and related merriment, which

occurs in several Burgundy locations. The **Festiventu,** in Calvi (Corsica), is a celebration of wind-related activities ranging from windsurfing to woodwinds. Nationwide **Armistice Day** ceremonies on November 11 commemorate veterans of World Wars I and II; in Paris there's a military parade down the Champs-Élysées. On the third Thursday in November, France—especially Paris—celebrates the arrival of the **Beaujolais Nouveau.** The **Salon des Caves Particulières** is a giant wine fair held in Paris at the end of the month. November is also the **Mois de la Photo,** with open photography exhibits in most galleries throughout France.

SMART TRAVEL TIPS

Half the fun of traveling is looking forward to your trip—but when you look forward, don't just daydream. There are plans to be made, things to learn about, serious work to be done. After all, finding out about your destination before you leave home means you won't spend time organizing everyday minutiae once you've arrived. You'll be more streetwise when you hit the ground as well, better prepared to explore the aspects of France that drew you here in the first place. The organizations in this section can provide information to supplement this guide; contact them for up-to-the-minute details, and consult the A to Z sections that end each chapter for facts on the various topics as they relate to France's many regions. Happy landings!

ADDRESSES

Addresses in France are fairly straightforward: there are the number and the street name. However, you may see an address with a number plus "bis," for instance, 20 bis rue Vavin: This indicates the next entrance or door down from 20 rue Vavin. In small towns a street number may not be given, as the site will be the dominant (or only) building on the block or square. In rural areas, however, a site may list only a route name, a number near the site, or sometimes just the name of the small village in which it is located.

In Paris a site's location in one of the city's 20 arrondissements is noted by its mailing code or, simply, the last one or two digits of that code (for example, Paris 75010 or 10^e, both of which indicate that the address is in the 10th arrondissement; Paris 75005 or 5e, for another example, indicates the address is in the 5th arrondissement). Because of its large size, Paris's 16th arrondissement has two numbers assigned to it: 75016 and 75116. Note that in France you enter a building on the *rez-de-chaussée* (RC or 0), as the ground floor is known, and you have to go up one floor to reach the first floor, or *premier étage*.

AIR TRAVEL

As one of the premier destinations in the world, Paris is serviced by many international carriers and a surprising number of U.S.–based airlines. **Air France** is the French flag carrier and offers numerous direct flights (often several per day) between Paris's Charles de Gaulle Airport and New York City's JFK Airport; Newark, New Jersey; Washington, DC's Dulles Airport; as well as the cities of Boston, Atlanta, Miami, Chicago, Houston, San Francisco, Los Angeles, Toronto, Montréal, and Mexico City. Most other North American cities are served through Air France partnerships with Delta and Continental Airlines. American-based carriers are usually less expensive but offer, on the whole, fewer nonstop flights. **Delta Airlines** is a popular U.S.–France carrier; departures for Paris leave Atlanta, Cincinnati, and New York City's JFK, although Delta's regional flights link airports throughout the southeastern United States and the Midwest with its main international hub in Atlanta. Travelers in the northeast and southwest of the United States often use **Continental Airlines,** whose nonstop Paris flights generally depart from Newark and Houston; in peak season they often offer daily departures. Another popular carrier is **United Airlines,** with nonstop flights to Paris from Chicago, Denver, Los Angeles, Miami, Philadelphia, Washington, DC, and San Francisco. **American Airlines** offers daily nonstop flights to Paris's Charles de Gaulle Airport from numerous cities, including New York City's JFK, Miami, Chicago, and Dallas/Fort Worth. **Northwest** offers a daily departure to Paris from its hub in Detroit; connections from Seattle, Minneapolis, and numerous other airports link up to Detroit. In Canada, Air France and **Air Canada** are the leading choices for departures from Toronto and Montréal; in peak season, departures are often daily. The new carrier **Zoom** offers discount long-haul flights from Toronto and Montréal twice weekly. From London, Air France, **British Airways,** and **British Midland,** are the leading carriers, with up to 15 flights daily in peak season. In addition, direct routes link Manchester, Edinburgh, and Southampton with Paris. **Ryanair,** an Irish charter company that connects Paris, London, and Dublin, is getting raves for its cheaper-

than-cheap flights. In France, Ryanair flights land at Beauvais airport, about one hour from Paris. A number of charter companies are cashing in on the booming inter-European travel market, offering short flights with no-frills service and exceptional fares. **EasyJet** has flights from Paris to Liverpool, London, Nice, Geneva, Barcelona, Marseille, Naples, Toulouse, and Belfast. It also connects Nice to Berlin for less than €30 one-way. **Virgin Express** links Nice to Brussels, Rome, Athens, Copenhagen, Geneva, Lisbon, Madrid and Malaga at attractive prices. **BMI Baby** has flights from Paris to Cardiff and Nottingham. Options are more limited for travelers to Paris from Australia and New Zealand, who usually wind up taking British Airways and **Qantas** flights to London, then connections to Paris.

There's also the quick and efficient option of using train transport via the Eurostar Express through the Channel Tunnel (⇨ The Channel Tunnel *and* Train Travel to and from Paris).

BOOKING

When you book, look for nonstop flights and remember that "direct" flights stop at least once. Try to avoid connecting flights, which require a change of plane. Two airlines may operate a connecting flight jointly, so ask whether your airline operates every segment of the trip; you may find that the carrier you prefer flies you only part of the way. To find more booking tips and to check prices and make online flight reservations, log on to www.fodors.com.

CARRIERS

🛪 Major Airlines **Air Canada** ☎ 888/247-2262 in the U.S. and Canada, 08-25-88-08-81 in France ⊕ www.aircanada.com. **Air France** ☎ 800/237-2747 in U.S., 08-20-82-08-20 in France ⊕ www.airfrance.com. **American Airlines** ☎ 800/433-7300 in U.S., 08-10-87-28-72 in France, 01-55-17-43-41 in Paris ⊕ www.aa.com. **British Airways** ☎ 800/247-9297 in U.S., 0870-8509-850 in the U.K., 08-25-82-50-40 in France ⊕ www.britishairways.com. **Continental** ☎ 800/231-0856 in U.S., 01-71-23-03-35 in France ⊕ www.continental.com. **Delta** ☎ 800/241-4141 in U.S., 08-00-30-13-01 in France ⊕ www.delta.com. **Northwest** ☎ 800/447-

4747 in the U.S., 08-90-71-07-10 in France ⊕ www.klm.com. **Qantas** ☎ 800/227-4500 in U.S., 08-20-82-05-00 in France ⊕ www.qantas.com. **United** ☎ 800/538-2929 in U.S., 08-10-72-72-72 in France ⊕ www.unitedairlines.com. **US Airways** ☎ 800/622-1015 in the U.S., 08-10-63-22-22 in France ⊕ www.usairways.com. **Zoom Air** ☎ 866/359-9666 in the U.S./Canada, 613/235-3666 from outside North America ⊕ www.flyzoom.com.

F U.K. to France Air France ☎ 0845-0845-111 in the U.K., 08-02-80-28-02 in France ⊕ www.airfrance.com. **BMI Baby** ☎ 0870-264-2229 in the U.K., 08-90-71-00-81 in France ⊕ www.bmibaby.com. **British Airways** ☎ 0870-8509-850 in the U.K., 08-25-82-50-40 in France ⊕ www.britishairways.com. **British Midland** ☎ 0870-6070-222, 0133-285-4854 in the U.K., 01-55-69-83-06 in France ⊕ www.flybmi.com. **EasyJet** ☎ 0990/292-929 in U.K., 08-25-08-25-08 in France ⊕ www.easyjet.com. **Ryan Air** ☎ 0990/292-929 in U.K., 08-92-55-56-66 in France ⊕ www.ryanair.com. **Virgin Express** ☎ 08-00-52-85-28 ⊕ www.virginexpress.com.

F Within France Air France (⊏⊐ Carriers, *above*).

CHECK-IN & BOARDING

Always **find out your carrier's check-in policy.** Plan to arrive at the airport about two hours before your scheduled departure time for domestic flights and 2½ to 3 hours before international flights. You may need to arrive earlier if you're flying from one of the busier airports or during peak air-traffic times. **Due to traffic-jams within the main airports, always allot at least an extra hour for the commute (via car, bus, or train)** when departing from the capital, since horrendous traffic tie-ups within Charles de Gaulle or Orly airport can seriously add to the time it takes to get to the ticket counter. Once you arrive at the airport from Paris, you'll often need to take the inter-airport bus to shuttle you from one terminal to another, and if there's traffic congestion, a serious case of nail-biting can result.

To avoid delays at airport-security checkpoints, try not to wear any metal. Jewelry, belt and other buckles, steel-toe shoes, barrettes, and underwire bras are among the items that can set off detectors.

Assuming that not everyone with a ticket will show up, airlines routinely overbook planes. When everyone does, airlines ask for volunteers to give up their seats. In return, these volunteers usually get a several-hundred-dollar flight voucher, which can be used toward the purchase of another ticket, and are rebooked on the next available flight out. If there are not enough volunteers, the airline must choose who will be denied boarding. The first to get bumped are passengers who checked in late and those flying on discounted tickets, so get to the gate and check in as early as possible, especially during peak periods.

Always **bring a government-issued photo I.D.** to the airport; even when it's not required, a passport is best.

CUTTING COSTS

The least expensive airfares to France are often priced for round-trip travel and must usually be purchased in advance. Airlines generally allow you to change your return date for a fee; most low-fare tickets, however, are nonrefundable. It's smart to call a number of airlines and check the Internet; when you are quoted a good price, book it on the spot—the same fare may not be available the next day, or even the next hour. Always check different routings and look into using alternate airports. Also, price off-peak flights, which may be significantly less expensive than others. Travel agents, especially low-fare specialists (⊏⊐ Discounts & Deals), are helpful.

Consolidators are another good source. They buy tickets for scheduled flights at reduced rates from the airlines, then sell them at prices that beat the best fare available directly from the airlines. (Many also offer reduced car-rental and hotel rates.) Sometimes you can even get your money back if you need to return the ticket. Carefully read the fine print detailing penalties for changes and cancellations, purchase the ticket with a credit card, and confirm your consolidator reservation with the airline.

When you fly as a courier, you trade your checked-luggage space for a ticket deeply subsidized by a courier service. There are restrictions on when you can book and how long you can stay. Some courier companies list with membership organizations, such as the Air Courier Association and the International Association of Air Travel Couriers; these require you to become a member before you can book a flight.

7 Consolidators AirlineConsolidator.com ☎ 888/468-5385 ⊕ www.airlineconsolidator.com, for international tickets. **Best Fares** ☎ 800/880-1234 or 800/576-8255 ⊕ www.bestfares.com; $59.90 annual membership. **Cheap Tickets** ☎ 800/377-1000 or 800/652-4327 ⊕ www.cheaptickets.com. **Expedia** ☎ 800/397-3342 or 404/728-8787 ⊕ www.expedia.com. **Hotwire** ☎ 866/468-9473 or 920/330-9418 ⊕ www.hotwire.com. **Now Voyager Travel** ✉ 1717 Ave. M, Brooklyn, NY 11230 ☎ 212/459-1616 📠 718/504-4762 ⊕ www.nowvoyagertravel.com. **One-travel.com** ⊕ www.onetravel.com. **Orbitz** ☎ 888/656-4546 ⊕ www.orbitz.com. **Priceline.com** ⊕ www.priceline.com. **Travelocity** ☎ 888/709-5983, 877/282-2925 in Canada, 0870/876-3876 in U.K. ⊕ www.travelocity.com.

7 Courier Resources AirCourier.org/Cheaptrips.com ☎ 800/211-5119 or 800/461-8856 ⊕ www.aircourier.org or www.cheaptrips.com; $34 annual membership. **International Association of Air Travel Couriers** ☎ 308/632-3273 ⊕ www.courier.org; $45 annual membership.

7 Discount Passes Air France (⇨ Carriers, *above*).

ENJOYING THE FLIGHT

State your seat preference when purchasing your ticket, and then repeat it when you confirm and when you check in. For more legroom, you can request one of the few emergency-aisle seats at check-in, if you're capable of moving obstacles comparable in weight to an airplane exit door (usually between 35 pounds and 60 pounds)—a Federal Aviation Administration requirement of passengers in these seats. Seats behind a bulkhead also offer more legroom, but they don't have under-seat storage. Don't sit in the row in front of the emergency aisle or in front of a bulkhead, where seats may not recline.

Ask the airline whether a snack or meal is served on the flight. If you have dietary concerns, request special meals when booking. These can be vegetarian, low-cholesterol, or kosher, for example. It's a good idea to pack some healthful snacks and a small (plastic) bottle of water in your carry-on bag. On long flights, try to maintain a normal routine, to help fight jet

lag. At night, get some sleep. By day, eat light meals, drink water (not alcohol), and **move around the cabin** to stretch your legs. For additional jet-lag tips consult *Fodor's FYI: Travel Fit & Healthy* (available at bookstores everywhere).

All airlines flying to France from the United Kingdom, Ireland, continental Europe and North America prohibit smoking on flights.

FLYING TIMES

Flying time to Paris is 7½ hours from New York, 9 hours from Chicago, 11 hours from Los Angeles, and 1 hour from London. Flying time between Paris and Nice is one hour.

HOW TO COMPLAIN

If your baggage goes astray or your flight goes awry, complain right away. Most carriers require that you **file a claim immediately.** The Aviation Consumer Protection Division of the Department of Transportation publishes *Fly-Rights,* which discusses airlines and consumer issues and is available online. You can also find articles and information on mytravelrights.com, the Web site of the nonprofit Consumer Travel Rights Center.

7 Airline Complaints Aviation Consumer Protection Division ✉ U.S. Department of Transportation, Office of Aviation Enforcement and Proceedings, C-75, Room 4107, 400 7th St. SW, Washington, DC 20590 ☎ 202/366-2220 ⊕ airconsumer.ost.dot.gov. **Federal Aviation Administration Consumer Hotline** ✉ For inquiries: FAA, 800 Independence Ave. SW, Washington, DC 20591 ☎ 800/322-7873 ⊕ www.faa.gov.

RECONFIRMING

Check the status of your flight before you leave for the airport. You can do this on your carrier's Web site, by linking to a flight-status checker (many Web booking services offer these), or by calling your carrier or travel agent. Always confirm international flights at least 72 hours ahead of the scheduled departure time.

AIRPORTS

There are two major gateway airports to France, both just outside the capital: Orly, 16 km (10 mi) south of Paris, and Charles de Gaulle—also known as Roissy—26 km (16 mi) northeast of the city. Orly has two terminals: Orly Ouest (domestic flights) and Orly Sud (international, regular, and charter flights). Roissy has three terminals: Aérogare 1 (foreign flights), Aérogare 2 (Air France flights), and Aérogare T-3 (discount airlines and charter flights). Terminal information should be noted on your ticket. Terminals within each airport are connected with a free shuttle service, called the *navette*. At Roissy there's a TGV station (from Terminal 2), where you can connect to trains going all over the country. Many airlines have less frequent flights to Lyon, Nice, Marseille, Bordeaux, and Toulouse. Or you can fly to Paris and get a connecting flight to other destinations in France.

ℱ Airport Information Charles de Gaulle/Roissy ☎ 01-48-62-22-80 in English ⊕ www.adp.fr. Orly ☎ 01-49-75-15-15 ⊕ www.adp.fr.

AIRPORT TRANSFERS: PARIS

Charles de Gaulle/Roissy: From Charles de Gaulle airport, **the least expensive way to get into Paris is on the RER-B line,** the suburban express train, which runs from 5:45 AM to 11 PM daily. Each terminal has an exit where the free RER shuttle bus (a white-and-yellow bus with the letters ADP in gray) will pass every 7–15 minutes to take you on the short ride to the nearby RER station: Terminal 2A and Terminal 2C (Exit 8), Terminal 2B and Terminal 2D (Exit 6), Terminal 2E (Exit 2.06), Terminal 2F (Exit 2.08). Trains to central Paris (Les Halles, St-Michel, Luxembourg) depart every 15 minutes. The fare (including métro connection) is €7.85, and journey time is about 30 minutes.

The **Air France shuttle service** is a comfortable option to get to and from the city— you don't need to have flown the carrier to use this. Line 2 goes from the airport to Paris's Charles de Gaulle Étoile and Porte Maillot from 5:45 AM to 11 PM. It leaves every 15 minutes and costs €12, which you can pay on board. Passengers arriving in Terminal 1 need to take Exit 34; Terminals 2B and 2D, Exit 6; Terminals 2E and 2F, Exit 3. Line 4 goes to Montparnasse and the Gare de Lyon from 7 AM to 9 PM.

Buses run every 30 minutes and cost €12. Passengers arriving in Terminal 1 need to look for Exit 34, Terminals 2A and 2C need to take either Exit C2, Terminals 2B and 2D Exit B1, and Terminals 2E and 2F Exit 3.

Another option is to take **Roissybus,** operated by the Paris Transit Authority, which runs between Charles de Gaulle and the Opéra every 20 minutes from 6 AM to 11 PM; the cost is €8.30. The trip takes about 45 minutes in regular traffic, about 90 minutes in rush-hour traffic.

Taxis are your least desirable mode of transportation into the city. If you are traveling at peak tourist times, you may have to stand in a very long line with a lot of other disgruntled European travelers (most of whom smoke). Journey times, and as a consequence, prices, are therefore unpredictable. At best, the journey takes 30 minutes but it can take as long as one hour.

Airport Connection is the name of just one of a number of van services that serve both Charles de Gaulle and Orly airports. Prices are set so there are no surprises even if traffic is a snail-paced nightmare. To make a reservation, call or fax your flight details at least one week in advance to the shuttle company and an air-conditioned van with a bilingual chauffeur will be waiting for you upon your arrival. Note these shuttle vans pick up and drop off other passengers.

Orly: From Orly Airport **the most economical way to get into Paris is to take the RER-C or Orlyrail line;** catch the free shuttle bus from the terminal to the train station. Trains to Paris leave every 15 minutes. Passengers arriving in either the South or West Terminal need to use Exit G. The fare is €5.45, and journey time is about 35 minutes. Another option is to **take the monorail service, Orlyval,** which runs between the Antony RER-B station and Orly Airport daily every four to eight minutes from 6 AM to 11 PM. Passengers arriving in the South Terminal should look for Exit K, those arriving in the West terminal, Exit W. The fare to downtown Paris is €8.85.

You can also **take an Air France bus** from Orly to Les Invalides on the Left Bank and Montparnasse; these run every 15 minutes from 6 AM to 11 PM (you need not have flown on Air France to use this service). The fare is €8, and journey time is between 30 and 45 minutes, depending on traffic. Those of you arriving in Orly South need to look for Exit K; those arriving in Orly West, Exit D. The Paris Transit Authority's **Orlybus is yet another option**; buses leave every 15 minutes for the Denfert-Rochereau métro station; the cost is €5.80. You can economize using **Jet Bus,** which shuttles you from the airport to Line 7, métro Villejuif Louis Arragan station for under €5. It operates daily from 6 AM to 10 PM; those arriving in Orly South look for Exit H, Quai 2; those arriving via Orly West need to find Exit C.

⚑ Taxis & Shuttles Air France Bus ☎ 08-92-35-08-20 recorded information in English ⊕ www.cars-airfrance.com. **Airport Connection** ☎ 01-43-65-55-55 🖷 01-43-65-55-57 ⊕ www.airport-connection.com. **Paris Airports Service** ☎ 01-55-98-10-80 🖷 01-55-98-10-89 ⊕ www.parisairportservice.com. **RATP (including Roissybus, Orlybus, Orlyval)** ☎ 08-92-68-41-14, €.35 per minute ⊕ www.ratp.com.

DUTY-FREE SHOPPING

Duty-free shopping at French airports is no longer available for those traveling *within* the boundaries of the European Community. You can purchase whatever you want at airport stores, of course, but only travelers *leaving* European territory will benefit from the duty-free prices.

BARGE & YACHT TRAVEL

Canal and river trips are popular in France, particularly along the picturesque waterways in Brittany, Burgundy, and the Midi. For further information, contact a travel agent; ask for a "Tourisme Fluvial" brochure at any French tourist office; or get in touch with one of the companies that organize barge trips. It's also possible to rent a barge or crewed sailboat to travel around the coast of France, particularly along the Côte d'Azur.

⚑ Domestic Barge Companies En-Bateau ☎ 04-67-94-38-73 ⊕ http://en-bateau.com. **Maine Anjou Rivières** ✉ Le Moulin, 49220 Che-

nille-Change ☎ 02-41-95-10-83 ⊕ www.maine-anjou-rivieres.com.

⚑ International Barge Companies Abercrombie & Kent ✉ 1520 Kensington Rd., Oak Brook, IL 60521 ☎ 630/954-2944 or 800/323-7308 🖷 630/954-3324. **Étoile de Champagne** ✉ 88 Broad St., Boston, MA 02110 ☎ 800/280-1492 🖷 617/426-4689. **European Waterways** ✉ 140 E. 56th St., Suite 4C, New York, NY 10022 ☎ 212/688-9489 or 800/217-4447 🖷 212/688-3778 or 800/696-4554. **French Country Waterways** ✆ Box 2195, Duxbury, MA 02331 ☎ 781/934-2454 or 800/222-1236 🖷 781/934-9048. **KD River Cruises of Europe** ✉ 2500 Westchester Ave., Purchase, NY 10577 ☎ 914/696-3600 or 800/346-6525 🖷 914/696-0833 ⊕ www.rivercruises.com. **Kemwel's Premier Selections** ✉ 106 Calvert St., Harrison, NY 10528 ☎ 914/835-5555 or 800/234-4000 🖷 914/835-5449.

BEACHES

Along the miles of French coast you'll find broad-brimmed hats, parasols, and opaque sunglasses—their modesty and discretion charmingly contradictory in view of (and we mean full view of) the frankly bare flesh that bobbles up and down the same miles of seashore. And not just the famous *seins nus* (topless women), but the bellies of gastronome *pépés* (grandfathers) as well. Naked children crouch over sand châteaux, their unself-consciousness a reflection of their elders' own. For the French the summer beach holiday is a sacred ritual, a counterbalance to the winter ski trip.

To avoid the July and August stampede, **go in June or September.** Ironic as it may be, France's most famous coastline has the country's worst beaches: sand along the Côte d'Azur is in shorter supply than pebbles. By far the finest French beaches are those facing north (toward the Channel) and west (toward the Atlantic). Many are so vast that you can spread out even at the most popular resorts (like Biarritz, Royan, Dinard, or Le Touquet). Brittany's beaches are the most picturesque, though the water can be chilly, even in summer.

If you're planning to devote a lot of time to beaches and haven't tackled the French coast before, get to **know the distinction between private and public.** France's waterfront is carved up into private frontage, often roped off and advertised by color-coordinated awnings, parasols, and mattresses. These private beaches frequently offer full restaurant and bar service and rent mattresses, umbrellas, and lounge chairs by the day and half-day. Dressing rooms and showers are included; some even rent private cabanas. Prices can run from €10 a day to €20 or more. Interspersed between these commercial beaches is plenty of public space.

BIKE TRAVEL

The French are great bicycling enthusiasts—witness the Tour de France—and there are many good bicycling routes in France. For about €8 a day (€12 for a 10-speed touring bike) you can **rent a bike from one of 30 train stations throughout the country**; you need to show your passport and leave a deposit of €155 or a Visa or MasterCard. Mountain bikes (known as VTT, or vélos touts-terrains) can be rented from many shops, as well as from some train stations. Tourist offices supply details on the more than 200 local shops that rent bikes, and the SNCF has a brochure entitled the "Guide du Train et du Vélo," available at any train station. Bikes may be taken as accompanied luggage from any station in France; most trains in rural areas do not charge for bikes (but inquire at the SNCF ticket agencies about which ones do). Free bike space works on a first-come, first-served basis; you must take your bike to the designated compartment for loading yourself, so plan accordingly.

For information about good bike routes, contact the Fédération Française de Cyclotourisme. The yellow Michelin maps (1:200,000 scale) are fine for roads, but for off-road bicycling you may want to get one of the Institut Géographique National's detailed, large-scale maps. Try their blue series (1:25,000) or orange series (1:50,000).

As many travelers have learned, one of the most satisfying ways to explore the French countryside is by bike. Happily, there are many bike-tour companies that truly deliver on their gorgeous *itinéraires* year after year—two of the most successful are

VBT and Butterfield & Robinson. To get a peek into one such bike tour, see the CloseUp Box on biking in the Loire Valley in Chapter 3.

Bike Maps Institut Géographique National (IGN) ⊠ 107 rue La Boétie, 75008 Paris ☎ 01-42-56-06-68 ⊕ www.ign.fr.

Bike Rentals SNCF (⇨ Train Travel, *below*).

Bike Routes Fédération Française du Cyclisme ⊠ 5 rue de Rome, 93561 Rosny-sous-Bois ☎ 01-49-35-69-00 ⊕ www.ffc.fr.

Bike Tours Backroads ⊠ 801 Cedar St., Berkeley, CA 94710-1800 ☎ 510/527-1555 or 800/462-2848 🖷 510/527-1444 ⊕ www.backroads.com. **Butterfield & Robinson** ⊠ 70 Bond St., Toronto, Ontario M5B 1X3 ☎ 416/864-1354 or 800/678-1147 🖷 416/864-0541 ⊕ www.butterfield.com. **Discover France Biking** ⊠ 1603 E. Gardenia Ave., Phoenix, AZ 85020 ☎ 800/960-2221 🖷 602/944-5934 ⊕ www.discoverfrance.com. **Europeds** ⊠ 761 Lighthouse Ave., Monterey, CA 93940 ☎ 415/388-2853 🖷 415/388-3290 ⊕ www.europeds.com. **VBT (Vermont Biking Tours)** ✆ Box 711, Bristol, VT 05443 ☎ 800/245-3868 ⊕ www.vbt.com.

BIKES IN FLIGHT

Most airlines accommodate bikes as luggage, provided they are dismantled and boxed; check with individual airlines about packing requirements. Some airlines sell bike boxes, which are often free at bike shops, for about $20 (bike bags can be considerably more expensive). International travelers often can substitute a bike for a piece of checked luggage at no charge; otherwise, the cost is about $100. Most U.S. and Canadian airlines charge $40–$80 each way.

BOAT & FERRY TRAVEL

BETWEEN THE U.K. & FRANCE

A number of ferry and hovercraft routes link the United Kingdom and France. Driving distances from the French ports to Paris are as follows: from Calais, 290 km (180 mi); from Boulogne, 243 km (151 mi); from Dieppe, 193 km (120 mi); from Dunkerque, 257 km (160 mi). The fastest routes to Paris from each port are via the N43, A26, and A1 from Calais and the Channel Tunnel; via the N1 from Boulogne; via the N15 from Le Havre; via the D915 and N1 from Dieppe; and via the A25 and A1 from Dunkerque.

🚢 Dover–Calais **Hoverspeed** ✉ International Hoverport, Marine Parade, Dover, Kent CT17 9TG ☎ 0870/460-7157 ⊕ www.hoverspeed.fr operates up to 15 crossings a day by a one-hour fast ferry or a two-hour ferry. **P&O European Ferries** ✉ Channel House, Channel View Rd., Dover, Kent CT17 9TJ ☎ 0870/598-0333 ⊕ www.poportsmouth.com has up to 3 sailings a day; the crossing takes about 75 minutes. **Seafrance** ✉ Eastern Docks, Dover, Kent CT16 1JA ☎ 0870/5711-71 ⊕ www.seafrance.net operates up to 15 sailings a day; the crossing takes about 90 minutes.

🚢 Portsmouth–Le Havre **P&O European Ferries** (⇨ Dover–Calais) has up to three sailings a day, and the crossing takes 5½ hours by day, 7½ by night.

FARES & SCHEDULES

Note that sample fares are difficult to assess because of the number of variables involved, including destination, season, and number of people traveling. Sample fare (high season): Dover–Calais, round-trip (within five days), €125–€185 for up to five adults plus car (this price doubles if the visit exceeds five days). Schedules and tickets are available at any travel agency throughout France or via the Internet.

BUSINESS HOURS

BANKS & OFFICES

Generally, **banks are open weekdays from 9 AM to 5 PM** (note that the Banque de France closes at 3:30 PM), and some banks are also open on Saturday. Most take a one-hour, or even a 90-minute, lunch break, except for those in Paris. In general, government offices and businesses are open 9 AM–5 PM. For information about post-office hours, *see* Mail & Shipping, *below.*

GAS STATIONS

Gas stations in cities and towns are generally open 8 AM–8 PM, Monday–Saturday, with the exception of those stations located in the major *portes,* or entryways into each city, which are open 24 hours a day, seven days a week, as are those along the highways.

MUSEUMS & SIGHTS

The usual opening times for museums and other sights are from 9:30 AM to 5 PM or 6 PM. Many close for lunch (noon–2 PM) outside Paris. Most are closed one day a week (generally Monday or Tuesday) and on national holidays: **check museum hours before you go.** National museums are free to the public the first Sunday of every month.

PHARMACIES

Pharmacies are generally open Monday–Saturday 8:30 AM–8 PM; on the door of every pharmacy is a list of those closest that are open Sunday or 24 hours.

SHOPS

Large stores in big towns are open from 9 AM or 9:30 AM until 7 PM or 8 PM. Smaller shops often open earlier (8 AM) and close later (8 PM) but take a lengthy lunch break (1 PM–4 PM), particularly in the south of France. Corner groceries frequently stay open until around 10 PM. Some Paris stores are beginning to stay open on Sunday, although it's still uncommon.

BUS TRAVEL

France's excellent train service means that long-distance buses are rare; **regional buses are found mainly where train service is spotty.** Excursions and bus tours are organized by the SNCF and other tour companies. Ask for a brochure at any major travel agent or contact the French Tourism Office (⇨ Visitor Information). Bus tours from the United Kingdom generally depart from London for Paris, the Atlantic Coast, Chamonix and the Alps, Grenoble, Lyon, and the Côte d'Azur. Note that **reservations are necessary on most long-distance buses.**

There's no central bus network servicing France because train service here is considered the best in the world, and if you are traveling off-season or have researched the best rates, train service can be just as economical as bus travel, if not more so. What a bus service saves in money, it often loses in both comfort and time. The largest international operator is Eurolines France, whose main terminal is in the Parisian suburb of Bagnolet (a half-hour métro ride from central Paris, at the end of métro Line 3). Eurolines runs many international routes to over 37 European destinations, including a route from London to Paris, usually departing at 8:30 AM, arriving at

5:30 PM; noon, arriving at 9 PM; and 9:30 PM, arriving at 7:30 AM. Fares are €68 round-trip (under-25 youth pass €57). Other Eurolines routes include: Amsterdam (7 hours, €70); Barcelona (15 hours, €170); and Berlin (10 hours, €150). There are also international-only arrivals and departures from Avignon, Bordeaux, Lille, Lyon, Toulouse, and Tours. If you are planning a grand tour, there are economical passes to be had—15-day passes run €285, a 30-day pass will cost €425. These passes offer unlimited coach travel to all Eurolines European destinations. Local bus information to the relatively rare rural areas where trains do not have access can be obtained from the SNCF.

🚩 **From the U.K. Eurolines** ✉ 28 av. Général-de-Gaulle, Bagnolet ☎ 08-36-69-52-52 in France, 020/7730-3499 in U.K. ⊕ www.eurolines.fr.

🚩 **Within France Paris Vision** ✉ 1 rue d'Auber, 75009 Paris ☎ 01-47-42-27-40 ⊕ www.parisvision.com. **SNCF** ✉ 88 rue St-Lazare, 75009 Paris ☎ 08-36-35-35-39 in English ⊕ www.sncf.fr.

CAMERAS & PHOTOGRAPHY

If you need to get your camera repaired, your best bet in Paris and other major cities is to go to FNAC (a book, record, and electronics store). You should be able to find a small camera repair shop in most small towns. Note that you may have to wait some time to get your camera fixed. The *Kodak Guide to Shooting Great Travel Pictures* (available at bookstores everywhere) is loaded with tips.

🚩 **Photo Help Kodak Information Center** ☎ 800/242-2424 ⊕ www.kodak.com.

EQUIPMENT PRECAUTIONS

Don't pack film or equipment in checked luggage, where it is much more susceptible to damage. X-ray machines used to view checked luggage are extremely powerful and therefore are likely to ruin your film. Try to ask for hand inspection of film, which becomes clouded after repeated exposure to airport X-ray machines, and keep videotapes and computer disks away from metal detectors. Always keep film, tape, and computer disks out of the sun. Carry an extra supply of batteries, and be prepared to turn on your camera,

camcorder, or laptop to prove to airport security personnel that the device is real.

FILM & DEVELOPING

In Paris and most major cities, the easiest place to get film developed and printed is a FNAC store. If you're in a smaller town and want your film developed, look for a store with a Kodak sign outside its door. Keep in mind that **it's expensive to develop and print film in France**—around $20 per 36-exposure roll.

VIDEOS

France uses SECAM, which is a different system from that used either in the United States (NTSC) or in the United Kingdom (PAL). Therefore, you won't be able to play the videotapes you bring from home on French equipment. In addition, you probably won't be able to use SECAM videotapes in your camera, so it's a good idea to **bring extra videotapes from home.**

CAR RENTAL

Though renting a car in France is expensive—about twice as much as in the United States—as is gas (€.90–€1.25 per liter), it can pay off if you're traveling with two or more people. In addition, renting a car gives you the freedom that trains cannot. Rates in Paris begin at about €35 a day and €200 per week for an economy car with air-conditioning, manual transmission, and unlimited mileage. The price doesn't usually take into account the 19.6% V.A.T. tax or, if you pick it up from the airport, the airport tax. You won't need a car in the capital, so **wait to pick up your rental until the day you leave Paris.**

🚩 **Major Agencies Alamo** ☎ 800/522-9696 ⊕ www.alamo.com. **Avis** ☎ 800/331-1084, 800/879-2847 in Canada, 0870/606-0100 in U.K., 02/9353-9000 in Australia, 09/526-2847 in New Zealand ⊕ www.avis.com. **Budget** ☎ 800/527-0700, 0870/156-5656 in U.K. ⊕ www.budget.com. **Dollar** ☎ 800/800-6000, 0800/085-4578 in U.K. ⊕ www.dollar.com. **Hertz** ☎ 800/654-3001, 800/263-0600 in Canada, 0870/844-8844 in U.K., 02/9669-2444 in Australia, 09/256-8690 in New Zealand ⊕ www.hertz.com. **National Car Rental** ☎ 800/227-7368, 0870/600-6666 in U.K. ⊕ www.nationalcar.com.

CUTTING COSTS

Renting a car through local French agencies has a number of serious disadvantages, notably price, as they simply cannot compete with the larger international companies. These giants combine bilingual service, the security of name recognition, extensive services (such as 24-hour hotlines), and automatic vehicles. However, Rent-a-Car Prestige can be useful if you are interested in luxury cars (convertible BMWs) or large family vans (Renault Espace, for example). Note that the big international agencies like Hertz and Avis offer better prices to those clients who make reservations in their home countries before they arrive in France; if you need to rent a car while in France, it even pays to call home and have a friend take care of it for you from there. So, to get the best deal, **reserve a car before you leave home.**

For a good deal, book through a travel agent who will shop around. Remember to ask about required deposits, cancellation penalties, and drop-off charges if you're planning to pick up the car in one city and leave it in another. If you're traveling during a holiday period, also make sure that a confirmed reservation guarantees you a car.

Do look into wholesalers, companies that do not own fleets but rent in bulk from those that do and often offer better rates than traditional car-rental operations. Prices are best during off-peak periods. Rentals booked through wholesalers often must be paid for before you leave home.

Local Agencies Autorent ✉ 98 bd. de la Convention, Montparnasse, 75015 Paris ☎ 01-45-54-22-45. **Easycar** ⊕ www.easycar.net. **Europcar** ☎ 08-03-35-23-52 ⊕ www.europcar.fr. **Locabest** ✉ 104 bd. Magenta, République, 75010 Paris ☎ 01-44-72-08-05 ⊕ www.locabest.fr/. **Rent-a-Car** ✉ 79 rue de Bercy, Bercy/Tolbiac, 75012 Paris ☎ 01-43-45-98-99 ⊕ www.rentacar.fr/.

Wholesalers Auto Europe ☎ 207/842-2000 or 800/223-5555 🖷 207/842-2222 ⊕ www.autoeurope.com. **Destination Europe Resources** (DER) ✉ 9501 W. Devon Ave., Rosemont, IL 60018 ☎ 800/782-2424 🖷 800/282-7474. **Europe by Car** ☎ 212/581-3040 or 800/223-1516 🖷 207/842-2124

or 866/726-6726 ⊕ www.europebycar.com. **Kemwel** ☎ 877/820-0668 or 800/678-0678 🖷 207/842-2147 ⊕ www.kemwel.com.

INSURANCE

When driving a rented car you are generally responsible for any damage to or loss of the vehicle. Collision policies that car-rental companies sell for European rentals typically do not cover stolen vehicles. Before you rent—and purchase collision or theft coverage—see what coverage you already have under the terms of your personal auto-insurance policy and credit cards.

REQUIREMENTS & RESTRICTIONS

In France you must be over 18 to rent a car, though rates may be higher if you're under 25. Foreign drivers should have an international driving permit (available at any U.S. branch of the AAA) although this is not required for Canadian and European Union nationals (*see* Rules of the Road *in* Car Travel, *below*).

SURCHARGES

Before you pick up a car in one city and leave it in another, ask about drop-off charges or one-way service fees, which can be substantial. Also inquire about early-return policies; some rental agencies charge extra if you return the car before the time specified in your contract, while others give you a refund for the days not used. To avoid a hefty refueling fee, fill the tank just before you turn in the car, but be aware that gas stations near the rental outlet may overcharge. It's almost never a deal to buy the tank of gas that's in the car when you rent it; the understanding is that you'll return it empty, but some fuel usually remains.

CAR TRAVEL

An unlimited third-party liability insurance policy is compulsory for all automobiles driven in France and will be issued to you automatically as part of your rental agreement. An International Driver's Permit is valid for temporary, not long-term use—less than 90 days—and is not required but can prove useful in emergencies such as traffic violations or auto accidents, particularly when a foreign language is involved. Drivers in France must be over 18 years old to drive, but there is no top age limit (if your faculties are intact).

EMERGENCY SERVICES

If your car breaks down on an expressway, **go to a roadside emergency telephone.** If you have a breakdown anywhere else, find the nearest garage or contact the police. There are also 24-hour assistance hotlines valid throughout France (available through rental agencies and supplied to you when you rent the car), but do not hesitate to call the police in case of any roadside emergency, for they are quick and reliable, and the phone call is free. There are special phones just for this purpose on all highways; you'll see them every few kilometers and they are picked out in bright orange–just pick up the phone and dial 17. The French equivalent of the AAA is the Club Automobile de l'Ile de France, but it only takes care of its members and is of little use to international travelers.
🚓 Police ☎ 17.

FROM THE U.K.

If you're driving from the United Kingdom to the Continent, you have a choice of either the Channel Tunnel or ferry services. Reservations are essential at peak times and are always a good idea, especially when going via the Chunnel. Cars don't drive in the Chunnel but are loaded onto trains (⇨ Boat & Ferry Travel, *above, and* Channel Tunnel & Train Travel, *below*).

GASOLINE

Gas is expensive, especially on expressways and in rural areas. When possible, **buy gas before you get on the expressway** and keep an eye on pump prices as you go. These vary enormously—anything from €.90 to €1.25 per liter. The cheapest gas can be found at *hypermarchés* (large supermarkets). Credit cards are accepted in every gas station. It's possible to go for miles in the country without passing a gas station—**don't let your tank get too low in rural areas.**

PARKING

Parking is a nightmare in Paris and often difficult in other large towns. Meters and ticket machines (pay and display) are common and work with parking cards (*cartes de stationnements*). Parking cards work like credit cards in the parking meters and come in three denominations: €10, €20, and €30. Since parking in Paris runs a whopping €2 per hour, you should invest in the €30 option if you can. Parking cards are available at any café posting the red TABAC sign. Insert your card into the nearest meter, choose the approximate amount of time you expect to stay, and you'll receive a green receipt, which must be clearly visible to the meter patrol; place it on the dashboard on the inside of the front window on the passenger side.

Parking is free on Sunday, national holidays, and in certain residential areas in August. Parking meters showing a dense yellow circle indicate a free parking zone during the month of August; if you do not see the circle, pay. Parking tickets are expensive, and there's no shortage of the blue-uniformed parking police. Parking lots, indicated by a blue sign with a white P, are usually underground and are generally expensive. In smaller towns, parking may be permitted on one side of the street only—alternating every two weeks—so pay attention to signs. In France, illegally parked cars are likely to be impounded, especially those blocking entrances or fire exits.

ROADS

The French road network is very extensive: 8,000 km of expressway and 808,000 km of main roads. For the fastest roads between two points, **look for roads marked A for autoroute.** A *péage* (toll) must be paid on most expressways: the rate varies but can be steep. The N (*route nationale*) roads—which are sometimes divided highways—and D (*route départementale*) roads are usually also wide and fast. Don't be daunted by smaller (C and V) roads, either.

There are excellent links between Paris and most French cities, but poor ones between the provinces (the principal exceptions are A26 from Calais to Reims, A62 between Bordeaux and Toulouse, and A9/A8 the length of the Mediterranean coast).

Though routes are numbered, **the French generally guide themselves from city to city and town to town by destination name.** When reading a map, keep one eye on the next big city toward your destination as well as the next small town; most snap decisions will have to be based on town names, not road numbers.

The major ring road encircling Paris is called the *périférique*, with the *périférique intérieur* going counterclockwise around the city, and the *périférique extérieur*, or the outside ring, going clockwise. Up to five lanes wide, the périférique is a major highway from which *portes* (gates) connect Paris to the major highways of France. The names of these highways function on the same principle as the métro, with the final destination as the determining point in the direction you must take. For instance, heading north, look for Porte de la Chapelle (direction Lille and Charles de Gaulle Airport); east, for Porte de Bagnolet (direction Metz and Nancy); south, for Porte d'Orléans (direction Lyon and Bordeaux); and west, for Porte d'Auteuil (direction Rouen and Chartres) or Porte de St-Cloud. Other portes include Porte de la Villette; Porte de Pantin; Porte de Bercy (A4 to Reims); Porte d'Italie; and Porte de Maillot (A14 to Rouen).

The major expressways into Paris are the A1, from the north/Great Britain; the A13, from Rouen, Normandy, and northwestern France; the A6, from Lyon, the French Alps, the Riviera, and Italy; the A10, from France's southwest and the Pyrénées; and the A4, from Nancy and Strasbourg in eastern France.

ROAD MAPS

If you plan on driving through France, **get a Michelin or IGN map** for each region you'll be visiting. The maps are available from most bookshops, gas stations, and magazine stores.

RULES OF THE ROAD

Drive on the right and **yield to drivers coming from streets to the right.** However, this rule does not necessarily apply at traffic circles, where you should watch out for just about everyone. You must **wear your seat belt,** and children under 12 may not travel in the front seat. Speed limits are 130 kph (80 mph) on expressways (*autoroutes*), 110 kph (70 mph) on divided highways (*routes nationales*), 90 kph (55 mph) on other roads (*routes*), 50 kph (30 mph) in cities and towns (*villes et villages*). French drivers break these limits, and police dish out hefty on-the-spot fines with equal abandon. Do not expect to find traffic lights in the center of the road, as French lights are usually on the right- and left-hand sides.

If you are driving through France during the traditional holiday months (Christmas, Easter, July–September) you might be asked to pull over by the Police National at busy intersections. You will have to show your papers (*papiers*)—including car insurance—and submit to an "alcotest" (you guessed it, a Breathalyzer test). The rules in France have become stringent due to the high incidence of accidents on the roads; anything above 0.5 grams of alcohol in the blood, which, according to your size, could simply mean two to three glasses of good wine, and you are over the limit. This does not necessarily mean a night in the clinker, but your driving privileges in France will be revoked on the spot and you will pay a hefty fine. Don't drink and drive, even if you're just crossing town to the sleepy little inn on the river. Local police are notorious for their vigilance.

Some important traffic terms and signs to note: SORTIE (exit); SENS UNIQUE (one-way); STATIONNEMENT INTERDITE (no parking); and IMPASSE (dead end). Blue rectangular signs indicate a highway; green rectangular signs indicate a major direction; triangles carry illustrations of a particular traffic hazard; speed limits are indicated in a circle with the maximum limit circled in red.

🚗 **Auto Clubs American Automobile Association** ☎ 800/564-6222 ⊕ www.aaany.com/travel/travel services/IDPform2.asp?. **Australian Automobile Association** ☎ 02/6247-7311. **Canadian Automobile Association (CAA)** ☎ 613/247-0117. **New Zealand Automobile Association** ☎ 09/377-4660. **Royal Automobile Club (RAC)** ☎ 0990/722-722 for membership, 0345/121-345 for insurance. **U.K. Automobile Association (AA)** ☎ 0990/500-600.

THE CHANNEL TUNNEL

Short of flying, taking the Eurostar train through the "Chunnel" is the fastest way to cross the English Channel: 3 hours from

London's central Waterloo Station to Paris's central Gare du Nord, 35 minutes from Folkestone to Calais, and 60 minutes from motorway to motorway. There's a vast range of prices for Eurostar—round-trip tickets range from €520 for first class to €105 for second class depending on when you travel. It's a good idea to **make a reservation if you're traveling with your car on a Chunnel train**; cars without reservations, if they can get on at all, are charged 20% extra.

🚩 **Car Transport Eurotunnel** ☎ 0870/535-3535 in U.K., 070/223210 in Belgium, 03-21-00-61-00 in France ⊕ www.eurotunnel.com. **French Motorail/ Rail Europe** ☎ 800/942-4866 or 800/274-8724 ⊕ www.raileurope.co.uk/frenchmotorail.

🚩 **Passenger Service Eurostar** ☎ 1233/617575, 0870/518-6186 in U.K. ⊕ www.eurostar.co.uk. **Rail Europe** ☎ 800/942-4866 or 800/274-8724, 0870/ 584-8848 U.K. inquiries and credit-card bookings ⊕ www.raileurope.com.

CHILDREN IN FRANCE

Be sure to plan ahead and **involve your youngsters** as you outline your trip. When packing, include things to keep them busy en route. On sightseeing days try to schedule activities of special interest to your children.

Getting around Paris and other major cities with a stroller can be a challenge, so **take your lightest folding stroller.** Many museums require you to check strollers at the entrance. There are some, like the Louvre in Paris, that will permit you to use one but, chances are, you'll be spending an inordinate amount of time maneuvering through crowds, waiting for one of the tiny elevators, and wishing you brought along a baby backpack or kangaroo pouch. In Paris few métro stations have escalators, so you're better off taking the bus in off-peak hours. *Fodor's Around Paris with Kids* (available in bookstores everywhere) can help you plan your days together.

If you are renting a car, don't forget to arrange for a car seat when you reserve. Playgrounds can be found off many highways. Most rest-stop bathrooms have changing tables. For general advice about traveling with children, consult *Fodor's*

FYI: Travel with Your Baby (available in bookstores everywhere).

🚩 **Family-Friendly Tour Operators Grandtravel** ✉ 6900 Wisconsin Ave., Suite 706, Chevy Chase, MD 20815 ☎ 301/986-0790 or 800/247-7651 for people traveling with grandchildren ages 7-17. **Families Welcome!/Great Destinations** ✉ 92 N. Main St., Ashland, OR 97520 ☎ 541/482-6121 or 800/326-0724 🖷 541/482-0660. **A Touch of France** ✉ 660 King Rd., Fords, NJ 08863 ☎ 800/738-5240.

🚩 **Local Information Paris Office of Tourism** ✉ 25 rue des Pyramides, 75002 Paris ☎ 08-92-68-30-00 ⊕ www.parisinfo.com.

EATING & DRINKING

The best restaurants in France do not welcome small children; except for the traditional family Sunday-noon dinner, fine dining is considered an adult pastime. Aim for more modest *auberges* (country inns), and if there's a choice, **consider having your meal in the café or brasserie** rather than in the linen-and-goblet-filled dining room. In cities, brasseries and cafés offer a casual option and the flexible meal times that children often require. If you get desperate, France has its share of McDonald's, Pizza Huts, and other fast-food restaurants. Very few mainstream restaurants have high chairs, but some do serve children's portions (*menu enfant*), usually spaghetti or the ubiquitous *steak-frites*, a mountain of fries with a thin steak or fat patty of ground beef, usually cooked extremely rare. If you're queasy about this, ask for it *bien cuit* (well done) or *à point* (medium). If your children go to bed early, **opt for your hot meal at noon** (there are cheaper prix-fixe menus then, too) and consider having a sandwich, quiche, a *croque monsieur* (a grilled ham-and-cheese sandwich), or pizza at a café or brasserie in the early evening; full-service restaurants usually do not serve before 7 PM.

FLYING

If your children are two or older, ask about children's airfares. As a general rule, infants under two not occupying a seat fly at greatly reduced fares or even for free. But if you want to guarantee a seat for an infant, you have to pay full fare. Consider flying during off-peak days and times; most airlines will grant an infant a seat without a ticket if there are available seats. When booking, confirm carry-on allowances if you're traveling with infants. In general, for babies charged 10% to 50% of the adult fare you are allowed one carry-on bag and a collapsible stroller; if the flight is full, the stroller may have to be checked or you may be limited to less.

Experts agree that it's a good idea to use safety seats aloft for children weighing less than 40 pounds. Airlines set their own policies: if you use a safety seat, U.S. carriers usually require that the child be ticketed, even if he or she is young enough to ride free, because the seats must be strapped into regular seats. And even if you pay the full adult fare for the seat, it may be worth it, especially on longer trips. Do **check your airline's policy about using safety seats during takeoff and landing.** Safety seats are not allowed everywhere in the plane, so get your seat assignments as early as possible.

When reserving, request children's meals or a freestanding bassinet (not available at all airlines) if you need them. But note that bulkhead seats, where you must sit to use the bassinet, may lack an overhead bin or storage space on the floor.

LODGING
If you're planning to stay in hotels, it's essential to book ahead. Many small hotels have only one or two rooms that sleep four (triples are much more common); if there are more of you, you'll have to book two neighboring rooms or a suite. Larger hotels often provide cribs free to guests with young children, which is not usually the case at inns and smaller hotels. Older children are charged at adult rates unless the hotel offers a special family rate. Be sure to **ask about the cutoff age for children's discounts** when booking.

Some hotel chains offer discounts for families and programs for children. Club Med is particularly family friendly: it has a "Baby Club" (from age four months) at its resort in Chamonix, and "Mini Clubs" (for ages 4–6 or 4–8, depending on the resort) and "Kids Clubs" (for ages eight and up during school holidays) at all its resort villages in France except at Val d'Isère.

Some clubs are only French-speaking. The Novotel chain allows up to two children under 15 to stay free in their parents' room. Sofitel hotels offer a free second room for children during July and August and over the Christmas period.

Another option: **consider a gîte, a short-term apartment or house rental,** or a home exchange (⇨ Lodging, *below*).
🚩 **Best Choices Club Med** ⌂ 40 W. 57th St., New York, NY 10019 ☎ 888/932-2582 ⊕ www.clubmed. com. **Novotel** ☎ 800/221-4542 ⊕ www.novotel. com. **Sofitel** ☎ 800/221-4542 ⊕ www.sofitel.com.

SIGHTS & ATTRACTIONS
Places that are especially appealing to children are indicated by a rubber-duckie icon (🦆) in the margin. There are plenty of diversions for the young, and **almost all museums and movie theaters have discounted rates.**

SUPPLIES & EQUIPMENT
Supermarkets carry several major brands of diapers (*couches*), universally referred to as Pampers (pawm-*paires*). Junior sizes are hard to come by, as the French toilet-train early. Baby formula is available in grocery stores or pharmacies. There are two types of formulas: *lait prémier age,* for infants 0–4 months, and *lait deuxieme age,* for four months or older. French formulas come in powder form and need to be mixed with a pure, low-mineral-content bottled water such as Evian or Volvic (the French *never* mix baby formula with tap water). American formulas are not available in France. If you're looking for treats for your little ones, some items to keep in mind are: *coloriage* (coloring books), *crayons de couleur* (crayons), *pate à modeler* (modeling clay), and *feutres* (magic markers).

TRANSPORTATION
SNCF allows children under four to travel free (provided they don't occupy a seat) or for €8 for a seat, and children 4–12 to travel at half fare with an accompanying adult. The Carte "Enfant Plus" (€63) allows children under 12 and as many as four accompanying adults to make an unlimited number of trips at as much as half the cost (though you are only guaranteed

at least 25% off on all trains). This card is worth your while only if you are planning on traveling extensively in France—it is valid for one year.

When traveling by train with children, you may want to travel first class, as there is more space and it's considerably calmer and cleaner than second-class space. Another option is to request an "*espace famille*" ("family space") in second class (when you make reservations), which consists of two sets of seats facing each other. Whatever you do, double—no, *triple*—check your train tickets to make sure your seats are together in a no-smoking train; the SNCF are notorious for bungling the details. For more information, *see* Train Travel, *below*.

COMPUTERS ON THE ROAD

If you use a major Internet provider, getting online in France shouldn't be difficult. Most hotels have in-room modem lines or wireless Internet access. You may, however, need an adapter for your computer for the European-style plugs (⇨ Electricity, *below*). As always, if you're traveling with a laptop, carry a spare battery and adapter. **Never plug your computer into any socket before asking about surge protection.** IBM sells a pen-size modem tester that plugs into a telephone jack to check if the line is safe to use.

🛛 Access Numbers in Paris **AOL**
☎ 01-41-45-81-00. **Compuserve** ☎ 08-03-00-60-00, 08-03-00-80-00, or 08-03-00-90-00.

CONSUMER PROTECTION

Whether you're shopping for gifts or purchasing travel services, **pay with a major credit card** whenever possible, so you can cancel payment or get reimbursed if there's a problem (and you can provide documentation). If you're doing business with a particular company for the first time, contact your local Better Business Bureau and the attorney general's offices in your state and (for U.S. businesses) the company's home state as well. Have any complaints been filed? Finally, if you're buying a package or tour, always consider travel insurance that includes default coverage (⇨ Insurance).
🛛 BBBs **Council of Better Business Bureaus** ✉ 4200 Wilson Blvd., Suite 800, Arlington,

VA 22203 ☎ 703/276-0100 🖷 703/525-8277 ⊕ www.bbb.org.

CUSTOMS & DUTIES

When shopping abroad, keep receipts for all purchases. Upon reentering the country, **be ready to show customs officials what you've bought.** Pack purchases together in an easily accessible place. If you think a duty is incorrect, appeal the assessment. If you object to the way your clearance was handled, note the inspector's badge number. In either case, first ask to see a supervisor. If the problem isn't resolved, write to the appropriate authorities, beginning with the port director at your point of entry.

IN AUSTRALIA

Australian residents who are 18 or older may bring home A$900 worth of souvenirs and gifts (including jewelry), 250 cigarettes or 250 grams of cigars or other tobacco products, and 2.25 liters of alcohol (including wine, beer, and spirits). Residents under 18 may bring back A$450 worth of goods. If any of these individual allowances are exceeded, you must pay duty for the entire amount (of the group of products in which the allowance was exceeded). Members of the same family traveling together may pool their allowances. Prohibited items include meat products. Seeds, plants, and fruits need to be declared upon arrival.
🛛 **Australian Customs Service** 🖅 Locked Bag 3000, Sydney International Airport, Sydney, NSW 2020 ☎ 02/6275-6666 or 1300/363-263, 02/8334-7444 or 1800/020-504 quarantine-inquiry line 🖷 02/8339-6714 ⊕ www.customs.gov.au.

IN CANADA

Canadian residents who have been out of Canada for at least seven days may bring in C$750 worth of goods duty-free. If you've been away fewer than seven days but more than 48 hours, the duty-free allowance drops to C$200. If your trip lasts 24 to 48 hours, the allowance is C$50; if the goods are worth more than C$50, you must pay full duty on all of the goods. You may not pool allowances with family members. Goods claimed under the C$750 exemption may follow you by mail; those claimed under the lesser exemptions must accompany you. Alcohol and tobacco products may be included in the seven-day and 48-hour exemptions but not in the 24-hour exemption. If you meet the age requirements of the province or territory through which you reenter Canada, you may bring in, duty-free, 1.5 liters of wine *or* 1.14 liters (40 imperial ounces) of liquor *or* 24 12-ounce cans or bottles of beer or ale. Also, if you meet the local age requirement for tobacco products, you may bring in, duty-free, 200 cigarettes and 50 cigars. Check ahead of time with the Canada Border Services Agency or the Department of Agriculture for policies regarding meat products, seeds, plants, and fruits.

You may send an unlimited number of gifts (only one gift per recipient, however) worth up to C$60 each duty-free to Canada. Label the package UNSOLICITED GIFT—VALUE UNDER $60. Alcohol and tobacco are excluded.

▪ Canada Customs and Revenue Agency ✉ 2265 St. Laurent Blvd., Ottawa, Ontario K1G 4K3 ☎ 800/461-9999 in Canada, 204/983-3500, 506/636-5064 ⊕ www.ccra.gc.ca.

IN FRANCE

There are two levels of duty-free allowance for travelers entering France: one for goods obtained (tax paid) within another European Union (EU) country and the other for goods obtained anywhere outside the EU or for goods purchased in a duty-free shop within the EU.

In the first category, you may import duty-free: 300 cigarettes or 150 cigarillos or 75 cigars or 400 grams of tobacco; 5 liters of table wine and (1) 1½ liters of alcohol over 22% volume (most spirits), (2) 3 liters of alcohol under 22% by volume (fortified or sparkling wine), or (3) 3 more liters of table wine, 90 milliliters of perfume, 375 milliliters of toilet water, and other goods to the value of €365 (€95 for those under 15).

In the second category, you may import duty-free: 200 cigarettes or 100 cigarillos or 50 cigars or 250 grams of tobacco (these allowances are doubled if you live outside Europe); 2 liters of wine and (1) 1 liter of alcohol over 22% volume (most

spirits), (2) 2 liters of alcohol under 22% volume (fortified or sparkling wine), or (3) 2 more liters of table wine, 60 milliliters of perfume, 250 milliliters of toilet water, and other goods to the value of €45 (€25 for those under 15).

▪ Direction des Douanes ✉ 16 rue Yves Toudic, 10ᵉ Paris ☎ 01-40-40-39-00 ⊕ www.douane.gouv.fr/.

IN NEW ZEALAND

All homeward-bound residents may bring back NZ$700 worth of souvenirs and gifts; passengers may not pool their allowances, and children can claim only the concession on goods intended for their own use. For those 17 or older, the duty-free allowance also includes 4.5 liters of wine or beer; one 1,125-ml bottle of spirits; and either 200 cigarettes, 250 grams of tobacco, 50 cigars, *or* a combination of the three up to 250 grams. Meat products, seeds, plants, and fruits must be declared upon arrival to the Agricultural Services Department.

▪ New Zealand Customs ✉ Head office: The Customhouse, 17–21 Whitmore St., Box 2218, Wellington ☎ 09/300-5399 or 0800/428-786 ⊕ www.customs.govt.nz.

IN THE U.K.

If you are a U.K. resident and your journey was wholly within the European Union, you probably won't have to pass through customs when you return to the United Kingdom. If you plan to bring back large quantities of alcohol or tobacco, check EU limits beforehand. In most cases, if you bring back more than 200 cigars, 3,200 cigarettes, 400 cigarillos, 10 liters of spirits, 110 liters of beer, 20 liters of fortified wine, and/or 90 liters of wine, you have to declare the goods upon return. Prohibited items include unpasteurized milk, regardless of country of origin.

▪ HM Customs and Excise ✉ Portcullis House, 21 Cowbridge Rd. E, Cardiff CF11 9SS ☎ 0845/010-9000, 0208/929-0152 advice service, 0208/929-6731, 0208/910-3602 complaints ⊕ www.hmce.gov.uk.

IN THE U.S.

U.S. residents who have been out of the country for at least 48 hours may bring home, for personal use, $800 worth of foreign goods duty-free, as long as they haven't used the $800 allowance or any part of it in the past 30 days. This exemption may include 1 liter of alcohol (for travelers 21 and older), 200 cigarettes, and 100 non-Cuban cigars. Family members from the same household who are traveling together may pool their $800 personal exemptions. For fewer than 48 hours, the duty-free allowance drops to $200, which may include 50 cigarettes, 10 non-Cuban cigars, and 150 ml of alcohol (or 150 ml of perfume containing alcohol). The $200 allowance cannot be combined with other individuals' exemptions, and if you exceed it, the full value of all the goods will be taxed. Antiques, which U.S. Customs and Border Protection defines as objects more than 100 years old, enter duty-free, as do original works of art done entirely by hand, including paintings, drawings, and sculptures. This doesn't apply to folk art or handicrafts, which are in general dutiable.

You may also send packages home duty-free, with a limit of one parcel per addressee per day (except alcohol or tobacco products or perfume worth more than $5). You can mail up to $200 worth of goods for personal use; label the package PERSONAL USE and attach a list of its contents and their retail value. If the package contains your used personal belongings, mark it AMERICAN GOODS RETURNED to avoid paying duties. You may send up to $100 worth of goods as a gift; mark the package UNSOLICITED GIFT. Mailed items do not affect your duty-free allowance on your return.

To avoid paying duty on foreign-made high-ticket items you already own and will take on your trip, register them with Customs before you leave the country. Consider filing a Certificate of Registration for laptops, cameras, watches, and other digital devices identified with serial numbers or other permanent markings; you can keep the certificate for other trips. Otherwise, bring a sales receipt or insurance form to show that you owned the item before you left the United States.

For more about duties, restricted items, and other information about international travel, check out U.S. Customs and Border Protection's online brochure, *Know Before You Go*. You can also file complaints on the U.S. Customs and Border Protection Web site, listed below.

U.S. Customs and Border Protection ✉ For inquiries and complaints, 1300 Pennsylvania Ave. NW, Washington, DC 20229 ☎ 877/227–5551, 202/354–1000 ⊕ www.cbp.gov ✉ For complaints, Customer Satisfaction Unit, 1300 Pennsylvania Ave. NW, Room 5.2C, Washington, DC 20229.

DISABILITIES & ACCESSIBILITY

Though the French government is doing much to ensure that public facilities provide for visitors with disabilities, it still has a long way to go.

Local Resources Association des Paralysés de France ✉ 22 rue du Père Guerin, 75013 Paris ☎ 01-40-78-69-00 ⊕ www.apf-asso.com for a list of Paris hotels.

LODGING

Only some hotels—particularly more modern ones—are equipped with ramps, elevators, and special toilet facilities. Lists of regional hotels include a symbol to indicate which hotels have rooms accessible to people using wheelchairs.

RESERVATIONS

When discussing accessibility with an operator or reservations agent, ask hard questions. Are there any stairs, inside *or* out? Are there grab bars next to the toilet *and* in the shower/tub? How wide is the doorway to the room? To the bathroom? For the most extensive facilities meeting the latest legal specifications, opt for newer accommodations. If you reserve through a toll-free number, consider also calling the hotel's local number to confirm the information from the central reservations office. Get confirmation in writing when you can.

SIGHTS & ATTRACTIONS

Only some monuments and museums—especially those constructed within the past decade—are equipped with ramps, elevators, and special toilet facilities.

TRANSPORTATION

The SNCF has special accommodations in the first-class compartments (for the usual second-class rate) on non-TGV and main-line rail services that have been reserved exclusively for people using wheelchairs; arrangements can be made for those passengers to be escorted on and off trains and assisted in making connections (this service must be requested in advance at 08–00–05–47–53).

Unfortunately, at this time very few métro stations in Paris and only some RER stations are wheelchair accessible. For information about accessibility, **get the RER and métro access guide,** available at most stations and from the Paris Transit Authority.

The Airhop shuttle company runs adapted vehicles to and from the airports; Orly–Paris costs €35 and Charles de Gaulle–Paris costs €45; this service is available Monday through Friday only. Reservations (in French) must be made in advance. Note that you must pay €2 for every 15 minutes there is a delay.

⚡ Complaints Aviation Consumer Protection Division (⇨ Air Travel) for airline-related problems. **Departmental Office of Civil Rights** ⊠ For general inquiries, U.S. Department of Transportation, S-30, 400 7th St. SW, Room 10215, Washington, DC 20590 ☎ 202/366–4648 🖷 202/366–9371 ⊕ www.dot.gov/ost/docr/index.htm. **Disability Rights Section** ⊠ NYAV, U.S. Department of Justice, Civil Rights Division, 950 Pennsylvania Ave. NW, Washington, DC 20530 ☎ ADA information line 202/514–0301 or 800/514–0301, 202/514–0383 TTY or 800/514–0383 TTY ⊕ www.ada.gov. **U.S. Department of Transportation Hotline** ☎ For disability-related air-travel problems, 800/778–4838 or 800/455–9880 TTY.

⚡ Local Resources **Airhop** ☎ 01-41-29-01-29. **Paris Transit Authority** ⊠ (RATP) kiosk, 54 quai de la Rapée, 75012 ☎ 08-36-68-77-14 ⊕ www.ratp.fr.

TRAVEL AGENCIES

In the United States, the Americans with Disabilities Act requires that travel firms serve the needs of all travelers. Some agencies specialize in working with people with disabilities.

⚡ Travelers with Mobility Problems **Access Adventures/B. Roberts Travel** ⊠ 206 Chestnut Ridge Rd., Scottsville, NY 14624 ☎ 585/889–9096 ⊕ www.brobertstravel.com ✎ dltravel@prodigy. net, run by a former physical-rehabilitation counselor. **CareVacations** ⊠ No. 5, 5110–50 Ave., Leduc,

Alberta, Canada, T9E 6V4 ☎ 780/986–6404 or 877/478-7827 🖷 780/986–8332 ⊕ www.carevacations. com, for group tours and cruise vacations. **Flying Wheels Travel** ⊠ 143 W. Bridge St., Box 382, Owatonna, MN 55060 ☎ 507/451–5005 🖷 507/451–1685 ⊕ www.flyingwheelstravel.com.

DISCOUNTS & DEALS

Be a smart shopper and compare all your options before making decisions. A plane ticket bought with a promotional coupon from travel clubs, coupon books, and direct-mail offers or purchased on the Internet may not be cheaper than the least expensive fare from a discount ticket agency. And always keep in mind that what you get is just as important as what you save.

DISCOUNT RESERVATIONS

To save money, look into discount reservations services with Web sites and toll-free numbers, which use their buying power to get a better price on hotels, airline tickets (⇨ Air Travel), even car rentals. When booking a room, always **call the hotel's local toll-free number** (if one is available) rather than the central reservations number—you'll often get a better price. Always ask about special packages or corporate rates.

When shopping for the best deal on hotels and car rentals, look for guaranteed exchange rates, which protect you against a falling dollar. With your rate locked in, you won't pay more, even if the price goes up in the local currency.

⚡ Airline Tickets **Air 4 Less** ⊕ www.air4less.com; low-fare specialist.

⚡ Hotel Rooms **Accommodations Express** ☎ 800/444–7666 or 800/277-1064. **Hotels.com** ☎ 800/246–8357 ⊕ www.hotels.com. **International Marketing & Travel Concepts** ☎ 800/790–4682 ⊕ www.imtc-travel.com. **Steigenberger Reservation Service** ☎ 800/223–5652 ⊕ www. srs-worldhotels.com. **Turbotrip.com** ☎ 800/473-7829 ⊕ www.turbotrip.com.

PACKAGE DEALS

Don't confuse packages and guided tours. When you buy a package, you travel on your own, just as though you had planned the trip yourself. Fly–drive packages, which combine airfare and car rental, are often a good deal. In cities, ask the local visitor's bureau about hotel and local transportation packages that include tickets to major museum exhibits or other special events. If you **buy a rail–drive pass,** you may save on train tickets and car rentals. All Eurailpass holders get a discount on Eurostar fares through the Channel Tunnel and often receive reduced rates for buses, hotels, ferries, sightseeing cruises, and car rentals.

EATING & DRINKING

All establishments must post their menus outside, so study them carefully before deciding to enter. Most restaurants have two basic types of menu: à la carte and fixed-price (prix-fixe or *un menu*). The prix-fixe menu is usually the best value, though choices are more limited. Most menus begin with a first course (*une entrée*), often subdivided into cold and hot starters, followed by fish and poultry, then meat; it's rare today that anyone orders something from all three. The restaurants we review in this book are the cream of the crop in each price category.

A few pointers on French dining etiquette: diners in France don't negotiate their orders much, so don't expect serene smiles when you ask for sauce on the side. Order your coffee after dessert, not with it. When you're ready for the check, ask for it: no professional waiter would dare put a bill on your table while you're still enjoying the last sip of coffee. And don't ask for a doggy bag; it's just not done. The French usually drink wine or mineral water—not soda or coffee—with their food. You may ask for a carafe of tap water if you don't want to order wine or pay for bottled water.

COSTS

The following is the price chart used throughout this book to determine price categories for all restaurants. Prices are per person for a main course at dinner, including tax (19.6%) and service; note that if a restaurant offers only prix-fixe (set-price) meals, it is given a price category that reflects the full prix-fixe price.

CATEGORY	ALL REGIONS EXCEPT	CORSICA & BASQUE COUNTRY
$$$$	over €30	over €25
$$$	€23–€30	€17–€25
$$	€17–€23	€12–€17
$	€11–€17	€8–€12
¢	under €11	under €8

MEALS & SPECIALTIES

What's the difference between a bistro and a brasserie? Can you order food at a café? Can you go to a restaurant just for a snack? The following definitions should help.

A **restaurant** traditionally serves a three-course meal (first, main, and dessert) at both lunch and dinner. Although this category includes the most formal, three-star establishments, it also applies to humble neighborhood spots. Don't expect to grab a quick snack. In general, restaurants are what you choose when you want a complete meal and when you have the time to linger over it.

Many say that **bistros** served the world's first fast food. After the fall of Napoléon, the Russian soldiers who occupied Paris were known to bang on zinc-top café bars, crying "*bistro*"—"quickly" in Russian. In the past, bistros were simple places with minimal decor and service. Although nowadays many are quite upscale, with beautiful interiors and chic clientele, most remain cozy establishments serving straightforward, frequently gutsy cooking.

Brasseries—ideal places for quick, one-dish meals—originated when Alsatians fleeing German occupiers after the Franco-Prussian War came to Paris and opened restaurants serving specialties from home. Pork-based dishes, *choucroute* (sauerkraut), and beer (*brasserie* also means brewery) were—and still are—mainstays here. The typical brasserie is convivial and keeps late hours. Some are open 24 hours a day—a good thing to know since many restaurants stop serving at 10:30 PM.

Like bistros and brasseries, **cafés** come in a confusing variety. Often informal neighborhood hangouts, cafés may also be veritable showplaces attracting chic, well-heeled crowds. At most cafés the regulars congregate at the bar, where coffee and drinks are cheaper than at tables. At lunch tables are set, and a limited menu is served. Sandwiches, usually with *jambon* (ham), *fromage* (cheese, often Gruyère or Camembert), or *mixte* (ham and cheese), are served throughout the day. *Casse croûtes* (snacks) are also offered. Cafés are for lingering, for people-watching, and for daydreaming. If none of these options fit the bill, head to the nearest **traiteur** (deli) for picnic fixings.

See the Menu Guide at the end of the book for guidance with menu items that appear frequently on French menus and throughout the reviews in this book.

MEALTIMES
Breakfast is usually served from 7:30 AM to 10 PM, lunch from noon to 2 PM, and dinner from 7:30 PM to 10 PM. Restaurants in Paris usually serve dinner until 10:30 PM. Unless otherwise noted, the restaurants listed in this guide are open daily for lunch and dinner.

PAYING
By French law, prices must include tax and tip (*service compris* or *prix nets*), but pocket change left on the table in basic places, or an additional 5% in better restaurants, is always appreciated. Beware of bills stamped SERVICE NOT INCLUDED in English.

RESERVATIONS & DRESS
Reservations are always a good idea; we mention them only when they're essential or not accepted. Book as far ahead as you can, and reconfirm as soon as you arrive. (Large parties should always call ahead to check the reservations policy.) We mention dress only when men are required to wear a jacket or a jacket and tie.

ELECTRICITY
To use electric-powered equipment purchased in the United States or Canada, **bring a converter and adapter.** The electrical current in France is 220 volts, 50 cycles alternating current (AC); wall outlets take continental-type plugs, with two round prongs.

If your appliances are dual-voltage, you'll need only an adapter. Don't use 110-volt outlets marked FOR SHAVERS ONLY for high-wattage appliances such as blow-dryers. Most laptops operate equally well on 110 and 220 volts and so require only an adapter.

EMBASSIES
If you need assistance in an emergency, you can go to your country's embassy. Proof of identity and citizenship are generally required to enter. If your passport has been stolen, get a police report, then contact your embassy for assistance.

🔝 **Australia Australian Embassy** ✉ 4 rue Jean-Rey, Invalides–Eiffel Tower, 15ᵉ Paris ☎ 01-40-59-33-00 Ⓜ Bir Hakeim ☉ Weekdays 9:15 AM–12:15 PM.

🔝 **Canada Canadian Embassy** ✉ 35 av. Montaigne, Champs-Élysées, 8ᵉ Paris ☎ 01-44-43-29-02 Ⓜ Franklin-D.-Roosevelt ☉ Weekdays 9 AM–noon and 2 PM–4:30 PM.

🔝 **New Zealand New Zealand Embassy** ✉ 7 ter rue Léonardo da Vinci, Trocadéro, 16ᵉ Paris ☎ 01-45-01-43-43 Ⓜ Victor Hugo ☉ Mon.–Thurs., 9 AM–1 PM and 2 PM–5:30 PM; Fri., 9 AM–1 PM and 2 PM–4 PM (early closing hours in July and Aug.).

🔝 **United Kingdom British Consulate** ✉ 18 bis rue d'Anjou, Louvre–Tuileries, 8ᵉ Paris ☎ 01-44-51-31-00 Ⓜ Madeleine ☉ Weekdays 9:30 AM–12:30 PM and 2:30 PM–5 PM ✉ 24 av. du Prado, 13006 Marseille ☎ 04-91-15-72-10 ☉ Weekdays 9 AM–noon and 2 PM–5 PM.

🔝 **United States U.S.Consulate** ✉ 2 rue St-Florentin, Louvre/Tuileries, 1ᵉʳ Paris ☎ 01-43-12-22-22 in English Ⓜ Concorde ☉ Weekdays 9 AM–1 PM ✉ Pl. Varian Fry, 13006 Marseille ☎ 04-91-54-92-00 ☉ Weekdays 9 AM–noon and 2 PM–5 PM.

EMERGENCIES
The National Medical System in France is excellent and was recently ranked number one by the World Health Organization, but there are certain things you must understand to get optimum care. For minor emergencies—the flu, food poisoning, a bad respiratory infection—you should contact a generalist who will actually visit you in your home or hotel, medical bag in hand, at any hour of the day or night, whether you are in the city or on the outskirts of a tiny town. At the moment,

hospital emergency rooms are undergoing a crisis and are to be used only for emergencies. They operate on a strict priority system, which could leave you with your high temperature or sprained ankle waiting for hours; in early 2004, a flu epidemic kept hospitals overwhelmed with an average wait of four hours.

France's emergency services are conveniently streamlined and universal and quite simple to use, so no matter where you are in the country you can dial the same phone numbers, listed below. Every town and village has a *médecin de garde* (on-duty doctor) for flus, sprains, tetanus shots, and similar problems. Larger cities have a remarkable service called "SOS Doctor" (or "SOS Dentist" for dental emergencies); just dial information (12) and they will put you through. To find out who's on call on any given evening, call any *généraliste* (general practitioner), and a recording will refer you to the available doctors and specialists. If you need an X-ray or emergency treatment, call an ambulance, and you'll be whisked to the hospital of your choice—or the nearest one. Note that outside Paris it's very difficult to find English-speaking doctors.

Pharmacies have an important role in French culture; they can be very helpful with minor health problems and come equipped with blood pressure machines and first aid kits. They also can be consulted for a list of practicing doctors in the area, nearby hospitals, private clinics, or health centers. Hotels are required to post emergency exit maps with multilingual instructions to be followed in case of fire on the inside door of every room. On the street the French phrases that may be needed in an emergency are: *Au secours!* (Help!), *urgence* (emergency), *samu* (ambulance), *pompiers* (firemen), *poste de station* (police station), *médecin* (doctor), and *hôpital* (hospital).

See also Emergencies *in* A to Z sections *in* some of the regional chapters for information on local hospitals.

🚑 Ambulance ☎ 15. Fire Department ☎ 18.
Police ☎ 17.

ENGLISH-LANGUAGE MEDIA
BOOKS
Paris has many bookstores selling English-language books (⇨ Shopping *in* Chapter 1), and you can probably find at least one bookstore in other major cities with English-language books. However, in most smaller towns you won't have much luck.

NEWSPAPERS & MAGAZINES
Besides a large variety of French newspapers and magazines, all kinds of English-language newspapers and magazines can be found at newsstands in larger cities and even in smaller towns, including: the *International Herald Tribune, USA Today,* the *New York Times,* the *European Financial Times,* the *London Times, Newsweek, The Economist, Vogue,* and *Elle.* In Paris you'll find a number of free English-language magazines with all kinds of listings, including events, bars, restaurants, shops, films, and museums: Look for *Time Out Paris, FUSAC,* the *Paris Free Voice,* and *Irish Eyes.*

RADIO & TELEVISION
Turn on the television, and you'll notice many American shows dubbed into French (Canal Jimmy, Cable Channel 8, presents American shows in their original, undubbed format). France has both national stations (TF1, France 2, France 3, La Cinq/Arte, and M6) and cable stations (most notably Canal+, France's version of HBO). Every morning at 7:05 AM, ABC News (from the night before) is aired on Channel 4. You can also find CNN, BBC World, and BBC Prime on cable.

You'll find all kinds of music on French radio stations—from rock to jazz to classical, depending on the time of day. For highway information 24/7 tune into 101.7 FM.

ETIQUETTE & BEHAVIOR
SMOKING
The French are smokers—there's no way around it. Just watch them light up their first cigarette after getting off the plane right under the *no smoking* sign at the airport. And they're notorious for disregarding the few no-smoking laws that do exist, with little retribution. Even in restaurants,

cafés, and train and métro stations that have no-smoking sections, you'll see people smoking. Even if you ask people to move or not to smoke, don't expect them to respond or respect your request. Your best bet for finding an environment as smoke-free as possible is to stick to the larger cafés and restaurants, where there is a greater likelihood of clearly defined smoking and no-smoking areas, or if you're lucky enough to enjoy good weather, to simply sit at an outside table.

SNCF trains have cars designated for smoking and no-smoking (specify when you make reservations), and these are some of the few places where the laws are respected. Some hotels, too, have designated no-smoking rooms; ask for these when reserving.

GAY & LESBIAN TRAVEL

The largest gay and lesbian communities in France are in Paris. A number of informative newspapers and magazines that cover the Parisian gay and lesbian scene are available at stores and kiosks in the city, notably *Lesbia Magazine* and *Têtu*.

Gay- & Lesbian-Friendly Travel Agencies Different Roads Travel ✉ 1017 N. LaCienega Blvd., Suite 308, West Hollywood, CA 90069 ☎ 310/289-6000 or 800/429-8747 (Ext. 14 for both) 🖷 310/855-0323 ✉ lgernert@tzell.com. **Kennedy Travel** ✉ 130 W. 42nd St., Suite 401, New York, NY 10036 ☎ 212/840-8659 or 800/237-7433 🖷 212/730-2269 ⊕ www.kennedytravel.com. **Now, Voyager** ✉ 4406 18th St., San Francisco, CA 94114 ☎ 415/626-1169 or 800/255-6951 🖷 415/626-8626 ⊕ www.nowvoyager.com. **Skylink Travel and Tour/Flying Dutchmen Travel** ✉ 1455 N. Dutton Ave., Suite A, Santa Rosa, CA 95401 ☎ 707/546-9888 or 800/225-5759 🖷 707/636-0951; serving lesbian travelers.

Organizations Act Up Paris ✉ 45 rue Sedaine, 11ᵉ ☎ 01-48-06-13-89. **Association des Médecins Gais** ☎ 01-48-05-81-71. **Centre Gai et Lesbien** ✉ 3 rue Keller, 11ᵉ ☎ 01-43-57-21-47.

HEALTH
For information about emergencies and hospitals, *see* Emergencies, *above*.

HIKING & WALKING
France has many good places to hike and an extensive network of mapped-out Grandes Randonnées (GRs, or long trails)

that range from easy to challenging. For details on hiking in France and guides to GRs in specific areas, contact the Club Alpin Français or the Fédération Française de la Randonnée Pédestre, which also publishes good topographical maps. The IGN maps sold in many bookshops are also invaluable (⇨ Bike Travel, *above*).

Hiking Organizations Club Alpin Français ✉ 24 av. Laumière, 75019 Paris ☎ 01-53-72-87-00 ⊕ www.clubalpin.com. **Fédération Française de la Randonnée Pédestre** ✉ 14 rue de Riquet, 75019 Paris ☎ 01-44-89-93-93 ⊕ www.ffrp.asso.fr.

Hiking & Walking Tours Abercrombie & Kent (⇨ Barge & Yacht Travel, *above*). **Backroads** ✉ 801 Cedar St., Berkeley, CA 94710-1800 ☎ 800/462-2848 🖷 510/527-1444. **Butterfield & Robinson** (⇨ Bike Travel, *above*). **Classic Adventures** (⇨ Bike Travel, *above*). **Country Walkers** ✉ Box 180, Waterbury, VT 05676-0180 ☎ 802/244-1387 or 800/464-9255 🖷 802/244-5661. **Mountain Travel-Sobek** ✉ 1266 66th St., Emeryville, CA 94608 ☎ 510/594-6000 or 888/687-6235. **Wilderness Travel** ✉ 1102 9th St., Berkeley, CA 94710 ☎ 510/558-2488 or 800/368-2794 🖷 510/558-2489 ⊕ www.wildernesstravel.com.

HOLIDAYS
With 11 national *jours feriés* (holidays) and five weeks of paid vacation, the French have their share of repose. In May there is a holiday nearly every week, so be prepared for stores, banks, and museums to shut their doors for days at a time. Be sure to **call museums, restaurants, and hotels in advance to make sure they will be open.**

Note that these dates are for the calendar year 2006: January 1 (New Year's Day); April 16 and 17 (Easter Sunday and Monday); May 1 (Labor Day); May 8 (V.E. Day); May 25 (Ascension); June 4 and 5 (Pentecost Sunday and Monday); July 14 (Bastille Day); August 15 (Assumption); November 1 (All Saints); November 11 (Armistice); December 25 (Christmas).

INSURANCE
The most useful travel-insurance plan is a comprehensive policy that includes coverage for trip cancellation and interruption, default, trip delay, and medical expenses (with a waiver for preexisting conditions).

Without insurance you'll lose all or most of your money if you cancel your trip, regardless of the reason. Default insurance covers you if your tour operator, airline, or cruise line goes out of business—the chances of which have been increasing. Trip-delay covers expenses that arise because of bad weather or mechanical delays. Study the fine print when comparing policies.

If you're traveling internationally, a key component of travel insurance is coverage for medical bills incurred if you get sick on the road. Such expenses aren't generally covered by Medicare or private policies. U.K. residents can buy a travel-insurance policy valid for most vacations taken during the year in which it's purchased (but check preexisting-condition coverage). British and Australian citizens need extra medical coverage when traveling overseas.

Always **buy travel policies directly from the insurance company**; if you buy them from a cruise line, airline, or tour operator that goes out of business you probably won't be covered for the agency or operator's default, a major risk. Before making any purchase, review your existing health and home-owner's policies to find what they cover away from home.

🚩 Travel Insurers In the U.S.: **Access America** ✉ 2805 N. Parham Rd., Richmond, VA 23294 ☎ 800/284-8300 🖷 804/673-1469 or 800/346-9265 ⊕ www.accessamerica.com. **Travel Guard International** ✉ 1145 Clark St., Stevens Point, WI 54481 ☎ 715/345-0505 or 800/826-1300 🖷 800/955-8785 or 715/345-1990 ⊕ www.travelguard.com.
🚩 In the U.K.: **Association of British Insurers** ✉ 51 Gresham St., London EC2V 7HQ ☎ 020/7600-3333 🖷 020/7696-8999 ⊕ www.abi.org.uk. In Canada: **RBC Insurance** ✉ 6880 Financial Dr., Mississauga, Ontario L5N 7Y5 ☎ 800/387-4357 or 905/816-2559 🖷 888/298-6458 ⊕ www.rbcinsurance.com. In Australia: **Insurance Council of Australia** ✉ Level 3, 56 Pitt St., Sydney, NSW 2000 ☎ 02/9253-5100 🖷 02/9253-5111 ⊕ www.ica.com.au. In Canada: **RBC Insurance** ✉ 6880 Financial Dr., Mississauga, Ontario L5N 7Y5 ☎ 800/387-4357 or 905/816-2559 🖷 888/298-6458 ⊕ www.rbcinsurance.com. In New Zealand: **Insurance Council of New Zealand** ✉ Level 7, 111-115 Custom-house Quay, Box 474, Wellington ☎ 04/472-5230 🖷 04/473-3011 ⊕ www.icnz.org.nz.

LANGUAGE

The truth of the matter is that, although most French people pretend to speak English, they, in fact, do not. So keep in mind that you are in France and France is full of French people who speak French. Needless to say, you'll find personnel in hotels that are multilingual, but if you find yourself in a small outdoor market in Arles and you want to buy 12 jars of lavender honey for the price of 11, you are going to have to be patient, speak slowly, and mime a lot. This is not to say that English-speaking visitors should shout English words very slowly and loudly in the hope that the French will suddenly understand them. Any effort, even a small one, to say hello, good-bye, or thank you in their language is always greatly appreciated. So even if your own French is terrible, try to master a few words. A simple, friendly *bonjour* (hello) will do, as will asking if the person you are greeting speaks English (*"Parlez-vous anglais?"*). Throwing yourself on their mercy does wonders, so you can always try to begin a conversation with *"Excusez-moi. Mon Française est très, très mauvaise. Mille pardons."* ("Excuse me. My French is very bad. A thousand pardons.") That way, you'll start out by acknowledging your shortcomings—and probably be all the more befriended for them. *See* the French Vocabulary & Menu Guide at the back of the book for more suggestions.

LANGUAGES FOR TRAVELERS

A phrase book and language-tape set can help get you started. *Fodor's French for Travelers* (available at bookstores everywhere) is excellent.

LODGING

The lodgings we list are the cream of the crop in each price category. We always list the facilities available—but we don't specify whether they cost extra: when pricing accommodations, always ask what's included and what costs extra. Properties indicated by a ✕⊡ are lodging establishments whose restaurant warrants a special trip.

APARTMENT & HOUSE RENTALS

If you want a home base that's roomy enough for a family and comes with cooking facilities, consider a furnished rental. These can save you money, especially if you're traveling with a group. Renting an apartment or a *gîte rural*—a furnished house in the country—for a week or month can also save you money. Home-exchange directories sometimes list rentals as well as exchanges.

The national rental network, the Fédération Nationale des Gîtes de France, rents all types of accommodations rated by ears of corn (from 1 to 4) based on a stringent criteria of comfort and quality. You can find listings for fabulous stone farmhouses renovated to perfection with lit swimming pools and their own olive groves or simple cottages located in the heart of wine country, in the vineyards themselves if you wish. Gîtes de France has listings for rural gîtes, B&Bs, lodges, group accommodations for hikers located near hiking paths, and campsites where you can put up your tent in the middle of French farmland with not a soul in sight. Gîtes are nearly always maintained by on-site owners, who greet you on your arrival and provide information on groceries, doctors, and nearby attractions. A nationwide catalog (€22) is available from the Fédération Nationale des Gîtes de France, listing gîtes for rent. If you know the region you want to visit, contact the departmental branch directly and order a photo catalog that lists every property. If you specify which dates you plan to visit, the office will narrow down the choice to rentals available for those days, but be sure to plan early, renting gîtes has become one of the most popular ways to discover France.

Individual tourist offices often publish lists of *locations meublés* (furnished rentals); these are often inspected by the tourist office and rated by comfort standards. Usually they are booked directly through the individual owner, which generally requires some knowledge of French. Rentals that are not classified or rated by the tourist office should be undertaken with trepidation, as they can fall well below your minimum standard of comfort.

Vacation rentals in France always book from Saturday to Saturday (with some offering weekend rates off-season). Most do not include bed linens and towels but make them available for an additional fee. Always check on policies on pets and children and specify if you need an enclosed garden for toddlers, a washing machine, a fireplace, etc. If you plan to have overnight guests during your stay, let the owner know; there may be additional charges. Insurance restrictions prohibit loading in guests beyond the specified capacity.

🏠 **International Agents At Home Abroad** 🖉 163 3rd Ave., No. 319, New York, NY 10003 ☎ 212/421-9165 🖷 212/533-0095 ⊕ www.athomeabroadinc.com. **Drawbridge to Europe** ✉ 98 Granite St., Ashland, OR 97520 ☎ 541/482-7778 or 888/268-1148 🖷 541/482-7779 ⊕ www.drawbridgetoeurope.com. **Hideaways International** ✉ 767 Islington St., Portsmouth, NH 03801 ☎ 603/430-4433 or 800/843-4433 🖷 603/430-4444 ⊕ www.hideaways.com, annual membership $145. **Hometours International** ✉ 1108 Scottie La., Knoxville, TN 37919 ☎ 865/690-8484 or 866/367-4668 🖉 hometours@aol.com ⊕ thor.he.net/~hometour/. **Interhome** ✉ 1990 N.E. 163rd St., Suite 110, North Miami Beach, FL 33162 ☎ 305/940-2299 or 800/882-6864 🖷 305/940-2911 ⊕ www.interhome.us. **Vacation Home Rentals Worldwide** ✉ 235 Kensington Ave., Norwood, NJ 07648 ☎ 201/767-9393 or 800/633-3284 🖷 201/767-5510 ⊕ www.vhrww.com. **Villanet** ✉ 1251 N.W. 116th St., Seattle, WA 98177 ☎ 206/417-3444 or 800/964-1891 🖷 206/417-1832 ⊕ www.rentavilla.com. **Villas and Apartments Abroad** ✉ 183 Madison Ave., Suite 201, New York, NY 10016 ☎ 212/213-6435 or 800/433-3020 🖷 212/213-8252 ⊕ www.vaanyc.com. **Villas International** ✉ 4340 Redwood Hwy., Suite D309, San Rafael, CA 94903 ☎ 415/499-9490 or 800/221-2260 🖷 415/499-9491 ⊕ www.villasintl.com.

🏠 **Local Agents Fédération Nationale des Gîtes de France** ✉ 59 rue St-Lazare, 75009 Paris ☎ 01-49-70-75-75 🖷 01-42-81-28-53 ⊕ www.gitesdefrance.fr. **French Government Tourist Office** (⇨ Visitor Information, *below*).

BED & BREAKFASTS

Chambres d'hôtes (bed-and-breakfasts) can mean simple lodging, usually in the hosts' home, with breakfast, but can also mean a beautiful room in an 18th-century château with gourmet food and a harpsichord in the living room. Chambres d'hôtes are most common in rural France, though they are becoming more so in Paris and other major cities. Check with local tourist offices or contact Gîtes de France, a national organization that lists B&Bs all over the country, or private reservation agencies. Often table d'hôte dinners (meals cooked by and eaten with the owners) can be arranged for an extra, fairly nominal fee. Note that your hosts at B&Bs, unlike those at hotels, are more likely to speak only French.

🛈 **Reservation Services Gîtes de France** ⊠ 59 rue St-Lazare, 75009 Paris ☎ 01-49-70-75-75 🖷 01-42-81-28-53 ⊕ www.gitesdefrance.fr. **Paris Bed & Breakfast** ☎ 800/872-2632.

CAMPING

French campsites have a good reputation for organization and amenities but are crowded in July and August. Many campsites welcome reservations, and in summer it makes sense to book in advance. The Fédération Française de Camping et de Caravaning publishes a guide to France's campsites (€16, plus shipping).

🛈 **Campsite Guide Fédération Française de Camping et de Caravaning** ⊠ 78 rue de Rivoli, 75004 Paris ☎ 01-42-72-84-08 ⊕ www.ffcc.fr.

COSTS

The following is the price chart used throughout this book to determine price categories for all hotels. Prices are for a standard double room in high season, including tax (19.6%) and service charge; rates for any board plans will be higher.

CATEGORY	ALL REGIONS EXCEPT	CORSICA & BASQUE COUNTRY
$$$$	over €190	over €175
$$$	€120–€190	€120–€175
$$	€80–€120	€70–€120
$	€50–€80	€40–€70
¢	under €50	under €40

HOME EXCHANGES

If you would like to exchange your home for someone else's, join a home-exchange organization, which will send you its updated listings of available exchanges for a year and will include your own listing in at least one of them. It's up to you to make specific arrangements.

🛈 **Exchange Clubs HomeLink USA** ⊠ 2937 N.W. 9th Terrace, Wilton Manors, FL 33311 ☎ 954/566-2687 or 800/638-3841 🖷 954/566-2783 ⊕ www.homelink.org; $75 yearly for a listing and online access; $45 additional to receive directories. **Intervac U.S.** ⊠ 30 Corte San Fernando, Tiburon, CA 94920 ☎ 800/756-4663 🖷 415/435-7440 ⊕ www.intervacus.com; $128 yearly for a listing, online access, and a catalog; $68 without catalog.

HOSTELS

No matter what your age, you can save on lodging costs by staying at hostels. In some 4,500 locations in more than 70 countries around the world, Hostelling International (HI), the umbrella group for a number of national youth-hostel associations, offers single-sex, dorm-style beds and, at many hostels, rooms for couples and family accommodations. Membership in any HI national hostel association, open to travelers of all ages, allows you to stay in HI-affiliated hostels at member rates; one-year membership is about $28 for adults (C$35 for a two-year minimum membership in Canada, £15 in the U.K., A$52 in Australia, and NZ$40 in New Zealand); hostels charge about $10–$30 per night. Members have priority if the hostel is full; they're also eligible for discounts around the world, even on rail and bus travel in some countries.

Paris's major public hostels are run by the Fédération Unie des Auberges de Jeunesse (FUAJ)—for about €20, a bed, sheets, shower, and breakfast are provided, with beds usually three to four to a room. Maisons Internationales des Jeunes Etudiants (MIJE) have the plushest hostels, sometimes in historic mansions. Private hostels have accommodations that run from pleasant, if spartan, double rooms to dormlike arrangements.

🛈 **Organizations Hostelling International–USA** ⊠ 8401 Colesville Rd., Suite 600, Silver Spring, MD 20910 ☎ 301/495-1240 🖷 301/495-6697 ⊕ www.hiusa.org. **Hostelling International–Canada** ⊠ 205 Catherine St., Suite 400, Ottawa, Ontario K2P 1C3 ☎ 613/237-7884 or 800/663-5777 🖷 613/237-7868 ⊕ www.hihostels.ca. **YHA England and Wales** ⊠ Trevelyan House, Dimple Rd., Matlock,

Derbyshire DE4 3YH, U.K. ☎ 0870/870-8808, 0870/770-8868, or 0162/959-2600 🖶 0870/770-6127 ⊕ www.yha.org.uk. **YHA Australia** ⊠ 422 Kent St., Sydney, NSW 2001 ☎ 02/9261-1111 🖶 02/9261-1969 ⊕ www.yha.com.au. **YHA New Zealand** ⊠ Level 1, Moorhouse City, 166 Moorhouse Ave., Box 436, Christchurch ☎ 03/379-9970 or 0800/278-299 🖶 03/365-4476 ⊕ www.yha.org.nz.

HOTELS & MOTELS

Rates are always by room, not per person. Often a hotel in a certain price category will have a few less-expensive rooms; it's worth asking about. In the off-season—usually November to Easter (except for southern France)—tariffs can be lower. It helps to inquire about promotional specials and weekend deals. Rates must be posted in all rooms (usually on the back of the door), with all extra charges clearly shown. You might try negotiating rates if you're planning on staying for a week or longer.

Assume all hotel rooms have air-conditioning, telephones, TV, and private bath unless otherwise noted. You should always **check what bathroom facilities the price includes.** When making your reservation, state your preference for shower (*douche*) or tub (*baignoire*)—the latter always costs more. Also when booking, **ask for a *grand lit* if you want a double bed.**

If you're counting on air-conditioning you should **make sure, in advance, that your hotel room is *climatisé*** (air-conditioned). If you throw open the windows, **don't expect screens** (*moustiquaires*). Nowhere in Europe are they standard equipment.

The quality of accommodations, particularly in older properties and even in luxury hotels, can vary greatly from room to room; **if you don't like the room you're given, ask to see another.**

Hotels operate on the European Plan (EP, with no meal provided) unless we note that they offer the Breakfast Plan (BP), Modified American Plan (MAP, with breakfast and dinner daily, known as *demi-pension*), or Full American Plan (FAP, or *pension complète,* with three meals a day); **board plans, which are usually an option offered in addition to the basic room plan, are generally only available with a minimum two- or three-night stay** and are, of course, more expensive than the basic room rate. Many noted hotels—especially those found in Provence, the Côte d'Azur, and the Loire Valley—have superb restaurants and, in such cases, room-and-board plans present an enjoyable game plan (one to be avoided if you wish to explore regional restaurants). Note that the hotel price charts in this book reflect basic room rates only. Inquire about board plans when making your reservations; details and prices are often stated on hotel Web sites.

It's always a good idea to **make hotel reservations in Paris and other major tourist destinations as far in advance as possible,** especially in late spring, summer, or fall. Faxing is the easiest way to contact the hotel (the staff is probably more likely to read English than to understand it spoken over the phone long-distance), though calling also works, while larger, more modern hotels now correspond using their e-mail address (always found on their Web site). But whether by fax, phone, or e-mail, you should specify the exact dates you want to stay at the hotel (don't forget to notify your hotel of a possible late check-in to prevent your room from being given away); the size of the room you want and how many people will be sleeping there; the type of accommodations you want (two twins, double, etc.); and what kind of bathroom (private with shower or bath, or both). You might also ask if a deposit (or your credit-card number) is required, and if so, what happens if you cancel. Request that the hotel fax you back so you have a written confirmation of your reservation.

If you arrive without a reservation, the tourist offices in major train stations and most towns can probably help you find a room.

Many hotels in France are small, often independently owned or family-run establishments. Some are affiliated with hotel groups, such as Logis de France, which can be relied on for comfort, character, and regional cuisine (look for its distinctive yellow-and-green sign). A Logis de France paperback guide is widely available in bookshops or from Logis de France. Two prestigious international groups with numerous converted châteaux and manor houses among its members are Relais & Châteaux and Small Luxury Hotels of the World; booklets listing members are available from these organizations. France also has some hotel chains. Examples in the upper price bracket are Frantel, Novotel, and Sofitel as well as Inter-Continental, Marriott, Hilton, Hyatt, Westin, and Sheraton. The Best Western, Campanile, Climat de France, Ibis, and Timhotel chains are more moderate. Typically, chains offer a consistently acceptable standard of modern features (modern bathrooms, TVs, etc.) but tend to lack atmosphere, with some exceptions (Best Western, for instance, tries to maintain the local character of the hotels it takes over).

RESERVING A ROOM

Here is a sample letter you can use when making a written reservation.

Cher (Dear) *Madame, Monsieur:*

Nous voudrions réserver une chambre pour (We wish to reserve a room for) ___ (number of) *nuit(s)* (nights), *du* (from) ___ (arrival date) *au* ___ (departure date), *à deux lits* (with twin beds), or *à lit-double* (with a double bed), or *une chambre pour une seule personne* (a room for a single person), *avec salle de bains et toilettes privées* (with a bathroom and private toilet). *Si possible, nous voudrains une salle de bains avec une baignoire et aussi une douche.* (If possible, we would prefer a bathroom with a tub as well as a shower—note that a bathroom with a tub can be more expensive than one with just a shower.) *Veuillez confirmer la réservation en nous communicant le prix de la chambre, et le dépot forfaitaire que vous exigez. Dans l'attente de votre lettre, nous vous prions d'agréer, Madame, Monsieur, l'expression de nos sentiments amicales.* (Can you please inform us about availabilties, the rate of room, and if any deposit is needed? With our friendliest greetings, we will wait your confirmation.)

🔢 **Toll-Free Numbers Best Western** ☎ 800/528-1234 ⊕ www.bestwestern.com. **Choice** ☎ 800/424-6423 ⊕ www.choicehotels.com. **Clarion** ☎ 800/424-6423 ⊕ www.choicehotels.com. **Comfort Inn** ☎ 800/424-6423 ⊕ www.choicehotels.com. **Four Seasons** ☎ 800/332-3442 ⊕ www.fourseasons.com. **Hilton** ☎ 800/445-8667 ⊕ www.hilton.com. **Holiday Inn** ☎ 800/465-4329 ⊕ www.ichotelsgroup.com. **Hyatt Hotels & Resorts** ☎ 800/233-1234 ⊕ www.hyatt.com. **Inter-Continental** ☎ 800/327-0200 ⊕ www.ichotelsgroup.com. **Marriott** ☎ 800/228-9290 ⊕ www.marriott.com. **Le Meridien** ☎ 800/543-4300 ⊕ www.lemeridien.com. **Quality Inn** ☎ 800/424-6423 ⊕ www.choicehotels.com. **Renaissance Hotels & Resorts** ☎ 800/468-3571 ⊕ www.renaissancehotels.com/. **Sheraton** ☎ 800/325-3535 ⊕ www.starwood.com/sheraton. **Westin Hotels & Resorts** ☎ 800/228-3000 ⊕ www.starwood.com/westin.

MAIL & SHIPPING

Post offices, or PTT, are found in every town and are recognizable by a yellow LA POSTE sign. They are usually open weekdays 8 AM–7 PM, Saturday 8 AM–noon, but the **main Paris post office** (⊠ 52 rue du Louvre, 1ᵉʳ) is open 24 hours, seven days a week.

OVERNIGHT SERVICES

Sending overnight mail from major cities in France is relatively easy. Besides DHL, Federal Express, and UPS, the French post office has overnight mail service, called Chronopost, which is much cheaper for small packages. Keep in mind that certain things cannot be shipped from France to the United States, such as perfume and any meat products.

🔢 **Major Services DHL** ⊠ 6 rue des Colonnes, Opéra-Grands Boulevards, 2ᵉ Paris ☎ 01-55-35-30-30 ⊠ 59 ave. Iéna, Trocadéro, 16ᵉ Paris ☎ 01-45-01-91-00 ⊕ www.dhl.com. **Federal Express** ⊠ 63 bd. Haussmann, Champs-Élysées, 8ᵉ Paris ☎ 01-40-06-90-16 ⊠ 2 rue 29 Juillet, Louvre-Tuileries, 1ᵉʳ Paris ☎ 01-49-26-04-6, 08-00-12-38-00 for information about pickups all over France ⊕ www.fedex.com. **UPS** ⊠ 34 bd. Malesherbes, Champs-Élysées, 8ᵉ Paris ⊠ 107 rue Réaumur, Beaubourg-Les Halles, 2ᵉ Paris ☎ 08-00-87-78-77 for information all over France ⊕ www.ups.com.

POSTAL RATES

Letters and postcards to the United States and Canada cost €.90 for 20 grams. Letters and postcards to the United Kingdom cost €.55 for up to 20 grams. Letters and postcards within France cost €.53. Stamps can be bought in post offices and in cafés displaying a red TABAC sign outside. It takes, on the average, five days for a letter to reach the United States, 5–6 days to Australia, 4–5 days to Canada, and three days to any location in Europe.

RECEIVING MAIL
If you're uncertain where you'll be staying, **have mail sent to the local post office,** addressed as "poste restante," or to American Express, but remember that during peak seasons American Express may refuse to accept mail. The French postal service has a €.45 per item service charge.

MONEY MATTERS
The following prices are for Paris; other cities and areas are often cheaper (with the notable exception of the Côte d'Azur). Keep in mind that it's less expensive to eat or drink standing at a café or bar counter than to sit at a table. Two prices are listed, *au comptoir* (at the counter) and *à salle* (at a table; sometimes orders cost even more if you're seated at a terrace table). Coffee in a bar: €1–€1.50 (standing), €1.50–€5 (seated) for an espresso; more for a café crème; beer in a bar: €2 (standing), €3–€6 (seated); Coca-Cola: €2–€3 a can; ham sandwich: €3–€5; 2-km (1-mi) taxi ride: €6; movie-theater seat: €9 (15%–33% cheaper on Monday and Wednesday); foreign newspaper: €1–€4.

Prices throughout this guide are given for adults. Substantially reduced fees are almost always available for children, students, and senior citizens. For information on taxes, *see* Taxes.

ATMS
Fairly common in Paris, other cities, most towns, and even some villages (as well as in airports and train stations), **ATMs are one of the easiest ways to get euros.** Don't, however, expect to find ATMs in rural areas. Banks usually offer excellent wholesale exchange rates through ATMs.

To get cash at ATMs in France, **your PIN must be four digits long.** Note that the machine will give you two chances to enter your correct PIN number; if you make a mistake on the third try, your card will be held, and you'll have to return to the bank the next morning to retrieve it. You may have better luck with ATMs with a credit or debit card that is also a Visa or Master-Card, rather than just your bank card. Note, too, that you may be charged by your bank for using ATMs overseas; inquire at your bank about charges. Before you go, it's a good idea to **get a list of ATM locations that you can use** in France from your bank.

CREDIT CARDS
France is a credit-card society. Credit cards are used for just about everything, from the automatic gas pumps (now starting to pop up all over the country), to the tolls on highways, payment machines in underground parking lots, stamps at the post office, and even the most minor purchases in the larger department stores. A restaurant or shop would either have to be extremely small or brand-new not to have some credit-card or debit-card capability. However, some of the smaller restaurants and stores do have a credit-card minimum, usually around €15, which normally should be clearly indicated; to be safe, ask before you order. Do not forget to take your credit-card receipt, as fraudulent use of credit-card numbers taken from receipts is on the rise.

Note that American Express isn't always accepted. Throughout this guide, the following abbreviations are used: **AE,** American Express; **DC,** Diners Club; **MC,** MasterCard; and **V,** Visa.

🔁 Reporting Lost Cards **American Express** ☎ 336/393-1111, call collect. **Diners Club** ☎ 303/799-1504, call collect. **MasterCard** ☎ 0800/90-1387. **Visa** ☎ 0800/90-1179, 410/581-9994 collect.

CURRENCY
On January 1, 2002, the new single European Union (EU) currency, the euro (€), became the official currency of the 12 countries participating in the European Monetary Union (with the notable exceptions of Great Britain, Denmark, and Sweden). The first thing you will notice is that the euro system has quite a lot of coins,

eight to be exact: 1 and 2 euros, plus 1, 2, 5, 10, 20, and 50 cents. All coins display their value on one side, while the other side is adorned with the national symbol of the issuing country. There are seven colorful notes: 5, 10, 20, 50, 100, 200, and 500 euros. Notes have illustrations of the principal architectural styles from antiquity onward on one side and a map of Europe on the other, and are the same in all countries. The first thing you must do when you change your money is memorize the coins as soon as you can (notes are much easier to grasp, as they start off at €5) and you'll undoubtedly find yourself quickly weighted down with all those coins. This was the first complaint most Europeans had about this new system, and this, in turn, led to the second complaint: euro coins, with their high nickel content, pose a problem for people with an allergic sensitivity to the mineral (if you're one of them, try to handle the coins as little as possible, and if you do come in contact with them, rinse your hands as soon as you can).

The advent of the euro makes any whirlwind grand European tour all the easier. From France, you'll glide across the borders of Austria, Germany, Italy, Spain, Holland, Ireland, Greece, Belgium, Finland, Luxembourg, and Portugal with no pressing need to run to the local exchange booth to change to yet another currency before you even had the time to become familiar with the last. You'll be able to do what drives many tourists crazy—to assess the value of a purchase (for example, to realize that eating a three-course meal in a small restaurant in Lisbon is cheaper than that ham sandwich you bought on the Champs Élysées). Initially, the euro had another benefit in that it was created as a direct competitor with the U.S. dollar and was envisioned to be, therefore, of nearly equal value. Unfortunately, exchange rates in 2004 and 2005 have seen the euro soar and the dollar take a hit. At press time, one euro equals U.S. $1.35.

Such are the ground rules when it comes to the euro and the old EU currencies. But you still have to **pay close attention to where you change your U.S. dollars and all other currencies that are not part of the EU community**—shop around for the best exchange rates (and also check the rates before leaving home) when it comes to non–EU currencies such as the dollar, the Japanese yen, and the British pound. The rates of conversion between the euro and other local currencies have been irrevocably fixed: 1 euro = 1.95 German marks; 1.39 Canadian dollars; 0.78 Irish punts; 13.76 Austrian schillings; 1.79 Australian dollars; 2.14 New Zealand dollars; 1,936.26 Italian lire; 40.33 Belgian francs; 166.38 Spanish pesetas; 2.20 Dutch guilders; 200.48 Portuguese escudos; 40.33 Luxembourg francs; 5.94 Finnish markkas; and 0.62 British pounds.

CURRENCY EXCHANGE

These days, the **easiest way to get euros is through ATMs**; you can find them in airports, train stations, and throughout the city. ATM rates are excellent because they are based on wholesale rates offered only by major banks. It's a good idea, however, to bring some euros with you from home and always to have some cash and traveler's checks as backup. For the best deal when exchanging currencies not within the Monetary Union purview (the U.S. dollar, the yen, and the British pound are examples), compare rates at banks (which usually have the most favorable rates) and booths and look for exchange booths that clearly state "no commission"; some exchange booths in tourist areas have been adding on a hefty €20—always confirm the rate with the teller before you hand over your money. The best rates are found at the Banque de France, but do expect a wait during busy summer months and be aware of the fact that it closes early (3:30 PM). You won't do as well at exchange booths in airports or rail and bus stations, in hotels, in restaurants, or in stores. To avoid lines at airport exchange booths, **get an initial amount of euros before you leave home**.

Exchange Services International Currency Express ✉ 427 N. Camden Dr., Suite F, Beverly Hills, CA 90210 ☎ 888/278-6628 orders 🖷 310/278-6410 ⊕ www.foreignmoney.com. **Travel Ex Currency Services** ☎ 800/287-7362 orders and retail locations ⊕ www.travelex.com.

TRAVELER'S CHECKS

Do you need traveler's checks? It depends on where you're headed. If you're going to rural areas and small towns, go with cash; traveler's checks are best used in cities. Lost or stolen checks can usually be replaced within 24 hours. To ensure a speedy refund, buy your own traveler's checks—don't let someone else pay for them: irregularities like this can cause delays. The person who bought the checks should make the call to request a refund.Note that with the prevalence of ATM cash machines in even the smallest French towns, you may find little, if no, need for traveler's checks.

PACKING

In your carry-on luggage, pack an extra pair of eyeglasses or contact lenses and enough of any medication you take to last a few days longer than the entire trip. You may also ask your doctor to write a spare prescription using the drug's generic name, as brand names may vary from country to country. In luggage to be checked, **never pack prescription drugs, valuables, or undeveloped film.** And don't forget to carry with you the addresses of offices that handle refunds of lost traveler's checks. Check *Fodor's How to Pack* (available at online retailers and bookstores everywhere) for more tips.

To avoid customs and security delays, carry medications in their original packaging. Don't pack any sharp objects in your carry-on luggage, including knives of any size or material, scissors, nail clippers, and corkscrews, or anything else that might arouse suspicion.

To avoid having your checked luggage chosen for hand inspection, don't cram bags full. The U.S. Transportation Security Administration suggests packing shoes on top and placing personal items you don't want touched in clear plastic bags.

CHECKING LUGGAGE

You're allowed to carry aboard one bag and one personal article, such as a purse or a laptop computer. Make sure what you carry on fits under your seat or in the overhead bin. Get to the gate early, so you can board as soon as possible, before the overhead bins fill up.

Baggage allowances vary by carrier, destination, and ticket class. On international flights, you're usually allowed to check two bags weighing up to 70 pounds (32 kilograms) each, although a few airlines allow checked bags of up to 88 pounds (40 kilograms) in first class. Some international carriers don't allow more than 66 pounds (30 kilograms) per bag in business class and 44 pounds (20 kilograms) in economy. On domestic flights, the limit is usually 50 to 70 pounds (23 to 32 kilograms) per bag. In general, carry-on bags shouldn't exceed 40 pounds (18 kilograms). Most airlines won't accept bags that weigh more than 100 pounds (45 kilograms) on domestic or international flights. Expect to pay a fee for baggage that exceeds weight limits. Check baggage restrictions with your carrier before you pack.

Airline liability for baggage is limited to $2,500 per person on flights within the United States. On international flights it amounts to $9.07 per pound or $20 per kilogram for checked baggage (roughly $640 per 70-pound bag), with a maximum of $634.90 per piece, and $400 per passenger for unchecked baggage. You can buy additional coverage at check-in for about $10 per $1,000 of coverage, but it often excludes a rather extensive list of items, shown on your airline ticket.

Before departure, itemize your bags' contents and their worth, and label the bags with your name, address, and phone number. (If you use your home address, cover it so potential thieves can't see it readily.) Include a label inside each bag and **pack a copy of your itinerary.** At check-in, make sure each bag is correctly tagged with the destination airport's three-letter code. Because some checked bags will be opened for hand inspection, the U.S. Transportation Security Administration recommends that you leave luggage unlocked or use the plastic locks offered at check-in. TSA screeners place an inspection notice inside searched bags, which are re-sealed with a special lock.

If your bag has been searched and contents are missing or damaged, file a claim with the TSA Consumer Response Center as soon as possible. If your bags arrive damaged or fail to arrive at all, file a written report with the airline before leaving the airport.

🛂 Complaints **U.S. Transportation Security Administration Contact Center** ☎ 866/289-9673 ⊕ www.tsa.gov.

PASSPORTS & VISAS

When traveling internationally, carry your passport even if you don't need one (it's always the best form of I.D.) and **make two photocopies of the data page** (one for someone at home and another for you, carried separately from your passport). If you lose your passport, promptly call the nearest embassy or consulate and the local police.

U.S. passport applications for children under age 14 require consent from both parents or legal guardians; both parents must appear together to sign the application. If only one parent appears, he or she must submit a written statement from the other parent authorizing passport issuance for the child. A parent with sole authority must present evidence of it when applying; acceptable documentation includes the child's certified birth certificate listing only the applying parent, a court order specifically permitting this parent's travel with the child, or a death certificate for the nonapplying parent. Application forms and instructions are available on the Web site of the U.S. State Department's Bureau of Consular Affairs (⊕ travel.state.gov).

ENTERING FRANCE

All Australian, Canadian, New Zealand, U.K., and U.S. citizens, even infants, need only a valid passport to enter France for stays of up to 90 days.

PASSPORT OFFICES

The best time to apply for a passport or to renew is in fall and winter. Before any trip, check your passport's expiration date, and, if necessary, renew it as soon as possible.

🛂 Australian Citizens Australian Department of Foreign Affairs and Trade: **Passports Australia** ☎ 131-232 ⊕ www.passports.gov.au.

🛂 Canadian Citizens **Passport Office** ✉ To mail in applications: 200 Promenade du Portage, Hull,

Québec J8X 4B7 ☎ 819/994-3500 or 800/567-6868 ⊕ www.ppt.gc.ca.

🛂 New Zealand Citizens **New Zealand Passports Office** ☎ 0800/22-5050 or 04/474-8100 ⊕ www.passports.govt.nz.

🛂 U.K. Citizens **U.K. Passport Service** ☎ 0870/521-0410 ⊕ www.passport.gov.uk.

🛂 U.S. Citizens **National Passport Information Center** ☎ 877/487-2778, 888/874-7793 TDD, TTY ⊕ travel.state.gov.

PUBLIC TRANSPORTATION

For information about public transportation in France, *see* A to Z sections *in* individual chapters.

RESTROOMS

Although most cafés reserve the right to limit use of their bathroom facilities to paying customers, most French are willing to ignore the frustrated glare of the waiter in an emergency. Bathrooms are often downstairs, are usually unisex (which means you may have to walk by urinals in use), are often just holes in the ground with porcelain pads on either side for your feet, and to top it all off, you'll probably have to pay a fee of 20–40¢. They are not the cleanest places in the world, especially for children, so it is in your best interest to be prepared and always carry a small box of tissues with you. In cities, your best bets may be fast-food chains, large department stores, and hotel lobbies. Do not be alarmed if you don't see any light switches—once the bathroom door is shut and locked, the lights will go on. You can also find pay-per-use toilet units on Parisian streets; these require 50¢ (small children, however, should not use these alone, as the self-sanitizing system works with weight-related sensors that might not sense the presence of a child). There are bathrooms in the larger métro stations and in all train stations for a cost of 50¢. Highway rest stops also have bathrooms, which are equipped with changing tables for babies and even showers during summer months.

SAFETY

Don't wear a waist pack, which pegs you as a tourist. Distribute your cash and any valuables (including your credit cards and passport) between a deep front pocket, an inside jacket or vest pocket, and a hidden money pouch. Do not reach for the money pouch once you're in public.

Beware of petty theft—purse snatching, pickpocketing, and pilfering from automobiles—throughout France, particularly in Paris and along the Côte d'Azur. Use common sense: avoid pulling out a lot of money in public; wear a handbag with long straps that you can sling across your body, bandolier style, with a zippered compartment for your money and passport. It's also a good idea to wear a money belt. When withdrawing money from cash machines, be especially aware of your surroundings and anyone standing uncomfortably close. If you feel uneasy, press the cancel button (*annuler*) and walk to an area where you feel more comfortable. Incidents of credit-card fraud are on the rise in France, especially in urban areas; be sure to collect your receipts, as these have recently been used by thieves to charge over the Internet, where a PIN number is not mandatory. Men should keep their wallets up front. Car break-ins, especially in isolated parking lots where hikers set off for the day, are on the rise. It makes sense to **take valuables with you or leave your luggage at your hotel.**

Although Paris is as safe as any major city, muggers do occasionally mark tourists in the city's métro system, especially at the tricky turnstiles; see the Métro Travel section in Paris A to Z in Chapter 1 for details. Note one cultural difference; a friendly smile or steady eye contact is often seen as an invitation to further contact; so, unfortunately, you should avoid being overly friendly with strangers—unless you feel perfectly safe.

SENIOR-CITIZEN TRAVEL

Older travelers (60 and older) can take advantage of many discounts, such as reduced admissions of 20%–50% to museums and movie theaters. For rail travel in France, the Carte Senior entitles travelers 60 years or older to discounts (⇨ Train Travel, *below*).

To qualify for age-related discounts, mention your senior-citizen status up front

when booking hotel reservations (not when checking out) and before you're seated in restaurants (not when paying the bill). Be sure to have identification on hand. When renting a car, ask about promotional car-rental discounts, which can be cheaper than senior-citizen rates.

Educational Programs Elderhostel ⊠ 11 Ave. de Lafayette, Boston, MA 02111-1746 ☎ 877/426-8056, 978/323-4141 international callers, 877/426-2167 TTY ⊟ 877/426-2166 ⊕ www.elderhostel.org. **Interhostel** ⊠ University of New Hampshire, 6 Garrison Ave., Durham, NH 03824 ☎ 603/862-1147 or 800/733-9753 ⊟ 603/862-1113 ⊕ www.learn.unh.edu.

SHOPPING

People in France like to bargain when they have a good feeling with the salesperson, even if the prices are clearly marked; it's one of the great pleasures of shopping in a country rich in small local businesses (in fact, the only places people don't bargain are in your typical large shopping center or big-name business). Bargaining is traditional in outdoor and flea markets, antiques stores, small jewelry shops, and art galleries, for example. If you're thinking of buying several items, or if you're simply in love with something a little bit too expensive, you've nothing to lose by cheerfully suggesting to the proprietor, "*Vous me faites un prix?*" ("How about a discount?"). The small business man will immediately size you up, and you'll have some good-natured fun.

SMART SOUVENIRS

When in France, think gourmet. For those who love to cook—or just love to taste—there are some simple gifts available in grocery stores or one of the many city and countryside outdoor markets: delicious mustard in a ceramic jar made following a traditional recipe from the 18th century costs about €4; organic jams made with whole cherries or figs from the south cost about €3 each; organic olive oils (with flavors ranging from thyme to truffle) will run about €15–€25 each; and a pot of organic lavender honey goes for €5. There's even gourmet salt, called *fleur de sel,* which comes from the coast of Brittany. Wonderful liqueurs include cognacs, armagnacs, or calvados—the fiery apple after-dinner *digestif* from Normandy—or one of the various fruit-flavored *eaux de vie* that Hemingway and Fitzgerald loved so much. These liquors can be found in any grocery or small liquor store and cost €16–€45. For the best quality, look for the tall slender bottles with handwritten labels and red-wax seals. For the champagne lover there are wonderful organic champagnes produced by smaller vineyards.

For other unique gift ideas, look to the museums. The Louvre, for example, has a museum shop that sells beautiful reproductions of a variety of masterpieces, from Greek figures to Egyptian heads, and ceramic Buddhas using the original molds. You can also purchase T-shirts here with charming vintage illustrations of Parisian life. Or look—surprise!—in the larger pharmacies for gift ideas from small French companies. For example, you could buy a small pot of all-natural Nuxe honey lip balm or the increasingly popular skin care products by Claudelie made from grape-seed extracts—French actresses swear by these. It's always interesting to look to the past: flea markets and *brocantes* (secondhand shops) sell Art Deco brooches, tiny eau-de-vie glasses, and evocative old copies of *Paris Match*. And there's always the chance of finding a stray bit of Quimper faïence. Another good bet is purchasing regional specialties, though your exports must be legal—madeleines, say, or nougat—as those savory sausages and glass jars of foie gras may be confiscated by customs. And for the hottest gift items going, just consult the latest issues of France's many style magazines, including *ELLE* and *Vogue*.

STUDENTS IN FRANCE

Studying in France is the perfect way to shake up your perception of the world, make international friends, and improve your language skills. You may choose to study through a U.S.–sponsored program, usually through an American university, or enroll in a program sponsored by a French organization. Do your homework: programs vary greatly in expense, academic quality, exposure to language, amount of contact with locals, and living conditions. Working through your local university is the easiest way to find out about study-abroad programs in France. Most universities have staff members who distribute information on programs at European universities, and they might be able to put you in touch with program participants.

Student bargains can be found almost everywhere—on train and plane fares, and for movie and museum tickets. Note, however, that you must be 26 or under.

🎫 I.D.s & Services STA Travel ✉ 10 Downing St., New York, NY 10014 ☎ 212/627-3111, 800/777-0112 24-hr service center 🖷 212/627-3387 ⊕ www.sta.com. **Travel Cuts** ✉ 187 College St., Toronto, Ontario M5T 1P7, Canada ☎ 800/592-2887 in the U.S., 416/979-2406 or 866/246-9762 in Canada 🖷 416/979-8167 ⊕ www.travelcuts.com.

🎫 Resources American Institute for Foreign Study ✉ River Plaza, 9 W. Broad St., Stamford, CT 06902 ☎ 203/869-9090 or 800/727-2437 🖷 203/863-6180. **American Council of International Studies (ACIS)** ✉ 343 Congress St., Suite 3100, Boston, MA 02210 ☎ 617/236-2051 or 800/888-2247. **Council on International Educational Exchange (CIEE)** ✉ 7 Custom House St., 3rd fl., Portland, ME 04101 ☎ 207/553-7600 or 800/407-8839 🖷 207/553-7699. **Institute of International Education (IIE)** ☎ 212/984-5413 ⊕ www.iie.org. **World Learning** ✉ Kipling Rd., Box 676, Brattleboro, VT 05302 ☎ 802/257-7751 or 800/336-1616 🖷 802/258-3248.

TAXES

All taxes must be included in posted prices in France. The initials TTC (*toutes taxes comprises*—taxes included) sometimes appear on price lists but, strictly speaking, they are superfluous. By law, **restaurant and hotel prices must include 19.6% taxes and a service charge.** If they show up as extra charges on your bill, complain.

VALUE-ADDED TAX

A number of shops offer V.A.T. refunds to foreign shoppers. You are entitled to an export refund of the 19.6% tax, depending on the item purchased, but it's often applicable only if your purchases in the same store reach a minimum of €430 (for U.K. and EU residents) or €184 (others, including U.S. and Canadian residents). In most instances, you need to fill out a form, which must then be tendered to a customs official at your last port of departure. Remember to **ask for the refund, as some stores—especially larger ones—offer the service only upon request,** and note that V.A.T. refunds can't be processed after you arrive back home. In the end, you often wind up getting a credit on your charge card.

When making a purchase, **ask for a V.A.T. refund form** and find out whether the merchant gives refunds—not all stores do, nor are they required to. Have the form stamped like any customs form by customs officials when you leave the country or, if you're visiting several European Union countries, when you leave the EU. Be ready to show customs officials what you've bought (pack purchases together, in your carry-on luggage); budget extra time for this. After you're through passport control, take the form to a refund-service counter for an on-the-spot refund (which is usually the quickest and easiest option), or mail it to the address on the form (or the envelope with it) after you arrive home.

A service processes refunds for most shops. You receive the total refund stated on the form. Global Refund is a Europe-wide service with 210,000 affiliated stores and more than 700 refund counters—located at major airports and border crossings. Its refund form is called a Tax Free Check. The service issues refunds in the form of cash, check, or credit-card adjustment. If you don't have time to wait at the refund counter, you can mail in the form to an office in Europe or Canada instead.

⚑ V.A.T. Refunds Global Refund Canada ⊕ Box 2020, Station Main Brampton, Ontario L6T 3S3 ☎ 800/993-4313 🖷 905/791-9078 ⊕ www.globalrefund.com.

TELEPHONES
AREA & COUNTRY CODES

The country code for France is 33. The first two digits of French numbers are a prefix determined by zone: Paris and Ile-de-France, 01; the northwest, 02; the northeast, 03; the southeast, 04; and the southwest, 05. Numbers that begin with 06 are for mobile phones (and are notori-

ously expensive). Pay close attention to the numbers beginning with 08; 08 followed by 00 is a toll-free number but 08–36 numbers are very costly, at least €.35 per minute.

CALLING FRANCE

Note that **when dialing France from abroad, drop the initial 0 from the number.** For instance, to call a telephone number in Paris from the United States, dial 011–33 plus the phone number minus the initial 0 (phone numbers in this book are listed with the full 10 digits, which you use to make local calls). To call France from the United Kingdom, dial 00–33, then dial the number in France minus the initial 0.

DIRECTORY & OPERATOR ASSISTANCE

To find a number **in France, dial 12 for information.** For international inquiries, dial 08–36–59–32–12 (you may request information for two numbers per call for a €3 service charge).

Another source of information is the Minitel, an online network similar to the Internet. You can find one—they look like a small computer terminal—in most post offices. Available free is an online phone book covering the entire country. To find information, hit the *appel* (call) key, then, when prompted, type the name you are looking for and hit *envoi* (return). It's also useful for tracking down services: choose *activité* (activity), tap in *piscine* (swimming pool), then Chartres, for example, and it will give you a list of all the pools in Chartres. Go to other lines or pages by hitting the *suite* (next) key. Newer models will connect automatically when you hit the book-icon key. To disconnect, hit *fin* (end).

INTERNATIONAL CALLS

To make a direct international call out of France, dial 00 and wait for the tone, then dial the country code (1 for the United States and Canada, 44 for the United Kingdom, 61 for Australia, and 64 for New Zealand) and the area code (minus any initial 0) and number.

Telephone rates have decreased recently in France owing to the fact that the French

Telecom monopoly finally has some stringent competition. As in most countries, the highest rates fall between 8 AM and 7 PM; you can expect to pay €.25 per minute for a call to the United States, Canada, or some of the closer European countries such as Great Britain, Belgium, Italy, and Germany. Rates are slashed by half when you make that same call between 7 PM and 8 AM, at just €.12 per minute, making it definitely worth the wait. There should be very little to compel you to call home with the help of international directory assistance, as it costs a hefty €6 per call; if this doesn't dissuade you, dial 00–33 plus the code of the country you'd like to call and a bilingual operator will come on line. Try not to make calls directly from your hotel either, unless you're using a phone card; they charge heavily for local calls and slap a service charge on for international calls. Your best bet is to buy a French phone card, a *télécarte,* which can be used from any phone and will end up saving you a bundle.

LOCAL CALLS
To make calls in the same city or town, or in the same region, dial the full 10-digit number.

LONG-DISTANCE CALLS
To call any region in France from another region, just dial the full 10-digit number.

LONG-DISTANCE SERVICES
AT&T, MCI, and Sprint access codes make calling long-distance relatively convenient, but you may find the local access number blocked in many hotel rooms. First ask the hotel operator to connect you. If the hotel operator balks, ask for an international operator, or dial the international operator yourself. One way to improve your odds of getting connected to your long-distance carrier is to travel with more than one company's calling card (a hotel may block Sprint, for example, but not MCI). If all else fails, call from a pay phone.
🌐 Access Codes **AT&T Direct** ☎ 08-00-99-00-11, 08-00-99-01-11, 800/874-4000 for information. **MCI WorldPhone** ☎ 08-00-99-00-19, 800/444-4444 for information. **Sprint International Access** ☎ 08-00-99-87, 800/793-1153 for information.

PHONE CARDS
The rare French person who doesn't have a mobile phone uses ***télécartes*** (phone cards), which you can buy just about anywhere, from post offices, tabacs, métro stations, magazine kiosks, small grocery stores, or any France Telecom office. These phone cards will save you money because the international rates they offer have been negotiated and are the best you will find. They will also save you time, as it's virtually impossible to find a phone that will take coins nowadays. There are two télécartes available; *une pétite* that costs €9 for 50 units or *une grande* that costs €16.25 for 120 units. Scratch the card to uncover your personal PIN, dial the toll-free number and the number you wish to reach (be it local or international) and the operator will tell you the exact amount of time you have to chat.

PUBLIC PHONES
Telephone booths can be found in airports, post offices, train stations, on the street, and often in cafés. You can use your own credit card or an international calling card; you must insert your credit card and punch in your PIN. Keep in mind that credit cards work on a €20 minimum—you will have exactly thirty days after the first call you put on your card to use up the credit. If you are using a phone card, simply dial the toll-free number on the back of the card, enter the identification number from the back of the card, and follow the instructions in English. At press time, prices were falling, and a local call made between 8 AM and 7 PM cost €.032 per minute. Low rates of €.016 per minute apply weekdays between 7 PM and 8 AM, all day Saturday and Sunday, and all national holidays.

TIME & DATES
The time difference between New York and Paris is six hours (so when it's 1 PM in New York, it's 7 PM in Paris). The time difference between London and Paris is one hour; between Sydney and Paris, 8–9 hours; and between Auckland and Paris, 12 hours. France, like the rest of Europe, uses the 24-hour (or "military") clock, which means that after noon you continue

counting forward: 13h00 is 1 PM, 14h00 is 2 PM, 22h30 is 10:30 PM. The European format for abbreviating dates is day/month/year, so 7/5/05 means May 7th, not July 5th.

TIPPING

The French have a clear idea of when they should be tipped. Bills in bars and restaurants include a service charge, but **it is customary to round out your bill with some small change** unless you're dissatisfied. The amount varies: anywhere from €.50, if you've merely bought a beer, to €1–€2 (or more) after a meal. Tip taxi drivers and hairdressers about 10%. In some theaters and hotels, coat-check attendants may expect nothing (if there is a sign saying POURBOIRE INTERDIT—tips forbidden); otherwise give them €.50–€1. Washroom attendants usually get €.50, though the sum is often posted.

If you stay in a hotel for more than two or three days, it is customary to leave something for the chambermaid—about €1.50 per day. In expensive hotels you may well call on the services of a baggage porter (bellboy) and hotel porter and possibly the telephone receptionist. All expect a tip: plan on about €1.50 per item for the baggage porter, but the other tips will depend on how much you've used their services—common sense must guide you here. In hotels that provide room service, give €1 to the waiter (this does not apply to breakfast served in your room). If the chambermaid does some pressing or laundering for you, give her €1 on top of the charge made. If the concierge has been very helpful, it is customary to leave a tip of €10–€20, depending on the type of hotel and the level of service.

Gas-station attendants get nothing for gas or oil but €.75 or €1.50 for checking tires. Train and airport porters get a fixed €1–€1.50 per bag, but you're better off getting your own baggage cart if you can (a €1 coin—refundable—is necessary in train stations only). Museum guides should get €1–€1.50 after a guided tour, and it is standard practice to tip tour guides (and bus drivers) €2 or more after an excursion, depending on its length.

TOURS & PACKAGES

Because everything is prearranged on a prepackaged tour or independent vacation, you spend less time planning—and often get it all at a good price.

BOOKING WITH AN AGENT

Travel agents are excellent resources. But it's a good idea to collect brochures from several agencies, as some agents' suggestions may be influenced by relationships with tour and package firms that reward them for volume sales. If you have a special interest, find an agent with expertise in that area. The American Society of Travel Agents (ASTA) has a database of specialists worldwide; you can log on to the group's Web site to find one near you. Make sure your travel agent knows the accommodations and other services of the place being recommended. Ask about the hotel's location, room size, beds, and whether it has a pool, room service, or programs for children, if you care about these. Has your agent been there in person or sent others whom you can contact? Do some homework on your own, too: local tourism boards can provide information about lesser-known and small-niche operators, some of which may sell only direct.

BUYER BEWARE

Each year consumers are stranded or lose their money when tour operators—even large ones with excellent reputations—go out of business. So check out the operator. Ask several travel agents about its reputation, and try to **book with a company that has a consumer-protection program.** (Look for information in the company's brochure.) In the United States, members of the United States Tour Operators Association are required to set aside funds ($1 million) to help eligible customers cover payments and travel arrangements in the event that the company defaults. It's also a good idea to choose a company that participates in the American Society of Travel Agents' Tour Operator Program; ASTA will act as mediator in any disputes between you and your tour operator.

Remember that the more your package or tour includes, the better you can predict the ultimate cost of your vacation. Make sure you know exactly what is covered, and beware of hidden costs. Are taxes, tips, and transfers included? Entertainment and excursions? These can add up.

🔢 Tour-Operator Recommendations **American Society of Travel Agents** (⇨ Travel Agencies). **CrossSphere-The Global Association for Packaged Travel** ✉ 546 E. Main St., Lexington, KY 40508 ☎ 859/226-4444 or 800/682-8886 🖷 859/226-4414 ⊕ www.CrossSphere.com. **United States Tour Operators Association (USTOA)** ✉ 275 Madison Ave., Suite 2014, New York, NY 10016 ☎ 212/599-6599 🖷 212/599-6744 ⊕ www.ustoa.com.

THEME TOURS

The following tour companies specialize in trips to France. The French Government Tourist Office (⇨ Visitor Information, *below*) publishes brochures on theme trips in France including "In the Footsteps of the Painters of Light in Provence" and "France for the Jewish Traveler." Also *see* Barge & Yacht Travel, Bike Travel, *and* Children in France, *above,* for more information about theme tours.

🔢 Food & Wine **DuVine Adventures** ✉ 124 Holland St., Suite 2, Somerville, MA 02144 ☎ 617/776-4441 or 888/396-5383 🖷 617/776-1660 ⊕ www.duvine.com. **European Culinary Adventures** ✉ 5 Ledgewood Way, Suite 6, Peabody, MA 01960 ☎ 978/535-5738 or 800/852-2625. **Le Cordon Bleu** ✉ 8 rue Léon Delhomme, 75015 Paris ☎ 01-53-68-22-50 🖷 01-48-56-03-77 ⊕ www.cordonbleu.net. **Ritz-Escoffier** ✉ 15 pl. Vendôme, 75001 Paris ☎ 800/966-5758 ⊕ www.ritzparis.com, in Paris's Ritz hotel. **La Varenne** ☎ Box 25574, Washington, DC 20007 ☎ 202/337-0073 or 800/537-6486 🖷 703/823-5438 ⊕ www.lavarenne.com.

🔢 Music **Dailey-Thorp Travel** ✉ Box 670, Big Horn, WY 82833 ☎ 307/673-1555 or 800/998-4677 🖷 307/674-7474.

TRAIN TRAVEL

The SNCF, France's national rail service, is fast, punctual, comfortable, and comprehensive. Traveling across France, you have various options: local trains, overnight trains with sleeping accommodations, and the high-speed TGV, the Trains à Grande Vitesse (very fast trains).

TGVs average 255 kph (160 mph) on the Lyon–southeast line and 300 kph (190 mph) on the Lille and Bordeaux–southwest lines and are the best and the fastest domestic trains. They operate between Paris and Lille/Calais, Paris and Brussels, Paris and Amsterdam, Paris and Lyon–Switzerland–Provence, Paris and Angers–Nantes, and Paris and Tours–Poitiers–Bordeaux. As with other main-line trains, a small supplement may be assessed at peak hours.

It's possible to get from one end of France to the other without traveling overnight, especially on TGVs. Otherwise, you have a choice between high-price *wagons-lit* (sleeping cars) and affordable *couchettes* (bunks, six to a compartment in second class, four to a compartment in first, with sheets and pillow provided, priced at around €15).

Try to **get to the station half an hour before departure** to ensure you'll have a good seat. Before boarding, you must **punch your ticket (but not Eurailpass) in one of the orange machines** at the entrance to the platforms, or else the ticket collector will fine you €15 on the spot.

In Paris there are six international rail stations: Gare du Nord (northern France, northern Europe, and England via Calais or Boulogne); Gare St-Lazare (Normandy and England via Dieppe); Gare de l'Est (Strasbourg, Luxembourg, Basel, and central Europe); Gare de Lyon (Lyon, Marseille, Provence, Geneva, and Italy); and Gare d'Austerlitz (Loire Valley, southwest France, and Spain). Note that Gare Montparnasse has taken over as the main terminus for trains bound for southwest France.

BETWEEN THE U.K. & FRANCE

Short of flying, taking the "Chunnel" by riding the Eurostar train is the fastest way to cross the English Channel: 35 minutes from Folkestone to Calais, 60 minutes from motorway to motorway, or 2 hours and 40 minutes from London's Waterloo Station to Paris's Gare du Nord. For more information, *see* The Channel Tunnel, *above.*

British Rail also has four daily departures from London's Victoria Station, all linking with the Dover–Calais–Boulogne ferry services through to Paris. There's also an overnight service on the Newhaven–Dieppe ferry. Journey time is about eight hours. Credit-card bookings are accepted by phone or in person at a British Rail travel center.

🚗 Car Transport **Eurotunnel** ☎ 0870/535-3535 in the U.K., 0810/63-03-04 in France ⊕ ww2. eurotunnel.com.

🚃 Passenger Service In the U.K.: **Eurostar** ☎ 0990/186-186 ⊕ www.eurostar.com. In the U.S.: **BritRail Travel** ☎ 866/274-8724 in the U.S. ⊕ www.britrail.com. **Rail Europe** ☎ 800/942-4866 ⊕ www.raileurope.com.

🚃 Passenger Service In the U.K.: **Eurostar** ☎ 0990/186-186 ⊕ www.eurostar.com. **InterCity Europe** ✉ Victoria Station, London ☎ 0990/848-848 for credit-card bookings. In the U.S.: **BritRail Travel** ☎ 800/677-8585. **Rail Europe** ☎ 800/942-4866 ⊕ www.raileurope.com.

CLASSES

There are two classes of train service in France; first (*première*) or second (*deux-ième*). First-class seats offer 50% more legroom, plusher upholstery, private reading lamps, and computer plugs on the TGV, not to mention the hush-hush environment for those of you who want to sleep. The price is also nearly double.

CUTTING COSTS

To save money, **look into rail passes.** But be aware that if you don't plan to cover many miles, you may come out ahead by buying individual tickets.

There are two kinds of rail passes: those you must purchase at home before you leave for France, including the France Rail Pass, the Eurail Selectpass (which replaces the old Europass), and those available in France from SNCF. EurailPasses are available through travel agents and a few authorized organizations, such as Rail Europe (*see* contact information *under* Rail Pass Agents, *below*). SNCF rail passes are available at any train station in France. It's important to note that your rail pass does not guarantee you a seat on the train you wish to ride. You need to **book seats ahead even if you're using a rail pass.**

If you plan to travel outside of Paris by train, **consider purchasing a France Rail**

Pass, which allows four days of unlimited train travel in a one-month period. If you travel solo, first class will run you $263, whereas second class is $229: you can add up to six days on this pass for $34 a day. For two people traveling together on a Saver Pass, the cost is $225, whereas in second class it is $195; additional days (up to 6) cost $29 each. Another option is the France Rail 'n Drive Pass (combining rail and rental car).

France is one of 17 countries in which **you can use EurailPasses,** which provide unlimited first-class rail travel in all of the participating countries for the duration of the pass. If you plan to rack up the miles, get a standard pass. These are available for 15 days ($588), 21 days ($762), one month ($946), two months ($1,338), and three months ($1,654). If your plans call for only limited train travel between France and another country, **consider a two-country pass** which costs less money than a EurailPass. With the two-country pass you'll get four flexible travel days between France and Italy, France and Spain, or France and Switzerland for $299. In addition to standard EurailPasses, **ask about special rail-pass plans.** Among these are the Eurail Selectpass Youth (for those under age 26) and the Eurail Selectpass Saver (which gives a discount for two or more people traveling together). Whichever of the above passes you choose, remember that **you must purchase your Eurail passes at home before leaving for France.** Another option is to **purchase one of the discount rail passes available only for sale in France** from SNCF. When traveling together, **two people (who don't have to be a couple) can save money with the Prix Découverte à Deux.** You'll get a 25% discount during "*périodes bleus*" (blue periods: weekdays and not on or near any holidays). Note that you have to be with the person you said you would be traveling with.

You can **get a reduced fare if you're a senior citizen (over 60).** There are two options: for the Prix Découverte Senior, all you have to do is show a valid I.D. with your age and you're entitled to up to a

25% reduction in fares in first and second class. The second, the Carte Senior, is better if you're planning on spending a lot of time traveling; it costs €49, is valid for one year, and entitles you to up to a 50% reduction on most trains with a guaranteed minimum reduction of 25%. It also entitles you to a 30% discount on trips outside of France.

With the Carte Enfant Plus, for €65 **children under 12 and up to four accompanying adults can get up to 50% off on most trains for an unlimited number of trips.** This card is perfect if you're planning on spending a lot of time traveling in France with your children, as it's valid for one year. You can also opt for the Prix Découverte Enfant Plus: when you buy your ticket, simply show a valid I.D. with your child's age and you can get a significant discount for your child and a 25% reduction for up to four accompanying adults.

If you purchase an individual ticket from SNCF in France and you're under 26, you automatically get a 25% reduction (a valid I.D., such as an ISIC card or your passport, is necessary). If you're going to be using the train quite a bit during your stay in France and **if you're under 26, consider buying the Carte 12–25** (€52), which offers unlimited 50% reductions for one year (provided that there's space available at that price; otherwise you'll just get the standard 25% discount).

If you don't benefit from any of these reductions and **if you plan on traveling at least 200 km (132 mi) round-trip and don't mind staying over a Saturday night, look into the Prix Découverte Séjour.** This ticket gives you a 25% reduction.

🚆 **Rail-Pass Agents CIT Tours Corp.** ☎ 800/248-7245 for rail, 800/248-8687 for tours and hotels. **Eurail** ⊕ www.eurail.com. **Rail Europe** ☎ 800/942-4866 in U.S. ⊕ www.raileurope.com.

FARES & SCHEDULES

You can **call for train information from any station or reserve tickets in any station.** Train schedules are available at stations or on the multilingual computerized schedule information network found at many stations. You can also make reservations and buy your ticket at the computer. Go to the Grandes Lignes counter for travel within France and to the Billets Internationaux desk if you're heading out of the country. Note that calling the SNCF's 08 number costs money (€0.34 per minute, and you often have to wait for minutes at a time), so it's better to go to the nearest station.

You must **always make a seat reservation for the TGV**—easily obtained at the ticket window or from an automatic machine. Seat reservations are reassuring but seldom necessary on other main-line French trains, except in summer and at certain busy holiday times. You also need a reservation for sleeping accommodations.

🚆 **Train Information BritRail Travel** ☎ 866/274-8724 in the U.S. ⊕ www.britrail.com. **Eurostar** ☎ 08-36-35-35-39 in France, 1233/617-575 or 0870/518-6186 in the U.K. ⊕ www.eurostar.com. **Rail Europe** ☎ 800/942-4866 in U.S. ⊕ www.raileurope.com. **SNCF** ✉ 88 rue St-Lazare, 75009 Paris ☎ 08-36-35-35-35 ⊕ www.sncf.fr/indexe.htm.

LUGGAGE DELIVERY SERVICE

With an advance arrangement, SNCF will pick up and deliver your luggage at a given time. For instance, if you're planning on spending a weekend in Nice, SNCF will pick up your luggage at your hotel in Paris in the morning before check out and deliver it to your hotel in Nice, where it will be awaiting your arrival. The cost is €15 for the first bag, and €10 for two additional bags, with a maximum of three bags per person.

🚆 **SNCF Luggage Delivery Service** ☎ 08-25-84-58-45 ⊕ www.sncf.fr.

TRAVEL AGENCIES

A good travel agent puts your needs first. Look for an agency that has been in business at least five years, emphasizes customer service, and has someone on staff who specializes in your destination. In addition, **make sure the agency belongs to a professional trade organization.** The American Society of Travel Agents (ASTA) has more than 10,000 members in some 140 countries, enforces a strict code of ethics, and will step in to mediate agent-client disputes involving ASTA members. ASTA also maintains a directory of agents on its Web site; ASTA's TravelSense.org, a trip-planning and travel-advice site, can also help to locate a travel agent who caters to your needs.

⁊ Local Agent Referrals **American Society of Travel Agents (ASTA)** ⊠ 1101 King St., Suite 200, Alexandria, VA 22314 ☎ 703/739–2782, 800/965–2782 24-hr hotline ⏚ 703/684–8319 ⊕ www.astanet.com and www.travelsense.org. **Association of British Travel Agents** ⊠ 68–71 Newman St., London W1T 3AH ☎ 020/7637–2444 ⏚ 020/7637–0713 ⊕ www.abta.com. **Association of Canadian Travel Agencies** ⊠ 130 Albert St., Suite 1705, Ottawa, Ontario K1P 5G4 ☎ 613/237–3657 ⏚ 613/237–7052 ⊕ www.acta.ca. **Australian Federation of Travel Agents** ⊠ Level 3, 309 Pitt St., Sydney, NSW 2000 ☎ 02/9264–3299 or 1300/363–416 ⏚ 02/9264–1085 ⊕ www.afta.com.au. **Travel Agents' Association of New Zealand** ⊠ Level 5, Tourism and Travel House, 79 Boulcott St., Box 1888, Wellington 6001 ☎ 04/499–0104 ⏚ 04/499–0786 ⊕ www.taanz.org.nz.

⁊ Local Agencies **Access Voyages** ⊠ 128 quai de Jemmapes, 10ᵉ ☎ 08-92-89-38-92 Ⓜ Jaurès. **American Express** ⊠ 11 rue Scribe, 8ᵉ ☎ 01-47-77-77-07 ⊠ 38 av. de Wagram, 8ᵉ ☎ 01-42-27-58-80. **Nouvelles Frontières** ⊠ 5 av. de l'Opéra, 1ᵉʳ ☎ 08-03-33-33-33 Ⓜ Pyramides ⊠ 14 av. de Verdun, 06000 Nice ⊠ 12 E. 33rd St. New York, NY 10016 ⏚ 212/779–1007. **Soltours** ⊠ 48 rue de Rivoli, 4ᵉ ☎ 01-42-71-24-34 Ⓜ Hôtel-de-Ville.

VISITOR INFORMATION

Learn more about foreign destinations by checking government-issued travel advisories and country information. For a broader picture, consider information from more than one country.

⁊ France Tourism Information **Maison de la France** ☎ 410/286-8310, weekdays 9-7 ⊕ www.francetourism.com. **Chicago** ⊠ 676 N. Michigan Ave., Chicago, IL 60611 ✎ fgto@mcs.net. **Los Angeles** ⊠ 9454 Wilshire Blvd., Suite 715, Beverly Hills, CA 90212 ✎ fgto@gte.net. **New York City** ⊠ 444 Madison Ave., 16th fl., New York, NY 10022 ✎ info@francetourism.com. **Canada** ⊠ 1981 Ave. McGill College, Suite 490, Montréal, Québec H3A 2W9. **U.K.** ⊠ 178 Piccadilly, London W1V OAL ☎ 171/6399-3500 ⏚ 171/6493-6594.

⁊ Local Tourist Offices *See* the A to Z sections *in* individual chapters for local tourist office telephone numbers and addresses.

⁊ Government Advisories **U.S. Department of State** ⊠ Overseas Citizens Services Office, 2100 Pennsylvania Ave. NW, 4th fl., Washington, DC 20520 ☎ 202/647–5225 interactive hotline, 888/407–4747 ⊕ www.travel.state.gov. **Consular Affairs Bureau of Canada** ☎ 800/267–6788 or 613/944–6788 ⊕ www.voyage.gc.ca. **U.K. Foreign and Commonwealth Office** ⊠ Travel Advice Unit, Consular Division, Old Admiralty Bldg., London SW1A 2PA ☎ 0870/606–0290 or 020/7008–1500 ⊕ www.fco.gov.uk/travel. **Australian Department of Foreign Affairs and Trade** ☎ 300/139–281 travel advisories, 02/6261–1299 Consular Travel Advice ⊕ www.smartraveller.gov.au or www.dfat.gov.au. **New Zealand Ministry of Foreign Affairs and Trade** ☎ 04/439–8000 ⊕ www.mft.govt.nz.

⁊ Tourism Web Sites **Tourism in France** ⊕ www.tourisme.fr with links to 3,500 tourist offices. **Bordeaux Tourist Office** ⊕ www.bordeaux-tourisme.com is the main site for this southwest France metropolis. **French Government Tourist Office** ⊕ www.francetourism.com is the national site for French tourism. **Lyon Tourist Office** ⊕ www.lyon-france.com is a helpful portal to this important hub of the country. **Monaco Tourist Office** ⊕ www.visitmonaco.com welcomes you to this glitzy resort in the south of France. **Normandy Tourist Board** ⊕ www.normandy-tourism.org is a great site for the region. **The Office du Tourisme et Congresses de Paris** ⊕ www.parisinfo.com is the main site for the Paris tourist office. **Provence Tourist Office** ⊕ www.visitprovence.com is a helpful site to all things Provençal. **Riviera Tourist Office** ⊕ www.crt-riviera.fr is one of the helpful overview sites devoted to the region. **Strasbourg Tourism Office** ⊕ www.strasbourg.com is devoted to one of the hubs of the Alsace-Lorraine region.

WEB SITES

Do check out the World Wide Web when planning your trip. You'll find everything from weather forecasts to virtual tours of famous cities. Be sure to visit Fodors.com (⊕ www.fodors.com), a complete travel-planning site. You can research prices and book plane tickets, hotel rooms, rental cars, vacation packages, and more. In addition, you can post your pressing questions in the Travel Talk section. Other

CONVERSIONS

DISTANCE

KILOMETERS/MILES

To change kilometers (km) to miles (mi), multiply km by .621. To change mi to km, multiply mi by 1.61.

km to mi	mi to km
1 = .62	1 = 1.6
2 = 1.2	2 = 3.2
3 = 1.9	3 = 4.8
4 = 2.5	4 = 6.4
5 = 3.1	5 = 8.1
6 = 3.7	6 = 9.7
7 = 4.3	7 = 11.3
8 = 5.0	8 = 12.9

METERS/FEET

To change meters (m) to feet (ft), multiply m by 3.28. To change ft to m, multiply ft by .305.

m to ft	ft to m
1 = 3.3	1 = .30
2 = 6.6	2 = .61
3 = 9.8	3 = .92
4 = 13.1	4 = 1.2
5 = 16.4	5 = 1.5
6 = 19.7	6 = 1.8
7 = 23.0	7 = 2.1
8 = 26.2	8 = 2.4

TEMPERATURE

METRIC CONVERSIONS

To change centigrade or Celsius (C) to Fahrenheit (F), multiply C by 1.8 and add 32. To change F to C, subtract 32 from F and multiply by .555.

°F	°C
0	-17.8
10	-12.2
20	-6.7
30	-1.1
32	0
40	+4.4
50	10.0
60	15.5
70	21.1
80	26.6
90	32.2
98.6	37.0
100	37.7

WEIGHT

KILOGRAMS/POUNDS

To change kilograms (kg) to pounds (lb), multiply kg by 2.20. To change lb to kg, multiply lb by .455.

kg to lb	lb to kg
1 = 2.2	1 = .45
2 = 4.4	2 = .91
3 = 6.6	3 = 1.4
4 = 8.8	4 = 1.8
5 = 11.0	5 = 2.3
6 = 13.2	6 = 2.7
7 = 15.4	7 = 3.2
8 = 17.6	8 = 3.6

GRAMS/OUNCES

To change grams (g) to ounces (oz), multiply g by .035. To change oz to g, multiply oz by 28.4.

g to oz	oz to g
1 = .04	1 = 28
2 = .07	2 = 57
3 = .11	3 = 85
4 = .14	4 = 114
5 = .18	5 = 142
6 = .21	6 = 170
7 = .25	7 = 199
8 = .28	8 = 227

LIQUID VOLUME

LITERS/U.S. GALLONS

To change liters (L) to U.S. gallons (gal), multiply L by .264. To change U.S. gal to L, multiply gal by 3.79.

L to gal	gal to L
1 = .26	1 = 3.8
2 = .53	2 = 7.6
3 = .79	3 = 11.4
4 = 1.1	4 = 15.2
5 = 1.3	5 = 19.0
6 = 1.6	6 = 22.7
7 = 1.8	7 = 26.5
8 = 2.1	8 = 30.3

CLOTHING SIZE

WOMEN'S CLOTHING

US	UK	EUR
4	6	34
6	8	36
8	10	38
10	12	40
12	14	42

WOMEN'S SHOES

US	UK	EUR
5	3	36
6	4	37
7	5	38
8	6	39
9	7	40

MEN'S SUITS

US	UK	EUR
34	34	44
36	36	46
38	38	48
40	40	50
42	42	52
44	44	54
46	46	56

MEN'S SHIRTS

US	UK	EUR
14½	14½	37
15	15	38
15½	15½	39
16	16	41
16½	16½	42
17	17	43
17½	17½	44

MEN'S SHOES

US	UK	EUR
7	6	39½
8	7	41
9	8	42
10	9	43
11	10	44½
12	11	46

planning tools include a currency converter and weather reports, and there are loads of links to travel resources.

⚑ Recommended Web Sites The **Centre du Monuments Nationaux** ⊕ www.monum.fr runs 200 monuments—from the Arc de Triomphe to Chambord—is chock full of information. If you are château-hopping, log on to www.chateauxandcountry.com for brief overview of hundreds of châteaux in France. **Eurail** ⊕ www.eurail.com has all the info about the many railway passes available for travel through France and Europe. **Eurostar** ⊕ www.eurostar.com is the main contact for the Chunnel train that connects Paris and London. **French Embassy** ⊕ www. france.diplomatie.fr is helpful for information on the French government. **French Ministry of Culture** ⊕ www.culture.fr provides a portal to all the cultural happenings and institutions throughout France. **French National Museums** ⊕ www.rmn.fr is the main site for the Réunion des musées nationaux, which administers the biggest and greatest museums in France. **Rail Europe** ⊕ www. raileurope.com gives you the scoop on many different discount rail passes through France and Europe. **SNCF** ⊕ www.sncf.fr/indexe.htm is the main clearinghouse for the French national railway network, invaluable for schedules and prices. **Weather Reports** ⊕ www.meteo.fr helps you track the highly variable weather in France.

Paris

WORD OF MOUTH

"Go to the Impressionist floor at the Musée D'Orsay. View the Renoirs on one side, the Monets on the other, and the Eiffel Tower straight through the window. Think how lucky you are to be in Paris!"

—Idsant

"As evening approaches, take one of the sunset cruises that leave from the Iles. Then return to the restaurant you chose earlier. Lastly, a late walk back to your hotel past Paris's softly-lit monuments and bridges. Sigh."

—JeanneB

Introduction by
Nancy Coons

Updated by
Jennifer Ditsler-
Ladonne, Rosa
Jackson, Lisa
Pasold,
Mathew
Schwartz, and
Heather
Stimmler-Hall

IF THERE'S A PROBLEM WITH A TRIP TO PARIS, it's the embarrassment of riches that faces you. No matter which aspect of Paris you choose— touristy, historic, fashion-conscious, pretentious-bourgeois, thrifty, or the legendary bohemian arty Paris of undying attraction—one thing is certain: you will carve out your own Paris, one that is vivid, exciting, ultimately unforgettable. Wherever you head, your itinerary will prove to be a voyage of discovery. But choosing the Paris of your dreams is a bit like choosing a perfume or cologne. Do you want something young and dashing, or elegant and worldly? How about sporty, or perhaps strictly glamorous? No matter: they are all here—be it perfumes, famous museums, legendary churches, or romantic cafés. Whether you spend three days or three months in this city, it will always have something new to offer you, which may explain why the most assiduous explorers of Paris are the Parisians themselves.

Veterans know that Paris is a city of vast, noble perspectives and intimate, ramshackle streets, of formal *espaces vertes* (green open spaces) and quiet squares. This combination of the pompous and the private is one of the secrets of its perennial pull. Another is its size: Paris is relatively small as capitals go, with distances between many of its major sights and museums invariably walkable.

For the first-timer there will always be several must-dos at the top of the list, but getting to know Paris will never be quite as simple as a quick look at Notre-Dame, the Louvre, and the Eiffel Tower. You'll discover that around every corner, down every *ruelle* (little street) lies a resonance-in-waiting. You can stand on the rue du Faubourg St-Honoré at the very spot where Edmond Rostand set Ragueneau's pastry shop in *Cyrano de Bergerac.* You can read the letters of Madame de Sévigné in her actual *hôtel particulier,* or private mansion, now the Musée Carnavalet. You can hear the words of Racine resound in the ringing, hair-raising diction of the Comédie Française. You can breathe in the fumes of hubris before the extravagant onyx tomb Napoléon designed for himself. You can gaze through the gates at the school where Voltaire honed his wit, and you can lay a garland on Oscar Wilde's poignant grave at Père-Lachaise Cemetery.

If this is your first trip, you may want to take a guided tour of the city— a good introduction that will help you get your bearings and provide you with a general impression before you return to explore the sights that particularly interest you. To help track those down, this chapter's exploration of Paris is divided into eight neighborhood walks. Each *quartier,* or neighborhood, has its own personality, which is best discovered by foot power. Ultimately, your route will be marked by your preferences, your curiosity, and your state of fatigue. You can wander for hours without getting bored—though not, perhaps, without getting lost. By the time you have seen only a few neighborhoods, drinking in the rich variety they have to offer, you should not only be culturally replete but downright exhausted—and hungry, too. Again, take your cue from Parisians and think out your next move in a sidewalk café. So you've heard stories of a friend who paid $6 for a coffee at a café. So what? What you're paying for is time, and the opportunity to watch the in-

1

A visit to Paris will never be quite as simple as a quick look at a few landmarks. Each *quartier* (neighborhood) has its own treasures, and you should be ready to explore them—an enticing prospect in this most elegant of cities. Outlined here are the main areas on which to concentrate, depending on the length of your stay. Bear in mind that the amount of time spent visiting monuments—and museums in particular—is not something you can predict with any certainty, nor would you want to. Just to see the city's larger museums, let alone its smaller ones, would probably take a whole week.

If you have
3 days

On your first day begin at the beginning: the Ile de la Cité, settled more than 2,000 years ago and home to the cathedral of **Notre-Dame ❶** ►. Take a cue from Victor Hugo and climb the 387 steps of one of its towers to the former haunts of its mythic hunchback, Quasimodo—you'll be rewarded by a great view of Paris framed by the stone gargoyles created by Viollet-le-Duc. Descend to explore the enchanting **Ancien Cloître Quartier ❷**, nestled next to the cathedral. Then head several blocks over to marvel at the **Sainte-Chapelle ❸**, a jewel box of Gothic art shimmering with hundreds of stained-glass panels. After visiting the nearby **Conciergerie ❹**—the last abode of Queen Marie-Antoinette—walk over the **Pont Neuf ❼**, which spans the Seine, and turn left to reach the greatest museum in the world—the **Louvre ❽** (keep in mind it's closed Tuesday), famed showcase for the *Winged Victory,* the *Venus de Milo,* and the haunting, ironic smile of the *Mona Lisa.* Afterward, exit into the calm, green **Jardin des Tuileries ❿**, immortalized by the Impressionists, then head west to the city's heart, place de la Concorde. Walk up the leafy lower reaches of the Champs-Élysées, heading over to the Seine and its most gorgeous bridge—the **Pont Alexandre III ⓯**—just in time for *l'heure bleue,* or dusk.

On Day 2 you're ready to tackle picture-postcard Paris. Start at the **Tour Eiffel ⓰**, then take in some culture at the **Palais de Chaillot ⓱** museums, or the nearby **Musée Guimet ⓲** (for great Asian art) and the **Musée d'Art Moderne de la Ville de Paris ⓴** (for fine modern art). For a blast of the purest Parisian glamour, check out the **Maison de Baccarat ⓳**. At the place de l'Alma opt for a ride on the **Bateaux Mouches ㉑** up and down the Seine. Head along avenue Montaigne—Dior is here along with numerous other temples of fashion—to the Champs-Élysées and up left to the **Arc de Triomphe.**

On Day 3 explore the Faubourg St-Honoré, Paris's legendary center of luxe, where world-class shopping and two of Paris's most beautiful urban set pieces—**place Vendôme ㉚** and the **Palais-Royal ㉟**—await. Continue north to hit the Grands Boulevards, famed for their sidewalk cafés, the glittering **Opéra Garnier ㊼**—still haunted by the Phantom?—and then enjoy a tranquil afternoon in the chic and rich residential neighborhood around **Parc Monceau ㊶**, with a stop at the art-filled mansions of the **Musée Nissim de Camondo ㊸** and the **Musée Jacquemart-André ㊹**.

If you have
5 days

Follow the three-day itinerary above, then on your fourth day begin at the **Musée d'Orsay** ⑦, where many of the most famous Impressionist paintings in the world are on view. Pay your respects to Napoléon at the nearby church of the **Hôtel des Invalides** ⑱ and then to the great sculptor Rodin, at the **Musée Rodin** ⑲, housed in one of the prettiest *hôtels particuliers* in the city. Head east along the boulevard St-Germain to the picturesque place Furstenberg to visit the **Musée Delacroix** ㉝, the haunt of another great artist and set on gorgeous place Furstenberg. South a few blocks is the **Jardin du Luxembourg** ㊆, perfect for a sylvan time-out. If you're not tired yet, stop in at the extraordinary **Musée National du Moyen-Age** ⑫, which graces the time-stained Hôtel de Cluny.

On your fifth day begin on the **Ile St-Louis** ㊉—the little island sitting next to the larger Ile de la Cité in the Seine. Although there are no major sights to see here, you'll find an enchanting neighborhood that has more than a touch of the time machine to it. Cross over the Seine to the Marais—one of the city's most venerable quarters, studded with great Baroque and Rococo mansions, many of which are now museums, including the **Musée Picasso** ㊽. Nearby is another mecca for modern-art lovers, the **Centre Pompidou** ㊾, although those with more traditional tastes will make a beeline for the **Musée Carnavalet** ㊿ (the Paris History Museum). Then, to give your less-than-bionic feet a well-deserved rest, head to the magnificent 17th-century square **place des Vosges** ㊻ to enjoy sunset on one of its park benches and dinner at one of the casual cafés lining the square.

If you have
7 days

On your sixth day take a vacation from your Paris vacation by heading out for a day trip to **Versailles,** built in bicep-flexing Baroque splendor. Don't forget to explore its vast park in order to take in the intimate Petit Trianon and Hameau, which was Marie-Antoinette's toy farm.

On your seventh day get up at dawn and hurry up to the Butte (mound) of Montmartre, which graces a dramatic rise over the city. Get here to see the sun rise over the entire city from your perch on place du Parvis, in front of the basilica of the **Sacré-Coeur** ㊝. Track the spirit of Toulouse-Lautrec through the streets and to the **Musée de Montmartre** ㊞. For your last afternoon, descend back into the city to either attack some of the city's "other" museums (the **Musée Cognacq-Jay** ㊻ and the **Musée Maillol** ㊿), to explore Montparnasse, or, for a unique *grande finale* to your trip, visit some "permanent" Parisians ensconced in noble marble splendor at legendary **Cimetière du Père-Lachaise** ㊡. Congratulations are in order: you've just finished a unique cram course in French culture and history.

---

tricate drama of Parisian street life unfold. Hemingway knew the rules; after all, he would have remained just another unknown sportswriter if the waiters in the cafés had hovered around him impatiently.

Exploring Paris

By Lisa Pasold and Mat Schwartz

As world capitals go, Paris is surprisingly compact. With the exceptions of the Bois de Boulogne and Montmartre, you can easily walk from one major sight to the next. The city is divided in two by the River Seine, with two islands (Ile de la Cité and Ile St-Louis) in the middle. Each bank of the Seine has its own personality; the Rive Droite (Right Bank), with its spacious boulevards and formal buildings, generally has a more genteel feel than the carefree Rive Gauche (Left Bank), to the south. The east–west axis from Châtelet to the Arc de Triomphe, via the rue de Rivoli and the Champs-Élysées, is the Right Bank's principal thoroughfare for sightseeing and shopping.

The city is divided into 20 *arrondissements* (districts). The last one or two digits of a city zip code (e.g., 75002) will tell you the arrondissement (in this case, the 2ᵉ, or 2nd). Although the best method of getting to know Paris is on foot, public transportation—particularly the métro system—is excellent. Buy the *Plan de Paris* booklet, a city map and guide with a street-name index that also shows métro stations. Note that all métro stations have detailed neighborhood maps displayed just inside the entrance.

This chapter is divided into eight Paris neighborhood walks. A few monuments and museums close for lunch between noon and 2, and many are closed on either Monday or Tuesday: check before you set off.

Numbers in the text correspond to numbers in the margin and on the Paris and Montmartre maps.

The Historic Heart: From Notre-Dame to the Place de la Concorde

No matter how you first approach Paris—historically, geographically, emotionally—it is the River Seine that summons all and that harbors two celebrated islands, the Ile de la Cité and the Ile St-Louis, both at the very center of the city. Of the two, it is the Ile de la Cité that forms the historic ground zero of Paris. It was here that the earliest inhabitants of Paris, the Gaulish tribe of the Parisii, settled in about 250 BC, calling their home Lutetia, meaning "settlement surrounded by water." Today it is famed for the great, brooding cathedral of Notre-Dame, the haunted Conciergerie, and the dazzling Sainte-Chapelle. If Notre-Dame represents Church, another major attraction of this walk—the Louvre—symbolizes State. A succession of French rulers was responsible for filling this immense structure with the world's greatest paintings and works of art. It's the largest museum in the world, as well as one of the easiest to get lost in. Beyond the Louvre lie the graceful Tuileries Gardens, the grand place de la Concorde—the very hub of the city—and the Belle Époque splendor of the Grand Palais and the Pont Alexandre III. All in all, this area comprises some of the most historic and beautiful sights to see in Paris.

a good walk

Place du Parvis—the square regarded by the French as *kilomètre zero,* the spot from which all distances to and from the city are officially measured—makes a fitting setting for **Notre-Dame de Paris** ❶ ▶, familiar and yet regal, like the gracious lady (as the priests will tell you) whose name it bears. Explore the interior, then toil up the steps to the towers for a grand view of the heart of Paris. To escape the crowds, relief is just a short—and magical—stroll away: the **Ancien Cloître** ❷, a nook of medieval Paris that is tucked behind the northern (or left-hand side as you face the cathedral) buttresses of Notre-Dame. Explore this storybook warren of streets, then head behind the cathedral to the Pont de l'Archevêché for the best view of Notre-Dame and proceed to cross over to the quai de la Tournelle (where Leslie Caron and Gene Kelly so memorably pas-de-deux-ed in *An American in Paris*) for a waterside vista.

Walk along the Seine embankment to the Pont au Double, cross over the Seine once again to place du Parvis, then head across the square and along rue de la Cité to rue de Lutèce, where you should make a left and walk to boulevard du Palais and the imposing Palais de Justice, the 19th-century Law Courts, which harbors the medieval **Sainte-Chapelle ❸**—a vision in shimmering stained glass—and the **Conciergerie ❹**, the prison where Marie-Antoinette awaited her appointment with the guillotine. At the end of quai de l'Horloge is the charming **place Dauphine ❺**. Opposite, on the other side of the Pont Neuf, is **square du Vert-Galant ❻**, with its proud equestrian statue of Henri IV. On the quay side of the square, *vedettes* (glass-top motorboats) start their tours along the Seine.

Cross the **Pont Neuf ❼**—the New Bridge, confusingly so called given that it's actually the oldest bridge in Paris—to the Rive Droite and make a left turn toward the **Louvre ❽**, the vast museum on the quai du Louvre, entering through the grand East Front and heading through the Cour Carrée to the I. M. Pei glass-pyramid entry. After viewing some of the greatest artworks in the world, exit through the **Carrousel du Louvre ❾** complex, a posh underground shopping mall, to the manicured lawns of the **Jardin des Tuileries ❿**, or Tuileries Gardens. Standing sentinel is the **Musée du Jeu de Paume ⓫**, host to outstanding exhibits of contemporary art. At the far end lies one of the world's grandest squares, **place de la Concorde ⓬**, centered by a grand Egyptian obelisk with a gilded top. Continue up the Champs-Élysées to avenue Winston-Churchill to the **Grand Palais ⓭**, whose back half houses the **Palais de la Découverte ⓮**, with Paris's planetarium and exhibits on science and technology. For a romantic finale, head back over to the Seine and the floridly beautiful **Pont Alexandre-III ⓯**.

TIMING   Allowing for toiling up towers, dancing down quays, and musing at *Mona Lisa,* this walk will take a full day—enabling you to reach Pont Alexandre-III just before sundown. Of course, if you want to do full justice to the vast collections of the Louvre, you could easily spend a week there and still not see everything. If you return to ogle the museum, visit in the mornings or late in the day, after 4 PM, when it's less crowded (note that it's closed Tuesday). But if this is your first exploration of Paris's historic heart, plan on spending your morning touring the Ile de la Cité sights, then, after your break for lunch, the afternoon at the Louvre.

What to See

❷ **Ancien Cloître Quarter.** Hidden in the shadows of Notre-Dame, this
Fodor'sChoice   adorable and often overlooked nook of Paris was thankfully spared when
★   Baron Georges Eugène Haussmann knocked down much of the Ile de la Cité in the 19th century. Enter the quarter—originally the area where seminary students boarded with the church canons—by heading north toward the Seine to reach rue Chanoinesse, once the seminary's cloister walk. Here, at No. 10, is the house that was once paradise to those fabled lovers of the Middle Ages, Héloïse and Abélard. That house, unfortunately, is completely renovated, but there are other houses here that

1

Beyond the Great Museums

Paris's museums range from the ostentatiously grand to the delightfully obscure—the French seem bent on documenting everything any of its citizens have ever done. Not just repositories of masterworks, the city's museums also reveal the endlessly fascinating nuances of French culture. It's fitting that the Musée d'Orsay, a Belle Époque former train station, houses the city's legacy of art from 1848 to 1914: railroads and other everyday phenomena were—shockingly so at the time—favorite subjects of the period's artists, especially the Impressionists, who enjoy pride of place under the glass-vaulted roof. And it was the French Revolution that opened the Louvre to the masses, so that all can now view the extraordinary collection amassed in good part by seven centuries of monarchs. A proletarian spirit also holds sway at the Centre Pompidou, where the world's largest collection of modern art is displayed; though opened in 1977, it has been so popular that a 2001 renovation means it is looking better than ever. In addition to these big three, other favorites include museums that began life not as museums, but as sumptuous houses. Many of these gilded time-machines are filled with salons aglitter with gilt *boiserie* (carved-wood panels), chandeliers, and flocked red-velvet walls literally oozing Parisian elegance. For these unique peeps into yesteryear, top bets include the decorative arts treasures found at the Musée Nissim de Camondo, the Musée Jacquemart-André, and the Musée Carnavalet. Skip through the centuries at some modern art museums, as both the Musée Rodin and the Musée Picasso are housed in historic hôtels particuliers—mansions built as private homes for the rich and famous. For a true trip back to the 17th, 18th or 19th century, discover overlooked jewels like the Hôtel Lauzun on the Ile St-Louis, the Atelier Delacroix on the place Furstenberg, and the Musée de la Vie Romantique, where the likes of Chopin and George Sand once rendezvoused, at the foot of Montmartre.

Bon Appétit!

As for dining, well . . . the French wrote the book. Paris is one of the world's great food capitals and a bastion of both classic and nouvelle French cuisine. Nonetheless, if you're coming from New York, London, or Los Angeles, where innovative restaurants abound, you may find the French capital a little staid. In fact, a battle is currently being waged here between the traditionalists and a remarkable new generation of chefs who are set on modernizing food preparation—forever changing the French culinary landscape in the process. But all chefs here agree with the French gastronome Anthelme Brillat-Savarin, who proclaimed, "Animals feed, men eat, but only wise men know the art of dining." Join them in the pursuit of this art and don't feel guilty if you spend as much time of your stay in Paris in its restaurants as in its museums. Give yourself over to the leisurely meal; two hours for a three-course menu is par, and you may, after relaxing into the routine, begin to feel pressed at less than three. Whether your dream meal is savoring truffle-studded foie gras served on Limoges china or sharing a baguette with *jambon* (ham) and Brie *sur l'herbe* (on the grass), eating in Paris can be a memorable experience. Needless to say, it's well worth splurging on a dinner of outstanding haute cuisine in historic, time-burnished splendor. But also keep in mind that many famous chefs have opened bistro annexes where you can sample their cooking for less. In addition, younger chefs are setting up shop in more affordable, outlying parts of Paris, where they are serving their own innovative version of bistro classics. End any proper meal with a sublime cheese course, then dessert (the more decadent and creamy the better), then an *express* (taken black, with sugar).

Splendid Shopping

Quotidian activities are elevated to high art in Paris, and shopping is no exception. Sophisticated city dwellers that they are—many natives live by the motto *bon chic, bon genre* ("well dressed, well bred")—Parisians approach this exercise as a ritual, and an elaborate ritual at that. Picking produce at the open-air markets on rue Mouffetard or rue Montorgueil or at the Marché d'Aligre, or searching for haute couture at Jean-Paul Gaultier, Sonia Rykiel, or Christian Dior, they cast a discerning eye on the smallest detail and demand the highest quality—which may explain why the city's shopkeepers are so famously grouchy. Browsing through old books and maps in the stalls of *bouquinistes* (secondhand booksellers) on quai de l'Hôtel de Ville along the Seine, or prowling through castoffs at the Marché aux Puces St-Ouen, Parisians show their practicality, their sense of economy, and their ability to turn even a piece of junk into an inventively chic treasure. The city's lairs of consumerism are celebrated—the fashion salons, venerable antiques shops around the rue de Beaune and rue Jacob, august fashion showrooms, and *grands magasins* (department stores) such as Le Bon Marché, Printemps, and the Galeries Lafayette, which flaunt Belle Époque extravagance and trendy designers.

---

date back to the Middle Ages. Although defaced by a modern police station and garage, this tiny warren of six streets still casts a spell, particularly at the intersection of rue des Ursins and rue des Chantres, where a lovely medieval palace, tiny flower garden, and quayside steps form a cul-de-sac where time seems to be holding its breath. ⊠ *Rue du Cloître-Notre-Dame north to the quai des Fleurs, Ile de la Cité* Ⓜ *Cité.*

❾ Carrousel du Louvre. Part of the early '90s Louvre renovation program, this subterranean shopping complex is centered on an inverted glass pyramid (overlooked by the regional Ile-de-France tourist office) and contains a wide range of stores, spaces for fashion shows, an auditorium, and a huge parking garage. At lunchtime, museum visitors rush to the mall-style food court, where fast food goes international. Note that you can get into or exit from the museum (and avoid some lines) by entering through the mall. ⊠ *Entrances on rue de Rivoli or by Arc du Carrousel, Louvre/Tuileries* Ⓜ *Palais-Royal.*

❹ Conciergerie. Bringing a tear to the eyes of *ancien régime* devotees, this is the famous prison in which dukes and duchesses, lords and ladies, and, most famously, Queen Marie-Antoinette were imprisoned during the Revolution before being carted off to the guillotine. Originally part of a royal palace, the turreted medieval building still holds Marie-Antoinette's cell; a chapel, embellished with the initials M. A., which was commissioned after the queen's death by her daughter, occupies the true site of her confinement. Out of one of these windows, the queen saw a notorious scene of the Revolution: her best friend, the Comtesse de Lamballe—lover of the arts and daughter of the richest duke in France—torn to pieces by a wild mob, her dismembered limbs then displayed on pikes. Elsewhere are the courtyard and fountain where victims of the Terror spent their final days playing piquet, writing letters to their loved ones, and waiting for the dreaded climb up the staircase to the Chamber of the Revolutionary Council to hear its final verdict. By the end of the Reign of Terror (1793–95), countless others fell foul of the revolutionaries, including their own leaders Danton and Robespierre. ⊠ *1 quai de l'Horloge, Louvre/Tuileries* ☎ *01–53–40–60–93* ⊕ *www.monum.fr* ✑ *€7.50, joint ticket with Sainte-Chapelle €10.40* ☉ *Daily 9:30–6* Ⓜ *Cité.*

⓭ **Grand Palais** (Grand Palace). With its curved glass roof, the Grand Palais is unmistakable when approached from either the Seine or the Champs-Élysées, and forms a turn-of-the-20th-century Beaux-Arts showpiece with the **Petit Palais,** located on the other side of avenue Winston-Churchill. Today, the adjoining galleries play host to major exhibitions, but the giant iron-and-glass interior of the Grand Palais itself is closed for renovation until 2007, when it will reopen as an exhibition space for contemporary art. Until then, some of the complex hosts major temporary art exhibitions. ⊠ *Av. Winston-Churchill, Champs-Élysées* ☎ *01–44–13–17–30* ⊕ *www.rmn.fr/galeriesnationalesdugrandpalais* ✑ *€11.10 until 1 PM with reservation, €10 after 1, no reservation* ☉ *Thurs.–Mon. 10–8, Wed. 10–10* Ⓜ *Champs-Élysées–Clemenceau.*

🐣 ⓾ **Jardin des Tuileries** (Tuileries Gardens). Monet and Renoir captured this gracious garden (really more of a long park) with paint and brush, Left Bank songstresses warble about its beauty, and all Parisians know it as a charming place to stroll and survey the surrounding cityscape. A palace once stood here on the site of a clay pit that supplied material for many of the city's tile roofs. (Hence the name *tuileries,* or tile works.) During the Revolution, Louis XVI and his family were kept in the Tuileries under house arrest. Now the Tuileries is a typically French garden: formal and neatly patterned, with statues, rows of trees, fountains with gaping fish, and gravel paths. No wonder the Impressionists liked it here—note how the gray, austere light of Paris makes green trees look even greener. ⊠ *Bordered by quai des Tuileries, pl. de la Concorde, rue de Rivoli, and the Louvre, Louvre/Tuileries* Ⓜ *Tuileries.*

need a break? Stop off for a snack or lunch at **Dame Tartine** (☎ 01–47–03–94–84), one of the two designer brasseries erected in the Tuileries in the late 1990s (it's on the left as you arrive from the place de la Concorde). With its glass-paneled walls and roof and light wood and aluminum accents, the restaurant is sober and airy. The cuisine is inventive and offers good value—try the lamb flan with tomato puree and a carafe of red Ventoux from the Rhône. You can also eat outdoors in the leafy shade.

❽ **Louvre.** Leonardo da Vinci's *Mona Lisa* and *Virgin and St. Anne,* **Fodor'sChoice** Veronese's *Marriage at Cana,* Giorgione's *Concert Champêtre,* Delacroix's ★ *Liberty Guiding the People,* Whistler's *Mother (Arrangement in Black and White)* . . . you get the picture. This is the world's greatest art mu-

JUMP TO THE HEAD OF THE LINE

Something to consider in the time vs. money balance: the **Carte Musées et Monuments** (Museums and Monuments Pass), which offers unlimited access to more than 65 museums and monuments.

You can get passes for one-, three-, or five-consecutive-day periods; the cost, respectively, is €15, €30, and €45.

Considering that most Paris museums cost under €10, you have to be serious about museum going to make this pay off, but there's one incredible plus: you get to jump to the head of the line by displaying it, a coup when there are 600 people lined up to get into the Musée d'Orsay.

The pass is available at Paris's tourist offices and métro stations and at all participating museums, and it comes with a handy info list of all the museums you can visit.

For more information, see www. intermusees.com.

---

seum—and the largest. Today, after two decades of renovations, the Louvre is now a coherent, unified structure, and search parties no longer need to be sent in to bring you out. Begun by Philippe-Auguste in the 13th century as a fortress, it was not until the reign of pleasure-loving François I, 300 years later, that the Louvre of today gradually began to take shape. Through the years Henri IV (1589–1610), Louis XIII (1610–43), Louis XIV (1643–1715), Napoléon I (1804–14), and Napoléon III (1852–70) all contributed to its construction. The recent history of the Louvre centers on I. M. Pei's glass pyramid, unveiled in March 1989, and numerous renovations.

The number one attraction—ever more so, since Dan Brown's *The Da Vinci Code* took over best-sellers lists the world over—is The Most Famous Painting in the World: Leonardo da Vinci's enigmatic **Mona Lisa** (*La Joconde*, to the French), painted in 1503–06 and now cynosure of all eyes in the museum's Salle des États, where it was ensconced in its own special alcove in 2005. To those who recall Théophile Gautier's words calling her "a sphinx of beauty," the portrait is a bit of a disappointment. Once you get in front of the videotaping tourists, you, too, may find yourself asking, "Is this it?" when faced with this 30″×18″ painting of an eyebrowless woman with yellowing skin and an annoyingly smug smile. However, the story behind her face—one that is still emerging—is fascinating. The portrait of the wife of one Francesco del Giocondo, a 15th-century Florentine millionaire, Leonardo's masterpiece is now believed to have been painted for her husband as a memorial after the lady's death. Some historians now maintain that her black garb is in honor of her baby who died in 1502. If so, however, this may be at odds with the famous smile, which critics point to as another example of Leonardo's famous wit: the family name Giocondo is derived from the Latin word for "jocundity," or humor. On nearby walls, don't miss some other High Renaissance masterworks: Leonardo's *Virgin and St. Anne* and Raphael's *La Belle Jardinière*.

The Louvre is packed with legendary collections, which are divided into seven sections: Asian antiquities; Egyptian antiquities; Greek and Roman antiquities; sculpture; paintings, prints, and drawings; furniture; and objets d'art. Don't try to see it all at once; try, instead, to make repeat visits—the admission is nearly half price on Sunday and after 3 PM on other days. (Unless you plan on going to a number of museums every day, the one-, three-, and five-day tourist museum passes probably aren't worth your money, since you could easily spend a whole day at the Louvre alone.) Some other highlights of the painting collection are Jan van Eyck's magnificent *The Madonna and Chancellor Rolin*, painted in the early 15th century; *The Lacemaker*, by Jan Vermeer (1632–75); *The Embarkation for Cythera*, by Antoine Watteau (1684–1721); *The Oath of the Horatii*, by Jacques-Louis David (1748–1825); *The Raft of the Medusa*, by Théodore Géricault (1791–1824); and *La Grande Odalisque*, by Jean-Auguste-Dominique Ingres (1780–1867).

The French crown jewels (in the Gallerie d'Apollon—a newly renovated 17th-century extravaganza) include the mind-boggling 186-carat Regent diamond. Atop the marble Escalier Daru is the Nike, or *Winged Victory of Samothrace*, which seems poised for flight at the top of the stairs (remember Audrey Hepburn's high-cheekboned take on this statue in *Funny Face?*), and other much-loved pieces of sculpture are Michelangelo's two *Slaves*, intended for the tomb of Pope Julius II. These can be admired in the Denon Wing, where a medieval and Renaissance sculpture section is housed partly in the former imperial stables. The Sully Wing's Greek Collection is home to the famous *Venus de Milo*—what archaeologist doesn't dream of unearthing her lost arms one day? In 1997 new rooms for Persian, Arab, Greek, and Egyptian art were opened, followed in 1999 by rooms for Italian and Spanish painting and French furniture and objets d'art from the period 1815–48. For fans of the Napoléon III style—the apotheosis of 19th-century, red-and-gilt opulence—be sure to see the galleries that once housed the Ministry of Finance. To get into the Louvre, you may have to wait in two long lines: one outside the Pyramide entrance portal and another downstairs at the ticket booths. You can avoid the first by entering through the Carrousel du Louvre, but you can't avoid the second. Your ticket (be sure to hold on to it) will get you into any and all of the wings as many times as you like during one day—and once you have your ticket you can skip the entry line. Once inside, you should stop by the information desk to pick up a free color-coded map and check which rooms are closed for the day. (Closures rotate through the week, so you can come back if something is temporarily unavailable.) Beyond this, you'll have all you need—shops, a post office, and places to eat. Café Marly may have an enviable location facing into the Cour Napoléon, but its food is decidedly lackluster. For a more soigné lunch, keep your appetite in check until you get to the museum's stylish Café Richelieu, or head outside the palace walls. There's also a full calendar of lectures, films, concerts, and special exhibits; some are part of the excellent lunch-hour series called Les Midis du Louvre. Most are not included in the basic ticket price—pick up a three-month schedule at the information desk or check online for information. Remember that the Louvre is closed on Tuesday. ⊠ *Palais du Louvre, Louvre/Tuileries* ☎ *01–40–20–53–17 information* ⊕ *www. louvre.fr* ✉ *€8.50, €6 after 6* PM *on Mon. and Wed. and all day Sun. Free 1st Sun. of month, €8.50 for special temporary exhibitions* ⊙ *Mon., Thurs., and weekends, 9–6, Wed. and Fri. 9* AM*–9:45* PM*. Some sections closed on certain days* Ⓜ *Palais-Royal.*

⓫ **Musée du Jeu de Paume.** At the entrance to the Tuileries Gardens, this museum is an ultramodern white-walled showcase for the Centre National de la Photographie, with excellent temporary exhibits of bold contemporary photography, video, and multimedia. Its adjoining sister museum, the **Musée de l'Orangerie**—home to Claude Monet's largest *Water Lilies*—has been closed for renovation. Though it was scheduled to open in fall 2004, workers discovered the ruins of a medieval wall underneath the building and the project was put on pause for further excavation. When it finally reopens, the Orangerie will display its selection of early-20th-century paintings, with works by Renoir, Cézanne, and Matisse, among other masters. ✉ *1 pl. de la Concorde, Louvre/ Tuileries* ☎ *01–47–03–12–51* ✉ *€6* ⊙ *Tues., Wed., and Fri. noon–7, Thurs. noon–9:30, weekends 10–7* Ⓜ *Concorde.*

▶ ❶ **Notre-Dame.** Looming above the large, pedestrian place du Parvis is la
Fodor'sChoice cathédrale de Notre-Dame, the most enduring symbol of Paris. Begun
★ in 1163, completed in 1345, badly damaged during the Revolution, and restored by Viollet-le-Duc in the 19th century, Notre-Dame may not be France's oldest or largest cathedral, but in terms of beauty and architectural harmony, it has few peers—as you can see by studying the facade from the open square. The doorways seem like hands joined in prayer, and the sculpted kings form a noble procession, while the rose window gleams, to wax poetic, like the eye of divinity. Above, the gallery breaks the lines of the stone vaults, and between the two high towers the flèche soars from the crossing of the transept. The cathedral was conceived by Bishop de Sully, who claimed he had seen the building in a vision. More pragmatically, Sully needed a cathedral in Paris so that he could compete with Abbot Suger's phenomenal cathedral in St-Denis, just north of the city. An army of stonemasons, carpenters, and sculptors came to work and live on the site, which had already seen a Roman temple, an early Christian basilica, and a Romanesque church. The chancel and altar were consecrated in 1182, but the magnificent sculptures surrounding the main doors were not put into position until 1240.

The facade divides neatly into three levels. At the first-floor level are the three main entrances, or portals: the Portal of the Virgin, on the left; the Portal of the Last Judgment, in the center; and the Portal of St. Anne, on the right. All three are surmounted by magnificent carvings—most of them 19th-century copies of the originals—of figures, foliage, and biblical scenes. Above these are the restored statues of the kings of Israel, the Galerie des Rois. Above the gallery is the great rose window and, above that, the Grande Galerie, at the base of the twin towers. The south tower houses the great bell of Notre-Dame, as tolled by Quasimodo, Victor Hugo's fictional hunchback. The 387-step climb to the top of the towers is worth the effort for a close-up of the famous gargoyles—most added in the 19th century by Viollet-le-Duc—as they frame an expan-

ON THE TRAIL OF *THE DA VINCI CODE*

HE DA VINCI CODE, Dan Brown's best-selling suspense novel, kicks off with a murder at one of Paris's greatest sights, the Louvre museum. Much of the ensuing action unfolds at real-life Parisian landmarks, so we've whipped up a tour to guide you to the highlights. Fair warning: the end of this tour includes a plot spoiler.

The book opens at that pinnacle of poshness, the **Ritz Paris** (✉ 15 place Vendôme, Louvre/Tuileries Ⓜ Opéra). Professor Robert Langdon is awoken by a late-night surprise visit. Lieutenant police inspector Bezu Fache, from the French equivalent of the FBI, tells him that the man with whom Langdon was supposed to meet earlier that day, Jacques Saunière, has been murdered.

From the Ritz, take rue de Castiglione out of the place Vendôme and hang a left on rue Saint Honoré to reach the **Palais-Royal** (✉ pl. du Palais-Royal, Louvre/Tuileries Ⓜ Palais-Royal). Under the arcades, keep your eyes on the ground to spot the bronze medallions marking the trail of the Rose Line. This line stands for the original zero-longitude line, which passed through Paris before being moved to Greenwich, England—and you'll cross its path again.

Next, cross the rue de Rivoli to reach the **Louvre** (✉ Palais du Louvre, Louvre/Tuileries Ⓜ Palais-Royal). Jacques Saunière's body is discovered in the Denon wing, not far from two of Leonardo da Vinci's greatest works. Near the body, the police have found an enigmatic message. With the help of Saunière's granddaughter, cryptologist Sophie Neveu, Langdon unravels the message: a series of clues that will lead the two on a quest for the Holy Grail.

The Denon wing houses the museum's Italian painting collection—including the works of the original Renaissance man, painter-engineer-inventor-anatomist Leonardo da Vinci. The Mona Lisa was Leonardo's own favorite creation. Langdon subscribes to some interesting theories about the painting's meaning; Saunière used it to leave behind a crucial clue before he died. La Joconde, as she's called in French, was moved into the freshly renovated Salle des États in 2005. Leonardo's enigmatic, androgynous St-John the Baptist hangs in Salle 5, along with the 1483 Virgin of the Rocks, the hiding place of another clue from Saunière.

Neveu and Langdon flee the Louvre, heading first to the rue de Rivoli and then down the Champs-Élysées to the Arc de Triomphe. On a clear day, you can see the Arc de Triomphe from the Arc du Carrousel, the arch standing between the Louvre and the Tuileries gardens. Langdon and Neveu zig-zag through the city to throw the police off their trail and eventually make their way to the fictional Depository Bank of Zurich. So instead of tracing their route, cross instead to the Rive Gauche via the Pont du Carrousel, to the left of the Arc du Carrousel if you're facing the Tuileries.

Head south on rue Bonaparte to **Saint-Sulpice** (✉ pl. Saint-Sulpice, Saint-Germain-des-Prés Ⓜ Saint-Sulpice). Silas, an albino monk-assassin, visits this church believing he'll find a keystone to unlock the secret of the Grail. Near the middle of the nave on the right side, next to a stone statue, you can locate one end of the narrow brass strip marking the Rose Line. You can retrace the monk's path north across the nave and transept to an obelisk next to the statue of St. Peter.

Ready for a break? Nab a table at one of the cafés on the square in front of Saint-Sulpice. Or, if you can't rest before the end of your Grail quest, turn back to the Rive Droite. Remember, your Louvre entry ticket is valid all day . . . .

sive view of the city. If some find both towers a bit top heavy, that's because they were designed to be topped by two needlelike spires, which were never built. The cathedral interior, with its vast proportions, soaring nave, and soft multicolor light dimly filtering through the stained-glass windows, inspires awe—visit early in the morning, when the cathedral is at its lightest and least crowded.

If your interest in the cathedral is not yet sated, duck into the **Musée de Notre-Dame** (⊠ 10 rue du Cloître-Notre-Dame, Ile de la Cité), across the street opposite the North Door. The museum's paintings, engravings, medallions, and other objects and documents chart the history of the cathedral. Interestingly, it was only after the publication of Victor Hugo's immensely popular novel featuring the hunchback Quasimodo that Parisians took notice of the cathedral's shabby condition. Then, architect Viollet-le-Duc began a renovation project that lasted through much of the 19th century. The cathedral spire is his invention; at the same time, Baron Haussmann demolished the warren of little buildings in front of the cathedral, creating place du Parvis. When it comes to views of Notre-Dame, no visit is complete without a riverside walk past the cathedral through **Square Jean-XXIII.** It offers a breathtaking sight of the east end of the cathedral, ringed by flying buttresses and surmounted by the spire. To put the cathedral in its proper medieval context, explore the super-charming **Ancien Cloître Quarter,** set just to the north of the cathedral. ⊠ *Pl. du Parvis, Ile de la Cité* ☎ *01–53–10–07–00* ⊕ *www.monum.fr* ⊠ *Cathedral free, towers €7, crypt €3.30, treasury €2.50, museum €2.50* ⊙ *Cathedral daily 8–7. Towers Apr.–Sept., daily 9:30–7:30; Oct.–Mar., daily 10–5:30. Treasury Mon.–Sat. 9:30–11:30 and 1–5:30. Crypt Tues.–Sun. 10–6. Museum Wed. and weekends 2:30–6* Ⓜ *Cité.*

⑭ Palais de la Découverte (Palace of Discovery). A planetarium, working models, and scientific and technological exhibits on such topics as optics, biology, nuclear physics, and electricity make up this science museum behind the Grand Palais. ⊠ *Av. Franklin-D.-Roosevelt, Champs-Élysées* ☎ *01–56–43–20–21* ⊠ *€6.50, €3.50 extra for planetarium* ⊙ *Tues.–Sat. 9:30–6, Sun. 10–7* Ⓜ *Champs-Élysées–Clemenceau.*

⑫ Place de la Concorde. This majestic square at the foot of the Champs-Élysées was laid out in the 1770s, but there was nothing in the way of peace or concord about its early years. Between 1793 and 1795 more than a thousand victims, including Louis XVI and Marie-Antoinette, were sent into oblivion at the guillotine, prompting Madame Roland's famous cry, "Liberty, what crimes are committed in thy name." The top of the 107-foot **Obelisk**—a present from the viceroy of Egypt in 1833—was regilded in 1998. The place continues to have politically symbolic weight. Demonstrations center here, since the Assemblée Nationale is right across the river and the Palais de l'Élysée (the French presidential palace) and the U.S. Embassy are just around the corner. Among the handsome, symmetrical 18th-century buildings facing the square is the Hôtel Crillon, originally built by Gabriel—architect of the Petit Trianon—as an 18th-century home for three of France's wealthiest families. At the near end of high-walled rue Royale is the legendary Maxim's restaurant, but unless you choose to eat here, you won't be able to see the riot of crimson velvets and florid Art Nouveau furniture inside. ⊠ *Champs-Élysées* Ⓜ *Concorde.*

⑤ Place Dauphine. The Surrealists loved place Dauphine, which they called "*le sexe de Paris*" because of its location—at the far-western end of the Ile de la Cité—and suggestive V-shape. Its origins were much more proper: built by Henri IV, it was named in homage to his successor, the dauphin, who grew up to become Louis XIII. The triangular square is lined with some charming 17th-century houses that the writer André Maurois felt represented the very quintessence of Paris and France. Take a seat on a park bench, enjoy a picnic, and see if you agree. ⊠ *Ile de la Cité* Ⓜ *Cité.*

⑮ Pont Alexandre-III (Alexander III Bridge). No other bridge over the Seine epitomizes the fin-de-siècle frivolity of the Belle Époque (or Paris itself) like the exuberant, bronze-lamp-lined Pont Alexandre-III. An urban masterstroke that seems as much created of cake frosting and sugar sculptures as stone and iron, it was built, like the Grand and Petit Palais nearby, for the 1900 world's fair and inaugurated by the ill-fated czar Nicholas II, and ingratiatingly named in honor of his father. ⊠ *Invalides* Ⓜ *Invalides.*

⑦ Pont Neuf (New Bridge). Crossing the Ile de la Cité, just behind square du Vert-Galant, is the oldest extant bridge in Paris, confusingly called the New Bridge, or Pont Neuf. It was completed in 1607 and was the first bridge in the city to be built without houses lining either side. ⊠ *Ile de la Cité* Ⓜ *Pont-Neuf.*

③ Sainte-Chapelle (Holy Chapel). Not to be missed and one of the most FodorsChoice magical sights in European medieval art, this Gothic chapel was built ★ by Louis IX (1226–70; later canonized as St. Louis) in the 1240s to house what he believed to be Christ's Crown of Thorns, purchased from Emperor Baldwin of Constantinople. A dark lower chapel is a gloomy prelude to the shimmering upper one, whose walls consist of little else but dazzling 13th-century stained glass. Think of it as an enormous magic lantern, illuminating 1,130 figures from the Bible, to create—as one writer put it—"the most marvelous colored and moving air ever held within four walls." Today, the magic of the chapel comes alive during the regular concerts held here; call to check the schedule. ⊠ *4 bd. du Palais, Ile de la Cité* ☎ *01–53–73–78–51* ⊕ *www.monum.fr* ⊠ *€6.10, joint ticket with Conciergerie €10.40* ☉ *Daily 9:30–6, entry closes at 5:30, or 4:30 from Nov. to Feb.* Ⓜ *Cité.*

⑥ Square du Vert-Galant. The equestrian statue of the Vert-Galant himself—amorous adventurer Henri IV—surveys this leafy square at the western end of the Ile de la Cité. Henri, king of France from 1589 until his assassination in 1610, is probably best remembered for his cynical remark that "*Paris vaut bien une messe*" ("Paris is worth a mass"), a reference to his readiness to renounce Protestantism to gain the throne of predominantly Catholic France. A fine spot to linger on a sunny afternoon, the square is also the departure point for the glass-top *vedettes* (tour boats) on the Seine (at the bottom of the steps to the right). ⊠ *Ile de la Cité* Ⓜ *Pont-Neuf.*

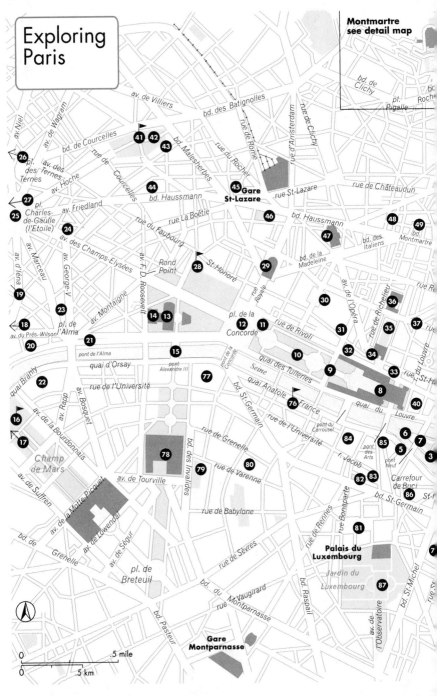

Exploring Paris

Montmartre
see detail map

bd. de Clichy

pl. Pigalle

bc Roch

av. de Villiers

bd. des Batignolles

rue de Rome

rue d'Amsterdam

rue de Clichy

av. Niel

av. de Wagram

bd. de Courcelles

41 42

43

bd. Malesherbes

rue du Rocher

26

pl. des Ternes

av. des Ternes

av. Hoche

rue de Courcelles

44

bd. Haussmann

45 **Gare St-Lazare**

rue St-Lazare

rue de Châteaudun

27

25 pl. Charles-de-Gaulle (l'Etoile)

24

av. Friedland

rue La Boétie

rue du Faubourg

46

bd. Haussmann

48

49 bd. Montmartre

av. des Champs-Elysées

av. F. D. Roosevelt

Rond Point

28 St-Honoré

47

bd. des Italiens

av. Marceau

av. George-V

19

23

pl. de l'Alma

14 13

29

rue Royale

30

av. de l'Opéra

36

rue Re

av. d'Iéna

18

20

av. du Prés.-Wilson

21

pl. de la Concorde

12

11

rue de Rivoli

31

rue de Richelieu

35

34

37

rue

pont de l'Alma

15

10

quai des Tuileries

32

33

rue du Louvre

quai Branly

22

quai d'Orsay

pont Alexandre III

77

Seine

quai Anatole France

76

9

8

40

rue St-H

av. Rapp

av. Bosquet

rue de l'Université

bd. St-Germain

rue de l'Université

quai du Louvre

16

17

Champ de Mars

av. de la Bourdonnais

rue de Grenelle

84

pont du Carrousel

85

pont des Arts

6

5

pont Neuf

7

3

av. de Suffren

78

bd. des Invalides

79

80 rue de Varenne

82 83

Carrefour de Buci

86

St-

bd. St-Germain

av. de la Motte-Picquet

av. de Lowendal

av. de Ségur

rue de Babylone

rue de Sèvres

rue de Rennes

rue Bonaparte

81

Palais du Luxembourg

7

bd. de Grenelle

pl. de Breteuil

bd. du Vaugirard

rue Montparnasse

bd. Raspail

Jardin du Luxembourg

87

av. de l'Observatoire

bd. St-Michel

bd. Pasteur

Gare Montparnasse

0 .5 mile

0 .5 km

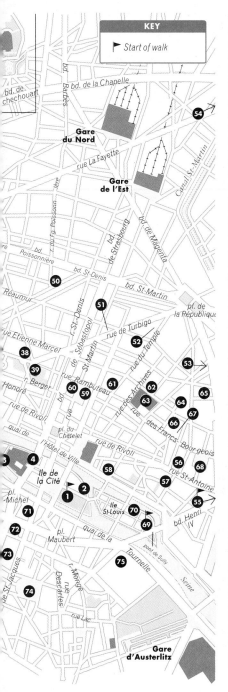

Monuments & Marvels: From the Eiffel Tower to the Arc de Triomphe

The Eiffel Tower (or Tour Eiffel, to use the French) lords over southwest Paris, and from nearly wherever you are on this walk you can see its jutting needle. For years many Parisians felt it was an iron eyesore and called it the Giant Asparagus, a vegetable that weighed 15 million pounds and grew 1,000 feet high. But gradually the tower became part of the Parisian landscape, entering the hearts and souls of Parisians and visitors alike. Thanks to its stunning nighttime illumination, topped by four 6,000-watt projectors creating a lighthouse beacon visible for 80 km (50 mi) around, it continues to make Paris live up to its moniker *La Ville Lumière*—the City of Light.

Water is the second highlight here: fountains playing beneath place du Trocadéro and boat tours along the Seine on a Bateau Mouche. Museums are the third; the area around Trocadéro is full of them. Style is the fourth, and not just because the buildings here are overwhelmingly elegant—but because this is also the center of haute couture, with the top names in fashion all congregated around avenue Montaigne, only a brief walk from the Champs-Élysées, to the north.

The 2-km (1-mi) Champs-Élysées was originally laid out in the 1660s by landscape gardener André Le Nôtre as parkland sweeping away from the Tuileries. In an attempt to reestablish this thoroughfare as one of the world's most beautiful avenues, the city has planted extra trees, broadened sidewalks, refurbished Art Nouveau newsstands, and clamped down on garish storefronts. One legacy of this much-advertised renovation are some excellent megastores, including Virgin (music and video) and Sephora (makeup and perfume), along with a few chic restaurants, plus an opulent branch of the pâtissier Ladurée. Site of most French national celebrations, the Champs-Élysées is the last leg of the Tour de France bicycle race, on the third or fourth Sunday in July, and the site of vast ceremonies on Bastille Day (July 14) and Armistice Day (November 11).

a good walk

The verdant expanse of the Champ de Mars, once used as a parade ground by the École Militaire (still in use as a military academy and therefore not open to the public), then as site of the world exhibitions, provides a thrilling approach to the iron symbol of Paris, the **Tour Eiffel** ⑯ ▶. As you get nearer, the Eiffel Tower's colossal bulk (it's far bigger and sturdier than pictures suggest) becomes increasingly evident.

Across the Seine from the Eiffel Tower, above stylish gardens and fountains on the heights of place du Trocadéro, is the Art Deco **Palais de Chaillot** ⑰, a cultural center containing three museums: an anthropology museum, a maritime museum, and a museum of French architecture (these collections are under renovation at press time). The area around place du Trocadéro is a feast for museum lovers. The **Musée Guimet** ⑱, on place d'Iéna, contains three floors of Indo-Chinese and Far Eastern art. If you're interested in glittering crystal, make a detour up avenue d'Iéna to the **Maison de Baccarat** ⑲, a small, Philippe Starck–designed funhouse museum. Otherwise, head down avenue du Président-Wilson, to the **Musée** d'Art Moderne de la Ville de Paris ⑳, which has temporary exhibits as well as a permanent collection of modern art and reopened in 2005 after a big makeover.

Continue down to bustling place de l'Alma, where a giant golden torch appears to be saluting the memory of Diana, Princess of Wales, who died in a car crash in the tunnel below in 1997 (in fact, this replica of the Statue of Liberty's flame was donated by Paris-based U.S. companies in 1989, in honor of the bicentennial of the French Revolution). Down the sloping side road just beyond the Pont de l'Alma (Alma Bridge) is the embarkation point of the **Bateaux Mouches** ㉑ and their tours of Paris by water. Across the Seine you'll see the long, low outline of the new **Musée du Quai Branly** ㉒, meant by architect Jean Nouvel to suggest the Tour Eiffel's shadow and now housing a rich cross-section of state-owned anthropological collections. From place de l'Alma head up the grand thoroughfare of avenue Montaigne, one of the leading showcases for the great haute-couture houses such as Dior, Chanel, Christian Lacroix, Prada, and Louis Vuitton. Get a different take on fashion by going over a block to avenue Marceau, where you'll find the **Fondation Pierre Bergé–Yves Saint Laurent** ㉓. The gallery fills what was once the designer Yves Saint Laurent's atelier; now it shows clothes for admiring and studying, not buying. After some dazzling window-shopping, continue on to the Rond-Point des Champs-Élysées, the main traffic nexus of Paris's most famous avenue. At No. 116 is the famous **Lido de Paris** ㉔ nightclub, opposite the venerable Le Fouquet's restaurant-café, once frequented by Orson Welles and James Joyce.

Local charm is not a highlight of this sector of western Paris, though renovation has gone some way toward restoring the avenue's legendary elegance, particularly as you head up the grand promenade to that icon of Paris, the **Arc de Triomphe** ㉕. Through the arch to the west lies the city's own Manhattan-on-the-Seine—the skyscraper complex of **La Défense** ㉖. For a more tranquil respite, head southwest from the Arc down Avenue Foch—one of Paris's most fashionable addresses—to the sylvan glades of Paris's largest park, the **Bois de Boulogne** ㉗.

TIMING   You can probably cover this walk in a couple of hours, but if you wish to ascend the Eiffel Tower, take a trip along the Seine, or visit any of the myriad museums along the way, you'd be best off allowing most of the day.

What to See

★ ㉕ **Arc de Triomphe.** Set on place Charles-de-Gaulle—known to Parisians as L'Étoile, or the Star (a reference to the streets that fan out from it)—the colossal, 164-foot Arc de Triomphe arch was planned by Napoléon but not finished until 1836, 20 years after the end of his rule. It's decorated with some magnificent sculptures by François Rude, such as the *Departure of the Volunteers,* better known as *La Marseillaise,* to the right of the arch when viewed from the Champs-Élysées. A small museum halfway up the arch is devoted to its history. France's Unknown Soldier is buried beneath the archway; the flame is rekindled every evening at 6:30. ⊠ *Pl. Charles-de-Gaulle, Champs-Élysées* ☎ *01–55–37–73–77*

⊕ *www.monum.fr* ⊠ €7 ⊙ *Apr.–Sept., daily 10* AM*–11* PM*; Oct.–Mar., daily 10* AM*–10:30* PM Ⓜ *Métro or RER: Étoile.*

♨ ㉑ **Bateaux Mouches.** If you want to view Paris in slow motion, hop on one of these famous motorboats, which set off on their hour-long tours of the city waters regularly (every half hour in summer) from place de l'Alma. Their route heads east to the Ile St-Louis and then back west, past the Tour Eiffel, as far as the Allée des Cygnes and its miniature version of the Statue of Liberty. Note that some travelers prefer to take this Seine cruise on the smaller Vedettes du Pont Neuf, which depart from square du Vert-Galant on the Ile de la Cité, as the Vedettes have a guide giving commentary in French and English, while the Bateaux Mouches have a loud recorded spiel in several languages. For the quietest journey, take the city-run Batobus, which has no commentary and allows you to get on and off at its various quayside stops. ⊠ *Pl. de l'Alma, Trocadéro/ Tour Eiffel* ☎ *01–40–76–99–99* ⊕ *www.bateaux-mouches.fr* ⊠ €7 Ⓜ *Alma-Marceau.*

㉗ **Bois de Boulogne.** Class and style have been associated with this 2,200-acre wood—known to Parisians as simply *Le Bois*—ever since it was landscaped into an upper-class playground by Baron Haussmann in the 1850s. Today the park is a happy escape for rowers, joggers, strollers, riders, and picnickers. Crowds head here for the racetracks of **Longchamp** and **Auteuil,** along with the **Roland Garros** stadium where the French Open tennis tournament is held in late May. After dark, ladies of the night festoon some sections. ⊠ *Main entrance at bottom of av. Foch, Bois de Boulogne* Ⓜ *Porte Maillot, Porte Dauphine, Porte d'Auteuil; Bus 244.*

★ ㉓ **Fondation Pierre Bergé–Yves Saint Laurent.** With his business partner, Pierre Bergé (who had the Napoléon-sized ego to include his name in this museum's name), iconic fashion designer Yves Saint Laurent reopened his former atelier in 2004—this time as a gallery and archive of his work. Temporary fashion-related exhibits rotate roughly every six months. Many of the signature looks are here, including the early 1960's Mondrian dress and the mid-1970s Russian peasant-luxe ball gowns. ⊠ *5 av. Marceau, Trocadéro/Tour Eiffel* ☎ *01–44–31–64–00* ⊕ *www.fondation-pb-ysl. net* ⊠ €5 ⊙ *Tues.–Sun. 11–6* Ⓜ *Alma-Marceau.*

㉖ **La Défense.** This is the skyscraper district of Paris, just west of the city (thankfully), across the Seine from Neuilly. Crowning the main plaza is the **Grande Arche de La Défense,** an enormous open cube of a building where tubular glass elevators whisk you 360 feet to the top. ⊠ *Parvis de La Défense, La Défense* ☎ *01–49–07–27–57* ⊠ €7 ⊙ *Daily 10–7* Ⓜ *Grande Arche de La Défense.*

㉔ **Lido de Paris.** Free-flowing champagne, songs in French and English, and topless razzmatazz pack in the crowds (mostly tourists) every night for the show at this famous nightclub, which has been around since 1946. Thanks to its return as a fashion show and party venue, the cabaret is recapturing a more polished crowd, but your chances of sitting next to a busload of Belgian tourists are still pretty high. Shows start at €80 (not including dinner). ⊠ *116 av. des Champs-Élysées, Champs-Élysées* ☎ *01–40–76–56–10* ⊕ *www.lido.fr* Ⓜ *George V.*

⑲ Maison de Baccarat. Famed modernist designer Philippe Starck brought an irreverent, Alice-in-Wonderland approach to the HQ of the venerable Baccarat crystal firm. Opened in 2003, the Baccarat museum plays on its building's Surrealist legacy; Cocteau, Dalí, Buñuel, and Man Ray were all frequent guests of the mansion's onetime owner, Countess Marie-Laure de Noailles. At the entrance, talking heads are projected onto giant crystal urns, and a lit chandelier is submerged in an aquarium. Other fairy-tale touches include a 46-foot-long crystal-legged dinner table and an 8-foot-high chair, perfect for seating a giant princess. Not all the marvels come from Starck though; Baccarat has created exquisite crystal pieces since Louis XV conferred his seal on the glassworks in 1764. Many of the company's masterworks are on display, from the soaring candlesticks made for Czar Nicholas II to the perfume flacon Dalí designed for Schiaparelli. The museum's Cristal Room café–restaurant attracts an appropriately glittering crowd, so book well in advance for lunch or dinner. ✉ *11 pl. des Etats-Unis, Trocadéro/Tour Eiffel* ☎ *01–40–22–11–00* ⊕ *www.baccarat.fr* ✉ *€7* ☉ *Mon.–Sat. 10–7* Ⓜ *Trocadéro.*

⑳ Musée d'Art Moderne de la Ville de Paris (City Museum of Modern Art). While the city's modern-art museum hasn't attracted a buzz comparable to that of its main Paris competitor, the Centre Georges Pompidou, it can give a more pleasant museum-going experience. Like the Pompidou, it shows temporary exhibits of painting, sculpture, installation and video art, plus a permanent collection of top-tier 20th-century works from around the world—but it happily escapes the Pompidou's overcrowding. At this writing, this leftover from the Exhibition of 1897 was closed for renovation (scheduled to finish up by late 2005). Once its vast, white-walled galleries are open, they'll again be an ideal backdrop for the bold statements of 20th-century art. The museum takes over, chronologically speaking, where the Musée d'Orsay leaves off; among the earliest works are Fauvist paintings by Vlaminck and Derain, followed by Picasso's early experiments in Cubism. Just next door, the **Palais de Tokyo** (✉ 13 av. du Président-Wilson ☎ 01–47–23–38–86 ⊕ www. palaisdetokyo.com ✉ €6 ☉ Tues.–Sun. noon–midnight), the Art Nouveau twin of the Musée d'Art Moderne, reemerged in 2002 as a trendy stripped-down space for contemporary arts. There is no permanent collection, just dynamic temporary exhibits, along with a bookstore and the hippest museum restaurant in town, Tokyo Eat. ✉ *11 av. du Président-Wilson, Trocadéro/Tour Eiffel* ☎ *01–53–67–40–00* ⊕ *www.paris. fr/musees/MAMVP/* ✉ *Permanent collection free, temporary exhibitions €7* ☉ *Tues.–Fri. 10–5:30, weekends 10–6:45* Ⓜ *Iéna.*

⑱ Musée Guimet. Prized by connoisseurs the world over, this museum was founded by Lyonnais industrialist Émile Guimet, who traveled around the world in the late 19th century amassing Indo-Chinese and Far Eastern objets d'art, plus a fabled collection of Cambodian art. Be sure to peer into the delicate round library (where you'd swear Guimet has just stepped out for tea) and toil up to the top floor's 18th-century ivory replica of a Chinese pavilion. ✉ *6 pl. d'Iéna, Trocadéro/Tour Eiffel* ☎ *01–56–52–53–00* ⊕ *www.museeguimet.fr* ☉ *Wed.–Mon. 10–5:45* Ⓜ *Iéna or Boissiére.*

㉒ Musée du Quai Branly. Architect Jean Nouvel is making another mark on the city's culturescape with this new museum, its long, flat shape stretching out next to the Seine. The museum, also known as the Musée des Arts Premiers, is scheduled to open in early 2006. It will gather together various state-held troves of African, Asian, and Oceanic art, including anthropological collections previously shown in the Louvre. ⊠ *Quai Branly Trocadéro/Tour Eiffel* ☎ *Not available at press time* ⊕ *www. quaibranly.fr* Ⓜ *Alma-Marceau.*

⑰ Palais de Chaillot (Chaillot Palace). This honey-color, Art Deco–culture center facing the Seine, perched atop tumbling gardens with sculpture and fountains, was built in the 1930s and houses three museums: the **Musée de l'Homme** (Museum of Mankind) with an array of prehistoric artifacts, now undergoing renovation as its collections are being prepared to be moved to the new Musée du Quai Branly (opening early 2006); the **Musée de la Marine** (Maritime Museum), with a collection of model ships, marine paintings, and naval paraphernalia salty enough to delight all fans of Patrick O'Brian's novels (and anyone who has ever thought of running away to sea); and the **Musée des Monuments Français** (Museum of French Monuments), which is undergoing renovation and will reopen in 2006, when it will share space with the Institut Français d'Architecture. This museum houses a gorgeously rich collection of medieval architectural and sculptural elements. The palace terrace, flanked by gilded statuettes (and often invaded by roller skaters and skateboarders), offers a wonderful picture-postcard view of the Tour Eiffel and is a favorite spot for fashion photographers. ⊠ *Pl. du Trocadéro, Trocadéro/Tour Eiffel* ☎ *01–44–05–72–72 Museum of Mankind, 01–53–65–69–69 Maritime Museum* ⊕ *www.mnhn.fr* 💷 *Museum of Mankind €7, Maritime Museum €6.50* ☉ *Museum of Mankind: Wed.–Fri. and Mon., 9:45–5:15; weekends 10–6:30; Maritime Museum: Wed.–Mon. 10–6* Ⓜ *Trocadéro.*

> **need a break?** You'll get a tremendous view of the Eiffel Tower and the Invalides dome with your ice cream, cocktail, or lunch at **Le Totem** (⊠ Pl. du Trocadéro, Trocadéro/Tour Eiffel ☎ 01–47–27–28–29), an elegant bar and restaurant in the south wing of the Palais de Chaillot.

★ ℭ ⌐ **⑯ Tour Eiffel** (Eiffel Tower). Known to the French as La Tour Eiffel (pronounced ef-*el*), Paris's most famous landmark was built by Gustave Eiffel for the World Exhibition of 1889, the centennial of the French Revolution, and was still in good shape to celebrate its own 100th birthday. Such was Eiffel's engineering wizardry that even in the strongest winds his tower never sways more than 4½ inches. Since its colossal bulk exudes a feeling of mighty permanence, you may have trouble believing that it nearly became 7,000 tons of scrap iron when its concession expired in 1909. At first many Parisians hated the structure, and only its potential use as a radio antenna saved the day (it still bristles with a forest of radio and television transmitters). Now it is the beloved symbol of Paris. If you're full of energy, stride up the stairs as far as the third deck. If you want to go to the top, you'll have to take the elevator. Today, the Tour is most breathtaking at night, when every girder is highlighted in a sparkling display originally conceived to celebrate the turn of the millennium. The glittering light show was so popular that the 20,000 lights were reinstalled for permanent use in 2003; the Tour does its electric shimmy for 10 minutes every hour on the hour, from 9 PM until 1 AM in winter and 2 AM in summer (why not take a seat on the grass of the Champs de Mars from 9 to 10 PM and see the lights dance twice?). If you really want to make an occasion of your visit, plan on reserving a table at Jules Verne, the tower's luxury restaurant, set on the second level. ⊠ *Quai Branly, Trocadéro/Tour Eiffel* ☎ *01–44–11–23–23* ⊕ *www.tour-eiffel.fr* ✉ *By elevator: 2nd fl. €4.10, 3rd fl. €7.50, 4th fl. €10.70. Climbing: 2nd and 3rd fl. only, €3.80* ☉ *June–Aug., daily 9 AM–midnight; Sept.–May, daily 9 AM–11 PM, stairs close at dusk in winter* Ⓜ *Bir-Hakeim; RER: Champ de Mars.*

Le Style, C'est Paris: The Faubourg St-Honoré

Fashions change, but the Faubourg St-Honoré, just north of the Champs-Élysées and the Tuileries, has been unfailingly chic since the early 1700s. The streets of this walk include some of the oldest in Paris. As you stroll from the President's Palace through arcaded streets and 19th-century passageways to the much-renovated market zone of Les Halles, you'll see all that is elegant in Paris, from architecture to fashion to food, all presented with typical Parisian insouciance. The centerpiece of the area is the stately place Vendôme; on this ritzy square, famous boutiques sit side by side with famous banks—but then elegance and finance have never been an unusual combination. It's not surprising to learn that one of the main arteries of the area, rue de Castiglione, was named after one of its former residents—the glamorous fashion-plate Countess de Castiglione, sent to plead the cause of Italian unity with Napoléon III. The emperor was persuaded (he was easily susceptible to feminine charms), and the area became a Kingdom of Woman: famous dressmakers, renowned jewelers, exclusive perfume shops, and the most chic hotel in Paris, the Ritz, made this *faubourg* (district) a symbol of luxury throughout the world. Today the tradition continues, with leading names in fashion found farther east on place des Victoires, close to what was, for centuries, the gastronomic heart of Paris: Les Halles (pronounced "lay-ahl"), once the city's main market. These giant glass-and-iron market halls were demolished in 1969 and replaced by a park and a modern shopping mall, the Forum des Halles, a dismal underground "shopping mall" now scheduled for a big makeover by a big name architect. The surrounding streets underwent a transformation and are now filled with shops, cafés, restaurants, and chic apartment buildings.

a good walk

Start in front of the most important home in France: the **Palais de l'Élysée** ㉘ ▶, or Presidential Palace. Crash barriers and gold-braided guards keep visitors at bay; in fact, there's more to see in the plethora of art galleries, luxury fashion boutiques, and Sotheby's fancy auction house lining rue du Faubourg–St-Honoré as you head east. At Hermès (where you can still order a hand-stitched saddle, along with silk scarves and Kelly bags), turn left onto rue Boissy-d'Anglas and cut right into Cité Berryer; this archway leads to "Village Royal," a shopping passage connecting to classy rue Royale. Looming to the left is the **Église de La Madeleine** ㉙, a sturdy Neoclassical edifice. The surrounding streets offer temptations such as the original branch of Laudrée pâtisserie (No.16 rue Royale) and Hédiard, a foodie's dream emporium (No. 21 place de la Madeleine), while Maxim's, the famed Art Nouveau restaurant, is found at number 3.

Take boulevard de la Madeleine, to the right as you face the church, then the first right down rue Duphot to Notre-Dame de l'Assomption, noted for its huge dome and solemn interior. Continue left on rue St-Honoré to rue de Castiglione and then head left to **place Vendôme** ㉚, one of the world's most soigné squares. Return to rue St-Honoré and follow it to the mighty church of **St-Roch** ㉛.

Take the next right onto rue des Pyramides and cross the place des Pyramides, with its gilded statue of Joan of Arc on horseback, to the northwest wing of the Louvre, site of the **Union Centrale des Arts Décoratifs** ㉜, with three separate museums dedicated to fashion, publicity, and the decorative arts. Stay on arcaded rue de Rivoli to the place du Palais-Royal. On the far side of the square is the **Louvre des Antiquaires** ㉝, a chic shopping mall housing upscale antiques stores. Just beyond Jean-Michel Othaniel's aluminum and psychedelic glass entrance canopy to the Palais-Royal Métro station, is the **Comédie Française** ㉞, the time-honored house for performances of classical French drama. To the right of the theater is the unobtrusive entrance to the **Palais-Royal** ㉟; its courtyard is an unexpected oasis in the heart of the city. Walk down to the far end of the garden and peek into the glossy 19th-century interior of Le Grand Véfour, one of the swankiest restaurants in the city. One block beyond the north exit of Palais-Royal, on the corner of rue de Richelieu and rue des Petits-Champs, stands what used to be France's main national library, the **Bibliothèque Nationale Richelieu** ㊱, now home to one of the world's largest photography archives. Next door are the connected passages of **Galerie Colbert** and **Galerie Vivienne,** two exquisite shopping arcades built in the mid-19th century, now filled with restaurants, luxury boutiques, and antiquarian booksellers. Continuing eastward on the rue des Petits-Champs brings you to the circular **place des Victoires** ㊲: that's Louis XIV riding the plunging steed in the center of the square. Head south down rue Croix-des-Petits-Champs, past the nondescript Banque de France on your right, and take the second street on the left to the circular **Bourse du Commerce,** or Commercial Exchange. Victor Hugo waggishly likened its roof to a jockey's cap without the peak. Alongside it is the 100-foot-high fluted **Colonne de Ruggieri.**

You don't need to scale Ruggieri's column to spot the bulky outline of the church of **St-Eustache** ㊳, a curious architectural hybrid of Gothic and Classical. The vast site next to St-Eustache is now occupied by a garden, the Jardin des Halles, and the modern **Forum des Halles** ㊴ shopping mall. Rue Berger leads from allée de St-Jean-de-Perse to the Square des Innocents, with its handsome Renaissance fountain. Head south along rue St-Denis from the far end of Square des Innocents to place du Châtelet, with its theaters, fountain, and the Tour St-Jacques, the tower looming up to your left. Turn right along the Seine to reach **St-**

Germain l'Auxerrois **40**, opposite the Louvre, once the French royal family's parish church.

TIMING With brief visits to churches and monuments, this walk should take from three to four hours. On a nice day you may want to linger in the gardens of the Palais-Royal, and on a cold day you may want to indulge in an unbelievably thick hot chocolate at the Angélina tearoom.

What to See

★ **36** **Bibliothèque Nationale Richelieu.** Housed in one of the grandest 17th-century Parisian mansions, France's longtime national library, named for the formidable 17th-century prime minister, Cardinal Richelieu, is shifting its public profile from books to photography. In spring 2003, a large exhibit space opened here to display the library's enormous photography collection. But you can also admire Robert de Cotte's 18th-century courtyard and peep into the magnificent 19th-century reading room (open only to researchers). Original manuscripts, engravings, coins, and prints are still here, and parts of these collections go on display from time to time. ⊠ *58 rue de Richelieu, Opéra/Grands Boulevard* ☎ *01–53–79–59–59* ⊕ *www.bnf.fr* 🎟 *€4–€8, depending on show* ⊙ *Tues.–Sun. 9–8* Ⓜ *Bourse.*

34 **Comédie Française.** Famous for its classical French drama, this theater company was founded in 1680 by Louis XIV, a king more interested in controlling theater than promoting it. This building opened in 1799 but burned almost to the ground a hundred years later; what you're looking at dates from 1900. The *comedienne* Sarah Bernhardt, who famously performed from palaces in St. Petersburg to tents in Texas, began her career here. Today, mannered productions of Molière, Racine, and Corneille appear regularly on the bill—enjoyable if you understand French and don't mind declamatory formal acting. ⊠ *Pl. Colette, Louvre/Tuileries* ☎ *01–44–58–15–15* Ⓜ *Palais-Royal.*

29 **Église de La Madeleine** (Church of La Madeleine). With its rows of uncompromising columns, this sturdy Neoclassical edifice—designed in 1814 but not consecrated until 1842—looks more like a Greek temple than a Christian church. In fact, La Madeleine, as it is known, was nearly selected as Paris's first train station (the site of the Gare St-Lazare, just up the road, was chosen instead). Inside, the walls are richly and harmoniously decorated; gold glints through the murk. The portico's majestic Corinthian colonnade supports a gigantic pediment with a frieze of the Last Judgment. ⊠ *Pl. de la Madeleine, Opéra/Grands Boulevards* ⊙ *Mon.–Sat. 7:30–7, Sun. 8–7* Ⓜ *Madeleine.*

39 **Forum des Halles.** Les Halles, the iron-and-glass halls that made up the central Paris food market, were closed in 1969 and replaced in the late '70s by the Forum des Halles, a mundane shopping mall. Nothing remains of either the market or the rambunctious atmosphere that led 19th-century novelist Émile Zola to dub Les Halles *le ventre de Paris* ("the belly of Paris"), although rue Montorgueil, behind St-Eustache, retains something of its original bustle. Plans are now underway to remodel Les Halles yet again, using a new design by hotshot French architect David Mangin. For really stylish shopping, wend your way northeast several blocks to rue Dussoubs and rue St-Denis to the 1835 covered gallery the **Passage du Grand-Cerf,** filled with crafts shops offering innovative selections of jewelry, paintings, and ceramics. ✉ *Main entrance: rue Pierre-Lescot, Beaubourg/Les Halles* ⊕ *www.forum-des-halles.com* ⊙ *Mon.–Sat. 10–7:30* Ⓜ *Les Halles; RER: Châtelet Les Halles.*

㉝ **Louvre des Antiquaires.** This "shopping mall" of superelegant antiques dealers, off place du Palais-Royal opposite the Louvre, is a minimuseum in itself. Its stylish glass-walled corridors—lined with Louis XVI *bois-eries* (antique wood paneling), Charles Dix bureaus, and the pretty sort of bibelots that would have gladdened the heart of Marie-Antoinette—deserve a browse whether you intend to buy or not. Don't wear your flip-flops in here. ✉ *Main entrance: Pl. du Palais-Royal, Louvre/Tuileries* ⊙ *Tues.–Sun. 11–7* Ⓜ *Palais-Royal.*

need a break?

Once patronized by Proust and Gertrude Stein (who loved the chocolate cake here), founded in 1903, **Angélina** (✉ 226 rue de Rivoli, Louvre/Tuileries ☎ 01–42–60–82–00) is an elegant *salon de thé* (tearoom), famous for its *chocolat africain,* a jug of incredibly thick hot chocolate served with whipped cream (irresistible even in summer). While it's still among the city's best chocolate hits, finicky Proust would probably sniff at the slightly shopworn air of the place today and reserve his affections for the ever-elegant teas served at historic **Ladurée,** a short walk to the east at 16 rue Royale.

▶ ㉘ **Palais de l'Élysée** (Élysée Palace). Madame de Pompadour, Napoléon, Joséphine, the Duke of Wellington, and Queen Victoria all stayed at this "palace," today the official home of the French president. It was originally constructed as a private mansion in 1718 and has housed presidents only since 1873. You can catch a glimpse of the palace forecourt and facade through the Faubourg St-Honoré gateway. ✉ *55 rue du Faubourg St-Honoré, Champs-Élysées* ⊙ *Not open to public* Ⓜ *Miromesnil.*

㉟ **Palais-Royal** (Royal Palace). One of the most Parisian sights in all of Paris, the Palais-Royal is especially loved for its gardens, where children play, lovers whisper, and senior citizens crumble bread for the sparrows, seemingly oblivious to the ghosts of history that haunt this place. The buildings of this former palace—royal only in that all-powerful Cardinal Richelieu (1585–1642) magnanimously bequeathed them to Louis XIII—date from the 1630s. In front of one of its shop fronts Camille Desmoulins gave the first speech calling for the French Revolution in 1789. Today the Palais-Royal is occupied by the French Ministry of Culture and private apartments (Colette and Cocteau were two lucky former owners), and its buildings are not open to the public. You can, however, visit its colonnaded courtyard and classical gardens, a tranquil oasis prized by Parisians. Around the exterior of the complex are famous arcades—notably the Galerie Valois—whose elegant shops have been attracting customers since the days when Thomas Jefferson used to come here for some retail therapy. ✉ *Pl. du Palais-Royal, Louvre/Tuileries* Ⓜ *Palais-Royal.*

30 Place Vendôme. Snobbish and self-important, this famous square is also gorgeous; property laws have kept away cafés and other such banal establishments, leaving the plaza stately and refined, the perfect home for the rich and famous (Chopin lived and died at No. 12; today's celebs camp out at the Hôtel Ritz, while a lucky few, including the family of the sultan of Brunei, actually own houses here). Mansart's rhythmic, perfectly proportioned example of 17th-century urban architecture still shines in all its golden-stone splendor. Napoléon had the square's central column made from the melted bronze of 1,200 cannons captured at the Battle of Austerlitz in 1805. There he is, perched vigilantly at the top. If you're feeling properly soigné, repair to Hemingway's Bar at the Hôtel Ritz and raise a glass to "Papa" (⇨ CloseUp Box, "Hemingway's Paris," below). Ⓜ *Opéra.*

37 Place des Victoires. This circular square, now home to many of the city's top fashion boutiques, was laid out in 1685 by Jules Hardouin-Mansart in honor of the military victories (*victoires*) of Louis XIV. The Sun King gallops along on a bronze horse in the center. Ⓜ *Sentier.*

38 St-Eustache. This huge church was built as the people's Right Bank reply to Notre-Dame, though St-Eustache dates from a couple of hundred years later. The church is a curious architectural hybrid: with the exception of the feeble west front, added between 1754 and 1788, construction lasted from 1532 to 1637, spanning the decline of the Gothic style and the emergence of the Renaissance. The vast, cathedral-like space is acoustically outstanding—composers such as Berlioz and Liszt liked to premiere works here. ⊠ *2 rue du Jour, Beaubourg/Les Halles* ☎ *01–46–27–89–21 concert information* ☉ *Daily 8–7* Ⓜ *Les Halles; RER: Châtelet–Les Halles.*

40 St-Germain l'Auxerrois. Until 1789, St-Germain was used by the French royal family as its parish church, in the days when the adjacent Louvre was a palace rather than a museum. The facade reveals the influence of 15th-century Flamboyant Gothic style, although the fluted columns around the choir, the area surrounding the altar, demonstrate the triumph of Classicism. ⊠ *Pl. du Louvre, Louvre/Tuileries* Ⓜ *Louvre-Rivoli.*

31 St-Roch. Designed by Lemercier in 1653 but completed only in the 1730s, this huge church is almost as long as Notre-Dame (138 yards), thanks to Hardouin-Mansart's domed Lady Chapel at the far end. ⊠ *Rue St-Honoré, Louvre/Tuileries* Ⓜ *Tuileries.*

32 Union Centrale des Arts Décoratifs (Decorative Arts Center). A must for lovers of fashion and the decorative arts, this northwestern wing of the Louvre building houses three high-style museums: the **Musée de la Mode,** devoted to costumes and accessories dating from the 16th century to today; the **Musée des Arts Décoratifs,** with furniture, tapestries, glassware, paintings, and other necessities of life from the Middle Ages through Napoléon's time and beyond—a highlight here are the sumptuous period-style rooms (undergoing renovations until mid-2006); and the **Musée de la Publicité,** with temporary exhibits of advertisements and posters. ⊠ *107 rue de Rivoli, Louvre/Tuileries* ☎ *01–44–55–57–50* ⊕ *www.ucad.fr* ⊡ €6 ☉ *Tues.–Sun. 11–6* Ⓜ *Palais-Royal.*

CloseUp

HEMINGWAY'S PARIS

"THERE IS NEVER ANY ENDING TO PARIS," wrote Ernest Hemingway, the legendary author. For the "Lost Generation" after World War I, his aperçu rang particularly true. Disillusioned by America's depression and prohibition, lured by favorable exchange rates and a booming artistic scene, many American writers, composers, and painters moved to Paris in the 1920s and 1930s. Heading this impressive list—F. Scott Fitzgerald, Gertrude Stein, Ezra Pound, e. e. cummings, Janet Flanner, and John dos Passos are just a few of the famous figures—was "Papa," who came to epitomize the flamboyant lifestyle of Gertrude Stein's "Lost Generation." He used her phrase—itself a lament made by one French bartender to bemoan the years, and chances, lost to the world war—to preface The Sun Also Rises, but he may or may not have liked it. "The hell with her lost-generation talk and all the dirty, easy labels," he wrote elsewhere.

Hemingway arrived in Paris with his first wife, Hadley, in December 1921, and made for the Left Bank—the Hôtel Jacob et d'Angleterre, to be exact (still operating at 44 rue Jacob). To celebrate their arrival, the couple went to the Café de la Paix for a meal they nearly couldn't afford. In 1922 the couple moved to 74 rue du Cardinal-Lemoine, then in early 1924 the couple and their baby son settled at 113 rue Notre-Dame des Champs. Nearby, he settled in at La Closerie des Lilas café to write much of The Sun Also Rises. The Closerie was "the nearest good café we had"—around the corner from Hemingway's "old friend," the 1853 statue of Marshal Michel ("Mike") Ney. This proved for Hemingway to be a time "when we were very young and very happy," as he wrote in A Moveable Feast. Not happy long. In 1926 Hemingway left Hadley and next year wedded his mistress Pauline Pfeiffer across town at St-Honoré-d'Eylau, then moved to 6 rue Férou, near the Musée du Luxembourg, whose Cézannes he revered. You can follow the steps of Jake and Bill in The Sun Also Rises as they "circle" the Ile St-Louis before the "steep walking . . . all the way up to the place de la Contrescarpe."

For gossip and books, Papa would visit Shakespeare & Co. at 12 rue de l'Odéon, owned by Sylvia Beach, an early buddy (the bookstore can now be found at 37 rue de la Bûcherie). Hemingway implied his sallies across the Seine to the upmarket Right Bank reflected a need for upmarket cocktails, but his first port of call was invariably the Guaranty Trust Company on 1 rue des Italiens, for money and mail. It was then on to, when flush, the bar of the Hôtel Crillon, or, when poor, either the Caves Mura, at 19 rue d'Antin, or Harry's Bar, still in brisk business at 5 rue Daunou. Hemingway's legendary association with the Hôtel Ritz, where he now has his own bar named for him, dates from the Liberation in 1944, when he strode in at the head of his platoon and "liberated" the joint by ordering 73 dry martinis. Here Hemingway asked Mary Welsh to become his fourth wife, and also righted the world with Jean-Paul Sartre, George Orwell, and Marlene Dietrich. A Moveable Feast tells how Hadley and Hemingway would stop at the Prunier restaurant in rue Duphot on their way back from the races, where you can still feast the night away.

Urban Kaleidoscope: The Grands Boulevards

The French have a word for it: *flâner*—to stroll, promenade, dawdle. Back in the 19th century, the Parisians made this a newly fashionable activity, thanks to the magisterial boulevards Baron Haussmann—the regional prefect who oversaw the reconstruction of the city in the 1850s and 1860s—had designed and laid out. The focal point of this walk is the uninterrupted avenue that runs in almost a straight line from St-Augustin, the city's grandest Second Empire church, to place de la République, whose very name symbolizes the ultimate downfall of the imperial regime. The avenue's name changes six times along the way, which is why Parisians refer to it as the *Grands Boulevards* (plural). The makeup of the neighborhoods along the Grand Boulevards changes steadily as you head east from the posh 8e arrondissement toward working-class east Paris. The *grands magasins* (department stores) at the start of the walk epitomize upscale Paris shopping and stand on boulevard Haussmann. The opulent Opéra Garnier, just past the grands magasins, is the architectural showpiece of the period (often termed Second Empire and corresponding to the rule of Napoléon III). Though big banks moved into the area between the World Wars, the Olympia concert hall has survived on the boulevard des Capucines, helping to keep alive *l'esprit boulevardier.* And recently, trendy cafés have sprouted up, attracting a fresh crop of fashionable wanderers to this perennially interesting strip.

a good walk

Take the métro to Monceau and step through gilt-top iron gates to enter the enchantingly idyllic **Parc Monceau** ㊶ ▶ by the domed Chartres Pavilion. At the middle of the park, head left to avenue Velasquez—lined by some of the most regal mansions in the city—past the **Musée Cernuschi** ㊷, with its distinguished collection of Chinese art from Neolithic pottery to contemporary paintings, to boulevard Malesherbes. Turn right on boulevard Malesherbes and right again on rue de Monceau to reach the **Musée Nissim de Camondo** ㊸, whose aristocratic interior reflects the upscale tone of this haughty part of Paris. More splendor awaits at the **Musée Jacquemart-André** ㊹, a grand 19th-century residence stuffed with antiques and Old Master paintings, which you can find by continuing down rue de Monceau and turning left onto rue de Courcelles, then left again onto boulevard Haussmann.

Continue eastward along the boulevard and cross the square to find the innovative iron-and-stone church of **St-Augustin** ㊺. Cross the square in front and turn left along boulevard Haussmann to Square Louis-XVI, the original burial spot of Louis XVI and Marie-Antoinette—the **Chapelle Expiatoire** ㊻ stands in their honor here now. Some 300 yards farther down boulevard Haussmann you'll find the grands magasins, Paris's most renowned department stores. First come the cupolas of Printemps, then Galeries Lafayette. Opposite looms the massive bulk of the **Opéra Garnier** ㊼, one of the most sumptuous theaters in the world.

Boulevard des Capucines, lined with cinemas and chain restaurants, heads east from in front of the Opera, becoming boulevard des Italiens before colliding with boulevard Haussmann. A left here down rue Drouot will take you to the **Hôtel Drouot** ㊽, Paris's central auction house. Rue Rossini leads from Drouot to rue de la Grange-Batelière. Halfway along on the right is the **Passage Jouffroy** ㊾, one of the many covered galleries that honeycomb the center of Paris. At the far end of the passage is the Musée Grévin, a waxworks museum. Cross boulevard Montmartre to passage des Panoramas, one of the city's oldest arcades; it was named for the panoramic scenes painted along the interior. You'll come out on rue St-Marc. Turn right, then left down rue Vivienne, to find the foursquare, colonnaded Bourse, the Paris Stock Exchange.

Head east along rue Réaumur, once the heart of the French newspaper industry—stationery shops still abound—and cross rue Montmartre. Take the second left up rue de Cléry, a narrow street that is the exclusive domain of fabric wholesalers. Continue up rue de Cléry as far as rue des Degrés—not a street at all but a 14-step stairway—then look for the crooked church tower of **Notre-Dame de Bonne-Nouvelle** ㊿, hemmed in by rickety housing. The porticoed entrance is around the corner on rue de la Lune, which leads back to the Grands Boulevards, by now going under the name of boulevard de Bonne-Nouvelle.

The Porte St-Denis, a triumphal arch, looms up ahead, and a little farther on is the smaller but similar Porte St-Martin. From here take rue St-Martin south past the Musée des Arts et Métiers, a technology museum housed partly in the former church of St-Martin. Then cross rue Réaumur to the high, narrow, late-Gothic church of **St-Nicolas des Champs** (51). Head left on rue de Turbigo, past the cloister ruins and Renaissance gateway that embellish the far side of St-Nicolas. Some 400 yards along on the right is the Baroque church of **Ste-Élisabeth** (52); shortly after, you'll reach place de la République. It's a short métro ride from here to either the city's most famous cemetery, the **Cimetière du Père-Lachaise** (53), or to the **Parc de La Villette** (54), with its postmodern science and music museums.

TIMING The distance between Parc Monceau and place de la République is almost 6 km (4 mi), which will probably take you four hours to walk, including coffee breaks and window-shopping. With museum visits and a good lunch, this could be stretched to an enjoyable day; keep in mind that the Musée Nissim de Camondo is closed on both Monday and Tuesday, though the Musée Jacquemart-André is open daily. Allot a few additional hours, if not a whole morning or afternoon, to visit the Père Lachaise Cemetery or the Parc de La Villette. Or return to these on another day.

What to See

㊻ **Chapelle Expiatoire.** Built in 1815, this expiatory chapel marks the original burial site of Louis XVI and Marie-Antoinette. After the deposed monarchs took their turns at the guillotine on place de la Concorde, their bodies were brought to a nearby mass grave. A loyalist marked their place, and their remains were eventually retrieved by Louis XVI's brother, Louis XVIII, who then ordered the monument. The Neoclassical mausoleum now emerges defiantly from the lush undergrowth of verdant square Louis-XVI off boulevard Haussmann, and its surprisingly subtle and moving tribute to royalty is in sharp contrast to

Napoléon's splashy memorial at the Invalides. ✉ *29 rue Pasquier, Opéra/Grands Boulevards* ☎ *01–44–32–18–00* ✉ *€2.50* ◷ *Thurs.–Sat. 1–5* Ⓜ *St-Augustin.*

⑤③ Cimetière du Père-Lachaise (Père-Lachaise Cemetery). Cemeteries may not be your idea of the ultimate attraction, but this is the largest and most interesting in Paris. It forms a veritable necropolis, with cobbled avenues and tombs competing in pomposity and originality. Named after the Jesuit father—Louis XIV's confessor—who led the reconstruction of the Jesuit Rest House in 1682, the cemetery houses the tombs of the famed medieval lovers Héloïse and Abelard; composer Chopin; artists Ingres and Georges Seurat; playwright Molière; writers Balzac, Proust, Colette, Wilde (usually covered in lipstick kisses), and (buried in the same grave) Gertrude Stein and Alice B. Toklas; popular French actress Simone Signoret and her husband, singer–actor Yves Montand; singer Edith Piaf; and rock-star Jim Morrison of the Doors. You can get a map at the entrance and track them down. ✉ *Entrances on rue des Rondeaux, bd. de Ménilmontant, rue de la Réunion, Père Lachaise* ⊕ *www.pere-lachaise.com* ◷ *Apr.–Sept., daily 8–6; Oct.–Mar., daily 8–5* Ⓜ *Gambetta, Philippe-Auguste, Père-Lachaise.*

④⑧ Hôtel Drouot. Paris's central auction house has everything from stamps and toy soldiers to Renoirs and 18th-century commodes. The 16 salesrooms make for fascinating browsing, and there's no obligation to bid. Although much of the auction action has moved to the glamorous Parisian venues of Sotheby's and Christie's, Drouot is still as lively as ever. ✉ *9 rue Drouot, Opéra/Grands Boulevards* ☎ *01–48–00–20–00* ⊕ *www.gazette-drouot.com* ◷ *Mid-Sept.–mid-July, viewings Mon.–Sat. 11–noon and 2–6, with auctions starting at 2* Ⓜ *Richelieu-Drouot.*

④② Musée Cernuschi. Despite extensive renovation delays, at press time this Asian art museum is expected to reopen by late 2005. A connoisseur's delight, the collection includes Chinese art from Neolithic pottery (3rd century BC) to funeral statuary, painted 8th-century silks, and contemporary paintings, as well as ancient Persian bronze objects. ✉ *7 av. Velasquez, Parc Monceau* ☎ *01–45–63–50–75* ⊕ *www.paris.fr/musees/* ✉ *Free* ◷ *Tues.–Sun. 10–5:40* Ⓜ *Monceau.*

★ ④④ Musée Jacquemart-André. Often compared to New York City's Frick Collection, this was one of the grandest private residences of 19th-century Paris. Built between 1869 and 1875, it found Hollywood fame when used as Gaston Lachaille's mansion in the 1958 musical *Gigi,* as a great stand-in for the floridly opulent home of a sugar millionaire played by Louis Jourdan. Edouard André and his painter-wife, Nélie Jacquemart, the house's actual owners, were rich and cultured, so art from the Italian Renaissance and 18th-century France compete for attention here. Note the freshly restored Tiepolo frescoes in the staircase and on the dining-room ceiling, while salons done in the fashionable "Louis XVI–Empress" style (favored by Empress Eugénie) are hung with great paintings, including Uccello's *Saint George Slaying the Dragon,* Rembrandt's *Pilgrims of Emmaus,* Jean-Marc Nattier's *Mathilde de Canisy,* and Jacques-Louis David's *Comte Antoine-Français de Nantes.* You can tour the house with the free English audioguide. The Tiepolo salon now contains a café, so why not lunch here and enjoy the Fragonard, Mantegna, and Chardin salads, named after great painters. ⊠ *158 bd. Haussmann, Parc Monceau* ☎ *01–45–62–11–59* ⊕ *www.musee-jacquemart-andre.com/jandre/* ☐ *€8* ⊙ *Daily 10–6* Ⓜ *St-Philippe-du-Roule or Miromesnil.*

> **need a break?** Opened by superchef Alain Ducasse and renowned baker Eric Kayser, **Be** (⊠ 73 bd. de Courcelles, Parc Monceau ☎ 01–46–22–20–20), a *boulangerie-épicerie,* is a hybrid bakery and corner store stocked with gastronomic grocery items like candied tomatoes and walnut oil from the Dordogne. Pick up a superlative sandwich to eat in the nearby Parc Monceau or, if the weather's not cooperating, grab a seat in the back and order soup.

㊽ Musée Nissim de Camondo. Molière made fun of the *bourgeois gentil-*
Fodor's Choice *homme,* the middle-class man who aspired to the class of his royal bet-
★ ters, but the playwright would have been in awe of Comte Moïse de Camondo, whose sense of style, grace, and refinement could have taught the courtiers at Versailles a thing or two. This immensely rich businessman built this grand *hôtel particulier* in the style of the Petit Trianon and proceeded to furnish it with some of the most exquisite furniture, *boiseries* (carved wood panels), and bibelots of the mid- to late 18th century. His wife and children (the museum is named after his son, who died in combat during World War I) then moved in and lent the house enormous warmth and charm. From ancien régime splendor, however, the family descended to the worst horrors of World War II: after the death of Count Moïse in 1935, the estate left the family's house and treasures to the government, while shortly thereafter family descendants were packed off to Auschwitz by the Nazis, where several of them were murdered. Today, the wealthy matrons of Paris have made this museum their own, and it shines anew with the beauty of the 18th century. No other house in Paris gives you such a sense of high French style as this one. ⊠ *63 rue de Monceau, Parc Monceau* ☎ *01–53–89–06–50* ⊕ *www.ucad.fr* ☐ *€6* ⊙ *Wed.–Sun. 10–5:30* Ⓜ *Villiers.*

㊿ Notre-Dame de Bonne-Nouvelle. This wide, soberly Neoclassical church, built in 1823–29, is tucked away off the Grands Boulevards. ⊠ *Rue de la Lune, Opéra/Grands Boulevards* Ⓜ *Bonne-Nouvelle.*

㊼ Opéra Garnier. Haunt of *Phantom of the Opera,* setting for Degas's fa-
Fodor's Choice mous ballet paintings, and still the most opulent theater in the world,
★ the Paris Opéra was begun in 1862 by Charles Garnier at the behest of Napoléon III. But it was not completed until 1875, five years after the emperor's abdication. Awash with Algerian colored marbles and gilt putti, it's said to typify Second Empire architecture: a pompous hodgepodge of styles with about as much subtlety as a Wagnerian cymbal crash. The composer Debussy famously compared it to a Turkish bathhouse, but lovers of pomp and splendor will adore it. To see the theater and lobby, you don't actually have to attend a performance: after paying an entry fee, you can stroll around at leisure and view the auditorium and the

Grand Foyer, whose grandeur reminds everyone that this was a theater for Parisians who attended the opera primarily to see and be seen. The **Musée de l'Opéra,** containing a few paintings and theatrical mementos, is unremarkable. Although technically the official home of the Paris Ballet, this auditorium usually mounts one or two full-scale operas a season, although most operas are presented at the drearily modern Opéra de la Bastille. ⊠ *Pl. de l'Opéra, Opéra/Grands Boulevards* ☏ *01–40–01–22–63* ⊕ *www.opera-de-paris.fr* ⊠ *€6* ⊙ *Daily 10–5* Ⓜ *Opéra.*

---

need a break? Few cafés in Paris are grander than the recently restored Belle Époque **Café de la Paix** (⊠ 5 pl. de l'Opéra, Opéra/Grands Boulevards ☏ 01–40–07–30–10). Once described as "the center of the civilized world," it was a regular meeting place for the glitterati of 19th- and 20th-century Paris; the prices are as grand as the setting.

▶ ❹ **Parc Monceau.** The most picturesque gardens on the Right Bank were laid out as a private park in 1778 and retain some of the fanciful elements then in vogue, including mock ruins and a faux pyramid. Captured in all its verdant glory in Vincente Minelli's *Gigi,* it remains today the green heart of one of Paris's most fashionable neighborhoods. The rotunda—known as the Chartres Pavilion—is surely the city's grandest public restroom; it started life as a tollhouse. ⊠ *Entrances on bd. de Courcelles, av. Velasquez, av. Ruysdaël, and av. van Dyck, Parc Monceau* Ⓜ *Monceau.*

☾ ❺ **Parc de La Villette.** Usually known simply as La Villette, this ambitiously landscaped, futuristic park (designed by noted modernist Bernard Tschumi) has several attractions, including the **Cité de la Musique.** This giant Postmodern musical academy also houses the **Musée de la Musique** (Museum of Musical Instruments). At the **Géode** cinema, which looks like a huge silver golf ball, films are shown on an enormous 180-degree curved screen. The science museum, the **Cité des Sciences et de l'Industrie,** contains dozens of interactive exhibits (though most displays are in French only). *Science Museum* ⊠ *30 av. Corentin-Cariou, Parc de la Villette* ☏ *01–40–05–80–00* ⊕ *www.cite-sciences.fr* ⊠ *Museum of Musical Instruments €7.50, Science Museum €7.50, Planetarium, €3* ⊙ *Museum of Musical Instruments Tues.–Sat. noon–6, Sun. 10–6; Science Museum Tues.–Sun. 10–6* Ⓜ *Porte de La Villette, Porte de Pantin.*

❹ **Passage Jouffroy.** Built in 1846, as its giant clock will tell you, this shops-filled passage was one of the favorite haunts of 19th-century dandies and flâneurs like the author Gérard de Nerval, who often strolled here in top hat and tails, with a large lobster on a pink-ribbon leash. ⊠ *Entrances on bd. Montmartre, rue de la Grange-Batelière, Opéra/Grands Boulevards* Ⓜ *Richelieu Drouot.*

❹ **St-Augustin.** This domed church was dexterously constructed in the 1860s within the confines of an awkward V-shape site. It represented a breakthrough in ecclesiastical engineering because the use of metal pillars and girders obviated the need for exterior buttressing. The resulting church feels surprisingly traditional despite its riotous kitchen-sink architecture of Renaissance, Byzantine, and other styles. Stand beside the statue of Joan of Arc to size up this impressive Second Empire aesthetic. ⊠ *Pl. St-Augustin, Opéra/Grands Boulevards* Ⓜ *St-Augustin.*

❺❷ Ste-Élisabeth. This studied essay in Baroque (1628–46) has brightly restored wall paintings and a wide, semicircular apse around the choir. ⊠ *Rue du Temple, République* Ⓜ *Temple.*

❺❶ St-Nicolas des Champs. The rounded arches and fluted Doric columns in the chancel of this church date from 1560 to 1587, a full century later than the pointed-arch nave (1420–80). ⊠ *Rue St-Martin, Opéra/Grands Boulevards* Ⓜ *Arts-et-Métiers.*

The Changing Face: The Marais & the Bastille

The Marais is one of the city's most historic and sought-after residential districts. Except for the architecturally whimsical Pompidou Center, the tone here is set by the gracious architecture of the 17th and 18th centuries (the Marais was spared the attentions of Haussmann, the man who rebuilt so much of Paris in the mid-19th century). Today most of the Marais's spectacular hôtels particuliers—loosely translated as "mansions," the onetime residences of aristocratic families—have been restored; many are now museums, including the noted Musée Picasso and Musée Carnavalet. There are hyper-trendy boutiques and cafés among the kosher shops in what used to be a predominantly Jewish neighborhood around rue des Rosiers.

The Marais, which means "marsh" or "swamp" (so don't be surprised by the sulfurous smell after heavy rainfall, even today), first became a fashionable address back when King Charles V moved his court here from the Ile de la Cité in the 14th century. However, it wasn't until Henri IV laid out place Royale, today the gorgeous place des Vosges, in the early 17th century, that the Marais became *the* place to live. All that came to an end on July 14, 1789, when the Bastille prison—once located on the eastern edge of the Marais—was stormed. Largely in commemoration of the bicentennial of the French Revolution, the Bastille area was renovated and became one of the trendiest sections of Paris. Galleries, shops, theaters, cafés, restaurants, and bars now fill formerly decrepit buildings and alleys. Strolling through the bustling Marais streets today, it's easy to appreciate the fabulous gold-hued facades of these buildings. Also keep your eyes peeled for open passages (*portes cochères*), leading to elegant courtyards that speak of times gone by. You may flee into one of them on weekends when massive crowds descend on the Marais. In the end, however, the squeak-through streets, noisy traffic jams, and half-pint sidewalks are part of the game.

A Good Walk

Make your starting point **place de la Bastille** ❺❺ ▶, easily accessible by the métro. Today the square is dominated by the Colonne de Juillet, the curving glass facade of the modern **Opéra de la Bastille.**

Walk down rue St-Antoine to the **Hôtel de Sully** ❺❻, now housing the Caisse Nationale des Monuments Historiques (National Treasury of Historic Monuments), at No. 62. Cross the road and pause at the mighty Baroque church of **St-Paul–St-Louis** ⑰. Take the left-hand side door out of the church into narrow passage St-Paul; then turn right onto rue St-Paul, past the grid of courtyards that makes up the Village St-Paul antiques-shops complex. Wend your way through the small streets to the quai de l'Hôtel-de-Ville.

Turn right on quai de l'Hôtel-de-Ville; *bouquinistes* (booksellers) line the Seine to your left. Pause by the Pont Louis-Philippe to admire the dome of the Panthéon floating above the skyline; then take the next right up picturesque rue des Barres to **St-Gervais–St-Protais** ⑱. Beyond the church stands the Hôtel de Ville, the city hall. From the Hôtel de Ville, cross rue de Rivoli and go up rue du Temple. On your right you'll pass one of the city's most popular department stores, the Bazar de l'Hôtel de Ville, or BHV, as it is known.

Take rue de la Verrerie, the first street on your left. Cross rue du Renard—pause to take in an impressive clash of architectural styles: to your left are the medieval silhouette of Notre-Dame; to your right, the gaudy colored pipes of the Centre Pompidou—and take the second right past the ornate 16th-century church of St-Merri. Rue St-Martin, which is lined with stores, restaurants, and galleries, leads to the **Centre Pompidou** ⑲. In front of the Pompidou Center is the **Atelier Brancusi** ㉀, the reconstituted studio of sculptor Constantin Brancusi. The adjacent Square Igor-Stravinsky merits a stop for its unusual modern fountain.

Cross rue Beaubourg behind the Pompidou Center to rue Rambuteau, then take the first left onto rue du Temple. The stimulating **Musée d'Art et d'Histoire du Judaïsme** ㉁ is in the Hôtel de St-Aignan, at No. 71. Farther up the street, at No. 79, pause to admire the Hôtel de Montmor, a large-windowed Baroque mansion. Take a right onto rue des Haudriettes. Just to the left at the next corner is the **Musée de la Chasse et de la Nature** ㉂, the Museum of Hunting and Nature, housed in one of the Marais's most stately mansions. Head right on rue des Archives, crossing rue des Haudriettes, and admire the medieval gateway with two fairy-tale towers, now part of the **Archives Nationales** ㉃, the archives museum, entered from rue des Francs-Bourgeois around to the left.

Continue past the Crédit Municipal (the city's grandiose pawnbroking concern), the Dôme du Marais restaurant (housed in a circular 18th-century chamber originally used for auctions), and the church of Notre-Dame des Blancs-Manteaux. A corner turret signals rue Vieille-du-Temple: turn left past the palatial Hôtel de Rohan (now part of the Archives Nationales), then right onto rue de la Perle, and down rue de Thorigny (opposite) to the palatial 17th-century Hôtel Salé, now the **Musée Picasso** ㉄. Church lovers may wish to detour up rue de Thorigny and along rue du Roi-Doré to admire the severe Neoclassical portico of **St-Denis-du-St-Sacrement** ㉅ and the Delacroix *Deposition* inside.

Backtrack along rue de Thorigny and cross place de Thorigny to rue Elzévir. Halfway along is the **Musée Cognacq-Jay** ㉆, a must if you love 18th-century furniture, porcelain, and paintings. Turn left at the end of the street onto rue des Francs-Bourgeois, then right into rue Pavée, past the cheerfully askew facade of the city history library, to reach rue des

Rosiers, with its excellent Jewish bakeries and falafel shops. Double back to rue des Francs-Bourgeois and turn right, then left to find rue de Sévigné and the **Musée Carnavalet** Ⓖ, the Paris history museum, in perhaps the prettiest edifice in the Marais. A short walk along rue des Francs-Bourgeois takes you to one of Paris's most historic squares, the **place des Vosges** Ⓖ, lined with covered arcades, and the most beautiful legacy of the French Renaissance still intact in Paris.

TIMING   This walk will comfortably take a morning or an afternoon. If you choose to spend an hour or two in any of the museums along the way, allow a full day. Be prepared to wait in line at the Picasso Museum. Note that some of the museums don't open until the afternoon and that many shops in the Marais don't open until late morning. If you're interested in Judaica, don't plan this tour for a Saturday, when almost all Jewish-owned and -related stores, museums, and restaurants are closed. The place to lunch? No question: a café table under the arcades lining the magnificent place des Vosges.

What to See

Ⓖ **Archives Nationales** (National Archives). If you're a serious history buff, you'll be fascinated by the thousands of intricate historical documents, dating from the Merovingian period to the 20th century, at the National Archives. But even if you're not into history, the buildings themselves are worth seeing, as the Archives are housed in the **Hôtel de Soubise,** one of the grandest of all 18th-century Parisian mansions, whose salons were among the first to show the Rococo, light-filled curving style that followed the heavier Baroque opulence of Louis XIV. ⊠ *60 rue des Francs-Bourgeois, Le Marais* ☎ *01–40–27–62–18* ⊕ *www.archivesnationales. culture.gouv.fr* ☒ *€3.05* ☾ *Mon. and Wed.–Fri. 10–5:45, weekends 1:45–5:45* Ⓜ *Rambuteau.*

Ⓖ **Atelier Brancusi** (Brancusi Studio). Romanian-born sculptor Constantin Brancusi settled in Paris in 1898 at age 22. This small, airy museum in front of the Pompidou Center contains four glass-front rooms that recreate Brancusi's studio, crammed with smooth, stylized works from all periods of his career. ⊠ *Pl. Georges-Pompidou, Beaubourg/Les Halles* ☎ *01–44–78–12–33* ☒ *€7, €10 including Centre Pompidou* ☾ *Wed.–Mon. 2–6* Ⓜ *Rambuteau.*

★ Ⓖ **Centre Pompidou.** Known as Beaubourg (for the neighborhood), this modern art museum and performance center is named for French president Georges Pompidou (1911–74), although the project was actually initiated by his art-loving wife. Designed by then-unknowns Renzo Piano and Richard Rogers, the Centre was unveiled in 1977, three years after Pompidou's death. Its radical purpose-coded colors and spaceship appearance scandalized Parisians, but they've learned to love the futuristic apparition. You approach the center across **place Georges-Pompidou,** a sloping piazza, where you'll find (if you look carefully enough) the **Atelier Brancusi.** The **Musée National d'Art Moderne** (Modern Art Museum, entrance on Level 4) has doubled in size to occupy most of the center's top two stories: one devoted to modern art—including major works by Matisse, the Surrealists, Modigliani, Duchamp, and Picasso—the other to contemporary art from the 1960s onward, including video installations. Also look for rotating exhibits of contemporary art. In addition, there are a public reference library, a language laboratory, an industrial design center, two cinemas, and a rooftop restaurant, Georges, which is noted for its great view of the skyline and Eiffel Tower. ⊠ *Pl. Georges-Pompidou, Beaubourg/Les Halles* ☎ *01–44–78–12–33* ⊕ *www.cnac-gp.fr* ⊠ *€10, including Atelier Brancusi; €7 for permanent collection only; €7–€9 for temporary exhibits; free 1st Sun. of month* ⊙ *Wed.–Mon. 11–9* Ⓜ *Rambuteau.*

need a break? Cross the plaza in front of the Pompidou and grab a table at **Café Beaubourg** (⊠ 100 rue St-Martin, Beaubourg/Les Halles ☎ 01–48–87–63–96), an early brainchild of French architecture star Christian de Portzamparc. Flawed service is redeemed by great people-watching and the large nonsmoking section on the ground floor, not to mention the well-designed bathrooms in the basement.

⑤⑥ Hôtel de Sully. The best surviving example of early Baroque in Paris, this mansion was built in 1624 with Flemish-inspired carving and a stately secret garden. Like much of the area, the hôtel fell into ruin until the 1950s, when it was rescued by the administration of French historic monuments, **Caisse Nationale des Monuments Historiques.** This is now the administration's head office, complete with an excellent bookshop featuring innumerable publications in French and English about Paris (be sure to look up at the shop's original Louis XIII ceiling). Guided visits to Paris sites and buildings begin here, though all are conducted in French. There are also photography exhibitions here, organized by the **Patrimoine Photographique,** an outpost of the Jeu de Paume museum. ⊠ *62 rue St-Antoine, Le Marais* ☎ *01–44–61–20–00* ⊕ *www.monum.fr* Ⓜ *St-Paul.*

⑥① Musée d'Art et d'Histoire du Judaïsme (Museum of Jewish Art and History). With its clifflike courtyard ringed by giant pilasters, Pierre Le Muet's Hôtel St-Aignan—completed in 1650—is one of the most awesome sights in the Marais. It opened as a museum in 1998 after a 20-year, $35 million restoration. The interior has been remodeled to the point of blandness, but the displays, including 13th-century tombstones excavated in Paris; wooden models of destroyed East European synagogues; a roomful of early Chagalls; and Christian Boltanski's stark, two-part tribute to Shoah (Holocaust) victims, are carefully presented. Nearby, at 17 rue Geoffroy-l'Asnier, is the extremely moving Mémorial du Martyr Juif Inconnu, adjacent to the Centre de Documentation Juive Contemporaine. France's Jewish population sank from 300,000 to 180,000 during World War II but has since grown to around 700,000, the largest in Europe. ⊠ *71 rue du Temple, Le Marais* ☎ *01–53–01–86–60* ⊕ *www.mahj.org* ⊠ *€6.10* ⊙ *Sun.–Fri. 11–6* Ⓜ *Rambuteau.*

★ **⑥⑦ Musée Carnavalet.** If it has to do with Paris, it's here. This collection is a fascinating hodgepodge of Parisian artifacts, from the prehistoric canoes used by Parisii tribes to the furniture of the bedroom where Marcel Proust wrote his evocative, legendarily long novel *In Search of Lost Time.* Material dating from the city's origins until 1789 is housed in Hôtel

Carnavalet, the setting for the most brilliant 17th-century salon in Paris, presided over by Madame de Sévigné, best known for the hundreds of letters she wrote to her daughter; they've become one of the most enduring chronicles of French high society in the 17th century. The section on the Revolution includes riveting models of guillotines and objects associated with the royal family's final days, including the king's razor and the chess set used by the royal prisoners at the approach of their own endgame. Lovers of the decorative arts will enjoy the period rooms here, especially those devoted to that most French of French styles, the 18th-century Rococo. Be sure to see the evocative re-creations of Proust's cork-lined bedroom, the late-19th-century Fouquet jewelry shop, and a room from the Art Nouveau monument the Café de Paris. ⊠ *23 rue de Sévigné, Le Marais* ☎ *01–44–59–58–58* ⊕ *www.paris.fr/musees/musee_carnavalet/* ⊠ *Free* ⊗ *Tues.–Sun. 10–5:30* Ⓜ *St-Paul.*

㉒ Musée de la Chasse et de la Nature (Museum of Hunting and Nature). This museum is in the grandly elegant Hôtel de Guénégaud, designed around 1650 by François Mansart. There's little descriptive information, and none in English, so the visit is only worthwhile if you're especially keen on the subject. ⊠ *60 rue des Archives, Le Marais* ☎ *01–42–72–86–42* ⊠ *€4.62* ⊗ *Wed.–Mon. 11–6* Ⓜ *Rambuteau.*

㉖ Musée Cognacq-Jay. Another rare opportunity to see how cultured and rich Parisians once lived, this 16th-century mansion contains an outstanding collection of 18th-century artwork in its wood-panel, boiseried rooms. Ernest Cognacq, founder of the department store La Samaritaine, and his wife, Louise Jay, amassed furniture, porcelain, and paintings—notably by Fragonard, Watteau, Boucher, and Tiepolo—to create one of the world's finest private collections of this period. ⊠ *8 rue Elzévir, Le Marais* ☎ *01–40–27–07–21* ⊕ *www.paris.fr/musees/cognacq_jay/* ⊠ *Free; temporary exhibits €4.60* ⊗ *Tues.–Sun. 10–5:40* Ⓜ *St-Paul.*

★ **㉔ Musée Picasso.** Housed in the 17th-century Hôtel Salé, this museum has the largest collection of Picassos in the world—and these are "Picasso's Picassos," not necessarily his most famous works but rather the paintings and sculptures the artist valued most. Arranged chronologically, the museum gives you a great snapshot (with English info panels) of the painter's life. There are also works by Cézanne, Miró, Renoir, Braque, Degas, and Matisse. The hôtel is showing some wear and tear of being one of the city's most popular museums; on peak summer afternoons this place is more congested than the Gare du Lyon. ⊠ *5 rue de Thorigny, Le Marais* ☎ *01–42–71–25–21* ⊕ *www.musee-picasso.fr* ⊠ *€5.50; €6.70 for temporary exhibits plus permanent collection; Sun. €4, free 1st Sun. of month* ⊗ *Wed.–Mon. 9:30–5:30* Ⓜ *St-Sébastien.*

▶ **㉟ Place de la Bastille.** Nothing remains of the infamous Bastille prison destroyed at the beginning of the French Revolution. In the midst of the large traffic circle is the **Colonne de Juillet** (July Column), commemorating the overthrow of Charles X in July 1830. As part of the countrywide celebrations for July 1989, the bicentennial of the French Revolution, the Opéra de la Bastille was erected, inspiring substantial redevelopment on the surrounding streets, especially along rue de Lappe and rue de la Roquette. What was formerly a humdrum neighborhood rapidly gained art galleries, clubs, and bars. **M** *Bastille.*

68 **Place des Vosges.** The oldest monumental square in Paris—and proba-
Fodor'sChoice   bly still its most nobly proportioned—the place des Vosges was laid out
★   by Henri IV at the start of the 17th century. Originally known as place Royale, it has kept its Renaissance beauty nearly intact, although its buildings have been softened by time, their pale pink brick crumbling slightly in the harsh Parisian air and the darker stone facings pitted with age. It was always a highly desirable address, reaching a peak of glamour in the early years of Louis XIV's reign, when the nobility were falling over themselves for the privilege of living here. The two larger buildings on either side of the square were originally the king's and queen's pavilions. The statue in the center is of Louis XIII. It's not the original; that was melted down in the Revolution, the same period when the square's name was changed in honor of the French département of the Vosges, the first in the country to pay the new revolutionary taxes. With its arcades, symmetrical pink-brick town houses, and trim green garden, bisected in the center by gravel paths and edged with plane trees, the square achieves harmony and balance: it's a pleasant place to tarry on a sultry summer afternoon. Better yet, grab an arcade table at one of the many cafés lining the square—even a simple cheese crêpe becomes a feast in this setting. At No. 6 is the **Maison de Victor Hugo** (Victor Hugo's home), where the workaholic French author, famed for *Les Misérables* and *The Hunchback of Notre-Dame,* lived between 1832 and 1848. Upstairs, in Hugo's original apartment, you can see the tall desk where he stood to write, along with furniture from several of his homes—including the Chinese-theme panels and woodwork he created for his mistress. ✉ *Maison de Victor Hugo, 6 pl. des Vosges, Le Marais* ☎ *01–42–72–10–16* ⊕ *www.paris-france.org/musees* ⊠ *Free* ☉ *Tues.–Sun. 10–5:45* **M** *St-Paul, Chemin-Vert.*

65 **St-Denis-du-St-Sacrement.** This severely Neoclassical edifice, dating from the 1830s, is a formidable example of architectural discipline, oozing restraint and monumental dignity (or banality, according to taste). The grisaille frieze and gilt fresco above the semicircular apse have clout if not subtlety; the Delacroix *Deposition* (1844), in the front right-hand chapel as you enter, has both. ✉ *Rue de Turenne, Le Marais* **M** *St-Sébastien.*

58 **St-Gervais–St-Protais.** This imposing church near the Hôtel de Ville is named after two Roman soldiers martyred by the emperor Nero in the 1st century AD. The church, a riot of Flamboyant style, went up between 1494 and 1598, making it one of the last Gothic constructions in the country; the facade, however, is an essay in 17th-century Classicism. ✉ *Pl. St-Gervais, Le Marais* ☎ *01–47–26–78–38 concert information* ☉ *Tues.–Sun. 6:30 AM–8 PM* **M** *Hôtel-de-Ville.*

57 **St-Paul–St-Louis.** The leading Baroque church in the Marais, with its elegant dome soaring 180 feet above the crossing, was begun in 1627 by the Jesuits and partly modeled on their Gesù church in Rome. Look for Delacroix's dramatic *Christ on the Mount of Olives* high up in the transept. ✉ *Rue St-Antoine, Le Marais* **M** *St-Paul.*

Across the Seine: The Ile St-Louis & the Latin Quarter

Set behind the Ile de la Cité is one of the most romantic spots in Paris, tiny Ile St-Louis. Of the two islands in the Seine—the Ile de la Cité is located just to the west—the St-Louis best retains the romance and loveliness of *le Paris traditionnel*. It has remained in the heart of Parisians as it has remained in the heart of every tourist who came upon it by accident, and without warning—a tiny universe unto itself, shaded by trees, bordered by Seine-side quais, and overhung with ancient stone houses. Up until the 1800s it was reputed that some island residents never crossed the bridges to get to Paris proper—and once you discover the island's quiet charm, you may understand why. South of the Ile St-Louis on the Left Bank of the Seine is the bohemian **Quartier Latin** (Latin Quarter), with its warren of steep, sloping streets, populated largely by Sorbonne students and academics. The name Latin Quarter comes from the old university tradition of studying and speaking in Latin, a tradition that disappeared during the Revolution. The university began as a theology school in the Middle Ages and later became the headquarters of the University of Paris; in 1968 the student revolution here had an explosive effect on French politics, resulting in major reforms in the education system. Most of the district's appeal is less emphatic: Roman ruins, tumbling street markets, the two oldest trees in Paris, and chance glimpses of Notre-Dame all await your discovery.

a good walk

Four bridges link the **Ile St-Louis** ㉙ ▶, the smaller of the city's two islands, to the mainland. Rue St-Louis-en-l'Ile runs the length of the island, bisecting it. Walk down this street and admire the strange, pierced spire of St-Louis-en-l'Ile, and stop off for an ice cream at Berthillon, at No. 31. In spring and summer walk to the northern edge of the island to quai d'Anjou to visit the historic and opulent **Hôtel de Lauzun** ㉘.

Head toward the west end of the island, which gloriously overlooks Notre-Dame, and cross the Pont St-Louis. Just across the bridge on the left, at the eastern tip of the Ile de la Cité, is the Mémorial de la Déportation, a starkly moving modern crypt dedicated to the French people who died in Nazi concentration camps. Head through the gardens to the left of Notre-Dame and take the Pont au Double across the Seine to Square René-Viviani. Behind the square are the church of St-Julien-le-Pauvre, built at the same time as Notre-Dame, and the tiny, elegant streets of the Maubert district. Turn left out of St-Julien, then make the first right, and cross rue St-Jacques to the elegantly proportioned church of **St-Séverin** ㉑. The surrounding streets are pedestrian-only, lined with a gauntlet of questionable restaurants fronted by waiters cajoling customers to try their towers of seafood or smash-your-plate Greek taverns. Take rue St-Séverin, a right on rue Xavier-Privas, and a left on rue de la Huchette to reach place St-Michel. Gabriel Davioud's grandiose 1860 fountain, depicting St. Michael slaying the dragon, is a popular meeting spot at the nerve center of the Left Bank.

Turn left up boulevard St-Michel and cross boulevard St-Germain. To your left, behind some forbidding railings, lurks a garden with ruins that date from Roman times. These belong to the **Musée National du Moyen-**

Age ⑫, the National Museum of the Middle Ages. The entrance is down rue Sommerard, the next street on the left. Cross place Paul-Painlevé in front of the museum up toward the **Sorbonne** ⑫, fronted by a small plaza where the Left Bank's student population congregates after classes. Continue uphill until you are confronted, up rue Soufflot on your left, by the menacing domed bulk of the **Panthéon** ⑫. On the far left corner of place du Panthéon is St-Étienne-du-Mont, a church whose facade is a mishmash of architectural styles. Head along rue Clovis to reach rue du Cardinal-Lemoine, which leads into rue des Fosses-St-Bernard, and head back toward the Seine and the glass-facade **Institut du Monde Arabe** ⑫, a center devoted to Arab culture. End your walk here with a cup of mint tea in the lovely rooftop café, where you'll have a grand view overlooking Paris.

TIMING   This walk can be fitted into a morning or afternoon or serve as the basis for a leisurely day's exploring—given that several sites, notably the Musée National du Moyen-Age, deserve a lengthy visit.

What to See

⑦ **Hôtel de Lauzun.** Offering a very rare view inside an Ile St-Louis mansion, a visit here permits you to see opulent salons that were among the first examples to introduce the 17th-century Baroque style in Paris. Later, the visionary poet Charles Baudelaire (1821–67) had his apartment here, where he kept a cache of stuffed snakes and crocodiles and where he wrote a large chunk of *Les Fleurs du Mal* (*The Flowers of Evil*). In 1848 poet Théophile Gautier moved in, making it the meeting place of the Club des Haschischines (Hashish Eaters' Club); novelist Alexandre Dumas and painter Eugène Delacroix were both members. At this writing, the building is undergoing restoration until mid-2005. In past years, between Easter and October, special weekend tours were organized 10–5:30, so call to see if the newly gilded doors are back open. ✉ *17 quai d'Anjou, Ile St-Louis* ☎ *01–43–54–27–14* Ⓜ *Pont-Marie.*

▶ ⑥ **Ile St-Louis.** One of the more fabled addresses in Paris, this tiny island has
FodorsChoice   long harbored the rich and famous, including Chopin, Daumier, Helena
★   Rubenstein, Chagall, and the Rothschild family, who still occupy the island's grandest house. In fact, the entire island displays striking architectural unity, stemming from the efforts of a group of early 17th-century property speculators led by Christophe Marie. The group commissioned leading Baroque architect Louis Le Vau (1612–70) to erect a series of imposing town houses. Other than some elegant facades and the island's highly picturesque quays along the Seine, there are no major sights here—just follow your nose and soak in the atmosphere. Study the plaques on the facades of houses describing who lived where when. An especially somber reminder adorns 19 quai de Bourbon: "Here lived Camille Claudel, sculptor, from 1899 to 1913. Then ended her brave career as an artist and began her long night of internment." Rodin's muse, she was committed to an insane asylum by her family where she was forbidden to practice her art. In your tour of the St-Louis, don't miss the views of Notre-Dame from the Quai d'Orleans, the historic Hôtel Lauzun museum, or, *bien sûr,* the Grand-Marnier ice-cream or Pamplemousse Rose sorbet at Berthillon, found on the center street of the island. Ⓜ *Pont-Marie.*

need a break?

Cafés all over town sell Berthillon, the haute couture of ice cream, but the **Berthillon** (⊠ 31 rue St-Louis-en-l'Ile, Ile St-Louis ☎ 01–43–54–31–61) shop itself is the place to go. More than 30 flavors are served; expect to wait in line. The shop is open Wednesday–Sunday.

⑦ Institut du Monde Arabe (Institute of the Arab World). Jean Nouvel's striking 1988 glass-and-steel edifice adroitly fuses Arabic and European styles. Note the 240 shutterlike apertures that open and close to regulate light exposure. Inside, the institute tries to do for Arab culture what the Pompidou Center does for modern art, with the help of a sound-and-image center, a vast library and documentation center, and an art museum. The top-floor café provides a good view of Paris. ⊠ *1 rue des Fossés-St-Bernard, Quartier Latin* ☎ *01–40–51–38–38* ⊕ *www.imarabe.org* ⊠ *Exhibitions €7, museum €3* ⊙ *Tues.–Sun. 10–6* Ⓜ *Cardinal Lemoine.*

★ **⑦ Musée National du Moyen-Age** (National Museum of the Middle Ages). Rivaling New York City's Cloisters as the greatest museum of medieval art in the world, the Musée Cluny—a name that is more popularly used—is housed in the 15th-century Hôtel de Cluny, erstwhile residence of the abbots of Cluny (the famous—but now largely destroyed—abbey in Burgundy). A stunning selection of tapestries, including the exquisite *Dame à la Licorne* (*Lady and the Unicorn*) series, headlines its exhibition of medieval decorative arts. Alongside the mansion are the city's Roman baths and the *Boatmen's Pillar,* Paris's oldest sculpture. ⊠ *6 pl. Paul-Painlevé, Quartier Latin* ☎ *01–53–73–78–00* ⊕ *www.musee-moyenage. fr* ⊠ *€5.50, free 1st Sun. of month, otherwise €4 on Sun.* ⊙ *Wed.–Mon. 9:15–5:45* Ⓜ *Cluny–La Sorbonne.*

⑦ Panthéon. Originally commissioned as a church by Louis XV as a mark of gratitude for his recovery from a grave illness in 1744, the Panthéon is now a monument to France's most glorious historical figures, including Voltaire, Zola, Rousseau, and dozens of French statesmen, military heroes, and other thinkers. Germain Soufflot's building was not begun until 1764, and was not completed until 1790, during the French Revolution, whereupon its windows were blocked and it was transformed into the national shrine it is today. Its newest resident is Alexandre Dumas, whose remains were interred there in November of 2002. ⊠ *Pl. du Panthéon, Quartier Latin* ☎ *01–44–32–18–00* ⊕ *www.monum.fr* ⊠ *€7* ⊙ *Apr.–Sept., daily 10–6:30; Oct.–Mar., daily 10–6* Ⓜ *Cardinal Lemoine; RER: Luxembourg.*

⑦ St-Séverin. This unusually wide, Flamboyant Gothic church dominates a Left Bank neighborhood filled with squares and pedestrian streets. Note the splendidly deviant spiraling column in the forest of pillars behind the altar. ⊠ *Rue des Prêtres St-Séverin, Quartier Latin* ⊙ *Weekdays 11–5:30, Sat. 11–10* Ⓜ *St-Michel.*

⑦ Sorbonne. Named after Robert de Sorbon, a medieval canon who founded a college of theology here in 1253, this is one of the oldest universities in Europe. The church and university buildings were restored by Cardinal Richelieu in the 17th century, and the maze of amphitheaters, lecture rooms, and laboratories, along with the surrounding courtyards and narrow streets, retains a hallowed air. You can visit the main courtyard on rue de la Sorbonne and peek into the main lecture hall, a major meeting point during the tumultuous student upheavals of 1968. The square is dominated by the noble university church with cupola and Corinthian columns. Inside is the white-marble tomb of that ultimate crafty cleric, Cardinal Richelieu himself. ⊠ *Rue de la Sorbonne, Quartier Latin* Ⓜ *Cluny–La Sorbonne.*

Toujours la Politesse: From Orsay to St-Germain-des-Prés

This walk covers the Left Bank, from the Musée d'Orsay in the stately 7ᵉ arrondissement to the chic and colorful area around St-Germain-des-Prés in the 6ᵉ. The Musée d'Orsay, in a daringly converted Belle Époque rail station on the Seine, houses one of the world's most spectacular arrays of Impressionist paintings. Farther along the river, the 18th-century Palais Bourbon—now home to the National Assembly—sets the tone for the 7ᵉ arrondissement. This is Edith Wharton territory—select, discreet *vieille France,* where all the aristocrats live in gorgeous, sprawling, old-fashioned apartments or *maisons particulières* (*very* private town houses). Embassies—and the Hôtel Matignon, residence of the French prime minister—line the surrounding streets, their majestic scale in total keeping with the Hôtel des Invalides, whose gold-leaf dome climbs heavenward above the regal tomb of Napoléon. The Rodin Museum—set in a gorgeous 18th-century mansion—is only a short walk away. This remains a district where manners maketh the man.

To the east, away from the splendor of the 7ᵉ, the boulevard St-Michel slices the Left Bank in two: on one side, the Latin Quarter; on the other, the Faubourg St-Germain, named for St-Germain-des-Prés, the oldest church in Paris. Ask Parisians and tourists alike and many venture that this is their favorite district in Paris, stuffed as it is with friendly cafés, soigné boutiques, and adorably quaint streets. The venerable church tower has long acted as a beacon for intellectuals, most famously during the 1950s when Albert Camus, Jean-Paul Sartre, and Simone de Beauvoir ate and drank existentialism in the neighborhood cafés. Today most of the philosophizing is done by tourists, yet a wealth of bookshops, art stores, and antiques galleries ensures that St-Germain, as the area is commonly known, retains its highbrow and very posh appeal. In the southern part of this district is the city's most colorful park, the Jardin du Luxembourg.

a good walk

Arrive at the **Musée d'Orsay** ㉖ ⊩ early (consider reservations) to avoid the crowds that pile in to see the museum's outstanding collections, including dozens of the world's most beloved Impressionist paintings. Many late-19th-century artists, including Manet and Monet, painted the train stations that were reshaping their city, so it's fitting that the museum occupies a revamped train station. Head west along rue de Lille to the **Palais Bourbon** ㉗, home of the Assemblée Nationale (French Parliament). There are sometimes outdoor photo exhibitions here on the Assemblée's railings, and there's a fine view across the Seine to place de la Concorde and the church of the Madeleine.

Rue de l'Université leads from the Assemblée to the grassy Esplanade des Invalides and an encounter with the **Hôtel des Invalides** ⓲, founded by Louis XIV to house invalid, or wounded, war veterans. The most impressive dome in Paris towers over the church at the Invalides—the Église du Dôme. From the church, double back along boulevard des Invalides and take rue de Varenne to the Hôtel Biron, better known as the **Musée Rodin** ⓳, where you can see a fine collection of Auguste Rodin's emotionally charged statues. The quiet, distinguished 18th-century streets between the Rodin Museum and the Parliament are filled with embassies and ministries.

Continue on to rue du Bac, turn left, then take a right onto rue de Grenelle, to the **Musée Maillol** ⓰, dedicated to the work of sculptor Aristide Maillol. Continue on rue de Grenelle past Edme Bouchardon's monumental 1730s Fontaine des Quatre Saisons (Four Seasons Fountain) to the carrefour de la Croix-Rouge, with its mighty bronze Centaur by the contemporary sculptor César. Take rue du Vieux-Colombier to place St-Sulpice, a spacious square whose north side is lined with cafés. Looming over the square is the enormous church of **St-Sulpice** ⓱.

Exit the church, head back across the square, and turn right on rue Bonaparte to reach **St-Germain-des-Prés** ⓲, Paris's oldest church. Across the cobbled place St-Germain-des-Prés is the café Les Deux Magots, one of the principal haunts of the intelligentsia after World War II. Two doors down boulevard St-Germain is the Café de Flore, another popular spot with the likes of Jean-Paul Sartre and Simone de Beauvoir. Follow rue de l'Abbaye, alongside the far side of the church, to rue de Furstenberg. The street opens out into place Furstenberg—a postcard-perfect square— where you'll find Eugène Delacroix's studio, the **Musée Delacroix** ⓳. Take a left on rue Jacob and turn right down rue Bonaparte to the **École Nationale des Beaux-Arts** ⓴, whose students can often be seen painting and sketching on the nearby quays and bridges.

Continue down to the Seine and turn right along the quay, past the **Institut de France** ⓵. With its distinctive dome, curved facade, and commanding position overlooking the Pont des Arts—immortalized in paintings by Renoir and Pissarro, this iron-and-wood footbridge linking the Louvre to the Institut de France is a favorite of painters, art students, and misty-eyed romantics moved by the views of the Ile de la Cité—the institute is one of the city's most impressive waterside sights. Continue along quai de Conti past the Hôtel des Monnaies, the former national mint. Head up rue Dauphine. Just 150 yards up, it's linked by the open-air passage Dauphine to rue Mazarine, which leads left to the carrefour de Buci, where you can find one of the best food markets in Paris. Where rue Dauphine crosses rue St-André-des-Arts, make a left for about a half a block to find the enchanting **Cour du Commerce St-André** ⓶, a relentlessly picturesque alleyway lined with cafés—a time-machine that will hurtle you back to 18th-century Paris. Here you will find the extraordinary Cour de Rohan courtyard, possibly Paris's most magical hideaway—if you're lucky, the gate will be open. Follow the Cour du Commerce St-André up to busy place de l'Odéon. Cross boulevard St-Germain and climb rue de l'Odéon to the colonnaded Théâtre de l'Odéon. Behind the theater lies the spacious **Jardin du Luxembourg** ㊲, one of the most stylish parks in the city.

TIMING   This walk could take from four hours to a couple of days, depending on how long you spend in the plethora of museums along the way. Aim for an early start—that way you can hit the Musée d'Orsay early, when crowds are smaller, then get to the rue de Buci street market when it's in full swing, in the late afternoon (the stalls are generally closed for lunch until 3 PM). Note that the Hôtel des Invalides is open daily, but Orsay is closed Monday. You might consider returning to one or more museums on another day or night—the Orsay is open late Thursday evening, along with its stylish restaurant.

What to See

㊶ **Cour du Commerce St-André.** Like an 18th-century engraving come to life, FodorsChoice   this exquisite, cobblestone-street arcade is one of Paris's loveliest sights. ★   Although it's been tatted up with some faux cafés, its shop signs, awnings, and outdoor tables make it a most festive tableau, where Napoléon himself still wouldn't look too out of place taking his coffee (as he did back when). One of the restaurants on the Cour is actually Paris's oldest café, **Le Procope** (☎ 01–40–46–79–00), opened in 1686 by an Italian named Francesco Procopio. Many of Paris's most famous literary sons and daughters imbibed here through the centuries, including Voltaire, Balzac, George Sand, Victor Hugo, and even Benjamin Franklin, who popped in whenever business brought him to Paris. The café started out as the Sardi's of its day, because the Comédie-Française was nearby. Racine and Molière were regulars. The place is still going strong, so you, too, can enjoy its period (though now gussied-up) trimmings and traditional menu. Just opposite Procope is that hidden 18th-century treasure that some call Paris's most beautiful spot: the **Cour de Rohan,** a series of three cloistered courtyards that found Hollywood immortality when Cecil Beaton picked it as the locale of Gigi's home in the famed Lerner and Loewe 1958 musical film *Gigi* ("Chez Mamita" is the house with the steep staircase directly on your left as you enter). The Cour is comprised of private residences so you may find its gates are sometimes closed. ⊠ *Linking bd. St-Germain and rue St-André-des-Arts, St-Germain-des-Prés* Ⓜ *Odéon.*

㊴ **École Nationale des Beaux-Arts** (National Fine Arts College). In three large mansions near the Seine, this school—today the breeding ground for painters, sculptors, and architects—was once the site of a convent, founded in 1608. Wander into the courtyard and galleries of the school to see the casts and copies of the statues stored here for safekeeping during the Revolution. ⊠ *14 rue Bonaparte, St-Germain-des-Prés* ☉ *Daily 1–7* Ⓜ *St-Germain-des-Prés.*

need a break?   If you are in search of the mysterious glamour of the Rive Gauche, you can do no better than to station yourself at one of the sidewalk tables—or at a window table on a wintry day—to watch the passing parade outside and in **Les Deux Magots** (⊠ 6 pl. St-Germain-des-Pre, St-Germain-des-Prés ☎ 01–45–48–55–25), the immortal old-fashioned St-Germain café named after the two Chinese figurines, or *magots.* Today, tourists crowd the tables, but in its yesteryear this was the place where Oscar Wilde drank his evening absinthe at a sidewalk table, Hemingway raised glasses with James Joyce, and those 1950s coffee enthusiasts Jean-Paul Sartre and Richard Wright often talked late into the night.

★ **78** **Hôtel des Invalides.** Famed as the final resting place of Napoléon, Les Invalides, as it is widely known, is an outstanding monumental Baroque ensemble, designed by Libéral Bruand in the 1670s at the behest of Louis XIV to house wounded, or invalid, soldiers. Although no more than a handful of old-timers live at the Invalides these days, the army link remains in the form of the **Musée de l'Armée,** a military museum. The **Musée des Plans-Reliefs,** also housed here, contains a fascinating collection of old scale models of French towns. The 17th-century **Église St-Louis des Invalides** is the Invalides's original church. More impressive is Jules Hardouin-Mansart's **Église du Dôme,** built onto the end of the church of St-Louis but blocked off from it in 1793. The showpiece here is that grandiose monument to glory and hubris, **Napoléon's Tomb.** ⊠ *Pl. des Invalides, Trocadéro/Tour Eiffel* ☎ *01–44–42–37–72 Army and Model museums* ⊕ *www.invalides.org* ✑ *€7* ⊘ *Église du Dôme and museums Apr.–Sept., daily 10–6; Oct.–Mar., daily 10–5. Closed 1st Mon. of every month* Ⓜ *La Tour-Maubourg.*

85 **Institut de France** (French Institute). Built to the designs of Louis Le Vau from 1662 to 1674, the institute's curved, dome-top facade is one of the Left Bank's most impressive waterside sights. It also houses one of France's most revered cultural institutions, the Académie Française, created by Cardinal Richelieu in 1635. Unfortunately, the interior is closed to the general public. ⊠ *Pl. de l'Institut, St-Germain-des-Prés* Ⓜ *Pont-Neuf.*

🎈 **87** **Jardin du Luxembourg** (Luxembourg Gardens). Immortalized in countless paintings, the Luxembourg Gardens possess all that is unique and befuddling about Parisian parks: swarms of pigeons, cookie-cutter trees, ironed-and-pressed dirt walkways, and immaculate lawns meant for admiring, not touching. The tree- and bench-lined paths offer a reprieve from the incessant bustle of the Quartier Latin, as well as an opportunity to discover the dotty old women and smooching university students who once found their way into Doisneau photographs. The park's northern boundary is dominated by the Palais du Luxembourg, surrounded by a handful of well-armed guards; they are protecting the senators who have been deliberating in the palace since 1958. Although the garden may seem purely French, the original 17th-century planning took its inspiration from Italy. When Maria de' Medici, widow of Henri IV, acquired the estate of the deceased Duke of Luxembourg in 1612 she decided to turn his mansion into a version of the Florentine Medici home, the Palazzo Pitti. Today, an adjacent wing of her former palace houses the **Musée de Luxembourg,** open only for special temporary exhibitions (often blockbuster in scale—a Titian show will be in residence autumn 2005 through winter 2006). One of the great attractions of the park is the **Théâtre des Marionnettes,** where on Saturday and Sunday at 11 and 3:15, and on Wednesday at 3:15 PM, you can catch one of the classic *guignols* (marionette shows) for a small admission charge. ⊠ *Bordered by bd. St-Michel and rues de Vaugirard, de Médicis, Guynemer, and Auguste-Comte, St-Germain-des-Prés* ⊕ *www.museeduluxembourg. fr* Ⓜ *Odéon; RER: Luxembourg.*

㊷ Musée Delacroix. The studio of artist Eugène Delacroix (1798–1863) contains only a small collection of his sketches and drawings. But if you want to pay homage to France's foremost Romantic painter, you'll want to visit this museum. Two other reasons to pay a call: the atelier is set on place Furstenberg, one of the tiniest, most romantic squares in Paris, while just beyond the museum rooms is the lovely backyard garden—an enchanting nook that is sure to bring out the poet in you. ⊠ *6 rue Furstenberg, St-Germain-des-Prés* ☎ *01–44–41–86–50* 🖬 €5 ⊙ *Wed.–Mon. 9:30–5* Ⓜ *St-Germain-des-Prés.*

FodorśChoice
★

㊵ Musée Maillol. Drawings, paintings, tapestries, and, above all, bronzes by Art Deco sculptor Aristide Maillol (1861–1944)—whose sleek, stylized nudes adorn the Tuileries—can be admired at this handsome town house, lovingly restored by his former muse, Dina Vierny. ⊠ *61 rue de Grenelle, St-Germain-des-Prés* ☎ *01–42–22–59–58* ⊕ *www.museemaillol. com* 🖬 €8 ⊙ *Wed.–Mon. 11–6* Ⓜ *Rue du Bac.*

★ ▶ **㊹ Musée d'Orsay.** In a spectacularly converted Belle Époque train station, the Orsay Museum—devoted to the arts (mainly French) spanning the period 1848–1914—is one of the city's most popular, thanks to the presence of the world's greatest collection of Impressionist and Postimpressionist paintings. Here you'll find Manet's *Déjeuner sur l'Herbe* (*Lunch on the Grass*), the painting that scandalized Paris in 1863 when it was shown at the Salon des Refusés, an exhibit organized by artists refused permission to show their work at the Academy's official annual salon, as well as the artist's provocative nude, *Olympia*. There is a dazzling rainbow of masterpieces by Renoir (including his beloved *Le Moulin de la Galette*), Sisley, Pissarro, and Monet. The Postimpressionists—Cézanne, van Gogh, Gauguin, and Toulouse-Lautrec—are on the top floor. On the ground floor you'll find the work of Manet, the powerful realism of Courbet, and the delicate nuances of Degas. If you prefer more academic paintings, look for Puvis de Chavannes's larger-than-life classical canvases. And if you're excited by more modern developments, look for the early-20th-century Fauves (meaning "wild beasts," the name given them by an outraged critic in 1905)—particularly Matisse, Derain, and Vlaminck.

The museum is arranged on three floors. Once past the ticket booths (get your tickets in advance through the Web site to avoid the lines), you can pick up an English-language audioguide along with a free color-coded map of the museum. Then step down the stairs into the sculpture hall. Here the vastness of the space complements a ravishing collection of French sculpture from 1840 to 1875. ⊠ *1 rue de la Légion d'Honneur, St-Germain-des-Prés* ☎ *01–40–49–48–14* ⊕ *www. musee-orsay.fr* 🖬 €7.50, €5.50 on Sun. ⊙ *Tues., Wed., Fri., and Sat. 10–6, Thurs. 10–9:45, Sun. 9–6* Ⓜ *Solférino; RER: Musée d'Orsay.*

If those *Déjeuner sur l'Herbe* paintings make you think about lunch, stop at the middle floor's **Musée d'Orsay Restaurant** (☎ 1–45–49–47–03) in the former train station's sumptuous dining room. Train food, however, this is not: An elegant lunch is available 11:30–2:30, high tea from 3:30–5:40 (except on Thursday, when dinner is served instead, from 7–9:30 PM). For a simpler snack anytime, visit the top-floor **Café des Hauteurs** and drink in its panoramic view across the Seine toward Montmartre.

★ ⓲ **Musée Rodin.** The exquisite 18th-century Hôtel Biron makes a gracious stage for the sculpture of Auguste Rodin (1840–1917). You'll doubtless recognize the seated *Le Penseur* (*The Thinker*), with his elbow resting on his knee, and the passionate *Le Baiser* (*The Kiss*). From the upper rooms, which contain some fine if murky paintings by Rodin's friend Eugène Carrière (1849–1906) and some fine sculptures by Rodin's mistress, Camille Claudel (1864–1943), you can see the large garden behind the house. Don't skip the garden: it is exceptional not only for its rosebushes and sculpture, but also its view of the Invalides dome with the Eiffel Tower behind and its superb cafeteria. ⊠ *77 rue de Varenne, Invalides/Eiffel Tower* ☎ *01–44–18–61–10* ⊠ *€5, Sun. €3, gardens only €1* ◷ *Easter–Oct., Tues.–Sun. 9:30–5:45; Nov.–Easter, Tues.–Sun. 9:30–4:45* Ⓜ *Varenne.*

⓱ **Palais Bourbon.** The most prominent feature of the home of the Assemblée Nationale (French Parliament) is its colonnaded facade, commissioned by Napoléon. ⊠ *Pl. du Palais-Bourbon, Invalides/Eiffel Tower* ◷ *During temporary exhibits only* Ⓜ *Assemblée Nationale.*

⓲ **St-Germain-des-Prés.** Paris's oldest church was first built to shelter a relic of the true cross brought from Spain in AD 542. The chancel was enlarged and the church then consecrated by Pope Alexander III in 1163; the tall, sturdy tower—a Left Bank landmark—dates from this period. The church stages superb organ concerts and recitals. ⊠ *Pl. St-Germain, St-Germain-des-Prés* ◷ *Weekdays 8–7:30, weekends 8 AM–9 PM* Ⓜ *St-Germain-des-Prés.*

⓳ **St-Sulpice.** Dubbed the "Cathedral of the Left Bank," this enormous 17th-century church is of note for the powerful Delacroix frescoes in the first chapel on the right. The 18th-century facade was never finished, and its unequal towers add a playful touch to an otherwise sober design. ⊠ *Pl. St-Sulpice, St-Germain-des-Prés* Ⓜ *St-Sulpice.*

Montmartre: The Citadel of Paris

On a dramatic rise above the city is Montmartre, site of the Sacré-Coeur Basilica and home to a once-thriving artist community. This was the quartier that Toulouse-Lautrec and Renoir immortalized with a flash of their brush and a tube of their paint. Although the great painters have long departed, and the fabled nightlife of Old Montmartre has fizzled down to some glitzy nightclubs and skin shows, Montmartre still exudes history and Gallic charm. Windmills once dotted Montmartre (often referred to by Parisians as *La Butte*, meaning "mound"). They were set up here not just because the hill was a good place to catch the wind—at more than

300 feet it's the highest point in the city—but because Montmartre was covered with wheat fields and quarries right up to the end of the 19th century. Today only two of the original 20 windmills remain. Visiting Montmartre means negotiating a lot of steep streets and flights of steps. The crown atop this urban peak, the Sacré-Coeur Basilica, is something of an architectural oddity, with a silhouette that looks more like that of a mosque than a cathedral. No matter: when viewed from afar at dusk or sunrise, it looks like Paris's "sculpted cloud."

Long a draw because of its bohemian–artistic history, Montmartre became even more popular after its starring role in the 2001 smash-hit films *Amélie* and *Moulin Rouge* (the latter entirely recreated on a film-set, though). Now you not only have to contend with art lovers seeking out Picasso's studio and Toulouse-Lautrec's favorite brothel, but movie fans looking for Amélie's café and *épicerie*. Yet you can still give the hordes on the place du Tertre the slip and discover some of Paris's most romantic and picturesque corners.

a good walk

Begin at place Blanche, landmarked by the **Moulin Rouge** ⑧ ▶, the windmill turned dance hall immortalized by Toulouse-Lautrec. Prior to the raucous time of the cancan was the dreamy age of Romanticism; to discover its exquisite 19th-century charm, you need only to visit the lovely **Musée de la Vie Romantique** ⑨, set three blocks south of place Blanche. Heading down rue Blanche until the third left onto rue Chaptal, this country-house-in-the-city was the former haunt of such greats as Georges Sand, Chopin, Ingres, and Delacroix. After savoring its delicate salons, backtrack up to place Blanche and then walk up lively rue Lepic from place Blanche. Few people notice the tiny Lux Bar at No. 12, with its original Art Nouveau woodwork and tiled murals from 1910—most are too busy looking across the street at the Café des Deux Moulins, where Amélie Poulain served coffee and brewed up schemes for helping strangers in the noted 2001 movie. Up rue Lepic you'll find the **Moulin de la Galette** ⑨⓪, atop its leafy hillock opposite rue Tholozé, once a path over the hill. Turn right down rue Tholozé, past Studio 28, the first cinema built expressly for experimental films. Continue down rue Tholozé to rue des Abbesses and turn left toward the triangular **place des Abbesses** ⑨①. Follow rue Ravignan as it climbs north, via place Émile-Goudeau, an enchanting little cobbled square, to the "cradle of Cubism," the **Bateau-Lavoir** ⑨②, or Boat Wash House, at its northern edge. Unfortunately the building burned in 1970 and is now rebuilt rather blandly. Painters Picasso and Braque had studios in the original building; this drab concrete edifice was built in its place (check out the historic photographs in the window of No. 11 bis for an idea of how it used to look). Continue up the hill via rue de la Mire to place Jean-Baptiste Clément, where Amedeo Modigliani had a studio.

The upper reaches of rue Lepic lead to rue Norvins, formerly rue des Moulins. At the end of the street to the left is stylish avenue Junot. (Detour here—illogically, it's labeled Impasses Girardon at this point—at No. 23 to the *boulodrome*, or bowling ground, a setting right out of a Marcel Pagnol novel, complete with pastis-drinking old men. The next passage along avenue Junot is the Villa Léandre cul-de-sac. At different times home to artist Max Ernst, actor Jean Marais, and actress Anouk

Aimée, the street's Anglo-Norman villas are among the most coveted bits of real estate in Paris.) On avenue Junot, continue right past the bars and tourist shops until you reach **place du Tertre** ⑨, the heart of Montmartre. Fight your way through to the southern end of the square for a breathtaking view of the city. Around the corner on rue Poulbot, the **Espace Salvador-Dalí** ⑨ houses works by Salvador Dalí, who once had a studio in the area. Return to place du Tertre. Looming behind is the scaly white dome of the Basilique du **Sacré-Coeur** ⑨. The cavernous interior is worth visiting for its golden mosaics; climb to the top of the dome for the view of Paris. Walk back toward place du Tertre. Turn right onto rue du Mont-Cenis and left onto rue Cortot, site of the **Musée de Montmartre** ⑨, which, like the Bateau-Lavoir, once sheltered an illustrious group of painters, writers, and assorted cabaret artists. Another famous Montmartre landmark is at No. 22: the bar-cabaret **Au Lapin Agile** ⑨, former haunt of Picasso.

TIMING Reserve a morning or afternoon (late afternoon if you want to catch Au Lapin Agile in the evening hours) for this walk: many of the streets are steep and slow. Include half an hour each at Sacré-Coeur and the museums (the Dalí museum is open daily, but the Montmartre museum is closed Monday). From Easter through September Montmartre is besieged by tourists. Two hints for avoiding the worst of the rush: come on a gray day, when Montmartre's sullen-tone facades suffer less than most others in the city; or visit during the afternoon and return to place du Tertre (maybe via the funicular) by the early evening, when the tourist buses will have departed.

What to See

⑨ **Au Lapin Agile.** One of the most picturesque spots in Paris, this legendary
Fodor's Choice bar-cabaret (sorry—open nights only) is a miraculous survivor from the
★ 19th century. It got its curious name—the Nimble Rabbit—when the owner, André Gill, hung up a sign (now in the Musée du Vieux Montmartre) of a laughing rabbit jumping out of a saucepan clutching a bottle of wine. Founded in 1860, this adorable maison-cottage was a favorite subject of painter Maurice Utrillo. Once owned by Aristide Bruant (immortalized in many Toulouse-Lautrec posters), it became the home-away-from-home for Braque, Modigliani, Apollinaire, and Vlaminck. The most famous habitué, however, was Picasso, who once paid for a meal with one of his paintings, then promptly went out and painted another, which he named after this place (it now hangs in New York's Metropolitan Museum, which purchased it for $50 million). Today the Lapin Agile manages to preserve at least something of its earlier flavor, unlike the Moulin Rouge. ⊠ *22 rue des Saules, Montmartre* ☎ *01–46–06–85–87* ⊕ *www.au-lapin-agile.com* ✉ *€20* ⊗ *Tues.–Sat. 9 PM–2 AM* Ⓜ *Lamarck-Caulaincourt.*

⑨ **Bateau-Lavoir** (Boat Wash House). Montmartre poet Max Jacob coined the name for the original building on this site (which burned down in 1970), saying it resembled a boat and that the warren of artists' studios within was perpetually paint-splattered and in need of a good hosing down. Wishful thinking, since the building only had one water tap. It was here that Pablo Picasso and Georges Braque made their first bold

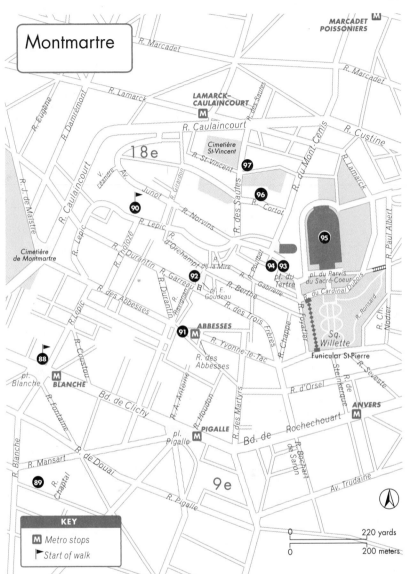

Montmartre

stabs at the concept of Cubism. The replacement building also contains art studios, but is the epitome of poured-concrete drabness. ✉ *13 pl. Émile-Goudeau, Montmartre* Ⓜ *Abbesses.*

❾❹ Espace Salvador-Dalí (Dalí Center). Some of Salvador Dalí's less familiar works are among the 25 sculptures and 300 etchings and lithographs housed in this museum, whose atmosphere is meant to approximate the experience of Surrealism. ✉ *11 rue Poulbot, Montmartre* ☎ *01–42–64–40–10* ⊕ *www.dali-espacemontmartre.com* 🎫 *€6* ⊙ *Daily 10–6:30* Ⓜ *Abbesses.*

❾⓪ Moulin de la Galette (Wafer Windmill). This is one of two remaining windmills in Montmartre. It was once the focal point of an open-air cabaret (made famous in a painting by Renoir). Rumor has it that in 1814 the miller Debray, who had struggled in vain to defend the windmill from invading Cossacks, was then strung up on its sails and spun to death by the invaders. Unfortunately, it's privately owned and can only be admired from the street below. ✉ *Rue Tholozé, Montmartre* Ⓜ *Abbesses.*

▶ **❽❽ Moulin Rouge** (Red Windmill). This world-famous cabaret was built in 1885 as a windmill, then transformed into a dance hall in 1900. Those wild, early days were immortalized by Toulouse-Lautrec in his posters and paintings. It still trades shamelessly on the notion of Paris as a city of sin: if you fancy a gaudy Vegas-style night out—sorry, admirers of the Baz Luhrmann film won't find any of its charm here—this is the place to go. The cancan, by the way—still a regular sight here—was considerably raunchier when Toulouse-Lautrec was around. ✉ *82 bd. de Clichy, Montmartre* ☎ *01–53–09–82–82* ⊕ *www.moulin-rouge.com* 🎫 *€80–€125* ⊙ *Shows nightly at 9 and 11* Ⓜ *Blanche.*

❾❻ Musée de Montmartre (Montmartre Museum). In its turn-of-the-20th-century heyday, Montmartre's historical museum was home to an illustrious group of painters, writers, and assorted cabaret artists. Foremost among them were Renoir and Maurice Utrillo. The museum also provides a view of the tiny **vineyard**—the only one in Paris—on neighboring rue des Saules. A token 125 gallons of wine are still produced here every year. ✉ *12 rue Cortot, Montmartre* ☎ *01–46–06–61–11* ⊕ *www.museedemontmartre. com* 🎫 *€5.50* ⊙ *Tues.–Sun. 11–6* Ⓜ *Lamarck-Caulaincourt.*

★ **❽❾ Musée de la Vie Romantique.** Lovers of all things "romantique" will enjoy visiting this tranquil, 19th-century countrified town house, set in a little park at the foot of Montmartre (head down rue Blanche from place Blanche; the third left is rue Chaptal). For years the site of Friday-evening salons hosted by the Dutch-born painter Ary Scheffer, the house often welcomed such guests as Ingres, Delacroix, Turgenev, Chopin, and Sand. The memory of author George Sand (1804–76)—real name Aurore Dudevant—haunts the museum. Portraits, furniture, and household possessions, right down to her cigarette box, have been moved here from her house in Nohant in the Loire Valley. There's also a selection of Scheffer's competent artistic output on the first floor. Take a moment to enjoy a cup of tea in the garden café. ✉ *16 rue Chaptal, Montmartre* ☎ *01–48–74–95–38* ⊕ *www.paris.fr/musees/* 🎫 *Free for permanent collection, exhibitions €4.50* ⊙ *Tues.–Sun. 10–5:40* Ⓜ *St-Georges.*

91 Place des Abbesses. The triangular square is typical of the picturesque, slightly countrified style that has made Montmartre famous. Now the hub of the local arts and fashion scene, the place is surrounded by trendy shops, sidewalk cafés, and shabby-chic restaurants, a prime habitat for the young, neo-bohemian crowd and a sprinkling of expats. The entrance to the Abbesses métro station, a curving, sensuous mass of delicate iron, is one of only two original Art Nouveau entrance canopies left in Paris. ⊠ *Montmartre* Ⓜ *Abbesses.*

93 Place du Tertre. This tumbling square (*tertre* means "hillock") regains its village atmosphere only in the winter, when the branches of the plane trees sketch traceries against the sky. At any other time of year you'll be confronted by crowds of tourists and a swarm of third-rate artists clamoring to do your portrait (if one of them whips up an unsolicited portrait, you are not obliged to buy it). **La Mère Catherine,** on one corner of the square, was a favorite with the Russian Cossacks who occupied Paris in 1814. They couldn't have suspected that by banging on the table and yelling "*bistro*" (Russian for "quickly"), they were inventing a new breed of French restaurant. ⊠ *Montmartre* Ⓜ *Abbesses.*

need a break? There are few attractive food options around place du Tertre; locals know to slip away to **La Divette du Moulin** (⊠ 98 rue Lepic at rue Orchampt, Montmartre ☎ 01–46–06–34–84) to regain a sense of camaraderie and rest their weary feet—there's tasty food or simply a decent cup of coffee, every day of the week.

★ **95 Sacré-Coeur.** Often compared to a "sculpted cloud" atop Montmartre, the Sacred Heart Basilica was erected as a sort of national guilt offering in expiation for the blood shed during the Paris Commune and Franco-Prussian War in 1870–71, and was largely financed by French Catholics fearful of an anticlerical backlash under the new republican regime. The basilica was not consecrated until 1919. Stylistically, the Sacré-Coeur borrows elements from Romanesque and Byzantine models. The gloomy, cavernous interior is worth visiting for its golden mosaics; climb to the top of the dome for the view of Paris. Try to visit at sunrise or long after sunset, as otherwise this area is crammed with bus groups, young lovers, postcard sellers, guitar-wielding Christians, and sticky-finger types; be extra cautious with your valuables. ⊠ *Pl. du Parvis-du-Sacré-Coeur, Montmartre* ☎ *01–53–41–89–00* ⌑ *Free, dome €4.50* ⊙ *Basilica daily 6:45 AM–11 PM; dome and crypt Oct.–Mar., daily 9–6; Apr.–Sept., daily 10–5* Ⓜ *Anvers.*

WHERE TO EAT

Updated by Rosa Jackson

Whether you get knee-deep in white truffles at Les Ambassadeurs or merely discover pistachio sausage (the poor man's foie gras) at a classic corner bistro, you'll discover that food in Paris is an obsession, an art, a subject of endless debate. From the edible genius of haute cuisine wizards Eric Frechon and Alain Ducasse to the sublime creations of Pierre Gagnaire (whose marriage of heated foie gras, pressed caviar, and Japanese seaweeds will make you purr), dining in Paris can easily leave you in a pleasurable stupor. And when it all seems a bit overwhelming, you can slip away to a casual little place for an earthy, bubbling cassoulet, have a midnight feast of the world's silkiest oysters, or even opt out of Gaul altogether for superb pasta, couscous, or an herb-bright Vietnamese stir-fry. Once you know where to go, Paris is a city where perfection awaits at all levels of the food chain.

Generally, restaurants are open from noon to about 2 and from 7:30 or 8 to 10 or 10:30. It's best to make reservations, particularly in summer, although the reviews only state when reservations are absolutely essential. If you want no-smoking seating, make this clear; the mandatory no-smoking area is sometimes limited to a very few tables. Brasseries have longer hours and often serve all day and late into the evening; some are open 24 hours. Assume a restaurant is open every day, unless otherwise indicated. Surprisingly, many prestigious restaurants close on Saturday as well as Sunday. July and August are the most common months for annual closings, although Paris in August is no longer the wasteland it once was. For help with the vocabulary of French cooking, see the Menu Guide at the end of this book. Places where a jacket and tie are de rigueur are noted. Otherwise, use common sense—jeans and T-shirts are not suitable in Paris restaurants, nor are shorts or running clothes, except in the most casual bistros and cafés.

Prices & Reservations

By French law, prices must include tax and tip (*service compris* or *prix nets*), but pocket change left on the table in basic places, or an additional 5% in better restaurants, is always appreciated. Beware of bills stamped "Service Not Included" in English or restaurants slyly using American-style credit-card slips, hoping that you'll be confused and add the habitual 15% tip. In neither case should you tip beyond the guidelines suggested above.

Here are a few key sentences for booking, if needed: "*Bonjour madame/monsieur* (ma'am, sir; say *bonsoir* after 6 PM). *Je voudrais faire une reservation pour X (1, un/une; 2, deux; 4, quatre; 6, six) personnes pour le diner* (evening)/ *le déjeuner* (lunch) *aujourd'hui à X heures* (today at X o'clock)/*demain à X heures* (tomorrow at X o'clock)/*lundi* (Monday), *mardi* (Tuesday), *mercredi* (Wednesday), *jeudi* (Thursday), *vendredi* (Friday), *samedi* (Saturday), *dimanche* (Sunday) *à X heures* (at X time). *Le nom est* (your own name). *Merci bien.*" Note that most wine bars do not take reservations; reservations are also unnecessary for brasserie and café meals at odd hours.

WHAT IT COSTS In euros				
	$$$$	**$$$**	**$$**	**$**	**¢**
AT DINNER	over €30	€23–€30	€17–€23	€11–€17	under €11

Prices are per person for a main course only at dinner, including tax (19.6%) and service; note that if a restaurant offers only prix-fixe (set-price) meals, it is given a price category that reflects the full prix-fixe price.

1er Arrondissement (Louvre/Les Halles)

CONTEMPORARY
$-$$$

✗ **Pinxo.** The word *pinxo* means "to pinch," which is how the food in this fashionable hotel restaurant is designed to be eaten—often with your fingers and off your dining companion's plate. (Each dish is served in three portions to allow for sharing.) Alain Dutournier, who also runs the more formal Le Carré des Feuillants nearby, drew on his southwestern roots to create this welcoming modern spot in black, plum, and dark wood. Freed from the tyranny of the entrée-*plat*-dessert cycle, you can nibble your way through such mini-dishes as marinated herring with Granny Smith apple and horseradish or squid cooked *à la plancha* (on a griddle) with ginger and chile peppers, then end, perhaps, with fresh pineapple and a piña colada sorbet. ✉ *Hôtel Plaza Paris Vendôme, 9 rue d'Alger, Louvre/Tuileries* ☎ *01–40–20–72–00* ▭ *AE, DC, MC, V* Ⓜ *Tuileries.*

FRENCH
$$$$
Fodor'sChoice
★

✗ **Le Grand Véfour.** Victor Hugo could stride in and still recognize this place—in his day, as now, a contender for the prize of most beautiful restaurant in Paris. Originally built in 1784, set in the arcades of the Palais-Royal, it has welcomed everyone from Napoléon to Colette to Jean Cocteau—many seats bear a plaque commemorating a famous patron. The mirrored ceiling and Restoration-era glass paintings of goddesses beguile the foodies as well as the fashionable who gather here to enjoy chef Guy Martin's delights. He hails from Savoie, so you'll find lake fish and mountain cheeses on the menu alongside such luxurious dishes as foie gras–stuffed raviolis. If you can't spring for the extravagant à la carte menu or the 10-course, €250 *menu plaisir,* try the lunchtime prix-fixe for €75. ✉ *17 rue Beaujolais, Louvre/Tuileries* ☎ *01–42–96–56–27* ⌁ *Reservations essential* ⌂ *Jacket and tie* ▭ *AE, DC, MC, V* ☉ *Closed weekends, and Aug. No dinner Fri.* Ⓜ *Palais-Royal.*

★ $$-$$$$

✗ **Restaurant du Palais-Royal.** Tucked away in the northeast corner of the magnificent Palais-Royal garden, this stylish modern bistro decorated in jewel tones serves food to match its stunning location under the palace arcades. Sole, scallops, and risotto—including a dramatic squid-ink and lobster version—are beautifully prepared, but juicy steak with *pommes Pont Neuf* is also a favorite of the expense-account lunchers who love this rather pricey place. Finish up with an airy *mille-feuille* pastry that changes with the seasons—berries in summer, chestnuts in winter. Be sure to book in advance, especially during the summer, when the terrace tables are hotly sought after. ✉ *Jardins du Palais-Royal, 110 Galerie Valois, Louvre/Tuileries* ☎ *01–40–20–00–27* ▭ *AE, DC, MC, V* ☉ *Closed Dec. and Jan., weekends Oct.–Apr., Sun. in summer* Ⓜ *Palais-Royal.*

$$
Fodor'sChoice
★

✗ **L'Ardoise.** This minuscule storefront painted white and decorated with enlargements of old sepia postcards of Paris is the very model of the contemporary bistros making waves in Paris. This one's claim to fame is chef Pierre Jay, who trained at La Tour d'Argent. His first-rate three-course menu for €31 tempts with such original dishes as scallops pan-fried with oyster mushrooms or a langoustine risotto (you can also order à la carte, but it's slightly less of a bargain). Just as enticing are the desserts, such as a superb *feuillantine au citron*—caramelized pastry leaves filled with lemon cream and lemon slices—and a boozy baba

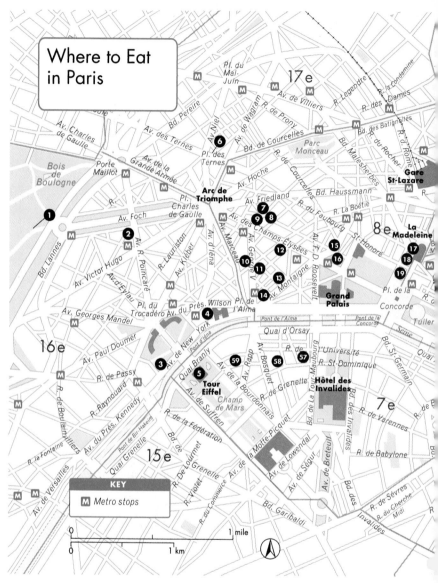

Where to Eat in Paris

KEY

Ⓜ *Metro stops*

0 — 1 mile
0 — 1 km

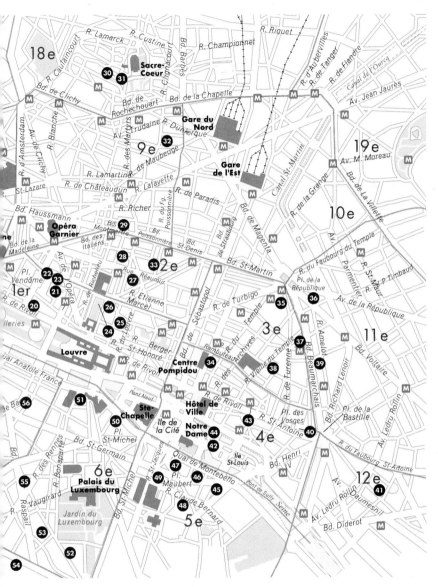

au rhum. With friendly waiters, service all weekend, and a small but well-chosen wine list, L'Ardoise would be perfect if it weren't often crowded and noisy. ✉ *28 rue du Mont Thabor, Beaubourg/Les Halles* ☎ *01–42–96–28–18* 🚍 *MC, V* 🕐 *Closed Mon., Aug., 1 wk at Christmas, 1 wk in May* Ⓜ *Concorde.*

$–$$ ✕ **Willi's Wine Bar.** Don't be fooled by the name—this English-owned spot is no modest watering hole but rather a stylish haunt for Parisian and foreign gourmands. The often original menu changes daily to reflect the market's offerings, and might include fresh scallops, foie gras prepared on the premises, *andouillette* (chitterling sausage), and crème brûlée or a bitter chocolate *terrine* (pudding). Owner Mark Williamson has a passion for Rhône Valley wines, reflected in the extensive list, and for Spanish sherries. ✉ *13 rue des Petits-Champs, Louvre/Tuileries* ☎ *01–42–61–05–09* 🚍 *MC, V* 🕐 *Closed Sun.* Ⓜ *Bourse.*

¢–$ ✕ **Rouge Tomate.** The name of this epicurean restaurant is misleading, since not all the tomatoes served here are red—the shop specializes in little-known varieties, with green, yellow and stripey varieties on display in summer. Off-season, the cook often uses homemade preserves (jars of homemade tomato sauces and jams are for sale in the shop). The airy space feels like a coffee shop and there is a quiet terrace for enjoying reasonably priced dishes such as a goat cheese and tomato terrine with confit tomatoes, tagliatelle with yellow tomato sauce, chicken and cumin, and a chocolate fondant with tomato-orange confit. ✉ *34 pl. du Marché St-Honoré, Louvre/Tuileries* ☎ *01–42–61–16–09* 🚍 *AE, MC, V* Ⓜ *Tuileries or Pyramides.*

2° Arrondissement (La Bourse/Opéra)

FRENCH ✕ **Chez Georges.** When you ask sophisticated Parisians—think bankers,
$$$ aristocrats, or antiques dealers—to name their favorite bistro, many choose Georges. The traditional bistro fare is good—herring, sole, kidneys, steaks, and *frites* (fries)—and the atmosphere is better. A wood-panel entry leads you to an elegant and unpretentious dining room where one long, white-clothed stretch of tables lines the mirrored walls and attentive waiters sweep efficiently along its entire length. ✉ *1 rue du Mail, Louvre/Tuileries* ☎ *01–42–60–07–11* 🚍 *AE, DC, MC, V* 🕐 *Closed Sun. and 3 wks in Aug.* Ⓜ *Sentier.*

$$–$$$ ✕ **Aux Lyonnais.** For Alain Ducasse it's not enough to run three of the
FodorsChoice world's most expensive restaurants (in Paris, Monte Carlo, and New
★ York) and an ever-expanding string of Spoon, Food & Wine fusion bistros. He also has a passion for the old-fashioned bistro, so he has resurrected this 1890s gem by appointing a terrific young chef to oversee the short, frequently changing, and reliably delicious menu of Lyonnais specialties (if you're watching your pennies, opt for the limited-choice €28 set menu). Dandelion salad with crisp potatoes, bacon, and silky poached egg, watercress soup poured over parsleyed frogs' legs, and a sophisticated rendition of coq au vin show he is no bistro dilettante. The decor hews to tradition, too; there's a zinc bar, an antique coffee machine, and original turn-of-the-20th-century woodwork. ✉ *32 rue St-Marc, Opéra/Grands Boulevards* ☎ *01–42–96–65–04* 🚍 *AE, MC, V* 🕐 *Closed Sat.–Mon.* Ⓜ *Bourse.*

PARIS NOW: THE NEW DINING TRENDS

WHAT ARE THE LATEST **FASHIONS** on the Paris dining scene? Not everyone wants a three-course blowout every time they go to a restaurant. While meals have long followed a predictable entrée-plat-dessert pattern, this is changing thanks to pioneering chefs such as Joël Robuchon. In his Atelier and his Table, the man once voted "chef of the 20th century" encourages dining in small or larger portions, according to your appetite. His opening hours even suggest that it's O.K. to graze outside traditional mealtimes—une révolution. Taking a similar approach is Alain Dutournier of Pinxo, who has actually persuaded Parisians to eat with their fingers and steal food off their companions' plates. Chefs are also developing a freer hand with spices, thanks to their experiences abroad. One of the first to successfully incorporate spices into French cuisine without falling into fusion follies was top chef Pascal Barbot at L'Astrance. During a stint in Australia, Barbot learned to juggle Asian flavors, then honed his French technique at L'Arpège. At Ze Kitchen Galerie, chef William Ledeuil puts the emphasis on presentation, drawing on ingredients from Chinatown and Middle Eastern grocery stores. Most recently, chef Michel Troisgros of the famed Roanne restaurant has created an innovative new menu for the bijou Hôtel Lancaster, introducing such bold dishes as frogs' legs with tamarind. Even as their palates grow more adventurous, however, the French are reembracing terroir. Nothing illustrates this better than the purchase of the turn-of-the-20th-century bistro Aux Lyonnais by superchef Alain Ducasse. Never one to miss a trend, Ducasse knows that Parisians will always love earthy regional food when it is prepared with care and served in a gorgeous setting.

$–$$$ ✕ **Le Vaudeville.** One of Jean-Paul Bucher's seven Flo brasseries, Le Vaudeville is filled with journalists, bankers, and locals *d'un certain âge* who come for its good-value assortment of prix-fixe menus and highly professional service. Shellfish, house-smoked salmon, and desserts such as profiteroles are particularly enticing. Enjoy the graceful 1920s decor— almost the entire interior of this intimate dining room is done in real or faux marble—and lively dining until 1 AM daily. ⊠ *29 rue Vivienne, Opéra/ Grands Boulevards* ☎ *01–40–20–04–62* ▤ *AE, DC, MC, V* Ⓜ *Bourse.*

☾ ¢ ✕ **La Ferme Opéra.** If your arm is aching from trying to flag down café waiters, take a break in this bright, super-friendly self-service restaurant not far from the Louvre, specializing in produce from the Ile de France region (around Paris). Inventive salads and sandwiches, quiches such as the three-cheese with pecan, hot dishes like chicken with dates and prunes served with polenta, and fruit crumbles, tarts, and cheesecakes are all impeccably fresh. ⊠ *55–57 rue St-Roch, Opéra/Grands Boule- vards* ☎ *01–46–33–35–36* ▤ *MC, V* Ⓜ *Pyramides.*

3ᵉ **Arrondissement (Beaubourg/Marais)**

CONTEMPORARY ✕ **Le Murano.** Last year, stylehounds made a beeline to Baccarat's Cristal
$$$–$$$$ Room; this year, they're trekking out to the new Murano Urban Resort

hotel in achingly chic northern Marais. There is nothing subtle about the showing-off that takes place in this "rock n' luxe" hotel's dining room, whose ceiling drips with white tubes of various lengths, so dress to the nines and go with plenty of attitude (or brace yourself with three test tubes of alcohol at the bar). The light-modern food will neither distract nor offend you—smoked salmon with too-pink tarama, sautéed squid, waffle potato chips—and the steep prices seem worth it for such a quintessentially Parisian fashion scene. If you can survive the once-over at the door, the good-humored dining room staff adds to the experience. ⊠ *13 bd. du Temple Marais* ☎ *01–42–71–20–00* ⚑ *Reservations essential* ▭ *AE, DC, MC, V* Ⓜ *Filles du Calvaire.*

FRENCH ✕ **Le Pamphlet.** Chef Alain Carrère's affordable and modern take on south-
★ **$$$** western French cooking—which is somewhat at odds with the rather sedate, dressed-up dining room—has made this Marais bistro popular with gourmets, tourists, and arty types from the neighborhood's galleries. The market-driven prix-fixe daily menu runs from first courses such as a carpaccio of duck breast or cream of lentil soup to entrées such as a juicy pork chop with béarnaise sauce and hand-cut frites. Finish up with a slice of tangy sheep's cheese or one of the comforting, calorific desserts. ⊠ *38 rue Debelleyme, Le Marais* ☎ *01–42–72–39–24* ⚑ *Reservations essential* ▭ *MC, V* ⊘ *Closed Sun. and 2 wks in Aug. No lunch Mon. or Sat.* Ⓜ *St-Sébastien Froissart.*

4e Arrondissement (Beaubourg/Marais/Ile St-Louis)

CONTEMPORARY ✕ **Georges.** Decorated in white and gray, with angular chairs and giant
$$$–$$$$ metallic shells, Georges stands in stark contrast to its graceful view of Paris from the top floor of the Centre Georges Pompidou. Staff are as sleek as the furniture, and at night the terrace has distinct snob appeal: come snappily dressed or suffer the consequences (you may be relegated to something resembling a dentist's waiting room). The menu headlines predictable Costes comfort food such as macaroni with morel mushrooms, but, sadly, most dishes are considerably less dazzling than the view. The exception are desserts by star pâtissier Stéphane Secco, whose YSL (as in Yves St-Laurent, darling) bitter chocolate cake is an event. Reservations are a must in the evening, whereas lunch is more casual. ⊠ *Centre Pompidou, 6th fl., rue Rambuteau, Beaubourg/Les Halles* ☎ *01–44–78–47–99* ▭ *AE, DC, MC, V* ⊘ *Closed Tues.* Ⓜ *Rambuteau.*

FRENCH ✕ **Bofinger.** One of the oldest, loveliest, and most popular brasseries in
☺ **$–$$$** Paris has generally improved since it joined the Flo group, known for its restorations of historic brasseries. Stake out one of the tables dressed in crisp white linen under the glowing Art Nouveau–glass cupola—this part of the dining room is nonsmoking—and enjoy classic brasserie fare such as oysters, seafood-topped choucroute, or lamb fillet (stick to simple fare as some of the more ambitious dishes can be simply odd). The prix-fixe includes a decent half bottle of red or white wine and there is an especially generous children's menu. ⊠ *5–7 rue de la Bastille, Bastille/Nation* ☎ *01–42–72–87–82* ▭ *AE, DC, MC, V* Ⓜ *Bastille.*

$–$$$ ✕ **Au Bourguignon du Marais.** The handsome, contemporary look of this Marais bistro and wine bar is the perfect backdrop for the good traditional fare and excellent Burgundies served by the glass and bottle. Always on the menu are Burgundian classics such as *jambon persillé* (ham in parsleyed aspic jelly), escargots, and *oeufs en meurette* (eggs poached in a red-wine sauce); more up-to-date picks include a cèpe mushroom velouté with poached oysters (though the fancier dishes are generally less successful). In summer, the terrace is the place to be. ✉ *19 rue de Jouy, Beaubourg/Les Halles* ☎ *01–48–87–15–40* 🖃 *AE, DC, MC, V* 🕙 *Closed weekends* Ⓜ *St-Paul.*

$–$$$ ✕ **Brasserie de l'Ile St-Louis.** Set on picturesque Ile St-Louis and opened in 1870—when Germany took over Alsace-Lorraine and its chefs decamped to the capital—this outpost of Alsatian cuisine remains a cozy cocoon filled with stuffed animal heads, antique fixtures fashioned from barrels, and folk-art paintings. The food is gemütlich, too: *coq-au-Riesling*, omelets with Muenster cheese, onion tarts, and *choucroutes garni* (sauerkraut studded with ham, bacon, and pork loin—one variant is made with smoked haddock). In warm weather, the crowds move out to the terrace overlooking the Seine and Notre-Dame. With the famed *glacier* Berthillon so close by, it's best not to bother with the pricey desserts here. ✉ *55 quai de Bourbon, Ile St-Louis* ☎ *01–43–54–02–59* 🖃 *DC, MC, V* 🕙 *Closed Wed. and Aug. No lunch Thurs.* Ⓜ *Pont Marie.*

$–$$
Fodor'sChoice
★
✕ **Mon Vieil Ami.** "Modern Alsatian" might sound like an oxymoron, but not once you've tasted the cooking of Antony Clémot, a young protegé of the celebrated Strasbourg chef Antoine Westermann. The updated medieval dining room of "My Old Friend"—stone walls, wooden beams, dark wood tables and panes of glass—provides a stylish setting for his inventive cooking, which showcases perfect produce. *Pâté en croûte,* with a knob of foie gras in the center, is hard to resist as a starter, while in a *salade tiède* of root vegetables with foie gras, the unusual vegetable varieties very nearly outshine the fattened liver. Long-cooked, wine-marinated venison also comes with succulent accompaniments of quince, prune, celery root, and chestnuts. If you don't want to go the whole hog, follow the lead of *les habitués* and order the €15 *plat du jour.* ✉ *69 rue St-Louis-en-l'Isle, Ile St-Louis* ☎ *01–40–46–01–35* 🖃 *AE, DC, MC, V* 🕙 *Closed Sun. No lunch Mon.* Ⓜ *Pont Marie.*

MIDDLE EASTERN
☺ **¢–$**
✕ **L'As du Fallafel.** Look no farther than the fantastic falafel stands on rue de Rosiers for some of the cheapest and tastiest meals in Paris: L'As (the Ace) is widely considered the best of the bunch. A falafel costs €5, but shell out a little extra money for the *spécial* with grilled eggplant, cabbage, hummus, tahini, and hot sauce. Though takeout is popular, it can be more fun (and a lot less messy) to eat off a plastic plate in the frenetic but fascinating fast-food style dining room, where you can watch the lightning-quick cooks at work. The fresh lemonade is the falafel's best match. ✉ *34 rue des Rosiers, Le Marais* ☎ *01–48–87–63–60* 🖃 *MC, V* 🕙 *Closed dusk Fri.–dusk Sat.* Ⓜ *St-Paul.*

5° Arrondissement (Latin Quarter)

CONTEMPORARY
★ **$–$$**
✕ **Le Pré Verre.** Chef Philippe Delacourcelle knows his cassia bark from his cinnamon, thanks to a long stint in Asia. He opened this sharp bistro (with purple-gray walls and photos of jazz musicians) in 2003 to showcase his unique culinary style, rejuvenating archetypal French dishes with Asian and Mediterranean spices. His bargain prix-fixe-only

menu changes constantly, but crisp salt cod with cassia bark and super-smooth smoked potato purée is a winner, as is an unlikely dessert of roasted figs with olives. ⊠ *8 rue Thénard, Quartier Latin* 🕾 *01–43–54–59–47* 🖃 *MC, V* ⊗ *Closed Sun., Mon., and 2 wks in Aug.* Ⓜ *Maubert-Mutualité.*

FRENCH
★ $$$$
✕ **La Tour d'Argent.** Beyond the wonderful if resolutely classic food, many factors conspire to make a meal at this venerable landmark memorable: the extraordinary wine cellar, considerate service, the grandeur of the dining room, and, of course, that privileged vista across the Seine to Notre-Dame. If the price of an à la carte meal makes you pause, you can't go wrong with the €70 lunch. You'll even be entitled to succulent slices of one of the restaurant's numbered ducks (the great duck slaughter began in 1919 and is now well past the millionth mallard, as your numbered certificate will attest). The most celebrated dish, *canard au sang* (duck in a blood-based sauce), is available à la carte or for a €22 supplement. Don't get too daunted by the wine list—more of a bible, really—for with the help of one of the sommeliers you can splurge a little (about €80) and perhaps taste a rare vintage Burgundy. The lunch crowd is remarkably casual, whereas evenings are a more formal affair, attracting a mix of suited tycoons and smoochy couples. ⊠ *15 quai de la Tournelle, Quartier Latin* 🕾 *01–43–54–23–31* ⬧ *Reservations essential* 🏛 *Jacket and tie* 🖃 *AE, DC, MC, V* ⊗ *Closed Mon. No lunch Tues.* Ⓜ *Cardinal Lemoine.*

★ $–$$$
✕ **Chez René.** Think there's nowhere left in Paris that serves *boeuf bourguignon,* coq au vin, and frogs' legs in a timeworn bistro setting—crisp white tablecloths, burgundy woodwork, waiters in black aprons? Then you haven't been to Chez René, whose specialty—aside from robust Burgundian classics—is reassuring continuity, as illustrated by the photos of the staff taken every decade that adorn the walls. ⊠ *14 bd. St-Germain, Quartier Latin* 🕾 *01–43–54–30–23* 🖃 *MC, V* ⊗ *Closed Sun., Mon., Christmas wk, and Aug. No lunch Sat.* Ⓜ *Maubert-Mutualité.*

★ $–$$
✕ **Le Reminet.** Chandeliers and mirrors add an unexpected grace note to this mellow bistro set in a narrow salon with stone walls run by a friendly couple. The menu can be outstanding, studded with winners like prawn ravioli with coconut milk and grilled lamb with a cumin-and-red-pepper crust. Desserts are equally inventive: don't even try to resist the mini baba au rhum with panfried winter fruits and *maniguette* (a.k.a. grains of paradise) pepper. Score a deal with the €13 prix-fixe lunch menu served on Monday, Thursday, and Friday, or the €17 dinner menu on Monday and Thursday (watch out for the restaurant's unusual opening days). The €50 tasting menu makes for a memorable indulgence. ⊠ *3 rue des Grands-Degrés, Quartier Latin* 🕾 *01–44–07–04–24* 🖃 *MC, V* ⊗ *Closed Tues. and Wed., 2 wks in Feb., and 2 wks in Aug.* Ⓜ *Maubert-Mutualité.*

$
✕ **Les Pipos.** The tourist traps along romantic rue de la Montagne Ste-Genevieve are enough to make you despair—and then you stumble across this bistro, bursting with chatter and laughter. Slang for students of the famous École Polytechnique nearby, Les Pipos is everything you could ask of a Quartier Latin bistro: the space is cramped, the food (such as Charolais steak and duck confit) is substantial (the cheese comes from

the Lyon market, though the Poilâne bread could be fr(
versation flows as freely as the wine. It gets crowded, s
snag a table. You can also stop in for a glass of wine and ₅ ᵣ
son in the late afternoon and watch the sun go down behind the Panthéon. ⊠ *2 rue de L'École Polytechnique, Quartier Latin*
☎ *01–43–54–11–40* ▭ *No credit cards* ⊘ *Closed Sun. and 2 wks in*
Aug. Ⓜ *Maubert-Mutualité.*

6° Arrondissement (St-Germain-des-Prés/ Latin Quarter)

CONTEMPORARY
$$–$$$

✖ **Ze Kitchen Galerie.** William Ledeuil made his name at the popular Les
Bouquinistes (a Guy Savoy baby bistro) before opening this pared-
down contemporary bistro in a loftlike space nearby. If the name isn't
exactly inspired, the cooking shows unbridled creativity and a sense of
fun: from a deliberately deconstructed menu featuring raw fish, soups,
pastas, and *à la plancha* plates, expect dishes such as a chicken wing,
broccoli, and artichoke soup with lemongrass or pork ribs with curry
jus and white beans (for best value, opt for one of the lunchtime prix-
fixes). Worldly eaters might find the flavors too subtle, but they are certainly adventurous for Paris. Ledeuil gives cooking classes in the compact
kitchen. The only thing missing is a no-smoking section. ⊠ *4 rue des*
Grands-Augustins, Quartier Latin ☎ *01–44–32–00–32* ▭ *AE, DC,*
MC, V ⊘ *Closed Sun. No lunch Sat.* Ⓜ *St-Michel.*

$$

✖ **Le Café des Délices.** There is a lot to like about this bistro, from the
Art Nouveau facade and the warm and spacious Asia-meets-Africa
decor (lots of dark wood and little pots of spices on each table) to the
polished service and mouthwatering food. Drop in for the bargain €15
lunch (the plat du jour with a glass of wine and coffee), or go for à la
carte dishes such as scallops with balsamic vinegar or blood pudding
flavored with cocoa. Tongue-in-cheek comfort-food desserts tout such
ingredients such as Chupa Chups lollipops and sugary cereal. Not every-
thing works, but the chef deserves credit for his adventurous approach.
⊠ *87 rue d'Assas, Montparnasse* ☎ *01–43–54–70–00* ▭ *AE, MC, V*
⊘ *Closed weekends* Ⓜ *Vavin.*

FRENCH
$$$$

✖ **Hélène Darroze.** Hélène Darroze has won a lot of followers—and
two Michelin stars—with her refined take on southwestern French
cooking, from the lands around Albi and Toulouse. You know it's not
going to be *la même chanson*—the same old song—as soon as you see
the contemporary Tse & Tse tableware, and her intriguingly modern touch
comes through in such dishes as duck foie-gras confit served with chut-
ney of exotic fruits, or a blowout of roast wild duck stuffed with foie
gras and truffles. Expect to spend a hefty €350 for two à la carte (with
drinks) upstairs, but there is a lunch menu at €68. The livelier down-
stairs bistro offers similar food in smaller tapas-style portions—how-
ever, inconsistent food and inexpert service mar what should be a more
relaxed experience. ⊠ *4 rue d'Assas, St-Germain-des-Prés*
☎ *01–42–22–00–11* ▭ *AE, DC, MC, V* ⊘ *Closed Sun. and Mon. No*
lunch Tues. Ⓜ *Sèvres Babylone.*

★ $$$$

✖ **Lapérouse.** Emile Zola, George Sand, and Victor Hugo were regulars,
and ladies are said to have mercilessly tested the authenticity of their

diamonds on the restaurant's mirrors, which still bear the scratches today—all this makes it hard not to fall in love with this 17th-century Seine-side town house. Chef Alain Hacquard seems to have found the right track with a daring (for Paris) spice-infused menu: his lobster, Dublin Bay prawn, and crayfish bisque is flavored with Szechuan pepper and a lemon vinaigrette. For the ultimate romantic meal, reserve a private salon where anything could happen (and probably has). The €30 "business menu," served at lunch in the beamed dining room overlooking the Seine, is a great value. ⊠ *51 quai des Grands Augustins, Quartier Latin* ☎ *01–43–26–68–04* ⚑ *Reservations essential* ▤ *AE, DC, MC, V* ☺ *Closed Sun., 3 wks in July, 1 wk in Aug. No lunch Sat.* Ⓜ *St-Michel.*

$–$$ ✕ **Le Timbre.** Working in a tiny open kitchen, Manchester native Chris Wright could teach many a French chef a thing or two about *la cuisine Française*. He works with only the finest suppliers—Le Comptoir Corrézien for truffles, La Poissonerie du Dôme for fish—to produce a constantly changing seasonal menu that keeps the locals coming back. A spring meal might begin with fat asparagus spears cut in half lengthwise and served with dabs of anise-spiked sauce, balsamic vinegar and Parmesan. A thick pork chop with confit petals of red onion is a lesson in how to retain the moisture in this cut of meat. The mille-feuille is spectacular, but it would be a shame to miss *le vrai et le faux fromage,* a two-year-old British cheddar juxtaposed with a farmer's goat cheese from the Ardèche. Black-and-white photos of Paris add real charm to the narrow dining room. ⊠ *3 rue Ste-Beuve, Montparnasse* ☎ *01–45–49–10–40* ▤ *MC, V* ☺ *Closed Sun. and 3 wks in Aug. No lunch Sat.* Ⓜ *Vavin.*

7e Arrondissement (Invalides/Eiffel Tower)

CONTEMPORARY ✕ **Petrossian.** Although young chef Sebastien Faré now mans the stoves,
★ **$$$$** Petrossian still jangles with the wildly imaginative style of his predecessor, Philippe Conticini. Conticini keeps his hand in as a consultant, which is good news for the restaurant's *gauche caviar* (luxe-loving Rive Gauche Socialist) clientele. In keeping with cost-conscious times, the restaurant has also introduced affordable limited-choice menus for €38 at lunch and €48 at dinner. Smoked fish and caviar star in house classics such as a breaded soft-boiled egg topped with caviar like a Fabergè egg, but other winning concoctions are risotto with squid ink and porcini and a Moroccan-inspired salad with crisp Dublin Bay prawns. Don't miss the "drinkable perfumes," an alluring series of vividly colored infusions of flowers, barks and roots; served cold in shot glasses, they cleanse the palate in preparation for the tongue-tickling desserts. ⊠ *18 bd. de La Tour–Maubourg, Invalides* ☎ *01–44–11–32–32* ▤ *AE, DC, MC, V* ☺ *Closed Sun., Mon., and 3 wks in Aug.* Ⓜ *La Tour–Maubourg, Invalides.*

FRENCH ✕ **Jules Verne.** A table at this all-black restaurant on the second level of
$$$$ the Tour Eiffel, 400 feet removed from the gritty reality of Parisian life, is one of the hardest to snag in Paris. At its best, Alain Reix's cooking justifies a wait of two months or more for dinner (lunch is more accessible), but lately his food has been a deflating experience. The wisest approach, then, is to go for the €53 lunch menu (weekdays only) and

expect good but not exquisite food, such as pigeon fricassee or squid with duck liver, an intriguing meeting of land and sea. There's always the exceptional view—the highlight of any meal here has to be the ride up the restaurant's private elevator. Arrive early to snag a window seat. ⊠ *Tour Eiffel, Trocadéro/Tour Eiffel* ☎ *01–45–55–61–44* ⚭ *Reservations essential* 🎩 *Jacket and tie* ⊟ *AE, DC, MC, V* Ⓜ *Bir-Hakeim.*

$$$–$$$$
Fodor'sChoice
★

✕ **L'Atelier de Joël Robuchon.** Famed chef Joël Robuchon had retired from the restaurant business for several years before opening this red-and-black-lacquered space with a bento-box-meets-tapas aesthetic and branches in Tokyo and Las Vegas. Seats line up around U-shape bars; this novel plan nudges neighbors to share recommendations and opinions. Robuchon's cooks whip up "small plates" for grazing (€12–€30) as well as full-size dishes. The menu changes frequently, but highlights have included an intense tomato jelly topped with avocado purée, thin-crusted mackerel tart, and his (inauthentic, but who's complaining?) take on carbonara with cream and bacon from Alsace. Reservations are now taken even for peak times and the entire restaurant is smoke-free. ⊠ *5 rue Montalembert, St-Germain-des-Prés* ☎ *01–42–22–56–56* ⊟ *MC, V* Ⓜ *Rue du Bac.*

★ $$–$$$

✕ **Au Bon Accueil.** To see what well-heeled Parisians like to eat these days, book a table at this extremely popular bistro as soon as you get to town; the dining room was redone in 2003 to open up the space, and the sidewalk tables have a Tour Eiffel view. The excellent, reasonably priced *cuisine du marché* (a daily, market-inspired menu, €25 at lunch and €29 at dinner) has made it a hit: typical of the winter fare is roast suckling pig with thyme and endives. ⊠ *14 rue de Montessuy, Trocadéro/Tour Eiffel* ☎ *01–47–05–46–11* ⚭ *Reservations essential* ⊟ *MC, V* ☽ *Closed weekends* Ⓜ *Pont de l'Alma.*

★ $

✕ **Le Café Constant.** Parisian thirty- and fortysomethings are a nostalgic bunch, which explains the popularity of this down-to-earth new address from chef Christian Constant. He was head chef at Le Crillon before opening his own restaurant, Le Violon d'Ingres, and then this more humble bistro, and seeing him relax in the dining room after the lunch rush you get the feeling that this is where he feels most at home. The menu reads like a French cookbook from the 1970s—who cooks veal cordon bleu these days?—and, with Constant overseeing the kitchen, the dishes taste even better than you remember. Creamy lentil soup with morsels of foie gras come with a modest €2 supplement, and artichoke salad is made with fresh, not bottled or frozen, hearts. A towering hunk of vacherin cheese brings this delightfully retro meal in traditional bistro surroundings—cream-colored walls, red banquettes, wooden tables—to a close. Show up early, since they don't take reservations. ⊠ *139 rue Saint-Dominique, Invalides* ☎ *01–48–04–88–28* ⊟ *MC, V* ☽ *Closed Sun. and Mon.* Ⓜ *Ecole Militaire or RER Pont de l'Alma.*

8ᵉ Arrondissement (Champs-Élysées/Louvre)

CONTEMPORARY
$$$$

✕ **Maison Blanche.** The celebrated Pourcel twin brothers preside over this edgy "White House," which basks in its show-off view across Paris from the top floor of the Théâtre du Champs-Élysées. Typical of the globe-trotting, southern-inspired (and not always successful) fare are the vegetable *pot au feu* with white Alba truffle (vegetarian dishes are special here), crisp-crusted scallop tart with crab and baby leeks, and French beef with an herb crust, mushrooms and shallots slow-cooked in Fitou wine. A side order of mashed potatoes, green beans or salad will set you back a sobering €10—this is a place for the fat of wallet and trim of figure, though there is a €45 lunch menu. In keeping with the snow-white setting, staff can be rather frosty. ☒ *15 av. Montaigne, Champs-Élysées* ☎ *01–47–23–55–99* ▭ *AE, MC, V* ☺ *No lunch weekends* Ⓜ *Franklin-D.-Roosevelt.*

$$$$ ✗ **La Table du Lancaster.** One of the most enduring names in French gas-
Fodor'sChoice tronomy—the family has run a world-famous restaurant in Roanne for
★ three generations—Troisgros has made its Paris debut in this stylish bou-tique hotel. Notoriously unpredictable as the weather is in Paris, try to sit in the stunning Asian-inspired courtyard with its red walls and bamboo trees—the perfect setting for tasting the Michel Troisgros' cosmopolitan cooking. Often drawing on humble ingredients, such as sardines, eel, or even pigs' ears, the food creates fascinating flavor and texture contrasts, as in silky sardines on crunchy melba toast, or tangy frogs' legs in tamarind. A classic from the menu in Roanne is cod in a seaweed bouillon on koshi-hikari rice, a subtle and sensual dish. Don't miss the desserts—the sugar tart with grapefruit slices is designed to bring out the child in the most sophisticated diner. ☒ *Hôtel Lancaster, 7 rue de Berri, Champs-Élysées* ☎ *01–40–76–40–18* ⌂ *Reservations essential* ▭ *AE, DC, MC, V* ☺ *Closed mid-July–mid-Aug. No lunch weekends.*

$$$–$$$$ ✗ **Market.** Celebrated New York–based Alsatian chef Jean-Georges Von-gerichten (think Vong, Mercer Kitchen, and Jean-Georges) set up shop in this strategic neighborhood to much fanfare, as this is his first restaurant in France. Put together with deceptively simple raw materials—burnt pine and stone offset with African masks—the dining room makes a soigné if sometimes noisy arena for well-traveled dishes such as truffled pizza, spiced sea bream, and sweet chestnut soufflé. The sometimes lacklus-ter food, however, suggests that the globe-trotting Vongerichten might be spreading himself too thin. This is a fine place for a breakfast meet-ing, however, over a plate of buttery pastries by star pâtissier Pierre Hermé (9–11 AM daily). ☒ *15 av. Matignon, Champs-Élysées* ☎ *01–56–43–40–90* ⌂ *Reservations essential* ▭ *AE, MC, V* Ⓜ *Franklin-D.-Roosevelt.*

$$$–$$$$ ✗ **Spoon, Food & Wine.** Star chef Alain Ducasse's bistro may be the grand-daddy of style-conscious restaurants around the Champs-Élysées, but its popularity shows no signs of waning. What draws the black-clad crowd are the playful, Asian- and American-inspired menu; the hypercool in-terior (white by day, plum by night); and the fact that it's so hard to get a dinner reservation. Fashion folk love this place for its many vegetable and pasta dishes and its irresistible desserts, particularly the Toble-Spoon, a takeoff on Toblerone. If you've sampled the Spoon concept elsewhere in the world, don't expect the same here; each branch is tai-lored to a particular city's tastes, and what looks exotic in Paris (bagels and bubble-gum ice cream) might seem humdrum in New York. ☒ *14 rue de Marignan, Champs-Élysées* ☎ *01–40–76–34–44* ⌂ *Reserva-*

tions essential ▱ *AE, MC, V* ☺ *Closed weekends, 4 wks in July–Aug., 2 wks in late Dec.* Ⓜ *Franklin-D.-Roosevelt.*

FRENCH   ✗ **Alain Ducasse au Plaza Athénée.** This posh hotel's previously sober din-
★ **$$$$**   ing room now glimmers with 10,000 crystals following a whirlwind revamp by decorator Patrick Jouin, who wanted the chandeliers to
seemingly "explode," projecting the organza that once shrouded them
toward the walls. Clementine-colored tablecloths and space-age cream-
and-orange chairs with pull-out plastic trays (a bit airplanelike) further
brighten up the room, providing a more cheerful setting for the cooking of young chef Christophe Moret. He still seems to be finding his foot-
ing in a dining room heavy with gastronomic expectations (sorry,
Ducasse really doesn't cook anymore)—some of the dishes taste too subtle, whereas in others strong flavors overwhelm more delicate ingredients. Even so, a meal here is delightfully luxe, starting with a heavenly
amuse-bouche of Dublin Bay prawn with caviar and a tangy lemon cream.
You can continue with a full truffle- and caviar-fest, or opt for slightly
more down-to-earth dishes such as lobster in spiced wine with quince
or saddle of lamb with small sautéed artichokes. If you find yourself hes-
itating over dessert, opt for the *baba au rhum comme à Monte-Carlo,*
which comes with a trolley of the finest rums to choose from. ✉ *Hôtel
Plaza Athenée, 27 av. Montaigne, Champs-Élysées* ☎ *01–53–67–66–65*
⌔ *Reservations essential* 🝓 *Jacket required* ▱ *AE, DC, MC, V* ☺ *Closed
weekends, 2 wks in late Dec., and mid-July–mid-Aug. No lunch
Mon.–Wed.* Ⓜ *Alma-Marceau.*

★ **$$$$**   ✗ **Les Ambassadeurs.** A former star—more of a comet, really—in the Alain
Ducasse galaxy, Jean-Francois Piége is now establishing his own identity in Le Crillon's hallowed 18th-century dining room, recently updated
in muted tones that offset the glistening marble and dripping chandeliers. Born in 1970, he is young enough to play with food—decon-
structing and reconstructing an egg to look like a square marshmallow,
its yolk studded with white truffle—and grown-up enough to serve unabashedly rich classics of French cooking, such as deboned squab stuffed
with foie gras. An expert at pairing langoustines and caviar, he has come
up with a new version for the Crillon, this time wrapping the ingredients in a delicate crêpe. À la carte, it's easily one of the city's priciest
restaurants, but there is a relatively democratic €70 lunch menu. Happily, the waiters will make you feel at home no matter what your budget. ✉ *Hôtel de Crillon, 10 pl. de la Concorde, Louvre*
☎ *01–44–71–16–17* ⌔ *Reservations essential* Ⓜ *Concorde.*

$$$$ ✗ **Lucas Carton.** Alain Senderens always sips wine while he's cooking,
Fodor'sChoice   but not to stay relaxed—he's the acknowledged French master of match-
★   ing wine with food. Each new dish on his menu was inspired by a wine,
which is listed next to it as the ideal accompaniment. He dreamed up
langoustines in a crunchy vermicelli shell to complement a Meursault
from Dury, while his *canard à l'Apicius* (duck roasted with honey and
spices) becomes all the more heavenly with a glass of Banyuls, a sweet
wine from southwestern France. Most customers are content to follow
his suggestions, and they can be sure the wines will always be served at
the optimum temperature—Senderens wants his wines to be as happy
as his customers in his sumptuous Art Nouveau dining room. ✉ *9 pl.*

de la Madeleine, Opéra/Grands Boulevards ☎*01–42–65–22–90* ⌕*Reservations essential* ▭ *AE, DC, MC, V* ⊘ *Closed Sun. and Aug. No lunch Sat. or Mon.* Ⓜ *Madeleine.*

$$$$ ✕ **Maxim's.** Count Danilo sang "I'm going to Maxim's" in Lehar's *The Merry Widow,* Leslie Caron was klieg-lighted here by Cecil Beaton for *Gigi,* and Audrey Hepburn adorned one of its banquettes with Peter O'-Toole in *How to Steal a Million.* In reality, Maxim's has lost some of its luster—the restaurant had its heyday 100 years ago during the Belle Époque, when *le tout Paris* swarmed here—but this exuberant Art Nouveau sanctuary still offers a taste of the good life under its breathtaking painted ceiling. It's just a shame that Maxim's is so jaw-droppingly expensive for food that would feel at home in a brasserie, like the Billy-bi mussel consommé with cream or braised sole in vermouth—a prix-fixe menu would attract a bigger crowd and make the room feel more festive. In a fit of cost cutting not reflected in the menu prices, a lone singing pianist has replaced the orchestra. ✉*3 rue Royale, Louvre/Tuileries* ☎ *01–42–65–27–94* ⌕ *Reservations essential* ▭ *AE, DC, MC, V* ⊘ *Closed Sun. and Mon. No lunch Sat.* Ⓜ *Concorde.*

$$$$ ✕ **Pierre Gagnaire.** If you want to venture to the frontier of luxe cooking today—and if money is truly no object (entrées can range from €90 to €200)—a meal here might be considered a must. Chef Pierre Gagnaire's work is at once intellectual and poetic, often blending three or four unexpected tastes and textures in a single dish. Just taking in the menu requires concentration, so complex are descriptions such as "suckling lamb from Aveyron: sweetbreads, saddle and rack; green papaya and turnip velouté thickened with Tarbais beans." If the businesslike gray-and-wood dining room feels refreshingly informal, especially at lunch, it also lacks the grandeur that you expect at this level. The uninspiring prix-fixe lunch, uneven service, and occasional ill-judged dishes linger as drawbacks and prices keep shooting skywards, making Pierre Gagnaire an experience only for the financial elite. ✉ *6 rue de Balzac, Champs-Élysées* ☎ *01–58–36–12–50* ⌕ *Reservations essential* ▭ *AE, DC, MC, V* ⊘ *Closed Sat. and 2 wks in July. No lunch Sun. and Aug.* Ⓜ *Charles-de-Gaulle–Étoile.*

$$$$
Fodor's Choice
★
✕ **Taillevent.** Once most traditional of all Paris luxury restaurants, this grande dame is basking in newfound freshness under brilliant chef Alain Solivérès, who draws inspiration from the Basque country, Bordeaux, and Languedoc for his daily-changing menu. Signatures such as the *boudin de homard* (an airy sausage-shape lobster soufflé) are now matched with choices such as a splendid spelt risotto with truffles and frogs' legs or panfried duck liver in Banyuls sauce with caramelized fruits and vegetables. One of the 19th-century paneled salons has been turned into a winter garden and new contemporary paintings adorn the walls. The service is flawless and the exceptional wine list is well priced. All in all, a meal here comes as close to the classic haute-cuisine experience as you can find in Paris today. Not surprisingly, you must reserve your table for dinner a month in advance; lunch is more accessible and there is even a €70 prix fixe, which is kept a bit of a secret. ✉ *15 rue Lamennais, Champs-Élysées* ☎ *01–44–95–15–01* ⌕ *Reservations essential* 🏛 *Jacket and tie* ▭ *AE, DC, MC, V* ⊘ *Closed weekends and Aug.* Ⓜ *Charles-de-Gaulle–Étoile.*

★ **$$$–$$$$**   ✕ **Flora.** Alain Passard-trained Flora Mikula made her name at Les Oli-
vades, a Provençal bistro in the 7ᵉ, before joining a gaggle of ambitious
restaurateurs in this platinum-card neck of the woods. Moving away
from the bistro register, she's turning out refined food with southern twists
in a dressed-up setting with plaster moldings and mirrors of various sizes
that feels much like a bourgeois apartment. Standout dishes on the fre-
quently changing seasonal menu are a scallop *tarte fine* with truffle vinai-
grette, roasted-apple mille-feuille with salted-caramel ice cream and a
spectacular Grand Marnier soufflé. Service, like the food, is impecca-
ble with the occasional minor slip-up, and the €60 tasting menu is a
terrific value. ✉ *36 av. George V, Champs-Élysées* ☎ *01–40–70–10–49*
🍴 *AE, MC, V* ✪ *Closed Sun. No lunch Sat.* Ⓜ *Franklin-D.-Roosevelt.*

$$–$$$ ✕ **La Fermette Marbeuf 1900.** Graced with one of the most mesmerizing
Belle Époque rooms in town—accidentally rediscovered during reno-
vations in the 1970s—this is a favorite haunt of French celebrities, who
adore the sunflowers, peacocks, and dragonflies of the Art Nouveau mo-
saic and stained-glass mise-en-scène. The menu rolls out a solid, updated
classic cuisine. Try the snails in puff pastry, saddle of lamb with *choron*
(a tomato-spiked béarnaise sauce), and bitter-chocolate fondant—but
ignore the rather depressing €30 prix-fixe unless you're on a budget.
Popular with tourists and businesspeople at lunch, La Fermette be-
comes truly animated around 9 PM. ✉ *5 rue Marbeuf, Champs-Élysées*
☎ *01–53–23–08–00* 🍴 *AE, DC, MC, V* Ⓜ *Franklin-D.-Roosevelt.*

$–$$ ✕ **Chez Savy.** Just off the glitzy avenue Montaigne, Chez Savy exists in
its own circa-1930s dimension, oblivious to the area's galloping fash-
ionization. The Art Deco cream-and-burgundy interior looks blissfully
intact (avoid the back room unless you're in a large group) and the waiters show not a trace of attitude, even offering to change a wine bottle
that's just a touch too chilled. Fill up on rib-sticking specialties from
the Auvergne in central France—lentil salad with bacon, beautifully
charred lamb with feather-light shoestring frites, poached peach with
sorbet—order a celebratory bottle of Mercurey, and feel smug that
you've found this place. ✉ *23 rue Bayard, Champs-Élysées*
☎ *01–47–23–46–98* 🍴 *AE, MC, V* ✪ *Closed weekends and Aug.*
Ⓜ *Franklin-D.-Roosevelt.*

9ᵉ Arrondissement (Opéra/Pigalle-Clichy)

FRENCH   ✕ **Les Vivres.** The brainchild of Jean-Luc André, chef at the elegant
$ Pétrelle next door, Les Vivres translates as "survival supplies" and many
locals now feel they couldn't live without it. Down the hill from Montmartre in a quiet residential street, this stylish dining room—like the French
country home you wish you had—serves lunch nonstop 11 AM–7 PM.
You'll always find seasonal vegetables, which are grilled, marinated or
slow-roasted, a savory tart, and hot dishes such as farmer's rabbit with
Nyons olives, *hachis parmentier* (shepherd's pie), or squid fricassee. ✉ *28
rue Pétrelle, Montmartre* ☎ *01–42–80–26–10* 🍴 *MC, V* ✪ *Closed
Sun.* Ⓜ *Anvers.*

♨ ¢   ✕ **Chartier.** People come here more for the bonhomie and the stunning
1896 interior than the cooking, which could be politely described as unambitious. This cavernous restaurant—the only original turn-of-the-cen-
tury *bouillon* to remain true to its mission of serving cheap, sustaining

food to the masses—enjoys a huge following. You may find yourself sharing a table with strangers as you study the long, old-fashioned menu of such standards as hard-boiled eggs with mayonnaise, pot-au-feu, and *blanquette de veau* (veal stew in a white sauce). ⊠ *7 rue du Faubourg-Montmartre, Opéra/Grands Boulevards* ☎ *01–47–70–86–29* ⌲ *Reservations not accepted* ▤ *MC, V* Ⓜ *Montmartre*.

11ᵉʳ Arrondissement (Bastille/République)

FRENCH
★ $$–$$$

✕ **Astier.** The prix-fixe menu (there's no à la carte) at this tried-and-true restaurant must be one of the best values in town, with a lunch menu for €22.50 and a second lunch menu and dinner menu for €27. Among the deftly prepared seasonal dishes are tomato and goat-cheese tart on curly endive, rabbit in mustard sauce with fresh tagliatelle, and *marquise au chocolat* (chocolate mousse cake). This is a great place to come if you're feeling cheesy, since it's locally famous for having one of the best *plateaux de fromages* (cheese plates) in Paris—a giant wicker tray lands on the table and you help yourself. The lengthy, well-priced wine list is a connoisseur's dream. ⊠ *44 rue Jean-Pierre Timbaud, République* ☎ *01–43–57–16–35* ⌲ *Reservations essential* ▤ *MC, V* ☉ *Closed weekends, Aug., Christmas wk, and Easter wk* Ⓜ *Parmentier*.

$–$$

✕ **Le Repaire de Cartouche.** In this split-level, dark-wood bistro between Bastille and République, young chef Rodolphe Paquin applies a disciplined creativity to earthy French regional dishes. The menu changes regularly, but typical are a salad of *haricots verts* (string beans) topped with tender slices of squid, scallops on a bed of diced pumpkin, juicy lamb with white beans, and old-fashioned desserts like custard with tiny madeleine cakes. ⊠ *99 rue Amelot, Bastille/Nation* ☎ *01–47–00–25–86* ⌲ *Reservations essential* ▤ *MC, V* ☉ *Closed Sun., Mon., and Aug.* Ⓜ *Filles du Calvaire*.

12ᵉ Arrondissement (Bastille/Nation)

FRENCH
★ $–$$

✕ **Le Square Trousseau.** This beautiful Belle Époque bistro is a favorite of the fashion set. Even models can't resist the peppered country pâté, slow-cooked lamb, or tender baby chicken with mustard and bread-crumb crust. Wines might seem a little pricey but are lovingly selected from small producers—you can also buy them, along with superb Spanish ham, at the restaurant's small boutique/wine bar next door. If you're on a budget, try the lunch menu at €20 or €25. ⊠ *1 rue Antoine Vollon, Bastille/Nation* ☎ *01–43–43–06–00* ▤ *AE, MC, V* ☉ *Closed Sun. and Mon., 3 wks in Aug., 1 wk at Christmas, and 2 wks in Feb.* Ⓜ *Ledru-Rollin*.

14ᵉ Arrondissement (Montparnasse)

FRENCH
$–$$$

✕ **La Coupole.** This world-renowned cavernous spot with Art Deco murals practically defines the term *brasserie*. La Coupole might have lost its intellectual aura since the Flo group's restoration, but it has been popular since the days when Jean-Paul Sartre and Simone de Beauvoir were regulars and is still great fun. Today it attracts a mix of bourgeois families, tourists, and elderly lone diners treating themselves to a dozen oysters. Expect the usual brasserie menu—including perhaps the largest shellfish platter in Paris—choucroute, a very un-Indian but tasty lamb curry, and some great over-the-top desserts. They don't take reservations after 8:30 PM Monday–Thursday and after 8 PM Friday–Sunday, so be prepared for a wait at the bar. ⊠ *102 bd. du Montparnasse, Montparnasse* ☎ *01–43–20–14–20* ⊟ *AE, DC, MC, V* Ⓜ *Vavin.*

16ᵉ Arrondissement (Trocadéro/Bois de Boulogne)

CONTEMPORARY
$$$$
Fodor'sChoice
★

✕ **Astrance.** Pascal Barbot may have risen to fame thanks to his restaurant's amazing-value food and casual atmosphere, but a few years later Astrance is resolutely haute with prices to match. Most diners put their faith in the chef by ordering his €150 tasting menu, which unfolds over two to three hours in a series of surprisingly light courses. Even à la carte a meal here now costs at least €100, but Barbot's cooking has such an ethereal touch that it's worth the month-long wait for a table at dinner. Barbot worked with Alain Passard at L'Arpège before opening his own restaurant and his dishes often draw on Asian ingredients, as in grilled lamb with miso-lacquered eggplant or a palate-cleansing white sorbet spiked with chile pepper and lemongrass. If you're looking for an affordable lunch menu, you'll sadly have to go elsewhere. ⊠ *4 rue Beethoven, Trocadéro/Tour Eiffel* ☎ *01–40–50–84–40* ⚓ *Reservations essential* ⊟ *AE, DC, MC, V* ⊘ *Closed Sat., Mon., and Aug.* Ⓜ *Passy.*

$$–$$$$
Fodor'sChoice
★

✕ **La Table de Joël Robuchon.** Despite its gold-leaf decor, this has been an unlucky address—this is the restaurant's third incarnation in as many years. Under Robuchon's expert leadership, however, success should be guaranteed. Chef Frédéric Simonin, who formerly worked with Ghislaine Arabian, brings northern and southern French touches to Robuchon's style in veal-rib chops with olives, broad beans, and tiny artichokes or, for dessert, the Total Rhubarbe, which raises this humble cold-weather stalk to sublime heights. As at L'Atelier you'll find a selection of small plates alongside more substantial dishes, but the seating arrangement is more conventional (no bar, just tables and chairs) and they accept reservations—though you should book weeks in advance. ⊠ *16 av. Bugeaud, Trocadéro/Tour Eiffel* ☎ *01–56–28–16–16* ⚓ *Reservations essential* ⊟ *MC, V* ⊘ *Closed Sun. and 2 wks in Aug. No lunch Mon. or Sat.* Ⓜ *Victor-Hugo.*

FRENCH
★ $$$$

✕ **Jamin.** This intimate if rather frilly restaurant where Joël Robuchon made his name serves brilliant food well away from the media spotlight. The best value is the lunch prix-fixe at €50, which entitles you to a generous meal with extras such as the sorbet trolley. The dinner prix-fixes at €95 and €130 also compare favorably with the offerings at other restaurants of Jamin's caliber. Benoît Guichard, Robuchon's second for many years, is a particularly marvelous *saucier* (sauce maker). The menu changes regularly, but Guichard favors dishes with a Mediterranean touch, such as sea bass with pistachios in fennel sauce and braised beef with cumin-scented carrots. ⊠ *32 rue de Longchamp, Trocadéro/Tour Eiffel* ☎ *01–45–53–00–07* ⚓ *Reservations essential* ⊟ *AE, DC, MC, V* ⊘ *Closed weekends, Aug., and 1 wk in Feb.* Ⓜ *Iéna.*

$$$$

✕ **Le Pré Catelan.** Live a Belle Époque fantasy by dining beneath the chestnut trees on the terrace of this fanciful landmark *pavillon* in the Bois de Boulogne. Among the winning dishes that have appeared on chef Frédéric Anton's menu are spit-roasted squab in a caramelized sauce, sweetbreads with morels and asparagus tips, and roasted pear on a caramelized waffle with bergamot ice cream. For a taste of the good life at a (relatively) gentle price, order the €55 lunch menu and soak up the opulent surroundings along with service that's as polished as the silverware. ✉ *Rte. de Surèsnes, Bois de Boulogne* ☎ *01–44–14–41–14* ⚬ *Reservations essential* 🎩 *Jacket and tie* ▭ *AE, DC, MC, V* ⊘ *Closed Sun., Mon., mid-Feb., and 1 wk in Nov.* Ⓜ *Porte Dauphine.*

17ᵉ Arrondissement (Monceau/Champs-Élysées)

FRENCH

★ $$$$

✕ **Guy Savoy.** Revamped with dark African wood, rich leather, and cream-color marble, Guy Savoy's luxury restaurant has stepped gracefully into the 21st century. Come here for a perfectly measured contemporary haute-cuisine experience, since Savoy's several bistros have not lured him away from his kitchen. The artichoke soup with black truffles, sea bass with spices, and veal kidneys in mustard-spiked jus reveal the magnitude of his talent, and his mille-feuille is an instant classic. Half portions allow you to graze your way through the menu—unless you choose a blowout feast for €210 or €285—and reasonably priced wines are available (though beware the cost of wines by the glass). Best of all, the atmosphere is joyful—Savoy senses that having fun is just as important as eating well. ✉ *18 rue Troyon, Champs-Élysées* ☎ *01–43–80–40–61* ▭ *AE, MC, V* ⊘ *Closed Sun., Mon., and mid-July–mid-Aug. No lunch Sat.* ⚬ *Reservations essential* 🎩 *Jacket and tie* Ⓜ *Charles-de-Gaulle–Étoile.*

18ᵉ Arrondissement (Montmartre)

FRENCH

$–$$

✕ **Chez Toinette.** Between the red lights of Pigalle and the Butte Montmartre, this cozy bistro with red walls and candlelight hits the romance nail on the head. In autumn and winter, game comes into play in longsimmered French dishes—choose from *marcassin* (young wild boar), venison, and pheasant. Regulars can't resist the crème brûlée and the raspberry tart. Prices have crept up, but Chez Toinette is still a rare find for this neighborhood. ✉ *20 rue Germaine Pilon, Montmartre* ☎ *01–42–54–44–36* ▭ *MC, V* ⊘ *Closed Sun. and Mon., Aug., and 2 wks at Christmas. No lunch* Ⓜ *Pigalle.*

$–$$

✕ **La Famille.** Inaki Aizpitarte, originally from the Basque region, opened this hip restaurant on a street known for its role in the film *Amélie*. Happily, La Famille is worth visiting for what it brings to the plate, not the screen. The spare space attracts the *bobo* (bohemian bourgeois) neighbors who are bringing a new energy to Montmatre. Aizpitarte's globetrotting menu might include pan-fried foie gras with miso sauce or chocolate custard with fiery Basque peppers. On the last Sunday of every month a tasting menu is served (the restaurant is closed the other Sundays). ✉ *41 rue des Trois-Frères, Montmartre* ☎ *01–42–52–11–12* ▭ *MC, V* ⊘ *Closed Sun. and Mon. No lunch* Ⓜ *Abbesses.*

Cafés & Salons de Thé

Along with air, water, and wine (Parisians eat fewer and fewer threecourse meals), the café remains one of the basic necessities of life in Paris; following is a small selection of cafés and *salons de thé* (tearooms) to whet your appetite. **Au Père Tranquille** (✉ 16 rue Pierre Lescot, Beaubourg/Les Halles, 1ᵉʳ ☎ 01–45–08–00–34 Ⓜ Les Halles) is one of the best places in Paris for people-watching. **Brasserie Lipp** (✉ 151 bd. St-Germain, St-

Germain-des-Prés, 6ᵉ ☎ 01–45–48–53–91 Ⓜ St-Germain-des-Prés),
with its turn-of-the-20th-century decor, was a favorite spot of Hemingway's; today television celebrities, journalists, and politicians come
here for coffee on the small glassed-in terrace off the main restaurant.
Café Beaubourg (✉ 43 rue St-Merri, Beaubourg/Les Halles, 4ᵉ
☎ 01–48–87–63–96 Ⓜ Hôtel-de-Ville), near the Pompidou Center and
designed by architect Christian de Portzamparc, is one of the trendiest
rendezvous spots for fashion and art types. **Café Marly** (✉ Cour Napoléon
du Louvre, 93 rue de Rivoli, Louvre/Tuileries, 1ᵉʳ ☎ 01–49–26–06–60
Ⓜ Palais-Royal), overlooking the main courtyard of the Louvre, is perfect for an afternoon break or a nightcap, though the food could be better. Note that ordinary café service shuts down during meal hours,
when overpriced, mediocre food is served. **La Charlotte en l'Ile** (✉ 24 rue
St-Louis-en-l'Ile, Ile St-Louis, 4ᵉ ☎ 01–43–54–25–83 Ⓜ Pont-Marie)
would be fancied by the witch who baked gingerbread children in
Hansel and Gretel—set with fairy lights, carnival masques, and de-
coupaged detritus, it's a tiny, storybook spot that offers more than 30
varieties of tea along with a sinfully good hot chocolate. **La Crémaillère**
(✉ 15 pl. du Tertre, Montmartre, 18ᵉ ☎ 01–46–06–58–59 Ⓜ Anvers)
is a veritable monument to fin-de-siècle art in Montmartre. **Les Editeurs**
(✉ 4 carrefour de l'Odéon, St-Germain-des-Prés, 6ᵉ ☎ 01–43–26–67–76
Ⓜ St-Germain-des-Prés), strategically placed near prestigious Rive
Gauche publishing houses, attracts passersby with red velour seats and
glossy books on display. The terrace just off the boulevard St-Germain
is great for people-watching, but not ideal for catching a waiter's eye.
Le Flore en l'Ile (✉ 42 quai d'Orléans, Ile St-Louis, 4ᵉ ☎ 01–43–29–88–27
Ⓜ Pont-Marie) is set on the Ile St-Louis and has a magnificent view of
the Seine. **Ladurée** (✉ 16 rue Royale, Opéra/Grands Boulevards, 8ᵉ
☎ 01–42–60–21–79 Ⓜ Madeleine) is pretty enough to bring a tear to
Proust's eye—this salon de thé has barely changed since 1862. You'll
dote on the signature lemon-and-caramel macaroons (there are other
outposts at 75 av. des Champs-Élysées and on the Left Bank at 21 rue
Bonaparte). **Ma Bourgogne** (✉ 19 pl. des Vosges, Le Marais, 4ᵉ
☎ 01–42–78–44–64 Ⓜ St-Paul) is a calm oasis for a coffee or a light
lunch away from the noisy streets and set on magical place des Vosges.
Mariage Frères (✉ 30 rue du Bourg-Tibourg, Le Marais, 4ᵉ
☎ 01–42–72–28–11 Ⓜ Hôtel-de-Ville) is an outstanding tea shop serving 500 kinds of tea, along with delicious tarts. **Le Vieux Colombier**
(✉ 65 rue de Rennes, St-Germain-des-Prés, 7ᵉ ☎ 01–45–48–53–81
Ⓜ St-Sulpice) is just around the corner from St-Sulpice and the Vieux
Colombier Theater.

WHERE TO STAY

Updated by
Heather
Stimmler-Hall

Winding staircases, flower-filled window boxes, concierges who seem
to have stepped from a 19th-century novel—all of these can still be found
in Paris hotels, and despite the scales being tipped in favor of the well-
heeled, overall there's good news for travelers of all budgets. Increased
competition means the bar for service and amenities has been raised everywhere. Many good-value establishments in the lower-to-middle price

ranges have updated their funky '70s wallpaper and "Why should I care, Madame?" attitudes, while still keeping their prices in check. Virtually every hotel is now equipped with cable TV to meet the needs of international guests. Now it's not uncommon for mid-range hotels to have a no-smoking floor, for inexpensive hotels to offer air-conditioning, and even for budget places to have planted an Internet terminal in their little lobbies. So, whatever price you're looking for, compared to most other cities Paris is a paradise for the weary traveler tired of dreary, out-of-date, or cookie-cutter rooms. The best hotels still emanate an unmistakable Paris vibe: weathered beamed ceilings, vaulted stone breakfast crypts, tall windows overlooking zinc rooftops, and leafy courtyards where you can sit and linger over your daily croissant and café.

Despite the huge choice of hotels, you should always reserve well in advance, especially if you're determined to stay in a specific place. You can do this by telephoning, faxing, or e-mailing ahead, then asking for confirmation of your reservation, detailing the duration of your stay, the price, the location and type of your room (single or double, twin beds or double), and the bathroom (shower—*douche*—or bath—*baignoire*—private or shared). Assume that hotel rooms have air-conditioning, TV, telephones, and private bath, unless otherwise noted. Remember that the *very* top Paris hotels retain their ranks among the world's priciest. Room rates at these legendary places can range from €400 to €700—and upward—for a night. These rates can artificially skew our price chart figures for, in truth, a **$$$** hotel listed below can be as reasonable as €160.

Prices

Almost all Paris hotels charge extra for breakfast, with prices ranging from €5 to more than €30 per person in luxury establishments. For anything more than the standard Continental breakfast of café au lait and croissants, the price will be higher. You may be better off finding the nearest café. Occasionally breakfast is included in the hotel rate—this is denoted below with a BP (Breakfast Plan) in the review. If not, presume all hotels reviewed operate on the EP (European Plan), with no breakfast included in the basic room rate. A nominal *séjour* (lodging) tax of €1.07 per person per night is charged to pay for promotion of tourism in Paris.

WHAT IT COSTS In euros				
	$$$$	**$$$**	**$$**	**$**	**¢**
FOR 2 PEOPLE	over €225	€150–€225	€100–€150	€75–€100	under €75

Prices are for two people in a standard double room in high season, including tax (19.6%) and service charge.

1ᵉʳ Arrondissement (Louvre/Les Halles)

$$$$ **Hôtel Costes.** Jean-Louis and Gilbert Costes's eponymous hotel is the darling of decorating magazines and a magnet for the sunglasses-at-night set. Nearly every room is swathed in enough pomegranate-red, $400-a-yard fabrics, swagging, and braided trim to choke a runway of supermodels. A seductive bar with its labyrinth of secluded nooks is *the* place in Paris to be seen trying not to be seen. For taste, many consider this the top Paris hotel, but better wear thick skin: unless you're an off-duty celeb, the army of perfectly coiffed hosts and hostesses has a knack for making you feel underdressed and unimportant. ⊠ *239 rue St-Honoré, Louvre/Tuileries, 75001* ☎ *01–42–44–50–50* 🖷 *01–42–44–50–01* ⊕ *www.hotelcostes.com* 🖙 *77 rooms, 5 suites* ⌁ *Restaurant, room service, in-room safes, minibars, cable TV, in-room VCRs, in-room data ports, indoor pool, gym, sauna, bar, babysitting, laundry service, meeting rooms, parking (fee), some pets allowed* 🖃 *AE, DC, MC, V.*

★ **$$$$**   🖭 **Hôtel Meurice.** With millions recently lavished on this famous hotel by its owner, the Sultan of Brunei, the Meurice sparkles as never before— and that's saying something, since it has welcomed royalty and celebrity since 1835. The restaurant—a fabled extravaganza of cream boiseries and glittering chandeliers—and the elaborately gilded 18th-century Rococo salons have been entirely restored, while the guest rooms are aswim in Persian carpets, marble mantelpieces, and ormolu clocks and are in either a gilded Louis XVI or Napoleonic-Empire style. Most have a Tuileries/Louvre or Sacré-Coeur view, but the massive Royal Suite takes in a 360-degree panorama (reportedly Paris's only). Goodies are extraordinary: the honey in the minibars is gathered from bees buzzing on the roof of the Opéra, while the health club includes grape-seed-based Caudalíe treatments such as "Cabernet Sauvignon" massages. ⊠ *228 rue de Rivoli, Louvre/Tuileries, 75001* ☎ *01–44–58–10–10* 🖷 *01–44–58–10–15* ⊕ *www.meuricehotel.com* 🖙 *160 rooms, 36 suites* ⌁ *2 restaurants, room service, in-room safes, minibars, cable TV, in-room data ports, health club, bar, laundry service, meeting rooms, no-smoking rooms* 🖃 *AE, DC, MC, V* Ⓜ *Tuileries, Concorde.*

★ **$$$$**   🖭 **Hôtel Ritz.** The majestic and legendary hotel founded in 1896 by Cesar Ritz is festooned with Napoleonic gilt, sparkling crystal chandeliers, and *qualité de Louvre* antiques. Yes, the glamour quotient declines precipitously in the back wing, but even if you get one of the humbler chambers, you could easily spend days without venturing past the main gates, thanks to the hotel's dazzling shops, bars, clubs, and restaurants. There's the luxe Espadon restaurant, which overlooks the prettiest dining courtyard in Paris; the famed Ritz Escoffier cooking school where you can learn the finer points of *gâteaux*; the Hemingway Bar, where Colin Field reigns as a world-ranked bartender; and the basement health club—a veritable Louis XIV temple of sweat. ⊠ *15 pl. Vendôme, Louvre/Tuileries, 75001* ☎ *01–43–16–30–30* 🖷 *01–43–16–36–68* ⊕ *www.ritzparis.com* 🖙 *107 rooms, 55 suites* ⌁ *3 restaurants, room service, in-room data ports, in-room safes, minibars, cable TV, indoor pool, health club, hair salon, 2 bars, shops, children's programs (ages 6-12), babysitting, parking (fee)* 🖃 *AE, DC, MC, V* Ⓜ *Opéra.*

$$$$ 🖭 **Hôtel de Vendôme.** With a discreet entrance on the posh Place Vendôme and tiny jewel-box of a lobby with inlaid marble and carved mahogany paneling, this hotel has all the comfort and luxury of its neighboring palace hotels without the ostentatious size. Rooms are handsomely done in French period styles from Louis XIV to Art Deco, with marble baths, antique furnishings, and hand-carved wood detailing throughout. Technical touches include wireless Internet access, flat-screen TVs, and a bedside console that controls the lights, curtains, music, and an electronic DO NOT DISTURB sign. The British-style restaurant and bar, decorated with leather chesterfields and wood paneling, fits in with the 19th-century vintage of this building. ⊠ *1 pl. Vendôme, Louvre/Tuileries, 75001* ☎ *01–55–04–55–00* ☒ *01–49–27–97–89* ⊕ *www.hoteldevendome. com* ↩ *18 rooms, 11 suites* ⚭ *Restaurant, room service, in-room data ports, in-room safes, minibars, cable TV, piano bar, Internet, some pets allowed (fee)* ⊟ *AE, DC, MC, V* Ⓜ *Concorde, Opéra.*

$$$ 🏨 **Hôtel Brighton.** Many of Paris's most prestigious palace hotels are found facing the Tuileries or the place de la Concorde. The Brighton breathes the same rarified air under the arcades for a fraction of the price. Smaller rooms with showers look onto a courtyard; street-facing chambers have balconies and a royal view onto the gardens and the Rive Gauche in the distance. Extensive renovations in early 2004 updated a third of the older rooms, but the hotel's still not completely wired for Internet service. ⊠ *218 rue de Rivoli, Louvre/Tuileries, 75001* ☎ *01–47–03–61–61* ☒ *01–42–60–41–78* ⊕ *www.esprit-de-france.com* ↩ *65 rooms* ⚭ *Dining room, in-room data ports, in-room safes, minibars, cable TV, laundry service, some pets allowed; no a/c in some rooms* ⊟ *AE, DC, MC, V* Ⓜ *Tuileries.*

$–$$ 🏨 **Hôtel Londres St-Honoré.** An appealing combination of character and comfort distinguishes this small, inexpensive hotel, which is a five-minute walk from the Louvre. Exposed oak beams, statues in niches, and rustic stone walls give this place an old-fashioned air. Though rooms have floral bedspreads and standard hotel furniture, they are pleasant, and the price is right. Note that the elevator only starts on the second floor. ⊠ *13 rue St-Roch, Louvre/Tuileries, 75001* ☎ *01–42–60–15–62* ☒ *01–42–60–16–00* ⊕ *www.123france.com* ↩ *21 rooms, 4 suites* ⚭ *Dining room, minibars, cable TV, Internet, some pets allowed, no-smoking rooms; no a/c in some rooms* ⊟ *AE, DC, MC, V* Ⓜ *Pyramides.*

¢ 🏨 **Hôtel Henri IV.** Princes once made the regal Ile de la Cité their home but even paupers can call it their home, thanks to one of Paris's most beloved (and popular) rock-bottom sleeps. Set in a 400-year-old building that once housed Henri IV's printing presses, it has a drab lobby and narrow staircase (five flights, no elevator) but guest rooms wear their age with pride. Nothing beats the top location, set on gorgeous place Dauphine and just a short stroll to the Louvre and Notre-Dame. Bathrooms are in the hallway; pay a little extra and get a room with a private shower. ⊠ *25 pl. Dauphine, Ile de la Cité, 75001* ☎ *01–43–54–44–53* ↩ *20 rooms, 7 with shower/bath* ⚭ *Dining room; no a/c, no room phones, no room TVs* ⊟ *MC, V* Ⓜ *Cité, St-Michel, Pont Neuf.*

2ᵉ Arrondissement (Bourse/Les Halles)

¢ 🏨 **Hôtel Tiquetonne.** Just off the Montorgueil market and a short hoof from Les Halles (and the slightly seedy rue St-Denis), this is one of the least expensive hotels in the city center. The so-old-fashioned-they're-vintage rooms aren't much to look at, nor do they offer amenities, but they're always clean and some are downright spacious. Book one of the top two floors facing the quiet, pedestrian rue Tiquetonne, not the loud, car-strangled rue Turbigo. ⊠ *6 rue Tiquetonne, Beaubourg/Les Halles, 75002* ☎ *01–42–36–94–58* 🖷 *01–42–36–02–94* 📠 *45 rooms, 33 with bath* ⚴ *Some pets allowed; no a/c, no room TVs* 🝙 *AE, MC, V* ☾ *Closed Aug. and last wk in Dec.* Ⓜ *Étienne Marcel.*

3ᵉ Arrondissement (Beaubourg/Marais)

★ **$$$$** 🏨 **Murano Urban Resort.** As the epicenter of Parisian cool migrates to the eastern sectors of the city, it's no surprise that a design-conscious hotel would follow. Opened in summer 2004 in the République area, set on the trendy northern edge of the Marais (known for its contemporary art galleries and gay-friendly tearooms), this cheeky hotel combines Austin Powers playfulness with seriously 007 gadgetry. A psychedelic elevator takes guests to ultraviolet-lit hallways, where they enter pristine white rooms via fingerprint sensor locks. White shag carpeting, black-slate bathrooms, Pop Art furniture, and bedside control panels keep guests amused until it's time for aperitifs. Two suites have private terraces with heated, countercurrent swimming pools. Stylish Parisians pack the hotel's vodka bar and sleek restaurant, where a live DJ holds court in the elevated booth and staff seem genuinely welcoming. Resort? Well, a spa is promised, along with an indoor heated pool. ⊠ *13 bd. du Temple, République, 75003* ☎ *01–42–71–20–00* 🖷 *01–42–71–21–01* ⊕ *www.muranoresort.com* 📠 *43 rooms, 9 suites* ⚴ *Restaurant, room service, in-room data ports, in-room safes, minibars, cable TV, in-room VCRs, indoor pool, health club, spa, bar, Internet, business services, parking (fee), some pets allowed, no-smoking floors* 🝙 *AE, DC, MC, V* Ⓜ *Filles du Calvaire.*

★ **$$$$** 🏨 **Pavillon de la Reine.** The former hangout of the Marais elite—Madame de Sévigné, Racine, La Fontaine, and Molière—this gorgeous place des Vosges mansion dating from 1612 competes with Ritz-level luxury but on a more intimate scale. *Entrez* through a spectacular courtyard-driveway into a luscious lobby that recalls a royal hunting lodge: massive beams overhead, tapestries, and a salon with the original 300-year-old fireplace. You can reserve a room in the older section, decorated in classy Louis XIII style, or opt for the modern yet reserved wing redone in 2001. For an absolutely royal feeling, ask for a duplex overlooking two flower-filled courtyards behind the historic Queen's Pavilion. Wireless Internet access has recently been introduced, as has a ground-floor wing of classy scarlet-and-gray rooms. ⊠ *28 pl. des Vosges, Le Marais, 75003* ☎ *01–40–29–19–19, 800/447–7462 in the U.S.* 🖷 *01–40–29–19–20* ⊕ *www.pavillon-de-la-reine.com* 📠 *30 rooms, 26 suites* ⚴ *Room service, in-room safes, minibars, cable TV, bar, Internet, free parking, some pets allowed* 🝙 *AE, DC, MC, V* Ⓜ *Bastille, St-Paul.*

¢ 🏨 **Hôtel Bellevue et du Chariot d'Or.** Here you have an old Belle Époque time traveler, proud to keep its dingy chandeliers and faded gold trimming as is. Budget groups from France and the Netherlands come for the clean but sans-frills rooms; some rooms sleep four. Halls are lined with stamped felt that helps muffle sound trickling up from the spacious marble-floor lobby and bar. There may be some quirks, like the hefty old-fashioned room keys and the bathtub/showers without curtains, but you're just a few blocks from hipper addresses in the heart of the Marais. Get here before the fashionista crowd turns it into a shabby-chic hang-

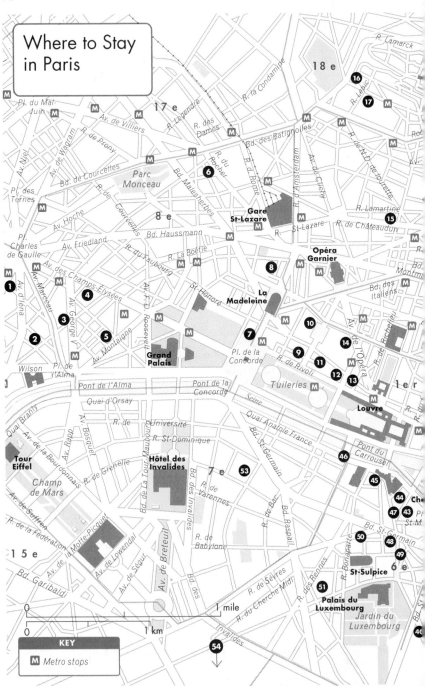

Where to Stay in Paris

18 e

17 e

Parc Monceau

8 e

Gare St-Lazare

Opéra Garnier

La Madeleine

Grand Palais

Pl. de la Concorde

Tuileries

Louvre

1 er

Tour Eiffel

Champ de Mars

Hôtel des Invalides

7 e

15 e

St-Sulpice

6 e

Palais du Luxembourg

Jardin du Luxembourg

KEY

Ⓜ Metro stops

0 _____ 1 mile

0 _____ 1 km

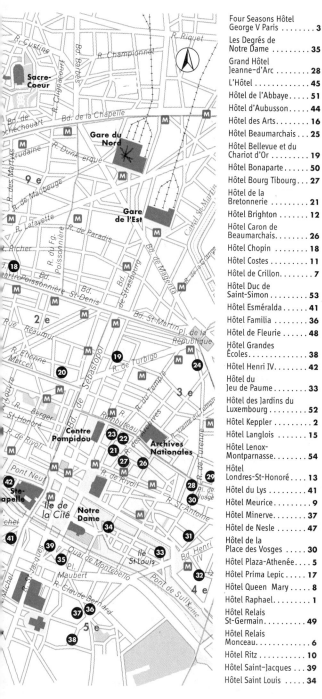

out. ✉ *39 rue de Turbigo, Beaubourg/Les Halles, 75003* ☎ *01-48-87-45-60* 🖷 *01-48-87-95-04* ⊕ *www.hotelbellevue75.com* ➟ *59 rooms* ⚐ *Cable TV, bar; no a/c* ▤ *AE, DC, MC, V* ⏧ *BP* Ⓜ *Réaumur-Sébastopol, Arts et Métiers.*

4° Arrondissement (Marais/Ile St-Louis)

$$$$ ⌨ **Hôtel du Jeu de Paume.** Set off the street by heavy doors and a small courtyard, the showpiece of this lovely 17th-century hotel on the Ile St-Louis is the stone-walled, vaulted lobby–cum–breakfast room. It stands on an erstwhile court where French aristocrats once played *jeu de paume,* an early version of tennis using the palms of their hands. The bright rooms are nicely done up in butter yellow or blue, with beamed ceilings and damask upholstery; however, the starker modern decor in the smaller rooms doesn't quite jibe with the style of the rest of the hotel. Superior rooms and suites open onto a sunny garden patio. ✉ *54 rue St-Louis-en-l'Ile, Ile-St-Louis, 75004* ☎ *01–43–26–14–18* 🖷 *01–40–46–02–76* ⊕ *www.jeudepaumehotel.com* ➟ *23 rooms, 5 suites* ⚐ *In-room safes, minibars, cable TV, exercise equipment, sauna, billiards, bar, Internet, some pets allowed; no a/c* ▤ *AE, DC, MC, V* Ⓜ *Pont Marie.*

★ $$$-$$$$ ⌨ **Hôtel Bourg Tibourg.** Scented candles and subdued lighting announce the designer-du-jour Jacques Garcia's theatrical mix of haremlike romance and Gothic contemplation. Royal blue paint and red velvet line the claustrophobic halls. The rooms are barely bigger than the beds, and every inch has been upholstered, tasseled, and draped in a cacophony of stripes, florals, and medieval motifs; Byzantine alcoves hold mosaic-tiled tubs. A stone staircase winds down to the cozy lounge where you can order drinks and plan your next tryst. A pocket-size garden has room for three tables, leafy plants, and a swath of stars above. ✉ *19 rue Bourg Tibourg, Le Marais, 75004* ☎ *01–42–78–47–39* 🖷 *01–40–29–07–00* ⊕ *www.hoteldubourgtibourg.com* ➟ *29 rooms, 1 suite* ⚐ *Dining room, in-room safes, minibars, cable TV, laundry service* ▤ *AE, DC, MC, V* Ⓜ *Hôtel de Ville.*

$$$ ⌨ **Hôtel Saint Merry.** Due south of the Pompidou Center is this small and
Fodor's Choice stunning Gothic hideaway, once the presbytery of the adjacent Saint Merry
★ church. In its 17th-century stone interior you can gaze through stained glass, relax on a church pew, or lean back on a headboard recycled from an old Catholic confessional. With a massive hardwood table, fireplace, and high ceiling, the suite is fit for a royal council. Room 9 is bisected by stone buttresses still supporting the church. he Saint Merry's lack of an elevator and 21st-century temptations like TV is also in keeping with its ascetic past (and keeps the place monkishly quiet). ✉ *78 rue de la Verrerie, Beaubourg/Les Halles, 75004* ☎ *01–42–78–14–15* 🖷 *01–40–29–06–82* ⊕ *www.hotelmarais.com* ➟ *11 rooms, 1 suite* ⚐ *In-room safes, some minibars, room service, laundry service, some pets allowed; no TV in some rooms, no a/c* ▤ *MC, V* Ⓜ *Châtelet.*

★ $$-$$$ ⌨ **Hôtel Caron de Beaumarchais.** The theme of this intimate hotel is the work of former next-door neighbor Pierre-Augustin Caron de Beaumarchais, supplier of military aid to American revolutionaries and author of *The Marriage of Figaro.* First-edition copies of his books adorn the public spaces, and the salons faithfully reflect the taste of 18th-century French nobility, right down to the wallpaper and 1792 pianoforte. Richly decorated with floral fabrics and white wooden period furnishings, the rooms have original wooden beams, hand-painted bathroom tiles, and gilded mirrors. Street-side rooms on the second through fifth floors are the largest, whereas smaller sixth-floor garrets under the mansard roof have beguiling views across Rive Droite rooftops. A future-forward touch: each room has a flat-screen TV. ✉ *12 rue Vieille-du-Temple, Le Marais, 75004* ☎ *01–42–72–34–12* 🖷 *01–42–72–34–63* ⊕ *www.carondebeaumarchais.com* ⤴ *19 rooms* ⌂ *In-room safes, minibars, cable TV, in-room data ports, Internet* ▭ *AE, DC, MC, V* Ⓜ *Hôtel de Ville.*

$$ 🏨 **Hôtel de la Bretonnerie.** This small hotel is in a 17th-century *hôtel particulier* (town house) on a tiny street in the Marais, a few minutes' walk from the Centre Pompidou and the bars and cafés of rue Vieille du Temple. Rooms are classified as either *chambres classiques* or *chambres de charme*, the latter being more spacious, and naturally pricier, but with more elaborate furnishings, like Louis XIII–style four-poster canopy beds and marble-clad bathtubs. Overall, the establishment is spotless, and the staff is welcoming. ✉ *22 rue Ste-Croix-de-la-Bretonnerie, Le Marais, 75004* ☎ *01–48–87–77–63* 🖷 *01–42–77–26–78* ⊕ *www.bretonnerie. com* ⤴ *22 rooms, 7 suites* ⌂ *In-room safes, minibars, cable TV, some in-room data ports, laundry service; no a/c* ▭ *MC, V* Ⓜ *Hôtel de Ville.*

$$ 🏨 **Hôtel de la Place des Vosges.** A loyal, eclectic clientele swears by this small, historic Marais hotel on a delightful street just off place des Vosges. The Louis XIII–style reception area and rooms with oak-beamed ceilings, rough-hewn stone, and a mix of rustic finds from secondhand shops evoke old Marais. ✉ *12 rue de Birague, Le Marais, 75004* ☎ *01–42–72–60–46* 🖷 *01–42–72–02–64* ⊕ *www.hotelplacedesvosges. com* ⤴ *16 rooms* ⌂ *Dining room, cable TV; no a/c* ▭ *AE, DC, MC, V* Ⓜ *Bastille.*

$$ 🏨 **Hôtel Saint Louis.** Louis XIII–style furniture, oil paintings, exposed beams, bare stone, and various antiques invite speculation about which duke may have owned this 17th-century building on the coveted Ile St-Louis. The older, unrenovated rooms seem worse for wear compared to the fresher ones, so it's best to request the newly remodeled rooms on the fourth and fifth floors. Minibalconies on the upper levels also have Seine views. ✉ *75 rue St-Louis-en-l'Ile, Ile St-Louis, 75004* ☎ *01–46–34–04–80* 🖷 *01–46–34–02–13* ⊕ *www.hotelsaintlouis.com* ⤴ *19 rooms* ⌂ *Dining room, in-room safes, cable TV, some pets allowed* ▭ *MC, V* Ⓜ *Pont Marie.*

$$ 🏨 **Hôtel Saint-Louis Marais.** Once an annex to a local convent, this 18th-century hôtel has retained its stone walls and beams while adding red-clay tile floors and antiques. A wooden-banistered stair leads to the small but proper rooms, decorated with basic red carpet and green bedspreads. (Those with heavy luggage, beware: no elevator.) The hotel's in Village St-Paul, a little tangle of medieval lanes just south of the well-traveled Marais that has an excellent English-language bookstore and is not yet overrun by tourists. ✉ *1 rue Charles V, Le Marais, 75004* ☎ *01–48–87–87–04* 🖷 *01–48–87–33–26* ⊕ *www.saintlouismarais.*

com ↻ *20 rooms* ⚭ *Dining room, in-room safes, cable TV, laundry service, Internet, some pets allowed; no a/c* ▤ *DC, MC, V* Ⓜ *Sully Morland, Bastille.*

$$ ▦ **Hôtel du Vieux Marais.** This pleasingly minimalist hotel with a turn-of-the-20th-century facade is on a quiet street in the heart of the Marais. Rooms are bright and impeccably clean, with contemporary oak furnishings, burgundy-leather seating, and velour curtains. Bathrooms are immaculately tiled in Italian marble, with walk-in showers or combination shower/bathtub. The staff is exceptionally friendly. ⊠ *8 rue du Plâtre, Le Marais, 75004* ☎ *01–42–78–47–22* 🖷 *01–42–78–34–32* ⊕ *www.vieuxmarais.com* ↻ *30 rooms* ⚭ *In-room safes, cable TV, Internet* ▤ *MC, V* Ⓜ *Hôtel de Ville.*

★ $ ▦ **Grand Hôtel Jeanne-d'Arc.** You'll get your money's worth at this hotel in an unbeatable location off the tranquil place du Marché Ste-Catherine, one of the city's lesser-known pedestrian squares. The 17th-century building has been a hotel for more than a century, and while rooms are on the spartan side they are well maintained, fairly spacious, and done in cheery Provençal colors (back rooms are dimmer). The welcoming staff is informal and happy to recount the history of this former market quartier. ⊠ *3 rue de Jarente, Le Marais, 75004* ☎ *01–48–87–62–11* 🖷 *01–48–87–37–31* ⊕ *www.hoteljeannedarc.com* ↻ *36 rooms* ⚭ *Cable TV, some pets allowed; no a/c* ▤ *MC, V* Ⓜ *St-Paul.*

5ᵉ Arrondissement (Latin Quarter)

★ $$–$$$ ▦ **Les Degrés de Notre Dame.** On a quiet street a few yards from the Seine, this cozy budget hotel is lovingly decorated with the owner's flea-market finds. The most expensive room, 501, occupies the entire top floor, with views of Notre Dame and room for four. There's no elevator, but colorful murals of Parisian scenes decorate the winding stairwell. The restaurant/bar, frequented by local Parisians, serves French and North-African specialties and has a large sidewalk terrace. ⊠ *10 rue des Grands Degrés, Quartier Latin, 75005* ☎ *01–55–24–88–88* 🖷 *01–40–46–95–34* ⊕ *www.lesdegreshotel.com* ↻ *10 rooms* ⚭ *Restaurant, in-room safes, bar; no a/c, no kids* ▤ *MC, V* ⵘ *BP* Ⓜ *Maubert-Mutualité.*

$$ ▦ **Hôtel Grandes Écoles.** Guests enter Madame Lefloch's country-style domain through two massive wooden doors. Distributed among a trio of three-story buildings, her baby-blue-and-white guest rooms and their flowery Louis-Philippe furnishings and lace bedspreads create a grandmotherly vibe, which may not be to everyone's taste. But the Grandes Écoles is legendary for its stunning interior cobbled courtyard and garden, which becomes the second living room and a perfect breakfast spot when *il fait beau.* Rooms 29 and 30 open directly onto the greenery and calm. ⊠ *75 rue du Cardinal Lemoine, Quartier Latin, 75005* ☎ *01–43–26–79–23* 🖷 *01–43–25–28–15* ⊕ *www.hotel-grandes-ecoles. com* ↻ *51 rooms* ⚭ *Room service, parking (fee), some pets allowed; no a/c, no room TVs* ▤ *MC, V* Ⓜ *Cardinal Lemoine.*

★ $$ ▦ **Hôtel des Jardins du Luxembourg.** Blessed with a personable staff and a smart, stylish look, this hotel, on an unbelievably calm cul-de-sac just a block from the Luxembourg Gardens, is an oasis for contemplation— even Freud stayed here for six weeks during the winter of 1885–86. A cheery hardwood-floored lobby with fireplace leads to smallish rooms furnished with wrought-iron beds, pastel bathroom tiles and contemporary Provençal fabrics. Ask for one with a balcony overlooking the street; the best room, No. 25, has dormer windows revealing a peekaboo view of the Eiffel Tower. It's also an easy commute to either airport or the Eurostar via the RER train that stops at the end of the street. ☒ *5 impasse Royer-Collard, Quartier Latin, 75005* ☎ *01–40–46–08–88* 🖷 *01–40–46–02–28* ⊕ *http://monsite.wanadoo.fr/jardinslux* ⮎ *26 rooms* ⚏ *In-room safes, minibars, sauna, Internet* ⊟ *AE, DC, MC, V* Ⓜ *RER: Luxembourg.*

★ **$$** ▦ **Hôtel Saint-Jacques.** Nearly every wall in this bargain hotel is bedecked with faux-marble and trompe-l'oeil murals. As in many old and independent Paris hotels, each room has unique features, furnishings, and layout. About half the rooms have tiny step-out balconies that give a glimpse of Notre-Dame and the Panthéon. Room 25 has a long round-the-corner balcony; also popular is the all-yellow room, No. 31, set right under the roof. ☒ *35 rue des Écoles, Quartier Latin, 75005* ☎ *01–44–07–45–45* 🖷 *01–43–25–65–50* ⊕ *www.hotel-saintjacques. com* ⮎ *35 rooms* ⚏ *Dining room, in-room safes, cable TV, Internet; no a/c* ⊟ *AE, DC, MC, V* Ⓜ *Maubert Mutualité.*

$–$$ ▦ **Hôtel Familia.** Owner Eric Gaucheron is proud of his hotel's nearly obsessive level of service and pace of renovations at this family-run show. The snug lobby has reproduction antique tapestries and hardwood furniture; rooms are snazzed up with murals of typical city scenes; and bathrooms have modern fixtures and tilework. Balconies give several rooms extra space; Nos. 61 and 62 have clear views to Notre-Dame. Cheaper rooms may strike you as too cramped for large suitcases, but each room has soundproofing and double-pane windows. ☒ *11 rue des Écoles, Quartier Latin, 75005* ☎ *01–43–54–55–27* 🖷 *01–43–29–61–77* ⊕ *www. hotel-paris-familia.com* ⮎ *30 rooms* ⚏ *Minibars, cable TV; no a/c* ⊟ *AE, MC, V* ¶Ⓞ¶ *BP* Ⓜ *Cardinal Lemoine.*

★ **$–$$** ▦ **Hôtel Minerve.** Fans of the Gaucheron family will be delighted to learn that the Minerve is now part of the Familia fold. Just next door to the Familia, and twice as big, the hotel has been completely refurbished in the inimitable Gaucheron style: flowers and breakfast tables on the balconies, frescoes in the spacious lobby, tapestries on the walls, and cherry-wood furniture in the rooms. It's less intimate than the Familia—but just as charming. ☒ *13 rue des Écoles, Quartier Latin, 75005* ☎ *01–43–26–26–04* 🖷 *01–44–07–01–96* ⊕ *www.hotel-paris-minerve. com* ⮎ *54 rooms* ⚏ *Internet; no a/c* ⊟ *AE, MC, V* ¶Ⓞ¶ *BP* Ⓜ *Cardinal Lemoine.*

$ ▦ **Hôtel Esméralda.** A Parisian flea market meets the Renaissance at this legendary shabby-chic hotel with superior views of Notre-Dame if you're lucky enough to get a front room. A vertiginous, ancient spiral staircase (no elevator) leads to a rabbit warren of low corridors, mismatched doors, and even funkier decor. Some rooms surprise with their marble fireplaces and chandeliers; others could be cleaner. The Esméralda's foyer may be its highlight: wood-beamed, strewn with art and tapestries, with classical music playing, it's right out of Flaubert's *Madame Bovary*. You'll decide whether it's "Paris charm" or "low-cost chaos." ☒ *4 rue*

St-Julien-le-Pauvre, Quartier Latin, 75005 ☎ *01–43–54–19–20*
🖷 *01–40–51–00–68* ⤶ *19 rooms, 4 without bath* ⚿ *Some pets allowed; no a/c, no room TVs* 🖃 *No credit cards* Ⓜ *St-Michel.*

6° Arrondissement (St-Germain)

$$$$
Fodor'sChoice
★

🖵 **L'Hôtel.** With its baroque mirrors, six-story circular atrium, gold-leaf
peacock murals, sinfully plush robes, and fax machines in the closets,
this super-fashionable hotel is a connoisseur's delight. Once an 18th-
century *pavillon d'amour* (inn for trysts), as a hotel it welcomed Oscar
Wilde, who in 1900 permanently checked out in Room 16, leaving behind a 2,600-franc bill ("Either this wallpaper goes or I do," were his
famous last words). Today, the hotel shines as never before thanks to
superstar decorator Jacques Garcia, who has outdone himself in the hyper-
chic restaurant—there are enough Second Empire sofas, oriental carpets,
Fortuny lamps, swagged screens, and gilded columns here to make even
Sarah Bernhardt feel at home. Upstairs, the guest rooms deliver 19th-
century pipe dreams, their sole downside being their snug size—but for
historic vibes, they can't be beat. Many of the rooms are essays in high-
style: one was Mistinguett's favorite and is a homage to Art Deco period, others are done in super-elegant Empire, and "Pondicherry" is a
dream of purple and gold hangings and Indo-Chinese furniture. Visit
the hotel's Web site to reserve your own showpiece. ⊠ *13 rue des
Beaux-Arts, St-Germain-des-Prés, 75006* ☎ *01–44–41–99–00*
🖷 *01–43–25–64–81* ⊕ *www.l-hotel.com* ⤶ *16 rooms, 4 suites* ⚿ *Restaurant, room service, in-room safes, minibars, cable TV, indoor pool,
steam room, piano bar, Internet, some pets allowed* 🖃 *AE, DC, MC,
V* Ⓜ *St-Germain-des-Prés.*

★ $$$$
🖵 **Hôtel d'Aubusson.** Dapper in their pin-stripe suits, the staff greets you
warmly at this 17th-century town house and former literary salon that
clings to its "country in the city" past. The showpiece is the stunning
salon spanned by massive beams and headed by a gigantic fireplace.
Decked out in rich burgundies, greens, or blues, the bedrooms are filled
with Louis XV- and Regency-style antiques; even the smallest rooms are
a good size by Paris standards. Behind the paved courtyard (where in
warmer weather you can have your breakfast or pre-dinner drink)
there's a second structure with three apartments handy for families. The
Café Laurent café/piano bar hosts jazz three time per week. ⊠ *33 rue
Dauphine, St-Germain-des-Prés, 75006* ☎ *01–43–29–43–43*
🖷 *01–43–29–12–62* ⊕ *www.hoteldaubusson.com* ⤶ *49 rooms* ⚿ *Room
service, in-room data ports, in-room safes, minibars, cable TV, some in-
room VCRs, piano bar, Internet, parking (fee), some pets allowed, no-
smoking floors* 🖃 *AE, DC, MC, V* Ⓜ *Odéon.*

★ $$$$
🖵 **Hôtel Relais St-Germain.** With a gracious staff and all the countrified
flowers, beams, and flea-market finds you could dream of, the Relais
St-Germain oozes with traditional 17th-century flavor. The rooms, done
in bright yellow and red printed fabrics and paints, are at least twice
the size of what you find at other hotels for the same price. Top-floor
rooms have balconies; some rooms have kitchenettes. Le Comptoir du
Relais, an adjacent café and former hangout of Hemingway, Picasso,
Joyce, and Matisse, is offered exclusively for hotel guests to breakfast
on coffee, croissants, and tartines. ⊠ *9 carrefour de l'Odéon, St-Ger-*

main-des-Prés, 75006 ☎*01–43–29–12–05* 📠*01–46–33–45–30* ⊕*www.hotelrsg.com* ↪ *21 rooms, 1 suite* ♿ *Room service, in-room safes, some kitchenettes, minibars, cable TV, bar, some pets allowed* 🚬 *AE, DC, MC, V* ⦿| *BP* Ⓜ *Odéon.*

★ **$$$$** 🏨 **Le Relais Christine.** This exquisite property was once a 13th-century abbey, but don't expect monkish quarters. You enter from the impressive stone courtyard into a lobby and fireside honor bar done up in rich fabrics, stone, wood paneling, and antiques. The cavernous breakfast room and adjacent fitness center flaunt their vaulted medieval stonework. The spacious, high-ceilinged rooms (many spanned by massive beams) offer a variety of classical and contemporary styles: Asian-themed wall fabrics or plain stripes, rich aubergine paints or regal scarlet-and-gold. Split-level lofts house up to five people, and several ground-level rooms open onto a lush garden with private patios and heaters. ✉ *3 rue Christine, St-Germain-des-Prés, 75006* ☎ *01–40–51–60–80, 800/525–4800 in the U.S.* 📠 *01–40–51–60–81* ⊕ *www.relais-christine.com* ↪ *33 rooms, 18 suites* ♿ *Room service, in-room safes, minibars, cable TV, some in-room VCRs, gym, hot tub, sauna, Internet, free parking, some pets allowed, no-smoking rooms* 🚬 *AE, DC, MC, V* Ⓜ *Odéon.*

$$$ 🏨 **Hôtel de l'Abbaye.** This hotel on a tranquil side street near St-Sulpice welcomes you with a cobblestone ante-courtyard and vaulted stone entrance. Paneled in bright wood, the rooms are spotless, if a little impersonal. The collision of modern and country design—fruit baskets and flat-screen TVs—may not be to everyone's taste, but it's all redeemed by the lobby's salons with vestiges of the original 18th-century convent and the spacious garden with fountain. Some first-floor rooms open onto it. Upper-floor accommodations have oak beams and sitting alcoves, and duplexes have lovely private terraces. The hotel has wireless Internet access. ✉ *10 rue Cassette, St-Germain-des-Prés, 75006* ☎ *01–45–44–38–11* 📠 *01–45–48–07–86* ⊕ *www.hotel-abbaye.com* ↪ *42 rooms, 4 suites* ♿ *In-room safes, cable TV, bar, Internet* 🚬 *AE, MC, V* ⦿| *BP* Ⓜ *St-Sulpice.*

$$$ 🏨 **Hôtel de Fleurie.** On a quiet side street near place de l'Odéon, a series of statues set into the facade invite you into this spiffy, super-pretty, family-run hotel. Antiques, Oriental rugs, and rich upholsteries fill the 18th-century building. The warm-colored rooms, mostly done in yellows with wood paneling and checked drapes, include amenities such as heated towel racks in the bathroom. Ask the helpful staff about freebies like museum passes that reward long stays. The location is ideal: equidistant from the Seine and Jardin du Luxembourg. ✉ *32–34 rue Grégoire-de-Tours, St-Germain-des-Prés, 75006* ☎ *01–53–73–70–00* 📠 *01–53–73–70–20* ⊕ *www.hotel-de-fleurie.tm.fr* ↪ *29 rooms* ♿ *Minibars, cable TV, in-room data ports, bar, Internet* 🚬 *AE, DC, MC, V* Ⓜ *Odéon.*

$$ 🏨 **Hôtel Bonaparte.** The congeniality of the staff only makes a stay in this intimate place more of a treat. Old-fashioned upholsteries, 19th-century furnishings, and paintings make the relatively spacious rooms feel comfortable and unpretentious. Rooms have empty refrigerators; you're invited to stock them with drinks and snacks. Services may be basic, but the location in the heart of St-Germain about 30 steps from place St-Sulpice is nothing short of fabulous. Light sleepers should request rooms overlooking the courtyard. ⊠ *61 rue Bonaparte, St-Germain-des-Prés, 75006* ☎ *01–43–26–97–37* 🖷 *01–46–33–57–67* 🗗 *29 rooms* ⌂ *In-room safes, refrigerators; no a/c in some rooms* ▭ *MC, V* 🍽️ *BP* Ⓜ *St-Germain-des-Prés.*

★ **$$** 🏨 **Hôtel du Lys.** To jump into an inexpensive Parisian fantasy, just climb the convoluted stairway to your room (there's no elevator) in this former 17th-century royal residence. Well-maintained by Madame Steffen, the oddly-shaped guest rooms have tiny nooks, weathered antiques, and exposed beams throughout. Breakfast is served in the lobby or in guest rooms. It may be modest, but it's extremely atmospheric. ⊠ *23 rue Serpente, Quartier Latin, 75006* ☎ *01–43–26–97–57* 🖷 *01–44–07–34–90* ⊕ *www.hoteldulys.com* 🗗 *22 rooms* ⌂ *In-room safes, cable TV, some pets allowed; no a/c* ▭ *MC, V* 🍽️ *BP* Ⓜ *St-Michel, Odéon.*

★ **$** 🏨 **Hôtel de Nesle.** This one-of-a-kind budget hotel is like a quirky and enchanting dollhouse. The services are bare-bones—no elevator, phones, or breakfast—but the payoff is in the petite rooms cleverly decorated by theme. Sleep in Notre-Dame de Paris, lounge in an Asian-style boudoir, spend the night with writer Molière, or steam it up in Le Hammam. Decorations include colorful murals, canopy beds, custom lamps, and clay tiles. Most rooms overlook an interior garden, and the dead-end street location keeps the hotel relatively quiet. If you book one of the rooms without a shower, you'll have to share the one on the second floor. ⊠ *7 rue de Nesle, St-Germain-des-Prés, 75006* ☎ *01–43–54–62–41* 🖷 *01–43–54–31–88* ⊕ *www.hoteldenesleparis.com* 🗗 *20 rooms, 9 with bath* ⌂ *Some pets allowed, no-smoking floors; no a/c, no room phones, no room TVs* ▭ *MC, V* Ⓜ *Odéon.*

7ᵉ Arrondissement (Tour Eiffel/Invalides)

★ **$$$$** 🏨 **Hôtel Duc de Saint-Simon.** If it's good enough for the notoriously choosy Lauren Bacall, you'll probably fall for the Duc's charms, too. Its hidden location between boulevard St-Germain and rue de Bac is one plus; another is the shady courtyard entry. Rooms in shades of yellow, green, pink, and blue teem with antiques and countrified floral and striped fabrics. Four rooms have spacious terraces overlooking the courtyard and the drooping wisteria. The 16th-century basement lounge is a warren of stone alcoves with a zinc bar and plush seating. To keep the peace, parents are discouraged from bringing children along. ⊠ *14 rue St-Simon, St-Germain-des-Prés, 75007* ☎ *01–44–39–20–20* 🖷 *01–45–48–68–25* ⊕ *www.hotelducdesaintsimon.com* 🗗 *29 rooms, 5 suites* ⌂ *In-room safes, cable TV, bar, parking (fee); no a/c in some rooms, no kids* ▭ *AE, DC, MC, V* Ⓜ *Rue du Bac.*

$$$ 🏨 **Hôtel Verneuil.** The Verneuil's location on a narrow street near the Seine is unbeatable. The rooms may be more petite than you'd hoped for, but each is painstakingly decorated. The white-cotton quilts on the beds, framed pressed flowers on the walls, and faux-marble trompe-l'oeil trim work and stained-glass windows in the hall make you feel you've arrived *chez grandmère.* Fans of Serge Gainsbourg can pilgrimage to his former home directly across the street. ⊠ *8 rue de Verneuil, St-Germain-des-Prés, 75007* ☎ *01–42–60–83–14* 🖷 *01–42–61–40–38* ⊕ *www. hotelverneuil.com* 🗗 *26 rooms* ⌂ *In-room safes, minibars, cable TV,* *bar, Internet, some pets allowed (fee); no a/c in some rooms* Ⓜ *RER: Musée d'Orsay.*

8ᵉ Arrondissement (Champs-Élysées)

★ $$$$ 🏨 **Four Seasons Hôtel George V Paris.** General Eisenhower's headquarters during the liberation of Paris is now owned by a Saudi prince and managed by the Four Seasons group—with a lineage like this, it is little wonder this place has many aficionados. The original Art Deco details and 17th-century tapestries have been restored, the bas-reliefs regilt, and the marble mosaic floors reconstructed stone by stone. Rooms are decked in yards of fabric and Louis XV trimmings; even the cheapest have crystal chandeliers, marble bathrooms, and soaking tubs. The Michelin three-star Le Cinq restaurant is one of Paris's most luxurious tables. The low-lit spa pampers guests with 11 treatment rooms, walls covered in toile de Jouy fabrics, and an indoor swimming pool surrounded by trompe l'oeil scenes from Marie-Antoinette's Versailles gardens. A relaxation room is available for guests who arrive before their rooms are ready. ⊠ *31 av. George-V, Champs-Élysées, 75008* ☎ *01–49–52–70–00* 🖷 *01–49–52–70–10* ⊕ *www.fourseasons.com* ➴ *184 rooms, 61 suites* ⌣ *2 restaurants, in-room safes, minibars, cable TV, in-room data ports, indoor pool, health club, hair salon, bar, shop, babysitting, children's programs (ages 6–12), business services, some pets allowed, no-smoking floors* ⊟ *AE, DC, MC, V* Ⓜ *George-V.*

$$$$ 🏨 **Hôtel de Crillon.** Home away from home for movie stars and off-duty celebrities, the Crillon has long been one of Paris's greatest hotels. It began life as a regal palace designed for Louis XV in 1758 by Jacques-Ange Gabriel to preside over the north side of the fabled place de la Concorde. In 1909 it became a hostelry and since then has played host to generations of diplomats and refined travelers. Most rooms are lavishly decorated with Rococo and Directoire antiques, crystal-and-gilt wall sconces, and gilt fittings. The sheer quantity of marble downstairs—especially in the highly praised Les Ambassadeurs restaurant—is staggering. ⊠ *10 pl. de la Concorde, Champs-Élysées, 75008* ☎ *01–44–71–15–00, 800/ 888–4747 in U.S.* 🖷 *01–44–71–15–02* ⊕ *www.crillon.com* ➴ *90 rooms, 57 suites* ⌣ *2 restaurants, room service, in-room safes, minibars, cable TV with movies, in-room data ports, gym, spa, 2 bars, babysitting, children's programs (ages 6–12), Internet, business services, no-smoking rooms* ⊟ *AE, DC, MC, V* Ⓜ *Concorde.*

$$$$ 🏨 **Hôtel Plaza-Athenée.** Once the favored Paris address for Grace Kelly and Jackie Kennedy, this 1911 palace hotel has reclaimed the luxury mantle from its peers in the past few years. The renaissance is partly due to the Le Relais Plaza restaurant's *années 30* restoration and Alain Ducasse's flagship Restaurant Plaza Athenée. May to September, all guests repair to the gorgeously red-parasoled La Cour Jardin since this courtyard restaurant has long been one of the prettiest sights in Paris. Most guest rooms have Regènce and Louis Seize–style accent pieces, while the top two floors go Art Deco. Interact with the unflagging energy of the 460 staff members and you'll see why the Athenée continues to be the choice of the Jagger-Paltrow set. ⊠ *25 av. Montaigne, Champs-Élysées, 75008* ☎ *01–53–67–66–65, 866/732–1106 in U.S.* 🖷 *01–53–67–66–66*

⊕ *www.plaza-athenee-paris.com* 🔖 *145 rooms, 43 suites △ 3 restaurants, room service, in-room safes, minibars, cable TV, health club, bar, babysitting, business services, some pets allowed, no-smoking rooms* ⊟ *AE, DC, MC, V* Ⓜ *Alma-Marceau.*

$$$$ 🏨 **Pershing Hall.** Formerly an American Legion hall, this circa-2001 boutique hotel designed by Andrée Putman champions masculine minimalism, with muted surfaces of wood and stone and even cooler attitudes to match. Rooms have stark-white linens, triptych dressing mirrors, slender tubelike lamps and tubs perched on round marble bases. The only trace of lightheartedness is the free minibars. All deluxe rooms and suites face the courtyard dining room whose west wall is a six-story hanging garden with 300 varieties of plants. The lounge bar serves drinks, dinner, and DJ-driven music until 2 AM. ✉ *49 rue Pierre Charron, Champs-Élysées, 75008* ☏ *01–58–36–58–00* 🖷 *01–58–36–58–01* ⊕ *www.pershinghall.com* 🔖 *20 rooms, 6 suites △ Restaurant, room service, in-room safes, minibars, cable TV, in-room VCRs, in-room data ports, health club, bar, babysitting, some pets allowed* ⊟ *AE, DC, MC, V* Ⓜ *George-V, Franklin-D.-Roosevelt.*

$$$ 🏨 **Hôtel Queen Mary.** A warm welcome (and a gentle price-tag) awaits you at this cheerfully elegant hotel, set just two blocks from the Place de la Madeleine and Paris's famous department stores. Sunny yellow walls, fabrics in burgundy, gold, and royal blue, and plush carpeting throughout soften the historic architectural detailing and high ceilings. Rooms are nicely appointed with large beds, and thoughtful extras like trouser presses, Roger & Gallet toiletries, and complimentary decanters of sherry. Guests mingle in the bar during happy hour, and breakfast can be served in the enchantingly trellised garden courtyard in summer. ✉ *9 rue Greffulhe, Opéra/Grands Boulevards, 75008* ☏ *01–42–66–40–50* 🖷 *01–42–66–94–92* ⊕ *www.hotelqueenmary. com* 🔖 *35 rooms, 1 suite △ Room service, in-room data ports, in-room safes, minibars, cable TV with movies, bar, Internet, some pets allowed* ⊟ *MC, V* Ⓜ *Madeleine.*

FodorśChoice
★

$$$ 🏨 **Hôtel Relais Monceau.** Within six blocks of the prim Parc Monceau, one of Paris's most soigné parks, this friendly and fashionable hotel is an oasis of refined tranquillity. Ivy-covered trellises surround the lovely breakfast garden. Warm tones make rooms cozy; the efficient and professional staff makes your stay easy. In 2004 the hotel refitted guest rooms and added wireless Internet, air-conditioning and conference facilities. ✉ *85 rue du Rocher, Parc Monceau, 75008* ☏ *01–45–22–75–11* 🖷 *01–45–22–30–88* ⊕ *www.relais-monceau.com* 🔖 *50 rooms, 1 suite △ In-room safes, minibars, cable TV, in-room data ports, bar, no-smoking rooms* ⊟ *AE, DC, MC, V* Ⓜ *Villiers.*

9ᵉ Arrondissement (Opéra)

$–$$ 🏨 **Hôtel Langlois.** After starring in *The Truth About Charlie* (a remake of *Charade*), this darling hotel gained a reputation as one of the most atmospheric budget sleeps in the city. Rates have creeped up, but the former circa-1870 bank retains its beautiful wood-paneled reception area and wrought-iron elevator. The individually decorated and spacious rooms are decked out with original glazed-tile fireplaces and period art. Rooms on the lower floors have the largest bathrooms, but those on the fifth

FodorśChoice
★

and sixth have wonderful views of Paris rooftops. Nos. 63 and 64 look out on Sacré-Coeur. ⊠ *63 rue St-Lazare, Opéra/Grands Boulevards, 75009* ☎ *01-48-74-78-24* 🖶 *01-49-95-04-43* ⊕ *www.hotel-langlois. com* ⇋ *24 rooms, 3 suites* ☼ *Minibars, cable TV, Internet, some pets allowed; no a/c* ⊟ *AE, MC, V* Ⓜ *Trinité.*

¢–$ 🖼 **Hôtel Chopin.** At the end of the passage Jouffroy—one of the many glass-roof shopping arcades built in Paris in the early 19th century—the Chopin recalls its 1846 birth date with a creaky-floored lobby and aged woodwork. The basic but comfortable rooms overlook the arcade's quaint boutiques or the rooftops of Paris. The decor leans heavily toward salmon walls and green carpets, but rooms on the first and second floors have blue toile de Jouy prints. The best rooms end in 7 (no. 407 overlooks the Grevin waxwork museum's ateliers), while the cheapest are the smaller rooms ending with a 2. ⊠ *10 bd. Montmartre (46 passage Jouffroy), Opéra/Grands Boulevards, 75009* ☎ *01-47-70-58-10* 🖶 *01-42-47-00-70* ⇋ *36 rooms* ☼ *Dining room, in-room safes, cable TV; no a/c* ⊟ *AE, MC, V* Ⓜ *Grands Boulevards.*

11er Arrondissement (Bastille)

$$ 🖼 **Hôtel Beaumarchais.** This bold hotel serves as a gateway to the hip student and artist neighborhood of Oberkampf and the 11er and 20^e arrondissements. Brightly colored vinyl armchairs, an industrial metal staircase, and glass tables mark the lobby. Out back a small courtyard is decked in hardwood, a look you'll rarely see in Paris. The rooms hum with primary reds and yellows, some with Keith Haring prints on the walls. Kaleidoscopes of ceramic fragments tile the bathrooms. The Beaumarchais lures in artsy budget travelers; for the price and attention to detail, the popularity is justified. ⊠ *3 rue Oberkampf, République, 75011* ☎ *01-53-36-86-86* 🖶 *01-43-38-32-86* ⊕ *www.hotelbeaumarchais. com* ⇋ *31 rooms* ☼ *Dining room, in-room safes, cable TV, some pets allowed; no a/c in some rooms* ⊟ *AE, MC, V* Ⓜ *Filles du Calvaire, Oberkampf.*

12e Arrondissement (Bastille/Gare de Lyon)

$$ 🖼 **Le Pavillon Bastille.** The transformation of this 19th-century hôtel particulier (across from the Opéra Bastille) into a mod, colorful, high-design hotel garnered both architectural awards and a fiercely loyal, hip clientele. Some clients take to the hotel's blue-and-gold color scheme, but others find it brash. ⊠ *65 rue de Lyon, Bastille/Nation, 75012* ☎ *01-43-43-65-65, 800/233-2552 in U.S.* 🖶 *01-43-43-96-52* ⇋ *24 rooms, 1 suite* ☼ *In-room safes, minibars, cable TV, in-room data ports, bar, Internet, some pets allowed, no-smoking floors* ⊟ *AE, DC, MC, V* Ⓜ *Bastille.*

14^e Arrondissement (Montparnasse)

$$ 🖼 **Hôtel Lenox-Montparnasse.** Few budget hotels this close to the famous Dôme and Coupole brasseries and the Jardin du Luxembourg offer this level of service and amenities for the price. A smooth head-to-toe face-lift gave the largest (and best) rooms tile fireplaces, white-painted exposed beams, and violet or beige color schemes. The small standard rooms—there's barely a suitcase-width between the wall and the foot of the bed—follow a more functional contemporary style, with rich col-

ors and print bedspreads. ✉ *15 rue Delambre, Montparnasse, 75014* ☎ *01–43–35–34–50* 🖷 *01–43–20–46–64* ⊕ *www.hotellenox.com* ➦ *46 rooms, 6 suites* ♦ *Room service, in-room safes, minibars, cable TV, in-room data ports, Internet, parking (fee), no-smoking rooms* ▭ *AE, DC, MC, V* Ⓜ *Vavin.*

16ᵉ Arrondissement (Arc de Triomphe/Le Bois)

★ **$$$$** 🖾 **Hôtel Raphael.** The landmark and soigné Raphael was built in 1925 to cater to travelers spending a season in Paris, so every space is generously sized for such long, lavish stays—the closets, for instance, have room for ball gowns and plumed hats. You'll feel *très* V.I.P entering the sumptuous oak-wood-and-chandeliered lobby. Guest rooms, most with king-size beds, are turned out in 18th- and early-19th-century antiques and have 6-foot windows, Oriental rugs, silk damask wallpaper, chandeliers, and ornately carved wood paneling. Bathrooms are remarkably large; most have claw-foot bathtubs and separate massage-jet showers. The roof terrace, topped with a summer restaurant, has a panoramic view of the city, with the Arc de Triomphe looming in the foreground. ✉ *17 av. Kléber, Trocadéro/Tour Eiffel, 75116* ☎ *01–53–64–32–00* 🖷 *01–53–64–32–01* ⊕ *www.raphael-hotel.com* ➦ *52 rooms, 38 suites* ♦ *2 restaurants, room service, in-room safes, some in-room hot tubs, minibars, cable TV, some in-room VCRs, in-room data ports, gym, sauna, bar, babysitting, Internet, meeting rooms, some pets allowed (fee), no-smoking floors* ▭ *AE, DC, MC, V* Ⓜ *Kléber.*

$$ 🖾 **Hôtel Keppler.** On the border of the 8ᵉ and 16ᵉ arrondissements, near the Champs-Élysées, is this small modern hotel in a 19th-century building. The prices are a bargain for this chic neighborhood. The spacious, airy rooms have simple furnishings and floral upholstery; upper-floor rooms face the Tour Eiffel. A big lounge and dining room provide plenty of hangout space. ✉ *12 rue Keppler, Champs-Élysées, 75016* ☎ *01–47–20–65–05* 🖷 *01–47–23–02–29* ⊕ *www.hotelkeppler.com* ➦ *49 rooms* ♦ *Dining room, in-room safes, cable TV, bar; no a/c* ▭ *AE, MC, V* Ⓜ *George V.*

18ᵉ Arrondissement (Montmartre)

$$ 🖾 **Hôtel Prima Lepic.** An impressive value, the Prima Lepic stands out among dozens of mediocre hotels in this perennial tourist zone. Elements from the original 19th-century building remain, such as vintage tiling in the entry and heavy-duty white iron furniture in the breakfast area. The bright rooms are full of spring colors and florals; the so-called Baldaquin rooms have reproduction canopy beds. Modern conveniences include wireless Internet access, in-room teapots and bathrobes, and some flat-screen TVs. Larger rooms are suitable for families but have very little natural light. Shop for your picnic on the thriving market street rue Lepic. ✉ *29 rue Lepic, Montmartre, 75018* ☎ *01–46–06–44–64* 🖷 *01–46–06–66–11* ⊕ *www.hotel-paris-lepic.com* ➦ *38 rooms* ♦ *In-room data ports, in-room safes, cable TV, babysitting; no a/c* ▭ *AE, DC, MC, V* Ⓜ *Blanche.*

$ 🖾 **Hôtel des Arts.** The location in the heart of Montmartre's winding streets would be reason enough to stay at this budget-priced hotel, but the scattering of antiques in the lounge, book cases in the lobby, and vintage cabaret scenes painted onto each elevator door give it a welcoming feel usually lacking in this price range. Rooms have red or green carpeting, modern wooden furnishings, and floral or plaid linens. No. 42 is a larger double with a balcony overlooking Paris, but the best views are from the 6th floor (these cost an additional €20). ⊠ *5 rue Tholozé, Montmartre, 75018* ☎ *01–46–06–30–52* 🖷 *01–46–06–10–83* ⊕ *www.arts-hotel-paris.com* 🛏 *50 rooms ♦ Dining room, room service, in-room safes, cable TV, Internet; no a/c* ☰ *AE, DC, MC, V* Ⓜ *Abbesses.*

NIGHTLIFE & THE ARTS

Updated by
Heather
Stimmler-Hall

With a heritage that includes the cancan, the Folies-Bergère, the Moulin Rouge, Mistinguett, and Josephine Baker, Paris is one city where no one has ever had to ask, "Is there any place exciting to go to tonight?" Today the city's nightlife and arts scenes are still filled with pleasures. Hear a chansonnier belt out Piaf, take in a *Victor/Victoria* show, catch a Molière play at the Comédie Française, or perhaps spot the latest supermodel at Johnny Depp's Man Ray. Detailed entertainment listings can be found in the weekly magazines **Pariscope, L'Officiel des Spectacles,** and **Zurban.** Also look for **Aden** and **Figaroscope,** Wednesday supplements to the newspapers *Le Monde* and *Le Figaro* respectively. The 24-hour hot line and the Web site of the **Paris Tourist Office** (☎ 08–92–68–30–00 in English [€0.34/min] ⊕ www.parisinfo.com) are other good sources of information about activities in the city.

The best place to buy tickets is at the venue itself; try to purchase in advance, as many of the more popular performances sell out. Also try your hotel or a ticket agency, such as **Opéra Théâtre** (⊠ 7 rue de Clichy, Montmartre, 9ᵉ ☎ 01–42–81–98–85 Ⓜ Trinité). Tickets for most concerts can be bought at **FNAC** (⊠ 1–5 rue Pierre Lescot, Forum des Halles, 3rd level down, Beaubourg/Les Halles, 1ᵉʳ ☎ 08–92–68–36–22 Ⓜ Châtelet–Les Halles). The **Virgin Megastore** (⊠ 52 av. des Champs-Élysées, Champs-Élysées, 8ᵉ ☎ 01–49–53–50–00 Ⓜ Franklin-D.-Roosevelt) also sells theater and concert tickets. Half-price tickets for many same-day theater performances are available at the **Kiosques Théâtre** (⊠ Across from 15 pl. de la Madeleine, Opéra/Grands Boulevards Ⓜ Madeleine ⊠ Outside Gare Montparnasse on pl. Raoul Dautry, Montparnasse, 15ᵉ Ⓜ Montparnasse-Bienvenüe); open Tuesday–Saturday 12:30 PM–8 PM and Sunday 12:30 PM–4 PM. Expect to pay a €3 commission per ticket and to wait in line.

The Arts

Classical Music

Classical- and world-music concerts are held at the **Cité de la Musique** (⊠ 221 av. Jean-Jaurès, Parc de la Villette, 19ᵉ ☎ 01–44–84–44–84 Ⓜ Porte de Pantin). The **Salle Pleyel** (⊠ 252 rue du Faubourg–St-Honoré, Champs-Élysées, 8ᵉ ☎ 08–25–00–02–52 ⊕ www.pleyel.com Ⓜ Ternes), a longtime regular venue for the Orchestre de Paris, is undergoing renovations and will be closed until early 2006. The **Théâtre des Champs-Élysées** (⊠ 15 av. Montaigne, Champs-Élysées, 8ᵉ

☎01–49–52–50–50 ⊕ www.theatrechampselysees.fr Ⓜ Alma-Marceau), an Art Deco temple and famed site of the premiere of Stravinsky's 1913 *Le Sacre du Printemps,* hosts concerts and ballet. **Churches** with classical concerts (often free) often hold concerts. For musical events at **Notre-Dame** (✉ Pl. du Parvis Notre-Dame, Ile de la Cité, 4ᵉ Ⓜ Cité) tickets are through **Musique Sacrée à Notre-Dame** (☎ 01–44–41–49–99). **Sainte-Chapelle** (✉ 4 bd. du Palais, Ile de la Cité, 1ᵉʳ ☎ 01–42–77–65–65 Ⓜ Cité), a Gothic tour-de-force of shimmering stained glass, holds memorable candlelighted concerts March through November; make reservations well in advance.

Dance

The biggest news on the French dance scene is the spanking new **Centre National de la Danse** (✉ 1 rue Victor Hugo, Pantin ☎ 01–41–83–27–27 ⊕ www.cnd.fr Ⓜ Hoche or RER: Pantin), which opened in 2004 in a former jailhouse on the canal of the Pantin suburb of Paris. Dedicated to teaching dance, it also has a regular program of performances open to the public. The super-spectacular 19th-century **Opéra Garnier** (✉ Pl. de l'Opéra, Opéra/Grands Boulevards, 9ᵉ ☎ 08–92–89–90–90 ⊕ www.opera-de-paris.fr Ⓜ Opéra) is home to the reputable Ballet de l'Opéra National de Paris and hosts other troupes like Merce Cunningham. Seat prices range €6–€57; note that many of the cheaper seats have obstructed views. The **Opéra de la Bastille** (✉ Pl. de la Bastille, Bastille/Nation, 12ᵉ ☎ 08–92–69–78–68 ⊕ www.opera-de-paris.fr Ⓜ Bastille) occasionally hosts major dance troupes, often modern and avant-garde in tenor. The **Théâtre de la Bastille** (✉ 76 rue de la Roquette, Bastille/Nation, 11ᵉʳ ☎ 01–43–57–42–14 Ⓜ Bastille) is where innovative modern-dance companies perform. At its two houses, the **Théâtre de la Ville** (✉ 2 pl. du Châtelet, Beaubourg/Les Halles, 4ᵉ ☎ 01–42–74–22–77 for both Ⓜ Châtelet ✉ 31 rue des Abbesses, Montmartre, 18ᵉ Ⓜ Abbesses) presents the leading stars of contemporary dance.

Film

Parisians are far more addicted to the cinema as an art form than even Londoners or New Yorkers, as evidenced by the number of movie theaters in the city. Many theaters, especially in principal tourist areas such as the Champs-Élysées, St-Germain-des-Prés, Les Halles, and the boulevard des Italiens near the Opéra, show first-run films in English. Check the weekly guides for a movie of your choice. Look for the initials *v.o.,* which mean *version originale,* that is, not dubbed. Cinema admission runs from €6 to €10; many theaters reduce rates slightly on Monday and for some morning shows. Most theaters will post two showtimes: the first is the *séance,* when commercials, previews, and sometimes short films start, and the second is the actual feature presentation time, which is usually 10–20 minutes later. Paris has many small cinemas showing classic and independent films, especially in the Latin Quarter. Screenings are often organized around retrospectives (check "Festivals" in weekly guides). For the *cinéphile* (movie lover) brought up on Fellini, Bergman, and Resnais, the main mecca is the famed **Cinémathèque Française** (✉ 51 rue de Bercy, Bercy, 12ᵉ ☎ 01–56–26–01–01 Ⓜ Bercy), which pioneered the preservation of early films. Its new home, designed by Frank

Gehry, is set to open in fall 2005 and will include a museum and video library, as well as four theaters. The **Balzac** (⊠ 1 rue Balzac, Champs-Élysées, 8ᵉ ☏ 01–45–61–10–60 Ⓜ George-V) frequently hosts talks by ★ directors before screenings. **La Pagode** (⊠ 57 bis rue de Babylone, Trocadéro/Tour Eiffel, 7ᵉ ☏ 08–92–89–28–92 Ⓜ St-François Xavier)—where else but in Paris would you find movies screened in an antique pagoda? A Far East fantasy, this structure was built in 1896 for the wife of the owner of the Le Bon Marché department store. Who can resist seeing a flick in the silk-and-gilt Salle Japonaise? Come early to have tea in the bamboo-fringed garden.

Opera

Paris offers some of the best opera in the world—and thousands know it. Consequently, getting tickets to a performance of the **Opéra National de Paris** at its two main venues, the Opéra de la Bastille and the Opéra Garnier, can be difficult on short notice, so it's a good idea to plan ahead. There's even been renewed interest since the 2004–2005 season under the new direction of Gérard Mortier, famous for his turnaround of the Salzburg Festival. Review a list of performances by checking the Web site www.opera-de-paris.com, getting a copy of the Paris Tourist Office's *Saison de Paris* booklet, or by writing to the **Opéra de la Bastille** (⊠ 120 rue de Lyon Bastille/Nation, 75576 Cedex 12 Paris) well in advance. Make your selection and send back the booking form, giving several choices of nights and performances. If the response is affirmative, just pick up and pay for your tickets before the performance (you can also pay for them by credit card in advance). For performances at either the Opéra de la Bastille or the Palais Garnier (for complete info on this theater, *see* Dance, *above*), seats go on sale at the box office two weeks before any given show or a month ahead by phone or online; you must go in person to buy the cheapest tickets. Last-minute discount tickets, if available, are offered 15 minutes before a performance for seniors and anyone under 28. The box office is open 11 to 6:30 PM daily. Prices for tickets start at €5 for standing places (at the Opéra Bastille, only) to €160. The **Opéra de la Bastille** (⊠ Pl. de la Bastille, Bastille/Nation, 12ᵉ ☏ 08–92–89–90–90 ⊕ www.opera-de-paris.fr Ⓜ Bastille), a modern auditorium, has taken over the role of Paris's main opera house from the Opéra Garnier. However, nothing beats seeing a grand production of a Verdi or Mozart opera within the 19th-century splendor of the Opéra Garnier, and the good news is that this historic house still hosts a limited number of Opéra National de Paris productions every season (information on these productions is contained within the Opera de Paris Web site listed above). Note that if a certain opera is presented, it's only mounted for a minirun of one to two weeks, not in a repertory schedule throughout the season. Cheaper seats in the Garnier house are sometimes—and notoriously—view-obstructed (partial-view in French is *visibilité partielle*). The opera season usually runs September through July. The **Opéra Comique** (⊠ 5 rue Favart, Opéra/Grands Boulevards, 2ᵉ ☏ 08–25–00–00–58 ⊕ www.opera-comique.com Ⓜ Richelieu-Drouot) is a lofty old hall where comic operas are often performed. **Théâtre Musical de Paris** (⊠ Pl. du Châtelet, Beaubourg/Les Halles, 1ᵉʳ ☏ 01–40–28–28–40 ⊕ www.chatelet-theatre.com Ⓜ Châtelet), better known as the Théâtre du Châtelet, puts on some of the finest opera productions in the city and regularly attracts international divas like Cecilia Bartoli and Anne-Sofie von Otter. It also plays host to classical concerts, dance performances, and the occasional play.

Theater

A number of theaters line the Grands Boulevards between Opéra and République, but there's no Paris equivalent of Broadway or the West End. Shows are mostly in French. Information about performances can be obtained on a Web site ⊕ www.theatreonline.fr, which lists 170 different theaters, offers critiques, and provides an online reservation service. **Bouffes du Nord** (⊠ 37 bis bd. de la Chapelle, Stalingrad/La Chapelle, 10ᵉ ☎ 01–46–07–34–50 Ⓜ La Chapelle) is the wonderfully atmospheric theater that is home to English director Peter Brook. The **Comédie-Française** (⊠ Pl. Colette, Louvre/Tuileries, 1ᵉʳ ☎ 01–44–58–15–15 ⊕ www.comedie-francaise.fr Ⓜ Palais-Royal) is a distinguished venue that stages classical French drama in the very regal surrounds of the 18th-century Palais-Royal. The legendary 19th-century **Odeon Théâtre de l'Europe** (⊠ ⊠ Pl. de l'Odéon, St-Germain-des-Prés, 6ᵉ ☎ 01–44–41–36–36 Ⓜ Odéon), once home to the Comédie Française, has today made pan-European theater its primary focus. A major renovation was scheduled to end in fall 2005. **Théâtre National de Chaillot** (⊠ 1 pl. du Trocadéro, Trocadéro/Eiffel Tower, 16ᵉ ☎ 01–53–65–30–00 Ⓜ Trocadéro) has two theaters dedicated to drama and dance. Since 2003, it has hosted the groundbreaking duo of Deborah Warner (director) and Fiona Shaw (actress) for several excellent English-language productions. **Théâtre du Palais-Royal** (⊠ 38 rue Montpensier, Louvre/Tuileries, 1ᵉʳ ☎ 01–42–97–59–81 Ⓜ Palais-Royal) is a sparkling 750-seat Italian theater bedecked in gold and purple. For children, one "theatrical" experience can be a delight—the **Marionnettes du Jardin du Luxembourg** (⊠ St-Germain-des-Prés ☎ 01–43–26–46–47 Ⓜ Vavin) stages the most traditional performances, including *Pinocchio* and *The Three Little Pigs*.

Nightlife

The City of Light truly lights up after dark. So, if you want to paint the town *rouge* after dutifully pounding the parquet in museums all day, there's a dazzling array of options to discover. The hottest spots are around Ménilmontant, the Bastille, and the Marais. The Left Bank is definitely a lot less happening. The Champs-Élysées is making a comeback, though the clientele remains predominantly foreign. Take note: the last métro runs between 12:30 AM and 1 AM (you can take a taxi, but they can be hard to find, especially on weekend nights). For information about dates for the dazzling one-night only soirees, keep an eye out for the free listings mag *Lylo* or flyers in bars.

Bars & Clubs

American Bar at La Closerie des Lilas (⊠ 171 bd. du Montparnasse, Montparnasse, 6ᵉ ☎ 01–40–51–34–50 Ⓜ Montparnasse) lets you drink in the swirling action of the adjacent restaurant and do it at a bar hallowed by plaques honoring such former habitués as Man Ray, Jean-Paul Sartre, and Samuel Beckett. Happily, many Parisians still call this watering hole their home away from home. A cherished relic from the days of Picasso and Modigliani, **Au Lapin Agile** (⊠ 22 rue des Saules, Montmartre, 18ᵉ ☎ 01–46–06–85–87 Ⓜ Lamarck-Caulaincourt), the fabled artists' hangout in Montmartre, is a miraculous survivor from the early 20th century. This is an authentic French cabaret of songs, poetry and humor in a publike setting where the audience comes and goes throughout the evening show (Tuesday–Sunday 9 PM–2 AM). The famous brasserie **Alcazar** (⊠ 62 rue Mazarine, St-Germain-des-Prés, 6ᵉ ☎ 01–53–10–19–99 Ⓜ Odéon) was Sir Terence Conran's first makeover of a Parisian landmark, and comes complete with a stylish bar on the first floor, where you can sip a glass of wine under the huge glass roof. From Wednesday to Saturday a DJ spins either lounge or Latin music. **Barramundi** (⊠ 3 rue Taitbout, Opéra/Grands Boulevards, 9ᵉ ☎01–47–70–21–21 Ⓜ Richelieu Drouot) is one of Paris's hubs of nouveau-riche chic. The lighting is dim, the copper bar is long, and the walls are artfully textured. **Le Bilboquet** (⊠ 13 rue St-Benoît, St-Germain-des-Prés, 6ᵉ ☎ 01–45–48–81–84 Ⓜ St-Germain-des-Prés) is the place to sip cocktails in a ritzy Belle Époque salon while a jazz combo sets the mood. The namesake of **Buddha Bar** (⊠8 rue Boissy d'Anglas, Champs-Élysées, 8ᵉ ☎ 01–53–05–90–00 Ⓜ Concorde), towering gold-painted Buddha contemplates enough Dragon Empress screens and colorful chinoiserie for five MGM movies. Although quite past its prime as a Parisian hot spot, it manages to remain packed in the evenings with an eclectic crowd. **Le Cab** (⊠ 2 pl. du Palais Royal, Louvre/Tuileries, 1ᵉʳ ☎ 01–58–62–56–25 Ⓜ Palais-Royal) heats up during Fashion Week with models, photographers and stylists bypassing the lesser beings at the velvet rope. **Café Charbon** (⊠ 109 rue Oberkampf, Oberkampf, 11ᵉʳ ☎ 01–43–57–55–13 Ⓜ St-Maur, Parmentier) is a beautifully restored 19th-century café with a trendsetting crowd that has made this place one of the mainstays of trendy Okerkampf. **Chez Prune** (⊠ 71 quai de Valmy, République, 10ᵉ ☎ 01–42–41–30–47 Ⓜ République) is one of the most charming cafés in Paris *and* it has one

★ of the best terraces right in front of the Canal St-Martin. **Harry's New York Bar** (⊠ 5 rue Daunou, Opéra/Grands Boulevards, 2ᵉ ☎01–42–61–71–14 Ⓜ Opéra), a cozy, wood-paneled hangout decorated with dusty college pennants and popular with expatriates, is haunted by the ghosts of Ernest Hemingway and F. Scott Fitzgerald. This place claims to have invented the Bloody Mary, and one way or another, the bartenders here do mix a mean one. Don't miss the piano bar downstairs where Gershwin composed "An American in Paris." The ravishing Asian–Art Deco **Man Ray** (⊠ 34 rue Marbeuf, Champs-Élysées, 8ᵉ ☎ 01–56–88–36–36 Ⓜ Franklin-D.-Roosevelt) keeps its profile high, not surprising given that it is owned by Johnny Depp, Sean Penn, and Simply Red's Mick Hucknall. The clientele come to flash their bling and don't bat an eye at the pricey drinks (starting at €10 for a Coke). **Wagg** (⊠ 62 rue Mazarine, St-Germain-des-Prés, 6ᵉ ☎ 01–55–42–22–00 Ⓜ Odéon), in a vaulted stone cellar that was Jim Morrison's hangout back when it was the Whiskey-a-Go-Go, has been turned into a small, sleek club run by the über-trendy London club Fabric, with large helpings of house techno music. It's beneath the popular Alcazar restaurant.

GAY & LESBIAN BARS & CLUBS Gay and lesbian bars and clubs are mostly concentrated in the Marais and include some of the most happening addresses in the city. Aimed at women, **Bliss Kfé** (✉ 30 rue du Roi de Sicile, Le Marais, 4ᵉ ☎ 01–42–78–49–36 Ⓜ St-Paul) is a buzzing bar in the heart of the Marais. The mostly male crowd at **L'Open Café** (✉ 17 rue des Archives, Le Marais, 4ᵉ ☎ 01–42–72–26–18 Ⓜ Hôtel-de-Ville) comes for the sunny decor and convivial ambience. **Le Vinyl** (✉ 25 bd. Poissonnière, Opéra/Grands Boulevards, 2ᵉ ☎ 01–40–26–8–30 Ⓜ Grands Boulevards) is a gay landmark. **Queen** (✉ 102 av. des Champs-Élysées, Champs-Élysées, 8ᵉ ☎ 08–92–70–73–30 Ⓜ George-V) is one of the hottest nightspots in Paris: although it's predominantly gay, everyone else lines up to get in, too.

HOTEL BARS

Fodor'sChoice
★

Some of Paris's best hotel bars mix historic pedigrees with hushed elegance—and others go for a modern, edgy luxe. Following are some perennial favorites. The super-chic bar at **L'Hôtel** (✉ 10 rue des Beaux-Arts, St-Germain-des-Prés, 6ᵉ ☎ 01–44–41–99–00 Ⓜ St-Germain-des-Prés) had stylemeister Jacques Garcia revamp its gorgeously historic decor. **Hôtel Le Bristol** (✉ 112 rue du Faubourg–St-Honoré, Champs-Élysées, 8ᵉ ☎ 01–53–43–43–42 Ⓜ Miromesnil) attracts the rich and powerful. **Hôtel Costes** (✉ 239 rue Saint-Honoré, Louvre/Tuileries, 1ᵉʳ ☎ 01–42–44–50–25 Ⓜ Tuileries) draws many big names in the fashion world during Collections weeks to its red-velvet interior. **Hôtel Plaza Athénée** (✉ 25 av. Montaigne, Champs-Élysées, 8ᵉʳ ☎ 01–53–67–66–00 Ⓜ Alma Marceau) is Paris's perfect chill-out spot; the bar was designed by Starck protegé Patrick Jouin. Hot/cool **Pershing Hall** (✉ 49 rue Pierre Charron, Champs-Élysées, 8ᵉ ☎ 01–58–36–58–00 Ⓜ George V) has a stylish lounge bar with muted colors and an enormous "wall garden" in the courtyard. Colin Field, the best barman in Paris, presides at the

★ **Ritz's Hemingway Bar** (✉ 15 pl. Vendôme, Louvre/Tuileries, 1ᵉʳ ☎ 01–43–16–33–65 Ⓜ Opéra), but with a dress code and cognac aux truffes on the menu, Hemingway might raise an eyebrow. Across the hallway is the hotel's Cambon Bar, a soigné setting where Cole Porter

★ composed "Begin the Beguine." **Murano Urban Resort** (✉ 13 bd. du Temple, République, 3ᵉ ☎ 01–42–71–20–00 ⊕ www.muranoresort. com Ⓜ République) is by far the hippest hotel bar *du jour,* with its never-ending black stone bar, candy-colored fabric wall panels, and is packed nightly with beautiful art and fashion types.

Cabaret

Paris's cabarets are household names, though mostly just tourists go to them these days. Prices range from €40 (simple admission plus one drink) to more than €125 (dinner plus show). **Crazy Horse** (✉ 12 av. George-V, Champs-Élysées, 8ᵉ ☎ 01–47–23–85–56 ⊕ www.lecrazyhorseparis. com Ⓜ Alma-Marceau) is one of the best-known cabarets, with pretty dancers and a new risqué routine called "teasing" that involves top hats, fishnets, dark pink lipstick, and little else. **Lido** (✉ 116 bis av. des Champs-Élysées, Champs-Élysées, 8ᵉ ☎ 01–40–76–56–10 ⊕ www.lido. fr Ⓜ George-V) stars the famous Bluebell Girls; the owners claim that no show in Las Vegas can rival it for special effects. **Le Limonaire** (✉ 21 rue Bergère, Opéra/Grands Boulevards, 9ᵉ ☎ 01–45–23–33–33 Ⓜ Grands

Boulevards), a small restaurant, simply oozes with Parisian charm. This is the kind of place where you could imagine Edith Piaf belting out "*Je ne regrette rien,*" and, in fact, imagination is often not required at 10 PM, Tuesday to Sunday, when the service stops and a singer takes to the floor. The house specialty is *la chanson française,* and one of its finest guest artists is the modern-day Little Sparrow, Kalifa. **Michou** (⊠ 80 rue des Martyrs, Montmartre, 18ᵉ ☎ 01–46–06–16–04 ⊕ www.michou.fr Ⓜ Pigalle) is owned by the always blue-clad Michou, famous in Paris circles. The men on stage wear extravagant drag—high camp and parody are the order of the day. That old favorite at the foot of Montmartre, **Moulin Rouge** (⊠ 82 bd. de Clichy, Montmartre, 18ᵉ ☎ 01–53–09–82–82 Ⓜ Blanche), mingles the Doriss Girls, the cancan, and a horse in an extravagant (and expensive) spectacle.

Jazz Clubs

For nightly schedules consult the specialty magazines *Jazz Hot, Jazzman,* or *Jazz Magazine.* Nothing gets going 'til 10 PM or 11 PM; entry prices vary widely from about €10 to more than €25. **Caveau de la Huchette** (⊠ 5 rue de la Huchette, Quartier Latin, 5ᵉ ☎ 01–43–26–65–05 Ⓜ St-Michel), one of the only surviving cellar clubs from the 1940s, is a Paris classic, big with swing dancers and Dixieland musicians. **Le Petit Journal** (⊠ 71 bd. St-Michel, Quartier Latin, 5ᵉ ☎ 01–43–26–28–59 Ⓜ Luxembourg ⊠ 13 rue du Commandant-Mouchotte, Montparnasse, 14ᵉ ☎ 01–43–21–56–70 Ⓜ Montparnasse Bienvenüe), with two locations, has long attracted the greatest names in French and international jazz. It now specializes in big band (Montparnasse) and Dixieland (St-Michel) jazz and also serves dinner 8:30–midnight.

Rock, Pop & World-Music Venues

Upcoming concerts are posted on boards in FNAC and Virgin Megastores. **L'Olympia** (⊠ 28 bd. des Capucines, Opéra/Grands Boulevards, 9ᵉ ☎ 08–92–68–33–68 ⊕ www.olympiahall.com Ⓜ Madeleine), a legendary venue once favored by Jacques Brel and Edith Piaf, still plays host to leading French vocalists. **Palais Omnisports de Paris-Bercy** (⊠ 8 bd. de Bercy, Bercy/Tolbiac, 12ᵉ ☎ 08–92–69–23–00 Ⓜ Bercy) is the largest venue in Paris; English and American pop stars shake their spangles here (we see you, Mademoiselle Spears). **Zénith** (⊠ Parc de la Villette, 19ᵉ ☎ 01–42–08–60–00 Ⓜ Porte-de-Pantin)—here's your chance to see White Stripes or Limp Bizkit while surrounded by screaming Parisians.

SPORTS & THE OUTDOORS

Bicycling

Updated by
Mathew
Schwartz

★

The amazingly popular **Tour de France** (⊕ www.letour.fr) consists of a grueling three weeks of pure physical torture as the world's best cyclists cover more than 2,000 mi of French terrain. The athletes finish in a blaze of adulation, as tradition requires and the winner no doubt merits, on the Champs-Élysées. The race usually begins the end of June or beginning of July and finishes in Paris sometime in July. Maps of Paris's main cycle paths can be found in the free brochure *Paris A Vélo,* available in any city hall or at one of the tourist offices. Paris's two large parks, the Bois de Boulogne and the Bois de Vincennes, are the best places for biking.

The following places rent bikes, and many of these establishments also organize guided excursions. **Bike 'n Roller** (⊠ 38 rue Fabert, Invalides/Eiffel Tower, 7ᵉ ☎ 01–45–50–38–27 ⊕ www.bikenroller.fr Ⓜ La Tour ★ Maubourg) hires bikes for €12 for three hours and €17 for the day. **Fat Tire Bike Tours** (⊠ 24 rue Edgar Faure, Trocadéro/Eiffel Tower, 15ᵉ ☎ 01–56–58–10–54 ⊕ www.FatTireBikeToursParis.com Ⓜ Dupleix), formerly Mike's Bike Tours, organizes fun guided trips around Paris daily from March to November and by appointment from December to February. Tours are peppered with historical information and give a great overview of the city; tours of Versailles are available, too. Day tours run €24, night tours €28. **Pariscyclo** (⊠ Rond Point de Jardin d'Acclimatation, Bois de Boulogne, 16ᵉ ☎ 01–47–47–76–50 Ⓜ Les Sablons) is the perfect place for bike rentals if you want to explore the Bois de Boulogne. Rentals are €5 for an hour, €10 for the day.

Spectator Sports

Information on upcoming events can be found in the weekly guide *Pariscope,* on posters around the city, or by calling the ticket agencies of **FNAC** (☎ 08–03–80–88–03). You'll find a popular ticket outlet in the **Virgin Megastore** (☎ 08–03–02–30–24). A wide range of sporting events takes place at the **Palais Omnisports de Paris-Bercy** (⊠ 8 bd. de Bercy, Bercy/Tolbiac, 12ᵉ ☎ 08–03–03–00–31 Ⓜ Bercy). Details of events are also on their Web site: www.bercy.com. The **Parc des Princes** (⊠ 24 rue du Cdt. Guilbaud, Passy-Auteuil, 16ᵉ ☎ 08–25–07–50–78 Ⓜ Porte de Saint-Cloud) is the site of the home matches of the city's soccer team, ★ Paris St-Germain. **Roland-Garros** (⊠ 2 av. Gordon Bennett, Bois de Boulogne, 16ᵉ ☎ 01–47–43–48–00 ⊕ www.frenchopen.com Ⓜ Porte d'Auteuil) is the venue for the French Open tennis tournament during the last week of May and first week of June. **Stade de France** (⊠ St-Denis ☎ 01–55–93–00–00 ⊕ www.stade-de-france.com Ⓜ La Plaine–Stade de France) is home to the French national soccer and rugby teams.

SHOPPING

Updated by
Jennifer Ditsler-
Ladonne

In the most beautiful city in the world, it's no surprise to discover that the local greengrocer displays his tomatoes as artistically as Cartier does its rubies. The capital of style, Paris has an endless panoply of delights to tempt shop-'til-you-droppers, from grand couturiers like Dior to the funkiest flea markets. Today every neighborhood seems to reflect a unique attitude and style: designer extravagance and haute couture characterize avenue Montaigne and rue Faubourg St-Honoré; classic sophistication pervades St-Germain; avant-garde style dresses up the Marais; while a hip feel suffuses the area around Les Halles. With the euro trouncing the dollar (at press time, at least), here are some words to remember: *soldes,* sale; *fripes,* secondhand clothing; *dépôt vent,* secondhand shop; and *dégriffé,* designer labels, often from last year's collection, for sale at a deep discount. And if you do decide to indulge on that special bauble, what better place to make that once-in-a-blue-moon splurge than Paris?

Most stores—excepting department stores and flea markets—stay open until 6 or 7 PM, but many take a lunch break sometime between noon and 2 PM. Many shops traditionally close on Sunday. If you're from outside the European Union, age 15 and over, and stay in France and/or the European Union for less than six months, you can benefit from Value Added Tax (V.A.T.) reimbursements, known in France as TVA, while the sum remitted to non-EU folk is known as the *détaxe* (détaxe forms must be shown and stamped by a customs official before leaving the country). To qualify, non-EU residents must spend at least €175 in a single store on a single day. Refunds vary from 13% to 19.6% and are mailed to you by check or credited to your charge card. Remember: If you want to check out—and shop—the latest and greatest that Paris has to offer, pick up the newest issues of style magazines at neighborhood kiosks (or, better yet, back home!): *French Vogue, Maison Française,* and *Elle Decor* are just a few of the publications that are filled with the newest finds and *en dit* (gossip).

Shopping by Neighborhood

Avenue Montaigne

Shopping doesn't come much more chic than on avenue Montaigne, with its graceful town mansions housing some of the top names in international fashion: **Chanel, Dior, Céline, Valentino, Krizia, Ungaro, Prada, Dolce & Gabbana,** and many more. Neighboring rue François 1er and avenue George-V are also lined with many designer boutiques: **Versace, Fendi, Givenchy,** and **Balenciaga.**

Champs-Élysées

Cafés and movie theaters keep the once-chic Champs-Élysées active 24 hours a day, but the invasion of exchange banks, car showrooms, and fast-food chains has lowered the tone. Four glitzy 20th-century arcade malls—**Galerie du Lido, Le Rond-Point, Le Claridge,** and **Élysées 26**—capture most of the retail action, not to mention the **Gap** and the **Disney Store.** Some of the big luxe chain stores—also found in cities around the globe—are here: **Sephora** has reintroduced a touch of elegance and the cool factor soared skyward when the mothership **Louis Vuitton** (on the Champs-Élysées proper) reopened in spring 2005 after a year of renovations.

The Faubourg St-Honoré

This chic shopping and residential area is also quite a political hub. It's home to the Élysée Palace as well as the official residences of the American and British ambassadors. The Paris branches of **Sotheby's** and **Christie's** and renowned antiques galleries such as **Didier Aaron** add artistic flavor. Boutiques include **Hermès, Lanvin, Gucci, Chloé,** and **Christian Lacroix.**

Left Bank

For an array of bedazzling boutiques with hyper-picturesque goods—antique toy theaters, books on gardening—and the most fascinating antiques stores in town, be sure to head to the area around rue Jacob, nearly lined with *antiquaires,* and the streets around super-posh place Furstenberg. After decades of clustering on the Right Bank's venerable shopping avenues, the high-fashion houses have stormed the Rive Gauche. The first to arrive were **Sonia Rykiel** and **Yves St-Laurent** in the late '60s. Some of the more recent arrivals include **Christian Dior, Giorgio Armani,** and **Louis Vuitton.** Rue des St-Pères and rue de Grenelle are lined with designer names.

Louvre–Palais Royal

The elegant and eclectic shops clustered in the 18th-century arcades of the Palais-Royal sell such items as antiques, toy soldiers, cosmetics, jewelry, and vintage designer dresses. There are even handmade gardening tools sold by a prince at **Le Prince Jardinier.**

Le Marais

The Marais is a mixture of many moods and many influences; its lovely, impossibly narrow cobblestone streets are filled with some of the most original, small name, nonglobal goods to be had—a true haven for the original gift—including the outposts of **Jamin Puech, The Red Wheelbarrow,** and **Sentou Galerie.** Avant-garde designers **Azzedine Alaïa** and Tsumori Chistato have boutiques within a few blocks of stately place des Vosges and the Picasso and Carnavalet museums. The Marais is also one of the few neighborhoods that has a lively Sunday shopping scene.

Opéra to La Madeleine

Two major department stores—**Printemps** and **Galeries Lafayette**—dominate boulevard Haussmann, behind Paris's ornate 19th-century Opéra Garnier. Place de la Madeleine tempts many with its two luxurious food stores, **Fauchon** and **Hédiard.**

Place Vendôme & Rue de la Paix

The magnificent 17th-century place Vendôme, home of the Ritz Hotel, and rue de la Paix, leading north from Vendôme, are where you can find the world's most elegant jewelers: **Cartier, Boucheron, Bulgari,** and **Van Cleef and Arpels.** The most exclusive, however, is the discreet **Jar's.**

Place des Victoires & Rue Étienne Marcel

The graceful, circular place des Victoires, near the Palais-Royal, is the playground of fashion icons such as **Kenzo,** while **Comme des Garçons** and Yohji Yamamoto line rue Étienne Marcel. In the nearby oh-so-charming Galerie Vivienne shopping arcade, **Jean-Paul Gaultier** has a shop that has been renovated by Philippe Starck, and definitely worth a stop.

Rue St-Honoré

A fashionable set makes its way to rue St-Honoré to shop at Paris's trendiest boutique, **Colette.** The street is lined with numerous designer names, while on nearby rue Cambon you'll find the wonderfully elegant **Maria Luisa** and the main **Chanel** boutique.

Department Stores

For an overview of Paris *mode,* visit *les grands magasins,* Paris's monolithic department stores. Most are open Monday through Saturday from about 9:30 AM to 7 PM, and some are open until 10 PM one weekday evening.

★ **Le Bon Marché** (✉ 24 rue de Sèvres, St-Germain-des-Prés, 7ᵉ
☎ 01–44–39–80–00 Ⓜ Sèvres-Babylone) has undergone a complete
face-lift and is now Paris's chicest department store, with an impressive
array of designers represented for both men and women. La Grande
Épicerie is one of the largest groceries in Paris and a gourmand's home
away from home. **Bazar de l'Hôtel de Ville** (✉ 52–64 rue de Rivoli,
Beaubourg/Les Halles, 4ᵉ ☎ 01–42–74–90–00 Ⓜ Hôtel de Ville), better known as BHV, has minimal fashion offerings but is noteworthy for
its enormous basement hardware store. **La Samaritaine** (✉ 19 rue de la
Monnaie, Louvre/Tuileries, 1ᵉʳ ☎ 01–40–41–20–20 Ⓜ Pont-Neuf or
Châtelet) has the Toupary restaurant with magnificent views of the
Seine. **Printemps** (✉ 64 bd. Haussmann, Opéra/Grands Boulevards, 9ᵉ
☎ 01–42–82–50–00 Ⓜ Havre-Caumartin, Opéra, or Auber) has everything plus a whopping six floors dedicated to men's fashion. **Galeries
Lafayette** (✉ 40 bd. Haussmann, Opéra/Grands Boulevards, 9ᵉ
☎ 01–42–82–34–56 Ⓜ Chaussée d'Antin, Opéra, or Havre-Caumartin)
is dangerous—the granddaddy of them all—everything you never even
dreamt of and then some.

Budget

Monoprix (✉ 21 av. de l'Opéra, Opéra/Grands Boulevards, 1ᵉʳ
☎ 01–42–61–78–08 Ⓜ Opéra ✉ 6 av. de la Plaine, Nation, 20ᵉ
☎ 01–43–73–17–59 Ⓜ Nation ✉ 50 rue de Rennes, St-Germain-des-
Prés, 6ᵉ ☎ 01–45–48–18–08 Ⓜ St-Germain-des-Prés) is the French
dime store par excellence—with scores of branches throughout the
city—and stocks inexpensive everyday items like toothpaste, groceries,
toys, and paper. It also carries inexpensive children's clothes and makeup
of surprisingly good quality.

Markets

The lively atmosphere that reigns in most of Paris's open-air food markets makes them a sight worth seeing even if you don't want or need to
buy anything. Every neighborhood has one, though many are open
only a few days each week. Sunday morning until 1 PM is usually a good
time to go. Many of the better-known markets are in areas you'd visit
for sightseeing; here's a list of the top bets. **Boulevard Raspail** (✉ Between
rue de Rennes and rue du Cherche-Midi, Quartier Latin, 6ᵉ Ⓜ Rennes),
has a great Sunday organic market. **Rue de Buci** (✉ St-Germain-des-Prés,
6ᵉ Ⓜ Odéon), in the chic and lively St-Germain-des-Prés quarter, is
closed Sunday PM and Monday. **Rue Mouffetard** (✉ Quartier Latin, 5ᵉ
Ⓜ Place Monge), near the Jardin des Plantes, is best on weekends. **Rue
Montorgueuil** (✉ Beaubourg/Les Halles, 1ᵉʳ Ⓜ Châtelet Les Halles) is closed
Monday. **Rue Lepic** (✉ Montmartre, 18ᵉ Ⓜ Blanche or Abbesses) is best
on weekends. The **Marché d'Aligre** (✉ Rue d'Aligre, Bastille/Nation,
12ᵉ Ⓜ Ledru-Rollin), open until 1 PM every day except Monday, is a bit
farther out but is the cheapest and probably most locally authentic
market in Paris; on weekends a small flea market is also held here.

On Paris's northern boundary, the **Marché aux Puces** (Ⓜ Porte de Clignancourt), which takes place Saturday through Monday, is a century-
old labyrinth of alleyways packed with antiques dealers' booths and

junk stalls spreading for more than a square mile; arrive early. On the southern and eastern sides of the city—at **Porte de Vanves** (Ⓜ Porte de Vanves) and Porte de Montreuil—are other, smaller flea markets. Vanves is a hit with the fashion set and specializes in smaller objects— mirrors, textiles, handbags, clothing, and glass. Arrive early if you want to find a bargain, the good stuff goes fast and stalls are liable to be packed up before noon.

Shopping Arcades

Paris's 19th-century commercial arcades, called *passages* or *galeries* are the forerunners of the modern mall. Glass roofs, decorative pillars, and mosaic floors give the passages character. The major arcades are on the Right Bank in central Paris. **Galerie Vivienne** (⊠ 4 rue des Petits-Champs, Opéra/Grands Boulevards, 2ᵉ Ⓜ Bourse) is home to a range of interesting shops, including **Jean-Paul Gautier's** Philippe Starck–designed fantasy, an excellent tearoom, and a quality wine shop. **Passage du Grand-Cerf** (⊠ Entrances on rue Dussoubs, rue St-Denis, Beaubourg/Les Halles, 4ᵉ Ⓜ Étienne-Marcel) is a pretty, glass-roofed gallery filled with crafts shops offering an innovative selection of jewelry, paintings, and ceramics. **Passage Jouffroy** (⊠ 12 bd. Montmartre, Opéra/Grands Boulevards, 2ᵉ Ⓜ Montmartre) is full of shops selling toys, postcards, antique canes, and perfumes. **Passage des Panoramas** (⊠ 11 bd. Montmartre, Opéra/Grands Boulevards, 2ᵉ Ⓜ Montmartre), built in 1800, is the oldest of them all. The elegant **Galerie Véro-Dodat** (⊠ 19 rue Jean-Jacques Rousseau, Louvre/Tuileries, 1ᵉʳ Ⓜ Louvre) has shops selling old-fashioned toys, contemporary art, and stringed instruments. It's best known, however, for its antiques stores.

Specialty Stores

Accessories, Cosmetics & Perfumes

By Terry (⊠ Galerie Véro-Dodat, Louvre/Tuileries, 1ᵉʳ ☎ 01–44–76–00–76 Ⓜ Louvre, Palais-Royal) is the brainchild of Yves Saint Laurent's former director of makeup, Terry de Gunzberg; it offers her own brand of "ready-to-wear" cosmetics as well as a personalized cosmetics service. **Christian Louboutin** (⊠ 19 rue Jean-Jacques Rousseau, Louvre/Tuileries, 1ᵉʳ ☎ 01–42–36–05–31 Ⓜ Louvre) is famous for his wacky but elegant shoes, trademark blood-red soles, and impressive client list (Caroline of Monaco, Catherine Deneuve, Elizabeth Taylor). **E. Goyard** (⊠ 233 rue St-Honoré, Louvre/Tuileries, 1ᵉʳ ☎ 01–42–60–57–04 Ⓜ Tuileries) has been making the finest luggage since 1853. **Jamin Puech** (⊠ 43 rue Madame, St-Germain-des-Prés, 6ᵉ ☎ 01–45–48–14–85 Ⓜ St-Sulpice ⊠ 68 rue Vieille-du-Temple, Le Marais, 3ᵉ ☎ 01–48–87–84–87 Ⓜ St-Paul) thinks of its bags as jewelry, not just a necessity. Nothing's plain-Jane here—everything is whimsical, unusual, and fun. **Loulou de la Falaise** (⊠ 7 rue de Bourgogne, Trocadéro/Tour Eiffel, 7ᵉ ☎ 01–45–51–42–22 Ⓜ Invalides) was the original muse of Yves Saint Laurent; she was at his side for more than 30 years of collections and designed his accessories line. Now this paragon of the fashion aristocracy has her own two-floor boutique filled with the best style around. **Sabbia Rosa** (⊠ 73 rue des Sts-Pères, St-Germain-des-Prés, 6ᵉ ☎ 01–45–48–88–37 Ⓜ St-Germain-des-Prés) sells French lingerie favored by celebrities like Catherine Deneuve and Claudia Schiffer. **Les Salons du Palais Royal Shiseido** (✉ Jardins du Palais-Royal, 142 Galerie de Valois, 25 rue de Valois, Louvre/Tuileries, 1ᵉʳ ☎ 01–49–27–09–09 Ⓜ Palais-Royal) is a magical place with marble floors and purple walls that exclusively sells the scents Serge Lutens dreams up for the Japanese cosmetics firm.

Bookstores (English-Language)

The scenic open-air bookstalls along the Seine sell secondhand books (mostly in French), prints, and souvenirs. Numerous French-language bookstores—specializing in a wide range of topics, including art, film, literature, and philosophy—are found in the Latin Quarter and around St-Germain-des-Prés. For English-language books try these stores: **Brentano's** (✉ 37 av. de l'Opéra, Opéra/Grands Boulevards, 2ᵉ ☎ 01–42–61–52–50 Ⓜ Opéra) is stocked with everything from classics to children's titles. **Galignani** (✉ 224 rue de Rivoli, Louvre/Tuileries, 1ᵉʳ ☎ 01–42–60–76–07 Ⓜ Tuileries) is especially known for its extensive collection of art and coffee-table books. **The Red Wheelbarrow** (✉ 22 rue St-Paul, Le Marais, 4ᵉ ☎ 01–42–77–42–17 Ⓜ St-Paul ✉ 13 rue St-Charles, Le Marais, 4ᵉ ☎ 01–40–26–76–20 Ⓜ St-Paul) is *the* anglophone bookstore—if it was written in English, they can get it. It also has a complete academic section and every literary review you can think of. **Shakespeare and Company** (✉ 37 rue de la Bûcherie, 5ᵉ, Quartier Latin ☎ 01–43–26–96–50 Ⓜ St-Michel), the sentimental Left Bank favorite, is named after the publishing house that first edited James Joyce's *Ulysses*. Nowadays, it specializes in expatriate literature. The staff tends to be rather pretentious, but the shelves of secondhand books hold real bargains. Poets give readings upstairs on Monday at 8 PM; there are also tea-party talks on Sunday at 4 PM. **Village Voice** (✉ 6 rue Princesse, St-Germain-des-Prés, 6ᵉ ☎ 01–46–33–36–47 Ⓜ Mabillon) hosts regular literary readings.

Clothing

MEN'S WEAR **Berluti** (✉ 26 rue Marbeuf, Champs-Élysées, 8ᵉ ☎ 01–53–93–97–97 Ⓜ Franklin-D.-Roosevelt) has been making the most exclusive men's shoes for more than a century. **Charvet** (✉ 28 pl. Vendôme, Opéra/Grands Boulevards, 1ᵉʳ ☎ 01–42–60–30–70 Ⓜ Opéra) is the Parisian equivalent of a Savile Row tailor. **Madélios** (✉ 23 bd. de la Madeleine, Opéra/Grands Boulevards, 1ᵉʳ ☎ 01–53–45–00–00 Ⓜ Madeleine) gathers up all kinds of menswear labels from classy (Dior, Kenzo) to quirky (Paul Smith) to casual (Diesel, Levi's).

WOMEN'S WEAR It doesn't matter, say the French, that fewer and fewer of their top couture houses are still headed by compatriots. It's the chic elegance, the classic ambience, the *je ne sais quoi,* that remains undeniably Gallic. Here are some meccas for Paris chic. **Azzedine Alaïa** (✉ 7 rue de Moussy, Le Marais, 4ᵉ ☎ 01–42–72–19–19 Ⓜ Hôtel-de-Ville) is the undisputed "king of cling" and a supermodel favorite. **Chanel** (✉ 42 av. Montaigne, Champs-Élysées, 8ᵉ ☎ 01–47–23–74–12 Ⓜ Franklin-D.-Roosevelt ✉ 31 rue Cambon, Louvre/Tuileries, 1ᵉʳ ☎ 01–42–86–26–00 Ⓜ Tuileries) is helmed by svelte Karl Lagerfeld who whips together nouvelle takes on all of Coco's favorites: the perfectly tailored tweed suit, a lean, soigné black dress, a quilted bag with the gold chain, a camellia brooch. **Christian Dior** (⊠ 30 av. Montaigne, Champs-Élysées, 8ᵉ ☎ 01–40–73–54–44 Ⓜ Franklin-D.-Roosevelt ⊠16 rue de l'Abbé, St-Germain-des-Prés, 6ᵉ ☎01–40–73–54–44 Ⓜ St-Germain-des-Prés) features the flamboyant John Galliano . . . so what if he pairs full-length body-skimming evening dresses with high-tops and a Davy Crockett raccoon hat? It's just fashion, darling. **Christian Lacroix** (⊠ 73 rue du Faubourg St-Honoré, Louvre/Tuileries, 8ᵉ ☎01–42–68–79–00 ⓂConcorde ⊠2 pl. St-Sulpice, St-Germain-des-Prés, 6ᵉ ☎ 01–46–33–48–95 Ⓜ St-Sulpice) masters color and texture to such an ultra-Parisian extent that his runway shows leave fans literally weeping with pleasure—and not just Eddy from *Absolutely Fabulous*. The rue du Faubourg St-Honoré location is the Lacroix epicenter; on the ground floor you'll find the ready-to-wear line "Bazar"; haute couture is through the courtyard. **Colette** (⊠ 213 rue St-Honoré, Louvre/Tuileries, 1ᵉʳ ☎ 01–55–35–33–90 Ⓜ Tuileries) is the most fashionable, most hip, and most hyped store in Paris (and possibly the world). The ground floor, which stocks design objects, gadgets, and makeup, is generally packed with fashion victims and the simply curious. Upstairs are handpicked fashions, accessories, magazines, and books, all of which ooze trendiness. Fashionistas adore hot and luxe **Dolce & Gabbana** (⊠22 av. Montaigne, Champs-Élysées, 8ᵉ ☎01–42–25–68–78 Ⓜ Alma-Marceau), who serve up a sexy young Italian widow with a side of moody boyfriend. **Jean-Paul Gaultier** (⊠44 av. George V, Champs-Élysées, 8ᵉ ☎ 01–44–43–00–44 Ⓜ George V ⊠ 6 Galerie Vivienne, Opéra/Grands Boulevards, 2ᵉ ☎01–42–86–05–05 Ⓜ Bourse) first made headlines with his celebrated corset with the ironic i-conic breasts for Madonna, but now sends fashion editors into ecstasy with his sumptuous haute couture creations. Designer Philippe Starck spun an *Alice in Wonderland* fantasy for the boutiques, with quilted cream walls and Murano mirrors. **Sonia Rykiel** (⊠ 175 bd. St-Germain, St-Germain-des-Prés, 6ᵉ ☎01–49–54–60–60 Ⓜ St-Germain-des-Prés ⊠ 70 rue du Faubourg St-Honoré, Louvre/Tuileries, 8ᵉ ☎01–42–65–20–81 ⓂConcorde) is the queen of French fashion. Since the '60s she's been designing stylish knit separates and has made black her color of preference.

Trendsetter **Antik Batik** (⊠ 18 rue de Turenne, Le Marais, 4ᵉ ☎01–48–87–95–95 ⓂSt-Paul) sells hippie-chic and ethnic-inspired clothing, bags, and shoes, which has made the label a hit with in-the-know Parisians and supermodels. **Didier Ludot** (⊠ Jardins du Palais-Royal, 24 Galerie Montpensier, Louvre/Tuileries, 1ᵉʳ ☎ 01–42–96–06–56 Ⓜ Palais-Royal) is one of the world's most famous vintage clothing dealers and an incredibly charming man to boot. (A tip: be nice to the dogs.) Check out the wonderful old Chanel suits, Balenciaga dresses, and Hermès scarves, and bring lots of money.

Gourmet Goodies

Fauchon (⊠ 26 pl. de la Madeleine, Opéra/Grands Boulevards, 8ᵉ ☎ 01–70–39–38–00 Ⓜ Madeleine) is the most famous and iconic of all Parisian food stores. **Ladurée** (⊠ 16 rue Royale, Louvre/Tuileries, 8ᵉ ☎ 01–42–60–21–79 Ⓜ Madeleine ⊠ 75 av. des Champs-Élysées,

Champs-Élysées, 8ᵉ ☏ 01–40–75–08–75 Ⓜ George V ✉ 21 rue Bonaparte, Quartier Latin, 6ᵉ ☏ 01–44–07–64–87 Ⓜ Odéon), founded in 1862, oozes Proustian period atmosphere—even at the new, large Champs-Élysées branch. But nothing beats the original tearoom on rue Royale, with its pint-size tables and frescoed ceiling.

PARIS A TO Z

To research prices, get advice from other travelers, and book travel arrangements, visit www.fodors.com.

AIR TRAVEL TO & FROM PARIS

CARRIERS Major carriers fly daily from the United States; Air France, British Airways, British Midland, and EasyJet fly regularly from London.

AIRPORTS & TRANSFERS

Paris is served by two international airports: Charles de Gaulle, also known as Roissy, 26 km (16 mi) northeast; and Orly, 16 km (10 mi) south. For telephone numbers, *see* Airports *in* this book's Smart Travel Tips section.

From Charles de Gaulle, the RER-B, the suburban commuter train, beneath Terminal 2, has trains to central Paris (Les Halles, St-Michel, Luxembourg) every 20 minutes; the fare is €7.85, and the journey takes 30 minutes. Note that you have to carry your luggage up from and down to the platform and that trains can be crowded during rush hour. **Remember you must retain the train ticket sold to you at Charles de Gaulle Airport since you will need it at the end of the ride to exit the métro system** once you are in the city center. Without a ticket stub, you will not be able to get the métro turnstiles to open to exit the subway system in Paris and you could wind up being ostensibly trapped in the station until a passerby can aid you (also see the note about métro mugging in the Métro Travel section below).

Buses operated by Air France (you need not have flown with the airline) run every 15 minutes between Roissy and western Paris (Porte Maillot and the Arc de Triomphe). The fare is €12, and the trip takes about 40 minutes, though rush-hour traffic may make it longer. Additionally, the Roissybus, operated by the RATP, runs directly between Roissy and rue Scribe by the Opéra every 15 minutes and costs €8.30. Taxis are readily available; the fare will be around €30–€40, depending on traffic, but traffic jams can make this a frustrating venture. Aeroports Limousine Service can meet you on arrival in a private car and drive you to your destination; reservations should be made two or three days in advance; MasterCard and Visa are accepted—readers report inordinate delays, however. The following minibus services can also meet you on arrival: Airport Shuttle, Paris Airports Service, and Parishuttle.

The RER-C line is one way to get to Paris from Orly Airport; there's a free shuttle bus from the terminal building to the train station, and trains leave every 15 minutes. The fare is €5.45 (métro included), and the train journey takes about 35 minutes. The Orlyval service is a shuttle train that runs direct from each Orly terminal to the Antony RER-B station every seven minutes; a one-way ticket for the entire trip into Paris is €8.85. Buses operated by Air France (you need not have flown with the airline) run every 12 minutes between Orly Airport, Montparnasse station, and Les Invalides. On the Left Bank, the fare is €8, and the trip can take from 30 minutes to an hour, depending on traffic. RATP also runs the Orlybus between the Denfert-Rochereau métro station and Orly every 15 minutes, and the trip costs €5.80. A 20-minute taxi ride costs about €20–€30. With reservations, Aeroports Limousine Service can pick you up at Orly, but readers report delays.

🛈 Taxis & Shuttles **Air France Bus** ☎ 08-92-35-08-20 recorded information in English €.35 per min ⊕ www.cars-airfrance.com. **Airport Connection** ☎ 01-43-65-55-55 🖶 01-43-65-55-57 ⊕ www.airport-connection.com. **Paris Airports Services** ☎ 01-55-98-10-80 🖶 01-55-98-10-89 ⊕ www.parisairportservice.com. **RATP (Paris Transit Authority: including Roissybus, Orlybus, Orlyval)** ⊠ 54 quai de la Rapée, 75012 Paris ☎ 08-92-68-77-14, €.35 per min ⊕ www.ratp.com.

BUS TRAVEL TO & FROM PARIS

Long-distance bus journeys within France are uncommon, which may be why Paris has no central bus depot. *See* Bus Travel *in* Smart Travel Tips A to Z for information on traveling to and from Paris by bus.

BUS TRAVEL WITHIN PARIS

Paris buses are marked with the route number and destination in front and with major stopping places along the sides. The brown bus shelters contain timetables and route maps. Maps are also found on each bus. To get off, press one of the red buttons mounted on all the silver poles that run the length of the bus and the *arrêt demandé* (stop requested) light directly behind the driver will light up. Use the rear door to exit.

TICKETS & SCHEDULES You can use your métro ticket on buses; if you have individual tickets (as opposed to weekly or monthly tickets), be prepared to validate your ticket in the red-and-gray machines on board the bus. Your best bet is to buy a *carnet* of 10 tickets for €10.50 at any métro station, or you can buy a single ticket on-board (exact change appreciated) for €1.40. You need to show (but not punch) weekly, monthly, and Paris-Visite/Mobilis tickets to the driver. Tickets can be bought on buses, in the métro, or in any bar/tabac store displaying the lime-green métro symbol above its street sign. Most routes operate from 6 AM to 8:30 PM; some continue until midnight. Eighteen *Noctambus,* or night buses, operate hourly (1 AM–6 AM) between Châtelet and various nearby suburbs.

🛈 Bus Information **RATP** ⊠ 54 quai de la Rapée, 75012 Paris ☎ 08-92-68-77-14, €.35 per min ⊕ www.ratp.com.

CAR RENTAL

Cars can be rented at both airports, as well as at locations throughout the city, including the ones listed below.

🛈 Local Agencies **Avis** ⊠ 60 rue de Ponthieu, Champs-Élysées, 8ᵉ ☎ 01-43-59-03-83 Ⓜ St-Philippe du Roule. **National/Citer** ⊠ 18 rue de Dunkerque, Gare du Nord, 10ᵉ ☎ 01-53-20-06-52 Ⓜ Gare du Nord. **Europcar** ⊠ 60 bd. Diderot, Bastille/Nation, 12ᵉ ☎ 08-25-82-54-63 Ⓜ Gare de Lyon. **Hertz** ⊠ 193 rue de Bercy, Bercy/Tolbiac, 12ᵉ ☎ 01-43-44-06-00 Ⓜ Gare de Lyon.

CAR TRAVEL

In a country as highly centralized as France, it's no surprise that expressways converge on the capital from every direction: A1 from the north (225 km [140 mi] from Lille); A13 from Normandy (225 km [140 mi] from Caen); A4 from the east (500 km [310 mi] from Strasbourg); A10 from the southwest (580 km [360 mi] from Bordeaux); and A7 from the Alps and the Riviera (465 km [290 mi] from Lyon). Each connects with the *périphérique*, the beltway, whose exits into the city are named (as *portes*), not numbered.

CHILDREN IN PARIS

Fodor's Around Paris with Kids (available in bookstores everywhere) can help you plan your days together.

BABYSITTING   Babysitting services can provide English-speaking babysitters on just a few hours' notice. The hourly rate is approximately $8 (three-hour minimum) plus an agency fee of around $12.

🔲 **Agencies Allo Assistance BabyChou** ☎ 01-43-13-33-23 ⊕ www.babychou.com. **Baby-Sitting Service** ✉ 4 rue Nationale, Boulogne BillanCt. ☎ 01-46-21-33-16 ⊕ www.babysittingservices.com.

EMBASSIES & CONSULATES

🔲 **Australia** ✉ 4 rue Jean-Rey, Trocadéro/Tour Eiffel, 15ᵉ ☎ 01-40-59-33-00 Ⓜ Bir Hakeim.

🔲 **Canada** ✉ 35 av. Montaigne, Champs-Élysées, 8ᵉ ☎ 01-44-43-29-00 Ⓜ Franklin-D.-Roosevelt.

🔲 **New Zealand** ✉ 7 terr. rue Léonardo da Vinci, Champs-Élysées, 16ᵉ ☎ 01-45-01-43-43 Ⓜ Victor-Hugo.

🔲 **United Kingdom** ✉ 18 bis rue d'Anjou, Champs-Élysées, 8ᵉ ☎ 01-44-51-31-00 Ⓜ Madeleine.

🔲 **United States** ✉ 2 rue St-Florentin, Champs-Élysées, 1ᵉʳ ☎ 01-43-12-22-22 Ⓜ Concorde.

EMERGENCIES

A 24-hour emergency service is available at American Hospital. Hertford British Hospital also has all-night emergency service. This guidebook does not list the major Paris hospitals, as the French government prefers an emergency operator to make the judgment call and assign you the best option. Note that if you are able to walk into a hospital emergency room by yourself, you are often considered "low priority." So if time is of the essence, the best thing to do is to call the fire department (☎ 18); a fully trained team of paramedics will usually arrive within five minutes. You may also dial for a Samu ambulance (☎ 15); there is usually an English-speaking physician available. In a less urgent situation, SOS Medecin (doctor) or SOS Dentiste services send a certified, experienced doctor or dentist to your door, a very helpful 24-hour service to use for common symptoms of high fever, toothache, or upset stomach). It's important to check with your insurance company before you leave for your trip to make sure that you are covered internationally.

🔲 **Doctors & Dentists SOS Dentist** ☎ 01-43-37-51-00. **SOS Medecin** ☎ 01-43-07-77-77. 🔲 **Emergency Services Ambulance** ☎ 15 or 01-45-67-50-50. **Police** ☎ 17.

🏥 **Hospitals American Hospital** ⊠ 63 bd. Victor-Hugo, Neuilly ☎ 01-46-41-25-25. **Hertford British Hospital** ⊠ 3 rue Barbès, Levallois-Perret ☎ 01-46-39-22-22.
🏥 **Late-Night & 24-Hour Pharmacies Dhéry** ⊠ Galerie des Champs, 84 av. des Champs-Élysées, Champs-Élysées, 8ᵉ ☎ 01-45-62-02-41 is open 24 hours. **Pharmacie Internationale** ⊠ 5 pl. Pigalle, Pigalle-Clichy, 9ᵉ ☎ 01-48-78-38-12. **Pharmacie Matignon** ⊠ 2 rue Jean-Mermoz, at the Rond-Point de Champs-Élysées, Champs-Élysées, 8ᵉ is open daily until 2 AM.

MÉTRO TRAVEL

The métro is by far the quickest and most efficient way to get around. Trains run from 5:30 AM until 1 AM (and be forewarned—this means the famous "last métro" can pass your station anytime after 12:30 AM). Stations are signaled either by a large yellow **M** within a circle or by their distinctive curly green Art Nouveau railings and archway entrances bearing the subway's full title (Métropolitain). It's essential to **know the name of the last station on the line you take,** as this name appears on all signs. A connection (you can make as many as you like on one ticket) is called a *correspondance*. At junction stations illuminated orange signs bearing the name of the line terminal appear over the correct corridors for correspondance. Illuminated blue signs marked SORTIE indicate the station exit. In general, the métro is safe, although try to avoid the larger, mazelike stations at Les Halles and République if you're alone late at night, and try and ride in the first car behind the conductor. Access to métro platforms is through an automatic ticket barrier. Slide your ticket in and pick it up and retrieve it as it pops up. **Keep your ticket during your journey; you will need it to leave the RER system,** and you'll be glad you have it in case you run into any green-clad inspectors when you are leaving—they can be very unpleasant and will impose a big fine on the spot if you do not have a ticket.

Speaking of unpleasant, many readers have written to us about being mugged in the métro system. A favorite mode is for muggers to "sandwich" you as you attempt to exit the rather tricky turnstiles; others make their attack on the lengthy escalators at the métro exits. Pickpockets are close enough and nimble-fingered enough (think Oliver Twist) to rob you in a split second. These pickpockets work in groups, never alone—one will divert your attention (think the Artful Dodger) while the other whisks away your wallet or your passport (which should not be in your back pocket or shoulder purse). Prevention of petty crime is the same all over the world. Just use discretion and caution while maintaining your physical comfort zone in crowded places. Happily, as large cities go, Paris remains—for the most part—a safe place.

FARES & SCHEDULES   All métro tickets and passes are valid for RER and bus travel as well; tickets cost €1.40 each, but it makes more sense to buy a *carnet* (10 tickets) for €10.50. If you're staying for a week or more, the best deals are the weekly or monthly *carte orange* (orange card), sold according to zone. Zones 1 and 2 cover the entire métro network; tickets cost €15.40 a week or €50.40 a month. If you plan to take suburban trains to visit places in the Ile-de-France, consider a four-zoner (Versailles, St-Germain-en-Laye; €25.20 a week) or a six-zoner (Rambouillet, Fontainebleau;

€34 a week). Weekly and monthly passes are available from rail and major métro stations, and require a passport-size photograph.

An alternative for métro travel is to purchase two-, three-, or five-day unlimited-travel tickets (*Paris Visite*). Unlike the *carte orange "hebdo"* (the weekly pass for unlimited travel beginning on a Monday and ending on a Sunday evening), the unlimited ticket is valid starting any day of the week and gives you discounts on a limited number of museums and tourist attractions. The prices are, respectively, €8.35, €13.70, and €26.65 for Paris only; for Paris and the suburbs, prices are nearly twice as much. The equivalent one-day ticket is called *mobilis* and costs €5.30 (Paris only) or €7–€18.40 (Paris plus suburbs).

⑦ Métro Information RATP ☎ 08-92-68-41-14 ⊕ www.ratp.fr.

TAXIS

On weekend nights after 11 PM it's nearly impossible to find a free taxi—you are best off asking hotel or restaurant staff to call you one, but, be forewarned; you will have to pay for them to come get you and, depending on where they are, the fare can quickly add up. If you want to hail a cab on your own, look for the taxis with their signs lit up (their signs will be glowing white as opposed to the taxis that are already taken whose signs will be a dull orange). There are taxi stands on almost every major street corner but again, expect a wait if it is a busy weekend night. Taxi stands are marked by a square dark blue sign with a white T in the middle. Daytime rates, denoted A (7 AM–7 PM), within Paris are €.62 per km (½ mi), and nighttime rates, B, are €1.06 per km. Suburban zones and airports, C, are €1.24 per km. There is a basic hire charge of €2 for all rides, a €1 supplement per piece of luggage, and a €.75 supplement if you're picked up at an SNCF station. Waiting time is charged at €26.23 per hour.

TOURS

BOAT TOURS Hour-long boat trips on the Seine can be fun if you're in Paris for the first time; the cost is €9–€15. A few lines (but not the Bateaux Mouches) serve lunch and dinner (for an additional cost); make reservations in advance. The massive, double-decker Bateaux Mouches boats (with commentary in seven languages) depart from the Pont de l'Alma (Right Bank) every half hour from April to September from 10 AM to 11 PM and approximately every three hours during the grey winter months from 11 AM to 9 PM. Bateaux Parisiens boats depart every half hour in summer and every hour in winter, starting at 10 AM; the last boat departs at 10 PM (11 PM in summer). Canauxrama organizes half- and full-day barge tours along the canals of east Paris. Vedettes du Pont-Neuf offer one-hour trips with live commentary in French and English; boats depart daily from square du Vert Galant every 30 to 60 minutes 10 AM to 10:30 PM (with a 90-minute lunch break from noon) March through October, and from 10:30 AM to 10 PM with a 2-hour lunch break November through February. Yachts de Paris organizes romantic 2½-hr "gourmand cruises" (for about €149) year-round. Yachts set off every evening at 7:45 PM while a team of uniformed officers and crew serve Chef Gérard Besson's three-course meal.

⑦ Fees & Schedules Bateaux Mouches ✉ Pont de l'Alma, Trocadéro/Tour Eiffel, 8ᵉ ☎ 01-42-25-96-10 ⊕ www.bateauxmouches.com Ⓜ Alma-Marceau. **Bateaux Parisiens**

⊠ Port de la Bourdonnais Trocadéro/Tour Eiffel, 7ᵉ ☎ 0825/01-01-01 ⊕ www. bateauxparisiens.com Ⓜ Trocadéro. Boats depart from **Canauxrama** ⊠ 13 quai de la Loire, Gare de l'Est, 19ᵉ ☎ 01-42-39-15-00 ⊕ www.canauxrama.com Ⓜ Jaurès ⊠ For information: Bassin de l'Arsenal, opposite 50 bd. de la Bastille, Bastille/Nation, 12ᵉ Ⓜ Bastille ☎ 01-42-39-15-00. **Vedettes du Pont-Neuf** ⊠ Below Sq. du Vert-Galant, Ile de la Cité, 1ᵉʳ ☎ 01-46-33-98-38 ⊕ www.vedettesdupontneuf.com Ⓜ Pont Neuf. **Yachts de Paris** ⊠ Port de Javel ☎ 01-44-54-14-70 ⊕ www.yachtsdeparis.com.

BUS TOURS For a 2-hour orientation tour by bus, the standard price is about €24. The two largest bus-tour operators are Cityrama and Paris Vision; for a more intimate—albeit expensive—tour of the city, Cityrama also runs several minibus excursions per day with a private multilingual tour operator for €54. Paris Vision runs nonstop two-hour tours with multilingual commentary available via individual headphones with over 10 languages for €19. Paris L'Open Tour gives tours in a double-decker bus with an open top; commentary is available in French and English on individual headphones. Get on or off at one of the 50 pickup points indicated by the lime-green sign posts; tickets may be purchased on-board and cost €24 for one day, €27 for unlimited use for two days. Les Cars Rouges offer double-decker London-style buses with nine stops—a ticket for two consecutive days is available for €22. RATP (Paris Transit Authority) also offers economical, commentary-free excursions; the Montmartrobus departs from métro Anvers and zips through the winding cobbled streets of Montmartre to the top of the hill for those of you who don't want to brave the walk; the trip is the price of one métro ticket (€1.40). The RATP Balabus Bb line goes from Gare du Lyon to the Grand Arch at La Défense passing by all major tourist attractions on the way for the price of one to three métro tickets. The Balabus Bb line runs Sunday and holidays from mid-April to September.

🚌 **Cityrama** ⊠ 4 pl. des Pyramides, 1ᵉʳ ☎ 01-44-55-61-00 ⊕ www.cityrama.com. **Les Cars Rouges** ☎ 01-53-95-39-53. **Paris L'Open Tour** ⊠ 13 rue Auber, 9ᵉʳ ☎ 01-42-66-56-56 ⊕ www.paris-opentour.com. **Paris Vision** ⊠ 214 rue de Rivoli, 1ᵉʳ ☎ 01-42-60-30-01 ⊠ 53 bis quai des Grands-Augustins, 6ᵉ ☎ 08-92-68-41-14 ⊠ Pl. de la Madeleine, 8ᵉ

WALKING TOURS The team at Paris Walking Tours offers a wide selection of tours, from neighborhood visits to museum tours and theme tours such as "Hemingway's Paris," "The Marais," "Montmartre," and "The Latin Quarter." A 2-hour tour costs about €10. A list of walking tours is also available from the Caisse Nationale des Monuments Historiques, in the weekly magazines available at any kiosk in the city *Pariscope* and *L'Officiel des Spectacles*, which list walking tours under the heading "*Conférences*" (most are in French, unless otherwise noted).

🚌 **Fees & Schedules Caisse Nationale des Monuments Historiques** ⊠ Bureau des Visites: Hôtel de Sully, 62 rue St-Antoine, Bastille/Nation, 4ᵉ ☎ 01-44-61-21-70 Ⓜ St-Paul. **Paris Walking Tours** ☎ 01-48-09-21-40 ⊕ www.paris-walks.com.

TRAIN TRAVEL

Paris has five international train stations: Gare du Nord (northern France, northern Europe, and England via Calais or the Channel Tunnel); Gare St-Lazare (Normandy and England via Dieppe); Gare de l'Est (Strasbourg, Luxembourg, Basel, and central Europe); Gare de Lyon (Lyon, Marseille, the Riviera, Geneva, Italy); and Gare d'Austerlitz (Loire Valley, southwest France, Spain). The Gare Montparnasse is used by the TGV *Atlantique* bound for Nantes or Bordeaux. Call 08–92–35–35–35 for information.

RER trains travel between Paris and the suburbs. When they go through Paris, they act as a sort of supersonic métro—they connect with the métro network at several points—and can be great time-savers. Access to RER platforms is through the same type of automatic ticket barrier (if you've started your journey on the métro, you can use the same ticket), but you'll need to have the same ticket handy to put through another barrier when you leave the system.

🚩 Train Information SNCF ☎ 08-91-36-20-20 ⊕ www.sncf.fr or www.transilien.com.

TRANSPORTATION AROUND PARIS

To help you find your way around, buy a *Plan de Paris par Ar-rondissement*, a city guide available at most kiosks, with separate maps of each district, including the whereabouts of métro stations and an index of street names. Maps of the métro/RER network are available free from any métro station and from many hotels. They are also posted on every platform, as are maps of the bus network. Bus routes are also marked at bus stops and on buses. The extensive public transportation system is the best way to get around. Don't use a car in Paris unless you have to. Parking is difficult—and expensive—and traffic can be awesome. Meters and ticket machines (pay and display) are common; meters and parking-ticket machines use parking cards (*cartes de stationnements*), which can be purchased at any café posting the red TABAC sign.

TRAVEL AGENCIES

🚩 Local Agent Referrals **Air France** ✉ 119 av. des Champs-Élysées, Champs-Élysées, 8ᵉ ☎ 01-42-99-21-99 Ⓜ Charles-de-Gaulle-Étoile. **American Express** ✉ 11 rue Scribe, Opéra/Grands Boulevards, 8ᵉ ☎ 01-47-77-70-00 Ⓜ Opéra. **Nouvelles Frontières** ✉ 13 av. de l'Opéra, Louvre/Tuileries, 1ᵉʳ ☎ 01-42-61-02-62 Ⓜ Pyramides. **Soltours** ✉ 46 rue de Rivoli, Le Marais, 4ᵉ ☎ 01-42-71-24-34 Ⓜ Hôtel-de-Ville. **Carlson Wagon Lit Travel** ✉ 31 rue Marbeuf, Champs-Élysées, 8ᵉ ☎ 08-26-82-54-68 Ⓜ Alma-Marceau.

VISITOR INFORMATION

There are over five branches of the Paris tourist office located at key points in the capital. Don't call with a question though—you'll get a host of generic recorded information that will cost you €.34 per minute.

🚩 **Espace du Tourisme d'Ile-de-France** ✉ Carrousel du Louvre, 99 rue de Rivoli, 75001 Paris Ⓜ Métro: Palais Royale/Musée du Louvre ☎ 08-26-16-66-66. **Office du Tourisme de la Ville de Paris** Opéra-Grands Magasins ✉ 11 rue Scribe Ⓜ Opéra ☎ 08-92-68-30-00 €.34 per min. **Office du Tourisme de la Ville de Paris** Gare du Lyon, Arrivals ✉ 20 bd Diderot Ⓜ Gare du Lyon ☎ 08-92-68-30-00 €.34 per min. **Office du Tourisme de la Ville de Paris** Pyramides ✉ 25 rue des Pyramides 75002 ☎ 08-92-68-30-00, €.34 per min Ⓜ Pyramides.

Ile-de-France

WORD OF MOUTH

"I'm not into overdone luxury so wasn't fond of most of Versailles, but way out back, after a wonderful walk through the gardens, is the Hameau of Marie-Antoinette—a little country village where she and her maids could "play" at being peasants. It is the most delightful little place with thatched houses, a little mill, a fascinating dovecote, and, best of all, there are farm animals all over the place."

—SalB

"The wonder of France, Chartres cathedral gives one a feeling of entering the Middle Ages with its cobblestone floor. The town is wonderful and there is a tour of the crypts and a great stained glass museum/school across the square from the cathedral."

—LaurenSuite

Introduction by
Nancy Coons

Updated by
Simon Hewitt

TO SOME OBSERVERS THE ILE-DE-FRANCE is the most heartwarming of all the French provinces. First, there's the pleasure of imagination fulfilled: there's something comfortingly familiar about the lanes bordered with silvery poplar trees, the golden haze in the air, the gray stone of a village steeple. And no wonder, for scores of painters have immortalized these very features. Corot began with the forest of Fontainebleau and the village of Barbizon. Camille Pissarro worked at Pontoise. Alfred Sisley's famous riverside canvases were painted at Moret-sur-Loing, near Fontainebleau. Claude Monet painted the Epte River. And Vincent van Gogh thrived (creatively, at least) and died in Auvers.

But aside from these things, just what is it that makes the Ile-de-France so attractive? Is it its proximity to the great city of Paris—or perhaps that it's so far removed? Had there not been this world-class cultural hub right nearby, would Monet have retreated to his Japanese gardens at Giverny? Or Paul Cézanne and Van Gogh to bucolic Auvers? Kings and courtiers to the game-rich forests of Fontainebleau, Rambouillet, and Dampierre? Would medieval castles and palaces have sprouted in the towns of Vincennes and St-Germain-en-Laye? Would abbeys and cathedrals have sprung skyward in Chartres, Senlis, and Royaumont?

If you asked Louis XIV, he wouldn't have minced his words: The city of Paris—yawn—was simply *démodé*—out of fashion. In the 17th century, the new power base was going to be Versailles, once a tiny village in the heart of the Ile-de-France, now the site of a gigantic château from which the Sun King's rays (Louis XIV was known as *le roi soleil*) could radiate, unfettered by rebellious rabble and European arrivistes. Of course, later heirs kept the lines open and restored the grandiose palace as the governmental hub it was meant to be—and commuted to Paris, well before the high-speed RER.

That, indeed, is the dream of most Parisians today: to have a foot in both worlds. Paris may be small as capital cities go, with just under 2 million inhabitants, but Ile-de-France, the region around Paris, contains more than 10 million people—a sixth of France's entire population. That's why on closer inspection the once rustic villages of Ile-de-France reveal cosseted gardens, stylishly gentrified cottages, and extraordinary country restaurants no peasant farmer could afford to frequent. And that's why Ile-de-France retains a sophisticated air, along with a glowing patina of history, not found in any of France's other patches of verdure.

The Ile-de-France is the ancient heartland of France, the core from which the French kings gradually extended their power over the rest of a rebellious, individualistic nation. Since the time when it was first wrested from savage Gauls by Julius Caesar, in 52 BC, the region has played a leading role in French history; its towns and villages intimately entwined with the course of national fact and legend. Charlemagne confirmed his power in France after generations had fought against the Romans near Soissons. There is Versailles, from which the three Louis gloriously reigned until the forces of Revolution dealt the French monarchy a death blow. And Napoléon, after ruling for a time from Malmaison, abdicated his rule in the courtyard at Fontainebleau.

The Ile-de-France is not really an *île* (island), of course. This green-forested buffer zone that enfolds Paris is only vaguely surrounded by the three rivers that meander through its periphery. But France's capital city seems to crown this genteel sprawl of an atoll, peppered with pretty villages, anchored by grandiose châteaux. The spokes of railway and freeway that radiate every which way from the Paris ring road all merge gently into this verdant countryside.

Ile-de-France strikes a mellow balance, offering a rich and varied cross-section of Gallic culture . . . a minisampling of everything you expect from France, and all within easy day trips from Paris. With cathedrals, châteaux, and places immortalized by great painters, what more could you wish for? Well, how about Goofy on parade along Main Street U.S.A.? Pirates of the Caribbean? And Disney's own answer to Versailles, the bubblegum-pink turrets of Sleeping Beauty's Castle? Yes, the much-maligned, now renascent Disneyland Paris has taken root, drawing sellout crowds of Europeans wanting a taste of the American Dream—and of American families stealing a day from their Louvre schedule. It's just another epic vision realized against the green backdrop of Ile-de-France.

Exploring Ile-de-France

A great advantage to exploring Ile-de-France is that all its major monuments are within a half-day's drive from Paris. Though small, Ile-de-France is so rich in treasures that a whole day of fascinating exploration may take you no more than 60 km (35 mi) from the capital. The four tours suggested in the Great Itineraries section include the major points of interest: southwest from Paris to Versailles and Chartres; northwest along the Seine to St-Germain and Giverny; north and east along the Oise Valley via Chantilly to Disneyland; and southeast from Vaux-le-Vicomte to Fontainebleau.

About the Restaurants & Hotels

Not surprisingly, given its proximity to Paris and relatively well-heeled population, the Ile-de-France has no shortage of good restaurants; prices are generally cheaper than those in the capital and eating hours a little earlier—some restaurants may refuse to accept diners who arrive after 9 PM. Be aware that many restaurants popular with the locals, and so not over-reliant on tourist trade, close for up to a month in July and August. Restaurants abound in the larger tourist towns like Versailles, Chartres, and Fontainebleau, but it's best to book ahead in the smaller towns like Chantilly, Senlis, Barbizon, or Auvers-sur-Oise, where choice is limited.

In summer, hotel rooms are at a premium, and making reservations is essential; almost all accommodations in the swankier towns—Versailles, Rambouillet, and Fontainebleau—are on the costly side. Take nothing for granted; picturesque Senlis, for instance, does not have a single hotel in its historic downtown area. Assume that all hotel rooms have air-conditioning, TV, telephones, and private bath, unless otherwise noted.

With so many legendary sights in the Ile-de-France—many of which are gratifying human experiences rather than just guidebook necessities—you could spend weeks visiting the region. But if you don't have that much time, try one of the following shorter itineraries. Spend from three to eight days exploring the area or take day trips from Paris—most sites are within easy reach of the capital by car or train.

Numbers in the text correspond to numbers in the margin and on the Ile-de-France, Versailles, and Fontainebleau maps.

2

If you have 3 days

For a full blast of kingly splendor, first head west from Paris to nearby **St-Germain-en-Laye** ㉘ ► and visit the château and the Prieuré Museum—don't forget to take a promenade on the palace's stately Grande Terrasse. Try to reach 🚉 **Versailles** ❶–⓱ for lunch and then visit France's largest château and its park. The next morning spend more time in Versailles, then drive 55 km (30 mi) northwest—or return to Paris and train it out—to 🚉 **Giverny** ㉜ to visit Monet's famous home and water-lily garden. For your last day, head south to destinations either spiritual or secular—either the regal châteaux of **Rambouillet** ⓴ or **Maintenon** ㉑ or past the wheat fields of the Beauce to 🚉 **Chartres** ㉒, where you can spend half a day exploring the sublime cathedral and Vieille Ville.

If you have 5 days

Take the expressway north from Paris to **Senlis** ㊴ ►, visit the Vieille Ville and cathedral, then head to 🚉 **Chantilly** ㊳ for the afternoon to visit its exquisite château, replete with fabled art collection, grand park, and a regal stable. The next morning follow the Oise Valley, stopping briefly in the painters' village of **Auvers-sur-Oise** ㊱ en route to 🚉 **Versailles** ❶–⓱. Spend the morning of your third day in Versailles or **Rambouillet** ⓴; try to be in 🚉 **Chartres** ㉒ by early afternoon. Spend the night there and drive to the palace at 🚉 **Fontainebleau** ㊺ –㊿ the following morning, perhaps visiting the romantic forest village of **Barbizon** ㊹ on your way. On Day 5 make sure to visit **Vaux-le-Vicomte** ㊸—the 17th-century château whose splendor inspired the building of Versailles.

If you have 8 days

Spend your first day in medieval **Senlis** ㊴ ► and aristocratic 🚉 **Chantilly** ㊳. On the second day, head down the Oise Valley, via **Auvers-sur-Oise** ㊱ to haunt Van Gogh's footsteps and on to 🚉 **St-Germain-en-Laye** ㉘, where the 17th-century palace and gardens await. Head northwest down the Seine Valley to Monet's beloved 🚉 **Giverny** ㉜ on the third day; spend the night here or in nearby 🚉 **Vernon** ㉝. The following day take the expressway to that showstopper, 🚉 **Versailles** ❶–⓱. On the fifth day, go southwest to feast your eyes (and perhaps your soul) on the sublime cathedral at 🚉 **Chartres** ㉒, with a stop in at regal **Rambouillet** ⓴ or **Maintenon** ㉑ if time allows. On Day 6 head to the painters' forest of **Barbizon** ㊹ and 🚉 **Fontainebleau** ㊺–㊿, Napoléon's favorite palace; make it your base for two nights. On Day 7 don't miss the 17th-century splendor at **Vaux-le-Vicomte** ㊸, and also fit in that Impressionist jewel, **Moret-sur-Loing** ㊻; finish up on Day 8 at **Disneyland Paris** ㊷.

WHAT IT COSTS In euros					
	$$$$	**$$$**	**$$**	**$**	**¢**
RESTAURANTS	over €30	€23–€30	€17–€23	€11–€17	under €11
HOTELS	over €190	€120–€190	€80–€120	€50–€80	under €50

Restaurant prices are per person for a main course at dinner, including tax (19.6%) and service; note that if a restaurant offers only prix-fixe (set-price) meals, it has been given the price category that reflects the full prix-fixe price. Hotel prices are for a standard double room in high season, including tax (19.6%) and service charge. Hotels operate on the European Plan (EP, with no meal provided) unless we note that they use the Breakfast Plan (BP), or also offer such options as Modified American Plan (MAP, with breakfast and dinner daily, known as *demi-pension*), or Full American Plan (FAP, or *pension complète*, with three meals a day). Inquire when booking if these all-inclusive mealplans (which always entail higher rates) are mandatory or optional.

Timing

With its extensive forests, Ile-de-France is especially beautiful in the fall, particularly October. May and June are good months, too, but July through August can be sultry and crowded. On a Saturday night in summer you can see a son-et-lumière show in Moret-sur-Loing and make a candlelight visit to Vaux-le-Vicomte. Be aware when making your travel plans that some places are closed one or two days a week: the châteaux of Versailles and Auvers are closed on Monday; the Musée Tavet-Delacour in Pontoise is closed both Monday and Tuesday; and the châteaux of Chantilly and Fontainebleau are closed Tuesday. In fact, as a rule, well-touristed towns make their *fermeture hebdomadaire* (weekly closing) on Monday or Tuesday, when museums, shops and markets may be closed—call ahead if in doubt. Disneyland Paris gets really crowded on summer weekends. So does Giverny (Monet's garden), which is at its best May through June and, like Vaux-le-Vicomte, is closed November to March.

SOUTHWEST FROM VERSAILLES TO CHARTRES

Not only is majestic Versailles one of the most unforgettable sights in Ile-de-France, it's also within easy reach of Paris, less than 30 minutes by either train or car (A13 expressway from Porte d'Auteuil). It's also the starting point for a visit to southwestern Ile-de-France, which is anchored by Chartres to the south and Dreux to the west.

Versailles

16 km (10 mi) west of Paris via A13.

You'll need no reminding that you're in the world's grandest palace when you arrive at Versailles—gold, gold, and more gold, multicolor marbles, and acres of Charles Le Brun–painted ceilings will greet your eye. Corridors still warm with the spirits of Louis XIV, Madame de Pompadour, and Marie-Antoinette remind you that this voluptuous glory served as preface to the blood-stained French Revolution. Less a monument than an entire world unto itself, its immensity is such that some visitors con-

The Impressionist Ile

Paris's Musée d'Orsay may have some of the most fabled Monet and Van Gogh paintings in the world, but the Ile de France has something (almost) better—the actual landscapes that were rendered into masterpieces by the brushes of many great Impressionist and Postimpressionist artists. At Giverny, Claude Monet's house and garden is a moving visual link to his finest daubs—its famous lily-pond garden, designed by the artist himself, gave rise to his legendary water-lilies series (some historians feel it was the other way around). Elsewhere, villages like Vétheuil—where the master liked to set up his easel—still look like three-dimensional "Monets." In Auvers-sur-Oise, Vincent van Gogh had a final burst of creativity before ending his life; the famous wheat field where he was attacked by crows and painted his last painting is just outside town. André Derain lived in Chambourcy, Camille Pissarro in Pontoise, Alfred Sisley in Moret-sur-Loing—all were inspired by the silvery sunlight that tumbles over these hills and towns. Earlier, Rousseau, Millet, and Corot paved the way for Impressionism with their penchant for outdoor landscape painting in the village of Barbizon, still surrounded by its romantic, quietly dramatic forest. A trip to any of these towns will provide lasting impressions.

La Vie de Châteaux

Dukes and counts began building châteaux in the 11th century, when they needed to watch over parts of the king's lands and protect themselves from each other. Sparse, cold, and uninviting (that being the point), châteaux—the French word for castles—began as drafty stone fortresses. By the 17th century, when the age of feudal wars came to a close, castles began to be seen as pleasure palaces, sumptuous inside and out. The rich and the powerful were mightily attracted to the Ile-de-France partly because its many forests—large portions of which still stand—harbored sufficient game to ensure hunters' satisfaction, even for bloated, pampered monarchs. First Fontainebleau, in manageable Renaissance proportions, then Versailles—the world's most vainglorious palace, designed in minion-crushing Baroque—reflected the royal desire to transform hunting lodges into palatial residences. Other châteaux that exude almost comparable grandeur are at Vaux-le-Vicomte and Chantilly. And there are another dozen châteaux not quite as grandiose but still grand—such as Dampierre, Rambouillet, Maintenon, Maisons-Laffitte, and Thoiry.

Loosen Your Belts

Ile-de-France's fanciest restaurants can be just as pricey as their Parisian counterparts. Close to the Channel for fresh fish, to lush Normandy for beef and dairy products, and to the rich agricultural regions of Picardy and the Beauce, Ile-de-France chefs have all the ingredients they could wish for, and shop for the freshest produce early each morning at the huge food market at Rungis, (18 km [10mi]) south of the capital. Traditional "local delicacies"—lamb stew, *pâté de Pantin* (pastry filled with meat), or pig's trotters—tend to be obsolete, though soft, creamy Brie, made regionally in Meaux and Coulommiers, remains queen of the cheeseboard.

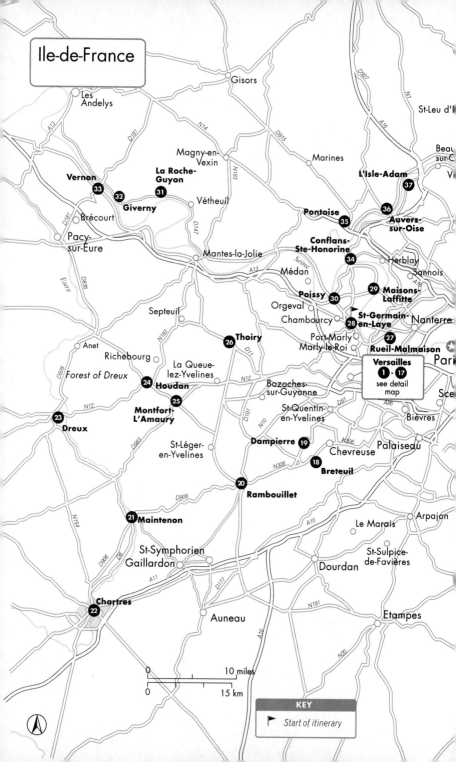

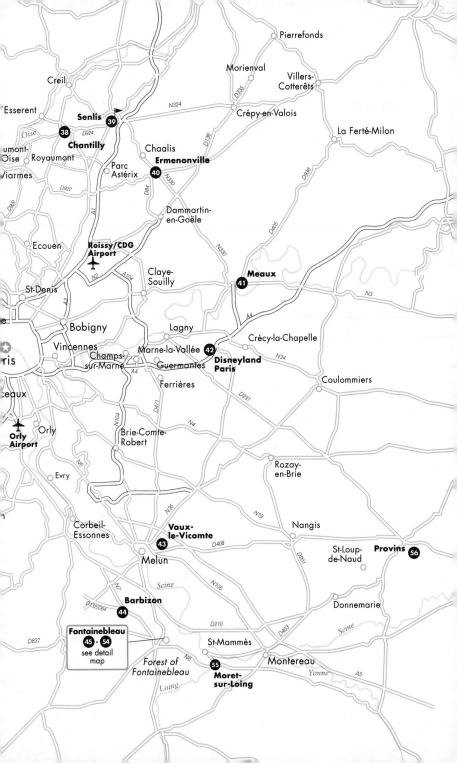

sider touring it more an ordeal than a pleasure. Even the Bourbon kings needed to escape its endless confines, and did so by building one of Europe's largest parks to surround the palace. So take a cue from them and remember: if the grandeur begins to overwhelm, the park outside the palace walls is the best place to come back down to earth.

The creation of Versailles is regarded by some historians as the result of a childhood shock suffered by the young king Louis XIV. With his mother, Anne of Austria, he was forced to flee Paris and was captured temporarily by a group of nobles, known as the Frondeurs. Louis developed a hatred for Paris and those Parisians who had sided with the conspirators. He lost no time in casting his cantankerous royal eye over Ile-de-France in search of a site for a new power base. Marshy, inhospitable Versailles became the object of his dreams. Down came his father's modest royal hunting lodge and up, up, and along rose a swank new palace.

The army of 20,000 noblemen, servants, and sycophants who moved into the huge **Château de Versailles** along with Louis is matched today by the battalions of visitors—three million a year. You may be able to avoid the crowds (and lines for tours) if you arrive here at 9 AM. The hard part is figuring out where you're supposed to go once you arrive. The main entrance is near the top of the courtyard to the right; there are different lines depending on tour, physical ability, and group status. Frequent guided tours in English visit the private royal apartments. More detailed hour-long tours explore the opera house or Marie-Antoinette's private parlors. You can go through the grandest rooms—including the Hall of Mirrors and Marie-Antoinette's stunningly opulent bedchamber—without a group tour (by means of yet another line). To figure out the system, pick up a brochure at the information office or ticket counter. If you plan on spending the day, keep in mind that you can purchase sandwiches in the town of Versailles (whether you can sneak them past the front-door guards is another question) or opt for luncheon at La Flotille restaurant by the Grand Canal.

Versailles was dreamed up as a gigantic palace flanked by avenues broader than the Champs-Élysées, all in bicep-flexing Baroque, on a scale designed by the 23-year-old Louis to dwarf the provocatively lavish château of Vaux-le-Vicomte that had recently been erected by his own finance minister. As time wore on and styles changed, Louis XIV's successors felt out of sync with this architectural inheritance. Louis XV exchanged the heavy red-and-gilt of Italianate Baroque for lighter, pastel-hued Rococo. In doing so, he transformed the daunting royal apartments into places to live rather than pose. The hapless Louis XVI cowered in the Petit Trianon, in the leafy depths of Versailles's gardens, out of the shadow of the mighty château. His queen, Marie-Antoinette, seems to have lost her senses well before she lost her head in 1793, by playing at being a peasant shepherdess amid the ersatz rusticity and perfumed flocks of sheep of the Hameau, a faux farm and village she had created just beyond the precincts of the Petit Trianon.

The château was built between 1662 and 1690 by architects Louis Le Vau and Jules Hardouin-Mansart. These days, a 17-year, $500-million-restoration program is underway, but most of the work is structural and unlikely to interfere with your visit. You arrive through gilt-iron gates from the huge place d'Armes. The center of the palace was the living quarters of the king and queen, and the two gigantic wings were occupied by the royal children and princes of the blood. Courtiers had to make do in the attics and distant apartments—while luxurious, Versailles proved to be as crowded and noisy as a tenement, much to the distress of the courtiers who had been commanded to forsake their country homes for this Pentagon-size dwelling. On the first floor of the château, dead center across the sprawling cobbled forecourt beyond the Sun King's statue, is **Louis XIV's bedchamber,** but the real headliner is the sparkling **Galerie des Glaces** (Hall of Mirrors). It was here, after France's capitulation, that Otto von Bismarck proclaimed the unified German Empire in 1871; and here that the Treaty of Versailles, asserting Germany's responsibility for World War I, was signed in 1919. The **Grands Appartements** (state apartments), which flank the Hall of Mirrors, retain most of their original Baroque decoration: gilt stucco, painted ceilings, and marble sculpture. Perhaps the most extravagant is the **Salon d'Apollon** (Apollo Chamber), the former throne room, dedicated to the sun god Apollo, Louis XIV's mythical hero. The **Petits Appartements** (private apartments), where the royal family and friends lived in relative seclusion, provide an intimate contrast.

In the north wing of the château are the solemn white-and-gold **Chapelle** (chapel), completed in 1710; the intimate **Opéra Royal** (Opera House), the first oval-shape hall in France, built by Jacques-Ange Gabriel for Louis XV in 1770 and entirely constructed of wood painted over to look like marble; and, connecting the two, the 17th-century **Galeries,** with exhibits retracing the château's history. The south wing contains the bombastic **Galerie des Batailles** (Hall of Battles), lined with gigantic canvases extolling French military glory. The former state rooms and sumptuous debate chamber of the **Aile du Midi** (South Wing) are also open to the public, with infrared headphones (English commentary available) recounting Versailles's parliamentary history. ☒ *Pl. d'Armes* ☎ *01–30–83–78–00* ⊕ *www.chateauversailles.fr* ☐ *Château €7.50, parliament exhibition €3 extra* ☉ *Apr.–Oct., Tues.–Sun. 9–6:30; Nov.–Mar., Tues.–Sun. 9–5:30. Tours of Opéra Royal and Petits Appartements every 15 mins (€6) from Entrance D.*

★ ❷ After the awesome feast of interior pomp, the **Parc de Versailles** (Versailles Park) is an ideal place to catch your breath. The 250-acre grounds, designed by André Le Nôtre, represent classical French landscaping at its most formal and sophisticated and include woods, lawns, flower beds, statues, artificial lakes, and fountains galore. The Three Fountains grove near the Bassin de Neptune was restored to its original glory in 2004, and an extensive tree-replacement scheme—necessary once a century—was launched in 1998 to recapture the full impact of Le Nôtre's artful vistas; replantings became all the more necessary after 10,000 trees were uprooted by a hurricane in 1999. The cost of that damage came to some $35 million, and American donors contributed 40% of that amount. The distances are vast—the Trianons themselves are more than a mile from

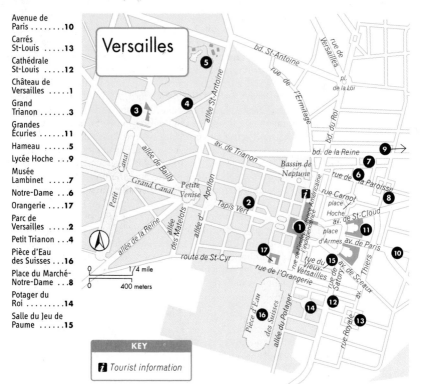

the château—so you might want to climb aboard a horse-drawn carriage (round-trip from the château to Trianon, €7, www.calechesversailles.com), take the electric train (€5.20 round-trip), or rent a bike from the **Grille de la Reine** near the Trianon Palace Hotel (€4.50 per hour) or from the **Petite-Venise** (☎ 01–39–66–97–66 🖃 €5.20 per hr, or €26 for 6 hrs) building at the top of the Grand Canal. You can also drive to the Trianons and Canal through the Grille de la Reine (€5.50 per car). The park is at its golden-leafed best in the fall but is also enticing in summer—especially on Sunday afternoon from mid-April through mid-October, when the fountains are in full flow. ☎ 01–30–83–77–88 for guided tour 🖃 Park free; gardens €3 from Apr.–Oct., free Nov.–Mar., €6 for Sun. fountain displays ☉ Daily 7 AM–8 PM or dusk.

❸ The **Grand Trianon**, built by Hardouin-Mansart in 1687, is a pink-marble pleasure palace which is occasionally used to entertain visiting heads of state. But most of the time it is open to visitors, who can admire its lavish interior and early-19th-century furnishings. ☎ 01–30–84–75–43 🖃 Joint ticket with Petit Trianon €5 ☉ Tues.–Sun. noon–5:30.

★ ❹ Art historians go weak in the knees when they tour the **Petit Trianon**—although you may wonder what all the hubbub is about. That was precisely the point: a bijou palace, this abode—built by the great Gabriel,

SAVE MARIE-ANTOINETTE

WAS MARIE-ANTOINETTE A luxury-mad butterfly flitting from ball to costume ball? Or was she a misunderstood queen who suffered a loveless marriage and became a prisoner of court etiquette at Versailles? Historians now believe the answer was the latter and point to her private retreats at Versailles as proof.

Here, in the northwest part of the royal park, far from the main palace, Marie-Antoinette created a tiny universe of her own: her comparatively dainty mansion called the Petit Trianon and its adjacent "farm," the still extant, still magnificently lovely Hameau ("hamlet"). In a life that took her from royal cradle to throne of France to guillotine, her happiest days were spent at Trianon.

For here she could live a life in the "simplest" possible way; here the queen could enter a salon and the game of cards would not stop; here women wore simple gowns of muslin without a single jewel; here she could be called "Toni." Toinette only wanted to be "Queen of Trianon," not queen of France. And considering the horrible, chamber-pot-pungent, gossip-infested corridors of Versailles, you can almost understand why.

From the first, Maria-Antonia (her actual name), was ostracized as an outsider, "l'Autrichienne," an Austrian. Married to Louis XVI—a well-meaning but wishy-washy husband—and shamed by her initial failure to deliver a royal heir, she grew to hate overcrowded Versailles and soon escaped to the Trianon, built from 1763–68 in the English "Adamesque" style by Jacques-Ange Gabriel for Madame de Pompadour, who died before it was finished. After becoming queen in 1774, Toinette refashioned the interior, banishing the gilt trip of Rococo. Instead, sober Neoclassical boiseries, distinguished Riesener and Carlin bureaus, and walls painted in that most dramatic of new shades—off-white—

revealed a sea change in taste. Today her spirit is still present, thanks in part to collectors who have saved her bibelots—including the ivory clock fashioned for her by Louis XVI himself—and furniture; her initials still can be seen on the wrought-iron railings of the staircase.

Beyond the Petit Trianon lay the queen's storybook Hameau, a mock-Norman village inspired by the peasant-luxe daydreams caught by Boucher on canvas and by Rousseau in literature. Here Marie-Antoinette lived out her romanticized idyll of "the simple life." With its water mill, genuine lake (Grand Lac), thatched-roof houses built in daub-and-wattle style, pigeon loft, and vegetable plots, this make-believe farm village was run by Monsieur Valy-Busard, a farmer, and his wife, who often helped the queen—outfitted as a Dresden shepherdess with a Sèvres porcelain crook—tend her flock of perfumed sheep.

As if to destroy any last link with reality, the queen built nearby a jewel-box theater (open by appointment). Here she acted in little plays, sometimes essaying the role of a servant girl. Only the immediate royal family, about seven or so titled friends, and her personal servants were permitted entry; disastrously, the entire officialdom of Versailles society was shut out—a move that only served to infuriate courtiers. This is how fate and destiny close the circle. For it was here at Trianon that a page sent by Monsieur de Saint-Priest found Marie-Antoinette on October 5, 1789, to tell her that Paris was marching on an already half-deserted Versailles.

A 21st-century version of Toinette is in the works, thanks to a film now being shot by Sofia Coppola and starring Kirsten Dunst. No matter how good this may turn out to be, it will always pale compared to the splendor of MGM's 1938 Marie Antoinette and Norma Shearer's star turn.

— Robert I. C. Fisher

architect of Paris's Place de la Concorde, upon command of Madame de Pompadour, Louis XV's amour—was a radical statement, since, for a royal residence, its design was so casual and unassuming. Here *le Bien-Aimé*—the Well-Beloved (as the king was called)—and his consort escaped from the pomp at Versailles, abandoning royal duties the better to play with lap dogs, translate poetry, and plan gala balls. *Joint ticket with Grand Trianon €5* ☉ *Tues.–Sun. noon–5:30.*

When La Pompadour died, the house passed to Queen Marie-Antoinette, who refurnished it in the Neoclassical style (made fashionable by the rediscovery of Pompeii) while painting its rooms in the pastel hues of Pierre-Joseph Redouté's flowers paintings. Here, across the Petit Lac **⑤** "Toinette" built her **Hameau** (hamlet; ☎ 01–30–83–77–43), a mock Normandy village where she could play out her idyll of peasant life, pretending to be a shepherdess tending her flock—which happened to be perfumed sheep. Nearby is the tiny jewel-box **Théâtre de la Reine** the queen often used to put on theatricals for her immediate family. The interior is a wonder of 18th-century luxe. Restored in the 1980s, it is now open by appointment only and probably remains the best place to channel the queen's spirit. As she was so happy to take the stage to enact the roles of maids in frothy comedies it is little wonder she lost sight of reality and the first rumblings of revolution (for more on this hapless figure, see the CloseUp box "Save Marie-Antoinette").

The town of Versailles itself—the capital of France from 1682 to 1789 and again from 1871 to 1879—is easily underestimated, despite its broad, leafy boulevards and majestic buildings. You may feel too tired from exploring the palace and park to spend time visiting the town—but it's worth some effort. Leave the château park by the Bassin de Neptune and turn right onto rue des Réservoirs, past the classical Théâtre Montansier. Up to the right you can make out Louis XIV's equestrian statue in the château courtyard; away in the other direction is the church spire of neighboring Le Chesnay. Rue Carnot, opposite, leads past the stately Écuries de la Reine, once the queen's stables, now the regional law courts, to octagonal place Hoche. Down rue Hoche to the left is **⑥** the powerful Baroque facade of **Notre-Dame,** built from 1684 to 1686 by Jules Hardouin-Mansart as the parish church for Louis XIV's new town. Around the back of Notre-Dame, on boulevard de la Reine (note the regimented lines of trees), are the elegant Hôtel de Neyret and the **⑦** **Musée Lambinet,** a sumptuous mansion from 1751, furnished with paintings, weapons, fans, and porcelain. ✉ *54 bd. de la Reine* ☎ *01–39–50–30–32* 💲 *€5* ☉ *Tues.–Sun. 2–5.*

Take a right onto rue Le Nôtre, then go left and right again into passage de la Geôle, a cobbled alley, lined with quaint antiques shops, that **⑧** climbs up to **place du Marché-Notre-Dame,** whose open-air morning market on Tuesday, Friday, and Sunday is famed throughout the region; there are also four 19th-century timber-roof halls with fish, meat, and spice stalls. Cross the square and head up rue de la Paroisse to avenue de St-**⑨** Cloud. Around to the left is the **Lycée Hoche,** whose domed, colonnaded chapel was once part of a convent built for Louis XV's queen, Maria Leszczynska, in 1767.

❿ Cross avenue de St-Cloud and head along rue Montbauron to **Avenue de Paris**; its breadth of 120 yards makes it wider than the Champs-Élysées, and its buildings are just as grand and even more historic. Note the mighty doorway at the **Hôtel de Police** on your left and then, at No. 21, the pretty **Hôtel du Barry.** Cross the avenue and return toward the château, past the **Hôtel des Menus-Plaisirs,** where the States General held its first session in May 1789. Just opposite, behind an imposing grille, is the elaborate 19th-century **Préfecture** (the regional government building), confronting the even larger—but uglier—stone-and-brick **Hôtel de Ville** (Town Hall). Avenue de Paris leads down to place d'Armes, a vast sloping plaza usually filled with tourist buses. Facing the château are the Trojan-size

⓫ royal stables. The **Grandes Écuries** (Grand Stables), to the right, house the **Musée des Carrosses** (Carriage Museum), open summer weekends only (€2), and the **Manège,** where you can see 28 white horses and their riders, trained by the great equine choreographer Bartabas, practicing every morning. ⊠ *1 av. de Paris* ☎ *01–39–02–07–14* 🎫 *€7* ⊘ *Tues.–Fri., 9–noon, weekends 11–2.*

Turn left from the Grandes Écuries, cross Avenue de Sceaux and Avenue de Paris, pass the imposing chancellery on the corner, and take rue de

⓬ Satory—a cute pedestrian shopping-street—to the domed **Cathédrale St-Louis,** with its twin-towered facade, built from 1743 to 1754 and enriched with a fine organ and paintings. Turn left down narrow rue du

⓭ Marché to reach the ramshackle but photogenic **Carrés St-Louis,** a prototype of 18th-century housing development.

⓮ Rue d'Anjou leads down to the 6-acre **Potager du Roi,** the lovingly restored, split-level royal fruit-and-vegetable garden created in 1683 by Jean-Baptiste de La Quintinye. ⊠ *Entrance at 4 rue Hardy* ☎ *01–39–24–62–62* 🎫 *€6.50* ⊘ *Apr.–Oct., daily 10–6.*

From the Potager du Roi, return up rue de Satory and take rue du Vieux-Versailles, just as old—in parts, actually decrepit—and full of charac-

⓯ ter as its name suggests. The **Salle du Jeu de Paume,** the indoor tennis court (built in 1686) where the Third Estate swore to transform absolutist France into a constitutional monarchy on June 20, 1789, is off to the right. ⊠ *1 rue du Jeu-de-Paume* ☎ *01–30–83–77–88* 🎫 *Free* ⊘ *Apr.–Oct., weekends 12:30–6:30.*

Rue de l'Indépendance-Américaine leads from the top of rue du Vieux-Versailles up to the château, where Louis XIV, quite uncoincidentally, is clearly visible on his prancing steed. Admire the sculpted porticoes and gilded Sun King emblems on the 17th- and 18th-century state build-

⓰ ings lining the street. In the other direction, it leads down to the **Pièce d'Eau des Suisses,** a large artificial lake. Opposite the lake is the stately

⓱ **Orangerie,** erected by Hardouin-Mansart from 1684 to 1686. From November through Easter the Orangerie serves as a hothouse, when it is packed with the orange and palm trees that are artfully moved to the front in summer. Two monumental flights of steps lead up to the château terrace above.

Where to Stay & Eat

★ **$$$$** ✕ **Les Trois Marches.** In the Trianon Palace hotel, celebrated chef Gérard Vié's take on *cuisine bourgeoise* is one of the most luxe around—you'll find it hard to wait for your meal after perusing the menu, studded with delights like turbot *galette* (cake) with onions and *pommes Anna*, cassoulet with Codiza sausages, and a sublime duck simmered with turnips and truffles. In pleasant weather, you can opt to dine on the long, attractive terrace. ⊠ *1 bd. de la Reine* ☎ *01–30–84–52–00* ⌂ *Reservations essential* ⍟ *Jacket and tie* ▭ *AE, DC, MC, V* ⊘ *Closed Sun., Mon., and Aug.*

$–$$ ✕ **Quai No. 1.** Fish and seafood rule supreme amid the sails, barometers, and model ships of this quaintly decked-out restaurant. Lobster and house-smoked salmon are specialties. Eating à la carte isn't too expensive, and there are good-value prix-fixe menus at €17 and €25. ⊠ *1 av. de St-Cloud* ☎ *01–39–50–42–26* ▭ *MC, V* ⊘ *Closed Mon. No dinner Sun.*

★ **$$$$** ✕⌂ **Trianon Palace.** A modern-day Versailles, this deluxe hotel is in a turn-of-the-20th-century creation of imposing size, filled with soaring rooms (including the historic Salle Clemenceau, site of the 1919 Versailles Peace Conference) and with a huge garden close to the château park. Once faded, the hotel is now aglitter with a health club (the pool idles beneath a glass pyramid) and Les Trois Marches restaurant, one of France's best. Try to avoid the newer annex, the Pavillon Trianon, and insist on the full treatment in the main building (and ask for one of the even-numbered rooms, which look out over the woods near the Trianons; odd-numbered rooms overlook the modern annex). ⊠ *1 bd. de la Reine, 78000* ☎ *01–30–84–51–20* 🖷 *01–30–84–50–01* ⊕ *www.trianonpalace.fr* ⇨ *165 rooms, 27 suites* ⌂ *Restaurant, minibars, cable TV, pool, health club, Internet, business services* ▭ *AE, DC, MC, V* ⍾ *BP.*

$ ⌂ **Le Cheval Rouge.** This unpretentious old hotel, built in 1676, is in a corner of the town market square, close to the château and strongly recommended if you plan to explore the town on foot. Some rooms around the old stable courtyard have their original wood beams. ⊠ *18 rue André-Chénier, 78000* ☎ *01–39–50–03–03* 🖷 *01–39–50–61–27* ⊕ *www.chevalrouge.fr.st* ⇨ *38 rooms* ⌂ *Cable TV, bar, some pets allowed (fee); no a/c* ▭ *AE, MC, V.*

$ ⌂ **Home St-Louis.** This family-run, three-story stone-and-brick hotel is a good, cheap, quiet bet—close to the cathedral and not too far from the château. ⊠ *28 rue St-Louis, 78000* ☎ *01–39–50–23–55* 🖷 *01–39–21–62–45* ⇨ *25 rooms* ⌂ *Some pets allowed; no a/c* ▭ *AE, MC, V.*

Nightlife & the Arts

The largest fountain in Versailles' château park, the Bassin de Neptune, becomes a spectacle of rare grandeur during the **Fêtes de Nuit** (☎ 01–30–83–78–88 for details), a light-and-fireworks show held every Saturday evening in July and September. Directed by Bartabas, the **Académie du Spectacle Equestre** (☎ 01–39–02–07–14) stages hour-long shows on weekend afternoons of horses performing to music—sometimes with riders, sometimes without—in the converted 17th-century

Manège (riding school) at the Grandes Écuries opposite the palace. The **Mois Molière** (☎ 01–30–97–84–48) in June heralds a program of concerts, drama, and exhibits inspired by the famous playwright. The **Théâtre Montansier** (☎ 01–39–24–05–06) has a full program of plays. The **Centre de Musique Baroque** (⊕ www.cmbv.com) often presents concerts of Baroque music in the château opera and chapel.

Shopping

Aux Colonnes (✉ 14 rue Hoche) is a highly rated *confiserie* (candy shop) with a cornucopia of chocolates and candies; it's closed Monday. **Les Délices du Palais** (✉ 4 rue du Maréchal-Foch) has all the makings for an impromptu picnic (cold cuts, cheese, salads); it's also closed Monday. **Le Gall** (✉ 15 rue Ducis) has a huge choice of cheeses—including one of France's widest selections of goat cheeses; it's closed Sunday afternoon and Monday. **Passage de la Geôle,** which is open Friday–Sunday 9–7 and is close to the town's stupendous market, houses several good antiques shops.

Breteuil

⓲ *27 km (17 mi) southwest of Versailles, 58 km (35 mi) southwest of Paris, 6 km (4 mi) south of Chevreuse on the N305.*

The elegant, mansard-roofed **Château de Breteuil,** built in 1610, houses Swedish porcelain, Gobelin tapestries, the richly inlaid Teschen Table encrusted with pearls and precious stones, and dozens of life-size wax figures—including onetime guests English king Edward VII and French novelist Marcel Proust. The vast wooded park has picnic areas, a playground, a pigeon loft, a maze, and more waxwork tableaux representing Puss in Boots, Tom Thumb, and other fairy-tale figures from the works of Charles Perrault. ☎ *01–30–52–05–11* ⊕ *www.chateaudebreteuil.fr* ✉ *Château and grounds €9.60, grounds only €6.50* ⊙ *Château Mon.–Sat. 2:30–6, Sun. 11–6; grounds daily 10–6.*

The surrounding **Chevreuse Valley** is a scenic region of hills and woods replete with old churches, abbeys, castles, and houses for the well-heeled. Lovers of 17th-century literature may enjoy exploring the **Chemin de Racine** (Racine Trail) lined with panels bearing verse by the great poet and dramatist. The path runs between Port-Royal, where Racine studied in the 1650s, and the pretty town of Chevreuse, where there's a regional museum and visitor center in the **Château de la Madeleine,** a hilltop castle (⊕ www.parc-naturel-chevreuse.org ⊙ daily 2–5:30). Also of note is handsome 13th-century church of **Notre-Dame de la Roche.**

Dampierre

⓳ *5 km (3 mi) northwest of Breteuil via D906 and D149, 21 km (13 mi) southwest of Versailles via D91.*

The unspoiled village of Dampierre is adorned with one of the most elegant family seats in Ile-de-France. The stone-and-brick **Château de Dampierre,** surrounded by a moat and set well back from the road, was rebuilt in the 1670s by Hardouin-Mansart for the Duc de Luynes. Much of the interior retains its 17th-century decoration—portraits, wood paneling, furniture, and works of art. But the main staircase, with its trompel'oeil murals, and the richly gilded **Salle des Fêtes** (ballroom) date from the 19th century. This second-floor chamber contains a huge wall painting by the celebrated artist Jean-Auguste-Dominique Ingres (1780–1867), an idealized evocation of the mythical Age d'Or (Golden Age)—fitting, perhaps, since this aristocratic family did many good deeds and was even beloved by locals and farmers during the French Revolution. The large park, fronted by gigantic gates, was planned by Versailles landscape architect André Le Nôtre. ⊠ *2 Grande-Rue* ☏ *01–30–52–53–24* ⊕ *www. chateau-de-dampierre.com* ⊠ *€8, grounds only €5.20* ☉ *Apr.–mid-Oct., Mon.–Sat. 2–6:30, Sun. 11–noon and 2–6:30.*

Rambouillet

➋⓿ *16 km (10 mi) southwest of Dampierre via D91 and D906, 32 km (20 mi) southwest of Versailles, 42 km (26 mi) southwest of Paris.*

Haughty Rambouillet, once favored by kings and dukes, is now home to affluent gentry and, occasionally, the French president. The **Château de Rambouillet** is surrounded by a magnificent 30,000-acre forest that remains a great place for biking and walking. Most of the château dates from the early 18th century, but the brawny **Tour François-I**er (François I Tower), named for the king who died here in 1547, was part of the fortified castle that stood on this site in the 14th century. Highlights include the wood-paneled apartments, especially the **Boudoir de la Comtesse** (Countess's Dressing Room); the marble-wall **Salle de Marbre** (Marble Hall), dating from the Renaissance; and the **Salle de Bains de Napoléon** (Napoléon's Bathroom), adorned with Pompeii-style frescoes. Compared to the muscular forecourt, the château's lakeside facade is a sight of unsuspected serenity and, as flowers spill from its balconies, cheerful informality. ☏ *01–34–83–00–25* ⊕ *www.monum.fr* ⊠ *€6.10* ☉ *Daily 10–11:30 and 2–5:30.*

An extensive **park**, with a lake with small islands, stretches behind the château, site of the extraordinary **Laiterie de la Reine** (Queen's Dairy), built for Marie-Antoinette, who, inspired by the writings of Jean-Jacques Rousseau, came here to escape from the pressures of court life, pretending to be a simple milkmaid. It has a small marble temple and grotto and, nearby, the shell-lined Chaumière des Coquillages (Shell Pavilion). The **Bergerie Nationale** (National Sheepfold) is the site of a more serious agricultural venture: The merinos raised here, prized for the quality and yield of their wool, are descendants of sheep imported from Spain by Louis XVI in 1786. A museum alongside tells the tale and evokes shepherd life. The park's exotic, storybook beauty once inspired Jean-Honoré Fragonard to paint one of the greatest landscape paintings of the 18th century, the *Fête at Rambouillet* (now in the Gulbenkian Museum in Lisbon), which tellingly depicts a gilded, courtier-filled barge about to enter a stretch of river torn by raging rapids. "*Apres moi, le deluge,*" indeed. ⊠ *Dairy and Shell Pavilion €3, Sheepfold €4* ☉ *Dairy Apr.–Sept., Wed.–Mon. 10–noon and 2–5:30; Oct.–Mar., Wed.–Mon. 10–noon and 2–3:30; Sheepfold mid-Jan.–mid-Dec., Wed.–Sun. 2–5.*

Some 4,000 models, some dating back to 1885, and more than 1,300 feet of track make the **Musée Rambolitrain** a serious model-train museum. It has historic steam engines, old-time stations, and a realistic points and signaling system. ⊠ *4 pl. Jeanne-d'Arc* ☎ *01–34–83–15–93* ✆ *€3.50* ☉ *Wed.–Sun. 10–noon and 2–5:30.*

Where to Eat

$–$$ ✕ **La Poste.** You can bank on traditional, unpretentious cooking at this lively former coaching inn right in the center of town. Service is good, as is the selection of prix-fixe menus (€20–€32). Chicken fricassee with crayfish is a specialty, along with game in season. ⊠ *101 rue du Général-de-Gaulle* ☎ *01–34–83–03–01* ▭ *AE, MC, V* ☉ *Closed Mon. No dinner Sun. or Thurs.*

Maintenon

㉑ *23 km (14 mi) southwest of Rambouillet via D906, 65 km (41 mi) southwest of Paris.*

Vestiges of Louis XIV, both atmospheric and architectural, make Maintenon an intriguing stopover on the road to Chartres. The **Château de Maintenon** once belonged to Louis XIV's second wife, Françoise Scarron—better known as Madame de Maintenon—whom he married morganatically in 1684 (as social inferiors, neither she nor her children could claim a royal title). She had acquired the château as a young widow 10 years earlier, and her private apartments are the focus of an interior visit. A round brick tower (16th century) and square 12th-century keep give the ensemble a muscular dignity. Mirrored in a canal that contains the waters of the Eure, this is one of the most picturesque châteaux in France. Inside, lush salons are done up in the Louis XIII style (or rather, in the Second Empire, 19th-century version of it), a homage to royal roots created by the Ducs de Noailles, one of France's most aristocratic families, which has maintained Maintenon as one of its family homes for centuries. ⊠ *Pl. Aristide-Briand* ☎ *02–37–23–00–09* ✆ *€6.20* ☉ *Apr.–Oct., Wed.–Mon. 2–6:30; Nov.–mid-Dec. and late Jan.–Mar., weekends 2–5:30.*

Looming at the back of the château garden and extending through the village almost from the train station to highway D6 are the unlikely ivy-covered arches of a ruined **aqueduct,** one of the Sun King's most outrageous projects. The original scheme aimed to provide the ornamental lakes in the gardens of Versailles (some 50 km [31 mi] away) with water from the River Eure. In 1684, 30,000 men were signed up to construct a three-tiered, 5-km (3-mi) aqueduct as part of the project. Many died in the process, and construction was called off in 1689.

Where to Stay & Eat

★ **¢–$** ✕ **Bistrot d'Adeline.** This small, rustic bistro on the main street close to the château in Maintenon offers a cheerful welcome and home cooking with sauces, stews, and *tête de veau* (calf's head) among the specialties. There's a good-value three-course set menu at lunchtime for just €11. ⊠ *3 rue Collin-d'Harleville* ☎ *02–37–23–06–67* ✑ *Reservations essential* ▭ *No credit cards* ☉ *Closed Sun., Mon., and part of Aug.*

$$$-$$$$ ×⊞ **Château d'Esclimont.** Graced with pointed turrets, *pièces d'eau*
Fodor'sChoice (moated pools), and a checkerboard facade, this 19th-century château—
★ built by the de La Rochefoucaulds—is well worth seeking out if you wish
to eat and sleep like an aristocrat. This member of the Relais & Châteaux
group is replete with luxuriously furnished guest rooms (many are loftily
dimensioned, others snug in corner turrets) adorned with reproduction
18th-century French pieces. Carved stone garlands, cordovan leathers,
brocades, and period antiques grace the public salons; the superbly
manicured grounds cradle a heated pool. The cuisine is sophisticated:
quail, lamb, lobster, and game in season top the menu at the restaurant,
La Rochefoucauld (dinner reservations are essential, and a jacket and
tie are required, as is a very fat wallet). ⊠ *2 rue du Château-d'Esclimont,
19 km (12 mi) southeast of Maintenon: take D116 to village of Gail-
lardon, keep an eye out for the imposing church, then turn left, 28700
St-Symphorien-le-Château* ☎ *02–37–31–15–15* 🖷 *02–37–31–57–91*
⊕ *www.esclimont.com* 🖙 *46 rooms, 6 suites* ♲ *Restaurant, minibars,
cable TV, 2 tennis courts, pool, fishing, Internet, helipad; no a/c* ▭ *AE,
DC, MC, V* ¶◎¶ *MAP.*

Chartres

❷❷ *19 km (12 mi) southwest of Maintenon via D906, 88 km (55 mi) south-
west of Paris.*

If Versailles is the climax of French secular architecture, perhaps
Chartres is its religious apogee. All the descriptive prose and poetry that
have been lavished on this supreme cathedral can only begin to sug-
gest the glory of its 12th- and 13th-century statuary and stained glass,
somehow suffused with burning mysticism and a strange sense of the
numinous. Chartres is more than a church—it's a nondenominational
spiritual experience.

If you arrive in summer from Maintenon across the edge of the Beauce,
the richest agrarian plain in France, you can see Chartres's spires rising
up from oceans of wheat. The whole town—with its old houses and pic-
turesque streets—is worth a leisurely exploration. From rue du Pont-
St-Hilaire there is an intriguing view of the rooftops below the cathedral.
Ancient streets tumble down from the cathedral to the river, lined most
weekends with bouquinistes selling old books and prints. Each year on
August 15, pilgrims and tourists flock here for the Procession du Voeu
de Louis XIII, a religious procession through the streets commemorat-
ing the French monarchy's vow to serve the Virgin Mary.

Fodor'sChoice Worship on the site of the **Cathédrale Notre-Dame,** better known as
★ Chartres Cathedral, goes back to before the Gallo-Roman period; the
crypt contains a well that was the focus of Druid ceremonies. In the late
9th century Charles II (known as the Bald) presented Chartres with what
was believed to be the tunic of the Virgin Mary, a precious relic that
went on to attract hordes of pilgrims. The current cathedral, the sixth
church on the spot, dates mainly from the 12th and 13th centuries and
was erected after the previous building, dating from the 11th century,
burned down in 1194. A well-chronicled outburst of religious fervor fol-

lowed the discovery that the Virgin Mary's relic had miraculously survived unsinged. Princes and paupers, barons and bourgeois gave their money and their labor to build the new cathedral. Ladies of the manor came to help monks and peasants on the scaffolding in a tremendous resurgence of religious faith that followed the Second Crusade. Just 25 years were needed for Chartres Cathedral to rise again, and it has remained substantially unchanged since.

The lower half of the facade survives from the earlier Romanesque church: this can be seen most clearly in the use of round arches rather than the pointed Gothic type. The **Royal Portal** is richly sculpted with scenes from the life of Christ—these sculpted figures are among the greatest created during the Middle Ages. The taller of the two spires (380 feet versus 350 feet) was built at the start of the 16th century, after its predecessor was destroyed by fire; its fanciful Flamboyant intricacy contrasts sharply with the stumpy solemnity of its Romanesque counterpart (access €3). The **rose window** above the main portal dates from the 13th century, and the three windows below it contain some of the finest examples of 12th-century stained-glass artistry in France.

Your eyes will need time to adjust to the somber interior. The reward is seeing the gemlike richness of the stained glass, with the famous deep Chartres blue predominating. The oldest window is arguably the most beautiful: **Notre-Dame de la Belle Verrière** (Our Lady of the Lovely Window), in the south choir. The cathedral's windows are being gradually cleaned—a lengthy, painstaking process—and the contrast with those still covered in the grime of centuries is staggering. It's worth taking a pair of binoculars along with you to pick out the details. If you wish to know more about stained-glass techniques and the motifs used, visit the small exhibit in the gallery opposite the north porch. For even more detail, try to arrange a tour (in English) with local institution Malcolm Miller, whose knowledge of the cathedral's history is formidable. (He leads tours twice a day Monday through Saturday; the cost is €10. You can reach him at the telephone number below.) The vast black-and-white labyrinth on the floor of the nave is one of the few to have survived from the Middle Ages; the faithful were expected to travel along its entire length (some 300 yards) on their knees. Guided tours of the **Crypte** start from the Maison de la Crypte opposite the south porch. You can also see a 4th-century Gallo-Roman wall and some 12th-century wall paintings. ⊠ *16 cloître Notre-Dame* ☎ *02-37-21-56-33* ⊕ *www.ville-chartres.fr* ▧ *Crypt €2.30* ☯ *Cathedral 8:30–7:30, guided tours of crypt Easter–Oct., daily at 11, 2:15, 3:30, 4:30, and 5:15; Nov.–Easter, daily at 11 and 4.*

The **Musée des Beaux-Arts** (Fine Arts Museum) is in a handsome 18th-century building just behind the cathedral that used to serve as the bishop's palace. Its varied collection includes Renaissance enamels, a portrait of Erasmus by Holbein, tapestries, armor, and some fine (mainly French) paintings from the 17th, 18th, and 19th centuries. There's also a room devoted to the forceful 20th-century landscapes of Maurice de Vlaminck, who lived in the region. ⊠ *29 cloître Notre-Dame* ☎ *02-37-36-41-39* ▧ *€2.50* ☯ *Wed.–Mon. 10–noon and 2–5.*

The Gothic church of **St-Pierre** (⊠ Rue St-Pierre), near the Eure River, has magnificent medieval windows from a period (circa 1300) not represented at the cathedral. The oldest stained glass here, portraying Old Testament worthies, is to the right of the choir and dates from the late 13th century. Exquisite 17th-century stained glass can be admired at the church of **St-Aignan** (⊠ Rue des Grenets), around the corner from St-Pierre.

Where to Stay & Eat

$$$ ✕ **La Vieille Maison.** Just 100 yards from the cathedral, in a pretty 14th-century building with a flower-decked patio, this restaurant is a fine choice for either lunch or dinner. Chef Bruno Letartre changes his menu regularly, often including such regional specialties as asparagus, rich duck pâté, and superb homemade foie gras. Prices, though justified, can be steep, but the €29 lunch menu is a good bet. ⊠ *5 rue au Lait* ☎ *02–37–34–10–67* ⊕ *www.lavieillemaison.fr.st* ☰ *AE, MC, V* ⊗ *Closed Mon. No dinner Sun.*

$–$$ ✕ **Moulin de Ponceau.** Ask for a table with a view of the River Eure, with the cathedral looming behind, at this 16th-century converted watermill. Choose from a regularly changing menu of French stalwarts such as rabbit terrine, trout with almonds, and tarte tatin. ⊠ *21 rue de la Tannerie* ☎ *02–37–35–30–05* ☰ *AE, MC, V* ⊗ *Closed 2 wks in Feb. No lunch Sat., no dinner Sun.*

$$–$$$ ▥ **Le Grand Monarque.** The most popular rooms in this 18th-century coaching inn, part of the Best Western chain, are in a separate turn-of-the-20th-century building overlooking a garden. The most atmospheric are tucked away in the attic. The restaurant, which has prix-fixe menus starting at €29, offers such delicacies as pheasant pie and roast duck with mushrooms. ⊠ *22 pl. des Épars, 28000* ☎ *02–37–18–15–15* ▤ *02–37–36–34–18* ⊕ *www.bw-grand-monarque.com* ◁ *55 rooms* ⌂ *Restaurant, minibars, cable TV, bar, Internet, some pets allowed (fee); no a/c in some rooms* ☰ *AE, DC, MC, V* ▯ *BP.*

Shopping

Vitrail (stained glass) being the key to Chartres's fame, you may want to visit the **Galerie du Vitrail** (⊠ 17 cloître Notre-Dame ☎ 02–37–36–10–03 ⊕ www.galerie-du-vitrail.com), which specializes in the noble art. Pieces range from small plaques to entire windows, and there are books on the subject in English and French.

Dreux

 35 km (22 mi) north of Chartres via N154, 74 km (46 mi) west of Paris.

Dreux, center of an independent province during the Middle Ages, enjoyed an upsurge in prosperity after being united to the French crown in 1556 (shortly after completion of the beefy belfry on the main square). The early 19th century conferred lasting glory on the town in the form of the burial chapel of the royal House of Orléans.

In 1816 the Orléans family, France's ruling house from 1830 to 1848, began the construction of a circular chapel-mausoleum on the hill behind the town center. The **Chapelle Royale St-Louis** is built in sugary but not unappealing neo-Gothic: superficial ornament rather than structural form recalls the medieval style. The magnificent interior prompts wonder with its Sèvres-manufactured "stained glass"—thin layers of glass coated with painted enamel (an extremely rare, fragile, and vivid technique)—and funereal statuary. Some of the **tombs**—an imploring hand reaching through a window to a loved one or an infant wrapped in a cloak of transparent gauze—may exude morbid sentimentality, but their technical skill and compositional drama outweigh the mawkishness. ⊠ 2 *sq. d'Aumale* 🕾 *02–37–46–07–06* ✇ *€6* ⊙ *Apr.–Nov., Wed.–Mon. 9–11:30 and 2:30–6.*

The church of **St-Pierre,** across the road from the belfry, is an interesting jumble of styles with pretty stained glass and a 17th-century organ loft. It presents a curious silhouette, with its unfinished classical towers cut off midway. ⊠ *Pl. Métézeau* 🕾 *02–37–42–06–89.*

Houdan

㉔ *20 km (12 mi) east of Dreux via N12, 54 km (34 mi) west of Paris.*

Although fast N12 now skirts around Houdan, the town grew up as a busy stop on the Paris–Dreux road. It is protected by a mighty 12th-century keep rising from the hilltop above two small rivers, the Opton and the Vesgre. Timber-frame houses along the main street (rue de Paris), including several former inns, recall Houdan's bygone status, as does the ornate church, which retains many of its original 17th- and 18th-century elements, including the pulpit, altarpiece, lectern, pews, and organ case. Houdan was also famed for its poultry market, and a succulent local breed of chicken with a fancy plumed crest—the *poularde de Houdan*—still survives.

Where to Eat

$$–$$$ ✕ **La Poularde.** This comfortable restaurant at the foot of the town is named for the local breed of chicken, often served here with truffles or morels. Braised beef and smoked-fish salad are other specialties, and there's a good-value lunch menu. The airy pastel dining room turns its back on the highway outside, looking out on a trim lawn instead. ⊠ *24 av. de la République* 🕾 *01–30–59–60–50* ⊕ *www.alapoularde.com* ▤ *MC, V* ⊙ *Closed Wed. and part of Aug. No dinner Sun. or Tues.*

Montfort-L'Amaury

㉕ *18 km (11 mi) east of Houdan via N12 and D76, 40 km (25 mi) west of Paris.*

Montfort-L'Amaury, with its 17th-century houses and twisting, narrow streets clustered around an old church, is one of the prettiest towns in Ile-de-France. It has a ruined hilltop castle, remnants of medieval ramparts, and a cloister-lined cemetery. Dominating the town square is the bulky Renaissance tower of the church of **St-Pierre–St-Paul.** Note the gargoyles around the far end and, inside, the 37 splendid Renaissance stained-glass windows.

Composer Maurice Ravel lived in Montfort from 1921 until his death in 1937; he composed his famous *Bolero* in 1928 in his Japanese-style garden. His house, now the **Musée Maurice-Ravel** (Ravel Museum), has been reconstituted with many of his mementos and furnishings (including his piano). ⊠ *Le Belvédère, 5 rue Maurice-Ravel* ☎ *01–34–86–00–89* ⊠ *€6.10* ⊙ *Guided visits only, weekends at 10, 11, 2:30, 3:30, 4:30 and 5:30, Wed.–Fri. 2:30–6 by appointment.*

Where to Stay & Eat

★ **$$–$$$** ✕▦ **Domaine du Verbois.** Greek goddesses set the tone here: bedrooms in this stately late-19th-century mansion in Neauphle-le-Château, 10 km (6 mi) east of Montfort and just a 20-minute drive from Paris, are named after them. The larger rooms are at the front; the smaller rooms at the back are quieter and overlook the pretty, tumbling garden. All rooms have reproduction 18th-century furniture and colorful Chinese rugs. The four-course set menu (€30) in the pink-walled dining room might include crawfish salad or turbot in champagne sauce. Genial owner Kenneth Boone is half-American. ⊠ *38 av. de la République, 10 km (6 mi) east of Montfort via N12–D11, 78640 Neauphle-le-Château* ☎ *01–34–89–11–78* 🖷 *01–34–89–57–33* ⊕ *www.hotelverbois.com* ⇌ *22 rooms* ⌂ *Restaurant, some minibars, cable TV, babysitting, Internet, some pets allowed (fee); no a/c* ⊟ *AE, DC, MC, V* ⊙ *Closed 2 wks Aug. No dinner Sun.* ▯◯▮ *MAP.*

Thoiry

❷❻ *11 km (7 mi) north of Montfort-L'Amaury via D76 and D11, 44 km (28 mi) west of Paris.*

Thoiry is most famous for its 16th-century château with beautiful gardens, a wild-animal preserve, and a gastronomy museum. The village makes an excellent day trip from Paris, especially if you're traveling with
ꚙ children. The showpiece remains the **Château de Thoiry,** built by Philibert de l'Orme in 1564. Its handsome Renaissance facade is set off by gardens landscaped in the disciplined French fashion by Le Nôtre, in this case with unexpected justification: the château is positioned directly in line with the sun as it sets in the west at the winter solstice (December 21) and as it rises in the east at the summer solstice (June 21). Heightening the effect, the central part of the château appears to be a transparent arch of light because of its huge glass doors and windows. Owners Vicomte Paul de La Panouse and his American wife Annabelle have restored the château and park, opening both to the public. The distinguished history of the La Panouse family—a Comte César even fought in the American Revolution—is retraced in the **Musée des Archives** (Archives Museum), where papal bulls and Napoleonic letters mingle with notes from Thomas Jefferson and Benjamin Franklin. You're allowed to wander at leisure, although it's best not to stray too far from the official footpath through the **Parc Zoologique** (animal preserve). Note that the parts of the reserve that contain the wilder beasts—deer, zebra, camels, hippos, bears, elephants, and lions—can be visited only by car. Tigers can be seen from the safety of a raised footbridge. Nearby is a children's play area with a burrow to wriggle through and a huge netted cobweb

to bounce around in. ☎ *01–34–87–52–25* ⊕ *www.thoiry.tm.fr* ▨ *Château only, €6, park and game reserve €20* ☯ *June–Sept., 10–6; Oct.–May, daily 10–5.*

ALONG THE SEINE TO GIVERNY

Renowned for its beauty as it weaves through Paris, the Seine River is no less appealing where it flows gently northwest toward Normandy. The terrace at the château St-Germain-en-Laye, residence of the French kings before Versailles, provides a memorable view of the valley, soon to break into a series of chalky cliffs beyond Mantes. Farther on, tucked away on the bank of the Epte (a tributary of the Seine), are Monet's home and fabled garden in Giverny.

Rueil-Malmaison

㉗ *8 km (5 mi) west of Paris on N13 via La Défense.*

Rueil-Malmaison is a slightly dreary western suburb of Paris, but the memory of the legendary pair Napoléon and Joséphine still haunts its château. Built in 1622, **La Malmaison** was bought by the future empress Joséphine in 1799 as a love nest for Napoléon and herself (they had married three years earlier). After the childless Joséphine was divorced by the heir-hungry emperor in 1809, she retired to La Malmaison and died here on May 29, 1814. The château has 24 rooms furnished with exquisite tables, chairs, and sofas of the Napoleonic period; of special note are the library, game room, and dining room. The walls are adorned with works by artists of the day, such as Jacques-Louis David, Pierre-Paul Prud'hon, and Baron Gérard. Take time to admire the clothes and hats that belonged to Napoléon and Joséphine, particularly the empress's gowns. Their carriage can be seen in one of the garden pavilions, and another pavilion contains a unique collection of snuffboxes donated by Prince George of Greece. The gardens themselves are delightful, especially the regimented rows of tulips in spring. ▨ *15 av. du Château* ☎ *01–41–29–05–55* ⊕ *www.chateau-malmaison.fr* ▨ *€4.50* ☯ *Wed.–Mon. 10–noon and 1:30–5.*

FodorsChoice ★

Currently being renovated, the **Bois Préau,** a smaller mansion dating from the 17th century, is close to La Malmaison (and can be visited on the same admission ticket). It was acquired by Joséphine in 1810, after her divorce, but was subsequently reconstructed in the 1850s. Today its 10 rooms, complete with furniture and objects from the Empire period, are devoted mainly to souvenirs of Napoléon's exile on the island of St. Helena. ▨ *Av. de l'Impératrice* ☎ *01–41–29–05–55* ☯ *Closed for renovation at this writing.*

St-Germain-en-Laye

㉘ *4 km (2½ mi) north of Marly-le-Roi via N186 and N13, 9 km (5½ mi) west of Rueil-Malmaison, 17 km (11 mi) west of Paris.*

The elegant town of St-Germain-en-Laye, encircled by forest perched behind Le Nôtre's Grande Terrace overlooking the Seine, has lost little of its original cachet, despite the invasion of wealthy former Parisians who commute to work on the RER.

If you're fond of the swashbuckling novels of Alexandre Dumas (who, incidentally, enjoyed the rare honor of reburial in the Paris Panthéon in 2002), then you'll enjoy the **Château de Monte-Cristo** (Monte Cristo Castle) at Port-Marly on the southern fringe of St-Germain (signposted to your left as you arrive from Marly-le-Roi). You may find that its fanciful exterior, where pilasters, cupolas, and stone carvings compete for attention, has crossed the line from opulence to tastelessness, but—as in such swashbuckling novels as *The Count of Monte Cristo* or *The Three Musketeers*—swagger, not subtlety, is what counts. Dumas built the château after his books' surging popularity made him rich in the 1840s. Construction costs and lavish partying meant he went broke just as quickly, and he skedaddled to a Belgian exile in 1849. The château contains pictures, Dumas mementos, and the luxurious Moorish Chamber, with spellbinding, interlacing plasterwork executed by Arab craftsmen (lent by the Bey of Tunis) and restored thanks to a donation from the late Moroccan king Hassan II. ⊠ *Av. du Président-Kennedy* ☎ *01–39–16–49–49* ⊕ *www.mairie-marlyleroi.fr* ✉ *€5* ◷ *Apr.–Oct., Tues.–Fri. 10–12:30 and 2–6, weekends 10–6; Nov.–Mar., Sun. 2–5.*

★ Next to the St-Germain RER train station is the stone-and-brick **Château de St-Germain**, with its dry moat, intimidating circular towers, and La Grande Terrasse, one of the most spectacular of all French garden set-pieces; the château itself dates from the 16th and 17th centuries. A royal palace has existed here since the early 12th century, when Louis VI—known as Le Gros (the Plump)—exploited St-Germain's defensive potential in his bid to pacify Ile-de-France. A hundred years later Louis IX (St. Louis) added the elegant **Sainte-Chapelle,** the château's oldest remaining section; note the square-topped, not pointed, side windows and the filled-in rose-window on the back wall. Charles V (1364–80) built a powerful defensive keep in the mid-14th century, but from the 1540s François I and his successors transformed St-Germain into a palace with more of a domestic than a warlike vocation. Louis XIV was born here, and it was here that his father, Louis XIII, died. Until 1682—when the court moved to Versailles—it remained the country's foremost royal residence outside Paris; several Molière plays were premiered in the main hall. Since 1867 the château has housed the impressive **Musée des Antiquités Nationales** (Museum of National Antiquities), holding a trove of artifacts, figurines, brooches and weapons, from the Stone Age to the 8th century. Behind the château is Andre Le Nôtre's **Grande Terrasse**, a terraced promenade lined by century-old lime trees. Directly overlooking the Seine, it was completed in 1673 and has rarely been outdone for grandeur or length. ⊠ *Pl. Charles-de-Gaulle* ☎ *01–39–10–13–00* ⊕ *www.musee-antiquitesnationales.fr/* ✉ *€4* ◷ *Wed.–Mon. 9–5:15.*

★ The quaint **Musée du Prieuré** (Priory Museum) is devoted to the work of the artist Maurice Denis (1870–1943) and his fellow Symbolists and to Nabis—painters opposed to the naturalism of their 19th-century Impressionist contemporaries. Denis found the calm of the former Jesuit priory, set above tiered gardens with statues and rose bushes, ideally suited to his spiritual themes, which he expressed in stained glass, ceramics, and frescoes as well as oils. ⊠ *2 bis rue Maurice-Denis* ☎ *01–39–73–77–87* 🎫 *€4* ⏱ *Tues.–Fri. 10–5:30, weekends 10–6:30.*

Where to Stay & Eat

$–$$ ✕ **La Feuillantine.** An imaginative, good-value prix-fixe menu has made this wood-beamed restaurant an often-crowded success. Gizzard salad, salmon with endive, and herbed chicken fricassee with morels are among the specialties. Try for a table near the window; those near the back of the restaurant can be a bit gloomy. ⊠ *10 rue des Louviers* ☎ *01–34–51–04–24* ⊕ *www.lafeuillantine.com* 🖅 *AE, MC, V.*

$$$$ ✕🏨 **La Forestière.** A quintessentially beautiful Ile-de-France country re-
Fodor'sChoice treat, this hotel, run by Philippe and Isabelle Cazaudehore, is St-Ger-
★ main's most stylish. The rambling house itself is a solid, shuttered-window affair. Its forest environs, 18th century–style furniture, and fine restaurant, the Cazaudehore (closed Monday, no dinner on Sunday from November to February), where chef Jacques Pactol majors in braised monkfish, pig's feet and truffle puree, contribute to a sense of well-being. Dining on the garden veranda on such delights as Pactol's melt-in-the-mouth "pearls" of foie gras and tiger prawns in a poultry "consommé" can prove a most seductive experience. ⊠ *1 av. du Président-Kennedy, 78100* ☎ *01–30–61–64–64* 🖶 *01–39–73–73–88* ⊕ *www.cazaudehore. fr* ➷ *25 rooms, 5 suites* ⚘ *Restaurant, minibars, cable TV, bar, some pets allowed (fee); no a/c* 🖅 *AE, DC, MC, V* ⑩ *BP.*

Nightlife & the Arts

The **Fête des Loges** (Loges Festival) is a giant fair and carnival held in the Forest of St-Germain from July to mid-August. Hordes of fans of cotton candy, roller coasters, and Ferris wheels turn up every year.

Maisons-Laffitte

㉙ *8 km (5 mi) northeast of St-Germain-en-Laye via D157, 16 km (10 mi) northwest of Paris.*

The riverside suburb of Maisons-Laffitte has an unusually high proportion of elegant villas, many of which were built with profits from the town's racetrack by the Seine (with its famous 2,200-yard straight) and training stables; 14 races are held between July and September.
★ The town's steep-roofed, early Baroque **Château de Maisons,** constructed by architect François Mansart from 1634 to 1651, is one of the most elegant but least known châteaux in Ile-de-France. This was not always the case: Sun King Louis XIV came to the housewarming party, and Louis XV, Louis XVI, the 18th-century writer Voltaire, and Napoléon all stayed here. The interior clearly met their exacting standards, thanks to the well-proportioned entrance vestibule with its rich sculpture; the winding **Escalier d'Honneur,** a majestic staircase adorned with paintings and statuary; and the royal apartments above them, with their parquet floors and wall paneling. The **Musée du Cheval de Course** (Racehorse Museum), in the basement, evokes the world of the turf. Unfortunately, the château's once regal grounds have

been greatly amputated by encroaching streets and highways. ✉ *2 av. Carnot* ☎ *01–39–62–01–49* ⊕ *www.monum.fr* ✉ € *6.10* ⊘ *Wed.–Mon. 10–12:30 and 2–5.*

Poissy

30 *8 km (4 mi) west of Maisons-Laffitte via D308, 21 km (13 mi) northwest of Paris.*

Three museums and its historic significance as the birthplace of France's saintly king Louis IX help Poissy—the name comes from *poisson* (fish), as you may deduce from the town's ubiquitous emblem—defy its reputation as an unfashionable industrial town. The remains of the font in which Louis was baptized in 1214 can still be seen in the **Église Notre-Dame,** a medieval church with two striking octagonal towers. The **Musée d'Art et d'Histoire** (Art and History Museum), in a stern brick mansion opposite the church, is packed with tools, sculptures, old postcards, and paintings tracking Poissy's history from its 6th-century origins to its medieval prosperity as a cattle market and vine-growing center to its latter-day position as a center for auto plants. ✉ *12 rue St-Louis* ☎ *01–39–65–06–06* ✉ *Free* ⊘ *Wed.–Sun. 9:30–noon and 2–5:30.*

Housed behind the turreted facade of the 14th-century royal priory, the **Musée du Jouet** (Toy Museum) has a collection of historical toys, games, automatons, puppets, electric trains, rocking horses, tin soldiers, and dollhouses. ✉ *1 enclos de l'Abbaye* ☎ *01–39–65–06–06* ✉ € *3.20* ⊘ *Tues.–Sun. 9:30–noon and 2–5:30.*

★ Rising on what look like stilts—in fact, slender concrete pillars—above an extensive lawn that stretched over 15 acres until a (not undistinguished) school was built alongside in the 1950s, the **Villa Savoye** is considered one of Le Corbusier's most accomplished designs. Industrialist Pierre Savoye and his wife spent weekends here beginning in 1931, but stopped coming in 1938—fed up with the leaky flat roof. The villa appears as an austere white block; this is intentionally misleading—the ground floor, in fact, curves around to the entrance, at the back. An oval funnel emerges from the roof, harboring a solarium. Inside, the visual teasing continues, with a spiral staircase whose vertical emphasis clashes with the gently sloping ramp that serves as the principal transition from floor to floor. Be warned: the villa's delights are hidden in more ways than one, and advance signposting is terrible. Head up from the Toy Museum and turn right at the lights opposite the cemetery: the villa is 700 yards up, at the crest of the hill on the right. ✉ *82 rue de Villiers* ☎ *01–39–65–01–06* ⊕ *www.monum.fr* ✉ € *4* ⊘ *Tues.–Sun. 10–1 and 2–5.*

en route As you begin to enter the region of the Ile-de-France the Impressionists made their own, cross the Seine at Vernouillet and follow D190 to **Mantes-la-Jolie.** As you arrive from Limay, look out for the old, now ruined bridge over the Seine once painted by Jean-Baptiste-Camille Corot. Another painter, the Postimpressionist Maximilien Luce, is the hero of the fine town museum alongside the 12th-century Église

Notre-Dame, whose twin -towered silhouette was another favorite Corot motif. The small, circular windows ringing the east end of the church are an unusual local architectural characteristic—you can also see them 11 km (7 mi) north, at the church in **Vétheuil**—a town immortalized in many a magnificent Monet canvas—where the road regains the riverbank beneath impressive chalk cliffs.

La Roche-Guyon

③ *7 km (4 mi) northwest of Vétheuil on D913, 45 km (28 mi) northwest of Poissy via D190 and D147, 69 km (43 mi) northwest of Paris.*

Ruins of a medieval cliff-top castle look down on the River Seine and the quaint village of La Roche-Guyon. A steep-climbing stairway, hewn through the rock, links the castle to the classical **château** below, constructed mainly in the 18th century. The château has impressive iron gates incorporating the arms of the owners, the la Rochefoucauld family; its main building is one story higher than ground level, behind an arcaded terrace that towers above the stables and grassy forecourt. An interior highlight is the *Story of Esther* tapestry series. ☒ *1 rue de l'Audience* ☎ *01–34–79–74–42* ⊕ *www.val-doise-tourisme.fr* ☒ *€7.50* ⊙ *Weekdays 10–6; weekends 10–7.*

Where to Eat

$$-$$$ ✕ **Le Moulin de Fourges.** Nestled in verdant countryside by the River Epte, 5 km (3 mi) north of La Roche-Guyon, this converted 18th-century water mill has a mouthwatering setting. Stéphane Lebar's cuisine varies from tuna with satay to duck with raspberry sauce. The €35 three-course menu is a good bet. ☒ *38 rue du Moulin, Fourges* ☎ *02–32–52–12–12* ⊕ *www.moulin-de-fourges.com* ⚱ *Reservations essential* ▤ MC, V ⊙ *Closed Mon. and Nov.–Mar. No dinner Sun.*

Giverny

㉜ *8 km (5 mi) west of La Roche-Guyon on D5, 70 km (44 mi) northwest of Paris.*

The small village of Giverny (pronounced jee-vair-knee), just beyond the Epte River, which marks the boundary of Ile-de-France, has become a place of pilgrimage for art lovers. It was here that Claude Monet lived for 43 years, until his death at the age of 86 in 1926. Although his house is now prized by connoisseurs of 19th-century interior decoration, it's his garden, with its Japanese-inspired water-lily pond and its bridge, that remains the high point for many—a 5-acre, three-dimensional Impressionist painting you can stroll around at leisure. Monet also immortalized the surrounding countryside's haystacks and poplar trees in oils, but these motifs have often been altered beyond recognition—the wheat fields are still there, but the wheat is now rolled up, while Monet's famous rows of poplar trees along the River Epte, near the village of Limetz, about 3 km (2 mi) south of Giverny, are completely overgrown. It's easy to get to Giverny from Paris—trains leave every couple of hours from Gare St-Lazare for the 50-minute ride to Vernon; buses and taxis meet the trains and whisk you to Giverny, or you can rent a bike from the café opposite the station (head town to the river and take the cycle path once you've crossed the Seine). Most make this a day trip, although Giverny has some jewel B&Bs, so you should consider an overnight or two. Vernon itself (*see below*) is a well-preserved old town with a magisterial Gothic church.

Fodor'sChoice
★
The **Maison et Jardin Claude-Monet** (Monet's House and Garden) has been lovingly restored. Monet was brought up in Normandy and, like many of the Impressionists, was captivated by the soft light of the Seine Valley. After several years in Argenteuil, just north of Paris, he moved downriver to Giverny in 1883 along with his two sons, his mistress, Alice Hoschedé (whom he later married), and her six children. By 1890 a prospering Monet was able to buy the house outright. With its pretty pink walls and green shutters, the house has a warm feeling that may come as a welcome change after the stateliness of the French châteaux. Rooms have been restored to Monet's original designs: the kitchen with its blue tiles, the buttercup-yellow dining room, and Monet's bedroom on the second floor. Only in the 1970s was the house fully and glamorously restored, thanks to the millions contributed by fans and patrons (who were often Americans). Reproductions of his works, and some of the Japanese prints he avidly collected, crowd its walls. During this era, French culture had come under the spell of Orientalism and these framed prints were often gifts from visiting Japanese diplomats, whom Monet had befriended in Paris.

Three years after buying his house and cultivating its garden—which the family called the "Clos Normand"—the prospering Monet purchased another plot of land across the lane to continue his gardening experiments, even diverting the Epte to make a pond. The resulting garden "*à la japonaise*" (reached through a tunnel from the "Clos"), with flowers spilling out across the paths, contains the famous "teagarden" bridge and water-lily pond, flanked by a mighty willow and rhododendrons. Images of the bridge and the water lilies—in French, *nymphéas*—in various seasons appear in much of Monet's later work. Looking across the pond, it's easy to conjure up the grizzled, bearded brushsmith dabbing at his canvases—capturing changes in light and pioneering a breakdown in form that was to have a major influence on 20th-century art.

The garden is a place of wonder, filled with butterflies, roosters, nearly 100,000 plants bedded every year and more than 100,000 perennials. No matter that nearly 500,000 visitors troop through it every year; they fade into the background thanks to all the beautiful roses, purple carnations, lady's slipper, aubrieta, tulips, beaded irises, hollyhocks, poppies, daises, lambs' ears, larkspur, and azaleas, to mention just a few of the blooms (note that the water lilies flower during the latter part of July and the first two weeks of August). Even so, during the height of spring, when the gardens are particularly popular, try to visit during midweek. If you want to pay your respects, Monet is buried in the family vault in Giverny's village church. ⊠ *84 rue Claude-Monet*

☎ *02–32–51–28–21* ⊕ *www.giverny.org* ✑ *Gardens and home €5.50, gardens only €4* ☉ *Apr.–Oct., Tues.–Sun. 10–6.*

After touring the painterly grounds of Monet's house, you may wish to see some real paintings at the airy **Musée Américain** (American Museum), farther along the road. Endowed by the late Chicago art patrons Daniel and Judith Terra, it displays works by American Impressionists who were influenced by Claude Monet. After the master made Giverny his home, other artists, including Willard Metcalf, Louis Ritter, Theodore Wendel, and John Leslie Breck, "discovered" Giverny, too (truth be known, Monet soon tired of being a cult figure). On-site are a restaurant and *salon de thé* (tearoom), as well as a garden "quoting" some of Monet's plant compositions. Head down the road to visit Giverny's landmark Hôtel Baudy (*see below*), now a restaurant and once the stomping grounds and watering hole of many of these 19th-century artists. ⊠ *99 rue Claude-Monet* ☎ *02–32–51–94–65* ⊕ *www.maag.org* ✑ *€5.50* ☉ *Apr.–Nov., Tues.–Sun. 10–6.*

Where to Stay & Eat

$–$$ ✕ **Les Jardins de Giverny.** This tile-floor restaurant, overlooking a rose garden, is a few minutes' walk from Monet's house. Enjoy the €20 menu or choose from a repertoire of inventive dishes such as foie gras spiked with calvados, duck in cider, or scallops with wild mushrooms. ⊠ *Chemin du Roy* ☎ *02–32–21–60–80* ☰ *AE, MC, V* ☉ *Closed Mon. and Dec.–Feb. No dinner Sun.–Fri.*

$ ✕ **Baudy.** Back in Monet's day, this pretty-in-pink villa, originally an *épicerie-buvette* (café-cum-grocer's store), was the hotel of the American painters' colony. Today, the rustic dining room and flowery patio, overlooked by a rose garden and the hut Cézanne once used as a studio, retain more historic charm than the very simple cuisine and busloads of tour groups. ⊠ *81 rue Claude-Monet* ☎ *02–32–21–10–03* ☰ *MC, V* ☉ *No dinner Sun. Closed Mon. and Nov.–Mar.*

★ $–$$ ⊞ **Giverny B&Bs.** Giverny's dire shortage of hotels is made up for by a plethora of enticing, stylish, and affordable B&Bs set up in many of the town's homes. Particularly notable are **Le Clos Fleuri** (⊠ 5 rue de la Dîme ☎☏ *02–32–21–36–51*), a Norman manor house set in a lovely garden and run by the Fouché family; **La Réserve** (⊠ Rue Blanche-Hoschedé ☎ *02–32–21–99–09*), about a mile outside town, an expansive residence surrounded by orchards and with gorgeous, antiques-adorned and wood-beamed guest apartments, some of which have fireplaces and canopy beds; and the residence of **Marie-Claire Boscher** (⊠ 1 rue du Colombier ☎☏ *02–32–51–39–70*), which used to be a hotel-restaurant that Monet frequented. Log onto the Web site www.giverny.org/hotels for all the details.

$ ⊞ **La Musardière.** Just a short stroll from chez Monet, this manor house (the name means "Place To Idle") has a cozy lobby, guest rooms with views overlooking a leafy garden, and its own restaurant-crêperie (no lunch Monday). ⊠ *123 rue Claude-Monet, 27620* ☎ *02–32–21–03–18* ☏ *02–32–21–60–00* ⇥ *10 rooms, 1 suite* ⌂ *Restaurant, tennis court, pool; no a/c* ☰ *AE, DC, MC, V* ☉ *Closed Nov.–Mar.* ❢⊘ *MAP.*

Vernon

③③ *5 km (3 mi) northwest of Giverny on D5, 73 km (46 mi) northwest of Paris.*

The Vieille Ville (old town) of Vernon, on the Seine, has a medieval church, which Monet painted from across the Seine, and several fine timber-frame houses (the most impressive, on rue Carnot, houses the tourist office). The church of **Notre-Dame** (⊠ Rue Carnot), across from the tourist office, has an arresting rose-window facade that, like the high nave, dates from the 15th century. Rounded Romanesque arches in the choir, however, attest to the building's 12th-century origins.

A few minor Monet canvases, along with other late-19th-century paintings, can be admired in the town museum, the **Musée Poulain.** This rambling old mansion is seldom crowded, and the helpful curators are happy to explain local history. ⊠ *12 rue du Pont* ☎ *02–32–21–28–09* ⬚ *€2.50* ⊙ *Tues.–Fri. 10–12:30 and 2–6, weekends 2–6.*

Where to Stay & Eat

$$–$$$ ✕ **Les Fleurs.** This small, white-walled restaurant in the center of Vernon looks unremarkable inside and out, but the food on your plate has far more personality—as you'll see with one bite of the roast salmon with herbs, or the snails in a Roquefort cheese sauce. Fresh flowers on the tablecloths add a colorful touch, and service is slick and friendly. ⊠ *71 rue Sadi-Carnot* ☎ *02–32–51–16–80* ⊟ *AE, MC, V* ⊙ *Closed Aug., part of Mar. and Mon. No dinner Sun.*

★ **$$–$$$** ✕⌂ **Château de Brécourt.** This 17th-century stone-and-brick château close to the expressway outside Vernon has high-pitched roofs, an imposing forecourt, and extensive grounds. Guest rooms follow the same exuberant turn-of-the-19th-century lines. Even if you're not staying here, you can dine on the inventive food in the august restaurant, Le Grand Siècle. Dishes such as lobster mousse and veal with truffles make it a popular spot—and it's even easy to get to from Giverny, which is just across the Seine from Vernon. As such châteaux-hotels go, a stay here is a relatively good value. ⊠ *Route de Brécourt, 8 km (5 mi) southwest of Vernon on D181–D75, 27120 Douains* ☎ *02–32–52–40–50* ⬚ *02–32–52–69–65* ⊕ *www.chateaudebrecourt.com* ⬧ *25 rooms, 5 suites* ⭑ *Restaurant, in-room hot tubs, minibars, tennis court, pool, sauna, some pets allowed (fee); no a/c* ⊟ *AE, DC, MC, V* ⟟⟙ *MAP.*

FROM THE OISE VALLEY TO DISNEYLAND PARIS

This area covers a broad arc, beginning northwest of Paris in Conflans–Ste-Honorine, where the Oise joins the Seine, then heading east along the Oise Valley to Chantilly, and continuing southeast through Meaux. In addition to being the old stomping grounds for several world-famous artists—Pissarro's canvases of Pontoise are among his best-known, while those Van Gogh painted in Auvers were his very last—the area is now the domain of Disneyland Paris.

Conflans–Sainte-Honorine

③④ *28 km (3 mi) northwest of Paris via A15 and D48.*

Conflans is the capital of France's inland waterway network. Barges arrive from as far afield as the ports of Le Havre and Dunkerque, on the Channel coast, and are often moored as many as six abreast along the 1½-km-long (1-mi-long) quayside, near the *conflans* (confluence) of the rivers Seine and Oise; one, the *Je Sers* (*I Serve*), is the boatmen's own church (open daily). From the hilltop church of St-Maclou there is a spectacular view of the boats. The **Musée de la Batellerie** (Waterways Museum) explains the historic role of the barges and waterways with the help of pictures and scale models. ✉ *3 pl. Jules-Gévelot* ☎ *01–39–72–58–05* 💶 *€4* 🕙 *Tues. 1:30–6, Wed.–Fri. 9–noon and 1:30–6, weekends 2–6 (Easter–Sept.) or 2–5 (Oct.–Easter).*

Pontoise

③⑤ *8 km (5 mi) north of Conflans–Ste-Honorine via N184 and N14, 29 km (19 mi) northwest of Paris via A15.*

A pleasant old town on the banks of the Oise, Pontoise is famous for its link with the Impressionists. The small **Musée Pissarro,** high up in the Vieille Ville, pays tribute to one of Pontoise's most illustrious past residents, Impressionist painter Camille Pissarro (1830–1903). The collection of prints and drawings is of interest mainly to specialists, but the view across the valley from the museum gardens will appeal to all. ✉ *17 rue du Château* ☎ *01–30–32–06–75* 🌐 *www.ville-pontoise.fr* 💶 *Free* 🕙 *Wed.–Sun. 2–6.*

The **Musée Tavet-Delacour,** housed in a turreted mansion in the center of Pontoise, stages good exhibitions and has a permanent collection that ranges from street scenes and landscapes by Norbert Goenutte and other local painters to contemporary art and the intriguing abstractions of Otto Freundlich. ✉ *4 rue Lemercier* ☎ *01–30–38–02–40* 🌐 *www.ville-pontoise.fr* 💶 *€4* 🕙 *Wed.–Sun. 10–12:30 and 1:30–6.*

Auvers-sur-Oise

③⑥ *7 km (4 mi) east of Pontoise via D4, 33 km (21 mi) northwest of Paris via N328.*

FodorsChoice
★

The tranquil Oise River valley, which runs northeast from Pontoise, retains much of the charm that attracted Camille Pissarro, Paul Cézanne, Camille Corot, Charles-François Daubigny, and Berthe Morisot to Auvers-sur-Oise in the second half of the 19th century. But despite this lofty company, it is the spirit of Vincent van Gogh that haunts every nook and cranny of this pretty riverside village. You can find out about his haunts and other Impressionist sites in Auvers by stopping in at the tourist office at Les Colombières, a 14th-century manor house, set on the rue de la Sansonne (closed from 12:30 to 2 PM every day). Short hikes outside the town center—sometimes marked with yellow trail signs—will lead you to rural landscapes once beloved by Pissarro and Cézanne, including the site of one of Van Gogh's last paintings, *Wheat Fields with Crows*. On July 27, 1890, the great painter laid his easel against a haystack, walked behind the Château d'Auvers, shot himself, then stumbled to the Auberge Ravoux, where the owner sent to Paris for the artist's brother, Theo. Van Gogh died on July 29th. The next day, using a hearse from neighboring Méry (because the priest of Auvers refused to provide his for a suicide victim), Van Gogh's body was borne up the hill to the village cemetery. His heartbroken brother died the following year and, in 1914, was re-buried alongside Vincent in his simple ivy-covered grave.

Van Gogh moved here from Arles in May 1890 to be nearer his brother. Little has changed here since that summer of 1890, during the last 10 weeks of Van Gogh's life, when he painted no fewer than 70 pictures. The whole village is peppered with plaques marking the spots that in-spired his art. The plaques bear reproductions of his paintings, enabling you to compare his final works with the scenes as they are today. His last abode has been turned into a shrine. You can also visit the medieval village church, subject of one of Van Gogh's most famous paintings, *L'Église d'Auvers*, and admire Osip Zadkine's powerful statue of Van Gogh in the village park.

Set opposite the village town hall, the Auberge Ravoux, the inn where Van Gogh stayed, is now the **Maison de van Gogh** (Van Gogh House). The inn opened in 1876 and owes its name to Arthur Ravoux, the land-lord from 1889-91. He had seven lodgers in all, including the minor Dutch painter Anton Hirsching; they paid 3.50 francs board and lodging, cheaper than the other inns in Auvers, where 6 francs was the going rate. A dingy staircase leads up to the tiny, spartan wood-floor attic where Van Gogh stored some of modern art's most famous pictures under his bed. A short film retraces Van Gogh's time at Auvers, and there is a well-stocked souvenir shop. Stop for a drink or for lunch in the ground-floor restaurant. ⊠ *8 rue de la Sansonne* ☎ *01-30-36-60-60* ⊕ *www. maison-de-van-gogh.com* ▣ *€5* ⊘ *Mar.–Nov., Tues.–Sun. 10–6.*

A major town landmark opened to the public for the first time in 2004: the house and garden of Van Gogh's closest friend in Auvers, Dr. Paul Gachet. Documents and souvenirs at the **Maison du Dr Gachet** evoke Van Gogh's stay in Auvers and Gachet's passion for the avant-garde art of his era. The good doctor was himself the subject of one of the artist's most famous portraits (and the world's second-most expensive paint-ing when it sold for $82 million in the late 1980s), the actual painting of which was reenacted in the 1956 Kirk Douglas biopic, *Lust for Life*. Friend and patron to many of the artists who settled in and visited Au-vers in the 1880s, among them Cézanne (who immortalized the doc-tor's house in a famous landscape), Gachet also taught them about engraving processes. The ivy covering Van Gogh's grave in the ceme-tery across town was provided by Gachet from this house's garden. ⊠ *78 rue du Dr-Gachet* ☎ *01-30-36-60-60* ▣ *€4* ⊘ *Tues.–Sun. 10–6.*

The elegant 17th-century village château—also depicted by Van Gogh—set above split-level gardens, now houses the **Voyage au Temps des Im-pressionnistes** (Journey Through the Impressionist Era). You'll receive a set of headphones (English available), with commentary that guides you past various tableaux illustrating life during the Impressionist years. Although there are no Impressionist originals—500 reproductions pop up on screens interspersed between the tableaux—this is one of France's most imaginative, enjoyable, and innovative museums. Some of the special effects—talking mirrors, computerized cabaret dancing girls, and a simulated train ride past Impressionist landscapes—are worthy of Disney. The museum restaurant, Les Canotiers—named after Renoir's famous painting of boaters—offers dishes favored by such artists as Morisot, Degas, and Manet, while more casual fare is offered at a recreation of a 19th-century *guinguette* (riverbank café). ⊠ *Rue de Léry* ☎ *01–34–48–48–40* ⊕ *www.chateau-auvers.fr* ⊡ *€10* ⊙ *May–Oct., Tues.–Sun. 10–8; Nov.–Apr., Tues.–Sun. 11–4:30.*

The landscape artist Charles-François Daubigny, a precursor of the Impressionists, lived in Auvers from 1861 until his death in 1878. You can visit his studio, the **Atelier de Daubigny,** and admire the mural and roof paintings by Daubigny and fellow artists Camille Corot and Honoré Daumier. ⊠ *61 rue Daubigny* ☎ *01–34–48–03–03* ⊡ *€5* ⊙ *Thurs.–Sun. 2–6:30.*

You may also want to visit the modest **Musée Daubigny** to admire the drawings, lithographs, and occasional oils by local 19th-century artists, some of which were collected by Daubigny himself. The museum is opposite the Maison de van Gogh, above the tourist office. ⊠ *Manoir des Colombières, rue de la Sansonne* ☎ *01–30–36–80–20* ⊡ *€4* ⊙ *Wed.–Sun. 2–5.*

Where to Eat

★ **$$–$$$** ✕ **Auberge Ravoux.** For total Van Gogh immersion, have lunch in the restaurant he patronized regularly more than 100 years ago, in the building where he finally expired. The €33, three-course menu changes regularly, but it's the genius loci that makes eating here special, with glasswork, lace curtains, and wall blandishments carefully modeled on the original designs. A magnificently illustrated book, *Van Gogh's Table* (published by Artisan), by culinary historian Alexandra Leaf and Fred Leeman, recalls Vincent's stay at the Auberge and describes in loving detail the dishes served there at the time. ⊠ *52 rue Général-de-Gaulle* ☎ *01–30–36–60–63* ⊲ *Reservations essential* ⊟ *AE, DC, MC, V* ⊙ *Closed Mon. and Nov.–Feb. No dinner Sun.*

L'Isle-Adam

㊲ *6 km (4 mi) northeast of Auvers-sur-Oise via D4, 40 km (25 mi) north of Paris via N1.*

Residentially exclusive L'Isle-Adam is one of the most picturesque towns in Ile-de-France. Paris lies just 40 km (25 mi) south, but it could be 100 mi and as many years away. The town has a sandy beach along one stretch of the River Oise (via rue de Beaumont); a curious pagodalike folly, the Pavillon Chinois de Cassan; and an unassuming local museum. The **Musée Louis-Senlecq,** on the main street behind the tall-towered town church, features the ceramic figures produced in L'Isle-Adam a century ago, and contains numerous attractive works by Jules Dupré and other local landscapists. ⊠ *46 Grande-Rue* 🕾 *01–34–69–45–44* ⊕ *www.ville-isle-adam.fr* 🎫 *€3.10* ⊙ *Wed.–Mon. 2–6.*

Where to Stay & Eat

$ ✕🖼 **Le Cabouillet.** The riverside Cabouillet aptly reflects the quiet charm of L'Isle-Adam, thanks to its pretty views over the Oise. You can savor these from each of its cozy rooms or from the chic restaurant, where the cooking can be inspired—have the crawfish in Sauternes sauce, if it's on the menu. ⊠ *5 quai de l'Oise, 95290* 🕾 *01–34–69–00–90* 🖷 *01–34–69–33–88* ⊕ *www.le-cabouillet.com* ➳ *5 rooms* ⚹ *Restaurant; no a/c* ⊟ *AE, DC, MC, V* ⊙ *Closed Mon. and late Dec.–early Feb. No dinner Sun.* ⏀❘ *MAP.*

Chantilly

㊳ *10 km (6 mi) northeast of Royaumont via D909, 23 km (14 mi) east of L'Isle-Adam via D4, 37 km (23 mi) north of Paris via N16.*

Celebrated for lace, cream, and the most beautiful medieval manuscript in the world—*Les Très Riches Heures du Duc de Berry*—romantic Chantilly has a host of other attractions: a faux Renaissance château with an eye-popping art collection, splendid Baroque stables, a classy racecourse, and a 16,000-acre forest.

Fodor'sChoice
★
Although its lavish exterior may be 19th-century Renaissance pastiche, the **Château de Chantilly,** sitting snugly behind an artificial lake, houses the outstanding **Musée Condé,** with illuminated medieval manuscripts, tapestries, furniture, and paintings. The most famous room, the **Santuario** (sanctuary), contains two celebrated works by Italian painter Raphael (1483–1520)—the *Three Graces* and the *Orleans Virgin*—plus an exquisite ensemble of 15th-century miniatures by the most illustrious French painter of his time, Jean Fouquet (1420–81). Farther on, in the **Cabinet des Livres** (library), is the world-famous book of hours whose title translates as *The Very Rich Hours of the Duc de Berry,* which was illuminated by the Brothers Limbourg with magical pictures of early 15th-century life as lived by one of Burgundy's richest lords (unfortunately, due to their fragility, painted facsimiles of the celebrated calendar illuminations are on display, not the actual pages of the book). Other highlights of this unusual museum are the **Galerie de Psyché** (Psyche Gallery), with 16th-century stained glass and portrait drawings by Flemish artist Jean Clouet II; the **Chapelle,** with sculptures by Jean Goujon and Jacques Sarrazin; and the extensive collection of paintings by 19th-century French artists, headed by Jean-Auguste-Dominique Ingres. In addition, there are grand and smaller salons, all stuffed with palace furniture, family portraits, and Sèvres porcelains, making this a must for lovers of the decorative and applied arts. 🕾 *03–44–62–62–62* ⊕*www.chateaudechantilly.com* 🎫*€7, including park* ⊙ *Mar.–Oct., daily 10–6; Nov.–Feb., Wed.–Mon. 10:30–12:45 and 2–5.*

Le Nôtre's **park** is based on that familiar French royal combination of formality (neatly planned parterres and a mighty, straight-banked canal) and romantic eccentricity (the waterfall and the Hameau, a mock-Norman village that inspired Marie-Antoinette's version at Versailles). You can explore on foot or on an electric train, and take a **hydrophile** (electric-powered boat) for a glide down the Grand Canal. ☎ *03–44–57–35–35* 🚃 *Park only €3, with boat €8, with train and boat €10; €15 joint ticket including château* ☉ *Mar.–Oct., daily 10–6; Nov.–Feb., daily 10:30–12:45 and 2–5.*

★ ☾ The palatial 18th-century **Grandes Écuries** (Grand Stables) by the racetrack, built by Jean Aubert in 1719 to accommodate 240 horses and 500 hounds for stag and boar hunts in the forests nearby, are the grandest stables in France. They're still in use as the home of the **Musée Vivant du Cheval** (Living Horse Museum), with 30 breeds of horses and ponies housed in straw-lined comfort—in between dressage performances in the courtyard or beneath the majestic central dome. The 31-room museum has a comprehensive collection of equine paraphernalia: everything from saddles, bridles, and stirrups to rocking horses, anatomy displays, and old postcards. There are explanations in English throughout. ⊠ *7 rue du Connétable* ☎ *03–44–57–40–40* ⊕ *www.musee-vivant-du-cheval.fr* 🚃 *€8* ☉ *Apr.–Oct., Wed.–Mon. 10:30–5:30; Nov.–Mar., Wed.–Fri. and Mon. 2–6, weekends 10:30–6:30.*

Where to Stay & Eat

$$–$$$ ✕ **La Capitainerie.** Housed in the stone-vaulted kitchens of the château's legendary 17th-century chef Vorace Vatel, with an open-hearth fireplace big enough for whole lambs or oxen to sizzle on the spit, this quaint restaurant is no ordinary museum cafeteria. Reflect at leisure on your cultural peregrinations over mouthfuls of grilled turbot or roast quail, and don't forget to add a good dollop of homemade crème de Chantilly to your dessert. ⊠ *In Château de Chantilly* ☎ *03–44–57–15–89* ▤ *MC, V* ☉ *Closed Tues.*

$–$$$ ✕ **La Ferme de Condé.** At the far end of the racetrack, in a building that originally served as an Anglican chapel, is one of the classiest restaurants in Chantilly. Dishes include roast suckling pig, duck with honey and spices, and lobster terrine. A €16 menu makes it a suitable lunch spot. There's a good wine list and choice of wine by the jug. ⊠ *42 av. du Maréchal-Joffre* ☎ *03–44–57–32–31* 🍴 *Reservations essential* ▤ *AE, DC, MC, V.*

$$$$ 🏨 **Dolce Chantilly.** Surrounded by forest and its own 18-hole golf course, this luxe, highly restored, and meetings-friendly hotel is set 1½ km (1 mi) northeast of the château. The marble-floor reception hall creates a glitzy impression not quite matched by the guest rooms, which are functional, modern, and a bit small. The De Par En Par brasserie, in the golf clubhouse, serves lunch for €16, and the deluxe Carmontelle has formal dining (pastry chef Hugues Lenté is a master at crème de Chantilly). ⊠ *Rte. d'Apremont, Vineuil–St-Firmin 60500* ☎ *03–44–58–47–77* 🖨 *03–44–58–50–11* ⊕ *www.chantilly.dolce.com* 🛏 *202 rooms, 4 suites* 🍴 *3 restaurants, minibars, cable TV, golf course, tennis court, pool, health club, babysitting, Internet* ▤ *AE, DC, MC, V* ⦿ *FAP.*

$ 🏨 **Campanile.** This functional, modern motel is in quiet Les Huit Curés, just north of Chantilly, on the edge of the forest (which compensates for the lack of interior atmosphere). There's a grill room for straightforward meals, with a buffet for appetizers, cheese, and desserts. You can dine outside on the terrace in summer. ⊠ *Rte. de Creil, on N16 toward Creil, Les Huit Cures 60500* ☎ *03–44–57–39–24*

☏ 03–44–58–10–05 ✒️45 rooms ⚐ Restaurant, bar, some pets allowed; no a/c ☰ AE, DC, MC, V.

Sports & the Outdoors

Since 1834 Chantilly's fabled racetrack, the **Hippodrome des Princes de Condé** (✉ Rte. de la Plaine-des-Aigles ☏ 03–44–62–44–00 ⊕ www. paristurf.tm.fr/chantil.html), has come into its own each June with two of Europe's most prestigious events: the **Prix du Jockey-Club** (French Derby) on the first Sunday of the month, and the **Prix de Diane** for three-year-old fillies the Sunday after.

Senlis

39 *10 km (6 mi) east of Chantilly via D924, 45 km (28 mi) north of Paris via A1.*

Senlis is an exceptionally well-preserved medieval town with crooked, mazelike streets dominated by the svelte, soaring spire of its Gothic cathedral. Be sure to also inspect the moss-tile church of St-Pierre, with its stumpy crocketed spire. You can enjoy a 40-minute tour of the Vieille Ville by horse and carriage, departing from in front of the cathedral, daily April–December (€30 for up to three people).

★ The **Cathédrale Notre-Dame** (✉ Pl. du Parvis), one of France's oldest and narrowest cathedrals, dates from the second half of the 12th century. The superb spire—arguably the most elegant in France—was added around 1240, and the majestic transept, with its ornate rose windows, in the 16th century.

The town's excellent **Musée d'Art** (Art Museum), built atop an ancient Gallo-Roman residence, displays archaeological finds ranging from Gallo-Roman votive objects unearthed in the neighboring Halatte Forest to the building's own excavated foundations (uncovered in the basement), including some macabre stone heads bathed in half light. Paintings upstairs include works by Manet's teacher Thomas Couture (who lived in Senlis) and a whimsical fried-egg still life by 19th-century realist Théodule Ribot. ✉ *Palais Épiscopal, pl. du Parvis-Notre-Dame* ☏*03–44–53–00–83* 🎟️*€4* ☉ *Thurs.–Mon. 10–noon and 2–6, Wed. 2–6.*

off the beaten path

PARC ASTÉRIX – A great alternative to Disneyland, and a wonderful day out for young and old, this Gallic theme park, 10 km (6 mi) south of Senlis via A1, opened in 1989 and takes its cue from a French comic-book figure whose adventures are set during the Roman invasion of France 2,000 years ago. Among the 30 rides and six shows that attract thundering herds of families each year are a mock Gallo-Roman village, costumed druids, performing dolphins, splash-happy water slides, and a giant roller coaster. ☏ *03–44–62–34–04* ⊕ *www. parcasterix.com* 🎟️ *€32* ☉ *Apr.–Aug., daily 10–6; Sept.–mid-Oct., Wed. and weekends 10–6.*

Where to Stay & Eat

$$–$$$ ✕ **Le Bourgeois Gentilhomme.** This pink-and-cream restaurant in old Senlis, named for dapper chef Philippe Bourgeois, serves such interesting dishes as pigeon with cabbage and bacon, fricassee of burbot with mushrooms, and crab lasagna with cress, to name but three. ⊠ *3 pl. de la Halle* ☎ *03–44–53–13–22* ▭ *AE, DC, MC, V* ⊘ *Closed Mon. and 2 wks in Aug. No lunch Sat., no dinner Sun.*

¢–$ ▦ **L'Hostellerie de la Porte-Bellon.** This old stone house with garden, just a five-minute walk from the cathedral and close to the bus station, is the closest you'll get to spending a night in the historic center of Senlis. The restaurant (no dinner Sunday) has menus at €15 and €20. ⊠ *51 rue Bellon, 60300* ☎ *03–44–53–03–05* ▤ *03–44–53–29–94* ⤳ *18 rooms* ⸖ *Restaurant, some pets allowed (fee); no a/c* ▭ *MC, V* ⊘ *Closed mid-Dec.–mid-Jan.* ⦿❘ *MAP.*

Ermenonville

➍⓪ *13 km (8 mi) southeast of Senlis via N330, 43 km (27 mi) northeast of Paris.*

A ruined abbey and children's amusement park, both nearby, add to the appeal of the village of Ermenonville, best known as the final haunt of the 18th-century French philosopher Jean-Jacques Rousseau. The Cistercian **Abbaye Royale de Chaalis**, just off N330 as you arrive from Senlis, has photogenic 13th-century ruins, a landscaped park, an orangery, and an 18th-century château. Inside are an eclectic collection of Egyptian antiquities and medieval paintings and three rooms displaying manuscripts and other mementos of Jean-Jacques Rousseau. ⊠ *Just off N330* ☎ *03–44–54–04–02* ▨ *Abbey and park €6.50; park only €3* ⊘ *Mar.–Oct., daily 10–5:30; Nov.–Feb., Sun. 10:30–12:30 and 1:30–5:30.*

The **Parc Jean-Jacques Rousseau**, a tranquil oasis in the center of Ermenonville, is famous as the initial resting place of the influential writer, who spent the last three months of his life in Ermenonville in 1778 and was buried on the Ile des Peupliers in the middle of the lake. Rousseau's ideas about natural equality made him a hero of the French Revolution, and in 1794 his body was removed to the Panthéon in Paris. ▨ *€2* ⊘ *Daily 2–5:30.*

Where to Stay & Eat

★ $$–$$$ ✕▦ **Château d'Ermenonville.** Right out of a storybook, this turreted 18th-century château opposite the Parc Jean-Jacques Rousseau has great style—it's surrounded by a lake, the main courtyard has a sculpted pediment and wrought-iron balconies, and the rooms are furnished with fin-de-siècle opulence. The menu changes regularly at the restaurant, La Table du Poète. ⊠ *60950 Ermenonville* ☎ *03–44–54–00–26* ▤ *03–44–54–01–00* ⊕ *www.chateau-ermenonville.com* ⤳ *38 rooms, 11 suites* ⸖ *Restaurant, minibars, Internet; no a/c* ▭ *AE, MC, V* ⦿❘ *MAP.*

Meaux

➍① *24 km (15 mi) southeast of Ermenonville via N330, 40 km (25 mi) east of Paris via N3.*

A sturdy cathedral and a well-preserved bishop's palace embellish Meaux, a dignified old market town on the banks of the Marne River.

An excellent Brie is produced locally. Above the Marne sits the **Cathé-drale St-Étienne,** which took more than 300 years to complete and is, consequently, a bit of a stylistic hodgepodge. The stonework in the soaring interior becomes increasingly decorative as you approach the west end, culminating in a notable Flamboyant Gothic rose window. The exterior is somewhat eroded and looks sadly battered—or pleasingly authentic, according to taste. A son-et-lumière show replete with medieval costumes is staged outside the cathedral on several weekends between mid-June and mid-September. ⊠ *Rue St-Étienne* ☎ *01–60–23–40–00 for details about son-et-lumière show* ⊕ *www.feerie.org* 🎫 *€15* ☉ *Daily 8–noon and 2–6.*

Disneyland Paris

☾ 🅸 42   *20 km (13 mi) southwest of Meaux via A140 and A4, 38 km (24 mi)*
Fodor'sChoice   *east of Paris via A4.*
★

Disneyland Paris (originally called Euro Disney) is probably not what you've traveled to France to experience. But if you have a child in tow, the promise of a day here may get you through an afternoon at Versailles or Fontainebleau. If you're a dyed-in-the-wool Disney fan, you'll want to make a beeline for the park to see how it has been molded to appeal to the tastes of Europeans (Disney's "Imagineers" call it their most lovingly detailed park). And if you've never experienced this particular form of Disney showmanship, you may want to put in an appearance if only to see what all the fuss is about. When it opened, few turned up to do so; today the place is jammed with crowds, and Disneyland Paris is here to stay—and grow, with **Walt Disney Studios** opened alongside it in 2002.

The Disneyland theme park is made up of five "lands": Main Street U.S.A., Frontierland, Adventureland, Fantasyland, and Discoveryland. The central theme of each land is relentlessly echoed in every detail, from attractions to restaurant menus to souvenirs. The park is circled by a railroad, which stops three times along the perimeter. **Main Street U.S.A.** goes under the railroad and past shops and restaurants toward the main plaza; Disney parades are held here every afternoon and, during holiday periods, every evening. Top attractions at **Frontierland** are the chilling Phantom Manor, haunted by holographic spooks, and the thrilling runaway mine train of Big Thunder Mountain, a roller coaster that plunges wildly through floods and avalanches in a setting meant to evoke Utah's Monument Valley. Whiffs of Arabia, Africa, and the West Indies give **Adventureland** its exotic cachet; the spicy meals and snacks served here rank among the best food in the park. Don't miss the Pirates of the Caribbean, an exciting mise-en-scène populated by eerily humanlike, computer-driven figures, or Indiana Jones and the Temple of Doom, a breathtaking ride that re-creates some of this luckless hero's most exciting moments.

Fantasyland charms the youngest parkgoers with familiar cartoon characters from such classic Disney films as *Snow White, Pinocchio, Dumbo,* and *Peter Pan.* The focal point of Fantasyland, and indeed Disneyland Paris, is Le Château de la Belle au Bois Dormant (Sleeping Beauty's Castle), a 140-foot, bubblegum-pink structure topped with 16 blue- and gold-tipped turrets. Its design was allegedly inspired by illustrations from a medieval *Book of Hours*—if so, it was by way of Beverly Hills. The castle's dungeon conceals a 2-ton scaly green dragon that rumbles in its sleep and occasionally rouses to roar—an impressive feat of engineering, producing an answering chorus of shrieks from younger children. **Discoveryland** is a futuristic eye-knocker for high-tech Disney entertainment. Robots on roller skates welcome you on your way to Star Tours, a pitching, plunging, sense-confounding ride based on the *Star Wars* films. In Le Visionarium, a simulated space journey is presented by 9-Eye, a staggeringly realistic robot. Space Mountain pretends to catapult riders through the Milky Way.

Walt Disney Studios opened next to the Disneyland Park in 2002. The theme park is divided into four "production zones." Beneath imposing entrance gates, and a 100-foot water-tower inspired by the one erected in 1939 at Disney Studios in Burbank, California, **Front Lot** contains shops, a restaurant and a studio re-creating the atmosphere of Sunset Boulevard. **Animation Courtyard** has Disney artists demonstrating the various phases of character animation; Animagique brings to life scenes from *Pinocchio* and *The Lion King*; while the Genie from *Aladdin* pilots Flying Carpets over Agrabah. **Production Courtyard** hosts the Walt Disney Television Studios; Cinémagique, a special-effects tribute to U.S. and European cinema; and a behind-the-scenes Studio Tram tour of location sites, movie props, studio decor and costuming, ending with a visit to Catastrophe Canyon in the heart of a film shoot. **Back Lot** majors in stunts. At Armageddon Special Effects you'll confront a flaming meteor shower aboard the Mir space station, then complete your visit at the giant outdoor arena with a Stunt Show Spectacular involving cars, motorbikes, and jet skis. ☎ *01–60–30–60–30* ⊕ *www.disneylandparis. com* ✉ *€40, €108 for 3-day Passport; includes admission to all individual attractions within Disneyland or Walt Disney Studios, but not meals; tickets for Walt Disney Studios are also valid for admission to Disneyland during last 3 opening hrs of same day* ☉ *Disneyland mid-June–mid-Sept., daily 9 AM–10 PM; mid-Sept.–mid-June, weekdays 10–8, weekends 9–8; Dec. 20–Jan. 4, daily 9–8; Walt Disney Studios daily 10–6* ▭ *AE, DC, MC, V.*

Where to Stay & Eat

$–$$$ ✕ **Disneyland Restaurants.** Disneyland Paris is peppered with places to eat, ranging from snack bars and fast-food joints to five full-service restaurants—all with a distinguishing theme. In addition, Walt Disney Studios, Disney Village, and Disney Hotels have restaurants open to the public. But since these are outside the park, it's not recommended that you waste time traveling to them for lunch. Disneyland Paris has relaxed its no-alcohol policy and now serves wine and beer in the park's sit-down restaurants, as well as in the hotels and restaurants outside the park. ☎ *01–60–45–65–40* ▭ *AE, DC, MC, V.*

$$$–$$$$ ▦ **Disneyland Hotels.** The resort has 5,000 rooms in six hotels, all a short distance from the park, ranging from the luxurious Disneyland Hotel to the not-so-rustic Camp Davy Crockett. Free transportation to the park

is available at every hotel. Packages including Disneyland lodging, entertainment, and admission are available through travel agents in Europe. ⌖ *Centre de Réservations, B.P. 100, cedex 4, 77777 Marne-la-Vallée* ☎ *01–60–30–60–30, 407/934–7639 in U.S.* 🖷 *01–49–30–71–00* ⌖ *All hotels have at least 1 restaurant, café, indoor pool, health club, sauna, bar, Internet* 🖃 *AE, DC, MC, V* ⍾⃝ *FAP.*

Nightlife & the Arts

Nocturnal entertainment outside the park centers on **Disney Village,** a vast pleasure mall designed by American architect Frank Gehry. Featured are American-style restaurants (crab shack, diner, deli, steak house), including **Billybob's Country Western Saloon** (☎ 01–60–45–70–81). Also in Disney Village is **Buffalo Bill's Wild West Show** (☎ 01–60–45–71–00 for reservations), a two-hour dinner extravaganza with a menu of sausages, spare ribs, and chili; performances by a talented troupe of stunt riders, bronco busters, tribal dancers, and musicians; plus some 50 horses, a dozen buffalo, a bull, and an Annie Oakley–style sharpshooter, with a golden-maned "Buffalo Bill" as emcee. A re-creation of a show that dazzled Parisians 100 years ago, it's corny but great fun. There are two shows nightly, at 6:30 and 9:30; the cost is €53 for adults, €33 for children under 12.

en route   Two châteaux just west of Disneyland merit a stop if you have time. The 17th-century **Château de Guermantes** (☎ 01–64–30–00–94), in Guermantes, 5 km (3 mi) north of Ferrières via D35, has Franco-Italianate decor and is open weekends from March through November. The name was immortalized in the figure of the Duchesse de Guermantes in Marcel Proust's *In Search of Lost Time,* but as it turns out, Proust simply liked the sound of the name and only visited the house after his book appeared and the last of the Guermantes had died. Two great names of the 18th-century—Robert de Cotte and Andre Le Nôtre—helped design the château; the showpiece is the gilt Grand Gallery, which was used in the James Bond film *Moonraker.* Aficionados of 18th-century French art and architecture should stop off between Paris and Disneyland at the bijou **Château de Champs-sur-Marne,** set in a magnificent park (✉ 31 rue de Paris, Champs-sur-Marne ☎ 01–60–05–24–43 ⊕ www.monum.fr ⊠ €6.10 ⊙ Wed.–Mon., 10–noon and 1:30–6).

SOUTHEAST TO FONTAINEBLEAU

Fontainebleau forms the hub of this heavily wooded southeast region of Ile-de-France. Nearby attractions include the grandeur of Vaux-le-Vicomte, a masterpiece of 17th-century architecture and garden design; or the pretty painters' villages of Barbizon and Moret-sur-Loing.

Vaux-le-Vicomte

 56 km (35 mi) southeast of Paris via A6, N104, A5, and N36; 5 km (3 mi) northeast of Melun via N36 and D215; 48 km south (30 mi) of Disneyland Paris via N36.

FodorśChoice ★ A manifesto for French 17th-century splendor, the **Château de Vaux-le-Vicomte** was built between 1656 and 1661 by finance minister Nicolas Fouquet. The construction program was monstrous: entire villages were razed, 18,000 workmen called in, and architect Louis Le Vau, painter Charles Le Brun, and landscape architect André Le Nôtre recruited at vast expense to prove that Fouquet's taste was as refined as his business acumen. The housewarming party was so lavish it had star guest Louis XIV, tetchy at the best of times, spitting jealous curses. He hurled Fouquet in the slammer and set about building Versailles to prove just who was top banana.

The high-roofed château, partially surrounded by a moat, is set well back from the road behind iron railings topped with sculpted heads. A cobbled avenue stretches up to the entrance, and stone steps lead to the vestibule, which seems small given the noble scale of the exterior. Charles Le Brun's captivating decoration includes the ceiling of the **Chambre du Roi** (Royal Bedchamber), depicting *Time Bearing Truth Heavenward,* framed by stuccowork by sculptors François Girardon and André Legendre. Along the frieze you can make out small squirrels, the Fouquet family's emblem—squirrels are known as *fouquets* in local dialect. But Le Brun's masterwork is the ceiling in the **Salon des Muses** (Hall of Muses), a brilliant allegorical composition painted in glowing, sensuous colors that some feel even surpasses his work at Versailles. On the ground floor the impressive **Grand Salon** (Great Hall), with its unusual oval form and 16 caryatid pillars symbolizing the months and seasons, has harmony and style even though the ceiling decoration was never finished. The state salons are redolent of *le style louisquartorzième,* thanks to the grand state beds, Mazarin desks, and Baroque marble busts—gathered together by the current owners of the château, the Comte et Comtesse de Vogüé—that replace the original pieces, which Louis XIV trundled off as booty to Versailles. In the basement, whose cool, dim rooms were used to store food and wine and house the château's kitchens, you'll find rotating exhibits about the château's past and life-size wax figures illustrating its history, including the notorious 19th-century murder-suicide of two erstwhile owners, the Duc et Duchess de Choiseul-Praslin. The house has been featured in many Hollywood films, including *The Man in the Iron Mask* and *Dangerous Liaisons.*

Le Nôtre's carefully restored **gardens** are at their best when the fountains are turned on (the second and final Saturday of each month from April through October, 3 PM–6 PM). Also visit the **Musée des Équipages** (Carriage Museum) in the stables, and inspect a host of carriages and coaches in wonderful condition. Perhaps the most beautiful time to visit the château and gardens are when they illuminated by thousands of candles during the Candlelight Evenings, held every Saturday night, from 8 to 11, from May 7th to October 15th. Get to Vaux by taking the train to Melun, then hopping on a local bus. ☎ *01–64–14–41–90* ⊕ *www.vaux-le-vicomte.com* ⊠ *€12, candlelight château visits €15; gardens only €7* ☉ *Apr.–Nov. 11, daily 10–6; candlelight visits May–mid-Oct., Sat. 8 PM–11.*

Where to Eat

¢–$ ✕ **L'Écureuil.** An imposing barn to the right of the château entrance has been transformed into this self-service cafeteria, where you can enjoy fine steaks (insist yours is cooked enough), coffee, or a snack beneath the ancient rafters of a wood-beam roof. The restaurant is open daily for lunch and tea, and for dinner during candlelight visits. ⊠ *Château de Vaux-le-Vicomte* ☎ *01–60–66–95–66* ▭ *MC, V.*

Barbizon

㊹ *17 km (11 mi) southwest of Vaux-le-Vicomte via Melun and D132/D64, 52 km (33 mi) southeast of Paris.*

On the western edge of the 62,000-acre Forest of Fontainebleau, the village of Barbizon retains its time-stained allure despite the intrusion of art galleries, souvenir shops, and busloads of tourists. The group of landscape painters known as the Barbizon School—Camille Corot, Jean-François Millet, Narcisse Diaz de la Peña, and Théodore Rousseau, among others—lived here from the 1830s on. They paved the way for the Impressionists by their willingness to accept nature on its own terms rather than using it as an idealized base for carefully structured compositions. Sealed to one of the famous sandstone rocks in the forest—which starts, literally, at the far end of the main street—is a bronze medallion by sculptor Henri Chapu, paying homage to Millet and Rousseau.

Corot and company would often repair to the Auberge Ganne after painting to brush up on their social life; the inn is now the **Musée de l'École de Barbizon** (Barbizon School Museum). Here you'll find documents of the village as it was in the 19th century, as well as a few original works. The Barbizon artists painted on every available surface, and even now you can see some originals on the upstairs walls. Two of the ground-floor rooms have been reconstituted as they were in Ganne's time—note the trompe-l'oeil paintings on the buffet doors. There's also a video on the Barbizon School. ⊠ *92 Grande-Rue* ☎ *01–60–66–22–27* ✆ *€6, joint admission with Maison-Atelier Théodore-Rousseau* ☉ *Mon. and Wed.–Fri. 10–12:30 and 2–5, weekends 10–5.*

Though there are no actual Millet works, the **Atelier Jean-François Millet** (Millet's Studio) is cluttered with photographs and mementos evoking his career. It was here that Millet painted some of his most renowned pieces, including *The Gleaners.* ⊠ *27 Grande-Rue* ☎ *01–60–66–21–55* ✆ *Free* ☉ *Wed.–Mon. 9:30–12:30 and 2–5:30.*

By the church, beyond the extraordinary village war memorial featuring a mustached ancient Gaul in a winged helmet, is the **Musée Théodore-Rousseau** (Rousseau's House-cum-Studio), in a converted barn. It is crammed with personal and artistic souvenirs and also has an exhibition space for temporary shows. ⊠ *55 Grande-Rue* ☎ *01–60–66–22–38* ✆ *€6, joint ticket with Barbizon School Museum* ☉ *Mon. and Wed.–Fri. 10–12:30 and 2–5, weekends 10–5.*

Where to Stay & Eat

$-$$ ✕ **Le Relais de Barbizon.** French country specialties are served at this rustic restaurant with a big open fire and a large terrace shaded by lime and chestnut trees. The four-course weekday menu is a good value, but wine here is expensive and cannot be ordered by the *pichet* (pitcher). Reservations are essential on weekends. ✉ *2 av. Général-de-Gaulle* ☎ *01–60–66–40–28* ☐ *MC, V* ☺ *Closed part of Aug., part of Feb., and Wed. No dinner Tues.*

★ **$** ✕🏨 **Les Alouettes.** This delightful, family-run 19th-century inn is set in 2 acres of leafy parkland, which the better rooms overlook. The interior is '30s style, and many rooms have oak beams. Lionel Ménard's rustic restaurant (reservations essential; no dinner Sunday), with its large open terrace, serves traditional French cuisine such as hare with mushrooms and lamb with eggplant. ✉ *4 rue Antoine-Barye, 77630* ☎ *01–60–66–41–98* 🖨 *01–60–66–20–69* 🛏 *22 rooms* ♨ *Restaurant, cable TV, bar, Internet, some pets allowed (fee); no a/c* ☐ *AE, DC, MC, V* ❚◯❚ *MAP.*

Fontainebleau

9 km (6 mi) southeast of Barbizon via N7, 61 km (38 mi) southeast of Paris via A6 and N7.

Like Chambord, in the Loire Valley, or Compiègne, to the north, Fontainebleau was a favorite spot for royal hunting parties long before the construction of one of France's grandest residences. Although not as celebrated as Versailles, this palace is almost as spectacular.

★ **45–54** The **Château de Fontainebleau** you see today dates from the 16th century, although additions were made by various royal incumbents through the next 300 years. The palace was begun under the flamboyant Renaissance king François I, the French contemporary of England's Henry VIII. The king hired Italian artists Il Rosso (a pupil of Michelangelo) and Primaticcio to embellish his château. In fact, they did much more: by introducing the pagan allegories and elegant lines of Mannerism to France, they revolutionized French decorative art. Their virtuoso frescoes and stuccowork can be admired in the **Galerie François-Ier** (Francis I Gallery) and in the jewel of the interior, the 100-foot-long **Salle de Bal** (ballroom), with its luxuriant wood paneling, completed under Henri II, François's successor, and a gleaming parquet floor that reflects the patterns on the ceiling. Like the château as a whole, the room exudes a sense of elegance and style—but on a more intimate, human scale than at Versailles: this is Renaissance, not Baroque. Henri II also added the decorative interlaced initials found throughout the palace. You might expect to see the royal *H* woven with a *C* (for Catherine de' Medici, his wife). Instead you'll find a *D*—indicating his mistress, Diane de Poitiers.

Napoléon's apartments occupied the first floor. You can see a lock of his hair, his Légion d'Honneur medal, his imperial uniform, the hat he wore on his return from Elba in 1815, and one bed in which he definitely did spend a night (almost every town in France boasts a bed in which the emperor supposedly snoozed). The **Salon Jaune** (Yellow

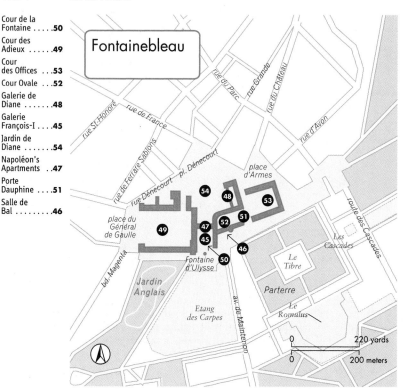

Room) of Joséphine is one of the best examples of the Empire style—the austere Neoclassical style promoted by the emperor. There's also a throne room—Napoléon spurned the one at Versailles, a palace he disliked, establishing his imperial seat in the former King's Bedchamber—and the Queen's Boudoir, also known as the Room of the Six Maries (occupants included ill-fated Marie-Antoinette and Napoléon's second wife, Marie-Louise). The sweeping **Galerie de Diane,** built during the reign of Henri IV (1589–1610), was converted into a library in the 1860s. Other salons have 17th-century tapestries and paintings and frescoes by members of the Fontainebleau School.

Although Louis XIV's architectural fancy was concentrated on Versailles, he commissioned Mansart to design new pavilions and had André Le Nôtre replant the gardens at Fontainebleau, where he and his court returned faithfully in the fall for the hunting season. But it was Napoléon who spent lavishly to make a Versailles, as it were, out of Fontainebleau. He held Pope Pius VII here as a captive guest in 1812, signed the second church-state concordat here in 1813, and, in the cobbled **Cour des Adieux** (Farewell Courtyard), said good-bye to his Old Guard on April 20, 1814, as he began his brief exile on the Mediterranean island of Elba. The famous **Horseshoe Staircase** that dominates the Cour des Adieux, once the

Cour du Cheval Blanc (White Horse Courtyard), was built by Androuet du Cerceau for Louis XIII (1610–43); it was down this staircase that Napoléon made his way slowly to take a final salute from his Vieille Garde. Another courtyard—the **Cour de la Fontaine** (Fountain Courtyard)—was commissioned by Napoléon in 1812 and adjoins the Étang des Carpes (Carp Pond). Across from the pond is the formal Parterre (flower garden) and, on the other side, the leafy Jardin Anglais (English Garden).

The **Porte Dauphine** is the most beautiful of the various gateways that connect the complex of buildings; its name commemorates the christening of the dauphin—the heir to the throne, later Louis XIII—under its archway in 1606. The gateway fronts the **Cour Ovale** (Oval Court), shaped like a flattened egg. Opposite the courtyard is the **Cour des Offices** (Kitchen Court), a large, severe square built at the same time as place des Vosges in Paris (1609). Around the corner is the informal **Jardin de Diane** (Diana's Garden), with peacocks and a statue of the hunting goddess surrounded by mournful hounds. ⊠ *Pl. du Général-de-Gaulle* ☎ *01–60–71–50–70* ⊕ *www.musee-chateau-fontainebleau.fr* ✍ *€5.50, Napoleon's Apartments €3 extra; gardens free* ☉ *Wed.–Mon. 9:30–5; gardens Apr.–Sept., daily 9–8:30; Oct.–Mar., daily 9–5.*

Where to Stay & Eat

$$–$$$ ✕ **Chez Arrighi.** This cozy, pink-walled, Art Deco restaurant near the château pulls in local gourmets with its three-course €18 menu that sometimes includes salmon or boeuf bourguignon. Jugged hare, pavé de biche (venison) and scallops with ginger and *roquette* salad are among seasonal specialties à la carte. ⊠ *53 rue de France* ☎ *01–64–22–29–43* ▭ *MC, V* ☉ *Closed Mon., no dinner Sun.*

★ **$$$$** ✕▥ **L'Aigle Noir.** This may be Fontainebleau's costliest hotel, but you can't go wrong if you request one of the rooms overlooking either the garden or the palace. They have late-18th- or early-19th-century reproduction furniture, creating a Napoleonic ambience. The restaurant, Le Beauharnais, serves subtle, imaginative cuisine—lamb with thyme and gentian, for instance (dinner only, except Sunday; restaurant closed most of August). There's a tranquil garden for alfresco dining in summer. Reservations are essential and jacket and tie are required. ⊠ *27 pl. Napoléon-Bonaparte, 77300* ☎*01–60–74–60–00* 🖶*01–60–74–60–01* ⊕ *www.hotelaiglenoir.fr* ⬫ *53 rooms, 3 suites* ⌂ *Restaurant, minibars, cable TV, pool, gym, sauna, some pets allowed (fee)* ▭ *AE, DC, MC, V* ⍾◯ *BP.*

$$$ ✕▥ **Napoléon.** This former post office close to the palace counts as one of the best local hotels. Pastel-color rooms have modern furniture and marble baths and look out onto terraces or the indoor patio. The plush restaurant, La Table des Maréchaux, with its golden wallpaper and crimson velvet seating, serves satisfying, deftly prepared classics, and the €25 menu is an excellent deal. ⊠ *9 rue Grande, 77300* ☎ *01–60–39–50–50* 🖶 *01–64–22–20–87* ⊕ *www.hotelnapoleon-fontainebleau.com* ⬫ *58 rooms* ⌂ *Restaurant, minibars, cable TV, Internet, some pets allowed (fee); no a/c* ▭ *AE, DC, MC, V* ⍾◯ *MAP.*

$$–$$$ ▥ **Londres.** Established in 1850, the Londres is a small, family-style hotel with Louis XV accents. Some balconies overlook the palace entrance and the Cour des Adieux, where Napoléon bade his troops an emotional farewell. The hotel's prim 19th-century facade is a registered landmark. ⊠ *1 pl. du Général-de-Gaulle, 77300* ☎ *01–64–22–20–21* 🖶 *01–60–72–39–16* ⊕ *www.hoteldelondres.com* ↩ *12 rooms* ⚲ *Restaurant, cable TV, bar, Internet; no a/c* ▭ *AE, DC, MC, V* ☉ *Closed 1 wk Aug. and mid-Dec.–early Jan.* ❢◯❢ *BP.*

Sports & the Outdoors

The Forest of Fontainebleau is laced with hiking trails; for more information ask for the *Guide des Sentiers* (trail guide) at the tourist office. Bikes can be rented at the Fontainebleau-Avon train station. The forest is also famed for its quirky rock formations, where many a novice alpinist first caught the climbing bug; for more information contact the **Club Alpin Français** (⊠ 24 av. Laumière, 75019 Paris ☎ 01–53–72–87–00).

Moret-sur-Loing

⑤⑤ *10 km (6 mi) southeast of Fontainebleau via N6, 72 km (45 mi) southeast of Paris.*

Close to the confluence of the Seine and Yonne rivers is the picturesque village of Moret-sur-Loing. It was immortalized by Impressionist painter Alfred Sisley, who lived here for 20 years, at 19 rue Montmartre (not open to the public), around the corner from the church. A narrow bridge, one of the oldest in France, leads across the Loing River (boat trips available) and provides a view of the village walls, rooftops, and church tower. If you've a sweet tooth, take note: Moret is renowned for its barley sugar.

Nightlife & the Arts

A good time to be in Moret is on a Saturday evening in summer (from mid-June through mid-September) for the riverside **Festival de Moret,** when 600 locals stage son-et-lumière pageants illustrating the town's history. ☎ 01–60–70–41-66 🎟 €16.

Provins

⑤⑥ *48 km (30 mi) northeast of Moret on N6/D403, 77 km (48 mi) southeast of Paris.*

On the hilltop site of a Roman camp, Provins developed into the third-largest town in France (after Paris and Rouen) in the Middle Ages as capital of the counts of Champagne, acquiring international renown for its fairs and as a rose-growing center. Provins is a UNESCO-listed World Heritage Site with 50 protected monuments bearing witness to its opulent past, including the 12th-century Gothic church of **St-Quiriace** with its incongruous 17th-century classical dome. There's plenty to see underground, too—a guided tour of the **Souterrains** takes in a small part of the 6 mi of tunnels that honeycomb the hill on which Provins is built. Contact the tourist office Web site for details: www.provins.net.

Climb up to the **Tour César,** a round, ivy-covered 11th-century keep atop a sturdy mound, for a panoramic view of the town and some of the best-preserved medieval ramparts in France. ⊠ *7 rue du Palais*

☎ *01–64–01–40–19* 🎟 *€3.40* ⏲ *Apr.–Oct., daily 10–6; Nov.–Mar., daily 2–5.*

The vaulted 13th-century **Grange aux Dîmes** (Tithe Barn), originally used as a covered market, houses a collection of waxwork displays evoking the crafts and merchants who brought medieval Provins wealth and fame, and shows a film retracing the town's history. ✉ *Rue St-Jean* 🎟 *€3.40* ⏲ *Apr.–Aug., daily 10–6; Sept.–Oct., daily 2–6; Nov.–Mar., weekends 2–5.*

Where to Stay & Eat

$–$$$$ ✕🏨 **Aux Vieux Remparts.** Set, as its name suggests, within the Vieille Ville walls (or ramparts), this thriving establishment (seven new rooms were added in 2002) has plush-carpeted rooms with contemporary furniture overlooking the leafy inner garden, where you can dine outdoors on balmy summer evenings. Otherwise the delectable talents of chef Lionel Seret—ranging from grilled scallops to rose-petal soufflé—are showcased in the adjacent half-timber 16th-century restaurant. ✉ *3 rue Couverte, 77160* ☎ *01–64–08–94–00* 📠 *01–60–67–77–22* 🌐 *www.auxvieuxremparts.com* *32 rooms* *Restaurant, minibars, cable TV, bar, Internet, some pets allowed (fee); no a/c* 💳 *AE, DC, MC, V* 🍽 *MAP.*

Nightlife & the Arts

Reconstituted **jousting tournaments** (☎ 01–64–60–26–26) and a mock attack on the town walls using medieval war machines are held most weekend afternoons in summer; call the tourist office for details.

ILE-DE-FRANCE A TO Z

To research prices, get advice from other travelers, and book travel arrangements, visit www.fodors.com.

AIRPORTS

Major airports in the Ile-de-France area are Charles de Gaulle, commonly known as Roissy, 25 km (16 mi) northeast of Paris, and Orly, 16 km (10 mi) south. Shuttle buses link Disneyland to the airports at Roissy, 56 km (35 mi) away, and Orly, 50 km (31 mi) distant; buses take 45 minutes and run every 45 minutes from Roissy, every 60 minutes from Orly (less frequently in low season), and cost €15.

Airport Information **Charles de Gaulle** ☎ 01-48-62-22-80 🌐 www.adp.fr. **Orly** ☎ 01-49-75-15-15 🌐 www.adp.fr.

BUS TRAVEL

While many of the major sights in this chapter have train lines connecting them on direct routes with Paris, the lesser towns and destinations pose more of a problem. You often need to take a local bus or taxi after arriving at a train station (for instance, to get to Senlis from Chantilly Gare SNCF, or Fontainebleau and Barbizon from Avon Gare SNCF, or Vaux-le-Vicomte from Melun Gare SNCF, or Giverny from Vernon Gare SNCF). Other buses travel outward from Paris's suburbs—the No. 158A bus, for instance, which goes from La Défense to St-Germain-en-Laye and Rueil-Malmaison.

CAR RENTAL

Cars can be rented from agencies in Paris or at Orly or Charles de Gaulle airports.

CAR TRAVEL

A13 links Paris (from the Porte d'Auteuil) to Versailles. You can get to Chartres on A10 from Paris (Porte d'Orléans). For Fontainebleau take A6 from Paris (Porte d'Orléans), or for a more attractive, although slower route through the Forest of Sénart and the northern part of the Forest of Fontainebleau, take N6 from Paris (Porte de Charenton) via Melun. A4 runs from Paris (Porte de Bercy) to Disneyland. Although a comprehensive rail network ensures that most towns in Ile-de-France can make comfortable day trips from Paris, the only way to crisscross the region without returning to the capital is by car. There's no shortage of expressways or fast highways, but be prepared for delays close to Paris and during the morning and evening rush hours.

EMERGENCIES

The American Hospital and the British Hospital are closer to Paris, and other regional hospitals are listed by town below.

🚩 **Ambulance** ☎ 15. **American Hospital** ✉ 63 bd. Victor-Hugo ☎ 01-47-45-71-00 in Neuilly. **British Hospital** ✉ 3 rue Barbès ☎ 01-47-58-13-12 in Levallois-Perret. **Chartres** ✉ 34 rue du Dr-Maunoury ☎ 02-37-30-30-30. **Melun** ✉ 2 rue Fréteau-de-Pény ☎ 01-64-71-60-00. **Versailles** ✉ 177 rue de Versailles, Le Chesnay ☎ 01-39-63-91-33.

TOURS

Cityrama organizes guided excursions to Giverny, Chartres, and Vaux-le-Vicomte (€60) from April through October. Cityrama and Paris Vision run half- and full-day trips to Versailles (€48–88), some combined with Chartres or Fontainebleau/Barbizon (€95).

🚩 **Cityrama** ✉ 4 pl. des Pyramides, 75001 Paris ☎ 01-44-55-61-00 ⊕ www.cityrama. com. **Paris Vision** ✉ 214 rue de Rivoli, 75001 Paris ☎ 01-42-60-30-01 ⊕ www. parisvision.com.

PRIVATE GUIDES Alliance Autos has bilingual guides who can take you on a private tour around the Paris area in a luxury car or minibus for a minimum of four hours for about €80 an hour (call to check details and prices). Euroscope runs minibus excursions to Versailles (€70) and Giverny (€75).

🚩 **Alliance Autos** ✉ 149 rue de Charonne, 75011 Paris ☎ 01-55-25-23-23. **Euroscope** ☎ 01-49-46-24-50 ⊕ www.euroscope.fr; contact your hotel for bookings.

TRAIN TRAVEL

Many sights can be reached by train from Paris. Both regional and main-line (Le Mans–bound) trains leave Gare Montparnasse for Chartres (50–70 minutes); the former also stop at Versailles, Rambouillet, and Maintenon. Gare Montparnasse is also the terminal for trains to Dreux (Granville line) and for the suburban trains that stop at Montfort-L'Amaury, the nearest station to Thoiry (35 minutes).

Some mainline trains from Gare St-Lazare stop at Mantes-la-Jolie (30 minutes) and Vernon (50 minutes) on their way to Rouen and Le Havre.

Suburban trains leave the Gare du Nord for L'Isle-Adam (50 minutes). Chantilly is on the main northbound line from Gare du Nord (the trip takes 25–40 minutes), and Senlis can be reached by bus from Chantilly. Fontainebleau—or, rather, neighboring Avon, 2 km (1½ mi) away (there is frequent bus service)—is 45 minutes from Gare de Lyon. To reach Vaux-le-Vicomte, head first for Melun, then take a taxi or local bus; to reach Giverny, rail it to Vernon, then use the taxi or local bus.

St-Germain-en-Laye is a terminal of the RER-A (commuter train) that tunnels through Paris (main stations at Étoile, Auber, Les Halles, and Gare de Lyon). The RER-A also accesses Poissy and Maisons-Laffitte and, at the other end, the station for Disneyland Paris (called Marne-la-Vallée–Chessy), within 100 yards of the entrance to both the theme park and Disney Village. Journey time is around 40 minutes, and trains operate every 10–30 minutes, depending on the time of day. The handiest of Versailles's three train stations is the one reached by the RER-C line (main stations at Austerlitz, St-Michel, Invalides, and Champ-de-Mars); the trip takes 30–40 minutes. Special *forfait* tickets, combining travel and admission, are available for several regional tourist destinations (including Versailles, Fontainebleau, and Auvers-sur-Oise).

A mainline TGV (Trains à Grande Vitesse) station links Disneyland to Lille, Lyon, Brussels, and London (via Lille and the Channel Tunnel). 🚊 Train Information **SNCF** ☎ 08-36-35-35-35 ⊕ idf.sncf.fr/GB. **TGV** ⊕ www.tgv.com.

VISITOR INFORMATION

Contact the Espace du Tourisme d'Ile-de-France (open Wednesday–Monday 10–7, www.pidf.com), under the inverted pyramid in the Carrousel du Louvre, for general information on the area. Information on Disneyland is available from the Disneyland Paris reservations office. Local tourist offices are listed below by town.

🚊 Tourist Information **Espace du Tourisme d'Ile-de-France** ✉ Pl. de la Pyramide-Renversée, 99 rue de Rivoli, 75001 Paris ☎ 08-03-81-80-00. **Disneyland Paris reservations office** ✆ B.P. 100, cedex 4, 77777 Marne-la-Vallée ☎ 01-60-30-60-30, 407/824-4321 in U.S. **Barbizon** ✉ 41 Grande-Rue ☎ 01-60-66-41-87 ⊕ www.barbizon-france.com. **Chantilly** ✉ 60 av. du Maréchal-Joffre ☎ 03-44-57-08-58 ⊕ www.ville-de-chantilly.fr. **Chartres** ✉ Pl. de la Cathédrale ☎ 02-37-18-26-26 ⊕ www.chartres-tourisme.com. **Fontainebleau** ✉ 4 rue Royale ☎ 01-60-74-99-99 ⊕ www.fontainebleau-tourisme.com. **Rambouillet** ✉ 1 pl. de la Libération ☎ 01-34-83-21-21 ⊕ www.ot-rambouillet.fr. **St-Germain-en-Laye** ✉ 38 rue au Pain ☎ 01-34-51-05-12 ⊕ www.ville-st-germain-en-laye.fr. **Senlis** ✉ Pl. du Parvis Notre-Dame ☎ 03-44-53-06-40 ⊕ www.ville-senlis.fr. **Versailles** ✉ 2 bis av. de Paris ☎ 01-39-24-88-88 ⊕ www.versailles.tourisme.com.

The Loire Valley

WORD OF MOUTH

"Chenonceau is the most famous Loire château and certainly one of the most beautiful, built straddling the lazy Cher River. The stomping grounds of Diane de Poitiers, a consort of the king, she was forced to down-trade it for Chaumont. During World War II, folks escaped from Nazi France by going through the castle to cross the Cher to the Vichy controlled part of France. The Chenonceaux rail station was recently relocated to now let you off right in front of the château, thus a day trip by rail from Paris is possible!"

—PalQ

"Best bit about Chambord: taking the boat tour around the château. We were the only ones on the boat and got a different perspective of the place."

—BTilke

Introduction by
Nancy Coons

Updated by
Robert I. C.
Fisher and
Simon Hewitt

A DIAPHANOUS AURA OF SUBTLY SHIFTING LIGHT plays over the luxuriant countryside of the Loire Valley, a region blessedly mild of climate, richly populated with game, and habitually fertile. Although it had always been viewed as prime real estate, the victorious Valois dynasty began to see new possibilities in the territory once the dust from the Hundred Years' War began to settle and the bastions of the Plantagenet kings lost some of their utility. This, they mused, was an ideal spot for a holiday home. Sketching, no doubt, on a tavern napkin at Blois, Louis XII dreamed of a tasteful blend of symmetry and fantasy, of turrets and gargoyles, while Anne of Brittany breathed down his neck for more closet space. In no time at all, the neighboring Joneses had followed suit, and by the 16th century the area was a showplace of fabulous châteaux *d'agrément,* or pleasure castles—palaces for royalty, yes, but also love nests for mistresses and status statements for arrivistes (Chenonceau was built by a tax collector). There were boxwood gardens endlessly receding toward vanishing points, moats graced with swans, parades of delicate cone-topped towers, frescoes, and fancywork ceilings. The glories of the Italian Renaissance, observed by the Valois while making war on their neighbor, were brought to bear on these mega-monuments with all the elegance and proportions characteristic of antiquity.

By the time François I took charge, extravagance knew no bounds: on a 13,000-acre forest estate, hunting parties at Chambord drew A-list crowds from the far reaches of Europe—and the availability of 430 rooms made weekend entertaining a snap. Queen Claudia hired only the most recherché Italian artisans: Chambord's famous double-helix staircase may, in fact, have been Leonardo da Vinci's design (he was a frequent houseguest there when not in residence in a manor on the Amboise grounds). From massive kennels teeming with hunting hounds at Cheverny to luxurious stables at Chaumont-sur-Loire, from endless allées of pollarded lime trees at Villandry to the fairy-tale towers of Ussé—worthy of Sleeping Beauty herself—the Loire Valley became the power base and social center for the New France, allowing the monarchy to go all out in strutting its stuff.

All for good reason. In 1519 Charles V of Spain, at the age of 19, inherited the Holy Roman Empire, leaving François and his New France—as well as England's Henry VIII—out in the cold. It was perhaps no coincidence that in 1519 François, in a grand stab at face-saving one-upmanship, commenced construction on his ultimate declaration of dominion, the gigantic château of Chambord. After a few skirmishes (the Low Countries, Italy), and no doubt a few power breakfasts, François was confident enough to entertain the emperor on his lavish Loire estates, and by 1539 he had married Charles V's sister.

Location is everything, as you realize when you think of Hyannisport, Kennebunkport, and Balmoral: homesteads redolent of dynasty, where natural beauty, idyllic views, an invigorating hunt with the boys, and a barefoot stroll in the great outdoors liberate the mind to think great thoughts and make history's decisions. Perhaps this is why French Revolution have-nots sacked so many of the châteaux of the Loire Valley; today most of the châteaux have been restored, and are maintained as museums in the public domain. Although these châteaux are testimony to France's most fabled age of kings, their pleasures, once restricted to royalty and members of the nobility, are now shared by the populace. Yet the Revolution and the efforts of latter-day socialists have not totally erased a lingering gentility in the people of the region, characterized by an air of refined assurance far removed from the shoulder-shrugging, chest-tapping French stereotypes. Here life proceeds at a pleasingly genteel pace, and you'll find a winning concentration of gracious country inns and discerning chefs, a cornucopia of local produce and game, and the famous, flinty wines of Sancerre—all regional blessings still truly fit for a king, but now available to his subjects as well.

Exploring the Loire Valley

Pick up the Loire River halfway along its course from central France to the Atlantic Ocean. Châteaux and vineyards will accompany you throughout a 340-km (210-mi) westbound course from the hilltop wine town of Sancerre to the bustling city of Angers. Towns punctuate the route at almost equal distances—Orléans, Blois, Tours, Saumur—and are useful bases if you're relying on public transportation. But don't let the lack of a car prevent you from visiting and overnighting in the lovely villages of the region because a surprising number can be accessed via train, bus, or taxi. Although you may be rushing around to see as many famous châteaux as possible, make time to walk through the poppy-covered hills, picnic along the riverbanks, and sample the famous local wines.

About the Restaurants & Hotels

In summer you will face an appetizing choice of places to eat along the Loire; play safe and book ahead, especially on weekends and in July and August. The off-season (October through Easter) is different—many of the Loire Valley villages that hum with life in the summertime return to hibernation once the tourist season ends. Note that many of the famed château-hotels have their own restaurants; these are usually superb, so if they expect—in summer, sometimes insist—that you eat dinner in their restaurant, by all means, say *oui*. Loire wines are among the most loved in France, and they are varied. Among the best are Savennières, Sancerre, and Cheverny, dry whites; Coteaux du Layon and Montlouis, sweet whites; Cabernet d'Anjou, rosé (often sweet); Bourgueil, Chinon, and Saumur-Champigny, reds; and Vouvray, white—dry, sweet, or sparkling.

Even before the age of the railway, the Loire Valley drew vacationers from far afield, so there are hundreds of hotels of all types. At the higher end are converted châteaux, but even these are not as pricey as you might think. At the lower end are small, traditional inns in towns and villages, usually offering terrific value for the money. The Loire Valley is a very popular destination, so make reservations well in advance. Assume all hotel rooms have air-conditioning, telephones, TV, and private bath, unless otherwise noted.

3

Strung like precious gems along the peaceful Loire and its tributaries, the royal and near-royal châteaux of the region are among the most fabled sights in France. From magical Chenonceau—improbably suspended above the River Cher—to mighty Chambord, from the *Sleeping Beauty* abode of Ussé to the famed gardens of Villandry, this parade of châteaux gloriously epitomizes France's golden age of monarchy. In Orléans, a dramatic chapter in the country's history unfolds: it was here that Joan of Arc had her most rousing successes against the English. With all these treasures, you need two weeks to cover the Loire Valley region in its entirety. But even if you don't have that long, you can still see many of the valley's finest châteaux in three days by concentrating on the area between Blois and Azay-le-Rideau. Six days will give you time to explore these châteaux in depth, as well as to visit Tours and Angers, two of the region's major cities. In 10 days you can follow the Loire from Orléans to Angers.

Numbers in the text correspond to numbers in the margin and on the Loire Valley, Orléans, and Tours maps.

If you have 3 days

Gateway to the central Loire Valley, **Tours** ① ▶ – ⑧ is the hub of Touraine. Although there are a few museums to catch and historic place Plumereau beckons, don't tarry in this big city—begin your tour of some of France's choicest real estate by taking an easy train ride away to **Chenonceau** ⑫, everyone's dream of a Loire Valley castle. If you want your own taste of *la vie de château*, backtrack by train or car to ⊡ **Montlouis-sur-Loire** ⑩ and the Broglie princes' gorgeous, neo-Renaissance Château de la Bourdaisière (a hotel but also open to day-trippers) or, for a more urban treat, continue on to the north side of the Loire and ⊡ **Blois** ⑰, where you'll find one of the earliest of the great châteaux. Spend the morning of your second day touring Blois, then move inland through the forest to spend the night at ⊡ **Chambord** ⑮—such a vast marble pile it seems more a city than a palace. On your third day, return to Blois, then head downstream to **Amboise** ⑪ to take in its massive château and, more delightfully, the Clos-Lucé mansion, the last home of Leonardo da Vinci. If you hustle—and trains can make the journey in around an hour—head instead to the edge of Touraine and spectacular **Chinon** ㉓ for an unforgettable dip into the Middle Ages. Connecting trains from Chinon can get you back to Paris via Tours by night.

If you have 6 days

Start by following the three-day itinerary. On the fourth day explore enchanting ⊡ **Chinon** ㉓, then head east to see two of the dreamiest fairy-tale châteaux—the Renaissance jewel of **Azay-le-Rideau** ⑳ and, a few miles away (buses are rare, so consider a taxi), ⊡ **Ussé** ㉒, which inspired Perrault to write *Sleeping Beauty*. On your fifth day, those without a car will need to return to Azay or Chinon, where you can wend your way to magical ⊡ **Fontevraud** ㉔, Europe's largest surviving abbey and a Romanesque wonder. Then head to the smart river town of **Saumur** ㉕, with its dramatic cliff-top castle and comprehensive train and bus connections.

If you have
10
days

Follow the six-day itinerary and, after exploring Saumur on your sixth day, stop off in nearby ▦ **Bourgueil** ㉙ to tour the vineyards or wine caves, making an overnight at the lovely Château de Réaux (save your pennies for this one; it is also open for touring by day-trippers). On your seventh day, a helpful train route can deposit you at the mighty citadel of **Langeais** ㉚ to ogle its sumptuous, tapestried interior. In the afternoon, continue northeast back to Tours, then head out (via bus or taxi if you have no car) to spectacular ▦ **Villandry** ⑲, famed for its enormous Renaissance château and garden parterres. On your eighth day, backtrack to Tours and train it to ▦ **Orléans** ㉛–㉞. After exploring this gateway city to the Upper Loire Valley and overnighting here, head out on your ninth morning to explore the region's sights—either the imposing abbey at **St-Benoît-sur-Loire** ㊲ or the storybook moated castle at **Sully-sur-Loire** ㊳ before ending up in the town of ▦ **Gien** ㊴, famed for its earthenware, to spend the night. Or, for a dazzling splurge, head south by car or train to the Franco-Scottish town of ▦ **Aubigny-sur-Nère** ㊷ and enjoy a stay at the seignorial hotel, the Château de la Verrerie. On your final morning, visit the hilltop wine town of Sancerre. After lunch, head back to Orléans, Paris, and reality.

WHAT IT COSTS In euros				
$$$$	**$$$**	**$$**	**$**	**¢**
RESTAURANTS over €30	€23–€30	€17–€23	€11–€17	under €11
HOTELS over €190	€120–€190	€80–€120	€50–€80	under €50

Restaurant prices are per person for a main course only, including tax (19.6%) and service; note that if a restaurant offers only prix-fixe (set-price) meals, it has been given the price category that reflects the full prix-fixe price. Hotel prices are for a standard double room in high season, including tax (19.6%) and service charge. Hotels operate on the European Plan (EP, with no meal provided) unless we note that they use the Breakfast Plan (BP), or also offer such options as Modified American Plan (MAP, with breakfast and dinner daily, known as *demi-pension*), or Full American Plan (FAP, or *pension complète*, with three meals a day). Inquire when booking if these all-inclusive mealplans (which always entail higher rates) are mandatory or optional.

Timing

The Loire, the last great European river left undammed, is at its best in May and June, when it still looks like a river; come midsummer, the water level can drop, revealing unsightly sandbanks. The valley divides France in two, both geographically and climatically: north of the Loire, France has the moist, temperate climate of northern Europe; southward lies the drier climate of the Mediterranean. It's striking how changeable the weather can be as you cross the Loire. The valley can be sultry in July and August, when most of the son-et-lumière shows take place and the tourist crowds arrive. October is a good off-season option, when all is mist and mellow fruitfulness along the Loire and the mysterious pools of the Sologne, as the trees turn russet and gold. Fall is also the best time to sample regional specialties such as wild mushrooms and game. On Sunday, when most shops are closed, try to avoid the main cities—Orléans, Tours, Angers.

3

Châteaux Country

Loire and *château* are almost synonymous; even the word *château*—part fortress, part palace, part mansion—has no English equivalent. There are châteaux in every region of France, but nowhere are they found clustered as thickly as in the Loire. Why? There are several reasons. By the early Middle Ages, strategically sited and prosperous towns had already grown up because of transport on the Loire, and fortresses—the first châteaux—were built by warlords for defense. The region was also a wildly productive land—the part between the Loire and the Cher has long been known as the "garden of France." In few other areas of France is *la douceur de la vie*, the sweetness of life, more alluring. Feudal lords grew rich; so did monks, building splendid abbeys. The early medieval Plantagenet kings, rulers of France and England, soon arrived (at Chinon and Fontevraud, to be exact). Under the later medieval Valois kings, the Loire became in effect the capital of France. Châteaux sprang up at their command thanks to the region's easily worked building stone, tufa, or *tuffeaux*. The parade of châteaux began with the medieval fortress at Angers, a brooding, muscular fort designed to withstand long sieges. Such castles were meant to look grim, advertising horrid problems for attackers and unpleasant conditions for prisoners in the dungeons. Elegance arrived at Saumur—the Duc de Berry adorned the sturdy fort with a riot of high pointed roofs, gilded steeples, iron weather vanes, and soaring pinnacles, creating a Gothic-style castle that Walt Disney would have been proud of. Decent-sized windows replaced the old cross-bow slits and love-sick princesses would lean out of these windows to gaze down on chivalric tournaments, with all the trappings of cloth-of-gold, and banquets with trumpeters. The time has arrived for every rich noble to insist on a decorative drawbridge and defensive tower or two to impress the neighbors.

By the Renaissance—brought to France by Charles VIII at the end of the 15th century—balance, harmony, and grace were brought to the fore by rich bankers and officials who, some super-romantic American art historians believe, wanted to wow their womenfolk by building châteaux that were homages to the death-defying chivalry of the past. Azay-le-Rideau may look Gothic from a distance, but its moat is actually the river Indre, and its purpose is to provide a pleasing reflection, adding a further symmetry to this jewel of architecture. This was literally a fairy-tale castle, not used to defend territories but to entertain and astonish guests with luxury. This style reached its peak at Chenonceau, the beautiful château that seems moored over the river Cher—designed by ladies, it was used mostly to host gala balls and famous VIPs. By the 17th century the line of great châteaux had come to an end—the locus of power had moved to the Ile de France and Paris. Cheverny, built between 1604 and 1634, seems only an exercise in classical Italianate symmetry. Although it has a wide facade, the building is only one room deep—the château had become a stage curtain and little more.

Son-et-Lumière

In summer, concerts, music festivals, fairs, and celebrated *son-et-lumière* (sound-and-light) extravaganzas are held on the grounds of several châteaux. These dramatic spectacles, mounted after dark, can take the form of historical pageants—with huge casts of people, all in period costume, and caparisoned horses, all floodlighted (some shows simulate shadows of flickering flames to conjure up the mobs of the French Revolution) and backed by music and commentary, sometimes in English; Amboise is the top example. Productions are more often shows with spoken commentary and dialogue but no visible figures, as at Chenonceau and Azay-le-Rideau. Other than at Amboise and Loches, don't expect a cast of thousands—most of the special effects are due to slide projections, smoke-machines, torches, and color spotlights, but they are breathtaking and unforgettable. Of course, to truly experience the château in all its splendor, be sure to stay at some of the many gorgeous château-hotels in the region.

ALONG THE LOIRE: FROM TOURS TO CHAMBORD

Halfway along the route of the Loire—the longest river in France—and just outside the city of Orléans, the river takes a wide, westward bend, gliding languidly through low, rich country known as the Val de Loire— or Loire Valley. In this temperate region—a 225-km (140-mi) stretch between Orléans and Angers—scores of châteaux built of local *tufa* (white limestone) rise from the rocky banks of the Loire and its tributaries: the rivers Cher, Indre, Vienne, and Loir (with no *e*).

The Loire is liquid history. For centuries the river was the area's principal means of transportation and an effective barrier against invading armies. Towns arose at strategic bridgeheads, and fortresses—the earliest châteaux—appeared on towering slopes. The Loire Valley was hotly disputed by France and England during the Middle Ages; it belonged to England (under the Anjou Plantagenet family) between 1154 and 1216 and again during the Hundred Years' War (1337–1453). It was the example of Joan of Arc, the Maid of Orléans (so called after the site of one of her most stirring victories), that crystallized French efforts to expel the English.

The Loire Valley's golden age came under François I (ruled 1515–47)— flamboyant contemporary of England's Henry VIII—whose salamander emblem can be seen in many châteaux, including Chambord, the mightiest of them. Although the nation's power base shifted to Paris around 1600, aristocrats continued to erect luxurious palaces along the Loire until the end of the 18th century.

Tours, the capital city of the province of Touraine, is the gateway to the entire region, not only for its central position but because the TGV high-speed train can deposit you there from Paris in little more than an hour. A string of fine châteaux dominates the Loire Valley east of Tours—Blois, Chaumont, and Amboise lead the way—but two of the area's most stunning monuments lie south of the Loire: romantic Chenonceau, with its arches half-straddling the River Cher, and colossal Chambord, its forest of chimneys and turrets visible above the treetops. By heading west-

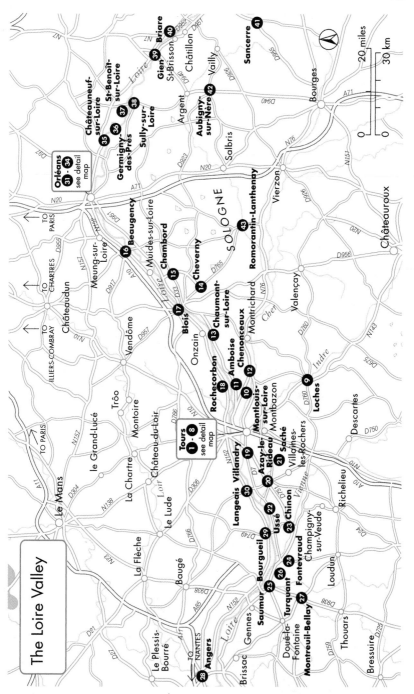

The Loire Valley

ward from Tours, on the other hand, you enter a storyland par excellence, address to such fairy-tale châteaux as Ussé and Azay-le-Rideau and the more muscular castles of Chinon and Saumur. From Angers you can drive northeast to explore the winding, intimate Loir Valley all the way to Châteaudun, just south of Chartres and the Ile-de-France; or continue along the Loire as far as Nantes, the southern gateway to Brittany.

Tours

240 km (150 mi) southwest of Paris.

Little remains of Tours's own château—one of France's finest cathedrals more than compensates—but the city serves as the transportation hub for the Loire Valley. Trains from Tours (and from its adjacent terminal at St-Pierre-de-Corps) run along the river in both directions, and regular bus services radiate from here; in addition, the city is the starting point for organized bus excursions (many with English-speaking guides). The town has mushroomed into a city of a quarter of a million inhabitants, with an ugly modern sprawl of factories, high-rise blocks, and overhead expressway junctions cluttering up the outskirts. But the timber-frame houses in **Le Vieux Tours** (Old Tours) and the attractive medieval center around place Plumereau were smartly restored after extensive damage in World War II.

Only two sturdy towers—the Tour Charlemagne and the Tour de l'Horloge (Clock Tower)—remain of the great medieval abbey built over the tomb of St. Martin, the city's 4th-century Bishop and patron saint. Most of the abbey, which once dominated the heart of Tours, was razed during the French Revolution. Today's bombastic neo-Byzantine church,

❶ the ☞ **Basilique St-Martin,** was completed in 1924. There's a shrine to St. Martin in the crypt. ☒ *Rue Descartes.*

❷ Old mosaics and Romanesque sculptures from the former abbey are on display in the **Musée St-Martin,** a small museum housed in a restored 13th-century chapel that adjoined the abbey cloisters. The museum retraces the life of St. Martin and the abbey's history. ☒ *3 rue Rapin* ☎ *02–47–05–64–48* ☝ *Free* ☉ *Mid-Mar.–mid-Nov., Wed.–Sun. 9:30–12:30 and 2–5:30.*

North from the Basilique St-Martin to the river is **Le Vieux Tours,** the lovely medieval quarter. A warren of quaint streets, wood-beam houses, and grand mansions once home to 15th-century merchants, it has been gentrified with chic apartments and pedestrianized streets—Tours's

❸ college students and tourists alike love to sit at the cafés lining **Place**

 Plumereau, once the town's *carroi aux chapeaux* (hat market). Lining the square, Nos. 1 through 7 form a magnificent series of half-timber houses; note the woodcarvings of royal moneylenders on Nos. 11 and 12. At the top of the square a vaulted passageway leads on to a cute medieval **Place St-Pierre-le-Puellier.** Running off the Place Plumereau are other streets adorned with historic houses, notably rue Briçonnet—No. 16 is the **Maison de Tristan** with a noted medieval staircase. ☒ *Bordered by rues du Commerce, Briçonnet, de la Monnaie, and du Grand-Marché.*

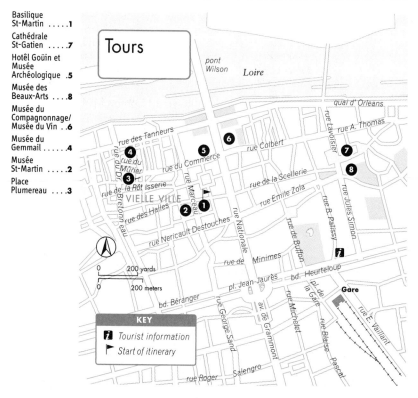

🖑 ❹ The **Musée du Gemmail,** in the imposing 19th-century Hôtel Raimbault, contains an unusual collection of three-dimensional colored-glass window panels. Depicting patterns, figures, and portraits, the panels are beautiful and intriguing—most of the gemlike fragments of glass came from broken bottles. Incidentally, Jean Cocteau coined the word *gemmail* by combining *gemme* (gem) with *émail* (enamel). ⊠ *7 rue du Mûrier* ☎ *02–47–61–01–19* ⊕ *www.gemmail.com* ☑ *€5* ⊙ *Mid-Mar.–mid-Oct., Tues.–Sun. 10–noon and 2–6:30.*

❺ The **Hôtel Gouin** (archaeology museum) is set in Tours's most extravagant example of early Renaissance domestic architecture (too bad its immediate vicinity was among the hardest hit by German bombs), its facade covered with carvings that seemed to have grown like Topsy. Inside are assorted oddities ranging from ancient Roman finds to the scientific collection of Dupin de Chenonceau (owner of the great château in the 18th century). The museum is closed in December. ⊠ *25 rue du Commerce* ☎ *02–47–66–22–32* ☑ *€4.50* ⊙ *Mid-May–Sept., daily 10–7; mid-Mar.–mid-May, daily 10–12:30 and 2–6:30; Oct., Nov., and Jan.–mid-Mar., daily 10–12:30 and 2–5:30.*

❻ The **Musée du Compagnonnage** (Guild Museum) and the **Musée du Vin** (Wine Museum) are both in the cloisters of the 13th-century church of

St-Julien. *Compagnonnage* is a sort of apprenticeship–cum–trade union system, and here you see the masterpieces of the candidates for guild membership: virtuoso craft work, some of it eccentric (an Eiffel Tower made of slate, for instance, or a château constructed of varnished noodles). ⊠ *8 rue Nationale* ☎ *02–47–61–07–93* 🖭 *Musée du Compagnonnage €4.20, Musée du Vin €2.60; joint ticket €5* ♡ *Wed.–Mon. 9–noon and 2–6.*

★ ❼ The **Cathédrale St-Gatien**, built between 1239 and 1484, reveals a mixture of architectural styles. The richly sculpted stonework of its majestic, soaring, two-tower facade betrays the Renaissance influence on local château-trained craftsmen. The stained glass dates from the 13th century (if you have binoculars, bring them). Also take a look at the little tomb with kneeling angels built in memory of Charles VIII and Anne of Brittany's two children; and the **Cloître de La Psalette** (cloister), on the south side of the cathedral. ⊠ *Rue Lavoisier* ☎ *02–47–47–05–19* ♡ *Daily 8–noon and 2–6.*

❽ The **Musée des Beaux-Arts** (Fine Arts Museum), in what was once the archbishop's palace, has an eclectic selection of furniture, sculpture, wrought-iron work, and pieces by Rubens, Rembrandt, Boucher, Degas, and Calder. It even displays Fritz the Elephant, stuffed in 1902. ⊠ *18 pl. François-Sicard* ☎ *02–47–05–68–73* 🖭 *€4* ♡ *Wed.–Mon. 9–12:45 and 2–6.*

Where to Stay & Eat

$–$$ ✕ **Les Tuffeaux.** This restaurant, between the cathedral and the Loire, is the city's best value. Chef Gildas Marsollier wins customers with delicious fennel-perfumed salmon, oysters in an egg sauce seasoned with Roquefort, and remarkable desserts. Gentle lighting and 17th-century wood-beam and stone-wall decor provide a soothing background. ⊠ *19 rue Lavoisier* ☎ *02–47–47–19–89* 🝱 *AE, MC, V* ♡ *Closed Sun. and part of July. No lunch Mon. or Wed.*

★ $$$–$$$$ ✕🖭 **Jean Bardet.** King of Tourangeau chefs, Jean Bardet has a propensity for quoting philosophers, is as happy as a rabbit in a garden (his is packed with heirloom blooms and plants), and is celebrated for showcasing exotic fruits and vegetables in his signature creations. Specials served up in his plush yellow dining salon on his eight-course, €110 *menu dégustation* (tasting menu) and the mighty à la carte menu might include pigeon with foie gras in cabbage-leaf papillote, baby eel in red wine, oysters poached in Muscadet on a puree of watercress, or roast lobster with duck gizzards. Reservations are essential (April to October, there is no lunch Saturday, Monday, and Tuesday; November to March, there is no lunch Saturday and Tuesday, no dinner Sunday, and it is closed Monday). If you want to enjoy what some might deem the ultimate luxury—a breakfast masterminded by Bardet—book one of the guest rooms upstairs at this stately Directoire-style mansion; all luxuriously mix-and-match antiques and modern touches in the distinctive Relais & Châteaux manner. ⊠ *Château Belmont, 57 rue Groison, 37100* ☎ *02–47–41–41–11* 🖶 *02–47–51–68–72* ⊕ *www.jeanbardet.com* 🛏 *16 rooms, 5 suites* ♗ *Restaurant, minibars, cable TV, pool, some pets allowed (fee)* 🝱 *AE, DC, MC, V* ♡ *Nov.–Mar., hotel closed Sun. evening and Mon.* ⍾⊙⍾ *MAP.*

★ $$–$$$$ ✕🖭 **Domaine de la Tortinière.** South of Tours atop a vast, sloping lawn, this storybook, toy-sized, neo-Gothic château comes complete with two fairy-tale towers and a heated, terraced pool. Built in 1861, La Tortinière is now nearing perfection in all things bright and beautiful. Guest rooms in the main building convey quiet, rustic luxury; the conversation pieces are those in the two turrets, while others delight with beamed ceilings. Most beds are so comfy it's hard to wake up. In recent years the owners have smartly done up the former stables, warehouses, and servants' quarters (all just a path away from the main building). Replete with Louis XVI chairs, taffeta curtains, chiffonière tables, plate-glass windows, and air-conditioning, these are almost as alluring as the rooms in the main château. The stylish rotunda restaurant looks out over the lawn and showcases David Chartier's cuisine, including *beuchelle tourangelle,* sautéed veal sweetbreads with morels in white wine (no dinner Sunday, November through March). The main lawn overlooks the Indre River, bordered by a line of towering oak trees that have been trimmed back to make a "frame." The sweet life, indeed. ⊠ *10 rte. de Ballan-Miré, 12 km (7 mi) south of Tours, 37250 Veigné* ☎ *02–47–34–35–00* 🖷 *02–47–65–95–70* ⊕ *www.tortiniere.com* 🛏 *30 rooms* ⚐ *Restaurant, minibars, cable TV, tennis court, pool; no a/c in some rooms* 🝙 *MC, V* ☉ *Closed mid-Dec.–late Feb.* ⫴ *MAP.*

$$ 🏨 **Central.** This Best Western hotel near the Musée du Compagnonnage, set back from the street behind a gravel court and terraced garden, provides a delightfully friendly city-center oasis. Inside, the welcome is vivacious, the lobby daguerreotype-charming, the guest rooms comfortable, and the clientele a pleasant mix of foreign students and happy travelers. This is your most convenient option for Place Plumereau and the historic center of Tours. ⊠ *21 rue Berthelot, 37000 Tours* ☎ *02–47–05–46–44* 🖷 *02–47–66–10–26* ⊕ *www.bestwesterncentralhoteltours.com/* 🛏 *38 rooms* ⚐ *Minibars, cable TV, bar, free parking, some pets allowed; no a/c in some rooms* 🝙 *AE, MC, V* ⫴ *BP.*

$$ 🏨 **Mondial.** Tucked away in the city center on a small leafy square 300 yards from the Loire, this is the closest hotel to historic half-timbered Place Plumereau, a five-minute walk away. The white-walled, post-war building has some rooms with floral-patterned quilts and curtains, others with pastel-shaded decor. All are on the small side but spotlessly clean and offer good value, and service is friendly. There's no restaurant but the brasserie Bure is right next door. ⊠ *3 pl. de la Résistance, 37000 Tours* ☎ *02–47–05–62–18* 🖷 *02–47–61–85–31* ⊕ *www. hotelmondialtours.com* 🛏 *19 rooms* 🝙 *AE, MC, V.*

Loches

❾ *39 km (24 mi) southeast of Tours via N143.*

Fodor'sChoice
★

One of the spokes that reaches into the southern reaches of Touraine (six daily buses and a few trains link this town to Tours), Loches is a fascinating prelude to the main hub of châteaux that border the Loire. A "Cité Royale," it came to be adorned with a bevy of gorgeously picturesque medieval and Renaissance-era structures. Set on a rocky spur overlooking the Indre valley, it is easy to see why it became the 11th-century fief of Foulques Nerra, the warrior Comte d'Anjou. Today, Loches is still dominated by its famous **Citadelle,** one of the most complete medieval fortifications extant, bristling with portcullises, posterns, keeps, and crenelated ramparts. Unlike Chinon's, which stand in ruins, sections of these defensive walls are well preserved and function as part of the town.

By the 15th century, however, Loches had become a pleasure dome. Charles VII and his famous amour, Agnés Sorel, set-up shop in the town château, the **Logis Royaux,** located on the north end of the citadel, and proceeded to set the style for much of courtly France. Notorious for her exceedingly low necklines, fabled as the "Dame de Beauté"—a name with a double meaning, since she was also the chatelaine of the nearby Château de Beauté—Agnés became a tastemaker extraordinaire. Her coterie included her husband, King René d'Anjou, and the great ministers Jacques Coeur and Étienne Chevalier, all of whom set the seal on the extravagantly showy Late Gothic style, best seen in the Italianate works of court painter Jean Fouquet. A copy of his panel portrait of Agnés, poised as a virtuous Virgin Mary (though semitopless), is displayed here opposite her beautiful alabaster tomb, where her recumbent figure is guarded by angels and lambs. Agnès died in 1450 at age 28, probably poisoned by Charles's son, the future Louis XI.

Great hostess that she was, Agnés might have cottoned to the château's son-et-lumière show, "Merlin the Magician," presented during July and August and featuring a goodly chunk of Loches' population in chivalric tableaux (note that the show's theme changes after several seasons). Elsewhere in town are other historic sights (some with separate admissions): the Donjon of Fouques Nerra; the Tour Ronde of Louis XI (with its horrifying dungeons and their *fillettes,* or cages); a medieval-style garden; the massive Romanesque church of Collegiale St-Ours (on rue Thomas-Pactius); a magnificent Renaissance-period Hôtel de Ville, built for François I; and the Maison Lansyer, beautifully set into the town ramparts and fitted out with 19th-century salons filled with the works of painter Emmanuel Lansyer (1835–93). Be sure to get a map of the town from the tourist office or the town's Web site (⊕ www. lochesentouraine.com)—nearly every street will lead you to medieval drawbridges, ancient houses (the Maison d'Agnés Sorel is at 19 rue du Château), and towering ramparts. Hidden away (27 km [15 mi]) to the northeast is a toy-sized Loches: Montrésor ("My Treasure"), also founded by Fouques Nerra, now presided over by an elegantly furnished château, and known far and wide as "one of the most beautiful villages in France." ⊠ *Pl. Charles-VII* ☎ *02–47–59–01–32* ⊕ *www. loches-tourainecotesud.com/* ⊠ *Donjon and Logis Royal:* €*7* ⊙ *Jan.–mid-Mar. and Oct.–Dec., daily 9:30–5; mid-Mar.–June and Sept., daily 9:30–6; July and Aug., daily 9–7.*

Montlouis-sur-Loire

❿ *11 km (7 mi) east of Tours on the south bank of the Loire.*

Like Vouvray—its sister town on the north side of the Loire—Montlouis is noted for its white wines. On place Courtemanche the **Cave Touristique** will help you learn all about the fine vintages produced by the wine-growers of Montlouis. On the eastern side of town is one of the most alluring châteaux of the region, **La Bourdaisière**. Although open to day-trippers for guided tours, this once-royal retreat and birthplace of noted 17th-century courtesan Gabrielle d'Estrées is today the enchanted hotel–domain of the Princes de Broglie.

Where to Stay

$$–$$$$ ⬚ **Château de la Bourdaisière.** Few other hotels so magically distill all the
Fodor'sChoice   grace, warmth, and elan of *la vie de château* as does this 15th-century,
★   100-carat jewel. Once the favored retreat of two kings, François I and Henri IV, today the presiding spirits are only slightly less royal: brother-Princes Philippe-Maurice and Louis-Albert de Broglie, scions of one of France's top families (two prime ministers and one Nobel Prize winner, at last count). Louis-Albert is one of Paris's most famed gardeners, who here cultivates 400 types of tomatoes in the château's *potager* (vegetable garden). It's not surprising, then, to find the three main public salons suavely done up in shades of tomato red, sumptuously offsetting such accents as an immense marble fireplace and large bouquets designed by the prince. You'll start your gawking, however, at the park entrance—motorists often stop to drink in the view of the neo-Renaissance castle perched atop its picture-perfect hill. Guest rooms range from the grand—*François-Premier* is a timber-roof cottage blown up to ballroom dimensions—to more standard-issue, yet always stylish, salons (garden-view rooms away from the gravel driveway are best). Other rooms are found in the adjoining 17th-century "stables" fitted out with a gardening shop and a tiny eatery that serves up dazzling salads and confections (lunch only, June–September). What more can you ask? What about an enormous secluded pool—a gift from heaven during hot summer days. Life-changingly gracious, La Bourdaisière makes a truly princely base for exploring the Loire. ⊠ *25 rue de la Bourdaisière, 37270* ☎ *02–47–45–16–31* 🖷 *02–47–45–09–11* ⊕ *www.chateaulabourdaisiere.com* ⇦ *17 rooms, 3 suites* ⅃ *Restaurant, tennis court, pool, shop; no a/c, room TV on request* ⊟ *MC, V* ⊗ *Closed Nov. 15–Mar. 15* ⊺⊙⊦ *BP.*

Amboise

❶ *13 km (8 mi) east of Montlouis via D751, 24 km (15 mi) east of Tours.*

The Da Vinci trail ends here in one of the more popular towns along the river. Site of Leonardo's final home, crowned with a royal château, and jammed with bustling markets and plenty of hotels and restaurants, Amboise is one of the major hubs of the Loire. On hot summer days, however, the plethora of tour-buses turn the Renaissance town into a carbon monoxide nightmare. So why come? The main château is soaked in history (and blood), while Leonardo's Clos-Lucé is a must-do on any Val de Loire itinerary.

The **Château d'Amboise** became a royal palace in the 15th and 16th centuries. Charles VII stayed here, as did the unfortunate Charles VIII, best remembered for banging his head on a low doorway lintel (you will be shown it) and dying as a result. The gigantic **Tour des Minimes** drops down the side of the cliff, enclosing a massive circular ramp designed to lead horses and carriages up the steep hillside. François I, whose long nose appears in so many château paintings, based his court here, inviting Leonardo da Vinci as his guest. The castle was also the stage for the Amboise Conspiracy, an ill-fated Protestant plot against François II; you are shown where the corpses of 1,200 conspirators dangled from the castle walls. This is one reason why the château feels haunted and forlorn—another is the fact that most of its interior furnishings have been lost. But don't miss the lovely grounds, adorned with a Flamboyant Gothic gem, the little chapel of St-Hubert with its carvings of the Virgin and Child, Charles VIII, and Anne of Brittany, and once graced by the tomb of Leonardo. ☎ 02–47–57–00–98 ⊕ *www.chateau-amboise.tm.fr* ✉ *€7.70* ☉ *Nov.–Mar., daily 9–noon and 2–4:45; Apr.–June, Sept., and Oct., daily 9–6; July and Aug., daily 9–7.*

★ ☙ If you want to see where "the 20th century was born"—as the posters would have it—head to the legendary **Clos Lucé**, about 600 yards up rue Victor-Hugo from the château. Here, in this handsome Renaissance manor, Leonardo da Vinci (1452–1519) spent the last four years of his life, tinkering away at inventions, amusing his patron, King François I, and gazing out over a garden that was planted in the most fashionable Italian manner. The basement contains working models, built by IBM engineers using the detailed sketches in the artist's notebooks, of some of Leonardo's extraordinary inventions; by this time, Leonardo had put away his paint box because of arthritis. Mechanisms on display include three-speed gearboxes, a military tank, a clockwork car, and a flying machine complete with designs for parachutes. Cloux, the house's original name, was given to Anne of Brittany by Charles VIII, who built a chapel for her that is still here. Some of the house's furnishings are authentically 16th century—indeed, thanks to the artist's presence, this house was one of the first places the Italian Renaissance made inroads in France: Leonardo's *Mona Lisa* and *Virgin of the Rocks*, both of which graced the walls here, were bought by the king, who then moved them to the Louvre. ✉ *2 rue du Clos-Lucé* ☎ *02–47–57–00–73* ⊕ *www.vinci-closluce.com* ✉ *€8.50* ☉ *Sept.–Dec. and Feb.–June, daily 9–6; July and Aug., daily 9–7; Jan., daily 10–5.*

Just 3 km (2 mi) south of Amboise on the road to Chenonceaux, the **Pagode de Chanteloup** is a remarkable sight—a 140-foot, seven-story Chinese-style lakeside pagoda built for the Duke of Choiseul in 1775. Children will adore puffing their way to the top for the vertigo-inducing views, but some adults will find the climb—and the 400-yard walk from the parking lot—a little arduous. Sadly, the adjoining lake and park have become the worse for wear. ✉ *Rte. de Bléré* ☎ *02–47–57–20–97* ✉ *€6.30* ☉ *Apr.–Sept., daily 10–6:30; Oct.–mid-Nov. and mid-Feb.–Mar., daily 10–noon and 2–5.*

Where to Stay & Eat

★ $$$ ✕⬚ **Château de Noizay.** Filled with mystery of the past—this was once the fabled redoubt of the Protestant plotters in the 1559 Amboise Conspiracy—this château is fitted out with Renaissance chimneys and salons, a parterre garden, and, best of all, one of the finest chefs around. Guest rooms are so regal you may feel like bowing or curtsying to the staff, so opt for the adjacent 19th-century "Clock House"—a gracious pastel-hued haven with lush air-conditioning. Noizay itself is a tiny, off-the-beaten-path treasure—don't miss the idyllic countryside hike down rue François-Poulenc, past the famous composer's pretty 18th-century house, a troglodyte hamlet, and endless poppy fields right out of a Monet painting. ⊠ *Rte. de Chançay, 8 km (5 mi) west of Tours, 37210 Noizay* ☎ *02–47–52–11–01* 🖨 *02–47–52–04–64* ⊕ *www. chateaudenoizay.com* ⤴ *14 rooms* ⚭ *Restaurant, minibars, cable TV, tennis court, pool; no a/c in some rooms* ⊟ *AE, MC, V* ⊗ *Closed mid-Jan.–mid-Mar.* ⦿ *FAP.*

$$–$$$
Fodor'sChoice
★
✕⊞ **Château de Pray.** Fifty years ago Loire Valley guide books praised this domain and, delightfully, things have gotten better. Like a Rolls Royce Silver Cloud, this hotel keeps purring along, offering many delights—a romantic, twin-towered château, Loire River vista, tranquil guest rooms (four of the less expensive are in a charming "Pavillon Renaissance"), and an excellent restaurant. The latter is set in two salons, one in Charles-Dix golds, the other lit with chandeliers and stained-glass windows, lined with tapestries, and centered around a sculpted-wood fireplace. Just outside is the lawn terrace, where tipsy guests assemble to toast their friends with magnums of Veuve Clicquot. ⊠ *Rte. de Chargé, 4 km (2 mi) east of Amboise, 37400* ☎ *02–47–57–23–67* 🖨 *02–47–57–32–50* ⊕ *http://praycastel.online.fr* ⤴ *17 rooms, 2 suites* ⚭ *Restaurant, cable TV, pool; no a/c* ⊟ *AE, MC, V* ⊗ *Closed Jan.* ⦿ *MAP.*

$
✕⊞ **Le Blason.** Two blocks behind Château d'Amboise and a five-minute walk from the town center, this small hotel is enlivened by its enthusiastic owners. The old building has rooms of different shapes and sizes: No. 229, for example, has exposed beams and a cathedral ceiling; No. 109 is comfortably spacious with a good view of the square. The on-site restaurant, L'Alliance (under different ownership), offers reasonably priced seasonal fare—roast lamb with garlic, and salmon carpaccio with mustard dressing, for instance. ⊠ *11 pl. Richelieu, 37400* ☎ *02–47–23–22–41* 🖨 *02–47–57–56–18* ⤴ *28 rooms* ⚭ *Restaurant, some pets allowed (fee)* ⊟ *AE, DC, MC, V* ⊗ *Closed mid-Jan.–early Feb.* ⦿ *MAP.*

$$$
Fodor'sChoice
★
⊞ **Le Vieux Manoir.** You'll know you're in great hands when you come down to an elegant and inviting breakfast in a glass conservatory filled with purring fellow guests. An ultimate welcome mat for anyone visiting the Loire Valley, this magnificent hotel is the creation of Gloria Belknap—a Californian whose immense style Edith Wharton would have cottoned to immediately. You'll have a hard time tearing yourself away from your guest room, as Gloria has turned loose some decorators extraordinaires on her inn: toile de Jouy screens, gilt-framed paintings, comfy Napoléon III covered-in-jute armchairs, time-worn armoires, and tables adorned with Shaker baskets make this place *House & Garden*–worthy. Each chamber—named after great French ladies, such as George Sand, Madame du Barry, and Colette—is a delight: a bleached redbrick chimney and red-and-white calico accent one, while ceiling beams and a French Provincial four-poster bed warm another. Larger groups can move into a separate (and proportionately pricier) 17th-century cottage, a cosseting maison filled with antiques and wood beams. But you'll probably spend more time in the book-filled library or in the main

salon—soaking up the wit and wisdom of Gloria and husband Bob—or by the fountain in the leafy garden. ⊠ *13 rue Rabelais, 37400* ☎🖶 *02–47–30–41–27* ⊕ *www.le-vieux-manoir.com* 🛏 *6 rooms, 1 cottage* ⚒ *No a/c, no room TVs* ⊟ *MC, V* ⦿ *BP.*

★ **$$–$$$** 🏨 **Le Manoir Les Minimes.** Picture-perfect and soigné as all get out, this gorgeously stylish hotel is lucky enough to preside over a Loire riverbank under the shadow of Amboise's great cliffside château. Set within its own compound and centered around a grass parterre, this quaintly shuttered manoir looks like it is on sabbatical from a Fragonard landscape—a *pavillon* in the 18th-century style, it is a refreshing change from the usual Renaissance castle-style so prevalent in these parts. Inside, the grand staircase (note: no elevator), dining room, and main salon are all a-dazzle in daffodil yellow silks and gilt-framed mirrors, with ruby accents of the Louis Seize sofas and bergères. The standard guest rooms are pleasant enough—three are set in an adjoining, trellised annex—but try to spring for the showpieces, such as the Suite Prestige in a stunning blue toile de Jouy, which are stunners. Happily, most rooms have charming views of the château, even the smaller dormer rooms on the top floor. Eric Deforges and Patrice Longet have made this hotel very *chez soi*, with all sorts of loving details—at night, you'll even find the weather forecast for the following day on your pillow. At dusk, cap it all off by stepping beyond the French doors to the manoir's exquisite gravel terrace to enjoy a Kir Royale. Life is beautiful, *non?* ⊠ *34 quai Charles Guinot, 37400* ☎ *02–47–30–40–40* 🖶 *02–47–30–40–77* ⊕ *www.manoirlesminimes. com* 🛏 *10 rooms, 8 suites* ⚒ *Minibars; no room TVs* ⊟ *MC, V.*

Chenonceaux

⑫ *12 km (8 mi) southeast of Amboise via D81, 32 km (20 mi) east of Tours.*

Fodor'sChoice Achingly beautiful, the **Château de Chenonceau** has long been considered
★ the "most romantic" of all the Loire châteaux, thanks in part to its showpiece—a breathtaking *galerie de bal* that spans the River Cher like a bridge (used as an escape point for French Resistance fighters during World War II, since all other crossings had been bombed). Set in the village of Chenonceaux (spelled with an *x*) on the River Cher, this was the fabled retreat for the *dames des Chenonceau*: Diane de Poitiers, Catherine de' Medici, and Mary, Queen of Scots. Happily spending at least half a day wandering through the château and grounds, you'll see that this monument has an undeniable feminine touch (the design was entirely overseen by women). During the peak summer season the château is open—unlike many others—all day. The only drawback is its popularity: if you want to avoid a roomful of schoolchildren, take a stroll on the grounds and come back to the house at lunchtime. Whatever hour, be sure to walk to the most distant point of the largest parterre garden—there you'll find a tiny bridge leading to a river lookout point where you'll find the most beautiful view of France's most glorious château.

More pleasure-palace than fortress, the château was built in 1520 by Thomas Bohier, a wealthy tax collector, for his wife, Catherine Briçonnet. When he went bankrupt, it passed to François I. Later, Henri II gave it to his mistress, Diane de Poitiers. After his death, Henri's not-so-understanding widow, Catherine de' Medici, expelled Diane to nearby Chaumont and took back the château. Before this time, Diane's five-arched bridge over the River Cher was simply meant as a grand ceremonial entryway leading to a gigantic château, a building never constructed. It was to Catherine, and her architect, Philibert de l'Orme, that historians owe the audacious plan to transform the bridge itself into the most unusual château in France. Two stories were constructed, including an enormous gallery that runs from one end of the château to the other—a grand space that became the stage set for some legendary galas. July and August are the peak months at Chenonceau: only then can you escape the maddening crowds by exiting at the far end of the gallery to walk along the opposite bank (weekends only), rent a rowboat to spend an hour just drifting in the river (where Diane used to enjoy her morning dips), and enjoy an evocative **son-et-lumière,** performed in the illuminated château gardens.

Before you go inside, pick up an English-language leaflet at the gate. Then walk around to the right of the main building to see the harmonious, delicate architecture beyond the formal garden—the southern part belonged to Diane de Poitiers, the northern was Catherine's—with the river gliding under the arches (providing superb "air-conditioning" to the rooms above). Inside the château are splendid ceilings, colossal fireplaces, scattered furnishings, and paintings by Rubens, del Sarto, and Correggio. The curatorial staff have delightfully dispensed with velvet ropes and adorned some of the rooms with bouquets designed in 17th-century style. As you tour the salons, be sure to pay your respects to former owner Madame Dupin, tellingly captured in Nattier's charming portrait: thanks to the affection she inspired among her proletarian neighbors, the château and its treasures survived the Revolution intact (her grave is enshrined near the northern embankment). The château's history is illustrated with wax figures in the **Musée des Cires** (Waxwork Museum) in one of the château's outbuildings. A cafeteria, tearoom, and the ambitious Orangerie restaurant handle the crowds' varied appetites. ☎ 02–47–23–90–07 ⊕ *www.chenonceau.com* ⊠ *Château €9.50 (includes Musée des Cires); son-et-lumière €8* ☽ *Feb.–May and Oct.–mid-Nov., daily 9–5:30; June–Sept., daily 9–7; Dec. and Jan., daily 9–4:30.*

Where to Stay & Eat

★ **\$\$–\$\$\$** ✕🖫 **Le Bon Laboureur.** In 1882 this ivy-covered inn won Henry James's praise and the famed author might be even more impressed today. Thanks to four generations of the Jeudi family, this remains one of the most stylish auberges in the Val de Loire. Charm is in abundance—many guest rooms are enchantingly accented in toile de Jouy fabrics, rustic wainscoting, tiny lamps, and Redouté pink-and-blue pastels. Those in the main house are comfortably sized (a few overlook the main street—avoid these if you are a light sleeper), those in the former stables are larger (some overlook a pert vegetable garden) and more renovated, but our favorites are the quaint rooms in the separate patio house near the terrace. Don't lose any time bagging a table in the "old" dining room (book this room, not the more modern ones), whose wood-beamed ceiling, glazed terra-cotta walls, and Louis XVI chairs are almost as elegant as chef Jean-Marie Burnet's cream of crayfish with basil, pike-perch with spices, or turbot with red pepper and fennel. And that is saying something: meals here are marvels. ✉ *6 rue du Dr-Bretonneau, 37150* ☎ *02–47–23–90–02* 🖷 *02–47–23–82–01* ⊕ *www.amboise.com/ laboureur* ↝ *24 rooms* ☖ *Restaurant, minibars, cable TV, pool, bicycles, bar, some pets allowed (fee); no a/c in some rooms* ▭ *AE, DC, MC, V* ☉ *Closed Jan.–mid-Feb. and mid-Nov.–mid-Dec.* ⦿⎮ *MAP.*

★ $ ✕⊡ **La Roseraie.** The Bon Laboureur may be Chenonceaux's most famous hostelry, but this runs close for charm, thanks in part to the joyful welcome of its English-speaking hosts, Laurent and Sophie Fiorito. But let's not forget the guest rooms, many of which are designed with florals, checks, and lace, or the copious meals served in the rustic dining room (where foie gras, duck with fruit and honey, and apple tart are among the specialties), or the pretty pool. Try to get a garden-side room, even if too many pink tablecloths and white chairs make the patio less than restful. If car traffic bothers you, be sure to avoid the rooms overlooking the main street. ✉ *7 rue du Dr-Bretonneau, 37150* ☎ *02–47–23–90–09* 🖷 *02–47–23–91–59* ⊕ *www.charmingroseraie. com* ↝ *17 rooms* ☖ *Restaurant, cable TV, pool, bar; no a/c* ▭ *AE, DC, MC, V* ☉ *Closed mid-Nov.–mid-Feb.* ⦿⎮ *BP.*

Chaumont-sur-Loire

⑬ *26 km (16 mi) northeast of Chenonceaux via D176/D62, 21 km (13 mi) southwest of Blois.*

★ Although a favorite of Loire connoisseurs, the 16th-century **Château de Chaumont** is often overlooked by visitors who are content to ride the conveyor belt of big châteaux like Chambord and Chenonceau, and it's their loss. Set on a dramatic bluff that towers over the river, Chaumont has always cast a spell—perhaps literally so. One of its fabled owners, Catherine de' Medici, occasionally came here with her court "astrologer," the notorious Ruggieri. In one of Chaumont's bell-tower rooms, the queen reputedly practiced sorcery (for her troubles, she foresaw the tragic deaths of all her three sons in a magic mirror, foretelling the historic downfall of the Valois dynasty). Whether Ruggieri still haunts the place (or Nostradamus, another on Catherine's guest list), there seem to be few castles as spirit-warm as this one.

Centerpiece of a gigantic park (a stiff walk up a long path from the little village of Chaumont-sur-Loire; cars and taxis can also leave you off at the top of the hill) and built by Charles II d'Amboise between 1465 and 1510, the château greets visitors with glorious, twin-tower *châtelets*—twin turrets that frame a double-drawbridge. The castle became the residence of Henri II. After his death his widow Catherine de' Medici took revenge on his mistress, the fabled beauty Diane de Poitiers, and forced her to exchange Chenonceau for Chaumont. Another "refugee" was the late-18th-century writer Madame de Staël. Exiled from Paris by Napoléon, she wrote *De l'Allemagne* (*On Germany*) here, a book that helped kickstart the Romantic movement in France. In the 19th century her descendants, the Prince and Princess de Broglie, set up regal shop, as you can still see from the stone-and-brick stables, where purebred horses (and one elephant) lived like royalty in velvet-lined stalls. The couple also renovated many rooms in the glamorous neo-Gothic style of the 1870s. Today, their sense of fantasy is retained in the castle's **Festival International des Jardins** (www.chaumont-jardins.com), held July to October every year in the extensive park and featuring the latest in horticultural invention. ☎ 02–54–51–26–26 ⊠ €6.10 ☉ Mid-Mar.–mid-Nov., daily 9:30–6; mid-Dec.–mid-Mar., daily 10–5.

Where to Stay & Eat

★ $$–$$$$ ✕⌂ **Domaine des Hauts-de-Loire.** Long a landmark of Loire luxe, this aristocratic outpost is across the river from Chaumont (which has a handy bridge) and some 4 km (2 mi) inland. Set in an 18th-century, turreted, vine-covered hunting lodge, it comes with the requisite grand salon furnished with 18th-century antiques, a lovely pool, an adorable swan lake, a helipad, 180 acres of forest for hikes, and the most blissful air-conditioning in all Touraine (a gift from heaven on sweltering summer days). Guest rooms are beige, suave, and tranquil; those in the adjacent carriage houses have exposed brick walls and gabled ceilings. The restaurant (closed Monday and no lunch Tuesday off-season) glows with mellow lights, white bouquets, and some dazzling dishes, showcased in a €90 prix-fixe menu. Later, contented patrons often repair to the salon for champagne to swap stories and toast their good luck at being here—and here. ⊠ Rte. de Mesland, across the Loire from Chaumont, 41150 Onzain ☎ 02–54–20–72–57 🖷 02–54–20–77–32 ⊕ www.domainehautsloire.com ⇆ 25 rooms, 10 suites ♨ Restaurant, minibars, cable TV, tennis court, pool, helipad ⊟ AE, DC, MC, V ☉ Closed Dec.–Feb. ⑩ MAP.

$–$$$ ✕⌂ **Hostellerie du Château.** Set on a bank of the Loire and directly opposite the road leading up to Chaumont's château, this quaint edifice was—rather uniquely for these parts—built in the early 20th century as a hotel pure and simple. Four-stories tall, fitted out with half-timbered eaves, the hotel conjures up the grace of earlier days. Today, happily, it's purring along as a reasonably priced option. The entry hall soars, the restaurant is cozy and friendly, and the staff is Chaumont-courteous. Who cares if the rooms are on the simple side and a bit worse for wear? However: the hotel does front the main road zipping through Chaumont (with loads of traffic) so be sure to bag a room on the side facing the Loire, or, failing that, along the side flanks of the hotel. ⊠ 2 rue Maréchal-de Lattre-de Tassigny, 41150 ☎ 02–54–20–98–04 🖷 02–54–20–97–98 ⊕ www.hostellerie-du-chateau.com ⇆ 28 rooms ♨ Restaurant, pool; no room phones ⊟ MC, V ☉ Closed Feb. ⑩ EP.

Cheverny

⑭ 24 km (15 mi) east of Chaumont, 14 km (9 mi) southeast of Blois.

Perhaps best remembered as Capitaine Haddock's mansion in the Tintin comic books, the **Château de Cheverny** is also iconic for its restrained 17th-century elegance. One of the last in the area to be built, it was finished in 1634, at a time when the rich and famous had mostly stopped building in the Loire Valley. By then, the taste for quaintly shaped châteaux had given way to disciplined Classicism; so here a white, elegantly proportioned, horizontally coursed, single-block facade greets you across manicured lawns. To emphasize the strict symmetry of the plan, a ruler-straight drive leads to the front entrance. The Louis XIII interior with its stridently painted and gilded rooms, splendid furniture, and rich tapestries depicting the Labors of Hercules is one of the few still intact in the Loire region. Despite the priceless Delft vases and Persian embroideries, it feels lived in. That's because it's one of the rare Loire Valley houses still occupied by a noble family. You can visit a small Tintin exhibition called *Le Secret de Moulinsart* (admission extra) and are free to contemplate the antlers of 2,000 stags in the Trophy Room: Hunting, called "venery" in the leaflets, continues vigorously here, with red coats, bugles, and all. In the château's kennels, hordes of hungry hounds lounge around dreaming of their next kill. Feeding times—*la soupe aux chiens*—are posted on a notice board, and you are welcome to watch the "ceremony" (delicate sensibilities beware: the dogs line up like statues and are called, one by one, to wolf down their meal from the trainer). From April through October, you can visit the château grounds by either boat or electric buggy, or get a bird's-eye view from 500 feet up in a charming hot-air balloon; purchase tickets on the spot. The château's village is officially named Cour-Cheverny. ☎ 02–54–79–96–29 ⊕ *www.chateau-cheverny. fr* 🎫 *€6.30, €10.70 with Tintin exhibition, €15.40 inc. boat-and-buggy rides* ☉ *Apr.–Sept., daily 9:15–6:15; Oct.–Mar., daily 9:45–5.*

Chambord

⑮
Fodor's Choice
★
★ ☾

17 km (11 mi) northeast of Cheverny via D102 and D112, 19 km (12 mi) east of Blois, 45 km (28 mi) southwest of Orléans.

The "Versailles" of the 16th century and the largest of the Loire châteaux, the **Château de Chambord** is the kind of place William Randolph Hearst might have built if he'd had the money. Variously dubbed "megalomaniacal" and "an enormous film-set extravaganza," this is one of the most extraordinary structures in Europe, set in the middle of a royal game forest, with just a cluster of buildings—barely a village—across the road. As you travel the gigantic highways that converge on the building, you first spot Chambord's incredible towers—19th-century novelist Henry James said they were "more like the spires of a city than the salient points of a single building"—rising above the forest. When the entire château breaks into view, it is an unforgettable sight.

With a facade that is 420 feet long, 440 rooms and 365 chimneys, a wall 32 km (20 mi) long to enclose a 13,000-acre forest (you can wander through 3,000 acres of it; the rest is reserved for wild boar and other game), this is one of the greatest buildings in France. Under François I, building began in 1519, a job that took 12 years and required 1,800 workers. His original grandiose idea was to divert the Loire to form a moat, but someone (perhaps his adviser, Leonardo da Vinci, who some feel may have provided the inspiration behind the entire complex) persuaded him to make do with the River Cosson. François I used the château only for short stays; yet when he came, 12,000 horses were required to transport his luggage, servants, and entourage. Later kings also used Chambord as an occasional retreat, and Louis XIV, the Sun King, had

Molière perform here. In the 18th century Louis XV gave the château to the Maréchal de Saxe as a reward for his victory over the English and Dutch at Fontenoy (southern Belgium) in 1745. When not indulging himself with wine, women, and song, the marshal planted himself on the roof to oversee the exercises of his personal regiment of 1,000 cavalry. Now, after long neglect—all the original furnishings vanished during the French Revolution—Chambord belongs to the state.

There's plenty to see inside. You can wander freely through the vast rooms, filled with exhibits (including a hunting museum)—not all concerned with Chambord, but interesting nonetheless—and lots of Ancien Régime furnishings. The enormous double-helix staircase (probably envisioned by Leonardo, who had a thing about spirals) looks like a single staircase, but an entire regiment could march up one spiral while a second came down the other, and never the twain would meet. But the high point here in more ways than one is the spectacular chimneyscape—the roof terrace whose forest of Italianate towers, turrets, cupolas, gables, and chimneys have been compared to everything from the minarets of Constantinople to a bizarre chessboard. The most eye-popping time to see this roof is at night, when the château is spectacularly illuminated. During the year there's a packed calendar of activities on tap, from performances of 17th-century dressage (horsemanship technique) by Les Écuries du Maréchal de Saxe to guided tours on bike or horseback and photo-safaris through the game preserve (during deer-rut season) to concerts to boating on the grand moat. A three-story-tall hall has been fitted out to offer lunches and dinners. ☎ 08–25–82–60–88 ⊕ *www.chambord.org* ⊡ €8.50 ☉ *Apr.–Sept., daily 9–6:15; Oct.–Mar., daily 9–5:15.*

Where to Stay & Eat

★ **$$$–$$$$** ✕ **Relais de Bracieux.** Masterminded by chef Bernard Robin, this is one of the Loire's top restaurants. Out of the gleaming kitchens comes sumptuous nouvelle cuisine: lobster with dried tomatoes or shepherd's pie with oxtail and truffles. Connoisseurs also savor Robin's simpler fare: carp, game in season, and salmon with beef marrow. Others delight in his opulent details—accompanying your dessert you may find a fairy-tale forest of mushrooms and elves spun in sugar. The dining room is white, traditional-modern, and luxe, while the attentive staff brings delicious tidbits to keep you busy between courses. ⊠ *1 av. de Chambord, 8 km (5 mi) south of Chambord, 9 km (6 mi) northeast of Cour-Cheverny on road to Chambord, Bracieux* ☎ *02–54–46–41–22* ⊕ *www. relaisdebracieux.com* ⚛ *Reservations essential* 🏠 *Jacket and tie* ⊟ *AE, DC, MC, V* ☉ *Closed mid-Dec.–late Jan. and Tues. and Wed.*

★ **$** ✕🏠 **Grand St-Michel.** The village of Chambord is as tiny as its château is massive. Its leading landmark is this historic hotel, a revamped country house set at the edge of the woods across the lawn from the château. Guest rooms once boasted fabled views of the palace but towering oak trees now block the view from all but two. No matter—this is a most enjoyable hotel, with a cozy lobby, solidly bourgeois guest rooms, and a 19th-century-flavored restaurant. Adorned with mounted deer heads, majolica serving platters, and thick curtains, this room has ambience to spare. The fare is local, hearty (including deer pâté, pike-perch with fennel, and game in the fall), attractively priced, and there's a pleasant café-terrace facing the château—just the place for reflection while sipping a drink. ⊠ *103 pl. St-Michel, 41250* ☎ *02–54–20–31–31* 🖷 *02–54–20–36–40* 🛏 *39 rooms, 38 with bath* ⚐ *Restaurant, tennis court, some pets allowed (fee); no a/c* ▤ *MC, V* ☺ *Closed mid-Nov.–mid-Dec.* ◉| *BP.*

\$\$\$ 🖽 **Château de Colliers.** Keep Chenonceau. You can have Chambord. For

Fodor's Choice a few lucky travelers, the most unforgettable château in the Loire proves

★ to be this tiny, overlooked treasure. Colliers may not have the showy pomp of the Loire's more famous château-hotels, but it has something more precious—*authenticité*. The home of Christian and Marie-France de Gélis (both of whom are charming and speak English), it was sold to their family in 1779 by the Marquis de Vaudreuil, first French governor of Louisiana. At the end of a long allée, this "pavillon Mansart" embraces you in a semicircular layout (the *collier,* or necklace). Ten family descendants study you from gilded Charles-Dix frames in the main salon, a room that is possibly the most beautiful in all the Loire: a confectionery vision of white Rococo moldings, glittering chandelier, with furniture that Madame Bovary would have loved. The breakfast room is covered with quaint 16th-century Italian frescoes, each guest room is a bouquet of antiques and comfy furniture, and—unique to this hotel—there is a vast river terrace that overlooks a magnificently pristine stretch of the Loire. Unfortunately, Monsieur and Madame de Gélis don't hold down the fort yearround any longer. While their housekeepers are friendly, they don't provide that distinctive family ambience. ⊠ *Rue Nationale, Muides-sur-Loire, 8 km (4 mi) northwest of Chambord; 17 km (10 mi) southwest of Blois, 41500* ☎ *02–54–87–50–75* 🖷 *02–54–87–03–64* 📧 *Chcolliers@aol.com* 🛏 *5 rooms* ⚐ *Pool; no a/c, no room TVs* ▤ *MC, V* ◉| *BP.*

The Outdoors

Rent a horse from the former stables, **Les Écuries du Maréchal de Saxe** (⊠ On grounds of Château de Chambord ☎ 02–54–20–31–01) and ride through the vast national park surrounding the château. From March through October you can hire a boat to explore the château moat and the **Grand Canal** (☎ 02–54–56–00–43 for details) linking it to the River Cosson.

Beaugency

❶ *24 km (15 mi) northeast of Chambord via D112 and D951.*

A clutch of historic towers and buildings around a 14th-century bridge over the Loire lends Beaugency its charm. The buildings in this town on the north bank of the river include the massive 11th-century **donjon** (keep), the Romanesque church of **Notre-Dame,** and the **Tour du Diable** (Devil's Tower), overlooking the river. The **Château Dunois** contains a regional museum with traditional costumes and peasant furniture. ⊠ *2 pl. Dunois* ☎ *02–38–44–55–23* ☺ *Closed for renovation at press time.*

Blois

⑰ *27 km (17 mi) southwest of Beaugency via N152, 54 km (34 mi) south-west of Orléans, 58 km (36 mi) northeast of Tours.*

Perched on a steep hillside overlooking the Loire, site of one of France's most historic châteaux, and birthplace of those delicious Poulain choco-lates and gâteaux (check out the bakeries along the main street of rue Denis-Papin and tour the nearby Poulain factory), the bustling old town of Blois is an alluring and convenient base, well served by train and high-way. A signposted route leads you on a walking tour of the **Vieille Ville** (Old Town)—a romantic honeycomb of twisting alleys, cobblestone streets, and half-timber houses—but it is best explored with the help of a map available from the tourist office. The historic highlight is place St-Louis, where you'll find the Maison des Acrobats (note the timbers carved with *jongleurs,* or jugglers), Cathédrale St-Louis, and Hôtel de Villebresme, but unexpected Renaissance-era galleries and staircases also lurk in tucked-away courtyards, such as the one in the Hôtel d'Alluye, built by Florimond Robertet, finance minister to three kings and the last patron to commission a painting from Leonardo da Vinci. The best view of the town, with its château and numerous church spires rising sharply above the river, can be had from across the Loire.

The massive **Château de Blois** spans several architectural periods and is among the valley's finest. Your ticket entitles you to a guided tour—given in English when there are enough visitors who don't understand French—but you are more than welcome to roam around without a guide if you visit between mid-March and August. Before you enter, stand in the court-yard to admire examples of four centuries of architecture. On one side stand the 13th-century hall and tower, the latter offering a stunning view of the town and countryside. The Renaissance begins to flower in the Louis XII wing (built between 1498 and 1503), through which you enter, and comes to full bloom in the François I wing (1515–24). The mas-terpiece here is the openwork spiral staircase, painstakingly restored. The fourth side consists of the Classical Gaston d'Orléans wing (1635–38). Upstairs in the François I wing is a series of enormous rooms with tremendous fireplaces decorated with the gilded porcupine, emblem of Louis XII, the ermine of Anne of Brittany, and, of course, François I's salamander, breathing fire and surrounded by flickering flames. Many rooms have intricate ceilings and carved, gilt paneling; there's even a sad little picture of Mary, Queen of Scots. In the council room the Duke of Guise was murdered by order of Henri III in 1588. In the **Musée des Beaux-Arts** (Fine Arts Museum), in the Louis XII wing, you'll find royal portraits, including Rubens's puffy portrayal of Maria de' Medici as France Personified. Most evenings May through September, **son-et-lumière** shows are staged (in English on Wednesday). Call 02–54–78–72–76 for details; admission is €10. ☎ 02–54–90–33–33 ⬙ €6.50 ⊙ *Mid-Mar.–Oct., daily 9–6; Nov.–mid-Mar., daily 9–12:30 and 2–5:30.*

Where to Stay & Eat

$$–$$$ ✕ **L'Espérance.** In a bucolic setting overlooking the Loire, chef Raphaël Guillot serves up inventive cuisine, like fried mangoes with lavender and five different kinds of scallop dishes. ✉ *189 quai Ulysse-Besnard* ☎ *02–54–78–09–01* ▭ *AE, MC, V* ⊘ *Closed Mon. and part of Aug. No dinner Sun.*

★ **$$**   ✕ **Au Rendez-Vous des Pêcheurs.** This friendly restaurant in an old grocery near the Loire has simple decor but offers excellent value for its creative cooking. Chef Christophe Cosme studied under Burgundy's late Bernard Loiseau and brings inventiveness to his fish and seafood specialties (try the crayfish and parsley flan) and desserts. ✉ *27 rue du Foix* ☎ *02–54–74–67–48* ⚐ *Reservations essential* ▭ *AE, MC, V* ⊘ *Closed Sun., Aug., and 2 weeks Jan. No lunch Mon.*

$$ ✕🖾 **Le Médicis.** Rooms at this smart little hotel 1 km (½ mi) from the château de Blois are comfortable, air-conditioned, and soundproof; all share a joyous color scheme but are individually decorated. The restaurant alone—done Renaissance-style with a coffered ceiling—makes a stay here worthwhile. Chef-owner Christian Garanger turns his innovative classic dishes into a presentation—*coquilles St-Jacques* (scallops) with bitter *roquette* lettuce, roast pigeon, and thin slices of roast hare with a black-currant sauce. The staff is cheerful and there are 250 wines to choose from (the restaurant does not serve dinner Sunday October–March). ✉ *2 allée François-Ier, 41000* ☎ *02–54–43–94–04* 🖶 *02–54–42–04–05* ⊕ *www.le-medicis.com* ⟿ *12 rooms* ⚏ *Restaurant, minibars* ▭ *AE, DC, MC, V* ⊘ *Closed Jan.* ⑩| *MAP.*

Rochecorbon

⑱   *5 km (3 mi) east of Tours on the north bank of the Loire.*

One of the poshest villages in the Loire, this is a favored forgetaway for Parisians and vacationers. Spread out along the Loire-bank N152 road, with a tiny center set with a church and fine restaurants, Rochecorbon is overshadowed by its immense cliff studded with curious troglodyte dwellings—caves-cum-cottages sculpted out of tufa, that milky-white porous stone which lines the Loire Valley (and was used to build so many great châteaux). Unfortunately, the town's Manoir des Basses-Rivières—an exquisite, 18th-century rock-face manor—has recently closed for a lengthy renovation. Other than weekend homes for harried urbanites, the town is also address to some of the Val de Loire's most distinctive hotels. Rochecorbon is the only place from which you can actually take a boat-ride excursion out on the Loire. The hour-long **Bateau-Promenade** glides you along a magnificently tranquil stretch of the river to Vouvray and back. Although the commentary on the boat is in French, the sights alone—riverside caves, deserted towers, distant châteaux (like Moncontour, made famous by Balzac)—make for a most enjoyable outing. ✉ *Observatoire, 56 quai de la Loire* ☎ *02–47–52–68–88* ⚐ *€10* ⊘ *July and Aug., daily 3, 4, and 5 PM; May, June, and Sept., weekends 4 and 5 PM.*

★

Once you find the little town center along the Quai de la Loire embankment, take the road leading into the highlands to discover "upper" Rochecorbon. Past the elegant L'Oubliette restaurant and a gorgeous church (elsewhere in town is the St. George Chapel, with Romanesque frescoes), the road gently mounts the tufa cliff to arrive at a vast plateau studded with Vouvray vineyards. The one attraction hereabouts is found two-thirds up along the route—the **Caves Rupestres,** an abandoned 600-year-old quarry now carved, in a folkloric-modern manner, with 34 wall bas-reliefs detailing the legends of wine in the region, which you can admire with a glass of the grape in your hand. ⊠ *Rue Vaufoynard* 🎟 *€5.30* ⊙ *Apr., weekends 2–6; May, June, Sept., and Oct., daily 2–6; July and Aug., daily 10:30–7.*

Rochecorbon makes its own wines and you can explore a vast group of underground galleries at the **Grandes Caves Saint-Roch,** along the main river road. Learn about the extraction of tufa stone, and the methods of cave mushroom-growing and silkworm-production, and taste the Blanc-Foussy whites. ⊠ *65 quai de la Loire* ☎ *02–47–52–57–70* 🎟 *Free* ⊙ *July and Aug., Tues.–Sat. 10–noon and 2–7; call ahead for details at other times.*

Where to Stay & Eat

★ **$$$–$$$$** ✕🏨 **Hôtel des Hautes Roches.** *Extraordinaire* is the word for some of the dozen luxe-troglodyte rooms at this famous hotel, which stud a towering cliff-face with their elegant sash windows, gas-lantern lamps, and finished marble steps. Don't expect decor à la Fred Flintstone: half the guest-room walls are Ice Age, but stylish fabrics, Louis Treize seating, and carved fireplaces are the main allurements. Some prefer rooms in the regular house—no cave-dwelling drama, but exquisitely comfortable and air-conditioned. The restaurant (closed Monday, no lunch Wednesday, no dinner Sunday) has an extremely staid decor, so most everyone repairs to the enchanting terrace to feast on a panoply of foie gras, fish and duck dishes, and architectonic desserts—one of the best kitchens in the Loire (don't forget to order a selection from the gigantic cheese tray brought out—at least one summer afternoon—by a boy who seems half the size of the tray). To top it all off, a sapphire pool tempts all during the Loire's *grandes chaleurs.* ⊠ *86 quai de la Loire, 37210 Rochecorbon* ☎ *02–47–52–88–88* 🖨 *02–47–52–81–30* ⊕ *www.leshautesroches.com/* 🛏 *15 rooms* 🍴 *Restaurant, minibars, cable TV, pool, some pets allowed (fee); no a/c in some rooms* ⊟ *AE, DC, MC, V* ⊙ *Closed mid-Jan.–mid-Mar.* ⦿❘ *MAP.*

THE STORYBOOK LOIRE: VILLANDRY TO LANGEAIS

To the west of Tours, breathtaking châteaux dot the Indre Valley between the regional capital and the historic town of Chinon on the River Vienne. This is the most glamorous part of the Val de Loire and the beauty pageant begins with the fabled gardens of the Château de Villandry. Your journey then continues on to the fairy-tale châteaux of Azay-le-Rideaux, Ussé, and Montreuil-Bellay. Further on, no one will want to miss the towns of Chinon, Saumur, Angers, Fontevraud, and Langeais, which contain sights that remain the quintessence of romantic medievalism. Along the way, you can savor such storybook delights as Saché—perhaps the Loire's prettiest town—Turquant, a troglodyte village, and the Château de Réaux, with its picture-perfect pepper-pot towers, moat, and swans.

Villandry

⑲ *18 km (11 mi) west of Tours via D7, 48 km (30 mi) northwest of Loches.*

Fodor'sChoice
★

Green-thumbers get weak in the knees at the mere mention of the **Château de Villandry,** a grand estate near the Cher River, thanks to its painstakingly re-laid 16th-century **gardens,** now the finest example of Renaissance garden design in France. These were originally planted in 1906 by Dr. Joachim Carvallo and Anne Coleman, his American wife, whose passion resulted in two terraces planted in styles that combine the French monastic garden with Italianate models depicted in historic Du Cerceau etchings. Seen from the cliffside walkway, the terraces look like flowered chessboards blown up to the nth power—a breathtaking sight.

Beyond the water garden and an ornamental garden depicting symbols of chivalric love is the famous *potager,* or vegetable garden. Organized in square patterns, purple cabbages, pumpkins, and pear trees catch the eye at every turn. In total, there are nearly 150,000 plantings, with two seasonal shows presented—the spring one is a veritable "salad." The fall one comes to fruition in late September or early October and is famed for its pumpkins. Flower lovers will rejoice in the main *jardin à la française* (French-style garden): framed by a canal, it is a vast carpet of rare and colorful blooms planted *en broderie* ("like embroidery"), set into patterns by box hedges and paths. The aromatic and medicinal garden, its plots neatly labeled in three languages, is especially appealing. Below an avenue of 1,500 precisely pruned lime trees lies an ornamental lake that is home to two swans: not a ripple is out of place. The château interior was restored in the mid-19th century; of particular note are the painted and gilt Moorish ceiling from Toledo and the collection of Spanish pictures. Note that the quietest time to visit is usually during the two-hour French lunch break, while the most photogenic is during the **Nuits des Mille Feux** (Nights of a Thousand Lights, usually held in early July), when paths and pergolas are illuminated with myriad lanterns and a dance troupe offers a tableau vivant. There are also a Baroque music festival in late August and a gardening weekend held in early September. ☎ *02–47–50–02–09* ⊕ *www.chateauvillandry.com* ✉ *Château and gardens €8, gardens only €6* ☉ *Château June–Sept., daily 9–6; Oct.–mid-Nov. and mid-Feb.–May, daily 9–5. Gardens June–Sept., daily 9–7:30; Oct.–May, daily 9–5:30.*

Where to Stay & Eat

¢–$ ✕▥ **Le Cheval Rouge.** Just a half-minute walk from the great château of Villandry, this is a fine, comfortable, and casual hotel-restaurant. Since it's set on a major traffic route, book one of the quieter rooms at the back. The restaurant (closed Monday) is popular with locals, who come for the surprisingly good and classic food and wine. Best bets are the terrine of foie gras, the calf sweetbreads, and the wood-fired-grill fare. ✉ *9 rue Principale, 37510* ☎ *02–47–50–02–07* ⊟ *02–47–50–08–77* ⊕ *www.lecheval-rouge.com* ⇋ *38 rooms* ⚿ *Restaurant, some pets allowed (fee); no room TVs* ⊟ *MC, V* ☉ *Closed Jan.* ⏀ *BP.*

Azay-le-Rideau

⑳ *11 km (7 mi) south of Villandry via D39, 27 km (17 mi) southwest of Tours.*

A largish town surrounding a sylvan dell on the banks of the River Indre, the pleasant town of Azay-le-Rideau is famed for its white-walled Renaissance pleasure palace, called "a faceted diamond set in the Indre Valley" by Honoré de Balzac. The 16th-century **Château d'Azay-le-Rideau** was created as a literal fairy-tale castle. When it was constructed in the Renaissance era (note the Greco-Roman stone detailing), the nouveau-riche treasurer Gilles Berthelot decided he wanted to add tall corner turrets, moat, and machicolations to conjure up the distant seigneurial past when knighthood was in flower and two families, the Azays and the Ridels, ruled this terrain. It was never a serious fortress—it certainly offered no protection to its builder when a financial scandal forced him to flee France shortly after the château's completion in 1529. For centuries the château passed from one private owner to another until it was finally bought by the State in 1905. Though the interior contains an interesting blend of furniture and artwork (one room is a homage to the Marquis de Biencourt who, in the early 20th century, led the way in renovating château interiors in sumptuous fashion—sadly, many of his elegant furnishings were later sold), you may wish to spend most of your time exploring the enchanting gardens, complete with a moatlike lake. Innovative son-et-lumière shows are held on the grounds from 10:30 PM, May through September. ☎ *02–47–45–42–04* ⊕ *www.chateau-france.com/azaylerideau.fr* ✉ *€6.10* ⊘ *Apr.–Sept., daily 9:30–6; Oct.–Mar., daily 10–12:30 and 2–5:30.*

★ Privately tended by Madame Béatrice de Andia—one of the grandes dames of the Loire—and her staff are the **Jardins de la Chatonnière,** a 15-acre garden that will make most emerald-green with envy. Framing the private, turreted Renaissance château are six spectacular visions, with each garden devoted to a theme, including L'Élégance, Le Silence, and L'Abondance, in the extraordinary shape of a gigantic leaf. ⊠ *Rte. D57, direction Lignières–Langeais, 4 km (2½ mi) north of Azay-le-Rideau* ☎ *02–47–45–40–29* ⊕ *www.lachatonniere.com* ✉ *€5* ⊘ *Apr.–Oct. 10–7.*

Where to Stay & Eat

$–$$$ ✕▥ **Le Grand Monarque.** Grand and elegant, this famous town landmark is about a three-minute walk from Azay's château. Some complain that its fame brings a captive audience, which can result in offhand service. However, rooms, which vary in size and style, have character; most are simple, with an antique or two, and many have exposed beams. Public salons are luxe and alluring, while the restaurant (which, from mid-October through late March, is closed Monday, and does not serve dinner Sunday or lunch Tuesday and Friday) serves high-style food. Weekend stays must include dinner. ⊠ *3 pl. de la République, 37190* ☎ *02–47–45–40–08* 🖷 *02–47–45–46–25* ⊕ *www.legrandmonarque.com* ⇄ *24 rooms* ⚖ *Restaurant, cable TV, bar, some pets allowed (fee); no a/c* ⊟ *AE, MC, V* ⊘ *Closed Dec.–mid-Feb.* ¶◎¶ *MAP.*

★ ¢–$ ⊞ **Biencourt.** Charmingly set on the pedestrian street that leads to Azay's château gates, this red-shuttered town house hides an authentic, 19th-century schoolhouse within a delightful courtyard-garden, now fitted out with cozily traditional guest rooms (and the stray blackboard and school desk). No matter if you can't land one of the conversation pieces in "La Classe"—the other chambers are fine enough, decorated in pastels as warm as the delightfully helpful owners, the Mariotons. The town has quite a few restaurant selections—if you just don't want to stroll around and pick, ask Cédric and Emmanuelle for the best. ⊠ 7 rue Balzac, 37190 ☎ 02–47–45–20–75 📠 02–47–45–91–73 ⊕ www.hotelbiencourt. com ⇨ 17 rooms, 12 with bath ⌂ No a/c in some rooms, no room TVs ⊟ MC, V ⊗ Closed mid-Nov.–late Feb. ⊠ EP.

The Outdoors

Rent bikes from **Leprovost** (⊠ 13 rue Carnot ☎ 02–47–45–40–94) to ride along the Indre; the area around Azay-le-Rideau is among the most tranquil and scenic in Touraine.

Shopping

Osier (wicker) products have been made for centuries in Villaines-les-Rochers, 6 km (4 mi) southeast of Azay-le-Rideau via D57. Willow reeds are cultivated in nearby fields and dried in the sun each May, before being transformed into sofas, cat baskets, or babies' rattles. In 1849, when the craft was threatened with extinction, the parish priest persuaded 65 small groups of basket weavers to form France's first agricultural workers' cooperative. The **Coopératif de la Vannerie** (⊠ 1 rue de la Cheneillère ☎ 02–47–45–43–03), which is open Saturday 10–noon and 2–7 and Sunday 2–7, is still going strong and offers a wide choice of wicker goods for sale.

Saché

㉑ *7 km (4½ mi) east of Azay-le-Rideau via D17.*

Fodor'sChoice
★

A crook in the road, a Gothic church, the centuries-old Auberge du XIIᵉ Siècle, an Alexander Calder stabile (the great American sculptor created a modern atelier nearby), and the country retreat of novelist Honoré de Balzac (1799–1850)—these few but choice elements all add up to Saché, one of the prettiest (and most undiscovered) nooks in the Val de Loire. If you are heading in to the town from the east, you are first welcomed by the **Pont-de-Ruan**—a dream-sequence of a flower-bedecked bridge, water mill, and lake that is so picturesque it will practically click your camera for you. Two kilometers (1 mi) further, you hit the center of Saché and the **Château de Saché,** which contains the **Musée Balzac.** If you've never read any of Balzac's "Comédie Humaine," you might find little of interest here; but if you have, and do, you'll return to such novels as *Cousin Bette* and *Eugénie Grandet* with fresh enthusiasm and understanding. Much of the landscape around here, and some of the people back then, found immortality by being fictionalized in many a Balzac novel. The present château, built between the 16th and 18th centuries, is more of a comfortable country house than a fortress. Born in nearby Tours, Balzac came here—to stay with

WHEEL ESTATE: BIKING IN THE LOIRE VALLEY

A FAIRY-TALE REALM PAR EXCELLENCE, the Loire Valley is studded with storybook castles, forests primeval, time-burnished towns, and—bien sûr—the famous châteaux de la Loire, which are strung like a strand of pearls across a countryside so serene it could win the Nobel peace prize. With magic at every curve in the road, Cinderella's glass coach might be the optimum way to get around, but the next best thing is to tour the Val de Loire by bike.

A car means you have to stop and get out to look around; on foot you don't cover ground. But the Loire's plateau and châteaux are custom-made for a group bike tour. There's nothing like seeing Chenonceaux with your head pumped full of endorphins, surrounded by 20 new best friends, and knowing you'll be spending the night in a pointed turret bedroom that savors of sleeping princesses. If you want to experience this region at its most blissful—but not blisterful!—take the VBT (Vermont Biking Tours) Loire Valley Tour. Many of the participants found it to be the most wonderful, truly ooooooooooolala travel experience they ever had in France.

Every morning, for six days, you sally forth not to kill dragons, but to cycle down village roads that look like Corot paintings, visit feudally luxurious châteaux, explore medieval towns like Chinon, and bike through the "sweet reasonableness" of this lovely landscape at 180 heartbeats a mile. Each day sees from two to four hours of biking (about 34 to 56 km/19 to 35 mi), with an option of either calling it quits at lunch and returning to your hotel or continuing on with the rack pack for the afternoon.

Our group's Captain Cycle joked that "real men don't ask for directions—at least not in English," but since the instructions and maps direct you along the route virtually pebble-to-pebble, this faux pas never arose. Just when the route would get too tranquil, a dazzling château was conveniently set around the bend.

In fact, your itinerary reads like the pages of a Perrault fairy tale, studded as it is with such legendary abodes as Azay-le-Rideau, Chenonceaux, Villandry, and Ussé, the latter literally the château that inspired Perrault to write "Sleeping Beauty." Feeling the time for Beauty's awakening was long since past, the Duc de Blacas, Ussé's longtime owner (movie-star handsome and a lawyer who once worked for years in America) has ravishingly renovated this symbol of Old France as a family home open to all. It's a good morning's work to see two châteaux, non?

You'll have an even better evening of it, thanks to VBT's splendid choice of châteaux-hotels. At the 16th-century La Bourdaisière, retreat of King François I, you'll feel a wand has been waved over you as you repair to the Richelieu-red dining room where you enjoy the group's first candlelit supper (our filet de carpe au Bourgueil was supper-lative). Audrey Hepburn's favorite, the Domaine de la Tortinière, fulfills anyone's "Queen-for-a-Stay" fantasies. Your final hotel, the Château de Rochecotte, was the 19th-century Xanadu of Prince de Talleyrand-Périgord. After all this, it is little wonder that most of the 20 bikers in the group were in a state of dumb intoxication after six days with **VBT** (✉ 614 Monkton Rd., Bristol, VT 05443 ☎ 800/245–3868 ⊕ www.vbt.com). And we're not talking about all the wine tastings.

— Robert I. C. Fisher

his friends, the Margonnes—during the 1830s, both to write such works as *Le Père Goriot* and to escape his creditors. The château houses substantial exhibits, ranging from photographs to original manuscripts to the coffeepot Balzac used to brew the caffeine that helped to keep him writing up to 16 hours a day. A few period rooms are here and impress with 19th-century charm, including a lavish emerald-green salon and the author's writing room. Be sure to study some of the corrected author proofs on display. Balzac had to pay for corrections and additions beyond a certain limit. Painfully in debt, he made emendations filling all the margins of his proofs, causing dismay to his printers. Their legitimate bills for extra payment meant that some of his books, best-sellers for nearly two centuries, failed to bring him a centime. Outside, the château is surrounded by a pretty park, overlooking a tiny vale. ☎ *02–47–26–86–50* ⊕ *www.chateaux-france.com/sache* 🎫 *€4.50* 🕓 *Wed.–Mon. 10–12:30 and 2–5.*

Where to Stay & Eat

★ **$$–$$$** ✕ **Auberge du XIIe Siècle.** You half expect Balzac himself to come strolling in the door of this half-timber, delightfully historic auberge, so little has it changed since the 19th century. Still sporting a time-stained painted sign on its exterior, its original exterior staircase, and nearly opposite the great author's country retreat, this inn still retains its centuries-old dining room, now warmed by a fireplace, bouquets, and rich wood tables. Beyond this room is a modern extension—all airy glass and white walls but not exactly what you're looking for in such historic surrounds. Balzac's ample girth attested to his great love of food, and he would no doubt enjoy the nouvelle spins on his classic *géline* chicken favorites served here today. But there's more, much more on tap—chefs Thierry Jimenez and Xavier Aubrun are exceedingly talented, as witness their *aiguillettes de canard rosées en réduction de Chinon* (slices of duck flavored in Chinon wine). Dessert is excellent, and so is the coffee, a refreshment Balzac drank incessantly (little wonder he created more than 2,000 characters). ✉ *1 rue du Château* ☎ *02–47–26–88–77* 💳 *MC, V* 🕓 *Closed 3 wks in Jan., 1 wk in June, 1 wk in Sept., 1 wk in Nov., and Mon. No dinner Sun., no lunch Tues.*

$$$ 🏠 **Chez Patrick Bernard.** Sadly, there are no hotels in Saché, but you can stay in one of three luxuriously renovated *gîtes* (furnished country houses) at an 18th-century farm owned by Patrick Bernard and his Norwegian wife Benny who speaks excellent English. The largest, in a converted barn, has room for six people, with a huge lounge area and mezzanine. The smallest can sleep four. All bedrooms have en suite bathrooms. From Saché, go north on a little road over the Indre river and follow the sign for La Sablonnière. The Bernards prefer to rent by the week in summer but call ahead and you may be able to book for a weekend or a night or two. ✉ *37190, Baulay* ☎ *02–47–26–86–92* ✉ *baulay@wanadoo.fr* 🛏 *3 houses with bath* 🚫 *No a/c* 💳 *No credit cards* 🍴 *EP.*

Ussé

Fodor'sChoice
★

🔟 *14 km (9 mi) west of Azay-le-Rideau via D17 and D7.*

The most beautiful castle in France is first glimpsed as you approach the **Château d'Ussé** (in the village of Rigny-Ussé) and an astonishing array of blue-slate roofs, dormer windows, delicate towers, and Gothic turrets greets you against the flank of the Forest of Chinon. Literature describes this château, overlooking the banks of the river Indre, as the original *Sleeping Beauty* castle; Charles Perrault—author of this beloved 17th-century tale—spent time here as a guest of the Count of Saumur and legend has it that Ussé inspired him to write the famous story. Though parts of the castle are from the 1400s, most of it was completed two centuries later. By the 17th century, the region was so secure one fortified wing of the castle was demolished to allow grand vistas over the valley and the castle gardens, newly built in the style Le Nôtre had made so fashionable at Versailles. Only Disney could have outdone this white-tufa marvel: the château is a flamboyant mix of Gothic and Renaissance styles—romantic and built for fun, not for fighting. Its history supports this playful image: it endured no bloodbaths—no political conquests or conflicts—while a tablet in the chapel indicates that even the French Revolution passed it by. Inside, a tour leads you through several sumptuous period salons, a 19th-century French fashion exhibit, and the Salle de Roi bedchamber built for a visit by King Louis XV (who never arrived—his loss, as the red-silk, canopied four-poster bed here is the stuff of dreams). At the end of the house tour, you can go up the fun spiral staircases to the *chemin de ronde* of the lofty towers; there are pleasant views of the Indre River from the battlements, and you will also find rooms filled with waxwork effigies detailing the fable of Sleeping Beauty herself. Kids will love this.

Before you leave, visit the exquisite Gothic-becomes-Renaissance chapel in the garden, built for Charles d'Espinay and his wife in 1523–35. Note the door decorated with pleasingly sinister skull-and-crossbones carvings. Just a few steps from the chapel are two towering cedars of Lebanon—a gift from the genius-poet of Romanticism, Viscount René de Chateaubriand, to the lady of the house, the Duchess of Duras. When her famous amour died in 1848, she stopped all the clocks in the house—à la Sleeping Beauty—"so as never to hear struck the hours you will not come again." The castle then was inherited by her relations, the Comte and Comtesse de la Rochejacquelin, one of the most dashing couples of the 19th century. Today, Ussé belongs to their descendant, the Duc de Blacas, who is as soigné as his castle. If you do meet him, proffer thanks, as every night his family floodlights the entire château, a vision that is one of the Loire Valley's dreamiest sights. Regarded as a symbol of *la vieille France*, Ussé can't be topped for fairy-tale splendor, so make this a must-do. ☎ *02–47–95–54–05* 🎟 *€9.50* ⊘ *Mid-Feb.–Mar. and Oct.–mid-Nov., daily 10–noon and 2–5:30; Apr., May, and Sept., daily 9–noon and 2–6:45; June–Aug., daily 9–6:30.*

Where to Stay & Eat

$$–$$$ ✕🏨 **Manoir de Bray & Monts.** A blissfully charming retreat, this handsome 1730s manor is set in the idyllic riverbank village of Bréhémont, on the south bank of the Loire halfway between Azay-le-Rideau and Rigny-Ussé. Under new owners Nelly and Eric Le Dreff, the cooking classes for which the manor was famous are no more, but you can still stay here and admire the magnificent staircase with its neo-Gothic iron banisters, and the exquisite and shady rose garden. Most of the guest rooms are redolent of antique charm, replete with toile de Jouy touches and pink-and-white floral accents. ✉ *10 rue Ridet, 3 km (2 mi) northeast of Rigny-Ussé, 3 km (1½) mi west of Azay-le-Rideau, 37130 Bréhémont* ☎ *02–47–96–70–47* 📠 *02–47–96–57–36* 🌐 *manoirdebrayetmonts.com* *9 rooms* *Restaurant, some minibars, bicycles, bar, some pets allowed (fee); no a/c, no room TVs* 💳 *MC, V* ⏲ *Closed mid-Nov.–mid-Feb.* *EP.*

★ ¢–$ ✕🏨 **Le Clos d'Ussé.** Thank heavens for this delightful inn. The best time to see the great Château d'Ussé is in early morning light or illuminated at night, and the easiest way to do that is to overnight in the village of Rigny-Ussé here at the home of the *famille* Duchemin. Eric runs the place, Muriel is in charge of the extremely cozy restaurant, while *grand-mère* offers a warm smile. Not surprisingly, families will adore this place, especially as three of the rooms are custom-built for them (and rather stylish, to boot). Best of all, a one-minute walk from the front door takes you to the castle gates. ✉ *7 rue Principale, 37420 Rigny-Ussé* ☎📠 *02–47–95–55–47* *8 rooms, 4 with bath* *Restaurant, bar, some pets allowed (fee); no a/c, no room phones* 💳 *MC, V* ⏲ *Closed Nov.–Feb.* *EP.*

Chinon

23 *13 km (8 mi) southwest of Rigny-Ussé via D7 and D16, 44 km (28 mi) southwest of Tours.*

Fodor'sChoice ★

The historic town of Chinon—birthplace of author François Rabelais (1494–1553)—is dominated by the towering ruins of its medieval castle, perched high above the River Vienne. The medieval heart of the town is a storybook warren of narrow, cobbled streets (some are pedestrian-only) lined with half-timber houses; its fairy-tale allure was effectively used to frame Josette Day when she appeared as Beauty in Jean Cocteau's 1949 film *La Belle et la Bête.* The main road of the historic quarter, rue Haute St-Maurice (a continuation of rue Voltaire, which begins at the central place du Général-de-Gaulle) is a virtual open-air museum; other towns may have one or two or three blocks lined with medieval and Renaissance houses, but this street runs, spectacularly, for more than 15 blocks. While there are some unprepossessing museums in town—the **Musée du Vieux Chinon,** in a medieval town house on rue Haute St-Maurice, the **Maison de la Rivière,** devoted to Chinon's maritime trade and set along the embankment, and the **Musée du Vin** (Wine Museum) on rue Voltaire—the medieval quarter remains the must-do, as a walk here catapults you back to the days of Rabelais. Because both the village and the château are on steep, cobbled slopes, it's a good idea to wear comfortable walking shoes. For a fun side trip in summer, a steam train chugs from Chinon 15 km (10 mi) south to **Richelieu,** the town founded and designed by Louis XIII's notorious cardinal (☎ 02–47–58–12–97 for details).

The vast **Château de Chinon,** a veritable fortress with walls 400 yards long, dates from the time of Henry II of England, who died here in 1189 and was buried at Fontevraud. Two centuries later the castle witnessed an important historic moment: Joan of Arc's recognition of the disguised Dauphin, later Charles VII; the castle was also one of the domiciles of Henri II and his warring wife, Eleanor of Aquitaine (Kate Hepburn's 1968 film *The Lion in Winter* was set, but not filmed, here). In the early 17th century the castle was partially dismantled by Cardinal Richelieu (1585–1642), who used many of its stones to build himself a new palace—itself now dismantled—in Richelieu, 21 km (13 mi) to the south. At Chinon everything is open to the elements, except the **Logis Royal** (Royal Chambers). Here there is a small museum containing a model of the castle when it was intact, various old tapestries, and precious stones. For a fine view of the region, climb the **Tour Coudray** (Coudray Tower), where in 1307 leading members of the crusading Knights Templar were imprisoned before being taken to Paris, tried, and burned at the stake. The **Tour de l'Horloge** (Clock Tower), whose bell has sounded the hours since 1399, contains the **Musée Jeanne d'Arc** (Joan of Arc Museum). There are sensational views from the ramparts over Chinon, the Vienne Valley, and, toward the back of the castle, the famous vineyard called Le Clos de l'Echo. ☎ 02–47–93–13–45 ⊠ €6 ☉ *Mid-Mar.–June and Sept., daily 9:30–6; July and Aug., daily 9–7; Oct., daily 9–6; Nov.–mid-Mar., daily 9:30–5.*

Where to Stay & Eat

$$$ ✕ **Au Plaisir Gourmand.** Jean-Claude Rigollet's tufa-stone 18th-century restaurant by the Vienne River is the finest in Chinon. Specialties served in the Renaissance-style dining room include crayfish salad, snails in garlic, jellied rabbit, *sandre* (pike-perch) with butter sauce, and braised oxtail in red wine. ⊠ *2 rue Parmentier* ☎ 02–47–93–20–48 ⊟ *AE, MC, V* ☉ *Closed Mon. and mid-Feb.–mid-Mar. No dinner Sun., no lunch Tues.*

$–$$ ✕▥ **France.** Right on Chinon's most charming square—a picture postcard come to life with splashing fountain and a bevy of cafés—this sweetly agreeable Best Western hotel, just two blocks from the medieval quarter, has been an hotel since 1577. Many regional notables lived here before the Revolution, when it became the Hôtel Lion d'Or, the first hostelry in the region. Guest rooms are comfortable and cozy; some overlook two tiny, flowerpot-bedecked courtyards, while others take in views that include Chinon's castle ruins. The ground-floor restaurant, Au Chapeau Rouge (closed Monday and no dinner Sunday) serves regional cuisine, and there's also a brasserie for cheaper snacks. The hotel staff is most congenial. ⊠ *47 pl. du Général-de-Gaulle, 37500* ☎ 02–47–93–33–91 ▨ *02–47–98–37–03* ⊕ *www.chinon-hoteldefrance-restaurant.com* ⤏ *30 rooms* ⌂ *Restaurant, brasserie; no a/c in some rooms* ⊟ *AE, DC, MC, V* ☉ *Closed Nov. and mid-Feb.–mid-Mar.* �ⓞⅠ *MAP.*

$ ▥ **Diderot.** With a facade that seems on sabbatical from an 18th-century François Boucher painting—ivy-covered stone, white shutters, mansard roof, dormer windows, rococo spiral staircase—this is Chinon's prettiest hotel. Inside, a corner bar and cozy stone breakfast room create a welcoming air, one strengthened by the Kazamias family, the hotel's owners, who relocated from Cyprus (and brought a bit of it with them, as the olive and laurel trees in the forecourt attest). Guest rooms are standard-issue—avoid the airless ones in the separate house on the back street. The hotel is in a nice residential area, about 10 blocks from the medieval quarter. ⊠ *7 rue Diderot, 37500* ☎ *02–47–93–18–87* 🖷 *02–47–93–37–10* ⊕ *www.hoteldiderot.com* ⇴ *28 rooms, including 4 in annex* ⬧ *No a/c, no room TVs* ▤ *AE, DC, MC, V* ⊗ *Closed mid-Dec.–mid-Feb.* ⍰ *EP.*

Nightlife & the Arts

Chinon stages a **Marché à l'Ancienne** (⊕ www.chinon.com) on the third Saturday of August, a free wine-tasting extravaganza with stalls, displays, and costumed locals recalling rural life of a hundred years ago. For details, contact the tourist office.

Fontevraud-l'Abbaye

㉔ *20 km (12 mi) northwest of Chinon via D751.*

A refreshing break from the worldly grandeur of châteaux, the small village of Fontevraud is crowned with the largest abbey in France, a magnificent complex of Romanesque and Renaissance buildings that were of central importance in the history of both England and France. Founded in 1101, the **Abbaye Royale de Fontevraud** had separate churches and living quarters for nuns, monks, lepers, "repentant" female sinners, and the sick. Between 1115 and the French Revolution in 1789, a succession of 39 abbesses—among them a granddaughter of William the Conqueror—directed operations. The great 12th-century **Église Abbatiale** (Abbey Church) contains the tombs of Henry II of England, his wife Eleanor of Aquitaine, and their son, Richard Coeur de Lion (the Lion-Hearted). Though their bones were scattered during the Revolution, their effigies still lie *en couchant* in the middle of the echoey nave. Napoléon turned the abbey church into a prison, and so it remained until 1963, when historical restoration work—still under way—began. The **Salle Capitulaire** (Chapter House), adjacent to the church, with its collection of 16th-century religious wall paintings (prominent abbesses served as models), is unmistakably Renaissance; the paving stones bear the salamander emblem of François I. Next to the long refectory is the famously octagonal **Cuisine** (kitchen), topped by 20 scaly stone chimneys led by the **Tour d'Evrault.** ⊠ *Pl. des Plantagenêts* ☎ *02–41–51–71–41* ⊕ *www.abbaye-fontevraud. com* ⚏ *€6.10* ⊗ *June–Sept., daily 9–6; Oct.–May, daily 10–5.*

After touring the Abbaye Royale, head outside the gates of the complex a few blocks to the north to discover one of the Loire Valley's most time-machine streets, the **Allée Sainte-Catherine.** Bordered by the Fontevraud park, headed by a charming medieval church, and lined with a few scattered houses (which now contain the town tourist office, a gallery that sells medieval illuminated manuscript pages, and the delightful Licorne restaurant), this street still looks like the 14th century aborning.

Fodor'sChoice
★

Where to Stay & Eat

★ **$$$–$$$$** ✕ **La Licorne.** A hanging shop sign adorned with a painted unicorn beckons you to this pretty-as-a-picture town-house restaurant just off Fontevraud's idyllic Allée Sainte-Catherine. Past a flowery garden and table-adorned terrace, tiny salons glow with happy folks feasting on some of the best food in the region: Loire salmon, guinea fowl in Layon wine, and lobster with fava beans should make most diners purr with contentment. ⊠ *31 rue Robert-d'Arbrissel* ☎ *02–41–51–72–49* ◇ *Reservations essential* ➡ *AE, DC, MC, V* ☉ *Closed Mon. No dinner Sun. and Wed.*

★ **$–$$** ✕🖭 **Hostellerie du Prieuré St-Lazare.** One of the more unusual hotels in the Loire Valley and set right within the medieval splendor of Fontevraud, this series of outbuildings was once the abbey's lepers' hospice. The entrance gives onto the vast *salle capitulaire* conference room and the cloisters now house a fine restaurant, Le Cloître (reservations essential), where such delicacies as swordfish simmered in Saumur-Champigny wine entice. In a snug side wing the erstwhile monks' cells have been transformed into small but alluring guest rooms, chic and bright in modern checks and fine wood accents. Staying here lets you explore the abbey grounds when its gates are closed to the public—an exceptional experience. ⊠ *Abbaye Royale, 49590* ☎ *02–41–51–73–16* 🖷 *02–41–51–75–50* ⊕ *www.hotelfp-fontevraud.com* ⟿ *52 rooms* ♨ *Restaurant, minibars; no a/c* ➡ *AE, MC, V* ☉ *Closed mid-Nov.–mid-Mar.* ❮❘ *MAP.*

Saumur

★ ㉕ *15 km (9 mi) northwest of Fontevraud via D947, 68 km (43 mi) west of Tours.*

Dominated by its mighty turreted castle high above the river and adorned with a particularly lovely historic quarter, ancient Saumur is one of the larger towns along the Loire and a key transportation hub for Anjou, the province just to the west of Touraine. Saumur is also known for its riding school and flourishing mushroom industry, which produces 100,000 tons per year. The same cool tunnels in which the mushrooms grow provide an ideal storage place for the local *mousseux* (sparkling wines); many vineyards hereabouts are open to the public for tours.

Regional government offices, wealthy wine producers, and the spiffy riding school all help make Saumur's natives some of the Loire's most stylish, nay, snobbish residents—chances are you'll get a blast of old-time French attitude, not just from the preppy ladies but a greater whiff from shopkeepers and waiters. Little seems to have changed over the centuries: Honoré de Balzac famously wrote up the surly side of the Saumurois in his *Eugénie Grandet.* Putting up with this *snobisme* may be worth it: Saumur's historic center is studded with elegant 19th-century town houses and the magnificent place St-Pierre, lorded over by the vast 14th-century church of St-Pierre and centerpiece of a warren of streets, cafés, and ice-cream parlors. Be sure to spend an hour or two exploring the *centre historique.*

If you arrive in the evening, the sight of the elegant, floodlighted, white 14th-century **Château de Saumur** takes your breath away. Look familiar? Probably because you've seen it in reproductions from the famous *Très Riches Heures* (Book of Hours) painted for the Duc de Berry in 1416 (now in the Musée Condé at Chantilly). Inside it's bright and cheerful, with a fairy-tale gateway and plentiful potted flowers. Owing to renovation of the castle walls, the two museums based here, the **Musée des Arts Décoratifs** (Decorative Arts Museum), and the **Musée du Cheval** (Equestrian Museum), will be closed through 2007. Until the museums reopen, visitors will only have access to the garden and terrace. However, for July and August, guided tours of some castle interiors can be arranged, 10:15–4:45. From the cliffside promenade beyond the carpark there's a thrilling vista of the castle on its bluff against the river backdrop. ⊠ *Esplanade du Château* ☏ *02–41–40–24–40* ⊕ *www.saumur-tourisme.net/chateausaumur.html* ⊠ *€2* ☾ *Wed.–Mon., 10–1 and 2–5.*

The **Cadre Noir de Saumur** (Riding School) is unique in Europe, with its 400 horses, extensive stables, five Olympic-size riding schools, and miles of specially laid tracks. Try for a morning tour, which includes a chance to admire the horses in training. During the **Carrousel de Saumur,** on the last two weekends in July, the horses put on a full gala display for enthusiastic crowds. ⊠*Rue de l'Abbaye* ☏*02–41–53–50–60* ⊕*www.cadrenoir.fr* ⊠*€7* ☾ *Guided tours only, Apr.–Sept., Tues.–Sat. 9:30–11 and 2–4.*

Saumur is the heart of one of the finest wine regions in France. To pay a call on some of the vineyards around the city, first stop into the **Maison du Vin** (House of Wine), for the full scoop on hours and directions; also consult the web site for Loire wines, www.vins-valdeloire.com. ⊠ *Quai Lucien-Gautier* ☏ *02–41–38–45–83* ☾ *Easter–mid-Nov., daily 10–5.*

Here are some of the top vineyards of the Saumur region. Note that Loire wine is not a practical buy—except for instant consumption—but if wine-tasting tours of vineyards inspire you, enterprising wine makers will arrange shipments. For sparkling Saumur wine try **Ackerman** (⊠ 19 rue Léopold-Palustre, St-Hilaire ☏ 02–41–53–30–20). **Veuve Amiot** (⊠ 21 rue Jean-Ackerman, St-Hilaire ☏02–41–83–14–14) is a long-established producer of Saumur wines. You can visit the cavernous premises of **Gratien-Meyer** (⊠ Rte. de Montsoreau ☏ 02–41–83–13–32 ⊠ €2.50 ☾ 9–noon and 2–6) on the east side of Saumur daily, April through September. Just southeast of Saumur, in Dampierre-sur-Loire, stop in at the **Château de Chaintres** (⊠ 54 rue de la Croix-de-Chaintre ☏ 02–41–52–90–54), where husky Krishna Lester, a hunky English eccentric, produces the region's finest red and enjoys expounding on the unexpected links between frogs in the throat, toads in the hole, and malolactic fermentation.

Where to Stay & Eat

$$–$$$ ✕⊞ **Anne d'Anjou.** The spectacular setting at the foot of Saumur castle may appeal to you most about this elegant 18th-century hotel—or maybe the flower-strewn courtyard, or perhaps the views of the Loire from some of the guest rooms. The finest retain their original, late-18th- and early-19th-century decoration, and one is even furbished to the designs of Percier and Fontaine, Napoléon's favorite architects. The restaurant Les Ménestrels (closed Sunday) is in a separate building—a lovingly

restored 16th-century house up against the castle cliff (⊠ 11 rue Raspail ☎ 02–41–67–71–10). The menu here changes regularly under the eye of virtuoso chef Christophe Hosselet, who has a penchant for perch with spring-onion fondue, and venison in season. ⊠ *32 quai Mayaud, 49400* ☎ *02–41–67–30–30* 🖷 *02–41–67–51–00* ⊕ *www.hotel-anneanjou.com* ➷ *45 rooms* ⚭ *Minibars, cable TV, some pets allowed (fee)* ▤ *AE, DC, MC, V* �🍽 *MAP.*

★ $–$$$ 🏨 **Saint-Pierre.** At the very epicenter of historic Saumur, this gorgeous little jewel is hidden beneath the medieval walls of the church of St. Pierre—look for the hotel's storybook entrance on one of the pedestrian *passages* that circle the vast nave. Once inside the 15th- to 17th-century house, you'll find a sweet reception area and suave staff to welcome you. Up the Renaissance corkscrew staircase (or modern mini-elevator) you'll find the astonishingly refined guest rooms. Designer fabrics, antique *pont* cabinets (forming a "bridge" over bed headboards), elegant wainscotting, Persian rugs, tuffeaux fireplaces, and bathrooms replete with Paloma Picasso designs make this a favored home-away-from-home for Saumur's most savvy visitors. The smaller rooms face the church but they also are quieter than those overlooking the road leading up to the castle. There is no restaurant, but just steps away is lovely place St-Pierre, lined with outdoor cafés. ⊠ *Rue Haute-Saint-Pierre, 49400* ☎ *02–41–50–33–00* 🖷 *02–41–50–38–68* ⊕ *www.saintpierresaumur.com* ➷ *15 rooms* ⚭ *Minibars, cable TV, some pets allowed (fee)* ▤ *AE, DC, MC, V* �🍽 *EP.*

en route   Along the river east of Saumur (that is, on the way back toward Tours) is a particularly scenic stretch of countryside. Here you will find the village of **Montsoreau,** famed for its riverside castle (now a museum devoted to the history of the Loire). Break for a meal at the excellent Diane de Méridor restaurant, just a few steps from the château. One town over is super-picturesque **Candes-St-Martin,** which perches over the confluence of the Loire and Vienne rivers and huddles within the shadows of its great Gothic church, consecrated to St. Martin of Tours, who died here.

Turquant

❷❻ *6 km (4 mi) west of Saumur via D947.*

FodorśChoice
★

A treasury of troglodyte dwellings, fairy-tale Turquant is picturesquely arranged around a limestone cliff landmarked by its striking blue windmill, the Moulin de la Herpinière, and the cave-mansion of La Grande Vignolle. Once used to quarry stone for the great châteaux, made into retreats for religious prophets and monks, recycled as storehouses for wines, and, in more recent centuries, transformed into unique houses, the tuffeaux caves that honeycomb the entire Loire Valley are among its most distinctive features. Among the more noted troglodyte towns—Rochecorbon, Rochemenier, Doué-la-Fontaine—the village of Turquant has some of the most amazing of these residences. Growing out of the sheer rock, these houses often boast rock doorways, sash windows, relief sculptures, everything but stone flowers (along the D947 route from Saumur to Turquant look out for the castle, complete with turrets and battlements, emerging from the cliff). Arriving in Turquant, you'll spot **La Grande Vignolle,** landmarked by its historic pigeon-loft tower. Now overseen by the Filleatreau wine company, the "Lordly Dwelling," parts of which date back to the 13th century, comprises several chambers carved out of the living rock, including a chapel, a ballroom, and a kitchen. Best of all is the elegant facade, adorned with horseshoe staircase and pepper-pot tower. ⊠ *Rte. de Montsoreau (D947)* ☎ *02–41–38–16–44* ⊕ *www.chez.com/turquant* ⊠ *Free* ⊙ *Easter–Oct., daily 10–6.*

A back road leads from La Grande Vignolle up the cliffside to the Turquant plateau of vineyards—on the way up look for the signs to **Le Val Hulin,** a cave that now holds the Troglo des Pommes Tapées, where you can see how dried and hammered apple slices—*pommes tapées*—are made. These were once the favored taste treat of Georges Clemenceau and the British Royal Navy. ⊠ *Le Val Hulin* ☎ *02–41–51–48–30* ⊠ *Free* ⊙ *July and Aug., Tues.–Sun. 10–noon, 2:30–6:30; June, Sept., Tues.–Sun. 2:30–6:30; Apr., Oct., Nov., weekends 2:30–6.*

Streets descending from the Turquant plateau are lined with many delightful rock-face houses. Once you get back down to ground level, head back to the highway to pass the village church of St-Aubin and the magnificent **Château de la Fessardière** (☎ 02–41–38–11–28 ⊕ www.chez.com/turquant). Head through its grand portal to find a small shop sometimes open, where you can check out the latest vintages of the Turquantois grape. For more information on the village, check out the Web site.

Where to Stay

$–$$ ⊠ **Demeure de la Vignole.** A cliffside domain to keep even the most
Fodor'sChoice picky atmosphere-hunters happy, this little kingdom—comprising an en-
★ chanting Renaissance-era *château troglodytique,* an elegant 15th-century manor house, and a medieval cave dwelling—is adjacent to the noted La Grand Vignolle museum. The manor is a mix of exposed tuffeaux rock face, rustic wood beams, tinkling chandeliers, *Maison Française* fabrics, and piquant antiques. Outside, a terrace framed by a grove of Van Gogh irises overlooks a grand stretch of Saumur-Champigny vineyards. Monique Bartholeyns—blond, sassy, and *sympathique*—oversees her hotel from her adjacent 1450 rock-château, believed to have once been home to Queen Marguerite d'Anjou. Even this residence may pale when compared to Monique's newest accommodation: the prehistoric "suite troglodyte," a duplex part and parcel (along with a rock ballroom) of the hillside cave dwelling. Upon special request, dinners will be served. Don't miss this delightful place. ⊠ *3 impasse Marguerite-d'Anjou, 49730* ☎ *02–41–53–67–00* 🖷 *02–41–53–67–09* ⊕ *www.demeure-vignole.com* ⇒ *8 rooms* ♢ *Cable TV, some pets allowed (fee); no a/c* ▭ *AE, DC, MC, V* ⊙ *Closed mid-Nov.–mid. Mar.* ⵏⵘ *BP.*

Montreuil-Bellay

㉗ *18 km (11 mi) south of Saumur via N147.*

Many people have a special place in their heart for Montreuil-Bellay, a small riverside town with many 18th- and 19th-century houses, lovely public gardens, and a leafy square next to its castle. The 15th-century

Château de Montreuil-Bellay has a grandiose exterior—majestic towers and pointed roofs—and a fascinating interior, with fine furniture and tapestries, a fully equipped medieval kitchen, and a chapel adorned with frescoes of angelic musicians. For a memorable view, take a stroll in the gardens; graceful white turrets tower high above the trees and rosebushes, and down below, the little River Thouet winds its lazy way to the Loire. ⊠ *Pl. des Ormeaux* ☎ *02–41–52–33–06* ✆ *€7* ☉ *Apr.–Oct., Wed.–Mon. 10–noon and 2–5:30.*

Angers

➋➑ *51 km (32 mi) northwest of Montreuil-Bellay via D761, 45 km (28 mi) northwest of Saumur, 88 km (55 mi) northeast of Nantes.*

The bustling city of Angers, on the banks of the Maine River, just north of the Loire, is famous for its towering castle filled with the extraordinary Apocalypse Tapestry. But it also has a fine Gothic cathedral, a selection of art galleries, and a network of pleasant, traffic-free streets around place Ste-Croix, with its half-timber houses. The town's principal sights lie within a compact square formed by the three main boulevards and the Maine.

★ The banded black-and-white **Château d'Angers,** built by St. Louis (1228–38), glowers over the town from behind turreted moats, now laid out as gardens and overrun with flowers and deer. As you explore the grounds, note the startling contrast between the thick defensive walls, defended by a drawbridge and 17 massive round towers in a distinctive pattern, and the formal garden, with its delicate white-tufa chapel, erected in the 16th century. For a sweeping view of the city and surrounding countryside, climb one of the castle towers. A well-integrated modern gallery on the castle grounds contains the great **Tenture de l'Apocalypse** (Apocalypse Tapestry), woven in Paris in the 1380s for the Duke of Anjou. Measuring 16 feet high and 120 yards long, its many panels show a series of 70 horrifying and humorous scenes from the Book of Revelation. In one, mountains of fire fall from heaven while boats capsize and men struggle in the water. Another has the beast with seven heads. ⊠ *2 promenade du Bout-du-Monde* ☎ *02–41–86–48–77* ⊕ *www.monum.fr* ✆ *€7* ☉ *May–Aug., daily 9:30–6:30; Sept.–Apr., daily 10–5:30.*

The **Cathédrale St-Maurice** (⊠ Pl. Monseigneur-Chappoulie) is a 12th- and 13th-century Gothic cathedral noted for its curious Romanesque facade and original stained-glass windows; bring binoculars to appreciate both fully.

The **Musée David d'Angers,** in a refurbished glass-roof medieval church, has a collection of dramatic sculptures by Jean-Pierre David (1788–1859), the city's favorite son. ⊠ *33 bis rue Toussaint* ☎ *02–41–05–38–90* ✆ *€4* ☉ *Tues.–Sun. 10–noon and 2–6.*

To learn about the heartwarming liqueur made in Angers since 1849, head to the **Distillerie Cointreau** on the east of the city. It has a museum and offers a guided visit of the distillery, which starts with an introductory film, moves through the bottling plant and alembic room, with its gleaming copper-pot stills, and ends with a tasting. ⊠ *Bd. des Breton-nières, St-Barthélémy d'Anjou* ☎ *02–41–31–50–50* ⊕ *www.cointreau. com* ⊠ *€5.50* ⊙ *Tours daily July and Aug. 10:30, 2:30, 3:30, and 4:30; May, June, Sept., and Oct., 10:30 and 3; Nov.–Apr., 3.*

Where to Stay & Eat

$$$–$$$$ ✕ **La Salamandre.** Chef Danie Louboutin's meticulously prepared classic cuisine ranges from lamb and duck with cranberries to calamari with crab sauce, served amid Renaissance-style allurements and under stained-glass windows. Opt for one of the reasonably priced prix-fixe menus. ⊠ *1 bd. du Maréchal-Foch* ☎ *02–41–88–99–55* ⊟ *AE, DC, MC, V* ⊙ *Closed Sun.*

$ ✕ **La Treille.** For traditional, simple fare at affordable prices, try this small two-story mom-and-pop restaurant off place Ste-Croix and across from Maison d'Adam, Angers's finest timber-frame house. The prix-fixe menu may start with a *salade au chèvre chaud* (warm goat-cheese salad), followed by confit of duck and an apple tart. The upstairs dining room draws a lively crowd; downstairs is quieter. ⊠ *12 rue Montault* ☎ *02–41–88–45–51* ⊟ *MC, V* ⊙ *Closed Sun.*

$$–$$$ ⊞ **Anjou.** In business since 1846, the Anjou, now part of the Best Western chain, has a vaguely 18th-century style, including stained-glass windows in the lobby. The spacious rooms have high ceilings, double doors, and modern bathrooms where terry robes await you. ⊠ *1 bd. du Maréchal-Foch, 49100* ☎ *02–41–88–24–82, 800/528–1324 in U.S.* ᕦ *02–41–87–22–21* ⊕ *www.hoteldanjou.fr* ⟿ *53 rooms* ᕦ *Restaurant, some pets allowed (fee); no a/c* ⊟ *AE, DC, MC, V* ⊚ *BP.*

$ ⊞ **Mail.** A stately lime tree stands sentinel outside this 17th-century mansion on a calm street between the Hôtel de Ville and the river. The smallish rooms are individually decorated in pastel shades. ⊠ *8 rue des Ursules, 49100* ☎ *02–41–25–05–25* ᕦ *02–41–86–91–20* ⊕ *www. destination-anjou.com/mail* ⟿ *26 rooms* ᕦ *Minibars, cable TV, some pets allowed (fee); no a/c* ⊟ *AE, DC, MC, V* ⊚ *EP.*

Nightlife & the Arts

July and August see the **Angers L'Eté** (Angers Summer) festival, with concerts at the Cloître Toussaint and Chapelle des Ursules; call ☎ 02–41–05–41–48 for details.

en route Heading 22 km (15 mi) south of Angers, stop off in the charming village of Brissac-Quincé to admire the tallest château in France, the **Château de Brissac** (⊕ www.chateau-brissac.fr) a towering pile of Mannerist, Baroque, and Classical motifs grafted onto a Gothic castle; inside, all is seignorial splendor, with tapestries, Venetian-glass chandeliers, and even a grand theater (whose crimson interior once hosted such eminences as Gounod, Massenet, and Debussy).

Bourgueil

★ ㉙ *66 km (41 mi) southeast of Angers via N147 and D10, 19 km (12 mi) north of Chinon.*

Connoisseurs like to say that Chinon's red wines taste of raspberries, those of Bourgueil—just across the Loire—smell of violets. If you want to test that, explore the caves and vineyards surrounding the quaint market town of Bourgueil; just north of the village in Chevrette is the **Cave Touristique de la Dive Bouteille,** a vast cavern presenting regional wines, open daily 10 to noon and 2 to 6 (a handy Web site is www.vinbourgueil.com). Headliner here is the Benedictine **Abbaye de Bourgueil,** where Father Baudry legendarily planted the region's first cabernet franc vine in 1089. Aesthetic attractions—although founded by the Benedictines in the 10th century, most structures here date from the far-from-holy 18th-century— are greatly outweighed by those of the nearby Romanesque abbey of Fontevraud, but there is a **Musée des Arts et Traditions Populaires** to explore in the abbey. ☎ 02–47–97–72–04 ☑ €5 ◷ *July and Aug., Wed.–Mon. 2–6; Apr.–June and Sept.–late Oct., weekends 2–6.*

Where to Stay

$$–$$$　🏨 **Château des Réaux.** Half-museum, half-hotel, and extravagantly em-
Fodor'sChoice　blazoned with checkered red-and-white brickwork, this historic mon-
★　ument is a must-see for its 15th-century moat, its fortified entrance, and its fairy-tale, pepper-pot towers (day-trippers can visit for a fee). But it comes into its own when you overnight as guests of charming Comtesse Florence de Bouille, whose family has lived here for more than a century. What with period salons dripping with atmosphere (family memorabilia, Louis Quinze sofas, Victorian tric-trac tables), storybook-stylish guest rooms, and three swans in residence (wait until you hear their nicknames), this place is a delight. The cheapest rooms are in the 19th-century cottage in the grounds. ⊠ *Port-Boulet, 5 km (2 mi) south of Bourgueil, 37140* ☎ *02–47–95–14–40* 🖷 *02–47–95–18–34* ⊕ *www.chateaux-france.com/reaux* ⤴ *12 rooms, 5 suites* ⚭ *Tennis court; no a/c, no room TVs* ▭ *AE, DC, MC, V* ⦿ *BP.*

> **off the beaten path**

LE MANS – Best known for its 24-hour automobile race in June (call 02–43–40–24–75 for details; the Web site is www.lemans.org), Le Mans is 92 km (58 miles) north of Bourgueil. From Bourgueil take D749, D15, D86, and D141 to Noyant, then D767 to Le Lude, and end on D307. Le Mans is a bustling city with Gallo-Roman ramparts, a well-preserved Old Quarter, and a magnificent cathedral—part Gothic, part Romanesque—perched precariously on a hilltop overlooking the River Sarthe.

Langeais

30 *19 km (12 mi) northeast of Bourgueil via D35 and N152.*

Sometimes unjustly overlooked, the **Château de Langeais**—a castle in the true sense of the word—will particularly delight those who dream of lions rampant, knights in shining armor, and the chivalric days of yore. Built in the 1460s, bearing a massive portcullis and gate, and never altered, it has an interior noted for its superb collection of medieval and Renaissance furnishings—fireplaces, tapestries, chests, and beds—which would make Guinevere and Lancelot feel right at home. Outside, gardens nestle behind sturdy walls and battlements. The town itself has other sites, including a Renaissance church tower, but chances are you won't want to move from the delightful outdoor cafés that face the castle entrance. Do follow the road a bit to the right (when looking at the entrance) to discover the charming historic houses grouped around a waterfall and canal. ☎ 02–47–96–72–60 ⚐ €6.50 ☉ Apr.–Sept., daily 9–6:30; Oct.–Mar., daily 10–5:30.

ORLÉANS & THE EASTERN LOIRE

Orléans probably has the biggest inferiority complex this side of Newark, New Jersey. The city pales pitifully in comparison with other cities of central France, so the townfolk cling to the city's finest moment—the coming of *la pucelle d'Orléans* (the Maid of Orleans), Joan of Arc, in 1429 to liberate the city from the English during the Hundred Years' War. There's little left from Joan's time, but the city is festooned with everything from her equestrian monument to a Jeanne d'Arc Dry Cleaners. Orléans remains the gateway to the upper Loire Valley, which has some intriguing destinations: the hilltop wine town of Sancerre, the ceramics center of Gien, the ancient abbey of St-Benoît, and the extraordinary canal bridge designed by Gustave Eiffel at Briare. Heading back to the central Loire Valley (or south to Bourges), you can enjoy a grand finale at one of the Loire's most gorgeous hotels—the Comte de Vogüé's Château de la Verrerie (near Aubigny-sur-Nère) and one of the finest restaurants in France, the Lion d'Or, in the moody Sologne region.

Orléans

112 km (70 mi) northeast of Tours, 125 km (78 mi) south of Paris.

Once hallowed by Joan of Arc, Orléans is today a thriving commercial city; sensitive urban renewal has done much to bring it back to life, especially the medieval streets between the Loire and the cathedral. The city has quite a history; as a natural bridgehead over the Loire it was long the focus of hostile confrontations and invasions. In 52 BC Julius Caesar slaughtered its inhabitants and burned it to the ground. Five centuries later Attila and the Huns did much the same. Next came the Normans; then the Valois kings turned it into a secondary capital. The story of the Hundred Years' War, Joan of Arc, and the Siege of Orléans is widely known. In 1429 France had hit rock bottom. The English and their Burgundian allies were carving up the kingdom. Besieged by the English, Orléans was one of the last towns about to yield, when a young Lorraine peasant girl, Joan of Arc, arrived to rally the troops and save the kingdom. During the Wars of Religion (1562–98), much of the cathedral was destroyed. A century ago ham-fisted town planners razed many of the city's fine old buildings. Both German and Allied bombs helped finish the job during World War II.

③ The **Cathédrale Ste-Croix** is a riot of pinnacles and gargoyles, both Gothic and pseudo-Gothic, embellished with 18th-century wedding-cake towers. After most of the cathedral was destroyed in the 16th century during the Wars of Religion, Henry IV and his successors rebuilt it. Novelist Marcel Proust (1871–1922) called it France's ugliest church, but most find it impressive. Inside are vast quantities of stained glass and 18th-century wood carvings, plus the modern **Chapelle de Jeanne d'Arc** (Joan of Arc Chapel), with plaques in memory of British and American war dead. ⊠ *Pl. Ste-Croix* ⊘ *Daily 9–noon and 2–6.*

❸❷ The modern **Musée des Beaux-Arts** (Fine Arts Museum) is across from the cathedral. Take the elevator to the top of the five-story building; then make your way down to see works by such artists as Tintoretto, Velázquez, Watteau, Boucher, Rodin, and Gauguin. The museum's richest collection is its 17th-century French paintings. ⊠ *1 rue Fernand-Rabier* ☎ *02–38–79–21–55* ⊕ *www.ville-orleans.fr/html/fr/beauxarts. html* 🖾 *€3, joint ticket with History Museum* ⊘ *Tues.–Sat. 9:30–12:15 and 1:30–5:45, Sun. 2–6:30.*

❸❸ The **Musée Historique** (History Museum) is housed in the **Hôtel Cabu,** a Renaissance mansion restored after World War II. It contains works of both "fine" and "popular" art connected with the town's past, including a remarkable collection of pagan bronzes of animals and dancers. These bronzes were hidden from zealous Christian missionaries in the 4th century and discovered in a sandpit near St-Benoît in 1861. ⊠ *Square de l'Abbé-Desnoyers* ☎ *02–38–79–25–60* 🖾 *€3, joint ticket with Arts Museum* ⊘ *July and Aug., Tues.–Sun. 10:30–12:15 and 1:30–6; Sept.–June, Wed. 1:30–5:45 and Sun. 2–6:15.*

❸❹ During the 10-day Siege of Orléans in 1429, 17-year-old Joan of Arc stayed on the site of the **Maison de Jeanne d'Arc** (Joan of Arc House). This faithful reconstruction of the house she knew contains exhibits about her life and costumes and weapons of her time. Several dioramas modeled by Lucien Harmey recount the main episodes in her life, from the audience at Chinon to the coronation at Reims, her capture at Compiègne, and her burning at the stake at Rouen. ⊠ *3 pl. du Général-de-Gaulle* ☎ *02–38–52–99–89* ⊕ *www.jeannedarc.com.fr* 🖾 *€2* ⊘ *May–Oct., Tues.–Sun. 10–12:30 and 1:30–6; Nov.–Apr., Tues.–Sun. 1:30–6.*

Where to Stay & Eat

★ **$$–$$$** ✕ **Les Antiquaires.** The understated elegance of this cozy, wood-beamed restaurant close to the river, with its red walls, cane-backed chairs, and brass chandeliers, is in telling contrast to Philippe Bardau's penchant for colorfully presented dishes with a Mediterranean flavor: mullet with eggplant, for instance, or sea bass with artichokes and fennel. ⊠ *4 rue au Lin* ☎ *02–38–53–63–48* ▤ *AE, MC, V* ⊘ *Closed Mon. No dinner Sun.*

$–$$ ✕🏨 **Le Rivage.** This small, white-walled hotel south of Orléans makes a pleasant base. Each of the compact rooms has a little balcony with a view of the tree-lined Loiret River; the bathrooms are tiny. The dining room (no lunch Saturday; no dinner Sunday, November through April) opens onto a terrace facing the river. The menu changes with the season—if you're lucky, chef François Tassin's memorable lobster salad with mango or glazed green-apple soufflé with apple marmalade will be on tap. There's always a huge cheese board. ⊠ *635 rue de la Reine-Blanche, 5 km (3 mi) south of Orléans, 45160 Olivet* ☎ *02–38–66–02–93* 🖨 *02–38–56–31–11* 🛏 *17 rooms* ⚬ *Restaurant, minibars, tennis court, bar, some pets allowed (fee)* ▤ *AE, DC, MC, V* ⊘ *Closed late Dec.–mid-Jan.* ⋈⋈ *MAP.*

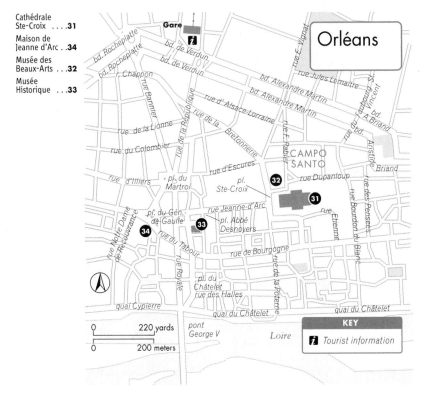

Nightlife & the Arts

The two-day **Fête de Jeanne d'Arc** (Joan of Arc Festival), on May 7 and 8, celebrates the heroic Maid of Orléans with a parade and religious procession.

Châteauneuf-sur-Loire

★ **35** *25 km (16 mi) southeast of Orléans via N460.*

The scenic village of Châteauneuf-sur-Loire has a delightful public park with giant tulip trees, magnolias, weeping willows, and rhododendrons, and is especially beautiful in late May and early June. Until the railroad arrived 130 years ago, the Loire was a working river, with boats transporting everything from wheat, salt, wine, and stone to wood, coal, and pottery. The **Musée de la Marine de la Loire** (Loire River Museum), housed in the former château stables, chronicles that era with documents, old photos, and a reconstituted 19th-century fishing boat equipped with ropes, nets, chests, eel pots, and harpoons. The cynosure remains an astonishingly elegant **octagonal rotunda**—once centerpiece of the château estate and now the town hall, it gracefully overlooks the river. ⊠ *1 pl. Aristide-Briand* ☎ *02-38-46-84-46* ⊠ *€3.50* ☉ *Apr.–Oct., Wed.–Mon. 10–6; Nov.–Mar., Wed.–Mon. 2–6.*

Germigny-des-Prés

36 *5 km (3 mi) southeast of Châteauneuf-sur-Loire via D60.*

The village of Germigny-des-Prés is famous for its church, one of the oldest in France. Around AD 800, Theodulf, an abbot of St-Benoît, built the tiny **Église de Germigny-des-Prés**—a Byzantine arrangement of round arches on square pillars, with indirect light filtering from smaller arches above the central square. The church was carefully restored to its original condition in the 19th century. Though Theodulf himself brought most of the original mosaics from Italy, only one—covered by plaster and not discovered until 1848—survives. Made of 130,000 cubes of colored glass, it shows the Ark of the Covenant transported by angels with golden halos. The Latin inscription asks us not to forget Theodulf in our prayers. ☎ *02–38–58–27–97* ☒ *Free* ☉ *Daily 9–noon and 2–5.*

St-Benoît-sur-Loire

37 *6 km (4 mi) southeast of Germigny-des-Prés.*

The highlight of St-Benoît-sur-Loire is its ancient abbey, among the finest Romanesque churches in France. Village signposts refer to it as LA BASILIQUE. St-Benoît (St. Benedict) was the founder of the Benedictine monastic order. In AD 650 a group of monks chose this safe and fertile spot for their new monastery, then returned to Monte Cassino, Italy, to retrieve the bones of St. Benedict with which to bless the site. Despite demands from priests at Monte Cassino for the return of the ★ bones, some of the relics remained here in the 11th-century **Abbaye St-Benoît.** Following the Hundred Years' War in the 14th and 15th centuries, the monastery fell into decline, and the Wars of Religion (1562–98) wrought further damage. During the French Revolution the monks dispersed, and all the buildings were destroyed except the abbey church itself. Monastic life here began anew in 1944, when the monks rebuilt their monastery and regained the church for their own use. The pillars of the tower porch are noted for their intricately carved capitals, and the choir floor is a gaudy patchwork of multicolor marble. Gregorian chants can be heard daily, at mass or at vespers, and Sunday services attract worshipers and music lovers from all around. ☎ *02–38–35–72–43* ☒ *Free* ☉ *Mass and vespers Sun. 11 AM and 6:15 PM, Mon.–Sat. noon and 6:15 PM* ☞ *Guided English-language tours of monastic bldgs. can be arranged; inquire at monastery shop.*

Sully-sur-Loire

38 *8 km (5 mi) southeast of St-Benoît-sur-Loire via D60, 48 km (30 mi) southeast of Orléans.*

Other châteaux may have Loire-side perches, but few have the picture-★ perfect allure of the **Château de Sully,** fitted out as it is with turrets and machicolated walkways and framed by a park and storybook moat. The spectacular medieval roof tips us off that the château dates from the first half of the 14th century. It also has a sturdy keep with the finest chestnut roof anywhere along the Loire—a vast structure in the form of an overturned boat, erected in 1400. Great families, including the de Sully and Béthune clans, once called this home; their illustrious friends included Voltaire, who enjoyed putting on plays here. Have your cameras ready for this one! ☎ 02–38–36–36–86 ✉ €5 ☉ Apr.–Sept. daily 10–6; Oct.–May, Tues.–Sun. 10–noon and 2–5.

Gien

㊴ *24 km (15 mi) southeast of Sully-sur-Loire via D951, 70 km (44 mi) southeast of Orléans.*

Ceramics and hunting are the twin historical attractions of the pleasant riverside town of Gien. Its redbrick château, completed in 1484, houses ★ the unexpectedly fine **Musée International de la Chasse** (International Hunting Museum). Exhibits trace the various types of hunt—shooting, trapping, fox-hunting with hounds—and the display of firearms ranges from harquebuses to rifles. Vast 18th-century hunting pictures by François Desportes and Jean-Baptiste Oudry line the stately hall under its superb beamed roof. ⊠ Pl. du Château ☎ 02–38–67–69–69 ✉ €5 ☉ June–Sept., daily 9–6; Oct.–May, Wed.–Mon. 10–noon and 2–5.

At the **Musée de la Faïencerie** (Earthenware Factory Museum), in an old paste store, admire local Gien earthenware (both old and new), with its distinctive deep blue glaze and golden decoration. Call ahead to arrange a tour of the factory; there's also a shop. ⊠ 78 pl. de la Victoire ☎ 02–38–67–00–05 ⊕ www.gien.com ✉ €3.50 ☉ May–Sept., daily 9–12:30 and 1:30–6:30; Oct.–Apr., daily 2–6.

Where to Stay & Eat

$ ✕▦ **La Poularde.** Some of the bedrooms at this friendly hostelry overlook the Loire; room No. 1 is the largest and lightest. The formal dining room (no lunch Monday, no dinner Sunday), with 18th-century style furniture and local Gien tableware, serves traditional French cuisine, notably *poularde de Bresse*, a succulent fatted chicken, from which the establishment takes its name, often fricasseed *aux morilles* (with morel mushrooms). Weekday menus start at €16, and the copious €27 menu is a good bet for dinner. There's a mountainous cheese board and an extensive selection of local wines. ⊠ 13 quai de Nice, 45500 ☎ 02–38–37–36–05 ⊟ 02–38–38–18–78 ⤶ 9 rooms ♺ Restaurant, some pets allowed (fee) ⊟ AE, DC, MC, V ☉ Closed 1st half Jan. ⦿ BP.

Briare

㊵ *10 km (6 mi) southeast of Gien via D952.*

The **Pont-Canal de Briare** is one of France's most famous bridges—in fact, a lamp-lined 700-yard aqueduct, held together by a mind-boggling 7 million bolts, built by Gustave Eiffel in 1890 (the year after his Paris tower) to transport the Canal Latéral de la Loire (Loire Side Canal) across the river to join the Canal de Briare. Walk along the span and admire the colorful riverboats along Briare's pretty quay; for those who want to live life along the Loire, there are houseboats available for rent here. (If you're interested in waterways, make a detour 10 km [6 mi] north of Briare to admire the abandoned but spectacular 17th-century seven-rise locks at **Rogny-les-Sept-Écluses.**)

Sancerre

41 *40 km (25 mi) south of Briare via D951, 120 km (75 mi) southeast of Orléans, 46 km (29 mi) northeast of Bourges.*

The hilltop town of Sancerre is a maze of old cobbled streets offering dramatic views of the mountainous vineyards producing flinty white wines and perky, lesser-known reds and rosés. The local setting challenges the Loire's reputation for soft pastures and gentle hills: the vineyards of Sancerre (like the town itself) stand on rugged, towering mounds and are among the most scenic in France. The main square, Nouvelle Place, was once the site of the grain market; here you'll find the tourist office, which has information about a walking tour of town. From Sancerre visit **Chavignol,** 3 km (2 mi) away, a wine village with a number of producers that have tastings and vintages for sale. Chavignol is also famed for its delicious small, round goat cheese, Crottin de Chavignol, which comes in both hard and soft varieties, depending on the time of year. This famous goat cheese, along with other local cheeses, is celebrated in Sancerre every April during the Fête du Crottin.

Where to Eat

★ ¢ ✕ **Auberge Joseph Mellot.** This wood-beam, checked-tile-floored house on the main town square, one of the oldest buildings in Sancerre and a restaurant since 1882, has been an inn for over a century and is a splendid setting for a budget meal. You can have an *assiette du pays* platter with local cheese, pâté, or salad from as little as €7; there's a two-course menu at €10 and three courses for €16. The Mellot family have been winemakers since 1513 and their Sancerre wine can be ordered by the glass. ✉ *16 Nouvelle-pl.* ☎ *02–48–54–20–53* ⊕ *www. joseph-mellot.fr* ▤ *No credit cards* ☯ *Closed Wed. and mid-Dec.–mid-Jan. No dinner Tues. or Sun.*

Aubigny-sur-Nère

42 *42 km (26 mi) northwest of Sancerre via D923, 30 km (18 mi) southwest of Gien.*

Graced with half-timber houses, this town was once the little kingdom of the royal Stuarts of Scotland, who were granted its charter by King Charles VII in 1423. With the noble Darnley family as presiding spirits, the town had been an obvious rallying point for Mary, Queen of Scots. Centuries later the town was made the duchy of the royal courtesan, Louise de Kéroualle, by Louis XIV. The town château now displays her famous tapestries and also contains the **Mémorial de l'Auld Alliance,** which details the history of the Franco-Scottish entente and the Scot Jacobite refugees who settled here. A Scottish fête is held every July 14th weekend. ✉ *Château d'Aubigny* ☎ *02–48–81–50–07* ▨ *€3* ☯ *Mid-June–mid-Sept., daily 2:30–7; mid-Sept.–mid-Nov. and Apr.–mid-June, weekends 2:30–6; mid-Nov.–Mar., Sun. 2:30–6.*

Where to Stay & Eat

★ **$$$–$$$$** ✕🏨 **Château de La Verrerie.** Set in the Forêt d'Ivoy next to its own mirror-lake, this turreted abode exudes fairy-tale elegance. Dating from the 15th century and once owned by royal Stuarts, it is now a famously elegant retreat run by Comte Béraud and Comtesse Florence de Vogüé, whose ancestors acquired the place in 1842. Guest rooms are spacious (six have twin beds, six are doubles) with high ceilings, family heirlooms, and sweeping views of the estate. A half-timber 17th-century cottage on the estate has been transformed into the **Maison d'Hélène** restaurant, an excellent spot for light lunches and sumptuous dinners (closed Tuesday and Wednesday). Don't forget to visit the château's delightful Renaissance chapel, with frescoes dating from 1525. ⊠ *11 km (7 mi) southeast of Aubigny, 18700 Oizon* ☎ *02–48–81–51–60 château, 02–48–58–24–27 restaurant* 🖷 *02–48–58–21–25* ⊕ *www.chateaux-france.com/verrerie* ⇆ *11 rooms, 1 suite* ⌂ *Restaurant, tennis court, some pets allowed (fee); no a/c, no room TVs* 🖃 *MC, V* ☉ *Closed mid-Dec.–late Jan.* ⦿❘ *BP.*

Romorantin-Lanthenay

❸ *60 km (38 mi) southwest of Aubigny-sur-Nère via D924, 45 km (28 mi) southeast of Blois.*

Silence rules in the flat, wooded Sologne region, famed for its game, mushrooms, asparagus, and hidden lakes. Pretty Romorantin-Lanthenay is the area's main town, which saw its heyday in the early 16th century during the turbulent youth of François I (who in 1517 commissioned Leonardo da Vinci to design a palace for his mother here, though it was never built). Some of the great Renaissance houses, including the Hôtel St-Pol where François had his head shaved by doctors after being hit by a burning log (and thereafter grew a beard, starting the fashion for them), are on rue du Milieu and rue de la Résistance.

Where to Stay & Eat

★ **$$$–$$$$** ✕🏨 **Grand Hôtel du Lion d'Or.** Along with Jean Bardet in Tours, this restaurant is considered a mandatory pilgrimage spot by Loire Valley gourmands. The Barrat family has owned this former post house since 1961, welcoming guests to fine accommodations and a renowned restaurant (no lunch Tuesday) where Didier Clément, married to Marie-Christine Barrat since 1980, simmers magical prawns in an exotic medieval spice called paradise seed, and hurls a *tabac de cuisine* (half a dozen ground spices) over his noisettes of lamb. In the inn, pale greens, blues, and pinks plus old stone and warm wood dominate, along with large beds and marble bathrooms; choose one overlooking the delightful courtyard. ⊠ *69 rue Georges-Clemenceau, 41200* ☎ *02–54–94–15–15* 🖷 *02–54–88–24–87* ⊕ *www.hotel-liondor.fr* ⇆ *12 rooms, 4 suites* ⌂ *Restaurant, minibars, cable TV* 🖃 *AE, DC, MC, V* ☉ *Closed mid-Feb.–late Mar., 2nd half Nov.* ⦿❘ *BP.*

THE LOIRE VALLEY A TO Z

To research prices, get advice from other travelers, and book travel arrangements, visit www.fodors.com.

AIRPORTS
The closest international airports are Paris's Charles de Gaulle and Orly, although Ryanair flies to Tours from London Stansted (⇨ Air Travel *in* Smart Travel Tips A to Z).

BIKE TRAVEL
With its nearly flat terrain, the Loire Valley is custom-built for traveling by bike; however, a single-day expedition visiting three or more châteaux would be difficult, except for professional bicyclists, considering the distances involved. *Vélos tout-terrain* (mountain bikes) are the sturdiest models. When renting, inquire about bike-repair kits. As Tours is the heart of the region, it is the best base.

🚲 Bike Rentals **Amster Cycles** ⊠ 5 rue du Rempart, Tours ☎ 02-47-61-22-23.

BUS TRAVEL
Local bus services are extensive and reliable, providing a link between train stations and scenic areas off the river; it's possible to reach many villages and châteaux by bus (although many routes are in place to service schoolchildren, meaning service is less frequent in the summer and sometimes all but nonexistent on Sunday). Inquire at tourist offices for information about routes and timetables, available in very handy form. The leading companies are Les Rapides du Val de Loire, based in Orléans; TLC, serving Chambord and Cheverny from Blois; Touraine Fil Vert, Fil Bleu, and CAT (Compagnies des Autocars de Touraine, which offers buses to Chenonceaux and Amboise from Tours), all of which serve the Touraine region; and Anjou Bus (Anjou region).

🚌 Bus Information **Anjou Bus** ⊠ Pl. de la Poissonnerie, Angers ☎ 02-41-88-59-25. **Fil Bleu** ⊠ Pl. Jean-Jaurès, Tours ☎ 02-47-66-70-70. **Les Rapides du Val de Loire** ⊠ 27-B bd. Marie-Stuart, Orléans ☎ 02-38-61-90-00 ⊕ www.rvl-info.com. **Touraine Fil Vert** ⊠ 10 rue Alexander-Fleming, Tours ☎ 02-47-47-17-18 ⊕ www.touraine-filvert.com. **TLC (Transports du Loir-et-Cher)** ⊠ 9 rue Alexandre-Vézin, Blois ☎ 02-54-58-55-44.

CAR RENTAL
🚗 Local Agencies **Avis** ⊠ 6 rue Jean-Moulin, Blois ☎ 02-54-45-10-61 ⊠ 13 rue Sansonnières, Orléans ☎ 02-38-62-27-04 ⊠ Pl. Gal-Leclerc, Tours ☎ 02-47-20-53-27. **Europcar** ⊠ 81 rue André-Dessaux, on N20 near Orléans at Fleury-les-Aubrais ☎ 02-33-73-00-40 ⊠ 76 rue Bernard-Palissy, Tours ☎ 02-47-64-47-76. **Hertz** ⊠ Chaussée St-Victor [on N7], Blois ☎ 02-54-74-03-03 ⊠ 57 rue Marcel-Tribut, Tours ☎ 02-47-75-50-00.

CAR TRAVEL
The Loire Valley is an easy drive from Paris. A10 runs from Paris to Orléans—a distance of around 125 km (80 mi)—and on to Tours, with exits at Meung, Blois, and Amboise. After Tours, A10 veers south toward Poitiers and Bordeaux. A11 links Paris to Angers and Saumur

via Le Mans. Slower but more scenic routes run from the Channel ports down through Normandy into the Loire region.

The easiest way to visit the Loire châteaux is by car; N152 hugs the riverbank and is excellent for sightseeing. You can rent a car in all the large towns in the region, or at train stations in Orléans, Blois, Tours, or Angers, or in Paris.

EMERGENCIES

🚺 **Ambulance** ☎ 15. **Regional hospitals** ✉ 4 rue Larrey, Angers ☎ 02-41-35-36-37 ✉ 14 av. de l'Hôpital, Orléans ☎ 02-38-51-44-44 ✉ 2 bd. Tonnellé, Tours ☎ 02-47-47-47-47.

TOURS

CHÂTEAU TOURS   Many châteaux insist that you follow one of their tours; try to get a booklet in English before joining, as most are in French. Bus tours of the main châteaux leave daily in summer from Tours, Blois, Angers, Orléans, and Saumur: ask at the relevant tourist office for latest times and prices (*see* Visitor Information, *below*). If you want to do the top châteaux with the convenience of a van tour, readers rave about Acco-Dispo, based in Amboise—usually three are included on the tour (for example, Chambord, Cheverny, and Chenonceau), at a cost of around €30 a person, with enticing side-stops and lunch spots provided along the way.

🚺 **Acco-Dispo Tours** ✉ 18 rue des Vallées, Amboise ☎ 06-82-00-64-51 ⊕ www.accodispo-tours.com.

HELICOPTERS & BALLOONS   Jet Systems makes breathtaking helicopter trips over the Loire Valley on Tuesday, Thursday, and weekends from the aerodrome at Dierre, just south of Amboise; cost ranges from €57 (10 minutes) to €229 (50 minutes) per person.

For a more leisurely airborne visit, contact France Montgolfière for details of their balloon trips over the Loire from Chinon; prices run €190–€245.

🚺 **Fees & Schedules** Jet Systems ☎ 02-47-30-20-21 ⊕ www.jet-systems.fr. **France Montgolfière** ☎ 02-54-71-75-70 ⊕ www.franceballoons.com.

PRIVATE GUIDES   The tourist offices in Tours and Angers (*see* Visitor Information, *below*) arrange city and regional excursions with personal guides.

WALKING TOURS   A walking tour of Tours sets out from the tourist office (*see* Visitor Information, *below*) every morning at 10 AM from mid-April through October (€6). English-speaking guides show you around Blois on a tour that starts from the château at 4 (€5).

TRAIN TRAVEL

The great writer Henry James used the train system to tour Touraine back in the late 19th century and found it a most convenient way to get around. Things have only gotten better since then. Thanks to superbly organized timetables, you can whisk around from château to château with little worry or stress. True, you may occasionally need to avail yourself of a quick taxi ride from the station to the château door, but compared to renting a car, this adds up to little bother and expense. As gateways to the regions, Tours and Angers are both served by the superfast TGV

(Trains à Grande Vitesse) from Paris (Gare Montparnasse). There are also TGV trains from Charles-de-Gaulle Airport direct to the Loire Valley: four per day to Angers (2 hours 10 minutes), one per day (around lunchtime) to Blois (1 hour 50 minutes) and Tours (2 hours 20 minutes). Express trains run every two hours from Paris (Gare d'Austerlitz) to Orléans (usually you must change at nearby Les Aubrais) and Blois. Note that trains for Gien leave from Paris's Gare de Lyon (direction Nevers) and that the nearest station to Sancerre is across the Loire at Tracy.

The Loire region's local train network is magnificent, and it's possible to reach many of the châteaux by train. The main line follows the Loire from Orléans to Angers; there are trains every two hours or so, stopping in Blois, Tours, and Saumur; trains stop less frequently in Onzain (for Chaumont), Amboise, and Langeais. There are branch lines with trains from Tours to Loches, Chenonceaux, Azay-le-Rideau, and Chinon, and to Vendôme and Châteaudun. Ask the SNCF for the brochure *Les Châteaux de la Loire en Train* for more detailed information. Helpful train-schedule brochures are available at most stations.

🚆 Train Information **SNCF** ☎ 08-36-35-35-35 ⊕ www.ter-sncf.com/uk/paysdelaloire.

TRAVEL AGENCIES

🚆 Local Agent Referrals **American Express** ⊠ 19 av. des Droits-de-l'Homme, Orléans ☎ 02-38-22-15-45. **Carlson Wagonlit** ⊠ 9 rue Marceau, Tours ☎ 08-26-82-55-24.

VISITOR INFORMATION

The Loire region has two area tourist offices, both of which are for written inquiries only. For Chinon and points east, contact the Comité Régional du Tourisme Centre-Val de Loire. For Fontevraud and points west, contact the Comité Régional du Tourisme des Pays-de-Loire. Other main tourist offices are listed below by town.

🚆 Tourist Information **Comité Régional du Tourisme Centre-Val de Loire** ⊠ 37 av. de Paris, 45000 Orléans ⊕ www.loirevalleytourism.com.

Amboise ⊠ Quai Général-de-Gaulle ☎ 02-47-57-01-37 ⊕ www.amboise-valdeloire. com. **Angers** ⊠ 7 pl. Kennedy ☎ 02-41-23-51-11 ⊕ www.ville-angers.fr. **Blois** ⊠ 3 av. du Dr-Jean-Laigret ☎ 02-54-90-41-41 ⊕ www.loiredeschateaux.com. **Fontevraud-L'Abbaye** ⊠ Pl. St-Michel ☎ 02-41-51-79-45. **Gien** ⊠ Pl. Jean-Jaurès ☎ 02-38-67-25-28 ⊕ www.tourisme.fr/tourist-office/gien.htm. **Montlouis-sur-Loire** ⊠ Pl. François-Mitterrand ☎ 02-47-45-00-16 ⊕ www.ville-montlouis37.fr. **Orléans** ⊠ 6 rue Albert-Ier ☎ 02-38-24-05-05 ⊕ www.ville-orleans.fr. **Rochecorbon** ⊠ Pl. de la Lanterne ☎ 02-47-52-80-22. **Saumur** ⊠ Pl. de la Bilange ☎ 02-41-40-20-60 ⊕ www.saumur-tourisme.com. **Tours** ⊠ 78 rue Bernard-Palissy ☎ 02-47-70-37-37 ⊕ www.ligeris.com.

Brittany

4

"The Emerald Coast (north coast) is beautiful, especially around Ploumanach where the rocks are rose-colored and the water green. Along all of the coastline is the "Sentier des Douaniers," the historic tax collector's trail which can still be followed on foot today."

—Klondik

"If you like markets, Dinard has a nice one. There is a small walk along the coast as well that leaves from the downtown beach. I have done it at sunset and it is spectacular, with great views of St-Malo."

—MorganB

Introduction by
Nancy Coons

Updated by
Christopher
Mooney

YOU FEEL IT EVEN BEFORE THE SHARP SALT AIR strikes your face from the west—a subliminal rhythm suspended in the mist, a subsonic drone somewhere between a foghorn and a heartbeat, seemingly made up of bagpipes, drums, and the thin, haunting filigree of a tin-whistle tune. This is Brittany, land of the Bretons, where Celtic bloodlines run deep as a Druid's roots into the rocky, sea-swept soil. Wherever you wander—along jagged coastal cliffs, through cobbled seaport streets, into burnished-oak cider pubs—you'll hear this primal pulse of Celtic music. France's most fiercely and determinedly ethnic people, the Bretons delight in celebrating their primeval culture—circle dancing at street fairs, the women donning starched lace-bonnet *coiffes* and the men striped fishermen's shirts at the least sign of a regional celebration. They name their children Erwan and Edwige, carry sacred statues in ceremonial religious processions called *pardons,* pray in Hobbit-scale stone churches decked with elfin, moon-faced gargoyles. And scattered over the mossy hillsides stand Stonehenge-like dolmens and menhirs (prehistoric standing stones), eerie testimony to a primordial culture that predated and has long outlived Frankish France.

Similarities in character, situation, or culture to certain islands across the Channel are by no means coincidental. Indeed, the Celts that migrated to this westernmost outcrop of the French landmass spent much of the Iron Age on the British Isles, where they introduced the indigenes to innovations like the potter's wheel, the rotary millstone, and the compass. This first influx of Continental culture to Great Britain was greeted with typically mixed feelings, and by the 6th century AD the Saxon hordes had sent the Britons packing southward, to the peninsula that became Brittany. So completely did they dominate their new, Cornwall-like peninsula (appropriately named Finistère, from *finis terrae,* or "land's end") that when in 496 they allied themselves with Clovis, the king of the Franks, he felt as if he'd just claimed a little bit of England. Nonetheless the Britons remained independent of France until 1532, only occasionally hiring out as wild and woolly warrior-allies to the Norsemen of Normandy.

Yet the cultural exchange flowed both ways over the Channel. From their days on the British Isles the Britons brought a folklore that shares with England the bittersweet legend of Tristan and Iseult; that weaves mystical tales of the Cornwall/Cornouaille of King Arthur and Merlin. They brought a language that still renders village names unpronounceable: Aber-Wrac'h, Tronoën, Locmariaquer, Poldreuzic, Kerhornaouen. And, too, they brought a way of life with them: half-timber seaside cider bars, their blackened-oak tables softened with prim bits of lace; stone cottages fringed with clumps of hollyhock, hydrangea, and foxglove, damp woolens and rubber boots set to dry in flagstone entryways; bearded fishermen in yellow oilskins heaving the day's catch into weather-beaten boats, terns and seagulls wheeling in their wake. It's a way of life that feels deliciously exotic to the Frenchman and—like the ancient drone of the bagpipes—comfortably, delightfully, even primally familiar to the Anglo-Saxon.

This cozy regional charm extends inland to Rennes, at 200,000 inhabitants the largest city of Bretagne (to use the French name), as well as to Dinan, Vannes, Quimper, and seaside St-Malo. Though many towns took a beating during the course of the Nazi retreat in 1944, most have been gracefully restored, their sweet whitewashed cottages once again anchoring the soil. And the countryside retains the heather-and-emerald moorscape, framed in forests primeval and bordered by open sea, that first inspired wandering peoples to their pipes.

Exploring Brittany

Even the French may feel they are in a foreign land when they visit Brittany, the triangular patch of northwestern France that juts far out into the Atlantic. Cut off as they are from mainstream culture, the Bretons have closer cultural affinities with the Celts across the Channel than with Parisians. Attractions by the score are to be found here—village fêtes, prehistoric megaliths, and picturesque medieval towns among them. Little wonder Brittany remains a favorite vacation destination for Brits—but don't worry about overcrowding: its vast beaches offer space to spread out, and there are more than enough castles to go around.

Brittany can be divided into two basic areas. The first is the northeast, stretching from Rennes—the traditional capital of Brittany—to St-Malo and along the Channel coast. The **Côtes d'Armor,** the long stretch of Brittany's northern coast, recounts the dramatic struggle between sea and granite shore. The coastline is loosely divided into two parts: the **Côte d'Emeraude** (Emerald Coast), stretching westward from Cancale, where cliffs are punctuated by golden, curving beaches and chin-high forests of fern; and the peaceful **Côte de Granit Rose** (Pink Granite Coast), including the stupefying area around Trébeurden, where Brittany's granite glows an otherworldly pink. In northern Brittany mighty medieval castles survey the land and quaint resort towns line the seacoast. In addition to the cosmopolitan pleasures of Rennes and St-Malo, highlights include the splendid gabled wooden houses of Dinan; Chateaubriand's home at Combourg; and Dinard, the elegant Belle Époque resort once favored by British aristocrats. Brittany's westernmost point is called **Le Finistère,** literally meaning "the end of the earth." Ties to ancient Celtic culture are strong here in Basse Bretagne (Lower Brittany); elders speak Breton, and Irish pubs replace French cafés. Heading southward you hit Brittany's second major area—the Atlantic coast between Brest and Nantes, where frenzied surf crashing against the cliffs alternates with sprawling beaches and bustling harbors. Between Lorient and Nantes is Brittany's breathtakingly beautiful **Le Morbihan** (Morbihan Coast), famed for its coast lined with sand, not rock. Hereabouts lies lively Quimper, with its fine cathedral and museum; Pont-Aven, a former artists' colony made famous by Gauguin; the pretty island of Belle-Ile; the prehistoric menhirs of Carnac; the 19th-century resort of La Baule; and the thriving city of Nantes.

Numbers in the text correspond to numbers in the margin and on the Brittany and Nantes maps.

About the Restaurants & Hotels

The region's two main cities, Rennes and Nantes, offer extensive dining options all year round, and serve dinner later than in smaller towns,

If you only have three days or so, concentrate on northeast Brittany. With five days you can explore the region in greater depth, including Rennes. With 10 days you can cover the entire region, if you don't dally too long in any one place. A car is necessary for getting to the small medieval towns and deserted coastline.

Numbers in the text correspond to numbers in the margin and on the Brittany and Nantes maps.

4

If you have 5 days

Choose either the medieval town of 🏰 **Dinan** ❹ ► or the fortified "pirates' city" port of 🏰 **St-Malo** ❽—surrounded on four sides by walls and on three by sea—as your base for exploring northeast Brittany. Dinan's obvious attractions are its medieval buildings. Lacking stoplights, the town built its Tour de l'Horloge to keep an eye on 16th-century traffic jams. For a small fee you can climb it and take a look at the pretty town yourself. Be sure to visit ancient **Dol-de-Bretagne** ❻—site of Mont Dol, where Satan and the Archangel Michael once did battle, and a great early Gothic cathedral—the Romantic writer and hero Vicomte Chateaubriand's boyhood home at **Combourg** ❺, or the 16th-century castle in La Bourbansais, all pleasant side trips from seaside **Dinard** ❾, the fashionable Edwardian-era resort. In addition, the magnificent rock island of **Mont-St-Michel** is only 50 km (30 mi) away to the north, within the confines of Normandy.

If you have 10 days

Make 🏰 **Rennes** ❷ ► your base for exploring the castles, châteaux, and fortresses in **Vitré** ❶ and **Montmuran** ❸, making an excursion to the Château de Caradeuc if you have time. On Day 3 stop in **Combourg** ❺ to see the Chateaubriand château or time-stained **Dol-de-Bretagne** ❻ on your way to the walled medieval town of 🏰 **Dinan** ❹ or the historic seaside port of 🏰 **St-Malo** ❽ for the night. Head west the following day on a scenic tour of the coast and spend the night in 🏰 **Trébeurden** ⓫, on the tip of the Corniche Bretonne. Start early the next day for quaint **Morlaix** ⓬, with its houses with richly sculpted facades. Continue west and briefly visit the splendid basilica at Le Folgoët. Stop for lunch in **Brest** ⓭, a huge, modern port town. By late afternoon plan on being in Locronan, where sails used to be made for French fleets. Try to reach picturesque 🏰 **Douarnenez** ⓯ by evening. On the sixth day head to earthenware-famous **Quimper** ⓰, with its lovely riverbank and cathedral. Stop briefly to see the offshore stronghold at **Concarneau** ⓱ and aim to reach Gauguin's getaway, 🏰 **Pont-Aven** ⓲ by the end of the day; then dine on oysters in nearby Riec-sur-Belon. On Day 7 drive down the Atlantic seaboard to the beaches of Quiberon and catch the ferry to the pretty island of 🏰 **Belle-Ile-en-Mer** ⓳. On Day 8 return to the mainland and meander along the coast through the beach resorts of **Carnac** ⓴ and La Trinité-sur-Mer, stopping in the medieval town of **Vannes** ㉒ and exploring the marshy parkland of La Grande Brière. Spend the night in Biarritz-like 🏰 **La Baule** ㉓. The following day head to tranquil, prosperous 🏰 **Nantes** ㉔–㉚ and take in its many sights.

where some restaurants close for some, if not all, of the off-season (November through March). Smaller towns around the coast may only have one or two restaurants, so don't be surprised if they're booked solid in July and August. Crêperies are the regional specialty, catering just as readily for those in quest of a quick snack as a three-course meal.

Brittany has plenty of small, appealing family-run hotels with friendly and personal service, as well as a growing number of luxury hotels and châteaux. Dinard, on the English Channel, and La Baule, on the Atlantic, are the area's two most expensive resorts. In summer expect crowds, so make reservations far in advance and confirm before arriving. Assume all hotel rooms have air-conditioning, TV, telephones, and private bath, unless otherwise noted.

WHAT IT COSTS In euros					
	$$$$	**$$$**	**$$**	**$**	**¢**
RESTAURANTS	over €30	€23–€30	€17–€23	€11–€17	under €11
HOTELS	over €190	€120–€190	€80–€120	€50–€80	under €50

Restaurant prices are per person for a main course at dinner, including tax (19.6%) and service; note that if a restaurant offers only prix-fixe (set-price) meals, it has been given the price category that reflects the full prix-fixe price. Hotel prices are for a standard double room in high season, including tax (19.6%) and service charge. Hotels operate on the European Plan (EP, with no meal provided) unless we note that they use the Breakfast Plan (BP), or also offer such options as Modified American Plan (MAP, with breakfast and dinner daily, known as *demi-pension*), or Full American Plan (FAP, or *pension complète*, with three meals a day). Inquire when booking if these all-inclusive mealplans (which always entail higher rates) are mandatory or optional.

Timing

The tourist season is short in Brittany. Long, damp winters keep visitors away, and many hotels are closed until Eastertime. Brittany is particularly crowded in July and August, when most French people are on vacation, so choose crowd-free June or September, or early October, when autumnal colors and crisp evenings make for an invigorating visit. Late summer, however, is the most festive time in Brittany: the two biggest pardons take place on July 26 (Ste-Anne d'Auray) and the last Sunday in August (Ste-Anne-la-Palud); the Celtic Festival de Cornouaille is held in Quimper in late July; and the Festival Interceltique invades Lorient in early August.

NORTHEAST BRITTANY & THE CHANNEL COAST

Northeast Brittany extends from the city of Rennes to the coast. The rolling farmland around Rennes is strewn with mighty castles in Vitré, Fougères, and Dinan—remnants of Brittany's ceaseless efforts to repel invaders during the Middle Ages and a testimony to the wealth derived from pirate and merchant ships. The beautiful Côte d'Émeraude (Emerald Coast) stretches west from Cancale to St-Brieuc, and the dramatic

4

Dining à l'armoricaine
Brittany is a land of the sea. Surrounded on three sides by water, it's a veritable mine of fish and shellfish. These aquatic delights, not surprisingly, dominate Breton cuisine, starting off with the famed *homard à l'armoricaine* (lobster with cream), a name derived from the ancient name for Brittany—Armorica—and not to be confused with Américaine. Other maritime headliners include *coquilles St-Jacques* (scallops); *cotriade,* a distinctive fish soup with potatoes, onions, garlic, and butter; and langoustines, which are something between a large shrimp and a lobster. Other popular meals include smoked ham and lamb, frequently served with green kidney beans. The lamb that hails from the farms on the little island of Ouessant, off the coast of Brest, are famed—called *pré-salé,* or "pre-salted, " they feed on sea-salted grass, which marinates their meat while their hearts are still pumping, so to speak. Try the regional *ragout de mouton* and you can taste the difference. Fried eel is a traditional dish in Nantes.

Brittany is particularly famous for its crêpes, served with sweet fillings, or as the heartier *galettes*—thicker, buckwheat crêpes served as a main course and stuffed with meat, fish, or regional lobster. What's the difference between the two? The dark galette crêpe has a deeper flavor best paired with savory fillings—like lobster and mushrooms, or the more traditional ham and cheese. A crêpe plain and simple is wafer-thin and made with a lighter batter, reserved traditionally for the sweet—strawberries and cream, apples in brandy, or chocolate, for example. Accompanied by a glass of local cider, they are an ideal light, inexpensive meal; as *crêpes dentelles* (lace crêpes) they make a delicious dessert. Incidentally, crêpes are eaten from the triangular tails up to save the most flavorful buttery part for last. Folklore, however, permits older folks to eat the best part first in case some awful tragedy prevents them from enjoying *"la part de Dieu." Kouign* are delectable sugar cakes made from yeast dough, while *kouign-amann* are the same thing with butter or cream. A *far breton* is a warm or cold flanlike dessert made with prunes. If your sweet tooth is yearning for more, search for the kind of candy called *berlingot* and the region's very delicious macaroons. Of course, nothing is easier than to strike up a conversation with the Bretons than over a glass of Calvados.

Pardons & Festivals
It has been said that there are as many Breton saints as there are stones in the ground. One of the great attractions of Brittany, therefore, remains its many festivals, *pardons,* and folklore events—most occur in the months of June through September, but all year long you can attend special events, particularly village pardons held on various saints' days: banners and saintly statues are borne in colorful parades, accompanied by hymns, and the entire event is capped by a feast. In February, the great Pardon of Terre-Neuve takes place at St-Malo, and in March, Nantes celebrates with a pre-Lenten carnival procession. In mid-May there is the notable pardon of St-Yves, patron saint of lawyers, at Tréguier. Another of the great pardons takes place at Rumengol on Trinity Sunday, which usually comes at the end of May or early June. June is also the month of St. John, honored by the ceremonial Feux de

St-Jean at Locronan and Nantes. July sees Quimper's Celtic Festival de Cornouaille and the famed pardon in Ste-Anne-d'Auray. August sees Lorient's Festival Interceltique, Pont-Aven's Festival of the Golden Gorse, Brest's bagpipe festival, and a big pardon in Ste-Anne-la-Palud. Another pardon held in Le Folgoët during September is probably the biggest. At the best of these celebrations, you may find yourself rubbing elbows with twenty bishops, numbers of Breton women in their traditional costumes, and thousands of pilgrims.

Water, Water, Everywhere
Brittany's best beaches will lure even the palest of sunbathers, especially those white-sand wonders that spangle the coastal waters along the southern Morbihan Coast. The best sandy beaches and a multitude of water sports are found in Dinard, Perros-Guirec, Trégastel-Plage (the latter two are near the town of Trébeurden), Douarnenez, Carnac, La Trinité-sur-Mer, and La Baule. As it turns out, wherever you go in Brittany, you will be near the coast and see the handiwork of the turbulent Atlantic Ocean, which gnaws at Brittany's peninsula, creating a seascape of wave-battered crags, isolated coves, and dozens of islands. Note that many "beaches" will comprise rock, not sand; exclusive beaches charge a fee, as is the custom in Europe.

Côte de Granit Rose (Pink Granite Coast) extends from Paimpol to Trébeurden and the Corniche Bretonne. Follow the coastal routes D786 and D34—winding, narrow roads that total less than 100 km (62 mi) but can take five hours to drive; the spectacular views that unfold en route make the journey worthwhile.

Vitré

❶ *32 km (20 mi) south of Fougères via D798 and D178.*

There's still a feel of the Middle Ages about the formidable castle, tightly packed half-timber houses, remaining ramparts, and dark alleyways of Vitré (pronounced vee-*tray*). Built high above the Vilaine Valley, the medieval walled town that spreads out from the castle's gates, though small, is the best preserved in Brittany, and utterly beguiling, though you'll have to put on extra-strong fantasy goggles to block out the many tourists who visit here. The castle stands at the west end of town, facing narrow, cobbled streets as picturesque as any in Brittany—rue Poterie, rue d'Embas, and rue Beaudrairie, originally the home of tanners (the name comes from *baudoyers,* or leather workers).

★ Rebuilt in the 14th and 15th centuries to protect Brittany from invasion, the fairy-tale, 11th-century **Château de Vitré** (Silverware Tower)—shaped in an imposing triangle with fat, round towers—proved to be one of the province's most successful fortresses: during the Hundred Years' War (1337–1453), the English repeatedly failed to take it, even when they occupied the rest of the town. It's a splendid sight, especially from the vantage point of rue de Fougères across the river valley below. Time, not foreigners, came closest to ravaging the castle, which has been heavily though tastefully restored during the past century. The **Hôtel de Ville** (town hall), however, is an unfortunate 1913 accretion to the castle courtyard. Visit the wing to the left of the entrance, beginning with the **Tour**

St-Laurent and its museum, which contains 15th- and 16th-century sculptures, Aubusson tapestries, and engravings. Continue along the walls via the **Tour de l'Argenterie**—which contains a macabre collection of stuffed frogs and reptiles preserved in glass jars—to the **Tour de l'Oratoire** (Oratory Tower). ☎ 02–99–75–04–54 ⊕ www.ot-vitre.fr/english/ ✉ €4 ⊗ Wed.–Fri. 10–noon and 2–5:30, Sat.–Mon. 2–5:30.

Fragments of the town's medieval ramparts include the 15th-century **Tour de la Bridolle** (✉ Pl. de la République), five blocks up from the castle. The church of **Notre-Dame** (✉ Pl. Notre-Dame), with its fine, pinnacled south front, was built in the 15th and 16th centuries.

Where to Stay

¢–$ 🏨 **Le Petit Billot.** Carved paneling and faded pastel tones give this small family-run hotel a delightful French provincial air. The hotel has an informal relationship with Le Potager, the restaurant right next door, which serves reliable, though rather unexciting, Breton cuisine. ✉ 5 pl. du Général-Leclerc, 35500 ☎ 02–99–75–02–10 🖷 02–99–74–72–96 ⊕ www.petit-billot.com ➲ 21 rooms, 5 with bath ⌂ Cable TV, Internet, some pets allowed (fee); no a/c ☰ AE, MC, V ⊗ Closed last wk of Dec. and 1st wk of Jan. ⫿❁ MAP.

Rennes

❷ 36 km (22 mi) west of Vitré via D857 and N157, 345 km (215 mi) west of Paris, 107 km (66 mi) north of Nantes.

Packed with students during the school year, studded with sterile 18th-century granite buildings, and yet graced with medieval houses, Rennes (pronounced wren) is the traditional gateway to Brittany. Since the province was joined to Paris in 1532, Rennes has been the site of squabbles with the national capital, many taking place in the Rennes' Palais de Justice, long the political center of Brittany and the one building that survived a terrible fire in 1720 that lasted a week and destroyed half the city. The remaining cobbled streets and 15th-century half-timber houses form an interesting contrast to the Classical feel of the cathedral and Jacques Gabriel's disciplined granite buildings, broad avenues, and spacious squares. Many of the 15th- and 16th-century houses in the streets surrounding the cathedral have been converted into shops, boutiques, restaurants, and crêperies. The cavalier manner in which the French go about running a bar out of a 500-year-old building can be disarming to New Worlders.

The **Parlement de Bretagne** (✉ Rue Nationale ☎ 02–99–67–11–11 ⊕ www.parlement-bretagne.com), the palatial original home of the Breton Parliament and now of the Rennes law courts, was designed in 1618 by Salomon de Brosse, architect of the Luxembourg Palace in Paris. It was the most important building in Rennes to escape the 1720 flames, but in 1994, following a massive demonstration by Breton fishermen demanding state subsidies, a disastrous fire broke out at the building, leaving it a charred shell. Fortunately, much of the artwork—though damaged—was saved by firefighters, who arrived at the scene after the building was already

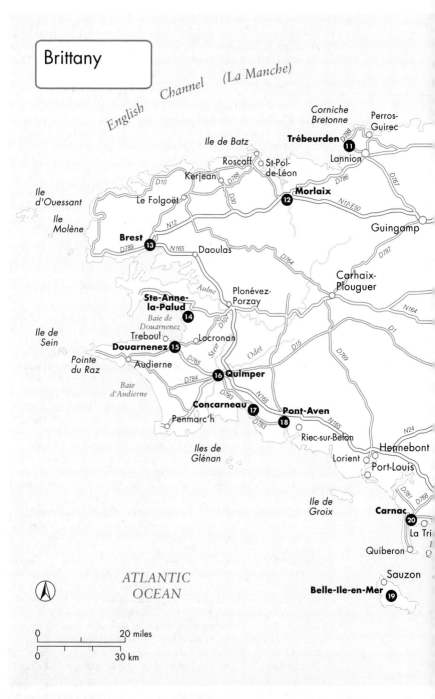

Brittany

English Channel (La Manche)

ATLANTIC
OCEAN

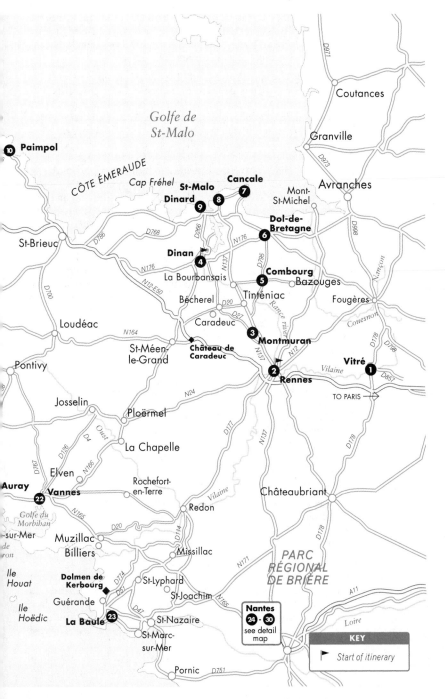

engulfed in flames. It was a case of the alarm that cried "fire" once too often; a faulty bell, which rang regularly for no reason, had led the man on duty to ignore the signal. Restoration has now been completed. Call ahead for information on guided tours in English.

The **Musée de Bretagne** (Museum of Brittany) has recently reopened in brand new headquarters designed by superstar architect Christian de Portzamparc and now occupies a vast three-part space that it shares with the Rennes municipal library and Espaces des Sciences. Portzamparc's layout harmonizes nicely with the organization of the museum's extensive ethnographic and archeological collection, which, chronologically ordered, depicts the everyday life of Bretons from prehistoric times up to the present. There is also a space devoted to the famous Dreyfus Affair; Alfred Dreyfus, an army captain who was wrongly accused of espionage and whose case was championed by Emile Zola, was tried a second time in Rennes in 1899. Service information was not available at press time; log on to the Web site for details. ⊠ *20 quai Émile-Zola* ⊕ *www. musee-bretagne.fr.*

The **Musée des Beaux-Arts** (Fine Arts Museum) contains works by Georges de La Tour, Jean-Baptiste Chardin, Camille Corot, Paul Gauguin, and Maurice Utrillo, to name a few. The museum is particularly strong in French 17th-century paintings and drawings and has an interesting collection of modern French artists. ⊠ *20 quai Émile-Zola* ☎ 02–99–28–55–85 ⊕ *www.mbar.org* ⊠ €4 ☉ *Wed.–Mon. 10–noon and 2–6.*

need a break?   **Thé au Fourneau** (⊠ 6 rue du Capitaine-Alfred-Dreyfus, near the Fine Arts Museum) is a cozy tearoom pleasantly cluttered with antiques, which serves chocolate cake, fruit crumble, excellent pastries, snacks, and salads. It's open weekdays 10–6:30.

A late-18th-century building in Classical style that took 57 years to construct, the **Cathédrale St-Pierre** looms above rue de la Monnaie at the west end of the *Vieille Ville* (Old Town), bordered by the Rance River. Stop in to admire its richly decorated interior and outstanding 16th-century Flemish altarpiece. ⊠ *Pl. St-Pierre* ☉ *Mon.–Sat. 8:30–noon and 2–5, Sun. 8:30–noon.*

★ Take a stroll through the lovely **Parc du Thabor** (⊠ Pl. St-Melaine), east of the Palais des Musées. It's a large, formal French garden with regimented rows of trees, shrubs, and flowers, and a notable view of the church of **Notre-Dame-en-St-Melaine**.

Where to Stay & Eat

$ ✕ **Piccadilly Tavern.** Around the corner from the Palais de Justice and next to the municipal theater is this oddly named brasserie that serves traditional Breton cuisine. Its huge, sunny terrace is the perfect place to people-watch while downing a half-dozen fresh oysters and an aperitif. The prix-fixe menu is € 12. ⊠ *15 Galeries du Théâtre* ☎ 02–99–78–17–17 ⊟ *MC, V.*

★ $$$ ✕⊡ **LeCoq-Gadby.** A 19th-century mansion with huge fireplaces and antiques sets the stage for this cozy retreat. Homey guest rooms have four-poster beds and floral covers, while hydrotherapy facilities, a hammam (steam room), a Jacuzzi, and a sauna are all available if you want to be pampered. Jean-Michel Boucault's cuisine must be good—French presidents have dined here on such delicacies as *pigeon fermier roti aux chataignes* (pigeon roasted with chestnuts). Book way in advance for this popular hotel and restaurant (which does not serve dinner Sunday). ⊠ *156 rue d'Antrain, 35700* ☎ *02–99–38–05–55* 🖷 *02–99–38–53–40* ⊕ *www.lecoq-gadby.com* 🗡 *11 rooms* ⚿ *Restaurant, minibars, cable TV, bar, Internet; no a/c* 🖃 *AE, DC, MC, V* 🍽 *MAP.*

$–$$$ 🏨 **Mercure Centre.** This stately 19th-century hotel is centrally located on a quiet, narrow backstreet close to the cathedral. Rooms overlook the street or a courtyard; all are modern and functional. ⊠ *6 rue Lanjuinais, 35000* ☎ *02–99–79–12–36* 🖷 *02–99–79–65–76* 🗡 *48 rooms* ⚿ *Cable TV, Internet, some pets allowed (fee)* 🖃 *AE, DC, MC, V* 🍽 *BP.*

★ ¢–$ 🏨 **Garden.** This picturesque, central hotel has an age-old wooden gallery overlooking a sunny inner courtyard where breakfast is served. Rooms are small but cheerful, with bright colors and antiques. ⊠ *3 rue Duhamel, 35000* ☎ *02–99–65–45–06* 🖷 *02–99–65–02–62* 🗡 *26 rooms* ⚿ *Some pets allowed; no a/c* 🖃 *AE, MC, V.*

Nightlife & the Arts

The streets around place Ste-Anne are jammed with popular student bars, most of them housed in fantastic medieval buildings with character to spare. If you feel like dancing the night away, head to **L'Espace** (⊠ 45 bd. de la Tour d'Auvergne ☎ 02–99–30–21–95). For the night owl, the **Pym's Club** (⊠ 27 pl. du Colombier ☎ 02–99–67–30–00) stays open all night, every night.

★ Brittany's principal theater is the **Opéra de Rennes** (⊠ Pl. de l'Hôtel de Ville ☎ 02–99–78–48–78). All kinds of performances are staged at the **Théâtre National de Bretagne** (⊠ 1 rue St-Hélier ☎ 02–99–31–12–31). The famous annual international rock-and-roll festival, **Les Transmusicales** (☎ 02–99–31–12–10 for information), happens the second week of December in bars around town and at the Théâtre National de Bretagne. The first week of July sees **Les Tombées de la Nuit** (☎ 02–99–67–11–11 for information), the "Nightfalls" Festival, featuring crowds, Celtic music, dance, and theater performances staged in old historic streets and churches around town.

Shopping

A lively **market** is held on Place des Lices on Saturday morning.

Montmuran

❸ *29 km (18 mi) northwest of Rennes via N137 and D221.*

The **Château de Montmuran** was once ground control to one of France's finest knights, Bertrand du Guesclin (1320–80). Commemorated in countless squares and hostelries across the province, du Guesclin sprang to prominence at the age of 17, when he entered a jousting tournament in disguise and successfully unseated several hoarier knights. He went on to lead the onslaught against the English during the Hundred Years'

War. An alley of oak and beech trees leads up to the main 17th-century building, which is surrounded by a moat and flanked by four towers, two built in the 12th century, two in the 14th. You can visit the towers and a small museum devoted to the castle's history. The château also has two pleasant guest rooms that are open from May to October. Call to reserve. ⊠ *Les Iffs* ☎ *02–99–45–88–88* ⊕ *www.chateau-montmuran. com* ⊠ *€4* ⊗ *June–Sept., Sun.–Fri. 2–6.*

CHÂTEAU DE CARADEUC – Ambitiously dubbed the Versailles of Brittany, this château, 8 km (5 mi) west of Montmuran just beyond Bécherel, is privately owned and not open to the public. But you can admire the statuary, flower beds, and leafy alleés in the surrounding park—Brittany's largest. ⊠ *Rte. de Chateaubriand* ☎ *02–99–66–77–76* ⊠ *€3* ⊗ *Apr.–June, daily 2–6; July and Aug., daily noon–6; Sept., weekends 2–6; Oct., Sun. 2–6.*

Dinan

❹ *29 km (18 mi) northwest of Montmuran via D27 and D68.*

Fodor'sChoice
★

During the frequent wars that devastated other cities in the Middle Ages, the merchants who ruled Dinan got rich selling stuff to whichever camp had the upper hand, well aware that loyalty to any side, be it the French, the English, or the Breton, would eventually lead to the destruction of their homes. The strategy worked: Today, Dinan is one of the best-preserved medieval towns in Brittany. Although there is no escaping the crowds here in summer, in the off-season or early morning Dinan feels like a time-warped medieval playground.

Like Montmuran, Dinan has close links with warrior-hero Bertrand du Guesclin, who won a famous victory here in 1359 and promptly married a local girl, Tiphaine Raguenel. When he died in the siege of Châteauneuf-de-Randon in Auvergne (central France) in 1380, his body was dispatched home to Dinan. Owing to the great man's popularity, only his heart completed the journey (it rests in the basilica); the rest of him was confiscated by devoted followers along the way.

Along place des Merciers, rue de l'Apport, and rue de la Poissonnerie, take note of the splendid gabled wooden houses. Rue du Jerzual, which leads down to Dinan's harbor, is also a beautifully preserved medieval street, divided halfway down by the town walls and the massive Porte du Jerzual gateway and lined with boutiques and crafts shops in 15th- and 16th-century houses. A few restaurants brighten the area around the harbor, and boats sail up the Rance River in summer (€22 round-trip, call ☎ 02–23–18–01–80 for details), but the abandoned warehouses mostly bear witness to the town's vanished commercial activity. Above the harbor, near Porte St-Malo, is the leafy Promenade des Grands Fossés, the best-preserved section of the town walls, which leads to the castle.

For a superb view of town, climb to the top of the medieval **Tour de l'Horloge** (Clock Tower). ⊠ *Rue de l'Horloge* ⊠ *€2.50* ⊗ *Apr.–June, daily 2–6; July–Sept., daily 10–6:30.*

Du Guesclin's heart lies in the north transept of the **Basilique St-Sauveur** (✉ Pl. St-Sauveur). The church's style ranges from the Romanesque south front to the Flamboyant Gothic facade and Renaissance side chapels. The old trees in the **Jardin Anglais** (English Garden) behind the church provide a nice frame. More spectacular views can be found at the bottom of the garden, which looks down the plummeting Rance Valley to the river below.

The stolidly built, fortresslike **Château,** at the end of the Promenade des Petits Fossés, has a two-story tower, the **Tour du Coëtquen,** and a 100-foot, 14th-century **donjon** (keep) containing a museum with varied displays of medieval effigies and statues, Breton furniture, and locally made lace coiffes (head coverings). ✉ *Porte de Guichet* ☎ *02–96–39–45–20* ⊕ *armorance.free.fr/dinan5.htm* ⬚ €*3.90* ☉ *June–Oct., daily 10–6:30; Nov., Dec., and Feb.–May, daily 1:30–5:30.*

Where to Stay & Eat

$–$$$ ✕ **Le Relais des Corsaires.** This riverbank spot is named for the old-time pirates who sporadically plundered Dinan and the Rance Valley. The mid-range prix-fixe menu provides an ample four-course meal of traditional French cuisine, with an emphasis on steak and fish. The welcoming proprietors, Sabine and Christian Boaumond, also have an informal, relaxed seafood restaurant, Au Petit Corsair, where you can compose your own seafood platter from the very fresh choices in the 15th-century building next door. ✉ *7 rue du Port* ☎ *02–96–39–40–17* ▤ *MC, V* ☉ *Closed mid-Nov.–mid-Feb.*

★ $$–$$$ ▥ **L'Avaugour.** Set on the town ramparts, with pretty sash windows, mansard roofs, and a Breton stone facade, this hotel has a sunny flower garden, which the best rooms—all were renovated in 2002—overlook, and where breakfast and afternoon tea are served. Start the day with the full buffet breakfast and a chat with the charming owner, Nicolas Caron, who enjoys speaking English and helping everyone plan day trips. There's a colorful street market opposite the hotel every Thursday. ✉ *1 pl. du Champ, 22100* ☎ *02–96–39–07–49* ▤ *02–96–85–43–04* ⊕ *www. avaugourhotel.com/around.htm* ⬚ *21 rooms, 3 suites* ♻ *Cable TV, Internet, some pets allowed (fee); no a/c* ▤ *AE, DC, MC, V* ☉ *Closed mid-Nov.–Dec. 20 and Jan.* ❍| *BP.*

¢–$ ▥ **Arvor.** The cobbled streets of the Vieille Ville are visible from this comfortable 18th-century hotel directly across from the town theater. Now under new management, it offers clean and simple rooms with friendly service. ✉ *5 rue Auguste-Pavie, 22100* ☎ *02–96–39–21–22* ▤ *02–96–39–83–09* ⬚ *23 rooms* ♻ *Cable TV, some pets allowed; no a/c* ▤ *MC, V* ☉ *Closed Jan.*

Nightlife & the Arts

In even years (including 2006), on the third weekend in July, medieval France is re-created with a market, parade, jousting tournament, and street music for **La Fête des Remparts** (Ramparts Festival), one of the largest medieval festivals in Europe.

Shopping

One of the leading craft havens in France, Dinan has attracted many wood-carvers, jewelers, leather workers, glass specialists, and silk painters, who have set up shop in the medieval houses that line the cobbled, sloping **rue de Jerzual**. Other delightful studios and artisan boutiques can be found on the nearby **rue de l'Apport, place des Merciers,** and **place des Cordeliers.**

| en route | Between Dinan and Combourg is the château **La Bourbansais,** built in the 1580s. Most of the interior furnishings (guided tours only) date from the 18th century, including the fine collection of porcelain and tapestries. Its extensive gardens contain a small zoo, a playground for children, a picnic area (with an on-site restaurant that serves simple sandwiches, steaks, french fries, and salads), and a pack of hunting hounds who perform a popular 20-minute show called *La Meute* from April through September. ⊠ *Pleugueneuc* ☎ *02–99–69–40–07* ⊕ *www.labourbansais.com* ☒ *€14* ⊗ *Apr.–Sept., daily 10–7; Oct.–Mar., daily 2–6.* |

Combourg

❺ *25 km (16 mi) southeast of Dinan via D794, 40 km (25 mi) north of Rennes.*

The pretty lakeside village of Combourg is dominated by the boyhood home of Romantic writer Viscount René de Chateaubriand (1768–1848), the thick-walled, four-tower **Château de Combourg** (Cat's Tower). Topped with "witches' cap" towers that the poet likened to Gothic crowns, the castle dates mainly from the 14th and 15th centuries. Here, quartered in the tower called "La Tour du Chat, " accompanied by roosting birds, a sinister quiet, and the ghost of a wooden-legged Comte de Combourg—whose false leg would reputedly get up and walk by itself—the young René succumbed to the château's moody spell and, in turn, became a leading light of Romanticism. His novel *Atala and René,* about a tragic love affair between a French soldier and a Native American maiden, was an international sensation in the mid-19th century, while his multivolume *History of Christianity* was required reading for half of Europe. The château grounds—ponds, woods, and cattle-strewn meadowland—are suitably mournful and can seem positively desolate when viewed under leaden skies. Its melancholy is best captured in Chateaubriand's famous *Mémoires d'outre-tombe* ("Memories from Beyond the Tomb"). Inside you can view neo-Gothic salons, the Chateaubriand archives, and the writer's severe bedroom up in the "Cat's Tower." ☎ *02–99–73–22–95* ⊕ *www.combourg.net* ☒ *€4, park only €1.50* ⊗ *Château open Apr.–Oct., Sun.–Fri. 2–5:30; park open Apr.–Oct., daily 9–noon and 2–6.*

FodorsChoice ★

| off the beaten path | **CHÂTEAU DE LA BALLUE –** This château, 18 km (11 mi) east of Combourg and dating from 1620, has sophisticated gardens that feature modern sculpture, leafy groves, columns of yew, a fernery, a labyrinth, and a Temple of Diana. To visit the interior, with its gleaming wood paneling and huge granite staircase, you'll have to stay the night—in one of the five large, beautifully decorated, fabric-swathed guest rooms (each with a four-poster bed), and dine with the |

dynamic English-speaking owners Alain Schrotter and Marie-France Barrère. Reserve well in advance and be sure to specify whether you'll be staying for dinner. Nineteenth-century writers Alfred de Musset, Honoré Balzac, and Victor Hugo all preceded you as guests. ⊠ *Bazouges-la-Pérouse* ☎ *02–99–97–47–86* 🖶 *02–99–97–47–70* 🖼 *Gardens* €8 ⊘ *May–Sept., daily 10:30–5:30.*

Where to Eat

★ $ ✕ **L'Écrivain.** Gilles Menier's inventive, light cuisine showcases mussels in flaky pastry flavored with chervil, cod with cream of coriander and a red-berry sauce, and apple crêpe with cider butter. Ask for a table in the intimate wood-panel dining room, with candles on the tables, rather than in the bustling larger hall, and take your *digestif* in the wood-panel bar with its oil paintings depicting scenes from Chateaubriand's life. Excellent fixed-price menus start at € 14. ⊠ *1 pl. St-Gilduin* ☎ *02–99–73–01–61* 🖃 *MC, V* ⊘ *Closed Thurs., 3 wks in Feb., and 2 wks in Oct. No dinner Wed. or Sun. Oct.–Apr.*

Dol-de-Bretagne

❻ *17 km (11 mi) north of Combourg via D795.*

The ancient town of Dol-de-Bretagne, which still has its original ramparts, looks out over the Marais de Dol, a marshy plain stretching across to Mont-St-Michel, 21 km (13 mi) northeast. For extensive views of the Marais as well as Mont-Dol—a 200-foot windmill-topped mound 3 km (2 mi) north and the legendary scene of combat between St. Michael and the Devil—walk along the **Promenade des Douves,** on the northern part of the original ramparts. Dol's picturesque main street is **Grande-Rue des Stuarts,** lined with medieval houses; the oldest, the **Maison des Palets,** at No. 17, has a chunky row of Romanesque arches.

The **Cathédrale St-Samson** (⊠ Pl. de la Cathédrale) is a damp, soaring, fortresslike bulk of granite dating mainly from the 12th to the 14th centuries. This mighty building shows the influence wielded by the bishopric of Dol in bygone days. The richly sculpted great porch, carved-wood choir stalls, and stained glass in the chancel warrant scrutiny.

The **Cathédraloscope** (Cathedral Museum), opposite the cathedral, uses models, frescoes, ground plans, and special lighting effects to explain the construction of France's cathedrals, their feats of engineering, and the evolution of the soaring Gothic style that is their chief characteristic. There are also sections on church liturgy and stained glass. ⊠ *Pl. de la Cathédrale* ☎ *02–99–48–35–30* 🖼 *€7.50* ⊘ *Apr.–Nov., daily 10–7.*

Cancale

❼ *22 km (14 mi) northwest of Dol via D155 and D76.*

If you enjoy eating oysters, be sure to get to Cancale, a picturesque fishing village renowned for its offshore *bancs d'huîtres* (oyster beds). You can sample the little brutes at countless stalls or restaurants along the quay. The **Musée de l'Huître et du Coquillage** (Oyster and Shellfish Museum) explains everything you ever wanted to know about farming oysters. ⊠ *Les Parcs St-Kerber, Plage de l'Aurore* ☎ *02–99–89–69–99* ☞ *€6.10* ⊙ *Guided 1-hr tours in English, mid-Feb.–Oct., daily at 2.*

Where to Stay & Eat

★ **$$$–$$$$**   ✕⊡ **Château Richeux.** One of three hotels owned by the famed Roellingers of Cancale's Relais Gourmand, the Château Richeux occupies an imposing turn-of-the-20th-century waterfront mansion built on the ruins of the du Guesclin family's 11th-century château, 4 mi (2½ km) south of Cancale. Request one of the rooms with large bay windows, which have stunning views of Mont-St-Michel. Le Coquillage, the hotel's small bistro (closed Monday, Tuesday, and Thursday lunch) specializes in local oysters and seafood platters served up in a relaxed, cozy atmosphere. ⊠ *Le Point du Jour, St-Méloir des Ondes, 35350* ☎ *02–99–89–64–76* 🖷 *02–99–89–18–49* ⊕ *www.maisons-de-bricourt. com* ⟿ *13 rooms* ♧ *Restaurant, cable TV, Internet; no a/c* ⊟ *AE, DC, MC, V* ⊺◉◖ *BP.*

$$$–$$$$
Fodor'sChoice
★   ✕⊡ **Le Relais Gourmand O. Roellinger.** The name of this place sounds the trumpet for chef Olivier Roellinger, who grew up in this grand 18th-century, St-Malo-style stone house and, fittingly for a town named "Oysters," came to master the *cuisine marine* of this region to perfection. Even those landlocked lubbers, Parisians, don't think twice about driving here just for dinner. Their 250-mi-long drive is worth it: Glowing murals, domed conservatory, stone fireplaces, spotlit trees, duck pond, and antique tiles all welcome them with a cozily imposing ambience. But the main attraction is Roellinger's way with seafood. He leaves *moules à la cancalaise* (mussels with butter)—the basic specialty of the region—in the dust with all sorts of culinary fireworks, such as the spiced consommé of cancalaises and foie gras or the John Dory steamed in seaweed and coconut milk. Luscious desserts all seduce, including farm raspberries with angelica, iced maingau, and "churned" milk. The restaurant is closed Tuesday and Wednesday. If you wish to stay the night, attractive rooms (with spectacular views across the oyster beds toward Mont-St-Michel) are available in the luxe **Les Rimains** cottage on rue des Rimains, a short walk away. ⊠ *1 rue Du-Guesclin, 35260* ☎ *02–99–89–64–76* 🖷 *02–99–89–88–47* ⊕ *www.maisons-de-bricourt.com* ⟿ *4 rooms* ♧ *Restaurant, cable TV, Internet; no a/c* ⊟ *AE, DC, MC, V* ⊙ *Closed mid-Dec.–mid-Mar.* ⊺◉◖ *BP.*

en route   Heading north from Cancale, past the attractive beach of Port-Mer, takes you to the jagged rock formations rising from the sea at the **Pointe de Grouin,** a magical spot for catching a sunset. From here follow D201 along the coast to St-Malo.

Shopping

Sublime tastes of Brittany—salted butter caramels, fruity sorbets, rare honeys, and heirloom breads—are sold in upper Cancale at the Roellingers' **Grain de Vanille** (⊠ 12 pl. de la Victoire ☎ 02–23–15–12–70). Tables beckon so why not sit a spell and enjoy a cup of "Mariage" tea and—Brittany in a bite—some cinnamon-orange-flavor *malouine* cookies?

NO MEAN CATCH!

TO THE GREAT SURPRISE OF MOST NORTH AMERICANS, *the humble canned sardine is a revered comestible—and justly so—among* French *gourmands. The best brands— Rodel, La Quibéronnaise, Gonidec and La Belle Illoise—are from Brittany, where the sardine industry was once the backbone of the Breton economy. The sardine tin, in fact, was invented by a Breton named Pierre-Joseph Colin (colin, incidentally, means hake; fish surnames are common in Brittany) in 1810. The preserved fish immediately made culinary history: Napoléon had thousands loaded into carts and brought to the Russian front where the tasty little fish, once extracted from their soldered cans with a hammer, must have helped soften the blow of France's defeat. The best cans of sardines, usually marked première catégorie or extra, are treated like bottles of fine wine, carefully dated (some cans are even* stamped with the name of the fishing boat credited with the catch), laid away in cellars for up to a decade and lovingly turned every few months for proper aging. Even the vocabulary for aged sardines is borrowed from oenology: one speaks of grands crus and millésimes. With the current trend toward "limited-edition" canned sardines, the oily fish has acceded to an even more exalted status. Once caught, they are put in salt, rinsed, hand-sorted by size, grilled, deep-fried and hand-packed in peanut or extra virgin cold-pressed olive oil. Purists take them straight, crushed onto a slice of buttered bread with the back of a fork, with perhaps the tiniest squeeze of lemon to bring out the oily flavors. Whichever way you wolf them down, vintage sardines are tender, delicately flavored, and deeply satisfying as a snack or an entire meal.*

St-Malo

8 *23 km (14 mi) west of Cancale via coastal D201.*

Fodor's Choice

★

Thrust out into the sea, bound to the mainland only by tenuous man-made causeways, romantic St-Malo—"the pirates' city"—has built a reputation as a breeding ground for phenomenal sailors. Many were fishermen, but St-Malo's most famous sea dogs were corsairs, pirates paid by the French crown to harass the Limeys across the Channel. Robert Surcouf and Duguay-Trouin were just two of these privateers who helped make this town rich through piratical pillages. Facing Dinard across the Rance Estuary, the stone ramparts of St-Malo have withstood the pounding of the Atlantic since the 12th century, the founding date of the town's main church, the **Cathédrale St-Vincent** (on rue St-Benoît). The ramparts were considerably enlarged and modified in the 18th century and now extend from the castle for more than 1½ km (1 mi) around the Vieille Ville—known as *intra-muros* (within the walls). The views are stupendous, especially at high tide. The town itself has proved less resistant: a weeklong fire in 1944, kindled by retreating Nazis, wiped out nearly all the old buildings. Restoration work was more painstaking than brilliant, but the narrow streets and granite houses of the Vieille Ville were satisfactorily re-created, enabling St-Malo to regain its role as a busy fishing port, seaside resort, and tourist destination. The ramparts themselves are authentic and the flames also spared houses along the Vieille Ville's rue de Pelicot. Battalions of tourists invade this quaint part of town in summer, so if you want to avoid crowds, don't come then.

At the edge of the ramparts is the 15th-century **château**, whose great keep and watchtowers command an impressive view of the harbor and coastline. It houses the **Musée d'Histoire de la Ville** (Town History Museum), devoted to local history, and the **Galerie Quic-en-Grogne**, a museum in a tower, where various episodes and celebrities from St-Malo's past are recalled by way of waxworks. ⊠ *Hôtel de Ville* ☎ *02–99–40–71–57* ☜ *€4.60* ☉ *Tues.–Sun. 10–noon and 2–6.*

Five hundred yards offshore is the **Ile du Grand Bé,** a small island housing the somber military tomb of the great Romantic writer Viscount René de Chateaubriand, who was born in St-Malo. The islet can be reached by a causeway at low tide *only.*

The "Bastille of Brittany," the **Fort National,** also offshore and accessible by causeway at low tide only, is a massive fortress with a dungeon constructed in 1689 by that military-engineering genius Sébastien de Vauban. ☎ *02–99–85–34–33* ☜ *€4* ☉ *June–Sept., daily; call ahead at other times* ☞ *Times of ½-hr guided tours depend on tides.*

You can pay homage to Jacques Cartier, who set sail from St-Malo in 1535 on a voyage in which he would discover the St. Lawrence River and found Québec, at his tomb in the church of **St-Vincent** (⊠ Grand-Rue). His statue looks out over the town ramparts, four blocks away, along with that of swashbuckling corsair Robert Surcouf (hero of many daring 18th-century raids on the British navy), eternally wagging an angry finger over the waves at England.

Where to Stay & Eat

$$–$$$ ✕ **Chalut.** The reputation of this small restaurant with nautical decor has grown since chef Jean-Philippe Foucat decided to emphasize fresh seafood. The succinct menus change as frequently as the catch of the day. Try the sautéed John Dory in wild-mushroom broth or the fresh lobster in lime. ⊠ *8 rue de la Corne-de-Cerf* ☎ *02–99–56–71–58* ☰ *AE, MC, V* ☉ *Closed Mon. No lunch Tues.*

¢–$ ✕ **Café de la Bourse.** Prawns and oysters are downed by the shovelful in this bustling brasserie in the Vieille Ville. Replete with wooden seats, ships' wheels, and posters of grizzled old sea dogs, it's hardly high design. But the large L-shape dining room makes amends with friendly service and a seafood platter for two that includes tanklike crabs flanked by an army of cockles, snails, and periwinkles. ⊠ *1 rue de Dinan* ☎ *02–99–56–47–17* ☰ *MC, V* ☉ *Closed Wed. Nov.–Easter.*

★ **$$$** ▦ **Elizabeth.** In a 16th-century town house built into the city wall, the Elizabeth, near the Porte St-Louis, is a little gem of sophistication in touristy St-Malo. North-facing rooms are modern, while the larger, recently renovated suites are tastefully furnished in period style. ⊠ *2 rue des Cordiers, 35400* ☎ *02–99–56–24–98* ☖ *02–99–56–39–24* ⊕ *www.st-*

malo-hotel-elizabeth.com ⤳ *14 rooms, 3 suites* ⌂ *Some pets allowed (fee); no a/c* ⊟ *AE, DC, MC, V* ⫧⊙⫧ *BP.*

$–$$ ⊞ **Kyriad.** Formerly the Blue Myriad Atlantis, the view of the sea is magnificent from the hotel's bar, terrace, and breakfast room. Rooms are airy, with modern furnishings; expect to pay around €10 extra for one with a sea view. ⊠ *49 chaussée du Sillon, 35400* ☎ *02–99–56–09–26* ⌨ *02–99–56–41–65* ⊕ *www.bleumarine.fr* ⤳ *55 rooms, 14 with bath* ⌂ *Minibars, cable TV, gym, sauna, bar, Internet, some pets allowed (fee); no a/c* ⊟ *AE, MC, V* ⫧⊙⫧ *BP.*

Nightlife & the Arts

Bar de l'Univers (⊠ 12 pl. Chateaubriand) is a nice spot to enjoy sipping a drink in a pirate's-lair setting. **La Belle Époque** (⊠ 11 rue de Dinan) is a popular hangout for all ages 'til the wee hours. **L'Escalier** (⊠ La Buzardière, rue de la Tour-du-Bonheur) is the place for dancing the night away. In summer, performances are held at the **Théâtre Chateaubriand** (⊠ 6 rue Groult-de-St-Georges ☎ 02–99–40–98–05). Bastille Day (July 14) sees the **Fête du Clos Poulet,** a town festival with traditional dancing. July and August bring a month-long religious music festival, the **Festival de la Musique Sacrée.**

Shopping

A lively outdoor **market** is held in the streets of Old St-Malo every Tuesday and Friday.

Dinard

❾ *13 km (8 mi) west of St-Malo via Rance Bridge.*

Fodor'sChoice
★

Dinard is the most elegant resort town on this stretch of the Brittany coast. Its picture-book perch on the Rance Estuary opposite the walled town of St-Malo lured the English aristocracy here in droves toward the end of the 19th century. What started out as a small fishing port soon became a seaside mecca of lavish Belle Époque villas (more than 400 still dot the town and shoreline), grand hotels, and a bustling casino. A number of modern establishments punctuate the landscape, but the town still retains something of an Edwardian tone. To make the most of Dinard's beauty, head down to the Pointe de la Vicomté, at the town's southern tip, where the cliffs offer panoramic views across the Baie du Prieuré and Rance Estuary, or stroll along the narrow promenade.

★ The **Promenade Clair de Lune** hugs the seacoast on its way toward the English Channel and passes in front of the small jetty used by boats crossing to St-Malo. In Dinard, the road weaves along the shore and is adorned with luxuriant palm trees and mimosa blooms, which, from July to the end of September, are illuminated at dusk with spotlights; strollers are serenaded with recorded music. The Promenade really hits its stride as it rounds the **Pointe du Moulinet** and heads toward the sandy **Plage du Prieuré,** named after a priory that once stood here. River meets sea in a foaming mass of rock-pounding surf: use caution as you walk along the slippery path to the calm shelter of the **Plage de l'Écluse,** an inviting sandy beach bordered by the casino and numerous stylish hotels. The coastal path picks up on the west side of Plage de l'Écluse, ringing the Pointe de la Malouine and the Pointe des Étêtés before arriving at the **Plage de St-Énogat.**

☺ The 24 pools and aquariums at the **Musée de la Mer** (Marine Museum) contain almost every known species of Breton sea creature, and stuffed local birds are also on display. One room is devoted to the polar expeditions of explorer Jean Charcot, one of the first men to chart the Antarctic. Closed for renovations at press time, the museum is scheduled to reopen in mid 2006. ✉ *17 av. George-V* ☎ *02–99–46–13–90* ✉ *€2.50* ⊗ *Mid-May–mid-Sept., daily 10:30–12:30 and 3:30–7:30.*

Where to Stay & Eat

$$–$$$ ✕ **La Salle à Manger.** Formerly of Paris's legendary Tour d'Argent, Chef Yannick Lalande serves up inventive Provençal cuisine, broadening its traditional olive oil–tomato-base repertoire to include balsamic vinegar reductions, sesame oil, even wasabi. The seasonal menu emphasizes market-fresh produce and, of course, local seafood. Chef Lalande also came up with the restaurant's home-sweet-home decor: lots of wood, forged iron, a cozy palette of Provençal red, orange, and yellow, and a fireplace. ✉ *25 bd. Féart* ☎ *02–99–16–07–95* ☰ *MC, V* ⊗ *Closed mid-Oct.–mid-Mar., Mon., and Sun. dinner.*

$–$$ ✕▦ **Printania.** This white-walled, family-run hotel is on the Clair de Lune Promenade. Rooms have regional furnishings and pictures of local scenes; the best ones have a balcony and sea view (ask for Room 101, 102, 211, or 311). Seafood and regional dishes are served in the paneled dining room. ✉ *5 av. George-V, 35800* ☎ *02–99–46–13–07* 🖷 *02–99–46–26–32* ⊕ *www.printaniahotel.com* ✍ *56 rooms* ♿ *Restaurant, bar; no a/c* ☰ *AE, MC, V* ⊗ *Closed mid-Nov.–mid-Mar.* ⊗ *FAP.*

★ **$$$–$$$$** ▦ **Villa Reine-Hortense.** All the aesthetical Napoléon-III glamour of 19th-century resort France is yours when you stay here at this *follie*—a villa built by the Russian Prince Vlassov in homage to his "queen," Hortense de Beauharnais (daughter of Napoléon's beloved Joséphine and mother to Emperor Napoléon III). A magical grand salon topped with a trompe l'oeil treillage, guest rooms with soaring, fairy-tale beds crowned with Empire-style canopies, and glamorous beach views are just some of the delights on tap here. The lucky guest who lands room No. 4 will even get to bathe in Queen Hortense's own silver-plated bathtub. ✉ *19 rue de la Malouine, 35800* ☎ *02–99–46–54–31* 🖷 *02–99–88–15–88* ⊕ *www.villa-reine-hortense.com* ✍ *8 rooms* ♿ *Bar; no a/c* ☰ *AE, MC, V.*

Nightlife

During July and August, stretches of the **Clair de Lune** promenade become a nighttime, son-et-lumière wonderland, thanks to spotlights and recorded music. The main nightlife activity in town is at the **casino** (✉ 4 bd. du Président-Wilson ☎ 02–99–16–30–30).

Sports & the Outdoors

For windsurfing, wander over to the **Wishbone Club** (✉ Digue de l'Écluse ☎ 02–99–88–15–20). Boats can be rented from the **Yacht Club** (✉ Promenade Clair de Lune ☎ 02–99–46–14–32).

Paimpol

⑩ *92 km (57 mi) west of Cap Fréhel via D786, 45 km (28 mi) northwest of St-Brieuc.*

Paimpol is one of the liveliest fishing ports in the area and a good base for exploring this part of the coast. The town is a maze of narrow streets lined with shops, restaurants, and souvenir boutiques. The harbor, where fishermen used to unload their catch from far-off seas, is its main focal point; today most fish are caught in the Channel. From the sharp cliffs you can see the coast's famous pink-granite rocks. For centuries, but no longer, Breton fishermen sailed to Newfoundland each spring to harvest cod—a long and perilous journey. The **Fête des Terres-Neuvas** is a celebration of the traditional return from Newfoundland of the Breton fishing fleets; it is held on the third Sunday in July.

Where to Stay

★ **$–$$** 🏨 **Repaire de Kerroc'h.** Built in the late 18th century by Corouge Kersau— one of the region's most notorious privateers—this delightful quayside structure (which looks transplanted from an urban street) overlooks the harbor and yacht marina. Beyond elegant sash windows lie rough-hewn stone walls, fireplaces, a lovely Neoclassical dining nook, while upstairs the spacious guest rooms use their artfully odd angles to best advantage. Most are decorated in an English style with flowered chintzes and wood accents; a favorite, Les Sept Isles, faces the street and has a view of the boats, whereas the Iles des Gizans double suite (with two bathrooms) is perfect for a large party traveling together. ✉ *29 quai Morand, 22500* ☎ *02–96–20–50–13* 🖶 *02–96–22–07–46* 🌐 *www.chateauxhotels.com/kerroch* 🛏 *12 rooms, 1 duplex* ⚗ *Internet; no a/c* ☰ *MC, V* ☩ *MAP.*

Trébeurden

⑪ *46 km (27 mi) west of Paimpol via D786 and D65, 9 km (6 mi) northwest of Lannion.*

Fodor's Choice
★

A small, pleasant fishing village that is now a summer resort town, Trébeurden makes a good base for exploring the pink-granite cliffs of the Corniche Bretonne, starting with the rocky point at nearby Le Castel. Take a look at the profile of the dramatic rocks off the coast near Trégastel and Perros-Guirec and use your imagination to see La Tête de Mort (Death's Head), La Tortoise, Le Sentinel, and Le Chapeau de Wellington (Wellington's Hat). The scene changes with the sunlight and the sweep and retreat of the tide, whose caprices can strand fishing boats among islands that were, only hours before, hidden beneath the sea. The ★ famous seaside footpath, the **Sentier des Douaniers** (🌐 www.perros-guirec. com or www.plouhinec-tourisme.com), starts up at the west end of the Trestraou beach in the resort town of **Perros-Guirec,** 3 km (2 mi) east of Trébeurden; from there this beautifully manicured, fence-lined, and gorgeously scenic path provides a two-hour walk eastward, through fern forests, past cliffs and pink granite boulders to the pretty beach at Ploumanac'h. If you keep your eye out, you might even spot one of the mythical, 900-year-old Korrigans—native sprites with pointed ears, beards, and hoof feet, who come out at night from seaside grottoes to dance around fires. From Perros-Guirec, you can take a boat trip out to the Sept Iles, a group of seven islets that are bird sanctuaries. On a hillside perch above **Ploumanac'h** is the village of La Clarté, home to the little Chapelle Notre Dame de la Clarté (pl. de la Chapelle), built of local pink granite and decorated with 14 stations of the cross painted by the master of the Pont-Aven school, Maurice Denis. During the **Pardon of la Clarté** (August 15), a bishop preaches an outdoor mass for the Virgin Mary, village girls wear Trégor costumes, and the statue of the Virgin Mary wears a gold crown (she wears a fake one for the rest of the year).

Five kilometers (3 mi) east of Trébeurden is **Cosmopolis,** home to the Radôme: a giant white radar dome, whose 340-ton antenna captured the first live TV satellite transmission from the United States to France in July 1962. Today the sphere houses one of Europe's largest planetariums, a museum retracing the history of telecommunications back to the first telegraph in 1792, and spectacular laser shows that employ 200 projectors to bring the history of satellite communication to life. ⊠ *Pleumeur-Bodou* ☎ *02–96–46–63–80* ⊕ *http://levillagegaulois.free. fr/* ☞ *€7* ☉ *Apr. and Sept., weekdays 11–6, weekends 2–6; May–June, daily 11–6; July and Aug., daily 11–7.*

Where to Stay & Eat

★ **$$$$** ✕⊡ **Manoir de Lan-Kerellec.** The beauty of the Breton coastline is embraced by this Relais & Châteaux hotel, where guest rooms are far more than just comfortable. Set long and cruiseliner-low, this renovated 19th-century Breton manor house has now been outfitted with dramatic windows—plate-glass, round, panoramic—so as to frame stirring vistas of the endless sea and the cliffs of the Côte de Granit Rose. The restaurant, whose circular dining room has a delightful model of the *St-Yves* ship suspended from its ceiling, mostly serves seafood, but the roast lamb is also good; it does not serve lunch Monday through Thursday and is closed Monday, October until Easter. ⊠ *11 allée Centrale, 22560* ☎ *02–96–15–00–00* 🖷 *02–96–23–66–88* ⊕ *www.relaischateaux.com* ☞ *18 rooms* 🖧 *Restaurant, cable TV, tennis court, Internet, some pets allowed (fee)* ⊟ *AE, DC, MC, V* ☉ *Closed mid-Nov.–mid-Mar.* ❖◯*MAP.*

Morlaix

② *45 km (28 mi) southwest of Trébeurden via D65 and D786, 56 km (35 mi) northeast of Brest.*

An unforgettable sight is the 19th-century stone railroad viaduct of Morlaix (pronounced mor-*lay*). At 300 yards long and 200 feet high, it spans the entire town. The Vieille Ville's attractive mix of half-timber houses, twisting streets, and shops deserves unhurried exploration. At its commercial heart is the pedestrian Grand'Rue, lined with quaint 15th-century houses. Look for the 16th-century, three-story Maison de la Reine Anne (Queen Anne House) on the adjacent rue du Mur—it's adorned with statuettes of saints. The town's museum, known as the **Musée des Jacobins** because it's in a former Jacobin church (note the early-15th-century rose window at one end), is just off rue d'Aiguillon, parallel to Grand'Rue; it has an eclectic collection ranging from religious statues to archaeological finds and modern paintings. ⊠ *Pl. des Jacobins* ☎ *02–98–88–68–88* ⌨ *€4* ⊙ *Daily 1:30–6.*

Beer at the **Brasserie des Deux Rivières** (Two Rivers Brewery)—named for the two rivers, the Jarlo and the Queffleuth, that flow through Morlaix—is brewed according to traditional English methods. You complete your visit to the brewery—whose long, narrow building was originally a rope factory—with a glass of dark, cask-conditioned *Coreff* ale. ⊠ *1 pl. de la Madeleine* ☎ *02–98–63–41–92* ⌨ *Free* ⊙ *July and Aug., tours weekdays 11 and 2. Call ahead at other times.*

Where to Stay & Eat

¢ ✕ **Tempo.** This relaxed, bustling brasserie by the marina on the northwest of town offers a good choice of quiches, salads and *plats du jour* in a glitzy modern decor. The outdoor terrace offers a front-row view of the boats. ⊠ *Bassin à Flot, Cours Beaumont* ☎ *02–98–63–29–11* ☰ *MC, V* ⊙ *Closed Sun. No lunch Sat.*

$–$$ ⊡ **Hôtel de L' Europe.** Rooms are spacious at this smartly renovated, centrally located hotel. It has been in existence since 1800, although the building itself is older, with some fine 17th-century wood paneling in the lobby and stairwell; previous guests range from the Queen of Portugal to General de Gaulle. ⊠ *1 rue d'Aiguillon, 29600* ☎ *02–98–62–11–99* 🖶 *02–98–88–83–38* ⊕ *www.hotel-europe-com.fr* ⤴ *60 rooms, 49 with bath* ⅍ *Cable TV, Internet, some pets allowed (fee); no a/c* ⊙ *Closed Christmas wk* ☰ *AE, DC, MC, V* ⑩ *BP.*

THE ATLANTIC COAST

What Brittany offers in the way of the sea handsomely makes up for its shortage of mountain peaks and passes. Its hundreds of miles of sawtooth coastline reveal the Atlantic Ocean in its every mood and form—from the peaceful cove where waders poke about hunting seashells to the treacherous bay whose waters swirl over quicksands in unpredictable crosscurrents; from the majestic serenity of the breakers rolling across La Baule's miles of golden-sand beaches to the savage fury of the gigantic waves that fling their force against jagged rocks 340 dizzy feet below the cliffs of Pointe du Raz. Brittany's Atlantic coast runs southeast from the down-to-earth port of Brest to the tony city of Nantes, at the mouth of the Loire River. The wild, rugged creeks around the little-visited northwestern tip of Finistère (Land's End) gradually give way to sandy beaches south of Concarneau. Inland, the bent trees and craggy rocks look like they've been bewitched by Merlin in a bad mood.

Brest

⑬ *56 km (35 mi) southwest of Morlaix, 240 km (150 mi) west of Rennes.*

Brest's enormous, sheltered bay is strategically positioned close to the Atlantic and the English Channel. You need not spend much time here: World War II left the city in ruins. Postwar reconstruction, resulting in long, straight streets of reinforced concrete, has given latter-day Brest the unenviable reputation of being one of France's drabbest cities. Its waterfront, however, offers dramatic views across the bay toward the Plougastel Peninsula, and is worth visiting for its handful of old buildings, its castle, and the **Monument Américain,** a pink-granite tower commemorating the American troops who landed here in 1917. The Pont de Recouvrance, which crosses the Penfeld River, is Europe's longest drawbridge at 95 yards. Boats leave from the Port du Commerce for the islands of Ouessant and Molène.

Begin your visit at one of the town's oldest monuments, the **Tour de la Motte-Tanguy,** next to the bridge. This bulky, round 14th-century tower, once used as a lookout post, contains a museum of local history with scale models of scenes of the Brest of yore. ⊠ *Square Pierre-Péron* ☎ *02–98–00–88–60* ⌧ *Free* ⊗ *Oct.–May, Wed., Thurs., and weekends 2–6; June–Sept., daily 10–noon and 2–7.*

Reopened in 2005 after extensive renovations, the medieval **château** across the bridge from the Tour Tanguy houses the **Musée de la Marine** (Naval Museum), which contains boat models, sculpture, pictures, and naval instruments. One section is devoted to the castle's 700-year history. The dungeons can also be visited. ☎ *02–98–22–12–39* ⊕ *www.musee-marine.fr* ⌧ *€5* ⊗ *Apr.–Sept., daily 10–6:30; Oct.–Mar., Wed.–Mon. 10–noon and 2–6.*

French, Flemish, and Italian paintings from the 17th to the 20th centuries and the regional Pont-Aven Postimpressionist school make up the collection at the **Musée des Beaux-Arts** (Fine Arts Museum). ⊠ *24 rue Traverse* ☎ *02–98–00–87–96* ⌧ *€4* ⊗ *Mon. and Wed.–Sat. 10–11:45 and 2–6, Sun. 2–6.*

The fauna and flora of the world's three ocean climates—temperate, polar, and tropical—are the themes of the exhibits at **Océanopolis,** one of the largest marine complexes in Europe, complete with a battery of pools and aquariums. Arrive at the park as early as you can, as it takes an entire day to do it justice. ⊠ *Rue Alain-Colas* ☎ *02–98–34–40–40* ⊕ *www. oceanopolis.com* ⌧ *€15* ⊗ *Apr.–early-Sept., daily 9–7; early-Sept.–Mar., Tues.–Sun. 10–5.*

---

off the beaten path

LE FOLGOËT – In early September pilgrims come from afar to Le Folgoët (⊕ www.folgoet.net), 24 km (15 mi) northeast of Brest, to attend the ceremonial religious procession known as the **pardon** and to drink from the Fontaine de Salaün, a fountain behind the church, whose water comes from a spring beneath the altar. The splendid church, known as the Basilique, has a sturdy north tower that serves as a beacon for miles around and, inside, a rare, intricately carved granite rood screen separating the choir and nave.

Where to Eat

$–$$$ ✕ **Maison de l'Océan.** This giant split-level brasserie by the waterfront mirrors the city of Brest: all earnest bustle with no frills. It serves the freshest seafood, or as they say here, the *top du top.* Try the delicious catch of the day or one of the traditional seafood platters. In the finest French tradition, the service remains hectically unflappable. ⊠ *2 quai de la Douane* ☎ *02–98–80–44–84* ⌲ *Reservations essential* ▭ *MC, V.*

en route | Stop in **Daoulas,** 16 km (10 mi) east of Brest, to admire its still-functioning 12th-century Augustinian abbey, with cloisters and herb garden. Then head south on N165 and D7 to the old weaving town of **Locronan,** 46 km (29 mi) away, and visit the 5th-century **Église St-Ronan** and the adjacent **Chapelle du Penity,** dominating the magnificently preserved ensemble of houses and main square.

Ste-Anne-la-Palud

⑭ *68 km (42 mi) south of Brest via N165, D887, D7, D61.*

Fodor's Choice
★

One of the great attractions of the Brittany calendar is the celebration of a religious festival known as a village *pardon*, replete with banners, saintly statues, a parade, bishops in attendance, women in folk costume, a feast, and hundreds of attendees. The seaside village of Ste-Anne-la-Palud has one of the finest and most authentic age-old pardons in Brittany, held on the last Sunday in August.

Where to Stay & Eat

$$$–$$$$ ✕▥ **Hotel de la Plage.** This former private house sits nestled in a cove on a quiet strip of sandy beach around the bay—a remote retreat perfect for long, restorative walks. Some of the comfortably furnished rooms face the sea. The hotel, however, has less of a feeling of Brittany than you might want. Alain Leduc's food is consistently good, especially the seafood dishes; reservations are essential, and a jacket is required. ⊠ *29550 Ste-Anne-la-Palud* ☎ *02–98–92–50–12* 🖷 *02–98–92–56–54* ⊕ *www.hotelplage.com* ⇄ *26 rooms, 4 suites* ⚭ *Restaurant, minibars, cable TV, tennis court, pool, sauna, beach, Internet, some pets allowed (fee)* ▤ *AE, DC, MC, V* ⊘ *Closed Nov.–Apr.* ⊚ *MAP.*

Douarnenez

⑮ *14 km (8 mi) south of Ste-Anne-la-Palud.*

Douarnenez is a quaint old fishing town of quayside paths and zigzagging narrow streets. Boats come in from the Atlantic to unload their catches of mackerel, sardines, and tuna. Just offshore is the Ile Tristan, accessible on foot at low tide (guided tours only, €5.50), and across the Port-Rhu channel is Tréboul, a seaside resort favored by French families.

☺ One of the three town harbors is fitted out with a unique **Port-Musée** (Port Museum). Along the wharves you can visit the workshops of boatwrights, sail makers, and other old-time craftspeople, then go aboard the historic trawlers, lobster boats, Thames barges, and a former lightship anchored alongside. On the first weekend in May you can sail on an antique fishing boat. ⊠ *Place de l'Enfer* ☎ *02–98–92–65–20* ⊕ *www.port-musee.org* ▧ *€4.60* ⊘ *June–Sept., daily 10–7; Oct., Apr., and May, Tues.–Sun. 10–12:30 and 2–6.*

Where to Stay & Eat

★ **$–$$** ✕▥ **Manoir de Moëllien.** Surrounded by extensive forested grounds, this textbook 17th-century stone Breton manor house, landmarked by a sturdy tower, and filled with precious antiques, makes an enviable choice. Another plus is the fine restaurant, famous for its local seafood dishes. Sample Bruno Garet's *terrine de poisson chaud* (warm seafood terrine) or the *duo de truites de mer* (poached sea trout). Rooms have terraces overlooking the garden, which makes for a peaceful country atmosphere. ✉ *12 km (7 mi) northeast of Douarnenez, 29550 Plonévez-Porzay* ☎ *02–98–92–50–40* 📠 *02–98–92–55–21* 🛏 *18 rooms* ♿ *Restaurant, some minibars, cable TV, bar, Internet, some pets allowed (fee); no a/c* 🖃 *AE, DC, MC, V* ⊘ *Closed mid-Nov.–mid-Mar.* ⁑ *FAP.*

★ $ ✕🖳 **Ty Mad.** In the 1920s artists and writers such as Picasso and Breton native Max Jacob frequented this small hotel in a quiet residential area near the beach in Tréboul. Under new management, this landmark was completely renovated in early 2005. Guest rooms are not large, but the sea views are great. A garden now adorns the property, and the separate house has been outfitted with a kitchen for larger groups and longer stays. Gérard Tanter's menu, served in the glass-enclosed restaurant, focuses on fresh produce sourced from neighboring farms and fish boats. ✉ *Plage St-Jean, 29100* ☎ *02–98–74–00–53* 📠 *02–98–74–15–16* ⊕ *www.tymad.com* 🛏 *17 rooms* ♿ *Restaurant, bar, some pets allowed; no a/c, no room TVs* 🖃 *MC, V* ⊘ *Closed Oct.–Easter* ⁑ *MAP.*

Quimper

🔟 *22 km (14 mi) southeast of Douarnenez via D765.*

A traditional crowd-puller, the twisting streets and tottering medieval houses of Quimper furnish rich postcard material, but lovers of decorative arts head here because this is the home of Quimperware, one of the more famous variants of French hand-painted earthenware pottery. The techniques were brought to Quimper by Normands in the 17th century, but the Quimperois customized them by painting typical local Breton scenes on the pottery. This lively and commercial town began life as the ancient capital of the Cornouaille province, founded, it is said, by King Gradlon 1,500 years ago. Quimper (pronounced cam-*pair*) owes its strange name to its site at the confluence (*kemper* in Breton) of the Odet and Steir rivers. Stroll along the banks of the Odet and through the **Vieille Ville,** with its cathedral. Then walk along the lively shopping street, rue Kéréon, and down narrow medieval rue du Guéodet (note the house with caryatids), rue St-Mathieu, and rue du Sallé.

The **Cathédrale St-Corentin** (✉ Pl. St-Corentin) is a masterpiece of Gothic architecture and the second-largest cathedral in Brittany (after Dol-de-Bretagne's). Legendary King Gradlon is represented on horseback just below the base of the spires, harmonious mid-19th-century additions to the medieval ensemble. The church interior remains very much in use by fervent Quimperois, giving the candlelit vaults a meditative air. The 15th-century stained glass is luminous. Behind the cathedral is the stately **Jardin de l'Évêché** (Bishop's Garden).

More than 400 works by such masters as Rubens, Corot, and Picasso mingle with pretty landscapes from the local Gauguin-inspired Pont-Aven school in the **Musée des Beaux-Arts** (Fine Arts Museum), next to the cathedral. Of particular note is a fascinating series of paintings depicting traditional life in Breton villages. ✉ *40 pl. St-Corentin*

☎ 02–98–95–45–20 ⬙ €4 ⊙ *July and Aug., daily 9–7; Sept.–June,*
Wed.–Mon. 10–noon and 2–6.

In the mid-18th century Quimper sprang to nationwide attention as a
pottery manufacturing center, when it began producing second-rate im-
itations of Rouen faïence, or ceramics with blue motifs. Today's more
colorful designs, based on floral arrangements and marine fauna, are
still often hand-painted. To understand Quimper's pottery past with the
help of more than 500 examples of "style Quimper, " take one of the
guided tours at the **Musée de la Faïence** (Earthenware Museum). ☒ *14*
rue Jean-Baptiste-Bousquet ☎ *02–98–90–12–72* ⊕ *www.quimper-*
faiences.com ⬙ *€4* ⊙ *Mid-Apr.–mid-Oct., Mon.–Sat. 10–6.*

Local furniture, ceramics, and folklore top the bill at the **Musée Départemental Breton** (Brittany Regional Museum). ☒ *1 rue du Roi-Grad-*
lon ☎ *02–98–95–21–60* ⬙ *€3.80* ⊙ *June–Sept., daily 9–6; Oct.–May,*
Tues.–Sun. 9–noon and 2–5.

Where to Eat

$$$ ✗ **L'Ambroisie.** This cozy little restaurant has soft-yellow walls, huge
contemporary paintings, and different settings at every table. Chef Gilbert
Guyon's traditional yet nouvelle menu is seasonal; local products are cho-
sen by hand. Try the buckwheat *galette* crêpe stuffed with lobster or the
pigeon roasted in apple liqueur with whipped potatoes and mushrooms.
The homemade desserts, like the *omelette norvégienne* with warm choco-
late and nougat ice cream in meringue, are delicious. ☒ *49 rue Élie-Fréron*
☎ *02–98–95–00–02* ⬚ *Reservations essential* ▭ *AE, MC, V* ⊙ *Closed*
Mon. and early July, 2 wks in Feb. No dinner Sun. except June–Aug.

Nightlife & the Arts

In late July, Quimper hosts the **Festival de Cornouaille** (☎ 02–98–55–53–53
⊕ www.festival-cornouaille.com), a nine-day Celtic extravaganza. More
than 250 artists, dancers, and musicians fill streets already packed with
the 4,000 people who come each year to enjoy the traditional street fair.

Shopping

Keep an eye out for such typical Breton products as woven and em-
broidered cloth, woolen goods, brass and wood objects, puppets, dolls,
and locally designed jewelry. When it comes to distinctive Breton folk
costumes, Quimper is the best place to look. The streets around the cathe-
dral, especially **rue du Parc**, are full of shops selling woolen goods (no-
tably thick marine sweaters). Faïence and a wide selection of hand-painted
pottery can be purchased at the **Faïencerie d'Art Breton** (☒ 16 bis rue du
Parc ☎ 02–98–95–34–13).

Concarneau

⓱ *22 km (14 mi) southeast of Quimper via D783.*

Concarneau is the third-largest fishing port in France. A busy industrial
town, it has a grain of charm and an abundance of tacky souvenir shops.
But it is worth visiting to see the fortified islet in the middle of the har-
bor. The **Ville Close**, which was regarded as impregnable from early me-
dieval times on, is entered by way of a quaint drawbridge. The fortifications

were further strengthened by the English under John de Montfort during the War of Succession (1341–64). Three hundred years later Sébastien de Vauban remodeled the ramparts into what you see today: 1 km (½ mi) long, with splendid views across the two harbors on either side. Held here during the second half of August is the **Fête des Filets Bleus** (Blue Net Festival), a weeklong folk celebration in which Bretons in costume swirl and dance to the wail of bagpipes. 🖼 *Ramparts €1 ☉ Easter–Sept., daily 10–7:30; Oct.–Easter, daily 10–noon and 2–5.*

The **Musée de la Pêche** (Fishing Museum), close to the island gateway, has aquariums and exhibits on fishing techniques from around the world. ✉ *3 rue Vauban* ☎ *02–98–97–10–20* 🖼 *€6 ☉ July and Aug., daily 9:30–8; Sept.–June, daily 10–noon and 2–6.*

Where to Eat

$$ ✕ **Chez Armande.** Rather than opting for one of the various tourist haunts in the Ville Clos, you might like to wander 300 yards down the waterfront for an excellent fish or seafood meal at Chez Armande. Specialties include *pot-au-feu de la mer au gingembre* (seafood in a clear ginger broth), *St-Pierre à la fricassée de champignons* (John Dory with fried mushrooms), and *homard rôti en beurre de corail* (roast lobster in coral butter). Try the *tarte de grand-mère aux pommes* (grandma's homemade apple pie) for dessert. ✉ *15 bis av. du Dr-Nicolas* ☎ *02–98–97–00–76* 🖃 *AE, MC, V ☉ Closed Tues. and Wed., mid-Dec.–early Jan., and 2 wks in Feb.*

Pont-Aven

18 15 km (9 mi) east of Concarneau via D783.

FodorśChoice ★

Long beloved by artists, this lovely village sits astride the Aven river as it descends from the Montagnes Noire to the sea, turning the town's mills along the way (there were once 14; now just a handful remain). Surrounded by one of Brittany's most beautiful stretches of countryside, Pont-Aven (⊕ www.pontaven.com) is a former artists' colony where, most famously, Paul Gauguin lived before he headed off to the South Seas. Wanting to break with traditional Western culture and values, in 1888 the lawyer-turned-painter headed to Brittany, a destination almost as foreign to Parisians as Tahiti. Economy was another lure: the Paris stock market had just crashed and, with it, Gauguin's livelihood, so cheap lodgings were also at the top of his list. Before long, Gauguin took to wearing Breton sweaters, berets, and wooden clogs; in his art he began to leave dewy, sunlit Impressionism behind for a stronger, more linear style. The town museum captures some of the history of the Pont-Aven School, whose adherents painted Breton landscapes in a bold yet dreamy style called Syntheticism.

One glance at the **Bois d'Amour** forest, set just to the north of town (from the tourist office, go left and walk along the river for five minutes), will make you realize why artists continue to come here. Past some meadows, you'll find Gauguin's inspiration for his famous painting *The Yellow Christ*—a wooden crucifix inside the secluded **Chapelle de Trémalo** (usually open, per private owners, from 9 to 7) just outside the Bois d'Amour woods. While in Brittany, Gauguin painted many of his earliest masterpieces, now given pride of place in great museums around the world. The **Musée Municipal** (Town Museum) has a photography exhibition documenting the Pont-Aven School, and works by its participants, such as Paul Sérusier, Maurice Denis, and Emile Bernard. After Gauguin departed for Tahiti, a group of Americans came here to paint, attracted by the light, the landscape, and the reputation. If the spirit of Gauguin and his hangers-on inspires you, the Maison de la Presse, right next to the bridge at 5 place Paul Gauguin, has boxes of 12 colored pencils and sketchbooks for sale. ⊠ *Pl. de l'Hôtel-de-Ville* ☎ *02–98–06–14–43* ✍ *€4* ⏲ *July and Aug., daily 10:30–12:30 and 2–7; Feb.–June and Sept.–Dec., daily 10–12:30 and 2–6.*

The crêperies and pizzerias that surround **place de l'Hôtel-de-Ville** cater to the lazy visitor, just emerging from the tourist office at **No. 5** (☎ 02–98–06–04–70); note the office's helpful list of chambers d'hôte accommodations offered by the residents in town. Instead, walk the few paces to **Le Moulin du Grand Poulguin** (⊠ 2 quai Théodore-Botrel ☎ 02–98–06–02–67), which provides a delightful setting in which to eat your crêpe on a terrace directly on the flowing waters of the Aven River in view of the footbridge. Those with a sweet tooth can just fill up on the buttery Traou Mad cookies at the **Biscuiterie** (⊠ 10 pl. Gauguin ☎ 02–98–06–01–03); they're baked with the local wheat of the last running windmill in Pont-Aven. After exploring the village, cool off (in summer) with a boat trip down the estuary.

Where to Stay & Eat

$$$–$$$$ ✕ **La Taupinière.** On the road from Concarneau, 2 mi (3 km) west of Pont-Aven, is this roadside inn with an attractive garden. Chef Guy Guilloux's open kitchen (with the large hearth he uses to grill fish, langoustine, crab, and Breton ham specialties) turns out local delicacies such as galette crêpes stuffed with spider crab. Splurge without guilt on the light homemade rhubarb and strawberry compote. ⊠ *Croissant St-André* ☎ *02–98–06–03–12* ✍ *Reservations essential* 🎩 *Jacket required* ▭ *AE, MC, V* ⏲ *Closed Mon., Tues., plus last 2 wks Mar. and mid-Sept.–mid-Oct.*

★ **$$** ✕⊡ **Hostellerie Le Moulin de Rosmadec.** You'll want to set up your easel in a second once you spot this pretty-as-a-picture, 15th-century stone water mill. Set at the end of a quiet street, the Sébilleaus' beloved hostelry sits in the middle of the rushing, rocky Aven River. Inside, atmospheric beamed ceilings, Breton stone fireplaces, and water views (you can hear the sound of water gently splashing over the stones beneath your window) cast their spell—but who can resist dining on the "island" terrace? Outside or inside, feast on the creations of a serious kitchen: the *sautée de langoustines,* duck in cassis, or lobster *grillé Rosmadec* are all winners. Reservations are essential; the restaurant does not serve dinner Sunday from September to June. If you're very lucky, you'll snag one of the four gently priced guest rooms available. ⊠ *Pl. Paul-Gauguin, 29930* ☎ *02–98–06–00–22* 🖶 *02–98–06–18–00* ⇥ *4 rooms* ⏛ *Restaurant, some pets allowed; no a/c* ▭ *MC, V* ⏲ *Closed Wed., last 2 wks Feb., and first 2 wks Oct.*

CloseUp
GAUGUIN & THE PONT-AVEN SCHOOL

SURROUNDED BY ONE OF BRITTANY'S most beautiful countrysides, Pont-Aven was a natural to become a "cité des artistes" in the heady days of Impressionism and Postimpressionism. It was actually the introduction of the railroad in the 19th century that put travel to Brittany in vogue, and it was here that Gauguin and other like-minded artists founded the noted Pont-Aven school. Inspired by the vibrant colors and lovely vistas to be found here, they created "synthétisme," a painting style characterized by broad patches of pure color and strong symbolism, in revolt against the dominant Impressionist school back in Paris. Gauguin arrived in the summer of 1886, happy to find a place "where you can live on nothing" (Paris's stock market had crashed and cost Gauguin his job). At Madame Gloanec's boarding house he welcomed a circle of painters to join him in his artistic quest for monumental simplicity and striking color.

Today Pont-Aven seems content to rest on its laurels. Although it's labeled a "city of artists," the galleries that line its streets display paintings that lack the unifying theme and common creative energy of the earlier works of art. The first Pont-Aven painters were American students who came here in the 1850s. The only one to gain recognition, Charles Fromuth, has some paintings on display in the town museum. Though Gauguin is not surprisingly absent (his paintings now go for millions), except for a few of his early zincographs, the exhibit Hommage à Gauguin is an interesting sketch of his turbulent life. Also on view in the museum are works by other near-great Pont-Aven artists: Maurice Denis, Emil Bernard, Emil Jordan, and Emmanuel Sérusier.

$-$$ 🏨 **Roz Aven.** Built into a rock face on the bank of the Aven, this efficiently run hotel has simple, clean rooms. You can choose a room in one of three locations: the 16th-century thatched cottage, the modern annex, or the *maison bourgeoise* with a river or garden view. Owner Yann Souffez speaks excellent English. He describes the furnishings as Louis XVI, but some might call them petit-bourgeois. ⊠ *11 quai Théodore-Botrel, 29930* ☎ *02–98–06–13–06* 🖷 *02–98–06–03–89* ⊕ *www.hotelpontaven.online.fr* 🛏 *23 rooms, 2 suites* ⚘ *Some minibars, bar, some pets allowed (fee); no a/c, no TV in some rooms* ⊟ *AE, MC, V* ⊗ *Closed Nov.–Feb.* ¶◯¶ *MAP.*

Belle-Ile-en-Mer

⑲ *45 mins by boat from Quiberon, 52 km (32 mi) southeast of Lorient.*

Fodor'sChoice
★

At 18 km (11 mi) long, Belle-Ile is the largest of Brittany's islands. It also lives up to its name: it's indeed beautiful, and less commercialized than its mainland harbor town, Quiberon. Because of the cost and inconvenience of reserving car berths on the ferry, cross over to the island as a pedestrian and rent a car—or, if you don't mind the hilly terrain, a bicycle.

Departing from Quiberon—a spa town with pearl-like beaches on the eastern side of the 16-km-long (10-mi-long) Presqu'île de Quiberon (Quiberon Peninsula), a stretch of coastal cliffs and beaches whose dramatic western coast, the Côte Sauvage (Wild Coast), is a mix of crevices and coves lashed by the sea—the ferry lands at **Le Palais,** crushed beneath a monumental Vauban citadel built in the 1680s. From Le Palais head northwest to **Sauzon,** the prettiest fishing harbor on the island; from here you can see across to the Quiberon Peninsula and the Gulf of Morbihan. Continue on to the **Grotte de l'Apothicairerie,** which derives its name from the local cormorants' nests, said to resemble apothecary bottles. At Port Goulphar is the **Grand Phare** (Great Lighthouse). Built in 1835, it rises 275 feet above sea level and has one of the most powerful beacons in Europe, visible from 120 km (75 mi) across the Atlantic. If the keeper is available and you are feeling well rested, you may be able to climb to the top.

Where to Stay & Eat

★ **$$$$** ✕☐ **Castel Clara.** Perched on a cliff overlooking the surf and the narrow Anse de Goulphar Bay, this '70s-era hotel was Francois Mitterrand's address when he vacationed on Belle-Ile. The hotel still retains its presidential glamour, with its renowned spa, saltwater pool, and spectacular room views. In the bright, airy restaurant, chef Christophe Hardouin specializes in seafood, caught just offshore. The John Dory baked in sea salt and the grilled sea bream are simple but delicious. Castel Clara's expansive wooden-decked terrace is the perfect lounging spot for cocktails at sundown. ✉ *Port-Goulphar, 56360* ☏ *02–97–31–84–21* 🖷 *02–97–31–51–69* ⊕ *www.castel-clara.com* ⇨ *33 rooms, 7 suites* ⚫ *Restaurant, minibars, cable TV, tennis court, pool, spa, Internet; no a/c* ⊟ *AE, DC, MC, V* ⊘ *Closed mid-Nov.–mid-Feb.* ❙◯❙ *MAP.*

Nightlife & the Arts

Every year, from the end of July to mid-August, Belle-Ile hosts **Lyrique-en-mer** (☏ 02–97–31–59–59 ⊕ www.belle-ile.net), an ambitious little festival whose heart is opera (the festival was founded by the American bass baritone, Richard Cowan) but which offers up a generous lyric menu of sacred music concerts, gospel, jazz, even the occasional sea shanty and Broadway musical number. Operas and concerts are performed by rising talents from around the world at various romantic locations around the island.

The Outdoors

The ideal way to get around to the island's 90 spectacular beaches is by bike. The best place to rent two-wheelers (and cars—this is also the island's Avis outlet) is at **Roue Libre** (✉ Rue du Pont Orgo ☏ 02–97–31–49–81).

Carnac

⑳ *19 km (12 mi) northeast of Quiberon via D768/D781.*

Fodor'sChoice
★

At the north end of Quiberon Bay, Carnac is known for its expansive beaches and its ancient stone monuments. Dating from around 4500

BC, Carnac's **menhirs** remain as mysterious in origin as their English contemporary, Stonehenge, although religious beliefs and astronomy were doubtless an influence. The 2,395 megalithic monuments that make up the three *alignements*—Kermario, Kerlescan, and Ménec—form the largest megalithic site in the world and are positioned with astounding astronomical accuracy in semicircles and parallel lines over about 1 km (½ mi). The site, just north of the town, is fenced off for protection, and you can examine the menhirs up close only October through March; in summer you must join a guided tour (☎ 02–97–52–29–81, some in English, €4). More can be learned at the **Archéoscope,** a visitor center where a 30-minute presentation involving slides, a video, and models explains the menhirs' history and significance. ⊠ *Alignements du Ménec* ☎ *02–97–52–07–49* ☑ *€6* ☉ *Mid-Feb.–mid-Nov., daily 10–5:30, English presentations at 10:30 and 2:30.*

Carnac also has smaller-scale dolmen ensembles and three *tumuli* (mounds or barrows), including the 130-yard-long, 38-foot-high **Tumulus de St-Michel,** topped by a small chapel with views of the rock-strewn countryside. ☑ *€2* ☉ *Easter–Oct.; guided tours of tumulus Apr.–Sept., daily 10, 11, 2, and 3:30.*

Auray

㉑ *16 km (10 mi) north of Carnac via D119/D768, 38 km (24 mi) southeast of Lorient.*

The ancient town of Auray grew up along the banks of the Loch River, best admired from the Promenade du Loch overlooking the quayside. Cross the river to explore the old, cobbled streets of the St-Goustan neighborhood. Tied alongside the quay, across the bridge, is the **Goélette St-Sauveur,** an old topsail schooner that once ferried coal from Wales. Today it houses a sailing museum with many unusual nautical artifacts. ⊠ *Pl. St-Sauveur* ☎ *02–97–56–63–38* ☑ *€3* ☉ *Easter–Sept., daily 10:30–12:30 and 2:30–7.*

Where to Eat

$$–$$$$ ✕ **La Closerie de Kerdrain.** Ebullient chef Fernando Corfmat presides over the kitchen in this large 17th-century town-center manor draped in wisteria. His seasonal menus highlight fresh ingredients prepared in innovative ways: sea-bass carpaccio with fresh green beans in Parmesan, scallops with hazelnuts, or breast of pigeon roasted in black pepper. The sweet-and-sour lemon pie with a *salade* of oranges in mango juice is the perfect way to end the meal. ⊠ *20 rue Louis-Billet* ☎ *02–97–56–61–27* 🖨 *02–97–24–15–79* ▭ *AE, DC, MC, V* ☉ *Closed Mon., 3 wks in Mar., and 3 wks in Dec. No dinner Sun.*

The Outdoors

Take a cruise down the Auray River on the **Navix-Vedettes du Golfe** (☎ 08–25–16–21–00); along the way you'll discover the lovely 16th-century Château du Plessis-Kaer and the tiny, tidal fishing port of Bono tucked between the steep banks and the oyster beds of the Pô estuary.

Vannes

★ ㉒ *18 km (11 mi) east of Auray via N165, 108 km (67 mi) southwest of Rennes.*

Scene of the declaration of unity between France and Brittany in 1532, historic Vannes is one of the few towns in Brittany to have been spared damage during World War II. Be sure to saunter through the Promenade de la Garenne, a colorful park, and admire the magnificent gardens nestled beneath the adjacent ramparts. Also visit the medieval wash houses and the cathedral; browse in the small boutiques and antiques shops in the pedestrian streets around pretty place Henri-IV; check out the Cohue, the medieval market hall now used as an exhibition center; and take a boat trip around the scenic Golfe du Morbihan.

The **Cathédrale St-Pierre** boasts a 1537 Renaissance chapel, a Flamboyant Gothic transept portal, and a treasury. ⊠ *Pl. de la Cathédrale* ☺ *Treasury mid-June–mid-Sept., Mon.–Sat. 2–6.*

Where to Stay & Eat

$$$–$$$$ ✕ **Richemont.** Step off the train and right into this popular spot, a haven of refinement where seafood reigns. Chef Régis Mahé prefers a small, seasonal menu with local hand-picked produce and fish so fresh they nearly swim to the plate. For a local specialty with a twist, try the buckwheat galette crêpe filled with lobster and pigeon and served with caramelized leeks. Attention chocolate lovers: save room for the warm chocolate tart with homemade salty caramel ice cream. ⊠ *24 pl. de la Gare* ☎ *02–97–42–61–41* 🖷 *02–97–54–99–01* ▭ *MC, V* ☺ *Closed Sun. and Mon.*

★ **$$$–$$$$** ✕🖩 **Domaine de Rochevilaine.** *Respirer le mer*—it sounds so much more luxurious than "Breathe the sea." At this stunning hotel, you will be able to do that exquisitely and so much more. Set on a magical *presqu'île* (peninsula) called the Pen Lan point, this enchanting collection of 15th- and 16th-century Breton stone buildings resembles a tiny village; one, however, that is surrounded by terraced gardens, has a spectacular spa, and offers grand vistas of the Bay of Vilaine. Once you step through the "Portail de la Verité"—a monumental 13th-century stone entryway—the interior allures with a mix of old and new, seen most elegantly in the restaurant, where Baroque ex-votos, Louis Treize chairs, rock-face fireplaces, and plate-glass windows make a suitable backdrop for the delicious creations of chef Patrice Caillaut, late of Ledoyen and Troisgros. He is noted for his *coucou de Rennes* (a tender hen roasted whole and sliced steaming at the table), while the noted Breton dessert of caramelized apples in pastry layers with cinnamon ice cream is a real treat. Delights continue in the guest rooms, asparkle with checked fabrics, veneered woods, and modern furnishings, while some have four-poster beds and private terraces. Most rooms face the ocean, so be sure to specify, especially if you want to call the 270-degree view from the Admiral's Room your own. To get your toes in the water, head to the alluring spa, the Aqua Phénica, replete with a full spectrum of seawater hydrotherapy facilities and gigantic indoor pool. ⊠ *Pointe de Pen-*

*Lan, 30 km (19 mi) southeast of Vannes, at tip of Pointe de Pen-Lan,
56190 Billiers* ☎ *02–97–41–61–61* 🖷 *02–97–41–44–85* ⊕ *www.
domainerochevilaine.com* ⥎ *32 rooms, 4 suites* ⚭ *Restaurant, minibars, cable TV, 3 pools (2 indoors), hot tub, sauna, Internet, some pets
allowed (fee); no a/c* ▭ *AE, DC, MC, V* ⊠ *FAP.*

$ ✕⊡ **Kyriad.** Set in an old, rustic building in town, this hotel attracts a
varied foreign clientele, drawn by the homey guest rooms—clean, bright,
and simple, with warm yellow walls—and the friendly and efficient staff.
Claude Le Lausque serves a traditional menu in the rustic Image Sainte-
Anne restaurant, with straightforward seasonal specialties like crab in
phyllo pastry, grilled sole, and fisherman's stew. No dinner is served Sunday, November through March. ⊠ *8 pl. de la Libération, 56000*
☎ *02–97–63–27–36* 🖷 *02–97–40–97–02* ⊕ *www.kyriad.com* ⥎ *33
rooms* ⚭ *Restaurant, minibars, cable TV, Internet; no a/c in some rooms*
▭ *AE, DC, MC, V* ⊠ *BP.*

La Baule

㉓ *72 km (45 mi) southeast of Vannes via N165 and D774.*

Star of the Côte d'Amour coast and gifted with a breathtaking 5-km (3-
mi) beach, La Baule is a fashionable resort town that can make you pay
dearly for your coastal frolics. Though it once rivaled Biarrtiz, today
tackiness has replaced sophistication, but you still can't beat that beach,
or the lovely, miles-long seafront promenade lined with hotels. Like Le
Touquet and Dinard, La Baule is a 19th-century creation, founded in
1879 to make the most of the excellent sandy beaches that extend
around the broad, sheltered bay between Pornichet and Le Pouliguen.
A pine forest, planted in 1840, keeps the shifting local sand dunes firmly
at bay. All in all, this can offer an idyllic stay for those who will enjoy
a day on the beach, an afternoon at the shops on avenue du Général-
de-Gaulle and avenue Louis-Lajarrige, and an evening at the Casino.

Where to Stay & Eat

★ $ ✕ **La Ferme du Grand Clos.** At this lively restaurant in an old farmhouse,
just 200 yards from the sea, you have to understand the difference between crêpe and galette to order correctly, since the menus showcase
both in all their forms. Or you can opt for the simple, straightforward
menu featuring food the owner likes to call *la cuisine de grand-mère*
(grandmother's cooking). Come early for a table; it's a very friendly and
popular place. ⊠ *52 av. du Maréchal-de-Lattre-de-Tassigny*
☎ *02–40–60–03–30* ▭ *MC, V* ☺ *Closed Oct. and Wed., Sept.–June.*

$–$$ ⊡ **Concorde.** This blue-shuttered, white-walled establishment numbers
among the least expensive good hotels in pricey La Baule. It's calm, comfortable, modernized, and a short block from the beach (ask for a room
with a sea view). ⊠ *1 bis av. de la Concorde, 44500* ☎ *02–40–60–23–09*
🖷 *02–40–42–72–14* ⊕ *www.hotel-la-concorde.com* ⥎ *47 rooms* ⚭ *Cable
TV, Internet; no a/c* ▭ *AE, DC, MC, V* ☺ *Closed Oct.–mid-Apr.*

★ $–$$ ⊡ **Hôtel de la Plage.** One of the few hotels on the beach in St-Marc-sur-
Mer, southeast of La Baule, this comfortable lodging was the setting for
Jacques Tati's classic comedy *Mr. Hulot's Holiday.* It has been updated
since and, *hélas,* the swinging door to the dining room is no longer there.

But the view of the sea and the sound of the surf remain. The restaurant—reserve a beachfront table in advance—serves seasonal fish specialties like the *choucroute de la mer* (seafood sauerkraut stew). ⊠ *37 rue du Commandant-Charcot, 10 km (6 mi) southeast of La Baule, 44600 St-Marc-sur-Mer* ☎ *02–40–91–99–01* 🖷 *02–40–91–92–00* ⊕ *www. hotel-de-la-plage-44.com* 🔊 *30 rooms* ♿ *Restaurant, cable TV, Internet; no a/c* ☰ *MC, V* ⊘ *Closed Jan.* ¶⊙¶ *FAP.*

Nightlife

Occasionally you see high stakes on the tables at La Baule's **casino** (⊠ 6 av. Pierre-Loti ☎ 02–40–11–48–28).

Nantes

72 km (45 mi) east of La Baule via N171 and N165, 108 km (67 mi) south of Rennes.

The writer Stendhal remarked of 19th-century Nantes, "I hadn't taken twenty steps before I recognized a great city." Since then, the river that flowed around the upper-crust Ile Feydeau neighborhood has been filled in and replaced with a rushing torrent of traffic, and now major highways cut through the heart of town. Still, Nantes is more than the sum of its traffic jams. The 15th-century château is still in relatively good shape, despite having lost an entire tower during a gunpowder explosion in 1800. The 15th-century cathedral floats heavenward as well. Its white stones, immense height, and airy interior make it one of France's best. Across the broad boulevard, cours des 50-Otages, is the 19th-century city. The unlucky Ile Feydeau, surrounded and bisected by highways, still preserves the tottering 18th-century mansion built with wealth from Nantes's huge slave trade. The Loire River flows along the southern edge of the Vieille Ville, making Nantes officially part of the Loire region, although historically it belongs to Brittany. In town you'll see many references to Anne de Bretagne, the last independent ruler of Brittany, who married the region away to King Charles VIII of France in 1491. Bretons have never quite recovered from the shock.

㉔ Built by the dukes of Brittany, who had no doubt that Nantes belonged in their domain, the **Château des Ducs de Bretagne** is a massive, well-preserved 15th-century fortress with a moat. François II, the duke responsible for building most of it, led a hedonistic life here, surrounded by ministers, chamberlains, and an army of servants. Numerous monarchs later stayed in the castle, where in 1598 Henri IV signed the famous Edict of Nantes advocating religious tolerance. As of this writing, the castle is expected to reopen in September 2006 after extensive renovations. ⊠ *4 pl. Marc-Elder* ☎ *02–51–17–49–00* 💶 *€3.10* ⊙ *Wed.–Sun. 10–6.*

㉕ The **Cathédrale St-Pierre–St-Paul** is one of France's last Gothic cathedrals, begun in 1434, well after most other medieval cathedrals had been completed. The facade is ponderous and austere, in contrast to the light, wide, limestone interior, whose vaults rise higher (120 feet) than those of Notre-Dame in Paris. ⊠ *Pl. St-Pierre* ☎ *02–40–47–84–64* 💶 *Free* ⊙ *Crypt Mon.–Sat. 10–12:30 and 2–6, Sun. 2–6:30.*

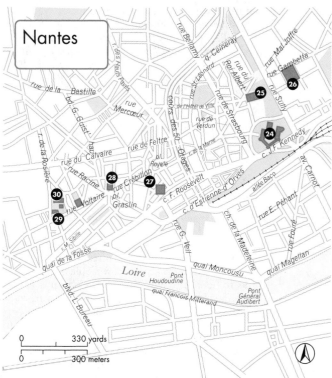

26 A fine collection of paintings from the Renaissance period onward, in-cluding works by Jacopo Tintoretto, Georges de La Tour, Jean-Auguste-Dominique Ingres, and Gustave Courbet, is at the **Musée des Beaux-Arts** (Museum of Fine Arts). ⊠ *10 rue Georges-Clemenceau* ☎ *02–40–41–65–65* ⊡ *€3.10* ☉ *Mon., Wed., and weekends 10–6, Thurs. 10–8.*

27 Erected in 1843, the **Passage Pommeraye** (⊠ *Rue Crébillon*) is an ele-**28** gant shopping gallery in the 19th-century part of town. The **Grand Théâtre** (⊠ Pl. Graslin), down the block from the Passage Pommeraye, was built in 1783.

29 The 15th-century **Manoir de la Touche** (⊠ Rue Voltaire) was once the abode ★ **30** of the bishops of Nantes. The mock-Romanesque **Musée Thomas-Dobrée** across the way was built by arts connoisseur Thomas Dobrée in the 19th century. On the facade he had chiseled the old Breton saying, ANN DIANAF A ROG AC'HANOUN ("The Unknown devours me"), and his vast collection offers proof, as it ranges from Old Master paintings to tapestries, from medieval manuscripts to Gothic goldwork, including the *coffret* reliquary of the heart of Anne de Bretagne; one room is de-voted to the Revolutionary War in Vendée. ⊠ *18 rue Voltaire* ☎ *02–40–71–03–50* ⊕ *www.nantes.fr* ⊡ *€3, free Sun.* ☉ *Tues.–Fri. 1:30–5:30, weekends 2:30–5:30.*

Where to Stay & Eat

$–$$$ ✕ **La Cigale.** Miniature palm trees, gleaming woodwork, colorful enamel tiles, and painted ceilings have led to the official recognition of La Cigale brasserie (built in 1895) as a *monument historique.* You can savor its Belle Époque blandishments without spending a fortune—the prix-fixe lunch menus are a good value. But the banks of fresh oysters and well-stacked dessert cart may tempt you to order à la carte. ⊠ *4 pl. Graslin* ☎ *02–51–84–94–94* ⌘ *Reservations essential* ▭ *MC, V.*

★ **$–$$$** ✕ **Villa Mon Rêve.** This cozy, yellow-walled restaurant is in delightful parkland off the D751 east of Nantes. Chef Gérard Ryngel concocts elegantly inventive regional fare (the roast duck in caramel and Muscadet is a good choice), with which you can sample one of more than 50 varieties of Muscadet, the local white wine. Request a table on the terrace when you reserve. ⊠ *Levée Divatte, 506 bd. de la Loire, 8 km (5 mi) east of Nantes, Basse-Goulaine* ☎ *02–40–03–55–50* ⊕ *www.villa-mon-reve. com* ▭ *AE, DC, MC, V* ⊗ *Closed part of Feb. and Nov.*

$–$$ ✕ **L'Embellie.** Sweet and simple, this spot lures diners with its modern, inventive attitude and friendly service. Chef Yvonnick Briand's "creative regional" cuisine extends to his own smokehouse for salmon and duck, so the foie gras is homemade—he likes to serve it light, atop a mesclun salad. The menu is dependent on Briand's daily trips to markets, so don't hesitate to try any of the fresh fish specials, such as the sea bass steamed in rosemary or other briny delights laced with French West Indian spices. Pineapple *croquant* with rum-laced creole ice cream makes a fitting finale. ⊠ *14 rue Armand-Brossard* ☎ *02–40–48–20–02* ▭ *AE, MC, V* ⊗ *Closed Sun. and 2nd wk in Aug. No dinner Mon.*

$$ ▥ **Pérouse.** Bare parquet floors, plain off-white walls, simple high-tech lighting, and minimal contemporary furnishings make rooms feel spacious; bathrooms are equally modern. The amiable staff speak fluent English. A pedestrian zone full of boutiques and restaurants is right outside the door, and place Royale is just 300 yards away. ⊠ *3 allée Dusquesne, 44000* ☎ *02–40–89–75–00* ▤ *02–40–89–76–00* ⊕ *www. hotel-laperouse* ⇆ *47 rooms* ⌂ *Minibars, cable TV, Internet, some pets allowed (fee)* ▭ *AE, DC, MC, V* ⎷⎔ *BP.*

Nightlife & the Arts

The informal **Pub Univers** (⊠ 16 rue Jean-Jacques Rousseau ☎ 02–40–73–49–55) has live-jazz concerts every other week. **Le Tie Break** (⊠ 1 rue des Petites-Écuries ☎ 02–40–47–77–00) is a popular piano bar. The **Théâtre Graslin** (⊠ 1 rue Molière ☎ 02–40–69–77–18) is Nantes's principal concert hall and opera house.

The Outdoors

You can take a 100-minute cruise along the pretty Erdre River, past a string of gardens and châteaux, with the **Bateaux Nantais.** There are also four-course lunch and dinner cruises that last about 2½ hours (€38). Call ahead to get the schedule for the special activities planned for children—treasure hunts, musical shows, or one of the Halloween dress-up cruises. ⊠ *Quai de la Motte Rouge* ☎ *02–40–14–51–14* ▧ *€10* ⊗ *June–Aug., Mon. and Fri. 3, weekends 3 and 5; May, Sept., and Oct., weekends 3.*

Shopping

The commercial quarter of Nantes stretches from place Royale to place Graslin. Various antiques shops can be found on rue Voltaire. The Devineau family has been selling wax fruit and vegetables at **Devineau** (⊠ 2 pl. Ste-Croix) since 1803; for €12, you can take home a basket of purple grapes or a cauliflower, as well as handmade candles and wildflower honey. For chocolate, head to **Gautier-Debotté** (⊠ 9 rue de la Fosse); try the local Muscadet grapes dipped in brandy and covered with chocolate.

BRITTANY A TO Z

To research prices, get advice from other travelers, and book travel arrangements, visit www.fodors.com.

AIRPORTS

Rennes, Brest, Nantes, Quimper, Dinard, and Lorient all have domestic airports. Air France (⇨ Air Travel *in* Smart Travel Tips A to Z) flies to them all, except Dinard.

BIKE TRAVEL

Bikes can be rented at most major train stations.

BUS TRAVEL

There are many bus routes linking Brittany, serviced by a bewildering number of bus companies. Buses connect the big city of Rennes (often via TIV and Cariane Atlantique Otages) with Nantes, St-Malo, Dinan (via CAT), Dinard (via CAT and TIV), Cancale (via TIV), Mont-St-Michel, Fougères, and Vitré (via TIV)—you can also bus to Mont-St-Michel from Fougères and (via Les Courriers Bretons) from St-Malo. Dinan is linked with Rennes (via TAE); Paimpol with St-Brieuc (via CAT); Morlaix with Roscoff (via Cars du Kreisker); Quimper with Brest (via CAT); Pont-Aven with Brest, Quimper, and Concarneau (via Transports Caoudal); Vannes with Quiberon (via Cariane Atlantique); and Carnac (via Transports Le Bayon). There are many other links, so, as always, check in with the regional tourist office or information window at a big gateway rail or bus station to get printed bus schedules.

🚍 Bus Information **Cariane Atlantique** ☎ 02-97-47-29-64. **Cariane Atlantique Otages-Nantes** ☎ 02-40-20-46-99. **Cars du Kreisker** ☎ 02-98-69-00-93. **CAT** ☎ 02-96-39-21-05. **Les Courriers Bretons** ☎ 02-99-19-70-80. **TIV** ☎ 02-99-26-11-11. **Transports Caoudal** ☎ 02-98-90-88-89. **Transports Le Bayon** ☎ 02-97-24-26-20.

CAR RENTAL

🚍 Local Agencies **Avis** ☎ 08-20-05-05-05 national reservations number in Paris ⊠ Pl. Rhin-et-Danube, La Baule ☎ 02-40-60-36-28 ⊠ Aéroport, Dinard ☎ 02-99-46-25-20 ⊠ 20 bis rue de Siam, Brest ☎ 02-98-44-63-02 ⊠ Rue Lourmel, Nantes ☎ 02-40-89-25-50 ⊕ www.avis.fr. **Europcar** ⊠ Pl. de la Gare, Rennes ☎ 02-23-44-02-73. **Hertz** ⊠ Rte. de Trégastel, Lannion ☎ 02-96-05-82-82 ⊠ 53 rue de la Gare, St-Brieuc ☎ 02-96-94-25-89.

CAR TRAVEL

Rennes, the gateway to Brittany, is 310 km (195 mi) west of Paris. It can be reached in about three hours via Le Mans and A81 and A11 (A11 continues southwest from Le Mans to Nantes). Rennes is linked by good roads to Morlaix and Brest (E50), Quimper (N24/N165), and Vannes (N24/N166). A car is a good idea if you want to see out-of-the-way places.

EMERGENCIES

🚩 **Hospitals Rennes** ✉ 2 rue Henri-Le-Guilloux, 35000 Rennes ☎ 02-99-28-43-21. **Brest** ✉ 5 av. Foch, 29200 Brest ☎ 02-98-22-33-33. **Nantes** ✉ 1 pl. Alexis-Ricordeau, 44000 Nantes ☎ 02-40-08-33-33.

SPORTS & THE OUTDOORS

For information on various regional activities such as sailing, hiking, camping, fishing, and daily excursions, contact the Regional Tourist Boards.

🚩 **Comité Départemental du Tourisme des Côtes-d'Armor** ✉ 7 rue St-Benoît, St-Brieuc ☎ 02-96-62-72-00 🖷 02-96-33-59-10 ⊕ www.cotesdarmor.com. **Comité Départemental du Tourisme de Finistère** ✉ 11 rue Théodore-Le Hars, Quimper ☎ 02-98-76-20-70 🖷 02-98-52-19-19 ⊕ www.finisteretourisme.com.

TOURS

Information about organized tours of Brittany is available from the very helpful Maison de la Bretagne in Paris.

🚩 **Fees & Schedules Maison de la Bretagne** ✉ 203 bd. St-Germain, 75007 Paris ☎ 01-53-63-11-50 🖷 01-53-63-11-57.

TRAIN TRAVEL

The high-speed TGV (Train à Grande Vitesse) departs 15 times daily from Paris (Gare Montparnasse) for both Nantes and Rennes, making this region easily accessible. The trip to either city takes about 2¼ hours. There are 8 daily TGVs to Brest (4½ hours) and 10 regional trains to St-Malo. To find out about other regional timetables and fares or to reserve your seat, contact the SNCF Web site. Most towns in this region are accessible by train, though you need a car to get to some of the more secluded spots. Some trains from Paris stop in Vitré before forking at Rennes on their way to either Brest (via Morlaix) or Quimper (via Vannes). Change at Rennes for Dol-de-Bretagne and St-Malo; at Dol-de-Bretagne for Dinan and Dinard (bus link); at Morlaix for Roscoff; at Rosporden, 19 km (12 mi) south of Quimper, for Concarneau (bus link); and at Auray for Quiberon (train service July and August only; otherwise, bus link).

🚩 **Train Information SNCF** ☎ 08-91-36-20-20 ⊕ www.ter-sncf.com/UK/bretagne.

TRAVEL AGENCIES

🚩 **Local Agent Referrals Havas** ✉ 33 rue Jean-Macé, Brest ☎ 02-98-80-05-43 ⊕ www.havasvoyages.com ✉ 14 rue Ville-Pépin, St-Malo ☎ 02-99-19-79-90. **Carlson Wagons-lit** ✉ 1 impasse Joseph-Marie-Fourage, Nantes ☎ 02-51-89-39-00 ✉ 2 rue Jules-Simon, Rennes ☎ 08-26-82-56-20.

VISITOR INFORMATION

The principal regional tourist offices are in Brest, Nantes, and Rennes.

🚩 Tourist Information **Brest** ✉ 8 av. Georges-Clemenceau ☎ 02-98-44-24-96 🖷 02-98-44-53-73 ⊕ www.mairie-brest.fr. **Nantes** ✉ 2 allée Baco ☎ 02-51-72-95-30 🖷 02-40-20-44-54 ⊕ www.cdt44.com. **Rennes** ✉ 11 rue St-Yves ☎ 02-99-67-11-11 🖷 02-99-67-11-10 ⊕ www.ville-rennes.fr. **Carnac** ✉ 74 av. des Druides ☎ 02-97-52-13-52 🖷 02-97-52-86-10 ⊕ www.ot-carnac.fr. **Concarneau** ✉ Quai d'Aiguillon ☎ 02-98-97-01-44 🖷 02-98-50-88-81 ⊕ www.ville-concarneau.fr. **Dinan** ✉ 9 rue du Château ☎ 02-96-87-69-76 🖷 02-96-87-69-77 ⊕ www.dinan-tourisme.com. **Dinard** ✉ 2 bd. Féart ☎ 02-99-46-94-12 🖷 02-99-88-21-07 ⊕ www.ot-dinard.com. **Dol-de-Bretagne** ✉ 3 Grande-Rue ☎ 02-99-48-15-37 ⊕ www.pays-de-dol.com. **Douarnenez** ✉ 2 rue du Dr-Mével ☎ 02-98-92-13-35 🖷 02-98-92-70-47 ⊕ www.douarnenez-tourisme.com. **La Baule** ✉ 8 pl. de la Victoire ☎ 02-40-24-34-44 🖷 02-40-11-08-10 ⊕ www.labaule.tm.fr. **Lorient** ✉ Maison de la Mer, quai de Rohan ☎ 02-97-21-07-84 🖷 02-97-21-99-44 ⊕ www.lorient-tourisme.com. **Morlaix** ✉ Pl. des Otages ☎ 02-98-62-14-94 ⊕ www.ville.morlaix.fr. **Pont-Aven** ✉ 5 place de l'Hôtel de Ville ☎ 02-98-06-04-70 🖷 02-98-06-17-25 ⊕ www.tourisme.fr/office-de-tourisme/pont-aven.htm. **Quiberon** ✉ 14 rue de Verdun ☎ 02-97-50-07-84 🖷 02-97-30-58-22 ⊕ www.quiberon.com. **Quimper** ✉ 7 rue Déesse ☎ 02-98-53-04-05 🖷 02-98-53-31-33 ⊕ www.quimper-tourisme.com. **St-Malo** ✉ Esplanade St-Vincent ☎ 02-99-56-64-48 🖷 02-99-56-67-00 ⊕ www.saint-malo-tourisme.com. **Trébeurden** ✉ Pl. de Crec'h Hery ☎ 02-96-23-51-64 🖷 02-96-15-44-87 ⊕ www.tourisme.fr/office-de-tourisme/trebeurden.htm. **Vannes** ✉ 1 rue Thiers ☎ 02-97-47-24-34 🖷 02-97-47-29-49 ⊕ www.mairie-vannes.fr. **Vitré** ✉ Pl. St-Yves ☎ 02-99-75-04-46 🖷 02-99-74-02-01 ⊕ www.ot-vitre.fr.

Normandy

WORD OF MOUTH

"I believe you make a mistake if you do not spend a night at Mont-St-Michel. The Mont is completely different after the daytrippers leave in the late afternoon. In the early evening you can see the tide come rushing back in to make the Mont an island again—this alone makes staying into the evening worthwhile. The soft gold glow of the lights throughout the village at night is very beautiful."

—LarryJ

"Trouville is absolutely tranquil and lovely. The Sunday morning flea market was so much fun. Deauville is nearby, more expensive, but lovely as well, and you can still visit Coco Chanel's first clothing store."

—Viajero2

Introduction by
Nancy Coons

Updated by
Simon Hewitt

SAY THE NAME "NORMANDY," and which Channel-side scenario comes to mind? Could it be long ships bristling with oars scudding into the darkness toward Hastings? Such ships were immortalized in the Bayeux Tapestry, which traces step-by-step the epic tale of William the Conqueror, who in 1066 sailed across the Channel to claim his right to England's throne. Or do you think of iron-gray convoys massing silently along the shore at dawn, lowering tailgates to pour troops of young Allied infantrymen into the line of German machine-gun fire? At Omaha Beach you may marvel at the odds faced by the handful of soldiers who in June 1944 were able to rise above the waterfront carnage to capture the cliff-top battery, paving the way for the Allies' reconquest of Europe.

Perhaps you think of Joan of Arc—imprisoned by the English yet burned at the Rouen stake by the Church she believed in? In a modern church you may light a candle on the very spot where, in 1431, the Maiden Warrior sizzled into history at the hands of panicky politicians and time-serving clerics: a dark deed that marked a turning point in the Hundred Years' War. Or are you reminded of the dramatic silhouette of Mont-St-Michel looming above the tidal flats, its cobbles echoing with the footfalls of medieval scholars? You may make a latter-day pilgrimage to the famous island-abbey, one of the most evocative monuments in Europe behind its crow's-nest ramparts.

The destinies of England and Normandie (as the French spell it) have been intertwined ever since William, duke of Normandy, insisted that King Edward the Confessor had promised him the succession to the English crown. When a royal council instead anointed the Anglo-Saxon Harold Godwinsson, the irate William stormed across the Channel with 7,000 well-equipped archers, well-mounted knights, and well-paid Frankish mercenaries. They landed at Pevensey Bay on September 28, 1066, and two weeks later, at Hastings, saw off a ragtag mix of battle-weary English troops hastily reinforced with peasant conscripts swinging stones tied to sticks. Harold met his maker, an arrow through his eye. William progressed to London and was crowned King of England on Christmas Day.

There followed nearly 400 years of Norman sovereignty in England. For generations England and Normandy vacillated and blurred, merged, and diverged. Today you'll still feel the strong flow of English culture over the Channel, from the Deauville horse races frequented by high-born ladies in gloves, to silver spoons mounded high with teatime cream; from the bowfront, slope-roof shops along the harbor at Honfleur to the black-and-white row houses of Rouen, which would seem just as much at home in the setting of *David Copperfield* as they would in *Madame Bovary*.

And just as in the British Isles, no matter how you concentrate on history and culture, sooner or later you'll find yourself beguiled by the countryside, by Normandy's rolling green hills dotted with dairy cows and half-timber farmhouses. Like the locals, you'll be tempted by seafood fresh off the boat, by sauces rich with crème fraîche, by cheeses

Named for the Norsemen who claimed this corner of Gaul and sent a famous conqueror over the Channel in 1066, and eternally tied in our memory to the D-Day landings, Normandy has always played shuttle diplomat in Anglo-French relations. From its half-timber houses to its green apple orchards to its rich dairy cream, it seems to mirror the culture of its English neighbor across the water. Treasures beckon: Mont-St-Michel, elegant Deauville, Rouen's great cathedral and museums, the legendary Bayeux Tapestry . . . and those warming glasses of calvados. With three days you can get a feel for the region. Five days gives you time to meander through the countryside and down the coast. And with nine days, if you don't spend much time in any one place, you can see most of Normandy.

5

Numbers in the text correspond to numbers in the margin and on the Normandy and Rouen maps.

**If you have
3 days**

Head straight to 🗺 **Rouen** ❺ ▶–⓯ and spend a day and a half in the region's cultural capital. Then follow the Seine Valley past the abbey of **Jumièges** ⓰ and the sights of **Caudebec-en-Caux** ⓲ including the Abbaye de St-Wandrille, then head west to 🗺 **Honfleur** ㉓, the fishing port that caught the Impressionists' eyes.

**If you have
9 days**

Follow the Seine en route from Paris to 🗺 **Rouen** ❺ ▶–⓯, visiting the gorgeous little villages of **Lyons-la-Forêt** ❷ and **Les Andelys** ❸. On the third day wind along the route des Abbayes to the abbeys of **Jumièges** ⓰ and St-Wandrille near **Caudebec-en-Caux** ⓲. Drive northwest to the fishing town of **Fécamp** ⓴, then head down the Côte d'Alabâtre to the spectacular cliffs of **Étretat** ㉑. Continue south, cross the Pont de Normandie, and spend the night in tony 🗺 **Honfleur** ㉓. On the next day travel along the Côte Fleurie to the fashionable seaside resorts of **Deauville-Trouville** ㉔ and Belle Époque **Houlgate** ㉕, reaching 🗺 **Caen** ㉖, site of some of World War II's fiercest fighting and William the Conqueror's fortress, by mid-afternoon. The following day visit Gold, Juno, and Sword beaches and historic **Arromanches-les-Bains** ㉗, then party in 🗺 **Bayeux** ㉘ overnight. Visit the storied Bayeux Tapestry and continue your exploration of the **D-Day beaches** ㉙–㉜ before continuing up the Cotentin coast to 🗺 **Cherbourg** ㉞. On Day 7 ramble south to the cathedral town of **Coutances** ㊱ and on to seafaring **Granville** ㊲, then continue to the majestic abbey on a rock, 🗺 **Mont-St-Michel** ㊳. Next morning hurry east to the Suisse Normande's rocky expanse of hills, passing through Clécy before stopping for a picnic lunch at the Roche d'Oëtre, a rock with a spectacular view of the Orne Valley. If time allows, take in William the Conqueror's hilltop castle at **Falaise** ㊴.

---

redolent of farm and pasture. And perhaps with cheeks pink from the apple-scented country air, you'll eventually succumb to the local antidote to northern damp and chill: a mug of tangy hard cider sipped by a crackling fire, and the bracing tonic of Normandy's famous apple brandy, calvados.

Exploring Normandy

You won't want to miss medieval Rouen, seaside Honfleur, or magnificent Mont-St-Michel. But if you get away from these popular spots you can lose yourself along the cliff-lined coast and in the green spaces inland, where the closest thing to a crowd is a farmer with his herd of brown-and-white cows. From Rouen northeast to the coast—the area known as Upper Normandy—medieval castles and abbeys stand guard above rolling countryside, while resort and fishing towns line the white cliffs of the Côte d'Alabâtre. Popular seaside resorts and the D-Day landing sites occupy the sandy beaches along the Côte Fleurie; apple orchards and dairy farms sprinkle the countryside of the area known as Lower Normandy. The Cotentin Peninsula to the west juts out into the English Channel. Central Normandy encompasses the peaceful, hilly region of La Suisse Normande, along the scenic Orne River.

About the Restaurants & Hotels

With Normandy a mecca for weekending Parisians throughout the year, especially between March and November, it makes sense to book your table in advance Friday dinner through Sunday lunch. The plus side to this is that Normandy differs from other French coastal regions in that, buoyed by this Parisian clientele, few restaurants close for more than a month in winter. You can therefore expect a good choice of restaurants throughout the region at any time, most of all in the lively cities of Rouen and Caen (though July and August here are the quietest months). Note that from October through Easter Mont-St-Michel offers a limited number of options for weekday lunch, and even fewer for dinner; in summer, on the other hand, it's packed, making advance reservations—or a very early arrival—essential.

Accommodations to suit every taste can be found throughout Normandy. The beach-resort season is short—late June through early September only—but weekends are busy most of the year, and especially during school holidays. In much of June and September lodging is usually available on short notice, and good discounts are given off-season, particularly for stays of more than a single night. If you are traveling in the summer months, reserve your hotel well in advance, request a written confirmation, and inform your hotel of any possible late check-in, or they may give your room away. Assume all hotel rooms have air-conditioning, telephones, TV, and private bath, unless otherwise noted.

WHAT IT COSTS In euros					
	$$$$	**$$$**	**$$**	**$**	**¢**
RESTAURANTS	over €30	€23–€30	€17–€23	€11–€17	under €11
HOTELS	over €190	€120–€190	€80–€120	€50–€80	under €50

Restaurant prices are per person for a main course at dinner, including tax (19.6%) and service; note that if a restaurant offers only prix-fixe (set-price) meals, it has been given the price category that reflects the full prix-fixe price. Hotel prices are for a standard double room in high season, including tax (19.6%) and service charge. Hotels operate on the European Plan (EP, with no meal provided) unless

5

Cuisine & Calvados

The Normans are notoriously heavy eaters. Between the warm-up and the main course traditionally comes the *trou normand* (Norman gap), a break for calvados—apple brandy (a typically Norman riddle asks, "Did the trou normand create calvados, or did calvados create the trou normand?"). Norman food isn't light; many dishes are prepared with cream sauces and apple flavoring—hence *à la normande* (with cream sauce or apples). Rich local milk makes excellent cheese: Pont-l'Évêque is made in the Pays d'Auge with milk still warm and creamy; Livarot uses milk that has stood a while—don't be put off by its pungent smell. Best known of them all is creamy Camembert, invented by a farmer's wife in the late 18th century. Normandy is not a wine-growing area, but produces excellent hard cider (the best comes from the Vallée d'Auge), calvados, and its lighter cousin *pommeau*, which is two-thirds apple juice and one-third calvados. Local specialties differ from place to place. Rouen is famous for its canard *à la rouennaise* (duck in blood sauce); Caen, for its *tripes à la mode de Caen* (tripe cooked with carrots in a seasoned cider stock); Mont-St-Michel, for *omelettes Mère Poulard* and *pré-salé* (salt-meadow lamb). Try *andouille de Vire,* a delicate, smoked chitterling sausage served in thin slices like salami. Fish and seafood lovers can feast on oysters, lobster, shrimp, and sole *dieppoise* (sole poached in a sauce with cream and mussels).

June 1944

One of the great events of modern history, the D-Day invasion of June 1944, was enacted on the beaches of Normandy—at Arromanches vestiges of the great artificial ports called "mulberries" still remain and in the town a diorama and description of the landings make those desperate days live again. Omaha Beach (site of an eye-opening museum), Utah Beach, as well as many sites on the Cotentin Peninsula, and the memorials to Allied dead, all bear witness to the furious fighting that once raged in this now-peaceful corner of France. Today, as seagulls sweep over the cliffs where American rangers scrambled desperately up ropes to silence murderous German batteries, visitors now wander through the blockhouses and peer into the bomb craters, the carnage of *Saving Private Ryan* thankfully now a distant, if still horrifying, memory.

Monet's Coast

Monet traveled to Normandy to immortalize on canvas the sea terraces at Le Havre and the ocean cliffs at Étretat—for good reason. Normandy has 600 km (375 mi) of some of the most striking coastline in France. Bordering the English Channel, there are major ports—Le Havre, Dieppe, and Cherbourg—plus coastal towns with seafaring pasts, like Honfleur (itself the subject of dozens of canvases by Boudin, a noted Impressionist), and fishing villages, like Fécamp. Sandwiched between are beaches and fashionable resort towns such as Cabourg, Deauville, and Étretat. Though the waters are chilly, you might be tempted to take a dip on a hot, sunny day, but don't try this at Mont-St-Michel, where the tide rushes in at lightning speed.

we note that they use the Breakfast Plan (BP), or also offer such options as Modified American Plan (MAP, with breakfast and dinner daily, known as *demi-pension*), or Full American Plan (FAP, or *pension complète*, with three meals a day). Inquire when booking if these all-inclusive mealplans (which always entail higher rates) are mandatory or optional.

Timing

July and August—when French families vacation—are the busiest months here, but also the most activity-filled: concerts are presented every evening at Mont-St-Michel, and the region's most important horse races are held in Deauville, culminating with the Gold Cup Polo Championship and the Grand Prix the last Sunday in August. June 6, the anniversary of the Allied invasion, is the most popular time to visit the D-Day beaches. If you're trying to avoid crowds, your best bet is late spring and early autumn, when it's still fairly temperate. May finds the apple trees in full bloom and miles of waving flaxseed fields spotted with tiny butter-yellow flowers. Some of the biggest events of the region take place during these seasons: at the end of May Joan of Arc is honored at a festival in Rouen, and there's jazz under the apple trees in Coutances; the first week of September in Deauville is the American Film Festival, and the last week sees the nationally acclaimed blues music festival in Lisieux. Winter offers quieter pleasures: the lush Normandy countryside rolling softly under a thick tent of clouds so low you can almost touch them; the strange desolate poetry of the empty D-Day beaches; intimate evenings in casinos with the fun-loving locals for company, or a good conversation with the less-harried hosts in a quiet country inn; and a last burning snifter of calvados in front of a roaring Norman hearth.

HAUTE NORMANDY

The French divide Normandy into two: Haute-Normandie and Basse-Normandie. Upper (Haute) Normandy is delineated by the Seine as it meanders northwest from Ile-de-France between chalky cliffs and verdant hills to Rouen—the region's cultural and commercial capital—and on to the port of Le Havre. Pebbly beaches and even more impressive chalk cliffs line the Côte d'Alabâtre from Le Havre to Dieppe. In the 19th century, the dramatic scenery and bathing resorts along the coast attracted and inspired writers and artists like Maupassant, Monet, and Braque. Lower (Basse) Normandy encompasses the sandy Côte Fleurie (Flowered Coast), stretching from the resort towns of Trouville and Deauville to the D-Day landing beaches and the Cotentin Peninsula, jutting out into the English Channel. Inland, lush green meadows and apple orchards form the heart of calvados country west of the pilgrim town of Lisieux. After the World War II D-Day landings, some of the fiercest fighting took place around Caen and Bayeux, as many monuments and memorials testify. To the south, in the prosperous Pays d'Auge, dairy farms produce the region's famous cheeses. The hilly Suisse Normande provides the region's most rugged scenery. Rising to the west is the fabled Mont-St-Michel. Our tour starts along the Seine Valley in Basse Normandie, then heads north to the Channel Coast, which we follow all the way from Dieppe to Mont-St-Michel. Here you can continue into Brittany or return east, cutting back inland to Falaise, Liseux, and Évreux.

Gisors

❶ *64 km (40 mi) northwest of Paris via A15 and D915, 35 km (24 mi) northeast of Vernon.*

Gisors, a peaceful market town in the Vexin region evoked by Impressionist painter Camille Pissarro (who lived just to the north in Eragny-sur-Epte), has several half-timber houses along the sloping rue de Vienne and a fine hilltop castle standing sentinel at the confines of Normandy. The town church, lovingly restored after being damaged in World War II, is a jumble of styles; the elaborate, two-towered 16th-century facade and florid vaulting in the side chapels clash with the sober choir, consecrated in 1249. The royal fleur-de-lis emblem keeps cropping up unexpectedly—carved on a spiral-patterned pillar, in a modern stained-glass window, or woven into the stone balustrade above the side chapels outside.

The **Château Fort** was begun in 1097 by the English king William Rufus, son of William the Conqueror, to defend Normandy's southeast frontier. This castle has two parts. One is the drumlike ring of curtain walls with a dozen towers, surrounded by a large ditch and enclosing a park of flowers and evergreens. The park is open daily without charge and offers a fine view of the church above the roofs of the old town. The other is the 70-foot artificial mound in the middle, the foursquare keep, with a staircase leading to the top—and also down to the dungeon. ⊠ *Pl. Blanmont* ☎ *02–32–55–59–36* ✉ *Guided tours of keep and dungeon €5* ☉ *Apr.–Sept., Wed.–Mon. 10–noon and 2–6; Oct.–Nov. and Feb.–Mar., weekends 10–noon and 2–5.*

In the pretty village of Boury-en-Vexin, 8 km (5 mi) southwest of Gisors, the steep-roofed **Château de Boury,** built in 1685 by Jules Hardouin-Mansart, displays the same monumental dignity as the architect's work at Versailles. The two-tiered facade, with arched ground-floor windows and Ionic pilasters above, surveys a trim lawn with cone-shape topiaries. The château has remained in the same family since it was built, which probably explains the prevailing homey, lived-in feel that complements its grand furniture, portraits, and crystal chandeliers. ⊠ *Boury-en-Vexin* ☎ *02–32–55–15–10* ✉ *€5* ☉ *July and Aug., Wed.–Mon. 2:30–6:30; mid-Apr.–June, Sept. and Oct., weekends 2:30–6:30.*

Lyons-la-Forêt

❷ *34 km (21 mi) northwest of Gisors, 36 km (23 mi) east of Rouen.*

Fodor'sChoice
★

Few villages in France are as pretty as Lyons-la-Forêt, built in a verdant clearing surrounded by a noble beech forest. Lyons has entire streets of rickety half-timber houses and, on its main square, a venerable market hall built of robust, medieval oak. In fact, the square is more of a tumbling triangle—all bustle in summer, but come winter, when most hotels and restaurants are shut, as forlorn as the leafless beech trees all around. Lyons is built on two levels, and if you arrive from Gisors, take care not to miss the lower road—a quilt of medieval black-and-white frontages leading to the village church and its life-size wooden statues.

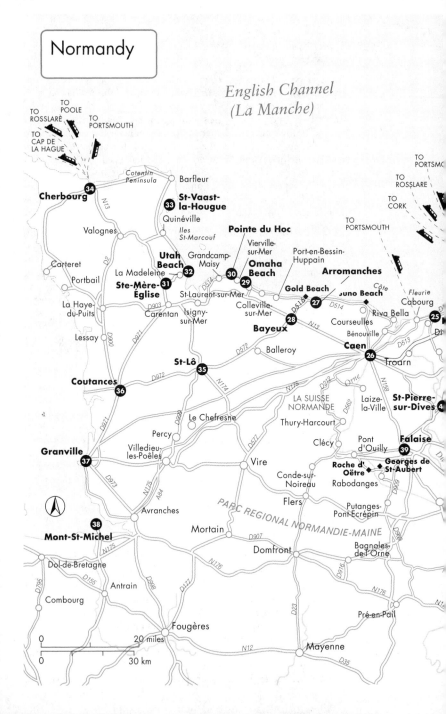

Normandy

English Channel
(La Manche)

TO
ROSSLARE
TO
POOLE
TO
PORTSMOUTH
TO
CAP DE
LA HAGUE

TO
PORTSMO
TO
ROSSLARE
TO
CORK
TO
PORTSMOUTH

*Cotentin
Peninsula*

Barfleur

Cherbourg **34**

N13

St-Vaast-
la-Hougue **33**

Quinéville

*Îles
St-Marcouf*

Valognes

Pointe du Hoc

Vierville-
sur-Mer

Port-en-Bessin-
Huppain

Carteret

D2

Utah
Beach **32**

Grandcamp-
Maisy

**Omaha
Beach**

Arromanches

Portbail

La Madeleine

Ste-Mère-
Église **31**

D514

30

29

Gold Beach

Côte

uno Beach

Fleurie

La Haye-
du-Puits

D903

St-Laurent-sur-Mer

Colleville-
sur-Mer

D516

27

D514

Riva Bella

Cabourg

25

Carentan

Isigny-
sur-Mer

28

Bayeux

Courseulles

Bénouville

Dı

Lessay

D900

D971

D572

Balleroy

N13

Caen **26**

D513

Troarn

St-Lô **35**

D972

N174

N175

D562

Orne

N158

D2

LA SUISSE
NORMANDE

Laize-
la-Ville

**St-Pierre-
sur-Dives** **4**

Coutances **36**

D971

D999

Le Chefresne

D577

Thury-Harcourt

D562

Clécy

Pont
d'Ouilly

Falaise

39

Percy

Villedieu-
les-Poêles

D524

Vire

Conde-sur-
Noireau

**Roche d'
Oëtre** ♦

♦ **Georges de
St-Aubert**

Rabodanges

D909

Granville **37**

D973

N175

A84

Flers

Putanges-
Pont-Ecrépin

D909

Avranches

PARC REGIONAL NORMANDIE-MAINE

Mortain

D907

Domfront

Bagnoles-
de-l'Orne

D916

N176

38

Mont-St-Michel

N175

D907

D23

Dol-de-Bretagne

D795

D155

Antrain

D898

D177

N176

N176

Pré-en-Pail

N1

Combourg

Fougères

0 ────── 20 miles
0 ────── 30 km

N12

Mayenne

D35

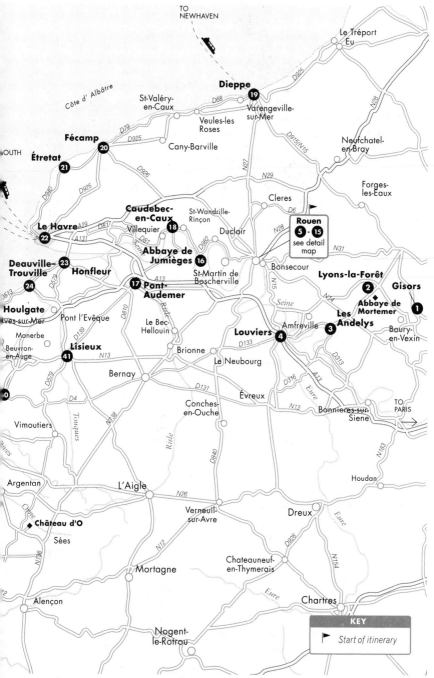

TO NEWHAVEN

Le Tréport
Eu

Dieppe 🄳

St-Valéry-
en-Caux

Côte d' Albâtre

Veules-les-
Roses

Varengeville-
sur-Mer

Neufchatel-
en-Bray

Fécamp 🄳

D79

D925

Cany-Barville

Forges-
les-Eaux

Étretat 🄳

D940 · D925 · D926

Cleres

D6

**Caudebec-
en-Caux** 🄳

St-Wandrille-
Rinçon

Rouen 🄳 - 🄳
see detail map

N31

Villequier

Duclair

Le Havre 🄳

**Abbaye de
Jumièges** 🄳

St-Martin de
Boscherville

Bonsecour

Lyons-la-Forêt 🄳

Gisors 🄳

**Deauville–
Trouville** 🄳

Honfleur

**Pont-
Audemer** 🄳

Seine

**Abbaye de
Mortemer**

**Les
Andelys** 🄳

Houlgate 🄳
ves-sur-Mer

Pont l'Evêque

Le Bec-
Hellouin

Amfreville

Boury-
en-Vexin

Manerbe

Beuvron-
en-Auge

Lisieux 🄳

N13

Brionne

Louviers 🄳

D133

Bernay

Le Neubourg

Vimoutiers

D131

Évreux

Conches-
en-Ouche

N13

Bonnieres-sur-
Siene

TO
PARIS

Argentan

L'Aigle

N26

♦ **Château d'O**

Sées

Verneuil-
sur-Avre

Dreux

Houdan

Mortagne

Chateauneuf-
en-Thymerais

Alençon

Eure

Chartres

Nogent-
le-Rotrou

KEY
▶ *Start of itinerary*

The scenic ruins of the Cistercian **Abbaye de Mortemer** are by a small lake in the heart of the forest, 5 km (3 mi) south of Lyons-la-Forêt. The 100-yard-long church was built at the start of the 13th century but destroyed during the Revolution. Some of the abbey buildings survive, including the large 15th-century pigeon loft that was also used as a prison. A small museum evokes aspects of monastic life. ⊠ *Rue de Mortemer, Lisors* ☎ *02–32–49–54–34* 🖅 *€5, €7 with museum* ☉ *Easter–Oct., daily 11–6:30; Nov.–Easter, daily 1:30–5:30.*

Where to Stay

$–$$$ 🏨 **La Licorne.** This venerable 17th-century inn at the top of the village square has comfortable rooms with rustic wooden furniture. The smaller rooms, Nos. 2, 3, and 9, are also the most reasonably priced. The owners will kindly direct you to nearby restaurants and to the town square for its wonderful bakery (you won't soon forget those croissants). ⊠ *27 pl. Isaac-Benserade, 27480* ☎ *02–32–49–62–02* 🖷 *02–32–49–80–09* 🛏 *19 rooms* ⚒ *Restaurant; no a/c* ⊟ *AE, DC, MC, V* ☉ *Closed Dec. 20–Jan. 25* ⏍ *MAP.*

Les Andelys

❸ *20 km (13 mi) southwest of Lyons-la-Forêt, 88 km (55 mi) northwest of Paris, 40 km (25 mi) southeast of Rouen.*

In one of the most picturesque loops of the Seine, the small town of Les Andelys, birthplace of France's leading classical painter, Nicolas Poussin, is set against magnificent chalky cliffs. The town is divided between riverside Petit Andely, with its 13th-century church of St-Sauveur and domed, 18th-century Hôpital St-Jacques, and bustling Grand Andely, whose Collégiale Notre-Dame gleams with a score of exquisite stained-glass windows created between 1540 and 1560. **Château Gaillard**, a formidable fortress built by England's King Richard the Lion-Hearted in 1196, overlooks Petit Andely from the cliff top, with spectacular views up- and down-river. Despite its solid defenses, the castle fell to French king Philippe-Auguste in 1204, after a lengthy siege during which it suffered considerable damage; further sections were torn down at the end of the 16th century, and only one of its five main towers remains intact. But the location and the history bring the ruins alive. ⊠ *Rue Richard-Coeur-de-Lion* ☎ *02–32–54–04–16* 🖅 *€3* ☉ *Mid-Mar.–mid-Nov., Thurs.–Mon. 10–1 and 2–6.*

Where to Stay & Eat

$–$$ ✕ **Le Grain de Sel.** Set on a quiet street at the foot of the hilltop château in Gaillon, 7 km (11 mi) south of Les Andelys, this beam-fronted restaurant is worth seeking out for its homey ambience, warm red decor, and good-value three-course menus (€19 and €27). Traditionalists will opt for such French staples as snails, oysters, and foie gras, while the more adventurous will be happy with more inventive specialities like scallops fried in cider butter or langoustine salad with chitterling sausage. ⊠ *12 rue Pierre-Brossolette, Gaillon* ☎ *02–32–53–51–10* ⊟ *MC, V* ☉ *Closed Sun. and part of Aug. No dinner Mon.–Wed.*

$–$$ ✕⊡ **La Chaîne d'Or.** This charming inn in Le Petit Andely, founded in 1751 within sight of Château Gaillard, has a terrace that overlooks the banks of the Seine (just the place to enjoy your predinner aperitif on warmer days). Rooms are large and bright; for time-burnished charm, request one with a view of the church or courtyard. In the airy, flower-laden restaurant (closed Monday, no dinner Sunday, no lunch Tuesday), Christophe Bouche's neoclassical Norman cuisine ranges from grilled lobster with truffles and olives to chicken with vanilla and cinnamon. ⊠ *27 rue Grande, 27700* ☎ *02-32-54-00-31* 🖷 *02-32-54-05-68* ↴ *10 rooms* ⚴ *Restaurant; no a/c* ▤ *AE, MC, V* ⊘ *Closed Jan.* ❑❙ *BP.*

en route
From Les Andelys head southwest to cross the Seine at Courcelles and reach **Gaillon,** a lively village with a twisting main street crushed beneath a hilltop château with turrets and roofs so abrupt that even the bravest pigeons think twice about landing on them. When it was built as the Archbishop of Rouen's summer palace in 1509, the **Château de Gaillon** was the first major Renaissance building in France. It was partly dismantled during the Revolution, and later used as a prison, but is slated to reopen to the public in 2006 after restoration lasting two decades. Only about half the original buildings remain, and the finest furniture and fittings were long ago transferred to the national Renaissance museum in Ecouen, north of Paris, but what's left is imposing enough. There are attractive views of the village rooftops from the terrace in front of the gatehouse and, further up the hill, wooded gardens with a panoramic view over the valley toward the Seine. From Gaillon take the scenic D82 to Ailly and the quaint village of **Acquigny** with its crafts shops and château park (open Easter–September, weekends 2–6), continuing on D7 to nearby Louviers.

Louviers

❹ *22 km (14 mi) west of Les Andelys via D313, 104 km (65 mi) north-west of Paris.*

Picturesque Louviers owed its medieval prosperity to the weaving of woolen cloth, and a good illustration of this wealthy past is the elaborate stonework of the town church, the **Eglise Notre-Dame,** whose intricately sculpted porch and gables show just why the late Gothic style of the 15th century is known as *flamboyant.* The Eure River splits scenically into several branches in downtown Louviers.

Where to Stay & Eat

$$–$$$ ✕⊡ **L'Hostellerie St-Pierre.** This hotel, a few miles east of Louviers by the Seine, is a good place to stay when on your way to Rouen. Room 27 has French doors that open onto a terrace with the best view of the river; its size, like that of most others, is modest but all have comfortingly traditional decor. You have the choice of two prix-fixe menus, ranging from €38 (four courses) to the epicurean five-course menu at €53, complete with a "trou Normand" calvados break. ⊠ *6 chemin de la Digue, 6 km (4 mi) east of Louviers, 27430 St-Pierre-du-Vauvray*

☎ 02–32–59–93–29 🖷 02–32–59–41–93 🌐 *www.hotel-saintpierre.com* ⇆ *14 rooms* ♿ *Restaurant, some pets allowed (fee); no a/c* ▭ *AE, MC, V* ⊙ *Closed mid-Nov.–mid-Mar.* 🍽 *MAP.*

en route

From Louviers head east to cross the Seine at St-Pierre-du-Vauvray. Stay on the right bank of the Seine for 8 km (5 mi) to Amfreville; then turn right up steep D508 to what is known as the **Côte des Deux Amants** (Lovers' Mount) for a spectacular view of the Seine Valley and its chalky cliffs. Follow the road to Pont St-Pierre, then head northwest on D138 toward Rouen, pausing in the suburb of **Bonsecours** to check out its 1840s hilltop **Basilique Notre-Dame,** a fine neo-Gothic church overlooking the Seine.

Rouen

32 km (20 mi) north of Louviers, 130 km (80 mi) northwest of Paris, 86 km (53 mi) east of Le Havre.

Fodor'sChoice ★

"O Rouen, art thou then to be my final abode!" was the agonized cry of Joan of Arc as the English dragged her out to be burned alive on May 30, 1431. The exact spot of the pyre is marked by a concrete and metal cross in front of the Église Jeanne-d'Arc, an eye-catching modern church on place du Vieux-Marché, just one of the many landmarks that make Rouen a fascinating destination. Although much of the city was destroyed during World War II, a wealth of medieval half-timber houses still lines the cobblestone streets, many of which are pedestrian-only—most famously rue du Gros-Horloge between place du Vieux-Marché and the cathedral, suitably embellished halfway along with a giant Renaissance clock. Rouen is also a busy port—the fifth largest in France.

Rouen is known as the City of a Hundred Spires, because many of its important edifices are churches. Lording it over them all is the highest spire in France, erected in 1876, a cast-iron tour-de-force rising 490 feet
5 above the crossing of the **Cathédrale Notre-Dame.** If you're familiar with the works of Impressionist artist Claude Monet, you will immediately recognize the cathedral's immense west facade, rendered in an increasingly hazy fashion in his series *Cathédrales de Rouen*—you can enjoy a ringside view and a coffee at the Brasserie Paul (just opposite) and the facade is illuminated by a free light show, based on Monet's canvases, for an hour June through mid-September every evening at nightfall. The original 12th-century construction was replaced after a devastating fire in 1200; only the left-hand spire, the **Tour St-Romain** (St. Romanus Tower), survived the flames. Construction on the imposing 250-foot steeple on the right, known as the **Tour de Beurre** (Butter Tower), was begun in the 15th century and completed in the 17th, when a group of wealthy citizens donated large sums of money for the privilege of continuing to eat butter during Lent. Interior highlights include the 13th-century choir, with its pointed arcades; vibrant stained glass depicting the crucified Christ (restored after heavy damage during World War II); and massive stone columns topped by some intriguing carved faces. The first flight of the famous **Escalier de la Librairie** (Library Stairway), attributed to Guillaume

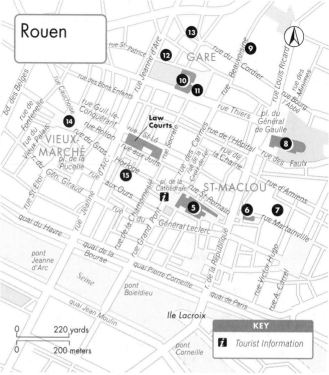

Pontifs (also responsible for most of the 15th-century work seen in the cathedral), rises from a tiny balcony just to the left of the transept. ⊠ *Pl. de la Cathédrale, St-Maclou* ☎ *02–32–08–32–40* ⏱ *Daily 8–6.*

6 The late-Gothic church of **St-Maclou**, across rue de la République behind the cathedral, bears testimony to the wild excesses of Flamboyant architecture; take time to examine the central and left-hand portals of the main facade, covered with little bronze lion heads and pagan engravings. Inside, note the 16th-century organ, with its Renaissance wood carving, and the fine marble columns. ⊠ *Pl. St-Maclou, St-Maclou* ☎ *02–35–71–71–72* ⏱ *Mon.–Sat. 10–noon and 2–6, Sun. 3–5:30.*

7 A former ossuary (a charnel house used for the bodies of plague victims), the **Aître St-Maclou** (⊠ 186 rue Martainville, St-Maclou) is a reminder of the plague that devastated Europe during the Middle Ages; these days it holds Rouen's Fine Art Academy. French composer Camille Saint-Saëns (1835–1921) is said to have been inspired by the ossuary when he was working on his *Danse Macabre.* The half-timber courtyard, where you can wander at leisure and maybe visit a picture exhibition, contains graphic carvings of skulls, bones, and gravediggers' tools.

8 A stupendous example of high Gothic architecture is the **Abbaye St-Ouen** next to the imposing Neoclassical City Hall. The abbey's stained-glass windows, dating from the 14th to 16th centuries, are the most spectacular grace notes of the spare interior, along with the 19th-century pipe organ, among the finest in France. ⊠ *Pl. du Général-de-Gaulle, Hôtel de Ville* ☎ *02–32–08–13–90* ⊙ *Mid-Mar.–Oct., Wed.–Mon. 8–12:30 and 2–6; Nov.–mid-Dec. and mid-Jan.–mid-Mar., Wed. and weekends 10–12:30 and 2–4:30.*

❾ Gallo-Roman glassware and mosaics, medieval tapestries and enamels, and Moorish ceramics vie for attention at the **Musée des Antiquités,** an extensive antiquities museum housed in a former monastery dating from the 17th century. ⊠ *198 rue Beauvoisine, Gare* ☎ *02–35–98–55–10* ▱ *€3* ⊙ *Mon.–Sat. 10–12:15 and 1:30–5:30, Sun. 2–6.*

❿ One of Rouen's cultural mainstays is the **Musée des Beaux-Arts** (Fine Arts Museum), which has a scintillating collection of paintings and sculptures from the 16th to the 20th centuries, including works by native son Géricault as well as by David, Rubens, Caravaggio, Velasquez, Poussin, Delacroix, Chassériau, Degas, and Modigliani, not to mention the impressive Impressionist gallery, with Monet, Renoir, and Sisley, and the Postimpressionist School of Rouen headed by Albert Lebourg and Gustave Loiseau. ⊠ *Square Verdrel, Gare* ☎ *02–35–71–28–40* ⊕ *www.rouen-musees.com* ▱ *€3* ⊙ *Wed.–Mon. 10–6.*

⓫ The **Musée Le Secq des Tournelles** (Wrought-Iron Museum), near the Musée des Beaux-Arts, claims to have the world's finest collection of wrought iron, with exhibits spanning from the 4th through 19th centuries. The displays, imaginatively housed in a converted medieval church, include many articles used in daily life, accessories, and professional instruments of surgeons, barbers, carpenters, clockmakers, and gardeners. ⊠ *2 rue Jacques-Villon, Gare* ☎ *02–35–88–42–92* ▱ *€2.30* ⊙ *Wed.–Mon. 10–1 and 2–6.*

⓬ A superb array of local pottery and European porcelain can be admired at the **Musée de la Céramique** (Ceramics Museum), in an elegant mansion near the Musée des Beaux-Arts. ⊠ *1 rue Faucon, Gare* ☎ *02–35–07–31–74* ▱ *€2.30* ⊙ *Wed.–Mon. 10–1 and 2–6.*

⓭ Sole remnant of the early 13th-century castle built by French king Philippe-Auguste, the beefy **Tour Jeanne-d'Arc,** a pointed-top circular tower, houses a small exhibit of documents and models charting the history of the castle where Joan of Arc was tried and held prisoner in 1430. ⊠ *Rue Bouvreuil, Gare* ☎ *02–35–98–55–10* ▱ *€1.50* ⊙ *Mon.–Sat. 10–12:30 and 2–6, Sun. 2–6.*

⓮ Dedicated to Joan of Arc, the **Église Jeanne d'Arc** (Joan of Arc Church) was built in the 1970s on the spot where she was burned to death in 1431. Not all is new, however: the church showcases some remarkable 16th-century stained-glass windows taken from the former Église St-Vincent, bombed out in 1944. The adjacent **Musée Jeanne-d'Arc** evokes Joan's history with waxworks and documents. ⊠ *33 pl. du Vieux-Marché, Vieux-Marché* ☎ *02–35–88–02–70* ⊕ *www.jeanne-darc.com* ▱ *€4* ⊙ *Daily 10–noon and 2–6:30.*

The friendly **L'Adelshoffen** (⊠ Pl. du Vieux-Marché, Vieux-Marché ☎ 02–35–70–25–22) offers zestful service and a splendid view of the picturesque market-square, scene of the burning of Joan of Arc, whose story is retraced in colorful frescoes on the café wall.

⑮ The name of the pedestrian rue du Gros-Horloge, Rouen's most popular street, comes from the **Gros-Horloge** itself, a giant Renaissance clock. In 1527 the Rouennais had a splendid arch built especially for it, and today its golden face looks out over the street. You can see the clock's inner workings from the 15th-century belfry. Though the street is crammed with stores, a few old houses, dating from the 16th century, remain. Wander through the surrounding **Vieux Rouen** (Old Rouen), a warren of tiny streets lined with more than 700 half-timber houses, many artfully transformed into fashionable shops. ⊠ *Rue du Gros-Horloge, Vieux-Marché* ☑ *€2* ⊙ *Wed.–Mon. 10–1 and 2–6.*

Where to Stay & Eat

$$$–$$$$ ✕ **La Couronne.** Behind a half-timber facade gushing geraniums, the "oldest inn in France," dating from 1345, is crammed with leather-upholstered chairs and a scattering of sculpture. The traditional Norman cuisine—lobster soufflé, sheep's feet, duck in blood sauce—makes few modern concessions and can be admired in the €28 menu. ⊠ *31 pl. du Vieux-Marché, Vieux-Marché* ☎ *02–35–71–40–90* ⊕ *www.lacouronne. com* ⊟ *AE, DC, MC, V.*

$$ ✕ **Chez Dufour.** Established since 1906 in an old street near the cathedral, this wood-beamed, stone-walled restaurant is a local institution.
Fodor's Choice Character is here a-plenty—model ships sway overhead, a variety of quirky
★ brass lamps bedeck the walls, the city's steepest, narrowest staircase leads up to the restrooms, and over-dressed bourgeois(es) arrive early to claim the best tables (in the corner beneath the large, pastel-paned windows). But it's the cuisine, even more than the ambience, that keeps them coming. Fish is a specialty—try the grilled sole or brill in cider nicely lubricated by some startlingly tasty Quincy (a white wine from south of the Loire). Among the welter of fixed-price menus, the choice extends from plump green asparagus, in lightly whisked butter sauce, to a sagging platter of Normandy cheeses, followed by a copious helping of home-made apple tart or chocolate profiteroles. ⊠ *67 rue St-Nicolas, St-Maclou* ☎ *02–35–71–90–62* ⊟ *AE, MC, V* ⊙ *Closed Mon., no dinner Sun.*

$–$$ ✕ **La Toque d'Or.** Overlooking the Église Jeanne d'Arc, this large, bustling restaurant has been renowned since time immemorial for Jean-Jacques Baton's Normandy classics such as veal with Camembert flamed in calvados, breast of duck glazed in cider, or spicy braised turbot. Try the excellent home-smoked salmon (they'll give you a tour of the smokehouse if you wish) and the Norman apple *tarte soufflée*. Cheaper meals are available in the *grill* upstairs. ⊠ *11 pl. du Vieux-Marché, Vieux-Marché* ☎ *02–35–71–46–29* ⊟ *AE, DC, V.*

$$ ✕▥ **Dieppe.** Established in 1880, the Dieppe remains up-to-date thanks to resolute management by five generations of the Guéret family. Staff members also are helpful, and they speak English. The compact rooms are cheerful and modern; street noise can be a problem, however, despite double-glazed windows. The restaurant, Les Quatre Saisons (no lunch Saturday), serves seasonal dishes with an emphasis on fish, such as the sole Michèle (poached in a light wine sauce), but is best known for its pressed duckling. ☒ *Pl. Bernard-Tissot, Gare, 76000* ☎ *02–35–71–96–00, 800/334–7234 for U.S. reservations* 🖃 *02–35–89–65–21* ⊕ *www.bestwestern.fr* ⤳ *41 rooms* ⟡ *Restaurant, cable TV, bar, some pets allowed; no a/c* ⊟ *AE, DC, MC, V* ❄❀ *MAP.*

$ ✕⊠ **Vieux Carré.** In the heart of Old Rouen, this cute hotel has small, practical, and comfortable rooms simply furnished with a taste for the exotic: lamps from Egypt, tables from Morocco, and 1940s English armoires. Ask for one of the rooms on the third floor for a view of the cathedral. Breakfast and lunch (but not dinner) are served in the leafy courtyard, weather permitting, or in the cozy little bistro (closed Monday) off the reception area. Lunches are light and simple, based on creative tourtes—tomato, olive, and Camembert, for example. Brunch is served both Saturday and Sunday until 2 PM. ☒ *34 rue Ganterie, Gare, 76000* ☎ *02–35–71–67–70* 🖃 *02–35–71–19–17* ⤳ *14 rooms* ⟡ *Restaurant, cable TV, Internet, some pets allowed; no a/c* ⊟ *AE, DC, MC, V.*

$$–$$$ ⊠ **Mercure Centre.** In the jumble of streets near the cathedral—a navigational challenge if you arrive by car—this modern chain hotel has small, comfortable rooms done in breezy pastels. This hotel is handy for exploring the old streets of the city center. ☒ *7 rue de la Croix-de-Fer, St-Maclou, 76000* ☎ *02–35–52–69–52* 🖃 *02–35–89–41–46* ⤳ *139 rooms* ⟡ *Cable TV, bar, parking (fee)* ⊟ *AE, DC, MC, V* ❄❀ *BP.*

$–$$ ⊠ **Cathédrale.** This hotel is in a medieval building on a narrow pedestrian street behind the cathedral. (You can sleep soundly, though: the cathedral bells do not boom out the hour at night.) Rooms are petite, but neat and comfortable. Breakfast is served in the beamed dining room. ☒ *12 rue St-Romain, St-Maclou, 76000* ☎ *02–35–71–57–95* 🖃 *02–35–70–15–54* ⊕ *www.hotel-de-la-cathedrale.fr* ⤳ *25 rooms* ⟡ *Cable TV, bar, Internet, parking (fee), some pets allowed (fee); no a/c* ⊟ *MC, V.*

Nightlife & the Arts

The **Fête Jeanne d'Arc** (Joan of Arc Festival) takes place on the Sunday nearest to May 30, with parades, street plays, concerts, exhibitions, and a medieval market. Evening **concerts** and organ recitals are held at St-Maclou in August and at St-Ouen throughout the year; details are available from the Rouen tourist office. Operas, plays, and concerts are staged at the **Théâtre des Arts** (☒ 7 rue du Dr-Rambert, Vieux-Marché ☎ 02–35–71–41–36 ⊕ www.operaderouen.com). Visit the popular local haunt **Bar de la Crosse** (☒ 53 rue de l'Hôpital, St-Maclou ☎ 02–35–70–16–68) for an aperitif and a good chat with some friendly Rouennais. At the **Big Ben Pub** (☒ 95 bis rue du Gros-Horloge, Vieux-Marché ☎ 02–35–88–44–50), relax with a glass of wine on the first floor, listen to music on the second, and on the third witness how the French do karaoke (not to be missed).

Abbaye de Jumièges

★ ⑯ *24 km (15 mi) west of Rouen, head west on D982 through Duclair and then exit left onto D143.*

Imposing ruins are all that is left of the once mighty Benedictine Abbaye de Jumièges, founded in 654 by St-Philbert, plundered by Vikings in 841, then rebuilt by William Longswood, duke of Normandy, around 940, though not consecrated until 1067. The French Revolution forced the evacuation of the remaining 16 monks, whereupon the abbey was auctioned off to a timber merchant, who promptly demolished part of the building to sell the stone. The imposing remains are especially impressive during the illuminated nighttime visits staged on Saturday in July and August. ⊠ *24 rue Guillaume-le-Conquérant* ☎ *02–35–37–24–02* ⊕ *www.monum.fr* ☎ *€4.60* ⊙ *Mid-Apr.–mid-Sept., daily 9:30–7; mid-Sept.–mid-Apr., daily 9:30–1 and 2:30–5:30.*

Pont-Audemer

⓱ *35 km (22 mi) southwest of Jumièges via ferry, D313 and N175; 53 km (33 mi) west of Rouen; 27 km (17 mi) southeast of Honfleur.*

Pont-Audemer, on the banks of the Risle River, luckily escaped destruction by warfare and bulldozers. Today many of its buildings are still as they were in the 16th century, when the town made its mark as an important trading center. Stroll along impasse St-Ouen and impasse de l'Épée, narrow streets by the church that are lined with timber-frame medieval houses. The pleasingly dilapidated church of **St-Ouen** has an unfinished single-tower facade and an entertaining clash of modern stained-glass windows and exuberant, late-medieval stonework. ⊠ *Rue de la République* ☎ *02–32–41–12–88.*

Where to Stay & Eat

★ **$$–$$$$** ✕⛺ **Belle-Isle sur Risle.** Idyllically set on a river island and, in summer, covered with romantic ivy tendrils, this turn-of-the-20th-century private manor makes you feel like a personal guest—an impression somehow heightened by a few rough edges. The newer, more modern rooms have wall-to-wall carpeting and department-store furniture, but the older ones have wooden floors with rugs and assorted traditional pieces; those on the first floor have balconies. The main reception salon has a special patina all its own, thanks to gilt-framed paintings and golden silk walls. In the restaurant, chef Loïc Rapper turns out foie gras with citrus fruit, honey-roast pigeon, and apple tart with mango. ⊠ *112 rte. de Rouen, 27500* ☎ *02–32–56–96–22* ☎ *02–32–42–88–96* ⊕ *www.bellile.com* ⇗ *18 rooms, 2 suites* ☖ *Restaurant, minibars, tennis court, pool, sauna, some pets allowed (fee); no a/c* ☱ *MC, V* ⌾ *MAP.*

Caudebec-en-Caux

⓲ *39 km (24 mi) northeast of Pont-Audemer via D139, 15 km (9 mi) northwest of Jumièges via D143/D982, 35 km (22 mi) northwest of Rouen.*

The riverside town of Caudebec-en-Caux is dominated by the spire of Notre-Dame-de-Caudebec, a wonderful medieval church with some of the most vivid 16th-century stained glass in Normandy. Don't miss the deep blood-reds of the window showing Pharaoh's army drowning in the Red Sea. The nearby **Musée de la Marine** charts the history of the Seine Valley with ship models, old photographs, and traditional costumes, and a section on the *mascaret*, the bore or tidal wave that used to power up the estuary during the equinox. ✉ *Av. Winston-Churchill* ☎ *02–35–95–90–13* 🏷 *€3.20* 🕐 *Wed.–Mon. 2–5:30.*

The **Musée Victor-Hugo**   he village of Villequier, 5 km (3 mi) west of Caudebec, occupies the prettily furnished riverside mansion where Hugo's daughter Léopoldine lived with her husband Charles Vacqueyrie. Pictures, letters, drawings, and documents evoke the great poet and his daughter, who, along with her husband, drowned when their boat was overturned by the Seine's notorious mascaret as they returned from Caudebec in September 1843. Léopoldine, who is buried in the village churchyard up the hill, was just 19. ✉ *Rue Ernest-Binet* ☎ *02–35–56–78–31* 🏷 *€3* 🕐 *Wed.–Sat. and Mon., 10–12:30 and 2–5:30. Sun. 2–5:30.*

The Benedictine **Abbaye de St-Wandrille**, 3 km (2 mi) east of Caudebec, is still active today, with 40 monks in residence. Founded in the 7th century, the abbey was sacked by the Normans and rebuilt in the 10th century—although what you see today is an ensemble of styles from the 11th through the early 18th centuries (mainly the latter). You can hear the monks sing their Gregorian chants at morning mass if you arrive early (9:45 AM weekdays, 10 AM Sunday and holidays), or wander at leisure in the gardens. Don't forget to visit the abbey shop down the hill; everything it sells—from floor polish to spiritual aids—is made by the monks. ✉ *2 rue St-Jacques* ☎ *02–35–96–23–11* ⊕ *www.st-wandrille.com* 🏷 *€3.50* 🕐 *Guided tours Apr.–Nov. 11, Tues.–Sat. at 3:30, Sun. at 11:30 and 3:30.*

Dieppe

19 *67 km (44 mi) north of Caudebec, 64 km (40 mi) north of Rouen.*

Bustling Dieppe, beneath its cliff-top castle, is part fishing and commercial port and part Norman seaside town—though its era in the fashionable spotlight is past, and the ramshackle church of St-Jacques, painted by Pissarro, has seen better days. Still, a year-round ferry service was reintroduced in 2001 to complement the summer-only jetfoil across the Channel to Newhaven, near Brighton. The seafront promenade, boulevard du Maréchal-Foch, separates an immense lawn from an unspoiled pebble beach where in 1942 many Canadian soldiers were killed during the so-called Jubilee Raid.

The 15th-century **Château-Musée** (Castle-Museum), overlooking the Channel at the western end of the bay, contains a well-known collection of ivories. In the 17th century Dieppe imported vast quantities of elephant tusks from Africa and Asia, and as many as 350 craftsmen settled here to work the ivory; their efforts can be seen in the form of ship models, nautical accessories, religious artifacts, and everyday objects. The museum also has some fine French paintings and a room devoted to sketches by Georges Braque. ✉ *Rue de Chastes* ☎ *02–35–84–19–76* 🏷 *€3* 🕐 *June–Sept., daily 10–noon and 2–6; Oct.–May, Mon. and Wed.–Sat. 10–noon and 2–5, Sun. 10–noon and 2–6.*

Where to Stay & Eat

$-$$ ✕🏨 **Auberge du Clos Normand.** This 15th-century inn in the tiny village of Martin-Église, 4 mi (6 km) southeast of Dieppe, is best known for its pretty garden, complete with a stream and flower-bedecked balconies. Even the bedrooms—which may seem a little chilly out of season—have flowery wallpaper, in the time-honored rural French tradition. The kitchen, all agleam with copper pots, is at one end of the restaurant (closed Sunday, no dinner Mon.), so you can glimpse the chef at work on his sturdy Norman dishes, with duck, sole, and chicken as specialties; round off your meal with a soufflé Grand-Marnier. ⊠ *22 rue Henri-IV, 76370* ☎*02–35–40–40–40* 🖷*02–35–04–48–49* ↪*8 rooms* ⚼ *Restaurant, cable TV; no a/c* ☰ *AE, MC, V* ⊘ *Closed mid-Nov.–mid-Dec.* ⑂⊙⊣ *MAP.*

Nightlife & the Arts

At night Dieppe's **casino** (⊠ 3 bd. de Verdun ☎ 02–35–82–33–60) at the Grand Hotel comes alive with shows and gambling. If you love jazz, come for the **Festival Européen de Jazz Traditionnel** (European Traditional Jazz Festival), held in mid-June in Luneray, 8 km (5 mi) southwest of Dieppe. During the second week of September, the **International Kite Festival** fills the skies with amazing high-flying contraptions. For information contact the Dieppe tourist office.

Fécamp

⑳ 🟢 *64 km (40 mi) southwest of Dieppe, 42 km (26 mi) northeast of Le Havre.*

★ The ancient cod-fishing port of Fécamp was once a major pilgrimage site. The magnificent abbey church, **Abbaye de La Trinité** (⊠ Rue Leroux), bears witness to Fécamp's religious past. The Benedictine abbey was founded by the Duke of Normandy in the 11th century and became the home of the monastic order of the Précieux Sang de la Trinité (Precious Blood of the Trinity—referring to Christ's blood, which supposedly arrived here in the 7th century in a reliquary from the Holy Land).

Fécamp is also the home of Benedictine liqueur. The **Palais de la Bénédictine** (Benedictine Palace), across from the tourist office, is a florid building dating from 1892 that mixes neo-Gothic and Renaissance styles. Watery pastiche or taste-tingling architectural cocktail? Whether you're shaken or stirred, this remains one of Normandy's most popular attractions. The interior is just as exhausting as the facade. Paintings, sculptures, ivories, advertising posters, and fake bottles of Benedictine compete for attention with a display of the ingredients used for the liqueur, and a chance to sample it. There's also a shop selling Benedictine products and souvenirs. ⊠ *110 rue Alexandre-le-Grand* ☎ *02–35–10–26–10* ⊕ *www.benedictine.fr* ⊠ *€5.60, including tasting* ⊙ *July and Aug., daily 10–7; Sept.–Dec., Feb.–June, daily 10–11:30 and 2–6* ⊙ *Closed Jan.*

Where to Stay & Eat

$ ✕ **L'Escalier.** This delightfully simple little restaurant overlooking the harbor serves traditional Norman cuisine, such as mussels in calvados and homemade fish soup. ⊠ *101 quai Bérigny* ☎ *02–35–28–26–79* ⚼ *Reservations essential* ☰ *DC, MC, V* ⊙ *Closed 2 wks in Nov.*

★ **$$–$$$** ✕⊡ **Les Hêtres.** Top chef Bertrand Warin runs this restaurant in Ingouville, east of Fécamp. Reservations are essential—as are jacket and tie—for the elegant 17th-century dining room (closed Monday and Tuesday, January through Easter), where half-timber walls and Louis XIII chairs contrast with sleek, modern furnishings. The five pretty guest rooms, each with old wooden furniture and engravings, are for diners only; the largest has a terrace overlooking the garden. ⊠ *24 rue des Fleurs, 28 km (17 mi) east of Fécamp, 76460 Ingouville* 🖀 *02–35–57–09–30* 🖷 *02–35–57–09–31* ⊕ *www.leshetres.com* ⤳ *5 rooms* ⚭ *Restaurant, cable TV, Internet, some pets allowed (fee); no a/c* ⊟ *MC, V* ⊙ *Closed Jan.* ⫷◎⫸ *MAP.*

$ ✕⊞ **Auberge de la Rouge.** The Enderlins welcome you to this little inn just south of Fécamp. Rooms overlook the garden and are actually good-size lofts that sleep four. The restaurant (closed Monday; no dinner Sunday) showcases modern classics by chef Thierry Enderlin, such as scallops with ham and leek shoots, and local specialties like roast turbot, veal and mushrooms in wine, or the duck with foie gras. Top it off, if you can, with a local favorite, soufflé *à la Bénédictine.* ⊠ *1 rue du Bois-de-Boclion, 1 km (½ mi) south of Fécamp, 76400 St-Léonard* 🖀 *02–35–28–07–59* 🖷 *02–35–28–70–55* ⊕ *www.auberge-rouge.com* ⤳ *8 rooms* ⚭ *Restaurant, minibars; no a/c* ⊟ *AE, DC, MC, V* ⫷◎⫸ *BP.*

$ ✕⊞ **La Ferme de la Chapelle.** The charm of this former priory lies neither in the simple, comfortable rooms around the courtyard, nor in its restaurant with its no-frills menu, but rather in its outstanding location high atop the cliffs overlooking Fécamp. There's a breathtaking, dramatic view over the entire coastline—explore it on an invigorating hike along the nearby coastal footpath. ⊠ *Côte de la Vierge, 76400* 🖀 *02–35–10–12–12* 🖷 *02–35–10–12–13* ⊕ *www.fermedelachapelle.fr* ⤳ *17 rooms, 5 studios* ⚭ *Restaurant, pool, some pets allowed (fee); no a/c* ⫷◎⫸ *MAP.*

Étretat

㉑ *17 km (11 mi) southwest of Fécamp via D940, 88 km (55 mi) northwest of Rouen.*

This large village, with its promenade running the length of the pebble beach, is renowned for the magnificent tall rock formations that extend out into the sea. The **Falaises d'Étretat** are white cliffs that are as famous in France as Dover's are in England—and have been painted by many artists, Claude Monet chief among them. At low tide it's possible to walk through the huge archways formed by the rocks to neighboring beaches. The biggest arch is at the **Falaise d'Aval,** to the south. For a breathtaking view of the whole bay, take the path up to the top of the Falaise d'Aval. From here you can hike for miles across the Manneporte Hills . . . or play a round of golf on one of Europe's windiest and most scenic courses, overlooking **L'Aiguille** (The Needle), a 300-foot spike of rock jutting out of the sea just off the coast. To the north towers the **Falaise d'Amont,** topped by the chapel of Notre-Dame de la Garde.

Fodor's Choice
★

Where to Stay & Eat

$ ✕ **Les Roches Blanches.** The exterior of this family-owned restaurant off the beach is a post–World War II concrete eyesore. But take a table by the window with a view of the cliffs, order Georges Trézeux's superb fresh seafood (try the sea bass roasted in calvados), and you'll be glad you came. Reservations are essential for Sunday lunch. ⊠ *Rue de l'Abbé-Cochet* 🖀 *02–35–27–07–34* ⊟ *MC, V* ⊙ *Closed Tues. and Wed. and mid-Nov.–mid-Jan.*

★ **$$$–$$$$** ✕▣ **Donjon.** This charming ivy-covered château, built in 1862 in a park overlooking the town, has lovely sea views. Rooms are individually furnished, spacious, comfortable, and quiet. For a spectacular view, request the Oriental Suite or the Horizon or Marjorie room. Jean-François Toulain's flamboyant cuisine, ranging from warm hare terrine to scallops and salmon in cider, is dished up in a cozy, romantic restaurant. Rooms are reserved on a half-board basis on weekends. ✉ *Chemin de St-Clair, 76790* ☎ *02–35–27–08–23* 🖶 *02–35–29–92–24* ⊕ *www.ledonjon-etretat.fr* ⇆ *21 rooms* ⚘ *Restaurant, some minibars, cable TV, pool, bar, Internet, some pets allowed (fee); no a/c* ▭ *AE, DC, MC, V* ⦿ *MAP.*

$–$$$ ✕▣ **Dormy House.** This unpretentious hotel is ideally located halfway up the Étretat cliffs. The rooms are simple and comfortable, but the real beauty is right out your bedroom window, thanks to views of *la mer*, so wonderful they would have Debussy humming in no time. The restaurant specializes in fresh fish and seafood platters, ranging from simple delights such as the sole stew to the full-scale *symphonie* of fish. Request a table near the window for a panoramic view of the coast. ✉ *Rte. du Havre, 76790* ☎ *02–35–27–07–88* 🖶 *02–35–29–86–19* ⊕ *www.dormy-house.com* ⇆ *61 rooms* ⚘ *Restaurant, Internet; no a/c* ▭ *AE, MC, V* ⦿ *MAP.*

¢–$$ ✕▣ **Résidence.** The cheapest rooms in this gorgeous 16th-century house in the heart of Étretat are pretty basic—both the bathroom and the shower are in the hallway—but the more expensive have in-room bathrooms, and one (€96) even has a Jacuzzi. The service is friendly; staff are young and energetic. The brasserie-type restaurant on the ground floor, Le Salamandre, is rather cutting-edge for the region; all products are certified organic, farm-raised, and homemade, from the vegetable terrine to the nougat ice cream. In winter a fire crackles in the hearth. ✉ *4 bd. du Président-René-Coty, 76790* ☎ *02–35–27–02–87* 🖶 *02–35–27–17–07* ⇆ *15 rooms* ⚘ *Restaurant, minibars; no a/c, no TV in some rooms* ▭ *AE, MC, V* ⦿ *BP.*

Sports

Don't miss the chance to play at **Golf d'Étretat** (✉ Rte. du Havre ☎ 02–35–27–04–89), where the breathtaking 6,580-yard, par-72 course drapes across the cliff tops of the Falaise d'Aval; it's closed Tuesday.

Le Havre

❷ *28 km (18 mi) southwest of Étretat via D940, 88 km (55 mi) west of Rouen, 200 km (125 mi) northwest of Paris.*

Le Havre, France's second-largest port (after Marseille), was bombarded 146 times during World War II. You may find the rebuilt city, with its uncompromising recourse to reinforced concrete and open spaces, bleak and uninviting; on the other hand, you may admire Auguste Perret's rational planning and audacious modern architecture. The hilly suburb of **Ste-Adresse**, just west of town, is resplendent with Belle Époque villas and an old fortress. It's also worth a visit for its beach, often painted by Raoul Dufy, and for its fine views of the sea and port, immortalized in a famous Monet masterpiece.

The **Musée André-Malraux,** the city art museum, is an innovative 1960s glass-and-metal structure surrounded by a moat, and includes an attractive sea-view café. Two local artists who gorgeously immortalized the Normandy coast are showcased here—Raoul Dufy (1877–1953), through a remarkable collection of his brightly colored oils, watercolors, and sketches; and Eugène Boudin (1824–98), a forerunner of Impressionism, whose compelling beach scenes and landscapes tellingly evoke the Normandy sea and skyline. ✉ *2 bd. Clemenceau* ☎ *02–35–19–62–62* ⊕ *www.ville-lehavre.fr* 🖾 *€3.80* ⊗ *Wed.–Mon. 11–6.*

★ The other outstanding building in Le Havre, and one of the most impressive 20th-century churches in France, is the **Église St-Joseph,** built to the plans of Auguste Perret in the 1950s. The 350-foot tower powers into the sky like a fat rocket. The interior is just as thrilling. No frills here: the 270-foot octagonal lantern soars above the crossing, filled almost to the top with abstract stained glass that hurls colored light over the bare concrete walls. ✉ *Bd. François-Ier* ☎ *02–35–42–20–03.*

Where to Stay & Eat

$$ ✕ **L'Odyssée.** With the port and fish market within netting distance, seafood is guaranteed to be fresh here. It's a no-frills place—the visual appeal is on your plate, in the pinks and greens of the smoked salmon and avocado sauce that accompany the chef's homemade fish terrine. Although it specializes in fresh fish, the Odyssée has its share of meat dishes—the breast of duck with three-pepper sauce is usually a winner. ✉ *41 rue du Général-Faidherbe* ☎ *02–35–21–32–42* ▤ *AE, MC, V* ⊗ *Closed Mon. and mid-Aug.–early Sept. No dinner Sun., no lunch Sat.*

$ 🏨 **Bordeaux.** The central location, overlooking the Bassin de Commerce, is this hotel's main plus—along with the welcoming owners. The light, airy rooms have modern furniture; the best have views of the port. As at all other hotels in Le Havre, prices are high for room size. ✉ *147 rue Louis-Brindeau, 76600* ☎ *02–35–22–69–44* 🖷 *02–35–42–09–27* ⊕ *www.bestwestern.fr* ➴ *30 rooms* ♻ *Some minibars, cable TV, bar, Internet, parking (fee); no a/c* ▤ *AE, DC, MC, V.*

HONFLEUR TO MONT-ST-MICHEL

Lower Normandy begins to the west of the Seine Estuary, near the Belle Époque resort towns of Trouville and Deauville, extending out to the sandy Côte Fleurie (Flower Coast), stretching northwest from the D-Day landing sites past Omaha Beach and on to Utah Beach and the Cotentin Peninsula, which juts out into the English Channel. After the World War II D-Day landings, some of the fiercest fighting took place around Caen and Bayeux, as many monuments and memorials testify. 2004 saw the 60th anniversary of the landings and the subsequent 80-day Battle of Normandy. Leading the honorary June 5th celebrations, Prince Charles inaugurated the British Garden at the Caen Memorial museum, a massive parachuting display took place at Sainte-Mère-Eglise (the site of the famous incident in The Longest Day), a replica of Philadelphia's Liberty Bell was set up at the landing beaches, and that night, L'Embrasement—fireworks set off simultaneously at 24 different sites along the

NORMANDY ON CANVAS

LONG BEFORE CLAUDE MONET created his Giverny lily pond by diverting the Epte River that marks the boundary with Ile-de-France, artists had been scudding into Normandy. For two watery reasons: the Seine and the sea. Just downstream from Vernon, where the Epte joins the Seine, Richard the Lionhearted's ruined castle at Les Andelys, immortalized by Paul Signac and Félix Vallotton, heralds the soft-lit, cliff-lined Seine Valley, impressionistically evoked by Albert Lebourg and Gustave Loiseau in the Arts Museum in Rouen—where Camille Corot once studied, and whose mighty cathedral Monet painted till he was pink, purple and blue in the face.

The Seine joins the sea at Le Havre, where Monet grew up, a protégé of Eugène Boudin, often termed the precursor of Impressionism. Boudin would boat across the estuary from Honfleur, where he hobnobbed with Gustave Courbet, Charles Daubigny, and Alfred Sisley at the Ferme St-Siméon. Le Havre in the 1860s was base-camp for Monet and his pals Frédéric Bazille and Johan Barthold Jongkind to explore the rugged coast up to Dieppe, with easels opened en route beneath the cliffs of Etretat.

The railroad from Gare St-Lazare (smokily evoked by Monet) put Dieppe within easy reach of Paris. Eugène Delacroix daubed seascapes here in 1852. Auguste Renoir visited Dieppe from 1878 to 1885; Paul Gauguin and Edgar Degas clinked glasses here in 1885; Camille Pissarro painted his way from Gisors to Dieppe in the 1890s. As the nearest port to Paris, Dieppe wowed the English too. Walter Sickert moved in from 1898 to 1905, and artists from the Camden Town Group he founded back in London often painted in Dieppe before World War I.

coast—lit up the sky. Heading south, in the prosperous Pays d'Auge, dairy farms produce the region's famous cheeses. Rising to the west is the fabled Mont-St-Michel. Inland, heading back toward central France, lush green meadows and apple orchards cover the countryside starting west of the market town of Lisieux—the heart of calvados country.

Honfleur

23
Fodor'sChoice
★
24 km (15 mi) southeast of Le Havre via A131 and the Pont de Normandie, 27 km (17 mi) northwest of Pont-Audemer, 80 km (50 mi) west of Rouen.

The colorful port of Honfleur has become increasingly crowded since the elegant Pont de Normandie suspension bridge—providing a direct link with Le Havre and Upper Normandy—opened in 1995 across the Seine. It's the world's largest cable-stayed bridge, supported by two concrete pylons taller than the Eiffel Tower and designed to resist winds of 160 mph. The town of Honfleur, full of half-timber houses and cobbled streets, was once an important departure point for maritime expeditions, including the first voyages to Canada in the 15th and 16th centuries. The 17th-century harbor is fronted on one side by two-story stone houses with low, sloping roofs and on the other by tall, narrow houses whose wooden facades are topped by slate roofs.

★ Soak up the seafaring atmosphere by strolling around the old harbor and paying a visit to the ravishing wooden church of **Ste-Catherine**, which dominates a tumbling square. The church, and ramshackle belfry across the way, were built by townspeople to show their gratitude for the departure of the English at the end of the Hundred Years' War, in 1453. ⊠ *Rue des Logettes* ☎ *02–31–89–11–83.*

Where to Stay & Eat

$–$$$ ✕ **La Terrasse de L'Assiette.** Gérard Bonnefoy, one of Honfleur's top chefs, offers has opened this new place, offering seasonal delights such as succulent scallops with hazelnut risotto and roast lamb from the salt marshes. ⊠ *8 pl. Ste-Catherine* ☎ *02–31–89–31–33* ☱ *AE, DC, MC, V* ⊘ *Closed Mon. No dinner Sun. except July and Aug.*

¢–$ ✕ **L'Ancrage.** Massive seafood platters top the bill at this bustling restaurant in a two-story 17th-century building overlooking the harbor. The cuisine is authentically Norman—simple but good. If you want a change, try the succulent calf sweetbreads. ⊠ *16 rue Montpensier* ☎ *02–31–89–00–70* ☱ *MC, V* ⊘ *Closed Wed. and last 2 wks in Mar. No dinner Tues. except July and Aug.*

★ **$$$–$$$$** ✕⌂ **Ferme St-Siméon.** The story goes that this 19th-century manor house was the birthplace of Impressionism, and that its park inspired Monet and Sisley. Rooms are opulent, with pastel colors, floral wallpaper, antiques, and period accents. Those in the converted stables are quieter but have less character. Be aware, however, that the high prices have more to do with the hotel's reputation than with the amenities it offers (although thalassotherapy treatment is among them). The sophisticated restaurant (closed Monday, no lunch Tuesday) specializes in fish; the cheese board does justice to the region. ⊠ *Rue Adolphe-Marais on D513 to Trouville, 14600* ☎ *02–31–81–78–00* ☷ *02–31–89–48–48* ⊕ *www.saint-simeon.com* ⊅ *31 rooms, 3 suites* ⌂ *Restaurant, minibars, cable TV, tennis court, pool, sauna; no a/c* ☱ *AE, MC, V* ⦿ *MAP.*

$$$–$$$$ ✕⌂ **Le Manoir de Butin.** An archetypal fin-de-siècle "villa," this dormer-roofed manor welcomes you with a pretty facade in the Anglo-Norman style. Perched on top of a small wooded hill just 200 meters from the sea, the hotel offers guest rooms with appetizing views, all traditionally and tastefully furnished, and with modern marble bathrooms. The room on the first floor has a four-poster bed and its own balcony. The restaurant (closed Wednesday, no lunch Thursday or Friday) specializes in seasonal fish dishes such as a light lobster consommé and braised freshwater cod. ⊠ *Phare du Butin, 14600* ☎ *02–31–81–63–00* ☷ *02–31–89–59–23* ⊕ *www.hotel-lemanoir.fr* ⊅ *10 rooms* ⌂ *Restaurant, cable TV, Internet, some pets allowed (fee); no a/c* ☱ *AE, MC, V* ⊘ *Closed Nov. and part of Jan.* ⦿ *MAP.*

★ **$$–$$$** ✕⌂ **L'Absinthe.** A 16th-century presbytery with stone walls and beamed ceilings houses a small and charming hotel and the acclaimed restaurant of the same name. Rooms are comfortable but small, except for the attic suite, which has a private living room. Rooms are equipped with large modern bathrooms and Jacuzzis. The elegant and cozy reception area is adorned with an imposing stone fireplace. Chef Antoine Ceffrey is famous for his seasonal seafood and fish dishes such as turbot grilled with leeks. On sunny days request a table on the terrace; the restaurant is closed for dinner on Monday. ⊠ *10 quai de la Quarantaine* ☎ *02–31–89–53–60* 📠 *02-31-89-48-48* ⊕ *www.absinthe.fr* ⟿ *6 rooms, 1 suite* ♿ *Restaurant, in-room hot tubs, cable TV, some pets allowed (fee); no a/c* ⊟ *DC, MC, V* ⊘ *Closed mid-Nov.–mid-Dec.* ⦿ *MAP.*

$–$$$ ✕🏨 **Le Clos St-Gatien.** Starting out as an old Norman half-timbered farmhouse, this hotel now sprawls over fifty rooms and a rather lush and glossy swimming pool terrace. Set just outside Honfleur, near the St-Gatien Forest, it remains a fine base for horseback riding (on-site facilities) or a round of golf at the nearby 18-hole course. Rooms in the main house are rustic, with exposed beams and traditional furniture; those in the annex lack character but have terraces that open out to the swimming pool. The restaurant (reservations pretty much essential) serves succulent Norman fare, such as blood sausage with roast apples, or grilled lamb with eggplant caviar. ⊠ *4 chemin des Bricoleurs, 14130* ☎ *02–31–65–16–08* 📠 *02-31-65-10-27* ⊕ *www.clos-st-gatien.fr* ⟿ *58 rooms* ♿ *Restaurant, 2 tennis courts, pool, gym, sauna, billiards* ⊟ *AE, MC, V.*

Nightlife & the Arts
The two-day **Fête des Marins** (Marine Festival) is held on Pentecost Sunday and Monday. On Sunday all the boats in the harbor are decked out in flags and paper roses, and a priest bestows his blessing at high tide. The next day, model boats and local children head a musical procession.

Deauville-Trouville

24 *16 km (10 mi) southwest of Honfleur via D513, 92 km (57 mi) west*
Fodor'sChoice *of Rouen.*
★

Twin towns on the beach, divided only by the River Touques, Deauville and Trouville compete for the title of Most Extravagant Norman Town. The two towns have distinctly different atmospheres, but it's easy (and common) to shuttle between them. Trouville—whose beaches were immortalized in the 19th-century paintings of Eugène Boudin (and Vincente Minelli's 1958 Oscar-winner, *Gigi*)—is the oldest seaside resort in France. In the days of Louis-Philippe, it was discovered by artists and the upper crust; by the end of the Second Empire it was the beach à la mode. Then the Duc de Mornay, half-brother of Napoléon III, and other aristos who were looking for something more exclusive, built their villas along the deserted beach across the Touques. Thus was launched Deauville, a vigorous grande dame who started kicking up her heels during the Second Empire, kept swinging through the Belle Époque, and is still frequented by a fair share of Rothschilds, princes, and French movie stars. Few of them ever actually get in the water here, since other attractions—casino, theater, music hall, polo, galas, racecourses (some of the world's most fabled horse farms are here), marina and regattas, palaces and gardens, and place Vendôme jewelry shops—compete. The Promenade des Planches—the boardwalk extending along the seafront and lined with deck chairs, bars, and striped cabanas—is the place for celebrity-spotting. With high-price hotels, designer boutiques, and one of the smartest gilt-edge casinos in Europe, Deauville's fashionable image still attracts the wealthy throughout the year.

Trouville—a short drive or five-minute boat trip across the Touques River from its more prestigious neighbor—remains more of a family resort, harboring few pretensions. If you'd like to see a typical French holiday spot rather than look for glamour, stay in Trouville. It, too, has a casino and boardwalk, an aquarium and bustling fishing port, plus a native population that makes it a livelier spot out of season than Deauville.

Where to Stay & Eat

$$$$
Fodor'sChoice
★

✕▦ **Normandy.** With a facade that is a riot of pastel-green timbering, checkerboard walls, Anglo-Norman balconies, and rooftop clochetons, the Normandy has long been one of the most beautiful landmarks of Deauville. Attracting well-heeled Parisians ever since it opened in 1912 (many of whom appreciated the underground passage to the town casino), it has kept them coming as its grand salons have been transformed by Jacques Garcia—France's chicest and most aristo decorator—and now overflow with needlepointed sofas, fin-de-siècle chandeliers, and opulent silks. The lobby is a Belle Époque blow-out, with soaring oak walls, a forest of columns, and islands of comfy, 19th-century style armchairs. The courtyard is an outdoor version, with a grassy patio surrounded by a spectacular panoply of turrets and balconies. Request a room with a sea view, and don't forget to ask about the special thalassotherapy rates with full or half-days of mud baths, salt massages, and soothing heated-seawater swims. Breakfast is served around the indoor pool. Creamy sauces are much in evidence in the mouthwatering Norman dishes served up in the restaurant, set in a grand hall which glitters like the salons of Versailles. ✉ *38 rue Jean-Mermoz, 14800 Deauville* ☎ *02–31–98–66–22, 800/223–5652 for U.S. reservations* 🖷 *02–31–98–66–23* ⊕ *www.lucienbarriere.com* 🛏 *272 rooms, 25 suites* ☖ *Restaurant, minibars, cable TV, indoor pool, sauna, bar, Internet, some pets allowed (fee); no a/c* ▤ *AE, DC, MC, V* ¶⧲ *BP.*

$–$$
▦ **Continental.** One of Deauville's oldest buildings is now this provincial hotel, close to the train station yet within easy walking distance of the town center and downtown Trouville. Rooms are small but simple, pristine, and reasonably priced for Deauville. ✉ *1 rue Désiré-Le-Hoc, 14800 Deauville* ☎ *02–31–88–21–06* 🖷 *02–31–98–93–67* ⊕ *www.hotel-continental-deauville.com* 🛏 *42 rooms* ☖ *Cable TV, Internet; no a/c* ▤ *AE, DC, MC, V* ☼ *Closed mid-Nov.–mid-Dec.*

Nightlife & the Arts

One of the biggest cultural events on the Norman calendar is the **American Film Festival,** held in Deauville during the first week of September. Formal attire is required at Deauville's **casino** (✉ 2 rue Edmond-Blanc ☎ 02–31–14–31–14). Trouville's **casino** (✉ Pl. du Maréchal-Foch ☎ 02–31–87–75–00) is slightly less highbrow than Deauville's. Night owls enjoy the smoky **Amazone** (✉ 13 rue Albert-Fracasse, Deauville); it's open until 5 AM. The **Y Club** (✉ 14 bis rue Désiré-le-Hoc, Deauville) is the place to go out dancing.

The Outdoors

At the **Club Nautique de Deauville** (✉ Quai de la Marine ☎ 02–31–88–38–19), hiring the smallest boat (16 feet) costs €25, although a day on an 80-foot yacht will set you back about €100 per person. Sailing boats large and small can also be rented from the **Club Nautique de Trouville** (✉ Digue des Roches Noires ☎ 02–31–88–13–59). Deauville becomes Europe's horse capital in August, when breeders jet in from around the world for its yearling auctions and the races at its two attractive **hippodromes** (racetracks). Head for the **Poney Club** (✉ Rue Reynolds-Mahn ☎ 02–31–98–56–24) for a wonderful horseback ride on the beach (the sunsets can be spectacular). They are open weekends and holidays, but be sure to call early to reserve your horse, or a pony for the little one.

Houlgate

㉕ *14 km (9 mi) southwest of Deauville via D513, 27 km (17 mi) northeast of Caen.*

Cheerful Houlgate, bursting with wood-beam, striped-brick Belle Époque villas and thatch-roof houses, paints a pretty picture, with the steep **Falaise des Vaches Noires** (Black Cow Cliffs) providing a rocky backdrop to the enormous sandy beach, which extends below the town casino. Leisure options include tennis, golf, and miniature golf, helping to make Houlgate a more personable alternative to neighboring **Cabourg,** evoked (as Balbec) by Marcel Proust in his epic *In Search of Lost Time.* Between the two resort towns is historic **Dives-sur-Mer,** with its oak-beam medieval market hall, rickety square, and chunky Gothic church. William the Conqueror set sail from Dives en route to England in 1066.

Where to Stay & Eat

★ ¢–$$ ✕▥ **1900.** Don't be misled by the tacky glass veranda: a wonderful dining room lurks within, with Art Nouveau lamps and a bronze and mahogany bar almost as old as the regiment of vari-sized calvados bottles that march across the top. Claire Lemarié is the good-humored *patronne*; her husband, André, is the deft cook with a penchant for fish and seafood (turbot, crayfish, and scallops); his pancake with orange zest makes a distinctive dessert (you need to order it at the start of your meal). Service from the young trainees, impeccable in their black-and-white aprons, is discreet and helpful. The kitschy bedrooms are small but comfortable. ✉ *17 rue des Bains, 14510* ☎ *02–31–28–77–77* 🖷 *02–31–28–08–07* 🛏 *18 rooms* ⚒ *Restaurant, some pets allowed; no a/c* 🖃 *AE, MC, V* ☉ *Closed Jan. and mid-Nov.–early Dec.* ⍟❘ *MAP.*

$$$–$$$$ ▥ **Grand Hôtel.** This luxurious white-stucco hotel, on the seafront in Cabourg, has a lively piano bar in summer. Many rooms have balconies overlooking the sea; Proust used to stay in No. 147, which has been carefully refurnished following his descriptions. In the restaurant, Le Balbec (closed Monday and Tuesday from November through March), you can dine on traditional French cuisine of high quality but no great imagination. ✉ *Promenade Marcel-Proust, 14390 Cabourg* ☎ *02–31–91–01–79* 🖷 *02–31–24–03–20* ⊕ *www.cabourg-web.com/ grandhotel* 🛏 *70 rooms* ⚒ *Restaurant, minibars, cable TV, golf course,*

2 tennis courts, horseback riding, piano bar, Internet, some pets allowed (fee); no a/c ⊟ AE, DC, MC, V ⏃⊘⟨ MAP.

Caen

26 *26 km (16 mi) southwest of Houlgate, 120 km (75 mi) west of Rouen,*
Fodor'sChoice *150 km (94 mi) north of Le Mans.*
★

With its abbeys and castle, Caen, a busy administrative city and the capital of Lower Normandy, is very different from the coastal resorts. William of Normandy ruled from Caen in the 11th century before he conquered England. Nine hundred years later, the two-month Battle of Caen in 1944 devastated much of the town in a fire that raged for 11 days. Today, the city is basically modern and commercial, with a vibrant student scene. The Caen Memorial, an impressive museum devoted to World War II, is considered a must-do by travelers interested in 20th-century history (many avail themselves of the excellent bus tours the museum sponsors to the D-Day beaches). But Caen's former grandeur can be seen in its extant historic monuments and along scenically restored rue Ecuyère and place St-Sauveur. A good place to begin exploring Caen is the **Hôtel d'Escoville,** a stately mansion in the city center built by wealthy merchant Nicolas Le Valois d'Escoville in the 1530s. The building was badly damaged during the war but has since been restored; the austere facade conceals an elaborate inner courtyard, reflecting the Italian influence on early Renaissance Norman architecture. The city **tourist office** is housed here and is an excellent resource. ⊠ *Pl. St-Pierre* ☎ *02–31–27–14–14* ⊕ *www.ville-caen.fr.*

Across the square, beneath a 240-foot spire, is the late-Gothic church of **St-Pierre,** a riot of ornamental stonework. Looming on a mound ahead of the church is the **château**—the ruins of William the Conqueror's fortress, built in 1060 and sensitively restored after the war. The castle gardens are a perfect spot for strolling, and the ramparts afford good views of the city. The citadel also contains two museums and the medieval church of **St-Georges,** used for exhibitions.

The **Musée des Beaux-Arts,** within the castle's walls, is a heavyweight among France's provincial fine-arts museums. Its Old Masters collection includes works by Poussin, Perugino, Rembrandt, Titian, Tintoretto, van der Weyden, and Paolo Veronese; there's also a wide range of 20th-century art. ⊠ *Entrance by castle gateway* ☎ *02–31–30–47–70* ⊟ *Free* ⊙ *Wed.–Mon. 9:30–6.*

The **Musée de Normandie** (Normandy Museum), in the mansion built for the castle governor, is dedicated to regional arts, such as ceramics and sculpture, plus some local archaeological finds. ⊠ *Entrance by castle gateway* ☎ *02–31–30–47–60* ⊕ *www.ville-caen.fr/mdn* ⊟ *Free* ⊙ *June–Sept., daily 9:30–6; Oct.–May, Wed.–Mon. 9:30–6.*

Fodor'sChoice Caen's finest church, of cathedral proportions, is part of the **Abbaye aux**
★ **Hommes** (Men's Abbey), built by William the Conqueror from local Caen stone (also used for Canterbury Cathedral, Westminster Abbey, and the Tower of London). The abbey was begun in Romanesque style in 1066

BILL CAME, SAW & CONQUERED

WHEN **WILLIAM THE BASTARD, DUKE OF NORMANDY**, was itching for action in 1066, he invaded England, and captured the English crown from King Harold in the Battle of Hastings. Overnight he became William the Conqueror. Ironically enough, the first town liberated by the British during the D-Day invasion was the town of Bayeux, where William's conquest of England is immortalized on the eponymous tapestry. Born in 1027, new Duke at eight, William survived an assassination attempt in Valognes and had to recapture Falaise Castle, where he was born, before ridding his duchy of feuding barons at the Battle of Val-ès-Dunes near Caen in 1047. In 1053 William snubbed a papal consanguinity ban to wed his distant cousin Matilda, daughter of the Count of Flanders. Alarmed by this new Norman-Flemish alliance, the King of France and Count of Anjou invaded Normandy. William defeated them at Mortemer in 1054. In 1059 new Pope Nicholas II gave William and Matilda his realpolitik blessing. Hoping to atone for having blown their chance at getting into heaven by their scandalous marriage, the lovebirds built the Abbaye aux Hommes and Abbaye aux Dames in Caen. His severe salvation anxiety calmed a bit, William stormed west in 1062 to snare Dol, Dinan, and the Mont-St-Michel. Next stop England. When Edward the Confessor, cousin of William's father, died childless in London in 1066, William raised a fleet of 700 ships, sailed up the coast and crossed the Channel to Hastings, where he whupped usurper Harold on October 14. William came, saw, conquered, and returned home to Normandy, dying of wounds in Rouen in 1087 after laying siege to Mantes (78 km/50 mi) up the Seine. He's buried in his manly abbey in Caen.

and added to in the 18th century; its elegant buildings are now part of City Hall and some rooms are brightened by the city's fine collection of paintings. Note the magnificent yet spare facade of the abbey church of **St-Étienne**, enhanced by two 11th-century towers topped by octagonal spires. Inside, what had been William the Conqueror's tomb was destroyed by 16th-century Huguenots during the Wars of Religion. However, the choir still stands; it was the first to be built in Norman Gothic style, and many subsequent choirs were modeled after it. ⊠ *Pl. Louis-Guillouard* ☎ *02–31–30–42–81* 🖃 *Church free, abbey tours €2* ⊗ *Tours daily at 9:30, 11, 2:30, and 4.*

The **Abbaye aux Dames** (Ladies' Abbey) was founded by William the Conqueror's wife, Matilda, in 1063. Once a hospital, the abbey—rebuilt in the 18th century—was restored in the 1980s by the Regional Council, which then promptly requisitioned it for office space; however, its elegant arcaded courtyard and ground-floor reception rooms can be admired during a (free) guided tour. You can also visit the squat **Église de la Trinité** (Trinity Church), a fine example of 11th-century Romanesque architecture, though its original spires were replaced by timid balustrades in the early 18th century. Note the intricate carvings on columns and arches in the chapel; the 11th-century crypt; and, in the choir, the back marble slab commemorating Queen Matilda, buried here in 1083. ⊠ *Pl. de la Reine-Mathilde* ☎ *02–31–06–98–98* ☜ *Free* ☉ *Guided tours daily at 2:30 and 4.*

★ The **Mémorial,** an imaginative museum erected in 1988 in the north side of the city, is a must-see if you're interested in World War II history. The stark, flat facade, with a narrow doorway symbolizing the Allies' breach in the Nazi's supposedly impregnable Atlantic Wall, opens onto an immense foyer containing a café, brasserie, shop, and British Typhoon aircraft suspended overhead. The museum itself is down a spiral ramp, lined with photos and documents charting the Nazi's rise to power in the 1930s. The idea—hardly subtle but visually effective—is to suggest a descent into the hell of war. The extensive displays range from wartime plastic jewelry to scale models of battleships, with scholarly sections on how the Nazis tracked down radios used by the French Resistance and on the development of the atomic bomb. A room commemorating the Holocaust, with flickering candles and twinkling overhead lights, sounds a jarring, somewhat tacky note. The D-Day landings are evoked by a tabletop Allied map of the theater of war and by a split-screen presentation of the D-Day invasion from both the Allied and Nazi standpoints. Softening the effect of the modern 1988 museum structure are tranquil gardens; the newest is the British Garden, inaugurated by Prince Charles in 2004.

Readers rave about the Mémorial's four-hour minibus tours of the D-Day beaches, run daily April–September. You can book on their Web site (under "Guided Tours") and even make a day trip out of Paris for this by catching the 9 AM out of Gare St-Lazare to Caen and returning on the 8 PM train. The museum itself is fittingly set 10 minutes away from the Pegasus Bridge and 15 minutes from the D-Day beaches. ⊠ *Esplanade Dwight-D.-Eisenhower* ☎ *02–31–06–06–44* ⊕ *www.memorial. fr* ☜ *€17* ☉ *Feb.–Oct., daily 9–7; Nov.–Dec. and late Jan., daily 9–6.*

Where to Stay & Eat

$$–$$$ ✕ **Le P'tit B.** On one of Caen's oldest pedestrian streets near the castle, this typical Norman 17th-century dining room—stone walls, beamed ceilings, and large fireplace–showcases the good-value regional cuisine of Cédric Mesnard. ⊠ *15 rue de Vaugueux* ☎ *02–31–93–50–76* ⌂ *Reservations essential* ☰ *MC, V* ☉ *Closed Mon.*

$–$$$ ✕▥ **Dauphin.** Despite being in the heart of the city, this hotel, in a former 12th-century priory, is surprisingly quiet. Some of the smallish rooms have exposed beams; those overlooking the street are soundproof; the ones in back look out on the courtyard. Service is friendly and efficient in the hotel and in the excellent though expensive restaurant (no lunch in summer). ⊠ *29 rue Gémare, 14000* ☎ *02–31–86–22–26* ⎙ *02–31–86–35–14* ⊷ *37 rooms* ⌂ *Restaurant, minibars, cable TV, bar; no a/c* ☰ *AE, DC, MC, V* ☉ *Closed 2 wks Nov. and part of Feb.* ❢⊙❢ *MAP.*

★ **$–$$** ✕▥ **Le Manoir d'Hastings.** Chef-owner José Aparicio's celebrated restaurant La Pommeraie is in this former 17th-century priory in Bénouville, close to Pegasus Bridge, northeast of Caen, the first French village to be liberated (by Anglo–Canadian troops) in June 1944. The decor is modern and nothing to write home about but the food takes center stage here: choose from great seasonal dishes prepared in the classic Norman manner, such as the sole stuffed with wild autumn mushrooms or the pigeon stuffed with marinated cabbage and homemade foie gras. You can stay overnight in one of the 16 cozy rooms. ⊠ *18 av. de la Côte-de-Nacre, 10 km (6 mi) northeast of Caen, 14970 Bénouville* ☎ *02–31–44–62–43* 🖷 *02–31–44–76–18* ⊕ *www.manoirhastings.com* ♨ *Reservations essential* ▤ *AE, DC, MC, V* ☉ *Closed Mon., mid-Nov.–mid-Dec., and mid-Feb. No dinner Sun.*

Shopping

A *marché aux puces* (flea market) is held on Friday morning on place St-Saveur and on Sunday morning on place Courtonne. In June, collectors and dealers flock to Caen's bric-a-brac and **antiques fair.**

The Outdoors

Take a barge trip along the canal that leads from Caen to the sea on the *Hastings* (⊠ Quai Vendeuvre ☎ 02–31–34–00–00); there are four daily departures: 9 AM, noon, 3 PM, and 7 PM.

---

en route

Early on June 6, 1944, the British 6th Airborne Division landed by glider and captured **Pegasus Bridge** (named for the division's emblem, showing Bellerophon astride his winged horse, Pegasus). This proved the first step toward the liberation of France from Nazi occupation. To see this symbol of the Allied invasion, from Caen take D514 north and turn right at Bénouville. The original bridge—erected in 1935—has been replaced by a similar but slightly wider bridge; but the original can still be seen at the adjacent **Mémorial Pegasus** visitor center (open daily February–November, €4). Café Gondrée by the bridge—the first building recaptured on French soil—is still standing, still serving coffee, and houses a small museum. A 40-minute son-et-lumière show lights up the bridge and the café at nightfall between June and September.

Five kilometers (3 mi) north of here, just beyond Ouistreham and its **Grand Bunker** museum recalling Hitler's Atlantic Wall, lie the easternmost D-Day landing beaches: **Sword Beach** extends to Luc-sur-Mer; **Juno Beach** to Courseulles; and **Gold Beach** to Arromanches. These flat, sandy beaches, stormed by British (Gold and Sword) and Canadian (Juno) troops, extend beneath pretty resort towns like Lion-sur-Mer, Langrune, and St-Aubin. Inland, slender church spires patrol the vast, flat horizon.

Arromanches-les-Bains

㉗ *31 km (19 mi) northwest of Caen, 10 km (6 mi) northeast of Bayeux.*

Little remains to mark the furious fighting waged hereabouts after D-Day. In the bay off Arromanches, however, some elements of the floating harbor are still visible. Head up to the terrace alongside Arromanches 360, high above the town on D65, to contemplate the seemingly insignificant hunks of concrete that form a broken offshore semicircle—and try to imagine the extraordinary technical feat involved in towing them across the Channel from England. General Eisenhower said that victory would have been impossible without this prefabricated harbor, which was nicknamed "Winston." The **Musée du Débarquement,** on the seafront, has models, mock-ups, and photographs depicting the creation of this technical marvel. ⊠ *Pl. du 6-Juin* ☎ *02–31–22–34–31* 📧 *€6.50* ⊙ *May–Sept., daily 9–7; Oct.–Dec. and Feb.–Apr., daily 10–12:30 and 1:30–4:30.*

Arromanches 360 is a striking modern movie theater with a circular screen—actually nine curved screens synchronized to show an 18-minute film (screenings at 10 past and 20 to the hour) titled *Le Prix de la Liberté* (*The Price of Freedom*). The film, which tells the story of the D-Day landings, is a mix of archival and more recent footage from major sites and cemeteries. Evocative music and sound effects serve as dramatic substitutes for spoken commentary. ⊠*Chemin du Calvaire* ☎*02–31–22–30–30* ⊕ *www.arromanches360.com* 📧 *€4* ⊙ *June–Aug., daily 9:10–6:40; May and Sept., 10:10–5:40; Oct.–Dec. and Feb.–Apr., daily 10:10–4:40.*

Where to Eat

¢–$ ✕ **Bistro d'Arromanches.** This brassy bistro has a warm and friendly aura and welcomes children—there is even a room upstairs with games and toys to keep them amused while Mommy and Daddy are enjoying the simple, classic fare. ⊠ *23 rue du Maréchal-Joffre* ☎ *02–31–22–31–32* 🗃 *MC, V* ⊙ *Closed Tues., Wed., and Jan.*

Bayeux

28 *10 km (6 mi) southwest of Arromanches via D516, 28 km (17 mi) northwest of Caen.*

Bayeux, the first town to be liberated during the Battle of Normandy, was already steeped in history—as home to a Norman Gothic cathedral and the world's most celebrated piece of needlework: the Bayeux Tapestry. Bayeux's medieval backcloth makes it a popular base, especially among British travelers, for day trips to other towns in Normandy. The old-world mood is at its most boisterous during the Fêtes Médiévales, a market-cum-carnival held in the streets around the cathedral on the first weekend of July. Bayeux makes one of the best bases for visitors to the World War II sites.

Fodor'sChoice ★ Really a 225-foot-long embroidered scroll stitched in 1067, the **Bayeux Tapestry,** known in French as the *Tapisserie de la Reine Mathilde* (Queen Matilda's Tapestry), depicts, in 58 comic strip–type scenes, the epic story of William of Normandy's conquest of England in 1066. The tapestry was probably commissioned from Saxon embroiderers by the count of Kent—who was also the bishop of Bayeux—to be displayed in his newly built cathedral, the Cathédrale Notre-Dame. Despite its age, the tapestry is in remarkably good condition; the extremely detailed, often homey scenes provide an unequaled record of the clothes, weapons, ships, and lifestyles of the day. It's showcased in the **Musée de la Tapisserie** (Tapestry Museum); for €1 you can rent headphones and listen to an English commentary about the tapestry, scene by scene. ⊠ *Centre Guillaume-le-Con-*

quérant, 13 bis rue de Nesmond ☎ *02–31–51–25–50* ⊕ *www.mairie-bayeux.fr* ☞ *€7.50, joint ticket with Musée Baron-Gérard* ☉ *May–Aug., daily 9–7; Sept.–Apr., daily 9:30–12:30 and 2–6.*

Housed in the Bishop's Palace beneath the cathedral, and fronted by a majestic plane tree planted in March 1797 and known as the Tree of Liberty, the **Musée Baron-Gérard** contains a fine collection of Bayeux porcelain and lace, ceramics from Rouen, a marvelous collection of pharmaceutical jars from the 17th and 18th centuries, and 16th- to 19th-century furniture and paintings by local artists. ⊠ *1 pl. de la Liberté* ☎ *02–31–92–14–21* ☞ *€2.60, joint ticket with Tapestry Museum €7.50* ☉ *Daily 10–12:30 and 2–6.*

Bayeux's mightiest edifice, the **Cathédrale Notre-Dame,** is a harmonious mixture of Norman and Gothic architecture. Note the portal on the south side of the transept that depicts the assassination of English archbishop Thomas à Becket in Canterbury Cathedral in 1170, following his courageous opposition to King Henry II's attempts to control the church. ⊠ *Rue du Bienvenu* ☎ *02–31–92–01–85* ☉ *Daily 9–6.*

Handmade lace is a specialty of Bayeux. The best place to learn about it and to buy some is the **Conservatoire de la Dentelle** near the cathedral, which has a good display. ⊠ *6 rue du Bienvenu* ☎ *02–31–92–73–80* ☞ *Free* ☉ *Mon.–Sat. 10–12:30 and 2–6.*

At the **Musée de la Bataille de Normandie** (Battle of Normandy Museum) exhibits trace the story of the struggle from June 7 to August 22, 1944. This modern museum near the British War Cemetery, sunk partly beneath the level of its surrounding lawns, contains some impressive war paraphernalia. ⊠ *Bd. du Général-Fabian-Ware* ☎ *02–31–51–46–90* ⊕ *www.normandiememoire.com* ☞ *€5* ☉ *May–mid-Sept., daily 9:30–6:30; mid-Sept.–Apr., daily 10–12:30 and 2–6.*

Fodor'sChoice ★ Sixteen kilometers (10 mi) southwest of Bayeux stands the **Château de Balleroy.** A connoisseur's favorite, it was built by architect François Mansart in 1626–36 and is a remarkably elegant 17th-century edifice. The *cour d'honneur* is marked by two stylish side pavilions—an architectural grace note adapted from Italian Renaissance models—which beautifully frame the small, but very seignorial, central mass of the house. Inside, the *salon d'honneur* is the very picture of Louis XIV decoration, while other rooms were recast in 19th-century chic by Malcolm Forbes, who bought the château in 1970. A gallery houses the fascinating **Musée des Ballons** (Balloon Museum), while the companion village was designed by Mansart in one of the first examples of town planning in France. ⊠ *Balleroy* ☎ *02–31–21–60–61* ⊕ *www.chateau-balleroy.com* ☞ *€7* ☉ *Mid-Mar.–June and Sept.–mid-Oct., Wed.–Mon. 10–6; July and Aug., daily 10–6.*

Where to Stay & Eat

$–$$$ ✕ **L'Amaryllis.** Pascal Marie's small restaurant has three prix-fixe menus, running €11–€28. The three-course dinner, with six selections per course, may include a half-dozen oysters, fillet of sole with a cider-based sauce, and pastries or chocolate gâteau for dessert. Lobster and skate with shallots lurk *à la carte.* ✉ *32 rue St-Patrice* ☎ *02–31–22–47–94* 🖃 *MC, V* ⊗ *Closed Mon., Sun. evening Nov.–Mar., and Jan.*

★ **$$$$** ✕🏨 **Château d'Audrieu.** This family-owned château, with an elegant 18th-century facade, fulfills a Hollywood notion of a palatial property: princely opulence, wall sconces, overstuffed chairs, and antiques. Rooms 50 and 51 have peaked ceilings with exposed-wood beams. The restaurant (closed Monday except for residents, with lunch served weekends only; smoking is not allowed) has an extensive wine list, and chef Cyril Haberland explores an exotic repertoire of dishes, like scallops with chestnuts and cranberry juice. ✉ *13 km (8 mi) southeast of Bayeux off N13, 14250 Audrieu* ☎ *02–31–80–21–52* 🖨 *02–31–80–24–73* ⊕ *www.chateaudaudrieu. com* ⤴ *29 rooms* ⚅ *Restaurant, minibars, cable TV, pool, bar, helipad; no a/c* 🖃 *AE, MC, V* ⊗ *Closed Dec.–mid-Feb.* �🍽 *MAP.*

$$ ✕🏨 **Grand Hôtel du Luxembourg.** The Luxembourg has small but adequate rooms; all but two face a courtyard garden. It has one of the town's best restaurants, Les Quatre Saisons (closed January), with a seasonal menu. Depending on the time of year, choose the honey-roasted ham with melted apples, or braised turbot with sage. ✉ *25 rue des Bouchers, 14400* ☎ *02–31–92–00–04, 800/528–1234 for U.S. reservations* 🖨 *02–31–92–54–26* ⊕ *www.adeauville.com/henri/hotelbayeux* ⤴ *24 rooms, 3 suites* ⚅ *Restaurant, cable TV, bar, dance club, Internet, some pets allowed (fee)* 🖃 *AE, DC, MC, V* 🍽 *MAP.*

★ **$$** 🏨 **Manoir du Carel.** The narrow slits serving as windows on the tower recall the origins of the 17th-century Manoir du Carel, set nicely halfway between Bayeux and the sea, which was originally constructed as a fortified manor during the Hundred Years' War. Owner Jacques Aumond enjoys welcoming American guests to his comfortable rooms with modern furnishings; public salons have 19th-century accents. The cottage on the grounds, ideal for families, has a kitchen plus a fireplace that masks a brick oven where villagers once had their bread baked. Note that pets are not allowed. ✉ *5 km (3 mi) northwest of Bayeux, 14400 Maisons* ☎ *02–31–22–37–00* 🖨 *02–31–21–57–00* ⊕ *www.bienvenue-au-chateau. com* ⤴ *3 rooms; 1 cottage* ⚅ *Tennis court; no a/c* 🖃 *DC, MC, V* 🍽 *BP.*

The Outdoors

Bicycles can be rented from **Family Home** (✉ 39 rue Général-de-Dais ☎ 02–31–92–15–22) for about €8 a day. Ask the tourist office for information about trails. The **Rassemblement International de Ballons** (International Balloon Festival; ☎ 02–31–21–60–61 information) takes place every two years in mid-June, 16 km (10 mi) southwest of Bayeux at the early-17th-century **Château de Balleroy.**

The D-Day Beaches

History focused its sights along the coasts of Normandy at 6:30 AM on June 6, 1944, as the 135,000 men and 20,000 vehicles of the Allied troops made land in their first incursion in Europe in World War II. The entire operation on this "Longest Day" was called Operation Overlord—the code name for the invasion of Normandy. Five beachheads (dubbed Utah, Omaha, Gold, Juno, and Sword) were established along the coast to either side of Arromanches. Preparations started in mid-1943, and British shipyards worked furiously through the following winter and spring building two artificial harbors (called "mulberries"), boats, and landing equipment; the other harbor, moored off Omaha Beach, was destroyed on June 19, 1944, by a violent storm. The British and Canadian troops that landed on Sword, Juno, and Gold on June 6, 1944, quickly pushed inland and joined with parachute regiments previously dropped behind German lines, before encountering fierce resistance at Caen, which did not fall until July 9. Today, the best way to tour this region is by car. Public buses from Bayeux have fairly infrequent service, so opt instead for one of the guided bus tours leaving from Caen (*see* Tours *in* Normandy A to Z, *below*).

★ ㉙ You won't be disappointed by the rugged terrain and windswept sand of **Omaha Beach,** 16 km (10 mi) northwest of Bayeux. Here you'll find the **Monument du Débarquement** (Monument to the Normandy Landings) and nearby, in Vierville-sur-Mer, the **U.S. National Guard Monument.** Throughout June 6th, Allied forces battled a hailstorm of German bullets and bombs, but by the end of the day they had taken the sector, although they had suffered grievous losses. In Colleville-sur-Mer is the hilltop **American Cemetery and Memorial,** designed by the landscape architect Markley Stevenson. It's a moving tribute to the fallen, with its Wall of the Missing (in the form of a semicircular colonnade), drum-like chapel, and avenues of holly oaks trimmed to resemble open parachutes. The crisply mowed lawns are studded with 9,386 marble tombstones; this is where Stephen Spielberg's fictional hero Captain John Miller was supposed to have been buried in *Saving Private Ryan.* You can look out to sea across the landing beach from a platform on the north side of the cemetery.

★ ㉚ The most spectacular scenery along the coast is at the **Pointe du Hoc,** 13 km (8 mi) west of St-Laurent. Wildly undulating grassland leads past ruined blockhouses to a cliff-top observatory and a German machine-gun post whose intimidating mass of reinforced concrete merits chilly exploration. Despite Spielberg's cinematic genius, it remains hard to imagine just how Colonel Rudder and his 225 men—only 90 survived—managed to scale the jagged cliffs with rope ladders and capture the German defenses in one of the most heroic and dramatic episodes of the war.

㉛ Head west around the coast on N13, pause in the town of **Carentan** to admire its modern marina and the mighty octagonal spire of the Église Notre-Dame, and continue northwest to **Sainte-Mère Église.** At 2:30 AM on June 6, 1944, the 82nd Airborne Division was dropped over Ste-Mère, heralding the start of D-Day operations. Famously, one parachutist—his name was John Steele—got stuck on the church tower (memorably recreated in the 1960 film *The Longest Day*); a dummy is strung up each summer to recall the event, and a stained-glass window inside the church honors American paratroopers. After securing their position at Ste-Mère, U.S. forces pushed north, then west, cutting off the Cotentin Peninsula on June 18 and taking Cherbourg on June 26. German defense proved fiercer farther south, and St-Lô was not liberated until July 19. Ste-Mère's symbolic importance as the first French village to be liberated from the Nazis is commemorated by the Borne 0 (Zero) outside the town hall—

a large, domed milestone marking the start of the Voie de la Liberté (Freedom Way), charting the Allies' progress across France.

The **Musée des Troupes Aéroportées** (Airborne Troops Museum), built behind the church in 1964 in the form of an open parachute, houses documents, maps, mementos, and one of the Waco CG4A gliders used to drop troops. ⊠ *Pl. du 6-juin-1944* ☏ *02–33–41–41–35* 🖂 €6 ☉ *Feb.–mid-Nov., daily 9:30–noon and 2–6.*

★ ㉜ Head east on D67 from Ste-Mère to **Utah Beach,** which, being sheltered from the Atlantic winds by the Cotentin Peninsula and surveyed by lowly sand dunes rather than rocky cliffs, proved easier to attack than Omaha. Allied troops stormed the beach at dawn and just a few hours later had managed to conquer the German defenses, heading inland to join up with the airborne troops. In **La Madeleine** (⊠ Plage de La Madeleine ☏ 02–33–71–53–35) inspect the glitteringly modern **Utah Beach Landing Museum** (⊠ Ste-Marie-du-Mont ☏ 02–33–71–53–35), whose exhibits include a W5 Utah scale model detailing the German defenses; it's open April–June and September–October, daily 9:30–noon and 2–6, and July and August, daily 9:30–6:30. Continue north to the **Dunes de Varreville,** set with a monument to French hero General Leclerc, who landed here. Offshore you can see the fortified **Iles St-Marcouf.** Continue to **Quinéville,** at the far end of Utah Beach, with its **museum** (⊠ Rue de la Plage ☏ 02–33–21–40–44) evoking life during the German Occupation; the museum is open April, May, and October, daily 10–noon and 2–6, and June–September, daily 9:30–6:30.

Where to Stay & Eat

$$$$ ✕🏨 **La Chenevière.** This grand 18th-century château, just inland from Port-en-Bessin, to the east of Omaha Beach, has rooms with modern furnishings, floor-to-ceiling windows, and flowered bedspreads. The restaurant (closed Monday, no lunch Tuesday) serves cuisine appropriate to its surroundings: chef Claude Esprabens specializes in scallops, while his roasted scampi with sesame seeds and fresh chanterelles is delicious. So is his warm sliced duck liver with raspberry sauce. ⊠ *Les Escures, 14520 Commes* ☏ *02–31–51–25–25* 🖷 *02–31–51–25–20* ⊕ *www.lacheneviere.fr* ⤳ *21 rooms* ⟁ *Restaurant, minibars, cable TV, bar, Internet, some pets allowed (fee); no a/c* ⊟ *AE, DC, MC, V* ☉ *Closed Jan.–mid-Feb.* ⍾ *MAP.*

$ ✕🏨 **Casino.** You can't get closer to the action. This handsome, postwar, triangular-gabled stone hotel, run by the same family since it was built in the 1950s, looks directly onto Omaha Beach. The bar is made from an old lifeboat, and it's no surprise that fish and regional cuisine with creamy sauces predominate in Bruno Clemençon's airy sea-view restaurant. ⊠ *Rue de la Percée, 14710 Vierville-sur-Mer* ☏ *02–31–22–41–02* 🖷 *02–31–22–41–12* ⤳ *12 rooms* ⟁ *Restaurant, bar, some pets allowed; no a/c* ⊟ *MC, V* ☉ *Closed mid-Nov.–late Mar.* ⍾ *MAP.*

St-Vaast-la-Hougue

③③ *14 km (9 mi) north of Quinéville D42/D14.*

The bustling harbor town of St-Vaast-la-Hougue has two waterfronts, one facing south toward its famous oyster beds, with Utah Beach beyond, the other to the west out toward the Channel. Between the two is a finger of land tipped by an imposing fort. Just offshore from St-Vaast is the **Ile de Tatihou,** a small island fortified by Vauban in 1692, along with the tiny Fort de l'Ilet, 200 yards to the south. Tatihou has a **Musée Maritime,** where you can admire objects salvaged from local shipwrecks and visit sprawling gardens where marine flora and exotic plants prosper in the temperate climate, along with thousands of seagulls and a hundred different species of migrating birds. ⊠ *Quai Vauban* ☎ *02–33–23–19–92* ⊕ *www.tatihou.com* ✆ *€7.60 round-trip boat ticket includes admission to museum and gardens.*

Cherbourg

③④ *37 km (23 mi) northwest of St-Vaast-la-Hougue via N13.*

Perhaps best known for Michel Legrand's haunting theme from the 1960s film musical *Les Parapluies de Cherbourg* (*The Umbrellas of Cherbourg*), Cherbourg is no longer the thriving transatlantic port of a Belle Époque heyday symbolized by the hyperelaborate facade of its 1882 **theater,** one of the few old monuments to survive World War II. Umbrellas are hardly the sunniest of city symbols, but the climate, though gusty, is generally mild, and it's fun to stroll around the grid of narrow lanes (many of them pedestrian-only) between the theater and the ramshackle **Église de la Trinité** (Holy Trinity Church) by the seafront—especially on Tuesday, Thursday, or Saturday, when the street market is in full swing.

It was back in 1686 that Vauban first spotted Cherbourg's potential as a defensive port beneath the rocky 360-foot Montagne du Roule, but it took the completion of a massive breakwater in 1853 before Cherbourg could harbor ocean-going ships. The first transatlantic liner docked in 1869; these days ferries ply the Channel to England (Portsmouth and Poole) and Ireland (Rosslare). You can take a short sea cruise around the bay from Port Chantereyne any afternoon from April through September (call 02–33–93–75–27 for details).

Cherbourg is also a major submarine base: more than 90 have been built here since 1899, and one, the *Redoutable,* is on display at the **Cité de la Mer** (Marine Center). You can tour the submarine with infrared commentary headsets; admire a barrage of designer fish-tanks; and plumb the depths of submarine history. There's also a salty sea shop and a brasserie-type restaurant. The converted maritime rail station, a supremely elegant Art Deco edifice designed by René Levasseur, is spectacularly illuminated at night, when the restaurant stays open long after the museum has docked. ⊠ *Quai Lawton-Collins* ☎ *02–33–20–26–26* ⊕ *www. citedelamer.com* ✆ *€14* ⊘ *June–Aug., daily 9:30–7; Sept.–Dec. and Feb.–May, daily 10–6.*

Uniforms, photographs, maps, flags, posters, and medals at the **Musée de la Libération** (Liberation Museum), on the hill above the town (excellent sea views), recall Cherbourg's pivotal role at the end of World War II, when it was the Allies' major bridgehead to France after the D-Day landings and the French terminus for the PLUTO seabed pipeline that pumped needed fuel under the Channel from the Isle of Wight. ⊠ *Fort du Roule* ☎ *02–33–20–14–12* ⌚ *€3* ☉ *Apr.–Sept., daily 10–6; Oct.–Dec., Tues.–Sun. 9:30–noon and 2–5:30.*

Thirty works by local-born painter Jean-François Millet (of *Angélus* renown) can be seen at the **Musée Thomas-Henry,** the town art museum, along with works by Murillo, "Velvet" Brueghel, David, and such talented 19th-century regional artists as Guillaume Fouace and Félix Bahot. Sculpture and ceramics complete the collection. ⊠ *Rue Vartel* ☎ *02–33–23–39–30* ⌚ *Free* ☉ *May–Sept., Tues.–Sun. 10–noon and 2–6; Oct.–Apr., Wed.–Sun. 2–6.*

Where to Stay & Eat

$$–$$$ ✕ **Vauban.** Warm, friendly, and family-owned, this spot is headed up by chef Daniel Imbert, who prefers to approach his cuisine with a light, modern touch, avoiding the cream that typifies classic Norman fare. The menu is seasonal, with set menus running €15–€38 and lots of fish and seafood temptations, such as the fresh *bar* (sea bass) with truffles or the coquilles St. Jacques with wild mushrooms. ⊠ *22 quai de Caligny* ☎ *02–33–43–10–11* 🖷 *02–33–43–15–18* ▤ *AE, MC, V* ☉ *Closed Mon., 2 wks Feb., 2 wks Nov. No dinner Sun.*

¢ ✕ **Faitout.** This cozy, paneled bistro in the shopping district near the Church of the Trinity packs in locals with its friendly service and traditional French cuisine. Stews, steaks, duck, smoked salmon, and mussels are high on the menu. ⊠ *25 rue de la Tour-Carrée* ☎ *02–33–04–25–04* ▤ *MC, V* ☉ *Closed Sun. No lunch Mon.*

¢–$ ⌂ **Ambassadeur.** This modernized quayside hotel offers good value, a central location, and an English-speaking staff. The better, and more expensive, rooms look out over the harbor. The Vauban restaurant, next door, is a calmer dinnertime alternative to the bustling Faitout. ⊠ *22 quai de Caligny, 50100* ☎ *02–33–43–10–00* 🖷 *02–33–43–10–01* ⊕ *www.ambassadeurhotel.com* ⇲ *40 rooms* ♨ *Internet; no a/c* ▤ *AE, MC, V* ☉ *Closed Dec. 24–Jan. 2.*

St-Lô

㉟ *78 km (49 mi) southeast of Cherbourg, 36 km (22 mi) southwest of Bayeux.*

St-Lô, perched dramatically on a rocky spur above the Vire Valley, was a key communications center that suffered so badly in World War II that it became known as the "capital of ruins." The medieval **Église Notre-Dame** bears mournful witness to those dark days: its imposing, spire-topped west front was never rebuilt, merely shored up with a wall of greenish stone. Reconstruction elsewhere, though, was wholesale. Some of it was spectacular, like the slender, spiral-staircase tower outside Town Hall; the circular theater; or the openwork belfry of the church of Ste-Croix. The town was freed by American troops, and its rebuilding was financed with U.S. support, notably from the city of Baltimore. The **Hôpital Mémorial France–États Unis** (France–United States Memorial Hospital), designed by Paul Nelson and featuring a giant mosaic by Fernand Léger, was named to honor those links.

St-Lô is capital of the Manche *département* (province) and, less prosaically, likes to consider itself France's horse capital. Hundreds of breeders are based in its environs, and the **Haras National** (National Stud) was established here in 1886. ⊠ *Av. du Maréchal-Juin* ☎ *02–33–77–88–77* ⊕ *www.haras-nationaux.fr* ✆ *€4* ☺ *June–Sept., daily 2–5:30, guided tours only.*

★ St-Lô's art museum, the **Musée des Beaux-Arts,** is the perfect French provincial museum. Its halls are airy, seldom busy, not too big, yet full of varied exhibits—including an unexpected masterpiece: *Gombault et Macée,* a set of nine silk-and-wool tapestries woven in Bruges around 1600 relating a tale about a shepherd couple, exquisitely showcased in a special circular room. Other highlights include brash modern tapestries by Jean Lurçat; paintings by Corot, Boudin, and Géricault; court miniatures by Daniel Saint (1778–1847); and the Art Deco pictures of Slovenian-born Jaro Hilbert (1897–1995), inspired by ancient Egypt. Photographs, models, and documents evoke St-Lô's wartime devastation. ⊠ *Centre Culturel, pl. du Champ-de-Mars* ☎ *02–33–72–52–55* ⊕ *http://lesamisdesmusees. free.fr* ✆ *€2.50* ☺ *Wed.–Mon. 10–noon and 2–6.*

Coutances

❸❻ *27 km (18 mi) southwest of St-Lô via D972.*

If you're interested in church architecture, you'll want to stop off in
★ Coutances. The largely 13th-century **Cathédrale Notre-Dame,** with its famous octagonal lantern rising 135 feet above the nave, is considered the most harmonious Gothic building in Normandy. On the outside, especially the facade, note the obsessive use of turrets, spires, slender shafts, and ultranarrow pointed arches squeezed senseless in their architectural pursuit of vertical takeoff. A further 200 yards down the street is the **Eglise St-Pierre,** topped by a chunky Renaissance pastiche of the cathedral lantern above a richly sculpted interior. The town's tumbling **Jardin des Plantes,** where an army of 12 gardeners tends 47,000 plants, is also worth a visit.

Where to Stay

¢ ▦ **Moulin Girard.** For English hospitality, cheerful conversation, and unusual, inexpensive accommodations, head to Brian and Pearl Mitchell's enchanting 200-year-old water mill. The main house has two small rooms, and there's also a miller's cottage with exposed beams and a two-bedroom suite—an ideal choice for a family or two couples. You can have your breakfast on the terrace overlooking the mill stream, or make arrangements for Pearl to whip up a four-course dinner (with wine) for €25. ⊠ *26 km (16 mi) southeast of Coutances; from Villedieu-les-Poêles make right on D98 as you enter Percy in the direction of Tessy-sur-Vire and then go right on D452 for Le Chefresne, 50410 Le Chefresne* ☎☎ *02–33–61–62–06* ➳ *2 rooms, 1 suite* ♿ *No a/c* ▭ *No credit cards* ❑| *MAP.*

Granville

③⑦ *30 km (19 mi) south of Coutances via D971, 107 km (67 mi) south-west of Caen.*

Proud locals like to call Granville the "Monaco of the North." It perches on a rocky outcrop and does have a seawater therapy center, but . . . the similarities end there. Free of casinos and sequins, Granville instead has a down-to-earth feel. Granite houses cluster around the church in the Vieille Ville, and the harbor below is full of working boats. From the ramparts there are fine views of the English Channel; catamarans breeze over to Jersey and the Iles Chausey daily in summer. Drive a few miles down the coast to find sandy beaches and a view of distant Mont-St-Michel.

Where to Eat

¢ ✕ **L'Echaugette.** There is an excellent choice of grills and pancakes, both sweet and savory, at this quaint little crêperie on a narrow street in the upper town. Pancakes au gratin and with scallops are specialties. ⊠ *24 rue St-Jean* ☎ *02–33–50–51–87* ▭ *No credit cards* ☉ *Closed Tues., Wed., and Nov.*

Nightlife & the Arts

The rambunctious **Carnaval de Granville** (⊕ www.ville-granville.fr) involves four days of parades and festivities, culminating each year on Shrove Tuesday. The **Grand Pardon des Corporations de la Mer**, a *pardon*, or religious festival, devoted to the sea, is celebrated on the last Sunday of July with a military parade, a regatta, and platefuls of shellfish.

The Outdoors

Granville is a center for aquatic sports; inquire about sailboat jaunts at the **Centre Régional de Nautisme** (⊠ Bd. des Amiraux ☎ 02–33–91–22–60). **Lepesqueux** (⊠ 3 rue Clément-Desmaisons ☎ 02–33–50–18–97) also rents boats and yachts.

Mont-St-Michel

③⑧ *44 km (27 mi) south of Granville via D973, N175, and D43; 123 km (77 mi) southwest of Caen; 67 km (42 mi) north of Rennes; 325 km (202 mi) west of Paris.*

Fodor'sChoice
★

Wrought by nature and centuries of tireless human toil, this sea-surrounded mass of granite adorned with the soul-lifting silhouette of the **Abbaye du Mont-St-Michel** may well be your most lasting image of Normandy. The abbey is perched on a 264-foot-high rock a few hundred yards off the coast: it's surrounded by water during the year's highest tides and by desolate sand flats the rest of the time. Be warned: tides in the bay are dangerously unpredictable. The sea can rise up to 45 feet at high tide and rushes in at incredible speed—more than a few ill-prepared tourists over the years have drowned. Also, be warned that there are patches of dangerous quicksand. A causeway—to be replaced in time by a bridge, allowing the bay waters to circulate freely—links Mont-St-Michel to the mainland. Leave your car in the parking lot (€2.50) along the causeway, outside the main gate. Just inside you'll find the tourist office, to the left, and a pair of old cannons (with cannonballs) to the right. If you're staying the night on Mont-St-Michel, take what you need in a small suitcase; you cannot gain access to your hotel by car. The Mont's tourist office is in the Corps de Garde des Bourgeois, just to the left of the island gates.

Legend has it that the Archangel Michael appeared in 709 to Aubert, Bishop of Avranches, inspiring him to build an oratory on what was then called Mont Tombe. The rock and its shrine were soon the goal of pilgrimages. The original church was completed in 1144, but further buildings were added in the 13th century to accommodate monks as well as the hordes of pilgrims who flocked here even during the Hundred Years' War, when the region was in English hands. During the period when much of western France was subjected to English rule, the abbey remained a symbol, both physical and emotional, of French independence. Because of its legendary origins and the sheer exploit of its centuries-long construction, the abbey became known as the *"Merveille de l'Occident"* (Wonder of the Western World). The granite used to build it was transported from the nearby Isles of Chausey and hauled up to the site. The abbey's construction took more than 500 years, from 1017 to 1521. The Romanesque choir was rebuilt in Gothic style during the 15th and 16th centuries and it was only thereabouts that the high Gothic spire was added—to step back several centuries, put your hand over your view of the spire and the abbey will, ipso facto, return to its original Romanesque squatness. The abbey's monastic independence was undermined during the 17th century, when the monks began to flout the strict rules and discipline of their order, drifting into a state of decadence that culminated in their dispersal and the abbey's conversion into a prison, well before the French Revolution. In 1874 the former abbey was handed over to a governmental agency responsible for the preservation of historic monuments. Emmanuel Frémiet's great gilt statute of St. Michael was added to the spire in 1897. Monks now live and work here again, as in medieval times: you can join them for daily mass at 12:15.

All year long, the hour-long guided tour in English (two a day and night in high season) and French (up to two an hour) takes you through the impressive Romanesque and Gothic abbey and the spectacular **Eglise Abbiatiale**, the abbey church which crowns the rock, as well as the **Merveille**, a 13th-century, three-story collection of rooms and passageways. La Merveille was built by King Philippe Auguste around and on top of the monastery; on its second floor is the Mont's grandest chamber, the **Salle des Chevaliers.** Another tour, which also includes the celebrated **Escalier de Dentelle** (Lace Staircase), and the pre-Roman and exquisitely evocative **Notre-Dame-sous-Terre** is longer, has a higher ticket price, and is only given in French. Invest in at least one tour while you are here—some of them get you on top of or into things you can't see alone. If you do go it alone, stop halfway up Grande-Rue at the medieval parish church of St-Pierre to admire the richly carved side chapel with its dramatic statue of St. Michael slaying the dragon. The **Grand Degré**, a steep, narrow staircase, leads to the abbey entrance, from which a wider flight of stone steps climbs to the **Saut Gautier Terrace** (named after a prisoner who jumped to his death from it) outside the sober, dignified church. After visiting the arcaded cloisters alongside, which offer vertiginous views of the bay, you can wander at leisure, and probably get lost, among the maze of rooms, staircases, and vaulted halls. Scattered through the Mont are four mini-museums, which share an admission ticket of €15. The **Logis Tiphaine** (☎ 02–33–60–23–34) is the home that Bertrand Duguesclin, a general fierce in his allegiance to the cause of French independence, for his wife Tiphaine in 1365. The **Musée Historique** (⊠ Chemin de la Ronde ☎ 02–33–60–07–01) traces the 1,000-year history of the Mont in one of its former prisons. The **Musée Maritime** (⊠ Grande Rue ☎ 02–33–60–14–09) explores the science of the Mont's tidal bay and has a vast collection of model ships. The **Archéoscope** (⊠ Chemin de la Ronde ☎ 02–33–60–14–09) explores the myths and legends of the Mont through a sound and light show. Some exhibits use wax figures fitted out in the most glamorous threads and costumes of the 15th century.

The island village, with its steep, narrow streets, is best visited out of season, from September to June. In summer the hordes of tourists and souvenir sellers can be stifling. Give yourself at least half a day here, and follow your nose. The mount is full of nooks, crannies, little gardens, and echoing views from the ramparts. When day-trippers depart, peace and quiet return to the Mont and you can appreciate its frightening grandeur. So make an overnight stay here, whatever the price. Time your visit a couple of days after the full moon to soak up sunsets over the Bay that touch lows of prestellar beauty. The Mont is spectacularly illuminated every night from dusk till midnight. ☎ 02–33–89–80–00 ⊕ *www. monum.fr ⌑ General admission: €7, with audioguide €11. Guided tours: €7. Museums: €15 ⊗ May–Aug., daily 9–7; Sept.–Apr., daily 9:30–6.*

Where to Stay & Eat

$$–$$$$ ✕⊡ **La Mère Poulard.** This legendary hotel consists of adjoining houses with three steep flights of narrow stairs. The restaurant's reputation derives partly from Mère Poulard's famous soufflélike omelet, partly from its convenient location (right by the gateway, so don't expect views from atop the Mont), and partly from the talent of chef Michel Bruneau, who established his reputation with his own restaurant in Caen. Room prices start low but ratchet upward according to size; the smallest rooms are bearable for an overnight stay, not longer. Walls throughout are plastered with posters and photographs of illustrious guests. You are usually requested to book two meals with the room. Reservations are essential for the restaurant in summer. ⊠ *Grande-Rue, 50116* ☎ *02–33–89–68–68* 🖷 *02–33–89–68–69* ⊕ *www.mere-poulard.com* 🖅 *40 rooms* ⌂ *Restaurant, minibars, cable TV, piano bar; no a/c* ⊟ *AE, DC, MC, V* ❙◎❙ *MAP.*

★ **$$** ✕⊡ **Manoir de la Roche Torin.** Run by the Barraux family, this pretty, slate-roofed, stone-walled manor set in 4 acres of parkland is a delightful alternative to the high cost of staying on Mont-St-Michel. Rooms are pleasantly old-fashioned, and the bathrooms modern. With walls of Normand stonework and its open fireplace, the restaurant (closed Tuesday, Wednesday, and Saturday lunch) has superb seafood and char-grilled *pré-salé* (salt-meadow lamb). In summer, aperitifs are served in the garden, with a view of Mont-St-Michel. ⊠ *34 rte. de la Roche-Torin, 9 km (5 mi) from Mont-St-Michel, 50220 Courtils* ☎ *02–33–70–96–55* 🖷 *02–33–48–35–20* ⊕ *www.manoir-rochetorin.com* ⮑ *15 rooms* ⚭ *Restaurant, minibars, bar, Internet, some pets allowed (fee); no a/c* ⊟ *AE, DC, MC, V* ☉ *Closed mid-Nov.–mid-Feb.* �🍽 *MAP.*

$$ ✕⊞ **Les Terrasses Poulard.** Run by the folks who own the noted Mère Poulard hotel, this ensemble of buildings is clustered around a small garden in the middle of the Mount. Rooms at this hotel are some of the best—with views of the bay and rustic-style furnishings—and most spacious on the Mount, although many require you to negotiate a labyrinth of steep stairways. ⊠ *Grande-Rue, opposite parish church, 50170* ☎ *02–33–89–02–02* 🖷 *02–33–60–37–31* ⊕ *www.terrasses-poulard. com* ⮑ *30 rooms* ⚭ *Restaurant, minibars, cable TV, billiards, library; no a/c* ⊟ *AE, DC, MC, V* 🍽 *MAP.*

$ ✕⊞ **Du Guesclin.** The courtesy of the staff, the comfy and clean guest rooms, and a choice of two restaurants make this well-maintained hotel a pleasant option. Downstairs try the casual brasserie for salads and sandwiches; upstairs the panoramic full-service restaurant has a wonderful view of the bay. ⊠ *Grande-Rue, 50170* ☎ *02–33–60–14–10* 🖷 *02–33–60–45–81* ⮑ *10 rooms* ⚭ *2 restaurants; no a/c* ⊟ *MC, V* ☉ *Closed Wed. and Nov.–Mar.* 🍽 *MAP.*

$$–$$$ ⊞ **Auberge St-Pierre.** You are not overwhelmed with choices on Mont-St-Michel when it comes to guest accommodations. However, this inn is a popular spot thanks to the fact that it's in a half-timber 15th-century building adjacent to the ramparts and has its own garden restaurant that offers seasonal specialties and interesting half-board rates. If you're lucky, you'll wind up in No. 16, which has a view of the abbey. The hotel annex, La Croix Blanche, has another nine rooms (shower only). ⊠ *Grande-Rue, 50170* ☎ *02–33–60–14–03* 🖷 *02–33–48–59–82* ⊕ *www.auberge-saint-pierre.fr* ⮑ *21 rooms* ⚭ *Restaurant, cable TV, Internet; no a/c* ⊟ *AE, MC, V* 🍽 *MAP.*

en route   From Mont-St-Michel head east on N176/D977 to the attractive hilltop towns of Mortain and Domfront, then north on D962, through Flers and Condé-sur-Noireau, to Clécy, a cute hilltop town on the fringe of **La Suisse Normande** (Norman Switzerland), a rocky expanse of hills and gullies. Stop for a drink at La Potinière Café (closed October–April), on the bank of the Orne River beneath Clécy, then drive south along the bank to Pont d'Ouilly, whose Hôtel du Commerce serves a good lunch. Take D167 to the Roche d'Oëtre, a rock with spectacular views of the craggy hills that give the region its name, and continue along D301 to the Gorges de St-Aubert, a dramatic river gorge, before taking D21 northeast to Falaise.

Falaise

❸❾ *132 km (82 mi) northeast of Mont-St-Michel, 32 km (20 mi) south of Caen.*

The memory of William the Conqueror, born here in 1027 as the illegitimate child of Duke Robert of Normandy and a local girl called La Belle Arlette, haunts the lively town of Falaise. William can be admired on a rearing bronze steed in the main square, and you can see the fountain where Robert is said to have first laid eyes on the lovely Arlette as she washed her clothes. Although Falaise was badly mauled during the Battle of Normandy, parts of the original town walls remain, as do the impressive medieval churches of St-Gervais, La Trinité, and Notre-Dame de Guibray. The foursquare **Château Guillaume-le-Conquérant** (Conqueror's Castle) glowers down from a spur above the town. Little has survived from the original building where William was born—but what remains is old enough. ⊠ *Pl. Guillaume-le-Conquérant* ☎ *02–31–41–61–44* 🖙 *€6* ☉ *Feb.–Dec., daily 10–6.*

⊙ At **Automates Avenue,** 300 clockwork toys and automatons, from the turn of the 20th century to the 1950s, are artfully presented in display windows evoking the streets of Paris. ⊠ *Bd. de la Libération* ☎ *02–31–90–02–43* 🖙 *€5* ☉ *Apr.–Sept., daily 10–12:30 and 1:30–6; Oct.–mid-Jan. and Feb.–Mar., weekends 10–12:30 and 1:30–6.*

off the beaten path

CHÂTEAU D'O – This château's storybook turrets, checkerboard walls, and improbably steep slate roofs rise above a moat patrolled by regal swans near Mortrée, 35 km (22 mi) southeast of Falaise. Inside, look out for the sculpted ermine emblem of the O family, distinguished both as royal courtiers and for possessing the shortest family name in France. With old houses, a stately town hall, and a majestic bishop's palace, nearby **Sées** exudes faded charm. The 200-foot spires of the **Cathédrale St-Latrin** are visible for miles around; note the exquisite late-13th-century stained glass in the soaring choir and the two rose windows in the transepts. ☎ *02–33–35–34–69* 🖙 *€5* ☉ *June–Sept., Wed.–Mon. 2–5.*

Historic **ALENÇON,** 22 km (16 mi) south of Sées via N138, has been a lace-making center since 1665; by the end of the 17th-century *point d'Alençon* (Alençon needlepoint lace) was de rigueur on women's and men's clothing. The **Musée des Beaux-Arts et de la Dentelle** has a sophisticated collection of lace from Italy, Flanders, and France, along with paintings from the French school that span the 17th to 20th centuries. ⊠ *Rue du Capitaine-Charles-Aveline* ☎ *02–33–32–40–07* 🖙 *€3* ☉ *Tues.–Sun. 10–noon and 2–6.*

Where to Eat

★ **$–$$** ✕**La Fine Fourchette.** Chef Gilbert Costil attracts local devotees with dishes combining color, flavor, and quantity. Salmon and tuna gazpacho, foie gras with hazelnut dressing, grilled turbot with lemon, and chocolate cake with pistachio cream stand out among his specialties. Alice Costil provides a gracious welcome. ⊠ *52 rue Georges-Clemenceau* ☎ *02–31–90–08–59* ▤ *AE, MC, V* ☉ *Closed Wed. and Feb. No dinner Tues.*

St-Pierre-sur-Dives

④⓪ *26 km (16 mi) northeast of Falaise on D511.*

St-Pierre-sur-Dives's main claim to fame is the finest medieval barn in Normandy; known as **Les Halles,** it was built in the 11th century, then enlarged in the 16th. It's best visited while the flower and food market is in full swing here on a Monday morning, when a lively cattle auction is held on the square outside. You can also admire the soaring medieval Eglise Abbatiale (abbey church), and visit its chapter house and cloisters; or explore the old tanners' district, with its washhouse and water mill.

en route For apple brandy, make a detour through the **Pays d'Auge,** north of St-Pierre-sur-Dives. This is the heart of calvados country: you don't need a fixed itinerary, just follow your nose and the minor roads, keeping an eye out for local farmers selling calvados. When you are buying calvados, or any regional product for that matter, always request the AOC label, *appéllation d'origine contrôlée,* which assures that the product is made from the finest local ingredients. One good distillery to seek out is the Grandval Calvados Distillery in **Cambremer,** 16 km (10 mi) north of St-Pierre.

Lisieux

41 *25 km (16 mi) northeast of St-Pierre-sur-Dives via D511, 82 km (51 mi) southwest of Rouen.*

Lisieux is the main market town of the prosperous and agriculturally bountiful Pays d'Auge region. Although the town emerged relatively unscathed from World War II, it has few historic monuments beyond the 12th- and 13th-century **Cathédrale St-Pierre.** (The tower to the left of the imposing facade is later than it looks—it's a rare example of 17th-century neo-Gothic reconstruction.) ⊠ *Pl. François-Mitterrand* ☎ *02–31–62–09–82.*

Lisieux's fame stems from St. Theresa (1873–97), who came here as a child, joined a convent at 15, and spent the last 10 years of her life as a Carmelite nun. Theresa was canonized in 1925, and in 1954 the **Basilique Ste-Thérèse**—one of the world's largest 20th-century churches, with a huge dome and an interior of colored marble—was built in her honor. From the cathedral walk up avenue Victor-Hugo and branch left onto avenue Jean-XXIII. A **son-et-lumière** show, running through 2,000 years of history, is presented at the basilica Monday–Saturday nights at 9:45 from June to September. The **Procession de la Vierge** (Virgin's Procession) is held on August 15. The **Procession de la Fête Ste-Thérèse** (St. Theresa's Day Parade) is on the last Sunday in September. ⊠ *Av. Jean-XXIII* ☎ *02–31–78–52–62* 🎫 *Son-et-lumière €6.*

Where to Stay & Eat

$–$$ ×🖾 **Espérance.** This imposing Art Deco hotel in the center of town has typical Norman elegance with its exposed beams and small balconies. Rooms are clean, simple, and, despite the location, quiet. The Pays d'Auge restaurant, on the first floor, has a traditional menu with regional specialties like seafood terrine, leg of duck with apple, and sole flamed in calvados. ⊠ *16 bd. St-Anne, 14100* ☎ *02–31–62–17–53* 🖨 *02–21–62–34–00* ⊕ *www.lisieux-hotel.com* 📞 *100 rooms* ⟷ *Restaurant, cable TV, bar, Internet, some pets allowed (fee); no a/c* ▤ *AE, DC, MC, V* ⊘ *Closed Nov.–late Mar.* ⫿❶ *MAP.*

NORMANDY A TO Z

To research prices, get advice from other travelers, and book travel arrangements, visit www.fodors.com.

AIR TRAVEL

CARRIERS   Air France flies to Caen from Paris. Ryanair flies from Dinard in Brittany, 35 mi west of Mont-St-Michel, to London's Stansted airport.

🛪 **Airlines & Contacts Air France** ☎ 08-02-80-28-02 for information ⊕ www.airfrance.com. **Ryanair** ⊕ www.ryanair.com for information.

AIRPORTS

Paris's Charles de Gaulle (Roissy) and Orly airports are the closest intercontinental links with the region. There are flights in summer from London to Deauville, and year-round service between Jersey and Cherbourg.

🛪 **Airport Information Caen** ☎ 02-31-71-20-10. **Cherbourg** ☎ 02-33-88-57-60. **Deauville** ☎ 02-31-65-65-65. **Rouen** ☎ 02-35-79-41-00.

BIKE & MOPED TRAVEL

You can rent bicycles at most major train stations for about €8 per day. Traveling with your bike is free on all regional trains and many national lines; be sure to ask the SNCF which ones when you're booking.

BOAT & FERRY TRAVEL

A number of ferry companies sail between the United Kingdom and ports in Normandy. Brittany Ferries travels between Caen (Ouistreham) and Portsmouth and between Poole and Cherbourg. The Dieppe-Newhaven route is covered both by boat, with a daily service from Transmanche, and by Hoverspeed, which runs daily in summer, weekends only in winter (and not at all January–mid-February). P&O goes between Le Havre and Portsmouth and between Cherbourg and Portsmouth.

FARES &   🛥 **Boat & Ferry Information Brittany Ferries** ☎ 08-03-82-88-28 ⊕ www.
SCHEDULES   brittany-ferries.com. **Hoverspeed** ☎ 08-20-00-35-55 ⊕ www.hoverspeed.
com. **P&O** ☎ 08-03-01-30-13 ⊕ www.poferries.com. **Transmanche**
☎ 08-00-65-01-00 ⊕ www.transmancheferries.com.

BUS TRAVEL

Three main bus systems cover the towns not served by trains. **CNA** (Compagnie Normande Autobus) runs around Upper Normandy from Rouen to the towns along the Côte d'Alabâtre, including Le Havre. **Autos-Cars Gris** runs buses from Fécamp to Le Havre, stopping in Étretat along the way. **Bus Verts du Calvados** covers the coast from Honfleur to Bayeux; They also run, during July and August, the special D-Day Circuit 44, which allows you to see as many D-Day sights as you can squeeze into one day—these buses depart from the train stations in Bayeux and Caen.

Bus routes connect many towns, including Rouen, Dieppe, Fécamp, Étretat, Le Havre, Caen, Honfleur, Deauville, Trouville, Cabourg, and Arromanches. For Mont-St-Michel, hook up with buses from nearby

Pontorson or from Rennes in adjacent Brittany. If you are traveling from Paris to the Mont, take the high-speed TGV train from Gare Montparnasse to Rennes (in high season, five departures a day), then a **Couriers Breton** bus transfer to the Mont. Tourist offices and train stations in Normandy will have printed schedules.

▸ Bus Information **Autos-Cars Gris** ☎ 02-35-28-19-88. **Bus Verts du Calvados** ☎02-31-44-77-44. **CNA** ☎ 02-35-52-92-92. **Les Couriers Breton** ☎02-99-19-70-70.

CAR RENTAL

▸ Local Agencies **Avis** ✉ 44 pl. de la Gare, Caen ☎ 02-31-84-73-80 ✉ 32 av. de Caen, Rouen ☎ 02-35-72-64-32. **Europcar** ✉ 6 rue du Dr-Piasecki, Le Havre ☎ 02-35-25-21-95.

CAR TRAVEL

From Paris A13 slices its way to Rouen in 1½ hours (toll €4.50) before forking to Caen (an additional hour, toll €6.70) or Le Havre (45 minutes on A131). N13 continues from Caen to Cherbourg via Bayeux in another two hours. From Paris, D915, the scenic route, will take you to Dieppe in about three hours.

The Pont de Normandie, between Le Havre and Honfleur, effectively unites Upper and Lower Normandy. A13/N13, linking Rouen to Caen, Bayeux, and Cherbourg, is the backbone of Normandy. At Caen the A84 forks off southwest toward Mont-St-Michel and Rennes.

EMERGENCIES

▸ Regional hospitals ✉ Av. de la Côte-de-Nacre, Caen ☎ 02-31-06-31-06 ✉ 29 av. Pierre-Mendès-France, Montivilliers, Le Havre ☎ 02-32-73-32-32 ✉ 1 rue Germont, Rouen ☎ 02-32-88-89-90.

SPORTS & THE OUTDOORS

▸ Canoeing & Kayaking **Fédération Française de Canoë-Kayak** ✉ 87 quai de la Marne BP 58, 94340 Joinville-le-Pont ☎ 01-48-89-39-89.
▸ Fishing **Conseil Supérieur de la Pêche** ✉ 134 av. Malakoff, 75016 Paris ☎ 01-45-02-20-20.
▸ Hiking **Comité Départemental de la Randonnée Pédestre de Seine-Maritime** ✉ 18 rue Henri-Ferric, 76210 Gruchet-le-Valasse ☎ 02-35-31-05-51.
▸ Horseback Riding **Ligue de Normandie des Sports Équestres** ✉ 181 rue d'Auge, 14000 Caen ☎ 02-31-84-61-87.

TOURS

The firm Wellcome arranges personalized driving tours with an English-speaking driver.

▸ Fees & Schedules **Wellcome** ✉ 130 rue Martainville, 76000 Rouen ☎ 02-35-07-79-79.

BUS TOURS Cityrama and Paris-Vision run full-day bus excursions from Paris to Mont-St-Michel for €140–€155, meals and admission included. This is definitely not for the faint of heart—buses leave Paris at 7:15 AM and return around 10:30 PM. In Caen, the Mémorial organizes four-hour English-language daily minibus tours of the D-Day landing beaches; the cost is €60, including entrance fees. Bus Fly runs a number of trips to the D-Day beaches and Mont-St-Michel; a full-day excursion to the D-Day beaches (8:30–6:00) runs about €55.

🚩Fees & Schedules **Bus Fly** ✉25 rue des Cuisiniers, 14400 Bayeux ☎02-31-22-00-08. **Cityrama** ✉ 4 pl. des Pyramides, 75001 Paris ☎ 01-44-55-61-00. **Mémorial** ☎ 02-31-06-06-44. **Paris-Vision** ✉ 214 rue de Rivoli, 75001 Paris ☎ 08-00-03-02-14.

TRAIN TRAVEL

From Paris (Gare St-Lazare), separate train lines head to Upper Normandy (Rouen and Le Havre or Dieppe) and Lower Normandy (Caen, Bayeux, and Cherbourg, via Évreux and Lisieux). Taking the train from Paris to Mont-St-Michel is not easy—count on about 3½ hours to get to the closest station (Pontorson), with another 15-minute bus or taxi ride to take you to the foot of the abbey (buses are directly in front of the station, with departures every 20 minutes).

Unless you are content to stick to the major towns (Rouen, Le Havre, Dieppe, Caen, Bayeux, Cherbourg), visiting Normandy by train may prove frustrating. You can sometimes reach several smaller towns (Fécamp, Deauville, Houlgate) on snail-paced branch lines, but the irregular intricacies of what is said to be Europe's most complicated regional timetable will probably have driven you nuts by the time you get there. **🚩 Train Information** **SNCF** ☎ 08-36-35-35-35 ⊕ www.ter-sncf.com/uk/haute-normandie.

TRAVEL AGENCIES

🚩 Local Agent Referrals **Havas** ✉57 quai George-V, Le Havre ☎ 02-32-74-75-76 ✉ 25 Grande-Rue, Alençon ☎ 02-33-82-59-00 ✉ 80 rue St-Jean, Caen ☎ 02-31-27-10-50.

VISITOR INFORMATION

The capital of each of Normandy's *départements*—Caen, Évreux, Rouen, St-Lô, and Alençon—has its own central tourist office. Other major Norman towns with tourist offices are listed below the département offices by name.

🚩 Tourist Information **Caen** ✉Pl. du Canada ☎02-31-27-90-30 🖨02-31-27-90-35 ⊕ www.ville-caen.fr for Calvados. **Rouen** ✉25 pl. de la Cathédrale ☎02-32-08-32-40 🖨 02-32-08-32-44 ⊕ www.rouentourisme.com for Seine-Maritime. **St-Lô** ✉Maison du Département, rte. de Villedieu ☎ 02-33-05-98-70 ⊕ www.manchetourisme.com/gb/ for Manche.

Bayeux ✉ Pont St-Jean ☎ 02-31-51-28-28 ⊕ www.bayeux-tourism.com. **Cherbourg** ✉ 2 quai Alexandre-III ☎ 02-33-93-52-02 ⊕ www.ot-cherbourg-cotentin.fr. **Dieppe** ✉Pont Jehan-An ☎02-35-84-11-77 ⊕www.dieppe-tourisme.com. **Falaise** ✉Le Forum, bd. de la Libération ☎ 02-31-90-17-26. **Fécamp** ✉ 113 rue Alexandre-le-Grand ☎ 02-35-28-51-01 ⊕ www.fecamp.com. **Le Havre** ✉ 186 bd. Clemenceau ☎ 02-32-74-04-04 ⊕ www.ville-lehavre.fr. **Honfleur** ✉ 9 rue de la Ville ☎ 02-31-89-23-30 ⊕ www.ville-honfleur.fr. **Lisieux** ✉ 11 rue d'Alençon ☎ 02-31-62-08-41 ⊕ www.ville-lisieux.fr. **Mont-St-Michel** ✉ Corps de Garde ☎ 02-33-60-14-30 ⊕ www.mont-saintmichel.com.

The North & Champagne

6

Introduction by
Nancy Coons

Updated by
Simon Hewitt

FLAT AS A CRÊPE AS FAR AS THE EYE CAN SEE and shimmering with hoar-frost, magpies wheeling over gnarl-fingered trees, and white-brick cottages punctuating an otherwise uninterrupted sight line to the horizon: this is the archetypal landscape of winter in the north of France, an evocative canvas that conjures up the great 16th-century paintings of Pieter Brueghel and reflects, as no history book can, how closely married this corner of France was—and is—to Flanders. Here, as in Belgium and the Netherlands, the iron grip of the Spanish Inquisition sent thinkers and threshers alike scrambling for cover. Here, also, numerous woolen mills spun the stuff of epic tapestries. And here, as well, the ill humors of the flatland air drove a people and a culture into golden, fire-lit interiors to seek comfort, as did their brethren to the east, in steaming platters of *moules-frites* (mussels and french fries), a mug of amber beer, and a warming swallow of juniper gin.

The landscape recalls images relentlessly epic: medieval stoneworkers in fingerless gloves raised radically new Gothic arches to improbable heights, running for cover when the naves failed to stand, while in the region's industrial areas the hollow-eyed miners immortalized in Émile Zola's *Germinal* descended into hellish black-coal portals. In Compiègne, Joan of Arc languished in prison after suffering wounds in mounted battle with the English. At Agincourt, Henry V rallied the British to gory victory, temporarily reversing William the Norseman's 349-year-long conquest. And in the Somme, wave upon wave of doughboy infantry slogged through the bomb-torn countryside to gain, lose, and ultimately regain a scrap of land.

Most people give the north of France a wide berth, roaring through the Channel ports at Boulogne and Calais on a beeline for Paris, en route to the south for a sunshine cure. But this underappreciated region, with its chiaroscuro of bleak exteriors and interior warmth, conceals treasures of art, architecture, history, and natural beauty that reward slow and pleasurable study. Just an hour's trip from Paris on the TGV, Lille beckons with its Palais des Beaux-Arts, whose collections of Old Masters are worthy in scale of the capital's. There are no fewer than 10 cathedrals still standing (though you might want to hover near the exits at Beauvais, whose nave, the tallest in France, makes some engineers nervous) and worth a visit. You may choose to relax on the relatively uncrowded beaches that wrap the coast from Dunkerque to the Bay of the Somme, or to wander through World War I battlefields and cemeteries whose scale is imponderable.

And then you can recover with Champagne. Head southeast toward Reims, and the sky clears, the landscape loosens and undulates, and the hills tantalize with the vineyards that produce the world's antidote to gloom, *à la méthode champenoise*. Between tasting tours at Reims and Épernay, you can contemplate Reims Cathedral, where Clovis was baptized and to which St. Joan dragged a recalcitrant Dauphin to be crowned. No wonder more and more British are using the Channel Tunnel to visit northern France for day and weekend trips.

France's northernmost out-thrust shows its Flemish roots in a Brueghelesque landscape, cozy Old Master interiors, and a violent history worthy of the images of Hieronymus Bosch. Add spectacular Gothic cathedrals, fine Flemish art in Lille, broad beaches, and Reims—the "Capital of Bubbly"—and you'll find that this overlooked region merits exploration. Count on at least five days to do justice to this vast treasury, starting at Beauvais, north of Paris. Only three days? Concentrate on the most scenic attractions of Picardy and Champagne.

Numbers in the text correspond to numbers in the margin and on the North and Champagne map.

If you have 3 days

Start in **Compiègne** ㉙ ▶ at its elegant Napoleonic palace, and then head to **Pierrefonds** ㉚ and its storybook castle. By dinnertime be in the hilltop cathedral town of ▣ **Laon** ㉔. After touring Laon the next morning, drive to the cathedral city of ▣ **Reims** ㉟–㊹ for the afternoon, the night, and maybe part of the third morning. Make the Champagne vineyards to the south—on the Montagne de Reims, along the Route du Vin, and in the Marne Valley west of **Épernay** ㉜—your final destination.

If you have 5 days

Begin with a day in the vibrant city of ▣ **Lille** ❹–⓯ ▶, home to France's largest art museum outside Paris. The next morning take in stately **Arras** ⑲ and the moving war cemeteries nearby en route to princely ▣ **Compiègne** ㉙. Devote Day 3 to the medieval splendor of **Pierrefonds** ㉚ and ▣ **Laon** ㉔ and Day 4 to ▣ **Reims** ㉟–㊹. Spend your last day touring the Montagne de Reims and the Route du Vin, and then head east from **Épernay** ㉜ to the historic town of **Châlons-en-Champagne** ㉝.

Exploring the North & Champagne

The region commonly referred to as northern France stretches from the Somme River up to the Channel Tunnel and includes the vibrant city of Lille, to the northeast. Champagne encompasses Reims and the surrounding vineyards and chalky plains. Picardy, to the south of the region, is traversed by the Aisne and Oise rivers. The hills and forests of the Ardennes lead northeast toward Belgium.

The north of France has a shared history with Flemish-speaking territories. Lille, France's northern metropolis, is the capital of what is known as French Flanders, which stretches northwest from the city to the coastal areas around Dunkerque and Gravelines. West of Lille extends the Côte d'Opale, the Channel coastline so named for the color of its sea and sky. To the southeast the grapes of Champagne flourish on the steep slopes of the Marne Valley and the Montagne de Reims, really more of a mighty hill than a mountain. Reims is the only city in Champagne—and one of France's richest tourist sites.

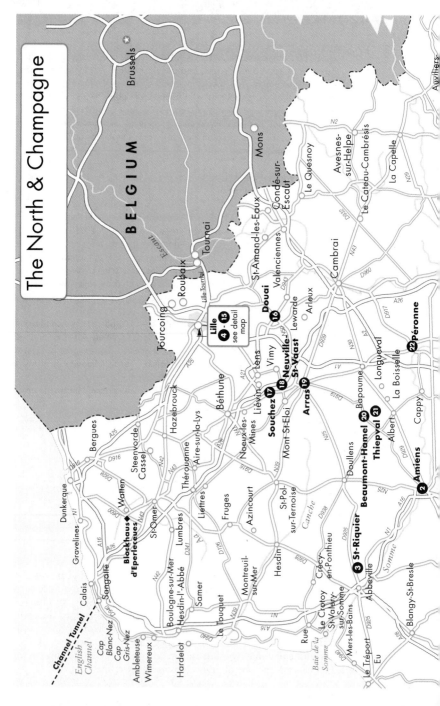

The North & Champagne

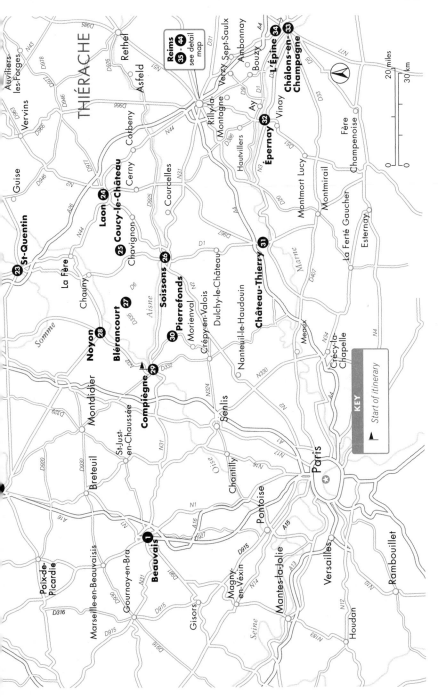

About the Restaurants & Hotels

With the exception of a handful of resort towns along the Channel Coast, this region is less dependent on tourism than many in France, and most restaurants are open year-round—although in Lille and Amiens, the two liveliest cities, each with large student populations, many restaurants close for two to three weeks in July and August. Typical of northern France are *estaminets*: part-brasserie, part-pub, where locals gather for a meal or just a snack, to accompany a higher standard of beer than commonly found elsewhere in France. Another regional specialty, handy if you're in a hurry, is the ubiquitous wayside *frites* van selling French fries and hot dogs.

Northern France is overladen with old, rambling hotels, often simple rather than pretentious; there are also luxurious châteaux with fine restaurants. Top quality is hard to come by, except in major cities such as Lille and Reims. Assume all hotel rooms have air-conditioning, TV, telephones, and private bath, unless otherwise noted.

	WHAT IT COSTS In euros				
	$$$$	**$$$**	**$$**	**$**	**¢**
RESTAURANTS	over €30	€23–€30	€17–€23	€11–€17	under €11
HOTELS	over €190	€120–€190	€80–€120	€50–€80	under €50

Restaurant prices are per person for a main course at dinner, including tax (19.6%) and service; note that if a restaurant offers only prix-fixe (set-price) meals, it has been given the price category that reflects the full prix-fixe price. Hotel prices are for a standard double room in high season, including tax (19.6%) and service charge. Hotels operate on the European Plan (EP, with no meal provided) unless we note that they use the Breakfast Plan (BP), or also offer such options as Modified American Plan (MAP, with breakfast and dinner daily, known as *demi-pension*), or Full American Plan (FAP, or *pension complète*, with three meals a day). Inquire when booking if these all-inclusive mealplans (which always entail higher rates) are mandatory or optional.

Timing

Compared to many other regions of France, the north remains relatively uncrowded in July and August, and the huge Channel beaches have room for everyone. If you're lucky enough to visit the Champagne region in the autumn, plan to drive along the Route du Vin through vineyards golden in the harvest sun. Champagne grapes are gathered in late September or early October (then pressed at once in *vendangeoirs* near the vineyards), and during this time you can even be hired as a grape-picker (according to law, the grapes that go into champagne must be picked by hand). But be sure to plan a visit to Reims and Champagne only between May and October; the region's ubiquitous vineyards are a dismal, leafless sight the rest of the year. The liveliest time in Lille is the first weekend in September, during its three-day street fair, La Grande Braderie. Other local fairs include the Dunkerque Carnival, in February, and the Giants' Carnival, in Douai in July. The wooded Ardennes, to the northeast, is attractive in fall, when local game highlights area menus.

6

The Capital of Bubbly

An uplifting landscape tumbles about Reims and Épernay, perhaps because its inhabitants treat themselves to a regular infusion of the local, world-prized elixir we know and love as champagne. Each year, millions of bottles of bubbly mature in hundreds of kilometers of chalk tunnels carved under the towns' streets. Whether or not you choose to buy a bottle, you should be able to land yourself a complimentary glass of champagne at the end of a tour. If you count yourself among the present-day crowds of case-toting bubblyphiles, you'll know that, unlike the great vineyards of Bordeaux and Burgundy, there are few country châteaux to go with the fabled names of this region— Mumm, Taittinger, Pommery, and Veuve-Clicquot. Most of the glory is to be found in *caves* and cellars.

Glorious Gothic

The hundreds of kilometers of chalk tunnels throughout the North, some dug by the ancient Romans as quarries, serve as the damp and moldy berth for millions of bottles of champagne, but they also gave up tons of blocks to create other treasures of the region: the magical and magnificent Gothic cathedrals of Northern France. Just a few are Amiens, the largest; Beauvais, the tallest; Noyon, the earliest; Abbeville, the last; Reims, the most regal; and Laon, with the most towers (and the most spectacular hilltop setting). Add in those at St-Omer, Soissons, St-Quentin, and Châlons-en-Champagne, along with the bijou churches in Rue, St-Riquier, and L'Épine, and fans of medieval architecture are in for a true feast.

Pigs & Potatoes

The cuisine of northern France is robust and hearty. In Flanders beer is often used as a base for sauces. French fries and mussels are featured on most menus; vans selling fries and hot dogs are a common sight; and large quantities of mussels and fish, notably herring, are consumed. Smoked ham and, in season, boar and venison are specialties of the eastern part of the region. Cheese aficionados will be keen to sample soft, square *Maroilles*, with its orange rind, and the spicy, pyramid-shape *boulette d'Avesnes*. To satisfy your sweet tooth, try macaroons and *bêtises de Cambrai* (minty lollipops). Ham, pigs' feet, gingerbread, and champagne-based mustard are specialties of the Reims area, as is ratafia, a sweet aperitif made from grape juice and brandy. To the north, a glass of *genièvre* (gin flavored with juniper berries, which is sometimes added to the dregs of a cup of black coffee to make a *bistouille*) is the classic way to finish a meal. In the old days champagne was treated as an aperitif or dessert wine, but it can be served throughout an entire meal, starting with the younger, lighter, and drier wines, and progressing gradually to the older, sweeter ones.

Beaches

Extending from Dunkerque to the Bay of the Somme is the Côte d'Opale, one long, sandy beach. It's sometimes short of sun, but not of space or beach sports, like *char à voile* (sand sailing). The climate is bracing, often windy, but there are wonderfully scenic spots along the cliffs south of Calais: Cap Gris Nez and Cap Blanc Nez. Le Touquet is one of France's fanciest coastal resort towns.

THE NORTH

Starting with Beauvais and Amiens (both easily accessible by expressway from Paris) and two of France's most splendorous Gothic cathedrals, follow the Somme Valley to the Channel. Unfortunately, the ports of Calais and Dunkerque are among France's uglier towns, but the old sections of Boulogne-sur-Mer have scenic appeal, as do the narrow streets of ancient Montreuil and the posh avenues of fashionable Le Touquet. After wheeling inland to church-and-museum-rich Lille, head south to the World War I battlefields between Arras and Albert, continuing southeast into Picardy with its hilltop castles and cathedrals.

Beauvais

① *80 km (50 mi) north of Paris.*

Beauvais and its neighbor Amiens have been rivals since the 13th century, when they locked horns over who could build the bigger cathedral. Beauvais lost—gloriously.

A work-in-progress preserved for all time, soaring above the characterless modern blocks of the town center, is the tallest cathedral in France: the **Cathédrale St-Pierre.** You may have an attack of vertigo just gazing up at its vaults, 153 feet above the ground. It may be the tallest, but not the largest. Paid for by the riches of Beauvais's wool industry, the choir collapsed in 1284, shortly after completion, and was only rebuilt with the addition of extra pillars. This engineering fiasco proved so costly that the transept was not attempted until the 16th century. It was worth the wait: an outstanding example of Flamboyant Gothic, with ornate rose windows flanked by pinnacles and turrets. It's also still standing— which is more than can be said for the megalomaniacal 450-foot spire erected at the same time. This lasted precisely four years; when it came crashing down, all remaining funds were hurled at an emergency consolidation program, and Beauvais's dream of having the largest church in Christendom vanished forever. Now the cathedral is starting to lean, and cracks have appeared in the choir vaults because of shifting water levels in the soil. No such problems bedevil the **Basse Oeuvre** (Lower Edifice; closed to the public), which juts out impertinently where the nave should have been. It has been there for 1,000 years. Fittingly donated to the cathedral by the canon Étienne Musique, the oldest surviving **chiming clock** in the world—a 1302 model with a 15th-century painted wooden face and most of its original clockwork—is built into the wall of the cathedral. Perhaps Auguste Vérité drew his inspiration from this humbler timepiece when, in 1868, he made a gift to his hometown of the gilded, templelike **astrological clock** (€4, displays at 11:40, 2:40 and 3:40, English headphones available). Animated religious figurines surrounded by all sorts of gears and dials emerge for their short program at erratic times, although there is a set schedule for visits with commentary. ⊠ *Rue St-Pierre* ☉ *May–Oct., daily 9–12:15 and 2–6:15; Nov.–Apr., daily 9–12:15 and 2–5:30.*

Fodor'sChoice
★

From 1664 to 1939 Beauvais was one of France's leading tapestry centers; it reached its zenith in the mid-18th century under the gifted artist Jean-Baptiste Oudry, known for his hunting scenes. Examples from all periods are in the modern **Galerie Nationale de la Tapisserie** (National Tapestry Museum). ⊠ *22 rue St-Pierre* ☎ *03–44–15–39–10* 🖭 *€4* ⊙ *Apr.–Sept., Tues.–Sun. 9:30–12:30 and 2–6; Oct.–Mar., Tues.–Sun. 10–12:30 and 2–5.*

One of the few remaining testaments to Beauvais's glorious past, the old Bishop's Palace is now the **Musée Départemental de l'Oise** (Regional Museum). Don't miss the beautifully proportioned attic story, Thomas Couture's epic canvas of the French Revolution, the 14th-century frescoes of instrument-playing sirens on a section of the palace's vaults, or the 1st-century brass *Guerrier Gaulois* (Gallic Warrior). The museum is scheduled to reopen in summer 2006 after enlargement and renovation. ⊠ *1 rue du Musée* ☎ *03–44–11–43–83* 🖭 *€2, free Wed.* ⊙ *Wed.–Mon. 10–noon and 2–6.*

Where to Eat

¢ ✗ **Le Marignan.** This lively brasserie near Beauvais town hall (make for the cozy upstairs dining-room if you'd prefer some peace and quiet) offers a choice of fish, chicken, and savory flans, plus a three-course lunchtime menu at just €11. Succulent desserts range from crème brûlée to almond and raspberry tart. ⊠ *1 rue Malherbe* ☎ *03–44–48–15–15* 🖃 *MC, V* ⊙ *Closed Mon., and late July–mid-Aug. No dinner Sun.*

Amiens

❷ *58 km (36 mi) north of Beauvais via N1 or A16.*

Although Amiens showcases some pretty brazen postwar reconstruction, epitomized by Auguste Perret's 340-foot Tour Perret, a soaring concrete stump by the train station, the city is well worth exploring. It has lovely Art Deco buildings in its traffic-free city center, as well as elegant, older stone buildings like the 18th-century Beffroi (belfry) and Neoclassical prefecture. Crowning the city is its great Gothic cathedral, which has survived the ages intact. Nearby is the waterfront quarter of St-Leu—with its small, colorful houses—rivaling the squares of Arras and streets of old Lille as the cutest city district north of Paris.

Fodor'sChoice ★ By far the largest church in France, the **Cathédrale Notre-Dame** could enclose Paris's Notre-Dame twice. It may lack the stained glass of Chartres or the sculpture of Reims, but for architectural harmony, engineering proficiency, and sheer size, it's without peer. The soaring, asymmetrical facade has a notable Flamboyant Gothic rose window, and is brought to life on summer evenings when a sophisticated 45-minute light show recreates its original color scheme. Inside, there is no stylistic disunity to mar the perspective, creating an overwhelming sensation of pure space. Construction took place between 1220 and 1264, a remarkably short period in cathedral-building spans. One of the highlights of a visit here is hidden from the eye, at least until you lift up some of the 110 choir-stall seats and admire the humorous, skillful misericord seat carvings executed between 1508 and 1518. ⊠ *Pl. Notre-Dame* ☎ *03–22–91–72–08* 🖭 *Free* ⊙ *Access to towers, Wed.–Mon. 3–4:30.*

The **Hôtel de Berny,** near the cathedral, is a steep-roof stone-and-brick mansion built in 1633. It's filled with 18th-century furniture, tapestries, and objets d'art. ⊠ *36 rue Victor-Hugo* ☎ *03–22–97–14–00* ✉ *€1.50* ⊙ *Oct.–Mar., Sun. 10–12:30 and 2–6; Apr.–Sept., Thurs.–Sun. 2–6.*

★ Behind an opulent columned facade, the **Musée de Picardie,** built 1855–67, looks like just another pompous offering from the Second Empire. Initial impressions are hardly challenged by its grand staircase lined with monumental frescoes by local-born Puvis de Chavannes, or its central hall with huge canvases, like Gérôme's 1855 *Siècle d'Auguste* and Maignon's 1892 *Mort de Carpeaux,* with flying muses wresting the dying sculptor from his earthly clay. One step beyond, though, and you're in a rotunda painted top to bottom in modern minimalist fashion by Sol LeWitt. The basement is filled with subtly lighted archaeological finds and Egyptian artifacts beneath masterly brick vaulting. On the top floor, El Greco leads the Old Masters, along with a humorous set of hunting scenes like Boucher's Rococo-framed *Crocodile Hunt,* from 1736. ⊠ *48 rue de la République* ☎ *03–22–97–14–00* ✉ *€4, free Sun.* ⊙ *Tues.–Sun. 10–12:30 and 2–6.*

Jules Verne (1828–1905) lived in Amiens for the last 35 years of his life, and his former home is now the **Maison Jules-Verne** (⊠2 rue Charles-Dubois ☎03–22–45–37–84 ⊕www.jules-verne.net ✉€3 ⊙Tues.–Sun. 10–12:30 and 2–6). It contains some 15,000 documents about Verne's life as well as original furniture and a reconstruction of the writing studio where he created his science-fiction classics. If you're a true Verne fan, you might want to visit his last resting place in the **Cimetière de la Madeleine** (⊠2 rue de la Poudrière), where he is melodramatically portrayed pushing up his tombstone as if enacting his own sci-fi resurrection.

Where to Stay & Eat

★ **$–$$$** ✕**Les Marissons.** In the scenic St-Leu section of Amiens, beneath the cathedral, this picturesque waterside restaurant serves creative takes on foie gras and regional ingredients: eel, duck pâté, turbot with apricots, rabbit with mint and goat cheese, and pigeon with black currants. To avoid pricey dining à la carte, order from the prix-fixe menus. ⊠ *68 rue des Marissons* ☎*03–22–92–96–66* ⊕*www.les-marissons.fr* ▭*AE, DC, MC, V* ⊙ *Closed Sun. and 3 wks in May. No lunch Sat.*

$–$$ ✕**Joséphine.** Despite its unprepossessing facade and drab front room, this good-value restaurant in central Amiens is a reliable choice. It serves solid fare (fish stew, a specialty) and has decent wines and a back room overlooking a garden courtyard. ⊠ *20 rue Sire-Firmin-Leroux* ☎ *03–22–91–47–38* ▭ *AE, MC, V* ⊙ *Closed Mon. and 3rd wk in Aug. No dinner Sun.*

$–$$ ▥ **Carlton.** This hotel near the train station has a stylish Belle Époque facade. In contrast, rooms are sober and functional, though light and airy, with spacious bathrooms. Foreign guests are common, and English is spoken. The brasserie-style restaurant, Le Bistrot, serves regional, mainly meat dishes. ⊠ *42 rue de Noyon, 80000* ☎ *03–22–97–72–22* 🖷 *03–22–97–72–00* ⊕ *www.lecarlton.fr* ⇝ *24 rooms* ⚐ *Restaurant, some pets allowed (fee); no a/c* ▭ *AE, DC, MC, V* ⊙❙ *BP.*

The Arts
The **Théâtre de Marionnettes** (✉31 rue Edouard-David ☎03–22–22–30–90) presents a rare glimpse of the traditional Picardy marionettes, known locally as Chés Cabotans d'Amiens. Shows are performed (in French), usually on Friday evening and Sunday afternoon (daily in August), with plot synopses printed in English.

St-Riquier

❸ *37 km (23 mi) northwest of Amiens via N1 and D32.*

★ The tumbling village of St-Riquier is dominated by its imposing abbey church. Magnificent **St-Riquier** has a majestic Flamboyant Gothic facade with a superbly sculpted 160-foot tower (illuminated on Friday and Saturday evenings), a 100-yard-long nave, and handsome 17th-century wrought-iron gates at the front of the choir.

Where to Stay & Eat
$$–$$$$ ✕⌗ **Jean de Bruges.** The 1473 abbot's house next to the church has been transformed into a small, stylish hotel owned by the folks who run the neighboring Bernadette-Stubbe wine tavern. Gleaming marble floors, white stonework, cream-color curtains, designer lighting, old carved furniture, and impressive modern art throughout make for stylish accents. Ask for airy Room 2, or Room 8, with a small terrace; all are named for former abbots. The glass-roof breakfast room leads to a patio used for afternoon tea. ✉ *18 pl. de l'Église, 80135* ☎ *03–22–28–30–30* 🖷 *03–22–28–00–69* ⊕ *www.hotel-jean-de-bruges.com* ⇖ *11 rooms* ⌂ *Restaurant, minibars, some pets allowed (fee); no a/c in some rooms* ⊟ *AE, MC, V* ☽ *Closed Jan.* ⏁ *MAP.*

Lille

▶ *116 km (65 mi) northeast of St-Riquier, 220 km (137 mi) north of Paris, 100 km (62 mi) west of Brussels.*

For a city supposedly reeling from the problems of its main industry— textiles—Lille is remarkably dynamic; years of ultra-stylish renovation culminated in the title of European City of Culture for 2004. After experiencing Flemish, Austrian, and Spanish rule, Lille passed into French hands for good in 1668. Lille (the name comes from *l'isle*, the island, in the Deûle River, where the city began) is a European crossroads— one hour by train from Paris and Brussels, under two from London. The shiny glass towers of the Euralille complex, a high-tech commercial center of dubious aesthetic merit, greet travelers arriving at the TGV station, Lille-Europe.

❹ The sumptuous church of **St-Maurice** (✉ Rue de Paris), just off place de la Gare, is a large, five-aisle structure built between the 14th and 19th **❺** centuries. The majestic **Porte de Paris** (✉ Rue de Paris), overlooked by the 340-foot brick tower of the **Hôtel de Ville,** is a cross between a mansion and a triumphal arch. It was built by Simon Vollant in the 1680s in honor of Louis XIV and was originally part of the city walls.

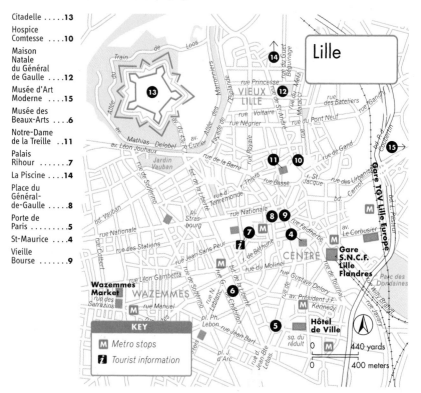

★ ❻ The **Museé des Beaux-Arts** is the country's largest fine arts museum outside Paris. It houses a noteworthy collection of Dutch and Flemish
paintings (Anthony Van Dyck, Peter Paul Rubens, Flemish Primitives,
and Dutch landscapists) as well as some charmingly understated still lifes
by Chardin, works by the Impressionists, and dramatic canvases by El
Greco, Tintoretto, Paolo Veronese, and Goya (including two of his
most famous—*Les Jeunes* and the ghastly *Les Vieilles*). A ceramics section displays some fine examples of Lille faïence (earthenware), and there's
a superbly lighted display of *plans reliefs* (18th-century scale models of
French towns) in the basement, with binoculars provided to help you
admire all the intricate detail. ⊠ *Pl. de la République* ☎ *03–20–06–78–00*
⊕ *www.musenor.com/gm/gmlillea.htm* ✉ *€4.60* ⊙ *Wed.–Thurs. and
weekends 10–6, Fri. 10–7, Mon. 2–6.*

❼ The late-15th-century **Palais Rihour** (Rihour Palace; ⊠ Pl. Rihour), built
for Philippe le Bon, duke of Burgundy, is famed for its octagonal turret
and staircase with intricate swirling-pattern brickwork. The city **tourist
office** is housed in the vaulted former guardroom on the ground floor.

Lille's most famous square, Grand'Place, is just one block from place Ri-
❽ hour and is now officially called **Place du Général-de-Gaulle.** The *Déesse*
(goddess), atop the giant column clutching a linstock (used to fire a can-

non), has dominated the square since 1845; she commemorates Lille's heroic resistance to an Austrian siege in 1792. Other landmarks include the handsome, gabled 1936 facade of *La Voix du Nord* (the main regional newspaper), topped by three gilded statues symbolizing the three historic regions of Flanders, Artois, and Hainaut; and the Furet du Nord, which outrageously claims to be the world's largest bookstore.

9 The elegant **Vieille Bourse** (Old Commercial Exchange), on one side of Grand'Place, was built in 1653 by Julien Destrées as a commercial exchange to rival those of the Low Countries. Note the bronze busts, sculpted medallions, and ornate stonework of its arcaded quadrangle.

The **Vieux Lille** (Old Lille) neighborhood dates mainly from the 17th and 18th centuries; most of its richly sculpted facades, often combining stone facings with pale pink brickwork, have been restored. Perhaps the most ornate building is the Maison de Gilles de La Boë on Place Louise-de-Bettignies, built in 1636 for a rich grocer.

10 The **Hospice Comtesse** (Countess Hospital), founded as a hospital in 1237 by Jeanne de Constantinople, countess of Flanders, was rebuilt in the 15th century after a fire destroyed most of the original structure. Local artifacts from the 17th and 18th centuries form the backbone of the museum now housed here, but its star attraction is the **Salle des Malades** (Sick Ward), featuring a majestic wooden ceiling. ⊠ *32 rue de la Monnaie* ☎ *03–28–36–84–00* 🖃 *€2.30* ☾ *Wed.–Fri. 10–12:30 and 2–6, weekends 10–6, Mon. 2–6.*

11 The cathedral of **Notre-Dame de la Treille** (⊠ Rue des Trois-Mollettes) stands on the spot of a medieval church dismantled during the Revolution. The present building was begun—in a suitably neo-Gothic style—in 1854. Construction was halted from 1869 to 1893, and by World War I only the choir was complete. The roof vaults were only finished in 1973, and the west front, with its dismal expanses of gray concrete, remained despairingly incomplete until a translucent marble facade was added in 1999.

12 General Charles de Gaulle (1890–1970), the former President of France, was born in Lille. His birthplace, the **Maison Natale du Général de Gaulle**, has been meticulously restored and is now a museum devoted to his memory. ⊠ *9 rue Princesse* ☎ *03–28–38–12–05* ⊕ *www.maison-natale-degaulle.org* 🖃 *€5.50* ☾ *Wed.–Sun. 10–noon and 2–5.*

13 Lille's gigantic **Citadelle** patrols the northwest of the city from the enchanting Bois de Boulogne Gardens, whose leafy walkways alongside photogenic streams attract hordes of strollers, cyclists, and joggers. The colossal walls of the citadel are immaculately preserved, no doubt because the site is still inhabited by the French military (you can only visit the interior on Sunday afternoon). It was constructed rapidly between 1667 and 1670; of course, that genius of military engineering Sébastien de Vauban got the commission. Some 60 million bricks were baked in record time, and the result is a fortified town in its own right. ☎ *03–20–21–94–21 for tourist office to arrange tours* 🖃 *€6.50* ☾ *Guided tours only, May–Sept. Sun. 3–5.*

★ ⑭ **La Piscine,** in the northeast suburb of Roubaix, is one of France's most unusual and visually exciting museums—it's housed in a converted swimming pool, opened 1932, closed 1985, transformed 2002, still complete with Art Deco mosaics, tile work, and giant half-moon stained-glass windows. The collection of 19th- and 20th-century art, sculpture, and textiles is imaginatively displayed along the waterside and in the former changing cubicles, while a subtle background soundtrack of swishing water and childlike yelps conjures up the public pool of yore. ⊠ *23 rue de l'Espérance* ☎ *03–20–69–23–60* ⊕ *museeroubaix.free.fr* ⊠ *€3* ⊙ *Tues.–Fri. 11–6, weekends 1–6.*

⑮ The **Musée d'Art Moderne,** in the leafy eastern suburb of Villeneuve d'Ascq, is a modern, sober brick building ringed by trim lawns alive with boxing bronze hares by Barry Flanagan and a giant Calder mobile. The outstanding picture collection ranges from the Cubists, Modigliani, and the Surrealists to Chaissac, Soulages, and postwar abstraction. A new extension, slated to open in 2006, contains a large collection of *Art Brut* (Outsider Art). ⊠ *1 allée du Musée* ☎ *03–20–19–68–68* ⊕ *www. nordnet.fr/mam* ⊠ *€6.50* ⊙ *Wed.–Mon. 10–6.*

Where to Stay & Eat

★ **$$$–$$$$** ✕ **L'Huîtrière.** Behind a magnificent Art Deco fish store lined with local Desvres tiles, this elegant seafood restaurant serves fresh, local seafood, simply prepared in regional (Flemish) style—turbot hollandaise, *waterzoï* (a mild, creamy fish stew), braised eel, scallops, and oysters. The clientele is well-heeled, the 18th-century decor with paneling and crystal chandeliers refined, and prices justifiably high. ⊠ *3 rue des Chats-Bossus* ☎ *03–20–55–43–41* ⊕ *www.huitriere.fr* ☐ *AE, DC, MC, V* ⊙ *Closed mid-July–late Aug. No dinner Sun.*

¢–$ ✕ **Le Lion Bossu.** Old bricks and beams distinguish the 17th-century interior of this restaurant in the heart of Old Lille, a cozy, old-fashioned spot serving simple, homey regional food. ⊠ *1 rue St-Jacques* ☎ *03–20–06–06–88* ☐ *AE, MC, V* ⊙ *Closed Sun. No lunch Mon.*

¢ ✕ **Les Brasseurs.** This dark, wood-paneled brasserie beside the Lille-Flandres station brews its own beer. Four types—blond (lager), amber, dark (stout), and white (wheat beer)—are available, and La Palette du Barman lets you sample all for €4. *Carbonnade flamande* (Flemish-style beef cooked in a sweet and sour sauce) and *flammekueches* (flattened bread dough topped with bacon and onions) are served. ⊠ *18 pl. de la Gare* ☎ *03–20–06–46–25* ☐ *MC, V.*

$$–$$$ 🛏 **Grand Hôtel Bellevue.** The former Hôtel de Bourbon, home to Mozart in 1765, is now an elegant central lodging near Grand'Place. Large, comfortable Art Deco rooms and modern bathrooms are complemented by the sort of deferential service you can no longer take for granted. The leather-lined bar is a good spot in which to rendezvous. ⊠ *5 rue Jean-Roisin, 59800* ☎ *03–20–57–45–64* 📠 *03–20–40–07–93* ⊕ *www. grandhotelbellevue.com* ⬐ *60 rooms* ⚘ *Minibars, bar, some pets allowed (fee); no a/c* ☐ *AE, DC, MC, V* ⎟⊙⎟ *BP.*

★ **$–$$** 🛏 **Brueghel.** The Brueghel, named in honor of one of the most famous of Flemish painting dynasties, is a picture of revived Art Deco charm; antiques are scattered throughout the corridors and rooms, many of which retain their original interwar furniture. The mood in the wood-panel lobby is friendly and welcoming, and that has made the hotel a favorite among visiting performers at the nearby opera house. The hotel is also handily placed for the Vieille Bourse and Grand'Place, as well as Lille's two train stations, and looks onto the pedestrian piazza around the venerable Gothic church of St-Maurice. ⊠ *3 parvis St-Maurice, 59000* ☎ *03–20–06–06–69* 🖷 *03–20–63–25–27* ⊕ *www.hotel-brueghel.com* 🖵 *66 rooms* ♿ *Bar, some Internet, some pets allowed (fee); no a/c* 🖃 *AE, DC, MC, V.*

Nightlife & the Arts

Jazz clubs, piano bars, nightclubs, and all kinds of performances are listed in *Lille by Night*, available at the Lille tourist office. Lille is at its liveliest during the first weekend of September, when the **Grande Braderie** summons folk from across northern Europe to one of the world's biggest street fairs, perhaps better described as one giant beer- and mussel-swilling party.

The Belle Époque **Opéra de Lille** (⊠ Rue Léon-Trulin ☎ 03–28–38–40–40 ⊕ www.opera-lille.fr/) reopened in 2003 after extensive renovation. The **Orchestre National de Lille** (⊠ 30 pl. Mendès-France ☎ 03–20–12–82–40 ⊕ www.onlille.com) is a well-respected symphony orchestra. The **Théâtre du Nord** (⊠ 4 pl. Général-de-Gaulle ☎ 03–20–14–24–24 ⊕ www.theatredunord.fr) is one of Lille's most prominent theaters.

Douai

⓰ *32 km (20 mi) west of Valenciennes, 35 km (22 mi) south of Lille.*

The industrial town of Douai is most noteworthy as the home of an elegant arts museum and to northern France's most famous **Beffroi** (belfry), whose turrets and pinnacles, climbing above the Town Hall, are immortalized in a painting, now in the Louvre, by Camille Corot. The sturdy tower, completed in 1410, rises 210 feet and is topped by a huge weather vane in the form of a Flanders Lion. The peal of bells—62 of them!—sounds the quarter hour with a selection of tunes. Climb the 193 steps to the top for a view of the town and the Scarpe River. ⊠ *Rue de la Mairie* ☉ *Sept.–June, Mon.–Sat. at 2, 3, 4, and 5, Sun. at 10, 11, 3, 4, and 5; July and Aug., daily at 10, 11, 2, 3, 4, and 5.*

off the
beaten
path

ARLEUX – Few herbs are more readily associated with France than *ail* (garlic), and France's unofficial garlic capital is Arleux, 11 km (7 mi) south of Douai; smoked garlic cloves are the local specialty. On the first weekend of September a Fête d'Ail (Garlic Festival) is held here. Just south of Arleux, the ponds and small lakes known as the Étangs de la Sensée provide a scenic backdrop for strolls and picnics.

The Artois Battlefields

The most poignant memories of World War I are evoked in the superbly maintained war cemeteries in the countryside between Lens and Arras.

Take A1 south from Lille toward Douai, then A21 west to Lens (where the Louvre II, the first regional offshoot of the Paris Louvre, is to open **⑰** in 2009), and head through Liévin and Angres to **Souchez.** Standing on a windswept hill 500 feet above the Artois plain is **Notre-Dame de Lorette,** a 30-acre cemetery with endless rows of white crosses, a pseudo-Byzantine church, an ossuary, and a huge tower with a small war museum. From the top there are extensive views of the surrounding countryside.

From Souchez head south on D937, past the beautiful circular cemetery of Cabaret Rouge, to **Neuville-St-Vaast,** whose Art Deco church is **⑱** a stately example of 1920s reconstruction. Just off D937 is gently sloping **La Targette,** one of the most serene and beautiful of all French war cemeteries. At the nearby crossroads of D937 and D49, opposite a stark war memorial in the form of a giant torch, is the small **Musée de la Guerre 1914–18** (World War I Museum), with a musty collection of posters, documents, costumes, and weapons. From Neuville take D55 east to **Vimy,** where there's a park commemorating the epic Canadian victory during World War I, or D49 west to the mournful, ruined, hilltop towers of **Mont-St-Éloi.**

Arras

⑲ *9 km (5½ mi) south of Mont-St-Eloi via D341, 11 km (7 mi) south of Vimy via N17, 54 km (34 mi) southwest of Lille.*

At first glance you might not guess that Arras, the capital of the historic Artois region between Flanders and Picardy, was badly mauled during World War I. In the Middle Ages, Arras was an important trading and tapestry-weaving center, its wealth reflected in two of the finest squares in the country—now home to lively markets on Wednesday and Saturday mornings. Other landmarks include the 18th-century theater, the Palais des États (former regional parliament), the octagonal place Victor-Hugo, and the former home of revolutionary firebrand Maximilien Robespierre. An hour-long audio guided tour of the city is available from the tourist office for a small fee.

★ Start your visit at the arcaded **Place des Héros,** the smaller of the two main squares, dominated by the richly worked—and much restored— Hôtel de Ville (Town Hall). You can take an elevator to the top of its ornate 240-foot **belfry** (€2.40) for a view that stretches as far as the ruined towers of Mont-St-Eloi, 10 km (6 mi) northwest, and you can join a guided tour through the **boves** (€3.80), a maze of underground chalk galleries quarried out back in the 10th century and then transformed into an underground city by 10,000 British troops during World War I. The tunnels run for miles in all directions—even, it is said, as far as Mont-St-Eloi. The tour lasts about an hour, and you'll need sturdy footwear to negotiate all the steep, damp stairs. ⊠ *Pl. des Héros* ⊗ *May–Sept., Mon.–Sat. 9–6:30, Sun. 10–1 and 2–6:30; Oct.–Apr., Mon.–Sat. 9–noon and 2–6, Sun. 10–12:30 and 3–6:30.*

Fodor'sChoice **Grand'Place,** linked to place des Héros by rue de la Taillerie, is a grand,
★ harmonious showcase of 17th- and 18th-century Flemish architecture. The gabled facades recall those in Belgium and Holland and are a re-

minder of the unifying influence of the Spanish colonizers of the Low Countries during the 17th century—though the oldest house here, now the Trois Luppars hotel at No. 49, actually dates from 1467.

The 19th-century **Cathédrale St-Vaast** (⊠ Rue des Teinturiers) is a stately Classical building in cool white stone, every bit as vast as its name (pronounced *va*) almost suggests. It was built between 1775 and 1830 to the designs of Contant d'Ivry; it was half-razed during World War I, although restoration was so diligent you'd never guess.

The **Musée des Beaux-Arts** (Fine Arts Museum), in the massive, regimented 18th-century abbey next to the cathedral, has a rich collection of objects and pictures, including cobalt-blue Arras porcelain; 19th-century landscapes by Camille Dutilleux and other local artists inspired by Camille Corot (also represented), who frequently visited the region; and two smiling 13th-century gilded wooden angels, the *Anges de Saudémont.* ⊠ *20 rue Paul-Doumer* ☎ *03–21–71–26–43* ⊕ *www.musenor. com/gm/gmarras.htm* ☑ *€4* ☉ *Wed.–Mon. 9:30–noon and 2–5:30.*

Where to Stay & Eat

★ $$$ ✕ **La Faisanderie.** In a former stable, this splendid restaurant serves memorable variations on international fare: *pied de veau* (calves' feet), pike baked with frogs' legs, and cod with local Arleux garlic. A loyal clientele supports its long-standing gastronomic reputation. ⊠ *45 Grand'Pl.* ☎ *03–21–48–20–76* ⚓ *Reservations essential* 🏛 *Jacket and tie* ▭ *AE, DC, MC, V* ☉ *Closed Aug. and Mon. No dinner Sun.*

$–$$ ✕ **La Rapière.** This lively, two-level bistro, with an airy ground-floor room and a more atmospheric, vaulted brick cellar, dishes up distinctly local cuisine, including andouillette (a kind of chitterling sausage) in pastry and *poule à la bière* (chicken in beer), as well as specialties like *flan de maroilles* (flan made with regional cheese) and homemade foie gras, all in a casual setting. ⊠ *44 Grand'Pl.* ☎ *03–21–55–09–92* ⊕ *www. larapiere.com* ▭ *AE, MC, V* ☉ *No dinner Sun.*

★ $$–$$$ ✕▢ **Univers.** Once an 18th-century Jesuit monastery, this stylish hotel has a pretty garden, pale pink brickwork, and a charming restaurant, Le Clusius, whose specialties range from fricasseed snails to pike-perch with sorrel (no dinner Sunday during January and February). Although centrally located, it's set well back from the main street and is an oasis of calm. The interior has been modernized but retains rustic provincial furniture. ⊠ *3 pl. de la Croix-Rouge, 62000* ☎ *03–21–71–34–01* 📠 *03–21–71–41–42* ⊕ *www.hotel-univers-arras.com* 🛏 *38 rooms* ⚘ *Restaurant, cable TV, bar, Internet, some pets allowed (fee); no a/c* ▭ *AE, MC, V* ⧆ *BP.*

The Somme Battlefields

32 km (20 mi) south of Arras near Albert.

The Battle of the Somme—a name forever etched into history as the site of one of the bloodiest battle campaigns of World War I—raged south of Arras, near Albert, from July through November 1916, leaving a million dead. During those five futile months, the Allies, including Irish, Canadian, Australian, and South African soldiers, progressed about 8

km (5 mi) along the hills above the Ancre River north of Albert. From Arras take D919 through gently rolling farmland, via Puisieux, and turn right on D415, through Beaumont, down to the north bank of the
20 Ancre River. Follow signs to the memorial of **Beaumont-Hamel,** where a bronze caribou—emblem of the Newfoundland regiments that fought here—gazes accusingly over trenches and undulating, still shell-shocked terrain. Across the Ancre and up the hill on the other side is the **Tour Ulster** (Ulster Tower), commemorating troops from Northern Ireland.

21 From the village of **Thiepval,** follow signs to the bombastic brick **British War Memorial,** a disjointed triumphal arch designed by Sir Edwin Lutyens, that looks as if it were made of giant Lego blocks. The names of 72,000 British soldiers are inscribed here, and an elegant visitor center-cum-museum (daily 10–5) opened alongside in 2004. From Thiepval, take D73 then D20 to Longueval, where the star-shaped South African **Delville Wood Memorial,** inspired by the Castle of Good Hope in Cape Town, overlooks a long lawn framed by a stately avenue of oaks.

Péronne

22 *17 km (11 mi) southeast of Longueval via D20 and N17.*

The small, brick town of Péronne was almost entirely razed in 1916. It
★ now contains, however, a fine World War I museum, the **Historial de la Grande Guerre.** Integrated into a ruined brick castle, this spacious modern museum has a thought-provoking spectrum of exhibits, from TV monitors playing old newsreels, to soldiers' uniforms strung out on the floor surrounded by machine guns, and a dim roomful of nightmarish war lithographs by Otto Dix. It also has a good gift shop, with books in English, and a café with views of what looks like a leafy-banked lake but is actually the Somme River languidly colliding with its tributary, the Cologne. ✉ *Pl. du Château* ☎ *03–22–83–14–18* 🌐 *www.historial.org* 🎫 *€7* ⏲ *May–Sept., daily 10–6; Oct.–Apr., Tues.–Sun. 10–6.*

Where to Stay & Eat

¢–$ ✕🏨 **Remparts.** Péronne makes a fine base for exploring the local battlefields and war cemeteries. This small hotel has long been an old-fashioned favorite among traveling salesmen, but redecorated rooms and increasingly inventive cuisine—snail ravioli with mushrooms or fish cooked with chicory and beetroot sauce—has helped the hotel broaden its appeal. A set menu at lunch runs €14.50, while complete dinners range from €16 to €40. ✉ *23 rue Beaubois, 80200* ☎ *03–22–84–01–22* 📠 *03–22–84–31–96* 🛏 *16 rooms* 🖒 *Restaurant, cable TV, some pets allowed (fee); no a/c* 💳 *AE, DC, MC, V* 🍽 *MAP.*

St-Quentin

23 *28 km (18 mi) southeast of Péronne via D44 and N29.*

Bustling St-Quentin, an industrial town rebuilt with considerable Art Deco panache after World War I (ask about a guided tour at the tourist office), is famed as the birthplace of 18th-century pastelist Maurice Quentin de La Tour—his work can be admired at the town museum.

Appearing to survey the town's sloping, pedestrian-only main square is the riotously sculpted, early-16th-century facade of the **Hôtel de Ville** (Town Hall; ⊠ Pl. de l'Hôtel de Ville), complete with arcades and gables and topped by an 18th-century campanile with an attractive peal of bells. The town's hilltop cathedral, officially styled **La Basilique** (⊠ Pl. de la Basilique) at the top of rue St-André, is topped by a 270-foot flèche, reconstructed in 1976. Most of the building, however, is resolutely medieval: the elegant 13th-century choir retains some original stained glass; the soaring nave, rising 112 feet, was added 200 years later (note the black-and-white labyrinth pattern embedded in the floor); the ornate organ case was designed by Berain in 1690.

Where to Stay & Eat

$ ╳🏨 **Château de Neuville.** If you're looking to escape the hustle and bustle of St-Quentin, one option is the 3½-km (2-mi) drive to the neighboring village of Neuville St-Amand, whose self-styled "château"—in fact a sturdy, century-old mansion with white walls, large windows, and dark-green shutters, set deep in a tree-studded park—offers impersonal service and rooms decked out in cool pastel shades. Those in the modern annex lack character but are slightly larger than those in the main block. The large-windowed restaurant, serving such delicacies as scrambled eggs with truffles or scallops and lobster with pasta, does not serve lunch on Saturday or Monday. ⊠ *Rue du Midi, 3 km (2 mi) southwest of St-Quentin off N44, 02100 Neuville St-Amand* 🕾 *03–23–68–41–82* 🖷 *03–23–68–46–02* ⊕ *www.chateauneuvillestamand.com* ⤶ *15 rooms* ⌂ *Restaurant, some minibars, bar, Internet; no a/c.*

off the
beaten
path

MUSÉE MATISSE – Artist Henri Matisse (1869–1954) was born in Le Cateau-Cambrésis, 35 km (21 mi) northeast of St-Quentin. The Matisse Museum, housed in the 18th-century **Palais Fénelon,** a former bishop's palace, contains a number of early oil paintings and sculptures, plus a superb collection of 50 drawings selected by Matisse himself; and 25 psychedelic abstract paintings by Auguste Herbin (1882–1960), who also hailed from the region. The museum reopened in 2002 after a three-year extension and renovation program. ⊠ *Palais Fénelon* 🖾 *03–27–84–64–50* 🗔 *€4.50* ⊙ *Wed.–Mon. 10–12:30 and 2–6.*

Laon

㉔ *40 km (25 mi) southeast of St-Quentin via A26.*

Thanks to its awesome hilltop site and the forest of towers sprouting from its ancient cathedral, lofty Laon basks in the title of the "crowned mountain." The medieval ramparts, virtually undisturbed by passing traffic, provide a ready-made itinerary for a tour of old Laon. Panoramic views, sturdy gateways, and intriguing glimpses of the cathedral lurk around every bend. There's even a funicular, which makes frequent trips (except on Sunday in winter) up and down the hillside between the station and the Vieille Ville.

Fodor'sChoice
★
The **Cathédrale Notre-Dame,** constructed between 1150 and 1230, is a superb example of early Gothic. The light interior gives the impression of order and immense length, and the first flourishing of Gothic architecture is reflected in the harmony of the four-tiered nave: from the bottom up, observe the wide arcades, the double windows of the tribune, the squat windows of the triforium, and, finally, the upper windows of the clerestory. The majestic towers can be explored during the guided visits that leave from the tourist office, housed in a 12th-century hospital on the cathedral square. The filigreed elegance of the five towers is audacious and rare. Look for the 16 stone oxen protruding from the tops, a tribute to the stalwart 12th-century beasts who carted up blocks of stone from quarries far below. Medieval stained glass includes the rose window dedicated to the liberal arts in the left transept, and the windows in the flat east end, an unusual feature for France although common in England. ⊠ *Pl. du Parvis* ☎ *Guided tours €6, audioguide €3* ☉ *Daily 8:30–6:30; guided tours Apr.–Sept., daily at 3* PM.

The **Musée Muncipal** (town museum) has some fine antique pottery and work by the local-born Le Nain brothers, Antoine, Louis, and Mathieu, active in the 17th century and abundantly represented in the Louvre. But its chief draw is the **Chapelle des Templiers** in the garden—a small, octagonal 12th-century chapel topped by a shallow dome. It houses fragments of the cathedral's gable and the chilling effigy of Guillaume de Harcigny, doctor to the insane king Charles VI, whose death from natural causes in 1393 did not prevent his memorializers from chiseling a skeletal portrait that recalls the Black Death. ⊠ *32 rue Georges-Ermant* ☎ *03–23–20–19–87* ☎ *€3.20* ☉ *June–Sept., Tues.–Sun. 11–6; Oct.–May, Tues.–Sun. 2–6.*

Where to Stay & Eat

$ ✕▦ **Bannière de France.** In business since 1685, this old-fashioned, uneven-floored hostelry is just five minutes from the cathedral. Lieselotte Lefèvre, the German patronne, speaks fluent English. Rooms are cozy and quaint. The restaurant's venerable dining room showcases sturdy cuisine (trout, lemon sole, guinea fowl) and good-value prix-fixe menus. ⊠ *11 rue Franklin-Roosevelt, 02000* ☎ *03–23–23–21–44* 🖶 *03–23–23–31–56* 🌐 *www.hoteldelabannieredefrance.com* ⇜ *18 rooms, 17 with bath* ☖ *Restaurant, cable TV, bar; no a/c* ⊟ *AE, DC, MC, V* ☉ *Closed mid-Dec.–mid-Jan.* ⎸❂⎹ *MAP.*

Coucy-le-Château

㉕ *28 km (18 mi) southwest of Laon via N2 and D5.*

Fodor'sChoice
★
The majestic hilltop fortress, or **château,** in Coucy-le-Château is but a glimmer of its former self—but it still casts a pretty intimidating shadow over the lush, rolling countryside of eastern Picardy. The 30-acre site, ringed with nearly 3 km (2 mi) of walls and no fewer than 31 towers, was developed by all-powerful warlords, the Enguerrands de Coucy, in the 12th century. They also erected the largest keep in Christendom, more than 210 feet high (Barbara Tuchman's *A Distant Mirror* provides fascinating background reading). The fortifications were partially disman-

tled by Mazarin in 1650 to prevent their use by rebels during the Fronde, later used as an open quarry after the Revolution, and then dynamited by retreating Germans in 1917. You can visit what's left of the keep and the vaulted cellars, and follow a path around the still-imposing town walls. ☎ 03–23–52–71–28 ☞ €4 ⊙ Daily 10–12:30 and 2–6.

Soissons

㉖ *19 km (12 mi) south of Coucy via D1.*

Although much damaged in World War I, Soissons commands attention for its two huge churches, one intact, one in ruins. The Gothic **Cathédrale Notre-Dame** was appreciated by Rodin, who famously declared that "there are no hours in this cathedral, but rather eternity." The interior, with its pure lines and restrained ornamentation, creates a more harmonious impression than the asymmetrical, one-towered facade. The most remarkable feature, however, is the rounded two-story transept, an element more frequently found in the German Rhineland than in France. Rubens's freshly restored *Adoration of the Shepherds* hangs on the other side of the transept. ⊠ *Pl. Fernand-Marquigny* ⊙ *Daily 9:30–noon and 2:30–5:30.*

The twin-spire facade, arcaded cloister, and airy refectory, constructed from the 14th to the 16th centuries, are all that is left of the hilltop abbey church of **St-Jean-des-Vignes,** which was largely dismantled just after the Revolution. Its fallen stones were used to restore the cathedral and neighboring homes. But the church remains the most impressive sight in Soissons, its hollow rose window peering out over the town like the eye of some giant Cyclops. ⊠ *Cours St-Jean-des-Vignes* ☞ *Free* ⊙ *Mon.–Sat. 9–noon and 2–6, Sun. 10–12:30 and 1:30–7.*

Partly housed in the medieval abbey of St-Léger, the **Musée de Soissons,** the town museum, has a varied collection of local archaeological finds and paintings, with fine 19th-century works by Gustave Courbet and Eugène Boudin. ⊠ *2 rue de la Congrégation* ☎ *03–23–59–15–90* ☞ *Free* ⊙ *Wed.–Mon. 10–noon and 2–5.*

Where to Stay & Eat

★ **$$$–$$$$** ✕◱ **Château de Courcelles.** This refined château by the Vesle River is run by easygoing Frédéric Nouhaud. Its pure, classical Louis XIV facade harmonizes oddly with the sweeping brass main staircase attributed to Jean Cocteau. Rooms vary in size and grandeur; the former outbuildings have been converted into large family-size suites. Wind down in the cozy bar next to a roaring fire while anticipating excellent fare, including seasonal game, prepared by chef Joel Orceau and served up in the stately dining room. A formal garden and pool are the gateway to 40 acres of parkland and a tree-shaded canal. ⊠ *8 rue du Château, 20 km (12 mi) east of Soissons via N31, 02220 Courcelles-sur-Vesle* ☎ *03–23–74–13–53* 🖶 *03–23–74–06–41* ⊕ *www.chateau-de-courcelles.fr* �’*11 rooms, 7 suites* ⸖ *Restaurant, minibars, cable TV, tennis court, pool, sauna, bar, some pets allowed (fee); no a/c* ▤ *AE, DC, MC, V* ◯◱ *MAP.*

¢–$ ✕◱ **Abbaye.** The shambling village of Longpont, on the northeast fringe of the Forest of Retz, boasts a ruined Cistercian abbey, a turreted 14th-century gateway, and this ivy-clad, foursquare hotel. The cavernous dining room welcomes all with massive wooden tables, a crackling fireplace, and generous portions of family cooking, much of it prepared over a charcoal grill, with mushrooms, game, and duck with cherries among the favorites. To work it all off, you can rent a bike from the hotel to explore the forest. Rooms are calm and look out over either the forest or the abbey ruins. ⊠ *8 rue des Tourelles, 14 km (9 mi) southwest of Soissons via N2/D17, 02600 Longpont* ☎ *03–23–96–02–44* 🖷 *03–23–96–10–60* ⤳ *11 rooms* ⚬ *Restaurant, bar; no a/c, no TV in some rooms* ⊟ *MC, V.*

Blérancourt

㉗ *23 km (14 mi) northwest of Soissons via D6.*

The village of Blérancourt is the home of the **Musée National de la Coopération Franco-Américaine** (Museum of Franco-American Cooperation). Two style-setting pavilions and monumental archways are all that remain of the original château, built in 1612–19 by the great architect Salomon de Brosse but largely demolished during the French Revolution. American Anne Morgan founded the museum in 1924. The airy, modern museum contains art and documents charting Franco-American relations, with a section on American involvement in World War I. A beguiling female portrait by Missouri Postimpressionist Richard Miller stands out: an American Mona Lisa. The trim gardens (open 8–7) include a bronze casting of the statue of George Washington by Jean-Antoine Houdon and an arboretum. ⊠ *33 pl. du Gal-Leclerc* ☎ *03–23–39–60–16* 🖾 *€3* ☉ *Wed.–Mon. 10–12:30 and 2–6.*

Noyon

㉘ *14 km (9 mi) northwest of Blérancourt via D934.*

Noyon is an often overlooked cathedral town that owed its medieval importance to the cult of 7th-century St. Eloi, patron of blacksmiths and a former town bishop. Its second famous son, the Protestant theologian John Calvin, was born here in 1509. The old streets around the cathedral are at their liveliest during the Saturday morning market.

Constructed between 1140 and 1290, the **Cathédrale St-Eloi** was one of the earliest attempts at building a full-fledged Gothic cathedral. This is evident in the four-story nave; the intermittent use of rounded as well as pointed arches; and the thin, pointed lancet (as opposed to rose) windows in the austere facade. Pause for a wry smile at the "piazza" in front of the cathedral, with its elegant town houses arranged in a semicircle in bashful imitation of St. Peter's in Rome; then head down the cobbled lane to the left of the facade to admire the timber-front 16th-century library behind the cathedral. ⊠ *Pl. du Parvis* ☉ *Daily 8–noon and 2–6.*

Where to Stay & Eat

$ ✕🏠 **St-Eloi.** Between the train station and the cathedral, this hotel charms with its provincial elegance. The redbrick and timber Victorian exterior, marble-lined reception area, and airy dining room are all staunchly French bourgeois. The spacious, pastel rooms have high ceilings; several have views of the interior courtyard. Avoid, however, the chain hotel–like annex. Several prix-fixe menus are available in the stylish restaurant, which does not serve Saturday lunch or Sunday dinner. ⊠ *81 bd. Carnot, 60400* ☎ *03–44–44–01–49* 🖷 *03–44–09–20–90* ⊕ *www.hotelsainteloi.fr* ⤳ *22 rooms* ⚒ *Restaurant, cable TV, bar, Internet, some pets allowed (fee); no a/c* ▤ *AE, DC, MC, V* ☉ *Closed mid-July–mid-Aug.* ❢❍❘ *MAP.*

Compiègne

㉙ *24 km (15 mi) southwest of Noyon via N32.*

Compiègne, a bustling town of some 40,000 people, is at the northern limit of the Forêt de Compiègne, on the edge of the misty plains of Picardy, which is prime hunting country, so you can be sure there's a former royal hunting lodge in the vicinity. The one here enjoyed its heyday in the mid-19th century under upstart emperor Napoléon III. But the town's history stretches farther back—to Joan of Arc, who was captured in battle and held prisoner here, and to its 15th-century Hôtel de Ville (Town Hall), with its jubilant Flamboyant Gothic facade; and farther forward—to the World War I armistice, signed in Compiègne Forest on November 11, 1918.

The 18th-century **Château de Compiègne** was restored by Napoléon I and favored for wild weekends by his nephew Napoléon III. The first Napoléon's legacy is more keenly felt: his state apartments have been refurbished using the original designs for hangings and upholstery, and bright silks and damasks adorn every room. Much of the mahogany furniture gleams with ormolu, and the chairs sparkle with gold leaf. Napoléon III's furniture looks ponderous in comparison. Behind the palace is a gently rising 4-km (2½-mi) vista, inspired by the park at Schönbrunn, in Vienna, where Napoléon I's second wife, Empress Marie-Louise, grew up. Also here is the **Musée du Second Empire**, a collection of Napoléon III–era decorative arts, including works by the caricaturist Honoré Daumier. Make time for the **Musée de la Voiture** and its display of carriages, coaches, and old cars, including the *Jamais Contente* (*Never Satisfied*), the first car to reach 100 kph (62 mph). ⊠ *Pl. du Général-de-Gaulle* ☎ *03–44–38–47–02* ⊕ *www.musee-chateau-compiegne.fr* 🎫 *€5.50* ☉ *Wed.–Mon. 10–6.*

FodorsChoice ★

A collection of 85,000 miniature soldiers—fashioned of lead, cardboard, and other materials—depicting military uniforms through the ages is found in the **Musée de la Figurine Historique** (Toy Soldier Museum). ⊠ *28 pl. de l'Hôtel-de-Ville* ☎ *03–44–40–72–55* 🎫 *€2* ☉ *Mar.–Oct., Tues.–Sat. 9–noon and 2–6, Sun. 2–6; Nov.–Feb., Tues.–Sat. 9–noon and 2–5, Sun. 2–5.*

Some 7 km (4 mi) east of Compiègne via N31 and D546, off the road to Rethondes, is the **Wagon de l'Armistice** (Armistice Railcar), a replica of the one in which the World War I armistice was signed in 1918. In 1940 the Nazis turned the tables and made the French sign their own surrender in the same place—accompanied by Hitler's infamous jig for joy—then tugged the original car off to Germany, where it was later destroyed. The replicated car is part of a small museum in a leafy clearing. ⊠ *Clairière de l'Armistice* ☎ *03–44–85–14–18* ☒ *€3* ⊙ *Apr.–Oct., Wed.–Mon. 9–noon and 2–6:30; Nov.–Mar., Wed.–Mon. 10–noon and 2–5.*

Where to Stay & Eat

$ ✕⊞ **Rotisserie du Chat.** This nice spot (no lunch Monday, no dinner Sunday) with its brass lights, plush curtains, and waiters in black tie, tries valiantly to be upper crust, while the brasserie serves a lighter, more casual fare. ⊠ *17 rue Eugène-Floquet, 60200* ☎ *03–44–40–02–74* ▭ *AE, MC, V.*

$ ⊞ **Harlay.** A family-run hotel in a foursquare stone building, the Harlay is conveniently sited by the bridge linking the rail station and downtown. Rooms are soberly decorated; the best overlook the River Oise and are sound-proofed with double-glazing. ⊠ *3 rue de Harlay, 60200* ☎ *03–44–23–01–50* ☖ *03–44–20–19–46* ↵ *20 rooms* ▭ *AE, DC, MC, V.*

Pierrefonds

③⓪ *14 km (9 mi) southeast of Compiègne via D973.*

Dominating the attractive lakeside village of Pierrefonds is its huge er-
Fodor's Choice satz medieval castle. Built on a huge mound in the 15th century, the **Château**
★ **de Pierrefonds** was comprehensively restored and re-created in the 1860s to imagined former glory at the behest of Emperor Napoléon III, seeking to cash in on the craze for the Middle Ages. Architect Viollet-le-Duc left a crenelated fortress with a fairy-tale silhouette, although, like the fortified town of Carcassonne, which he also restored, Pierrefonds is more a construct of what Viollet-le-Duc thought it should have looked like than what it really was. A visit takes in the chapel, barracks, and the majestic keep holding the lord's bedchamber and reception hall, which is bordered by a spiral staircase whose lower and upper sections reveal clearly what is ancient and modern in this former fortress. Don't miss the plaster casts of tomb sculptures from all over France in the cellars, and the **Collection Monduit**—industrially produced, larger-than-life lead decorations made by the 19th-century firm that brought the Statue of Liberty to life. ☎ *03–44–42–72–72* ☒ *€6.10* ⊙ *Mon.–Sat. 9:30–12:30 and 2–5:30, Sun. 9:30–5:30.*

off the beaten path

MORIENVAL – This village, 6 km (4 mi) south of Pierrefonds via D335, is known for its modest 11th-century Romanesque church, one of the key buildings in architectural history. It was here, in the 1120s, that masons first hit on the idea of using stone vaults supported on "ribs" springing diagonally from column to column, an architectural breakthrough that formed the structural basis of the Gothic style. The trend was soon picked up at the great basilica of St-Denis near Paris and swept through northern France during the years that followed.

Where to Stay & Eat

¢–$ ✕🖫 **Le Relais Brunehaut.** Just down the valley from Pierrefonds, in the hamlet of Chelles, is this quaint hotel-restaurant with a view of the abbey church next door. It's made up of a tiny ensemble of stucco buildings bordered by several acres of pleasant park and a small duck-populated river. An old wooden water mill in the dining room and the good, simple seasonal fare make eating here a pleasure. The dining room is closed Monday and Tuesday year-round, and on Wednesday and Thursday from mid-November through late April. ✉ *3 rue de l'Église, 5 km (3 mi) east of Pierrefonds on D85, 60350 Chelles* ☎ *03–44–42–85–05* 🖷 *03–44–42–83–30* 🛏 *7 rooms* ⚭ *Restaurant; no a/c* ═ *MC, V* ⭐ *MAP.*

CHAMPAGNE

Champagne, a place name that has become a universal synonym for joy and festivity, is a word of humble origin. Like *campagna,* its Italian counterpart, it is derived from the Latin *campus,* which means "open field." In French campus became *champ,* with the old language extending this to *champaign,* for "battlefield, " and *champaine,* for "district of plains." *Battlefield* and *plains* both accurately describe the province, as Champagne is crisscrossed by Roman roads along which defenders and invaders have clashed for two millennia.

Today, of course, the province is best known for its champagne vineyards, which start just beyond Château-Thierry, 96 km (60 mi) northeast of Paris, and continue along the towering Marne Valley to Épernay. Cheerful villages line the Route du Vin (Wine Road), which twines north to Reims, the capital of bubbly. As you head farther northeast, rolling chalk hills give way to the rugged Ardennes Forest, straddling the Belgian border. For a handy Web source for many of the great Champagne *maisons* (houses) of the region, log on to www.umc.fr.

Château-Thierry

③ *96 km (60 mi) northeast of Paris via A4, 40 km (25 mi) south of Soissons.*

Built along the Marne River beneath the ruins of a hilltop castle that dates from the time of Joan of Arc, and within sight of the American **Belleau Wood** War Cemetery, Château-Thierry is best known as the birthplace of the French fabulist Jean de La Fontaine (1621–95). The 16th-century mansion where La Fontaine was born is now a museum, the **Musée Jean de La Fontaine,** furnished in the style of the 17th century. It contains La Fontaine's bust, portrait, and baptism certificate, plus editions of his fables magnificently illustrated by Jean-Baptiste Oudry (1755) and Gustave Doré (1868). ✉ *12 rue Jean-de-La-Fontaine* ☎ *03–23–69–05–60* 🖃 *€3.20* ⊙ *Wed.–Mon. 10–noon and 2–5.*

Épernay

③ *50 km (31 mi) east of Château-Thierry via D3/N3.*

Unlike Reims with its numerous treasures, the town of Épernay, on the south bank of the Marne, appears to live only for champagne. Unfortunately, no relation exists between the fabulous wealth of Épernay's illustrious wine houses and the drab, dreary appearance of the town as a whole. Most champagne firms are spaced out along the long, straight avenue de Champagne, and although their names may provoke sighs of wonder, their facades are either functional or overdressy. The attractions are underground.

Of the various champagne houses open to the public, **Mercier** offers the best deal; its sculpted, labyrinthine cellars contain one of the world's largest wooden barrels (with a capacity of more than 215,000 bottles). A tour of the cellars takes 45 minutes in the relative comfort of a small train. A glass of champagne is your post-visit reward. ⊠ 68–70 av. de Champagne 🕾 03–26–51–22–22 ⊕ www.champagne-mercier.fr 🖃€6.50 🕙 Weekdays 9:30–11:30 and 2–4:30 🕙 Closed mid-Dec.–mid-Feb.

To understand how the region's still wine became sparkling champagne, head across the Marne to **Hautvillers.** Here the monk Dom Pérignon (1638–1715)—upon whom, legend has it, blindness conferred the gifts of exceptional taste buds and sense of smell—invented champagne as everyone knows it by using corks for stoppers and blending wines from different vineyards. Dom Pérignon's simple tomb, in a damp, dreary Benedictine abbey church (now owned by Moët et Chandon), is a forlorn memorial to the hero of one of the world's most lucrative drink industries.

Where to Stay & Eat

$$$$ ✕ꔮ **La Briqueterie.** Épernay is short on good hotels, so it's worth driving south to Vinay to find this luxurious manor. The spacious rooms are modern; ask for one overlooking the extensive gardens. The chef has the Mediterranean on his mind, hence the lobster and prawns in citrus sauce. For more regional fare try the Champagne snails with herbed butter and, for dessert, the *crêpe soufflée au marc de champagne* (a crepe filled with pastry cream and flavored with brandy). ⊠ 4 rte. de Sézanne, 6 km (4 mi) south of Épernay, 51530 Vinay 🕾 03–26–59–99–99 🖷 03–26–59–92–10 ⊕ www.labriqueterie.com 🛏 40 rooms, 2 suites ⚲ Restaurant, minibars, cable TV, pool, gym, sauna, bar, Internet, some pets allowed (fee) 🖃 AE, MC, V 🕙 Closed late Dec. 🍽 BP.

Nightlife & the Arts

The leading wine festival in the Champagne region is the **Fête St-Vincent** (named for the patron saint of vine growers), held on either January 22 or the following Saturday in Ambonnay, 24 km (15 mi) east of Épernay.

Châlons-en-Champagne

㉝ 34 km (21 mi) southeast of Épernay via N3.

Strangely enough, the official administrative center of the champagne industry is not Reims or Épernay but Châlons-en-Champagne. Yet this large town is mainly of interest for its vast cathedral and smaller, early Gothic church.

★ With its twin spires, Romanesque nave, and early Gothic choir and vaults, the church of **Notre-Dame-en-Vaux** bears eloquent testimony to Châlons's

"BROTHER, COME QUICKLY, I'M DRINKING STARS"

SO EXCLAIMED DOM PÉRIGNON UPON FIRST SIPPING the bubbling beverage that he invented through luck and alchemy. The blind 17th-century Benedictine monk was the first to discover the secret of its production at the Abbey of Hautvillers by combining the still wines of the region and storing the mix in bottles. Today, the world's most famous sparkling wine comes from this region's vineyards, along the towering Marne Valley between Épernay and Château-Thierry and on the slopes of the Montagne de Reims between Épernay and Reims.

Champagne firms—Veuve-Clicquot, Mumm, Pommery, Taittinger, and others—welcome you into their chalky, mazelike cellars. Most of the big houses give tours of their caves (cellars), accompanied by informative lectures on the champagne production process. The quality of the tours is inconsistent, ranging from hilarious to despairingly tedious, though a glass of champagne at the end makes even the most mediocre worth it (some would say). On the tours, you'll discover that champagne is not made so differently from the way the Dom did it three centuries ago. Chardonnay, pinot noir, and sometimes Pinot Meunier grapes ferment separately and are then mixed into each house's distinctive blend and bottled. The use of a bottle is key.

Previously, wines were only stored in large barrels and the effervescence caused by fermentation escaped. When bottles replaced barrels, the wines' natural sparkle was kept imprisoned until they were opened. Left tilted almost upside down in chilly underground tunnels, the heavy-walled bottles are frequently turned by "riddlers, " men who spend three years learning exactly how to turn bottles in order to nudge the sediment down into the neck. After a while the bottles are opened, the sediment shoots out, a small quantity of liqueur is added, and the corks are tied down for good with wire. It takes about three years of fermentation to produce the proper level of fizz, alcohol, and taste. Only wine from Champagne can properly be called champagne; otherwise, it's sparkling wine.

Irritatingly, champagne costs about as much in Champagne as it does in Chicago, but there are some wine stores in the region that can usually recommend excellent but unknown champagnes for half the price of the big names. Vin mousseux and Crémant are inferior products that don't conform to the champagne cartel's strict regulation. Remember that you can tell a lot about champagne just by looking at the label. The words brut, sec, demi-sec, and doux tell you how sweet the drink is; brut is driest and doux is sweetest. The words vintage or millésime mean you might wish to pick a cheaper bottle because this one was made entirely from grapes harvested during a single good year, and you're going to have to pay for it. Champagnes made from a mixture of grapes from different years are more common and less expensive. No matter if pricey or basic, brut or doux, the Champagne region fixates obsessively on the bubbly brew and you'll find the popping of champagne corks builds to quite a roar as you travel the Route du Vin, a road that leads to many local champagne houses and dégustations (tastings) as it threads through the countryside south of Reims. Remember to ask for a coupe of champagne, never a verre (glass).

medieval importance. The small **museum** beside the excavated cloister contains outstanding medieval statuary. ✉ *Rue Nicolas-Durand* ☎ *03–26–64–03–87* ✇ *€5* ⊘ *Apr.–Sept., Wed.–Mon. 10–noon and 2–6; Oct.–Mar., Wed.–Fri. 10–noon and 2–5, weekends 10–noon and 2–6.*

The 13th-century **Cathédrale St-Étienne** (✉Rue de la Marne) is a harmonious structure with large nave windows and tidy flying buttresses; the exterior effect is marred only by the bulky 17th-century Baroque west front.

Where to Stay & Eat

$$–$$$ ✕▥ **Angleterre.** Rooms at this stylish spot in central Châlons have elaborate decor and marble bathrooms; those in the back are quietest. In the outstanding restaurant (closed Sunday; no lunch Monday or Saturday), chef Jacky Michel's creations include quail with foie gras and red mullet with artichoke, as well as the seasonal dessert *tout-pommes*, featuring five variations on the humble apple. Breakfast is a superb buffet. ✉ *19 pl. Monseigneur-Tissier, 51000* ☎ *03–26–68–21–51* 🖷 *03–26–70–51–67* ⊕ *www.hotel-dangleterre.fr* ⇆ *25 rooms* ♿ *Restaurant, minibars, bar, Internet, some pets allowed (fee)* ▤ *AE, DC, MC, V* ⊘ *Closed mid-July–early Aug. and late Dec.–early Jan.* ⦅◯⦆ *BP.*

> **en route**   The grapes of Champagne flourish on the steep slopes of the Montagne de Reims—more of a forest-topped plateau than a mountain—northwest of Châlons. Take D1 northwest, then turn right on D37 to Ambonnay to join the Route du Vin (Wine Road). This winds around the vine-entangled eastern slopes of the Montagne through such pretty wine villages as the aptly named **Bouzy** (known for its fashionable if overpriced red), **Verzy, Mailly-Champagne, Chigny-les-Roses,** and **Rilly-la-Montagne.**

L'Épine

🔟 *7 km (4½ mi) east of Châlons via N3.*

The tiny village of L'Épine is dominated by its church, the twin-towered Flamboyant Gothic **Basilique de Notre-Dame de l'Épine.** The church's facade is a magnificent creation of intricate patterns and spires, and the interior exudes elegance and restraint.

Where to Stay & Eat

★ **$$–$$$** ✕▥ **Aux Armes de Champagne.** The highlight of this cozy former coaching inn (just opposite the town church, so ask for a table with a view) is the restaurant, with its renowned champagne list and imaginative, often spectacular cuisine by chef Philippe Zeiger. Among his specialties are artichokes with local goat cheese, and red mullet prepared with juice from roast veal. (From November through March, the restaurant is closed Monday, and no dinner is served Sunday.) Rooms are furnished with solid, traditional reproductions, wall hangings, and thick carpets. No. 21, with wood beams, is the most atmospheric. ✉ *31 av. du Luxembourg, 51460* ☎ *03–26–69–30–30* 🖷 *03–26–69–30–36* ⊕ *www. aux-armes-de-champagne.com* ⇆ *37 rooms, 2 suites* ♿ *Restaurant, minibars, cable TV, tennis court, bar, Internet; no a/c* ▤ *AE, DC, MC, V* ⊘ *Closed Jan.–mid-Feb.* ⦅◯⦆ *BP.*

Reims

44 km (27 mi) northwest of Châlons via N44, 144 km (90 mi) north-east of Paris.

Although many of its historic buildings were flattened in World War I and replaced by drab, modern architecture, those that do remain are of royal magnitude. Top of the list goes to the city's magnificent cathedral, in which the kings of France were crowned until 1825, while the Musée des Beaux-Arts has a stellar collection, including the famed Jacques-Louis David painting of Marat in his bath. Reims sparkles with some of the biggest names in champagne production, and the thriving industry has conferred wealth and sometimes an arrogant reserve on the region's inhabitants. Nevertheless, the maze of champagne cellars constitutes another fascinating sight of the city. Several champagne producers organize visits to their cellars, combining video presentations with guided tours of their cavernous, hewn-chalk underground warehouses. For a complete list of champagne cellars, head to the **tourist office** (⊠ 2 rue Guillaume-de-Machault ☎ 03–26–77–45–25) near the cathedral. A handy Web site that lists many of the leading houses is another way to plan your visits: www.umc.fr.

㉟ The tour of the cavernous **Taittinger** cellars is the most spectacular of the champagne producer visits. It includes a champagne *dégustation* (tasting) afterward. ⊠ 9 pl. St-Nicaise ☎ 03–26–85–84–33 ⊕ www.taittinger.fr ⊠ €7 ⊗ Mar.–Nov., daily 9:30–noon and 2–4:30; Dec.–Feb., weekdays 9:30–noon and 2–4:30.

㊱ **Piper-Heidsieck** offers the most amusing champagne tours in a little electric chariot, complete with zillions of bubbles, a "scene" from *Casablanca*, and even the ghost of Monsieur Heidsieck. ⊠ 51 blvd. Henry-Vasnier ☎ 03–26–84–43–44 ⊕ www.piper-heidsieck.com ⊠ €7 ⊗ Daily 9:30–11:45 and 2–5; Closed Jan. and Feb.

㊲ The 11th-century **Basilique St-Rémi** honors the 5th-century saint who gave his name to the city. Its interior seems to stretch into the endless distance, an impression created by its relative murk and lowness. The airy four-story Gothic choir contains some fine original 12th-century stained glass. Like the cathedral, the basilica puts on indoor **son-et-lumière** shows every Saturday evening at 9:30 from late June to early October. They are preceded by a tour of the building and are free. ⊠ 53 rue St-Rémi ☎ 03–26–85–31–20 ⊗ Daily 8–7.

★ ㊳ The **Palais du Tau** (formerly the Archbishop's Palace), alongside the cathedral, houses an impressive display of tapestries and coronation robes, as well as several statues rescued from the cathedral facade before they fell off. The second-floor views of the cathedral are terrific. ⊠ 2 pl. du Cardinal Luçon ☎ 03–26–47–81–79 ⊠ €4.10 ⊗ July and Aug., Tues.–Sun. 9:30–6:30; Sept.–June, Tues.–Sun. 9:30–12:30 and 2–5:30.

㊴ The **Musée des Beaux-Arts** (Museum of Fine Arts), two blocks southwest of the cathedral, has an outstanding collection of paintings: no fewer than 27 Corots are here, as well as Jacques-Louis David's unforgettable

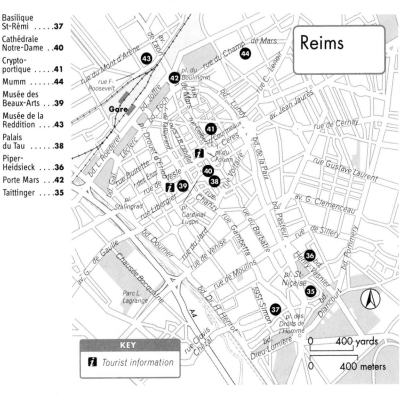

KEY

i Tourist information

0   400 yards

0   400 meters

portrait of the revolutionary polemicist Jean-Paul Marat, stabbed to death in his bath by Charlotte Corday in 1793. ⊠ *8 rue Chanzy* ☎ *03–26–47–28–44* ☑ *€3, joint ticket with Salle de Reddition* ⊗ *Wed.–Mon. 10–noon and 2–6.*

40   The **Cathédrale Notre-Dame** was the age-old setting for the coronations

Fodor's Choice   of the French kings. Clovis, king of the Franks in the 6th century, was

★   baptized in an early structure on this site; Joan of Arc led her recalcitrant Dauphin here to be crowned King Charles VII; Charles X's coronation, in 1825, was the last. The east-end windows have stained glass by Marc Chagall. Admire the vista toward the west end, with an interplay of narrow pointed arches. The glory of Reims's cathedral is its facade: it's so skillfully proportioned that initially you have little idea of its monumental size. Above the north (left) door hovers the *Laughing Angel,* a delightful statue whose famous smile threatens to melt into an acid-rain scowl; pollution has succeeded war as the ravager of the building's fabric. With the exception of the 15th-century towers, most of the original building went up in the 100 years after 1211. A stroll around the outside reinforces the impression of harmony, discipline, and decorative richness. The east end presents an idyllic sight across well-tended lawns. Spectacular **son-et-lumière** shows are performed both inside (small charge) and outside (free) the cathedral on Friday and Saturday evenings from July to mid-September. ⊠ *Pl. du Cardinal-Luçon* ⊙ *Daily 7:30–7:30.*

④① The Gallo-Roman **Cryptoportique,** an underground gallery and crypt, now a semi-subterranean passageway, was constructed around AD 200 under the forum of what was Reim's predecessor, the Roman town of Durocortorum. ⊠ *Pl. du Forum* ☏ *03–26–85–23–36* ⊙ *Mid-June–mid-Sept., Tues.–Sun. 2–6.*

④② The **Porte Mars** (⊠ Rue de Mars), an unlikely but impressive 3rd-century Roman arch adorned by worn bas-reliefs depicting Jupiter, Romulus, and Remus, looms up across from the train station.

④③ The **Musée de la Reddition** (Surrender Room), near the train station, also known as the Salle du 8-Mai-1945, is a well-preserved map-covered room used by General Eisenhower as Allied headquarters at the end of World War II. It was here that General Alfred Jodl signed the German surrender at 2:41 AM on May 7, 1945. Fighting officially ceased at midnight the next day. ⊠ *12 rue Franklin-Roosevelt* ☏ *03–26–47–84–19* ⊠ *€3, joint ticket with the Musée des Beaux-Arts* ⊙ *Wed.–Mon. 10–noon and 2–6.*

④④ **Mumm** is the closest champagne house to the centre ville, about a 10-minute walk north from the cathedral. This is one of the few champagne houses to give out free samples after a tour, which is usually on the bland side (the tour, that is). ⊠ *34 rue du Champ-de-Mars* ☏ *03–26–49–59–70* ⊕ *www.mumm.com* ⊠ *€7* ⊙ *Mar.–Oct., daily 9–11 and 2–5; Nov.–Feb., daily 2–5.*

Where to Stay & Eat

$-$$ ✕ **Vigneron.** This little brasserie in a 17th-century mansion is cozy and cheerful, with two tiny dining rooms displaying a jumble of champagne-related paraphernalia. The food is delightful as well: relatively cheap, distinctly hearty, and prepared with finesse. Try the pigs' feet or andouillettes slathered with delicious mustard made with champagne. ⊠ *1 pl. Paul-Jamot* ☏ *03–26–79–86–86* ▭ *MC, V* ⊙ *Closed weekends, late Dec.–early Jan., and most of Aug.*

★ $$$$ ✕▦ **Les Crayères.** The top attraction at this hotel—a late-19th-century château surrounded by a hilly park and with a gilt-trimmed interior—is Gérard Boyer, one of the country's most highly rated chefs, whose imaginative dishes range from wild mushrooms in cream to scallops with endive confit. The extensive wine list pays homage to Reims's champagne heritage. The restaurant is closed Monday, and no luncheon is offered Tuesday; reservations and jacket and tie are all essential. ⊠ *64 bd. Henry-Vasnier, 51100* ☏ *03–26–82–80–80* ⊟ *03–26–82–65–52* ⊕ *www. gerardboyer.com* ⊅ *19 rooms* ⟁ *Restaurant, minibars, cable TV, tennis court, bar, Internet, some pets allowed (fee)* ▭ *AE, DC, MC, V* ⊙ *Closed late Dec.–mid-Jan.* ⫯◌⫯ *BP.*

$$-$$$ ✕▦ **La Paix.** A modern eight-story hotel, 10 minutes' walk from the cathedral, La Paix has simple, pastel-colored rooms with 18th- and 19th-century reproductions, a pretty garden, and an incongruous chapel. Its brasserie-style restaurant serves mainly grilled meats and seafood. ⊠ *9 rue Buirette, 51100* ☏ *03–26–40–04–08* ⊟ *03–26–47–75–04* ⊅ *106*

rooms ⚹ *Restaurant, minibars, cable TV, pool, bar, some pets allowed (fee)* ⊟ *AE, DC, MC, V* ⦵| *BP.*

$–$$ ✕⊞ **Le Cheval Blanc.** This hotel, owned for five generations by the hospitable Robert family, is in the small village of Sept-Saulx, southeast of Reims. Guest rooms overlook a parklike glade on the Vesle River—some are quite small, but the newer suites are larger and have modern furnishings. Restaurant specialties include St-Pierre fish seasoned with Chinese pepper and pigeon with dried raisins. There's no lunch on Wednesdays. ⊠ *Rue du Moulin, 24 km (15 mi) southeast of Reims via D8, 51400 Sept-Saulx* ☎ *03–26–03–90–27* ⊞ *03–26–03–97–09* ⊕ *www. chevalblanc-sept-saulx.com* ⬎ *25 rooms* ⚹ *Restaurant, minibars, cable TV, tennis court, fishing, Internet; no a/c* ⊟ *AE, DC, MC, V* ⦵ *Closed Tues. Oct.–Mar., and Feb.* ⦵| *MAP.*

THE NORTH & CHAMPAGNE A TO Z

To research prices, get advice from other travelers, and book travel arrangements, visit www.fodors.com.

AIRPORTS

If you are coming from the United States and most other destinations, count on arriving at Paris's Charles de Gaulle or Orly airport. Charles de Gaulle offers easy access to the northbound A1 and the TGV line for Lille. If coming from the U.K., consider the direct flights to Lille-Lesquin from Heathrow or to Le Touquet from Brighton and from Lydd (near Folkestone).

BOAT & FERRY TRAVEL

Ferry and hovercraft companies travel between northern France and the United Kingdom. Companies traveling between Calais and Dover include Hoverspeed, P&O Stena, and Seafrance. SpeedFerries operate a fast catamaran service between Boulogne and Dover, and Norfolk Line operates between Dunkerque and Dover. For more information, *see* Boat & Ferry Travel *in* Smart Travel Tips A to Z.

BUS TRAVEL

The main bus operator in Picardy is **Courriers Automobiles Picards** (⊠ Rue de la Vallée, Amiens ☎ 03–22–92–27–03); their main hub is the Gare Routière in Amiens. In the Champagne region, services are run by STDM Trans-Champagne; the main hub is Reims, where buses depart from the train station. Some sample bus links include Amiens to Arras (via Courriers Automobiles Picards) and Boulogne to Calais (via Cariane Littoral, the main operator for services along the Channel coast). There are many other links, so always check with the regional tourist office or information window at a big gateway rail or bus station to get printed bus schedules.

🖪 Bus Information **Cariane Littoral** ⊠ 10 rue d'Amsterdam, 62100 Calais ☎ 03-21-34-74-40 ⊟ 03-21-97-73-33. **Courriers Automobiles Picards** ⊠ B.P. 59, ZAC La Haute Borne, 80136 Rivéry ☎ 03-22-91-46-82 ⊟ 03-22-70-70-71. **STDM Trans-Champagne** ⊠ 86 rue des Fagnières, 51000 Châlons-en-Champagne ☎ 03-26-65-17-07.

CAR RENTAL

Be aware that the Avis offices at the Calais car ferry and Hoverport terminals may not always be staffed. Look for instructions on how to use the red phones provided in these offices to reach the central office in the town of Calais, which will handle your rental.

📱 **Local Agencies Avis** ✉ 36 pl. d'Armes, Calais 📞 03-21-34-66-50 ✉ Calais car ferry terminal 📞 03-21-96-47-65 ✉ Calais Hoverport 📞 03-21-96-66-52 ✉ Cour de la Gare, Reims 📞 03-26-47-10-08. **Europcar** ✉ Gare Lille-Europe, av. Le Corbusier, Lille 📞 03-20-06-01-46 ✉ Gare Lille-Flandre, rue de Tournai 📞 03-20-06-10-04. **Hertz** ✉ 5 bd. d'Alsace-Lorraine, Amiens 📞 03-22-91-26-24 ✉ 10 bd. Daunou, Boulogne-sur-Mer 📞 03-21-31-53-14.

CAR TRAVEL

Two highways head north from Paris. Busy A1 passes close to Compiègne and Arras (where A26 branches off to Calais) before reaching Lille. Journey time is about 1 hour and 40 minutes to Arras and 2½ hours to Lille. The quieter A16 leads from L'Isle-Adam, north of Paris, up to Beauvais and Amiens, before veering northwest to Abbeville and around the coast to Boulogne, Calais, and Dunkerque. Journey time is about 90 minutes to Amiens and 2½ hours to Boulogne. If you're arriving by car via the Channel Tunnel, you'll disembark at Coquelles, near Calais, and join A16 not far from its junction with A26, which heads to Arras (75 minutes) and Reims (2½ hours). A4 heads east from Paris to Reims; allow 90 minutes to two hours, depending on traffic.

EMERGENCIES

🚑 **Ambulance** 📞 15. **Regional hospitals** ✉ 1 pl. Victor-Pauchet, Amiens 📞 03-22-66-80-00 ✉ 8 av. Henri-Adnot, Compiègne 📞 03-44-23-60-00 ✉ 51 bd. de Belfort, Lille 📞 03-20-87-48-48 ✉ American Hospital, 47 rue Cognac-Jay, Reims 📞 03-26-78-78-78.

TOURS

Service des Visites Guidées in Boulogne's Château-Musée arranges trips to Boulogne's old town and port for groups of up to 30 people; the cost for two hours totals €60 for two or more.

📱 **Fees & Schedules Service des Visites Guidées** ✉ Rue Bernet, Boulogne-sur-Mer 📞 03-21-80-56-78.

BUS TOURS The Lille Tourist Office is a mine of information about companies that operate bus tours through northern France. Loisirs-Accueil Nord organizes bus trips to Boulogne and Flanders and can arrange fishing, walking, and beer-tasting tours.

📱 **Fees & Schedules Lille Tourist Office** ✉ 42 pl. Rihour 📞 03-20-21-94-21 🌐 www.lilletourism.com. **Loisirs-Accueil Nord** ✉ 6 rue Gauthier-de-Châtillon, Lille 📞 03-20-57-59-59.

TRAIN TRAVEL

It's easy to get around the region by train. Most sites can be reached by regular train service, except for the war cemeteries and the castle in Pierrefonds. TGV (Trains à Grande Vitesse) trains speed from Paris (Gare du Nord) to Lille (255 km [165 mi]) in just one hour. A separate TGV service links Paris (Gare du Nord) to Arras (50 minutes) and Dunkerque (two hours). The Paris–Boulogne–Calais train chugs unhurriedly around the coast, taking nearly three hours to cover 300 km (185 mi) via Amiens, Abbeville, and Étaples (bus links to nearby Le Touquet and Montreuil). There are also frequent daily services from Paris (Gare du Nord) to Beauvais and to Compiègne, Noyon, and Laon (taking up to two leisurely hours to cover 140 km [87 mi]). Regular trains cover the 170 km (105 mi) from Paris (Gare de l'Est) to Reims, via Château-Thierry, in 1½ hours. Cross-country services connect Reims to Épernay, Châlons, and Amiens (via Laon). Eurostar trains, via the Channel Tunnel, link London to Lille in under two hours; some stop at Fréthun, just outside Calais.

🚆 Train Information **SNCF** ☎ 08-36-35-35-35 ⊕ www.ter-sncf.com/uk/nord-pas-de-calais.

TRAVEL AGENCIES
🚆 Local Agent Referrals **Carlson Wagonlit** ✉ 1 rue Paul-Bert, Calais ☎ 03-21-34-79-25 ✉ 9 rue Faidherbe, Lille ☎ 08-26-82-55-03.

VISITOR INFORMATION
The principal regional tourist offices in Amiens, Lille, and Reims are good sources of information about the region. Other, smaller towns also have their own tourist offices, listed below by town.

🚆 Tourist Information **Abbeville** ✉ 1 pl. de l'Amiral-Courbet ☎ 03-22-24-27-92 ⊕ www.ville-abbeville.fr. **Amiens** ✉ 6 bis rue Dusevel ☎ 03-22-71-60-50 ⊕ www.amiens.com/tourisme. **Arras** ✉ Hôtel de Ville, pl. des Héros ☎ 03-21-51-26-95 ⊕ www.ville-arras.fr. **Beauvais** ✉ 1 rue Beauregard ☎ 03-44-45-08-18. **Boulogne-sur-Mer** ✉ Forum Jean-Noël, quai de la Poste ☎ 03-21-31-68-38 ⊕ www.tourisme-boulognesurmer.com. **Calais** ✉ 12 bd. Clemenceau ☎ 03-21-96-62-40 ⊕ www.ot-calais.fr. **Compiègne** ✉ Pl. de l'Hôtel-de-Ville ☎ 03-44-40-01-00 ⊕ www.compiegne.fr. **Eu** ✉ 41 rue Paul-Bignon ☎ 02-35-86-04-68 ⊕ www.ville-eu.fr. **Laon** ✉ Pl. du Parvis ☎ 03-23-20-28-62 ⊕ www.ville-laon.fr. **Le Touquet** ✉ Palais de l'Europe, pl. de l'Hermitage ☎ 03-21-06-72-00 ⊕ www.letouquet.com. **Lille** ✉ 42 pl. Rihour ☎ 03-20-21-94-21 ⊕ www.lilletourism.com. **Montreuil-sur-Mer** ✉ 21 rue Carnot ☎ 03-21-06-04-27 ⊕ www.montreuil62.net. **Noyon** ✉ Pl. de l'Hôtel-de-Ville ☎ 03-44-44-21-88 ⊕ www.noyon.com/tourisme. **Pierrefonds** ✉ Rue Louis-d'Orléans ☎ 03-44-42-81-44. **Reims** ✉ 2 rue Guillaume-de-Machault ☎ 03-26-77-45-25 ⊕ www.reims-tourisms.com. **Soissons** ✉ 16 pl. Fernand-Marquigny ☎ 03-23-53-17-37 ⊕ www.ville-soissons.fr.

Alsace-Lorraine

7

WORD OF MOUTH

"If you happen to be a fan of art and architecture, you'll be in hog heaven in Nancy—both for its 18th-century architecture and for its Art Nouveau treasures of the early 1900s. Stop at the Tourist Office on the place Stanislas and pick up brochures for walking tours with architectural itineraries of both."

—MaisonMetz

"When I went to Strasbourg, I kept the car and drove the Alsace wine route and saw the quaint towns Ribeauvillé and Riquewihr. These have got to be the most picturesque villages in France— and a nice day trip from Strasbourg!"

—Richarddab

Introduction by
Nancy Coons

Updated by
Christopher
Mooney

WHO PUT THE HYPHEN IN ALSACE-LORRAINE? The two regions, long at odds physically and culturally, were bonded when Kaiser Wilhelm sliced off the Moselle chunk of Lorraine and sutured it, à la Dr. Frankenstein, to Alsace, claiming the unfortunate graft as German turf. Though their names to this day are often hyphenated, Alsace and Lorraine have always been two separate territories, with distinctly individual characters. It's only their recent German past that ties them together—it wasn't until 1879, as a concession after France's surrender in 1871, that the newly hyphenated "Alsace-Lorraine" became part of the enemy's spoils. At that point the region was systematically Teutonized—architecturally, linguistically, culinarily (" . . . ve haff our own vays of cookink sauerkraut!")—and the next two generations grew up culturally torn. Until 1918, that is, when France undid its defeat and reclaimed its turf. Until 1940, when Hitler snatched it back and reinstated German textbooks in the primary schools. Until 1945, when France once again triumphantly raised the *bleu-blanc-rouge* over Strasbourg.

But no matter how forcefully the French tout its hard-won Frenchness, Alsace's German roots go deeper than the late 19th century, as one look at its storybook medieval architecture will attest. In fact, this strip of vine-covered hills squeezed between the Rhine and the Vosges mountains was called Prima Germania by the Romans, and belonged to the fiercely Germanic Holy Roman Empire for more than 700 years. Yet west of the Vosges, Lorraine served under French and Burgundian lords as well as the Holy Roman Empire, coming into its own under the powerful and influential dukes of Lorraine in the Middle Ages and Renaissance. Stanislas, the duke of Lorraine who transformed Nancy into a cosmopolitan Paris of the East, was Louis XV's father-in-law. Thus Lorraine's culture evolved as decidedly less German than its neighbor to the southeast.

But that's why these days most travelers find Alsace more exotic than Lorraine: its gabled, half-timber houses, ornate wells and fountains, oriels (upstairs bay windows), storks' nests, and carved-wood balustrades would serve well as a stage set for the tale of William Tell and satisfy a visitor's deepest craving for well-preserved Old World atmosphere. Strasbourg, perhaps France's most fascinating city outside Paris, offers all this ambience, and urban sophistication as well. And throughout Alsace, hotels are well scrubbed, with tile bathrooms, good mattresses, and geraniums spilling from every windowsill. Although the cuisine leans toward wursts and sauerkraut, sophisticated spins on traditional fare have earned it a reputation—perhaps ironic, in some quarters—as one of the gastronomic centers of France. In fact, it has been crudely but vividly put that Alsace combines the best of both worlds: one dines in France but washes up, as it were, in Germany.

Lorraine, on the other hand, has suffered over the last 20 years, and a decline in its northern industry and the miseries of its small farmers have left much of it tarnished and neglected—or, as others might say, kept it unspoiled. Yet Lorraine's rich caches of verdure, its rolling countryside

Only the Rhine River separates Germany from Alsace-Lorraine, a region that often looks and even sounds German. But its heart—after all, its natives were the first to sing the "Marseillaise"—is passionately French. In Alsace, wind along the Route du Vin through vineyards and storybook villages, then explore Strasbourg, which for all its medieval charms rivals Paris in history and haute cuisine. In mellow Lorraine, trace Joan of Arc's childhood, then discover the elegant 18th-century town of Nancy. Great art treasures—the Grünewald altarpiece at Colmar is one—also entice, as do hikes in the forested wilds of Franche-Comté. You can cover most of Alsace-Lorraine and Franche-Comté in about nine days. With six days you can see the northern part of Lorraine, from Verdun to Nancy, and most of Alsace. Three days will give you just enough time to explore Alsace, including the cosmopolitan city of Strasbourg.

Numbers in the text correspond to numbers in the margin and on the Lorraine, Alsace, Nancy, and Strasbourg maps.

If you have
3 days

Explore Alsace, beginning with a day and night in the delightful city of 🖼 **Strasbourg** ㉗–㊵ ⌐. The next day start out early, cruising south along the Route du Vin to pretty **Obernai** ㊶; the charming villages of **Barr** ㊸, **Andlau** ㊹, and **Dambach-la-Ville** ㊺; and the dramatic castle in **Haut-Koenigsbourg** ㊼. Spend the night in the wine town of 🖼 **Ribeauvillé** ㊽ or medieval 🖼 **Riquewihr** ㊾. On Day 3 soak up the art and atmosphere in **Colmar** ㊿, whose museum headlines the world-famous Grünewald altarpiece.

If you have
8 days

Begin in memory-haunted **Verdun** ⑲ ⌐ and 🖼 **Metz** ⑳; then head south through Lorraine to the crumbling cathedral town of **Toul** ㉒ and to Joan of Arc's birthplace in 🖼 **Domrémy-la-Pucelle** ㉔. Spend Days 3 and 4 in 🖼 **Nancy** ①–⑱ and discover its dazzling treasures of 18th-century and Art Nouveau architecture. On Day 5 make 🖼 **Strasbourg** ㉗–㊵ your goal, with the Rohan Palace and Petite France perched at the top of your list. On the sixth day follow the Route du Vin to **Obernai** ㊶—perhaps choose lunch here at the famed L'Ami Fritz or opt instead for a once-in-a-lifetime dinner tonight in **Sélestat** ㊻ at the legendary L'Auberge de L'Ill. Overnight nearby in ravishing 🖼 **Ribeauvillé** ㊽. On the seventh day, tour the town, then spend the afternoon at the nearby castle of **Haut-Koenigsbourg** ㊼. Forge on to quaint 🖼 **Riquewihr** ㊾ and your hotel. On Day 8 head to 🖼 **Colmar** ㊿ to see its splendid Unterlinden Museum. Spend the night here, and why not take a last look at Grünewald's great altarpiece the next morning before you return home?

dotted with *mirabelle* (plum) orchards and crumbling-stucco villages, abbeys, fortresses, and historic cities (majestic Nancy, verdant Metz, war-ravaged Verdun) offer a truly French view of life in the north. Its borders flank Belgium, Luxembourg, and Germany's mellow Mosel (Moselle in French). Home of Baccarat and St-Louis crystal (thanks to limitless supplies of firewood from the Vosges Forest), the birthplace of Gregorian chant, Art Nouveau, and Joan of Arc, Lorraine-the-underdog has long had something of its own to contribute. Although it may lack the Teutonic comforts of Alsace—it subscribes to the more laissez-faire school of innkeeping (concave mattresses, dusty bolsters, creaky floors)—it serves its regional delicacies with flair: *tourte Lorraine* (a pork-and-beef pie), madeleines (shell-shape butter cakes), mirabelle plum tarts, and the famous local quiche.

Exploring Alsace & Lorraine

These two regions of eastern France border three countries. Alsace, the smallest region, occupies a narrow strip of territory between the Vosges mountains and Germany, across the Rhine river. The capital of Alsace, Strasbourg, is the largest city in the region and one of the most attractive in France. The large town holding down the southern stretch of the region is historic Colmar. To the west of Alsace, across the Vosges and sharing a northern frontier with Germany and Luxembourg, is Lorraine. The largest city here, Nancy, also has considerable charm. North of Nancy is Metz, a picturesque town, and to the west lies Verdun. Most visitors begin exploring this region to the west—nearest Paris—where the battlegrounds of Verdun provide a poignant introduction to Lorraine. Linger in the artistic city of Nancy and then head east to Strasbourg (145 km [90 mi]), a city of such historic and cultural importance that it's worth exploring in depth. From here, tour the rest of Alsace, following the photogenic Route du Vin (Wine Road) to Colmar.

About the Restaurants & Hotels

Strasbourg and Nancy may be known as two of France's more expensive cities, but you wouldn't know it by the eating scene: no matter where you are, you can find down-to-earth eating spots with down-to-earth prices. Most notably, the regional *Weinstubes* (pronounced *veen*-shtoob), cozier and more wine-oriented than the usual French brasserie, are to be found in most Alsace towns and villages. In Alsace's capital, Strasbourg, along with Nancy and Metz, the two cities of Lorraine, as well as the villages along Alsace's pretty wine road, you'll need to arrive early (soon after noon, before eight) to be sure of a restaurant table in July and August. Out of season is a different matter throughout. As for food, these regions are typically French in their appreciation of fine foods, breads, and outdoor cafés, but a love of beer and beer pubs betrays that strong German influence.

Accommodations are easier to find in Lorraine than in Alsace, where advance reservations are essential in summer. Alsace is rich in *gîtes,* country houses that can be rented. Throughout Alsace, hotels are models of good housekeeping. Lorraine tends to lack the Teutonic comforts of Alsace but is coming around as renovations get under way. Assume that all hotel rooms have air-conditioning, TV, telephones, and private bath, unless otherwise noted.

Beyond Quiche Lorraine

A bottle of sharp Savagnin, a pink slab of air-dried ham, a patty of silky Vacherin Mont d'Or melted over potatoes: You don't need pink linens to dine on this primal mountain food, just a hiker's appetite, perhaps whetted by exploring the forested ranges of the region. Alsace cooking tends to be hearty and influenced by its Germanic origins—*choucroute* (sauerkraut served with ham and sausages) and *baeckoffe* (a meat-and-potato casserole) are two mainstays—but there is sophistication, too: foie gras accompanied by a glass of *vendanges tardives* (late-harvested) Gewürztraminer, and trout and chicken cooked in Riesling, the classic wine of Alsace. Snails and seasonal game are other favorites, as are Muenster cheese, salty *bretzel* loaves, and briochelike *kouglof* bread. Geese are very popular, especially if they're stuffed with apples or chestnuts! Carp fried in bread crumbs is a specialty of southern Alsace. Another regional favorite is the *tarte flambée*, a thin-crusted, pizzalike thing, topped with everything from fresh cream and cheese to mushrooms and fish. Desserts are also rich, most notably the *Kougelhopf*, a buttery upside-down cake cooked in a round pan and commonly served with kirsch, the local liqueur made from cherries. Lorraine, renowned for quiches, is also famous for its madeleines, *dragées* (almond candies), macaroons, and the lovely little *mirabelle*, a small yellow plum juicy with heady, perfumed nectar. Lorraine shares the Alsatian love of pastry and fruit tarts, served as often at 4 in the afternoon, with coffee, as an after-dinner dessert.

A Glass of Gewürztraminer

Wine is an object of worship in Alsace, and any traveler down the region's Route du Vin will want to become part of the cult. Just because Alsatian vintners use German grapes, don't expect their wines to taste like their counterparts across the Rhine. German vintners aim for sweetness, creating wines that are best appreciated as an aperitif. Alsatian vintners, on the other hand, eschew sweetness in favor of strength, and their wines go wonderfully with knock-down, drag-out meals. The main wines you need to know about are Gewürztraminer, Riesling, muscat, pinot gris, and sylvaner, all white wines. The only red wine produced in the region is the light and delicious pinot noir.

Gewürztraminer, which in Germany is an ultrasweet dessert wine, has a much cleaner, drier taste in Alsace, despite its fragrant bouquet. It is best served with the richest of Alsace dishes, such as goose. Riesling is the premier wine of Alsace, balancing a hard flavor with a certain gentleness. Pinot gris, also called tokay, and muscat are known as the Noble Wines of Alsace. With a grapy bouquet and clean finish, the dry muscat does best as an aperitif. Tokay is probably the most full-bodied of Alsatian wines. Sylvaner falls below those grapes in general acclaim, tending to be lighter and a bit dull. You'll discover many of these wines as you drive along the Route du Vin as it makes its way between Mulhouse and Strasbourg.

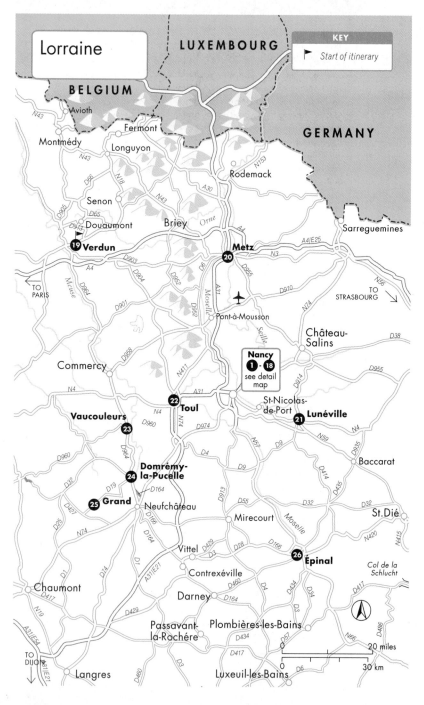

WHAT IT COSTS In euros					
	$$$$	**$$$**	**$$**	**$**	**¢**
RESTAURANTS	over €30	€23–€30	€17–€23	€11–€17	under €11
HOTELS	over €190	€120–€190	€80–€120	€50–€80	under €50

Restaurant prices are per person for a main course at dinner, including tax (19.6%) and service; note that if a restaurant offers only prix-fixe (set-price) meals, it has been given the price category that reflects the full prix-fixe price. Hotel prices are for a standard double room in high season, including tax (19.6%) and service charge. Hotels operate on the European Plan (EP, with no meal provided) unless we note that they use the Breakfast Plan (BP), or also offer such options as Modified American Plan (MAP, with breakfast and dinner daily, known as *demi-pension*), or Full American Plan (FAP, or *pension complète*, with three meals a day). Inquire when booking if these all-inclusive mealplans (which always entail higher rates) are mandatory or optional.

Timing

Outside tourist-packed high summer, June and September are the warmest and sunniest months. Many of the region's towns and villages, especially the wine villages of Alsace, stage summer festivals, including the spectacular pagan-inspired burning of the three pine trees in Thann (late June), the Flower Carnival in Sélestat (mid-August), and the wine fair in Colmar (first half of August). Some of the region's top sights, however—notably Haut-Koenigsbourg—can be besieged by tourists in July and August, so if you're there then, try to visit early in the morning. Although Lorraine is a lusterless place in winter, the Vosges mountains make attempts at being ski venues—plentiful snow cannot always be guaranteed—while Strasbourg pays tribute to the Germanic tradition with a Christmas fair.

NANCY

For architectural variety, few French cities match Nancy, which is in the heart of Lorraine, 300 km (190 mi) east of Paris. Medieval ornamentation, 18th-century grandeur, and Belle Époque fluidity rub shoulders in the town center, where the bustle of commerce mingles with stately elegance. Its majesty derives from a long history as domain to the powerful dukes of Lorraine, whose double-barred crosses figure prominently on local statues and buildings. Never having fallen under the rule of the Holy Roman Empire or the Germans, this Lorraine city retains an eminently Gallic charm.

The city is at its most sublimely French in its harmoniously constructed squares and buildings, which, as vestiges of the 18th century, have the quiet refinement associated with the best in French architecture. Curiously enough, it was a Pole, and not a Frenchman, who was responsible for much of what is beautiful in Nancy. Stanislas Leszczynski, ex-king of Poland and father of Marie Leczinska (who married Louis XV of France) was given the Duchy of Lorraine by his royal son-in-law on the understanding that on his death it would revert to France. Stanislas installed himself in Nancy and devoted himself to the glorious embellishment of the city. Today place Stanislas remains one of the loveliest and most perfectly proportioned squares in the world, with place de la

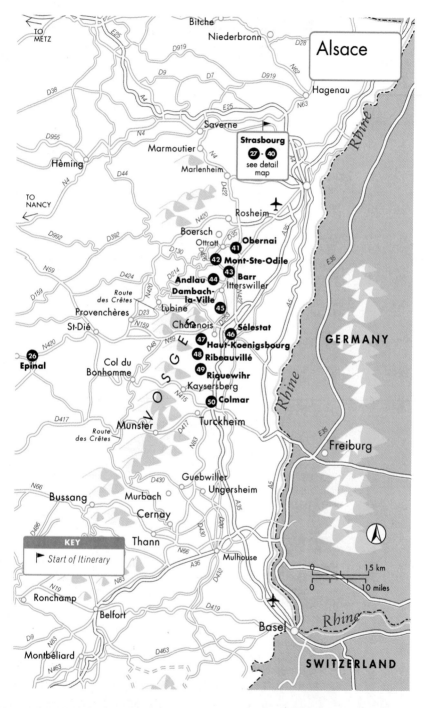

TO
METZ

Bitche

Niederbronn

D28

Alsace

D919

D919

D9

D7

D919

N62

Hagenau

D38

A4

E25

N63

D955

Saverne

E25

Strasbourg
27 - 40
see detail
map

TO
NANCY

Marmoutier

N4

Marlenheim

D422

▶

Hèming

D44

Rosheim

✈

N420

D992

D392

Boersch

D35

41 Obernai

Ottrott

D130

42 Mont-Ste-Odile

E35

N59

D424

D214

43 Barr

Andlau 44

Itterswiller

Route
des Crêtes

D420

**Dambach-
la-Ville**

D422

Provenchères

D23

Lubine

45

D159

N159

Châtenois

46 Sélestat

St-Dié

N59

D48

47 Haut-Koenigsbourg

GERMANY

26
Epinal

N420

48 Ribeauvillé

Col du
Bonhomme

V
O
S
G
E

49 Riquewihr

Kaysersberg

Rhine

50 Colmar

D417

Route
des Crêtes

D417

Turckheim

A5

Munster

N83

E35

Freiburg

N66

D430

Guebwiller

Bussang

Murbach

Ungersheim

A35

Freiburg

D486

Cernay

D430

D20

Thann

N66

N83

A36

Mulhouse

N19

N83

D462

Ronchamp

0   1,5 km

0   10 miles

D9

N63

D419

✈

Belfort

Rhine

Montbéliard

N463

D463

Basel

SWITZERLAND

KEY

▶ *Start of Itinerary*

Carrière—reached through Stanislas's Arc de Triomphe—with its elegant, homogeneous 18th-century houses, its close rival for this honor.

The Historic Center

Concentrated northeast of the train station, this neighborhood—rich in architectural treasures as well as museums—includes classical place Stanislas and the shuttered, medieval *Vieille Ville* (Old Town).

a good walk

Begin your walk at the symbolic heart of Nancy, **place Stanislas** ❶ ▶, one of the grandest architectural set-pieces of the 18th century. The crown jewel of the city, enclosed by gold-and-black gates and Neoclassical buildings, the huge public square is bordered by many of the city's main institutions, including the art museum, the Hôtel de Ville (Town Hall), the Opéra, the tourist office, outdoor cafés, fountains, and a triumphal arch. On its western corner is the **Musée des Beaux-Arts** ❷, the Fine Arts Museum, fitted out with treasures from Rubens to great Daum glass. Cross place Stanislas diagonally and head south down rue Maurice Barrès to the Baroque **Cathédrale** ❸. On leaving, turn left on rue St-Georges and right up rue des Dominicains, stopping to admire the elegant stonework on No. 57, the Maison des Adams, named for the sculptors who lived in (and decorated) the edifice in the 18th century.

Recross place Stanislas and go through the monumental Arc de Triomphe, entering into peaceful **place de la Carrière** ❹, another square that is a triumph of elegant symmetry. At the colonnaded Palais du Gouvernement, former home of the governors of Lorraine, turn right into the vast, formal city park known as **La Pépinière** ❺. From the park's entrance at the foot of place de la Carrière, head straight under the arches and into the Vieille Ville. Dominating the square is the mighty basilica of **St-Epvre** ❻, which compensates for the absence of a Gothic cathedral in Nancy.

Head immediately right up picturesque Grande-Rue, with its antiques shops, bookstores, and artisanal bakeries behind brightly painted facades. On your right is the **Palais Ducal** ❼, one wing of which is a spectacular example of Flamboyant Gothic. Here's the main branch of the Musée Historique Lorraine, an ambitious complex that covers art—Georges de la Tour, Jacques Callot, Jacques de Bellange are the best known of Lorraine's great masters—as well as fascinating regional lore. The neighboring **Musée des Arts et Traditions Populaires** ❽ occupies the Couvent des Cordeliers, combining a folk-arts museum and a Gothic chapel. At the end of Grande-Rue is the delightfully imposing **Porte de la Craffe** ❾, the last of Nancy's medieval fortifications.

TIMING Depending on how much time you spend in the museums, this walk could take an hour or a whole day. Note that all the museums are closed on Tuesday.

Sights to See

❸ **Cathédrale.** This vast, frigid edifice was built in the 1740s in a ponderous Baroque style, eased in part by the florid ironwork of Jean Lamour. Its most notable interior feature is a murky 19th-century fresco in the

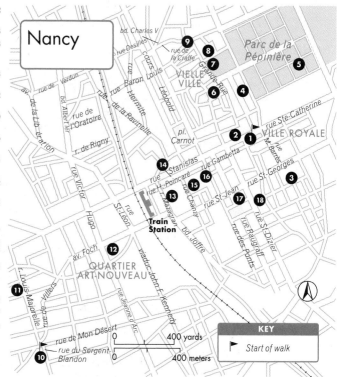

dome. The **Trésor** (Treasury) contains minute 10th-century splendors carved of ivory and gold. ✉ *Rue St-Georges, Ville Neuve.*

★ ❽ Just up the street from the Palais Ducal, the quirky, appealing **Musée des Arts et Traditions Populaires** (Museum of Folk Arts and Traditions) is housed in the **Couvent des Cordeliers** (Convent of the Franciscans, who were known as Cordeliers until the Revolution). It re-creates how local people lived in pre-industrial times, using a series of evocative rural interiors. Craftsmen's tools, colorful crockery, somber stone fireplaces, and dark waxed-oak furniture accent the tableaulike settings. The dukes of Lorraine are buried in the crypt of the adjoining **Église des Cordeliers,** a Flamboyant Gothic church; the *gisant* (reclining statue) of Philippa de Gueldra, second wife of René II, executed in limestone in flowing detail, is a moving example of Renaissance portraiture. The octagonal Ducal Chapel was begun in 1607 in the Renaissance style, modeled on the Medici Chapel in Florence. ✉*66 Grande-Rue, Vieille Ville* ☎*03–83–32–18–74* 💶*€3.10; €4.60 joint ticket with Musée Lorrain* ☉ *Wed.–Mon. 10–12:30 and 2–6.*

❷ **Musée des Beaux-Arts** (Fine Arts Museum). In a splendid building that now spills over into a spectacular modern wing, a broad and varied collection of art treasures lives up to the noble white facade designed by Emmanuel Héré. Among the most striking are the freeze-the-moment realist tableaux painted by native son Emile Friant at the turn of the 20th century. A sizable collection of Lipschitz sculptures includes portrait busts of Gertrude Stein, Jean Cocteau, and Coco Chanel. You'll also find 19th- and 20th-century paintings by Monet, Manet, Utrillo, and Modigliani; a Caravaggio *Annunciation* and a wealth of Old Masters from the Italian, Dutch, Flemish, and French schools; and impressive glassworks by Nancy native Antonin Daum. The showpiece is Rubens's massive *Transfiguration.* Good commentary cards in English are available in every hall. ⊠ *Pl. Stanislas, Ville Royale* ☎ *03–83–85–30–72* ⊕ *www.ot-nancy.fr/Decouverte/ musees/mba.htm* 🎫 *€4.57; €5.34 for joint ticket with Musée de l'École* 🕙 *Wed.–Mon. 10:30–6.*

★ **❼ Palais Ducal** (Ducal Palace). This palace was built in the 13th century and completely restored at the end of the 15th century and again after a fire at the end of the 19th century. The main entrance to the palace, and the **Musée Lorrain** (Lorraine History Museum), which it now houses, is 80 yards down the street from the spectacularly flamboyant Renaissance portal. A spiral stone staircase leads up to the palace's most impressive room, the **Galerie des Cerfs** (Stags Gallery). Exhibits here (including pictures, armor, and books) recapture the Renaissance mood of the 16th century—one of elegance and merrymaking, with an undercurrent of stern morality: an elaborate series of huge tapestries, *La Condemnation du Banquet* (Condemnation of the Banquet), expounds on the evils of drunkenness and gluttony. Exhibits showcase Stanislas and his court, including "his" oft-portrayed dwarf; a section on Nancy in the revolutionary era; and works of Lorraine native sons, including a collection of Jacques Callot engravings and a handful of works by Georges de La Tour. ⊠ *64 Grande-Rue, Vieille Ville* ☎ *03–83–32–18–74* 🎫 *€3.10; €4.60 joint ticket with Musée des Arts et Traditions* 🕙 *Wed.–Mon. 10–12:30 and 2–6.*

☾ **❺ La Pépinière.** This picturesque, landscaped city park has labeled ancient trees, a rose garden, playgrounds, a carousel, and a small zoo. ⊠ *Entrance off pl. de la Carrière, Vieille Ville.*

★ **❹ Place de la Carrière.** Spectacularly lined with pollarded trees and handsome 18th-century mansions (another successful collaboration between King Stanislas and Emmanuel Héré), this elegant rectangle leads from place Stanislas to the colonnaded facade of the **Palais du Gouvernement** (Government Palace), former home of the governors of Lorraine. ⊠ *Vieille Ville.*

★ ▶ **❶ Place Stanislas.** With its severe, gleaming-white Classical facades given a touch of Rococo jollity by fanciful wrought gilt-iron railings, this perfectly proportioned square will probably remind many of Versailles. The square is named for Stanislas Leszczynski, twice dethroned as king of Poland but offered the Duchy of Lorraine by Louis XV (his son-in-law) in 1736. Stanislas left a legacy of spectacular buildings, undertaken between 1751 and 1760 by architect Emmanuel Héré and ironwork genius Jean Lamour. The sculpture of Stanislas dominating the square went up in the 1830s, when the square was named after him. Framing the exit, and marking the divide between the Vieille Ville and the *Ville Neuve* (New Town), is the **Arc de Triomphe**, erected in the 1750s to honor Louis XV. The facade trumpets the gods of war and peace; Louis's portrait is here. Fitting showpiece of the southern flank of the square is the 18th-century **Hôtel de Ville**, Nancy's Town Hall, where the handiwork of Lamour can also be seen to stunning effect on the wrought-iron handrail of the *grand escalier* (grand staircase) leading off the lobby. You could get a closer view when the building was open to the public on summer evenings (July and August, 10:30 to 11 PM) but, at press time, was closed for major renovations in honor of the 250th anniversary of the place Stanislas. Hopefully, by late 2005 you will once again be allowed to mount the staircase and enter the Salle des Fêtes from whose windows the full beauty of the place Stanislas may truly be savored. ⊠ *Ville Royale.*

❾ **Porte de la Craffe.** A fairy-tale vision out of the late Middle Ages, this gate is the only remains of Nancy's medieval fortifications. With its twin *châtelet* towers looming at one end of the Grande-Rue, built in the 14th and 15th centuries, this arch served as a prison through the Revolution. Above the main portal is the Lorraine Cross, comprising a thistle and cross. ⊠ *Vieille Ville.*

❻ **St-Epvre.** A 275-foot spire towers over this splendid neo-Gothic church rebuilt in the 1860s. Most of the 2,800 square yards of stained glass were created by the Geyling workshop in Vienna; the chandeliers were made in Liège, Belgium; many carvings are the work of Margraff of Munich; the heaviest of the eight bells was cast in Budapest; and the organ, though manufactured by Merklin of Paris, was inaugurated in 1869 by Austrian composer Anton Bruckner. ⊠ *Pl. du Général-de-Gaulle, Vieille Ville.*

Art Nouveau Nancy

FodorśChoice
★

Think of *"l'Art Nouveau"* and many will conjure up the rich Parisian salons of Paris's Maxim's restaurant, the lavender-hue Prague posters of Alphonse Mucha, and the stained-glass dragonflies and opalescent vases that, to this day, remain the darlings of such collectors as Barbra Streisand. All of that beauty was born, to a great extent, in 19th-century Nancy. Inspired and coordinated by the glass master Émile Gallé, the local movement was formalized in 1901 as L'École de Nancy—from there, it spread like wildfire through Europe, from Naples to Monte-Carlo to Prague. The ensuing flourish encompassed the floral *pâte de verre* (literally, glass dough) works of Antonin Daum and Gallé; the Tiffany-esque stained-glass windows of Jacques Gruber; the fluidity of Louis Majorelle's furniture designs; and the sinuous architecture of Lucien Weissenburger, Émile André, and Eugène Vallin. Thanks to these artists, Nancy's downtown architecture gives the impression of a living garden suspended above the sidewalks.

a good walk

The magical **Musée de l'École de Nancy** ❿ ➤ is the best place to immerse yourself in the fanciful style that crept into interiors and exteriors throughout Nancy. To get to the museum from the busy shopping street rue St-Jean (just up rue des Dominicains from place Stanislas), take Bus 5 or 25 uphill and get off at place Painlevé. From the museum turn left down rue du Sergent-Blandan and walk about four blocks to **Villa Ma-**

jorelle ⑪. Cut east to place de la Commanderie and head up **avenue Foch ⑫** to admire the colorful structures at Nos. 71, 69, and 41. Hike over the Viaduct Kennedy and the *gare* (train station), turn left past the department store Printemps, and follow rue Mazagran to the **Brasserie l'Excelsior ⑬**. Turn right toward **No. 40 rue Henri-Poincaré ⑭**. Turn right and walk past **No. 9 rue Chanzy ⑮** (now the Banque Nationale de Paris). Head left to find **No. 2 rue Bénit ⑯**, with its ornate metal structure. Head south to rue St-Jean; at the corner of **rue Raugraff ⑰** are two bay windows, remnants of stores that were once here. Continue down rue St-Jean and turn right to find **Nos. 42–44 rue St-Dizier ⑱**. Many more Art Nouveau addresses are scattered throughout the city; you can get a detailed map at the tourist office.

TIMING Allow a full morning to linger in the Musée de l'École de Nancy and then, during the course of about an hour and a half, wander back circuitously toward the Vieille Ville, stopping to admire Art Nouveau masterworks along the way.

Sights to See

⑫ **Avenue Foch.** This busy boulevard lined with mansions was built for Nancy's affluent 19th-century middle class. At No. 69, the occasional pinnacle suggests Gothic influence on a house built in 1902 by Émile André, who designed the neighboring No. 71 two years later. No. 41, built by Paul Charbonnier in 1905, bears ironwork by Majorelle. ⊠ *Quartier Art-Nouveau.*

⑬ **Brasserie l'Excelsior.** This bustling brasserie has a severely rhythmic facade that is invitingly illuminated at night. The popular restaurant continues to evoke the turn of the 20th century, both in its historic decor and its fin-de-siècle perfume. ⊠ *5 rue Mazagran, Quartier Art-Nouveau.*

★ ▶ ⑩ **Musée de l'École de Nancy** (School of Nancy Museum). The only museum in France devoted to Art Nouveau is housed in an airy turn-of-the-last-century garden–town house. It was built by Eugène Corbin, an early patron of the School of Nancy. There isn't a straight line in the house; pianos ooze, bedsteads undulate; the wood itself, hard and burnished as it is, seems to have melted and re-formed. Re-created rooms and original works of art by local Art Nouveau stars Gallé, Daum, Muller, and Walter all allure. Gallé (1846–1904) was the engine that drove the whole Art Nouveau movement. He called upon artists to resist the imperialism of Paris, follow examples in nature (not those of Greece or Rome), and use a variety of techniques and materials. Many of their gorgeous artifacts are on view here. ⊠ *36 rue du Sergent-Blandan, Quartier Art-Nouveau* ☎ *03–83–40–14–86* ⊕ *www.ecole-de-nancy.com* ⊡ *€4.60; €6.10 for joint ticket with Musée des Beaux-Arts* ☉ *Mon. 2–6, Wed.–Sun. 10:30–6.*

⑯ **No. 2 rue Bénit.** This elaborately worked metal exoskeleton, the first in Nancy (1901), exudes functional beauty. The fluid decoration reminds you of the building's past as a seed supply store. Windows were worked by Gruber; the building was designed by Henry-Barthélemy Gutton, while Victor Schertzer conceived the metal frame. ⊠ *Quartier Art-Nouveau.*

⑮ No. 9 rue Chanzy. Designed by architect Émile André, this lovely structure—now a bank—can be visited during business hours. You can still see the cabinetry of Majorelle, the decor of Paul Charbonnier, and the stained-glass windows of Gruber. ⊠ *Quartier Art-Nouveau.*

⑭ No. 40 rue Henri-Poincaré. The Lorraine thistle and brewing hops weave through this undulating exterior, designed by architects Émile Toussaint and Louis Marchal. Victor Schertzer conceived this metal structure in 1908, after the success of No. 2 rue Bénit. Gruber's windows are enhanced by the curving metalwork of Majorelle. ⊠ *Quartier Art-Nouveau.*

⑱ Nos. 42–44 rue St-Dizier. Eugène Vallin and Georges Biet left their mark on this graceful 1903 bank. ⊠ *Quartier Art-Nouveau* ☉ *Weekdays 8:30–5:30.*

⑰ Rue Raugraff. Once there were two stores here, both built in 1901. The bay windows are the last vestiges of the work of Charles Vallin, Émile André, and Eugène Vallin. ⊠ *At corner of rue St-Jean, Quartier Art-Nouveau.*

★ ⑪ Villa Majorelle. This villa was built in 1902 by Paris architect Henri Sauvage for Majorelle himself. Sinuous metal supports seem to sneak up on the unsuspecting balcony like swaying cobras, and there are two grand windows by Gruber: one lighting the staircase (visible from the street) and the other set in the dining room on the south side of the villa (peek around from the garden side). ⊠ *1 rue Louis-Majorelle Quartier Art-Nouveau.*

Where to Stay & Eat

★ $$–$$$ ✕ **Le Capucin Gourmand.** With a chic decor making the most of Nancy's Art Nouveau pâte de verre, including a giant chandelier and glowing mushroom lamps on the tables, this landmark puts its best foot forward under chef Hervé Fourrière. Soigné specialties include a light lobster lasagna with mushrooms, beef marrow served in the bone with truffles and white beans, and a trio of fresh mango desserts. The choice of Toul wines is extensive. ⊠ *31 rue Gambetta, Ville Royale* ☎ *03–83–35–26–98* ☖ *Reservations essential* ▤ *AE, DC, MC, V* ☉ *Closed Mon. and Aug. No lunch Sat. No dinner Sun.*

$$ ✕ **La Gastrolâtre.** Under the inspired direction of chef Patrick Tanesy, this stylish checked-cloth bistro off place Stanislas serves sophisticated regional cooking. Combinations include a meat-and-potato *baeckoffe* casserole with foie gras, mullet with pigs' feet, and authentic *bouchée à la reine* (pastry shell with creamed meat), complete with cock's comb, sweetbreads, and morel mushrooms. Reserve ahead for summer terrace dining. ⊠ *1 pl. de Vaudemont, Vieille Ville* ☎ *03–83–35–51–94* ▤ *MC, V* ☉ *Closed Sun., 2 wks Aug., first wk of May, late Dec.–early Jan. No lunch Mon. No dinner Thurs.*

¢–$ ✕ **Le P'tit Cuny.** If you were inspired by the rustic exhibits of the Musée des Arts et Traditions Populaires, cross the street and sink your teeth into authentic Lorraine cuisine in the form of choucroute, *tête de veau* (calf's head), or tangy veal *tourte* (pie). ⊠ *95 Grande-Rue, Vieille Ville* ☎ *03–83–32–85–94* ▤ *MC, V* ☉ *Closed Sun. and Mon.*

★ **$$$-$$$$** ✕⏹ **Grand Hôtel de la Reine.** This hotel is every bit as grand as place Stanislas, on which it stands; the magnificent 18th-century building is officially classified as a historic monument. Rooms are in a suitably regal Louis XV style; the most luxurious overlook the square. The restaurant, Le Stanislas (closed Sunday November–April; no lunch Saturday), aglitter with chandeliers and carved-wood boiseries and run with elan by Olivier Hubert, has four- and five-course menus at €43 and €55. Showstoppers here include Lobster Bavaroise, duck in Vosges honey, and a supreme of melted chestnuts served with a morel mushroom caramel sauce. ⊠ *2 pl. Stanislas, Ville Royale, 54000* ☎ *03–83–35–03–01* 🖷 *03–83–32–86–04* ⊕ *www.concorde-hotels.com* ⇆ *42 rooms* ⚘ *Restaurant, minibars, cable TV, bar, some pets allowed (fee)* ⊟ *AE, DC, MC, V* ⧖ *BP.*

$-$$ ⏹ **Guise.** Deep in the shuttered Vieille Ville, this hotel is in an 18th-century nobleman's mansion with a magnificent stone-floor entry. Three and a half years of renovation were completed in 2002 and rooms are now furnished with period pieces. Breakfast on the once-grand main floor and an excellent location make this a good choice if you're a bargain-hunting romantic. ⊠ *18 rue de Guise, Vieille Ville, 54000* ☎ *03–83–32–24–68* 🖷 *03–83–35–75–63* ⊕ *www.hoteldeguise.com* ⇆ *42 rooms, 6 junior suites* ⚘ *Some pets allowed (fee); no a/c* ⊟ *MC, V* ⧖ *BP.*

¢ ⏹ **Carnot.** This somewhat generic downtown hotel, with 1950s-style comforts and mostly tiny rooms, is handy to cours Léopold parking and backs up on the Vieille Ville. Corner rooms are sizable, rooms in the rear quiet. ⊠ *4 cours Léopold, Vieille Ville, 54000* ☎ *03–83–36–59–58* 🖷 *03–83–37–00–19* ⇆ *33 rooms* ⚘ *Bar, some pets allowed (fee); no a/c, no TV in some rooms* ⊟ *MC, V.*

Nightlife & the Arts

On summer evenings (June–September) at 10 PM, place Stanislas comes alive with a **sound-and-light show,** and the doors of the magnificent Hôtel de Ville are opened to the public (€2.30). Nancy's **Orchestre Symphonique & Lyrique** (⊠ 1 rue Ste-Catherine, Ville Royale ☎ 03–83–85–30–65) is a highly-rated classical orchestra.

Le Chat Noir (⊠ 63 rue Jeanne-d'Arc, Ville Neuve ☎ 03–83–28–49–29) draws a thirtysomething crowd to retro-theme dance parties. **Métro** (⊠ 1 ter rue du Général-Hoche, Ville Neuve ☎ 03–83–40–25–13) is a popular dance club. **La Place** (⊠ 9 pl. Stanislas, Ville Royale ☎ 03–83–35–24–14) attracts a young upscale crowd that comes to dance.

Shopping

Daum (⊠ 17 rue des Cristalleries, Vieille Ville ☎ 03–83–30–80–20) sells deluxe crystal and examples of the city's traditional Art Nouveau pâte de verre. **Librairie Lorraine** (⊠ 93 Grande-Rue, Vieille Ville ☎ 03–83–36–79–52), across from the Musée des Arts et Traditions Populaires, is an excellent bookstore devoted entirely to Lorraine history and culture.

LORRAINE

In long-neglected Lorraine there are hidden treasures worth digging up. You can study the evolution of Gregorian chant in the municipal museum in Metz, where it was first codified. You can observe the luster of Baccarat crystal at its ancient factory, and the consummate artistry of Daum glassware in Nancy, where it sprang from the roots of Art Nouveau. You can stand on the unquiet earth of Verdun, and hear the church bells in which Joan of Arc discerned voices challenging her to save Orléans. Throughout Lorraine you'll find the statue of the region's patron saint, St. Nicholas—old St. Nick himself—with three children in a *saloir* (salting tub). Every December 6, Lorraine schoolchildren reenact the legend: a greedy butcher slaughters and salts down three children as hams, but when St. Nicholas drops by his place for a meal, he discovers the dastardly deed and brings them back to life.

Verdun

▶ ⓳ *96 km (60 mi) northwest of Nancy, 264 km (165 mi) east of Paris.*

A key strategic site along the Meuse Valley, Verdun is known, above all, for the 10-month battle between the French and the Germans in World War I that left more than 350,000 dead and nine villages wiped off the map. Both sides fought with suicidal fury, yet no significant ground was gained or lost. The French declared victory once they regained the 10 km (6 mi) the Germans had taken, but bloody scrapping continued until the Armistice, leaving a total of more than 700,000 dead. To this day, the scenes of battle are scarred by bomb craters, stunted vegetation, and thousands of unexploded mines and shells, rendering the area permanently uninhabitable.

The most shocking memorial of the carnage is the **Ossuaire de Douaumont,** 10 km (6 mi) north of the city. The bizarre, evocative structure—a little like a cross, a lot like a bomb—rears up over an endless sea of graves, its ground-level windows revealing undignified heaps of human bones harvested from the killing fields. Climb to the top of the tower (€1) for a view of the cemetery. In the basement a film is shown that dwells on the agony of the senseless butchery. ☎ *03–29–84–54–81* ⊕ *www.verdun-douaumont.com* ✉ *Slide show €3* ⊙ *Mar. and Oct., daily 9–noon and 2–5:30; Apr., daily 9–6; May–Aug., daily 9–6:30; Sept., daily 9–noon and 2–6; Nov., daily 9–noon and 2–5.*

The square, modern **Mémorial de Verdun** (Verdun Memorial), in the town of Fleury-devant-Douaumont, is a World War I museum with emotionally charged texts and video commentary, as well as uniforms, weapons, and the artwork of soldiers (Art Nouveau vases hammered from artillery shells). ☎ *03–29–84–35–34* ✉ *€7* ⊙ *Mid-Apr.–Dec., daily 9–6; Feb. and Mar., daily 9–noon and 2–6.*

Where to Stay & Eat

$–$$$ ✕▥ **Le Coq Hardi.** This large, steep-roof, half-timber hotel, built in 1827 on the bank of the Meuse, is a Lorraine landmark, with comfy, unpretentious rooms and a familial welcome. Young chef Frédèric Engel has brought a breath of fresh air to the place. His training at Buerehiesel and Crocodile in Strasbourg shows, blending fashionable Mediterranean touches with Lorraine tradition: frothy pea-soup "cappuccino" with Spanish ham, pig's foot stuffed with foie gras, and raspberry-lemon gratin. The restaurant is not open for dinner Friday and Sunday. ⊠ *8 av. de la Victoire, 55100* ☎ *03–29–86–36–36* 🖷 *03–29–86–09–21* ⊕ *www.coq-hardi.com* ⟿ *35 rooms* ⚭ *Restaurant, minibars, cable TV, bar, some pets allowed (fee); no a/c* ▭ *AE, DC, MC, V* ⭑◯⭑ *BP.*

Metz

★ ⑳ *64 km (40 mi) east of Verdun via D3, 56 km (35 mi) north of Nancy, 160 km (100 mi) northwest of Strasbourg.*

Despite its industrial background, Metz, the capital of the Moselle region, is one of France's greenest cities: parks, gardens, and leafy squares frame an imposing mix of military and classical architecture, all carved out of the region's yellow sandstone. At the Vieille Ville's heart is one of the finest Gothic cathedrals in France.

The **Musée de la Cour d'Or** (Museum of the Golden Courtyard), two blocks up from the cathedral in a 17th-century former convent, has a wide-ranging collection of French and German paintings from the 18th century on; military arms and uniforms; and religious works of art stored in the **Grenier de Chèvremont,** a granary built in 1457. Best by far are the stelae, statuary, jewelry, and arms evoking the city's Gallo-Roman and Merovingian past. Not to be missed: the ethereal reconstruction of the ancient chapel of St-Pierre-aux-Nonnains. Unfortunately, the museum's labyrinth of stairways excludes wheelchairs, strollers, and poor navigators. ⊠ *2 rue du Haut-Poirier* ☎ *03–87–68–25–00* ▱ *€4.60* ☽ *Wed.–Mon. 9–5.*

★ At 137 feet from floor to roof, the **Cathédrale St-Étienne** is one of France's tallest; and thanks to nearly 1½ acres of window space, one of the most luminous. The narrow, sloping 13th- to 14th-century nave channels the eye toward the dramatically raised 16th-century choir, whose walls have given way to richly colored, gemlike glass created by masters old and modern, including artist Marc Chagall. The oldest windows—on the right rear wall of the transept above the modern organ—date from the 12th century, their dark, mosaiclike simplicity a stark contrast to the ethereal stained glass of modern times. A pair of symmetrical 290-foot towers flank the nave, marking the division between the two churches that were merged to form the cathedral. The **Grand Portal,** beneath the large rose window, was reconstructed by the Germans at the turn of the 20th century; the statues of the prophets include, on the right, *Daniel,* sculpted to resemble Kaiser Wilhelm II (his unmistakable upturned mustache was snapped off in 1940). ⊠ *Pl. des Armes.*

The lively **Marché Couvert** (Market Hall) was built as a bishop's palace at the end of the 18th century, but the Revolution saw it converted to its current, more practical use as a home to smelly, farm-cured cheeses and still-flopping seafood. At the bottom of the slope down rue d'Estrées from the market, veer left and cut right over the rushing river for picturesque views of bridges and flower-laden balconies. ⊠ *Pl. de la Cathédrale* ☉ *Closed Sun. and Mon.*

Take in the broad perspective of grand Classical symmetry on the **place de la Comédie,** with its turn-of-the-last-century Protestant temple. The curving sandstone buildings date from the 18th century and include the opera and theater.

The small, heavily restored church of **St-Pierre-aux-Nonnains** has round stones and rows of red bricks thought to date from the 4th century, predating Attila the Hun's sacking of Metz and helping the city lay claim to the oldest church in France. But you may want to skip the church itself: the best of the rare Merovingian ornaments salvaged from the 6th-century version of the chapel are displayed in a full reproduction in the Musée de la Cour d'Or, demonstrating as chronologies never can how early Christian times mixed the cultures and tastes of Celts, Romans, and Gauls. ⊠ *Rue Poncelet* ☉ *Weekends.*

Where to Stay & Eat

$$–$$$ ✕ **La Dinanderie.** Chef Claude Piergiorgi serves inventive cuisine—scallops with delicate bacon threads, farm pigeon in salt crust, and pear gratin with gingerbread ice cream—with dependable flair. The intimate restaurant is across the Moselle, a 10-minute hike from the cathedral. ⊠ *2 rue de Paris* ☎ *03–87–30–14–40* ▤ *AE, MC, V* ☉ *Closed Sun., Mon., and 3 wks Aug.*

$–$$ ✕ **Le Pont St-Marcel.** Murals, dirndl skirts, and rib-sticking old-style cuisine make this a culinary plunge into Lorraine culture. There's quiche, of course, but also stewed rabbit, *potée* (boiled pork and cabbage), and carp. The list of Lorraine wines (from Toul) is encyclopedic, with the oak-cured red from Laroppe worth the splurge. In summer reserve a spot on the tiny terrace on the river. ⊠ *1 rue du Pont St-Marcel* ☎ *03–87–30–12–29* ▤ *AE, DC, MC, V.*

¢ ✕ **La Dauphiné.** Come to this unpretentious barrel-vaulted lunch spot for *tourte Lorraine* (meat pie), a plat du jour with delicious gratin potatoes, and a generous slice of fruit tart. Locals claim permanent lunch stations, but there's room upstairs, too. It's between the cathedral and the museum. ⊠ *8 rue du Chanoine-Collin* ☎ *03–87–36–03–04* ▤ *MC, V* ☉ *Closed Sun. No dinner Mon.–Thurs.*

★ $ 🏨 **Cathédrale.** From its waxed plank floors, ironwork banister, beamed ceilings, and French windows to its views of the cathedral, this gem of a hotel is reason enough to spend the night in Metz. The country-chic bedspreads, linen drapes, and hand-painted furniture are the work of the friendly owner; she collected all the antiques, too. The hotel is expanding, with an additional 10 rooms in the annex a few doors down the street. Breakfast is served in the Baraka. ⊠ *25 pl. de Chambre, 57000* ☎ *03–87–75–00–02* 🖷 *03–87–75–40–75* ⊕ *www.hotelcathedrale-metz.fr* ⇨ *20 rooms* ♤ *Restaurant, cable TV, bar, Internet, some pets allowed (fee); no a/c* ▤ *AE, DC, MC, V* ⧆ *BP.*

Lunéville

㉑ *30 km (19 mi) southeast of Nancy via N4.*

Lunéville rose to prominence at the start of the 18th century when Duke Léopold of Lorraine had the château built by Mansart's pupil Germain Boffrand, who also designed the Baroque town church of St-Jacques (of note for its carved pulpit and choir stalls). The château's glory days, however, came under King Stanislas, who held court here from 1735 to 1760, treating Lunéville as his own (scaled-down) version of Versailles. After Stanislas died, Lorraine reverted to the French crown, and Lunéville lost its luster. The château gardens have been painstakingly restored but, tragically, the château itself was devastated by fire at the start of 2003 and is likely to be closed to the public for several years.

The small industrial town of St-Nicolas-de-Port, 18 km (11 mi) northwest of Lunéville, is saved from mediocrity by its colossal basilica. Legend has it that a finger of St. Nicholas was brought to the town during the 11th-century Crusades. Sheltering such a priceless relic, the **Basilique de St-Nicolas-de-Port** (1495–1555) was rapidly besieged by pilgrims (including Joan of Arc, who came to ask St. Nicholas's blessing on her famous journey to Orléans). The simplified column capitals and elaborate rib vaulting are shining examples of Flamboyant Gothic enjoying a final fling before the gathering impetus of the Renaissance, as are the 280-foot onion-dome towers, almost symmetrical but, as was the Gothic wont, not quite. Inside, the slender, freestanding 90-foot pillars in the transept are the highest in France.

Where to Stay & Eat

★ **$$$** ✕▦ **Château d'Adoménil.** Quite a magnificent sight, this steep-roofed, pink-walled, ivy-covered 18th-century château makes a super-stylish base for visiting Nancy, Baccarat, and St-Nicolas-de-Port. Under flamboyant owner Michel Million, chef Cyril Leclerc has developed a gastronomic signature that is both elegant and rustic (the restaurant is closed Sunday and Monday from November to April and offers no lunch Tuesday), ranging from roast pike-perch with wild mushrooms to grilled foie gras and frogs'-leg omelet, perfect with a bottle of Côtes de Toul, the tangy local wine. Rooms in the château have weighty regional furniture; those in the annex—the converted stable—offer a mix of modern and Neoclassical designs. Outside, a gentle parkland and lake await your contemplative strolls. ⊠ *54300 Rehainviller, 5 km (3 mi) southwest of Lunéville* ☎ *03–83–74–04–81* 🖶 *03–83–74–21–78* ⊕ *www.relaischateaux.com/adomenil* ⤴ *14 rooms* ♺ *Restaurant, pool, Internet* ▭ *AE, DC, MC, V* ⊗ *Closed Jan.–mid-Feb.* ¶❁ *MAP.*

Toul

㉒ *21 km (13 mi) west of Nancy via A31.*

The Vieille Ville of Toul, behind mossy, star-shape ramparts, has been a bishopric since AD 365 and merited visits from the Frankish king Clovis to study the Christian faith; from Charlemagne in passing; and from a young, premilitary Joan of Arc, who was sued in the Toul court for breach of promise when she tossed aside a beau for the voice of God. In 1700, under Louis XIV, the military engineer Vauban built the thrusting ramparts around the town.

The ramshackle streets of central Toul haven't changed much for centuries—not since the embroidered twin-tower facade, a Flamboyant Gothic masterpiece, was woven onto the **Cathédrale St-Étienne** in the second half of the 15th century. The cathedral's interior, begun in 1204, is long (321 feet), airy (105 feet high), and more restrained than its exuberant facade. On one side of the cathedral are the 14th-century **cloisters,** and on the other is a pleasant **garden** behind the **Hôtel de Ville** (Town Hall), built in 1740 as the Bishop's Palace. ⊠ *Pl. d'Armes* ⊙ *Weekdays 9:30–noon, 2:30–6; weekends 10–noon, 2–4.*

The **Musée Municipal** (Town Museum), in a former medieval hospital, has a well-preserved Salle des Malades (Patients' Ward) dating from the 13th century. Archaeological finds, ceramics, tapestries, and medieval sculpture are on display. ⊠ *25 rue Gouvion-St-Cyr* ☎ *03–83–64–13–38* 🎫 *€2.60* ⊙ *Mar.–Oct., Wed.–Mon. 10–noon and 2–6; Nov.–Feb., Wed.–Mon. 2–6.*

Where to Eat

$$–$$$ ✕ **Le Dauphin.** In a bleak industrial neighborhood and with a dated decor, this grand restaurant seems out of place in humble Toul. But the modern and imaginative cooking of Christophe Vohmann draws kudos for its exotic touches and balance of flavor—opt for the langoustines with ginger and radishes or the local foie gras with artichokes. ⊠ *65 allée Gaumiron* ☎ *03–83–43–13–46* ▭ *AE, DC, MC, V* ⊙ *Closed Mon. and mid-July–mid-Aug. No dinner Sun. and Wed.*

Vaucouleurs

㉓ *24 km (15 mi) southwest of Toul on D960.*

Above the modest main street in the market town of Vaucouleurs, you can see ruins of Robert de Baudricourt's ancient medieval castle and the Porte de France, through which Joan of Arc led her armed soldiers to Orléans. The barefoot Maid of Orléans spent a year within these walls, first wheedling an audience with Baudricourt and then, having convinced him of the necessity of her mission, learning to ride and to sword-fight.

Where to Stay & Eat

¢ ✕🏠 **Relais de la Poste.** On the main street, this simple hotel has quiet rooms and a pleasant, intimate restaurant (closed Friday–Sunday in November–May). The good regional menu is served noon and night. A friendly family cooks, serves the meals, and checks you in. ⊠ *12 av. André-Maginot, 55140* ☎ *03–29–89–40–01* 🖷 *03–29–89–40–93* ⬆ *9 rooms* ♿ *Restaurant, bar, Internet; no a/c* ▭ *AE, MC, V* ⊙ *Closed last 2 wks Dec.*

Domrémy-la-Pucelle

㉔ *19 km (12 mi) south of Vaucouleurs on D964.*

Joan of Arc was born in Domrémy-la-Pucelle in a stone hut in either 1411 or 1412. You can see it as well as the church where she was baptized, the actual statue of St. Marguerite before which she prayed, and the hillside where she tended sheep and first heard voices telling her to take up arms and save France from the English. The humble stone-and-stucco **Maison Natale Jeanne d'Arc** (Joan of Arc's Birthplace)—an irregular, slope-roof, two-story cottage—has been preserved with style and reverence. The modern museum alongside, the **Centre Johannique,** shows a film (French only) while mannequins in period costume present Joan of Arc's amazing story. After she heard mystical voices, Joan walked 19 km (12 mi) to Vaucouleurs. Dressed and mounted like a man, she led her forces to lift the siege of Orléans, defeated the English, and escorted the unseated Charles VII to Reims, to be crowned king of France. Military missions after Orléans failed—including an attempt to retake Paris—and she was captured at Compiègne. The English turned her over to the Church, which sent her to be tried by the Inquisition for witchcraft and heresy. She was convicted and burned at the stake in Rouen. No matter: as a figure she remains pivotal to her "époque de transformation." Thanks to her and other leaders, civilization began to evolve from the medieval to the modern. ⊠ *2 rue de la Basilique* ☎ *03–29–06–95–86* ☞ *€3* ☉ *Apr.–Sept., daily 9–noon and 1:30–6:30; Oct.–Mar., Wed.–Mon. 9:30–noon and 2–5.*

FodorsChoice ★

The ornate late-19th-century **Basilique du Bois-Chenu** (Bois Chenu Basilica), high up the hillside above Domrémy, boasts enormous painted and mosaic panels expounding on her legend in glowing Pre-Raphaelite tones. Outside lurk serene panoramic views over the emerald, gently rolling Meuse Valley. If you are traveling to Domrémy without a car, you need to train it to either Nancy or Toul, then bus it to Neufchâteau to catch one of the two daily buses to Domrémy.

Where to Stay

¢ 🏠 **Jeanne d'Arc.** Stay next door to Joan of Arc's childhood church and wake to the bells that accompanied her voices. Accommodations are considerably less evocative, in jazzy '60s tile and paneling, but bathrooms are spotless and breakfasts (in-room only) generous. ⊠ *1 rue Principale, 88630* ☎ *03–29–06–96–06* ☞ *12 rooms* ♨ *No a/c, no room TVs* ☰ *MC, V* ☉ *Closed mid-Nov.–Mar.*

Grand

㉕ *20 km (12 mi) southwest of Domrémy; from Bois-Chenu follow signs down country roads.*

In the tiny, enigmatic hamlet of Grand, a natural spring developed into a center for the worship of the Gallo-Roman sun god Apollo-Grannus. It was important enough to draw the Roman emperors Caracalla and Constantine. Thus Grand today is a treasure trove of classical ruins. At the edge of the village the remains of a giant **amphitheater** that once seated

20,000 have been reconstructed as an imposing outdoor theater; displays illustrate its history. In a tiny museum in the centre of the village there is an expressive floor **mosaïque** with marvelously realistic animal details. Surrounding this mosaic are scraps of exotic stone and relics transported from across two continents, bearing witness to this isolated village's opulent past. ☎ *03–29–06–63–43* ◻ *Amphitheater and mosaic €3* ⊘ *Apr.–Sept., daily 9–noon and 2–7; Oct.–mid-Dec. and mid-Jan.–Mar., daily 10–noon and 2–5.*

Épinal

㉖ *96 km (60 mi) southeast of Grand via Neufchâteau and Mirecourt, 72 km (45 mi) south of Nancy.*

On the Moselle River at the feet of the Vosges, Épinal, a printing center since 1735, is famous throughout France for boldly colored prints, popular illustrations, and hand-colored stencils. **Cité de l'image,** opened in 2003, combines a new public exhibition space with the private museum of the town's most famous printing workshop, l'Imagerie d'Epinal. ⊠ *42 quai de Dogneville* ☎ *03–29–81–48–30* ◻ *€7* ⊘ *Oct.–June, Mon–Sat. 9:30–noon and 2–6, Sun. 10–noon and 2–6; July–Sept., Mon–Sat. 9:30–12:30 and 1:30–6:30, Sun. 10–12:30 and 1:30–6.*

On an island in the Moselle in the center of Épinal, the spectacular ★ **Musée Départemental d'Art Ancien et Contemporain** (Museum of Antiquities and Contemporary Art) is in a renovated 17th-century hospital, whose ancient classical traces are still visible under a dramatic barrel-vaulted skylight. The crowning jewel here is *Job Lectured by His Wife,* one of the greatest works of Georges de la Tour, the painter whose candlelit scenes constitute Lorraine's most memorable artistic legacy. Other Old Masters, including works by Rembrandt, Fragonard and Boucher, are on view, once part of the famous collection of the Princes of Salm. The museum also contains one of France's largest collections of contemporary art, as well as Gallo-Roman artifacts, rural tools, and local faïence. ⊠ *1 pl. Lagarde* ☎ *03–29–82–20–33* ◻ *€4.60* ⊘ *Wed.–Mon. 10–12:30 and 1:30–6.*

The small but bustling Vieille Ville is anchored by the lovely old **Basilique St-Maurice,** a low gray-stone basilica blending Romanesque and Gothic styles. Its deep 15th-century entry porch prepares you for passing into dark, sacred space. ⊠ *Pl. St-Goëry* ☎ *03–29–82–58–36.*

STRASBOURG

Though centered in the heart of Alsace 490 km (304 mi) east of Paris, and drawing appealingly on Alsatian Gemütlichkeit (coziness), the city of Strasbourg is a cosmopolitan French cultural center and, in many ways, the unofficial capital of Europe. Against an irresistible backdrop of old half-timber houses, waterways, and the colossal single spire of its red-sandstone cathedral, which seems to insist imperiously that you pay homage to its majestic beauty, Strasbourg is an incongruously sophisticated mix of museums, charming neighborhoods like La Petite France, elite schools (including that notorious hothouse for blooming politicos, the École Nationale d'Administration, or National Administration School), international think tanks, and the European Parliament. The *strasbourgeoisie* have a lot to be proud of.

The Romans knew Strasbourg as Argentoratum before it came to be known as Strateburgum, or City of (Cross) Roads. After centuries as part of the Germanic Holy Roman Empire, the city was united with France in 1681, but retained independence regarding legislation, education, and religion under the honorific title Free Royal City. Since World War II Strasbourg has become a symbolic city, embodying Franco-German reconciliation and the wider idea of a united Europe. The city center is effectively an island within two arms of the River Ill; most major sites are found here, but the northern districts also contain some fine buildings erected over the last 100 years, culminating in the Palais de l'Europe.

Note to drivers: the configuration of downtown streets makes it difficult to approach the center via the autoroute exit marked STRASBOURG CENTRE. Instead, hold out for the exit marked PLACE DE L'ÉTOILE and follow signs to CATHÉDRALE/CENTRE VILLE. At place du Corbeau, veer left across the Ill, and go straight to the place Gutenberg parking garage, a block from the cathedral.

The Historic Heart

This central area, from the cathedral to picturesque Petite France, concentrates the best of Old Strasbourg, with its twisting backstreets, flower-lined courts, tempting shops, and inviting Weinstubes (wine taverns).

a good walk

Begin at place Gutenberg and head up rue des Hallebardes. To see a bit of Strasbourg's appealing combination of cozy Weinstubes, medieval alleys, and chic shops, turn left up rue des Orfevres (marked RUE PITTORESQUE); then circle right down rue Chaudron and again down rue du Sanglier. Head back right down rue des Hallebardes and onto place de la Cathédrale, passing the landmark Maison Kammerzell. Emerging from this close-packed warren of dark-timber buildings and narrow streets, you'll confront the magnificent **Cathédrale Notre-Dame** ㉗ ▶. Continue across the square to the **Musée de l'Oeuvre Notre-Dame** ㉘, with its collection of statuary. Leaving the museum, turn right and approach the vast neighboring palace, the **Palais Rohan** ㉙. Once the headquarters of the powerful prince-bishops, the Rohans, it now houses the art and archaeology museums.

Once out of the château's entry court, double back left and turn left again, following rue des Rohan to the river. From here you can take a boat tour of the Vieille Ville. Veer right away from the water and cross place du Marché aux Cochons-de-Lait (Suckling Pig Market Square) and place de la Grande Boucherie (Grand Slaughterhouse Square) to reach the **Musée Historique** ㉚, with its collection of paintings, weapons, and furniture from Strasbourg (reopening 2006 after renovations). Across the street is the modern glass entrance to the **Ancienne Douane** ㉛, the former customs house, now a vast venue for temporary exhibitions. Over

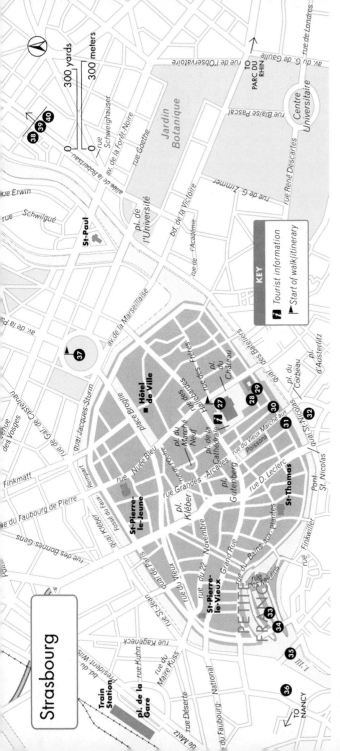

Strasbourg

KEY

i Tourist information

▲ Start of walk/itinerary

Ancienne Douane **31**
Barrage Vauban **35**
Cathédrale
Notre-Dame **27**
European
Parliament **39**
Musée Alsacien **32**

Musée d'Art
Moderne et
Comtemporain **36**
Musée Historique **30**
Musée de l'Oeuvre
Notre-Dame **28**
Orangerie **40**

Palais de l'Europe **38**
Palais Rohan **29**
Petite France **33**
Place de la
République **37**
Ponts Couverts **34**

the Ill, cross Pont du Corbeau and veer right to the **Musée Alsacien** ㉜, where you can get a glimpse of how Alsatian families used to live.

Now cross back over the river on the Pont St-Nicolas and follow the riverside promenade west to the picturesque quarter of **Petite France** ㉝. At Pont St-Martin, take rue des Dentelles to rue du Bain aux Plantes. Explore the alleys, courtyards, cafés, and shop windows as you work your way west. Eventually you'll reach the four monumental **Ponts Couverts** ㉞. Just beyond the bridges lies the grass-roof dam, the **Barrage Vauban** ㉟. Climb to the top; from here you'll see a gleaming glass-frame building, the **Musée d'Art Moderne et Contemporain** ㊱.

TIMING Allow at least a full day to see Strasbourg—perhaps visiting the Vieille Ville and cathedral in the morning, ending at 12:30 with the astronomical clock, and then lunch on a nearby backstreet. The afternoon might allow a museum stop and time to wander through Petite France. Two days would allow more museum time; a third day would allow you to take in the monumental sights on place de la République and the Palais de l'Europe.

Sights to See

㉛ **Ancienne Douane** (Old Customs House). In 2000, a terrible fire ravaged this old customs house set on the Ill River; extensive repairs are expected to continue until 2007. When operational, the airport-hangar scale and flexible walls here lend themselves to enormous expositions of Old Master paintings as well as archaeology and history. ⊠ *1 rue de Vieux-Marché-aux-Poissons* ☎ *03–88–52–50–00* ✆ *Call ahead.*

㉟ **Barrage Vauban** (Vauban Dam). Just beyond the Ponts Couverts is the grass-roof Vauban Dam, built by its namesake in 1682. Climb to the top for wide-angle views of the Ponts Couverts and, on the other side, the Museum of Modern Art. Then stroll through its echoing galleries, where magnificent cathedral statuary lies scattered among pigeon droppings. ⊠ *Ponts Couverts* ✆ *Free* ☉ *Mid-Oct.–mid-Mar., daily 9–7; mid-Mar.–mid-Oct., daily 9–8.*

★ ☾ ⚑ ㉗ **Cathédrale Notre-Dame.** Rosy, ornately carved Vosges sandstone masonry covers the facade of this most novel and Germanic of French cathedrals, a triumph of Gothic art begun in 1176. Not content with the outlines of the walls themselves, medieval builders lacily encased them with slender stone shafts. The off-center **spire**, finished in 1439, looks absurdly fragile as it tapers skyward some 466 feet; you can climb 330 to the base of the spire to take in sweeping views of the city, the Vosges Mountains, and the Black Forest.

The interior presents a stark contrast to the facade: it is older (mostly finished by 1275), and the nave's broad windows emphasize the horizontal rather than the vertical. Note Hans Hammer's ornately sculpted pulpit (1484–86) and the richly painted 14th- to 15th-century organ loft that rises from pillar to ceiling. The left side of the nave is flanked with richly colored Gothic windows honoring the early leaders of the Holy Roman Empire—Otto I and II, and Heinrich I and II. The **choir** is not ablaze with stained glass but framed by chunky Romanesque masonry.

The elaborate 16th-century **Chapelle St-Laurent,** to the left of the choir, merits a visit; turn to the right to admire the **Pilier des Anges** (Angels' Pillar), an intricate column dating from 1230.

Just beyond the pillar, the Renaissance machinery of the 16th-century **Horloge Astronomique** (Astronomical Clock) whirs into action daily at 12:30 PM (but the line starts at the south door at 11:45 AM): macabre clockwork figures enact the story of Christ's Passion. ⊠ *Pl. de la Cathédrale* ▧ *Clock €1, spire platform €3* ☯ *Cathedral open daily 7–11:30 and 12:40–7.*

㉜ Musée Alsacien (Alsatian Museum). In this labyrinthine half-timber home, with layers of carved balconies sagging over a cobbled inner courtyard, local interiors have been faithfully reconstituted. The diverse activities of blacksmiths, clog makers, saddlers, and makers of artificial flowers are explained with the help of old-time craftsmen's tools and equipment. ⊠ *23 quai St-Nicolas* ☎ *03–88–52–50–00* ▧ *€4* ☯ *Wed.–Mon. 10–6.*

㊱ Musée d'Art Moderne et Contemporain (Modern and Contemporary Art Museum). A magnificent sculpture of a building (designed by architect Adrien Faiensilber) that sometimes dwarfs its contents, this spectacular museum frames a relatively thin collection of new, esoteric, and unsung 20th-century art. Downstairs, a permanent collection of Impressionists and Modernists up to 1950 is heavily padded with local heroes but happily fleshed out with some striking furniture; all are juxtaposed for contrasting and comparing, with little to no chronological flow. Upstairs, harsh, spare works must work hard to live up to their setting; few contemporary masters are featured. Drawings, watercolors, and paintings by Gustave Doré, a native of Alsace, are enshrined in a separate room. ⊠ *1 pl. Hans-Jean Arp* ☎ *03–88–23–31–31* ▧ *€4.50* ☯ *Tues.–Wed. and Fri.–Sun. 11–7, Thurs. noon–10.*

㉚ Musée Historique (Local History Museum). This museum, in a step-gabled slaughterhouse dating from 1588, is closed for extensive renovation and not expected to reopen before 2006. It contains a collection of maps, armor, arms, bells, uniforms, traditional dress, printing paraphernalia, and two huge relief models of Strasbourg. ⊠ *2 rue du Vieux-Marché-aux-Poissons.*

★ **㉘ Musée de l'Oeuvre Notre-Dame** (Cathedral Museum). There's more to this museum than the usual assembly of dilapidated statues rescued from the cathedral before they fell off (you'll find *those* rotting in the Barrage Vauban). Sacred sculptures stand in churchlike settings, and secular exhibits are enhanced by the building's fine old architecture. Subjects include a wealth of Flemish and Upper Rhine paintings, stained glass, gold objects, and massive, heavily carved furniture. ⊠ *3 pl. du Château* ☎ *03–88–32–88–17* ▧ *€3* ☯ *Tues.–Sun. 10–6.*

★ **㉙ Palais Rohan** (Rohan Palace). The exterior of Robert de Cotte's massive Neoclassical palace (1732–42) may be starkly austere, but there's plenty of glamour inside. Decorator Robert le Lorrain's magnificent ground-floor rooms are led by the great **Salon d'Assemblée** (Assembly Room) and the book- and tapestry-lined **Bibliothèque des Cardinaux** (Cardinals' Library). The library leads to a series of less august rooms that house the **Musée des Arts Décoratifs** (Decorative Arts Museum) and its elaborate display of ceramics. This is a comprehensive presentation of works by Hannong, a porcelain manufacturer active in Strasbourg from 1721 to 1782; dinner services by other local kilns reveal the influence of Chinese porcelain. The **Musée des Beaux-Arts** (Fine Arts Museum), also in the château, includes masterworks of European painting from Giotto and Memling to El Greco, Rubens, and Goya. Downstairs, the **Musée Archéologique** (Archaeology Museum) displays regional archaeological finds, including gorgeous Merovingian treasures. ⊠ *2 pl. du Château* ☏ *03–88–52–50–00* ◻ *€4 each museum* ⊙ *Wed.–Mon. 10–6.*

㉝ Petite France. With its gingerbread half-timber houses that seem to lean precariously over the canals of the Ill, its shops, and inviting little restaurants, this is the most magical neighborhood in Strasbourg. Historically Alsatian in style, "Little France"—the district is just southwest of the center ville—is filled with Renaissance buildings that have survived plenty of wars. Wander up and down the tiny streets that connect rue du Bain-aux-Plantes and rue des Dentelles to Grand-Rue, and stroll the waterfront promenade.

FodorśChoice
★

㉞ Ponts Couverts (Covered Bridges). These three bridges, distinguished by their four stone towers, were once covered with wooden shelters. Part of the 14th-century ramparts that framed Old Strasbourg, they span the Ill as it branches into four fingerlike canals.

Beyond the Ill

If you've seen the center and have time to strike out in new directions, head across the Ill to view two architectural landmarks unrelated to Strasbourg's famous medieval past: place de la République and the Palais de l'Europe.

a good
walk

North of the cathedral, walk up rue des Hallebardes and turn left on rue du Dôme. Take a right onto place Broglie (pronounced "broiy*e*") and continue up this main thoroughfare across the river to the striking circle of red-sandstone buildings on **place de la République** ㊲ ▶. Back at the river, head for a bus stop on avenue de la Marseillaise and take Bus no. 23 to the **Palais de l'Europe** ㊳ for a guided tour (by appointment, arranged in advance). You may also want to visit the sleek **European Parliament** ㊴, just across the river. From here, plunge into the greenery of the **Orangerie** ㊵. Indulge in a three-hour lunch at the stellar Buerehiesel or have a picnic on a bench.

TIMING   Basing your schedule on your tour appointment at the Palais de l'Europe, allow about a half day for this walk; if need be, you can while away the wait in the Orangerie.

Sights to See

㊳ European Parliament. This sleek building testifies to the growing importance of the governing body of the European Union, which used to make do with rental offices in the Palais de l'Europe. Eurocrats continue to commute between Brussels, Luxembourg, and Strasbourg, hauling their staff and files with them. One week per month, visitors can slip into the hemicycle and witness the tribune in debate, complete with simultaneous translation. ☒ *Behind the Palais de l'Europe* ☎ 03–88–17–52–85 ☞ *Free* ☉ *Call ahead to verify Parliament in session.*

⓵ Orangerie. Like a private backyard for the Eurocrats in the Palais de l'Europe, this delightful park is laden with flowers and punctuated by noble copper beeches. It contains a lake and, close by, a small reserve of rare birds, including flamingos and noisy local storks. ☒ *Av. de l'Europe.*

⓷ Palais de l'Europe. Designed by Paris architect Henri Bernard in 1977, this Continental landmark is headquarters to the Council of Europe, founded in 1949 and independent of the European Union. A guided tour introduces you to the intricacies of its workings and may allow you to eavesdrop on a session. Arrange your tour by telephone in advance; appointments are fixed according to language demands and usually take place in the afternoon. Note: You must provide a *pièce d'identité* (I.D.) before entering. ☒ *Av. de l'Europe* ☎ 03–90–21–49–40 *for appointments* ☞ *Free* ☉ *Guided tours by appointment weekdays.*

▶ ⓷ Place de la République. The spacious layout and ponderous architecture of this monumental *cirque* (circle) have nothing in common with the Vieille Ville except for the local red sandstone. A different hand was at work here—that of occupying Germans, who erected the former Ministry (1902); the Academy of Music (1882–92); and the Palais du Rhin (1883–88). The handsome neo-Gothic church of **St-Paul** and the pseudo-Renaissance **Palais de l'Université** (University Palace), constructed between 1875 and 1885, also bear the German stamp. Heavy turn-of-the-20th-century houses, some reflecting the whimsical curves of the Art Nouveau style, frame **allée de la Robertsau,** a tree-lined boulevard that would not look out of place in Berlin.

Where to Stay & Eat

★ $$$$ ✕ Le Buerehiesel. This lovely Alsatian farmhouse, reconstructed in the lovely Orangerie park, warrants a pilgrimage if you are willing to pay for the finest cooking in Alsace. Antoine Westermann stands in the upper echelon of chefs while remaining true to the ingredients and specialties of his native Alsace: *schniederspaetzle* (onion-perfumed ravioli) with frogs' legs, steamed sea bass served with marinated vegetables, braised goose, and plum tarte tatin with vanilla ice cream. Two smaller salons are cozy, but most tables are set in a modern annex that is mostly glass and steel. In any event, plump European *parlementaires* come on foot; others might come on their knees. ☒ *4 parc de l'Orangerie* ☎ 03–88–45–56–65 ⌨ *Reservations essential* ▭ *AE, DC, MC, V* ☉ *No lunch; closed Tues. and Sun., 3 wks Jan., and 1st half Aug.*

★ $$$$ ✕ Chez Yvonne. Behind red-checked curtains you'll find artists, tourists, lovers, and heads of state sitting elbow-to-elbow in this classic Weinstube. All come to savor steaming platters of local specialties: watch for duck confit on choucroute, and *tête de veau* (calf's head) in white wine. Warm Alsatian fabrics dress tables and lamps, the china is regional, the photos historic, and the ambience chic—and no kitsch. ⊠ *10 rue du San-glier* ☎ *03–88–32–84–15* ⌔ *Reservations essential* ▤ *AE, MC, V* ⊗ *Closed Sun. and 1st half Aug. No lunch Mon.*

★ $$$$ ✕ **Au Crocodile.** As one of the temples of Alsatian-French haute cuisine, this has the expected grand salon—asparkle with skylights and a spectacular 19th-century mural showing the *strasbourgeoisie* at a country fair—an exhaustive wine list, and some of the most dazzling dishes around, courtesy of master chef Émile Jung. Fittingly for a restaurant founded in the early 1800s, you'll get a real taste of the-way-Alsace-was here but given a nouvelle spin. Delights include truffle turnover, warmed goose liver with rhubarb, lobster with vermicelli and pink pepper, bitter-chocolate cherry cake, and grapefruit sorbet with a green tea "cigarette." Even more urban finesse is given to the theme menus that are occasionally offered (recent homages include those to the Brothers Goncourt, Goethe, and Gutenberg). As for the crocodile, it refers to a stuffed specimen brought back by a Strasbourg general from Napoléon's Egyptian campaign which took pride of place in a tavern that centuries later became this luxe outpost, today more central than the Buerehiesel and nearly as revered. The wine cellar is vast and has plenty of tokay pinot gris, Riesling, and other luscious Alsatian vintages to choose from. ⊠ *10 rue de l'Outre* ☎ *03–88–32–13–02* ⊕ *www.au-crocodile.com* ⌔ *Reservations essential* ⋒ *Jacket and tie* ▤ *AE, DC, MC, V* ⊗ *Closed Sun. and Mon., late Dec.–early Jan., and 3 wks in July.*

$$ ✕ **St-Sépulcre.** Shared plank tables, a jovial red-vested patron (with a nose to match), and a wisecracking waitstaff enhance the convivial welcome at this no-frills, down-home Weinstube. A massive ham sits casually on the counter, and slabs of it find their way onto every platter—even the salads. A crock of crunchy pickles, chewy bread, and a cereal bowl heaped with fresh horseradish accompany every order except dessert. ⊠ *15 rue des Orfèvres* ☎ *03–88–32–39–97* ▤ *MC, V* ⊗ *Closed Sun., Mon., and 2nd half July.*

$–$$ ✕ **Maison Kammerzell.** This restaurant glories in its richly carved, half-timber 16th-century building—probably the most familiar house in Strasbourg. Fight your way through the tourist hordes on the terrace and ground floor to one of the atmospheric rooms above, with their gleaming wooden furniture and stained-glass windows. Foie gras and choucroute are best bets, though you may want to try the chef's pet discovery, choucroute with freshwater fish. ⊠ *16 pl. de la Cathédrale* ☎ *03–88–32–42–14* ▤ *AE, DC, MC, V.*

★ ¢ ✕ **Suzel.** This cozy little tearoom, just off rue Bain-aux-Plantes in Petite France, mixes rustic-chic blandishments (blue gingham, artfully arranged bric-a-brac, rows of potted boxwood) with excellent and unpretentious regional food. There's rabbit stew with dumplings, fresh trout, baeckoffe, fruit tarts, and good wines. It's also marvelous for an atmospheric afternoon tea break. Too bad it's closed nights. ⊠ *2 rue des Moulins* ☎ *03–88–23–10–46* ▤ *MC, V* ⊗ *Closed Mon. No dinner.*

★ $$$$ ▥ **Régent-Petite France.** Opposite the Ponts Couverts and surrounded by rushing canals, this centuries-old former ice factory—replete with noble pediment and mansard roofs—has been transformed into a boldly modern luxury hotel. Delightfully set in the heart of Strasbourg's quaintest quarter, La Petite France, the hotel welcomes you with a spacious marble vestibule, vivid graffiti art, and Le Pont Tournant, an eye-popping modernistic restaurant done up in white, pinks, and reds (enjoy its summer tables over the torrent). Upstairs, Philippe Starck–inspired sculptural room furnishings contrast sharply with the half-timber houses and roaring river viewed from nearly every room. There's no skimping on the amenities—both the beds and the bathrooms are divine. ⊠ *5 rue des Moulins, 67000* ☎ *03–88–76–43–43* 🖷 *03–88–76–43–76* ⊕ *www. regent-hotels.com* ⮠ *72 rooms* ᗐ *Restaurant, minibars, cable TV, bar, Internet, some pets allowed (fee)* ⊟ *AE, DC, MC, V* ⯑ *MAP.*

$$–$$$ 🖭 **Rohan.** Across from the cathedral on a picturesque pedestrian street, this modest little hotel has a welcoming air and a marvelous sense of French style, from the Louis XV furniture to the gilt mirrors. Though swagged in rich fabrics, rooms are fully modern, with impeccable all-tile baths. ⊠ *17 rue Maroquin, 67000* ☎ *03–88–32–85–11* 🖷 *03–88–75–65–37* ⊕ *www.hotel-rohan.com* ⮠ *36 rooms* ᗐ *Minibars, cable TV, Internet, parking (fee), some pets allowed (fee)* ⊟ *AE, DC, MC, V.*

$–$$$ 🖭 **Cathédrale.** Expansion and renovation have brought this superbly positioned hotel more than up to par. A sleek marble lobby abuts lounges, a bar, and breakfast room that are rich with ancient beams and sandstone. Rooms feature dark timbers, and most have windows framing a view of the 16th-century half-timbered Maison Kammerzell or the cathedral. For summer drinks and breakfast, there's a Belle Époque–garden courtyard cloistered from the outside world. ⊠ *12 pl. de la Cathédrale, 67000* ☎ *03–88–22–12–12* 🖷 *03–88–23–28–00* ⊕ *www. hotel-cathedrale.fr* ⮠ *47 rooms* ᗐ *Minibars, cable TV, bar, some Internet, some pets allowed (fee)* ⊟ *AE, DC, MC, V* ⯑ *BP.*

$–$$ 🖭 **Gutenberg.** In a 250-year-old mansion just off place Gutenberg, this sturdy urban hotel has rooms with fresh, old-fashioned wallpaper, chandeliers, and built-in wood cabinetry. Charming little fifth-floor lofts reveal roof timbers. The skylit breakfast room is inviting. The location is sweet and just a few blocks from the cathedral. ⊠ *31 rue des Serruriers, 67000* ☎ *03–88–32–17–15* 🖷 *03–88–75–76–67* ⊕ *www.hotel-gutenberg.com* ⮠ *42 rooms* ᗐ *Internet; no a/c in some rooms* ⊟ *MC, V* ⊘ *Closed 1st 2 wks in Jan.* ⯑ *BP.*

Nightlife & the Arts

The annual **Festival de Musique** (Music Festival; ⊠ 1 av. de la Marseillaise ☎ 03–88–39–64–10) is held from June to early July at the Palais des Congrès and the cathedral; contact the **Amis de la Musique** (☎03–88–15–44–66) for information. The **Opéra du Rhin** (⊠ 19 pl. Broglie ☎03–88–75–48–23) has a sizable repertoire. Classical concerts are staged by the **Orchestre Philharmonique** (⊠ Palais des Congrès ☎ 03–88–15–09–09).

The Vieille Ville neighborhood east of the cathedral, along rue des Frères, is the nightlife hangout for university students and twentysomethings; among its handful of heavily frequented bars is **La Laiterie** (⊠ 13 rue Hohwald ☎ 03–88–23–72–37), a new multiplex concert hall showcasing art, workshops, and music ranging from electronic to post-rock and reggae. **Le Chalet** (✉ 376 rte. de la Wantzenau ☎ 03–88–31–18–31) is the biggest and most popular disco, but it's some 10 km (6 mi) northeast of the city center.

The Outdoors

The **Port Autonome de Strasbourg** (☎ 03–88–84–13–13) organizes 75-minute boat tours along the Ill four times a day in winter and up to every half hour from 9:30 to 9, April–October. Boats leave from behind the Palais Rohan; the cost is €6.30.

Shopping

The lively city center is full of boutiques, including chocolate shops and delicatessens selling locally made foie gras. Look for warm paisley linens and rustic homespun fabrics, Alsatian pottery, and local wines. Forming the city's commercial heart are **rue des Hallebardes,** next to the cathedral; **rue des Grandes Arcades,** with its shopping mall; and **place Kléber.** An **antiques market** takes place behind the cathedral on rue du Vieil-Hôpital, rue des Bouchers, and place de la Grande Boucherie every Wednesday and Saturday morning.

ALSACE

The Rhine River forms the eastern boundary of both Alsace and France. But the best of Alsace is not found along the Rhine's industrial waterfront. Instead it's in the Ill Valley at the base of the Vosges, southwest of cosmopolitan Strasbourg. Northwest is Saverne and the beginning of the **Route du Vin,** the great Alsace Wine Road, which winds its way south through the Vosges foothills, fruitful vineyards, and medieval villages that would serve well as stage-sets for Rossini's *William Tell.* Signs for the road help you keep your bearings on the twisting way south, and you'll find limitless opportunities to stop at wineries and sample the local wares. The Wine Road stretches 170 km (100 mi) between Thann and Marienheim and is easily accessible from Strasbourg or Colmar. Many of the towns and villages have designated "vineyard trails" winding between towns (a bicycle will help you cover a lot of territory). Riquewihr and Ribeauville—accessible by bus from Colmar—are connected by an especially picturesque route. Along the way, stop at any *"Dégustation"* sign for a free tasting and pick up brochures on the "Alsace Wine Route" at any tourist office.

Obernai

❹ *30 km (19 mi) southwest of Strasbourg via A35/ N422.*

Many visitors begin their saunter down the Route du Vin at Obernai, a thriving, colorful Renaissance market town named for the patron saint of Alsace. Head to the central town enclosed by the ramparts to find some particularly Nikon-friendly sites, including a medieval belfry, Renaissance well, and late-19th-century church. Place du Marché, in the heart of town, is dominated by the stout, square 13th-century **Kapelturm Beffroi** (Chapel Tower Belfry), topped by a pointed steeple flanked at each corner by frilly openwork turrets added in 1597. An elaborate Renaissance well near the belfry, the **Puits à Six-Seaux** (Well of Six Buckets), was constructed in 1579; its name recalls the six buckets suspended from its metal chains. The twin spires of the parish church of **St-Pierre–St-Paul** compete with the belfry for skyline preeminence. They date, like the rest of the church, from the 1860s, although the 1504 Holy Sepulchre altarpiece in the north transept is a survivor from the previous church. Other points of interest include the flower-bedecked **place de l'Etoile** and the **Hôtel de Ville,** whose council chamber and historic balcony can be viewed.

Where to Stay & Eat

★ **$–$$** ✕▦ **L'Ami Fritz.** White-shuttered, flower-bedecked, with sunny yellow walls, this welcoming inn combines style, rustic warmth, and three generations of family tradition. Set several miles west of Obernai, this picture-perfect freestone residence of the 18th century continues its allurements inside, thanks to pretty, impeccable guest rooms decked in toile de Jouy and homespun checks (opt for rooms in the main hotel, not in the adjacent annex). Top attraction here is the fine restaurant, where you can feast on Patrick Fritz's sophisticated twists on regional specialties, including feather-light blood sausage in flaky pastry, a delicate choucroute of grated turnips, strudel of black pudding, fillet of zander with beer-flavored choucroute, or the gratinéed freshwater fish braised in Sylvaner. Don't miss the fruity red wine, an Ottrott exclusive, or taking a gander at the town's two medieval castles. The restaurant is closed Wednesday. ✉ *8 rue des Châteaux, 5 km (3 mi) west of Obernai, 67530 Ottrott* ☎ *03–88–95–80–81* 🖷 *03–88–95–84–85* ⊕ *www.amifritz.com* ⇌ *22 rooms* ♿ *Restaurant, minibars, pool, Internet, some pets allowed (fee); no a/c in some rooms* ▭ *AE, DC, MC, V* ⊙ *Closed last two wks July, mid-Jan.–mid-Feb., and Wed.* ❮❯⎮ *MAP.*

¢ ✕▦ **Cloche.** Leaded glass, dark oak, and Hansi-like murals set the tone in this sturdy half-timber 14th-century landmark on Obernai's market square. Standard local dishes and blackboard specials draw locals on market days. Rooms are well equipped and country-pretty; two double-decker duplex rooms accommodate four. ✉ *90 rue Général-Gouraud, 67210* ☎ *03–88–95–52–89* 🖷 *03–88–95–07–63* ⊕ *www.la-cloche.com* ⇌ *20 rooms* ♿ *Restaurant, bar, Internet; no a/c* ▭ *AE, DC, MC, V* ⊙ *Closed 2 wks in Jan.* ❮❯⎮ *MAP.*

Shopping

Dietrich (✉ 58 and 74 rue du Général-Gouraud ☎ 03–88–95–57–58) has a varied selection of Beauvillé linens, locally hand-blown Alsatian wine glasses, and Obernai-patterned china.

Mont-Ste-Odile

★ ㊷ *12 km (8 mi) southwest of Obernai via Ottrott.*

Mont-Ste-Odile, a 2,500-foot hill, has been an important religious and military site for 3,000 years. The eerie 9½-km-long (6-mi-long) **Mur Païen,** up to 12 feet high and, in parts, several feet thick, rings the summit; its mysterious origins and purpose still baffle archaeologists. The Romans established a settlement here and, at the start of the 8th century Odile, daughter of Duke Etichon of Obernai, who had been born blind, founded a convent on the same spot after receiving her sight while being baptized. The relatively modern convent is now a workaday hostelry for modern pilgrims on group retreats. Odile—the patron saint of Alsace—died here in AD 720; her sarcophagus rests in the 12th-century **Chapelle Ste-Odile.** The spare, Romanesque **Chapelle de la Croix** adjoins St-Odile.

Barr

43 *11 km (7 mi) southeast of Mont-Ste-Odile, 8 km (5 mi) south of Obernai.*

Surrounded by vineyards that harvest some of the finest vintages of Sylvaner and Gewürztraminer wines, Barr is a thriving, semi-industrial town surrounded by vines, with some charming narrow streets lined with half-timbered houses (notably rue des Cigognes, rue Neuve, and the tiny rue de l'Essieu), a cheerful 17th-century Hôtel de Ville, and a decorative arts museum. Most buildings date from after a catastrophic fire in 1678; the only medieval survivor is the Romanesque tower of St-Martin, the Protestant church. Admire original furniture, local porcelain, earthenware, and pewter at the **Musée de la Folie Marco,** in a mansion built by local magistrate Félix Marco in 1763. One section of the museum explains the traditional process of *schlittage*: sleds, bearing bundles of freshly sawed tree trunks, once slid down the forest slopes over a "corduroy road" made of logs. ⊠ *30 rue du Dr-Sultzer* ☎ *03–88–08–94–72, 03–88–08–66–65 winter* 🖃 *€3.10* ☉ *July–Sept., Wed.–Mon. 10–noon and 2–6; May–June, Oct.–Jan., weekends 10–noon and 2–6; closed Feb.–Apr.*

Andlau

44 *3 km (2 mi) southwest of Barr on the Route du Vin.*

Andlau has long been known for its magnificent abbey. Built in the 12th century, the **Abbaye d'Andlau** has the richest ensemble of Romanesque sculpture in Alsace. Sculpted vines wind their way around the doorway as a reminder of wine's time-honored importance to the local economy. A statue of a female bear, the abbey mascot—bears used to roam local forests and were bred at the abbey until the 16th century—can be seen in the north transept. Legend has it that Queen Richarde, spurned by her husband, Charles the Fat, founded the abbey in AD 887 when an angel enjoined her to construct a church on a site to be shown to her by a female bear.

Where to Stay & Eat

$$ ✕🏨 **Arnold.** This yellow-wall, half-timber hillside hotel overlooks the cute wine village of Itterswiller; most rooms have views across the vines. The cheapest rooms, on the top floor, have a shower and no balcony; the priciest have a bath and a balcony facing south. The wood-beam lobby with its wrought-iron staircase has the same quaint charm as the hotel restaurant (no dinner Sunday, May to November) across the street, with its old winepress and local Alsace wines served by the jug; home-made foie gras and venison in cranberry sauce top the menu, along with sauerkraut and *baeckoffe.* ✉ *98 rte. des Vins, 3 km (2 mi) south of Andlau on D253, 67140 Itterswiller* ☎*03–88–85–50–58* 🖷*03–88–85–55–54* ⊕ *www.hotel-arnold.com* ➫ *30 rooms* ⌂ *Restaurant, minibars, cable TV, Internet, some pets allowed (fee); no a/c* ▭ *AE, MC, V* ☉ *Closed 2 wks Feb.* ⵔ *MAP.*

Dambach-la-Ville

45 *8 km (5 mi) southeast of Andlau via Itterswiller.*

One of the prettiest villages along the Alsace Wine Road, Dambach-la-Ville is a fortified medieval town protected by ramparts and three powerful 13th-century gateways. It is particularly rich in half-timber, high-roof houses from the 17th and 18th centuries, clustered mainly around **place du Marché** (Market Square). Also on the square is the 16th-century **Hôtel de Ville** (Town Hall). As you walk the charming streets, notice the wrought-iron signs and roof-top oriels.

Where to Stay & Eat

¢ ✕ ⵔ **Le Raisin d'Or.** Set around the corner from the village church and halfway up the street that climbs straight into the vineyards, this unpretentious hotel is where you'll get a down-to-earth welcome and a hearty meal in a typical Alsace dining room (closed Monday and Tuesday) with heavy wooden tables and checked tablecloths. Hearty fare like sauerkraut, sausage meat, and potatoes will make you feel like the cook is one of those geese-stuffers. Rooms are on the small side, with functional dark-wood furnishings, but the best have balconies overlooking the street. ✉ *28 bis rue Clemenceau, 67650* ☎ *03–88–92–48–66* 🖷 *03–88–92–61–42* ⊕ *www.au-raisin-dor.com* ➫ *8 rooms* ⌂ *Restaurant, minibars, bar; no a/c* ▭ *DC, MC, V* ☉ *Closed mid-Dec.–early Jan., Feb.* ⵔ *MAP.*

Sélestat

46 *9 km (5½ mi) southeast of Dambach via D210 and N422, 47 km (29 mi) southwest of Strasbourg.*

Sélestat, midway between Strasbourg and Colmar, is a lively, historic town with a Romanesque church and a library of medieval manuscripts (and, important to note, a railway station with trains to and from Strasbourg). Head directly to the Vieille Ville and explore the quarter on foot. The church of **St-Foy** (✉ Pl. du Marché-Vert) dates from between 1155 and 1190; its Romanesque facade remains largely intact (the spires were added in the 19th century), as does the 140-foot octagonal tower over the crossing. Sadly, the interior was mangled over the centuries, chiefly by the Jesuits; their most inspired legacy is the Baroque pulpit of 1733 depicting the life of St. Francis Xavier. Note the Romanesque bas-relief next to the baptistery, originally the lid of a sarcophagus. Among the precious medieval and Renaissance manuscripts on display at the **Bibliothèque Humaniste** (Humanist Library), a major library founded in 1452 and installed in the former Halle aux Blés, are a 7th-century lectionary and a 12th-century Book of Miracles. ☒ *1 rue de la Bibliothèque* ☏ *03–88–58–07–20* ☑ *€3.50* ☉ *Sept.–June, Mon. and Wed.–Fri. 9–noon and 2–6, Sat. 9–noon; July and Aug., Mon. and Wed.–Fri. 9–noon and 2–6, weekends 9–noon and 2–5.*

Nightlife & the Arts

The colorful **Corso Fleuri** (Flower Carnival) takes place on the second Sunday in August, when the town decks itself—and the floats in its vivid parade—with a magnificent display of dahlias.

Haut-Koenigsbourg

47 *11 km (7 mi) west of Sélestat via D159.*

One of the most popular spots in Alsace is the romantic, crag-top castle of Haut-Koenigsbourg, originally built as a fortress in the 12th century. The ruins of the **Château du Haut-Koenigsbourg** were presented by the town of Sélestat to German emperor Wilhelm II in 1901. The château looked just as a kaiser thought one should, and he restored it with some diligence and no lack of imagination—squaring the main tower's original circle, for instance. The site, panorama, drawbridge, and amply furnished imperial chambers may lack authenticity, but they are undeniably dramatic. ☏ *03–88–82–50–60* ☑ *Château €6.20* ☉ *Nov.–Feb., daily 9:30–noon and 1–4:30; Mar., Apr., and Oct., daily 9–noon and 1–5:30; May, June, and Sept., daily 9–6; July and Aug., daily 9–6:30.*

Ribeauvillé

48 *13 km (8 mi) south of Haut-Koenigsbourg via St-Hippolyte, 16 km (10 mi) southwest of Sélestat.*

The beautiful half-timber town of Ribeauvillé, surrounded by rolling vineyards and three imposing châteaux, produces some of the best wines in Alsace. (The Trimbach family has made Riesling and superb Gewürztraminer here since 1626.) The town's narrow main street, crowded with Weinstubes, pottery shops, bakeries, and wine sellers, is bisected by the 13th-century **Tour des Bouchers**, a clock-belfry completed (gargoyles and all) in the 15th century. Storks' nests crown several towers in the village, while streets are adorned with quaint shop signs, fairy-tale turrets, and tour guides herding the crowds with directions in French and German. Make for the place de la Marie and its Hôtel de Ville to see its famous collection of silver-gilt 16th-century tankards and chalices. The place is also a good place to perch come every first Sunday in September, when the town hosts a grand parade to celebrate the **Jour des Menetriers** (Fete of the Minstrels), a day when at least one fountain here spouts free Riesling.

Where to Stay & Eat

¢–$ ✕ **Zum Pfifferhüs.** This is a true-blue Weinstube, with yellowed murals, glowing lighting, and great local wines available by the glass. The cooking is pure Alsace, with German-scale portions of choucroute, ham hock, and fruit tarts. No smoking here. ☒ *14 Grand-Rue* ☏ *03–89–73–62–28* ✍ *Reservations essential* ▤ *MC, V* ☉ *Closed Wed. and Thurs., Feb., and 2 wks in July.*

$$$$ ✕🖬 **L'Auberge de l'Ill.** England's late Queen Mother, Marlene Dietrich,
Fodor'sChoice   and Montserrat Caballé are just a few of the famous who have feasted
★   at this culinary temple, but, oddly, this place has never been as famous
as it should be, the long trek from Paris to the half-timbered village of
Illhaeusern perhaps the reason. Still, you need to book weeks in advance
to snare a table in this classic yet casual dining room. Master chef Paul
Haeberlin marries grand and Alsatian cuisine, with the emphasis on proper
marriage, not passionate love. The results are wonderful enough: Salmon
soufflé, lamb chops in dainty strudel, and showstoppers like *le homard
Prince Wladimir,* or lobster with shallots braised in champagne and crème
fraîche. Germanic-Alsatian flair is particularly apparent in such dishes
as the truffled *baeckoffa* (baker's oven), a casserole-terrine of lamb and
pork with leeks. The kitchen's touch is incredibly light (though not nouvelle, thank you), so you can even enjoy such master desserts as white
peaches in vanilla syrup served in a chocolate "butterfly" with champagne sabayon sauce. If you want to enjoy the pleasant surroundings
of the auberge, with its terraced lawns, romantic trees, and famous flowing brook, opt for an overnight in one of the guest rooms in the new
Hôtel des Berges, set behind the restaurant and designed to evoke an
Alsatian tobacco barn, replete with Havenese woods, rooms named after
famous cigars, and a lulling and lovely country-luxe decor. ✉ *2 rue de
Collonges, 10 km (6 mi) east of Ribeauville, Illhaeusern 68970*
☎ *03–89–71–89–00* 🖷 *03–89–71–82–83* ⊕ *www.auberge-de-l-ill.com*
📭 *6 rooms* ⚹ *Restaurant, minibars, cable TV, some pets allowed (fee)*
▭ *AE, DC, MC, V* ⊗ *Closed Mon. and Tues., 1st wk Jan., and Feb.*

$$–$$$ 🖬 **Seigneurs de Ribeaupierre.** On the edge of Ribeauvillé's old quarter,
this gracious half-timber inn offers a warm regional welcome with a touch
of flair. It has exposed timbers in pastel tones, sumptuous fabrics, and
slick bathrooms upstairs, as well as a fire crackling downstairs on your
way to the generous breakfast. ✉ *11 rue du Château, 68150*
☎ *03–89–73–70–31* 🖷 *03–89–73–71–21* 📭 *10 rooms* ⚹ *Bar; no a/c,
no room TVs* ▭ *AE, MC, V* ⊗ *Closed Jan. and Feb.* ⦿ *BP.*

$–$$ 🖬 **Tour.** In the center of Ribeauvillé and across from the Tour des Bouch-
ers, this hotel, with an ornate Renaissance fountain outside its front door,
is a good choice for experiencing the atmospheric town by night. Rooms
and amenities are modern; those on the top floor have exposed timbers
and wonderful views of ramshackle rooftops. ✉*1 rue de la Mairie, 68150*
☎ *03–89–73–72–73* 🖷 *03–89–73–38–74* ⊕ *www.hotel-la-tour.com*
📭 *33 rooms* ⚹ *Hot tub, sauna, bar, some Internet; no a/c* ▭ *AE, DC,
MC, V* ⊗ *Closed early Jan.–mid-Mar.*

Shopping

Find rich paisley Alsatian tablecloths discounted at the factory outlet
for **Beauvillé** (✉ *19 rte. de Ste-Marie-aux-Mines* ☎ *03–89–73–74–74*),
at the foot of forested hills just past the town center.

Riquewihr

㊾   *5 km (3 mi) south of Ribeauvillé.*

Fodor'sChoice
★

With its dormer windows fit for a Rapunzel, hidden cul-de-sacs home
to Rumpelstiltskins, and unique once-upon-a-time spell, Riquewihr is

the showpiece of the Wine Route and a living museum of the quaint architecture of old Alsace. Its steep main street, ramparts, and winding back alleys have scarcely changed since the 16th century, and could easily serve as a film set. Merchants cater to the sizable influx of tourists with a plethora of kitschy souvenir shops; bypass them to peep into courtyards with massive wine presses, to study the woodwork and ornately decorated houses, to stand in the narrow old courtyard that was once the Jewish quarter, or to climb up a narrow wooden stair to the ramparts. You would also do well to settle into a Weinstube to sample some of Riquewihr's famous wines. Just following your nose down the heavenly romantic streets will reward your eye with bright blue, half-timbered houses, storybook gables, and storks'-nest towers. The facades of certain houses dating from the late Gothic period take pride of place, including the Maison Kiener (1574), the Maison Priess (1686), and the Maison Liebrich (1535), but the Tower of Thieves and the Postal Museum, ensconced in the château of the duke of Württemberg, are also fascinating.

Where to Stay & Eat

★ ¢–$$ ✕ **Au Tire-Bouchon.** "The Corkscrew" is the best Weinstube in town to feast on Alsatian varieties of choucroute garni, including some rare delights like the *verte* (or green, flavored with parsley) version and the blowout "Choucroute Royale." This extravaganza is garnished with seven different kinds of wursts and meats and served with a half-bottle of mulled champagne plopped in the center of a mound of sauerkraut. The bottle is then poured by the waitress, with great flourish, over the entire dish. There are also fine Muscats, great breads, and fragrant onion tarts to savor. With communal tables and kind service, this is heartily recommended. If booked up, try the nearby Auberge du Schoenebourg. ✉ *29 rue du Génèral-de-Gaulle* ☎ *03–89–47–91–61* 🖃 *AE, MC, V.*

$ ✕🛏 **Sarment d'Or.** This cozy little hotel stands apart for its irreproachable modern comforts tactfully dovetailed with stone, dark timbers, and thick walls. The restaurant downstairs offers firelight romance and delicious cuisine—foie gras, frogs' legs in garlic cream, and breast of duck in pinot noir; it's closed Monday and does not serve dinner Sunday or lunch Tuesday. ✉ *4 rue du Cerf, 68340* ☎ *03–89–86–02–86* 🖷 *03–89–47–99–23* ⇥ *9 rooms* ⚅ *Restaurant; no a/c* 🖃 *MC, V* ⊗ *Closed Jan.–mid-Feb. and first 2 wks of July* 🍴 *MAP.*

★ $–$$ 🛏 **Hôtel de la Couronne.** Like an illustration out of the Brothers Grimm, this hotel is set in a 17th-century house with central tower and side wings. Its steep mansard roof, country shutters, and rusticated stone trim beautifully blend into the heart of medieval Riquewihr—the only modern note will be your car (allowed to drive to the hotel even though the town center is pedestrianized). Inside, several rooms have grand timber beams and folkloric wall stencils, making this a truly charming base to tour a truly charming town. ✉ *5 rue de la Couronne, 68340* ☎ *03–89–49–03–03* 🖷 *03–89–49–01–01* ⊕ *www.hoteldelacouronne.com* ⇥ *40 rooms* ⚅ *No a/c* 🖃 *AE, MC, V.*

SAUERKRAUT & CHOUCROUTE

TO EMBARK ON A FULL GASTRONOMIC EXCURSION into the hearty, artery-clogging terrain of Alsatian cuisine, your tour should probably start with flammekueche—a flat tart stuffed with bacon, onions, cream cheese, and heavy cream. The next stop is baeckaoffa, marinated pork, mutton, and beef simmered in wine with potatoes and onions, sometimes with a round of creamy Muenster cheese melted on top. And to finish up, land with a thud on a hefty slice of Kougelhopf, a butter-rich ring-shaped brioche cake with almonds and raisins. If, however, you have neither the constitution nor the inclination for such culinary heft, there is one dish that sums up the whole of Alsatian cuisine: choucroute garnie. Borrowed from the Germans, who call it sauerkraut, the base definition of choucroute is cabbage pickled in brine. In more elaborate terms, this means quintal d'Alsace, a substantial variety of local white cabbage, shredded and packed into crockery and left to ferment with salt and juniper berries for at least two months. Beyond this, any unanimity regarding the composition of choucroute garnie breaks down. The essential ingredients, however, seem to be sauerkraut, salted bacon, pork sausages, juniper berries, white wine, onions, cloves, black peppercorns, garlic, lard or goose fat, potatoes, and salt pork—pig's knuckles, cheeks, loin, shanks, feet, shoulder, and who knows what else? No matter—the taste is unforgettable, especially if you have the version served up at Au Tire-Bouchon in Riquewihr. There, the "Choucroute Royale" is lavished with seven different kinds of meat, served with a half bottle of mulled champagne set in the center, which is then poured by the waitress over the entire dish.

Colmar

50 *13 km (8 mi) southeast of Riquewihr via D3/ D10, 71 km (44 mi) southwest of Strasbourg.*

Forget that much of Colmar's architecture is modern (because of the destruction wrought by World Wars I and II): the heart of this proud merchant town—an atmospheric maze of narrow streets lined with Renaissance houses restored to the last detail—outcharms Strasbourg. Especially as you wander along the calm canals that wind through **La Petite Venise** (Little Venice), an area of bright Alsatian houses with colorful shutters and window boxes that's south of the center of town. Here, amid weeping willow trees that shed their tears into the eddies of the Lauch River and half-timbered houses gaily bedecked with geraniums and carnations, you have the sense of being in a tiny village. Elsewhere, the Vieille Ville streets fan out from the beefy towered church of **St-Martin**. Each shop-lined backstreet winds its way to the 15th-century customs house, the **Ancienne Douane,** and the square and canals that surround it. The **Maison Pfister** (Pfister House; ⊠ 11 rue Mercière), built in 1537, is the most striking of Colmar's many old dwellings. Note its decorative frescoes and medallions, carved balcony, and ground-floor arcades. Up the street from the Ancienne Douane on the Grand'Rue, the **Maison aux Arcades** (Arcades House) was built in 1609 in High Renaissance style with a series of arched porches (arcades) anchored by two octagonal towers.

FodorśChoice
★
The cultural highlight of Colmar is the **Musée d'Unterlinden,** once a medieval Dominican convent and hotbed of Rhenish mysticism, and now an important museum. Its star attraction is one of the greatest art works of the 16th century, the *Issenheim Altarpiece* (1512–16), by Matthias Grünewald, majestically displayed in the convent's Gothic chapel. Originally painted for the convent at Issenheim, 22 km (14 mi) south of Colmar near Guebwiller, the multipanel retable (altarpiece) is framed with two-sided wings, which unfold to show the Crucifixion and Incarnation, with side panels illustrating the Annunciation and the Resurrection. Other panels depict the life of St. Anthony, notably the Temptation. Grünewald's altarpiece, replete with its raw realism (note the chamber pots, boil-covered bellies, and dirty linen), was believed to have miraculous healing powers over ergotism, a widespread disease in the Middle Ages. Produced by the ingestion of fungus-ridden grains, the malady caused its victims to experience delusional fantasies. Hallucinogenic, indeed, is the word to describe the proto-Expressionist power of Grünewald's tortured faces and poses, whose emotional power made a direct appeal to the pain-racked victims living out their last days at the convent. Arms and armor, stone sculpture, ancient winepresses and barrels, and antique toys cluster around the enchanting 13th-century cloister. Upstairs are fine regional furnishings and a collection of Rhine Valley paintings from the Renaissance, including Martin Schongauer's opulent 1470 altarpiece painted for Jean d'Orlier. ⊠ *1 rue Unterlinden* ☎ *03–89–20–15–50* ⊠ *€7* ☉ *May–Oct., daily 9–6; Nov.–Apr., Wed.–Mon. 9–noon and 2–5.*

★ The **Église des Dominicains** (Dominican Church) houses the Flemish-influenced *Madonna of the Rosebush* (1473), by Martin Schongauer (1445–91), the most celebrated painting by the noted 15th-century German artist. This work, stolen from St-Martin's in 1972 and later recovered and hung here, has almost certainly been reduced in size from its original state but retains enormous impact. The grace and intensity of the Virgin match that of the Christ child; yet her slender fingers dent the child's soft flesh (and his fingers entwine her curls) with immediate intimacy. Schongauer's text for her crown is: ME CARPES GENITO TUO O SANTISSIMA VIRGO ("Choose me also for your child, o holiest Virgin"). ⊠ *Pl. des Dominicains* ☎ *03–89–24–46–57* ⊠ *€1.30* ☉ *Apr.–Dec., daily 10–1 and 3–6.*

The **Musée Bartholdi** (Bartholdi Museum) is the birthplace of Frédéric-Auguste Bartholdi (1834–1904), the local sculptor who designed the Statue of Liberty. Exhibits of Bartholdi's works claim the ground floor; a reconstruction of the artist's Paris apartments and furniture are upstairs; and, in adjoining rooms, the creation of Lady Liberty is explored. ⊠ *30 rue des Marchands* ☎ *03–89–41–90–60* ⊠ *€4* ☉ *Mar.–Dec., Wed.–Mon. 10–noon and 2–6.*

Where to Stay & Eat

★ **$$$–$$$$**   ✗ **Au Fer Rouge.** If you want a delicious feast of Old Colmar, head to this cobblestone square to find an adorable 17th-century Alsatian *colombage* (dovecote) mansion, replete with carved timber beams, oil paintings, stained glass, leaded windows, copper tankards, and flower window boxes. Even better, the kitchen is manned by a chef happy to leapfrog from yesteryear to tomorrow by offering nouvelle versions of classic standards. Patrick Fulgraff's salads are *"gourmandise d'oie"* (garnished with goose), his *croustillant au camembert* is topped with aspics and creams, his rabbit sausage comes with grilled polenta, and his wine list has one foot in Alsace and the other in France. Be sure to sit in the main floor salon and avoid the lackluster basement room. All in all, very much the best restaurant in Colmar. ✉ *52 Grand'rue* ☎ *03–89–41–37–24* ⊕ *www.au-fer-rouge.com* ▱ *AE, MC, V* ⊗ *Closed Sun. and Mon.*

$–$$ ✗ **Chez Hansi.** Named for the Rockwell-like illustrator whose beclogged folk children adorn most of the souvenirs of Alsace, this hypertraditional beamed tavern in the Vieille Ville serves excellent down-home classics such as choucroute and pot-au-feu, prepared and served with a sophisticated touch despite the waitresses' dirndls. ✉ *23 rue des Marchands* ☎ *03–89–41–37–84* ▱ *MC, V* ⊗ *Closed Wed., Thurs., and Jan.*

¢–$ ✗ **Au Koïfhus.** Not to be confused with the shabby little Koïfhus on rue des Marchands, this popular landmark serves huge portions of regional standards, plus changing specialties: roast quail and foie gras on salad, game stews with spaetzle (dumplings), and freshwater fish. Choose between the big, open dining room, glowing with wood and warm fabric, and a shaded table on the broad, lovely square. ✉ *2 pl. de l'Ancienne-Douane* ☎ *03–89–23–04–90* ▱ *DC, MC, V* ⊗ *Closed Thurs. and Jan.*

★ **$$–$$$$**   ✗▣ **Hostellerie le Maréchal.** A maze of narrow, creaky corridors connects the series of Renaissance houses that make up this romantic riverside inn. Built in 1565 in the fortified walls that encircle the Vieille Ville, the Maréchal has rooms that are small but lavished with extravagant detail, from glossy rafters to rich brocades to four-poster beds—ask for the Wagner or Bach rooms. A vivid color scheme—scarlet, sapphire, candy pink—adds to the Vermeer atmosphere. This is not a high-tech luxury hotel: it's an endearing, quirky, lovely old place hanging over a Petite Venise canal. The gastronomic restaurant, A l'Echevin, offers such dishes as terrine of rouget, leeks, truffles, and pigeon breast and foie gras crisped in pastry. Dine in salons or on a terrace perched over the river. ✉ *4 pl. des Six-Montagnes-Noires, 68000* ☎ *03–89–41–60–32* 🖷 *03–89–24–59–40* ⊕ *www.hotel-le-marechal.com* 🖙 *30 rooms* ♤ *Restaurant, minibars, cable TV, a/c, Internet, some pets allowed (fee)* ▱ *AE, DC, MC, V* ⦿ *MAP.*

$–$$ ✗▣ **Rapp.** In the Vieille Ville, just off the Champ de Mars, this solid, modern hotel has business-class comforts, a professional and welcoming staff, and a good German-scale breakfast. There's even an extensive indoor-pool complex, including sauna, steam bath, and workout equipment—all included in the low price. The restaurant is closed on Friday and does not serve lunch Saturday. ✉ *1 rue Weinemer, 68000*

☎ *03–89–41–62–10* 🖷 *03–89–24–13–58* ⊕ *www.rapp-hotel.com* 🛏*42 rooms* ⚫ *Restaurant, cable TV, pool, gym, sauna, bar; no a/c* ⊟*AE, DC, MC, V* ☙ *Closed July and 2 wks in Jan.*

The Arts

During the first half of August, Colmar celebrates with its annual **Foire Régionale des Vins d'Alsace,** an Alsatian wine fair in the Parc des Expositions. Events include folk music and theater performances and, above all, the tasting and selling of wine.

off the beaten path

ECOMUSÉE DE HAUTE-ALSACE – Great for kids, this open-air museum near Ungersheim, southeast of Guebwiller (via D430), is really a small village created from scratch in 1980, including 70 historic peasant houses and buildings typical of the region. The village is crisscrossed by donkey carts and wagons, and behind every door lie entertaining demonstrations of the old ways. An off-season visit is a study in local architecture; in high season the place comes alive. Small restaurants, snack bars, a playground, and a few amusement rides are scattered about for breaks. Inexpensive lodging is available on-site. ☎ *03–89–74–44–74* 🖷 *€15* ⊕ *www. ecomusee-alsace.com* ☙ *July and Aug., daily 9–7; Apr.–June and Sept., daily 9:30–6; Mar. and Oct., daily 10–5; Nov.–Feb., daily 10:30–5.*

ALSACE-LORRAINE A TO Z

To research prices, get advice from other travelers, and book travel arrangements, visit www.fodors.com.

AIRPORTS

Most international flights to Alsace land at Mulhouse-Basel Airport, on the Franco-Swiss border; some others at Entzheim, near Strasbourg. Metz-Nancy and Mirecourt (Vittel/Épinal) also have tiny airports for charter- and private-plane landings.

BUS TRAVEL

The two main bus companies are Les Rapides de Lorraine, based in Nancy, and Compagnie des Transports Strasbourgeois, based in Strasbourg. Various regional bus lines can connect you with towns and villages such as Mont-St-Odile, and those departing from Colmar for the towns along the Route du Vin, such as Riquewihr and Ribeauvillé; getting there when you want is another problem entirely. Bus routes run to Metz and Verdun from Nancy; Nancy, Strasbourg, and Colmar all have city buses. There are many other routes throughout Alsace and Lorraine, so always check in with the regional tourist office or information window at a gateway rail or bus station to get printed bus schedules.

🚍 Bus Information **Les Rapides de Lorraine** ✉ 52 bd. d'Austrasie, 54000 Nancy ☎ 03-83-32-34-20. **Compagnie des Transports Strasbourgeois** ✉ 14 rue de la Gare-aux-Marchandises, 67200 Strasbourg ☎ 03-88-77-70-70.

CAR RENTAL

🚗 Local Agencies **Avis** ✉ 7 pl. Flore, Besançon ☎ 03-81-80-91-08 ✉ Pl. de la Gare, Strasbourg ☎ 03-88-32-30-44. **Europcar** ✉ 18 rue de Serre, Nancy ☎ 03-83-37-57-24. **Hertz** ✉ 7 pl. Thiers, Nancy ☎ 03-83-32-13-14 ✉ Pl. Flore, Besançon ☎ 03-81-47-43-23.

CAR TRAVEL

A4 heads east from Paris to Strasbourg, via Verdun, Metz, and Saverne. It is met by A26, descending from the English Channel, at Reims. A31 links Metz to Nancy, continuing south to Burgundy and Lyon.

N83/A35 connects Strasbourg, Colmar, and Mulhouse. A36 continues to Belfort and Besançon. A4, linking Paris to Strasbourg, passes through Lorraine via Metz, linking Lorraine and Alsace. Picturesque secondary roads lead from Nancy and Toul through Joan of Arc country and on to Épinal. Several scenic roads climb switchbacks over forested mountain passes through the Vosges, connecting Lorraine to Alsace and Alsace to Belfort; a quicker alternative is the tunnel *under* the Vosges at Ste-Marie-aux-Mines, linking Sélestat to Lunéville and Épinal. Alsace's Route du Vin, winding from Marlenheim, in the north, all the way south to Thann, is the ultimate in scenic driving.

EMERGENCIES

🚑 Ambulance ☎ 15. **Hôpital Central** ✉ 29 av. du Mal-de-Lattre-de-Tassigny, 54000 Nancy ☎ 03-83-85-85-85. **Hôpital Civil** ✉ 1 pl. de l'Hôpital, 67000 Strasbourg ☎ 03-88-11-67-68.

LODGING

APARTMENT & VILLA RENTALS
Contact Gîtes de France for its brochure on "Gîtes de France" in the Jura. The list includes both bed-and-breakfasts and houses for rent.

🏠 Local Agents **Gîtes de France** ✉ 8 rue Louis Rousseau, 39016 Lons-le-Saunier ☎ 03-84-87-08-88 ⊕ www.gitesdefrance.com.

SPORTS & THE OUTDOORS

A guide to bicycling in the Lorraine is available from the Comité Départemental de Cyclisme. For a list of signposted trails in the Vosges foothills, contact the Sélestat Tourist Office (*see* Visitor Information, *below*).

🚴 Bicycling **Comité Départemental de Cyclotourisme de Meurthe et Moselle** ✉ 2 rue des Marguerites, 54700 Blénod-lès-Pont-à-Mousson ☎ 03-83-82-26-58 ⊕ http://cd54ffct.chez.tiscali.fr/

🐴 Horseback Riding **Délégation Départementale de Tourisme Équestre** ✉ 4 rue des Violettes, 67201 Eckbolsheim ☎ 03-88-77-39-64.

TOURS

Walking tours of Strasbourg's Vieille Ville are directed by the tourist office (*see* Visitor Information, *below*) for €6 and depart at 2:30 every Saturday afternoon in low season, daily at 10:30 in July and August. For Colmar and its enchanting environs, take a highly recommended van tour with Les Circuits d'Alsace—castles, villages, and vineyards make for an exhilarating itinerary.

🚐 Les Circuits d'Alsace ✉ 6 pl. de la Gare, 68000 Colmar ☎ 03-89-41-90-88 ⊕ www.alsace-travel.com. **Strasbourg minitrain tours** ☎ 03-88-77-70-03.

TRAIN TRAVEL

Mainline trains leave Paris (Gare de l'Est) every couple of hours for the four-hour, 500-km (315-mi) journey to Strasbourg. Some stop in Toul, and all stop in Nancy, where there are connections for Épinal. Trains run three times daily from Paris to Verdun and more often to Metz (around three hours to each). Mainline trains stop in Mulhouse (four to five hours) en route to Basel.

Several local trains a day run between Strasbourg and Mulhouse, stopping in Sélestat and Colmar; some continue to Belfort and Besançon. Local trains occasionally link Besançon to Arbois. Other towns, such as Obernai and Montbenoît are accessible, with planning, by train. But without any bus connection you'll need a car to visit smaller villages and the region's spectacular natural sights.

🚆 Train Information **SNCF** ☎ 08-36-35-35-35 ⊕ www.ter-sncf.com/uk/alsace/default.htm.

TRAVEL AGENCIES

🚆 Local Agent Referrals **Havas Voyages** ✉ 23 rue de la Haute-Montée, Strasbourg ☎ 03-88-32-99-77. **Carlson Wagons-lit** ✉ 30 pl. Kléber, Strasbourg ☎ 03-88-32-16-34 ✉ 2 rue Raymond-Poincaré, Nancy ☎ 03-83-35-06-97.

VISITOR INFORMATION

The principal regional tourist offices are in Nancy and Strasbourg. Other tourist offices are listed by town below the principal offices.

🚆 Tourist Information **Nancy** ✉ 14 pl. Stanislas ☎ 03-83-35-22-41 ⊕ www.ot-nancy.fr. **Strasbourg** ✉ 17 pl. de la Cathédrale ☎ 03-88-52-28-28 ⊕ www.strasbourg.com ✉ Pl. de la Gare ☎ 03-88-32-51-49; there's also a city tourist office at the train station.

Colmar ✉ 4 rue Unterlinden ☎ 03-89-20-68-95 ⊕ www.ville-colmar.fr. **Guebwiller** ✉ 73 rue de la République ☎ 03-89-76-10-63. **Lons-le-Saunier** ✉ 1 rue Louis-Pasteur ☎ 03-84-24-65-01. **Lunéville** ✉ Pl. du Château ☎ 03-83-74-06-55 ⊕ www.ville-luneville.fr. **Metz** ✉ Pl. d'Armes ☎ 03-87-55-53-76 ⊕ www.mairie-metz.fr. **Obernai** ✉ 59 rue du Général-Gouraud ☎ 03-88-95-64-13 ⊕ www.obernai.fr. **Saverne** ✉ 37 Grand'Rue ☎ 03-88-91-80-47. **Sélestat** ✉ 10 bd. Leclerc ☎ 03-88-58-87-20. **Toul** ✉ Parvis de la Cathédrale ☎ 03-83-64-11-69 ⊕ www.ot-toul.fr. **Verdun** ✉ Pl. de la Nation ☎ 03-29-86-14-18 ⊕ www.verdun-tourisme.com.

Burgundy

WORD OF MOUTH

"Beaune is a classic wine town a little north on the train. Though heavily used by tourists it has some incredible glazed tile roofs to see, two or three nice museums, and wine, wine, wine."
—IndyTravel

"Vézelay is a medieval village on a hilltop about two hours from Paris and two hours' drive from Beaune, if you go by the winding roads through wonderful villages. The Basilica Ste-Madeleine is the focal point—nuns and monks still worship there, and we were lucky to be inside right at noon prayers and heard astonishing singing. Vézelay also seems to be an artists' haven, for obvious reasons, and you can spend the day in their shops."

—Heather7

Introduction by
Nancy Coons

Updated by
Simon Hewitt

DRAIN TO THE DREGS BURGUNDY'S FULL-BODIED VISTAS: rolling hillsides carpeted in emerald green, each pasture crosshatched with hedgerows, patterned with cows, quilted with vineyards. Behind a massive quarried-stone wall, a château looms, seemingly untouched by time, the only signs of human habitation the featherbeds airing from casement windows and a flock of sheep mowing the grounds. In the villages, tightly clustered houses—with roofs of slate from the days when they protected against brigands—circle the local church, its spire a lightning rod for the faithful. On a hilltop high over the patchwork of green rises a patrician edifice of white rock, a Romanesque church whose austerity and architectural purity hark back to the early Roman temples on which it was modeled. And deep inside a musty *cave* or perhaps a wine cellar redolent of cork and soured grapes, a row of glasses gleams like a treasured necklace, their garnet contents waiting to be swirled, sniffed, and savored.

Although you may often fall under the influence of extraordinary wine during a sojourn in Burgundy—in French, Bourgogne—the beauty surrounding you will be no boozy illusion. Passed over by revolutions, both political and industrial, left unscarred by world wars, and relatively inaccessible thanks to necessarily circuitous country roads, the region still reflects the pastoral prosperity it enjoyed under the Capetian dukes and kings.

Those were the glory days—when self-sufficient Burgundy held its own against the creeping spread of France and the mighty Holy Roman Empire—a period characterized by the expanding role of the dukes of Bourgogne. Consider the Capetians, history-book celebrities all: there was Philippe le Hardi (the Bold), with his power-brokered marriage to Marguerite of Flanders. There was Jean sans Peur (the Fearless), who murdered Louis d'Orléans in a cloak-and-dagger affair in 1407 and was in turn murdered, in 1419, on a dark bridge while negotiating a secret treaty with the future Charles VII. There was Philippe le Bon (the Good), who threw in with the English against Joan of Arc, and then Charles le Téméraire, whose temerity stretched the boundaries of Burgundy—already bulging with Flanders, Luxembourg, and Picardy—to include most of Holland, Lorraine, Alsace, and even parts of French-speaking Switzerland. He met his match in 1477 at the Battle of Nancy, where he and his boldness were permanently parted. Nonetheless, you can still see Burgundian candy-tile roofs in Fribourg, Switzerland, his easternmost conquest.

Yet the Capetians in their acquisitions couldn't hold a candle to the "light of the world": the great Abbaye de Cluny, founded in 910, grew to such overweening ecclesiastical power that it dominated the European Church on a papal scale for some four centuries. It was Urban II himself who dubbed it *"la Lumière du Monde."* And like the Italian popes, Cluny, too, indulged a weakness for worldly luxury and knowledge, both sacred and profane. In nearby Clairvaux, St-Bernard himself vented his outrage, chiding the monks who, although sworn to chastity and poverty, kept mistresses, teams of horses, and a library of unfathomable depth that codified classical and Eastern lore for all posterity—that is, until it was destroyed in the Wars of Religion, its wisdom lost for all time. The abbey itself met a similar fate, its wealth of quarry stone ransacked after the French Revolution.

Neighboring abbeys, perhaps less glorious than Cluny but with more humility than hubris, fared better. The stark geometry of the Cistercian abbeys—Clairvaux, Cîteaux—stand in silent rebuke to Cluny's excess. The basilicas at Autun, Vézelay, and Paray le Monial remain today in all their noble simplicity, yet manifest some of the finest Romanesque sculpture ever created; the tympanum at Autun rejects all time frames in its visionary daring. Anchored between Autun and Vézelay rises the broad massif of the Morvan, its dewy green flanks densely wooded in oak and beech. Hidden streams, rocky escarpments, dark forests, and meadows alive with falcons and hoopoes—a hiker's dream—are protected today by the Parc Naturel Régional du Morvan.

It's almost unfair to the rest of France that all this history, all this art, all this natural beauty comes with delicious refreshments. As if to live up to the extraordinary quality of its Chablis, its Chassagne-Montrachet, its Nuits-St-Georges, its Gevrey-Chambertin, Burgundy flaunts some of the best good, plain food in the world. Two poached eggs in savory wine sauce, a slab of ham in aspic, a dish of beef stew, a half-dozen earthy snails—no frills needed—just the pleasure of discovering that such homely material could resonate on the tongue, and harmonize so brilliantly with the local wine. This is simplicity raised to Gallic heights, embellished by the poetry of one perfect glass of pinot noir paired with a licensed and diploma'd *poulet de Bresse* (Bresse chicken), sputtering in unvarnished perfection on your white-china plate. Thus you may find that food and drink entries take up as much space in your travel diary as the sights you see. And that's as it should be in such well-rounded, full-bodied terrain.

Exploring Burgundy

Arriving in Burgundy from Paris by car, we suggest you grand-tour it from Sens to Autun, with rewarding detours to the town of Troyes, in Champagne to the east, and the hilly forests of the Morvan, in the west. In Northern Burgundy, the accents are thinner than around Dijon, and sunflowers cover the countryside instead of vineyards. Near Auxerre, many small, unheard-of villages boast a château or a once-famous abbey; they happily see few tourists, partly because public transportation is more than a bit spotty. Highlights of Northern Burgundy include Sens's great medieval cathedral, historic Troyes, Auxerre's Flamboyant Gothic cathedral, the great Romanesque sculptures of the basilica at Vézelay and cathedral at Autun, and the lakes of the Morvan Regional Park.

Go next to the wine country in the southeast of Burgundy, which begins at Dijon, home to three noted churches and some fine museums, including the Chartreuse de Champmol and its great *Well of Moses* sculpture, and stretches south down the Saône Valley through charming Beaune to Mâcon. The area includes the prestigious Côte de Nuits and Côte de Beaune, where great wines are produced from the pinot noir and chardon-

Having done its duty by producing a wealth of what many consider the world's greatest wines and harboring an abundance of magnificent Romanesque abbeys, Burgundy hardly needs to be beautiful—but it is. Its hedgerowed countryside and densely forested Morvan, its manor houses and scattered villages, its numerous vineyards, all deserve to be rolled on the palate and savored. Like glasses filled with Clos de Vougeot, the sights here—from the stately hub of Dijon to the medieval sanctuaries of Cluny and Clairvaux—invite the wanderer to tarry and partake of their mellow splendor. If you have only three days, take in Burgundy's most interesting city—Dijon—and town, Beaune. With five days you can explore the northwest part of the region, from Sens to Beaune. Eight days will give you time to trawl the Morvan and Burgundy's finest vineyards.

8

Numbers in the text correspond to numbers in the margin and on the Burgundy, Troyes, and Dijon maps.

If you have 3 days Start with the age-old capital of Burgundy, 🔟 **Dijon** ㉗– ㊳ ▶—one-time haunt of the dukes of Burgundy, who were among the richest people in the late Middle Ages and who bequeathed to the city a dazzling legacy of art, goldsmithery, and tapestry. Then it's on to medieval 🔟 **Beaune** ㊶ to view its majestic Hospice, founded by Chancellor Rolin, the great patron of Jan van Eyck and Rogier van der Weyden, whose *Last Judgment* altarpiece takes pride of place here. En route, visit the famous Burgundy vineyards around **Clos de Vougeot** ㊴—if you're here in September or October, you may be in time for the *vendanges* (grape harvest).

If you have 5 days Coming from Paris, stop first in the small town of **Sens** ❶ ▶, with its vast cathedral and 13th-century Palais Synodal. Then head for the serene abbey in **Pontigny** ⓯ and the Ancien Hôpital in **Tonnerre** ⓲. End the day tasting the famous white wine in 🔟 **Chablis** ⓱ and spend the night there. Begin Day 2 with a visit to **Auxerre** ⓰ and its cathedral before going on to the famous basilica in **Vézelay** ㉓. Stay overnight in pretty 🔟 **Avallon** ㉒, with its medieval church of St-Lazare. Get to 🔟 **Dijon** ㉗– ㊳ on Day 3 and stay two nights. On Day 5 take a short run along the wine-producing Côte d'Or to 🔟 **Beaune** ㊶.

If you have 9 days Make 🔟 **Troyes** ❷ ▶ – ⓮, with its medieval pedestrian streets, your first stop. On Day 2 head south to see the Renaissance château of **Ancy-le-Franc** ⓴ and the Cistercian **Abbaye de Fontenay** ㉑. End the day in 🔟 **Dijon** ㉗– ㊳. Give yourself two nights in Dijon, then head to 🔟 **Beaune** ㊶ and spend the night there before driving south along the Saône Valley to medieval **Tournus** ㊺ and the abbey of St-Philibert, then across to 🔟 **Cluny** ㊻ and its ruined abbey. The next day drive north to see the cathedral and Roman remains in **Autun** ㊸, the **Château de Sully** ㊷, and end the day with a feast in 🔟 **Saulieu** ㉕. On Day 7 drive through the wooded hills of the **Morvan** ㉔ before spending the night in 🔟 **Vézelay** ㉓. Stop off in **Avallon** ㉒ before reaching 🔟 **Auxerre** ⓰—a good base for exploring **Chablis** ⓱ and its towering vineyards on your final day, before heading up to **Sens** ❶.

nay grapes. Next comes the Côte Chalonnaise, around Mercurey, then, still farther south, around Mâcon, the fine white wines of St-Véran and Pouilly-Fuissé. Throughout this killer countryside, small towns with big wine names draw tourists to their cellars. Farther south, fruity gamay (red) heralds neighboring Beaujolais, Cluny and Tournus add more spice to Burgundy's reputation for tasty church architecture.

About the Restaurants & Hotels

Welcome to the land of the Appellation d'Origine Contrôlée (AOC), an organization that slaps its mark onto quality products according to sacred rules of food and wine cultivation. In Burgundy this means that the *poulet de Bresse* (Bresse chicken), *boeuf Bourguignon* (beef stew with vegetables, braised in red Burgundy wine), *coq au vin* (chicken stewed in red wine), or escargots (snails) you ordered came from a pure lineage and were raised on natural ingredients before landing on your dinner table. And don't forget to down your victuals with a drink invented by a monk from Dijon—the kir, a mix of local crème de cassis (black-currant liqueur) and white Aligoté wine. Keep in mind some restaurants close the last two weeks in August and go into winter hibernation for January.

Burgundy is seldom overrun by tourists, so finding accommodations is not usually a problem. But it's still wise to make advance reservations, especially in the wine country (from Dijon to Beaune). Note that nearly all country hotels have restaurants, and you are usually expected to eat at them. Some towns have a large number of inexpensive hotels. In Dijon you can find them around place Émile-Zola; in Beaune look around place Madeleine; in Auxerre they're tucked away in the streets heading down from the cathedral; in Tournus and Avallon check out the *Vieille Ville* (Old Town). Assume all hotel rooms have air-conditioning, TV, telephones, and private bath, except when noted.

	WHAT IT COSTS In euros				
	$$$$	**$$$**	**$$**	**$**	**¢**
RESTAURANTS	over €30	€23–€30	€17–€23	€11–€17	under €11
HOTELS	over €190	€120–€190	€80–€120	€50–€80	under €50

Restaurant prices are per person for a main course at dinner, including tax (19.6%) and service; note that if a restaurant offers only prix-fixe (set-price) meals, it has been given the price category that reflects the full prix-fixe price. Hotel prices are for a standard double room in high season, including tax (19.6%) and service charge. Hotels operate on the European Plan (EP, with no meal provided) unless we note that they use the Breakfast Plan (BP), or also offer such options as Modified American Plan (MAP, with breakfast and dinner daily, known as *demi-pension*), or Full American Plan (FAP, or *pension complète*, with three meals a day). Inquire when booking if these all-inclusive mealplans (which always entail higher rates) are mandatory or optional.

Timing

May in Burgundy is lovely, as are September and October, when the sun is still warm on the shimmering golden trees and the grapes, now ready for harvesting, are scenting the air with anticipation. This is when the grapevines are colorful and the *caves* (wine cellars) are open for busi-

8

Beyond Boeuf Bourguignon
"Tonton Moutarde" (Uncle Mustard) is what one young Parisian sophisticate affectionately used to call her Dijon relative, who was actually in the mustard business. For many French people, mention of Burgundy's capital conjures up images of round, rosy, merry men enjoying large suppers of boeuf à la bourguignonne and red wine. And admittedly, chances are that in any decent restaurant you'll find at least one *Dijonnais* true to the stereotype. These days, however, Dijon is not quite the wine-mustard capital of the world it used to be as mustard production has been displaced by the more profitable colza plant, from which cooking oil is made. You'll find several people continue to make it by hand (importing the seed from Canada) in Dijon, but the happy fact remains that mustard finds its way into many regional specialties, including the sauce that usually accompanies andouillettes (chitterling sausages). Dijon ranks with Lyon as the gastronomic capital of France and Burgundy's hearty traditions help explain why. It all began in the early 15th century when Jean, Duc de Berry, arrived here, built a string of castles, and proceeded to make food, wine, and art top priorities for his courtiers. Today, Parisian gourmands consider a three-hour drive a small price to pay for the cuisine of Beaune's Jean Crotet or Vézelay's Marc Meneau.

Game, freshwater trout, coq au vin, *poulet au Meursault* (chicken in white wine sauce), snails, and, of course, beef *à la Bourguignonne* (incidentally, this dish is only called boeuf bourguignon when you are *not* in Burgundy) number among the region's specialties. The queen of chickens is the *poulet de Bresse,* which hails from east of the Côte d'Or and can be as pricey as a bottle of fine wine. Sausages—notably the *rosette du Morvan* and others served with a potato puree—are great favorites. Ham is a big item, especially around Easter, when garlicky *jambon persillé*—ham boiled with pig's trotters and served cold in jellied white wine and parsley (no wonder it is now found throughout the summer months) often tops the menu. Also look for *saupiquet des Amognes*—a Moravian delight of hot braised ham served with a spicy cream sauce. *Pain d'épices* (gingerbread) is the dessert staple of the region. Like every other part of France, Burgundy has its own cheeses. The Abbaye de Cîteaux, birthplace of Cistercian monasticism, has produced its mild cheese for centuries. Chaource and hearty Époisses also melt in your mouth—as do Bleu de Bresse and Meursault. Meat and poultry are often served in rich, wine-base sauces.

Heavenly Mansions
From the sober splendor of well-preserved Fontenay to the majestic ruins of Cluny and the isolated remains of Pontigny and Clairvaux, the abbeys, basilicas, and cathedrals of Burgundy evoke the region's storied past. Reminders of medieval religious luminaries—notably Thomas à Becket and Bernard of Clairvaux—are everywhere, laying a mantle of history over the region. Many of the region's greatest structures were built in the Romanesque style (11th–12th centuries) rather than the Gothic (13th–15th centuries) often prevalent elsewhere in France.

Rich Wines, Rich Past Some prefer Bordeaux, others insist that Burgundy is an oenophile's nirvana, to be accorded religious reverence. Indeed, this used to be literally the case, for the region's wine husbandry was perfected in large part by the great monasteries of the region, including Cluny and Cîteaux; the Cistercians founded the Clos de Vougeot, a great favorite of the 17th-century writer and gourmand Rabelais. The first evidence of vineyards in Cluny dates from 330 BC. Centuries later, during the Holy Roman Empire, nobility often gave vineyards to the church. The monks tasted and analyzed the wines and recorded the nuances of the different plots of land. Detailed maps were drawn, indicating the temperatures and miniclimates of the plots. The term *clos* (an ancient word for climate) comes from the names given these climates by the monks.

Each part of Burgundy produces wine of distinctive quality: Chablis (steely white wine), Côte de Nuits (rich and full-flavored red wine), Côte de Beaune (delicately flavored red and white wines), Côte Chalonnaise (whites and full-flavored reds), Irancy (earthy reds), St-Bris (flinty whites), Pouilly-Fuissé (fruity whites). The famous vineyards south of Dijon—the Côte de Nuits and Côte de Beaune—are among the world's most distinguished and picturesque. Don't expect to unearth many bargains in the vineyards themselves, however. The best place to sample a goodly selection is in the Marché aux Vins in Beaune, a scenic old town dominated by the patterned-tile roofs of its medieval Hôtel-Dieu (hospital).

ness. Many festivals also take place around this time. Note that some restaurants and hotels close down for a month or more in winter.

NORTHWEST BURGUNDY

In the Middle Ages, Sens, Auxerre, and Troyes (officially in the neighboring Champagne region), came under the sway of the Paris-based Capetian kings, who erected mighty Gothic cathedrals in those towns. Outside these major centers of northwest Burgundy, countryside villages are largely preserved in a rural landscape that seems to have remained the same for centuries. Here "life in the fast lane" is considered a reference to the Paris-bound A6 expressway. If you're driving down from Paris, we suggest you take the A6 into Burgundy (or alternatively the A5 direct to Troyes) before making a scenic clockwise loop around the Parc du Morvan.

Sens

▶ ❶ *112 km (70 mi) southeast of Paris on N6.*

It makes sense for Sens to be your first stop in Burgundy, since it's only 90 minutes by car from Paris on N6, a fast road that hugs the pretty Yonne Valley south of Fontainebleau. Historically linked more with Paris than with Burgundy, Sens was for centuries the ecclesiastical center of

Fodor'sChoice France and is still dominated by its **Cathédrale St-Étienne,** once the French
★ sanctuary for Thomas à Becket and a model for England's Canterbury Cathedral. You can see the cathedral's 240-foot south tower from way off; the highway forges straight past it. The pompous 19th-century

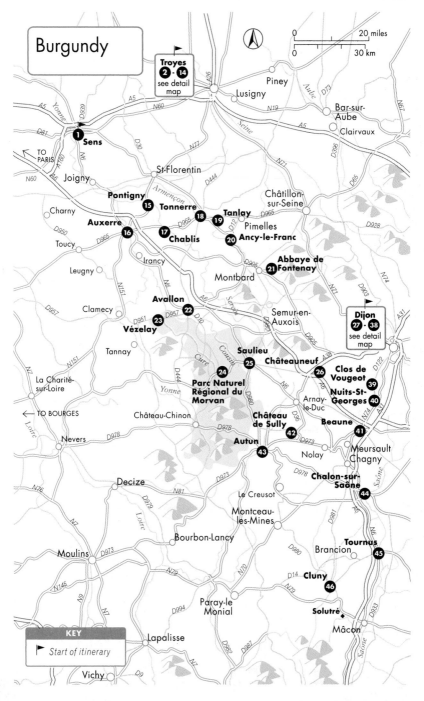

buildings lining the narrow main street—notably the meringue-like Hôtel de Ville—can give you a false impression if you're in a hurry: the streets leading off it near the cathedral (notably rue Abelard and rue Jean-Cousin) are full of half-timber medieval houses. On Monday the cathedral square is crowded with merchants' stalls, and the beautiful late-19th-century market hall—a distant cousin of Baltard's former iron-and-glass Halles in Paris—throbs with people buying meat and produce. A smaller market is held on Friday morning.

Begun around 1140, the cathedral once had two towers; one was topped in 1532 by an elegant though somewhat incongruous Renaissance campanile that contains two monster bells; the other collapsed in the 19th century. Note the trefoil arches decorating the exterior of the remaining tower. The gallery, with statues of former archbishops of Sens, is a 19th-century addition, but the statue of St. Stephen, between the doors of the central portal, is thought to date from late in the 12th century. The vast, harmonious interior is justly renowned for its stained-glass windows; the oldest (circa 1200) are in the north transept and include the stories of the Good Samaritan and the Prodigal Son; those in the south transept were manufactured in 1500 in Troyes and include a much-admired *Tree of Jesse*. Stained-glass windows in the north of the chancel retrace the story of Thomas à Becket: Becket fled to Sens from England to escape the wrath of Henry II before returning to his cathedral in Canterbury, where he was murdered in 1170. Below the window (which shows him embarking on his journey in a boat, and also at the moment of his death) is a medieval statue of an archbishop said to have come from the site of Becket's home in Sens. Years of restoration work have permitted the display of his *aube* (vestment) in the annex to the Palais Synodal. ⊠ *Pl. de la République* 🕿 *03–86–64–15–27.*

The roof of the 13th-century **Palais Synodal** (Synodal Palace), alongside Sens's cathedral, is notable for its yellow, green, and red diamond-tile motif—incongruously added in the mid-19th century by medieval monument restorer Viollet-le-Duc. Its six grand windows and vaulted Synodal Hall are outstanding architectural features; the building now functions as an exhibition space. Annexed to the Palais Synodal is an ensemble of Renaissance buildings with a courtyard offering a fine view of the cathedral's Flamboyant Gothic south transept, constructed by master stonemason Martin Chambiges at the start of the 16th century (rose windows were his specialty, as you can appreciate here). Inside is a museum with archaeological finds from the Gallo-Roman period, including the *trésor de Villethierry,* a cache of bronze jewelry unearthed during the construction of the A5 highway; exceptional stelae depicting various trades; and the remains of Roman baths discovered in situ 20 years ago. The cathedral treasury, now on the museum's second floor, is one of the richest in France, comparable to that of Conques. It contains a collection of miters, ivories, the shrouds of St. Sivard and St. Loup, and sumptuous reliquaries. But the star of the collection is Thomas à Becket's restored brown- and silver-edged linen robe. His chasuble, stole, and sandals are too fragile to display. 🕿 *03–86–64–46–22* 🖭 €3.50 🕒 *June–Sept., Wed.–Mon. 10–noon and 2–6; Oct.–May, Wed. and weekends 10–noon and 2–6, Mon. and Thurs.–Fri. 2–6.*

Where to Stay & Eat

$$–$$$ ✕ **Clos des Jacobins.** With its lemon-yellow walls and exceptional fish specialties, this restaurant in the center of town strikes a happy balance between elegant and casual. Try the €18 lunch *menu du marché*, which may include *matelotte d'oeufs pochés à l'Irancy* (poached eggs in Irancy wine sauce), and *blanc de turbot au Noilly-Prat* (turbot with dry vermouth). ✉ *49 Grande-Rue* ☎ *03–86–95–29–70* ⊕ *www.restaurantlesjacobins. com* ▤ *AE, MC, V* ⊘ *Closed Wed. No dinner Sun. or Tues.*

★ **$$–$$$** ✕▥ **La Lucarne aux Chouettes.** There's nothing Hollywoodesque about actress Leslie Caron's charmingly rustic riverside hotel and restaurant, the "Owl's Nest," set in four 17th-century buildings. The lovely whitewash-brick dining room, with its ingenious twisted rope chandeliers, has a homey-meets-elegant feel, as do the rooms: the "Loft" is an enormous wood-beamed aerie atop the house (the bathroom is in the room itself, just as it was in the rip-roaring days of the 1680s), while "The Suite" glows with a portrait of Sarah Bernhardt. The legendary hostess (the beloved Lili-Gigi-Fanny of everyone's memories) is often on hand to extend a warm greeting, although she does still depart for rare film shoots. In summer enjoy the terrace over the Yonne. The town itself, a *bastide* (fortified town, built on a grid pattern), is entered and exited via sturdy, angular 13th- and 14th-century gateways. ✉ *7 quai Bretoche, 12 km (7 mi) south of Sens on N6, 89500 Villeneuve-sur-Yonne* ☎ *03–86–87–18–26* 🖷 *03–86–87–22–63* ⊕ *www.lesliecaron-auberge.com* 🛏 *4 rooms* ⌂ *Restaurant, cable TV; no a/c* ▤ *AE, MC, V.*

$–$$ ✕▥ **Paris & Poste.** Owned for the last several decades by the Godart family, the modernized Paris & Poste, which began life as a canon's house in 1776 (before becoming a post house in 1796), is a convenient and pleasant stopping point. Rooms are clean, spacious and well equipped; most open onto a patio (No. 42 is especially nice). But it's the traditional red-and-gold restaurant, which serves great home-smoked salmon (closed Monday, no dinner Sunday); the padded, green leather armchairs in the lounge; and the little curved wooden bar that give this place its comfy charm. Better, the dishes of chef-owner Phillipe Godard exhibit real flair. ✉ *97 rue de la République, 89100* ☎ *03–86–65–17–43* 🖷 *03–86–64–48–45* ⊕ *www.hotel-paris-poste.com* 🛏 *30 rooms* ⌂ *Restaurant, cable TV, free parking; no a/c in some rooms* ▤ *AE, DC, MC, V.*

★ **$$$** ▥ **Château de Prunoy.** Though it's a little out of the way, this château and park—built by one of Louis XVI's finance ministers—is spectacular enough to be worth the trip. Grand public rooms are a stylish blend of Louis Seize gilt-trimmed antiques and grandmother's knickknackery, although many of the guest rooms seem to be the suave result of an elegant decorator (but do avoid the one designed as a Japanese teahouse). Quirky flea-market finds help make it all very *chez soi*, right down to the presence of the owner's friendly Labradors. Dinner is not especially grand but the dining salon itself is country-adorable. ✉ *40 km (25 mi) southwest of Sens, 40 km (25 mi) northwest of Auxerre on N6 to D943 to D18, 89120 Prunoy* ☎ *03–86–63–66–91* 🖷 *03–86–63–77–79* ⊕ *www.chateaudeprunoy.com* 🛏 *14 rooms, 5 suites* ⌂ *Restaurant, tennis court, pool, gym, sauna; no a/c* ▤ *AE, DC, MC, V.*

Troyes

★ ▶ *64 km (40 mi) east of Sens, 150 km (95 mi) southeast of Paris.*

The inhabitants of Troyes would be dismayed if you mistook them for Burgundians. Troyes is the historic capital of the counts of Champagne; as if to prove the point, its historic town center is shaped like a champagne cork. It was also the home of the late-12th-century writer Chrétien (or Chrestien) de Troyes who, in seeking to please his patrons Count Henry the Liberal and Marie de Champagne, penned the first Arthurian legends. Few, if any, other French town centers contain so much to see. A web of enchanting pedestrian streets with timber-frame houses, magnificent churches, fine museums, and a wide choice of restaurants make the Old Town—Vieux Troyes—especially appealing. The center of Troyes is divided by the boulevard Dampierre, a broad, busy thoroughfare. On one side is the quiet cathedral quarter, on the other the more upbeat commercial part.

Keep your eyes peeled, instead, for the delightful architectural accents that make Troyes unique: *essentes,* geometric chestnut tiles that keep out humidity and are fire resistant; and sculpted *poteaux* (in Troyes they are called *montjoies*), carvings at the joint of corner structural beams. There's a lovely one of Adam and Eve next door to the Comtes de Champagne hotel. Along with its neighbors Provins and Bar-sur-Aube, Troyes was one of Champagne's major fair towns in the Middle Ages. The wool trade gave way to cotton in the 18th century, and today Troyes draws busloads of shoppers from all over Europe to scour for bargains at its outlet clothing stores.

The dynamic **tourist office** (⊠ 16 bd. Carnot ☎ 03–25–82–62–70 ⊕ www.ot-troyes.fr) has information and sells €12 passes that admit you to the town's major museums, with a free audioguide and champagne tasting thrown in.

② Although Troyes is on the Seine, it's the capital of the Aube *département* (province) administered from the elegant **Préfecture** behind its gleaming gilt-iron railings.

③ Across the Bassin de la Préfecture, an arm of the Seine, is the **Hôtel-Dieu** (hospital), fronted by superb 18th-century wrought-iron gates topped with the blue-and-gold fleurs-de-lis emblems of the French monarchy. Around the corner is the entrance to the **Apothicairie de l'Hôtel-Dieu,** a former medical laboratory, the only part of the Hôtel-Dieu open to visitors. Inside, time has been suspended: floral-painted boxes and ceramic jars containing medicinal plants line the antique shelves. ⊠ *Quai des Comtes-de-Champagne* ☎ *03–25–80–98–97* ⊠ *€2* ☉ *July and Aug., Wed.–Mon. 10–6; Sept.–June, Wed. and weekends 10–noon and 1:30–5:45.*

★ **④** The **Musée d'Art Moderne** (Modern Art Museum) is housed in the 16th- to 17th-century former bishop's palace. Its magnificent interior, with a wreath-and-cornucopia carved oak fireplace, ceilings with carved wood beams, and a Renaissance staircase, now contains the Lévy Collection—one of the finest provincial collections in France, including Art Deco glassware, tribal art, and an important group of Fauve paintings

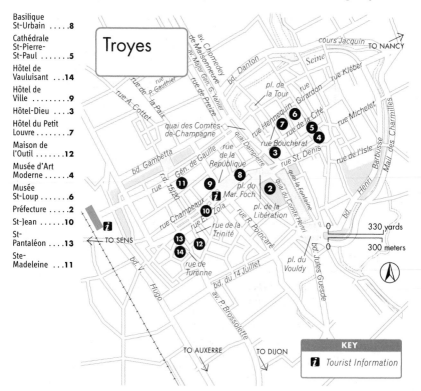

by André Derain and others. ✉ *Palais Épiscopal, pl. St-Pierre* ☎ *03–25–76–26–80* ⊕ *www.ville-troyes.fr/premiere.htm* ✎ €*5* ⊙ *Tues.–Sun. 11–6.*

Noted monument of Flamboyant Gothic—a style regarded as the last gasp
❺ of the Middle Ages—the **Cathédrale St-Pierre–St-Paul** dominates the heart of Troyes; note the incomplete single-tower west front, the small Renaissance campaniles on top of the tower, and the artistry of Martin Chambiges, who worked on Troyes's facade (with its characteristic large rose window) around the same time as he did the transept of Sens. At night the floodlit features burst into dramatic relief. The cathedral's vast five-aisle interior, refreshingly light thanks to large windows and the near-whiteness of the local stone, dates mainly from the 13th century. It has fine examples of 13th-century stained glass in the choir, such as the *Tree of Jesse* (a popular regional theme), and richly colored 16th-century glass in the nave and west front rose window. The choir stalls and organ were requisitioned from Clairvaux Abbey. One of the chapels contains black-basalt tombstones marking the remains of Count Henry I of Champagne, carved in 1792 after the count's palace was destroyed, and the cathedral treasury displays such curiosities as a piece of St. Bernard of Clairvaux's skull. The arcaded triforium above the pillars of the choir was one of the

first in France to be glazed rather than filled with stone. Across the street from the cathedral, behind an iron fence, is an unusual, lopsided, late-medieval **grange aux dîmes** (tithe barn) with a peaked roof. It is used as a warehouse by the winemaker next door. ⊠ *Pl. St-Pierre* ☎ *03–25–76–98–18* 🖾 *Free* ☉ *July–mid-Sept., daily 9–1 and 2–7; mid-Sept.–Feb., daily 10–noon and 2–4; Mar.–June, daily 10–noon and 2–5.*

★ ❻ The former 18th-century abbey of St-Loup to the side of the cathedral now houses the **Musée St-Loup,** an arts and antiquities museum, noted for its superlative collection of Old Master paintings. Exhibits are devoted to natural history, with impressive collections of birds and meteorites; local archaeological finds, especially gold-mounted 5th-century jewelry and a Gallo-Roman bronze statue of Apollo; medieval statuary and gargoyles; and the paintings from the 15th to 19th centuries, including works by Rubens, Anthony Van Dyck, Antoine Watteau, François Boucher, and Jacques-Louis David. ⊠ *1 rue Chrestien-de-Troyes* ☎ *03–25–76–21–68* 🖾 *€4* ☉ *Sept.–June, Wed.–Mon. 10–noon and 2–6; July and Aug., Wed.–Mon. 10–noon and 2–7.*

❼ The **Hôtel du Petit Louvre** (⊠ Rue Boucherat) is a handsome, 16th-century former coaching inn.

★ ❽ The **Basilique St-Urbain** was built between 1262 and 1286 by Pope Urban IV, who was born in Troyes. St-Urbain is one of the most remarkable churches in France, a perfect culmination of the Gothic quest to replace stone walls with stained glass. Its narrow porch frames a 13th-century *Last Judgment* tympanum, whose highly worked elements include a frieze of the dead rising out of their coffins (note the grimacing skeleton) and an enormous crayfish, a testament to the local river culture. Inside, a chapel on the south side houses the *Vièrge au Raisin* (*Virgin with Grapes*), clutching Jesus with one hand and a bunch of Champagne grapes in the other. ⊠ *Pl. Vernier* ☎ *03–25–73–37–13* 🖾 *Free* ☉ *July and Aug., daily 10:30–7; 1st 2 wks in Sept., daily 10:30–5; mid-Sept.–June, daily 10–noon and 2–4.*

❾ Place du Maréchal-Foch, the main square of central Troyes, is flanked by cafés, shops, and the delightful facade of the **Hôtel de Ville** (Town Hall). In summer the square is filled with people from morning to night.

❿ The clock tower of the church of **St-Jean** is an unmistakable landmark. England's warrior king Henry V married Catherine of France here in 1420. The church's tall 16th-century choir contrasts with the low nave, constructed earlier. ⊠ *Pl. du Marché au Pain* ☎ *03–25–73–06–96* 🖾 *Free* ☉ *July and Aug., daily 10:30–7; 1st 2 wks in Sept., daily 10:30–5; mid-Sept.–June, daily 10–noon and 2–4.*

⓫ **Ste-Madeleine,** the oldest church in Troyes, is best known for its elaborate triple-arched stone rood screen separating the nave and the choir. Only six other such screens still remain in France—most were dismantled during the French Revolution. This filigreed Flamboyant Gothic beauty was carved with panache by Jean Gailde between 1508 and 1517. ⊠ *Rue de la Madeleine* ☎ *03–25–73–82–90* 🖾 *Free* ☉ *July and Aug., daily 10:30–7; 1st 2 wks in Sept., daily 10:30–5; mid-Sept.–June, daily 10–noon and 2–4.*

🕐 ⓬ There's a practical reason why the windows of the **Maison de l'Outil** (Tool and Craft Museum) are filled with bizarre and beautiful outsize models—like a winding staircase and a globe on a swivel. It's the display venue for the "showpieces" created by apprentice Compagnons de Devoir, members of the national craftsmen's guild whose school is in Troyes. The museum, in the 16th-century Hôtel de Mauroy, also contains a collection of paintings, models, and tools relevant to such traditional wood-related trades as carpentry, clog making, and barrel making—including a medieval anvil, called a *bigorne.* ⊠ *7 rue de la Trinité* ☎ *03–25–73–28–26* 🖙 *€6.50* 🕐 *Daily 10–6.*

⓭ The 16th- to 18th-century church of **St-Pantaléon** primarily serves the local Polish community. A number of fine canopied stone statues, many of them the work of the Troyen Dominique le Florentin, decorator to François I, are clustered around its pillars. ⊠ *Rue de Turenne* ☎ *03–25–73–06–99* 🖙 *Free* 🕐 *July and Aug., daily 10:30–12:30 and 2:30–6:30; 1st 2 wks in Sept., daily 10:30–12:30 and 2:30–5:30; mid-Sept.–June, daily 10–noon and 2–4.*

★ 🕐 ⓮ The charmingly turreted 16th- to 17th-century **Hôtel de Vauluisant** houses two museums: the **Musée Historique** (History Museum) and the **Musée de la Bonneterie** (Textile Museum). The former traces the development of Troyes and southern Champagne, with a particularly magnificent selection of religious sculptures and paintings of the late-Gothic era; the latter outlines the history and manufacturing procedures of the town's 18th- to 19th-century textile industry. ⊠ *4 rue Vauluisant* ☎ *03–25–42–33–33* ⊕ *www.ville-troyes.fr/premiere.htm* 🖙 *Joint ticket for both museums €5* 🕐 *Sept.–June, Wed.–Sun. 10–noon and 2–6; July and Aug., Wed.–Mon. 10–6.*

Where to Stay & Eat

The pleasure of Troyes is its historic town center, Le Vieux Troyes. This is where you want your hotel to be—or at least within walking distance of it. If you want to dine informally, it's also the area to find a restaurant, especially along rue Champeaux.

$–$$$ ✕ **Le Vivien.** Despite the subdued elegance of the airy modern dining-room, with its padded wooden chairs and crisp white tablecloths, many diners at this friendly restaurant prefer to eat outside, on the terrace overlooking the leafy pedestrian square beside St-Rémy's church. Although chef Jean-Michel Jadot counts venison in grape juice, and bacon, pea and potato flan among his specialties, he is best known for his fish and seafood dishes, like fried pike-perch, or prawns and scallops flambéed in brandy. Prix-fixe menus at €18, €28, and €38 offer three, four, or five delicious courses respectively. ⊠ *7 pl. St-Rémy* ☎ *03–25–73–70–70* ⚑ *Reservations essential* 🖃 *AE, MC, V* 🕐 *Closed Mon. and second half Sept. No dinner Sun.*

¢–$ ✕ **La Taverne de l'Ours.** This popular, convivial brasserie has faux Art Nouveau and neo-Gothic furbelows, brass globe lamps, and plushy seating alcoves. It also has delicious, hearty cuisine, such as roast *cochon de lait* (suckling pig) straight off the spit. The €11 lunch menu is a real bargain, and even tastier when accompanied by the grapey, dark pink rosé *des Riceys* from the Champagne–Burgundy border. Happily, this place is open year-round. ✉ *2 rue Champeaux* ☎ *03–25–73–22–18* 🖃 *AE, MC, V.*

$$–$$$ 🏨 **Le Champ des Oiseaux.** "There are places like moments; those which
Fodor'sChoice permanently imprint memories," declaims the lyrical Web site for this
★ *chic et charmant* hotel. Le Champ comes through on that promise. Idyl-
lically situated in ancient Troyes and named after the city's centuries-old
roosting haunts of storks, this ensemble of three vine-clad pink-and-
yellow 15th- and 16th-century houses (their bright colors are part of a
town campaign to "medievalize" half-timber facades) seem ready to re-
ceive Manon Lescaut on the run. A daub-and-wattle facade abuzz with
the pattern of timbered logs and a storybook courtyard, graced with a
fairy-tale staircase, overhanging porch, and cobblestone patio, all set the
scene for the charm within. Tin chandeliers, Nantes silks and calico hang-
ings, 15th-century scrollwork panels, beamed roofs right out of the *Re-
turn of Martin Guerre,* and more traditional luxe touches make the
interiors a joy. The guest salon is set in a vaulted cave-wine cellar fitted
out with the latest in soigné furniture. The biggest guest room, the Suite
Médiévale, is under the oak-beam eaves, while the Salle Bleue (Blue
Room) looks worthy of the cover of *Maison Française.* Downstairs is a
lovely breakfast room with a stone fireplace. ✉ *20 rue Linard-Gonthier,*
10000 ☎*03–25–80–58–50* 🖷*03–25–80–98–34* ⊕*www.champdesoiseaux.*
com 🛏*9 rooms, 3 suites* 🗋 *Cable TV, Internet; no a/c* 🖃 *AE, MC, V.*

$$ 🏨 **Relais St-Jean.** This calm half-timber hotel, in the pedestrian zone near
the church of St-Jean, has fully equipped, good-size rooms with airy mod-
ern decoration, white-and pastel-colored walls, and floral-patterned
curtains. Some rooms are connected by a path running through the second floor's tree-filled atrium. Black-leather chairs and mirrored walls
in the bar contrast rudely with the wicker and plants of an adjoining
room, but have a drink here, and good-natured owner Pierre Rinaldi
will gladly stop to chat. The hotel has no restaurant, but just along the
street is the friendly **Valentino** (✉ 35 rue Paillot-de-Montabert
☎ 03–25–73–14–14), which has dining in its courtyard. ✉ *49 rue Paillot-de-Montabert, 10000* ☎ *03–25–73–89–90* 🖷 *03–25–73–88–60*
⊕ *www.relais-st-jean.com* 🛏 *25 rooms* 🗋 *Minibars, bar, Internet*
🖃 *AE, DC, MC, V* ☉ *Closed mid-Dec.–early Jan.*

¢–$ 🏨 **Comtes de Champagne.** In Vieux Troyes's former mint is this bargain
hotel. The topsy-turvy 16th-century building has a quaint inner courtyard with large vines and a philodendron, and slightly shabby rooms
with faded floral wallpaper and iron bedsteads. Ask for the largest
room, on the second floor, one of the few with its own bath. The two
couples who comanage, the Gribourets and the Picards, are friendly folk.
✉*56 rue de la Monnaie, 10000* ☎*03–25–73–11–70* 🖷*03–25–73–06–02*
🛏 *35 rooms, 5 with bath* 🖃 *MC, V.*

Shopping

If there's an ideal place for a shopping spree, it's Troyes. Many clothing manufacturers are just outside town, clustered together in two large
suburban malls: **Marques Avenue**, in St-Julien-les-Villas (take N71 toward
Dijon); and **Marques City** and the American outlet store **McArthur Glen**,
in Pont-Ste-Marie (take N77 toward Chalons-sur-Marne). Ralph Lau-

ren and Calvin Klein at McArthur Glen face off with Laura Ashley at Marques Avenue and Doc Martens at Marques City, to name a few of the shops. The malls are open Monday 2–7, Tuesday–Friday 10–7, and Saturday 9:30–7.

off the beaten path

CLAIRVAUX – Although much of it has been replaced by a sprawling 19th-century prison, the Abbaye de Clairvaux, 64 km (40 mi) east of Troyes via N19, was once the Cistercian mother abbey of Champagne and northern Burgundy. St. Bernard, a native of Fontaine-les-Dijon, founded Clairvaux (meaning "bright valley") only two years after his entry into Cîteaux, in 1115, and three years before establishing the community of Fontenay, in 1118. Subsequently known as Bernard of Clairvaux, he went on to condemn the behavior of Pierre Abélard, preach the Second Crusade in Vézelay, and decry the lavish pomp of Cluny. The 12th-century vaulted halls of the lay brothers' dormitory remain, as do parts of the once-flourishing 18th-century abbey. ⊠ *Off N19, watch for signs* ☎ *03–25–27–88–17* ⊙ *May–Oct., Sat. only. Guided tours at 2, 3, 4, and 5* ☞ *Bring I.D.*

Pontigny

⓯ *60 km (37 mi) south of Troyes, 56 km (35 mi) southeast of Sens.*

Pontigny can easily be mistaken for another drowsy, dusty village, but its once proud **Abbaye de Pontigny** is as large as many cathedrals. In the 12th and 13th centuries it sheltered three archbishops of Canterbury, including St. Thomas à Becket (from 1164 to 1166). His path to refuge from the king of England was followed by his successor, Stephen Langton (here from 1207 to 1215), and, lastly, Edmund of Abingdon—whose body, naturally mummified in the years following his death in 1240, has been venerated (as St. Edmund) by centuries of English pilgrims to Pontigny. His Baroque tomb, whose occupant is supposedly very much intact, can be seen at the rear of the church, although peeking through one of the openings is now strictly forbidden. The abbey was founded in 1114, and the current church finished around 1150. By Burgundian standards the church and lay brothers' quarters (all that remain) were precociously Gothic—the first buildings in the region to have rib vaults. Inside, note the beautiful, late-17th-century Baroque choir stalls, carved with garlands and angels. On the grassy lawn next to the church is a large, plate-shape 12th-century **fountain** with 31 spigots and sculpted Gothic feet—one of the few functioning medieval abbey fountains remaining in Europe. ☎ *03–86–47–54–99* ☒ *Free, €3.50 for guided tour* ⊙ *June–Oct., daily 9–7; Nov.–May, daily 10–5, except during services.*

Auxerre

⓰ *21 km (13 mi) southwest of Pontigny, 58 km (36 mi) southeast of Sens.*

Fodor'sChoice
★

Auxerre is a beautifully laid-out town with three imposing and elegant churches perched above the Yonne River. Its steep, undulating streets are full of massively photogenic, half-timber houses in every imaginable style and shape. Yet this harmonious, architecturally interesting town is underappreciated, perhaps because of its location, midway between Paris and Dijon.

Fanning out from Auxerre's main square, **place des Cordeliers** (just up from the cathedral), are a number of venerable, crooked, steep streets lined with half-timber and stone houses. The best way to see them is to start from the riverside on the quai de la République, where you find the tourist office (and can pick up a handy local map), and continue along the quai de la Marine. The medieval arcaded gallery of the **Ancien Evêché** (Old Bishop's Palace), now an administrative building, is just visible on the hillside beside the tourist office. At **9 rue de la Marine** (which leads off one of several riverside squares) are the two oldest houses in Auxerre, dating from the end of the 14th century. Continue up the hill to rue de l'Yonne, which leads into the **rue Cochois**. Here, at No. 23, is the appropriately topsy-turvy home and shop of a *maître verrier* (lead-glass maker). Closer to the center of town, the most beautiful of Auxerre's many *poteaux* (the carved tops of wooden corner posts) can be seen at **8 rue Joubert**: the building dates from the late 15th century and its Gothic tracery windows, acorns, and oak leaves are an open-air masterpiece.

The town's dominant feature is the ascending line of three magnificent churches—St-Pierre, St-Étienne, and St-Germain—and the **Cathédrale St-Étienne**, in the middle, rising majestically above the squat houses around it. The 13th-century choir, the oldest part of the edifice, contains its original stained glass, dominated by brilliant reds and blues. Beneath the choir, the frescoed 11th-century Romanesque crypt keeps company with the treasury, which has a panoply of medieval enamels, manuscripts, and miniatures. A 75-minute son-et-lumière show focusing on Roman Gaul is presented every evening from June to September. ⊠ *Pl. St-Étienne* ☎ *03–86–52–31–68* 🖃 *Crypt and treasury €3 each; €6 Passport ticket allows entry to crypt and treasury plus St-Germain* ☉ *Easter–Nov., Mon.–Sat. 9–noon and 2–6, Sun. 2–6.*

North of place des Cordeliers is the former **Abbaye de St-Germain,** which stands parallel to the cathedral some 300 yards away. The church's earliest aboveground section is the 12th-century Romanesque bell tower, but the extensive underground crypt was inaugurated by Charles the Bald in 859 and contains its original Carolingian frescoes and Ionic capitals. It's the only monument of its kind in Europe—a labyrinth retaining the plan of the long-gone church built above it—and was a place of pilgrimage until Huguenots burned the remains of its namesake, a Gallo-Roman governor and bishop of Auxerre, in the 16th century. Several hundred years of veneration had already seen the burial of 33 bishops of Auxerre as close to the central tomb of St-Germain as they could physically get. The frescoes are a testimony to the brief artistic sophistication of the Carolingian Renaissance: witness St. Stephen running from a stone-hurling crowd toward the disembodied hand of God, a date-bearing palm tree, and the reversed images of a young bishop and an old one teaching each other. ⊠ *Pl. St-Germain* ☎ *03–86–51–09–74* 🖃 *€4.30* ☉ *Guided tours of crypt Oct.–Apr., daily 10, 11, and 2–5; May–Sept., daily every ½ hr between 10 and 5:30.*

Where to Stay & Eat

$–$$$ ✕ **La Chamaille.** This restaurant is remarkably low-key for its culinary aspirations. The mood is set by a babbling brook running through the garden and the exposed brick walls in the dining room. Try the rabbit in a rich brown sauce and pastry. You'll be hard-pressed to find room for the apple flan, but you must—it's delectable. Prices are reasonable, especially for the four-course menu, which includes a half bottle of regional wine, for €35. ⊠ *4 rte. de Boiloup, 10 km (6 mi) south of Auxerre, Chevannes* ☎ *03–86–41–24–80* ⊕ *http://perso.wanadoo.fr/ lachamaille* ⌕ *Reservations essential* ⊟ *AE, MC, V* ⊘ *Closed Mon. and Tues.*

$–$$$ ✕ **Le Jardin Gourmand.** As its name implies, this restaurant in a former manor house has a pretty garden (*jardin*) where you can eat in summer. The interior is accented by sea-green and yellow panels and is equally congenial and elegant. Terrine of pheasant breast is a specialty, and hope that the superb snails with barley and chanterelles is available. The staff is discreet and friendly. ⊠ *56 bd. Vauban* ☎ *03–86–51–53–52* ⊟ *AE, MC, V* ⊘ *Closed Mon.*

★ $ ▦ **Château de Ribourdin.** Retired farmer Claude Brodard began building his *chambres d'hôte* (bed-and-breakfast) in an old stable six years ago, and the result is cozy, comfortable, and reasonably priced. Château de la Borde is the smallest, sunniest, and most intimate room; all overlook Monsieur Brodard's fields. Homemade preserves—cassis, quince, and carrot—are served at breakfast. ⊠ *8 rte. de Ribourdin, 8 km (5 mi) southwest of Auxerre on D1, 89240 Chevannes* ☎ *03–86–41–23–16* ⇨ *5 rooms* ⌕ *Pool; no a/c, no room phones, no room TVs* ⊟ *No credit cards* ⦿⎮ *BP.*

$ ▦ **Normandie.** Set in a rather grand 19th-century mansion, the vine-covered Normandie is in the center of Auxerre, just a short walk from the cathedral. Rooms are unpretentious and clean. There's a billiard room, and the terrace is a nice place to relax after a long day of sightseeing. ⊠ *41 bd. Vauban, 89000* ☎ *03–86–52–57–80* 🖷 *03–86–51–54–33* ⊕ *www.hotelnormandie.fr* ⇨ *47 rooms* ⌕ *Gym, sauna, bar; no a/c, no room phones, no room TVs* ⊟ *AE, DC, MC, V.*

Chablis

⑰ *16 km (10 mi) east of Auxerre.*

The pretty village of Chablis nestles amid the towering vineyards that produce its famous white wine on the banks of the River Serein and is protected, perhaps from an ill wind, by the massive, round, turreted towers of the Porte Noël gateway. Although in America Chablis has become a generic name for cheap white wine, it's not so in France: there it's a bone-dry, slightly acacia-tasting wine of tremendous character, with the Premier Cru and Grand Cru wines standing head to head with the best French whites. Prices in the local shops tend to be inflated, so your best bet is to buy directly from a vineyard; keep in mind that most are closed Sunday. The town's **Maison de la Vigne et du Vin** can provide information on nearby cellars where you can take tours and taste wine. ⊠ *28 rue Auxerroise* ☎ *03–86–42–42–22* ⊕ *www.bivb.com.*

Where to Stay & Eat

★ **$–$$** ✕🖬 **Hostellerie des Clos.** The moderately priced, simple yet comfortable rooms at this inn have floral curtains and wicker tables with chairs. But most of all, come here for chef Michel Vignaud's cooking, some of the best in the region. He uses Chablis as a base for sauces to accompany his bream with shellfish or fried veal kidneys. ✉ *18 rue Jules-Rathier, 89800* ☎ *03–86–42–10–63* 🖷 *03–86–42–17–11* ⊕ *www.hostellerie-des-clos.fr* ↪ *26 rooms, 10 suites* ♻ *Restaurant, minibars, cable TV, sauna, Internet* ▤ *AE, MC, V* ⊘ *Closed late Dec.–mid-Jan.* ¶◯| *MAP.*

Tonnerre

⑱ *16 km (10 mi) northeast of Chablis.*

Although its name means "thunder," the tiny town of Tonnerre is better known for its quiet streets and views. It was mostly rebuilt after a devastating fire in 1556. A good spot from which to survey the 16th-century reconstruction and the Armançon Valley is the terrace of the church of **St-Pierre.** The town's chief attraction, the high-roof **Vieil Hôpital,** or Hôtel-Dieu (hospital), was built in 1293 and has survived the passing centuries—flames and all—largely intact. The main room, the **Grande Salle,** is 280 feet long and retains its oak ceiling; it was designed as the hospital ward and after 1650 served as the parish church. The original hospital church leads off from the Grande Salle; in the adjoining **Chapelle du Revestière,** a dramatic 15th-century stone group represents the *Entombment of Christ.* ✉ *Rue du Prieuré* ☎ *03–86–55–14–48* 🖃 *€4* ⊘ *June–Sept., Wed.–Mon. 10–noon and 1:30–6:30; Apr., May, Oct., and Nov., weekends 1:30–6:30.*

Tanlay

⑲ *10 km (6 mi) east of Tonnerre.*

Fodor'sChoice A masterpiece of the French early Baroque, the **Château de Tanlay,** built
★ around 1550, is a miraculous survivor due to the fact, unlike most aristos who fled the countryside to take up the royal summons to live at Versailles, the Marquis and Marquise de Tanlay opted to live here among their village retainers. Spectacularly adorned with rusticated obelisks, pagodalike towers, the finest in French Classicist ornament, and a "grand canal," the château is centered around a typical *cour d'honneur.* Inside, the Hall of Caesars vestibule, framed by wrought-iron railings, leads to a wood-panel salon and dining room filled with period furniture. A graceful staircase climbs to the second floor, which has the showstopper—a gigantic gallery frescoed in Italianate trompe l'oeil. A small room in the tower above was used as a secret meeting-place by Huguenot Protestants during the 1562–98 Wars of Religion; note the cupola with its fresco of scantily clad 16th-century religious personalities. ☎ *03–86–75–70–61* ⊕ *www.chateaudetanlay.com* 🖃 *Guided tours €8; grounds only €2.50* ⊘ *Apr.–Oct., Wed.–Mon. 9:30, 10:30, 11:30 and 2:15, 3:15, 4:15, 5:15.*

Where to Stay

¢ 🖼 **Poste.** Set in the lovely hilltop farming village of Cruzy-le-Chatel, 12 km (7 mi) from Tanlay, this inn comes with its own walled garden. Rooms are large and filled with family furnishings; beds sag a little. Nonetheless, the rooms are good value for the money, especially the one at the end of the hall, whose exposed timbers and crossbeams form a sort of loft. ⊠ *30 rue de la Ville, 89740 Cruzy-le-Chatel* ☎ *03–86–75–23–27* 🛏 *4 rooms, 2 with bath* ▤ *No credit cards* ⫿○⫿ *BP.*

Ancy-le-Franc

⑳ *14 km (9 mi) southeast of Tanlay.*

It may be strange to find a textbook example of the Italian Renaissance in Ancy-le-Franc but in mid-16th-century France the court had taken up this import as the latest rage. So, quick to follow the fashion and gain kingly favor, the Comte de Tonnerre decided to create a family seat using all the artists François I (1515–47) had imported from Italy to his court at Fontainebleau. Built from Sebastiano Serlio's designs, with interior blandishments by Primaticcio, the **Château d'Ancy-le-Franc** is an important example of Italianism, less for its plain, heavy exterior than for its sumptuous rooms and apartments, many—particularly the magnificent Chambre des Arts (Art Gallery)—with carved or painted walls and ceilings and original furnishings. Here, Niccolo dell'Abate and other court artists created rooms filled with murals, depicting the signs of the zodiac, the Battle of Pharsala, and the motif of Diana in Her Bath (much favored by Diane de Poitiers, sister of the Comtesse de Tonnerre)— some of the finest examples of French Mannerism. Such grandeur won the approval of the Sun King, Louis XIV, no less, who once stayed in the Salon Bleu (Blue Room). ⊠ *Pl. Clermont-Tonnerre* ☎ *03–86–75–14–63* ⊕ *www.chateau-ancy.com* 🖃€8 🕙 *Early Apr.–mid-Nov., guided château tours Wed.–Mon. at 10:30, 11:30, 2, 3, 4, and 5; last one at 4 Oct.–mid-Nov.*

FodorśChoice
★

Abbaye de Fontenay

㉑ *32 km (20 mi) southeast of Ancy-le-Franc.*

FodorśChoice
★

The best-preserved of the Cistercian abbeys, the Abbaye de Fontenay, was founded in 1118 by St. Bernard. The same Cistercian criteria applied to Fontenay as to Pontigny: no-frills architecture and an isolated site—the spot was especially remote, for it had been decreed that these monasteries could not be established anywhere near "cities, feudal manors, or villages." The monks were required to live a completely self-sufficient existence, with no contact whatsoever with the outside world. By the end of the 12th century the buildings were finished, and the abbey's community grew to some 300 monks. Under the protection of Pope Gregory IX and Hughes IV, duke of Burgundy, the monastery soon controlled huge land holdings, vineyards, and timberlands. It prospered until the 16th century, when religious wars and administrative mayhem hastened its decline. Dissolved during the French Revolution, the abbey was used as a paper factory until 1906. Fortunately, the historic buildings emerged unscathed. The abbey is surrounded by extensive, immaculately-tended gardens dotted with the fountains that gave it its name. The church's solemn interior is lightened by windows in the facade and by a double row of three narrow windows, representing the Trinity, in the choir. A staircase in the south transept leads to the wood-roofed dormitory (spare a thought for the bleary-eyed monks, obliged to stagger down for services in the dead of night). The chapter house, flanked by a majestic arcade, and the scriptorium, where monks worked on their manuscripts, lead off from the adjoining cloisters. ⊠ *Marmagne* ☎ *03–80–92–15–00* ⊕ *www.abbayedefontenay.com* ⊠ *€8.70* ⊙ *Apr.–Oct., 10–5:30; Nov.–Mar., daily 10–noon and 2–5.*

Avallon

㉒ *44 km (28 mi) southwest of the Abbaye de Fontenay.*

Avallon is on a spectacular promontory jutting over the Vallée du Cousin. Its old streets and ramparts are pleasant places to stroll, and its medieval market-town ambience is appealing. It has enough cafés, bars, and shops to seem lively, yet it's small enough that you can quickly become familiar with it and turn it into your base for exploring the region. The main sight is the work of Romanesque stone carvers whose imaginations ran riot on the portals and 15th-century belfry of the venerable church of **St-Lazare.**

Where to Stay & Eat

★ ¢–$ ✕**Relais des Gourmets.** You can no longer stay at the former Hôtel de Paris, which dates from the days when Avallon was a stopping-off point for stagecoaches, but you can still get a great meal at a reasonable price. This is the liveliest restaurant in Avallon, with excellent regionally inspired cuisine and an especially attractive patio in summer. The €17 weekday menu, with wine, is a sumptuous steal. ⊠ *47 rue de Paris* ☎ *03–86–34–18–90* ▤ *AE, MC, V* ⊙ *Closed Sun. night and Mon.*

$$–$$$ ✕▥**Moulin des Ruats.** Once an old flour mill, the Moulin des Ruats became a family hotel in 1924 and is now a comfortable country inn run by Jocelyne Rossiand and her husband-chef Jean-Pierre. Guest rooms are pretty country-French in style; some have balconies overlooking the Cousin River. Ask for one that has been renovated; No. 11, for instance, with its exposed beams and a cozy alcove. The restaurant, fronting the river, serves traditional Burgundian fare with a strong Provençal accent (it's closed Monday, and serves lunch only on Sunday). Be forewarned that dishes can be uneven: you're better off choosing simple rather than complex preparations, although you can't go wrong with the foie gras salad. ⊠ *4 km (2½ mi) southwest of Avallon, 89200 Vallée du Cousin* ☎ *03–86–34–97–00* ▤ *03–86–31–65–47* ⊕ *www.hostellerie-moulin-ruats.fr* ⇥ *24 rooms, 1 suite* ⌂ *Restaurant; no a/c* ▤ *AE, DC, MC, V* ⊙ *Closed Dec. and Jan.* ▥⊘ *MAP.*

$ ▥**Avallon-Vauban.** This sturdy, flower-bedecked stone mansion is close to the historic town center and has airy, pastel-shaded rooms with cherrywood furniture. The quietest rooms overlook the spacious garden. ⊠ *53 rue de Paris, 89200* ☎ *03–86–31–66–31* ▤ *03–86–34–36–99* ⊕ *www. avallonvaubanhotel.com* ⇥ *26 rooms* ⌂ *No a/c* ▤ *AE, DC, V.*

Vézelay

❷ *16 km (10 mi) west of Avallon.*

In the 11th and 12th centuries one of the most important places of pilgrimage in the Christian world, hilltop Vézelay today is a picturesque, somewhat isolated, village. Its one main street, rue St-Étienne, climbs steeply and stirringly to the summit and its medieval basilica, world-famous for its Romanesque sculpture. In summer you have to leave your car at the bottom and walk up. Off-season you can drive up and look for a spot to park in the square.

It's easy to ignore this tiny village, but don't: hidden under its narrow *ruelles* (small streets) are Romanesque cellars that once sheltered pilgrims and are now opened to visitors by home owners in summer. Sections of several houses have arches and columns dating from the 12th and 13th centuries: don't miss the hostelry across from the tourist office and, next to it, the house where Louis VII, Eleanor of Aquitaine, and the king's religious supremo Abbé Suger stayed when they came to hear St. Bernard preach the Second Crusade in 1146.

In the 11th and 12th centuries the celebrated **Basilique Ste-Madeleine** was one of the focal points of Christendom. Pilgrims poured in to see the relics of St. Mary Magdalene (in the crypt) before setting off on the great trek to the shrine of St. James at Santiago de Compostela, in northwest Spain. Several pivotal church declarations of the Middle Ages were made from here, including St. Bernard's preaching of the Second Crusade (which attracted a huge French following) and Thomas à Becket's excommunication of English king Henry II. By the mid-13th century the authenticity of St. Mary's relics was in doubt; others had been discovered in Provence. The basilica's decline continued until the French Revolution, when the basilica and adjoining monastery buildings were sold by the state. Only the basilica, cloister, and dormitory escaped demolition, and were falling into ruin when ace restorer Viollet-le-Duc, sent by his mentor Prosper Merimée, rode to the rescue in 1840 (he also restored the cathedrals of Laon and Amiens and Paris's Notre-Dame).

Today the UNESCO-listed basilica has recaptured much of its glory and is considered to be one of France's most prestigious Romanesque showcases. The exterior tympanum was redone by Viollet-le-Duc (have a look at the eroded original as you exit the cloister), but the narthex (circa 1150) is a Romanesque masterpiece. Note the interwoven zodiac signs and depictions of seasonal crafts along its rim, similar to those at both Troyes and Autun. The pilgrims' route around the building is indicated by the majestic flowers over the left-hand entrance, which metamorphose into full-blown blooms on the right; an annual procession is still held on July 22. Among the most beautiful scenes on the nave capitals is one of Moses grinding grain (symbolizing the Old Testament) into flour (the New Testament), which St. Paul collects in a sack.

The basilica's exterior is best seen from the leafy terrace to the right of the facade. Opposite, a vast, verdant panorama encompasses vines, lush valleys and rolling hills. In the foreground is the Flamboyant Gothic spire of St-Père-sous-Vézelay, a tiny village 3 km (2 mi) away that is the site of Marc Meneau's famed restaurant. ⊠ *Pl. de la Basilique* ☎ *03–86–33–39–50* ⊕ *www.vezelaytourisme.com* ✑ *Free, donation of €3 for guided visit* ☉ *Daily 8–8, except during offices Mon.–Sat. 12:30–1:15 and 6–7, Sun. 11–12:15.*

Just 10 km (6 mi) out of Vézelay in the small town of Bazoches-du-Morvan is the **Château de Bazoches,** the former home of Sébastien de Vauban. Built in the 12th century in the stolid form of a trapezium with four storybook towers and a keep, the building was bought by Vauban in 1675 with the money Louis XIV awarded him for devising the parallel trenches successfully used in the siege of Maastricht. Vauban transformed the building into a fortress and created many of his military engineering designs here. Vauban is considered the "father of civil engineering" and his innovations influenced innumerable forts throughout France. His designs and furnishings of his day are on display. ⊠ *Bazoches-du-Morvan* ☎ *03–86–22–10–22* ⊕ *www.chateau-bazoches.com* ✑ *Free* ☉ *Late Mar.–early Nov., daily 9:30–noon and 2:15–6.*

Where to Stay & Eat

¢–$ ✕ **Bougainville.** One of the few affordable restaurants in this well-heeled town is in an old house with a fireplace in the dining room and the requisite Burgundian color scheme of brown, yellow, and ocher. Philippe Guillemard presides in the kitchen, turning out such regional favorites as hare stew, crayfish, escargot ragout in chardonnay sauce, and venison with chestnuts. He has also devised a vegetarian menu—a rarity in Burgundy—with deeply satisfying dishes like terrine of Époisses cheese and artichokes. ⊠ *26 rue St-Etienne* ☎ *03–86–33–27–57* ▤ *MC, V* ☉ *Closed Tues., Wed., and mid-Nov.–mid-Feb.*

★ $$$–$$$$ ✕▥ **L'Espérance.** Heading one of the greatest kitchens in Burgundy, chef Marc Meneau is justly renowned for his original creations, such as roast veal in a bitter caramel-based sauce and turbot in a salt-crust *croûte*. The setting—by a stream and a large, statue-filled garden with Vézelay in the background—is exquisite. Note that the restaurant is closed Tuesday mid-September through mid-June and there is no lunch Wednesday. Accommodations, which vary in price, come in a trinity of delights: charming rooms overlooking the garden; full suites in a renovated mill by the trout stream; and rooms in the annex, the Pré des Marguerites, are done up in a cozy *style anglais.* ⊠ *St-Père-en-Vézelay, 89450 St-Père* ☎ *03–86–33–39–10* ▤ *03–86–33–26–15* ⊕ *www.marc-meneau.com* ⌂ *Reservations essential* ⇥ *44 rooms* ↺ *Restaurant, minibars, cable TV, pool, Internet; no a/c in some rooms* ▤ *AE, DC, MC, V* ☉ *Closed Feb.* ❙⊙❙ *MAP.*

$–$$$ ✕▥ **Poste & Lion d'Or.** On a small square in the lower part of town is this old-fashioned, rambling hotel. A terrace out front welcomes you; the good-size rooms have traditional chintzes. The comfortable restaurant is a popular spot with locals, who come for the regional fare, such as roast partridge in black-currant sauce and rabbit casserole. ⊠ *Pl. du Champ de Foire, 89450* ☎ *03–86–33–21–23* ▤ *03–86–32–30–92* ⊕ *www.laposte-liondor.com* ⇥ *39 rooms* ↺ *Restaurant, bar; no a/c* ▤ *AE, MC, V* ☉ *Closed mid-Nov.–mid-Mar.* ❙⊙❙ *MAP.*

$$–$$$ ▢ **Pontot.** With Vézelay's limited lodging you would do well to book ahead, especially for this historic fortified house with sumptuous little rooms and a lovely garden. Another advantage is the hotel's location in the center of the village halfway up the hill. ⊠ *Pl. du Pontot, 89450* ☎ *03–86–33–24–40* 📠 *03–86–33–30–05* 🛏 *10 rooms* ♿ *No a/c, no room TVs* ▭ *DC, MC, V* ☻ *Closed mid-Nov.–mid-Apr.*

The Morvan

❷❹ *South of Vézelay.*

The vast **Parc du Morvan** encompasses a 3,500-square-km (1,350-square-mi) chunk of Burgundy. A network of roads and **Grandes Randonnées** (GRs, or Long Trails) winds around the park's lush forests, granite outcrops, photogenic lakes, idyllic farms, and tiny villages. Hiking in the Morvan is not strenuous, but it is enchanting: every turn down a trail provides a new idyllic scene. Numerous itineraries through the park are mapped and marked (maps for specific trails are available from local tourist offices). About 50 5- to 15-km (3- to 9-mi) routes are good for day hikes; another dozen trails of over 100 km (60 mi) each are good for much longer walks.

Quarré-les-Tombes, one of the prettiest villages peppering the park, is so named because of the empty prehistoric stone tombs eerily arrayed in a ring around its church. Eight kilometers (5 mi) south of Quarré-les-Tombes is the **Rocher de la Pérouse,** a mighty rocky outcrop worth scrambling up for a view of the park and the Cure and Cousin valleys.

Some 25 **gîtes d'étape** (simple B&Bs, also known as *chambres d'hôte*) en route provide for overnight stays (☎ 03–86–78–74–93 reservations). Twenty-one gîtes have facilities for you and your horse to stay overnight. For the pamphlet "Le Morvan à Cheval," which lists stables and gîtes for overnight accommodations, contact the **Parc Naturel Régional du Morvan** (⊠ Maison du Parc, St-Brisson ☎ 03–86–78–79–00 📠 03–86–78–74–22). Horses can be rented from several stables: **La Ferme des Ruats** (⊠ Off N6, between St-Emilion and Bussières ☎ 03–86–33–16–57); **Le Triangle** (⊠ Usy ☎ 03–86–33–32–78); and **La Vieille Diligence** (⊠ Rive Droite, Lac des Settons, 58230 Montsauche ☎ 03–86–84–55–22).

Saulieu

❷❺ *29 km (17 mi) southeast of Quarré-les-Tombes.*

Saulieu's reputation belies its size: it is renowned for good food (Rabelais, that roly-poly 16th-century man of letters, extolled its gargantuan hospitality) and Christmas trees (a staggering million are packed and sent off from the area each year). The town's **Basilique St-Andoche** (⊠ Pl. du Docteur Roclore) is almost as old as that of Vézelay, though less imposing and much restored. Note the Romanesque capitals. The **Musée François-Pompon,** adjoining the basilica, is a museum partly devoted to the work of animal-bronze sculptor Pompon (1855–1933), whose smooth, stylized creations seem contemporary but predate World War

II. The museum also contains Gallo-Roman funeral stones, sacred art, and a room devoted to local gastronomic lore. ⊠ *Rue Sallier* ☎ *03–80–64–19–51* 🎫 *€4* ⊙ *Apr.–Sept., Wed.–Mon. 10–12:30 and 2–6; Oct.–Mar., Wed.–Mon. 10–12:30 and 2–5:30.*

Where to Stay & Eat

★ **$$$$** ✕🏠 **Relais Bernard Loiseau.** Originally a historic coaching auberge, this is now one of the region's finest hotels and restaurants, celebrated as the home base for chef Bernard Loiseau, one of France's culinary superstars, who took his life in early 2003. Loiseau made his mark by offering up a feather-light nouvelle version of rich Burgundian fare, and he is sorely missed. Despite this tragedy, the restaurant (no lunch Wednesday) and hotel continue to receive guests under the direction of Dominique Loiseau and chef Patrick Bertron. The setting is exquisite: a chapel-like wood-beam dining room with a lush flower garden radiating around it. Guest rooms combine exposed beams and glass panels with cheerful traditional furnishings; a newer annex has the most comfortable (and air-conditioned) rooms, while the more stylish accommodations (styles range from Louis XVI to Empire) are in the main house. Some are tiny (one is complete with porthole window), some are luxurious (one has a comfy balcony overlooking the countryside)—no matter which you book, try to get a room facing the garden courtyard. ⊠ *2 rue d'Argentine, off N6, 21210 Saulieu* ☎ *03–80–90–53–53* 🖷 *03–80–64–08–92* ⊕ *www.bernard-loiseau.com* ↘ *33 rooms* ♻ *Restaurant, cable TV, health club, Internet, meeting room; no a/c in some rooms* 🖃 *AE, DC, MC, V* ⊙ *Closed Tues.* 🍴 *BP.*

$ ✕🏠 **Chez Camille.** Small, quiet, and friendly sum up this hotel in a 16th-century house with an exterior so ordinary you might easily pass it by. But within, rooms have period furniture and original wooden beams; ask for No. 22 or No. 23, the most dramatic, with a beamed ceiling that looks like spokes in a wheel. Traditional Burgundian fare—duck and boar are specialties—makes up the menu in the glass-roof restaurant with its green wicker chairs. ⊠ *1 pl. Édouard-Herriot, on N6 between Saulieu and Beaune, 21230 Arnay-le-Duc* ☎ *03–80–90–01–38* 🖷 *03–80–90–04–64* ⊕ *http://chez-camille.fr* ↘ *11 rooms* ♻ *Restaurant, cable TV, Internet; no a/c* 🖃 *AE, DC, MC, V* 🍴 *MAP.*

Châteauneuf

㉖ *36 km (23 mi) east of Saulieu.*

The hilltop village of Châteauneuf catches your eye from A6. Turn off at Pouilly-en-Auxois and take any one of the three narrow, winding roads up, and you'll suddenly feel you've entered the Middle Ages. The town's modest 15th-century church ministered to as many as 500 souls when the village was at its zenith. In the last few years tourists have discovered the charm of this village, so try to avoid it on weekends. The **château,** built in the 12th and 15th centuries (with some later modifications), commands a broad view over rolling farmland as far as the eye can see. Clustered behind the château are houses for ordinary folk, at least a score of them notable for their 14th- and 15th-century charm, where today only about 80 people live. One of these, the charming **Mon-**

sieur Simon (☎ 03–80–49–21–59), is so proud of his village that he gladly takes small groups on tours of the sights. ☎ *03–80–49–21–89* 🖃 *€4.60* ⊗ *Apr.–Sept., Tues.–Sun. 9:30–12:30 and 2–6; Oct.–Mar., Tues.–Sun. 10–noon and 2–6.*

Where to Stay & Eat

$$$–$$$$ ✕🏨 **Château La Chassagne.** Feel like a king or a queen for a night at this stylish domain 12 km (7 mi) from Châteauneuf, close to the junction of A38 and A6; you can even arrive by private plane or helicopter and be picked up in a Rolls-Royce. Rooms have high ceilings and are spacious; the modern iron-and-cane furnishings are obviously expensive, but of somewhat questionable taste. The grounds include a golf range, tennis court, and swimming pool. Nouvelle cuisine is served in the restaurant, but the chef seems to focus more on artistic presentation than creative flavoring. ⊠ *900 chemin de Chassagne, 21410 Pont-de-Pany* ☎ *03–80–49–76–00* 🖷 *03–80–49–76–19* ⊕ *www.chateau-chassagne. com* 🛏 *11 rooms* 🍴 *Restaurant, cable TV, driving range, 2 tennis courts, pool; no a/c* ☰ *AE, DC, MC, V* ⊗ *Closed Nov.–Mar.* ⦿ *MAP.*

¢–$ ✕🏨 **Hostellerie du Château.** This hotel is in an ancient timbered building in the shadow of the town castle. The restaurant serves classical Bourgogne fare—roasted Époisses (local cow's-milk cheese) on a salad bed with walnuts, noisettes of lamb with thyme, and coq au vin; it's closed Tuesday and doesn't serve dinner Monday, except in July and August. Rooms vary considerably—from small to commodious; the best have a view of the castle. ⊠ *Rue du Centre, 21320* ☎ *03–80–49–22–00* 🖷 *03–80–49–21–27* ⊕ *www.hostellerie-chateauneuf.com* 🛏 *17 rooms* 🍴 *Restaurant; no a/c, no room phones, no room TVs* ☰ *AE, DC, MC, V* ⊗ *Closed late Nov.–early Feb.*

DIJON

38 km (23 mi) northeast of Châteauneuf, 315 km (195 mi) southeast of Paris.

The erstwhile wine-mustard center of the world, site of an important university, and studded with medieval art treasures, Dijon—linked to Paris by expressway (A6/A38) and the high-speed TGV (Train à Grande Vitesse)—is the age-old capital of Burgundy. Throughout the Middle Ages, Burgundy was a duchy that led a separate existence from the rest of France, culminating in the rule of the four "Grand Dukes of the West" between 1364 and 1477—Philippe le Hardi (the Bold), Jean Sans Peur (the Fearless), Philippe le Bon (the Good), and the unfortunate Charles le Téméraire (the Foolhardy, whose defeat by French king Louis XI at Nancy spelled the end of Burgundian independence). A number of monuments date from this period, including the Palais des Ducs (Ducal Palace), now largely converted into an art museum. The city has magnificent half-timber houses and *hôtels particuliers,* some rivaling those in Paris. There's also a striking trio of central churches, built one following the other for three distinct parishes—St-Bénigne, its facade distinguished by Gothic galleries; St-Philibert, Dijon's only Romanesque church (with Merovingian vestiges); and St-Jean, an asymmetrical building now used as a theater.

Dijon's fame and fortune outlasted its dukes, and the city continued to flourish under French rule from the 17th century on. It has remained the major city of Burgundy—and the only one with more than 150,000 inhabitants. Its site, on the major European north–south trade route and within striking distance of the Swiss and German borders, has helped maintain its economic importance. It's also a cultural center—just a portion of its museums are mentioned below. And many of the gastronomic specialties that originated here are known worldwide, although unfortunately the Dijon traditions have largely passed into legend. They include snails (now, shockingly, mainly imported from the Czech Republic), mustard (the handmade variety is a lost art), and cassis (a black-currant liqueur often mixed with white wine—preferably Burgundy Aligoté—to make *kir,* the popular aperitif).

The Historic Center

a good walk

Begin at the **Palais des Ducs** ㉗ ⌐, Dijon's leading testimony to bygone splendor; these days it contains a major art museum. Cross to the left side of place de la Libération and take rue des Bons-Enfants, where you'll find the **Musée Magnin** ㉘, with exhibits of furniture and paintings. Continue on to rue Philippe-Pot to see the elegant **Chambre des Métiers** ㉙. Just south of here is the **Palais de Justice** ㉚, with its elaborate Baroque facade. Turn onto rue Jean-Baptiste-Liégeard, where the imposing pink-and-yellow limestone Hôtel Legouz de Gerland watches over the street from its distinctive *échauguettes* (watchtowers). Return to rue de la Liberté to get to the church of **St-Michel** ㉛. West of here, behind the palace, is **Notre-Dame** ㉜, one of the city's oldest churches. The rue Verrerie, behind Notre-Dame and the Palais des Ducs, is lined with half-timber houses. Facing the church on rue de la Chouette is the elegant **Hôtel de Vogüé** ㉝. Walk from here to the somewhat plain **Cathédrale St-Bénigne** ㉞. In the former abbey of St-Bénigne is the **Musée Archéologique** ㉟. The former Cistercian convent houses the **Musée de la Vie Bourguignonne & d'Art Sacré** ㊱. Behind the train station is the **Musée d'Histoire Naturelle** ㊲, in the lovely Jardin de l'Arquebuse, the botanical garden. More links with Dijon's medieval past can be found west of the town center, beyond the train station, just off avenue Albert-Ier, including the gateway to the celebrated **Chartreuse de Champmol** ㊳, where the spotlight is held by the Claus Sluter masterpiece, the *Puits de Moïse* (*Well of Moses*).

What to See

㉞ **Cathédrale St-Bénigne.** The chief glory of this comparatively austere cathedral is its atmospheric 11th-century crypt—a forest of pillars surmounted by a rotunda. ✉ *Pl. St-Bénigne.*

㉙ **Chambre des Métiers.** This stately mansion with Gallo-Roman stelae incorporated into the walls (a quirky touch) was built in the 19th century. ✉ *Rue Philippe-Pot.*

★ ㊳ **Chartreuse de Champmol.** All that remains of this former charterhouse—a half-hour walk from Dijon's center and now surrounded by a psychiatric hospital—are the exuberant 15th-century gateway and the *Puits de Moïse* (*Well of Moses*), one of the greatest examples of late-medieval

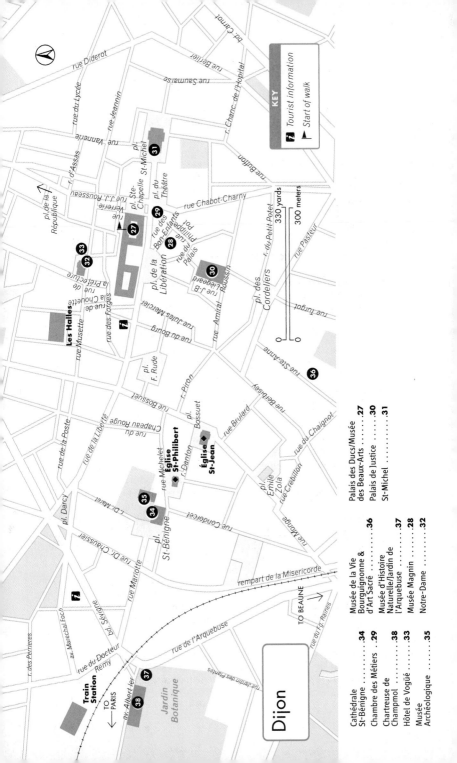

Dijon

KEY

ℹ️ *Tourist information*

▲ *Start of walk*

Cathédrale
St-Bénigne **34**

Chambre des Métiers . . . **29**

Chartreuse de
Champmol **38**

Hôtel de Vogüé **33**

Musée
Archéologique **35**

Musée de la Vie
Bourguignonne &
d'Art Sacré **36**

Musée d'Histoire
Naturelle/Jardin de
l'Arquebuse **37**

Musée Magnin **28**

Notre-Dame **35**

Palais des Ducs/Musée
des Beaux-Arts **27**

Palais de Justice **30**

St-Michel **31**

CloseUp

BURGUNDY BIGTIME

WITH NO CITY LARGER THAN THE CAPITAL DIJON (population 150,000), Burgundy seems the sleepy epitome of La France Profonde. Yet Dijon is one of the richest cities in France, and top European medieval painter Rogier van der Weyden stars down the road in Beaune. How come? Because, from 1369 to 1477, Burgundy hit the big time as an independent European power. In 1369, Philip II of Burgundy, then a minor duchy smaller than today's administrative region, married Marguerite de Flandre. She brought Nevers, Franche-Comté, and French Flanders with her as dowry. Burgundy prospered. In 1435, the Peace of Arras, signed with France, recognized Burgundy's further claims to Belgium, Picardy, and the Netherlands. The Duchy now extended up past Amsterdam to the Friesian Islands—the nearest the Burgundians ever came to regaining their Viking roots. Burgundy's

capital moved from Dijon to Brussels where, in 1436, Van der Weyden was appointed official city painter. In 1443 the art-loving Burgundian Chancellor Nicolas Rolin commissioned the Last Judgment from Van der Weyden that still hangs in Beaune's Hôtel Dieu. Burgundy bought Luxembourg off the Habsburgs the same year. Everything in the vineyard looked rosy, but there was just one problem: the northern and southern ends of Burgundy remained asunder, with Lorraine in between. When Charles the Bold succeeded Philip the Good in 1467, conquering Lorraine was top priority. Charles snatched part of Lorraine in 1475, but was slain two years later laying siege to Nancy. French King Louis XI seized the chance to invade Burgundy to annex it for the French crown. Charles' daughter Mary married Maximilian of Habsburg, taking Flanders and Holland with her. The Duchy of Burgundy had passed into the wine-vat of history.

sculpture. The well was designed by Flemish master Claus Sluter, who also created several other masterpieces during the late 14th and early 15th centuries, including the tombs of the dukes of Burgundy. If you closely study Sluter's six large sculptures, you will discover the Middle Ages becoming the Renaissance right before your eyes. Representing Moses and five other prophets, they are set on a hexagonal base in the center of a basin and remain the most compellingly realistic figures ever crafted by a medieval sculptor.

㉝ Hôtel de Vogüé. This stately 17th-century mansion has a characteristic red, yellow, and green Burgundian tile roof—a tradition whose disputed origins lie either with the Crusades and the adoption of Arabic tiles or with Philip the Bold's wife, Marguerite of Flanders. ⊠ *Rue de la Chouette.*

㉟ Musée Archéologique (Antiquities Museum). This museum, in the former abbey buildings of the church of St-Bénigne, traces the history of the region through archaeological finds. ⊠ *5 rue du Dr-Maret* ☎ *03–80–30–88–54* ✆ *Free* ☉ *June–Sept., Wed.–Mon. 9:30–6; Oct.–May, Wed.–Sun. 9–12:30 and 1:35–6.*

㊱ Musée de la Vie Bourguignonne & d'Art Sacré (Museum of Burgundian Traditions & Religious Art). Housed in the former Cistercian convent, one museum contains religious art and sculpture; the other has crafts and artifacts from Burgundy, including old storefronts saved from the streets of Dijon that have been reconstituted, Hollywood moviemaking style, to form an imaginary street. ⊠ *17 rue Ste-Anne* ☎ *03–80–44–12–69* ⌚ *Free* ☉ *May–Sept., Wed.–Mon. 9–6; Oct.–Apr., Wed.–Mon. 9–noon and 2–6.*

㊲ Musée d'Histoire Naturelle (Natural History Museum). The museum is in the impressive botanical garden, the **Jardin de l'Arquebuse,** a pleasant place to stroll amid the wide variety of trees and tropical flowers. ⊠ *1 av. Albert-Ier* ☎ *03–80–76–82–76 museum, 03–80–76–82–84 garden* ⌚ *Free* ☉ *Museum Wed.–Fri. and Mon. 9–noon and 2–6; weekends, 2–6; garden daily 7:30–6; until 8 PM in summer.*

㉘ Musée Magnin. In a 17th-century mansion, this museum showcases a private collection of original furnishings and paintings from the 16th to the 19th centuries. ⊠ *4 rue des Bons-Enfants* ☎ *03–80–67–11–10* ⌚ *€3* ☉ *Tues.–Sun. 10–noon and 2–6.*

㉜ Notre-Dame. One of the city's oldest churches, Notre-Dame stands out with its spindlelike towers, delicate arches gracing its facade, and 13th-century stained glass. Note the windows in the north transept tracing the lives of five saints, as well as the 11th-century Byzantine cedar Black Virgin. ⊠ *Rue de la Préfecture.*

> **need a break?**
>
> A pieman in Burgundy? Come taste his wares! For a quick *grignotage* (nibble) between meals or full-on Sunday brunch, **Simple Simon** (⊠ 4 rue de la Chouette) is the best address in town, and the only one in the entire region to offer such non-Burgundian delicacies as cheese and onion pie and buttered scones. Run by expat Brits, this is the ideal spot for a break or breakfast.

▶ **㉗ Palais des Ducs** (Ducal Palace). The elegant, classical exterior of the former palace can best be admired from the half-moon place de la Libération and the Cour d'Honneur. The **kitchens** (circa 1450), with their six huge fireplaces and (for its time) state-of-the-art aeration funnel in the ceiling, and the 14th-century **chapter house** catch the eye, as does the 15th-century **Salle des Gardes** (Guard Room), with its richly carved and colored tombs and late-14th-century altarpieces. The palace now houses one of France's major art museums, the **Musée des Beaux-Arts** (Fine Arts Museum). Here are displayed the magnificent tombs sculpted by celebrated artist Claus Sluter for dukes Philip the Bold and his son John the Fearless—note their dramatically moving mourners, hidden in shrouds. These are just two of the highlights of a rich collection of medieval objects and Renaissance furniture gathered here as testimony to Marguerite of Flanders, wife of Philip the Bold, who brought to Burgundy not only her dowry, the rich province of Flanders (modern-day Belgium), but also a host of distinguished artists—including Rogier van der Weyden, Jan van Eyck, and Claus Sluter. Their artistic legacy can be seen in this collection, as well as at several of Burgundy's other museums and monuments. Among the paintings are works by Italian Old Masters and

FodorśChoice ★

French 19th-century artists, such as Théodore Géricault and Gustave Courbet, and their Impressionist successors, notably Édouard Manet and Claude Monet. ⊠ *Rue Rameau* ☎ *03–80–74–52–70* 🖃 *Free* 🕙 *Wed.–Mon. 10–5.*

㉚ Palais de Justice. The meeting place for the old regional Parliament of Burgundy serves as a reminder that Louis XI incorporated the province into France in the late 15th century. ⊠ *Rue du Palais.*

㉛ St-Michel. This church, with its chunky Renaissance facade, fast-forwards 300 years from Notre-Dame. ⊠ *Pl. St-Michel.*

Where to Stay & Eat

As a culinary capital of France, Dijon has many superb restaurants, with three areas popular for casual dining. One is around place Darcy, a square catering to all tastes and budgets: choose from the bustling Concorde brasserie, the quiet bar of the Hôtel de la Cloche, the underground Caveau de la Porte Guillaume wine-and-snack bar, or—for your sweet tooth— the Pâtisserie Darcy. For a really inexpensive meal, try the cafeteria Le Flunch on boulevard de Brosses (near place Darcy). Two other areas for casual dining in the evening are place Émile-Zola and the old market (Les Halles), along rue Bannelier.

★ **$$$$** ✗ **Stéphane Derbord.** From starters like crawfish tails with anise or duck foie gras with gingerbread, to entrées like sizzling Charolais beef with ham and onions, and to desserts such as rice pudding topped with caramelized spices, the talented Derbord, the city's rising gastronomic star, ensures dinner in this Art Deco restaurant is an elegantly refined affair. ⊠ *10 pl. Wilson* ☎ *03–80–67–74–64* ⊕ *www.restaurantstephanederbord.fr* 🍴 *Reservations essential* 👔 *Jacket and tie* 🖃 *MC, V* 🕙 *Closed Sun., early Jan., and Aug. No lunch Mon. or Tues.*

★ **$$$–$$$$** ✗ **Le Pré aux Clercs.** This bright and beautiful Napoléon III–style restaurant is the perfect showcase for chef Jean-Pierre Billoux's golden touch, which can turn the lowliest farmyard chicken into a palate-plucking pièce de résistance. Most house specialties are inventive, like the langoustines with sherry vinaigrette or, to finish with, the roast pear with spices. The welcome is always convivial, and the wine list reads like a who's who of the region's best—but not necessarily best-known—winemakers. The €36 lunch menu (including wine) is a startling introduction to modern Burgundian cuisine. ⊠ *13 pl. de la Libération* ☎ *03–80–38–05–05* 🍴 *Reservations essential* 🖃 *AE, DC, MC, V* 🕙 *Closed Mon. No dinner Sun.*

★ **$$–$$$** ✗ **La Dame d'Aquitaine.** In a happy marriage between two of France's greatest gastronomic regions, chef Monique Saléra, from Pau, and her Dijonnais husband create a wonderful blend of regional cuisines. The foie gras and duck, in confit or with cêpes, come from Saléra's native region; the coq au vin, snails, and *lapin à la moutarde* (rabbit with mustard) from her husband's Burgundy; the *magret de canard aux baies de cassis* (duck breast with cassis berries) is a hybrid. The moderate prixfixe menus, starting at €19, offer succulent value. ⊠ *23 pl. Bossuet* ☎ *03–80–30–45–65* 🍴 *Reservations essential* 🖃 *AE, DC, MC, V* 🕙 *Closed Sun. No lunch Mon.*

$$–$$$ ✕ **Les Oenophiles.** A collection of superbly restored 17th-century buildings belonging to the Burgundian Company of Wine Tasters forms the backdrop to this pleasant restaurant. It is lavishly furnished but also quaint (candlelight in the evening). The food is good, especially the roast pheasant with mushrooms, the langoustines with ginger, and the nougat-and-honey dessert. After dinner you can visit the small wine museum in the cellar. ⊠ *18 rue Ste-Anne* ☎ *03–80–30–73–52* ✍ *Reservations essential* ☖ *Jacket required* ▭ *AE, DC, MC, V* ☻ *No dinner Sun.*

$–$$ ✕ **Le Bistrot des Halles.** Of the many restaurants in the area, this one is the best value. Well-prepared dishes range from escargots to boeuf Bourguignon with braised endive. Dine either at the sidewalk tables or inside, where traditional French decor—mirrors and polished wood—predominates. ⊠ *10 rue Bannelier* ☎ *03–80–49–94–15* ▭ *MC, V* ☻ *No dinner Sun.*

$$$ ✕☷ **Hostellerie du Chapeau Rouge.** A piano player in the bar and an elegant staircase give this hotel a degree of charm that the rooms, though clean and well appointed, lack. The restaurant, renowned as a haven of classic regional cuisine, serves snails cooked in basil and stuffed pigeon. The staff and owner William Frachot are attentive. ⊠ *5 rue Michelet, 21000* ☎ *03–80–50–88–88* ☷ *03–80–50–88–89* ⊕ *www.bourgogne. net/chapeaurouge* ✍ *26 rooms, 4 suites* ☖ *Restaurant, bar, Internet* ▭ *AE, DC, MC, V.*

$$$–$$$$ ☷ **La Cloche.** In use since the 19th century, La Cloche is a successful cross between a luxury chain and a grand hotel. The entry hall is imposing, and the gleaming bar has stylish leather-covered chairs. Rooms are large and plush; try to get one overlooking the tiny, tranquil back garden with its reflecting pool. The garden is also the backdrop for the stylish restaurant, Les Jardins de la Cloche, but you may wish to opt for the more relaxed Les Caves de la Cloche in the cellar, which offers French sing-alongs with dinner. ⊠ *14 pl. Darcy, 21000* ☎ *03–80–30–12–32* ☷ *03–80–30–04–15* ⊕ *www.hotel-lacloche.com* ✍ *53 rooms, 15 suites* ☖ *2 restaurants, minibars, cable TV, gym, sauna, bar, Internet, no-smoking floor* ▭ *AE, DC, MC, V.*

$–$$ ☷ **Wilson.** This hotel's "bones" are 17th century, set as it is in a fetching timber-frame post house, but inside rooms are modern, airy, light, and accented with wooden beams and Louis Treize chairs. Another plus—the hotel is connected by a walkway to Stéphane Derbord's noted restaurant. ⊠ *Pl. Wilson, 21000* ☎ *03–80–66–82–50* ☷ *03–80–36–41–54* ⊕ *www.wilson-hotel.com* ✍ *27 rooms* ☖ *Internet, parking (fee); no a/c* ▭ *AE, MC, V.*

¢–$ ☷ **Le Jacquemart.** In old Dijon, in a neighborhood known for its antiques shops, Le Jacquemart is housed in an 18th-century building with a steep staircase, high-ceilinged rooms of variable comfort, and rustic furniture. It's a quiet, restful spot and thus very popular, so make sure you book well in advance. ⊠ *32 Rue Verrerie, 21000* ☎ *03–80–60–09–60* ☷ *03–80–60–09–69* ⊕ *www.hotel-lejacquemart.fr* ✍ *32 rooms* ☖ *Internet, parking (fee); no a/c* ▭ *MC, V.*

Nightlife & the Arts

Dijon stages **L'Été Musical** (Musical Summer), a predominantly classical music festival in June; the tourist office can supply the details. For three days in June the city hosts **Arts in the Streets** (☎ 03–80–65–91–00 for information), an event at which dozens of painters exhibit their works. During the **Bell-Ringing Festival,** in mid-August, St-Bénigne's bells chime and chime. In September Dijon puts on the **Festival International de Folklore.** November in Dijon is the time for the **International Gastronomy Fair.**

New Galaxy (✉ 8 bis rue Marceau ☎ 03–80–70–03–69) caters to a slightly youngish clientele. **Cinquième Avenue** (✉ Centre Dauphine ☎ 03–80–30–60–63 ☉ Wed.–Sat.) is a popular Dijon disco. The **Bar Messire** (✉ 3 rue Jules-Mercier ☎ 03–80–30–16–40) attracts an older crowd.

Shopping

The auction houses in Dijon are good places to prospect for antiques and works of art. Tempting food items—mustard, snails, and candy (including snail-shape chocolates–*escargots de Bourgogne*) can easily be found in the pedestrian streets in the heart of Dijon.

en route A31 connects Dijon to Beaune, 40 km (25 mi) south. But if you prefer a leisurely route through the vineyards, chug along D122, the **Route des Grands Crus,** past venerable properties such as Gevrey-Chambertin, Chambolle-Musigny, and Morey-St-Denis, to Clos de Vougeot.

WINE COUNTRY

Burgundy—Bourgogne to the French—has given its name to one of the world's great wines. Although many people will allow a preference for Bordeaux, others for Alsace, Loire, or Rhône wines, some of the leading French gourmets insist that the precious red nectars of Burgundy have no rivals, and treat them with reverence. So for some travelers a trip to Burgundy's Wine Country takes on the feel of a spiritual pilgrimage. East of the Parc du Morvan, the low hills and woodland gradually open up, and vineyards, clothing the contour of the land in orderly beauty, appear on all sides. The vineyards' steeply banked hills stand in contrast to the region's characteristic gentle slopes. Burgundy's most famous vineyards run south from Dijon through Beaune to Mâcon along what has become known as the Côte d'Or (*or* doesn't mean gold here, but is an abbreviation of *orient,* or east). Here you can go from vineyard to vineyard tasting the various samples (both the powerfully tannic young reds and the mellower older ones). Purists will remind you that you're not supposed to drink them but simply taste them, then spit them into the little buckets discreetly provided. But who wants to be a purist?

The Côte d'Or is truly a golden slope for wine lovers, branching out over the countryside in four great vineyard-*côtes* (slopes or hillsides) in southern Burgundy. The northernmost, the Côte de Nuits, sometimes called the "Champs-Élysées of Burgundy," is the land of the unparalleled Grand Cru reds from the pinot noir grape. The Côte de Beaune, just to the south, is known for both full-bodied reds and some of the best dry whites in the world. Even farther south is the Côte Chalonnaise.

Although not as famous, it produces bottle after bottle of chardonnay almost as rich as its northern neighbors. Finally, the Côte Mâconnaise, the largest of the four côtes, brings its own quality whites to the market. There are hundreds of vintners in this region, many of them producing top wines from surprisingly small parcels of land. To connect these dots, consult the regional tourist offices for full information of the noted wine routes of the region. The 74-km (50-mi) Route des Grands Crus ranges from Dijon to Beaune and Santenay. You can extend this route southward by the Route Touristique des Grands Vins, which travels some 98 km (60 mi) in and around Chalon-sur-Saône. Coming from the north, you can tour the areas (covered above) around Auxerre and Chablis on the Route des Vignobles de l'Yonne. Whether touring by car, bike, or barge (several outfitters offer luxe barge cruises through the vineyard region waterways), you may wish to learn how to tell a Meursault from a Puligny-Montrachet by signing up with one of the English-language wine classes offered at the Ecole des Vins de Bourgogne in Beaune.

Clos de Vougeot

39 *16 km (10 mi) south of Dijon.*

FodorśChoice The reason to come to Vougeot is to see its *grange viticole* (wine-making barn) surrounded by its famous vineyard—a symbolic spot for all Burgundy aficionados. The **Château du Clos de Vougeot** was constructed in the 12th century by Cistercian monks from neighboring Cîteaux—who were in need of wine for mass and also wanted to make a diplomatic offering—and completed during the Renaissance. It's best known as the seat of Burgundy's elite company of wine lovers, the Confrérie des Chevaliers du Tastevin, who gather here in November at the start of an annual three-day festival, Les Trois Glorieuses. Josephine Baker slurped here once. You can admire the château's cellars, where ceremonies are held, and ogle the huge 13th-century grape presses, uncertain marvels of medieval engineering. ☎ 03–80–62–86–09 ⊕ *www.tastevin-bourgogne.com* 🎫 €3.50 🕐 *Apr.–Sept., daily 9–6:30; Oct.–Mar., daily 9–11:30 and 2–5:30.*

Near Clos de Vougeot at St-Nicolas-lès-Cîteaux is the **Abbaye de Cîteaux,** where the austere Cistercian order was founded in 1098 by Robert de Molesmes. The abbey has housed monks for more than 900 years. ✉ *Off D996, signs point the way along a short country road that breaks off from the entry road to Château de Gilly* ☎ 03–80–61–32–58 🎫 €7 🕐 *May–early Oct., Tues.–Sat. 9:15–noon and 1:45–4:45; Sun. after 10:30 mass* ✆ *Guided tours available.*

Where to Stay & Eat

$$$–$$$$ ✕🏨 **Château de Gilly.** Considered by some an obligatory stop on their tour of Burgundy's vineyards, this château, just 2 mi from Vougeot, has almost become too popular for its own good (a conference center onsite doesn't help things). Formerly an abbey and a government-run avant-garde theater, the château does show some glorious vestiges worthy of its Relais & Châteaux parentage: painted ceilings, a gigantic vaulted crypt-cellar (now the dining room), suits of armor. Guest rooms have magnificent beamed ceilings and lovely views, though the least expensive have standard-issue fabrics, reproduction furniture, and ordinary bathrooms. The restaurant's menu includes pastries made with Cîteaux's famous handmade cheese and pike-perch with a *pain d'épices* (gingerbread) crust. An "elegant form of dress" is requested for dinner. ⊠ *Gilly-lès-Cîteaux, 21640* ☎ *03–80–62–89–98* 🖷 *03–80–62–82–34* ⊕ *www. chateau-gilly.com* 🖘 *36 rooms, 12 suites* ⚐ *Restaurant, cable TV, tennis court, pool, Internet, meeting room; no a/c* ⊟ *AE, DC, MC, V* ☉ *Closed Feb.* ⍟⍟ *MAP.*

Nuits-St-Georges

❹⓪ *21 km (13 mi) south of Dijon, 5 km (3 mi) south of Clos de Vougeot.*

Wine has been made in Nuits-St-Georges since Roman times; its "dry, tonic, and generous qualities" were recommended to Louis XIV for medicinal use. There isn't much to see or do here—it mostly serves as a good stop while visiting the surrounding area.

Where to Stay & Eat

$ ✕ **La Toute Petite Auberge.** Vosne-Romanée, the greatest vine village on the Côte, also entices with one of the most charming restaurants in Burgundy. No surprises on the menu (jambon persillé, coq au vin, crème brûlée), but everything is excellent and prices are more than reasonable. As you would expect, the wine list is top-notch. ⊠ *Vosne-Romanée, on the N74, 2 km (1 mi) north of Nuits-St-George* ☎ *03–80–61–02–03* ⚐ *Reservations essential* ⊟ *MC, V* ☉ *Closed Aug. No lunch Mon.*

¢–$ ✕ **Au Bois de Charmois.** Three kilometers (2 mi) out of Nuits-St-Georges, on the way toward Meuilley, is this marvelous little inn serving local fare at tasty prices—a three-course lunch (sample the huge plate of garlicky frogs' legs) is a finger-lickin' €12.50. An even less-expensive menu is available at lunch on weekdays. It's especially pleasant to sit in the courtyard under the ancient trees, though on chilly, gray days the small dining room is full of good cheer. ⊠ *Rte. de la Serrée* ☎ *03–80–61–04–79* ⊟ *MC, V* ☉ *Closed Mon.*

★ $$–$$$ 🏨 **Domaine Comtesse Michel de Loisy.** Comtesse Christine de Loisy is an institution unto herself in the Nuits-St-Georges area: an internationally traveled, erudite *dame d'un certain âge,* who is also a well-known oenologist and local historian. Rooms in her eclectic *hôtel particulier* are furnished with fine antiques, tapestries, chintz-covered walls, and Oriental carpets, and memorably temper grandeur with old-fashioned charm. Four of the five have a view of the flower-filled courtyard or the magnificent winter garden. Happily, the domain offers an optional two-day program of wine tastings, Burgundy-focused meals, and vineyard excursions. ⊠ *28 rue du Général-de-Gaulle, 21700* ☎ *03–80–61–02–72* 🖷 *03–80–61–36–14* 🖘 *5 rooms* ⚐ *No a/c, no room TVs* ⊟ *AE, MC, V* ☉ *Closed mid-Nov.–mid-Mar.* ⍟⍟ *BP.*

$ 🏨 **Albizzia.** The Dufouleur family, Burgundian wine growers since the sixteenth century, run this charming chambre d'hôte in the small village of Quincey, just outside Nuits-St-George. Facing the night-lit church in the village square, the B&B is in an old stone farmhouse, entirely renovated, with two very cozy double rooms. Breakfast in summer is served in the beautiful garden, and wine tastings (with local cheeses) are held year-round in the Dufouleur cellar. ☒ *Grande Rue, Quincey, 4 km (2½ mi) south of Nuits-St-George, 21700* ☏ *03–80–61–13–23* 🖷 *03–80–61–13–23* 🖘 *2 rooms* ⚭ *No a/c, no room TVs* ▭ *AE, MC, V* ⦿ *BP.*

Beaune

41 *19 km (12 mi) south of Nuits-St-Georges, 40 km (25 mi) south of*
Fodor'sChoice *Dijon, 315 km (197 mi) southeast of Paris.*
★

Beaune is sometimes considered the wine capital of Burgundy because it's at the heart of the region's vineyards, with the Côte de Nuits to the north and the Côte de Beaune to the south. In late November, Les Trois Glorieuses, a three-day wine auction and fête at the Hospices de Beaune, pulls in connoisseurs and the curious from France and abroad. Despite the hordes, Beaune remains one of France's most attractive provincial towns, teeming with art above ground and wine barrels down below.

Some of the region's finest vineyards are owned by the **Hospices de Beaune** (better known to some as the **Hôtel-Dieu**), founded in 1443 as a hospital to provide free care for men who had fought in the Hundred Years' War. A visit to the Hospices (across from the tourist office) is one of the highlights of a stay in Beaune; its tiled roofs and Flemish architecture have become icons of Burgundy, and the same glowing colors and intricate patterns are seen throughout the region. The interior looks medieval but was repainted by 19th-century Gothic restorer Viollet-le-Duc. Of special note are the **Grand' Salle,** more than 160 feet long, with the original furniture, a great wooden roof, and the picturesque **Cour d'Honneur.** The Hospices carried on its medical activities until 1971— its nurses still wearing their habitlike uniforms—and the hospital's history is retraced in the museum, whose wide-ranging collections contain some weird medical instruments from the 15th century. You can also see a collection of tapestries that belonged to the repentant founder of the Hospices, ducal chancellor Nicolas Rolin, who hoped charity would relieve him of his sins—one of which was collecting wives. Outstanding are both the tapestry he had made for Madame Rolin III, with its repeated motif of "my only star," and one relating the legend of St. Eloi and his miraculous restoration of a horse's leg. But the star of the collection is Rogier Van der Weyden's stirring, gigantic 15th-century masterpiece *The Last Judgment,* commissioned for the hospital by Rolin. The intense colors and mind-tripping imagery were meant to scare the illiterate patients into religious submission. Notice the touch of misogyny; more women are going to hell than to heaven, while Christ, the judge, remains completely unmoved. A son-et-lumière show is presented every evening April through October. ☒ *Rue de l'Hôtel-Dieu* ☏ *03–80–24–45–00* ⊕ *www.hospices-de-beaune.com* 🎫 *€5.50* ☯ *Late Mar.–mid-Nov., daily 9–6:30; mid-Nov.–Mar., daily 9–11:30 and 2–5:30.*

A series of tapestries relating the life of the Virgin hangs in Beaune's main church, the 12th-century **Collégiale Notre-Dame.** ☒ *Just off av. de la République.*

★ To many, the liquid highlight of a visit to Burgundy is a visit to the **Marché aux Vins** (Wine Market) where, in flickering candlelight, and armed with your own *tastevin* (which you get to keep as a souvenir), you can taste a tongue-tingling, mind-spinning array of regional wines in the atmospheric setting of barrel-strewn cellars and vaulted passages. The selection runs from young Beaujolais to famous old Burgundies and there's no limit on how much you drink. Other Beaune tasting houses include Cordelier on the rue de l'Hôtel-Dieu and the Caves Patriarche on the rue du Collège. ⊠ *Rue Nicolas-Rolin* ☎ *03–80–25–08–20* ♨ *€10* ☉ *Daily 9:30–noon and 2–5:45.*

If you're going to spend a fortune on a bottle of Romanée-Conti and want to know how to savor it, sign up for one of the wine classes offered by the **Ecole des Vins de Bourgogne,** sponsored by the Bureau Interprofessionel des Vins de Bourgogne (B.I.V.B.) They offer several choices, ranging from a two-hour intro to a full weekend jammed with trips to vineyards and cellars in Macon and Chablis. ⊠ *6 rue du 16ème Chasseur* ☎ *03–80–26–35–10* 🖷 *03–80–26–35–11* ⊕ *www.bivb.com.*

> **need a break?**
>
> For a break and a snack of handmade pain d'épices (gingerbread) in all shapes and incarnations, stop by **Mulot & Petitjean** (⊠ Pl. Carnot). This famed pastry shop has a 200-year-old history.

Where to Stay & Eat

★ **$$$$** ✕ **Bernard Morillon.** This famous restaurant, in a stylish 18th-century town house that shares a courtyard (where you can dine in summer) with the neighboring Cep hotel, is embellished with old furniture and works of art, and considered by many top critics to be the best table in Beaune. Quiet-spoken chef Bernard Morillon lets his cooking—and his ebullient wife Régine, who welcomes guests as if they were old family friends—do the talking. Warm oyster soup with poached quail eggs, fillet of local Charolais beef with foie gras, and Poulet de Bresse (that famous succulent regional chicken) simmered in red wine, are among Bernard's mouthwatering delights. Service is as polished as the gleaming silverware, and as warm-hearted as the Burgundy wine list. ⊠ *31 rue Maufoux* ☎ *03–80–24–12–06* ⏚ *Reservations essential* ⊟ *AE, DC, MC, V* ☉ *Closed Jan. and Mon.–Sun. No lunch Tues. or Wed.*

$$$–$$$$ ✕ **L'Écusson.** Don't be put off by its unprepossessing exterior: this is a comfortable, friendly, thick-carpeted restaurant with good-value prix-fixe menus. Showcased is chef Jean-Pierre Senelet's sure-footed culinary mastery with dishes like boar terrine with dried apricot and juniper berries, and roast crayfish with curried semolina and ratatouille. ⊠ *2 rue du Lieutenant-Dupuis* ☎ *03–80–24–03–82* ⏚ *Reservations essential* ⊟ *AE, DC, MC, V* ☉ *Closed Sun. No lunch Mon.*

$–$$ ✕ **La Grilladine.** Chef Jean-Marc Jacquel's cuisine, though not elaborate, is good, hearty Burgundy fare: boeuf Bourguignon and oeufs en meurette. The prix-fixe menus are extremely reasonable. Warm and cheerful, the room allures with rose-pink tablecloths, exposed stone walls, and an ancient beam supporting the ceiling. ⊠ *17 rue Maufoux* ☎ *03–80–22–22–36* ⏚ *Reservations essential* ⊟ *MC, V* ☉ *Closed Mon. and late Nov.–mid-Dec.*

THROUGH THE GRAPEVINE

THROUGHOUT THE VILLAGES OF THE DIFFERENT CÔTES, *wine tastings abound. Some we've imbibed at include* **Caveau Napoléon** *(⊠ 12 rue Noisot ☎ 03–80–52–45–48) in Fixin, which specializes in Côte de Nuits-Villages and a Fixin Premier Cru. Only 2 km (1 mi) south is Gevrey-Chambertin, where you can sample one of 10 wines—including sparkling white Crémant de Bourgogne—at* **Caveau du Chapître** *(⊠ 1 rue de Paris ☎ 03–80–51–82–82). Still a couple of miles farther south in the celebrated village of Vougeot, you will come upon the* **Grande Cave** *(⊠ R.N. 74 ☎ 03–80–62–87–13), which offers a trip through the cellars of the old castle of Vougeot as well as a chance to try a drop of wine from the barrels of the nearby* **Maison l'Hériter** *(⊠ Rue des Clos Prieurs ☎ 03–80–62–86–58), one of the most distinguished wine houses in the Côte de Nuits. Most vineyards here are separated into patches of land called "clos"—a word redolent of Burgundian history. The first evidence of vineyards in the region dates from 300 BC in Cluny. Centuries later, during the Holy Roman Empire, nobility often gave vineyards to the church, giving control of fairly large properties to the monks at this holy center of Christendom. The monks made a life of recording everything, and so they did with the vineyards. They tasted and analyzed the wines and recorded the nuances of the different plots of land. Detailed maps were drawn, indicated the temperatures and miniclimates of the plots. The term "clos" (an ancient word for climate) may derive from the name given these climates by the monks. Here's hoping you'll enjoy quite a few clos calls yourself on your trip through Bourgogne.*

★ **$$$$** ✗⌂ **Hostellerie de Levernois.** An idyllically elegant and gracious country manor, this Relais & Châteaux property, smartly run by Jean-Louis and Susanne Bottigliero, gleams with light from its large picture windows. The cuisine, under new chef Vincent Maillard, who previously worked at the Carlton in Cannes and the Louis XV in Monaco, is of the highest standard. The lodgings in the modern annex overlooking the landscaped garden are most up-to-date. Meals are occasions to be savored, but they are also expensive; prix-fixe menus begin at €65 and may spotlight duck with foie gras and truffles or langoustines with mustard vinaigrette. ⊠ *Rte. de Verdun-sur-le-Doubs, 3 km (2 mi) east of Beaune, 21200 Levernois* ☎ *03–80–24–73–58* 📠 *03–80–22–78–00* ⊕ *www.levernois.com* ⤳ *15 rooms, 1 suite* ⌂ *Restaurant, minibars, cable TV, Internet* ▤ *AE, DC, MC, V* ⊗ *Closed Feb.–mid-Mar.* ⦿ *MAP.*

$–$$ ✗⌂ **Hôtel Central.** This well-run establishment with modernized rooms, just 100 yards from the Hospices, lives up to its name. The stone-walled restaurant (closed Wednesday November to Easter) is cozy—some might say cramped—and the consistently good cuisine is popular with locals, who come to enjoy oeufs en meurette and coq au vin. Service is efficient, if a little hurried. ⊠ *2 rue Victor-Millot, 21200* ☎ *03–80–24–77–24*

🛏 *03–80–22–30–40* 🛏 *20 rooms, 18 with bath* 🍴 *Restaurant, minibars, cable TV; no a/c in some rooms* 🟰 *MC, V* ☺ *Closed late Nov.–mid-Dec.*

$$$ **Château de Chorey.** To really soak up the flavor of the vineyards, stay at this family winery and B&B 2 km (1 mi) north of Beaune. Guest rooms are up a circular stone staircase; furnishings are from the attic. Though it's a bit rustic and casual, it's the kind of place where you can open the windows and let the country air, perfumed by grapes, waft in. A good breakfast is served but no dinner; you may have a chance to try their wine before going out to eat in Beaune. ⌂ *2 rue Jacques-Germain, 21200 Chorey-les-Beaune* ☎ *03–80–22–06–05* 🖶 *03–80–24–03–93* 🛏 *7 rooms* 🍴 *Some minibars, parking (fee); no a/c* 🟰 *MC, V* ☺ *Closed Dec.–Apr.* ❢|*BP.*

★ **$$$** **Hôtel Le Cep.** This venerable town-center hotel might be considered the shining showpiece among Beaune's myriad hostelries. It's actually an ensemble of buildings spanning the 14th–16th centuries, oozing history from every arcade of its Renaissance courtyard, yet all rooms—named for different Burgundy wines—have been luxuriously modernized, and decorated with crystal chandeliers and individual panache; some have wood beams, others canopied or four-poster beds. Those on the top story offer views over Beaune's famed multicolored tile roofs. Breakfast is served in a vaulted cellar; there's no hotel restaurant as such, but the lip-smackerous Bernard Morillon operates right next door. ⌂ *27 rue Maufoux, 21200* ☎ *03–80–22–35–48* 🖶 *03–80–22–76–80* ⊕ *www.hotel-cep-beaune.com* 🛏 *46 rooms, 11 suites* 🍴 *Minibars, cable TV, bar* 🟰 *AE, DC, MC, V.*

$ **Hôtel de la Cloche.** In a 15th-century residence in the heart of town, this hotel has rooms furnished with care by owners Monsieur and Madame Lamy, both of whom are always on hand to assist. The best rooms, those with a full bath, are more expensive; the smaller yet delightful attic rooms, each with a shower and separate toilet, are less. Breakfast is served on the garden terrace in summer. Note that some readers raise alarms that La Cloche has become a bit shopworn—but the price is certainly right. ⌂ *42 pl. Madeleine, 21200* ☎ *03–80–24–66–33* 🖶 *03–80–24–04–24* 🛏 *22 rooms* 🍴 *Restaurant, minibars, cable TV, Internet, parking (fee)* 🟰 *AE, MC, V* ☺ *Closed late Dec.–mid-Jan.* ❢|*MAP.*

The Arts

In July Beaune celebrates its annual **International Festival of Baroque Music,** which draws big stars of the music world. On the third Sunday in November at the Hospices is Beaune's famous wine festival, **Les Trois Glorieuses** (⊕ www.bourgogne.net/vente/1vente.html). For both festivals, contact **Beaune's Office de Tourisme** (⌂ 1 rue de l'Hôtel-Dieu ☎ 03–80–26–21–35 🖶 03–80–25–04–81 ⊕ www.beaune-burgundy.com).

Château de Sully

🅜 *35 km (19 mi) west of Beaune.*

"The Fontainebleau of Burgundy" was how Madame de Sévigné described this turreted Renaissance château, proclaiming the inner court, whose Italianate design was inspired by Sebastiano Serlio, as the latest in chic. The building is magnificent, landmarked by four lantern-topped corner towers that loom over a romantic moat filled with the waters of the River

Drée. Originally constructed by the de Rabutin family and once owned by Gaspard de Saulx-Tavannes—an instigator of the St. Bartholomew's Day Massacre, August 24, 1572, he reputedly ran through Paris's streets yelling, "Blood, blood! The doctors say that bleeding is as good for the health in August as in May!"—the château was partly reconstructed in elegant Régence style in the 18th century. Maurice de MacMahon, the Irish-origin president of France from 1873 to 1879, was born here in 1808. ☎ 03–85–82–09–86 ⊕ *www.chateaudesully.com* ✆ *Guided tours €6, grounds €3* ۩ *Château 45-min guided tours Apr.–Oct., 10:30–4:30. Grounds daily 10–noon and 2–6.*

Autun

Fodor'sChoice
★

43 *20 km (12 mi) southwest of Sully, 48 km (30 mi) west of Beaune.*

One of the most richly endowed *villes d'art* in Burgundy, Autun is a great draw for fans of both Gallo-Roman and Romanesque art. The name derives from Augustodonum—city of Augustus—and it was Augustus Caesar who called it "the sister and rival of Rome itself." You may still see traces of the Roman occupation—dating from when Autun was much larger and more important than it is today—in its well-preserved archways, Porte St-André and Porte d'Arroux, and the Théâtre Romain, once the largest arena in Gaul. Parts of the Roman walls surrounding the town also remain and give a fair indication of its size in those days. The significance of the curious Pierre (or "stone") de Couhard, a pyramidlike Roman construction, baffles archaeologists. Logically enough, this Roman outpost became a center for the new 11th-century style based on Roman precedent, the Romanesque, and its greatest sculptor, Gislebertus, left his precocious mark on the town cathedral. Several centuries later, Napoléon and his brother Joseph studied here at the military academy.

★ Autun's principal monument is the **Cathédrale St-Lazare,** a Gothic cathedral in Classical clothing. It was built between 1120 and 1146 to house the relics of St. Lazarus; the main tower, spire, and upper reaches of the chancel were added in the late 15th century. Lazarus's tricolor tomb was dismantled in 1766 by canons: vestiges of exquisite workmanship can be seen in the neighboring Musée Rolin. The same canons also did their best to transform the Romanesque-Gothic cathedral into a Classical temple, adding pilasters and other ornaments willy-nilly. Fortunately, the lacy Flamboyant Gothic organ tribune and some of the best Romanesque stonework, including the inspired nave capitals and the tympanum above the main door, emerged unscathed. Jean Ingres's painting *The Martyrdom of St. Symphorien* has been relegated to a dingy chapel in the north aisle of the nave. The *Last Judgment* carved in stone above the main door, was plastered over in the 18th century, which preserved not only the stylized Christ and elongated apostles but also the inscription GISLEBERTUS HOC FECIT (Gislebertus did this). Christ's head, which had disappeared, was found by a local canon shortly after World War II. Make sure to visit the cathedral's **Salle Capitulaire,** which houses Gislebertus's original capitals, distinguished by their relief carvings. The cathedral provides a stunning setting for **Musique en Morvan,** a festival of classical music held in July. ⊠ *Pl. St-Louis.*

The **Musée Rolin,** across from the cathedral, was built by Chancellor Nicholas Rolin, an important Burgundian administrator and famous art patron (he's immortalized in one of the Louvre's greatest paintings, Jan van Eyck's *Madonna and the Chancellor Rolin*). The museum is noteworthy for its early Flemish paintings and sculpture, including the magisterial *Nativity* painted by the Maître de Moulins in the 15th century. But the collection's star is a Gislebertus masterpiece, the *Temptation of Eve*, which originally topped one of the side doors of the cathedral. Try to imagine the missing elements of the scene: Adam on the left and the devil on the right. ⊠ *5 rue des Bancs* ☎ *03–85–52–09–76* ✆ €*3.20* ⊗ *Oct.–Mar., Wed.–Sat. 10–noon and 2–5, Sun. 10–noon and 2:30–5; Apr.–Sept., Wed.–Mon. 9:30–noon and 1:30–6.*

The **Théâtre Romain,** at the edge of town on the road to Chalon-sur-Saône, is a historic spot for lunch. Pick up the makings for a picnic in town and eat it on the stepped seats, where as many as 15,000 Gallo-Roman spectators perched during performances two millennia ago. In August a Gallo-Roman performance—the only one of its kind—is put on by locals wearing period costumes. The peak of a Gallo-Roman pyramid can be seen in the foreground. Elsewhere on the outskirts of town are the remains of an ancient Roman Temple of Janus.

Where to Stay & Eat

$$ ✕⌂ **St-Louis & Poste.** This Best Western hotel, in a former post house, is noteworthy more for its history than its pretensions to elegance. It has Mexican wrought-iron furnishings and a remarkable family-size suite—it was while making a speech from this room's balcony in 1815 on his way back to Paris that Napoléon was rebuffed by crowds; George Sand also stayed here. The staff is friendly and helpful, and the restaurant, La Rotonde, is one of Autun's best. ⊠ *6 rue de l'Arbalète, 71400* ☎*03–85–52–01–01* 🖷*03–85–86–32–54* ⃔*38 rooms* ⌂*Restaurant, minibars, cable TV, Internet, no-smoking rooms; no a/c* ▭*AE, DC, MC, V.*

$–$$ ✕⌂ **Les Ursulines.** Placed above the Roman ramparts of the old city, this converted 17th-century convent offers spacious, well-kept rooms overlooking a geometric, French-style garden. The restaurant, adorned with plush green carpets, floral-patterned curtains, and cane-backed Louis XV-style chairs, and run by Paul Bocuse protégé Bruno Schlewitz, is worth a trip in itself, especially for the escargots with dried tomatoes and garlic confit. Some guest rooms have fine views of the surrounding Morvan hills, and breakfast is served in the historic chapel area. ⊠ *14 rue Rivault, 71400* ☎ *03–85–86–58–58* 🖷 *03–85–86–23–07* ⊕ *www. hotelursulines.fr* ⃔ *40 rooms, 3 apartments* ⌂ *Minibars, cable TV, Internet, no-smoking rooms; no a/c* ▭ *AE, DC, MC, V.*

Chalon-sur-Saône

㊹ *42 km (25 mi) southeast of Autun, 29 km (18 mi) south of Beaune.*

Chalon-sur-Saône's medieval heart is close to the bank of the Saône River, around the former Cathédrale St-Vincent (now a parish church), which displays a jumble of styles. This area was reconstructed to have an old-world charm, but the rest of Chalon is modern and commercial—the cultural and shopping center of southern Burgundy. Chalon is best known as the birthplace of Nicéphore Niepce (1765–1833), whose early experiments, developed further by Jacques Daguerre, qualify him as the father of photography. The **Musée Nicéphore Niepce,** occupying an 18th-century house overlooking the Saône, retraces the early history of photography and motion pictures with the help of some pioneering equipment. It also includes a selection of contemporary photographic work and a lunar camera used during the U.S. Apollo program. But the star of the museum is the primitive camera used to take the very first photograph in 1816. ⊠ *28 quai des Messageries* 🕾 *03–85–48–41–98* 🖃 *€3.10.* ☾ *Sept.–June, Wed.–Mon. 9:30–11:45 and 2–5:45; July and Aug., Wed.–Mon. 10–5:45.*

Where to Stay & Eat

$ ✕🖾 **St-Georges.** Close to the train station and town center, this friendly, white-walled hotel is tastefully modernized and has many spacious rooms. Its cozy restaurant is known locally for its efficient service and menus of outstanding value, with such specialties as veal kidney with mustard; it's closed in early August and does not serve lunch Saturday. ⊠ *32 av. Jean-Jaurès, 71100* 🕾 *03–85–90–80–50* 🖷 *03–85–90–80–55* ⊕ *www.lesaintgeorges71.fr* ➭ *48 rooms* ♿ *Restaurant, minibars, cable TV, Internet* ⊟ *AE, DC, MC, V* ⦿ *MAP.*

The Arts

For two weeks in July all of Chalon becomes a stage as street-theater groups from around the world come to perform in the annual **Chalon dans la Rue** (Chalon in the Street) festival.

Tournus

★ ❹⑤ *27 km (17 mi) south of Chalon-sur-Saône.*

Tournus, which retains much of the charm of the Middle Ages and the Renaissance and has one of Burgundy's most spectacular and best-preserved Romanesque buildings, has long been overshadowed as a tourist attraction by other medieval Burgundian towns. But it's worth a stop, and it's also a great spot for a picnic, especially along the left bank (*rive gauche*) of the Saône River. The **tourist office** (⊠ 2 pl. Carnot 🕾 03–85–51–13–10) has a map of the town's many *traboules*—its hidden covered walkways—which are fun to explore.

The 17th-century **Hôtel-Dieu** (hospital) reopened in 1999 after extensive renovation. Particularly noteworthy is its pharmacy. In one wing is the **Musée de Greuze,** displaying the work of painter Jean-Baptiste Greuze (1725–1805), a native of Tournus, as well as pieces by other painters past and present, sculpture, and archaeological finds. ⊠ *Rue de l'Hôpital* 🕾 *03–85–51–23–50* 🖃 *€5* ☾ *Apr.–Nov., Wed.–Mon. 10–6.*

The abbey church of **St-Philibert,** despite its massiveness—unadorned cylindrical pillars more than 4 feet thick support the nave—is spacious and light. No effort was made to decorate or embellish the interior, whose sole hint of frivolity is the alternating red-and-white stones in the nave arches. The crypt—with its chapels containing 12th-century frescoes of

Christ in Majesty and the *Virgin with Child*—and former abbey buildings, including the cloister and magnificent 12th-century refectory, can also be visited. ⊠ *Pl. de l'Abbaye.*

Where to Stay & Eat

$–$$ ✕▥ **Rempart.** This hotel, originally a 15th-century guardhouse built on the town ramparts, has an elegant foyer and dining room incorporating Romanesque pillars. Rooms are modern and functional. Double-glazed windows keep out traffic noise. At the restaurant, prix-fixe dinners begin at €29; in the bistrot, menus start at €16. House specialties include frogs' legs, Bresse chicken, and Charolais beef. ⊠ *2 av. Gambetta, 71700* ☎ *03–85–51–10–56* 🖷 *03–85–40–77–22* ⊕ *www.lerempart. com* ⇨ *31 rooms, 6 suites* ♨ *Restaurant, minibars, bar* ▤ *AE, DC, MC, V* ⊚| *MAP.*

★ **$** ✕▥ **Aux Terrasses.** For an enjoyable meal of the region's products at reasonable prices—such as chef Michel Carrette's fricassee of peppered rabbit—this is the place. (The restaurant is closed Sunday dinner and Monday.) Many French, German, and Dutch travelers stop here for dinner and a night's rest. Rooms are reasonably large and comfortable, with standard floral decor. ⊠ *18 av. du 23-Janvier, 71700* ☎ *03–85–51–01–74* 🖷 *03–85–51–09–99* ⇨ *18 rooms* ♨ *Restaurant* ▤ *MC, V* ☺ *Closed early Jan.–early Feb.* ⊚| *MAP.*

en route   The best way to reach Cluny from Tournus is to use picturesque D14. Along the way you pass the fortified hilltop town of **Brancion**, with its old castle and soaring keep, before turning left at Cormatin.

Cluny

 36 km (22 mi) southwest of Tournus, 24 km (15 mi) northwest of Mâcon.

The village of Cluny is legendary for its medieval abbey, once the center of a vast Christian empire and today one of the most towering of medieval ruins. Although most of the fabled complex was destroyed by the mobs of the French Revolution, one soaring transept of this mammoth church remains standing, today one of the most magnificent sights of Romanesque architecture. Looming as large as Cluny does, art historians have written themselves into knots tracing the fundamental influence of its architecture in the development of early Gothic style. Founded in the 10th century, the **Ancienne Abbaye** was the largest church in Europe until the 16th century, when Michelangelo built St. Peter's in Rome. Cluny's medieval abbots were as powerful as popes; in 1098 Pope Urban II (himself a Cluniac) assured the head of his old abbey that Cluny was the "light of the world." That assertion, of dubious religious validity, has not stood the test of time—after the Revolution the abbey was sold as national property and much of it used as a stone quarry. Today Cluny stands in ruins, a reminder of the vanity of human grandeur. The ruins, however, suggest the size and gorgeous super-romantic glory of the abbey at its zenith, and piecing it back together in your mind is part of the attraction.

FodorŚChoice
★

In order to get a clear sense of what you are looking at, start at the **Porte d'Honneur,** the entrance to the abbey from the village, whose classical architecture is reflected in the pilasters and Corinthian columns of the **Clocher de l'Eau-Bénite** (a majestic bell tower), crowning the only remaining part of the abbey church, the south transept. Between the two are the reconstructed monumental staircase, which led to the portal of the abbey church, and the excavated column bases of the vast narthex. The entire nave is gone. On one side of the transept is a national horse-breeding center (*haras*) founded in 1806 by Napoléon and constructed with materials from the destroyed abbey; on the other is an elegant pavilion built as new monks' lodgings in the 18th century. The gardens in front of it once contained an ancient lime tree (destroyed by a 1982 storm) named after Abélard, the controversial philosopher who sought shelter at the abbey in 1142. Off to the right is the 13th-century *farinier* (flour mill), with its fine oak-and-chestnut roof and collection of exquisite Romanesque capitals from the vanished choir. The **Musée Ochier,** in the abbatial palace, contains Europe's foremost Romanesque lapidary museum. Vestiges of both the abbey and the village constructed around it are conserved here, as well as part of the Bibliothèque des Moines (Monks' Library). ☎ *03–85–59–15–93* ⊕ *www.monum.fr* 🎫 *€6.10* ◷ *Sept.–Apr., daily 9:30–noon and 1:30–5; May–Aug., daily 9:30–6:30.*

The village of Cluny was built to serve the abbey's more practical needs, and several fine Romanesque houses around the rue d'Avril and the rue de la République, including the so-called **Hôtel de la Monnaie** (Abbey Mint; ⊠ 6 rue d'Avril ☎ 03–85–59–25–66), are prime examples of the period's different architectural styles. Parts of the town ramparts, the much-restored 11th-century defensive **Tour des Fromages** (⊠ 6 rue Mercière ☎ 03–85–59–05–34), now home to the tourist office, and several noteworthy medieval churches also remain.

Where to Stay & Eat

$–$$ ✕🏠 **Hôtel Bourgogne.** This old-fashioned hotel was built in 1817, where parts of the abbey used to be. It has a small garden and an atmospheric restaurant with sober pink palette and comfort cuisine, such as *volaille de Bresse au Noilly et morilles* (Bresse chicken with Noilly Prat and morels). The evening meal is mandatory in July and August, and the restaurant is closed on Tuesday and Wednesday. ⊠ *Pl. de l'Abbaye, 71250* ☎ *03–85–59–00–58* 🖷 *03–85–59–03–73* ⊕ *www.hotel-cluny.com* 🛏 *13 rooms, 3 suites* ⚒ *Restaurant, bar; no a/c in some rooms* 🖃 *AE, DC, MC, V* ◷ *Closed Dec.–Feb.* ⍇ *MAP.*

¢–$ ✕🏠 **Hôtel Abbaye.** This modest hotel is a five-minute walk from the center. The three rooms to the right of the dining room are the best value. The restaurant serves rich, hearty local fare that's less elaborate than at the Bourgogne but better; if you're feeling adventurous, try the *pâté en croûte de grenouilles au Bleu de Bresse* (frog and Bresse blue-cheese pie). The prix-fixe menus are very reasonable, and the restaurant is closed Monday and doesn't serve dinner Sunday. ⊠ *14 ter av. Charles-de-Gaulle, 71250* ☎ *03–85–59–11–14* 🖷 *03–85–59–09–76* 🛏 *14 rooms* ⚒ *Restaurant; no a/c* 🖃 *AE, MC, V* ◷ *Closed mid-Jan.–mid-Feb.* ⍇ *MAP.*

The Arts

The ruined abbey of Cluny forms the backdrop of the **Grandes Heures de Cluny** (☎ 03–85–59–26–29 for details), a classical music festival held in August.

BURGUNDY A TO Z

To research prices, get advice from other travelers, and book travel arrangements, visit www.fodors.com.

AIRPORTS

Dijon Airport serves domestic flights between Paris and Lyon.

☷ Airport Information **Dijon Airport** ☎ 03-80-67-67-67.

BIKE & MOPED TRAVEL

Details about recommended bike routes and where to rent bicycles (train stations are a good bet) can be found at most tourist offices. La Peurtantaine arranges bicycle tours of Burgundy.

☷ Bike Tours **La Peurtantaine** ✉ Morvan Découverte, Le Bourg, 71550 Anost ☎ 03-85-82-77-74.

BUS TRAVEL

Local bus services are extensive; where the biggest private companies, Les Rapides de Bourgogne and TRANSCO, do not venture, the national SNCF routes often do. TRANSCO's No. 44 bus travels through the Côte d'Or wine region, connecting Dijon to Beaune via Vougeot and Nuits-St-Georges. The buses of Les Rapides des Bourgogne connect Auxerre to Chablis, Avallon, and Vézelay, and run between Autun, Beaune, Dijon, and Chalon-sur-Saône's train station, where you can take an SNCF bus over to Cluny. Another SNCF route connects Saulieu, Montbard (near Fontenay), Autun, and Avallon. Cars Taboreau operate in the Parc du Morvan. Always inquire at the local tourist office for timetables and ask your hotel concierge for information.

☷ Bus Information **Les Rapides de Bourgogne** ✉ 3 rue des Fontenottes, Auxerre ☎ 03-86-94-95-00. **TRANSCO** ✉ Rue des Perrières, Dijon ☎ 03-80-42-11-00. For SNCF, see Train Information, *below*.

CAR RENTAL

☷ Local Agencies **Avis** ✉ 5 av. du Maréchal-Foch, Dijon ☎ 03-80-43-60-76. **Europcar** ✉ 47 rue Guillaume-Tell, Dijon ☎ 03-80-43-28-44. **Hertz** ✉ 78 cours de la Gare, Dijon ☎ 03-80-53-14-00.

CAR TRAVEL

Although bus lines do service smaller towns and scenic byways, traveling through Burgundy by car allows you to explore its meandering country roads at leisure. A6 is the main route through the region; A6 heads southeast from Paris through Burgundy, past Sens, Auxerre, Chablis, Avallon, Saulieu, and Beaune, continuing on to Mâcon, Lyon, and the south. A38 links A6 to Dijon, 290 km (180 mi) from Paris; the trip takes around three hours, depending on traffic. A31 heads down from Dijon to Beaune, a distance of 45 km (27 mi). The uncluttered A5 links Paris to Troyes, where the A31 segues south to Dijon.

SPORTS & THE OUTDOORS

From April to November, Air Escargot arranges hot-air balloon rides over the countryside.

🏐 Hot-Air Ballooning **Air Escargot** ✉ Chemin du 6-septembre, 71150 Remigny ☎ 03-85-87-12-30 ⊕ www.air-escargot.com.

TOURS

For general information on tours in Burgundy, contact the regional tourist office, the Comité Régional du Tourisme. Tours of Beaune with a guide and a wine tasting can be arranged in advance through the Beaune tourist office. Gastronomic weekends, including wine tastings, are organized by Bourgogne Tour.

🏐 **Beaune tourist office** ✉ Rue de l'Hôtel-Dieu ☎ 03-80-26-21-30. **Bourgogne Tour** ✉ 11 rue de la Liberté, 21000 Dijon ☎ 03-80-30-49-49. **Comité Régional du Tourisme** ⌖ B.P. 1602, 21035 Dijon Cedex ☎ 03-80-50-90-00.

TRAIN TRAVEL

The TGV zips out of Paris (Gare de Lyon) to Dijon (75 minutes), Mâcon (100 minutes), and on to Lyon (two hours). Trains run frequently, though the fastest Paris–Lyon trains do not stop at Dijon or go anywhere near it. Some TGVs stop at Le Creusot, between Chalon and Autun, 90 minutes from Paris. There is also TGV service directly from Roissy Airport to Dijon (1 hour 50 minutes). Sens is on a mainline route from Paris (45 minutes). The region has two local train routes: one linking Sens, Joigny, Montbard, Dijon, Beaune, Chalon, Tournus, and Mâcon and the other connecting Auxerre, Avallon, Saulieu, and Autun. If you want to get to smaller towns or to vineyards, use bus routes or opt for the convenience of renting a car.

🏐 Train Information **SNCF** ☎ 08-36-35-35-35 ⊕ www.ter-sncf.com/uk/bourgogne.

TRAVEL AGENCIES

🏐 Local Agent Referrals **Air France** ✉ 29 pl. Darcy, Dijon ☎ 03-80-42-89-90. **Carlson-Wagonlit** ✉ 8 av. du Maréchal-Foch, Dijon ☎ 03-80-45-26-26.

VISITOR INFORMATION

Following are principal regional tourist offices, listed by town, as well as addresses of other tourist offices in towns mentioned in this chapter.

🏐 Tourist Information **Autun** ✉ 2 av. Charles-de-Gaulle ☎ 03-85-86-80-38 ⊕ www.autun.com. **Auxerre** ✉ 1 quai de la République ☎ 03-86-52-06-19 ⊕ www.ot-auxerre.fr. **Avallon** ✉ 4 rue Bocquillot ☎ 03-86-34-14-19. **Beaune** ✉ Rue de l'Hôtel-Dieu ☎ 03-80-26-21-30 ⊕ www.beaune-burgundy.com. **Cluny** ✉ 6 rue Mercière ☎ 03-85-59-05-34 ⊕ www.perso.wanadoo.fr/otcluny. **Dijon** ✉ 34 rue des Forges ☎ 03-80-44-11-44 ⊕ www.ot-dijon.fr. **Mâcon** Principal regional tourist office ✉ 1 pl. St-Pierre ☎ 03-85-21-07-07. **Sens** ✉ Pl. Jean-Jaurès ☎ 03-86-65-19-49. **Tournus** ✉ 2 pl. Carnot ☎ 03-85-51-13-10. **Troyes** ✉ 16 bd. Carnot ☎ 03-25-82-62-70 ⊕ www.ot-troyes.fr ✉ Rue Mignard ☎ 03-25-73-36-88. **Vézelay** ✉ Rue St-Pierre ☎ 03-86-33-23-69.

Lyon &
the Alps

WORD OF MOUTH

"We visited Vienne last summer for a concert during the festival. Modern jazz in a 2,000-year-old amphitheater—wow! The setting is magical."
—Ian

"With the best of all worlds intersecting there—Alps, Mediterranean, Massif Central, and Beaujolais wine country—Lyon has an endless energy and cultural richness that would inspire me to stay forever."
—Cheyne

"Take a 'hop-on, hop-off' type of boat from town to town along Lake Annecy. Annecy itself is lovely and filled with crêperies along a pretty canal, boutiques, galleries, and entertainment (jugglers, musicians, etc.) in the summer."
—Weadles

Introduction by
Nancy Coons

Updated by
George Semler

AS THE NOBLE RHÔNE COURSES DOWN from Switzerland, flowing out of Lake Geneva and being nudged west and south by the flanking Jura Mountains and the Alps, it meanders through France at its bracing best. Here you'll find the pretty towns and fruity purple wines of Beaujolais, the brawny, broad-shoulder cuisine of Lyon, the extraordinary beauty of the Alps, and friendly wine villages sitting high on the steep hills bordering the Rhône as it flows to the Mediterranean. To the west, deep gorges cut grooves through a no-man's-land of ragged stone and pine: the Ardèche. History is to be found here, but the kind that treads lightly: the ruins at Vienne mark, with more grace than pomp, the region's Gallo-Roman roots, while Lyon's gigantic amphitheater and intimate Odéon confirm Roman Lugdunum's 2,000 years of bright cultural history.

So relax and dig into the *terroir,* the earth. Strike up a flirtation with saucy Beaujolais, the region's pink-cheeked country lass-in-a-glass, blushing modestly next to Burgundy, its high-toned neighbor. The very names of Beaujolais's robust wines conjure up a wildflower bouquet: Fleurie, Chiroubles, Juliénas, St-Amour. Glinting purple against red-checked linens in a Lyonnais *bouchon,* they flatter every delight listed on the blackboard menu: a salty chew of sausage, a crunch of bacon, a fat boudin noir bursting from its casing, a tangle of country greens in a tangy mustard vinaigrette, or a taste of crackling roast chicken.

If you are what you eat, then Lyon itself is real and hearty, as straightforward and unabashedly simple as a *poulet de Bresse.* Yet the refinements of world-class opera, theater, and classical music also happily thrive in Lyon's gently patinated urban milieu, one strangely reminiscent of 1930s Paris—lace curtains in painted-over storefronts, elegant bourgeois town houses, deep-shaded parks, and low-slung bridges lacing back and forth over the broad, lazy Saône and Rhône rivers. Far from the madding immensity of Paris, immerse yourself in what feels, tastes, and smells like the France of yore.

When you've had your fill of this, pack a picnic of victuals to tide you over and take to the hills. If you head west, the Gorges de l'Ardèche will land you in a craggy world of stone villages; if you head northeast, you'll ease into the Alps, a land of green-velvet slopes and icy mists, ranging from the modern urban hub of Grenoble and the crystalline lake of Annecy to the state-of-the-art ski resorts of Chamonix and Megève. The grand finale: awe-inspiring Mont-Blanc, at 15,700 feet Western Europe's highest peak. End your day's exertions on the piste or the trail with a bottle of gentian-perfumed Suze, repair to your fir tree–enclosed chalet, and dress down for a hearty mountain-peasant supper of raclette, fondue, or cheesy *ravioles,* all in the company of a crackling fire.

Grouped together in this guide solely for geographic convenience, Lyon and the Alps are as alike as chocolate and broccoli. Lyon is fast, congested, and saturated with culture (and smog). Lyon may be the gateway to the Alps, but otherwise the two halves of the region could be on different continents. While in the bustling city, it's hard to believe the pristine Alps are only an hour's train ride away from this rich metropolis. Likewise, while in a small Alpine village you could almost forget that France has any large cities at all—much less one of the biggest and noisiest just on the other side of the mountains. When leaving Lyon, few travelers can resist paying a call on the Alps. Everything you imagine when you hear their name—soaring snowcaps, jagged ridges, crystalline lakes—is true. Their major outpost—Grenoble—buzzes with Alpine talk, propelling visitors away from city life and into the great Alpine high.

Exploring Lyon & the Alps

East-central France can be divided into two areas: the Alps and "not the Alps." The second area includes Lyon—a magnet for the surrounding region, including the vineyards of Beaujolais—and the area south of Lyon, dominated by the mighty Rhône as it flows toward the Mediterranean. This chapter is divided into four chunks: Lyon, France's "second city"; Beaujolais and La Dombes—where hundreds of wine *caves* alternate with glacier-created lakes and towns built of *pierres dorées,* soft, golden-tone stones that come from the local hillsides; the Rhône Valley, studded with quaint villages and hilltop castles; and Grenoble and the Alps, where you'll often find down-home friendliness on tap at sky-high ski resorts.

About the Restaurants & Hotels

Lyon's famous bouchons are, of course, irresistible in their checkered-tablecloth cozy atmosphere. The fare, however, is notoriously heavy, featuring creamy pike dumplings and pork and the like. The answer? Stick to soups and salads and other heretical bouchon specialties and live to dine again that day, or the next. Of course, you're also here to enjoy the region's famous restaurants, which rank right up there with Paris's—after all, the area has not one but two culinary shrines: Lyon's Paul Bocuse and Megève's La Ferme de Mon Père, the latter masterminded by Marc Veyrat. Since the luxe here can get very luxe, remember that prix-fixe menus are usually a fine way to keep tabs from soaring into the empyrean. House wines in Lyon are served in the traditional pot-de-Lyon, thick-bottomed bottles designed not to fool the customer, but to mock the government functionaries that (unsuccessfully) tried to limit the wine intake of the 19th-century silk workers. The pot-de-Lyon wine is unbeatable for price-value, but otherwise undistinguished.

Hotels, inns, bed-and-breakfasts, *gîtes d'étapes* (hikers' way stations), and *tables d'hôte* run the gamut from grande luxe to spartanly rustic in this ample region. Many hotels come complete with dining rooms and they expect you to have at least your evening meal there, especially in summer; in winter they up the ante and hope travelers will take all three meals. Assume all hotel rooms have air-conditioning, TV, telephones, and private bath, unless otherwise noted.

9

In this diverse region you can ski in the shadow of Mont Blanc, hike the trails over Alpine slopes, sail across idyllic Lake Annecy, and enjoy a broad palette of Lyon's cultural offerings. You can visit the Roman sites and medieval towns—evocative reminders of pre-modern eras—or take a heady trip along the Beaujolais Wine Road to discover the region's refreshingly unaffected vintages. As you plan your trip, remember that although you can make good time along the highways, you'll have to slow down on lesser roads and in the Alps. In more rural and mountainous regions avoid making your daily itineraries too ambitious.

Numbers in the text correspond to numbers in the margin and on the Lyon & the Alps map, the Lyon map, and the Grenoble map.

If you have 3 days

To enjoy some of France's best cooking, best museums, and theater, concentrate on 🗺 **Lyon** ①–㉚ ▶, but also spend a day heading down the Rhône to see a vineyard in Côte Rôtie or the Roman ruins in **Vienne** ㊱. For mountains and the wide open spaces, spend your second two days around the gorgeous lake in 🗺 **Annecy** ㊾ or in the Alps, using 🗺 **Megève** ㊽—where off-piste action outpaces the skiing—as your base. Of course, you'll want to save your euros for a blow-out at either one of Marc Veyrat's restaurants in Annecy and Megève.

If you have 7 days

Stay in 🗺 **Lyon** ①–㉚ ▶ for at least two days. If you love wine, travel up the Saône Valley, through the villages along the **Beaujolais Wine Road,** and then, for your third night, head to 🗺 **Bourg-en-Bresse** ㉝, landmarked by its Flamboyant Gothic church, or medieval 🗺 **Pérouges** ㉟. On Day 4 make 🗺 **Annecy** ㊾, with its medieval Vieille Ville, your destination; be sure to drive around the lake to lovely Talloires; stay the night in either one. The next day travel along the narrow roads connecting small villages via mountain passes in the Alps. Stop in the fashionable mountain resort town of **Megève** ㊽—home to Marc Veyrat's culinary shrine, La Ferme de Mon Père—before driving on to elegant 🗺 **Chambéry** ㊿. On Day 6 visit the abbey of **Grande Chartreuse** ㊿; then either go to **Grenoble** ㊸–㊾ to see the Grenoble Museum's fabulous collection or zip via the autoroute to 🗺 **Valence** ㊶ to view its Vieille Ville's cathedral and art museum. On the final day, drive through the spectacular Ardèche Gorge if you're heading for Provence. Or return to Lyon via **Vienne** ㊱ to see the Roman sites or Côte du Rhône vineyards.

WHAT IT COSTS In euros					
	$$$$	**$$$**	**$$**	**$**	**¢**
RESTAURANTS	over €30	€23–€30	€17–€23	€11–€17	under €11
HOTELS	over €190	€120–€190	€80–€120	€50–€80	under €50

Restaurant prices are per person for a main course at dinner, including tax (19.6%) and service; note that if a restaurant offers only prix-fixe (set-price) meals, it has been given the price category that reflects the full prix-fixe price. Hotel prices are for a standard double room in high season, including tax (19.6%) and service charge. Hotels operate on the European Plan (EP, with no meal provided) unless we note that they use the Breakfast Plan (BP), or also offer such options as Modified American Plan (MAP, with breakfast and dinner daily, known as *demi-pension*), or Full American Plan (FAP, or *pension complète*, with three meals a day). Inquire when booking if these all-inclusive mealplans (which always entail higher rates) are mandatory or optional.

Timing

Midsummer can be hot and sticky. The best time of year in Lyon and the Rhône Valley is autumn, when the lakes are still warm, the grape harvest is under way, and festivals are all over the place. Note, however, that many of Lyon's hotels book early for September and October, when masses of delegates arrive for conventions. Winter tends to be dreary, though the crystal mist hovering over the Rhône can be beautiful. In the Alps summer is the time to hike, explore isolated villages, and admire the vistas; in winter the focus is on snow and skiing. Many hotels in the Alps are closed in early spring and late autumn.

LYON

Lyon and Marseille each claim to be France's "second city." In terms of size and industrial importance, Marseille probably deserves that title. But for tourist appeal, Lyon, 462 km (287 mi) southeast of Paris, is the clear winner. Easily accessible by car or by train, Lyon's speed and scale are human in ways that Paris may have lost forever. Lyon has its share of historic buildings and quaint *traboules* (from the Latin *trans-ambulare*, or walk-through), which are the passageways under and through town houses dating from the Renaissance (in Vieux Lyon) and the 19th century (in La Croix Rousse). Originally designed as dry, high-speed shortcuts for silk weavers delivering their wares, these passageways were used by the French Resistance during World War II to elude German street patrols. The city's setting at the confluence of the Saône and the Rhône is a spectacular riverine landscape overlooked from the heights to the west by the imposing Notre-Dame de Fourvière church and from the north by the hilltop neighborhood of La Croix Rousse. And when it comes to dining, you will be spoiled for choice—Lyon has more good restaurants per square mile than any other European city except Paris.

Lyon's development owes much to its riverside site halfway between Paris and the Mediterranean, and within striking distance of Switzerland, Italy, and the Alps. Lyonnais are proud that their city has been important for more than 2,000 years: Romans made their Lugdunum (the name means "hill of the crow"), the second largest Roman city after Rome itself, capital of Gaul around 43 BC. The remains of the Roman theater and the Odéon, the Gallo-Roman music hall, are among the most spectacular Roman ruins in the world. In the middle of the city is the Presqu'île, a fingerlike peninsula between the rivers, only half a dozen blocks wide and about 10 km (6 mi) long, where modern Lyon throbs with shops, restaurants, museums, theaters, and a postmodern Jean Nouvel–designed opera house. West of the Saône is Vieux Lyon (Old Lyon), with its peaceful Renaissance charm and lovely traboules and patios; above

9

Dining with Bocuse & Veyrat

Haute cuisine today owes a great deal to the renovations of Lyonnais master chef Paul Bocuse. Back in the mid-1970s he unleashed his revolutionary dishes on an unsuspecting world, taking a stodgy, moribund tradition and creating fireworks by fusing unlikely ingredients, lighting up sauces, and putting the grand classics of Escoffier into jogging shoes. The amazing thing is that he did it all in traditional Lyon. For centuries, dining here has not been for the fainthearted. Indeed, most people throw out the dieter's notebook and roll up their sleeves in this city—everyone knows it's time to *eat!* Food lovers have long celebrated Lyon's cuisine and still rank it among the most complete and diverse in the world. The flavors are strong and cholesterol-heavy, the portions are trencherman-huge (oddly enough, many of these time-honored dishes were created by women, one reason so many Lyon dining establishments are affectionately called La Mère). Typical dishes are *sabodet,* a sausage made of pig's head; *gâteau de foie de volaille* (chicken liver pudding); *museau vinaigrette* (pickled beef muzzle); and the daunting *tête de veau* (calf's head). There are also such exquisitely light delicacies as *quenelles* (poached fish dumplings, often in sauce Nantua), which appear on tables in restaurants from the truly elegant to the truly simple. Lyon is most famous for its traditional *bouchons* (taverns), with homey wooden benches, zinc counters, and paper table coverings, that serve salads, pork products like garlicky *rosette* sausage, and sturdy main courses such as tripe, veal stew, and *andouillette* (chitterling sausage). Also the word for cork, *bouchon* in this case refers to the handfuls of straw used by grooms to *bouchonner* (rub down) horses after a day's ride. Taverns supplied piles of straw at the door and sold simple fare to horsemen. Unfortunately, the bouchon tradition has led to a host of modern-day fakes, so look for the little plaque at the door showing Gnafron, a Grand Guignol character, raising a glass of the grape, signifying a seal of approval from the town's historical association.

If you're not enthralled by traditional Lyonnais fare (only so much pork tripe and pike dumpling can be consumed in a day), turn to the full rainbow of Lyon's vast modern and postmodern culinary wealth, best seen in the absolutely extraordinary creations of Megève's poet-chef, Marc Veyrat: butter and creams from the north, Charolais beef to the west, olive oil, seafood from the Rhône estuary and the Mediterranean to the south, and game and highland delicacies from the Alps to the east. For a full account of this chef's fireworks, see our reviews of his La Maison de Marc Veyrat in Annecy and his La Ferme de Mon Père in Mègeve. The Dombes is rich in game and fowl; the chicken is famous, especially *poulet de Bresse,* traditionally cooked with cream. Thrush, partridge, and hare star along the Rhône. Local cheeses include St-Marcellin, Roquefort, Beaufort, Tomme, and goat's-milk Cabecou. Privas has its *marrons glacés* (candied chestnuts), Montélimar its nougats. Alpine rivers and lakes supply abundant pike and trout. When in the Alps don't forget to try a raclette, cheese melted over potatoes. Mountain herbs yield liqueurs and aperitifs such as tangy, dark Suédois; the sweet, green Chartreuse; and bittersweet Suze (made from gentian).

Le Beaujolais Nouveau

Many of France's most accessible and friendly wines hail from the 40-km (25-mi) north–south stretch of land known as the "Vignobles de Beaujolais" found about 30 km (20 mi) north of Lyon. Beaujolais wine is made exclusively from the *gamay noir à jus blanc* grape. The region's 10 best wines—Brouilly, Côte-de-Brouilly, Chénas, Chiroubles, Fleurie, Julienas, Morgon, St-Amour, Moulin-à-Vent, and Régine—are all labeled "Grands Crus," a more complex version of the otherwise light, fruity Beaujolais. Although the region's wines get better with age, many Beaujolais wines are drunk nearly fresh off the vine; every third Thursday in November marks the arrival of the Beaujolais Nouveau, a bacchanalian festival that also showcases regional cuisine.

Powder-Perfect Skiing

If you're going to work off all the highly calorific Lyonnais cuisine, there's no better way than by taking to the fabled ski runs of the region. Skiing can be a costly pastime, but if you're committed to the sport, the Alps are unbeatable, with verticals up to 9,240 feet and seemingly endless networks of pistes, most above the tree line. While some resorts (Tignes, Les Arcs) have year-round skiing, skiers seeking the true Alpine experience will head straight for the better-known resorts in Chamonix and Megève. These places are so big you can stay in them for one week and never cross your own tracks. One ideal situation is to gather a few friends together and rent an apartment for a week; contact the local tourist office for rental information. The longer you stay, the better chance you can get a cut in prices on lift tickets, equipment, even lodging. But if time is of the essence, you can always enjoy a short ski stint with one-day packages leaving from Grenoble for Chamrouse and Les Deux Alps. For most resorts, the ski season lasts from December through April. Which only leads us to remind you that these regions make almost more delightful destinations in summer.

---

it is the old Roman district of Fourvière. To the north is the hilltop Croix Rousse District, where Lyon's silk weavers once operated their looms in lofts designed as workshop dwellings, while across the Rhône to the east is a mix of older residential areas, the famous Halles de Lyon market, and the ultramodern Part-Dieu business and office district with its landmark *gratte-ciel* (skyscraper) beyond.

All in all, Lyon is a city of ups and downs: from the Presqu'île to the top of the Croix Rousse or from Vieux Lyon to the top of the Roman Fourvière, from a simple bouchon with checked tablecloths to a stunningly haute-cuisine establishment such as Paul Bocuse (this is where the superstar chef became world famous) or Leon de Lyon. Consider taking advantage of the Clés de Lyon (Keys to Lyon), a three-day museum pass costing €14.

Vieux Lyon & Fourvière

Vieux Lyon—one of the richest groups of urban Renaissance dwellings in Europe—has narrow cobblestone streets, 15th- and 16th-century mansions, lovely *traboules* (passageways) and patios, small museums, and the cathedral. When Lyon became an important silk weaving town in the 15th century, Italian merchants and bankers built dozens of Renaissance-style town houses. Officially catalogued as national monuments, the courtyards and passageways are open to the public during the morning. The excellent Renaissance Quarter map of the traboules and courtyards of Vieux Lyon, available at the tourist office and in most hotel lobbies, offers the city's most gratifying exploring (use the silver buttons at the top of entryway door-buzzer panels to gain access). Above Vieux Lyon, in hilly Fourvière, are the remains of two Roman theaters and the Basilique de Notre-Dame, visible from all over the city.

a good walk

Start your walk armed with free maps from the Lyon tourist office on Presqu'île's **place Bellecour** ❶ ➤. Cross the square and head north along lively rue du Président-Herriot; turn left onto place des Jacobins and explore rue Mercière and the small streets off it. Cross the Saône on the Passerelle du Palais de Justice (Palace of Justice Footbridge); now you are in Vieux Lyon. Facing you is the old Palais de Justice. Turn right and then walk 200 yards along quai Romain Rolland to No. 17, where there's a traboule that leads to No. 9 rue des Trois Maries. Take a right to get to small place de la Baleine. Exit the square on the left (north) side and then go right on historic **rue St-Jean** ❷. All along rue St-Jean are traboules and patios leading into lovely courtyards with spiral staircases and mullioned windows. Head up to cobblestoned place du Change; on your left is the **Loge du Change** ❸ church. Take rue Soufflot and turn left onto rue de Gadagne. The Hôtel de Gadagne now houses two museums: the **Musée Historique de Lyon** ❹, with medieval sculpture and local artifacts, and the Musée de la Marionnette, a puppet museum.

Walk south along **rue du Boeuf** ❺, parallel to rue St-Jean, with its many traboules, courtyards, and spiral staircases. Just off tiny place du Petit-Collège, at No. 16, is the **Maison du Crible** ❻, with its pink tower. Cut through the traboule at 31 rue du Boeuf into rue de la Bombarde and go left to get to the **Jardin Archéologique** ❼, a small garden with two excavated churches. Alongside the gardens is the solid **Cathédrale St-Jean** ❽, itself an architectural history lesson. The *ficelle* (funicular railway) runs from the cathedral to the top of Colline de Fourvière (Fourvière Hill). Take the Montée de Fourvière to the **Théâtres Romains** ❾, the well-preserved remnants of two Roman theaters. Overlooking the theaters is the semi-subterranean **Musée de la Civilisation Gallo-Romaine** ❿, a repository for Roman finds. Continue up the hill and take the first right to the mock-Byzantine **Basilique de Notre-Dame-de-Fourvière** ⓫.

Return to Vieux Lyon via the Montée Nicolas-de-Lange, the stone stairway at the foot of the metal tower, the **Tour Métallique** ⓬. You will emerge alongside the St-Paul train station. Venture onto rue Juiverie, off place St-Paul, to see two splendid Renaissance mansions, the **Hôtel Paterin** ⓭, at No. 4, and the **Hôtel Bullioud** ⓮, at No. 8. On the northeast side of place St-Paul is the church of **St-Paul** ⓯. Behind the church, cross the river on the Passarelle St-Vincent and take a left on quai St-Vincent; 200 yards along on the right is the **Jardin des Chartreux** ⓰, a small park. Cut through the park up to cours du Général Giraud and then turn right to place Rouville. Rue de l'Annonciade leads from the square to the **Jardin des Plantes** ⓱, the botanical gardens.

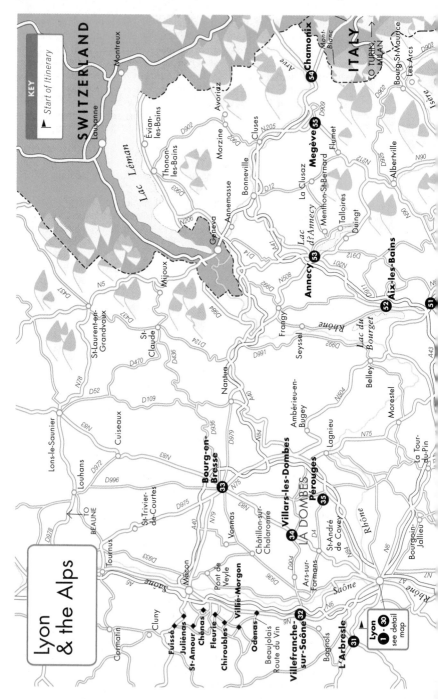

Lyon & the Alps

KEY

▲ Start of Itinerary

SWITZERLAND

Lausanne
Montreux

Évian-les-Bains
Thonon-les-Bains

Lac Léman

Geneva
Annemasse

Avoriaz
Morzine
Bonneville
Cluses

Chamonix **54**
Mont-Blanc

ITALY
TO TURIN,
MILAN →

Bourg-St-Maurice
Les-Arcs

Megève **55**
Flumet
Albertville

La Clusaz
Menthon-St-Bernard
Talloires
Duingt
Lac d'Annecy

Annecy **53**

Aix-les-Bains **52**

51

Frangy
Seyssel
Lac du Bourget
Belley
Morestel

St-Laurent-en-Grandvaux
St-Claude

Nantua

Ambérieu-en-Bugey
Lagnieu
La Tour-du-Pin

Lons-le-Saunier
Cuiseaux

Bourg-en-Bresse **33**

Villars-les-Dombes
Pérouges **35**
LA DOMBES **34**

Louhans
St-Trivier-de-Courtes

TO BEAUNE

St-André
de Covey

Cormatin
Cluny

Tournus

Mâcon
Pont de Veyle
Vonnas
Châtillon-sur-Chalaronne

Ars-sur-Formans

Bourgoin-Jallieu

Rhône

Fuissé
Juliénas
St-Amour
Chénas
Fleurie
Chiroubles
Villié-Morgon
Odenas
Beaujolais
Route du Vin

Villefranche-sur-Saône **32**

Bagnols

L'Arbresle **31**

Lyon **1 - 30**
see detail map

Saône

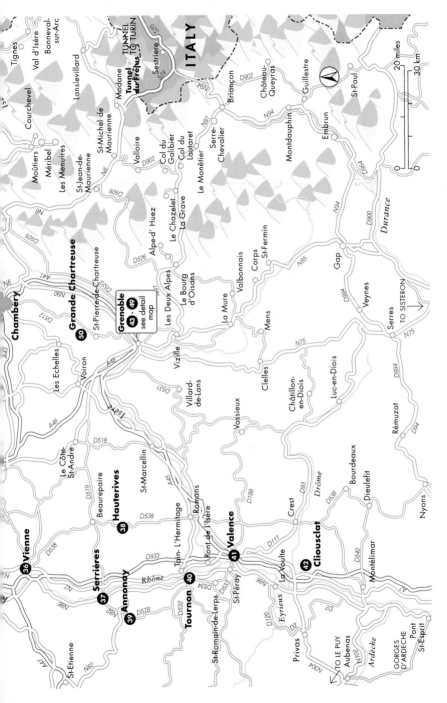

TIMING Spend the morning ambling around Vieux Lyon's traboules and patios. After a trip to the top of the Fourvière hill for a look at the basilica and the Roman ruins, have lunch in one of Vieux Lyon's many bouchons. (There's also the Restaurant de Fourvière [☎ 04–78–25–21–15], a spectacular restaurant overlooking all of Lyon next to the basilica.) In the afternoon explore the Croix Rousse District and its traboules and museums. Note that most museums are closed Monday.

What to See

⓫ **Basilique de Notre-Dame-de-Fourvière.** The rather pompous late-19th-century basilica, at the top of the ficelle, is—for better or worse—the symbol of Lyon. Its mock-Byzantine architecture and hilltop site make it a close relative of Paris's Sacré-Coeur. Both were built to underline the might of the Roman Catholic Church after the Prussian defeat of France in 1870 gave rise to the birth of the anticlerical Third Republic. The excessive gilt, marble, and mosaics in the interior underscore the Church's wealth, although they masked its lack of political clout at that time. One of the few places in Lyon where you can't see the basilica is the adjacent terrace, whose panorama reveals the city—with the cathedral of St-Jean in the foreground and the glass towers of the reconstructed Part-Dieu business complex glistening behind. For a yet more sweeping view, climb the 287 steps to the basilica observatory. ⊠ *Pl. de Fourvière, Fourvière* 🖼 *Observatory €2* ⊙ *Observatory Easter–Oct., daily 10–noon and 2–6; Nov.–Easter, weekends 2–6. Basilica daily 8–noon and 2–6.*

❽ **Cathédrale St-Jean.** Solid and determined—having withstood the sieges of time, revolution, and war—the cathedral's stumpy facade is stuck almost bashfully onto the nave. Although the mishmash inside has its moments—the fabulous 13th-century stained-glass windows in the choir and the varied window tracery and vaulting in the side chapels—the interior lacks drama and harmony. Still, it is an architectural history lesson. The cathedral dates from the 12th century, and the chancel is Romanesque, but construction on the whole continued over three centuries. The 14th-century astronomical clock, in the north transept, is a marvel of technology very much worth seeing. It chimes a hymn to St. John on the hour at noon, 2, 3, and 4 as a screeching rooster and other automatons enact the Annunciation. History majors will want to know that in 1600 Henri IV came to Lyon to meet his Italian fiancée, Marie de' Medici, en route from Marseille; he took one look at her, gave her the okay, and they were married immediately in this cathedral. To the right of the Cathédrale St-Jean stands the 12th-century **Manécanterie** (choir school). ⊠ *70 rue St-Jean, Vieux Lyon* ☎ *04–78–92–82–29.*

⓮ **Hôtel Bullioud.** This Renaissance mansion, close to the Hôtel Paterin, is noted for its courtyard, with an ingenious gallery (1536) built by Philibert Delorme, one of France's earliest and most accomplished exponents of Classical architecture. He also worked on several spectacular châteaux in central France, including those at Fontainebleau and Chenonceau. ⊠ *8 rue Juiverie, off pl. St-Paul, Vieux Lyon.*

⓭ **Hôtel Paterin.** This is a particularly fine example of the type of splendid Renaissance mansion found in the area. ⊠ *4 rue Juiverie, off pl. St-Paul, Vieux Lyon.*

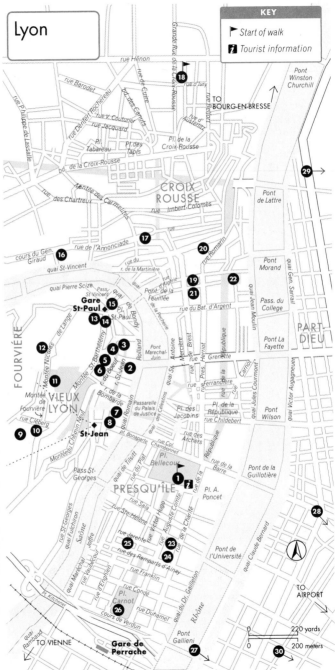

Lyon

KEY

▶ Start of walk

🛈 Tourist information

7 Jardin Archéologique (Archaeological Garden). This garden contains the excavated ruins of two churches that succeeded one another on this site. The foundations of the churches were unearthed during a time when apartment buildings—constructed here after churches had been destroyed during the Revolution—were being demolished. One arch still remains and forms part of the ornamentation in the garden. ✉ *Entrance on rue de la Bombarde, Vieux Lyon.*

16 Jardin des Chartreux. This garden is just one of several small, leafy parks in Lyon. It's a peaceful place to take a break while admiring the splendid view of the river and Fourvière Hill. ✉ *Entrance on quai St-Vincent, Presqu'île.*

17 Jardin des Plantes (Botanical Garden). In the peaceful, luxurious Botanical Garden are remnants of the once-huge **Amphithéâtre des Trois Gauls** (Three Gauls Amphitheater), built in AD 19. ✉ *Entrance on rue de la Tourette, Vieux Lyon* ⊘ *Dawn–dusk.*

3 Loge du Change. Originally a center for the money-changing activities that took place here in the late 15th and 16th centuries, the building was constructed by Simon Gourdet in the mid-16th century and completely redesigned in 1747 by Jean-Baptiste Roche, using plans supplied by his famous colleague Jacques-Germain Soufflot, the architect of Paris's Panthéon. After serving as an inn during the French Revolution, the Loge became a Protestant church in 1803, and is now one of Vieux Lyon's prime concert venues. ✉ *Pl. du Change, Vieux Lyon.*

6 Maison du Crible. This 17th-century mansion is one of Lyon's oldest. In the courtyard you can glimpse a charming garden and the original Tour Rose—an elegant pink tower. The higher the tower in those days, the greater the prestige—this one was owned by the tax collector—and it's not so different today. ✉ *16 rue du Boeuf, off pl. du Petit-Collège, Vieux Lyon* ✎ *Free* ⊘ *Daily 10–noon and 2–6.*

10 Musée de la Civilisation Gallo-Romaine (Gallo-Roman Civilization Museum). Since 1933, systematic excavations have unearthed vestiges of Lyon's opulent Roman precursor. The statues, mosaics, vases, coins, and tombstones are excellently displayed in this semisubterranean museum next to the Roman theaters. The large, bronze Table Claudienne is inscribed with part of Emperor Claudius's address to the Roman Senate in AD 48, conferring senatorial rights on the Roman citizens of Gaul. ✉ *17 rue Clébert, Fourvière* ☎ *04–72–38–81–90* ⊕ *www.museesgallo-romains.com* ✎ *€4* ⊘ *Tues.–Sun. 10–5.*

4 Musée Historique de Lyon (Lyon Historical Museum). This museum is housed in the city's largest ensemble of Renaissance buildings, the Hôtel de Gadagne, built between the 14th and 16th centuries. Medieval sculpture, furniture, pottery, paintings, and engravings are on display. Also housed here is the **Musée de la Marionnette** (Puppet Museum), tracing the history of marionettes, beginning with Guignol and Madelon (Lyon's Punch and Judy, created by Laurent Mourguet in 1795). ✉ *1 pl. du Petit-Collège, Vieux Lyon* ☎ *04–78–42–03–61* ✎ *€4* ⊘ *Wed.–Mon. 10:45–6.*

▶ ❶ **Place Bellecour.** Shady, imposing place Bellecour is one of the largest squares in France and is Lyon's fashionable center, midway between the Saône and the Rhône. Classical facades erected along its narrower sides in 1800 lend architectural interest. The large, bronze equestrian statue of Louis XIV, installed in 1828, is the work of local sculptor Jean Lemot. On the south side of the square is the **tourist office** (☎ 04–72–77–69–69). ⊠ *Presqu'île.*

❺ **Rue du Boeuf.** Like the parallel rue St-Jean, rue du Boeuf has lovely traboules, courtyards, spiral staircases, towers, and facades. The traboule at No. 31 rue du Boeuf hooks through and out on to rue de la Bombarde. No. 36 has a notable courtyard. At No. 19 is the standout Maison de l'Outarde d'Or, so named for the great bustard, a goose-like game bird, depicted in the coat of arms over the door. The late-15th-century house and courtyard inside have spiral staircases in the towers, which were built as symbols of wealth and power. The Hotel Tour Rose at No. 22 has, indeed, a beautiful *tour rose* (pink tower) in the inner courtyard. At the corner of place Neuve St-Jean and rue du Boeuf is the famous sign portraying the bull for which rue du Boeuf is named, the work of the Renaissance Italy–trained French sculptor Jean de Bologne. No. 18 contains Antic Wine, the emporium of English-speaking Georges Dos Santos, "the flying sommelier, " who is a wealth of information (throw away this book and just ask Georges). No. 20 conceals one of the rare open-shaft spiral staircases allowing for a view all the way up the core. At No. 16 is the Maison du Crible, and No. 14 has another splendid patio. ⊠ *Vieux Lyon.*

FodorśChoice
★

❷ **Rue St-Jean.** Once Vieux Lyon's major thoroughfare, this street leads north from place St-Jean to place du Change, where money changers operated during medieval trade fairs. Many area streets were named for their shops, still heralded by intricate iron signs. The elegant houses along the street were built for illustrious Lyonnais bankers and Italian silk merchants during the French Renaissance. The traboule at No. 54 leads all the way through to rue du Boeuf No. 27. Beautiful Renaissance courtyards can be visited at No. 50, No. 52, and No. 42. At No. 27 rue St-Jean an especially lovely traboule winds through to No. 6 rue des 3 Maries. No. 28 has a pretty courtyard; No. 24, the Maison Laurencin, has another; Maison Le Viste at No. 21 has a splendid facade. The courtyard at No. 18 merits a close look. The houses at No. 5 place du Gouvernment and No. 7 and No. 1 rue St-Jean also have facades you won't want to miss. ⊠ *Vieux Lyon.*

❻ **St-Paul.** The 12th-century church of St-Paul is noted for its octagonal lantern, its frieze of animal heads in the chancel, and its Flamboyant Gothic chapel. ⊠ *Pl. St-Paul, Vieux Lyon.*

❾ **Théâtres Romains** (Roman Theaters). Two ruined, semicircular Roman-built theaters are tucked into the hillside, just down from the summit of Fourvière. The **Grand Théâtre,** the oldest Roman theater in France, was built in 15 BC to seat 10,000. The smaller **Odéon,** with its geometric flooring, was designed for music and poetry performances. Lyon International Arts Festival performances are held here each September. ⊠ *Colline Fourvière, Fourvière* ☞ *Free* ☉ *Daily 9–dusk.*

⑫ Tour Métallique (Metal Tower). Beyond Fourvière Basilica is this skeletal metal tower built in 1893 and now a television transmitter. The stone staircase, the **Montée Nicolas-de-Lange**, at the foot of the tower, is a direct but steep route from the basilica to the St-Paul train station. ✉ *Colline Fourvière, Fourvière.*

Presqu'île & the Croix Rousse District

Presqu'île, the peninsula flanked by the Saône and the Rhône, is Lyon's modern center, with fashionable shops, a trove of restaurants and museums, and squares graced by fountains and 19th-century buildings. This is the core of Lyon, where you'll be tempted to wander the streets from one riverbank to the other and to explore the entire stretch from the Gare de Perrache railroad station to the place Bellecour and up to place des Terreaux.

The hillside and hilltop district north of place des Terreaux, the Croix Rousse District, is flanked by the Jardins des Plantes on the west and the Rhône on the east. It once resounded to the clanking of looms churning out the exquisite silks and other cloth that made Lyon famous. By the 19th century more than 30,000 *canuts* (weavers) worked on looms on the upper floors of the houses. So tightly packed were the buildings that the only way to transport fabrics was through the traboules, which had the additional advantage of protecting the fine cloth in poor weather.

a good walk

Armed with a detailed map, available from the Lyon Tourist Office, you could spend hours "trabouling" on the Croix Rousse hillside, which is still busy with textile merchants despite the demise of the old-style cottage industry of silk weaving. In the very northern part of the Croix Rousse District you can see ancient looms at the **Maison des Canuts ⑱** ▶. For an impromptu tour of the area, walk along rue Imbert-Colomès. At No. 20, turn right through the traboule that leads to rue des Tables Claudiennes and right again across place Chardonnet. Take the Passage Mermet alongside the church of St-Polycarpe; then turn left onto rue Leynaud. A traboule at No. 32 leads to the Montée St-Sébastien. Here's a transfixing trompe l'oeil on the Mur des Canuts, a large wall painted with depictions of local citizens both seated and walking up a passageway of steps. Exit the Croix Rousse District by taking rue Romarin down to **place des Terreaux ⑲**.

The sizable place des Terreaux has two notable buildings: on the north side is the **Hôtel de Ville ⑳**, the Town Hall; on the south side is the elegant **Musée des Beaux-Arts ㉑**, the art museum. To reach the barrel-vaulted **Opéra de Lyon ㉒**, walk east across place des Terreaux and through the ground floor of the Hôtel de Ville (go around if it's closed). For a culinary delight, detour to the east over the Rhône by walking south along the boulevard de la République; at place Regaud turn left and head over the Pont Lafayette for a 2 km (1½ mi) walk to **Les Halles de Lyon,** the city's main produce market—in a city where food is worshipped, this is one of its many temples. Backtrack over the river and check out Lyon's fashionable shops by walking down the pedestrian-only rue de la République and cross place Bellecour. Continue 300 yards farther (now rue de la Charité) to the **Musée des Arts Décoratifs** ㉓, a decorative arts museum. Next door is the **Musée Historique des Tissus** ㉔, a textile museum.

Now cut west across rue des Remparts d'Ainay to the **Basilique de Saint-Martin d'Ainay** ㉕, the abbey church of one of the oldest monasteries in the Lyon region. The lovely, archaic **Voûte d'Ainay** just past the church was the former gateway to the abbey. Just outside to the left is the much-filmed and -photographed restaurant Comptoir Abel Bar, also known as À La Voûte d'Ainay. Continue south to **place Carnot** ㉖ and the Gare de Perrache railway and subway station.

After crossing the Rhône on Pont Galliéni and going up avenue Berthelot, visit the **Centre d'Histoire de la Résistance et de la Déportation** ㉗, which focuses on Lyon's Resistance movement during World War II. If you're a film buff, head to the **Institut Lumière** ㉘. From the center walk east along avenue Berthelot to avenue Jean-Jaurès; take a right and then a left on grande rue de Guillotière, then another right on rue Premier-Film. To return to Presqu'île, walk west to Pont de la Guillotière.

If you've seen all of Lyon's main cultural sights and want to indulge your children, take the métro from Perrache train station to Masséna and the **Parc de la Tête d'Or** ㉙, which has a small zoo and pony rides. If you're an architecture buff, take the métro from place Bellecour to Monplaisir-Lumière (it's a bit of a long trip) and walk 10 minutes south along rue Antoine to the **Musée Urbain Tony Garnier** ㉚, usually referred to as the Cité de la Création.

TIMING It will take you at least five hours to explore Presqu'île and the Croix Rousse District. A full day would be even better. The Musée des Beaux-Arts deserves at least two hours, the Musée des Arts Décoratifs and the Musée Historique des Tissus another 45 minutes each. The explorations east of the Rhône might entail another half day. Note that most museums are closed Monday; the Musée des Beaux-Arts is open Monday but closed Tuesday.

What to See

㉕ **Basilique de Saint-Martin d'Ainay.** The abbey church of one of Lyon's most ancient monasteries, this fortified church dates back to a 10th-century Benedictine abbey and a 9th-century sanctuary before that. The millenary, circa-1000 energy field is palpable around this hulking structure, especially near the rear of the apse where the stained-glass windows glow richly in the twilight. One of the earliest buildings in France to be classified a national monument, in 1844, its interior murals and frescoes are disappointingly severe compared to the quirky, rough exterior. ✉ *Place de l'Abbaye d'Ainay, Presqu'île* ☎ *04–78–72–10–03* ✉ *Free* ☉ *Daily 9–1 and 4–7.*

㉗ **Centre d'Histoire de la Résistance et de la Déportation** (Museum of the History of the Resistance and the Deportation). During World War II, especially after 1942, Lyon played an important role in the Resistance movement against the German occupation of France. Displays include equipment, such as radios and printing presses, photographs, and exhibits recreating the clandestine lives and heroic exploits of Resistance fighters. ⊠ *14 av. Berthelot, Part-Dieu* ☎ *04–78–72–23–11* ⌨ *€4* ⊙ *Wed.–Sun. 9–5:30.*

②⓪ Hôtel de Ville (Town Hall). Architects Jules Hardouin-Mansart and Robert de Cotte redesigned the very impressive facade of the Town Hall after a 1674 fire. The rest of the building dates from the early 17th century. ⊠ *Pl. des Terreaux, Presqu'île.*

off the
beaten
path

LES HALLES DE LYON – For a sensory feast you won't soon forget, walk over west of the Rhône to Les Halles de Lyon, the city's main produce market, especially on Saturday, Sunday, or a holiday morning when the place crackles with excitement. On the left bank of the Rhône on Part-Dieu's Cours Lafayette, the market offers everything from pristine lettuce to wild mushrooms to poulet de Bresse to caviar, from 150 kinds of cheese at the Alain Martinet stand to the *"Rolls de l'huitre"* (Rolls-Royce of oysters) at Chez Georges. The *salons de dégustation* (tasting rooms) are in fact raging restaurants with a joie de vivre hard to surpass in Lyon, or anywhere else. Maison Monestir, le Jardin des Halles, Chez Léon, Au Patio are all good, but Maison Rousseau, with its raised platforms amid the produce for serving oysters and snails with marvelous bread, St-Marcellin cheese, and a white Côtes du Rhône, stands out.

②⑧ Institut Lumière. On the site where the Lumière brothers invented the first cinematographic apparatus, this museum has daily showings of early films and contemporary movies as well as a permanent exhibit about the Lumières. Researchers may access the archives, which contain numerous films, books, periodicals, director and actor information, photo files, posters, and more. ⊠ *25 rue Premier-Film, Part-Dieu* ☎ *04–78–78–18–95* ⊕ *www.institut-lumiere.org* ⌨ *€4* ⊙ *Tues.–Fri. 9–12:30 and 2–6, weekends 2–6.*

▶ ⟳ **①⑧ Maison des Canuts** (Silk Weavers' Museum). Despite the industrialization of silk and textile production, old-time Jacquard looms are still in action at this historical house in the Croix Rousse. The weavers are happy to show children how to operate a miniature loom. ⊠ *12 rue d'Ivry, La Croix Rousse* ☎ *04–78–28–62–04* ⌨ *€3* ⊙ *Sept.–July, weekdays 8:30–noon and 2–6:30, Sat. 9–noon and 2–6; Aug., Tues.–Fri. 8:30–noon and 2–6:30, Sat. 9–noon and 2–6.*

★ **②③ Musée des Arts Décoratifs** (Decorative Arts Museum). Housed in an 18th-century mansion, this museum has fine collections of silverware, furniture, objets d'art, porcelain, and tapestries. ⊠ *34 rue de la Charité, Presqu'île* ☎ *04–78–38–42–00* ⌨ *€6, joint ticket with the nearby Musée Historique des Tissus* ⊙ *Tues.–Sun. 10–5:30.*

★ **②① Musée des Beaux-Arts** (Fine Arts Museum). In the elegant 17th-century Palais St-Pierre, once a Benedictine abbey, this museum has one of France's largest collections of art after that of the Louvre, including Rodin's *Walker,* Byzantine ivories, Etruscan statues, and Egyptian artifacts. Amid Old Master, Impressionist, and modern paintings are works by the tight-knit Lyon School, characterized by exquisitely rendered flowers and overbearing religious sentimentality. Note Louis Janmot's *Poem of the Soul,* immaculately painted visions that are by turns heavenly, hellish, and downright spooky. ✉ *Palais St-Pierre, 20 pl. des Terreaux, Presqu'île* ☎ 04–72–10–17–40 ✉ €4 ☾ *Wed.–Mon. 10:30–6.*

need a break? For an adorable perch over the Rhône and a perfect sunset observation point, **Pieds Humides** (✉ 15 Quai Victor Augagneur, Part-Dieu)—literally, "damp feet"—is a nonpareil little kiosk for a coffee, a *pot de vin,* or a passable *plat du jour.*

㉔ Musée Historique des Tissus (Textile History Museum). On display is a fascinating exhibit of intricate carpets, tapestries, and silks, including Asian tapestries from as early as the 4th century, Turkish and Persian carpets from the 16th to the 18th centuries, and 18th-century Lyon silks, so lovingly depicted in many portraits of the time and still the star of many costume exhibits mounted throughout the world today. ✉ *34 rue de la Charité, Presqu'île* ☎ 04–78–38–42–00 ✉ *€6, joint ticket with Musée des Arts Décoratifs* ☾ *Tues.–Sun. 10–5:30.*

㉚ Musée Urbain Tony Garnier (Tony Garnier Urban Museum). Known also as the Cité de la Création (City of Creation), this project was France's first attempt at low-income housing. Over the years, tenants have tried to bring some art and cheerfulness to their environment: 22 giant murals depicting the work of Tony Garnier, the turn-of-the-20th-century Lyon architect, were painted on the walls of these huge housing projects, built in 1920 and 1933. Artists from around the world, with the support of UNESCO, have added their vision to the creation of the ideal housing project. To get there, take the métro from place Bellecour to Monplaisir-Lumière and walk 10 minutes south along rue Antoine. ✉ *4 rue Serpollières, Part-Dieu* ☎ 04–78–75–16–75 ✉ *€4* ☾ *Daily 2–6.*

㉒ Opéra de Lyon. The barrel-vaulted Lyon Opera, a reincarnation of a moribund 1831 building, was designed by star French architect Jean Nouvel and built in the early 1990s. It incorporates a columned exterior, soaring glass vaulting, Neoclassical public spaces, an all-black interior down to and including the bathrooms and toilets, and the latest backstage magic. High above, looking out between the heroic statues lined up along the parapet, is a small restaurant, Les Muses. ✉ *Pl. de la Comédie, Presqu'île* ☎ 04–72–00–45–00, 04–72–00–45–45 *for tickets* ⊕ *www.opera-lyon.org.*

㉙ Parc de la Tête d'Or (Golden Head Park). On the bank of the Rhône, this 300-acre park encompasses a lake, pony rides, and a small zoo. It's ideal for an afternoon's outing with children. Take the métro from Perrache train station to Masséna. ✉ *Pl. du Général-Leclerc, quai Charles-de-Gaulle, Cité Internationale* ✉ *Free* ☾ *Dawn–dusk.*

㉖ Place Carnot. Spread out in front of the Perrache train station built in 1857, this bustling square holds an excellent Christmas market from early December through New Year's. The two main monuments represent La République and (the seated figure) the City of Lyon. The Brasserie Georges, dating from 1836, has hosted legendary personalities from Mistinguet to Jacques Brel and Johnny Halliday. ✉ *Presqu'île.*

⑲ Place des Terreaux. The four majestic horses rearing up from a monumental 19th-century fountain in the middle of this large square are by Frédéric-Auguste Bartholdi, who sculpted New York Harbor's Statue of Liberty. The 69 fountains embedded in the wide expanse of the square are illuminated by fiber-optic technology at night. The notable buildings on either side are the Hôtel de Ville and the Musée des Beaux-Arts. ⊠ *Presqu'île.*

Where to Stay & Eat

★ **$$$$** ✕ **Auberge de l'Île.** For a pretty one-hour walk up the river Saône's right bank and a return down the other, the Ile Barbe is a lush and leafy enclave to keep in mind. Alex Ansanay's lovely restaurant, whether outside on the terrace or inside the graceful former 17th-century monastery refectory, serves smart, contemporary cuisine based on fresh market products prepared with originality. Look for game in the fall and winter. The wine list is strong in local Côtes du Rhône and Macon treasures. ⊠ *L'Ile Barbe, Collonges au Mont-D'Or* ☎ *04–78–83–99–49* ⚑ *Reservations essential* ⊟ *AE, MC, V* ☉ *Closed Sun., Mon.,and Aug. 1–24.*

★ **$$$$** ✕ **Léon de Lyon.** Chef Jean-Paul Lacombe's innovative uses of the region's butter, cream, and foie gras put this restaurant at the forefront of the city's gastronomic scene. Dishes such as fillet of veal with celery and leg of lamb with fava beans are memorable; suckling pig comes with foie gras, onions, and a truffle salad. Alcoves and wood paneling in this 19th-century house add charm to the mix. Evening prix-fixe menus are €115 and €170, with a lunch menu at €61. ⊠ *1 rue Pléney, Presqu'île* ☎ *04–72–10–11–12* ⚑ *Reservations essential* 🖾 *Jacket required* ⊟ *AE, DC, MC, V* ☉ *Closed Sun., Mon., and 1st 3 wks Aug.*

★ **$$$$** ✕ **Matthieu Viannay.** This bright young star in Lyon's dining scene has attracted the attention and admiration of this demanding gastronomical city's food critics and cuisine cognoscenti with daring new recipes combining originality, conceptual simplicity, and authenticity of ingredients. His escargots in bone-marrow croquette are as spare and novel as the stripped out stone-and-wood decor of this contemporary enclave, set in the upper Les Brotteaux district (east of the Rhône and up-river from Pont Morand behind the Opera). ⊠ *47 av. Foch, Les Brotteaux* ☎ *04–78–89–55–19* ⚑ *Reservations essential* ⊟ *AE, MC, V* ☉ *Closed weekends except holidays; Aug.; and Dec. 29–Jan. 5.*

$$$$ ✕ **Nicholas Le Bec.** Ever since walking off with the 2002 Gault-Millau Chef
Fodor'sChoice of the Year honors, Nicolas Le Bec has been hot as a pistol, whether at
★ his past spot, Les Loges, or here in this cozy hideaway near Place Bellecour. With a constantly changing menu responding to the seasons, the market, and the chef's abundant curiosity, there is always a new take on anything from artichokes to risotto in this postmodern culinary antithesis of traditional Lyonnais bouchon cooking. Le Bec's past triumphs include his duck foie gras with black figs and his roast crayfish with purple artichokes, and fans keep packing this place to see what new wonders he has up his sleeve. ⊠ *14 rue Grolée, Presqu'île* ☎ *04–78–42–15–00* ⊕ *www.nicholaslebec.com* ⚑ *Reservations essential* ⊟ *AE, MC, V* ☉ *Closed Sun., Mon., and Aug. 1–16.*

$$$$ ✗ **Paul Bocuse.** Parisians hop the TGV to dine at this culinary shrine in
Fodor'sChoice Collonges-au-Mont-d'Or, then snooze back to the capital. Whether Bo-
★ cuse—who kick-started the "new" French cooking back in the 1970s
and became a superstar in the process—is here or not, the legendary black-
truffle soup in pastry crust he created in 1975 to honor President Gis-
card d'Estaing will be. So will the frogs'-leg soup with watercress, the
green bean-and–artichoke salad with foie gras, or the Bresse wood-pi-
geon "tripled": drumstick in puff pastry with young cabbage, breast
roasted and glazed in cognac, and an aromatic dark pâté of the innards.
For a mere €158 for two, the *volaille de Bresse truffée en vessie "Mere
Fillioux"* (Bresse hen cooked in a pig bladder with truffles) comes to
the table looking something like a basketball—the bladder is removed
and discarded revealing a poached chicken within. Like the desserts, the
grand dining room is done in traditional style. Call ahead if you want
to find out whether Bocuse will be cooking, and book far in advance.
⊠ *50 quai de la Plage, Collonges-au-Mont-d'Or, Pont de Collonges Nord*
☎ *04-72-42-90-90* ⊕ *www.bocuse.fr* ⌫ *Reservations essential* 🏛 *Jacket
required* ⊟ *AE, DC, MC, V.*

$$$–$$$$ ✗ **Les Loges.** This lovely dining room, lavishly appointed with mahogany
chairs, modern art, and a giant medieval hearth, serves a range of culi-
nary delights reflecting Lyon's fame as the crossroads of cuisines influ-
enced by the Mediterranean to the south, the Alps to the east, and the
Massif Central to the west. Chef Anthony Bonnet's *poitrine de veau* (breast
of veal) with asparagus and essence of almonds or his *foie gras poèlé
au coing* (sauteed duck or goose liver with quince) are two specialties
to look for, though the menu is in constant flux according to markets
and seasons. ⊠ *6 rue du Boeuf, Vieux Lyon* ☎ *04-72-77-44-44* ⊟ *AE,
DC, MC, V* ☾ *Closed Sun., Mon., and Aug. 4–26.*

$$–$$$$ ✗ **L'Alexandrin.** Chef Alex Alexanian's take on nouvelle cuisine is everything to every mouth. If succulent game is your weakness, this is the place,
especially during hunting season. If you're tired of oversaturated Lyonnais cuisine, try the special "*fruits et légumes*" menu, a creative feast of
fresh goodies selected each morning from Les Halles market, just around
the corner. Whether a dish is based on veal, rabbit, or sole, Alexanian's
touch is always light on calories and heavy on flavor. ⊠ *83 rue Moncey,
Part-Dieu* ☎ *04-72-61-15-69* ⊟ *MC, V* ☾ *Closed Sun., Mon., and
July 29–Aug. 20.*

★ **$$–$$$** ✗ **L'Étage.** Hidden over place des Terreaux, this semi-secret upstairs din-
ing room prepares some of Lyon's finest new cuisine. A place at the window (admittedly hard to come by), overlooking the facade of the Beaux
Arts academy across the square, is a moment to remember, especially if
it's during the December 8th Festival of Lights. ⊠ *4 pl. des Terreaux,
Presqu'île* ☎ *04-78-28-19-59* ⊟ *AE, DC, MC, V* ☾ *Closed Feb.,
July 22–Aug. 22, Sun., and Mon.*

$$–$$$ ✗ **Le Nord.** Should you want to keep some change in your pocket and
still sample cooking by Paul Bocuse–trained-and-supervised chefs, lunch
at one of his four bistros distributed around Lyon's cardinal points. Specialties include dishes from the *rotissoire* and excellent fish and seafood.
Bocuse's other spots are **Le Sud** (⊠ 11 pl. Antonin-Poncet, Presqu'île
☎ 04-72-77-80-00), the rollicking **L'Est** (⊠ Gare des Brotteaux 14,

Les Brotteaux ☎ 04–37–24–25–26) in the old 19th-century Brotteaux train station, and **L'Ouest** (✉ Quai du Commerce 1, Villefranche ☎ 04–78–35–63–13). ✉ *18 rue Neuve, Presqu'île* ☎ *04–72–10–69–69* ▭ *AE, DC, MC, V.*

$–$$$ ✕ **Café des Fédérations.** For 80 years this sawdust-strewn café with homey red-check tablecloths has reigned as one of the city's leading bouchons. It may have overextended its stay, however, by trading on past glory. Some readers report a desultory hand in the kitchen, and native Lyonnais seem to head elsewhere. Others say Raymond Fulchiron not only serves deftly prepared local classics like *boudin blanc* (white-meat sausage) but also stops by to chat with you, making you feel at home. ✉ *8 rue du Major-Martin, Presqu'île* ☎ *04–78–28–26–00* ▭ *AE, DC, MC, V* ☾ *Closed weekends and Aug.*

★ $–$$$ ✕ **Les Muses.** High up under the glass vault of the Opéra de Lyon designed by Jean Nouvel, this small restaurant looks out past the backs of sculptures of the eight Muses over the Hôtel de Ville. The quality and variety of the creative contemporary cuisine makes it hard to decide between the choices offered, but the salmon in butter sauce with watercress mousse is a winner. ✉ *Pl. Comédie (Opéra de Lyon, 7th floor), Presqu'île* ☎ *04–72–00–45–58* ⌘ *Reservations essential* ▭ *AE, MC, V* ☾ *No dinner Sun.*

$–$$ ✕ **Anticipation.** Light, creative dishes using the region's famed specialties (such as poulet de Bresse) are carefully prepared here by John Rosiak, a former cook at Georges Blanc. The homey feel makes it a place where you can settle in for an evening of good fare and fun. ✉ *8 rue Chavanne, Presqu'île* ☎ *04–78–30–91–92* ▭ *AE, MC, V* ☾ *Closed Mon. No dinner Sun.*

$–$$ ✕ **Chez Hugon.** This typical bouchon-tavern with red-check tablecloths is behind the Musée des Beaux-Arts and is one of the city's top-rated insider spots. Practically a club, it's crowded with regulars, who keep busy trading quips with the owner while Madame prepares the best *tablier de sapeur* (tripe marinated in wine and fried in breadcrumbs) in town. Whether you order the hunks of homemade pâté, the stewed chicken in wine vinegar sauce, or the plate of *ris de veau* (sweetbreads), your dinner will add up to good, inexpensive food and plenty of it. ✉ *12 rue Pizay, Presqu'île* ☎ *04–78–28–10–94* ▭ *MC, V* ☾ *Closed weekends and Aug.*

$–$$
Fodor'sChoice
★
✕ **Comptoir Abel.** This charming 400-year-old house is one of Lyon's most frequently filmed and photographed taverns. Simple wooden tables in wood-paneled dining rooms, quirky art on every wall, heavy-bottomed *pot lyonnais* wine bottles: every detail is obviously pampered and lovingly produced. The *salade lyonnaise* (green salad with homemade croutons and sautéed bacon, topped with a poached egg) or the *rognons madère* (kidneys in a madeira sauce) are standouts. ✉ *25 rue Guynemer, Presqu'île* ☎ *04–78–37–46–18* ▭ *AE, DC, MC, V* ☾ *Closed Sat., Sun., and Dec. 22–Jan. 2.*

$–$$ ✕ **Les Lyonnais.** This popular brasserie, decorated with photographs of local celebrities, is particularly animated. The simple food—chicken simmered for hours in wine, meat stews, and grilled fish—is served on bare wood tables. A blackboard announces plats du jour, which are less expensive than items on the printed menu. Try the *caille aux petits* *legumes* (quail with vegetables) for a change from heavier bouchon fare such as *la quenelle* (pike dumpling) or *l'andouillette* (sausage). ⊠ *1 rue Tramassac, Vieux Lyon* ☎ *04–78–37–64–82* ▭ *MC, V* ☉ *Closed Aug. and 1st wk Jan.*

$ ✕ **Jura.** The rows of tables, the 1934 mosaic-tile floor, and the absence of anything pretty gives this place the feel of a men's club. The mustachioed owner, looking as if he stepped out of the turn-of-the-20th-century prints on the walls, acts gruffly but with a smile, as his wife rushes around. The game and steak dishes are robust, as is the *cassoulet des escargots* (stew of beans, mutton, and snails). For dessert, stick with the fine cheese selection. ⊠ *25 rue Tupin, Presqu'île* ☎ *04–78–42–20–57* ▭ *MC, V* ☉ *Closed weekends May–Sept., Sun. and Mon. Oct.–Apr.*

★ $ ✕ **Mâchonnerie.** The word *mâchon* comes from the morning snack of the silk weaver or *canut*, and has come to mean the typical food of the Lyon region. This is one of Lyon's most respected popular bistros, under the *ficelle*, the funicular up to the Fourvière hill. Try the *andouillettes* (sausage). ⊠ *36 rue Tramassac, Vieux Lyon* ☎ *04–78–42–24–62* ▭ *AE, DC, MC, V* ☉ *No lunch weekdays. Closed Sun.*

$ ✕ **Le Vivarais.** Robert Duffaud's simple, tidy restaurant is an outstanding culinary value. Don't expect napkins folded into flower shapes—the excitement is on your plate, with dishes like *lièvre royale* (hare rolled and stuffed with foie gras and a hint of truffles). ⊠ *1 pl. du Dr-Gailleton, Presqu'île* ☎ *04–78–37–85–15* 🖘 *Reservations essential* ▭ *AE, MC, V* ☉ *Closed Sat. lunch and Sun., and July 27–Aug. 19, Dec. 25–Jan. 1.*

¢–$ ✕ **Brasserie Georges.** This inexpensive brasserie at the south end of rue de la Charité next to the Perrache train station is one of the city's largest and oldest, founded in 1836 but now in a palatial Art Deco building. Meals range from hearty veal stew or sauerkraut and sausage to more refined fare. The kitchen could be better—stick with the great standards, such as *saucisson brioché* (sausage in brioche stuffed with truffled foie gras)—but the ambience is as delicious as it comes. ⊠ *30 cours Verdun, Perrache* ☎ *04–72–56–54–54* ▭ *AE, DC, MC, V.*

★ ¢–$ ✕ **Café 203/Café 100 Tabac.** These two clever sister bistros near the opera are young, hot, and happening. One is named for the Peugeot 203 (an antique model of which is parked outside), and the other is a play on "100/sans" (100 percent–without) tobacco—yes, you read it here: a smoke-free restaurant in Europe. The Italianate cuisine is fresh and original, fast, inexpensive, and delicious. For a quick pre- or post-opera meal, this is the spot. ⊠ *9 rue du Garet, Presqu'île* ✉ *23 rue de l'Arbre Sec, Presqu'île* ☎ *04–78–42–24–62* ▭ *AE, DC, MC, V* ☉ *Closed Sun. No lunch weekdays from Sept. to Easter.*

★ $$$$ ✕▥ **La Cour des Loges.** King Juan Carlos of Spain, Celine Dion, and the Rolling Stones have all graced this most eye-popping of Lyon hotels. Spectacularly renovated around a glassed-in Renaissance courtyard, this former Jesuit convent is now an extravaganza of glowing fireplaces, Florentine crystal chandeliers, Baroque credenzas, high-beamed ceilings, mullioned windows, guest rooms swathed in Venetian red and antique Lyon silks, suites that are like artist ateliers, and Phillipe Starck bathrooms. The restaurant, **Les Loges,** is one of Lyon's most graceful dining rooms, with, in addition, a cellar-level wine bar and a café-picerie with a lovely vaulted ceiling. ⊠ *6 rue du Boeuf, Vieux Lyon, 69005* ☎ *04–72–77–44–44* 🖷 *04–72–40–93–61* ⊕ *www.courdesloges.com* ⤳ *52 rooms* ⚘ *Restaurant, tapas bar, minibars, cable TV, pool, health club, bar, meeting rooms, parking (fee)* ⊟ *AE, DC, MC, V.*

★ **$$$$** ✕⊡ **La Tour Rose.** Philippe Chavent's silk-swathed Vieux Lyon hotel occupies a Renaissance-period convent set around a gorgeous Florentine-style courtyard under a rose-washed tower. The glass-roof restaurant occupies a former chapel and offers views of the hanging garden overhead. Each guest room is named for a famous silk-weaving concern and decorated in its goods; taffetas, plissés, and velvets cover walls, windows, and beds in daring, even startling styles. The signature specials here—smoked-duck soup, skate in oyster coulis, hibiscus sorbet—are well worth all the extra louis d'or. Six apartments with kitchenettes in an adjacent annex provide excellent value for longer stays. ⊠ *22 rue du Boeuf, Vieux Lyon, 69005* ☎ *04–78–92–69–10* 🖷 *04–78–42–26–02* ⊕ *www.tour-rose.com* ⤳ *12 rooms, 6 apartments* ⚘ *Restaurant, minibars, cable TV, bar, meeting rooms, parking (fee), some pets allowed* ⊟ *AE, DC, MC, V.*

★ **$$$$** ⊡ **Villa Florentine.** High above the *Vieille Ville* (Old Town), near the Roman theaters and the basilica, this pristine hotel was once a 17th-century convent—and everyone knows the sisters always enjoyed the best real estate in town. It has beamed and vaulted ceilings, terraces, and particularly marvelous views, which are seen to best advantage from the pool and the excellent restaurant, Les Terrasses de Lyon. In time-warp fashion, 17th-century Italianate architectural details are contrasted with the latest in bright postmodern Italian furnishings. ⊠ *25–27 Montée St-Barthélémy, Fourvière, 69005* ☎ *04–72–56–56–56* 🖷 *04–72–40–90–56* ⊕ *www.villaflorentine.com* ⤳ *11 rooms, 8 suites* ⚘ *Restaurant, café, minibars, cable TV, pool, bar, Internet, meeting rooms, parking (fee), some pets allowed (fee)* ⊟ *AE, DC, MC, V.*

$$$–$$$$ ⊡ **Boscolo Grand Hôtel.** This Belle Époque hotel off place de la République has a courteous and efficient staff. Rooms have high ceilings, mostly modern furnishings, and one special piece such as an armoire or writing desk. Erté prints try hard to set a stylish tone in the guest rooms, the Rhône is just across the street, and tour groups are kept happy and content. ⊠ *11 rue Grôlée, Presqu'île, 69002* ☎ *04–72–40–45–45* 🖷 *04–78–37–52–55* ⊕ *www.boscolohotels.com* ⤳ *140 rooms* ⚘ *Restaurant, cable TV, bar, meeting rooms, parking (fee), some pets allowed (fee)* ⊟ *AE, DC, MC, V* ⦿| *BP.*

$$$ ⊡ **Globe et Cécil.** This impeccably bright and clean hotel tucked in just one block north of place Bellecour is in the very heart of Lyon. The rooms are as cheery and fresh as the lobby; the staff is effervescent and pleasant, and the cost-value ratio is a definite boon to the soul (and wallet). What this place may lack in time-varnished charm it compensates for with crisp, polite efficiency and comfort. ⊠ *21 rue Gasparin, Presqu'île, 69002* ☎ *04–78–42–58–95* 🖷 *04–72–41–99–06* ⊕ *www.globeetcecilhotel.com* ⤳ *60 rooms* ⚘ *Cable TV, bar, parking (fee), some pets allowed* ⊟ *AE, DC, MC, V* ⦿| *BP.*

$$$ 🏨 **Phénix Hotel.** This little hotel in Vieux Lyon is a winning combina-
FodorsChoice tion of location, charming staff, tastefully decorated rooms, and mod-
★ erate prices. Overlooking the Saône at the upstream edge of Vieux Lyon, the hotel's modern design and decor is gracefully juxtaposed with its 16th-century ceiling beams and Renaissance facade. Some rooms have fireplaces, and the smallish upper floor rooms are charmingly built into the eaves and rooftop dormers. ⊠ *7 Quai Bondy, Vieux Lyon, 69005* 🕾 *04–78–28–24–24* 🖷 *04–78–28–62–86* ⊕ *www.hotel-le-phenix.fr* 🛏 *36 rooms ₺ Breakfast room, cable TV, bar, meeting rooms, parking (fee), some pets allowed (fee)* ⊟ *AE, DC, MC, V* ⏀⏀ *BP.*

$$ 🏨 **Hôtel des Artistes.** This intimate hotel on an elegant square opposite the Théâtre des Célestins has long been popular among stage and screen artists; black-and-white photographs of actors and actresses adorn lobby walls. Rooms are smallish but modern and comfortable, and the friendly reception and great location appeal to all comers. ⊠ *8 rue Gaspard-André, Presqu'île, 69002* 🕾 *04–78–42–04–88* 🖷 *04–78–42–93–76* 🛏 *45 rooms ₺ Minibars; no a/c* ⊟ *AE, DC, MC, V.*

$ 🏨 **Citôtel Dubost.** This little gem is a lot better than a first glance might indicate. Rooms are small but impeccable; the art hanging around the walls is generic but good; the breakfast bread, croissant, and coffee is uniformly excellent, and the staff is friendly and helpful. The one-minute walk to Lyon's slick subway line at Gare Perrache can be handy in rain or in haste, though the walk to the other end of Presqu'île is an entertaining 45-minute gallop not to miss. ⊠ *19 pl. Carnot, Presqu'île, 69002* 🕾 *04–78–42–00–46* 🖷 *04–72–40–96–66* 🛏 *56 rooms ₺ Some pets allowed* ⊟ *AE, DC, MC, V.*

$ 🏨 **Hôtel Bayard.** Rooms at this hotel in the heart of town each have a distinctive look. One favorite, No. 2, overlooks the large square and has a canopy bed. For a group, opt for No. 15, which sleeps four. Only breakfast is served, but there are dozens of restaurants nearby. ⊠ *23 pl. Bellecour, Presqu'île, 69002* 🕾 *04–78–37–39–64* 🖷 *04–72–40–95–51* ⊕ *www.hotelbayard.com* 🛏 *22 rooms ₺ Cable TV, bar, parking (fee); no a/c* ⊟ *MC, V.*

★ $ 🏨 **Hôtel du Théâtre.** The friendly and enthusiastic owner is sufficient reason to recommend this small hotel. But its location and reasonable prices make it even more commendable. Rooms are simple but clean; those overlooking place des Célestins not only have a theatrical view but also a bathroom with a tub. Those facing the side have a shower only. Breakfast is included. ⊠ *10 rue de Savoie, Presqu'île, 69002* 🕾 *04–78–42–33–32* 🖷 *04–72–40–00–61* 🛏 *21 rooms ₺ Bar, parking (fee); no a/c* ⊟ *AE, DC, MC, V.*

Nightlife & the Arts

Lyon is the region's liveliest arts center; check the weekly *Lyon-Poche*, published on Wednesday and sold at newsstands, for cultural events and goings-on at the dozens of discos, bars, and clubs.

For darts and pints and jazz on weekends, head to the **Albion Public House** (⊠ 12 rue Ste-Catherine, Presqu'île 🕾 04–78–28–33–00), where they even accept British pounds. The low-key, chic **L'Alibi** (⊠ 13 quai Romain-

CloseUp

LYON'S DANCE BLOWOUT

YON'S BIENNALE DE LA DANCE *throws France's second city into perpetual motion for nearly three weeks every other September (on even-numbered years). Brainchild of Lyon choreographer Guy Darmet, 2002's tenth edition, entitled "Terra Latina—From the Rio Grande to Tierra del Fuego," brought together some 600 dancers and choreographers from 11 Latin American countries with another eight contemporary dance troupes invited from France. The 2004 chapter of the biennale featured dance companies from all over Europe, with an emphasis on new members of the European Union such as Poland, Hungary, Bulgaria, Slovakia, and the Czech Republic. The result, no matter which even year you choose, is a nonpareil dance blow-out at the confluence of the Saône and Rhône rivers. At each biennale, in addition to the more than 100 performances scheduled in the city's finest venues such as the Jean*

Nouvel opera house, the Maison de la Danse, and the cookie box-like Théâtre des Célestins, popular highlights include the tumultuous 4,500-dancer street parade that roars down the left bank of the Rhône on the festival's first Sunday, and the three Saturday night dance galas held in the graceful Brotteaux train station, the Halle Tony Garnier, or the Place des Terreaux. Collective dance classes for thousands and spontaneous outbursts of tango, salsa, or nearly any other genre of rhythmic movement ever devised, pop up all over town, while newspaper front pages feature little else. With the world's largest dance festival budget ($5,000,000) and two decades of solid success under his belt, Darmet's spectacular celebration of modern and contemporary dance in one of Europe's most exciting cities is still gaining momentum. The Web site www. biennale-de-lyon.org has all the exciting details.

Roland, Vieux Lyon ☎ 04–78–42–04–66) has a laser show along with the music. **Bar Live** (✉ 13 pl. Jules Ferry, Vieux Lyon ☎ 04–72–74–04–41) is in the old Brotteaux train station and is the current drinking haunt. Romantics rendezvous at the **Bar de la Tour Rose** (✉ 22 rue du Boeuf, Vieux Lyon ☎ 04–78–37–25–90).

Bouchon aux Vin (✉ 64 rue Mercière, Presqu'île ☎ 04–78–42–88–90) is a wine bar with 30-plus vintages. **La Cave des Voyageurs** (✉ 7 pl. St-Paul–St-Barthélémy, Vieux Lyon ☎ 04–78–28–92–28), just below the St-Paul train station, is a cozy place to try some top wines. Computer jocks head into cyberspace at **Le Chantier** (✉ 18–20 rue Ste-Catherine, Presqu'île ☎ 04–78–39–05–56), while their friends listen to jazz and nibble on tapas. Caribbean and African music pulses at **Le Club des Iles** (✉ 1 Grande-Rue des Feuillants, Presqu'île ☎ 04–78–39–16–35). Live jazz is played in the stone-vaulted basement of **Hot Club** (✉ 26 rue Lanterne, Presqu'île ☎ 04–78–39–54–74). A gay crowd is found among the 1930s blandishments at **La Ruche** (✉ 22 rue Gentil, Presqu'île ☎ 04–78–39–03–82). **Villa Florentine** (✉ 25 Montée St-Barthélémy, Fourvière ☎ 04–72–56–56–56) is a quiet spot for sipping a drink to the strains of a harpist, who plays on Friday and Saturday.

Café-Théâtre de L'Accessoire (✉ 26 rue de l'Annonciade, Presqu'île ☎ 04–78–27–84–84) is a leading café-theater where you can eat and drink while watching a review. **Le Complexe du Rire** (✉ 7 rue des Capucins, Presqu'île ☎ 04–78–27–23–59) is a lively satirical and comic review above place des Terreaux. The café-theater **Espace Gerson** (✉ 1 pl. Gerson, Vieux Lyon ☎ 04–78–27–96–99) presents revues in conjunction with dinner. The **Opéra de Lyon** (✉ 1 pl. de la Comédie, Presqu'île ☎ 04–72–00–45–45 ⊕ www.opera-lyon.org) presents plays, concerts, ballets, and opera from October to June. Lyon's Société de Musique de Chambre performs at **Salle Molière** (✉ 18 quai Bondy, Vieux Lyon ☎ 04–78–28–03–11).

Early fall sees the unforgettably spectacular **Biennale de la Danse** (Dance Biennial), which takes place in even-numbered years. See our CloseUp Box, "Lyon's Dance Blow-Out" (www.biennale-de-lyon.org/) for the full scoop. September is the time for the **Foire aux Tupiniers** (☎ 04–78–37–00–68), a pottery fair. October brings the **Festival Bach** (☎ 04–78–72–75–31). The **Biennale d'Art Contemporain** (Contemporary Art Biennial; ☎ 04–78–30–50–66) is held in odd-numbered years in October. The **Festival du Vieux Lyon** (☎ 04–78–42–39–04) is a music festival in November and December. On December 8, the Fête de La Immaculée Conception (Feast of the Immaculate Conception), startling lighting creations transform the city into a fantasy for the marvelous **Fête de Lumière**, Lyon's Festival of Lights.

Shopping

Lyon has the region's best shopping; it's still the nation's silk-and-textile capital, and all big-name designers have shops here—for their chic clothing emporia try the stores on rue du Président Édouard-Herriot and rue de la République in the center of town. Lyon's biggest shopping mall is the **Part-Dieu Shopping Center** (✉ Rue du Dr-Bouchut, Part-Dieu ☎ 04–72–60–60–62), where there are 14 movie theaters and 250 shops. France's major department stores are well represented in Lyon. **Galeries Lafayette** (✉ in Part-Dieu Shopping Center, Part-Dieu ☎ 04–72–61–44–44 ✉ 6 pl. des Cordeliers, Presqu'île ☎ 04–72–40–48–00 ✉ 200 bd. Pinel, Villeurbanne ☎ 04–78–77–82–12) has always brought Parisian flair to its outlying branches. **Printemps** (✉ 42 rue de la République, Presqu'île ☎ 04–72–41–29–29) is the Lyon outpost of the big Paris store.

Captiva (✉ 10 rue de la Charité, Perrache ☎ 04–78–37–96–15) is the boutique of a young designer who works mainly in silk. **Les Gones** (✉ 33 rue Leynaud, La Croix Rousse ☎ 04–78–28–40–78), in the Croix Rousse, is a boutique carrying the work of several young designers. The workshop of **Monsieur Georges Mattelon** (✉ Rue d'Ivry, Presqu'île ☎ 04–78–28–62–04) is one of the oldest silk-weaving shops in Lyon. Lyonnais designer **Clémentine** (✉ 18 rue Émile-Zola, Presqu'île) is good for well-cut, tailored clothing. **Étincelle** (✉ 34 rue St-Jean, Vieux Lyon) has trendy outfits for youngsters.

For antiques, wander down **rue Auguste-Comte** (✉ From pl. Bellecour to Perrache). **Image en Cours** (✉ 26 rue du Boeuf, Vieux Lyon) sells superb engravings. **La Maison des Canuts** (⊠ 10–12 rue d'Ivry, Croix Rousse) carries local textiles. Fabrics can also be found at the **Boutique des Soyeux Lyonnais** (⊠ 3 rue du Boeuf, Vieux Lyon).

For arts and crafts there are several places where you can find irresistible objects. Look for Lyonnais puppets on **place du Change.** For new art, try the **Marché des Artistes** (Artists' Market; ⊠ Quai Romain-Rolland, 5e, Vieux Lyon) every Sunday morning from 7 to 1. Held on Sunday morning is another **Marché des Artisans** (Crafts Market; ⊠ Quai Fulchiron, 5e, Vieux Lyon). A **Marché aux Puces** (Flea Market; ⊠ Take Bus 37; 1 rue du Canal, Villeurbanne) takes place on Thursday and Saturday mornings 8–noon and on Sunday 6–1. For **secondhand books** try the market along quai de la Pêcherie (2e) near place Bellecour, held every Saturday and Sunday 10–6.

Food markets are held from Tuesday through Sunday on boulevard de la Croix-Rousse (4e), at Les Halles on cours Lafayette (3e), on quai Victor Augagneur (3e), and on quai St-Antoine (2e). For up-to-the-minute information on food, restaurants, and great wines, don't miss the (prize-winning and English-speaking) "flying sommelier, " Georges Dos Santos at **Antic Wine** (⊠ 18 rue du Boeuf, Vieux Lyon ☎ 04–78–37–08–96). A wine shop with an excellent selection is **À Ma Vigne** (⊠ 18 rue Vaubecour, Presqu'île ☎ 04–78–37–05–29). **Cave de la Côte** (⊠ 5 rue Pleney, Presqu'île ☎ 04–78–42–93–20) also has good wines. For chocolates head to **Bernachon** (⊠ 42 cours Franklin-Roosevelt, Les Brotteaux); some say it's the best *chocolaterie* in France. For fragrances, photos, furniture, philosophy, and comprehensive Oriental tea culture, **Cha Yuan** (⊠ 7–9 rue des Remparts d'Ainay, Presqu'île) is the best boutique in Lyon, with more than 300 varieties of tea on sale from all over the world. **Eléphant des Montagnes** (⊠ 43 rue Auguste Comte, Presqu'île), not far from Perrache station, has treasures from Nepal, Afghanistan, India, and the Himalayas, lovingly retrieved by Pierre Chavanne. **La Boîte à Dessert** (⊠ 1 rue de l'Ancienne-Préfecture, Presqu'île) makes luscious peach turnovers. For culinary variety, shop **Les Halles** (⊠ 102 cours Lafayette, Part-Dieu). **Pignol** (⊠ 17 rue Émile-Zola, Presqu'île) is good for meats and sandwich-makings. **Reynon** (⊠ 13 rue des Archers, Presqu'île) is the place for charcuterie.

BEAUJOLAIS & LA DOMBES

North of Lyon along the Saône are the vineyards of Beaujolais, a thrill for any oenophile. In the area around Villefranche, small villages—perhaps comprising a church, a bar, and a boulangerie—pop up here and there out of the rolling vine-covered hillsides. Lyon's tourist office has a decent map of the Beaujolais region; even better is the "Vignobles de Beaujolais" map, available in Villefranche's tourist office. Beaujolais wine is made exclusively from the *gamay noir à jus blanc* grape. The region's best wines are all labeled "Grand Cru," a more complex version of the otherwise light, fruity Beaujolais. For the price of one bottle, you can spend an afternoon getting a wealth of knowledge (and a little buzz) by visiting one of the village *caves* (cellars where wine is made, stored, and sold), from big-time tourist operators to mom-and-pop stops. Make sure the ones you pick have DÉGUSTATION signs out front. Signs that say VENTE EN DIRECT (sold directly from the property) and VENTE AU DÉTAIL (sold by the bottle) are also good indicators.

East of the Saône is the fertile land of La Dombes, where ornithologists flock to see migratory bird life. North of La Dombes and east of the Beaujolais wine villages is Bourg-en-Bresse, famous for its marvelous church and a breed of poultry that delights gourmands; it makes a good base after Lyon. South toward the Rhône, the great river of southern France, is the well-preserved medieval village of Pérouges.

L'Arbresle

31 *16 km (10 mi) northwest of Lyon.*

If you love modern architecture, don't miss Éveux, outside L'Arbresle. Here the stark, blocky Dominican convent of **Ste-Marie de la Tourette** protrudes over the hillside, resting on slender pillars that look like stilts and revealing the minimalist sensibilities of architect Le Corbusier, who designed it in 1957–59. ☎ 04–74–01–01–03 ⊠ €5 ۞ *July and Aug., daily 9–noon and 2–6; Sept.–June, weekends 2–6.*

Villefranche-sur-Saône

32 *6 km (4 mi) east of Ars-sur-Formans, 31 km (19 mi) north of Lyon.*

The lively industrial town of Villefranche-sur-Saône is the capital of the Beaujolais region and is known for its *vin nouveau* (new wine). Thanks to marketing hype, this youthful, fruity red wine is eagerly gulped down around the world every year on the third Thursday of November.

Where to Stay & Eat

$–$$$ ✕ **Juliénas.** This simple little restaurant delivers what other, pricier restaurants in town don't, won't, or can't: bistro fare that does honor to traditional Beaujolais cookery. All the all-stars are here: andouillette, hot sausage, pork with tarragon, and, for dessert, a luscious *île flottante*. ("Floating Island" merengue). The prix-fixe menu, served lunch and dinner, is one of the best deals in the region. ⊠ *236 rue d'Anse* ☎ *04–74–09–16–55* ▭ *AE, MC, V* ۞ *Closed Mon. No dinner Sun.*

★ **$$$$** ✕▥ **Château de Bagnols.** This intimate and exquisite 13th-century castle southwest of Villefranche is filled with period glassware, fabrics, and porcelain to go with the antique furniture. The 17th- and 18th-century murals were inspired by Lyon's textile industry. Rooms are huge, as are the baronial bathrooms. Those in the main château evoke the 18th century, while the ones in La Résidence, converted stables, and carriage houses, are rustic-contemporary. Wine tastings are held in the beautiful stone *cuvage* (wine-pressing room). ⊠ *15 km (9 mi) southwest of Villefranche on D38 to Tarare, 69620 Bagnols* ☎ *04–74–71–40–00* 🖷 *04–74–71–40–49* ⊕ *www.bagnols.com* ➥ *16 rooms, 5 apartments* ⚬ *Restaurant, minibars, cable TV, pool, bar, library, some pets allowed* ▭ *AE, DC, MC, V* ۞ *Closed Jan.–Mar.*

Beaujolais Route du Vin

Fodor'sChoice ★ *16 km (10 mi) north of Villefranche-sur-Saône, 49 km (30 mi) north of Lyon.*

Not all Beaujolais wine is promoted as *vin nouveau,* despite the highly successful marketing campaign that has made Beaujolais nouveau synonymous with French wine and the new grape harvest from Tokyo to Timbuktu (celebrated in full force on the third Thursday of November annually around the world). Wine classed as "Beaujolais Villages" is higher in alcohol and produced from a clearly defined region northwest of Villefranche. Beaujolais is made from one single variety of grape, the *gamay noir à jus blanc.* However, there are 12 different appellations: Beaujolais, Beaujolais Villages, Brouilly, Chénas, Chiroubles, Côte de Brouilly, Fleurie, Juliénas, Morgon, Moulin à Vent, Régnié, and St-Amour. The Beaujolais Route du Vin (Wine Road), a narrow strip 23 km (14 mi) long, is home to nine of these deluxe Beaujolais wines, also known as *grands crus.* Most villages have a *cave* (communal cellar) or *coopérative* where you can taste and buy. The **École Beaujolaise des Vins** (Beaujolais School of Wine; ⊠ Villefranche ☎ 04–74–02–22–18 🖷 04–74–02–22–19 ⊕ www.beaujolais.com) organizes lessons in wine tasting and on creating your own cellar.

In the southernmost and largest *vignoble* (vineyard) of the Beaujolais crus is **Odenas,** producing Brouilly, a soft, fruity wine best consumed young. In the vineyard's center is towering Mont Brouilly, a hill whose vines produce a tougher, firmer wine classified as Côte de Brouilly. From Odenas take D68 via St-Lager to **Villié-Morgon,** in the heart of the Morgon vineyard; robust wines that age well are produced here. At Monternot, east of Villié-Morgon, you will find the 15th-century **Château de Corcelles,** noted for its Renaissance galleries, canopied courtyard well, and medieval carvings in its chapel. The guardroom is now an atmospheric tasting cellar. ⊠ *Off D9 from Villié-Morgon* ☎ *04–74–66–72–42* ☉ *Mon.–Sat. 10–noon and 2:30–6:30.*

From Villié-Morgon D68 wiggles north through several more wine villages, including **Chiroubles,** where a rare, light wine best drunk young is produced. The wines from **Fleurie** are elegant and flowery. Well-known **Chénas** is favored for its two crus: the robust, velvety, and expensive Moulin à Vent and the fruity and underestimated Chénas. The wines of **Juliénas** are sturdy and a deep color; sample them in the cellar of the town church (closed Tuesday and lunchtime), amid bacchanalian decor. **St-Amour,** west of Juliénas, produces light but firm reds and a limited quantity of whites. The famous white Pouilly-Fuissé comes from the area around **Fuissé.**

Bourg-en-Bresse

❸❸ *30 km (18 mi) east of St-Amour on N79, 81 km (49 mi) northeast of Lyon.*

Cheerful Bourg-en-Bresse is esteemed among gastronomes for its fowl—striking-looking chickens, the *poulet de Bresse,* with plump white bodies, bright blue feet and red combs (adding up to France's *tricolore,* or national colors). The town's southeasternmost district, Brou, is its most interesting and the site of a singular church. This is a good place to stay before or after a trip along the Beaujolais Wine Road.

The **Église de Brou,** a marvel of the Flamboyant Gothic style, is no longer in religious use. The church was built between 1506 and 1532 by Margaret of Austria in memory of her husband, Philibert le Beau, Duke of Savoy, and their finely sculpted tombs highlight the rich interior. **Son-et-lumière** shows—on Easter and Pentecost Sunday and Monday, and on Thursday, Saturday, and Sunday from May through September—are magical. A massive restoration of the roof has brought it back to its 16th-century state with the same gorgeous, multicolor, intricate patterns found throughout Burgundy. The museum in the nearby **cloister** stands out for its paintings: 16th- and 17th-century Flemish and Dutch artists keep company with 17th- and 18th-century French and Italian masters, 19th-century artists of the Lyon School, Gustave Doré, and contemporary local painters. ⊠ *63 bd. de Brou* ☎ *04-74-22-83-83* 🎟 *€5* ☉ *Apr.–Sept., daily 9–12:30 and 2–6:30; Oct.–Mar., daily 9–noon and 2–5.*

Where to Stay & Eat

★ **$–$$$$** ✕ **L'Auberge Bressane.** Overlooking the Brou church, the modern, polished dining room and chef Jean-Pierre Vullin's cuisine are a good combination. Frogs' legs and Bresse chicken with wild morel–cream sauce are specialties; also try the *quenelles de brochet* (poached-fish dumplings). Jean-Pierre wanders through the dining room ready for a chat while his staff provides excellent service. Don't miss the house aperitif, a champagne cocktail with fresh strawberry puree. The wine list has 300 vintages. ⊠ *166 bd. de Brou* ☎ *04-74-22-22-68* ♠ *Reservations essential* 🖃 *AE, DC, MC, V* ☉ *Closed Tues. except holidays.*

$$–$$$ ✕ **La Petite Auberge.** This cozy flower-decked inn is in the countryside on the outskirts of town. Madame Bertrand provides games for children. Chef Philippe Garnier has a subtle way with mullet (he grills it in saffron butter) and Bresse chicken (browned in tangy cider vinegar). ⊠ *St-Just, rte. de Ceyzeriat* ☎ *04-74-22-30-04* 🖃 *MC, V* ☉ *Closed Jan. and Tues. No dinner Mon.*

★ **$$$–$$$$** ✕🏠 **Georges Blanc.** Set in the village of Vonnas and one of the great culinary addresses in all Gaul, this simple 19th-century inn full of antique country furniture makes a fine setting for poulet de Bresse, truffles, and lobster, all featured on this legendary menu. The wizard here is Monsieur Blanc, whose culinary DNA extends back to innkeepers dating from the French Revolution. He made his mark in the 1980s with a series of cookbooks, notably *The Natural Cuisine of Georges Blanc.* Today, he serves up his traditional-yet-nouvelle delights in a vast dining room (closed Monday and Tuesday; no lunch Wednesday), renovated—overly so, some might say—in a stately style replete with Louis Treize–style chairs, fireplace, and floral tapestries. Wine connoisseurs will go weak in the knees at the cellar here, overflowing with 130,000 bottles. The 30 guest rooms range from (relatively) simple to luxurious. It's worth the trip from Bourg-en-Bresse, but be sure you bring deep pockets. However, a block south you can also repair to Blanc's cheaper and more casual restaurant, **L'Ancienne Auberge,** most delightfully set in a 1900s "Fabrique de Limonade" soda-water plant and now festooned with antique bicycles and daguerrotypes. ⊠ *Pl. du Marché, 19 km (12 mi) from Bourg-en-Bresse, 01540 Vonnas* ☎ *04–74–50–90–90* 🖶 *04–74–50–08–80* ⊕ *www.georgesblanc.com* ⌂ *Reservations essential* ↩ *38 rooms* ⌂ *Restaurant, minibars, cable TV, tennis court, pool, meeting rooms, helipad, some pets allowed* ▤ *AE, DC, MC, V* ☺ *Closed Jan.*

Villars-les-Dombes

❸❹ *29 km (18 mi) south of Bourg-en-Bresse, 37 km (23 mi) north of Lyon.*

Villars-les-Dombes is the unofficial capital of La Dombes, an area once covered by a glacier. When the ice retreated, it left a network of lakes and ponds that draws anglers and bird-watchers today. The 56-acre **Parc des Oiseaux,** one of Europe's finest bird sanctuaries, is home-sweet-home to 400 species of birds (some 2,000 individuals from five continents); 435 aviaries house species from waders to birds of prey; and tropical birds in vivid hues fill the indoor birdhouse. Allow two hours. Admission fees, which vary according to season, are most expensive from May through October. ⊠ *Off N83* ☎ *04–74–98–05–54* ⊕ *www.parc-des-oiseaux.com* 🖪 *€8–€12* ☺ *Daily 9:30–dusk.*

Pérouges

★ **❸❺** *21 km (13 mi) southeast of Villars-les-Dombes, 36 km (22 mi) northeast of Lyon.*

Wonderfully preserved (though a little too precious), hilltop Pérouges, with its medieval houses and narrow cobbled streets surrounded by ramparts, is just 200 yards across. Hand-weavers first brought it prosperity; the industrial revolution meant their downfall, and by the late 19th century the population had dwindled from 1,500 to 12. Now the government has restored the most interesting houses, and a potter, bookbinder, cabinetmaker, and weaver have given the town a new lease on life. A number of restaurants make Pérouges a good lunch stop.

Encircling the town is **rue des Rondes;** from this road you can get fine views of the countryside and, on clear days, the Alps. Park your car by the main gateway, **Porte d'En-Haut,** alongside the 15th-century fortress-church. Rue du Prince, the town's main street, leads to the **Maison des Princes de Savoie** (Palace of the Princes of Savoy), formerly the home of the influential Savoie family that once controlled the eastern part of France. Note the fine watchtower. **Place de la Halle,** a pretty square with great charm, around the corner from the Maison des Princes de Savoie, is the site of a lime tree planted in 1792. The **Musée du Vieux Pérouges** (Old Pérouges Museum), to one side of the place de la Halle, contains local artifacts and a reconstructed weaver's workshop. The medieval **garden** is noted for its array of rare medicinal plants. ⊠ *Pl. du Tilleul* ☎ *04–74–61–00–88* 🖪 *€5* ☺ *May–Sept., daily 10–noon and 2–6.*

Where to Stay & Eat

★ **$$–$$$$** ✕⬚ **L'Ostellerie du Vieux Pérouges.** "The Old Man of Pérouges" is uniquely comprised of four medieval stone residences set around its main showpiece—an extraordinary corbelled, 14th-century timber-frame house now home to the inn's restaurant. Here, regional delights are served up on pewter plates by waitresses in folk costumes, recipes handed down from the days of Charles VII inspire the cook, and everybody partakes of the famous "pancake of Pérouges" dessert. The sweet taste will linger in your guest room, thanks to some time-burnished accents, such as antiques, gigantic stone hearths, and glossy wood floors and tables. Rooms in the geranium-decked 15th-century Au St-Georges et Manoir manor are more spacious—but also nearly twice the cost—than those in L'Annexe and have marble bathrooms and period furniture (one or two rooms even have their own garden). At the lower end of the scale, however, the rooms are fairly simple and threadbare. ⬚ *Pl. du Tilleul, 01800 Pérouges* ☎ *04–74–61–00–88* 🖷 *04–74–34–77–90* ⬚ *www. ostellerie.com* ⬩ *28 rooms* ⬩ *Restaurant, minibars, cable TV, bar, meeting rooms, some pets allowed; no a/c* 🖃 *AE, DC, MC, V.*

THE RHÔNE VALLEY

At Lyon, the Rhône, joined by the Saône, truly comes into its own, plummeting south in search of the Mediterranean. The river's progress is often spectacular, as steep vineyards conjure up vistas that are more readily associated with the river's Germanic cousin, the Rhine. All along the way, small-town vintners invite you to sample their wines. Early Roman towns like Vienne and Valence reflect the Rhône's importance as a trading route. To the west is the rugged, rustic Ardèche *département* (province), where time seems to have slowed to a standstill.

Vienne

36 *27 km (17 mi) south of Lyon via A7.*

Fodor'sChoice
★

One of Roman Gaul's most important towns, Vienne became a religious and cultural center under its count-archbishops in the Middle Ages and retains considerable historic charm despite being a major road and train junction. The tourist office anchors cours Brillier in the leafy shadow of the Jardin Public (Public Garden). The €7 Passport admits you to most local monuments and museums; it's available at the tourist office or at the first site that you visit.

On quai Jean-Jaurès, beside the Rhône, is the church of **St-Pierre.** Note the rectangular 12th-century Romanesque bell tower with its arcaded tiers. The lower church walls date from the 6th century. Although religious wars deprived the cathedral of **St-Maurice** of many of its statues, much original decoration is intact; the portals on the 15th-century facade are carved with Old Testament scenes. The cathedral was built between the 12th and 16th centuries, with later additions, such as the splendid 18th-century mausoleum to the right of the altar. A frieze of the zodiac adorns the entrance to the vaulted passage that once led to the cloisters but now opens onto place St-Paul.

★ Place du Palais is the site of the remains of the **Temple d'Auguste et de Livie** (Temple of Augustus and Livia), accessible via place St-Paul and rue Clémentine; they probably date in part from Vienne's earliest Roman settlements (1st century BC). The Corinthian columns were walled in during the 11th century, when the temple was used as a church; in 1833 Prosper Mérimée intervened to have the temple restored. The last vestige of the city's sizable Roman baths is a **Roman gateway** (⊠ Rue Chantelouve) decorated with delicate friezes.

★ The **Théâtre Romain** (Roman Theater), on rue de la Charité, is one of the largest in Gaul (143 yards across). It held 13,000 spectators and is only slightly smaller than Rome's Theater of Marcellus. Rubble buried Vienne's theater until 1922; excavation has uncovered 46 rows of seats, some marble flooring, and the frieze on the stage. Concerts take place here in summer. ⊠ *7 rue du Cirque* ☎ *04–74–85–39–23* ⊠ *€6* ☉ *Apr.–Aug., daily 9–12:30 and 2–6; Sept.–mid-Oct., Tues.–Sun. 9–12:30 and 2–6; mid-Oct.–Mar., Tues.–Sat. 9:30–12:30 and 2–5, Sun. 1:30–5:30.*

Rue des Orfèvres (off rue de la Charité) is lined with Renaissance facades and distinguished by the church of **St-André-le-Bas,** once part of a powerful abbey. If possible, venture past the restoration now in progress to see the finely sculpted 12th-century capitals (made of Roman stone) and the 17th-century wood statue of St. Andrew. It's best to see the cloisters during the music festival held here and at the cathedral from June to August. ⊠ *Cour St-André* ☎ *04–74–85–18–49* ⊠ *€5* ☉ *Apr.–mid-Oct., Tues.–Sun. 9:30–1 and 2–6; mid-Oct.–Mar., Tues.–Sat. 9:30–12:30 and 2–5, Sun. 2–6.*

Across the Rhône from the town center is the excavated **Cité Gallo-Romaine** (Gallo-Roman City), covering several acres. Here you can find villas, houses, workshops, public baths, and roads, all built by the Romans. ⊠ *€5* ☉ *Daily 9–6.*

Where to Stay & Eat

$$–$$$$ ✗ **Le Bec Fin.** With its understatedly elegant dining room and an inexpensive weekday menu, this unpretentious enclave opposite the cathedral is a good choice for lunch or dinner. Red meat, seafood, and freshwater fish are well prepared here. Try the turbot cooked with saffron. ⊠ *7 pl. St-Maurice* ☎ *04–74–85–76–72* ⌘ *Reservations essential* ▭ *AE, DC, MC, V* ☉ *Closed July 1–17, Dec. 23–Jan. 2, and Mon. No dinner Sun. or Wed.*

★ **$$$–$$$$** ✗▥ **La Pyramide.** Back when your grandmother's grandmother was making the grand tour, La Pyramide was *le must*—Fernand Point had perfected haute cuisine for a generation and became the first superstar chef, teaching a regiment of students who went on to glamorize dining the world over. Many decades later, La Pyramide has dropped its museum status and now offers contemporary classics by acclaimed chef Patrick Henriroux, accompanied by a peerless selection of wines featuring local stars from the nearby Côte Rôtie and Condrieu vineyards. Both classical and avant-garde dishes triumph here, from *crème souf-*

flée de crabe au croquant d'artichaut (cream crab soufflé with crunchy artichoke) to the *veau de lait aux légumes de la vallée* (suckling veal with vegetables from the Drôme valley). Rooms are graceful and comfortable in this relaxed setting. ⊠ *14 bd. Fernand-Point, 38200* ☎ *04–74–53–01–96* 🖷 *04–74–85–69–73* ⊕ *www.relaischateaux.com/ pyramide* ⇆ *21 rooms* ♻ *Restaurant, minibars, cable TV, bar, meeting rooms, some pets allowed* ⊟ *AE, DC, MC, V.*

Serrières

37 *32 km (20 mi) south of Vienne, 59 km (37 mi) south of Lyon.*

Riverboats traditionally stop at little Serrières, on the Rhône's west bank. Life on the water is depicted at the **Musée des Mariniers du Rhône** (Boatmen's Museum), in the wooden-roof Gothic chapel of St-Sornin. ☎ *04–75–34–01–26* 🖂 *€6* ⏲ *Apr.–Oct., weekends 3–6.*

Where to Stay & Eat

★ **$$$$** ✕🖭 **Schaeffer.** Guest rooms here are decorated in contemporary style, but the real draw is the dining room (closed Monday; no dinner Sunday), where chef Bernard Mathé invents variations on traditional French dishes: smoked duck cutlet in lentil stew or lamb with eggplant in anchovy butter. The number of desserts is overwhelming, but pistachio cake with bitter chocolate is the clear winner. Reservations are essential for the restaurant. Menus run from €40 to €60. ⊠ *Quai Jules Roche, 07340* ☎ *04–75–34–00–07* 🖷 *04–75–34–08–79* ⊕ *www.hotel-schaeffer.com* ⇆ *11 rooms* ♻ *Restaurant, minibars, cable TV, bar, meeting rooms, some pets allowed* ⊟ *AE, DC, MC, V* ⏲ *Closed 1st 3 wks Jan.*

Hauterives

38 *28 km (17 mi) east of Serrières, 40 km (25 mi) south of Vienne.*

Hauterives would be just another quaint village on the eastern side of the Rhône if not for the **Palais Idéal,** one of Western Europe's weirdest constructions. A fantasy constructed entirely of stones (called *galets*) from the nearby Galaure River, it was the life's work of a local postman, Ferdinand Cheval (1836–1924), who was haunted by visions of faraway mosques and temples. One of many wall inscriptions reads "1879–1912: 10,000 days, 93,000 hours, 33 years of toil." ☎ *04–75–68–81–19* 🖷 *04–75–68–88–15* 🖂 *€6* ⏲ *Mid-Apr.–mid-Sept., daily 9–7; mid-Sept.–mid-Apr., daily 9:30–5:30.*

Where to Stay & Eat

¢–$ ✕🖭 **Le Relais.** A stone's throw from the Palais Idéal, this rustic inn is a good place for a meal—and a night's stay, if desirable. Rooms are small and could use refurbishing in the not-too-distant future. Owner Roland Graillat is better as a chef—roast partridge and delicately seasoned frogs' legs are good bets. From September to June the restaurant is closed Monday and does not serve dinner Sunday. ⊠ *Pl. de l'Église, 26390* ☎ *04–75–68–81–12* 🖷 *04–75–68–92–42* ⇆ *17 rooms* ♻ *Restaurant, café, minibars, cable TV, bar; no a/c* ⊟ *AE, DC, MC, V* ⏲ *Closed Jan. and Feb.* 🍽 *MAP.*

Annonay

39 *44 km (27 mi) south of Vienne, 43 km (27 mi) southeast of St-Étienne.*

The narrow streets and passageways of central Annonay are full of character. The town, which grew up around the leather industry, is best known as the home of Joseph and Étienne Montgolfier, who, in 1783, invented the hot-air balloon (known in French as a *montgolfière*). The first flight was on June 4, 1783, from place des Cordeliers (although a commemorating obelisk is on avenue Marc-Seguin); the flight lasted a half hour and reached 6,500 feet.

Local history and folklore are evoked at the **Musée Vivarais César Filhol,** between the Mairie (Town Hall) and the church of Notre-Dame. ⊠ *15 rue Béchetoille* ☎ *04–75–33–24–51* ✉ €*5* ⊙ *July and Aug., Tues.–Sun. 3–6; Sept.–June, Wed. and weekends 3–6.*

Tournon

40 *37 km (23 mi) southeast of Annonay, 59 km (37 mi) south of Vienne.*

Tournon is on the Rhône at the foot of granite hills. Its hefty **Château,** dating from the 15th and 16th centuries, is the chief attraction. The castle's twin terraces have wonderful views of the Vieille Ville, the river, and—towering above Tain-l'Hermitage across the Rhône—the steep vineyards that produce Hermitage wine, one of the region's most refined— and costly—reds. In the château is a museum of local history, the **Musée Rhodanien** (or du Rhône). ⊠ *Pl. Auguste-Faure* ☎ *04–75–08–10–23* ✉ €*5* ⊙ *June–Aug., Wed.–Mon. 10–noon and 2–6; Apr., May, Sept., and Oct., Wed.–Mon. 2–6.*

⏲ A ride on one of France's last steam trains, the **Chemin de Fer du Vivarais,** makes an adventurous two-hour trip 33 km (21 mi) along the narrow, rocky Doux Valley to Lamastre and back to Tournon. ⊠ *Departs from Tournon station* ☎ *04–78–28–83–34* ✉ *Round-trip* €*20* ⊙ *June–Aug., daily 10 AM; May and Sept., weekends 10 AM.*

Where to Stay & Eat

$$–$$$ ✕▦ **Michel Chabran.** This modern interpretation of Drôme-style stone-and-wood design has floral displays, airy picture windows over the garden, and guest rooms with a touch of contemporary Danish influence. Next to the main road, sleeping with the windows open can make for a noisy nigh—though the air-conditioning largely solves that. The restaurant (closed Monday from January through April; no dinner Sunday) serves a truffle menu from December to March and imaginative and light fare such as mille-feuille de foie gras with artichokes and lamb from Rémuzat. ⊠ *29 av. du 45ᵉ Parallèle, on left (east) bank of the Rhône, 10 km (6 mi) south of Tournon via N7 and 7 km (4½ mi) north of Valence, 26600 Pont de l'Isère* ☎*04–75–84–60–09* ▤*04–75–84–59–65* ⊕*www.chateauxhotels. com/chabran* ⤴ *12 rooms* ⚴ *Restaurant, café, minibars, cable TV, pool, meeting room, some pets allowed* ▤ *AE, DC, MC, V* ❙❁❙ *MAP.*

$$ ✕▦ **Reynaud.** Tain-l'Hermitage, across the Rhône from Tournon, entices with this fine inn and restaurant. The dining room (closed Monday; no dinner Sunday) is comfortable and traditional, the river magnificent. Rooms are on the small side but cozy and tastefully furnished. The classic cuisine is excellent, with specialties from poached egg with foie gras to pigeon fillet in black-currant sauce. ⊠ *82 av. du Président-Roosevelt, Tain-l'Hermitage, 07300* ☎ *04–75–07–22–10* 🖷 *04–75–08–03–53* ➝ *13 rooms* ♨ *Restaurant, minibars, cable TV, pool, bar* ⊟ *AE, DC, MC, V* ☉ *Closed 1 wk in Aug.*

en route
From Tournon's place Jean-Jaurès, slightly inland from the château, follow signs to the narrow, twisting **Route Panoramique**; the views en route to the old village of **St-Romain-de-Lerps** are breathtaking. In good weather the panorama at St-Romain includes 13 départements, Mont Blanc to the east, and arid Mont Ventoux to the south. D287 winds down to St-Péray and Valence; topping the **Montagne de Crussol**, 650 feet above the plain, is the ruined 12th-century **Château de Crussol**.

Valence

④ *17 km (11 mi) south of Tournon, 92 km (57 mi) west of Grenoble, 127 km (79 mi) north of Avignon.*

Largish Valence, the Drôme département capital, is the region's market center. Steep-curbed alleyways called *côtes* extend into the Vieille Ville from the Rhône. At the center of the Vieille Ville is the cathedral of **St-Apollinaire**. Although begun in the 12th century in the Romanesque style, it's not as old as it looks: parts of it were rebuilt in the 17th century, with the belfry rebuilt in the 19th. The **Musée des Beaux-Arts** (Fine Arts Museum), next to the cathedral of St-Apollinaire, in the former 18th-century bishops' palace, displays archaeological finds as well as sculpture and furniture and drawings by landscapist Hubert Robert (1733–1808). ⊠ *Pl. des Ormeaux* ☎ *04–75–79–20–80* 🎫 *€5* ☉ *Mon., Tues., Thurs., and Fri. 2–6, Wed. and weekends 9–noon and 2–6.*

Where to Stay & Eat

$$$–$$$$
Fodor's Choice
★
×🖾 **Pic.** Kubla Khan would have decamped from Xanadu in a minute for this Drôme pleasure palace. The Maison Pic has been a culinary landmark for decades, although its (too?) glossy Relais & Château makeover into a full-scale hotel has nearly obliterated any traces of its time-stained past. Not that you will complain—much of the decor is to die for: vaulted white salons, red-velvet sofas, 18th-century billiard tables, gigantic Provençal (that's where the Pic family came from) armoires, lovely gardens, and an eye-popping pool make this a destination in itself. The famous restaurant (closed Monday; no dinner Sunday) is going stronger than ever—try the truffle-flavored *galettes* (pancakes) with asparagus or bass with caviar (served either "avec modération" or "passionnément") to see how Anne-Sophie, great-granddaughter of the founding matriarch, is continuing the family legacy. Dine in the cardinal-red dining room seated on Louis Seize–style bergères or, in summer, on the shaded terrace, then retire upstairs to the guest rooms, done in a mix of rustic antiques and high-style fabrics. A café, the Auberge du

Pin, also entices (with much lower prices). ✉ *285 av. Victor-Hugo, 26000* ☎ *04–75–44–15–32* 🖷 *04–75–40–96–03* ⊕ *www.pic-valence. com* ⤶ *12 rooms, 3 apartments* ⌂ *Restaurant, café, minibars, cable TV, pool, bar, meeting rooms, some pets allowed* ▭ *AE, DC, MC, V.*

Shopping

In the small town of Romans, 15 minutes northeast of Valence via D532, is a score of retail outlets for designer shoes. Romans, with its tradition of leather making, has become the major factory center for the production of high-quality shoes. Many of the top European designers are represented, and their products may be had at bargain prices from any number of stores. **Charles Jourdan** (✉ Galerie Fan Halles ☎04–75–02–32–36) is perhaps the highest-quality brand name represented in Romans. **Chaussures Tchlin** (✉ Quai Chopin ☎04–75–72–51–41) is a longtime mainstay for French shoes. **Stephane Kelian** (✉ 11 pl. Charles-de-Gaulle ☎ 04–75–05–23–26) is a name that speaks hip and high style.

| en route | The prettiest route between Valence and Privas is N86, on the right bank of the Rhône; after 16 km (10 mi) and just before La Voulte, turn onto the scenic D120, which follows the Eyrieux Valley as far as Les Ollières-sur-Eyrieux; then turn south along D2, under the thick canopy of horse-chestnut trees. |

Cliousclat

㊷ *21 km (13 mi) south of Valence, 27 km (17 mi) north of Montélimar.*

Less than 10 km (6 mi) off A7 and N7, the roads running south from Valence to Montélimar and on to Provence, is the delightful, tiny village of Cliousclat. It's built on a hillside, with room for just one narrow street running through it. There's not much to do or see, but its charming atmosphere and its gorgeous views make it very appealing. While you're here, however, drop in at the small **Histoires de Poteries** (Pottery History Museum) to see the work of local potters. You might want to buy some of the lovely wares, too. ☎ *04–75–63–15–60* 🎟 *€5* ⊘ *Apr.–June, Tues.–Sun. 2–7; July and Aug., daily 10–1 and 2–8; Sept., Tues.–Sun. 10–noon and 2–7; Oct., Tues.–Sun. 2–6.*

Where to Stay & Eat

★ **$–$$** ✕▥ **La Treille Muscate.** Between Lyon and Avignon there's no better place to spend a night than at this gem of a hotel, a symphony of muted 18th-century pastels, Provençal furnishings, and a decidedly rustic-luxe air. Lovingly collected antiques and clay-tile floors with throw rugs make each room different. Room No. 11 has a huge terrace overlooking fields to the Rhône. The restaurant (closed Wednesday) gets kudos from all the critics, and you can't lose with the Sisteron lamb, Mediterranean fish, or homemade foie gras. The friendly owner, Madame de Laître, speaks English fluently but politely refrains from doing so until you have exhausted your French. ✉ *26270 Cliousclat* ☎ *04–75–63–13–10* 🖷 *04–75–63–10–79* ⊕ *www.latreillemuscate.com* ⤶ *12 rooms* ⌂ *Restaurant, café, minibars, cable TV* ▭ *AE, DC, MC, V* ⊘ *Closed mid-Dec.–Feb.* ⦿ *BP, MAP.*

GRENOBLE & THE ALPS

This is double-treat vacationland: in winter some of the world's best skiing is found in the Alps; in summer chic spas, shimmering lakes, and hilltop trails offer additional delights. The Savoie and Haute-Savoie départements occupy the most impressive territory; Grenoble, in the Dauphiné, is the gateway to the Alps and the area's only city, occupying the nexus of highways from Marseille, Valence, Lyon, Geneva, and Turin.

The skiing season for most French resorts runs from December 15 to April 15. By late December resorts above 3,000 feet usually have sufficient snow. January is apt to be the coldest—and therefore the least popular—month; in Chamonix and Megève, this is the time to find hotel bargains. At the high-altitude resorts the skiing season lasts until May. In summer the lake resorts, as well as the regions favored by hikers and climbers, come into their own. Let's not forget that this is the region where Stendhal was born, and where the great 18th-century philosopher Jean-Jacques Rousseau lived out his old age. Worldly pleasures also await: incredibly charming Annecy, set with arcaded lanes and quiet canals in the old quarter around the lovely 16th-century Palais de l'Isle; the Old Master treasures on view at Grenoble's Musée; and the fashionable lakeside promenades of spa towns like Aix-les-Bains are just some of the civilized enjoyments to be discovered here.

Grenoble

104 km (65 mi) southeast of Lyon, 138 km (86 mi) northeast of Montélimar.

Capital of the Dauphiné (Lower Alps) region, Grenoble sits at the confluence of the Isère and Drac rivers and lies within three *massifs* (mountain ranges): La Chartreuse, Le Vercors, and Belledonne. This cosmopolitan city's skyscrapers seem intimidating by homey French standards. But along with the city's nuclear research plant, they bear witness to the fierce local desire to move ahead with the times, and it's not surprising to find one of France's most noted universities here. Grenoble's main claim to fame is as the birthplace of the great French novelist Henri Beyle (1783–1842), better known as Stendhal, author of *The Red and the Black* and *The Charterhouse of Parma*. The heart of the city forms a crescent around a bend of the Isère, with the train station at the western end and the university all the way at the eastern tip. As it fans out from the river toward the south, the crescent seems to develop a more modern flavor. The hub of the city is **place Victor Hugo,** with its flowers, fountains, and cafés, though most sights and nightlife are near the Isère in place St-André, place de Gordes, and place Notre-Dame; avenue Alsace-Lorraine, a major pedestrian street lined with modern shops, cuts right through it. The layout of the city is very tricky, so it is best to stop into the city tourist office for detailed maps and directions.

Near the center curve of the River Isère is a **Téléphérique** (cable car), starting at quai St-Stéphane-Jay, which whisks you over the River Isère

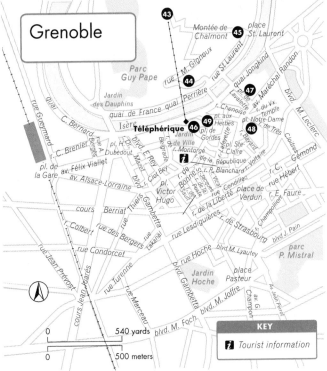

🐌 **43** and up to the hilltop and its **Fort de la Bastille,** where there are splendid views and a good restaurant. Walk back down via the footpath through the Jardin Dauphinoise. 🎫 €6 round-trip ⊙ Apr.–Oct., daily 9 AM–midnight; Nov., Dec., Feb., and Mar., daily 10–6.

On the north side of the River Isère is rue Maurice-Gignoux, lined with gardens, cafés, mansions, and a 17th-century convent that contains the **44 Musée Dauphinois,** featuring the history of mountaineering and skiing. The Premiers Alpins section explores the evolution of the Alps and its inhabitants. The museum restaurant is one of Grenoble's best. ✉ 30 rue Maurice-Gignoux ☎ 04–76–85–19–01 🎫 Free ⊙ Nov.–Apr., Wed.–Mon. 10–6; May–Oct., Wed.–Mon. 10–7.

45 The church of **St-Laurent,** near the Musée Dauphinois, has a hauntingly ancient 6th-century crypt—one of the country's oldest Christian monuments—supported by a row of formidable marble pillars. Closed for archaeological research at press time, the church is scheduled to reopen sometime in 2006. ✉ 2 pl. St-Laurent ☎ 04–76–44–78–68 🎫 Free ⊙ Wed.–Mon. 8–noon and 2–6.

On the south side of the River Isère and nearly opposite the cable-car stop is the Jardin de Ville—an open space filled with immense plane trees—

where a handsome conical tower with slate roof marks the **Palais Lesdiguières.** This was built by the right hand of King Henri IV, the Duc de Lesdiguières (1543–1626), and possibly the prototype for Stendhal's voraciously egoistic protagonists (as Constable of France, the duke had a reign of terror, marrying his young lover Marie Vignon—31 years his junior—after having her husband assassinated). A master urbanist, Lesdiguières did much to establish the Grenoble you see today, so it may

46 only be apt his palace is now the **Musée Stendhal,** where family portraits trace the life of Grenoble's greatest writer amidst elegant wooden furniture turned out by the Hache family dynasty of famous woodworkers. Although some of the city's residents will be surprised that non-natives know who Stendhal (much less Henri Beyle) is, there is no denying that this great author remains Grenoble's most famous native son. Copies of original manuscripts and major memorabilia will please fans,

Fodor'sChoice   who will wish to then pay a call to the **Maison Stendhal,** at 20 Grande
★   Rue, Stendhal's grandfather's house and the place where the author spent the "happiest days of his life"; you can also take a stroll back over to the **Jardin de Ville,** where the author met his first "love" (basically unrequited), the actress Virginie Kubly. The city tourist office distributes a **"Stendhal Itinerary"** that also includes the author's birthplace, at 14 rue Hébert, now a repository for memorabilia on the Resistance and deportations of World War II. ☒ *1 rue Hector-Berlioz* ☏ *04–76–54–44–14* ⊕ *www.armance.com/tourisme.html* ☒ *Free* ⊗ *Oct.–June, Tues.–Sun. 2–6; July–Sept., Tues.–Sun. 9–noon and 2–6.*

Several blocks east of the Musée Stendhal is place de Lavalette, on the south side of the river where most of Grenoble is concentrated, and site

★ **47** of the **Musée de Grenoble,** formerly the Musée de Peinture et de Sculpture (Painting and Sculpture Museum). Founded in 1796 and since enlarged, it's one of France's oldest museums and the first to concentrate on modern art (Picasso donated his *Femme Lisant* in 1921); a modern addition incorporates the medieval Tour de l'Isle (Island Tower), a Grenoble landmark. The collection includes 4,000 paintings and 5,500 drawings, among them works from the Italian Renaissance, Rubens, Flemish still lifes, Zurbaran, and Canaletto; Impressionists such as Renoir and Monet; and 20th-century works by Matisse (*Intérieur aux Aubergines*), Signac, Derain, Vlaminck, Magritte, Ernst, Miró, and Dubuffet. Modern-art lovers should also check out the **Centre National d'Art Contemporain** (☒ 155 cours Berriat ☏ 04–76–21–95–84). Behind the train station in an out-of-the-way district, it is noted for its distinctive warehouse museum and cutting-edge collection. ☒ *5 pl. de Lavalette* ☏ *04–76–63–44–44* ⊕ *www.museedegrenoble.fr/* ☒ *€5* ⊗ *Wed. 11–10, Thurs.–Mon. 11–7.*

48 Despite its 12th-century exterior, the 19th-century interior of the **Cathédrale Notre-Dame** is somewhat bland. But don't miss the adjoining bishop's house, now a museum on the history of Grenoble; the main treasure is a noted 4th-century baptistery. ☒ *Pl. Notre-Dame* ☒ *Free* ⊗ *Museum: Wed.–Mon. 10–noon and 2–5.*

49 **Place St-André** is a medieval square, now filled with umbrella-shaded tables and graced with the **Palais de Justice** on one side and the **Église St-**

André on the other. For a tour of Grenoble's oldest and most beautiful streets, wander the area between Place aux Herbes and the **Halles Ste-Claire,** the splendid glass-and-steel-covered market in place Ste-Claire, several blocks southeast. Facing the market's spouting fish fountain, at the end of the street is the Baroque Lyçee Stendhal entryway. A tour of Grenoble's four Sunday markets begins at L'Estacade food and flea market around the intersection of Avenue Jean Jaurès and the train tracks, followed by Les Halles, Place aux Herbes, and Place St-André.

Where to Stay & Eat

★ $$$–$$$$ ✕ **L'Auberge Napoléon.** Frédéric Caby's culinary haven in a meticulously restored town house (once inhabited by Napoléon Bonaparte himself) is where chef Agnès Chotin, one of France's top *cuisinères* (lady chefs) puts together the best table in Grenoble. Specializing in *terroir* (that is, unique to the region) creations ranging from *daube de sanglier en aumonière croustillante* (wild boar stewed in port wine with lemon crust) or *crème de potiron* (cream of squash soup), Mlle. Chotin proposes a foie menu that is nearly as wicked and wonderful as her regional *cru* chocolate dessert offering. ⊠ *7 rue Montorge* ☎ *04-76-87-53-64* ⊕ *www.auberge-napoleon.fr* ⊟ *AE, DC, MC, V* ☉ *No lunch except Sat. Closed Sun., May 1–8, Aug. 25–Sept. 7, and Jan. 2–7.*

¢–$ ✕ **Café de la Table Ronde.** The second-oldest café in France, junior only to the Procope in Paris, this was a favorite haunt of Henri Beyle (aka Stendhal) as well as the spot where Choderlos de Laclos sought inspiration for (or perhaps a rest from) his 1784 *Liaisons Dangereuses.* Traditionally known for gatherings of *les mordus* (literally the "bitten, " or passionate ones), the café still hosts poetry readings and concerts and serves dinner until nearly midnight. ⊠ *7 pl. St-André* ☎ *04-76-44-51-41* ⊟ *AE, DC, MC, V.*

★ $$$–$$$$ ✕▦ **Park Hôtel Grenoble.** Grenoble's finest hotel, with spacious corner rooms over the leafy Parc Paul Mistral, is more than comfortable. This smoothly run establishment attends to your every need with skill and good cheer, from recommendations around town to dinner in front of a roaring fire in Le Parc, the excellent restaurant. Try the sumptuous *foie gras de canard poelé aux figues* (duck liver sautéed with figs) and the *tournedos de charolais aux morilles* (Charolais beef with morels) with a Château Fombrauge, Saint Emilion '95 grand cru. ⊠ *10 pl. Paul Mistral, 38000* ☎ *04-76-85-81-23* ▦ *04-76-46-49-88* ⊕ *www.park-affaires.com* ➦ *40 rooms, 12 apartments* ♧ *Restaurant, minibars, cable TV, hot tubs, bar, meeting rooms, parking (fee), some pets allowed (fee)* ⊟ *AE, DC, MC, V.*

★ $$$ ✕▦ **Chavant.** Dining under the watchful eye of the charming Danièle Chavant is a pleasure at this ivy-covered mansion—note that the dining room is closed Saturday lunch, Sunday dinner, and Monday—in Bresson, a 15-minute drive south of town (out Avenue J. Perrot to Avenue J. Jaurès, which becomes route D269). The lobster smothered in truffles is wonderfully wicked and wholly delicious, while the *civet de biche en robe d'automne* (venison with apples, potatoes, and turnips in a daube sauce) is unforgettable. Rooms are elegant and spacious, overlooking meadows and forests beyond the lush garden and pool. ☒ *Rue Bresson, 8 km (5 mi) south of Grenoble, 38320 Bresson* ☎ *04–76–25–25–38* 🖷 *04–76–62–06–55* ⊕ *www.chavant.fr* ↪ *7 rooms* ♿ *Restaurant, minibars, cable TV, pool, meeting rooms, some pets allowed (fee); no a/c* ☰ *AE, DC, MC, V* ☉ *Closed Dec. 25–31.*

$ 🏨 **Europe.** This modest hotel at the edge of old Grenoble on a corner of Place Grenette is handy for its central location. As it is an easy walk from the river, the Jardin de Ville, and the city museums, once you're ensconced here, you're set to explore the town. Rooms are adequate and the staff is helpful. ☒ *22 pl. Grenette, 38000* ☎ *04–76–46–16–94* 🖷 *04–76–43–13–65* ⊕ *www.hoteleurope.fr* ↪ *45 rooms* ♿ *Minibars, cable TV, health club, parking (fee)* ☰ *AE, DC, MC, V.*

Nightlife & the Arts

Look for the monthly *Grenoble-Spectacles* for a list of events around town. **La Soupe aux Choux** (☒ 7 rte. de Lyon) is the spot for jazz. **Cinq Jours de Jazz** is just that—five days of jazz—in February or March. In summer, classical music characterizes the **Session Internationale de Grenoble-Isère.**

Sports & the Outdoors

The **Maison de la Randonnée** (☒ 7 rue Voltaire ☎ 04–76–51–76–00) can provide you with information on places to hike around Grenoble.

en route	For a loop through French history, drive 11 km (6 mi) south on Route D5 for **Uriage-Les-Bains,** home of the legendary Grand Hotel with its excellent Les Terrasses restaurant, once playground for the likes of Coco Chanel and Sacha Guitry. From there it's only another 10 km (6 mi) to the **Château de Vizille,** a gorgeous castle, park, and Museum of the French Revolution. Another 13 km (8 mi) south on N85 climbs to **Laffrey** and **La Prairie de la Rencontre** (Plain of the Encounter) where Napoléon faced down a detachment of his former troops sent to stop him on his return from Elba in 1815.

For a brief glimpse of the Alps, take N91 out of Grenoble toward Briançon, past the spectacular mountain scenery of **L'Alpe d'Huez,** **Les Deux Alpes,** and the **Col du Galibier.** Or take D512 north from Grenoble for 17 km (11 mi), fork left, and follow small D57-D as far as you can (only a few miles) before leaving your car for the 30-minute climb to the top of the 6,000-foot **Charmant Som peak.** Your reward will be a stunning view of the Grande Chartreuse Monastery to the north. If you're heading to Provence and using Grenoble as your gateway through the Alps, be sure to take N85, the Route Napoléon, which cuts through the mountains and presents some majestic scenery. From spring through fall the valleys are lush with greenery; in winter they are snow-covered bowls attracting skiers. Along the way you'll pass many small villages tucked inside mountain ridges, which guard them from winter winds.

Grande Chartreuse

50 *23 km (14 mi) north of Grenoble; head north on D512 and fork left 8 km (5 mi) on D520-B just before St-Pierre-de-Chartreuse.*

St. Bruno founded this 12-acre monastery in 1084; it later spawned 24 other charterhouses in Europe. Burned and rebuilt several times, it was stripped of possessions during the French Revolution, when the monks were expelled. On their return they resumed making their sweet liqueur, Chartreuse, the 132-plant–based formula that is today known to only a few monks. Sold worldwide, Chartreuse is a main source of income for the monastery. Enclosed by wooded heights and limestone crags, the monastery is austere and serene. Although it is not open to visitors, you can see the road that goes to it. The **Musée de la Correrie,** near the road to the monastery, has exhibits on monastic life and sells the monks' distillation. ☎ *04–76–88–60–45* 🎫 *€5* ⏲ *Easter–Oct., daily 10–noon and 2–6.*

Chambéry

51 *44 km (27 mi) northeast of Voiron, 40 km (25 mi) north of St-Pierre-de-Chartreuse, 55 km (34 mi) north of Grenoble.*

As for centuries—when it was once the crossroads for merchants from Germany, Italy, and the Middle East—elegant old Chambéry remains the region's shopping hub. Townspeople congregate for coffee and people-watching on pedestrians-only **place St-Léger.** The town's highlight is the 14th-century, mammoth **Château des Ducs de Savoie,** fitted out with one of Europe's largest carillons. Its Gothic **Ste-Chapelle** has good stained glass and houses a replica of the Turin Shroud. Elsewhere, the city allures with a Vieille Ville festooned with historic houses—from medieval to Premier Empire—a Musée des Beaux-Arts, and the Fountain of the Elephants. ✉ *Rue Basse du Château* ☎ *No phone* 🎫 *€5* ⏲ *Guided tours May, June, and Sept., daily at 10:30 and 2:30; July and Aug., daily at 10:30, 2:30, 3:30, 4:30, and 5:30; Mar., Apr., Oct., and Nov., Sat. at 2:15, Sun. at 3:30.*

Where to Stay & Eat

★ **$$–$$$$** ✕🏨 **Château de Candie.** If you wish to experience "la vie Savoyarde" in all its pastel-hue, François Boucher–charm, head to this towering centuries-old manor on a hill east of Chambéry. Its large restaurant is famous for its wedding feasts but anyone can delight in its special treats, such as the rabbit terrine with shallot compote and an *escalope de fruits de mer,* where the copious seafood is arranged in the shape of a lobster. Even more delicious are the guest rooms, which range from blow-out magnificent—the chandeliered nuptial chamber has a canopied red-velvet bed—to rooms done up in a sweet peasant-luxe decor. Owner Lhostis Didier, an avid antiques collector, spent four years renovating, so rooms feature an array of delights—antique panels of boiserie, honey-gold beams, a grandfather clock, carved armoires, a 19th-century "psyché" mirror, and glorious regional fabrics. Better yet are views ranging over the neighboring Chartreuse monastery and villages. So who can blame you for lingering

MONK-EYING AROUND

The formula for the green, 110-proof liqueur Chartreuse is a secret, entrusted to three monks at the **Chartreuse Distillery** (✉ 10 blvd. Edgar Kofler ☎ 04–76–05–81–77), located in Voiron, set 26 km (16 mi) west of St-Pierre-de-Chartreuse and 27 km (17 mi) northwest of Grenoble (making for a 20-minute bus ride from Grenoble). The liqueur was originally presented to the monastery in 1605 as a health elixir by Marshall d'Estrées and is known to use a combination of plants and herbs. You can visit the distillery and its museum at the original site of the monastery, founded by St. Bruno in 1084. Free tours (in French) are given June through September, daily 8:30 to 11:30 and 2 to 5:30. From October to May, tours are held weekdays 8:30–11:30 and 2–5:30. Happily, tastings are always free and offer a perfect time to contemplate the soberer meanings of the maxim, "Eat, drink, and be merry."

over the lavish breakfast? ✉ *Rue du Bois de Candie, 6 km (4 mi) east of Chambéry, 73000 Chambéry-le-Vieux* ☎ *04–79–96–63–00* 🖷 *04–79–96–63–10* ⊕ *www.chateaudecandie.com* ⇥ *17 rooms, 3 apartments* ⚐ *Restaurant, minibars, cable TV, pool, bar, meeting rooms, some pets allowed (fee); no a/c* ▭ *AE, MC, V* ❑ *MAP.*

Aix-les-Bains

🗗 *14 km (9 mi) north of Chambéry, 106 km (65 mi) east of Lyon.*

The family resort and spa town of Aix-les-Bains takes advantage of its position on the eastern side of **Lac du Bourget,** the largest natural freshwater lake in France, with a fashionable lakeshore esplanade. Although the lake is icy cold, you can sail, fish, play golf and tennis, or picnic on the 25 acres of parkland at the water's edge. (Try to avoid it on weekends, when it gets really crowded.) The main town of Aix is 3 km (2 mi) inland from the lake itself. Its sole reason for being is its thermal waters. Many small hotels line the streets, and streams of the weary take to the baths each day; in the evening, for a change of pace, they play the slot machines at the casino or attend tea dances. The Roman Temple of Diana (2nd to 3rd centuries AD) now houses the **Musée Archéologique** (Archaeology Museum); enter via the tourist office on place Mollard. The ruins of the original Roman baths are underneath the present **Thermes Nationaux** (National Thermal Baths), built in 1934. ◷ *Guided tours only Apr.–Oct., Mon.–Sat. at 3; Nov.–Mar., Wed. at 3.*

off the beaten path

ABBAYE DE HAUTECOMBE – You can tour this picturesque spot, a half-hour boat ride from Aix-les-Bains, every day but Tuesday; mass is celebrated in French daily at noon and at 6 PM.
☎ *04–79–54–26–12* ⊕ *www.chemin-neuf.org/hautecombe* 🎟 *€10* ◷ *Departures from Grand Pont, Mar.–June, Sept. and Oct., daily at 2:30; July and Aug., daily at 9:30, 2, 2:30, 3, 3:30, and 4:30.*

Annecy

⑤ *33 km (20 mi) north of Aix-les-Bains, 137 km (85 mi) east of Lyon, 43*
Fodor'sChoice *km (27 mi) southwest of Geneva.*
★

Jewel-like Annecy is on crystal-clear **Lac d'Annecy** (Annecy Lake), surrounded by snow-tipped peaks. Though the canals, flower-decked
bridges, and cobbled pedestrian streets are filled on market days—Tuesday and Friday—with shoppers and tourists, the town is still tranquil.
Does it seem to you that the River Thiou flows backward, that is, out
of the lake? You're right: it drains the lake, feeding the town's canals.
Most of the Vieille Ville is now a pedestrian zone lined with half-timber houses. Here is where the best restaurants are, so you'll probably
be back in the evening.

★ Meander through the Vieille Ville, starting on the small island in the River
Thiou, at the 12th-century **Palais de l'Isle** (Island Palace), once site of
courts of law and a prison, now a landmark. Like a stone ship, the small
islet perches in mid-stream, surrounded by cobblestone quais and it remains one of France's most picturesque (and photographed) sites. It houses
the **Musée d'Histoire d'Annecy** and is where tours of the old prisons
and cultural exhibitions begin. ☎ *04–50–33–87–30* ⊠ *€4* ☉ *June–Sept.,
daily 10–6; Oct.–May, Wed.–Mon. 10–noon and 2–6.*

★ Crowning the city is one of the most picturesque castles in France, the
medieval **Château d'Annecy.** Set high on a hill opposite the Palais and
bristling with stolid towers, the complex is landmarked by the Tour Perrière, which dominates the lake, and the Tour St-Paul, Tour St-Pierre, and
Tour de la Reine (the oldest, dating from the 12th century), which overlook the town. All give storybook views over the town and countryside.
Dwellings of several eras line the castle courtyard, one of which contains
a small museum on Annecy history and how it was shaped by the Ne-
meurs and Savoie dynasties. ☎ *04–50–33–87–31* ⊠ *€4* ☉ *June–Sept.,
daily 10–6; Oct.–May, Wed.–Mon. 10–noon and 2–6.*

A drive around Lake Annecy—or at least along its eastern shore, which
is the most attractive—is a must; set aside a half day for the 40-km (25-
mi) trip. Picturesque **Talloires,** on the eastern side, has many hotels and
restaurants. Just after Veyrier-du-Lac, keep your eyes open for the privately owned medieval **Château de Duingt.** Continue around the eastern
Fodor'sChoice shore to get to the magnificently picturesque **Château de Menthon-St-**
★ **Bernard.** The exterior is the stuff of fairy tales; the interior is even better. The castle's medieval rooms—many adorned with tapestries,
Romanesque frescoes, Netherlandish sideboards, and heraldic motifs—
have been lovingly restored by the owner, who can actually trace his an-
cestry directly back to St. Bernard. All in all, this is one of the loveliest
dips into the Middle Ages you can make in eastern France. You can get
a good view of the castle by turning onto the Thones road out of Veyrier.
☎ *04–50–60–12–05* ⊠ *€4* ☉ *July and Aug., daily 2–4:30; May, June,
and Sept., Tues., Thurs., and weekends 2–4:30; Oct.–Apr., Thurs. and
weekends 2–4:30.*

Where to Stay & Eat

¢–$$ ✕ **L'Étage.** This small second-floor restaurant serves inexpensive local fare—from cheese and beef fondue to grilled freshwater fish from Lake Annecy, and raclette made from the local Reblochon cheese. Minimal furnishings and plain wooden tables give it a rather austere look, but the often lively crowd makes up for it by creating true bonhomie. ⊠ 13 rue Paquier ☎ 04–50–51–03–28 ⊟ AE, DC, MC, V.

$$$$ ✕🏨 **L'Impérial Palace.** Though the Palace, across the lake from the town center, is Annecy's leading hotel, it lacks depth of character. In contrast to its Belle Époque exterior, the spacious, high-ceiling guest rooms are done in the subdued colors so loved by contemporary designers. The better rooms face the public gardens on the lake; waking up to breakfast on the terrace is a great way to start the day. Service is professional, but you pay for it. Fine cuisine is served in the stylish La Voile; the food in Le Jackpot Café, in the casino, is acceptable and less costly. ⊠ 32 av. Albigny, 74000 ☎ 04–50–09–30–00 🖷 04–50–09–33–33 ⊕ www.lac-annecy.com ⤷ 91 rooms, 8 suites ⸝ 2 restaurants, minibars, cable TV, health club, bar, casino ⊟ AE, DC, MC, V ⦿ MAP.

★ $$$$ ✕🏨 **La Maison de Marc Veyrat.** Formerly known as L'Auberge de l'Éridan, this elegant Third Empire mansion offers guest rooms with spectacular views of Lake Annecy, but most everyone will be too knocked out by what's going on in the dining room to even notice. Veyrat, the only six-starred Michelin chef on the planet—three here and three for his restaurant in Megève (*see below* for a perspective on his house style)—performs miracles with local Alpine produce, most of which the self-taught shepherd handpicks himself during daily treks through the idyllic mountain pastures that surround the hotel. The hikes are part of the Veyrat myth, as is the signature black hat he wears 24 hours a day. The menu changes according to the seasons, the chef's whims, and what the mountain hikes bring in. The results are once-in-a-lifetime events. To wit: his hot and cold Foie Gras with Fig Purée, Bitter Chocolate, and Bitter Orange Juice; or his Crayfish and Roquefort Sabayon with Queen of the Meadow Froth; or his Roasted Langoustines with Hogweed Semolina; or his amazing desserts—"The Dish of Our Adolescence"— such as his oven-baked cream-pots of Chicory, Wild Fern, Verbena, and Pansy, or his sublime molasses sorbet. At these prices, it had better be sublime. The sorbet is €60 while his Degreased Kidneys with Goutweed and Wild Lovage flavored with Coffee Bonbons is €106, the average rate for many of his entrées. The restaurant is closed Monday and Tuesday (but open Tuesday for dinner in July and August); there is no lunch served Monday to Friday. Upstairs, super-expensive guest rooms and suites—many done in a luxe-châlet style—await those who just want to retire and digest the feast. Note Veyrat closes up shop here November to May 15 to move to his Megève outpost, La Ferme de Mon Père. ⊠ 13 Vieille route des Pensières, 5½ km (3½ mi) from Annecy on D909, Veyrier-du-Lac 74290 ☎ 04–50–60–24–00 🖷 04–50–60–23–00 ⊕ www.marc-veyrat.com ⤷ 11 rooms ⸝ Restaurant, minibars, cable TV, bar, some pets allowed (fee) ⊟ AE, DC, MC, V ⦿ Closed Nov. 1–May 15.

$$–$$$ **Hôtel du Palais de l'Isle.** Steps away from the lake, in the heart of Old
Fodor'sChoice Annecy, and directly overlooking one of the most enchanting corners
★ of the town (if not Europe) is this delightful small hotel. Happily, some
of the hotel rooms directly look out on the "prow" of the magical stone
Palais. Without destroying the building's ancient feel, rooms have a cheery,
contemporary look and Philippe Starck furnishings; some have a view
of the Palais de l'Isle. Rates reflect the size of the room. Breakfast is served.
Though the area is pedestrian-only, you can drive up to unload luggage.
⊠ *13 rue Perrière, 74000* ☎ *04–50–45–86–87* 🖶 *04–50–51–87–15*
⊕ *www.hoteldupalaisdelisle.com* 🛏 *34 rooms* ♨ *Cable TV, some pets
allowed (fee); no a/c* ⊟ *AE, MC, V.*

Sports & the Outdoors

Bikes can be rented at the **train station** (⊠ Pl. de la Gare). Mountain bikes
are available from **Loca Sports** (⊠ 37 av. de Loverchy ☎ 04–50–45–44–33).
Sports Passion (⊠ 3 av. du Parmelan ☎ 04–50–51–46–28) is a convenient
source for cyclists. From April through October you can take an hour-
long cruise around Lake Annecy on the **M.S. Libellule** (⊠ Compagnie des
Bateaux du Lac d'Annecy, 2 pl. aux Bois ☎ 04–50–51–08–40) for €9.

Chamonix-Mont-Blanc

54 *94 km (58 mi) east of Annecy, 83 km (51 mi) southeast of Geneva.*

Chamonix is the oldest and biggest of the French winter-sports resort towns.
It was the site of the first Winter Olympics, held in 1924. As a ski resort,
however, it has its limitations: The ski areas are spread out, none is very
large, and the lower slopes often suffer from poor snow conditions. On
the other hand, some runs are extremely memorable, such as the 20-km
(12-mi) run through the **Vallée Blanche** or the off-trail area of **Les Grands
Montets.** And the situation is getting better: many lifts have been added,
improving access to the slopes as well as lessening lift lines. In summer
it's a great place for hiking, climbing, and enjoying outstanding views.
If you're heading to Italy via the Mont Blanc Tunnel, Chamonix will be
★ your gateway. The world's highest **cable car** soars 12,000 feet up the Aiguille du Midi, providing positively staggering views of 15,700-foot **Mont
Blanc,** Europe's loftiest peak. Be prepared for a lengthy wait, both going
up and coming down—and wear warm clothing. 🎟 *€35 round-trip*
🕐 *May–Sept., daily 8–4:45; Oct.–Apr., daily 8–3:45.*

Where to Stay & Eat

$$$–$$$$ ✕ **Hameau Albert 1er.** At Chamonix's most desirable hotel, rooms are
furnished with elegant reproductions, and most have balconies. Many,
such as No. 33, have unsurpassed views of Mont Blanc. Choose between
rooms in the original building or Alpine lodge–style accommodations—
with touches of contemporary rustic elegance—in the complex known
as le Hameau. The dining room also has stupendous Mont Blanc views.
Pierre Carrier's cuisine is best characterized as perfectly prepared and
presented, though sometimes not so interesting or original. ⊠ *119 im-
passe du Montenvers, 74400* ☎ *04–50–53–05–09* 🖶 *04–50–55–95–48*
⊕ *www.hameaualbert.fr* 🛏 *17 rooms, 12 suites, 3 chalets, 12 rooms
in farmhouse* ♨ *2 restaurants, minibars, cable TV, pool, health club,*

bar, meeting rooms, parking (fee), some pets allowed (fee) ⊟ *AE, DC, MC, V* ⊘ *Closed 2 wks in May, 3 wks in Nov.* ⊺⊙⊺ *FAP.*

$$$–$$$$ ✕⊞ **Mont-Blanc.** In the center of town, this Belle Époque hotel has catered to the rich and famous since 1878. Family owned, it is permeated by a sense of well-being; the staff is warm and efficient. High ceilings give guest rooms a majestic feel, accentuated by warm, pale colors, and period pieces. Most rooms look onto Mont Blanc or Mont Brevant. Dining on chef Morand's creations in the restaurant, Le Matafan, is a refined pleasure. Besides classic French dishes (try the succulent crayfish with shallots and chanterelle mushrooms), many foods available only locally are served, such as a delicious lake fish known as *fera.* ⊠ *62 allée Majestic, 74400* ☎ *04–50–53–05–64* 🖷 *04–50–55–89–44* ⊕ *www. chamonixhotels.com* ⇗ *32 rooms, 8 apartments* ♿ *Restaurant, minibars, cable TV, 2 tennis courts, pool, bar, parking (fee), some pets allowed (fee)* ⊟ *AE, DC, MC, V* ⊘ *Closed Nov.* ⊺⊙⊺ *MAP.*

$–$$ ⊞ **L'Auberge Croix-Blanche.** In the heart of Chamonix, this small inn has modest and tidy rooms, each with a good-size bathroom—from one you can even lie in the tub and look out the window at Mont Blanc. Make sure you ask for one of the newly renovated rooms. The hotel has no restaurant, but right next door is the Brasserie de L'M, where reasonably priced Savoie specialties are served. The hotel shuttle bus can take you to the slopes. ⊠ *87 rue Vallot, 74404* ☎ *04–50–53–00–11* 🖷 *04–50–53–48–83* ⇗ *35 rooms* ♿ *Minibars, cable TV, bar; no a/c* ⊟ *AE, DC, MC, V* ⊘ *Closed May 2–June 14.*

Nightlife

Chamonix is a lively place at night with its discos and late-night bars. A popular place to start or end the evening is at the **Casino** (⊠ Pl. de Saussure ☎ 04–50–53–07–65), which has a bar, a restaurant, roulette, and blackjack. Entrance to the casino is €12, though entry is free to the slot machine rooms.

Sports & the Outdoors

Contact the **Chamonix Tourist Office** for information on skiing in the area. Want to try bobsledding? Two approximately 3,000-foot-long runs are open winter and summer at **Parc de Loisirs des Planards** (☎ 04–50–53–08–07). Chamonix's indoor **skating rink** (☎ 04–50–53–12–36) is open year-round, Thursday–Tuesday 3–6 and Wednesday 3–11. Admission is €4, and skates are €4. The **Sports Centre Olympide** (☎ 04–50–53–09–07) has an indoor-outdoor Olympic-size pool.

Megève

⑤⑤ *35 km (22 mi) west of Chamonix, 69 km (43 mi) southeast of Geneva.*

The smartest of the Mont Blanc stations, idyllic Alpine Megève is not only a major ski resort but also a chic winter watering hole that draws royalty, celebrities, and fat wallets from all over the world (many will fondly recall Cary Grant bumping into Audrey Hepburn here in the opening scenes of the 1963 thriller *Charade*). The aprés-ski amusements tend to submerge the skiing here because the slopes are comparatively easy, and beginners and skiers of only modest ability will find Megève more to their liking than Chamonix. This may account for Megève's having one of France's largest ski schools. Ski passes purchased here cover the slopes not only around Megève but also in Chamonix. In summer the town is a popular spot for golfing and hiking. From Megève the drive along N212 to Albertville goes along one of the prettiest little gorges in the Alps.

Where to Stay & Eat

$$$$ ✕⌂ **La Ferme de Mon Père.** "Environmental cuisine conveys a real mes-
Fodor'sChoice sage; the message of well-being." So proclaims the new culinary mes-
★ siah and wunderkind, Marc Veyrat. Little wonder that this superb Savoyard inn has become one of Europe's latter-day culinary shrines, packed with critics and millionaires fighting to pay top dollar to taste the creations of this mega-talented chef. Past and future collide in the dazzling surroundings—a Savoyard farmhouse that looks like it was put together by a Ralph Lauren on mushrooms. Farm implements, drying hams, old pots, and even moss growing out of the rough-hewn floorboards all add up to Farmhouse Chic with an edge. Amusing is the bread cart—an antique crib. Not amusing, however, are the stables that Veyrat has concocted for resident cows, goats, sheep, and chickens—they can be seen through glass panels in the floor, allowing animals and humans to eye each other as one devours the other. Foodies insist that Veyrat's creations—fir-sap soup, bass cooked on slate, eggs infused with lichen and nutmeg, coquilles St-Jacques served up with a puree of dates in an essence of pink grapefruit, lobster with lovage and licorice root—hurtle the lessons of Escoffier far into the 21st century. There are those, however, who will carp that Alpine haute cuisine is at best merely a question of distance above sea level, and at worst an oxymoron. Still, his creations are extraordinary events—who can resist his Jar of Forgotten Vegetables, with Savoie Truffles and Master Dalí's Preferred Juice, or his Pan Fried Langoustine, with Sour Passion Fruit and Virtual Lichen Semolina (other signature dishes are found in our review for his La Maison de Marc Veyrat in Annecy)? Extraordinary, too, are his house-mortgaging prices: appetizers go for around €70, main courses, €110, and desserts, €60, while his special tasting menus run €270 and €360. The restaurant is closed Monday; there is no lunch served Monday to Friday. Upstairs are guest rooms that are the last word in Alpine luxe. Note that from mid-April to mid-December, Veyrat and his chefs close this hotel and move to La Maison in Annecy. ✉ *367 rte. du Crêt, 74120* ☎ *04–50–21–01–01* 🖷 *04–50–21–43–43* ⊕ *www.marc-veyrat.com* 🛏 *6 rooms, 3 apartments* ♨ *Minibars, cable TV, bar, some pets allowed (fee); no a/c* ⊟ *AE, DC, MC, V* ⊗ *Closed Apr. 16–Dec. 15.*

$$$$ ✕⌂ **Les Fermes de Marie.** By reassembling four Alpine chalets brought down from the mountains and decorating rooms with old Savoie furniture (shepherds' tables, sculptured chests, credenzas), Jocelyne and Jean-Louis Sibuet have created a luxury hotel with a delightfully rustic feel. Both a summer and winter resort, it has shuttle-bus service to ski lifts in season and a spa providing a wide range of services in this most tranquil of settings. In the kitchen, chef Christophe Cote creates fine cuisine based on local products. ✉ *Chemin de Riante Colline, 74120* ☎ *04–50–93–03–10* 🖷 *04–50–93–09–84* ⊕ *www.c-h-m.com* 🛏 *69 rooms* ♨ *3 restaurants,* minibars, cable TV, pool, gym, spa, bar, some pets allowed (fee); no a/c ⊟ AE, DC, MC, V ☉ Closed Apr., May, Oct. and Nov. ⑩ MAP.

$$ ▦ **Les Cîmes.** This tiny, reasonably priced hotel offers small, neat rooms and a pleasant little restaurant. Simple food is served, such as roast lamb or grilled fish. Breakfast is included in room rates. The hotel's only drawback is its location on a main street entering Megève, which can be a little noisy. ⊠ 341 av. Charles Feige, 74120 ☎ 04–50–21–11–13 🖷 04–50–58–70–95 ⊕ www.hotellescimes.com ⤶ 8 rooms ♨ Restaurant, minibars, cable TV, parking (fee); no a/c ⊟ AE, DC, MC, V ⑩ BP, FAP, MAP.

Sports & the Outdoors

For information about skiing in the area, contact the **Megève Tourist Office.** In summer you can play at the 18-hole **Megève Golf Course** (⊠ Golf du Mont d'Arbois ☎ 04–50–21–29–79).

LYON & THE ALPS A TO Z

To research prices, get advice from other travelers, and book travel arrangements, visit www.fodors.com.

AIR TRAVEL

CARRIERS   Air France, British Airways, and many other major carriers have connecting services from Paris into Aéroport-Lyon-Saint-Exupéry in Satolas. Only domestic airlines, such as Air France, fly into Grenoble Airport.

AIRPORTS

The region's international gateway airport is Aéroport-Lyon-Saint-Exupéry, 26 km (16 mi) east of Lyon, in Satolas. There are domestic airports at Grenoble, Valence, Annecy, Chambéry, and Aix-les-Bains.

To get between the Aéroport-Lyon-Saint-Exupéry and downtown Lyon take the Satobus, a shuttle bus that goes to the city center between 5 AM and 9 PM and to the train station between 6 AM and 11 PM; journey time is 35–45 minutes, and the fare is €6.92. There's also a bus from Satolas to Grenoble; journey time is just over an hour, and the fare is €18. A taxi into Lyon costs about €30. Taking a taxi from the small Grenoble airport to downtown Grenoble is expensive, but it may be your only option.

🚹 Airport Information **Aéroport-Lyon-Saint-Exupéry** ☎ 04–72–22–72–21 for information. **Satobus** ☎ 04–72–22–71–28.

BUS TRAVEL

Where there's no train service, SNCF often provides bus transport. Buses cover the entire region, but Lyon and Grenoble are the two main bus hubs for long-distance (national and international) routes. From these towns, buses go to the smaller towns. Many ski centers, such as Chamonix, have shuttle buses connecting them with surrounding villages. Tourist destinations, such as Annecy, have convenient bus links with Grenoble. There are many other routes, so always check in with the regional tourist office or information window at a gateway rail or bus station to get printed bus schedules.

🚹 Bus Information **SNCF** ☎ 02-38-53-94-75 ⊕ www.sncf.com.

CAR RENTAL

🚹 Local Agencies **Avis** ✉ 1 av. du Dr-Desfrançois, Chambéry ☎ 04-79-33-58-54 🖶 04-79-15-13-63 ✉ In Aéroport-Lyon-Saint-Exupéry. **Hertz** ✉ 16 rue Émile-Gueymard, Grenoble ☎ 04-76-43-12-92 🖶 04-76-47-97-26 ✉ 11 rue Pasteur, Valence ☎ 04-75-44-39-45 🖶 04-75-44-76-88.

CAR TRAVEL

A6 speeds south from Paris to Lyon (463 km [287 mi]). The Tunnel de Fourvière, which cuts through Lyon, is a classic hazard, and at peak times you may sit idling for hours. Lyon is 313 km (194 mi) north of Marseille on A7. To get to Grenoble (568 km [352 mi] from Paris) from Lyon, take A43. Coming from the south, take A7 to Valence and then swing east on A49 to Grenoble. Access to the Alps is easy from Geneva or Italy (via the Tunnel du Mont Blanc at Chamonix or the Tunnel du Fréjus from Turin). Another popular route into the Alps, especially coming north from Provence, is from Sisteron via N85.

ROAD CONDITIONS Regional roads are fast and well maintained, though smaller mountainous routes can be difficult to navigate and high passes may be closed in winter.

EMERGENCIES

In case of an emergency, call the fire department or the police. Samu, in Lyon, provides emergency medical aid and ambulance service. Lyon has several all-night pharmacies. One of the largest, with an equivalence chart of foreign medicines, is Pharmacie Blanchet. In Grenoble contact Europ'ambulance.

🚹 **Police** ☎ 17. **Fire department** ☎ 18. **Europ'ambulance** ☎ 04-76-33-10-03 Grenoble. **Pharmacie Blanchet** ✉ 5 pl. des Cordeliers ☎ 04-78-37-81-31 Lyon. **Samu** ☎ 04-72-33-15-15 Lyon.

TOURS

BOAT TOURS Navig-Inter arranges daily boat trips from Lyon along the Saône and Rhône rivers.

🚹 Fees & Schedules **Navig-Inter** ✉ 13 bis quai Rambaud, 69002 Lyon ☎ 04-78-42-96-81.

BUS TOURS Philibert runs bus tours of the region from April to October starting in Lyon.

🚹 Fees & Schedules **Philibert** ✉ 24 av. Barthélémy-Thimonier, B.P. 16, 69300 Caluire ☎ 04-72-23-10-56 🖶 04-72-27-00-97.

WALKING TOURS The Lyon tourist office organizes walking tours of the city in English, as well as minibus tours.

🚹 Fees & Schedules **Lyon Tourist Office** ✉ Pl. Bellecour ☎ 04-72-77-69-69.

TRAIN TRAVEL

The high-speed TGV (Train à Grande Vitesse) to Lyon leaves Paris (from Gare de Lyon) hourly and arrives in just two hours. There are also six TGVs daily between Paris's Charles de Gaulle Airport and Lyon. The TGV also has less frequent service to Grenoble, where you can connect to local SNCF trains headed for villages in the Alps. South of Lyon the TGV goes to Avignon and then splits and goes either to Marseille or Montpellier. The trips from Lyon to Marseille and Lyon to Montpellier take about 1½ hours. Major rail junctions include Grenoble, Annecy, Valence, Chambéry, and Lyon, with frequent train service to other points.

🚂 Train Information **SNCF** ☎ 08-36-35-35-35 ⊕ www.ter-sncf.com/uk/rhone-alpes/default.htm.

TRANSPORTATION AROUND LYON

Lyon's good subway system serves both of the city's train stations. A single ticket costs €1.23, and a 10-ticket book is €10.46. A day pass for bus and métro is €3.69 (available from bus drivers and the automated machines in the métro). Lyon Espace Affaires runs a fleet of well-kept taxi-vans in the city.

🚂 **Lyon Espace Affaires** ☎ 04-78-39-26-11.

TRAVEL AGENCIES

🚂 Local Agent Referrals **American Express** ⊠ 6 rue Childebert, 69002 Lyon ☎ 04-72-77-74-50. **Carlson Wagons-lit** ⊠ 2 bd. des Alpes, 38240 Melan ☎ 04-76-04-24-00 🖨 04-76-04-24-02.

VISITOR INFORMATION

Contact the Comité Régional du Tourisme Rhône-Alpes for information on Lyon and the Alps. The Maison du Tourisme deals with the Isère département and the area around Grenoble. Local tourist offices for towns mentioned in this chapter are listed by town below.

🚂 Tourist Information **Comité Régional du Tourisme Rhône-Alpes** ⊠ 78 rte. de Paris, 69260 Charbonnières-les-Bains ☎ 04-72-59-21-59 🖨 04-72-59-21-60 ⊕ www.rhonealpes-tourisme.com. **Maison du Tourisme** ⊠ 14 rue de la République, B.P. 227, 38019 Grenoble ☎ 04-76-42-41-41 🖨 04-76-00-18-98 ⊕ www.grenoble-isere-tourisme.com. **Annecy** ⊠ Centre Bonlieu, 1 rue Jean-Jaurès ☎ 04-50-45-00-33 ⊕ www.lac-annecy.com/. **Aubenas** ⊠ Centre Ville ☎ 04-75-89-02-03 ⊕ www.aubenas-tourisme.com/. **Bourg-en-Bresse** ⊠ 6 av. d'Alsace-Lorraine ☎ 04-74-22-49-40 ⊕ www.bourg-en-bresse.org/. **Chambéry** ⊠ 24 bd. de la Colonne ☎ 04-79-33-42-47 ⊕ www.chambery-tourisme.com/. **Chamonix** ⊠ 85 pl. du Triangle de l'Amitié ☎ 04-50-53-00-24 ⊕ www.chamonix.com/. **Courchevel** ⊠ La Croisette ☎ 04-79-08-00-29 ⊕ www.courchevel.com/. **Évian-les-Bains** ⊠ Pl. d'Allinges ☎ 04-50-75-04-26 ⊕ www.evian.fr/. **Grenoble** ⊠ 14 rue de la République ☎ 04-76-42-41-41 ⊕ www.ville-grenoble.fr/ 🚉 Train station ☎ 04-76-54-34-36. **Lyon** ⊠ Pl. Bellecour ☎ 04-72-77-69-69 ⊕ www.lyon-france.com/ 🚉 Av. Adolphe Max near cathedral ☎ 04-72-77-69-69 🚉 Perrache train station. **Megève** ⊠ Rue Monseigneur Conseil ☎ 04-50-21-27-28 ⊕ www.megeve.com/. **Montélimar** ⊠ Allées Provençales ☎ 04-75-01-00-20 ⊕ www.montelimar-tourisme.com/. **Privas** ⊠ 3 rue Elie-Reynier ☎ 04-75-64-33-35 ⊕ www.paysdeprivas.com/. **Tournon** ⊠ Mairie de Tournon ☎ 04-75-08-10-23 ⊕ www.ville-tournon.com/. **Valence** ⊠ Parvis de la Gare ☎ 04-75-44-90-40 ⊕ www.tourisme-valence.com/. **Vienne** ⊠ Cours Brillier ☎ 04-74-53-80-30 ⊕ www.vienne-tourisme.fr/.

The Massif Central

WORD OF MOUTH

"O. K., when you're tired of Lyon (to be so lucky!), Le Puy-en-Velay is an amazing destination and easily accessible by train. Its 10th-century church, perched in the air on a volcanic spire, is unbelievable—and the street west from the cathedral is claimed to be one of France's most picturesque."

—Indytravel

"I recommend Conques, an adorable town that's closed to cars and has a marvelous cathedral. Rodez, the area's largest city, is also very charming. And if you really want to treat yourselves, visit Restaurant Michel Bras in the quaint town of Laguiole."

—Petitpois

Introduction by
Nancy Coons

Updated by
Simon Hewitt

NOT FOR NOTHING IS THIS REGION termed *massif.* Stretching over a vast landscape that manages to border both Beaune and Avignon as well as Toulouse and Limoges, it covers a truly massive portion of the nation. But what's here? The answer to that question is: very little you've ever heard of. If the points of France's topographic star are its outthrust limbs—Alsace, Provence, the Basque Country, Bretagne—then this is the country's underbelly: raw, unprotected, and unrevealed. Its biggest city? Clermont-Ferrand, best known as the home of the Michelin Tire Man. Its most (in)famous city? Vichy, whose dubious distinction it is to bear the name of the Nazi puppet government Pétain established there.

While there are urbane pleasures to be found hereabouts—such as the gateway city of Bourges, which is graced with a fabulous Gothic cathedral and the medieval mansion of Jacques Coeur, and Roanne's culinary shrine La Maison Troisgros—this region is home to another side of France, usually the last one you might choose to explore. For aside from the occasional bicycle-with-baguette ride, few outsiders know natural France, the nation of rugged country carved deep with torrential rivers and sculpted with barren and beautiful landscapes just begging to be hiked, climbed, or surveyed from horseback. Windswept plains are punctuated with tiny villages cut into time-ravaged stone. Here and there, the silhouettes of volcanic cones pierce the horizon and speak of a landscape still forming, even as the rivers continue their work of gouging out canyons of dizzying depth. The Gorges du Tarn is one of France's most famous natural landmarks, and the extinct volcano of Puy de Dôme one of its most admired phenomena.

Battles have raged across this rugged land since the dawn of history: Romans versus Arvernes (the original Celtic settlers), Gauls versus Visigoths, Charlemagne versus Saracens, the dukes of Bourbon versus François I, and Huguenots versus Catholics in the Wars of Religion. Small wonder, then, that the Auvergnois kept to themselves during the French Revolution, thereby managing to escape much of its mayhem. Collaborating with Hitler under Pétain's Vichy-based government spared the region from the destructive forces of World War II. Thus little was lost— though, some might add, little was there in the first place.

This is truly *La France Profonde,* or deepest France, sought by lovers of natural beauty, overlooked for the most part by seekers of art museums and grand châteaux. But before you turn the page in search of a more tourist-intensive region, take note of a simple truth: the more rural the region, the better the cheese. And any area that proffers crusty yellow Cantal, redolent of volcanic ash; nutty-smooth St-Nectaire; mild and tangy Bleu d'Auvergne; and the world-famous Roquefort, salty-sharp and sheepy . . . well, perhaps the landscape hasn't gone to waste after all. As the lucky travelers who venture to discover the Massif Central realize, there are few greater pleasures than a day's hard hiking in France's deepest backcountry, then sitting down at night to a local roadhouse feast. After all, the way to France's heart is almost always through its stomach, and the Massif Central is indeed the nation's heartland.

Exploring the Massif Central

The Massif Central is roughly demarcated by Burgundy, the Rhône River, Languedoc-Roussillon, and the Dordogne. France's central highlands offer dramatic, untouched terrain, quiet medieval villages, imposing castles, and few large towns. Clermont-Ferrand (population 150,000), the capital of the Auvergne region, is the only major metropolis, hemmed in by the extinct volcanoes that form the Parc National des Volcans. Farther south lies canyon country, with the intimidating Gorges du Tarn, and the magnificent Cévennes Mountains, favorite destinations for nature lovers. Though not geographically part of the Massif Central, the ancient town of Bourges serves a convenient gateway to the region when coming from Paris.

About the Restaurants & Hotels

Although Troisgros in Roanne has long been one of the finest restaurants in France, and the region's major towns and cities (such as Bourges, Vichy, and Clermont-Ferrand) more than hold their own gastronomically, you'll discover that once you get out into mountainside villages, all you really need is a tasty wood-stove pizza, fragrant melting Bleu d'Auvergne cheese, and a warm fire. And perhaps a taste of some *verveine du Puy,* a local green liquor, to accompany your picnic. Keep in mind many restaurants in the smaller villages start their annual hibernation in November.

Because the region was difficult to reach for so long, you will not find a broad selection of accommodations. The larger towns generally have modest hotels, the villages have small inns, and a few châteaux dot the countryside. In July and August rates are higher and rooms are at a premium, so be sure to make reservations in advance. Many hotels are closed from November to March. Assume all rooms have air-conditioning, TV, telephones, and private bath, unless otherwise noted.

WHAT IT COSTS In euros					
	$$$$	**$$$**	**$$**	**$**	**¢**
RESTAURANTS	over €30	€23–€30	€17–€23	€11–€17	under €11
HOTELS	over €190	€120–€190	€80–€120	€50–€80	under €50

Restaurant prices are per person for a main course at dinner, including tax (19.6%) and service; note that if a restaurant offers only prix-fixe (set-price) meals, it has been given the price category that reflects the full prix-fixe price. Hotel prices are for a standard double room in high season, including tax (19.6%) and service charge. Hotels operate on the European Plan (EP, with no meal provided) unless we note that they use the Breakfast Plan (BP), or also offer such options as Modified American Plan (MAP, with breakfast and dinner daily, known as *demi-pension*), or Full American Plan (FAP, or *pension complète,* with three meals a day). Inquire when booking if these all-inclusive mealplans (which always entail higher rates) are mandatory or optional.

Timing

Autumn, when the sun is still warming the shimmering, golden trees, and early spring, May particularly, when the wildflowers are in bloom,

Continental France's wildest region, the Massif Central, offers a Top 10 medley of land masses, including windswept plains, snowcapped mountains, volcanic plateaus, and romantic forests. This is a country of early-to-bed and early-to-rise, the better to take delight in the great outdoors, where unblemished landscapes and spectacular panoramas seem to appear around nearly every turn. Because the Massif Central is so large, it's almost impossible to see everything in a short trip. But with 3–10 days you can get a fair sense of the region.

Numbers in the text correspond to numbers in the margin and on the Massif Central map.

10

If you have

4 days

Begin your first day in the former, short-lived capital of France, ▣ **Bourges** ❶ ▶, a medieval city adorned with one of the tallest Gothic cathedrals in the country, and one of its most beautiful medieval town houses; spend the night there or in nearby ▣ **St-Amand-Montrond** ❷ at the Château de la Commanderie. On Day 2 explore Bourbonnais country, with stops in **Bourbon-l'Archambault** ❸ for its weathered mansions. Head to medieval ▣ **Moulins** ❹ to gape at its Flamboyant Gothic cathedral and overnight at one of the hotels here. On Day 3 drive through the Parc National des Volcans to see its natural marvel, the extinct volcano of **Puy de Dôme** ❿; then visit the Romanesque church in **Orcival** ⓫. Backtrack north on the fourth day to enjoy a feast at the famed restaurant Troisgros in **Roanne** ❼.

If you have

9 days

You can cover much of the region by car if you don't mind a lot of driving. Begin with lunch in **Bourges** ❶ ▶ and then head to the Château de la Commanderie, near ▣ **St-Amand-Montrond** ❷, to stay the night. The second day explore **Bourbon-l'Archambault** ❸ and ▣ **Moulins** ❹, home of the Bourbons and another good place to spend a night. On Day 3 pass through the spa town of **Vichy** ❻ on your way to **Thiers** ❽ to ponder its House of the Seven Deadly Sins; stop in ▣ **Roanne** ❼ for the night and try to dine at the superb Troisgros restaurant. On the fourth day drive south to the most spectacular of the lava peak towns, **Le Puy** ⓮, and then on to overnight near the ▣ **Gorges du Tarn** ㉓ and its natural chasms that do their best to conjure up a mini Grand Canyon. On Day 5 explore the gorge, then head for the **Gorges de la Jonte** ㉕ on your way back westward toward **Millau** ㉒. If you want to really get off the beaten track, continue east through the Canyon de la Dourbie to two tiny villages evocative of Shangri-la, Cantobre and La Couvertoirade. On Day 6 head over to **Rodez** ㉑ to see its pink-sandstone cathedral en route to the famed medieval basilica in **Conques** ⓴. By nightfall get to ▣ **Aurillac** ⓱ or enchanting ▣ **Salers** ⓰. Spend Day 7 exploring the *cols* (passes) and valleys in this area and the sparse lands around **Laguiole** ⓲—home to the famous auberge of Michel Bras—and the perched village of **St-Flour** ⓯. On Day 8 travel through the **Parc National des Volcans** around the celebrated **Puy de Dôme** ❿, perhaps spending the night in ▣ **St-Nectaire** ⓬ or ▣ **Montpeyroux** ⓭. On your last day make your way to the region's urban center, ▣ **Clermont-Ferrand** ❾.

are the best times to visit central France. In summer the *canicule* (literally, dog days) can be oppressive, and the sky is often cloudy; in winter it's cold, and a snowstorm can make a catastrophic intrusion, unless the thought of getting snowed in by a cozy fire somewhere in France's central highlands appeals to you.

BOURGES & AUVERGNE

Historic Bourges, capital of the Berry region, is the gateway to Auvergne as you arrive from Paris. The northern part of Auvergne is known as the Bourbonnais, after the dynasty of French kings that it spawned. The heart of Auvergne is the Parc National des Volcans around Clermont-Ferrand, with its *puys* (craggy lava outcrops) and extinct volcanoes resembling giant grassy cones. Medieval villages perch on hilltops, and outdoor markets bring the narrow streets to life. Good restaurants, informative museums, and venerable churches are to be found throughout the area. Everywhere you go, religious architecture harmonizes with the terrain, be it a mountain crest, as at St-Nectaire, or the hollow of a green valley nestling its church, as at Orcival.

Bourges

▶ ❶ *240 km (150 mi) south of Paris, 70 km (42 mi) west of Nevers, 150 km (95 mi) east of Tours.*

Fodor'sChoice
★

Find your way to Bourges, and you'll find yourself at the center of France. Modern times have largely passed it by. The result: a stunningly preserved market town with a spectacularly high cathedral and streets lined with timber-frame houses right out of the Middle Ages. Pedestrians-only rue Mirabeau and rue Coursarlon are particularly appealing places to stroll and shop. In the early 15th century the town was home-base for France's most flamboyant art patron and fashion plate, Jean, Duc de Berry, who spent lavishly on castles, jewels, and art. Later in the 15th century, Bourges served as temporary capital for Charles VII, who had been forced to flee invading English forces. The town hero at that time was Jacques Coeur, the son of a local furrier, who amassed a fortune as the king's finance minister. His lavish early-Renaissance mansion still stands as one of central France's foremost sights.

★ Approaching the town, you'll see the soaring towers of the 13th-century **Cathédrale St-Étienne,** one of the skyscrapers of the Middle Ages. The architects who completed the nave in 1280 really pushed the envelope, as shown by the side aisles flanking the nave, which rise to an astonishing 65 feet—high enough to allow windows to be placed above the level of the second side aisles. The central portal is a sculpted masterpiece: cherubim, angels, saints, and prophets cluster mightily in the archway. The interior is sleek, elegant, and imbued with the quest for heaven-hugging vertical thrust. Admire the magnificent stained-glass windows and the pillars painted in royal blue and gold—testimony to the great wealth and power this church once enjoyed, also seen in the window-lit crypt with its monstrously fat pillars. ⊠ *Place Étienne-Dolet* ☺ *Daily 8–6.*

10

The Rocky Road

"The countryside here alone would cure me, " wrote France's great 17th-century woman of letters, the Marquise de Sévigné, when she came to this region to enjoy its famed medicinal waters and mountainside spas. She was on to something—travelers since the days of ancient Rome have marveled at this land of exotic volcanic peaks and impressive gorges. Today, for those who would not do battle with glaciers and crevasses, there are peaceful excursions across pastures and along the grassy tops of volcanic mountains. Since there is more oxygen here than in the Alps—the highest peak measures in at 6,561 feet here, compared to 15,000 feet in the Alps—biking, mountain biking (mountain bikes are known as *vélos tout terrain,* or VTT; bikes can be rented at train stations in most towns), and mountain climbing are popular. For serious hiking, strike out along the extensive network of trails that crisscrosses the Parc National des Volcans, centered around the Puy de Dôme. For gentler walking from village to village and valley to valley, follow the Monts du Cantal. During winter there's limited skiing around Le Mont-Dore and Mt. Aigoual in the Causses, a desolate, windy limestone plateau scattered with dormant cone-shaped craters, lakes, and "plugs" (enormous stone outcrops). Mountains loom to the east of Clermont-Ferrand (the Massif Central's only large city), beyond giant granite rocks and heather-clad hills. Wide "fallaway" panoramic views are plentiful over russet valleys sprinkled with spare vegetation. The landscape here suggests an ancient Chinese painting, with broad plateaus broken by humped domes or *puys* above fertile valleys. Here, the ultimate destination is the town of Le Puy-en-Velay—a rocky needle and two big volcanic trays springing up from the plain, crowned by a church built of polychrome lava.

The Hearty Kitchen

Food in the Massif Central is fuel for the body; fine dining it is often not. But there are many regional specialties to savor: *aligot* (puree of potatoes with Tomme de Cantal cheese and garlic), *cousinat* (chestnut soup), *sanflorin* (fried pork and herbs in pastry), and *salmis de colvert cévenol* (wild duck sautéed in red wine and onions). Rivers teem with trout and the natives love serving it up swimming in butter. Regional produce can be transmogrified into glorious haute cuisine, as you will discover dining on Aubrac beef and wild boar at the famed hostelry of Michel Bras in Laguiole. This is also a land of cheeses famous throughout the world—Roquefort, creamy Bleu d'Auvergne, Gaperon with garlic, and nutty St-Nectaire. In summer, bakers stuff *myrtilles* (blueberries) into tangy pies and tarts. And, if you have a sweet tooth, search out the barley sugar of Vichy.

★ Once showplace for the immensely wealthy Jacques Coeur, the **Palais Jacques-Coeur** is one of Europe's most important 15th-century secular buildings, an important landmark showing the transformation of the late-Gothic style into that of the Renaissance. Bearing witness to this are the vaulted chapel, the wooden ceilings covered with original paintings, the grandly picturesque courtyard, and the dining room with its tapestries and massive fireplace. There are few furnishings to be seen,

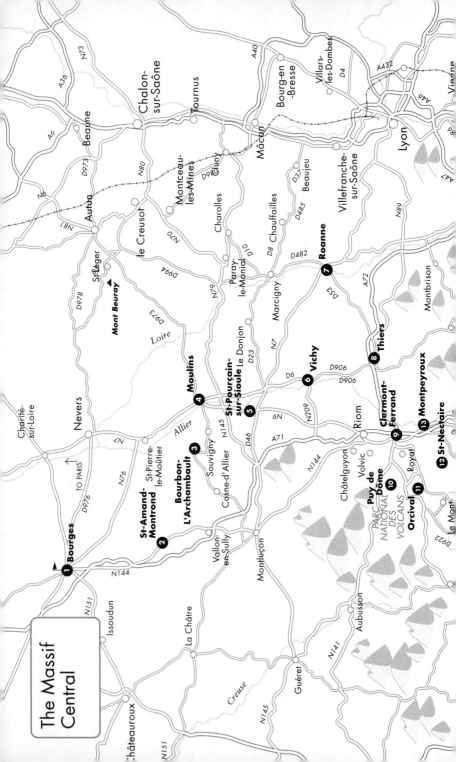

The Massif Central

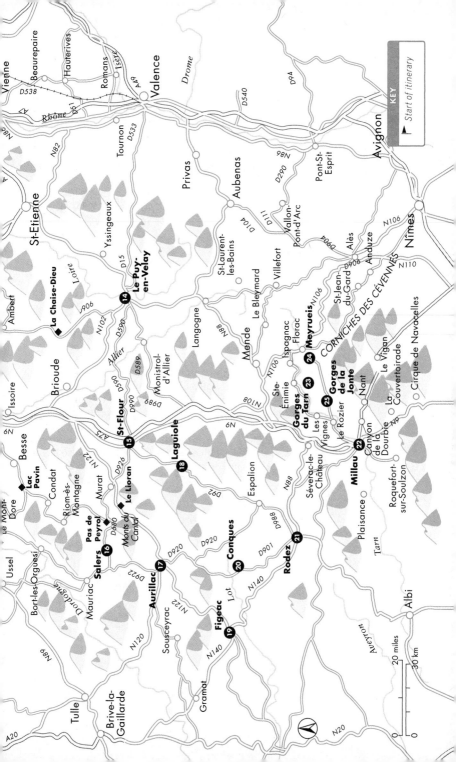

but the building itself more than makes up for this, from its carved and frescoed walls to its sculpture-covered facade (spot the celebrated stone carvings of courtiers staring out of "windows"). The palace's aristocratic elegance was such that several Vanderbilts used it as a model when they commissioned their Fifth Avenue mansions. The building's stairways, galleries, and service vestibules indicate that convenience and comfort were as important as luxury. As well as being Charles VII's finance minister, Coeur was a great art patron (along with Jean, Duc de Berry, he sponsored some of the finest 15th-century illuminated books of hours) and helped spread a taste for the Italian Renaissance. ⊠ *Rue Jacques-Coeur* ☎ *02–48–24–06–87* ⊕ *jacques-coeur.bourges.net* ⊠ *€6.10* ⊙ *Guided tours only in French (English text provided) at 9:45, 11, 2:15, 3:15, and 4:15.*

Where to Stay & Eat

★ ¢ ✕ **Le Comptoir de Paris.** The red exterior of this cozy bar–restaurant beckons from afar; inside, the all-wood interior is warm and welcoming. On the prettiest square in Bourges, surrounded by magnificent medieval houses, this is a very popular and lively spot, especially in the bar area, where dinner is served until 10:30 every night but Sunday. Menus run from €12 to €15. The food is creative and tasty, the portions generous. If you're feeling adventurous, try the *andouillette* (grilled-pork chitterlings). ⊠ *1 rue Jean-Girard* ☎ *02–48–24–17–16* ⊟ *AE, MC, V* ⊙ *Closed Sun.*

$$–$$$$ ✕⌧ **Bourbon.** Set on beautiful grounds close to Bourges's medieval quarter, this former 17th-century abbey combines the grandeur of vaulted ceilings with the modern comfort of contemporary furnishings, a conference center, and an Internet connection in every room. Adjacent to the hotel is its restaurant, L'Abbaye Saint-Ambroix. Chef Pascale Auger has a light, innovative touch with fish and does playful desserts such as strawberries with rosemary. The restaurant also has an extensive wine cellar for intrepid tipplers. ⊠ *60 rue Jean-Jaurès, 18000* ☎ *02–48–70–80–00* ⌧ *02–48–70–21–22* ⌧ *59 rooms* ⌂ *Restaurant, minibars, cable TV, bar, Internet, meeting room, parking (fee); no a/c* ⊟ *AE, DC, MC, V* ⦿⊙ *MAP.*

$–$$ ⌧ **Angleterre.** This foursquare hotel in the center of town near the palace is popular with business travelers. As it is part of the Best Western chain, its rooms compensate for their lack of character with soothing modern conveniences. ⊠ *1 pl. des Quatre-Piliers, 18000* ☎ *02–48–24–68–51* ⌧ *02–48–65–21–41* ⊕ *www.bestwestern.fr* ⌧ *31 rooms* ⌂ *Restaurant, minibars, cable TV, bar; no a/c* ⊟ *AE, DC, MC, V.*

St-Amand-Montrond

❷ *44 km (27 mi) south of Bourges.*

The small market town of St-Amand-Montrond is a convenient stopping point as you head south into the Massif Central. If time permits, visit the **Musée St-Vic** (town museum), housed in a 16th-century mansion, for an account of the region's history from the Stone Age to the present. ⊠ *10 pl. Philibert-Audebrand* ☎ *02–48–96–55–20* ⊠ *€2.10* ⊙ *Mon. and Wed.–Sat. 10–noon and 2–6, Sun. 2–6.*

Also worth exploring is the town park with its ruined hilltop **Château** (castle).

off the beaten path

ABBAYE DE NOIRLAC – Twenty kilometers (12 mi) northwest of St-Amand, this abbey, constructed in 1150, remains one of the finest examples of medieval monastic architecture in France. The abbey church, with its 13th- and 14th-century arcades flanking the south cloister, is still intact, as are the monastery, the chapter house, and the monks' hall. ⊠ *Noirlac, 18200 Bruère-Allichamps* ☎ *02–48–62–01–01* ⊠ *€5.50* ☉ *Feb.–Sept., daily 9:45–12:30 and 2–5; Oct.–Dec., Wed.–Mon. 9:45–noon and 2–5.*

Where to Stay & Eat

$ ✕⌂ **Poste.** The main draw of this 16th-century hostelry is the restaurant—where reasonably priced, delicious food is prepared with loving care and fresh ingredients from imaginative recipes (note that it's closed Sunday and does not serve dinner Monday). Rooms are small and plainly furnished, but perfectly adequate. ⊠ *9 rue du Dr-Vallet, 18200* ☎ *02–48–96–27–14* ⊟ *02–48–96–97–74* ⊃ *18 rooms* ⌂ *Restaurant; no a/c* ⊟ *AE, MC, V* ☉ *Closed Nov.–Mar.* ⎮◉⎮ *MAP.*

★ $$$ ⌂ **Château de la Commanderie.** You won't regret going out of your way to reach this impressive medieval château, 11 km (7 mi) northwest of St-Amand-Montrond. The storybook main building, built of gleaming white stone, has large, elegant bedrooms, a mansard roof, turrets, and towers. Dinner can be arranged with the owners, Laura and Umberto Ronsisvalle, in the paneled dining room. Expect well-prepared family fare, often including perfectly aged Charolais beef. ⊠ *9 le Bourg, 18200 Farges-Allichamps* ☎ *02–48–61–04–19* ⊟ *02–48–61–01–84* ⊃ *6 rooms, 2 suites* ⌂ *Dining room; no a/c, no room phones, no room TVs* ⊟ *AE, MC, V* ⎮◉⎮ *MAP.*

Bourbon-L'Archambault

❸ *54 km (34 mi) southeast of St-Amand-Montrond.*

Since Roman days, Bourbon-L'Archambault has been renowned for its healing waters: during the 17th–19th centuries it became a ritzy thermal spa-town, welcoming such glitterati as Talleyrand, France's powerful foreign minister. The weathered buildings and the ruined 14th-century **Château**—once quarters for visiting nobility, with three towers still standing—retain faded appeal and invite you to ruminate on long-gone glories. ⊠ *Rue du Château* ☉ *Mid-Apr.–mid-Oct., daily 2–6.*

Where to Stay & Eat

★ $ ✕⌂ **Grand Hôtel Montespan-Talleyrand.** Napoléon's foreign minister, Charles-Maurice de Talleyrand, used to stay here every August when he came to take the waters—just one member of an A-list 19th-century clientele. The hotel is a converted trio of houses with a sumptuous (tapestries and antiques) reading room, covered passageway to the bathhouse, and a swimming pool set amid formal French gardens. The rooms are large, some have wooden beams, but for true grandeur, spring for one of the apartment-size suites. The service is very accommodating, one reason many of the guests here become habitués. The restaurant's food is heavy, but consistently good. ⊠ *1 pl. des Thermes, 03160* ☎ *04–70–67–00–24* 🖷 *04–70–67–12–00* ⊕ *www.hotel-montespan. com* ⇨ *45 rooms, 4 suites* ⚲ *Restaurant, pool, gym; no a/c* ▭ *AE, MC, V* ⊘ *Closed Nov.–Apr.* ◉| *MAP.*

¢ 🖼 **Les Trois Puits.** Like any good French inn, Les Trois Puits (*puits* is regional jargon for "welcome") offers no-frills lodgings and warm, friendly service. Rooms are comfortable, the bathrooms unusually spacious, and the restaurant serves honest and hearty fare. ⊠ *Rue des Trois-Puits, 03160* ☎ *04–70–67–08–35* 🖷 *04–70–67–97–39* ⇨ *10 rooms* ⚲ *Restaurant; no a/c* ▭ *AE, MC, V.*

Moulins

❹ *24 km (15 mi) east of Bourbon-L'Archambault.*

★ Once the capital of the dukes of Bourbon, Moulins has a compact medieval center dominated by its cathedral. The oldest part of the **Cathédrale Notre-Dame** (⊠ Rue de Paris) is the Flamboyant Gothic, late-15th-century choir, famed for its stained-glass windows, designed as picture books for illiterate peasants, enabling them to follow the story of Louis IX (St-Louis) and the Crusades. The cathedral's other medieval treasure is the triptych by the Maître de Moulins—one of the greatest, although anonymous, artists of early Renaissance France— painted toward the end of the 15th century. The painter mixed classicizing style with realistic detail—notice the Virgin is not as richly clothed as the duke and duchess of Bourbon, the nobles who commissioned the painting. The town's belfry, known as the **Jacquemart** (⊠ Pl. de l'Hôtel-de-Ville), was built in 1232 and rebuilt in 1946 after it ignited during a fireworks display. The **Musée du Bourbonnais** (Regional Folklore Museum), in a 15th-century mansion next door to the Jacquemart, is filled with costumes, farming implements, and old-time household utensils. ⊠ *4 pl. de l'Ancien-Palais* ☎ *04–70–44–39–03* 🖾 *€4* ⊘ *Sun.–Tues. 2–6:30, Wed. 9:30–noon and 2–6:30, Sat. 10:15–noon and 2–6:30.*

Where to Stay & Eat

$–$$ ✕ **Cours.** Easily the best in town, Patrick Bourhy's elegant, vine-fronted restaurant serves classic dishes with creative twists, such as roast quail with foie gras and sea bass with thyme and garlic. Service is impeccable, and the wine list is balanced and sanely priced. The €17 prix-fixe menu, often including trout or duck, is outstanding. ⊠ *36 cours Jean-Jaurès* ☎ *04–70–44–25–66* ⊕ *http://perso.wanadoo.fr/patrick.bourhy* ▭ *MC, V* ⊘ *Closed Wed. and 1st 2 wks July.*

★ $–$$ ✕🖼 **Paris.** This family-owned hotel, just a block from the town's medieval quarter, is a genuine delight—traditional France at its very best. Service is welcoming and efficient. Rooms are suitably large, with high ceilings and 19th-century antiques. The menus range from the weekday lunchtime special at €25 to a €50 feast, usually including a hearty slab of Charolais beef. ⊠ *21 rue de Paris, 03000* ☎ *04–70–44–00–58* 🖷 *04–70–34–05–39* ⊕ *www.hoteldeparis-moulins.com* ⇨ *22 rooms,*

5 suites ⚬ Restaurant, minibars, cable TV, pool ⊟ *AE, DC, MC, V* ⊗ *Closed 1st 3 wks Jan. and last 2 wks June* |⊙| *MAP.*

St-Pourçain-sur-Sioule

❺ *32 km (20 mi) south of Moulins.*

The attractive village of St-Pourçain-sur-Sioule, with its medieval abbey church nestling snugly among old houses at the top of the hill, is best known for its wines—mainly fruity reds and rosés, made from the gamay grape. Vines were first planted here 2,000 years ago, making this one of the oldest vine-growing centers in France.

Where to Stay & Eat

$$–$$$ ✕⊞ **Château de Boussac.** Although the beefy turrets and gigantic moat reflect its defensive origins, this low-lying, squat château-inn, 10 km (6 mi) southwest of St-Pourçain on D987, is fully modernized and, despite doubling as a working Charolais cattle-ranch, surprisingly quiet. Copious breakfasts are served in guest rooms, which are furnished with antiques and named for their predominant color. In the evening you can sometimes enjoy an aperitif with the Marquis and Marquise de Longueil before tucking into an extensive €43 table d'hôte feast (advance arrangements required). ✉ *03140 Target* ☎ *04–70–40–63–20* 📠 *04–70–40–60–03* ⊕ *http://longueil.club.fr* ⤳ *3 rooms* ⚬ *Restaurant; no a/c, no room TVs* ⊟ *AE, MC, V* ⊗ *Closed Dec.–Mar.* |⊙| *MAP.*

¢–$ ✕⊞ **Le Chêne Vert.** This traditional hotel is clean, comfortable, and well-serviced. Rooms are large, prettily decorated and most have been fully modernized. Tasty, uncomplicated fare is served on crisp white tablecloths in the yellow-walled dining room—veal kidneys in mustard, superb Charolais beef, rabbit in aspic—all to be washed down with excellent St-Pourçain. ✉ *35 bd. Ledru-Rollin, 03500* ☎ *04–70–47–77–00* 📠 *04–70–47–77–39* ⤳ *29 rooms* ⚬ *Restaurant, bar; no a/c* ⊟ *AE, MC, V* ⊗ *Closed 2 wks Jan. and Sun. in winter.*

Vichy

❻ *30 km (19 mi) south of St-Pourçain, 350 km (215 mi) south of Paris.*

Vichy, one of the few large towns in the region, does not have the depth of character you'd expect from a place whose mineral waters attracted the Romans and, later, Paris haute society. Nobles such as Madame de Sévigné and her friend, the Duchess of Angoulême, started the trend in the 17th century; Napoléon III graced the scene in the mid-19th century, then the arrival of the railroad attracted the middle classes. When France fell to the Germans in 1940 and was divided under direct and indirect German control, the country's collaborationist government, under Marshal Pétain, moved to Vichy, using its hotels as embassies and ministries. The stay of the puppet government left a stain of infamy on the town. Vichy is still trying to overcome its past, as well as the perception that it's only a place for retirement. A stretch of the River Allier has been transformed into a lake, and large conference facilities and thermal baths have been built. Although there are no old, famous buildings to admire, you'll want to pay a visit, and drink a cup of spa water, at the Art Nouveau **Hall des Sources** (Pump Room) at one end of the leafy Parc des Sources. Across the park is the ornate **Grand Casino,** which contains an opera house. Shops and stately mansions ring the park, along with the **Office de Tourisme** (✉ 19 rue du Parc ☎ 04–70–98–71–94), where you can pick up a map showing the buildings used by the Pétain government.

Where to Stay & Eat

$–$$ ✕ **Alambic.** A master with local produce, chef-owner Jean-Jacques Barbot creates such dishes as fish, caught fresh from nearby streams, grilled with endives, and lentil salad using the famous tiny *lentilles du Puy.* Fixed-priced menus start at €25. ✉ 8 rue Nicolas-Larbaud ☎ 04–70–59–12–71 ⌂ *Reservations essential* ▤ MC, V ⊘ *Closed late Feb.–early Mar., late Aug.–early Sept., and Mon. No lunch Tues.*

¢–$ ▥ **Arverna.** This hotel in an 18th-century building in the center of town is an excellent value for the money. The owner, who has traveled the world extensively, provides a friendly welcome. Rooms are modest but functional (Nos. 101 and 102 are the best); bathrooms are clean. ✉ 12 *rue Desbrest, 03200* ☎ 04–70–31–31–19 ⎙ 04–70–97–86–43 ⇥ 22 *rooms, 4 suites* ⌂ *Cable TV, parking (fee); no a/c* ▤ AE, DC, MC, V ⊘ *Closed Dec. 15–Jan. 5.*

Roanne

❼ *64 km (40 mi) east of Vichy, 87 km (54 mi) west of Lyon, 390 km (245 mi) south of Paris.*

Industrial Roanne, a textiles center that grew up as a hub for river transportation, will probably be on your itinerary for only one reason—the world-famous Troisgros restaurant.

Where to Stay & Eat

$$$$ ✕▥ **Troisgros.** For more than four decades one of the most revered
Fodor'sChoice restaurants in France, Troisgros is an obligatory pilgrimage stop for food-
★ ies (book weekends two months in advance) interested in the mainstays of haute cuisine. Happily, you'll find the old magic is still here—quite a feat for a place that first set up shop in Roanne's station hotel in 1930. The third generation is now at the helm, and they have learned their lessons well: lightly sautéed foie gras with grilled groundnuts, frogs'-leg lasagna, regional cheeses, and the most celebrated dessert trolley in France are just a few highlights. Service is impeccable, with a waiter-to-diner ratio of three to one. You don't have to deprive your heirs to dine here, however: you can also enjoy the Troisgros's buffet breakfast—a dazzling spread—and the Grand Dessert, a high tea served in mid-afternoon. The restaurant is closed Tuesday and Wednesday, and reservations are essential. This is now officially La Maison Troisgros, for the family now owns the adjacent hotel as well. As in the restaurant, decor here is modern, so if you're out for charm, escape to the hotel's lovely garden-courtyard. ✉ *Pl. Jean-Troisgros, across from train station, 42300* ☎ 04–77–71–66–97 ⎙ 04–77–70–39–77 ⊕ *www.troisgros.fr* ⇥ 18 *rooms* ⌂ *Restaurant, minibars, cable TV* ▤ AE, DC, MC, V ⊘ *Closed Tues., Wed., mid-Feb.–early Mar., and 1st 2 wks Aug.*

Thiers

8 *60 km (38 mi) southwest of Roanne, 47 km (29 mi) northeast of Clermont-Ferrand.*

Built on a steep hill, Thiers is a slightly grimy yet intriguing 18th- and 19th-century town famous for its cutlery. It supplies 70% of France's carving and cutting needs, producing everything from table knives to daggers. In the old days, while the River Durolle turned the massive grindstones, craftsmen would lie on planks over the icy water to hone their blades on the stone. Today's factories use less exotic methods, but the tourist office gives demonstrations of the old way (as well as maps and information). Be prepared for stiff walking—the streets run only up and down! Follow rue Conchette, then rue Bourg to appealing place du Pirou, where there's a wonderful example of ancient half-timber architecture, the 15th-century **Maison du Pirou** (Pirou House). At 11 rue de Pirou is the **Maison des Sept Péchés Capitaux** (House of the Seven Deadly Sins)— look at the carvings on the ends of the beams, and you'll know why it is so named. On rue de la Coutellerie are old knife-making workshops and the 15th-century **Maison de la Coutellerie** (Cutlery House), a small museum and workshop with demonstrations covering five centuries of knife making. ⊠ *58 rue de la Coutellerie* ☎ *04–73–80–58–86* ▱ *€4.50* ☾ *Oct.–Dec. and Feb.–May, Tues.–Sun. 10–noon and 2–6; June and Sept., daily 10–noon and 2–6:30; July and Aug., daily 10–6:30.*

Where to Eat

$ ╳**Le Coutelier.** Housed in a former *coutelier*'s (cutler's) shop, this restaurant is filled with old Thiers cutlery. The fare is traditional Auvergne style— dishes such as lentils with bacon and sausage, chicken cooked in wine, and, most traditional of all, *truffade* (a potato dish with ham, cheese, and green salad). ⊠ *4 pl. du Palais* ☎ *04–73–80–79–59* ▤ *MC, V* ☾ *Closed June. No dinner Mon.–Thurs. in winter, no dinner Mon. in summer.*

Clermont-Ferrand

9 *40 km (24 mi) southwest of Thiers, 400 km (250 mi) south of Paris.*

Known to historians as the hometown of Vercingétorix, who rallied the Arvernes to defeat Julius Caesar in 52 BC (and who is immortalized in Astérix comic books), Clermont-Ferrand is the only large city in Auvergne. A bustling, modern commercial center that is home to the Michelin tire company's headquarters, Clermont-Ferrand probably won't draw you for more than a few hours. But the city serves as an ideal transfer point to the rest of Auvergne. It has some good museums and a small Old Quarter dominated by its cathedral. The Gothic **Cathédrale Notre-Dame-de-l'Assomption** (⊠ Pl. de la Victoire) was constructed of especially durable black volcanic stone that enabled the pillars to be unusually slender. It's famed for its stained glass and its two spires, added in the 19th century to the design of ace restorer Eugène Viollet le Duc, who also lengthened the nave while he was at it.

The older **Notre-Dame-du-Port** (⊠ Rue du Port) was built of sandstone and has an entirely different feel from the cathedral. Though founded in the 6th century, it dates mainly from the 11th and 12th centuries and is Romanesque in style. Note the raised choir with its carved capitals illustrating The Fall and the struggle between Good and Evil.

Housed in a former Ursuline convent, the **Musée d'Art Roger-Quillet** (Arts Museum) has a beautifully designed exhibit on the history of painting and sculpture. ⊠ *Pl. Louis-Deteix* ☎ *04–73–16–11–30* 🔛 *€4.10* 🕐 *Tues.–Sun. 10–6.*

Where to Stay & Eat

★ **$$$–$$$$** ✕ **Bernard Andrieux.** Chef Bernard Andrieux cooks deceptively simple dishes such as salmon with truffle sauce and *escalope de foie chaud de canard* (hot scalloped-duck liver). The restaurant's elegance—cream-color walls, white linens, and well-spaced tables—reflects the prices (the least expensive prix-fixe menu is €28), but not the suburban location. ⊠ *Rte. de la Baraque, Durtel, 3 km (2 mi) northwest of Clermont-Ferrand on D141A* ☎ *04–73–19–25–00* 🖶 *04–73–19–25–04* ⊟ *AE, DC, MC, V* 🕐 *Closed Sun. mid-Aug.–mid-July, 1st wk in May, school holidays in Feb., and Mon.*

★ **$$$–$$$$** ✕ **Clavé.** The finest restaurant in the *centre ville* is tucked away on a little street near the law courts. The decor—plain walls, good modern paintings, subtle lighting—has as much understated style as the chic waiters. Chef Jean-Claude Leclerc numbers ravioli of foie gras and pigeon with chanterelles among his specialties, but his touch is at its deftest with vegetables. Just taste the salad of green beans and candied tomatoes that he drapes alongside roast langoustines to form a culinary still life that looks almost too good to eat. ⊠ *12 rue St-Adjutor* ☎ *04–73–36–46–30* 🖶 *04–73–31–30–74* ⊟ *AE, MC, V* 🕐 *Closed Sun. and 2nd half Aug.*

$ 🏨 **Lyon.** With its exposed timbers, this centrally located hotel stands out in contrast to the surrounding buildings made of volcanic stone and concrete, but don't expect much more than clean rooms and perfunctorily efficient service. ⊠ *16 pl. de Jaude, 63000* ☎ *04–73–17–60–80* 🖶 *04–73–17–60–81* 🛏 *32 rooms* ♿ *Restaurant; no a/c* ⊟ *AE, DC, MC, V* �🍽 *MAP.*

Parc National des Volcans

★ *The Puy de Dôme is 15 km (9 mi) west of Clermont-Ferrand.*

★ Stretching 150 km (90 mi) from north to south, the **Parc National des Volcans** (National Volcano Park) contains 80 or so dormant volcanoes, with all kinds of craters, dikes, domes, prismatic lava flows, caldera cones, and basaltic plateaus dotting the terrain. The volcanoes are (relatively) young; the most recent is only 6,000 to 8,000 years old, which explains why their shapes are so well preserved.

The most famous *puy* (peak) of all is also the most convenient to visit **❿** from Clermont-Ferrand, 15 km (9 mi) to the east. At 4,800 feet, the **Puy**

Fodor's Choice **de Dôme,** is the highest volcano in the Mont-Dôme range, and one heck
★ of a 6 km (4 mi) climb—just ask the Tour de France bike riders, who are relieved they only have to visit every few years. If you're not up for the hike to the top, take an excursion bus from Clermont-Ferrand (such as those run by Voyages Maisonneuve). The road to the peak is paved, so

if you want hard-core nature, you're out of luck. Luckily, once you are at the top there are trails in every direction—one two-hour hike takes you to a cone-shape crater. The Romans built a temple to Mercury here; its ruins were uncovered in 1872. The number of tourists, especially in July and August, is tremendous—the Puy de Dôme is one of the most visited sights in France. Count on spending most of the day here, and bring your walking shoes so that you can follow the trails up to magnificent panoramas. If you're set on a bird's-eye view, parasailing, hot-air ballooning, and hang gliding can be arranged. ▤ *€4.50 per car except July and Aug., when access is by shuttle bus only, €3* ☉ *Mar. and Nov., daily 8–6; Apr. and Oct., daily 8–8; May–Sept., daily 7 AM–10 PM; Dec., weekends 7–5:30.*

★ ☺ A new volcano visitor center called **Vulcania** opened 16 km (10 mi) northwest of Clermont-Ferrand in 2002. Occupying the site of an extinct volcano, the center consists of an artificial volcanic cone, 90-feet high, and a crater dug into lava rock to a depth of 125 feet, lined with shimmering, stainless-steel scales designed to evoke the interior of a volcano. Video displays and spectacular lighting effects provide a razzmatazz introduction to fiery geology. ▢ *Rte. de Mazaye, St-Ours-les-Roches* ☎ *08–20–82–78–28* ⊕ *www.vulcania.com* ▤ *€19.50* ☉ *July and Aug., daily 9–7; Apr.–June, daily 9–6; Feb., Mar., and Sept.–mid-Nov., Wed.–Sun. 9–6.*

Orcival

⓫ *13 km (8 mi) southwest of Puy de Dôme, 22 km (14 mi) southwest of Clermont-Ferrand.*

To house pilgrims making the long trek from Le Puy to Santiago de Compostela in Spain, five Romanesque hospices—St-Austremoine d'Issoire, Notre-Dame-du-Port, Notre-Dame d'Orcival, St-Nectaire, and St-Saturnin—were erected in Auvergne in the 12th century. Of these, **Notre-Dame d'Orcival** (1146–78), with its octagonal spire rising proudly above the sleepy village square, remains the most famous. Step inside to inspect the unusual statue of the silver-clad Madonna bearing an adult-looking child, just behind the high altar made of serpentine and granite.

★

en route | From Orcival take D27 south, which joins D983, for a beautiful ride over the **Col de Guéry** pass, at 4,800 feet.

St-Nectaire

⓬ *16 km (10 mi) southwest of Orcival, 44 km (27 mi) southwest of Clermont-Ferrand.*

Dominating the upper part of the former spa town of St-Nectaire is its 12th-century Romanesque church—you may want to give thanks here after surviving the challenging drive over the passes, and admire the superb carved and gilded 12th-century bust of St-Baudime. Another reward is St-Nectaire's superb, soft, nutty-tasting cheese, made locally since the 3rd century.

Where to Stay

$–$$ ⊡ **Les Bains Romains.** On the site of the former Roman baths, in a dignified 19th-century building, is this attractive, modern hotel in the lower town. Soaring ceilings in the palatial public areas, picture windows in the bar, and the pastel-shaded restaurant create a pleasant, airy feel. Part of the reliable Mercure chain, the hotel has all the amenities, from cable TV to direct-dial phones and in-room modem lines. The grounds in back, rising protectively from the hotel, include a tranquil arboretum. ⊠ *Les Bains Romains, 63710* ☎ *04–73–88–57–00* 🖶 *04–73–88–57–02* 🛏 *71 rooms* ⚊ *Restaurant, minibars, cable TV, in-room data ports, pool, health club, hot tub, bar, Internet; no a/c* ⊟ *AE, DC, MC, V* ⊺⊙⫯ *MAP.*

Montpeyroux

⓭ *20 km (12 mi) east of St-Nectaire, 23 km (13 mi) south of Clermont-Ferrand.*

Well into the 19th century, this granite-walled, hilltop village—perched on a knoll just 8 km (5 mi) from the A75 expressway—boasted 450 inhabitants, most of whom tended the surrounding vineyards. Then came phylloxera. The vines were destroyed and the population dwindled to 125. The village's once-proud medieval homes fell into disrepair. It was not until the 1970s that Montpeyroux's scenic potential was recognized and a revival began. Now the village has 360 residents, restored houses, and an annual flower festival in the third week in May. There isn't actually that much to see here, except for the circular 13th-century keep and a restaurant or two. But the sense of history, and the panoramic views across to the distant volcanic mountains, create a mood of serenity.

Where to Stay

$ ⊡ **Chez Astruc.** Owner M. Astruc's enthusiasm for the village—he is its mayor—and his knowledge of the area make staying at this charming four-story inn a pleasure. The Astrucs live on the top floor; guest rooms—not large but pleasant if a bit fussy—are on the lower three floors. Ask to stay on the second floor, where two rooms have balconies and views of the countryside. ⊠ *Rue du Donjon, 63114* ☎ *04–73–96–69–42* 🛏 *5 rooms* ⚊ *No a/c, no room TVs* ⊟ *No credit cards.*

Le Puy-en-Velay

⓮ *108 km (68 mi) southeast of Montpeyroux.*

Fodor's Choice
★

★ Built around three *puys* (lava outcrops) that rise from the fertile valley like elongated pyramids, Le Puy-en-Velay presents the most astonishing **cityscape** in France. The monuments perched daringly atop these oversize pumice stones are the not-so-subtle beacons of power and religion that has made Le Puy a major pilgrimage destination since the days of Charlemagne, and one of the four principal departure points for the great medieval pilgrim road to Santiago de Compostela in Spain. The lowest of the peaks is crowned with a statue of St. Joseph and the Infant Jesus; the highest with an 11th-century chapel dedicated to St-Michel. The third hosts a huge red statue of the Virgin that may strike some as a tacky Biblical cousin of the Statue of Liberty.

The city's sturdiest religious monument is the hilltop Romanesque cathedral of **Notre-Dame-du-Puy,** begun in the early 5th century by Bishop Scutarious on the site of a Gallo-Roman temple. The cathedral was enlarged continuously until the end of the 12th century to accommodate pilgrim crowds. Admire the black-and-white banded stonework of the Byzantine facade; inside, note the Black Madonna on the high altar, a copy of the figure burned by revolutionaries in 1794. The origin of this first statue—perhaps a figure of Isis transformed into a Madonna, perhaps a statue carved by an Arab craftsman in Le Puy—remains a mystery. The cathedral sits squarely between the adjoining 11th-century cloisters and the baptistery, oozing history at the top of a lengthy flight of steps rising from the steep streets of the medieval *haute ville* (upper town). The rest of Le Puy seems shabbily provincial in comparison, overrun with overpriced boutiques selling the last remains of the town's once-great *dentelle-* (lace-) making tradition. ⊠ €2 *for cloister* ☉ *Cathedral daily 9:30–noon and 2–7; cloister daily 9:30–noon and 2–4.*

Just to the north of the cathedral you'll see the huge red statue of Notre-Dame de France (Our Lady of France) atop the **Rocher Corneille.** The hollow statue (you can venture inside) was built in 1860 using Russian cannons captured during the Crimean War, and melted down on their return to France. The view from the base of the 75-foot statue extends beyond the red roofs of the town to the castle of Polignac, 4 mi distant. ⊠ €3 ☉ *Mid-Mar.–early Sept., daily 9–6; Oct.–mid-Mar., daily 10–5.*

The 10th-century **Chapelle de St-Michel d'Aiguilhe,** perched on what was once the vent of an old volcano, also has a view that justifies a stiff climb. Notice the white, black, and red tiles on the facade, reflecting a blend of Romanesque and Islamic traditions. Come early to beat the backup along the winding staircase. ⊠ €1 ☉ *Mid-June–mid-Sept., daily 9–7; mid-Sept.–mid-Dec. and mid-Mar.–mid-June, daily 10–noon and 2–5; mid-Dec.–mid-Mar., daily 2–5.*

Where to Stay & Eat

$–$$ ✕▣ **Régina.** In the town center (ask for a room at the rear), the hotel's building dates from the late 19th century, but renovations made in the 1990s, including updates like Internet connections and Jacuzzis, have kept clientele equipped with all the modern essentials. A big selling point of the hotel is the restaurant, with its cozy interior and veranda, which makes it one of the prettiest addresses in town year-round. Succulent specialties range from Charolais beef with port and squash puree, to roast turbot with carrot butter, while the pick of the inventive sweets is the date zabaglione with orange and kiwi. ⊠ *34 bd. du Mal-Fayolle, 43000* ☎ *04–71–09–14–71* 🖷 *04–71–09–18–57* ⊕ *www.hotelrestregina.com* ⌫ *27 rooms* ⚐ *Restaurant, some in-room hot tubs, minibars, cable TV, Internet* ▭ *AE, MC, V.*

St-Flour

15 *96 km (60 mi) west of Le Puy.*

St-Flour is a medieval enclave perched on the edge of an escarpment 2,800 feet above sea level, with cliffs dropping down on three sides toward the more recent *ville basse* (lower town). Narrow cobblestone streets meander between 16th- and 17th-century buildings in the ancient *ville haute* (upper town). The **Musée de la Haute-Auvergne** (Auvergne Museum), in the former bishop's palace, presents some local archaeological finds but is mostly filled with artifacts and furnishings used by residents over the last 300 years. ✉ *1 pl. d'Armes* ☎ *04–71–60–22–32* 💶 *€3.50* 🕙 *Mid-Apr.–mid-Oct., daily 9–noon and 2–6; mid-Oct.–mid-Apr., weekdays 9–noon and 2–6, Sat. 10–noon and 2–6.*

Across the square from the Musée de la Haute-Auvergne is the **Musée Alfred-Douet.** The 13th-century building, renovated in the 16th century, has on display tapestries and furnishings from the 16th, 17th, and 18th centuries. The objects are laid out just as they might have been when the building was occupied by the consul-general. ✉ *17 pl. d'Armes* ☎ *04–71–60–44–99* 💶 *€3.50* 🕙 *Mid-Apr.–mid-Oct., daily 9–noon and 2–6; mid-Oct.–mid-Apr., weekdays 9–noon and 2–6, Sat. 10–noon and 2–6.*

Where to Stay

¢–$ 🏨 **Europe.** The choice of hotels in St-Flour's ville haute is limited; the family-run Europe is the best. A long, horizontal building on the edge of town, it overlooks the valley below and the hills beyond—this view being a large part of the hotel's appeal. Ask for a room—and in the restaurant, a table—with a view of the valley. Rooms, though not large, are old-fashioned, homey, and comfortable. ✉ *12 cours Ternes, 15100* ☎ *04–71–60–03–64* 🖨 *04–71–60–03–45* ⊕ *www.saint-flour-europe. com* 🛏 *44 rooms* ♿ *Restaurant, cable TV, minibars, bar; no a/c* ⊟ *AE, DC, MC, V* ◎ *MAP.*

---

en route   Take D926 northwest from St-Flour to Murat, then D680 toward Salers via the **Pas de Peyrol,** at nearly 5,200 feet Auvergne's highest pass. Leave your car in the parking lot and make the 30-minute climb
★   to the summit of the **Puy Mary,** 5,800 feet above sea level. The views of 13 valleys radiating from the mountain are stupendous.

Salers

⑯   *20 km (13 mi) west of the Pas de Peyrol, 68 km (43 mi) west of St-Flour.*

Fodor'sChoice
★

Medieval Salers, perched on a bluff above the Maronne Valley, is filled with visitors—little wonder, since the town casts a spell on most travelers. In the 15th century the people of Salers, feeling isolated in the country, began building protective ramparts and the town subsequently won the right to govern itself. Many 15th- and 16th-century houses of black lava stone remain, given over to boutiques and small restaurants. Although this was once an important cattle-market town, farming today plays a smaller role than tourism—though you may wake to the sound of cowbells and hooves clattering over **Grande-Place** on market days.

About 15 km (9 mi) south of Salers, the valley ridges are so fetching that you could spend a day or two exploring the region's tiny, winding roads. The *cols* (mountain passes) are high enough (plus or minus

3,000 feet) to have snow in the winter, but are relatively gentle, and provide eye-tingling views of the valleys below. Wend your way down D35 to **Fontanges,** with its tiny chapel hollowed out of a limestone bluff topped by a white Madonna, then on to St-Projet and, via D43 and D60, to the pretty hillside village of Tournemire. The **Château d'Anjony** here is worth a visit. ☎ 04-71-47-61-67 💶 €5.20 ⊙ Mid-Feb.–mid-Nov., daily 2–6:30.

Where to Stay & Eat

★ $ ✕🏠 **Hôtel des Remparts.** From its position atop the ramparts, this hotel has spectacular panoramic views and snazzily red-vested waitresses vying to greet you with a gentian-based cocktail upon arrival. Rooms are simple and functional. The management likes to quote half-pension rates, which you should resist if you are staying for more than one night. ⊠ Esplanade de Barrouze, 15140 ☎ 04-71-40-70-33 📠 04-71-40-75-32 ⊕ www.salers-hotel-remparts.com 📨 18 rooms ♿ Restaurant; no a/c ⊟ MC, V ⊙ Closed late Oct.–late Dec. ⊗ FAP.

★ $$ 🏠 **Château de la Vigne.** Monsieur and Madame du Fayet de la Tour's château-inn retains elements of its past roles as an 8th-century Merovingian castle and medieval fortress, with frescoed walls and lava-stone staircase, though it was rebuilt in the 15th century. Family coats of arms, a fabulous Louis Treize four-poster, and stained-glass windows decorate the best guest room, called the *Troubadour,* where Jean-Jacques Rousseau is said to have stayed in 1767. Elsewhere furnishings are stylish and bathrooms fully modernized. A table d'hôte dinner of regional dishes is served in the splendid dining room for €25 a head (plus wine)—be sure to request dinner when you make your booking. ⊠ 16 km (10 mi) from Salers, 15700 Ally ☎☎ 04-71-69-00-20 ⊕ www.chateaudelavigne.com 📨 4 rooms ♿ No a/c, no room TVs ⊟ No credit cards ⊙ Closed Nov.–Easter ⊗ MAP.

Aurillac

🔟 44 km (27 mi) south of Salers, 160 km (100 mi) southwest of Clermont-Ferrand.

The administrative center and market town of Aurillac, on the edge of the Monts du Cantal, bustles by day and becomes a sleepy country village at night. The dinky town center has an old cheese market, ancient houses, and narrow streets that twist along the banks of the River Jordanne. Locals and tourists spend their days at the cafés on place du Palais-de-Justice, the leafy main square. Stop by the tourist office here for a free walking-tour map—well worth following.

At the **Musée d'Art et d'Archéologie** (Art & Antiquities Museum), remains of a Gallo-Roman temple and various religious objects are on display. A unique collection of umbrellas from the past three centuries—about half of all French umbrellas are made in Aurillac—is also housed here. ⊠ Centre Pierre-Mendès-France, 1 pl. des Carmes ☎ 04-71-45-46-10 💶 €2.50 ⊙ Feb.–June, Sept., and Oct., Tues.–Sat. 10–noon and 2–6; July and Aug., Sun. 2–6.

Where to Stay & Eat

$–$$ ✕ **Poivre et Sel.** This intimate, friendly bistro serves a refined version of Auvergne fare. It is a good place to try Salers beef, as well as other regional dishes such as *salmis de colvert cévenol* (ragout of duck). Five prix-fixe menus are offered, from €11 to €30. ⊠ *4 rue du XIV-Juillet* ☎ *04–71–64–20–20* ▤ *MC, V* ☾ *Closed Sun. and Mon.*

$–$$ ▦ **Bordeaux.** There are advantages to this Best Western hotel—its central location, its private garage, and its professional staff. Otherwise, rooms are what you'd expect from this chain—compact but clean, functional, and adequate, though some have views of the gardens of the Palais de Justice. ⊠ *2 av. de la République, 15000* ☎ *04–71–48–01–84* ▤ *04–71–48–49–93* ⊕ *www.hotel-de-bordeaux.fr* ⬎ *30 rooms, 3 suites* ⟋ *Cable TV, bar, Internet; no a/c in some rooms* ▤ *AE, DC, MC, V* ☾ *Closed late Dec.–early Jan.*

CANYON COUNTRY

Breathtaking gorges carved into the limestone plateaus known as the Causses mark the landscape here. Millennia ago, pressure caused fractures and cleavages that trapped torrential rains. Through thousands of years the swirling waters ate into the mass of stone, gouging out the canyons and caves and the underground rivers and lakes that are today such wonders to the tourist, boatman, and geologist. The most famous of these are the Gorges du Tarn, a wilderness filled with sudden views of dramatic silhouettes of red and yellow cliffs. The lovely, old, rural towns make perfect bases for exploring the area, which also headlines some great medieval churches.

Laguiole

⓲ *80 km (50 mi) southeast of Aurillac.*

On the high basalt plateau, Laguiole is more than 3,000 feet above sea level. In winter the wind roars across the land, piling up snow on ski trails; in summer the sun scorches it; in spring and fall the angled sunlight dances on the granite outcroppings. The town is known for its hardy breed of Aubrac cattle; for its distinctive cheese made from unpasteurized cows' milk, flavored by the varied local flora; and for its springhinged pocket knife. You can visit the futuristic factory, the **Forge de Laguiole** (⊠ rte. de l'Aubrac ☎ 05–65–48–43–34), an unmistakable landmark with its giant knife protruding from the roof like a silver fin. This is where they make Laguiole knives, which have a slightly curved handle and a long blade; buy one here or in town (but don't carry it home on board the plane).

Where to Stay & Eat

$$$$ ✕▦ **Michel Bras.** Despite the flowery prose used by Monsieur Bras to de-
FodorśChoice   scribe his contemporary hotel–restaurant, it does not really "mold itself
★   perfectly into the countryside, " but stands on a promontory like a spaceship about to be launched. To be fair, the rooms are bright and comfortable and the views of the granite outcrops are haunting. But the main draw is Michel Bras's unique creations—foie gras with apricots and honey vine-

gar and asparagus with truffle vinaigrette—as well as his more classic Aubrac beef and wild boar dishes. The six-course €89 Evasion menu is worth every last lip-smacking centime. Note that the restaurant is closed Mondays and there is no luncheon served, except in July and August. ⊠ *Rte. de l'Aubrac, 12210* ☎ *05–65–51–18–20* 🖷 *05–65–48–47–02* ⊕ *www.michel-bras.com* ↩ *15 rooms* ᇊ *Restaurant, minibars, cable TV, Internet* ▤ *AE, DC, MC, V* ۞ *Closed Nov.–Easter.*

$ ✕⌨ **Auguy.** A good alternative to the high-price Michel Bras, the Auguy has basic, standard-issue rooms. Ask for one of the quieter ones away from the street. Owner Isabelle Auguy is a creative cook who uses her grandparents' rustic recipes, but gives them a lighter touch. The foie gras salad is a delight, as are the Aubrac beef and the fresh trout. The restaurant is closed Monday and does not serve dinner Sunday. ⊠ *2 allée de l'Amicale, 12210* ☎ *05–65–44–31–11* 🖷 *05–65–51–50–81* ↩ *20 rooms* ᇊ *Restaurant, minibars, cable TV, bar, Internet; no a/c* ▤ *AE, DC, MC, V* ۞ *Closed Dec. and Jan.* ⎥◯⎢ *MAP.*

Figeac

🔟 *64 km (40 mi) southwest of Aurillac, 100 km (62 mi) west of Laguiole.*

The old town of Figeac, which has a lively Saturday-morning market, was once a major stopping point for pilgrims heading toward Santiago de Compostela in Spain. Many of the 13th-, 14th-, and 15th-century houses have been carefully restored; note their octagonal chimneys and *soleilhos* (open attics used for drying flowers and wood). The elegant 13th-century **Hôtel de la Monnaie,** a block from the Célé River, is a characteristic old Figeac house. Probably used as a money-changing office in the Middle Ages, today it houses the **tourist office** and a museum of sculpture, coins, and antiquities. ⊠ *Pl. Vival* ☎ *05–65–34–06–25* 🖾 *€2* ۞ *July and Aug., daily 10–1 and 2–7; Sept.–June, daily 10–noon and 2:30–6.*

Jean-François Champollion (1790–1830), the first man to decipher Egyptian hieroglyphics, was born in Figeac. The **Musée Champollion** (leave place Vival on rue 11-Novembre, take the first left, and follow it as it veers right) contains a copy of the Rosetta stone, discovered in the Nile Delta in 1799, whose twin texts in Egyptian and Ancient Greek enabled Champollion to decode Pharaonic writing in 1821. A varied collection of Egyptian antiquities is also on display. (Note that the museum is closed for renovation and extension through late 2006.) ⊠ *5 impasse Champollion* ☎ *05–65–50–31–08* 🖾 *€3.20* ۞ *July and Aug., daily 10–noon and 2:30–6:30; Mar.–June, Sept., and Oct., Tues.–Sun. 10–noon and 2:30–6:30; Nov.–Feb., Tues.–Sun. 2–6.*

Where to Stay & Eat

★ **$$$–$$$$** ✕⌨ **Château du Viguier du Roy.** Everything—the tower, the cloister, the gardens, the wood beams, the tapestries, and the canopy beds—in this 14th-century palace, once the residence of the king's *viguier* (representative), has been painstakingly restored. Rooms throughout are regal. The restaurant, La Dinée du Viguier, serves excellent prix-fixe meals. ⊠ *52 rue Emile-Zola, 46100* ☎ *05–65–50–05–05* 🖷 *05–65–50–06–06* ⊕ *www.chateau-viguier-figeac.com* ↩ *18 rooms, 3 suites* ᇊ *Restaurant,* minibars, cable TV, pool, Internet, no-smoking rooms ⊟ AE, DC, MC, V ✆ Closed mid-Oct.–mid-Apr. ⏐⊚⏐ MAP.

$$ 🏠 **Domaine des Villedieu.** This lovely farmhouse 10 km (6 mi) from Figeac on D13, dates partly from the 16th century and is lovingly run by the Villedieu family. Not only are there cozy rooms in ancient (restored) outbuildings such as the former bakery, stables, and barn, but you can also look forward to a fireside dinner of cassoulet in a bubbling earthenware casserole accompanied by homemade foie gras and a local Cahors wine. ⊠ Les Olives, Vallée du Célé, 46100 Boussac ☎ 05–65–40–06–63 🖷 05–65–40–09–22 ⊕ www.villedieu.com ⏎ 5 rooms ⚒ Dining room, pool; no a/c, no room TVs ⊟ DC, MC, V ⏐⊚⏐ MAP.

---

en route
Leave Figeac on the road to Rodez and head left on narrow D52, which leads through the beautiful Lot Valley to D901, and hence to Conques.

Conques

㉔ *44 km (27 mi) east of Figeac.*

Fodor'sChoice
★

The pretty ochre houses of Conques harmonize perfectly with the surrounding rocky gorge. The village was put on the map by its Benedictine abbey, whose outstanding Romanesque church was one of the principal stopping points on the pilgrimage route between Le Puy and Santiago de Compostela. Outside town are several destinations that can make for delightful side trips. You can travel through the Lot Valley to **Entraygues** with its 13th-century bridge and 16th-century houses; to the old medieval town of **Estaing**, hugging the banks of the Lot River, with its picturesque bridge and old castle; to nearby **Espalion**, beloved by fishermen and artists for its red stone bridge and Renaissance riverside château; to the tiny fortified village of **St-Côme d'Olt**, with its tortuous cobbled streets; or to **Bozouls**, precariously clinging to the edge of a deep canyon.

★ Begun in the early 11th century, the leading monument in Conques, the abbey church of **Ste-Foy,** had its heyday in the 12th and 13th centuries, whereafter the torrent of pilgrims, and their revenue, ran dry. The two centuries of success were due to the purloined relics of Ste-Foy (St. Faith), a 13-year-old Christian girl martyred in 303 in Agen, where her remains were jealously guarded. A monk from Conques revered them so highly that he traveled to Agen, joined the community of St. Faith, and won their trust. After 10 years they put him in charge of guarding the saint's relics, whereupon he stole them and brought them back to Conques. Devastated by Huguenot hordes, the church languished until the mid-19th century, when the writer and government conservationist Prosper Mérimée stepped in to salvage it. Ste-Foy clings to a hill so steep that even driving and walking—let alone building—are still precarious activities. The church's interior is high and dignified; the ambulatory was given a lot of wear by medieval pilgrims, who admired the church's most precious relic, a 10th-century wooden **statue of Ste-Foy** encrusted with gold and precious stones. You can see this statue—prized by connoisseurs of medieval art the world over—in the **Trésor** (treasury), off the recently restored cloister. 🎟 €6 Trésor (joint ticket with Musée Joseph-

Fau) ⊙ *Apr.–Sept., daily 9:30–12:30 and 2–6:30; Oct.–Mar., daily 10–noon and 2–6.*

The **Musée Joseph-Fau** (Trésor II), opposite the pilgrims' fountain near Ste-Foy, houses a collection of 17th-century furniture, neo-Gothic reliquaries, and tapestries from Ste-Foy Abbey. 💶€6 *(joint ticket with church Trésor)* ☎05–65–72–92–28 ⊙ *Apr.–Sept., daily 9:30–12:30 and 2–6:30; Oct.–Mar., daily 10–noon and 2–6.*

Rodez

㉑ *40 km (25 mi) southeast of Conques.*

Rodez, capital of the Aveyron département, stands on a windswept hill. At its center is the pink-sandstone **Cathédrale Notre-Dame** (13th–15th centuries). Its sober bulk is lightened by decorative upper stories, completed in the 17th century, and by the magnificent 285-foot bell tower. The renovated **Cité** district, once ruled by medieval bishops, lies behind the cathedral. On tiny place de l'Olmet, just off place du Bourg, is the 16th-century **Maison d'Armagnac**, a fine Renaissance mansion with a courtyard and an ornate facade covered with medallion emblems of the counts of Rodez. The extensively modernized **Musée Denys-Puech**, an art museum named for a local painter, is just east of the wide boulevard that circles the Vieille Ville. ⊠*Pl. Clemenceau* ☎*05–65–77–89–60* 💶*€4 (free Fri.)* ⊙ *Wed.–Sat. 10–noon and 2–6, Sun. and Tues. 2–6.*

Where to Stay & Eat

$–$$ ✕ **Goûts & Couleurs.** In an intimate, pastel-color atmosphere, enjoy the à la carte selections or the prix-fixe seasonal menus (€28 and €58), which have such selections as pan-fried calf's liver stuffed with cabbage, or rabbit with fresh herbs. In summer lunch and dinner are served on the beautiful terrace. ⊠ *38 rue de Bonald* ☎ *05–65–42–75–10* ⊟ *MC, V* ⊙ *Closed Sun., Mon., and mid-Jan.–mid-Feb.*

★ ¢ ✕▥ **La Diligence.** It's worth seeking out this hotel–restaurant, 10 km (6 mi) northwest of Rodez via N140, to savor the talents of chef Joël Delmas, whose specialties include succulent mille-feuille of lamb kidneys and a superb banana and coconut tart (restaurant closed Sunday night and Monday). Equally impressive are the prices: prix-fixe lunches start at €14. Rooms, furnished in modern style, are not luxurious, but they are adequate and modestly priced. ⊠ *Rte. de Rodez, 12330 Nuces* ☎ *05–65–72–60–20* 🖷 *05–65–71–86–63* 🛏 *6 rooms* ⚑ *Restaurant; no a/c* ⊟ *MC, V* ⊙ *Closed 1st 2 wks Jan.*

Millau

㉒ *66 km (41 mi) southeast of Rodez.*

Millau, a good jumping-off point for exploring the magnificent gorges that cut through the limestone *causses* (plateaus), sprang to international
★ fame in 2004 with the opening of the **Viaduc de Millau,** the breathtaking viaduct designed by British architect Sir Norman Foster to whisk the A75 expressway across the Tarn (⊕ www.viaducdemillau.com). With its seven slender, hyper-modernistic, concrete pillars rising to a height

of 800 feet, this is one of the world's most breathtaking bridges, and stunningly illuminated at night. Millau's inhabitants, used to cashing in on bottle-necked motorists, are scared that potential visitors will now whiz by, but give yourself time to wander through the Old Quarter, especially around place du Maréchal-Foch, with its medieval arcades. Browse through the shops on place du Mandarous and place de la Tine for leather goods, by-products of all those sheep producing the milk for Roquefort cheese. In Roman times Millau produced pottery and sent its vases as far afield as Scotland. Some of these artifacts, collected from the nearby archaeological site, are in the **Musée de Millau.** ⊠ *Hôtel de Pégayrolles, pl. du Mal-Foch* ☎ *05–65–59–01–08* ☞ *€5* ☉ *Apr.–Sept., daily 10–noon and 2–6; Oct.–Mar., Mon.–Sat. 10–noon and 2–6.*

Where to Stay & Eat

$ ⚹⌧⊡ **Château de Creissels.** This hotel in an ancient 12th-century fort, 3 km (2 mi) outside town on D992, has 15 old rooms furnished in simple country style, and 18 modern rooms with less character but balconies overlooking the garden and the small village of Creissels. Dinner is served in the medieval allure of the vaulted cellar. ⊠ *Pl. du Prieur, 12100 Creissels* ☎ *05–65–60–31–79* ☒ *05–65–61–24–63* ⊕ *http://chateau-de-creissels.com* ☞ *33 rooms* ⚹ *Restaurant; no a/c* ⊟ *AE, DC, MC, V* ☉ *Closed mid-Dec.–mid-Feb.* ¶⊙ *MAP.*

The Outdoors

Mountain bikes, a good way to explore the gorges, can be rented from **William Orts** (⊠ 21 bd. de l'Ayrolle ☎ 05–65–61–14–29).

off the beaten path

THE GORGES DE LA DOURBIE – Southeast from Millau is one of the region's most peaceful river canyons, the verdant, meadow-bordered **Gorges de la Dourbie,** extending from Millau 40 km (25 mi) to Nant. Follow the gorge to the hilltop hamlet of **St-Véron** and the ruined castle once owned by the Marquis de Montcalm. Father on, where the Trévezel joins the Dourbie, beautiful **Cantobre** clings as if by magic to the cliff. Its tiny houses are prized and even its name says it is extraordinary, as it derives from *quant obra:* "some masterpiece." Past Cantobre is a fertile valley and the pleasant town of **Nant,** with its arcaded 14th-century market and impressively austere church of St-Pierre, built in 1135. Another 16 km (10 mi) south of Nant is the intact medieval village of **La Couvertoirade,** home to the Knights Templar in the 12th century and later the Knights of St. John, who built the encircling ramparts about 1450. Now classified as one of France's most beautiful villages, it is home to craftsmen and pretty stone houses; you can visit the fortress, the church, and a small historical museum, all of which are usually open daily (10 to noon and 2 to 4), for a small fee.

Gorges du Tarn

❷❸ *Extends from Le Rozier (21 km [13 mi] northeast of Millau) to Florac,*
Fodor'sChoice *83 km (52 mi) to the northeast.*
★

Though not quite as awesome as the Grand Canyon, the Gorges du Tarn (Tarn River Gorge) has dramatic beauty. The D907 runs along the foot of the gorge, 2,000 feet below the cliff top, from **Le Rozier,** where the Tarn River is joined by the swirling waters of the Jonte. Follow the road to **Les Vignes,** where the gorge opens into a little valley, and detour up D995, along some challenging switchbacks, and follow signs along the cliff top to the **Point Sublime,** where the views justify the name. Return to Les Vignes and follow the gorge as it grows ever more dramatic, with sheer cliffs and rock faces dappled with grays, whites, and blues.

At the **Cirque des Baumes** the cliffs form a natural amphitheater. Soon after, though, come **Les Détroits** (the straits), the gorge's narrowest and fastest-flowing section. Just past **La Malène,** note the 15th-century **Château de la Caze,** with its imposing parade of turrets. Beyond the castle, just before the village of St-Chély-du-Tarn, is the **Cirque de Pournadoires,** and catercorner to it is another, larger natural amphitheater. On summer nights it's the site of a son-et-lumière show. You may feel the gorge looks even more impressive in the light of day.

Ste-Énimie, the gorge's only town, is mired under a flood of tourists in summer. In its little church, ceramic tiles tell the 7th-century legend of Ste-Énimie, the beautiful sister of King Dagobert. When she was about to marry, she fell ill with leprosy and was scorned by her suitor. On the advice of an angel she was cured at the Fountain of Burle, where she then founded a convent. Its ruins can still be seen, as can the fountain. From Ste-Énimie, the road winds through the valley, opening out just before the small market town of **Florac.**

Where to Stay & Eat

¢ ✕▦ **Le Vallon.** Locals are drawn year-round by the simple yet good fare at this restaurant-inn in the touristy village of Ispagnac, between Florac and Ste-Enimie. Prix-fixe menus range from €10 to €25; €15 buys you a very respectable four-course repast, which might include an omelet, a salad, a casserole, and some cheese. Rooms are simple, clean, and inexpensive. ⊠ *Rue Neuve, 48320 Ispagnac* ☎ *04–66–44–21–24* 🖷*04-66-44-26-05* ⊕*www.camping-cerisiers.com* ⤇*24 rooms* ⌂*Restaurant, bar; no a/c* ▤ *AE, MC, V* ☯ *Closed late Dec. and Jan.* ⑩ *MAP.*

Sports & the Outdoors

For kayaking down the Gorges du Tarn, contact **Canoë Canyon** (⊠ Rte. de Millau, Ste-Énimie ☎ 04–66–48–50–52). You can choose from a variety of trips, ranging from a half-day, 11-km (7-mi) paddle to a four-day trip that takes you 72 km (45 mi).

en route Between Florac and St-Jean-du-Gard, the **Corniche des Cévennes** road winds its way through spectacular scenery. Follow D907 from Florac; then take a left on D983 toward St-Laurent-de-Trèves. From here the road ascends the **Col du Rey,** high above the valley.

Meyrueis

❷❹ *35 km (22 mi) southwest of Florac.*

The Jonte and Bétuzon rivers join at the village of Meyrueis (2,300 feet), whose warm days and cool nights make it a perfect base for exploring the Gorges du Tarn, Gorges de la Jonte, and other nearby caves, causses, and cirques. Meyrueis itself has a medieval tower, some ancient fortifications, which house the tourist office, as well as a ruined château high above. The narrow streets of the oldest part of town, once within the walls, conceal a minuscule Jewish quarter and a noble house you can stay in.

Where to Stay & Eat

★ **$$–$$$** ✕🏨 **Château d'Ayres.** A Benedictine monastery before the Wars of Religion, this aristocratic manor house has been transformed into a marvelous country retreat. A serene pool reflects the vine-covered building, and spacious grounds include a tennis court and pool. Inside are comfortable public spaces and two dining rooms where delightful Auvergne meals are served: Aubrac beef and Mt. Aigoual mushrooms are just some of the regional riches. Up the broad stone staircase are spacious, high-ceiling guest rooms. ⊠ *Rte. d'Ayres, 1½ km (1 mi) east of Meyrueis by D57, 48150* 🕾 *04–66–45–60–10* 🖷 *04–66–45–62–26* ⊕ *www.chateau-d-ayres.com* 🛏 *20 rooms, 7 suites* △ *Restaurant, minibars, cable TV, tennis court, pool, horseback riding; no a/c* ▭ *AE, DC, MC, V* ⊗ *Closed mid-Nov.–late Mar.* ❙◯❙ *MAP.*

¢ 🏨 **St-Sauveur.** This sturdy 18th-century mansion, with stone arches and parquet floors, is tastefully furnished with antiques and offers excellent value for the money. The guest rooms are on the small side; the best look out over the courtyard, where you can dine in some style beneath the fanning branches of a giant, century-old sycamore. Otherwise, repair to the charming dining room lined with floral wallpapers and lit with a chandelier to dine on regional specialties. ⊠ *2 pl. Jean-Sêquier, 48150* 🕾 *04–66–45–62–12* 🖷 *04–66–45–65–94* 🛏 *10 rooms* △ *Restaurant, cable TV; no a/c* ▭ *AE, DC, MC, V* ⊗ *Closed Nov.–mid-Mar.* ❙◯❙ *MAP.*

Gorges de la Jonte

㉕ *Runs from Meyrueis 21 km (13 mi) west to Le Rozier, 21 km (13 mi) northeast of Millau.*

The splendid Gorges de la Jonte (Jonte River Gorge) is narrower than the Gorges du Tarn. Start from the village of **Meyrueis,** where the gorge is at its broadest. It soon narrows, and the eroded limestone cliffs form strange pinnacles. A good spot to stop for a snack is **Les Douzes** halfway along. Soon after comes the deepest part of the gorge; past **Truel,** a cluster of houses clinging to the cliff face forms a lookout, where the view opens to reveal two levels of cliffs—**Les Terrasses de Truel**—then closes again before Le Rozier. Four kilometers (2½ mi) from Le Rozier, at St-Pierre des Tripiers, a sign to the right directs you up to the **Belvédère des Vautours,** a natural reserve for birds of prey. In the 1980s, the feisty feathered flappers were reestablished on the causse, offering you a rare chance to see them in their proper habitat—as well as marvel at the cliff-hanging views. 🕾 *05–65–62–69–69* ⊕ *www.vautours-lozere.com* ✉ *€6* ⊗ *Mid-Mar.–Nov., daily 10–6.*

THE MASSIF CENTRAL A TO Z

To research prices, get advice from other travelers, and book travel arrangements, visit www.fodors.com.

AIR TRAVEL

The major airport for the region, at Clermont-Ferrand, has regularly scheduled Air France flights to Paris (CDG), Bordeaux, Biarritz, Lille, Lyon, Marseille, Metz, Montpellier, Nantes, Nice, Strasbourg, and Toulouse, and direct international flights to Amsterdam, Basle, Brussels, Geneva, and Milan. Air France also flies from Lyon and Paris's Orly Airport to Rodez, and Ryanair flies to Rodez from London Stansted.

🛪 Airlines & Contacts **Air France** ☎ 08-20-82-08-20. **Ryanair** ☎ 08-92-55-56-66.

AIRPORTS

Clermont-Ferrand has the major regional airport; there's also a small airport in Rodez.

🛪 Airport Information **Clermont-Ferrand** ☎ 04-73-62-71-00. **Rodez** ☎ 05-65-76-02-00.

BUS TRAVEL

Where there's no train service, the SNCF often provides bus transport. Contact local tourist offices for schedules and advice for this national service plus the two main regional outfits, T2C Transports Urbains and Voyages Coudert.

🛪 Bus Information **SNCF** ☎ 08-36-35-35-35 ⊕ www.sncf.com. **T2C Transports Urbains** ⊠ 17 bd. Robert-Schumann, 63000 Clermont-Ferrand ☎ 04-73-28-56-56. **Voyages Coudert** ⊠ 7 pl. Hippolyre-Renoux, 63013 Clermont-Ferrand ☎ 04-73-92-00-40.

CAR RENTAL

🛪 Local Agencies **Avis** ⊠222 bd. Étienne-Clémentel, Clermont-Ferrand ☎04-73-25-72-06 🖨04-73-25-86-34 ⊠Clermont-Ferrand Airport ☎04-73-91-18-08 🖨04-73-61-06-93 ⊠ Clermont-Ferrand train station ☎04-73-91-72-94 🖨04-73-90-74-11. **Europcar** ⊠Rue Émile-Loubet ☎04-73-92-70-26 🖨04-73-90-28-10 ⊠ Clermont-Ferrand Airport ☎04-73-92-70-26. **Hertz** ⊠71 av. de l'Union-Soviétique, Clermont-Ferrand ☎04-73-14-47-99 🖨04-73-90-46-47 ⊠ Clermont-Ferrand Airport ☎04-73-62-71-93 🖨04-73-62-71-96.

CAR TRAVEL

There's only one way fully to explore the region, and that is by car. The region's beauty is best discovered on the small roads that twist through the mountains and along the gorges. Take A10 from Paris to Orléans, then A71 into the center of France. From Paris, Bourges is 230 km (137 mi), and Clermont-Ferrand is 380 km (243 mi). Coming from Lyon it takes less than 90 minutes to drive the 180 km (111 mi) on A72 to Clermont-Ferrand. Entry into Auvergne from the south is mostly on small curving national roads, or by the A75, linking Béziers and Montpellier to Clermont-Ferrand via the spectacular Viaduc de Millau.

SPORTS & THE OUTDOORS

Rafting trips of the Gorges du Tarn can be arranged through Association Le Merlet.

🚩 Canoeing, Kayaking & Rafting **Association Le Merlet** ⊠ Rte. de Nîmes, St-Jean du Gard ☎ 04-66-85-18-19.

TRAIN TRAVEL

The fastest way from Paris to Clermont-Ferrand, the capital of Auvergne, is on the direct train from Gare de Lyon; the journey takes 3½ hours. Regular SNCF trains also go from Paris to Bourges and from Nantes, Limoges, Toulouse, Brive, Bordeaux, and Nîmes to Clermont-Ferrand.

🚩 Train Information **SNCF** ☎ 08-36-35-35-35 ⊕ www.ter-sncf.com/uk/auvergne/default.htm.

TRAVEL AGENCIES

🚩 Local-Agent Referrals **Voyages Maisonneuve** ⊠ 24 rue Georges-Clemenceau, 63000 Clermont-Ferrand ☎ 04-73-93-16-72 🖶 04-73-93-22-99.

VISITOR INFORMATION

The main tourist office for the region is the Comité Régional du Tourisme d'Auvergne. **Comité Régional du Tourisme d'Auvergne** (⊠ 44 av. des Etats-Unis, 63000 Clermont-Ferrand ☎ 04–73–29–49–49 🖶 04–73–34–11–11 ⊕ www.crt-auvergne.fr). Other departmental and regional tourist offices are listed below by town.

🚩 Departmental Tourist Offices **Allier** ⊠ 6 rue Jean-Vidal, 03400 Yzeure ☎ 04-70-46-81-50 ⊕ www.allier-tourisme.com. **Aveyron** ⊠ 17 rue Aristide-Briand, 12000 Rodez ☎ 05-65-75-55-70. **Cantal** ⊠ 11 rue Paul-Doumer, 15000 Aurillac ☎ 04-71-63-58-00 ⊕ www.cdt-cantal.fr. **Cher** ⊠ 5 rue de Sérau Ct., 18000 Bourges ☎ 02-48-48-00-10. **Haute-Loire** ⊠ 1 pl. Monseigneur-de-Galard, 43000 Le Puy-en-Velay ☎ 04-71-07-41-54 ⊕ www.mididelauvergne.com. **Lot** ⊠ 107 quai Eugène-Cavaignac, 46000 Cahors ☎ 05-65-35-07-09 ⊕ www.tourisme-lot.com. **Lozère** ⊠ 14 bd. Henri-Bourrillon, 48000 Mende ☎ 04-66-65-60-00. **Puy-de-Dôme** ⊠ Pl. de la Bourse, 63000 Clermont-Ferrand ☎ 04-73-42-20-50 ⊕ www.planetepuydedome.com. 🚩 Local Tourist Offices **Bourbon-l'Archambault** ⊠ 1 pl. de Thermes, 03160 ☎ 04-70-67-09-79 ⊕ www.bourbon-archambault.auvergne.net. **Montpeyroux** ⊠ Les Pradets-Lebourg, 63114 ☎ 04-73-96-68-80. **Moulins** ⊠ 11 rue François-Péron, 03006 ☎ 04-70-44-14-14 ⊕ www.moulins.auvergne.net. **Orcival** ⊠ Le Bourg, 63210 ☎ 04-73-65-92-25. **St-Amand-Montrond** ⊠ Pl. de la République, 18200 ☎ 02-48-96-16-86. **St-Nectaire** ⊠ Les Grands Thermes, 63710 ☎ 04-73-88-50-86 ⊕ www.ville-saint-nectaire.fr. **St-Pourçain-sur-Sioule** ⊠ 13 pl. du Maréchal-Foch, 03500 ☎ 04-70-45-32-73. **Thiers** ⊠ 1 pl. Pirou, 63300 ☎ 04-73-80-65-65.

Provence

WORD OF MOUTH

"While in Gordes, be sure to visit the Abbaye de Śenanque. It's surrounded by the most amazing lavender fields in bloom in July."

—Mamc

"We loved the Camargue, with the beautiful grasses, flamingos, and storks, and the wild horses and bulls—we spent a full day there, having dinner in Aigues Mortes (which actually was, for us, a disappointment)."

—IkraKauer

"Do yourself a favor: get up, go to Pont du Gard, have lunch in the main square of Uzès, drive to Nîmes to see the Roman arena and Maison Carré, then back to Avignon. A full and perfect day."

—Vedette

Introduction by
Nancy Coons

Updated by
Sarah Fraser

AS YOU APPROACH PROVENCE there's a magical moment when you finally leave the north behind: cypresses and red-tile roofs appear; you hear the screech of cicadas and breathe the scent of wild thyme and lavender. Along the highway, oleanders bloom on the center strip against a backdrop of austere, sun-filled landscapes, the very same that inspired the Postimpressionists.

Then you notice a hill town whose red roofs skew downhill at Cubist angles, sun-bleached and mottled with age. Your eye catches the rhythm of Romanesque tiles overlapping in sensual, snaking rows, as alike and yet as varied as the reeds in a panpipe, their broad horizontal flow forming a foil for the contrasting verticals of the cypresses, and the willowy puffs of the silvery olive. Overhead, the sky is an azure prism thanks to the path of the famous mistral—a fierce, cold wind that razors through the Rhône Valley. Sheep bells *tonk* behind dry rock walls, while your ear picks up from the distance the roar of the sea. The Phoenicians, the Greeks, and the Romans recognized a new Fertile Crescent and founded vital civilizations here, whose traces seem to have been untouched by millennia of clean, dry air. Nowhere else in France, and rarely in the Western world, can you touch antiquity with this intimacy—its exoticism, its purity. This is Provence the primordial, eternal and alive.

But there's another Provence in evidence today, a disarming culture of *pastis* (an anise-based aperitif), *pétanque* (lawn bowling), and shady plane trees, where dawdling is a way of life, where you may plant yourself in a sidewalk café and listen to the trickling fountain, putter aimlessly down narrow cobbled alleyways, heft melons in the morning marketplace and, after a three-hour lunch, take an afternoon snooze in the cool shade of a 500-year-old olive tree.

Until the cell phone rings, that is. Because ever since Peter Mayle abandoned the London fog and described with sensual relish a life of unbuttoned collars and espadrilles in his best-selling *A Year in Provence,* the world has beaten a path here. Now Parisians are heard in the local marketplaces passing the word on the best free-range rabbit, the purest olive oil, the lowest price on a five-bedroom *mas* (farmhouse) with vineyard and pool. And a chic *bon-chic-bon-genre* city crowd languishes stylishly at the latest country inn and makes an appearance at the most fashionable restaurant. Ask them, and they'll agree: ever since Princess Caroline of Monaco moved to St-Rémy, Provence has become the new Côte d'Azur.

But chic Provence hasn't eclipsed idyllic Provence, and it's still possible to melt into a Monday-morning market crowd, where blue-aproned *paysannes* scoop fistfuls of mesclun into willow baskets, matron-connoisseurs paw through bins containing the first Cavaillon asparagus, a knot of *pépés* in workers' blues takes a pétanque break . . . welcoming all into the game.

Relax and join them—and plan to stay around a while. There are plenty of sights to see: some of the finest Roman ruins in Europe, from the Pont du Gard to the arenas at Arles and Nîmes; the pristine Romanesque abbeys of Senanque and de Montmajour; bijou chapels and weathered mas; the

Peter Mayle's book *A Year in Provence* prescribes just that, but even a year might not be long enough to soak up all the charm of this captivating region. In three days you can see three representative (and very different) towns: Arles, Avignon, and St-Rémy; with seven days you can easily add the Camargue, the Luberon, and Aix-en-Provence; with 10 days you can add Vaison-la-Romaine and Marseille. The following are suggested itineraries for touring the area; another option is to base yourself in one place and take day trips from there.

To make the most of your time in the region, plan to divide your days between big-city culture, backcountry tours, and waterfront leisure. If you must, you can "do" Provence at an if-this-is-Tuesday breakneck pace, but its rural roads and tiny villages will amply reward a more leisurely approach. Provence is as much a way of life as a region charged with tourist must-sees, so you should allow time to enjoy its old-fashioned pace.

Numbers in the text correspond to numbers in the margin and on the Provence, Nîmes, Arles, Avignon, and Marseille maps.

If you have 3 days

The best gateway to the region is **Avignon** ㉗–㉞ ▶, where tiny, narrow streets cluster around the 14th-century Palais des Papes, as if still seeking the protection afforded them when this massive structure represented the supreme Christian authority of the world, back in the 14th century. Then make an afternoon outing west to the **Pont du Gard** ㉟ aqueduct, a majestic relic from the ancient Romans that strikes all as more a work of art than a practical construction. On Day 2 stop briefly in **Nîmes** ⑭–㉒ to see the antiquities of the Arènes and the Maison Carrée—a striking contrast to this busy commercial center—then head into atmospheric old 🎬 **Arles** ①–⑩, inspiration to Van Gogh, who captured the delicate, pointed features of the Arlésienne in some of his finest portraits. On Day 3 drive through the countryside, stopping at the **Abbaye de Montmajour** ㉓—whose cloisters are a particularly charming spot when the oleander trees are in bloom—and the medieval hill town of **Les Baux-de-Provence** ㉔; stay overnight in 🎬 **St-Rémy-de-Provence** ㉕, with its Roman ruins and recognizable Van Gogh landmarks.

If you have 7 days

Visit **Orange** ㊲ ▶ on your first day before stopping to see the **Pont du Gard** ㉟— both the ancient Roman theater in Orange and the famous aqueduct will allow you to travel back two millennia in time. Spend two nights in 🎬 **Avignon** ㉗–㉞ and don't forget to visit the Bridge of St-Bénézet (made famous in the old song "Sur le pont d'Avignon"). In the morning stop briefly in **Nîmes** ⑭–㉒ on your way to the fortified town of **Aigues-Mortes** ⑬ and make a slight detour through the Camargue to 🎬 **Arles** ①–⑩. The next morning explore Arles's Roman remains. Try to get to the rocky perch of **Les Baux-de-Provence** ㉔ by lunchtime and then continue to 🎬 **St-Rémy-de-Provence** ㉕ to see where Van Gogh set up his easel. On day five wend your way through **L'Isle-sur-la-Sorgue** ㊶ to **Gordes** ㊸, in the Luberon Mountains, one of Provence's most famous *villages perchés* (perched villages). Spend the night in the hilltop village of **Bonnieux** ㊼ and drive over the windswept spine of the Luberon on your way south to

⊡ **Aix-en-Provence** ㊽–㊴; spend two days there visiting the marvelous 18th-century mansions, the museums, and its cours Mirabeau, which is to Aix what the Champs-Élysées is to Paris.

If you have
10
days

To the seven-day itinerary, add a day visiting ruins in the Rhône-side Roman market town of **Vaison-la-Romaine** ㊳ ☞ and drive the winding back roads of the neighboring Mont Ventoux region, whose fruited plains lead to forested heights. Or make a broader sweep through the Camargue to include the eccentric seaside town of **Stes-Maries-de-la-Mer** ⑫, its gloomy Romanesque church (full of Gypsy tributes to the two St. Marys and their servant girl Sarah). Then take the time to experience the urban vitality of **Marseille** ㊶–㊽, or cool your heels at the gentrified seaside retreat of ⊡ **Cassis** ㊿.

feudal châteaux at Tarascon and Beaucaire; the monolithic Papal Palace in old Avignon; and everywhere vineyards, pleasure ports, and sophisticated city museums. But allow yourself time to feel the rhythm of modern Provençal life, to listen to the pulsing *breet* of the insects, smell the *parfum* of a tiny country path, and feel the air of a summer night on your skin. . . .

Exploring Provence

Bordered to the west by the Languedoc and melting to the south and east into the blue waters of the Mediterranean, Provence falls easily into four areas. The Camargue is at the heart of the first, flanked by Nîmes and Van Gogh's picturesque Arles to the east. Here, the Camargue's hypnotic plane of marsh grass stretching to the sea is interrupted only by an explosion of flying flamingos or a modest stampede of stocky bulls led by latter-day cowboys. Northeast of Arles, the rude and rocky Alpilles jut upward, their hillsides green with orchards and olive groves; here you'll find feudal Les Baux and the Greco-Roman enclave of St-Rémy, now fashionable with the Summer People. The third area, which falls within the boundaries of the Vaucluse, begins at Avignon and extends north to Orange and Vaison-la-Romaine, then east to the forested slopes of the Luberon, where you'll find the countryside made famous by Peter Mayle—hilltop towns like Ménerbes, Roussillon, and Gordes are the jewels in a landscape studded with blue-black forests, sun-bleached rocks, and golden perched villages. The fourth area encompasses Cézanne country, east of the Rhône, starting in Aix-en-Provence, then winding southward to big-city Marseille—tough, gorgeous, and larger than life—and east along the Mediterranean coast to the idyllic Iles d'Hyères. Note: a very handy Web resource to all the villages of Provence is ⊕ www.provencebeyond.com/villages.

About the Restaurants & Hotels

You'll eat late in the south, rarely before 1 for lunch, usually after 9 at night. In summer, shops and museums may shut down until 3 or 4, as much to accommodate lazy lunches as for the crowds taking sun on the beach. But a late lunch works nicely with a late breakfast—and that's another southern luxury. As morning here is the coolest part of the day and the light is at its sweetest, hotels and cafés of every class take pains to make breakfast memorable and whenever possible served outdoors. Complete with tables in the garden with sunny-print cloths and a nosegay of flowers, accompanied by birdsong, and warmed by the cool morning sun, it's one of the three loveliest meals of the day.

Accommodations in Provence range from luxurious villas to elegantly converted mas to modest city-center hotels. Reservations are essential for much of the year, and many hotels are closed in winter. Assume all hotel rooms have air-conditioning, TV, telephones, and private bath, unless otherwise noted.

WHAT IT COSTS In euros					
	$$$$	**$$$**	**$$**	**$**	**¢**
RESTAURANTS	over €30	€23–€30	€17–€23	€11–€17	under €11
HOTELS	over €190	€120–€190	€80–€120	€50–€80	under €50

Restaurant prices are per person for a main course at dinner, including tax (19.6%) and service; note that if a restaurant offers only prix-fixe (set-price) meals, it has been given the price category that reflects the full prix-fixe price. Hotel prices are for a standard double room in high season, including tax (19.6%) and service charge. Hotels operate on the European Plan (EP, with no meal provided) unless we note that they use the Breakfast Plan (BP), or also offer such options as Modified American Plan (MAP, with breakfast and dinner daily, known as *demi-pension*), or Full American Plan (FAP, or *pension complète,* with three meals a day). Inquire when booking if these all-inclusive mealplans (which always entail higher rates) are mandatory or optional.

Timing

Spring and fall are the best months to experience the dazzling light, rugged rocky countryside, and fruited vineyards of Provence. Though the lavender fields show peak color in mid-July, summertime here is beastly hot; worse, it's always crowded on the beaches and connecting roads. Winter has some nice days, when the locals are able to enjoy their cafés and their town squares tourist-free, but it often rains, and the razor-sharp mistral wind can cut to the bone.

ARLES & THE CAMARGUE

Sitting on the banks of the Rhône River, with a *Vieille Ville* (Old Town) where time seems to have stood still since 1888—the year Vincent van Gogh immortalized the city in his paintings—Arles remains both a vibrant example of Provençal culture and the gateway to the Camargue, a wild and marshy region that extends south to the Mediterranean. Arles, in fact, once outshone Marseille as the major port of the area before sea gave way to sand. Today it competes with nearby Nîmes for the title "Rome of France," thanks to its magnificent Roman theater and Arènes (amphitheater). Just west and south of these landmarks, the Camargue is a vast watery plain formed by the sprawling Rhône delta and extending over 800 square km (300 square mi)—its landscape remains one of the most extraordinary in France.

Arles

36 km (22 mi) south of Avignon, 31 km (19 mi) east of Nîmes, 92 km (57 mi) northwest of Marseille, 720 km (430 mi) south of Paris.

If you were obliged to choose just one city to visit in Provence, lovely little Arles would give Avignon and Aix a run for their money. It's too chic to become museumlike yet has a wealth of classical antiquities and Romanesque stonework, quarried-stone edifices and shuttered town houses, and graceful, shady Vieille Ville streets and squares. Throughout the year there are pageantry, festivals, and cutting-edge arts events. Its panoply of atmospheric restaurants and picturesque small hotels makes it the ideal headquarters for forays into the Alpilles and the Camargue.

A Greek colony since the 6th century BC, little Arles took a giant step forward when Julius Caesar defeated Marseille in the 1st century BC. The emperor-to-be designated Arles a Roman colony and lavished funds and engineering know-how on it. It became an international crossroads by sea and land and a market to the world, with goods from Africa, Arabia, and the Far East. The emperor Constantine himself moved to Arles and brought with him Christianity.

The remains of this golden age are reason enough to visit Arles today, yet its character nowadays is as gracious and low-key as it once was cutting-edge. Seated in the shade of the plane trees on place du Forum or strolling the rampart walkway along the sparkling Rhône, you'll see what enchanted Gauguin and drove Van Gogh frantic with inspiration.

Note: If you plan to visit many of the monuments and museums in Arles, buy a *visite generale* ticket for €12. This covers the entry fee to the Musée de l'Arles et des Provence Antiques and any and all of the other museums and monuments (except the independent Museon Arlaten, which charges €4 each). The ticket is good for the length of your stay.

★ ❶ Though it's a hike from the center, a good place to set the tone and context for your exploration of Arles is at the state-of-the-art **Musée de l'Arles et des Provence Antiques** (Museum of Ancient Arles and Provence). The bold, modern triangular structure (designed by Henri Ciriani) lies on the site of an enormous Roman *cirque* (chariot-racing stadium). The permanent collection includes jewelry, mosaics, town plans, and 4th-century carved sacophagi from *Les Alyscamps*. You'll learn all about Arles in its heyday, from the development of its monuments to details of daily life in Roman times. Ask for the English-language guidebook. ⊠ *Presqu'île du Cirque Romain* ☎ *04–90–18–88–88* ⊕ *www.arles-antique.org* ☒ *€5.50* ☉ *Mar.–Oct., daily 9–7; Nov.–Feb., daily 10–5.*

❷ A good way to plunge into post-Roman Arles is through the quirky old **Museon Arlaten** (Museum of Arles). Created by the father of the Provençal revival, turn-of-the-20th-century poet Frédéric Mistral, it enshrines a seemingly bottomless collection of regional treasures ranging from 18th-century furniture and ceramics to a mixed-bag collection of toothache-prevention cures. Following Mistral's wishes, women in full Arlésienne costume oversee the labyrinth of lovely 16th-century halls. ⊠ *29 rue de la République* ☎ *04–90–93–58–11* ☒ *€4, free 1st Sun.*

11

Shopping à la Folklorique

Some of the smallest villages have their predatory claws unfurled these days, with every house a storefront overflowing with doodads and gewgaws on Provençal themes. Pottery mugs with good-luck cicadas and coasters of the famous sunflowers are the bastard children of legitimate crafts and products that are intrinsically Provence—*boutis,* intricately quilted cotton throws; richly textured Provençal fabrics in 18th-century reproduction paisley prints, put to legitimate use as skirts, curtains, and tablecloths; marvelously mild and natural *savon de Marseille* (Marseille soap); artisanal olive oils from the Alpilles; and if you acquire the taste, the sometimes exquisitely rendered *santons,* tiny terra-cotta figurines first made for Provençal Christmas crèches. The best *santonniers* have studios in Aubagne.

Roman to Romanesque

This isn't Gothic cathedral country, but a treasure trove of smaller church gems offers a moving, more intimate alternative. Provence is peppered with churches, châteaux, and abbeys, a surprising concentration of them pure Romanesque of the 12th and 13th centuries. Signs point to ÉGLISE ROMANE XIIÈME—meaning Romanesque. *Romain* refers to Roman remains, which you'll also find throughout Provence (in fact, its name comes from the Roman *provincia,* or "the province"). The most beautifully preserved are concentrated around the Rhône, their main shipping artery. There are two arenas (in Arles and Nîmes), the ancient Hellenistic settlement outside St-Rémy (Glanum), the miraculously preserved temple in Nîmes (Maison Carrée), a theater in Orange, and two villages in Vaison-la-Romaine. The granddaddy of all Roman treasures is the Pont du Gard, the magnificent multitier aqueduct straddling the Gardon River west of Avignon.

La Cuisine de Soleil

Universally emulated for its winning combination of simplicity, healthy ingredients, and vivid sun-kissed flavors, Provençal cooking glories in olive oil, garlic, tomatoes, olives, and the ubiquitous wild herbs that crunch underfoot. France's greatest chefs scour lively markets for melons still warm from the morning sun, and buy glistening olives by the pailful. You can't lose when you start with an icy pastis, the pale yellow, anise-based aperitif; smear your toast with *tapenade,* a delicious paste of olives, capers, and anchovies; heap aioli, a garlicky mayonnaise, on your fresh fish; and rub thyme and garlic on your lamb. No meal is complete without a round of goat cheese, sun-ripened fruit, and a chilled bottle of rosé from the surrounding hills.

Markets

Browsing through the *marché couvert* (covered food market) in Avignon is enough to make you regret all the tempting restaurants around. At nearly all Provençal markets, seafood, poultry, olives, melons, and asparagus cry out to be gathered in a basket, arranged lovingly in pottery bowls, and later cooked in their purest form. For picnics, stock up on tubs of tapenade and *anchoïade* (anchovy spread), dried game sausage, tangy marinated seafood, and tiny pucks of withered goat cheese. And antiques and *brocantes* (collectibles) are never far away, sometimes providing the most authentic local souvenirs. Many antiques stores are located in L'Isle-sur-la-Sorgue, also home to the finest Sunday morning flea market.

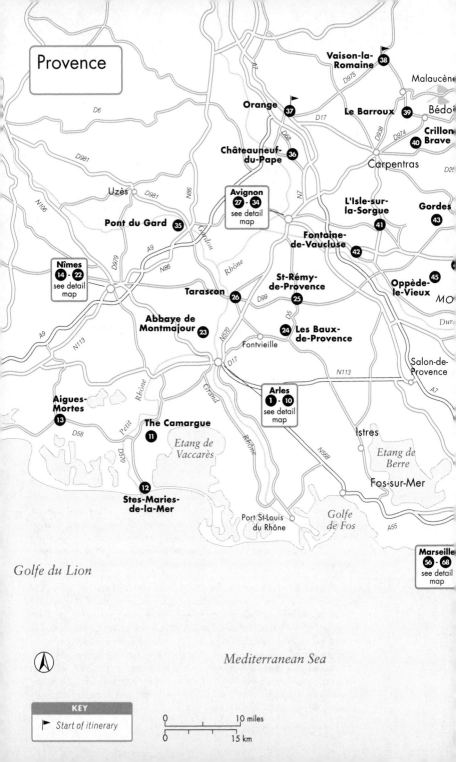

Provence

Malaucène

Vaison-la-Romaine 38

Orange 37   D17   **Le Barroux** 39   Bédo

D975

Châteauneuf-du-Pape 36   **Crillon Brave** 40

Carpentras   D25

Uzès   **L'Isle-sur-la-Sorgue** 41   **Gordes** 43

Pont du Gard 35

Avignon 27 - 34   see detail map   **Fontaine-de-Vaucluse** 42

Nîmes 14 - 22   see detail map   **St-Rémy-de-Provence** 25   **Oppède-le-Vieux** 45   MO

Tarascon 26   D99   Dur

Abbaye de Montmajour 23   Fontvieille   **Les Baux-de-Provence** 24   Salon-de-Provence

Istres

Aigues-Mortes 13   **Arles** 1 - 10   see detail map   N113

Etang de Berre

The Camargue 11   Etang de Vaccarès   Fos-sur-Mer

Stes-Maries-de-la-Mer 12   Port St-Louis du Rhône   Golfe de Fos

Marseille 56 - 68   see detail map

Golfe du Lion

Mediterranean Sea

KEY
► *Start of itinerary*

0 ————— 10 miles
0 ————— 15 km

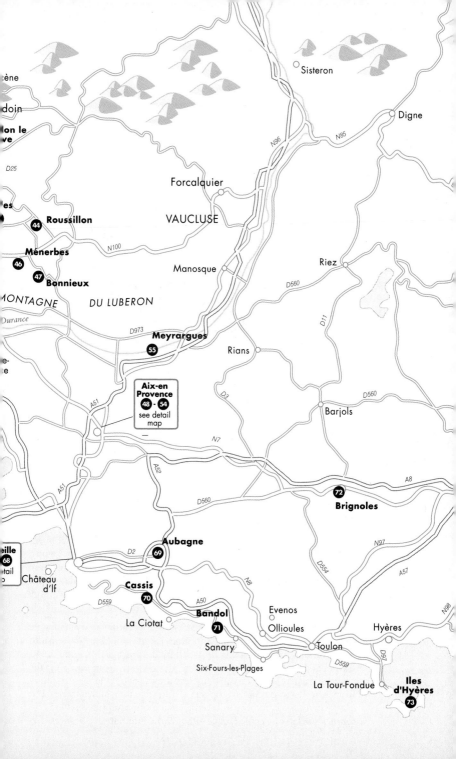

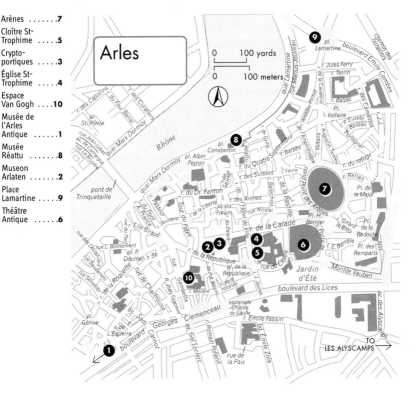

of every month ☉ *Apr., May, Sept., daily 9:30–12:30 and 2–6; June–Aug., daily 9–1 and 2–6:30; Oct.–Mar., Tues.–Sun. 9:30–12:30 and 2–5.*

At the entrance to a 17th-century Jesuit college you can access the ancient ❸ underground galleries called the **Cryptoportiques.** Dating from 30 BC to 20 BC, this horseshoe of vaults and pillars buttressed the ancient forum from belowground. Used as a refuge for Resistance members in World War II, these galleries still have a rather ominous atmosphere. Yet openings let in natural daylight, and artworks of considerable merit and worth were unearthed here, adding to the mystery of the original function of these passages. ✉ *Rue Balze* ☎ *04–90–49–36–74* 💶 *€3.50* ☉ *May–Sept., daily 9–noon and 2–7; Oct., daily 9–noon and 2–6; Nov.–Feb., daily 10–noon and 2–5; Mar. and Apr., weekends, 9–noon and 2–6.*

Classed as a world treasure by UNESCO, the extraordinary Romanesque ★ ❹ **Église St-Trophime** (✉ Pl. de la République) alone would justify a visit to Arles, though it's continually upstaged by the antiquities around it. Its transepts date from the 11th century and its nave from the 12th; the church's austere symmetry and ancient artworks (including a stunning Roman-style 4th-century sarcophagus) are fascinating in themselves. But it's the church's superbly preserved Romanesque sculpture on the 12th-century **portal**—its entry facade—that earns international respect. Re-

VAN GOGH'S ARLES & ST-RÉMY

I T WAS THE LIGHT THAT DREW VINCENT VAN GOGH *to Arles. For a man raised under the iron-gray skies of the Netherlands and the gaslight pall of Paris, Provence's clean, clear sun was a revelation. In his last years he turned his frenzied efforts toward capturing the resonance of ". . . golden tones of every hue: green gold, yellow gold, pink gold, bronze or copper colored gold, and even from the yellow of lemons to the matte, lusterless yellow of threshed grain." Arles, however, was not drawn to Van Gogh. Though it makes every effort today to make up for its misjudgment, Arles treated the artist very badly during the time he passed here near the end of his life—a time when his creativity, productivity, and madness all reached a climax.*

It was in 1888 that he settled in to work in Arles with an intensity and tempestuousness that first drew, then drove away his companion Paul Gauguin, with whom he had dreamed of founding an artists' colony. Astonishingly productive—he applied a pigment-loaded palette knife to some 200 canvases in that year alone—he nonetheless lived within intense isolation, counting his sous, and writing his visions in lengthy letters to his long-suffering, infinitely patient brother Theo. Often heavy-drinking, occasionally whoring, Vincent alienated his neighbors, driving them to distraction and ultimately goading them to action.

In 1889 the people of Arles circulated a petition to have him evicted, a shock that left him more and more at a loss to cope with life and led to his eventual self-commitment to an asylum in nearby St-Rémy. The houses he lived in are no longer standing, though many of his subjects remain as he saw them (or are restored to a similar condition). But with a little imagination you can glean something of Van Gogh's Arles from a tour of the modern town. In fact, the city has provided

helpful markers and a numbered itinerary to guide you between landmarks. You can stand on the place Lamartine, where his famous Maison Jaune stood until it was destroyed by World War II bombs. Starry Night may have been painted from the quai du Rhône just off place Lamartine, though another was completed at St-Rémy. The Café La Nuit on place Forum is an exact match for the terrace platform, scattered with tables and bathed in gaslight under the stars, from the painting Terrace de café le Soir; Gauguin and Van Gogh used to drink here.

Both the Arènes and Les Alyscamps were featured in paintings, and the hospital where he broke down and cut off his ear lobe is now a kind of shrine, its garden reconstructed exactly as it figured in Le Jardin de l'Hôtel-Dieu. The drawbridge in Le pont de Langlois aux Lavandières has been reconstructed outside of town, at Port-de-Bouc, 3 km (2 mi) south on D35.

About 25 km (16 mi) away is St-Rémy-de-Provence, where Van Gogh retreated to the asylum St-Paul-de-Mausolée. Here he spent hours in silence, painting the cloisters. On his ventures into town he painted the dappled lime trees at the intersection of boulevard Mirabeau and boulevard Gambetta.

And on the route between the towns and, in fact, in traveling anywhere nearby, you'll see the orchards whose spring blooms ignite joyous explosions of yellow and cream, olive groves twisting like dancers in silver and green, ocher houses and red roofs, star-spangled crystalline skies—the stuff of inspiration.

cent restorations have made it even more vivid. Particularly noteworthy is the frieze of the Last Judgment with chain-bound souls being dragged off to Hell or, on the contrary, being lovingly delivered into the hands of the saints.

5 Tucked discreetly behind St-Trophime is a peaceful haven, the **Cloître St-Trophime** (St-Trophime Cloister). A Romanesque treasure worthy of the church, it's one of the loveliest cloisters in Provence. A sturdy walkway above offers up good views of the town. ☎ 04–90–49–36–74 ⌨ €3.50 ⊙ *May–Sept., daily 9–7; Oct., Mar., and Apr., daily 9–6; Nov.–Feb., daily 10–5.*

Directly up rue de la Calade from place de la République are the pic-
6 turesque ruins of the **Théâtre Antique** (Ancient Theater), built by the Romans under Augustus in the 1st century BC. It is here that the noted Venus of Arles statue, now in the Louvre, was dug up and identified. Now overgrown and a pleasant, parklike retreat, it once served as an entertainment venue to some 20,000 spectators. Today it serves as a concert stage for the Festival d'Arles, in July and August, and site of the Recontres Internationales de la Photographie (Photography Festival), from early July to mid-September. ⊠ *Rue de la Calade* ☎ 04–90–49–36–74 ⊕ *www. rip-arles.org* ⌨ €3 ⊙ *May–Sept., daily 9–noon and 2–7; Oct., daily 9–noon and 2–6; Nov.–Feb, daily 10–11.:30 and 2–4:30; Mar. and Apr., daily 9–noon and 2–5.*

7 Rivaled only by the even better-preserved version in Nîmes, the **Arènes** (Arena) dominates old Arles. Its four medieval towers are testimony to its transformation from classical sports arena to feudal fortification in the Middle Ages. Younger than Arles's theater, it dates from the 1st century AD, and unlike the theater, seats 20,000 to this day. Its primary function is as a venue for the traditional spectacle of the corridas, or bullfights, which take place annually during the *féria pascale,* or Easter festival. Nearby is the **Fondation Van Gogh** (⊠ 24 bis rond point des Arènes ☎ 04–90–93–08–08 ⊙ Daily 10–7 ⌨ €7), where you can savor works by various modern and contemporary artists, including Francis Bacon and Doisneau, inspired by Van Gogh. ⊠ *Rond Point des Arènes* ☎ 04–90–49–36–74 ⌨ €4 ⊙ *May.–Sept., daily 9–7; Oct., daily 9–noon and 2–6; Nov. and Dec., daily 10–noon and 2–5; Mar. and Apr., daily 9–noon and 2–5.*

Though it makes every effort today to make up for its past misjudgment of him, Arles treated Vincent van Gogh very badly during the time he passed here near the end of his life. It was 1888 when he settled in to work in Arles with an intensity and tempestuousness that drove away his colleague and companion Paul Gauguin and alienated his neighbors. In 1889 the people of Arles circulated a petition to have him evicted, a shock that left him more and more at a loss to cope with life and led to his voluntary commitment to an insane asylum in nearby St-Rémy. Thus Arles can't boast a single Van Gogh painting—even so, did they have to name their art museum after Jacques Réattu, a local painter of confirmed mediocrity? The **Musée Réattu** lavishes three rooms on his turn-of-the-19th-century ephemera but redeems itself with a decent collection of 20th-century art including some daubs by Dufy and Gauguin. There's also an impressive collection of 57 drawings done by Picasso in 1971, including one delightfully tongue-in-cheek depiction of noted muse and writer Lee Miller in full Arles dress. The best thing about the Réattu may be the building itself, a Knights of Malta priory dating from the 15th century. ⊠ *Rue Grand Prieuré* ☎ *04–90–49–38–34* 🎫 *€4* ⊙ *Apr.–Sept., daily 10–12:30 and 2–7:30; Oct.–Mar., daily 1–5.*

You'll have to go to Amsterdam to view Van Goghs. But the city has provided helpful markers and a numbered itinerary to guide you from one landmark to another—many of them recognizable from his beloved canvases. Van Gogh resided in Arles from February 1888 to May 1889 and did about 300 drawings and paintings while here. You can stand ❾ on **Place Lamartine** (between the rail station and the ramparts), which is the site of his residence here, the now-famous Maison Jaune (Yellow House); it was destroyed by bombs in 1944. The artist may have set up his easel on the quai du Rhône, just off place Lamartine, to capture the view that he transformed into his legendary *Starry Night.* Eight other sites are included on the city's "Promenade Vincent van Gogh," linking sight to canvas, including the Place du Forum; the Trinquetaille bridge; Rue Mireille; the Summer Garden on the Boulevard des Lices; and the road along the Arles à Bouc canal.

The most strikingly resonant site, impeccably restored and landscaped to match one of Van Gogh's paintings, is the courtyard garden of what ❿ is now the **Espace van Gogh** (⊠ Pl. Dr. Félix Rey), featured in *Le Jardin de l'Hôtel-Dieu.* This was the hospital to which the tortured artist repaired after cutting off his earlobe—contrary to myth, he didn't cut off his entire ear and, in fact, made the desperate gesture in homage to Gauguin, whom he had come to idolize, following the fashion in Provençal bullrings for a matador to present his lady love with an ear from a dispatched bull—and its cloistered grounds have become something of a shrine for visitors. For more information about Van Gogh, see the Close-Up Box, "Van Gogh in Arles and St-Rémy," *above*

off the beaten path

LES ALYSCAMPS – Though this romantically melancholy Roman cemetery lies away from the Vieille Ville, it's worth the hike—certainly, Van Gogh thought so, as several of his famous canvases prove. This long necropolis amassed the remains of the dead from antiquity to the Middle Ages. Greek, Roman, and Christian tombs line the long shady road that was once the entry to Arles—the Aurelian Way. ☎ *04–90–49–36–74* 🎫 *€3.50* ⊙ *May–Sept., daily 9–noon and 2–7; Mar., Apr., Oct., daily 9–noon and 2–6; Nov.–Feb., daily 10–noon and 2–5.*

Where to Stay & Eat

★ **$$$$** ✕ **La Chassagnette.** Sophisticated yet down-home comfortable, this restaurant is the fashionable address in the area (14 km [8 mi] south of Arles). Stone walls, a stunning wood and green-marble bar, burnt-sienna tiles, Provençal chairs, and comfortable settees brightened by colorful pillows make for a fetching setting. Better, the dining area extends outdoors, where large family-style picnic tables can be found under a wooden slate canopy overlooking extensive gardens. Using ingredients that are certified organic and grown right on the property, innovative master chef Luc Rabanel serves up open-rotisserie style prix-fixe menus that are a refreshing mix of modern and classic French-country cuisine. ⊠ *Rte. du Sambuc, 14 km (8 mi) south of Arles on the D36* ☎ *04–90–97–26–96* ⚑ *Reservations essential* ▤ *MC, V* ☽ *Closed Tues. and Nov.–mid-Dec. No lunch Wed.*

$$$–$$$$ ✕ **Brasserie Nord-Pinus.** With its tile-and-ironwork interior, tastefully framed black-and-white photos, crisp white tablecloths, and its terrace packed with all the right people, this cozy-chic retro brasserie showcases the light and unpretentious cooking of chef Eric Griés: zucchini-flower risotto with fresh goat cheese, oven-cooked bass, or wild king prawns sautéed with pepper and cognac are some signature dishes. Immaculate service and a nicely balanced wine list only add to its charm. ⊠ *Pl. du Forum* ☎ *04–90–93–44–44* ⚑ *Reservations essential* ▤ *AE, DC, MC, V* ☽ *Closed Feb. and Wed. in Nov.–Mar.*

$$–$$$ ✕ **L'Affenage.** A vast smorgasbord of Provençal hors d'oeuvres draws loyal locals to this former fire-horse shed. They come here for heaping plates of grilled vegetables, tapenade, chickpeas in cumin, and a slab of ham carved off the bone. In summer you can opt for just the first-course buffet and go back for thirds; reserve a terrace table out front. ⊠ *4 rue Molière* ☎ *04–90–96–07–67* ⚑ *Reservations essential* ▤ *AE, MC, V* ☽ *Closed Sun. and 3 wks in Aug. No lunch Mon.*

$–$$ ✕ **La Gueule du Loup.** Serving as hosts, waiters, and chefs, the ambitious couple that owns this restaurant tackles serious cooking—lamb with eggplant and red-pepper puree, monkfish and squid in saffron, or chestnut mousse perfumed with almond milk top the delights here. Jazz music and vintage magic-act posters add color and warmth to the old Arles stone-and-beam rooms. ⊠ *39 rue des Arènes* ☎ *04–90–96–96–69* ⚑ *Reservations essential* ▤ *MC, V* ☽ *Closed Sun. and Mon. Oct.–Mar.; closed Sun. Apr.–Sept. No lunch Mon.*

$$$$ ▥ **Jules César.** Once a Carmelite convent but styled like a Roman palace, this pleasant landmark anchors the lively (sometimes noisy) boulevard des Lices. Don't be misled by the rather imposing lobby as this place turns out to be a friendly, traditional hotel. Rooms have high arched ceilings and massive Provençal armoires softened by plush carpets and burnished reds and oranges. Some windows look over the pool; others over the pretty cloister, where breakfast is served under a vaulted stone arcade. The restaurant, unexpectedly intimate for its size, has nice, simply prepared dishes—try the lobster risotto or the grilled steak. A meal plan is available with a minimum stay of three nights. ⊠ *Bd. des Lices, 13200* ☎ *04–90–52–52–52* 📠 *04–90–52–52–53* ⊕ *www.hotel-julescesar. fr* ⇨ *53 rooms, 5 suites* ⚲ *2 restaurants, minibars, cable TV, pool, Internet, parking (fee), some pets allowed (fee)* ▤ *AE, DC, MC, V* ☽ *Closed mid-Nov.–late Dec.* ⊙ *BP, MAP.*

$$$–$$$$ ▥ **L'Hôtel Particulier.** Once owned by the Baron of Chartrouse, this extraordinary 18th-century *hôtel particulier* (mansion) is delightfully intimate and carefully discreet behind a wrought-iron gate. Decor is sophisticated yet charmingly simple: stunning gold-framed mirrors, white-brocaded chairs, marble writing desks, artfully hung curtains, and hand-painted wallpaper. Rooms look out onto a beautifully landscaped garden; even if you take the five-minute walk into the center of town you can come back, stretch out by the pool, and listen to the birds chirp. ⊠ *4 rue de la Monnaie, 13200* ☎ *04–90–52–51–40* 🖷 *04–90–96–16–70* ⊕ *www.hotel-particulier.com* ⨠ *8 rooms* ♿ *Minibars, cable TV, pool, Internet, some pets allowed (fee)* ⊟ *AE, DC, MC, V.*

★ **$$$–$$$$** ▦ **Nord-Pinus.** The adventurer and mail-order genius J. Peterman would feel right at home in this eclectic and quintessentially Mediterranean hotel on place du Forum; Picasso certainly did. Richly atmospheric, the salon is dramatic with angular wrought iron, heavy furniture, colorful ceramics, and a standing collection of Peter Beard's black-and-white photographs. Rooms are individually decorated: wood or tiled floors, large bathrooms, handwoven rugs, and tasteful (if somewhat exotic) artwork are cleverly set off to stylish art director–chic advantage. Although it's hard to beat the low-key and accommodating service, this hotel may not be for everyone: traditionalists should head for the more mainstream luxuries of the Jules César. ⊠ *Pl. du Forum, 13200* ☎ *04–90–93–44–44* 🖷 *04–90–93–34–00* ⊕ *www.nord-pinus.com* ⨠ *26 rooms* ♿ *Some minibars, cable TV, bar, parking (fee), some pets allowed* ⊟ *AE, DC, MC, V.*

$ ▦ **Le Cloître.** Built as a private home, this grand old medieval building has luckily fallen into the hands of a couple devoted to making the most of its historic details—with their own bare hands. They've chipped away plaster from pristine quarry-stone walls, cleaned massive beams, restored tile stairs, and mixed natural chalk and ocher to plaster the walls. ⊠ *16 rue du Cloître, 13200* ☎ *04–90–96–29–50* 🖷 *04–90–96–02–88* ⊕ *www.members.aol.com/hotelcloitre* ⨠ *30 rooms* ♿ *Parking (fee), some pets allowed (fee); no a/c in some rooms, no TV in some rooms* ⊟ *AE, MC, V* ☺ *Closed Nov.–mid-Mar.*

★ **$** ▦ **Muette.** With 12th-century exposed stone walls, a 15th-century spiral stair, weathered wood, and an Old Town setting, a hotelier wouldn't have to try very hard to please. But the couple that owns this place does: hand-stripped doors, antiques, sparkling blue-and-white-tile baths, hair dryers, good mattresses, Provençal prints, and fresh sunflowers in every room show they care. ⊠ *15 rue des Suisses, 13200* ☎ *04–90–96–15–39* 🖷 *04–90–49–73–16* ⊕ *perso.wanadoo.fr/hotel-muette* ⨠ *18 rooms* ♿ *Cable TV, parking (fee), some pets allowed* ⊟ *AE, MC, V* ☺ *Closed last 2 wks of Feb.*

Nightlife & the Arts

To find out what's happening in and around Arles (even as far away as Nîmes and Avignon), the free weekly **Le César** lists films, plays, cabarets, and jazz and rock events. It's distributed at the tourist office and in bars, clubs, and cinemas. In high season the cafés stay lively 'til the wee hours; in winter the streets empty out by 11. **Le Cargo de Nuit** (⊠ 7 av. Sadi-Carnot ☎ 04–90–49–55–99) is the main venue for live jazz, reggae, and rock, with a dance floor next to the stage. Though Arles seems to be one big sidewalk café in warm weather, the place to tipple is the hip bar **Le Cintra,** in the Hôtel Nord-Pinus.

The Camargue

⑪   *19 km (12 mi) east of Aigues-Mortes, 15 km (9 mi) south of Arles.*

Fodor'sChoice
★

Stretching to the horizon for about 800 square km (309 square mi), the vast alluvial delta of the Rhône known as the Camargue is an austere, unrelievedly flat marshland, scoured by the mistral and swarmed over by mosquitoes. Between the endless flow of sediment from the Rhône and the erosive force of the sea, its shape is constantly changing. Even the Provençal poet Frederic Mistral described it in bleak terms: "*Ni arbre, ni ombre, ni âme*" ("Neither tree, nor shade, nor a soul").

Yet its harsh landscape harbors a concentration of exotic wildlife unique in Europe, and its isolation has given birth to an ascetic and ancient way of life that transcends national stereotype. This strange region is worth discovering, slowly, either on foot or on horseback—especially as its wildest reaches are inaccessible by car. People find the Camargue intriguing, birds find it irresistible. Its protected marshes lure some 400 species, including more than 160 in migration. As you drive the scarce roads that barely crisscross the Camargue, you'll usually be within the boundaries of the **Parc Regional de Camargue** (⊕ www.parc-camargue. fr). Unlike state and national parks in the United States, this area is privately owned and utilized following regulations imposed by the French government. The principal owners are the *manadiers* (the Camargue equivalent of small-scale ranchers) and their *gardians* (a kind of open-range cowboy), who keep it for grazing their wide-horn bulls and their dappled-white horses. When it's not participating in a bloodless bullfight (mounted players try to hook a red ribbon from its horns), a bull may well end up in the wine-rich regional stew called *gardianne de taureau*. Riding through the marshlands in leather pants and wide-rimmed black hats and wielding long prongs to prod their cattle, the gardians themselves are as fascinating as the wildlife. Their homes—tiny and whitewashed—dot the countryside.

The easiest place to view bird life is in a private reserve just outside the regional park called the **Parc Ornithologique du Pont de Gau** (Pont du Gau Ornithological Park). On some 150 acres of marsh and salt lands, birds are welcomed and protected (but in no way confined); injured birds are treated and kept in large pens, to be released if and when able to survive. A series of boardwalks (including a short, child-friendly inner loop) snakes over the wetlands, the longest leading to an observation blind, where a half hour of silence, binoculars in hand, can reveal unsuspected satisfactions. ☎ 04–90–97–82–62 ⊕ *www.parc-ornitho.com* ✉ €6 ۞ *Oct.–Mar., daily 10–sunset; Apr.–Sept., daily 9–sunset.*

Where to Stay & Eat

★ **$$$$**   ✕⊞ **Le Mas de Peint.** In a 17th-century farmhouse on some 1,250 acres of Camargue ranch land, this quietly sophisticated jewel of a hotel may just be the ultimate mas (traditional rural Provençal house) experience. A study in country elegance, rooms showcase beautifully preserved 400-year-old wood beams, carefully polished stone floors, and creamy linen fabrics all tastefully complemented by brass beds, claw-foot bathtubs, and natural, soft Provençal colors. The small restaurant (reservations essential), charmingly decorated with checked curtains, paysan chairs, and fresh roses on every table, is worth the trip even if you can't stay the night. The prix-fixe menu (€34–€45), changing daily, features sophisticated specialties often using homegrown products—roasted tuna flank with escargots à la provençale, or grilled game hen with roasted baby potatoes and exquisite cinnamon-flavored beets. A meal plan is available with a minimum stay of three nights. ⊠ *Le Sambuc, 20 km (12 mi) south of town, 13200* ☎ *04–90–97–20–62* 🖷 *04–90–97–22–20* ⊕ *www.masdepeint.com* ⤴ *8 rooms, 3 apartments* ⌂ *Restaurant, minibars, cable TV, pool, horseback riding, some pets allowed (fee)* ▤ *AE, DC, MC, V* ⊘ *Closed mid-Jan.–mid-Mar., mid-Nov.–mid-Dec.* ❘◯❙ *MAP.*

Stes-Maries-de-la-Mer

⑫ *18 km (10 mi) south of the Camargue, 129 km (80 mi) west of Marseille, 39 km (24 mi) south of Arles.*

The principal town within the confines of the Parc Régional de Camargue, Stes-Maries is a beach resort with a fascinating history. Provençal legend has it that around AD 45 a band of the very first Christians were rounded up and set adrift at sea without provisions in a boat without a sail. Their stellar ranks included Mary Magdalene, Martha, and Mary Salome, mother of apostles James and John; Mary Jacoby, sister of the Virgin; and Lazarus, not necessarily the one risen from the dead. Joining them in their fate was a dark-skinned servant girl named Sarah. Miraculously, their boat washed ashore at this ancient site, and the grateful Marys built a chapel in thanks. These days, new attention has been focused on Stes-Maries's great pilgrimage church due to an underlying theme of Dan Brown's megabest-seller, *The Da Vinci Code,* which contends that Mary Magdalene was betrothed to Jesus and bore him a child, whose descendants can be traced down through to the modern day. Historians, almost to the letter, contend that most of Brown's "facts" border on fantasy. More pointedly, the French media now notes that this genealogical "royal line" was first glommed onto by 19th-century, third-tier Provençal aristocrats in order to enhance their blue blood connections, and was then taken up and trumpeted by 20th-century French ultra-conservative religious/political groups. In any event, the pilgrims attracted to Stes-Maries aren't all lighting candles to the two St. Marys: Sarah has been adopted as an honorary saint by the Gypsies of the world. Two extraordinary festivals (⊕ www.saintesmariesdelamer.com) celebrating the Marys take place every year in Stes-Maries, one on May 24–25 and the other on the Sunday nearest October 22. In addition, the town honors the arrival of the Marys with its *navette,* a small pastry baked in the shape of the boat.

★ What is most striking to a visitor entering the damp, dark, and forbidding fortress-church, **Église des Stes-Maries,** is its novel character. Almost devoid of windows, its tall, barren single nave is cluttered with florid and sentimental ex-votos (tokens of blessings, prayers, and thanks) and primitive and sentimental artworks depicting the famous trio. Another oddity brings you back to the 21st century: a sign on the door forbids visitors from entering *torso nu* (topless). For outside its otherworldly role Stes-Maries is first and foremost a beach resort: dead flat, white-washed, and more than a little tacky. Unless you've made a pilgrimage here for the sun and sand, don't spend much time in the town center; if you've chosen Stes-Maries as a base for viewing the Camargue, stay in one of the discreet mas outside its city limits.

Where to Stay

★ **$$$** ☒ **Mas de Cacharel.** A haven for nature lovers, this quiet, laid-back re-treat is nestled in the middle of 170 acres of private marshland. The Wild West–like ranch setting is enhanced by simple whitewashed buildings and rather sparse decor; rooms are furnished with terra-cotta tiles, jute rugs, and white cotton throws, and large picture windows gaze out over hauntingly beautiful stretches of rose-colored reeds. A rather cavernous dining hall—complete with Provençal chairs and an enormous hand-carved fireplace—is really just a gathering place for sharing stories, local wine, and a hearty €17 plate of selected meats, fresh tomatoes, and regional goat cheese. ☒ *4 km (2½ mi) north of town on D85, 13460* ☎ *04–90–97–95–44* 🖷 *04–90–97–87–97* ⊕ *www.hotel-cacharel.com* ⤶ *16 rooms* ⚭ *Pool, horseback riding, bar, some pets allowed; no a/c, no room TVs* ☰ *MC, V.*

Aigues-Mortes

⓭ *16 km (10 mi) northwest of Stes-Maries-de-la-Mer, 41 km (25 mi) south of Nîmes, 48 km (30 mi) southwest of Arles.*

Like a tiny illumination in a medieval manuscript, Aigues-Mortes is a precise and perfect miniature fortress-town contained within symmet-rical crenellated walls, its streets laid out in geometric grids. Now awash in a flat wasteland of sand, salt, and monotonous marsh, it was once a major port town from which no less than St-Louis himself (Louis IX) set sail in the 13th century to conquer Jerusalem. In 1248 some 35,000 zealous men launched 1,500 ships toward Cyprus, engaging the infidel on his own turf and suffering swift defeat; Louis himself was briefly taken prisoner. A second launching in 1270 led to more crushing loss, and Louis succumbed to the plague.

Louis's state-of-the-art **fortress-port** remains astonishingly well pre-served. Its stout walls now contain a small Provençal village milling with tourists, but the visit is more than justified by the impressive scale of the original structure. ☒ *Porte de la Gardette* ☎ *04–66–53–61–55* 🖷 *€6.10* ⊙ *Easter–late May, daily 10–6; late May–mid-Sept., daily 9:30–7; mid-Sept.–Easter, daily 10–5.*

It's not surprising that the town within the rampart walls has become tourist oriented, with the usual plethora of gift shops and postcard stands. But **place St-Louis,** where a 19th-century statue of the father of the fleur-de-lis reigns under shady pollards, has a mellow village feel. The pretty, bare-bones **Église Notre-Dame des Sablons,** on one corner of the square, has a timeless air (the church dates from the 13th cen-tury, but the stained glass is ultramodern).

Where to Stay & Eat

★ **$$** ✕⛺ **Les Arcades.** Long a success as an upscale seafood restaurant, this beautifully preserved 16th-century house now has large, airy rooms, some with tall windows overlooking a green courtyard. Pristine white-stone walls, color-stained woodwork, and rubbed-ocher walls frame antiques and lush fabrics. Classic cooking includes lotte (monkfish) in saffron and poached turbot in hollandaise and the house specialty: hot oysters in a creamy herbed-butter sauce. Breakfast is included in the hotel price. ✉ *23 bd. Gambetta, 30220* ☏ *04–66–53–81–13* 🖷 *04–66–53–75–46* ⊕ *www.les-arcades.fr* ⤴ *9 rooms* ♿ *Restaurant, pool, Internet, some pets allowed (fee)* ▭ *AE, MC, V* ☉ *Closed 1st 2 wks of Mar., 1st 2 wks of Oct.* ♚ *BP.*

$$–$$$ ⛺ **Les Templiers.** In a 17th-century residence within the ramparts, this delightful hotel sets an atmospheric stage with stone, stucco, and terra-cotta floors. Two lovely suites in the building next door look out over the garden and pool. Furnishings are elegant, classically simple and soft-ened with antiques. On the ground floor are two small cozy sitting areas; breakfast, weather permitting, is served in the quiet oasis of a flower-filled garden courtyard. ✉ *23 rue de la République, 30220* ☏ *04–66–53–66–56* 🖷 *04–66–53–69–61* ⤴ *14 rooms, 2 suites* ♿ *Pool, Internet, parking (fee), some pets allowed (fee)* ▭ *AE, MC, V.*

Nîmes

35 km (20 mi) north of Aigues-Mortes, 43 km (26 mi) south of Avignon, 121 km (74 mi) west of Marseille.

If you've come to the south seeking Roman treasures, you need look no further than Nîmes (pronounced *neem*): The Arènes and Maison Carrée are among continental Europe's best-preserved antiquities. But if you've come seeking a more modern mythology—of lazy, graceful Provence—give Nîmes a wide berth. It's a feisty, rundown rat race of a town, with jalopies and Vespas roaring irreverently around the ancient temple. Its medieval Vieille Ville has none of the gentrified grace of those in Arles or St-Rémy. Yet its rumpled and rebellious ways trace directly back to its Roman incarnation, when its population swelled with newly victorious soldiers, flaunting arrogant behavior after their conquest of Egypt in 31 BC.

Already anchoring a fiefdom of pre-Roman *oppida* (elevated fortresses) before ceding to the empire in the 1st century BC, this ancient city grew to formidable proportions under the Pax Romana. Its next golden age bloomed under the Protestants, who established an anti-Catholic stronghold here and wreaked havoc on iconic architectural treasures—not to mention the papist minority. Their massacre of some 200 Catholic citizens is remembered as the Michelade; many of those murdered were priests sheltered in the *évêché* (bishop's house), now the Museum of Old Nîmes.

★ ⑭ The **Arènes** (Arena) is considered the best-preserved Roman amphitheater in the world. A miniature of the Colosseum in Rome (note the small carv-ings of Romulus and Remus—the wrestling gladiators—on the exterior and the intricate bulls' heads etched into the stone over the entrance on the north side), it stands more than 520 feet long and 330 feet wide, and has a seating capacity of 24,000. Bloody gladiator battles and theatrical wild-boar chases drew crowds to its bleachers. Nowadays its most colorful use is the **corrida**, the bullfight that transforms the arena (and all of Nîmes) into a sangria-flushed homage to Spain. ⊠ *Bd. Victor-Hugo* ☎ *04–66–02–80–80* ✆ *€4.65; joint ticket to Arènes and Tour Magne €5.65* ⊗ *May–Sept., daily 9–6:30; Oct.–Apr., daily 9–noon and 2–5.*

⓯ The **Musée des Beaux-Arts** (Fine Arts Museum) has now been beautifully restored by architect Jean-Michel Wilmotte. Centerpiece of this early-20th-century building is the skylit atrium and a vast ancient Roman mosaic of a marriage ceremony that provides intriguing insights into the Roman aristocratic lifestyle. Temporary exhibitions (such as one devoted to Cleopatra) offer fascinating glimpses into history, but it is the varied collection of Italian, Flemish, and French paintings (notably Rubens's *Portrait of a Monk*) that is the particularly interesting mainstay of the collection. ⊠ *Rue de la Cité-Foulc* ☎ *04–66–67–38–21* ✆ *€4.55* ⊗ *Tues.–Sun. 10–6.*

⓰ The **Musée Archéologique et d'Histoire Naturelle** (Museum of Archaeology and Natural History) is housed in an old Jesuit college and has a wonderful collection of local archaeological finds, including sarcophagi and beautiful pieces of Roman glass. A treasure trove of statues, busts, friezes, tools, coins, and pottery complete the collection. ⊠ *Bd. de l'Admiral-Courbet* ☎ *04–66–76–74–80* ✆ *€4.45* ⊗ *Tues.–Sun. 10–6.*

Destroyed and rebuilt in several stages, with particular damage by rampaging Protestants who slaughtered eight priests from the neighboring **⓱** évêché, the **Cathédrale Notre-Dame et St-Castor** (⊠ Pl. aux Herbes) still shows traces of its original construction in 1096. A remarkably preserved Romanesque frieze portrays Adam and Eve cowering in shame, the gory slaughter of Abel, and a flood-wearied Noah. Inside, look for the 4th-century sarcophagus (third chapel on the right) and a magnificent 17th-century chapel (in the apse).

⓲ The **Musée du Vieux Nîmes** (Museum of Old Nîmes), in the 17th-century bishop's palace opposite the cathedral, has embroidered garments in exotic and vibrant displays. Look for the 14th-century jacket made of blue-serge de Nîmes, the famous fabric from which Levi-Strauss first fashioned blue jeans. ⊠ *Pl. aux Herbes* ☎ *04–66–76–73–70* ✆ *€5.50* ⊗ *Tues.–Sun. 10–6.*

Lovely and forlorn in the middle of a busy downtown square, the **★ ⓳** exquisitely preserved **Maison Carrée** (Square House) strikes a timeless balance between symmetry and whimsy, purity of line and richness of decor. Modeled on the Temple to Apollo in Rome, adorned with magnificent marble columns and elegant pediment, it remains one of the most noble surviving structures of ancient Roman civilization anywhere. Built around 5 BC and dedicated to Caius Caesar and his grandson Lucius, it has survived subsequent use as a medieval meeting hall, an Augustine church, a storehouse for Revolutionary archives, and a horse shed. The interior of the great structure serves as a venue for temporary exhibitions as well as a display for photos and drawings of current ar-

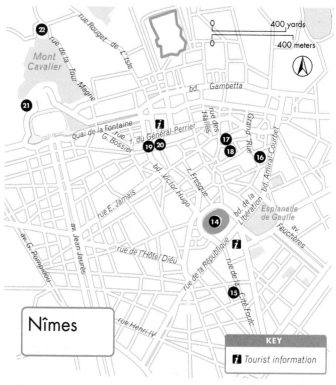

Nîmes

KEY

Tourist information

chaeological work. Most notably, there is a splendid ancient Roman fresco of Cassandra (being dragged by her hair by a hunter) that was discovered in 1992 and has been lovingly restored. ✉ *Bd. Victor-Hugo* ☎ *04–66–36–26–76* ✉ *Free* ☉ *Mid-Mar.–mid-Oct., daily 9–7; mid-Oct.–mid-Mar., daily 10–5.*

The glass-fronted Carré d'Art (directly opposite the Maison Carrée) was designed by British architect Sir Norman Foster as its neighbor's stark contemporary mirror: it literally reflects the Maison Carrée's creamy symmetry and figuratively answers it with a feather-light deconstructed colonnade. Homages aside, it resembles an airport terminal. It now houses

⓴ the **Musée d'Art Contemporain** (Contemporary Art Museum), featuring art dating from 1960 onward from artists such as Arman, and temporary exhibitions of newer works by artists like Javier Perez. The chic café on the top floor serves good coffee and has great views—stop here before heading off to the public library section which has a great collection of old manuscripts. ✉ *Pl. de la Maison Carrée* ☎ *04–66–76–35–70* ✉ *€4.75* ☉ *Tues.–Sun. 10–6.*

㉑ The shattered Roman ruin known as the **Temple de Diane** (Temple of Diana) dates from the 2nd century BC. The temple's function is unknown, though it is thought to have been part of a larger Roman complex that is still unexcavated. In the Middle Ages Benedictine nuns occupied the building before it was converted into a church. Destruction came during the Wars of Religion.

② The **Tour Magne** (Magne Tower), at the far end of the Jardin de la Fontaine, is all that remains of a tower the emperor Augustus had built on Gallic foundations; it was probably used as a lookout post. Despite a loss of 30 feet in height over the course of time, it still provides fine views of Nîmes for anyone energetic enough to climb the 140 steps. ⊠ *Quai de la Fontaine* ☎ *04–66–67–65–56* ⊡ *Tour Magne €2.45, joint ticket with Arènes €5.55* ☉ *Mid-Mar.–mid-Oct., daily 9–7; mid-Oct.–mid-Mar., daily 10–4:45.*

Where to Stay & Eat

★ **$$$$** ✕ **Chez Jacotte.** Duck into a Vieille Ville back alley and into this cross-vaulted grotto that embodies Nîmes's Spanish-bohemian flair. Candle-light flickering on rich tones of oxblood, ocher, and cobalt enhances the warm welcome from the staff. Mouthwatering goat-cheese-and-fig gratin, mullet crisped in olive oil and basil, herb-crusted oven-roasted lamb, and seasonal fruit crumbles show off a flair with local ingredients. ⊠ *15 rue Fresque, impasse* ☎ *04–66–21–64–59* ♨ *Reservations essential* ☐ *MC, V* ☉ *Closed Sun. and Mon. No lunch Sat.*

$$–$$$ ✕ **Le Jardin d'Hadrien.** This chic enclave, with its quarried white stone, ancient plank-and-beam ceiling, and open fireplace, would be a culinary haven even without its lovely hidden garden, a shady retreat for summer meals. Fresh cod crisped in salt and olive oil, zucchini flowers filled with *brandade* (the creamy, light paste of salt cod and olive oil), and a frozen parfait perfumed with licorice all show chef Alain Vinouze's subtle skills. Prix-fixe menus are €18 and €24. ⊠ *11 rue Enclos Rey* ☎ *04–66–22–07–01* ♨ *Reservations essential* ☐ *AE, MC, V* ☉ *Closed Wed. No dinner Tues.; July and Aug. closed Sun., no lunch Mon.*

$–$$$ ✕ **Vintage Café.** This popular Vieille Ville wine bar draws a loyal crowd of oenophiles for serious tastings and compatible regional viands using fresh ingredients straight from the marketplace—traditional foie gras, hot lentil salad with smoked haddock, and pan-fried bull steak. Exhibitions by local painters, bright ceramics, and warm-color lamplight enhance the artful Mediterranean decor. Summer nights on the terrace are idyllic. Better to make reservations on the weekend. ⊠ *7 rue de Bernis* ☎ *04–66–21–04–45* ☐ *MC, V* ☉ *Closed Sun. and Mon. No lunch Sat.*

$$ ⊡ **La Baume.** In the heart of scruffy Vieux Nîmes, this noble 17th-century hôtel particulier has been reincarnated as a stylish hotel with an architect's eye for mixing ancient detail with modern design. The balustraded stone staircase is a protected historic monument, and stenciled beamed ceilings, cross vaults, and archways counterbalance rich ocher tones, swags of raw cotton, leather, and halogen lighting. ⊠ *21 rue Nationale, 30000* ☎ *04–66–76–28–42* ☐ *04–66–76–28–45* ⊕ *www. new-hotel.com* ☜ *34 rooms* ♨ *Minibars, cable TV, bar, parking (fee), some pets allowed (fee)* ☐ *AE, DC, MC, V.*

Shopping

The only commercial maker of authentic brandade, Nîmes's signature salt-cod-and-olive-oil paste, is **Raymond** (⊠ 24 rue Nationale

☎ 04–66–67–20–47). It's paddled fresh into a plastic carton or sold in sealed jars so you can take it home. **L'Huilerie** (✉ 10 rue des Marchands ☎ 04–66–67–37–24) is a delightful treasure house of teas and spices that shows off great gift ideas, including smartly packaged mustards, honeys, and olive oils.

THE ALPILLES & THE RHÔNE FORTRESSES

The low mountain range called the Alpilles (pronounced ahl-*pee*-yuh) forms a rough-hewn, rocky landscape that rises into nearly barren limestone hills, the flanking fields silvered with ranks of twisted olive trees and alleys of gnarled *amandiers* (almond trees). There are superb antiquities in St-Rémy and feudal ruins in Les Baux. West of the Alpilles, the fortresses of Tarascon and Beaucaire guard the Rhône between Avignon and the sea.

Abbaye de Montmajour

㉓ *35 km (20 mi) southeast of Nîmes, 5 km (3 mi) northeast of Arles, 17 km (11 mi) south of Tarascon.*

An extraordinary structure looming over the marshlands north of Arles, this magnificent Romanesque abbey stands in partial ruin. Begun in the 12th century by a handful of Benedictine monks, it grew according to an ambitious plan of church, crypt, and cloister. Under the management of corrupt lay monks in the 17th century, it grew more sumptuous; when those lay monks were ejected by the Church, they sacked the place. After the Revolution it was sold to a junkman, and he tried to pay the mortgage by stripping off and selling its goods. A 19th-century medieval revival spurred its partial restoration, but its 18th-century portions remain in ruins. Ironically, because of this mercenary history, what remains is a spare and beautiful piece of Romanesque architecture. The **cloister** rivals that of St-Trophime in Arles for its balance, elegance, and air of mystical peace: Van Gogh was drawn to its womblike isolation and came often to the abbey to paint and reflect. The interior, renovated by Rudi Ricciotti, is now used for temporary exhibitions. ☎ 04–90–54–64–17 ▥ €6.10 ◷ Apr.–Sept., daily 9–7; Oct.–Mar., Wed.–Mon. 10–1 and 2–5.

Les Baux-de-Provence

★ **㉔** *17 km (10 mi) west of Montmajour, 18 km (11 mi) northeast of Arles, 29 km (18 mi) south of Avignon.*

When you first search the craggy hilltops for signs of Les Baux-de-Provence (pronounced lay-*bo*), you may not quite be able to distinguish between bedrock and building, so naturally do the ragged skyline of towers and crenellation blend into the sawtooth jags of stone. This tiny château-village ranks as one of the most visited tourist sites in France, a tour-de-force blend of natural scenery and medieval ambience of astonishing beauty. From this intimidating vantage point, the lords of Les Baux ruled throughout the 11th and 12th centuries over one of the largest fiefdoms in the south. Only in the 19th century did Les Baux find new purpose: the mineral bauxite, valued as an alloy in aluminum production, was discovered in its hills and named for its source. A profitable industry sprang up that lasted into the 20th century before fading into history.

Today Les Baux offers two faces to the world: its beautifully preserved medieval village and the ghostly ruins of its fortress, once referred to as the *ville morte* (dead town). In the village, lovely 12th-century stone houses, even their window frames still intact, shelter the shops, cafés, and galleries that line the steep cobbled streets. At the edge of the village is a cliff that offers up a stunning view over the Val d'Enfer (Hell's Valley) said to have inspired Dante's *Inferno*. Further along is the **Cathedral des Images** (⊠ Val d'Enfer, petite route de Mailliane ☎ 04–90–54–38–65 ▦ €7 ⊙ mid-Feb.–Sept., daily 10–7; Oct.–mid-Jan, daily 10–6). The setting is a vast old bauxite quarry, with 20-meter high stone walls, which makes a dramatic setting for the thousands of images projected onto its walls. Up above, the 17-acre cliff-top sprawl of ruins is contained under the umbrella name the **Château des Baux.** At the entry, the Tour du Brau contains the **Musée d'Histoire des Baux,** a small collection of relics and models. Its exit gives access to the wide and varied grounds, where Romanesque chapels and towers mingle with skeletal ruins. The tiny **Chapelle St-Blaise** shelters a permanent music-and-slide show called *Van Gogh, Gauguin, Cézanne au Pays de l'Olivier,* which features artworks depicting olive orchards in their infinite variety. In July and August there are fascinating medieval exhibitions: people dressed up in authentic costumes, displays of medieval crafts, and even a few jousting tournaments complete with handsome knights carrying fluttering silk tokens of their beloved ladies. ☎ 04–90–54–55–56 ⊕ *www.chateau-baux-provence.com* ▦ €7 with audioguide ⊙ Mar., Apr., May, Sept., and Oct., daily 9–6:30; June–Aug., daily 9–8; Nov. and Feb., daily 9–6; Dec. and Jan., daily 9–5.*

Where to Stay & Eat

$$$$
Fodor'sChoice
★ ✕▦ **L'Oustau de la Baumanière.** Sheltered by rocky cliffs below the village of Les Baux, this long-famous hotel, with its formal landscaped terrace and broad swimming pool, has a guest book studded with names like Winston Churchill, Elizabeth Taylor, and Pablo Picasso. The interior is luxe-Provençal chic, thanks to tile floors, arched stone ceilings, and brocaded settees done up in Canovas and Halard fabrics. Guest rooms—breezy, private, and beautifully furnished with antiques—have a contemporary flair, but the basic style remains archetypal Baux. These rooms are set in three buildings on broad landscaped grounds, the best of which are in the enchanting Le Manoir. As for the famed Baumanière restaurant (reservations essential), chef Jean-André Charial's hallowed reputation continues to attract culinary pilgrims (too many, it would appear from the noisy crowds that drive up the nearby road to the hotel). You can't blame them: the Oustau legacy is a veritable museum of Provençal tradition, but one that has been given a nouvelle face-lift—lobster cooked in Châteauneuf-du-Pape and set on a bed of polenta is a typical dazzler. Note that from November to December and in March

the restaurant is closed Wednesday and doesn't serve lunch Thursday; during January and February both the hotel and restaurant are closed. You can try a less expensive Oustau experience 1 km (½ mi) away at **La Cabro d'Or** (☎ 04–90–54–33–21 🖷 04–90–54–45–98 ⊕ www. lacabrodor.com). Run by the same owners, it's cheaper (€200–€340), more rustic, more private, and don't be surprised to see a billy-goat wander by your guest-room window. Meal plans for both hotels are available with a two-night minimum stay. ✉ *Val d'Enfer, 13520* ☎ *04–90–54–33–07* 🖷 *04–90–54–40–46* ⊕ *www.oustaudebaumaniere. com* ➯ *18 rooms, 9 suites, 3 apts.; 30 rooms in La Cabro* ↱ *Restaurant, minibars, cable TV, 2 tennis courts, pool, horseback riding, some pets allowed (fee)* ▭ *AE, DC, MC, V* ☼ *Closed Jan. and Feb.; La Cabro closed Nov.–mid-Dec.* ⍟❘ *MAP.*

$–$$ ✕🖼 **La Reine Jeanne.** At this modest inn majestically placed right at the entrance to the village, you can stand on balconies and look over rugged valley views worthy of the châteaux up the street. Rooms are small, simple, and—despite the white vinyl–padded furniture—lovingly decorated. Reserve in advance for one of the two rooms with a balcony, though even one of the tiny interior rooms gives you the chance to spend an evening in Les Baux after the tourists have drained away. Good home-style cooking is served in the restaurant, which has views both from inside and outside on the pretty terrace. ✉ *Grande Rue Baux, 13520* ☎ *04–90–54–32–06* 🖷 *04–90–54–32–33* ⊕ *www. la-reinejeanne.com* ➯ *10 rooms* ↱ *Restaurant, cable TV, some pets allowed (fee)* ▭ *MC, V* ☼ *Closed Jan.*

$$$–$$$$ 🖼 **Mas de L'Oulivié.** Built to look ancient, with recycled roof tiles and hand-waxed chalk walls, this mas is clarity itself, with a cool, clean look and a low-key aura. There's no upscale restaurant—just easy and unpretentious lunches by the pool (grilled meats, salads, and goat cheese). Eight rooms on the upper floor of the main house are pretty enough, with floral-print curtains and rich carpets, but ask for one with doors opening onto the lavender gardens and olive groves. ✉ *2 km (1 mi) after the exit Les Baux, D278F direction Fontvieille-Arles, 13520* ☎ *04–90–54–35–78* 🖷 *04–90–54–44–31* ⊕ *www.masdeloulivie.com* ➯ *25 rooms, 2 suites* ↱ *Restaurant, minibars, cable TV, tennis court, pool, bar, Internet, some pets allowed (fee)* ▭ *AE, DC, MC, V* ☼ *Closed mid-Mar.–mid-Nov.*

St-Rémy-de-Provence

②⑤ *8 km (5 mi) north of Les Baux, 24 km (15 mi) east of Arles, 19 km (12*
Fodor'sChoice *mi) south of Avignon.*
★

Something felicitous has happened in this market town in the heart of the Alpilles—a steady infusion of style, of art, of imagination—all brought by people with a respect for local traditions and a love of Provençal ways. Here more than anywhere you can meditate quietly on antiquity, browse redolent markets with basket in hand, and enjoy urbane galleries, cosmopolitan shops, and specialty food boutiques. An abundance of choices in restaurants, mas, and even châteaux awaits you;

the almond and olive groves conceal dozens of stone-and-terra-cotta *gîte* vacation homes, many with pools.

First established by an indigenous Celtic-Ligurian people who worshiped the god Glan, the village Glanum was adopted and gentrified by the Greeks of Marseille in the 2nd and 3rd centuries BC. Rome moved in to help ward off Hannibal, and by the 1st century BC Caesar had taken full control. The Via Domitia, linking Italy to Spain, passed by its doors, and the main trans-Alpine pass emptied into its entrance gate. Under the Pax Romana there developed a veritable city, complete with temples and forum, luxurious villas, and baths. The Romans eventually fell, but a town grew up next to their ruins, taking its name from their protectorate Abbey St-Remi, in Reims. It grew to be an important market town, and wealthy families built fine mansions in its center—among them the family de Sade (whose black-sheep relation held forth in the Lubéron at Lacoste). Another famous native son was the eccentric doctor, scholar, and astrologer Michel Nostradamus (1503–66), who is credited by some as having predicted much of the modern age. Perhaps the best known of St-Rémy's residents was the ill-fated Vincent van Gogh. Shipped unceremoniously out of Arles at the height of his madness (and creativity), he committed himself to the asylum St-Paul-de-Mausolé.

To approach Glanum, you must park in a dusty roadside lot on D5 south of town (toward Les Baux). But before crossing, you'll be confronted with two of the most miraculously preserved classical monuments in France, simply called **Les Antiques.** Dating from 30 BC, the **Mausolée** (mausoleum), a wedding-cake stack of arches and columns, lacks nothing but its finial on top, yet it is dedicated to a Julian (as in Julius Caesar), probably Caesar Augustus. A few yards away stands another marvel: the **Arc Triomphal,** dating from AD 20.

Across the street from Les Antiques and set back from D5, a slick visitor center prepares you for entry into the ancient village of **Glanum** with scale models of the site in its various heydays. A good map and an English brochure guide you stone by stone through the maze of foundations, walls, towers, and columns that spread across a broad field; helpfully, Greek sites are noted by numbers, Roman ones by letters. ⊠ *Off D5, direction Les Baux, info phone at Hôtel de Sade* ☎ *04–90–92–64–04* ✒ *€5; €6.50 includes entry to Hôtel de Sade* ☉ *Apr.–Sept., daily 9–7; Oct.–Mar., daily 9–noon and 2–5.*

★ You can cut across the fields from Glanum to **St-Paul-de-Mausolée,** the lovely, isolated asylum where Van Gogh spent the last year of his life (1889–90). But enter it quietly: it shelters psychiatric patients to this day—all of them women. You're free to walk up the beautifully manicured garden path to the church and its jewel-box Romanesque **cloister,** where the artist found womblike peace. ⊠ *Route des Baux; next to Glanum, off D5, direction Les Baux* ☎ *04–90–92–77–00* ✒ *€3.40* ☉ *May–Sept., daily 9:30–7; Oct.–Apr., daily 10:45–4:45.*

Within St-Rémy's fast-moving traffic loop, a labyrinth of narrow streets leads you away from the action and into the slow-moving inner sanctum of the **Vieille Ville.** Here trendy, high-end shops mingle pleasantly with local life, and the buildings, if gentrified, blend in unobtrusively.

Make your way to the **Hôtel de Sade,** a 15th- and 16th-century private manor now housing the treasures unearthed from the ruins of Glanum. The de Sade family built the house around remains of 4th-century baths and a 5th-century baptistery, now nestled in its courtyard. ⊠ *Rue du Parage* ☎ *04–90–92–64–04* ☜ *€2.50; €6.50 includes Glanum entry* ⊗ *Feb.–Mar. and Oct., Tues.–Sun. 10–noon and 2–5; Apr.–Sept., Tues.–Sun. 10–noon and 2–6; Nov. and Dec., Wed. and weekends 10–noon and 2–5.*

Where to Stay & Eat

$–$$$$ ✕ **La Maison Jaune.** This modern retreat in the Vieille Ville draws crowds of summer people to its pretty roof terrace, with accents of sober stone and lively contemporary furniture both indoors and out. The look reflects the cuisine: with vivid flavors and a cool, contained touch, chef François Perraud prepares grilled sardines with crunchy fennel and lemon confit, and veal lightly flavored with olives, capers, and celery. ⊠ *15 rue Carnot* ☎ *04–90–92–56–14* ⚐ *Reservations essential* ▭ *MC, V* ⊗ *Closed Mon. No dinner Sun. No lunch Tues.*

$–$$$ ✕ **La Gousse d'Ail.** It may have moved to larger premises around the corner, but thankfully, this intimate, indoor Vieille Ville hideaway and family-run bistro remains fundamentally the same. It continues to live up to its name (the Garlic Clove), serving robust, highly flavored southern dishes in hearty portions. Try the house specialties: grilled bull steak with creamed garlic or a powerful garlic-almond pesto. Aim for Thursday night, when there's Gypsy music and jazz. ⊠ *6 blvd. Marceau* ☎ *04–90–92–16–87* ▭ *AE, DC, MC, V* ⊗ *Closed mid-Nov.–mid-Mar. No lunch Thurs. and Sat.*

★ **$–$$** ✕ **L'Assiette de Marie.** Marie Ricco is a collector, and she's turned her tiny restaurant into a bower of attic treasures. Seated at an old school desk, you choose from the day's specials, all made with Marie's Corsican-Italian touch—marinated vegetables with tapenade, a cast-iron casserole of superb pasta, satiny *panetone* (flan). ⊠ *1 rue Jaume Roux* ☎ *04–90–92–32–14* ⚐ *Reservations essential* ▭ *MC, V* ⊗ *Closed Thurs., and Nov.–Mar.*

$$$–$$$$ ✕▥ **Domaine de Valmouriane.** In this genteel mas-cum-resort, peacefully isolated within a broad park, overstuffed English-country decor mixes cozily with cool Provençal stone and timber. The grounds are impressive and are dotted with some picture-perfect cypress trees; inside, much has been restored, so all is comfort and ease, if not the height of authenticity. The restaurant is masterminded by chef Pascal Volle, who is determined to please with fresh game, seafood, local oils, and truffles; his ravioli foie gras is sheer decadence. But it's the personal welcome from Philippe and Martin Capel that makes you feel like an honored guest. The pool, surrounded by a slate walk and delightful gardens, is most inviting. ⊠ *Petite rte. des Baux (D27), 13210* ☎ *04–90–92–44–62* ☎ *04–90–92–37–32* ⊕ *www.valmouriane.com* ⇆ *14 rooms* ⚘ *Restaurant, minibars, cable TV, tennis court, pool, hot tub, steam room, billiards* ▭ *AE, DC, MC, V* ⑩ *FAP, MAP.*

★ **$$–$$$** ✕▦ **Bistrot d'Eygalières.** Belgian chef Wout Bru's understated restaurant in nearby Eygalières is quickly gaining a reputation (and stars) for its elegant, light, and subtly balanced cuisine, like sole with goat cheese, lobster salad with candied tomatoes, and foie-gras carpaccio with summer truffles. The wine list is both eclectic and thorough, though prices are a bit on the high side. Guest rooms are very chic, very comfortable; Wout's wife, Suzy, has a wonderful eye and a welcoming disposition. Book well ahead. ⊠ *Rue de la République, Eygalières, 10 km (6 mi) southeast of St-Rémy-de-Provence on D99 then D24, 13810* ☎*04–90–90–60–34* 🖷*04–90–90–60–37* ⊕*www.chezbru.com* ⚓*Reservations essential* ⟿ *2 rooms, 2 suites* ⚒ *Restaurant, minibars, some pets allowed, free parking* ⊟ *AE, MC, V.*

$$$–$$$$ ▦ **Mas de Cornud.** An American stewards the wine cellar and an Egyptian runs the kitchen, but the attitude is pure Provence: David and Nito Carpita have turned their fairly severe, stone, black-shuttered farmhouse, just outside St-Rémy, into a B&B filled with French country furniture and objects from around the world. The welcome is so sincere you'll feel like one of the family in no time. Table d'hôte dinners, cooking classes, and tours can be arranged. Breakfast is included and the minimum stay is two nights. ⊠ *Rte. de Mas-Blanc, 13210* ☎ *04–90–92–39–32* 🖷 *04–90–92–55–99* ⊕ *www.mascornud.com* ⟿ *5 rooms, 1 suite* ⚒ *Dining room, pool, free parking, some pets allowed (fee); no a/c* ⊟ *No credit cards* ⊙ *Closed Jan. and Feb.* ¶❂ *BP, MAP.*

★ **$$–$$$** ▦ **Château de Roussan.** In a majestic park shaded by ancient plane trees, this yellow-stone 18th-century château (once the property of Nostradamus' brother) is a helter-skelter of brocantes and bric-a-brac, and the bathrooms have an afterthought air about them. Cats outnumber the staff. Yet if you're the right sort for this place—backpackers, romantic couples on a budget, lovers of atmosphere over luxury—you'll blossom in this three-dimensional costume-drama scene. Meal plans are available with a two-night minimum stay. ⊠ *D99, rte. de Tarascon, 13210* ☎ *04–90–92–11–63* 🖷 *04–90–92–50–59* ⊕ *www.chateau-de-roussan. com* ⟿ *22 rooms* ⚒ *Restaurant, cable TV, babysitting, some pets allowed (fee)* ⊟ *AE, DC, MC, V* ¶❂ *MAP.*

★ **$$–$$$** ▦ **Mas des Carassins.** A textbook example of a Provençal mas, this rambling 19th-century farmhouse is done with an impressive amount of style. Guest rooms come with stonework walls and wrought-iron canopy beds but you may wish to sleep under the stars since the mas is beautifully surrounded with thyme bushes, pots of lemon and orange trees, fountains, pools, and centuries-old olive trees. *Bien sûr,* you'll want to enjoy the copious lunch outside at a shady and intimate table. ⊠*1 chemin Gaulois, 13810* ☎ *04–90–92–15–48* 🖷 *04–90–92–63–47* ⊕ *www. hoteldescarassins.com* ⟿ *14 rooms* ⚒ *Restaurant, minibars, cable TV, pool, some pets allowed (fee)* ⊟ *AE, MC, V.*

Shopping

Every Wednesday morning St-Rémy hosts one of the most popular and picturesque **markets** in Provence, during which place de la République and narrow Vieille Ville streets overflow with fresh produce, herbs, and olive oil by the vat, as well as fabrics and brocantes (antiques).

Tarascon

㉖ *16 km (10 mi) west of St-Rémy, 17 km (11 mi) north of Arles, 25 km (15 mi) east of Nîmes.*

Tarascon's claim to fame is as the haunt of the mythical Tarasque, a monster that was said to emerge from the Rhône to gobble up children and cattle. Luckily, St. Marthe, who washed up at Stes-Maries-de-la-Mer, tamed the beast with a sprinkle of holy water, after which the inhabitants slashed it to pieces. This dramatic event is celebrated on the last weekend in June with a parade, and was immortalized by Alphonse Daudet, who lived in nearby Fontvieille, in his tales of a folk hero known to all French schoolchildren as *Tartarin de Tarascon.* Unfortunately, a saint has not yet been born who can vanquish the fumes that emanate from Tarascon's enormous paper mill, and the hotel industry is suffering for it.

★ Nonetheless, with the walls of its formidable **Château** plunging straight into the roaring Rhône, this ancient city on the river presents a daunting challenge to Beaucaire, its traditional enemy across the water. Begun in the 13th century by the noble Anjou family on the site of a Roman *castellum,* it grew through the generations into a splendid structure, crowned with both round and square towers and elegantly furnished. Complete with a moat, a drawbridge, and a lovely faceted spiral staircase, it retains its beautiful decorative stonework and original window frames. ☎04–90–91–01–93 ⌂ Bd. de Roi Réné ⊕*www.casteland.com* ☒ €6.10 ⊙ *Apr.–Sept., daily 9–7; Oct.–Mar., daily 10:30–5.*

AVIGNON & THE VAUCLUSE

Anchored by the magnificent papal stronghold of Avignon, the Vaucluse spreads luxuriantly east of the Rhône. Its famous vineyards—Châteauneuf-du-Pape, Gigondas, Vacqueyras, Beaumes-de-Venise—seduce connoisseurs, and its Roman ruins in Orange and Vaison-la-Romaine draw scholars and arts lovers. Arid lowlands dotted with orchards of olives, apricots, and almonds give way to a rich and wild mountain terrain around the formidable Mont Ventoux and flow into the primeval Luberon, made a household name by Peter Mayle. The hill villages around the Luberon—Gordes, Roussillon, Oppède, Bonnieux—are as lovely as any you'll find in the south of France.

Avignon

24 km (15 mi) northeast of Tarascon, 82 km (51 mi) northwest of Aix-en-Provence, 95 km (59 mi) northwest of Marseille, 224 km (140 mi) south of Lyon.

From its famous Palais des Papes (Papal Palace), where seven exiled popes camped between 1309 and 1377 after fleeing from the corruption and civil strife of Rome, to the long, low bridge of childhood song fame stretching over the river, you can beam yourself briefly into 14th-century Avignon, so complete is the context, so evocative the setting. Yet the town is anything but a museum; it surges with modern ideas and energy and thrives within its ramparts as it did in the heyday of the popes—and,

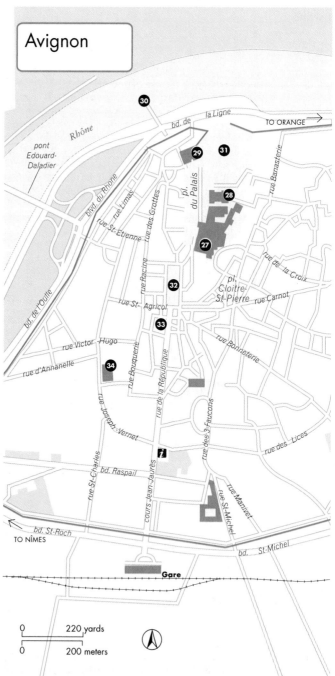

like those radical church lords, is sensual, cultivated, and cosmopolitan, with a taste for laic pleasures. Avignon remained papal property until 1791, and elegant mansions bear witness to the town's 18th-century prosperity.

★ **㉗** The colossal **Palais des Papes** creates a disconcertingly fortresslike impression, underlined by the austerity of its interior. Most of the original furnishings were returned to Rome with the papacy, others were lost during the French Revolution. Some imagination is required to picture its earlier medieval splendor, awash with color and with worldly clerics enjoying what the 14th-century Italian poet Petrarch called "licentious banquets." On close inspection, two different styles of building emerge at the palace: the severe **Palais Vieux** (Old Palace), built between 1334 and 1342 by Pope Benedict XII, a member of the Cistercian order, which frowned on frivolity, and the more decorative **Palais Nouveau** (New Palace), built in the following decade by the artsy, lavish-living Pope Clement VI. The Great Court, entryway to the complex, links the two.

The main rooms of the Palais Vieux are the **Consistory** (Council Hall), decorated with some excellent 14th-century frescoes by Simone Martini; the **Chapelle St-Jean** (original frescoes by Matteo Giovanetti); the **Grand Tinel,** or Salle des Festins (Feast Hall), with a majestic vaulted roof and a series of 18th-century Gobelin tapestries; the **Chapelle St-Martial** (more Giovanetti frescoes); and the **Chambre du Cerf,** with a richly decorated ceiling, murals featuring a stag hunt, and a delightful view of Avignon. The principal attractions of the Palais Nouveau are the **Grande Audience,** a magnificent two-nave hall on the ground floor, and, upstairs, the **Chapelle Clémentine,** where the college of cardinals once gathered to elect the new pope. ⊠ *Pl. du Palais* ☎ *04–90–27–50–00* ⊕ *www.palais-des-papes.com* ✒ *€7.50 entry includes choice of guided tour or individual audioguide; €8.50 includes audioguided tour to pont St-Bénézet* ☉ *Oct.–Mar., daily 9:30–5:45; Apr.–Nov., daily 9–7; July, during theater festival, daily 9–9.*

㉘ The **Cathédrale Notre-Dame-des-Doms,** first built in a pure Provençal Romanesque style in the 12th century, was quickly dwarfed by the extravagant palace that rose beside it. It rallied in the 14th century with the addition of a cupola—which promptly collapsed. As rebuilt in 1425, it's a marvel of stacked arches with a strong Byzantine flavor and is topped nowadays with a gargantuan Virgin Mary lantern—a 19th-century afterthought—whose glow can be seen for miles around. ⊠ *Pl. du Palais* ☎ *04–90–86–81–01* ☉ *Mon.–Sat. 7–7, Sun. 9–7.*

㉙ The **Petit Palais**—the former residence of bishops and cardinals before Pope Benedict built his majestic palace—houses a large collection of Old Master paintings. The majority are Italian works from the early-Renaissance schools of Siena, Florence, and Venice—styles with which the Avignon popes would have been familiar. Later key works to seek out include Sandro Botticelli's *Virgin and Child* and Venetian paintings by Vittore Carpaccio and Giovanni Bellini. ⊠ *Pl. du Palais* ☎ *04–90–86–44–58* ⊕ *www.mairie-avignon.fr* ✒ *€6* ☉ *Oct.–May, Wed.–Mon. 9:30–1 and 2–5:30; June–Sept., Wed.–Mon. 10–1 and 2–6.*

★ ㉚ The **Pont St-Bénézet** (St. Bénézet Bridge) is the subject of the famous children's song: "*Sur le pont d'Avignon on y danse, on y danse . . .*" ("On the bridge of Avignon one dances, one dances . . ."). Unlike London Bridge, this one still stretches its arches across the river, but only partway: half was washed away in the 17th century. Its first stones allegedly laid with the miraculous strength granted St-Bénézet in the 12th century, it once reached all the way to Villeneuve. ⊠ *Port du Rochre* ⊕ *www.mairie-avignon.fr* ☒ *€3.50.*

㉛ From the entrance to the Pont St-Bénézet, walk along the ramparts to a spiral staircase leading to the hilltop garden known as **Rocher des Doms**
Fodor'sChoice (Rock of the Domes). Set with grand Mediterranean pines, this park on
★ a bluff above town is dotted with statuary, lined with an elegant stone balustrade, and offers extraordinary views of the palace, the rooftops of Old Avignon, the Pont St-Bénézet, and formidable Villeneuve across the Rhône. On the horizon loom Mont Ventoux, the Luberon, and Les Alpilles. Often called the "cradle of Avignon," the rock's grottos were among the first human habitations in the area. Today, the park also has a fairly fake lake, home to some swans. ⊠ *Montée du Moulin off pl. du Palais* ⊕ *www.avignon-et-provence.com.*

㉜ The **Place de l'Horloge** (Clock Square) is the social nerve center of Avignon, where the concentration of bistros, brasseries, and restaurants draws swarms of locals to the shade of its plane trees.

㉝ Housed in a pretty little Jesuit chapel on the main shopping street, the
Musée Lapidaire gathers a collection of classical sculpture and stonework from Gallo-Roman times (1st and 2nd centuries), as well as pieces from the Musée Calvet's collection of Greek and Etruscan works. There is a notable depiction of *Tarasque of Noves*—the man-eating monster immortalized by Alphonse Daudet—but most items are haphazardly labeled and insouciantly scattered throughout the noble chapel, itself slightly crumbling but awash with light. ⊠ *27 rue de la République* ☎ *04–90–85–75–38* ☒ *€2* ☉ *Wed.–Mon. 10–1 and 2–6.*

㉞ Worth a visit for the beauty and balance of its architecture alone, the fine old **Musée Calvet** contains a rich collection of antiquities and classically inspired works. Recent acquisitions are Neoclassical and Romantic and almost entirely French, including works by Manet, Daumier, and David. The main building itself is a Palladian-style jewel in pale Gard stone dating from the 1740s; the garden is so lovely that it may distract you from the paintings. ⊠ *65 rue Joseph-Vernet* ☎ *04–90–86–33–84* ☒ *€6* ☉ *Wed.–Mon. 10–1 and 2–6.*

Where to Stay & Eat

$$–$$$$ ✕ **Brunel.** Stylishly decorated in a hip, contemporary retro-bistro style with urbane shades of gray (look for the Philippe Starck chairs), this Avignon favorite entices with the passionate Provençal cooking of Avignon-born and -bred chef Roger Brunel. This is down-home bistro cooking based on a sophisticated larder: parchment-wrapped mullet with eggplant, peppers, and tomatoes, pigeon roasted with basil, and caramelized apples in tender pastry. The prix-fixe menu is €38. ⊠ *46* *rue de la Balance* ☎ *04–90–85–24–83* ⌔ *Reservations essential* ▭ *MC, V* ⊘ *Closed Sun. and Mon.*

$–$$$ ✗ **La Compagnie des Comptoirs.** Glassed into the white stone cloister of the trendy complex called Les Cloître des Arts is the culinary haven of celebrated Porcel twins of Le Jardin de Sens fame (in Montpellier). Contemporary decorator Imaad Rahmouni did the interior, bringing together classic simplicity with modern elegance: in summer the 15th-century walls are artfully draped with Indian fabrics. Menu selections are beautifully presented and offer flavor mixtures from India, Italy, and Morocco: who can resist chicken breast wrapped in hazelnuts baked with prunes and *trompette des morts* mushrooms, or the dessert of cubed banana and pineapple served on softened fresh vanilla? ⊠ *83 rue Joseph-Vernet* ☎ *04–90–85–99–04* ⌔ *Reservations essential* ▭ *AE, MC, V* ⊘ *Closed Mon. in Oct.–Apr.*

★ **$–$$$** ✗ **Le Grand Café.** Behind the Papal Palace and set in a massive former army supply depot—note the carefully preserved industrial decay—this urban-chic entertainment complex combines an international cinema, a bar, and this popular bistro. Gigantic 18th-century mirrors and dance-festival posters hang on crumbling plaster and brick, and votive candles half-light the raw metal framework—an inspiring environment for intense film talk and a late supper of apricot lamb on a bed of semoule, goat cheese, or marinated artichokes. The prix-fixe dinner menu is €30. ⊠ *La Manutention, cours Maria Casares* ☎ *04–90–86–86–77* ▭ *MC, V* ⊘ *Closed Jan. and Sun.–Mon.*

¢–$ ✗ **Maison Nani.** Crowded inside and out with trendy young professionals, this pretty lunch spot serves stylish home cooking in generous portions without the fuss of multiple courses. Choose from heaping salads sizzling with fresh meat, enormous kebabs, and a creative quiche du jour. It's just off rue de la République. ⊠ *29 rue Théodore Aubanel* ☎ *04–90–82–60–90* ▭ *No credit cards* ⊘ *Closed Sun. No dinner Mon.–Thurs.*

★ **$$$$** ✗🏠 **Hôtel de la Mirande.** A designer's dream of a hotel, this *petit palais* permits you to step into 18th-century Avignon, thanks to painted coffered ceilings, sumptuous antiques, and other superb *grand siècle* touches (those rough sisal mats on the floors were the height of chic back in the Baroque era). The central lounge is a skylit and jazz-warmed haven. Upstairs, guest rooms are both gorgeous and comfy, with extraordinary baths and even more extraordinary handmade wall coverings. The costume-drama dining room provides an idyllic setting for the restaurant's sophisticated cuisine. Look for friendly Friday-night cooking classes from chef Jerome Verrière in the massive downstairs "country" kitchen. ⊠ *Pl. de la Mirande, 84000* ☎ *04–90–85–93–93* 🖷 *04–90–86–26–85* ⊕ *www.la-mirande.fr* ⇆ *19 rooms, 1 suite* ⌂ *Restaurant, minibars, cable TV, bar, Internet, meeting room, parking (fee), some pets allowed (fee)* ▭ *AE, DC, MC, V.*

$$$–$$$$ ✗🏠 **Hôtel d'Europe.** Once host to guests like Victor Hugo, Napoléon Bonaparte, and Emperor Maximilian, this vine-covered 16th-century home is regally discreet and classic. In a walled court shaded by trees, the splendor continues inside with Aubusson tapestries, porcelains, and Provençal antiques. Guest rooms are mostly emperor-size, with two suites overlooking the Papal Palace. The highly acclaimed restaurant, La Vieille Fontaine, is certainly one of Avignon's finest; during the festival period, tables in the courtyard are highly coveted and are top places to preen while enjoying such delights as hot duck foie gras with peaches. ✉ *12 pl. Crillon, 84000* ☎ *04–90–14–76–76* 🖷 *04–90–14–76–71* ⊕ *www.hotel-d-europe.fr* ↝ *44 rooms* ⟁ *Restaurant, minibars, cable TV, Internet, meeting room, parking (fee), some pets allowed (fee)* ═ *AE, DC, MC, V.*

$–$$$ 🏨 **Du Palais des Papes.** Despite its mere two-star rating, this is a remarkably solid, comfortable hotel, just off the place de Palais. With chic ironwork furniture and rich fabrics, the exposed-stone-and-beam decor fulfills fantasies of a medieval city—but one with good tile baths. ✉ *1 rue Gérard-Philippe, 84000* ☎ *04–90–86–04–13* 🖷 *04–90–27–91–17* ⊕ *www.hotel-avignon.com* ↝ *26 rooms, 6 suites* ⟁ *Restaurant, minibars, cable TV, bar; no a/c in some rooms* ═ *AE, DC, MC, V.*

★ $ 🏨 **Hôtel du Blauvac.** Just off rue de la République and place de l'Horloge, this 17th-century nobleman's home has been lovingly decorated while keeping much of the original structures intact. Rooms have pristine exposed stonework, aged-oak details, and lovely tall windows; many of which, alas, look onto backstreet walls. Pretty fabrics and a warm, familial welcome more than compensate, however. ✉ *11 rue de la Bancasse, 84000* ☎ *04–90–86–34–11* 🖷 *04–90–86–27–41* ⊕ *www.hotel-blauvac.com* ↝ *16 rooms* ⟁ *Cable TV, Internet, free parking; no a/c* ═ *AE, DC, MC, V.*

$ 🏨 **Hôtel de Mons.** Tatty and almost intolerably eccentric, this is a neo-Gothic budget flophouse after Edward Gorey's own heart, first built as a 13th-century chapel. Transformation took some maneuvering, but guest rooms with baths (with '70s-style decor) have been fitted into crooked nooks and crannies, while retaining some period detail (slanting spiral stairs, quarried stone). Breakfast is served in a groin-vaulted crypt. Location is everything: it's two steps off place de l'Horloge. And it's dirt cheap. ✉ *5 rue de Mons, 84000* ☎ *04–90–82–57–16* 🖷 *04–90–85–19–15* ⊕ *www.hoteldemons.com* ↝ *11 rooms* ⟁ *Cable TV, some pets allowed; no a/c* ═ *AE, MC, V.*

Nightlife & the Arts

Held annually in July, the Avignon festival, known officially as the **Festival Annuel d'Art Dramatique** (Annual Festival of Dramatic Art; ☎ 04–90–27–66–50 tickets and information) has brought the best of world theater to this ancient city since 1947. Some 300 productions take place every year; the main performances are at the Palais des Papes.

Within its fusty old medieval walls, Avignon teems with modern nightlife well into the wee hours. Having recently joined the masses near place Pie, **The Red Lion** (✉ 21 rue St-Jean-les-Vieux ☎ 04–90–86–40–25) serves Guinness, Stella, and Beck on tap and is hugely popular with students and the English-speaking crowd. At **AJMI** (Association Pour le Jazz et la Musique Improvisée; ✉ 4 rue Escaliers Ste-Anne ☎ 04–90–86–08–61), in La Manutention, you can hear live jazz acts of some renown. Avignon's trendy twenty- and thirtysomethings come to dance at **the Red Zone** (✉ 25 rue Carnot ☎ 04–90–27–02–44). On Wednesday, the ladies are invited to run the bar. At the cabaret **Dolphin Blues** (✉ Chemin de L'île

Piot ☏ 04–90–82–46–96), a hip mix of comedy and music dominates the repertoire, and there's children's theater as well. **Le Rouge Gorge** (✉ 10 bis rue Peyrollerie, behind palace ☏ 04–90–14–02–54) presents a dinner show and after-dinner dancing every Friday and Saturday night.

Shopping

Avignon has a cosmopolitan mix of French chains, youthful clothing shops (it's a college town), and a few plummy shops. **Rue St. Agricole** is where to find Parisian designers Lacroix and Hermès, and **rue des Marchands** off place Carnot is another, more mainstream shopping stretch. But **rue de la République** is the main artery, with chic street fashion names like Zara.

Pont du Gard

㉟ *22 km (13 mi) southwest of Avignon, 37 km (23 mi) southwest of*
Fodor'sChoice *Orange, 48 km (30 mi) north of Arles.*
★

No other architectural sight in Provence rivals the Pont du Gard, a mighty, three-tiered aqueduct nearly midway between Nîmes and Avignon. Erected some 2,000 years ago as part of a 48-km (30-mi) canal supplying water to the Roman settlement of Nîmes, it is astonishingly well preserved. In the early morning the site offers an amazing blend of natural and classical beauty—the rhythmic repetition of arches resonates with strength, bearing testimony to an engineering concept relatively new in the 1st century AD, when it was built under Emperor Claudius. Later in the day crowds become a problem, even off-season. At the visitor center, a film and a multimedia display detail the history of the aqueduct; in addition, there is a nifty children's area and an interactive exhibition about life in Roman times, archaeology, nature, and water. You can approach the aqueduct from either side of the Gardon River. If you choose the south side (Rive Droite), the walk to the *pont* (bridge) is shorter and the views arguably better from here (and the tour buses seem to stay on the Rive Gauche). Note there have been reports of break-ins in the parking area, so get a spot close to the booth. Although access to the spectacular walkway along the top of the aqueduct is now off-limits, the bridge itself is still a breathtaking experience. ✉ *Concession Pont-du-Gard* ☏ *04–66–37–50–99* 🎟 *€10, including parking* ☉ *Oct.–Apr., daily 10–6; May–Sept., daily 9:30–7.*

Châteauneuf-du-Pape

㊱ *18 km (11 mi) north of Avignon, 23 km (14 mi) west of Carpentras.*

The countryside around this very famous wine center is a patchwork of rolling vineyards. Imposing gates and grand houses punctuate the scene, as symmetrical and finely detailed as the etching on a wine label, and signs beckon you to follow the omnipresent smell of fermenting grapes to its source.

Once the table wine of the Avignon popes, who kept a fortified summer house here (hence the name of the town, which means "new castle of the pope"), the vineyards of Châteauneuf-du-Pape had the good fortune to be wiped out by phylloxera in the 19th century—good in that its revival as a muscular and resilient mix of up to 13 varietals has moved it to the forefront of French wines. To learn more, stop in at the **Musée des Outils de Vignerons Père Anselme,** a private collection of tools and equipment displayed in the *caveau* (wine cellar) of the Brotte family. ⊠ *Rte. d'Avignon* ☎ *04–90–83–70–07* 🔾 *Free* ⊙ *Daily 9–noon and 2–6.*

If you're disinclined to spend your holiday sniffing and sipping in a dark basement, climb the hill to the ruins of the **Château.** Though it was destroyed in the Wars of Religion and its remaining donjon blasted by the Germans in World War II, it still commands magnificent views.

Where to Stay & Eat

$–$$ ✕ **Le Pistou.** This friendly little restaurant serves sophisticated cooking by a chef in love with things Provençal, from marketing to cooking all day to cheerfully writing his whims on the menu-cum-blackboard. A regular feature? The mouthwateringly delicious *soup au pistou.* The welcome is warm, and the fixed-price menus start at the low end of our price level. ⊠ *15 rue Joseph-Ducos* ☎ *04–90–83–71–75* 🔾 *Reservations essential* ☰ *MC, V* ⊙ *Apr.—Sept., closed Mon., no dinner Sun., no lunch Tues.; Oct.–Mar., closed Mon., no dinner weekends, no lunch Tues.*

$–$$ ✕🛏 **La Garbure.** With eight rooms decked out in soft pastel ruffles and a low-price *menu terroir* (prix-fixe menu of regional specialties), this pretty inn aims to please. Look for potted quail in Carpentras truffles and stuffed rabbit with subtle thyme sauce (the restaurant is closed Sunday, October through June, and does not serve Sunday lunch in season, July–September). ⊠ *3 rue Joseph-Ducos, 84230* ☎ *04–90–83–75–08* 📠 *04–90–83–52–34* ⊕ *www.la-garbure.com* 🛏 *8 rooms* 🍽 *Restaurant, minibars, cable TV, some pets allowed* ☰ *MC, V* ⊙ *MAP.*

Orange

③⑦ *10 km (6 mi) north of Châteauneuf-du-Pape, 31 km (19 mi) north of Avignon, 193 km (121 mi) south of Lyon.*

Even less touristy than Nîmes and just as eccentric, the city of Orange (pronounced oh-*rawnzh*) nonetheless draws thousands every year to its ★ spectacular **Théâtre Antique,** a colossal Roman theater built in the time of Caesar Augustus. Its vast stone stage wall, bouncing sound off the facing hillside, climbs four stories high, and the niche at center stage contains the original statue of Augustus, just as it reigned over centuries of productions of classical plays. Today this theater provides a backdrop for world-class theater and opera. ⊠ *Pl. des Frères-Mounet* ☎ *04–90–51–17–60* 🔾 *€7.50 with audioguide, includes entry to Espace Culturel* ⊙ *Apr.–Sept., daily 9:30–6; Oct.–Mar., daily 9:30–noon and 1:30–5.*

Privitization required that the small Musée Municipal (Town Museum) change its name. As the **Espace Culturel** (Cultural Space), it is now a joint venture with the Théâtre Antique. A touristy boutique offers theater figurines and books; the displays include antiquities unearthed around Orange, including three detailed marble *cadastres* (land-survey maps) dating from the 1st century. Upstairs are Provençal fabrics manufactured in local mills in the 18th century and a collection of faïence pharmacy jars. ⊠ *Pl. des Frères-Mounet* ☎ *04–90–51–18–24* ◪ *€7.50, joint ticket to Théâtre Antique* ◷ *Apr.–Sept., daily 9:30–6; Oct.–Mar., daily 9:30–noon and 1:30–5.*

North of the city center is the **Arc de Triomphe,** which once straddled the Via Agrippa between Lyon and Arles. Three arches support a heavy double attic (horizontal top) floridly decorated with battle scenes and marine symbols, references to Augustus's victories at Actium. The arch, which dates from about 20 BC, is superbly preserved, particularly the north side, but to view it on foot, you'll have to cross a roundabout seething with traffic. ⊠ *North of center on av. de l'Arc, in direction of Gap.*

Where to Stay & Eat

$–$$$ ✗ **La Yaka.** At this intimate, unpretentious bistro you are greeted by the beaming owner, who is also your host and waiter, then pampered with specialties that are emphatically *style grandmère* (like Grandma used to make: rabbit stew, *caillette,* or pork-liver meat loaf, and even canned peas with bacon). It's all served up in charming stone-and-beam rooms. ⊠ *24 pl. Sylvain* ☎ *04–90–34–70–03* ▤ *MC, V* ◷ *Closed Wed. and Nov. No dinner Tues.*

$–$$$ ▦ **Arène.** On a quiet square in the Vieille Ville center, this comfortable old hotel has attentive owners and a labyrinth of rooms done in rich colors and heavy fabrics. The nicest ones look out over the square. As it's built of several fine old houses strung together, there's no elevator, but a multitude of stairways compensates. ⊠ *Pl. de Langues, 84100* ☎ *04–90–11–40–40* ▤ *04–90–11–40–45* ⊕ *www.avignon-et-provence. com/hotel-arene* ⇜ *30 rooms* ⚭ *Minibars, cable TV, Internet, parking (fee), some pets allowed* ▤ *AE, DC, MC.*

The Arts

Every July **Les Chorégies d'Orange** (☎ 04–90–34–24–24 ▤ 04–90–11–04–04 ✑ Chorégies, B.P. 205, Cedex, 84107 Orange) echo tradition and present operatic and classical music spectacles under the summer stars. Write for information well in advance; unfortunately, there is no main web site.

Vaison-la-Romaine

❸❽ *27 km (17 mi) northeast of Orange, 30 km (19 mi) northeast of Avignon.*

This ancient town thrives as a modern market center yet retains an irresistible Provençal charm, with medieval backstreets, lively squares lined with cafés, and, as its name implies, the remains of its Roman past. Vaison's well-established Celtic colony joined forces with Rome in the 2nd century BC and grew to powerful status in the empire's glory days. No gargantuan monuments were raised, yet the luxurious villas surpassed even those of Pompeii.

There are two broad fields of **Roman ruins,** both in the center of town: before you pay entry at either of the ticket booths, pick up a map (with English explanations) at the **Maison du Tourisme et des Vins** (☎ 04–90–36–02–11), which sits between them; it's open July and August, daily 9–12:30 and 2–6:45; September–June, Monday–Saturday 9–noon and 2–5:45. Like a tiny Roman forum, the **Maison des Messii** (Messii House) spreads over the field and hillside in the heart of town. Its skeletal ruins of villas, landscaped gardens, and museum lie below the ancient theater, all of which are accessed next to the booth across from the tourist office. Closest to the entrance, the foundations of the Maison des Messii retain the outlines of its sumptuous design. A formal garden echoes a similar landscape of the time; wander under its cypresses and flowering shrubs to the **Musée Archéologique Théo-Desplans** (Théo-Desplans Archaeology Museum). In this streamlined venue the accoutrements of Roman life have been amassed and displayed by theme: pottery, weapons, representations of gods and goddesses, jewelry, and sculpture. Cross the park behind the museum to climb into the bleachers of the 1st-century **theater,** which is smaller than Orange's but is still used today for concerts and plays. Across the parking lot is the **Quartier de la Villasse,** where the remains of a lively market town evoke images of main-street shops, public gardens, and grand private homes, complete with floor mosaics. The most evocative image of all is in the area of the *thermes* (baths): a neat row of marble-seat toilets. In July and August guided nocturnal visits (€5, start 10 PM) are a must and come replete with eerie backlighting and clever narration. ⊠ *Av. Général-de-Gaulle at pl. du 11 Novembre* ☎ *04–90–36–02–11* ⊠ *Ruins, museum, and cloister €7; €5 each* ☉ *Museum June–Sept., daily 9:30–6; Mar.–May and Oct., daily 10–12:30 and 2:30–6; Nov.–Feb., daily 10–11:30 and 2–4. Villasse June–Sept., daily 9:30–noon and 2–6; Mar.–May and Oct., daily 10–12:30 and 2–6; Nov.–Feb., daily 10–noon and 2–4:30.*

Take the time to climb up into the **Haute Ville,** a medieval neighborhood perched high above the river valley. Its 13th- and 14th-century houses owe some of their beauty to stone pillaged from the Roman ruins below, but their charm is from the Middle Ages.

If you're in a medieval mood, stop into the sober Romanesque **Cathé-drale Notre-Dame-de-Nazareth,** based on recycled fragments and foundations of a Gallo-Roman basilica. Its richly sculpted **cloister** is the key attraction. ⊠ *Av. Jules-Ferry* ☉ *June–Sept., daily 9:30–noon and 2–5:30; Mar.–May and Oct., daily 10–noon and 2–5:30; Nov.–Feb., daily 10–noon and 2–4.*

One last highlight: the remarkable single-arch **Pont Romain** (Roman Bridge), built in the 1st century, stands firm across the Ouvèze River.

Fodor's Choice
★

While Vaison has centuries-old attractions, the most popular for Americans may well now be **Patricia Wells's Cooking Classes.** A living monument of Provence, the celebrated food critic first made her name known through posh food columns and *The Food Lover's Guide to France.* Firsthand, she now introduces people to the splendors of French cooking in her lovely farmhouse near Vaison through week-long cooking seminars—luxe ($3,000 a student), eight students only, and set over Madame Wells's own Chanteduc vineyards. The truffle workshop is usually sold out, so book early. ⊕ *www.patriciawells.com.*

Where to Stay & Eat

$$$$ ✕ **Le Moulin à Huile.** Innovative chef Robert Bardot shows off his superb culinary talents by mixing creative regional cuisine with a touch of the exotic—top creations include the veal marinated in spiced milk, ginger, and cloves, or the unusual roasted peach with strawberry coulis. His impressive prix-fixe menus are served in an old, beautifully restored *moulin* (mill) by the Pont Romain, with a lovely garden terrace and a fairly spectacular view over the old city. ⊠ *Rte. de Malaucene* ☎ *04–90–36–20–67* 🚍 *AE, MC, V* ⊗ *Closed Mon. No dinner Sun.*

★ **$$–$$$** ✕▥ **Le Beffroi.** Crowned with a centuries-old stone clock tower and set on a cliff top in the Vieille Ville, this elegant grouping of 16th-century homes makes a fine little hotel. The extravagant salon decked out in period style leads to the sizable rooms with beams and antiques; the big corner rooms have breathtaking views. From April through October, dine on local specialties under the fig tree in the intimate enclosed garden court. The hotel restaurant, La Fontaine, has real flair—as one taste of their foie gras ravioli or duck in lavender honey will prove. By day you can enjoy a simple salad on the garden terrace or take a dip in the rooftop pool. Meal plans are available only with a two-night minimum stay. ⊠ *Rue de l'Évêché, 84110* ☎ *04–90–36–04–71* 🗐 *04–90–36–24–78* ⊕ *www. le-beffroi.com* ⇗ *22 rooms* ⚬ *Restaurant, minibars, cable TV, pool, some pets allowed (fee); no a/c* 🚍 *AE, DC, MC, V* ⊗ *Closed mid-Feb.–mid-Mar.* ⎟⊙⎟ *MAP.*

$$ ▥ **Évêché.** In the medieval part of town, this turreted 16th-century former bishop's palace has just four small rooms. The warm welcome and rustic charm—delicate fabrics, exposed beams, wooden bedsteads—have garnered a loyal following among travelers who prefer B&B character over modern luxury. Room rates include breakfast. ⊠ *Rue de l'Évêché, 84110* ☎ *04–90–36–13–46* 🗐 *04–90–36–32–43* ⊕ *eveche. free.fr* ⇗ *4 rooms, 1 suite* ⚬ *Some pets allowed* 🚍 *No credit cards* ⎟⊙⎟ *BP.*

Le Barroux

❸❾ *16 km (10 mi) south of Vaison-la-Romaine, 34 km (21 mi) northeast*
Fodor'sChoice *of Avignon.*
★

Of all the marvelous hilltop villages stretching across the south of France, this tiny ziggurat of a town may be unique: it's 100% boutique-and-gallery-free and has only one tiny old *épicerie* (small grocery) selling canned goods, yellowed postcards, and today's *Le Provençal.* You are forced, therefore, to look around you and listen to the trickle of the ancient fountains at every labyrinthine turn. The **château** is its main draw, though its perfect condition reflects a complete restoration after a World War II fire. Grand vaulted rooms and a chapel date from the 12th century, and other halls serve as venues for contemporary art exhibits. ☎ *04–90–62–35–21* ▱ *€3.50* ⊗ *Apr.–June, weekends 10–7; July–Sept., daily 10–7; Oct., daily 2–6.*

Where to Stay & Eat

$ ✕▥ **Les Géraniums.** Though it has simple, pretty rooms, many with views sweeping down to the valley, this family-run auberge emphasizes its restaurant. A broad garden terrace stretches along the cliffside, where you can sample herb-roasted rabbit, a truffle omelet, and local cheeses. New rooms in the annex across the street take in panoramic views, and half-pension is strongly encouraged. ⊠ *Pl. de la Croix, 84330* ☎ *04–90–62–41–08* ▨ *04–90–62–56–48* ↵ *22 rooms* ⚲ *Restaurant, bar, some pets allowed (fee)* ▤ *AE, DC, MC, V* ⊘ *Closed mid-Nov.–mid-Mar.* ⊚ *MAP.*

Crillon le Brave

40 *12 km (7 mi) south of Malaucène (via Caromb), 21 km (13 mi) south-east of Vaison-la-Romaine.*

The main reason to come to this tiny village, named after France's most notable soldier-hero of the 16th century, is to stay or dine at its hotel, the Hostellerie de Crillon le Brave. But it's also pleasant—perched on a knoll in a valley shielded by Mont Ventoux, with the craggy hills of the Dentelles in one direction and the hills of the Luberon in another. Today the village still doesn't have even a *boulangerie* (bakery), let alone a souvenir boutique.

Where to Stay & Eat

$$$–$$$$ ✕▥ **Hostellerie de Crillon le Brave.** The views from the interconnected hilltop houses of this Relais & Châteaux property are as elevated as its prices, but for this you get a rarefied stage-set of medieval luxury. A cozy-chic southern touch informs book-filled salons and brocante-trimmed guest rooms, some with terraces looking out onto infinity. In the stone-vaulted dining room, stylish French cuisine is served. Wine tastings and regional discovery packages encourage longer stays. ⊠ *Pl. de l'Église, 84410* ☎ *04–90–65–61–61* ▨ *04–90–65–62–86* ⊕ *www.crillonlebrave. com* ↵ *35 rooms* ⚲ *Restaurant, minibars, cable TV, tennis court, pool, massage, babysitting, Internet, some pets allowed (fee); no a/c in some rooms* ▤ *AE, DC, MC, V* ⊘ *Closed Jan.–mid-Mar.*

L'Isle-sur-la-Sorgue

41 *18 km (11 mi) south of Malaucène, 41 km (25 mi) southeast of Orange, 26 km (16 mi) east of Avignon.*

FodorsChoice
★

Crisscrossed with lazy canals and alive with moss-covered waterwheels that once drove its silk, wool, and paper mills, this old valley town retains a gentle appeal—except, that is, on Sunday, when it transforms itself into a Marrakech of marketeers, its streets crammed with antiques and brocantes, its cafés swelling with crowds of bargain seekers making a day of it. There are also street musicians, food stands groaning under mounds of rustic breads, vats of tapenade, and cloth-lined baskets of spices, and miles of café tables offering ringside seats to the spectacle. On a non-market day life returns to its mellow pace, with plenty of antiques dealers open year-round, as well as fabric and interior design shops, bookstores, and food stores for you to explore. The token sight to see is L'Isle's 17th-century church, the **Collégiale Notre-Dame-des-Anges,** extravagantly decorated with gilt, faux marble, and sentimental frescoes. Its double-colonnaded facade commands the center of the Vieille Ville.

Where to Stay & Eat

$$$–$$$$ ✕ **La Prévôté.** With all the money you saved bargaining on that chipped Quimper vase, splurge on lunch at this discreet, pristine spot hidden off a backstreet courtyard. The cuisine has won top awards for chef Roland Mercier—try his cannelloni stuffed with salmon and goat cheese, or tender duckling with lavender honey. The prix-fixe menus start at €26 and top out at €60. ⊠ *4 bis rue Jean-Jacques-Rousseau* ☎ *04–90–38–57–29* ⬟ *Reservations essential* ▭ *MC, V* ☉ *Closed Tues. and Wed. in Dec.–June. No dinner Wed. in July and Aug.*

$–$$$ ✕ **Lou Nego Chin.** In winter you sit shoulder to shoulder in the cramped but atmospheric dining room (chinoiserie linens, brightly hued tiles), but in summer tables are strewn across the quiet street, on a wooden deck along the river. Ask for a spot at the edge so you can watch the ducks play, then order the inexpensive house wine and the menu du jour, often a hearty omelet Provençal, goat-cheese salad, or a good, garlicky stew. ⊠ *12 quai Jean Jaurès* ☎ *04–90–20–88–03* ⬟ *Reservations essential* ▭ *DC, MC, V* ☉ *Closed Wed. No dinner Tues. in Oct.–Apr.*

★ $–$$ ✕⊞ **Le Mas de Cure-Bourse.** This graceful old 18th-century post-coach stop is well outside the fray, snugly hedge-bound in the countryside amid 6 acres of fruit trees and fields. Rooms are freshly decked out in Provençal prints and painted country furniture. You can be served sophisticated home cooking with a local touch. Half-pension is strongly encouraged, although the restaurant is closed Monday, and lunch is not served Tuesday. ⊠ *Rte. de Caumont, 84800* ☎ *04–90–38–16–58* ⬟ *04–90–38–52–31* ⬳ *13 rooms* ⬥ *Restaurant, pool, free parking; no a/c* ▭ *MC, V* ☉ *Closed 1st 3 wks in Nov., 1st 2 wks in Jan.* ⧄ *MAP.*

$ ✕⊞ **La Gueulardière.** After a Sunday glut of antiquing along the canals, you can dine and sleep just up the street in a hotel full of collectible finds, from the school posters in the restaurant to the oak armoires and brass beds that furnish the simple lodgings. Each room has French windows that open onto the enclosed garden courtyard, where you can enjoy a private breakfast in the shade. ⊠ *1 cours René Char, 84800* ☎ *04–90–38–10–52* ⬟ *04–90–20–83–70* ⬳ *5 rooms* ⬥ *Restaurant, some pets allowed, free parking; no a/c* ▭ *AE, MC, V* ☉ *Closed mid-Dec.–mid-Jan.*

Shopping

The famous **L'Isle-sur-la-Sorgue Sunday morning flea market** takes place from the Place Gambetta up the length of Avenue des Quatre Otages. Of the dozens of antiques shops in L'Isle, one conglomerate concentrates some 40 dealers under the same roof: **L'Isle aux Brocantes** (⊠ 7 av. des Quatre Otages ☎ 04–90–20–69–93); it's open Saturday–Monday. Higher-end antiques are concentrated next door at the twin shops of **Xavier Nicod et Gérard Nicod** (⊠ 9 av. des Quatre Otages ☎ 04–90–38–35–50 or 04–90–38–07–20). **Maria Giancatarina** (⊠ 4 av. Julien Guigue, across from train station ☎ 04–90–38–58–02) showcases beautifully restored linens, including *boutis* (Provençal quilts). A major group of antiquaires are found at **Hôtel Dongler** (⊠ 9 esplanade Robert Vasse ☎ 04–90–38–63–63). A tempting selection is on view at **Le Quai de la Gare** (⊠ 4 av. Julien Guigue ☎ 04–90–20–73–42). A popular source is **Village des Antiquaires de la Gare** (⊠ 2 bis av. de l'Égalité ☎ 04–90–38–04–57).

Fontaine-de-Vaucluse

42 *8 km (5 mi) east of L'Isle-sur-la-Sorgue, 33 km (20 mi) east of Avignon.*

★ The **Fontaine de Vaucluse,** for which the town is named, is a strange and beautiful natural phenomenon that has been turned into a charming, albeit slightly tacky, tourist center—like a tiny Niagara Falls—and should not be missed if you're either a connoisseur of rushing water or a fan of foreign kitsch. There's no exaggerating the magnificence of the *fontaine* itself, a mysterious spring that gushes from a deep underground source that has been explored to a depth of 1,010 feet . . . so far. Framed by towering cliffs, a broad, pure pool wells up and spews dramatically over massive rocks down a gorge to the village, where its roar soothes and cools the tourists who crowd the riverfront cafés. You must pay to park and then run a gauntlet of souvenir shops and tourist traps on your way to the top. But even if you plan to make a beeline past the kitsch, do stop in at the legitimate and informative **Moulin Vallis-Clausa.** A working paper mill, it demonstrates a reconstructed 15th-century waterwheel that drives timber crankshafts to mix rag pulp, while artisans roll and dry thick paper *à l'ancienne* (in the old manner). ☎ *04–90–20–34–14* ☉ *Sept.–June, daily 9–noon and 2–5:30; July and Aug., daily 9–7:30.*

A number of divers, including Jacques Cousteau, have unsuccessfully attempted to find the source of Vaucluse's "fountain." Their efforts are detailed along with other interesting glimpses into the geological wonders that have been found in the area at the **Monde Souterrain de Norbert Casteret** (Subterranean World Museum), found on the path leading to the Fontaine de Vaucluse. ✉ *Chemin de la Fontaine* ☎ *04–90–20–34–13* 🎫 *€4* ☉ *Feb.–May, Sept., and Nov., daily 10–noon, 2–6; June–Aug., daily 10–noon, 2–5.*

Fontaine has its own ruined **château,** perched romantically on a forested hilltop over the town and illuminated at night. First built around the year 1000 and embellished in the 13th century by the bishops of Cavaillon, it was destroyed in the 15th century and now forms little more than a saw-tooth silhouette against the sky.

The Renaissance poet Petrarch, driven mad with unrequited love for a beautiful married woman named Laura, retreated to this valley to nurse his passion in a cabin with "one dog and only two servants." Sixteen years in this wild isolation didn't ease the pain, but the serene landscape inspired him to poetry. The small **Musée de Fontaine de Vaucluse Pétrarch,** built on the site of his stay, displays prints and engravings of the virtuous lovers. ☎ *04–90–20–37–20* 🎫 *€3.50* ☉ *Apr. and May, Wed.–Mon. 10–noon and 2–6; June–Sept., Wed.–Mon. 10–12:30 and 1:30–6; Oct., weekends 10–noon and 2–5.*

Where to Stay & Eat

$ ✕🏨 **Le Parc.** In a spectacular riverside locale in the shadow of the ruined château, this solid old hotel has basic, comfortable rooms (whitewashed stucco, all-weather carpet) with clean bathrooms and no creaks; five of them offer river views. The restaurant (closed Wednesday) spreads along the river in a pretty park, with tables shaded by trellises heavy with grapes and trumpet vine. Moderately priced daily menus include river-fresh salmon. ⊠ *Rue de Bourgades, 84800* ☎ *04–90–20–31–57* 🖨 *04–90–20–27–03* ➘ *12 rooms* ◇ *Restaurant, some pets allowed (fee); no a/c* ☰ *AE, DC, MC, V* ⊘ *Closed Nov.–mid-Feb.* ⭗ *MAP.*

en route	Gordes is only a short distance from Fontaine de Vaucluse, but you need to wind your way south, east, and then north on D100A, D100, D2, and D15 to skirt the impassable hillside. It's a lovely drive through dry, rocky country covered with wild lavender and scrub oak and may tempt you to a picnic or a walk.

Gordes

❹❸ **Fodor'sChoice** ★ *16 km (10 mi) southeast of Fontaine-de-Vaucluse, 35 km (22 mi) east of Avignon.*

Gordes was once merely an unspoiled hilltop village; it's now a famous unspoiled hilltop village surrounded by luxury vacation homes, modern hotels, restaurants, and B&Bs. No matter: the ancient stone village still rises above the valley in painterly hues of honey gold, and its mosaiclike cobbled streets—lined with boutiques, galleries, and real-estate offices—still wind steep and narrow to its Renaissance château—making this certainly one of the most beautiful and picturesque towns in Provence. The only way to see the interior of the **château** is to view its ghastly collection of photo paintings by pop artist Pol Mara, who lived in Gordes. It's worth the price of admission to look at the fabulously decorated stone fireplace, created in 1541. ☎ *04–90–72–02–75* 🎟 *€4* ⊘ *Daily 10–noon and 2–6.*

Just outside Gordes, on a lane heading north from D2, follow signs to the **Village des Bories.** Found throughout this region of Provence, the bizarre and fascinating little stone hovels called *bories* are concentrated some 20 strong in an ancient community. Their origins are provocatively vague: built as shepherds' shelters with tight-fitting, mortarless stone in a hivelike form, they may date to the Celts, the Ligurians, even the Iron Age—and were inhabited or used for sheep through the 18th century. ☎ *04–90–72–03–48* 🎟 *€5.50* ⊘ *Daily 9–sunset or 8, whichever comes earlier.*

If you've dreamed of Provence's famed lavender fields, head to a wild valley some 4 km (2½ mi) north of Gordes (via D177) to find the beautiful 12th-century Romanesque **Abbaye de Sénanque,** which floats above a redolent sea of lavender (in full bloom in July and August). Begun in 1150 and completed at the dawn of the 13th century, the **church** and adjoining **cloister** are without decoration, but still touch the soul with their chaste beauty. In this orbit, the gray-stone buildings seem to have special resonance—ancient, organic, with a bit of the borie about it. Next door, the enormous vaulted **dormitory** contains an exhibition on the abbey's construction, and the **refectory** shelters a display on the history of Cistercian abbeys. ☎ *04–90–72–05–72* 🎟 *€6* ⊘ *Mar.–Oct., Mon.–Sat. 10–noon and 2–6, Sun. 2–6; Nov.–Feb., weekdays 2–5, weekends 2–6.*

Where to Stay & Eat

$$–$$$$ ✕ **Le Comptoir du Victuailler.** Across from the château, this tiny but deluxe bistro entices with daily *aioli*, a smorgasbord of fresh cod and lightly steamed vegetables crowned with the garlic mayonnaise. Evenings are reserved for intimate, formal indoor meals à la carte—roast Luberon lamb, beef with truffle sauce. The '30s-style bistro tables and architectural lines are a relief from Gordes's ubiquitous rustic-chic. ⊠ *Pl. du Château* ☎ *04–90–72–01–31* 🖾 *Reservations essential* ▭ *MC, V* ☉ *Closed Wed., Sept.–May. No dinner Tues., mid-Jan.–Easter. Closed mid-Nov.–mid-Dec.*

$$$–$$$$ ✕▦ **La Bastide de Gordes.** Spectacularly perched on Gordes' hilltop, the newly renovated Bastide is big, yet intimately-scaled, with architectural origins going back to the 16th century. The hotel, with its superb restaurant (and impressive, 20,000-bottle wine cellar), is surrounded by manicured lawns and a broad, elegantly appointed terrace that provides welcome shade in the summer heat. The guest-room furnishings are traditional and comfortable, with a few *haut Provençal* accents. The clientele is turning increasingly upscale and international, attracted by the Bastide's latest addition, a three-level Daniel Jouvance spa, whose luxe amenities include a Roman-style steam room, Japanese baths, state-of-the-art treatment rooms, ionization chamber, and a chromatic pool with breathtaking views of the Valleé de Gordes. ⊠ *Le Village 84220* ☎ *04–90–72–12–12* 🖾 *04–90–72–05–20* ⊕ *www. bastide-de-gordes.com* ➥ *39 rooms, 6 suites* 🖒 *Restaurant, bar, spa, 2 pools (1 indoor), Internet* ▭ *AE, MC, V* ☉ *Closed Jan and 1st 2 wks of Feb.*

$$$ ✕▦ **Le Ferme de la Huppe.** This 17th-century stone farmhouse with a well in the courtyard, a swimming pool in the garden, and rooms with pretty prints and secondhand finds is in the countryside outside Gordes. Dine poolside on three styles of roast lamb, prepared by the proprietors' son, Gerald Konings, but reserve ahead: the restaurant (closed Thursday) is as popular as the hotel. Meal plans are available with a minimum stay of three nights. ⊠ *Les Pourquiers, 3 km (2 mi) east of Gordes, R.D.156, 84220* ☎ *04–90–72–12–25* 🖾 *04–90–72–01–83* ⊕ *www. laprovence.com/lahuppe* ➥ *9 rooms* 🖒 *Restaurant, pool, some pets allowed (fee); no a/c in some rooms* ▭ *MC, V* ☉ *Closed end Nov.–mid-Mar.* ⏀ *MAP.*

$$$–$$$$ ▦ **Domaine de l'Enclos.** This cluster of private stone cottages has newly laid antique tiles and fresh faux-patinas that keep it looking fashionably old. There are panoramic views and a pool, babysitting services and swing sets, and an aura that is surprisingly warm and familial for an inn of this sophistication. ⊠ *Rte. de Sénanque, 84220* ☎ *04–90–72–71–00* 🖾 *04–90–72–03–03* ⊕ *www.domaine-enclos.com* ➥ *12 rooms, 5 apartments* 🖒 *Restaurant, minibars, cable TV, tennis court, pool, some pets allowed (fee)* ▭ *AE, MC, V* ⏀ *MAP.*

$$$–$$$$ ▦ **Les Romarins.** At this small hilltop inn on the outskirts of Gordes you can gaze at the town across the valley while having breakfast on a sheltered terrace in the morning sun. Rooms are clean, well lighted, and feel spacious—ask for either No. 1, in the main building, from whose white-curtained windows you can see forever, or the room with a terrace in the atelier. Oriental rugs, antique furniture, and a pool add to your contentment. ⊠ *Rte. de Sénanque, 84220* ☎ *04–90–72–12–13* 🖷 *04–90–72–13–13* ⊕ *www.hoteldesromarins. com* ⇆ *13 rooms* ♨ *Minibars, cable TV, pool, some pets allowed (fee)* ☰ *AE, MC, V.*

Roussillon

㊹ *10 km (6 mi) east of Gordes, 45 km (28 mi) east of Avignon.*

Fodor's Choice
★

In shades of deep rose and russet, this quintessential and gorgeous hilltop cluster of houses blends into the red-ocher cliffs from which its stone was quarried. The ensemble of buildings and jagged, hand-cut slopes is equally dramatic, and views from the top look out over a landscape of artfully eroded bluffs that Georgia O'Keeffe would have loved. Unlike neighboring hill villages, there's little of historic architectural detail here; the pleasure of a visit lies in the richly varied colors that change with the light of day, and in the views of the contrasting countryside, where dense-shadowed greenery sets off the red stone with Cézannesque severity. There are pleasant *placettes* (tiny squares) to linger in nonetheless, and a Renaissance fortress tower crowned with a clock in the 19th century; just past it, you can take in expansive panoramas of forest and ocher cliffs.

The area's famous vein of natural ocher, which spreads some 25 km (15 mi) along the foot of the Vaucluse plateau, has been mined for centuries, beginning with the ancient Romans, who used it for their pottery. You can visit the old **Usine Mathieu de Roussillon** (Roussillon's Mathieu Ochre Works) to learn more about ocher's extraction and its modern uses. There are explanatory exhibits, ocher powders for sale, and guided tours in English on advance request. ⊠ *On D104 southeast of town* ☎ *04–90–05–66–69* ☼ *Mar.–Nov., daily 10–7.*

From Rousillon's reds it is a drive of some 40 km (25 mi) west to discover the epicenter of Haute-Provence's fabled lavender in the sleepy, dusty town of Forcalquier. In the 12th century, this was known as the capital city of Haute-Provence and was called the *Cité des Quatre Reines* ("the City of the Four Queens") since the four daughters of the ruler of this region, Raimond Béranger V (Eleanor of Aquitaine among them), all married royals. Relics of this former glory can be glimpsed in the Vieille Ville of Forcalquier, notably its Cathédrale Notre-Dame and the Couvent des

Fodor's Choice
★

Cordeliers. However, everyone heads here to marvel at the **lavender fields of Forcalquier,** which burst into bloom with *Lavandula vera,* true wild lavender, during the last two weeks of July only. Contact the Forcalquier's **tourist office** (⊠ 13 place Bourguet ☎ 04–92–75–25–30 ⊕ www. forcalquier.com) for information on all things lavender, then get saddled up on a bicycle for a trip into the countryside at the town's Moulin de Sarret. If you wish to enjoy a fine meal and reserve (way in advance) a room, contact the town's most historic inn, the **Hostellerie des Deux Lions** (⊠ 11 pl. du Bourguet ☎ 04–92–75–25–30). For a workshop on lavender, meet **Monique Claessens** (☎ 04–92–73–06–76), located in the village of Mane, but found often at her stand in the vibrant Monday market

CloseUp

THE LAVENDER ROUTE

UNPREPOSSESSING, FRAGRANT, AND TINY, this flower not only enchants all who behold it but manages to bring in big tourist dollars along la "Route de la Lavande" (the Lavender Route), a wide blue-purple swath that connects over 2,000 producers across the Drôme, the plateau du Vaucluse, and the Alpes-de-Haute-Provence.

Once described as the "soul of Haute-Provence," lavender has colored the high plains and brought prosperity and clean smells to village life since the Middle Ages. The word itself comes from Latin lavare, which means "to wash"; since its discovery in ancient, unrecorded times, it has been indiscriminately used for anything from perfume to cleansers to tonics for the prevention of freckles.

And for good reason: today's trend for natural remedies has proven its innate properties and given it well-deserved recognition. Not only a disinfectant, a calmative against stress, preventative for migraines and sunburn, and effective in treating rheumatism and vertigo, lavender also smells good. Stylish body care product producers like the Body Shop and Occitaine were quick to catch on and perfumers Dior and Gautier soon followed suit.

Today, there are literally hundreds of beauty products that use some form of lavender or lavender essence, and consumers are madly buying. They are also—when visiting the Côte d'Azur and Provence—madly frolicking through the fields.

To do so yourself, go in season, June to early September (although the harvest doesn't start until July). **L'Association des Routes de la Lavande** (☎ 04–75–26–65–91 ⊕ www.routes-lavande.com) has itineraries that zigzag across the range. And the range is quite large: broken up into six main regions, they comprise the Vallée de la Drôme et Diois; the Drôme Provençal; the Pays de Sault, Mont Ventoux, and Luberon; the Pays du Buëch; the Pays de Forcalquier and Montagne de Lure; and the Pays de Digne, from the Plateau de Valensole to Verdon. All through this area there are countless events, hikes, and workshops, featuring everything from touring with a donkey to seminars on "blue gold" and lavender honey.

The very popular **Moulin de Savoirs** (☎ 04–75–28–15–94) has guided walks through the fields in the Drôme Provençal and runs workshops about lavender, its properties, and its essential oil. You can buy wine and lavender products at the famed **Ferme Lavanicole Château du Bois** (✉ Les Espagnols, Largarde d'Apt ☎ 04–90–76–91–23). Finally, see lavender distilled at the **Distillerie "Lavande 1100"** (✉ D34 between Sault and Apt ☎ 04–90–75–01–42).

The most generous patches of color are along the edge of Mont Ventoux, near Forcalquier, and the plateau de Valensole. Here, the fields are simply glorious. Arranged in nodding little rows, the lavender seems to stripe the landscape, maturing from baby blue to deep mauve amidst a haze of bees. A walk or a bicycle ride—in season—is like being transported into a magical world, one usually only found on a picture-perfect postcard.

(8 AM–noon) in Forcalquier. For routes through the fields, contact **Les Routes de la Lavande** ✉ *2 av. de Venterol, 26111 Nyons* ☎ *04–75–26–65–91* 🖷 *04–75–26–32–67.*

Where to Stay & Eat

★ $$$ ✕🖾 **Mas de Garrigon.** An exquisite hotel, tastefully decorated in classic Provençal style, the Garrigon has spacious rooms, a cozy library, and views of the surrounding ocher cliffs. It also showcases the best restaurant (by far) in Roussillon—which is a good thing, as the management takes it very personally if you pass on their demi-pension offer. So don't: the food is superb—monkfish in salt crust, straw-baked lamb with rosemary jus, inventive vegetable courses, plus wonderful desserts—and the family welcome is warm and genuine. ✉ *Rte. de St-Saturnin-d'Apt, 3 km (2 mi) north on the D2, 84220* ☎ *04–90–05–63–92* 🖷 *04–90–05–70–01* ⊕ *www.masdegarrigon-provence.com* 🛏 *8 rooms, 1 suite* 🖒 *Cable TV, pool, free parking* ▭ *AE, DC, MC, V* ¶❍¶ *MAP.*

$–$$$ 🖾 **Ma Maison.** In the valley 4 km (2½ mi) below Roussillon, this isolated 1850 mas has been infused with a laid-back, cosmopolitan style by its artist-owners. Wicker-backed chairs mix with oriental rugs, wrought iron, and fluffy white bedspreads. There's a big saltwater pool, a massive country kitchen, and an idyllic garden complete with lovely breakfast tables romantically set under sprawling, shady branches. Breakfast is included. ✉ *Quartier Les Devens, 84220* ☎ *04–90–05–74–17* 🖷 *04–90–05–74–63* ⊕ *www.mamaison-provence.com* 🛏 *3 rooms, 2 suites* 🖒 *Pool, some pets allowed (fee); no a/c* ▭ *MC, V* ☼ *Closed mid-Oct.–mid-Mar.* ¶❍¶ *BP.*

Oppède-le-Vieux

45 *25 km (15 mi) southeast of Avignon, 15 km (9 mi) southwest of Gordes.*

A Byronesque tumble of ruins arranged against an overgrown rocky hillside, Oppède's charm—or part of it—lies in its preservation. Taken over by writers and artists who have chosen to live here and restore but not develop it, the village has a café or two but little else. Bring a lunch, wander, and contemplate. Follow signs toward Oppède; you'll occasionally be required to follow signs for Oppède-le-Village, but your goal will be marked with the symbol of *monuments historiques*: Oppède-le-Vieux. Cross the village square, pass through the old city gate, and climb up steep trails past restored houses to the church known as **Notre-Dame-d'Alydon.** First built in the 13th century, its blunt buttresses were framed into side chapels in the 16th century; you can still see the points of stoned-in Gothic windows above. The marvelous hexagonal bell tower sprouts a lean, mean gargoyle from each angle. It once served as part of the village's fortifications. Head left past the cliff-edge wall, plunge into the rock tunnel, and clamber up to the ruins of the **château,** built in the 13th century and then transformed in the 15th century. From the left side of its great square tower, look down into the dense fir forests of the Luberon's north face.

Ménerbes

⁴⁶ *5 km (3 mi) east of Oppède-le-Vieux, 30 km (19 mi) southeast of Avignon.*

The town of Ménerbes clings to a long, thin hilltop over this sought-after valley, looming over the surrounding forests like a great stone ship. At its prow juts the **Castellet**, a 15th-century fortress. At its stern looms the 13th-century **Citadelle.** These redoubtable fortifications served the Protestants well during the Wars of Religion—until the Catholics wore them down with a 15-month siege. A campanile tops the Hôtel de Ville (Town Hall) on pretty **place de l'Horloge** (Clock Square), where you can admire the delicate stonework on the arched portal and mullioned windows of a Renaissance house. Just past the tower on the right is an overlook taking in views toward Gordes, Roussillon, and Mont Ventoux.

Seven kilometers (4 mi) east of Ménerbes is the eagle's-nest village of Lacoste, presided over by the once magnificent Château de Sade, erstwhile retreat to the notorious Marquis de Sade (1740–1814) when he wasn't on the run from authorities. For some years, the wealthy Paris couturier Pierre Cardin has been restoring the castle wall by wall and under his generous patronage the **Festival Lacoste** takes place here throughout the months of July and August. A lyric, musical, and theatrical extravaganza, events (and their dates) change yearly, ranging from outdoor poetry recitals to ballet to colorful operettas. ⊠ *Carrières du Château, Lacoste* ☎ *04–90–75–93–12* ⊕ *www.lacoste.easyclassic.com* ✍ *€20–€140.*

Where to Stay

★ **$$$** 🔟 **Hostellerie Le Roy Soleil.** In the imposing shadow of the Luberon, this luxurious country inn has pulled out all stops on comfort and decor: marble and granite bathrooms, wrought-iron beds, and coordinated fabrics. But the integrity of its 17th-century building, with thick stone walls and groin vaults and beams, redeems it just short of pretentiousness and makes it a lovely place to escape to. ⊠ *Rte. des Beaumettes, 84560* ☎ *04–90–72–25–61* 🖷 *04–90–72–36–55* ⊕ *www.roy-soleil. com* 🛏 *10 rooms, 9 suites* ⚼ *Restaurant, minibars, cable TV, tennis court, pool, bar, free parking, some pets allowed (fee)* ▭ *AE, MC, V* ⊗ *Closed Nov.–mid-Mar.* ¶⊙¶ *FAP.*

Bonnieux

★ **⁴⁷** *11 km (7 mi) south of Roussillon, 45 km (28 mi) north of Aix-en-Provence.*

The most impressive of the Luberon's hilltop villages, Bonnieux rises out of the arid hills in a jumble of honey-color cubes that change color subtly as the day progresses. The village is wrapped in crumbling ramparts and dug into bedrock and cliff. Most of its sharply raked streets take in wide-angle valley views, though you'll get the best view from the pine-shaded grounds of the 12th-century church, reached by stone steps that wind past tiny niche houses.

Where to Stay & Eat

$$$–$$$$ ✕ **Le Fournil.** In an old bakery in a natural grotto deep in stone, lighted by candles and arty torchères, this restaurant would be memorable even without its trendy look and stylishly presented Provençal cuisine. Try the adventurous dishes such as the crisped pigs'-feet *galette* (patty) and check out the informed wine list. ✉ *5 pl. Carnot* ☎ *04–90–75–83–62* 🖷 *04–90–75–96–19* ⚠ *Reservations essential* 🖃 *MC, V* ☯ *Closed Mon. and Tues.; Dec. and Jan.*

★ **$$$** ✕ **Auberge de la Loube.** The chef's inclusion in a Peter Mayle book hasn't gone to his toque: for simple, unpretentious Provençal food perfectly prepared, nothing beats this idyllic little restaurant in the neighboring hamlet of Buoux. Meals are served on a covered terrace out back. The gargantuan starters are famous and fabulous, as are house specialties like scrambled eggs with truffles and roasted leg of lamb. Sunday lunch is a feast worthy of Pagnol. ✉ *Quartier la Loube–Buoux* ☎ *04–90–74–19–58* 🖷 *04–90–74–19–58* ⚠ *Reservations essential* 🖃 *No credit cards* ☯ *Closed Wed., Thurs., and Jan.*

★ **$–$$$** 🏠 **Hostellerie du Prieuré.** Not every hotel has its own private chapel, but this gracious inn occupies an 18th-century abbey, right in the village center. A pleasantly warm glow quietly surrounds you from the firelit salon to the dining room burnished with Roussillon ocher. Summer meals and breakfasts are served in the enclosed garden oasis. Rooms have plush carpets and antiques. The Coutaz family has been in the hotel business since Napoléon III, and it shows. ✉ *In center of village, 84480* ☎ *04–90–75–80–78* 🖷 *04–90–75–96–00* 🌐 *www.esprit-de-france.com* ⟿ *10 rooms* ⚬ *Restaurant, tennis court, free parking, some pets allowed (fee); no a/c* 🖃 *MC, V* ☯ *Closed Nov.–Feb.* ❢ *FAP, MAP.*

★ **$–$$** 🏠 **Le Clos du Buis.** At this B&B, whitewash and quarry tiles, lovely tiled baths, and carefully juxtaposed antiques create a regional look in the guest rooms. Public spaces, with scrubbed floorboards, a fireplace, and exposed stone, are free for your use around the clock. It even has a pool and a pretty garden, and it's all overlooking the valley from the village center. ✉ *Rue Victor Hugo, 84480* ☎ *04–90–75–88–48* 🖷 *04–90–75–88–57* 🌐 *www.leclosdubuis.com* ⟿ *7 rooms* ⚬ *Pool, free parking, some pets allowed (fee); no a/c* 🖃 *MC, V* ☯ *Closed mid-Nov.–mid-Dec. and mid-Jan.–mid-Feb.* ❢ *BP.*

AIX-EN-PROVENCE & THE MEDITERRANEAN COAST

The southeastern part of this area of Provence, on the edge of the Côte d'Azur, is dominated by two major towns: Aix-en-Provence, considered the main hub of Provence and the most cultural town in the region; and Marseille, a vibrant port town that combines seediness with fashion and metropolitan feistiness with classical grace. For a breathtaking experience of the dramatic contrast between the azure Mediterranean sea and the rocky, olive tree–filled hills, take a trip along the coast east of Marseille and make an excursion to the Iles d'Hyères.

Aix-en-Provence

★ *48 km (29 mi) southeast of Bonnieux, 82 km (51 mi) southeast of Avignon, 176 km (109 mi) west of Nice, 759 km (474 mi) south of Paris.*

Gracious, cultivated, and made all the more cosmopolitan by the presence of some 30,000 international university students, the lovely old town of Aix (pronounced *ex*) was once the capital of Provence. The vestiges of that influence and power—fine art, noble architecture, and graceful urban design—remain beautifully preserved today. That and its thriving market, vibrant café life, and world-class music festival make Aix vie with Arles and Avignon as one of the towns in Provence that shouldn't be missed.

The Romans were first drawn here by mild thermal baths, naming the town Aquae Sextiae (Waters of Sextius) in honor of the consul who founded a camp near the source in 123 BC. Just 20 years later some 200,000 Germanic invaders besieged Aix, but the great Roman general Marius flanked them and pinned them against the mountain known ever since as Ste-Victoire. Marius remains a popular local first name to this day.

Under the wise and generous guidance of Roi René (King René) in the 15th century, Aix became a center of Renaissance arts and letters. At the height of its political, judicial, and ecclesiastic power in the 17th and 18th centuries, Aix profited from a surge of private building, each grand *hôtel particulier* (mansion) vying to outdo its neighbor. Its signature *cours* (courtyards) and *places* (squares), punctuated by grand fountains and intriguing passageways, date from this time.

It was into this exalting elegance that artist Paul Cézanne (1839–1906) was born, though he drew much of his inspiration from the raw countryside around the city and often painted Ste-Victoire. A schoolmate of Cézanne's made equal inroads: the journalist and novelist Émile Zola (1840–1902) attended the Collège Bourbon with Cézanne and described their friendship as well as Aix itself in several of his works. You can still sense something of the ambience that nurtured these two geniuses in the streets of modern Aix.

48 Under the deep shade of tall plane trees whose branches interlace over the street, **Cours Mirabeau** prevails as the city's social nerve center. One side of the street is lined with dignified 18th-century hôtels particuliers; you can view them from a comfortable seat in one of the dozen or so cafés and restaurants that spill onto the sidewalk on the other side.

49 In the **Musée du Vieil Aix** (Museum of Old Aix), an eclectic assortment of local treasures resides in a 17th-century mansion, from faïence to *santons* (terra-cotta figurines) to ornately painted furniture. The building itself is lovely, too. ✉ *17 rue Gaston-de-Saporta* ☎ *04–42–21–43–55* 🖵 *€4* 🕐 *Apr.–Oct., Tues.–Sun. 10–noon and 2:30–6; Nov.–Mar., Tues.–Sun. 10–noon and 2–5.*

50 The **Musée des Tapisseries** is housed in the 17th-century **Palais de l'Archevêché** (Archbishop's Palace) and showcases a sumptuous collection of tapestries that once decorated the walls of the bishops' quarters. Their

taste was excellent: there are 17 magnificent hangings from Beauvais and a series on the life of Don Quixote from Compiègne. Temporary exhibitions offer interesting sneak peeks into contemporary textile art. In the broad courtyard, the main opera productions of the Festival International d'Art Lyrique take place. ✉ *Pl. de l'Ancien-Archevêché* ☏ *04–42–23–09–91* 💶 *€2* 🕐 *Wed.–Mon. 10–5.*

★ ❺❶ The **Cathédrale St-Sauveur** (✉ Rue Gaston de Saporta) juxtaposes so many eras of architectural history, all clearly delineated and preserved, it's like a survey course in itself. It has a double nave, Romanesque and Gothic side by side, and a Merovingian (5th-century) **baptistery,** its colonnade mostly recovered from Roman temples built to honor pagan deities. Shutters hide the ornate 16th-century carvings on the **portals,** opened by a guide on request. The guide can also lead you into the tranquil Romanesque **cloister** next door, so that you can admire its carved pillars and slender columns. As if these treasures weren't enough, the cathedral also houses an extraordinary 15th-century triptych painted by Nicolas Froment in the heat of inspiration following his travels in Italy and Flanders. Called the *Triptyque du Buisson Ardent* (*Burning Bush Triptych*), it depicts the generous art patrons King René and Queen Jeanne kneeling on either side of the Virgin, who is poised above a burning bush.

These days, to avoid light damage, it's only opened for viewing on Tuesday from 3 to 4.

❺❷ The 12th-century **Église St-Jean-de-Malte** (⊠ Intersection of rue Cardinale and rue d'Italie) served as a chapel of the Knights of Malta, a medieval order of friars devoted to hospital care. It was Aix's first attempt at the Gothic style. It was here that the counts of Provence were buried throughout the 18th century; their tombs (in the upper left) were attacked during the Revolution and have been only partially repaired.

need a break? Just behind the Palais de la Justice is the colorful world of bric-a-brac collectibles and bookstands of place Verdun (stalls open Tuesday, Thursday, and Saturday). The best place to people-watch is from the sunny terrace of **Le Verdun** (⊠ 20 pl. St-de Verdun ☎ 04–42–27–03–24). Light snacks are served all day.

❺❸ In the graceful Quartier Mazarin, the **Musée Granet** is set below the cours Mirabeau. Once the Ecole de Dessin (Art School) that granted Cézanne a second prize in 1856, this former priory of the Eglise St-Jean-de-Malte is now an art museum. There are eight of Cézanne's paintings upstairs as well as a nice collection of his watercolors and drawings. You'll also find works by Rubens, David, and a group of sentimental works by the museum's founder, François Granet. At press time, the museum was closed for an ambitious renovation project that will eventually double the exhibition area. Reopening is scheduled for early 2006. ⊠ *13 rue Cardinale* ☎ *04–42–26–84–55* 🎫 *€2* ☉ *Wed.–Mon., 10–noon and 2–6.*

★ **❺❹** Just north of the Vieille Ville loop is the **Atelier Cézanne** (Cézanne Studio). After the death of his mother forced the sale of the painter's beloved country retreat, known as Jas de Bouffan, he had this studio built just above the town center. In the upstairs work space Cézanne created some of his finest paintings, including *Les Grandes Baigneuses* (*The Large Bathers*). But what is most striking is its collection of simple objects that once featured prominently in the portraits and still-lifes he created—redingote, bowler hat, ginger jar, and all—displayed as if awaiting his return. ⊠ *9 av. Paul-Cézanne* ☎ *04–42–21–06–53* ⊕ *www.atelier-cezanne.com* 🎫 *€5.50* ☉ *Apr.–Sept., daily 10–noon and 2:30–6; Oct.–Mar., daily 10–noon and 2–5.*

Where to Stay & Eat

★ **$$$$** ✕ **Le Clos de la Violette.** Whether you dine under the chestnut trees or in the airy, pastel dining room, you'll get to experience the cuisine of one of the south's top chefs, Jean-Marc Banzo. He spins tradition into gold, from poached crab set atop a humble white-bean-and-shrimp salad to grilled red mullet with squid-stuffed cabbage. The restaurant isn't far from the Atelier Cézanne, outside the Vieille Ville ring. ⊠ *10 av. de la Violette* ☎ *04–42–23–30–71* ⊕ *www.closdelaviolette.fr* 🍴 *Reservations essential* 👔 *Jacket required* 🖃 *AE, MC, V* ☉ *Closed Sun. No lunch Mon. and Wed.*

$–$$$ ✕ **Les Bacchanales.** Despite being positioned on a tourist-trap street off cours Mirabeau, this is a pleasant, intimate restaurant with inviting decor of daub-filled beams, yellow-ocher stucco, and Louis XIII chairs. The broad range of fixed-price menus may include smoked salmon with rosemary and green onion cream, *rouget* (red mullet) perfumed with sage and fennel, and crushed almonds flavored with marinated cherries. As the name implies, wine figures large here, and the list is extensive. ⊠ *10 rue de la Couronne* ☎ *04–42–27–21–06* ▤ *AE, MC, V* ⊙ *Closed Tues. No lunch Wed. and Sat.*

¢–$$ ✕ **Antoine Coté Cour.** Filled with trendy insiders and fashion conscious Aixois, this lively Italian restaurant has floor-to-ceiling windows that give almost every table a view of the plant-filled courtyard. Delicious smells wafting out from the open kitchen make the restaurant literally hum in hungry anticipation. Pastas are superb; try the mushroom and prosciutto ham fettuccine or the gnocchi à la Provençal. ⊠ *19 cours Mirabeau* ☎ *04–42–93–12–51* ▤ *DC, MC, V* ⊙ *Closed Sun. No lunch Mon.*

★ ¢–$$ ✕ **Brasserie Les Deux Garcons.** Cézanne and Emile Zola used to chow down here back when, so who cares if the food is rather ordinary. Eating isn't what you came for. Instead, revel in the exquisite gold-ivory *style Consulate* decor, which dates from the restaurant's founding in 1792. It is not so hard to picture the greats—Mistinguett, Churchill, Sartre, Picasso, Delon, Belmondo, and Cocteau—enjoying their demitasse under these mirrors. Better, savor the linen-decked sidewalk tables that look out to the cours Mirabeau, the fresh flowers, and the white-swathed waiters serving espressos in tiny gilt-edge cups. At night, the upstairs turns into a cozy, dimly lit piano bar buzzing with an interesting mix of local jazz lovers, tourists, and students. ⊠ *53 cours Mirabeau* ☎ *04–42–26–00–51* ▤ *AE, MC, V.*

$$$$ ▥ **Le Pigonnet.** Cézanne painted Ste-Victoire from what is now the large
FodorśChoice flower-filled garden terrace of this enchanting abode, and the likes of
★ Princess Caroline, Iggy Pop, and Clint Eastwood have spent a few nights under the luxurious roof of this family-owned, Old World, country-style hotel. Spacious and filled with light, each room is a marvel of decoration: baby-soft plush rugs, beautifully preserved antique furniture, rich colors of burnt reds, autumn yellows, and delicate oranges. The restaurant's terrace spills out onto a sculpted green, but the inside dining salon is equally pleasant on a rainy day, thanks to its softly draped yellow curtains and large picture windows. For sheerest Provençal luxe, this place can't be beat. ⊠ *5 av. du Pigonnet, 13100* ☎ *04–42–59–02–90* ▤ *04–42–59–47–77* ⊕ *www.hotelpigonnet.com* ⇆ *52 rooms, 1 apartment* ⚐ *Restaurant, minibars, cable TV, pool, some pets allowed (fee)* ▤ *AE, MC, V.*

★ $$$$ ▥ **Villa Gallici.** Perched on a hill overlooking the pink roofs of Aix, this former archbishop's palace was transformed into a homage to *le style provençal* thanks to the wizardry of three designers, Gilles Dez, Charles de Montemarco, and Daniel Jouvre. But this is the Provence that Parisian aristocrats enjoyed back in the 19th-century—don't come here for sunbaked walls, white tiles, and urns with cactus. Instead, hued in the lavenders and blues, ochres and oranges of Aix, rooms swim in the most gorgeous Souleiado and Rubelli fabrics and trim. If a Louis Seize chair covered in gingham check gets to be a bit much, just step outside to the Florentine-style garden, shaded by ancient cypress and plane trees. A pool beckons, as does Marcel, the cat. This hilltop garden retreat stands serenely apart from the city center on the outskirts of town (offering great views), and that means the shops of Cours Mirabeau are a 15-minute walk away. But who will want to leave the villa? After all, you have to choose between tea by the pool or luncheon on the terrace. That noted, some readers say the food needs work. ✉ *Av. de la Violette, 13100* ☎*04–42–23–29–23* 🖷*04–42–96–30–45* ⊕*www.villagallici. com* 🛏 *18 rooms, 4 suites, 3 duplexes* ⚒ *Restaurant, cable TV, pool, Internet, some pets allowed (fee), free parking* ▤ *AE, DC, MC, V.*

$–$$$ 🏨 **Nègre-Coste.** Its prominent cours Mirabeau position and its lavish public areas make this 18th-century town house a popular hotel. Provençal decor and newly tiled bathrooms live up to the lovely ground-floor salons. Large windows open up to the cours Mirabeau, perfect for people-watching with a morning cup of coffee; quieter ones at the back look over the rooftops to the cathedral. ✉ *33 cours Mirabeau, 13100* ☎ *04–42–27–74–22* 🖷 *04–42–26–80–93* ⊕ *www.hotelnegrecoste.com* 🛏 *36 rooms, 1 suite* ⚒ *Minibars, cable TV, parking (fee)* ▤ *AE, MC, V.*

★ **$–$$** 🏨 **Quatre Dauphins.** In the quiet Mazarin quarter, this modest but impeccable lodging inhabits a noble hôtel particulier. Its pretty, comfortable little rooms have been spruced up with *boutis* (Provençal quilts), Les Olivades fabrics, quarry tiles, jute carpets, and hand-painted furniture. The house-proud but unassuming owner-host bends over backward to please. ✉*55 rue Roux-Alphéran, 13100* ☎*04–42–38–16–39* 🖷*04–42–38–60–19* 🛏*13 rooms* ⚒ *Some pets allowed (fee)* ▤ *MC, V.*

$–$$ 🏨 **St-Christophe.** With so few midprice *hôtels de charme* in Aix and a distinct shortage of regional style, you might as well opt for this glossy art deco–style hotel, where the comfort and services are remarkable for the price. Rooms are slickly done in deep jewel tones, and the top-floor rooms have artisanal tiles in the bathrooms. Meal plans are available with a three-night minimum stay. ✉ *2 av. Victor-Hugo, 13100* ☎*04–42–26–01–24* 🖷*04–42–38–53–17* ⊕*www.hotel-saintchristophe. com* 🛏 *58 rooms, 7 suites* ⚒ *Restaurant, cable TV, parking (fee), some pets allowed (fee)* ▤ *AE, MC, V* ◉ *BP, MAP.*

Nightlife & the Arts

To find out what's going on in town, pick up a copy of the events calendar *Le Mois à Aix* or the bilingual city guide *Aix la Vivante* at the tourist office. **Le Scat Club** (✉ 11 rue de la Verrerie ☎ 04–42–23–00–23) is the place for live soul, funk, reggae, rock, blues, and jazz. **The Bistrot Aixois** (✉ 37 cours Sextius ☎ 04–42–27–50–10) is the hottest student night spot, with young yuppies lining up to get in. For a night of playing roulette and the slot machines, head for the **Casino Municipal** (✉ 2 bis av. N.-Bonaparte ☎ 04–42–26–30–33).

Every July during the **Festival International d'Art Lyrique** (International Opera Festival; ☎ 04–42–17–34–00 for information), you can see world-class opera productions in the courtyard of the Palais de l'Archevêché.

Shopping

Aix is a market town, and a sophisticated **food and produce market** sets up every morning on place Richelme; just up the street, on place Verdun, is a good high-end *brocante* (collectibles market) Tuesday, Thursday, and Saturday mornings. A famous Aixois delicacy is *calissons*, a blend of almond paste and glazed melon in almond shapes. The most picturesque shop specializing in calissons is **Bechard** (✉ 12 cours Mirabeau). **Leonard Parli** (✉ 35 av. Victor-Hugo), near the train station, also offers a lovely selection of calissons.

In addition to its old-style markets and jewel-box candy shops, Aix is a modern shopping town—perhaps the best in Provence. The winding streets of the Vieille Ville above cours Mirabeau—centered around **rue Clemenceau, rue Marius Reinaud, rue Espariat, rue Aude,** and **rue Maréchal Foch**—have a head-turning parade of goods.

Meyrargues

55 *12 km (7 mi) northwest of Aix-en-Provence on the N96.*

A picturesque village dominated by a feudal fortress, Meyrargues has been a pilgrimage stop for more than nine centuries. The fortress, transformed into a château in the 17th century and into a four-star hotel in 1952, remains the chief attraction, but the little town nestled beneath the château's monumental flight of steps is perfectly charming in itself. The clay santons, or terra-cotta figurines, from the village factory are much coveted, the surrounding woods are great for horseback riding, and Monsieur Sallier's wines (Château de Vauclaire, Coteaux d'Aix) are among the most *buvable* (drinkable) in the region. There are two ancient chapels in the village, and three arches of a Roman aqueduct that once fed Aix-en-Provence still stand in a valley just behind the château's cemetery.

Where to Stay & Eat

★ **$$-$$$$** ✕▢ **Château de Meyrargues.** A Celtic outpost in 600 BC, a military fortress in AD 900: few places, even in France, have as much history as the Château de Meyrargues. Fewer still take paying guests. Constructed over six centuries, the imposing château, with its massive stone walls and staircase, is a truly formidable sight, perched high above the Durance Valley, lording over the medieval village from the top of a rocky outcrop, surrounded by hills of pine. The views are breathtaking, as are the spacious, Provençal-decorated rooms and luxurious baths. If you can't stay the night, at least try to fit in lunch or dinner in the excellent restaurant. ✉ *13650 Traverse St-Pierre, Meyrargues* ☎ *04-42-63-49-90* ⊟ *04-42-63-49-92* ⊕ *www.chateau-de-meyrargues.com* ⇥ *8 rooms, 3 suites* ♿ *Restaurant, minibars, 2 tennis courts, pool* ⊟ *AE, MC, V* ⊘ *Closed Nov.* ⃝ *FAP, MAP.*

Marseille

31 km (19 mi) south of Aix-en-Provence, 188 km (117 mi) west of Nice, 772 km (483 mi) south of Paris.

Marseille may sometimes be given a wide berth by travelers in search of a Provençal idyll, but it's their loss. Miss it and you miss one of the vibrant, exciting cities in France. With its Cubist jumbles of white stone rising up over a picture-book seaport, bathed in light of blinding clarity and crowned by larger-than-life neo-Byzantine churches, the city's neighborhoods teem with multiethnic life, its souklike African markets reek deliciously of spices and coffees, and its labyrinthine Vieille Ville is painted in broad strokes of saffron, cinnamon, and robin's-egg blue. Feisty and fond of broad gestures, Marseille is a dynamic city, as cosmopolitan now as when the Phoenicians first founded it, and with all the exoticism of the international shipping port it has been for 2,600 years. Vital to the Crusades in the Middle Ages and crucial to Louis XIV as a military port, Marseille flourished as France's market to the world—and still does today.

The heart of Marseille is clustered around the Vieux Port—immortalized in all its briny charm in the 1961 Leslie Caron film version of *Fanny*. The hills to the south of the port are crowned with mega-monuments, such as Notre-Dame de la Garde and Fort St-Jean. To the north lies the ramshackle hilltop Vieille Ville known as Le Panier. East of the port you'll find the North African neighborhood and, to its left, the famous thoroughfare called La Canebière. South of the city, the cliff-top waterfront highway leads to obscure and colorful ports and coves.

Note: If you plan on visiting many of the museums in Marseille buy a museum *passport* for €8 at the tourism office. It covers the entry fee into all the museums in Marseille.

56 One of many museums devoted to Marseille's history as a shipping port, is the **Musée de la Marine et de l'Economie de Marseille** (Marine and Economy Museum). Inaugurated by Napoléon III in 1860, this impressive building houses both the museum and the city's Chamber of Commerce. The front entrance and hallway are lined with medallions celebrating the ports of the world with which the city has traded, or trades still. The museum charts the maritime history of Marseille from the 17th-century onward with paintings and engravings. It's a model-lover's dream with hundreds of steamboats and schooners, all in miniature. ⊠ *Palais de la Bourse, 7 La Canebière, La Canebière* ☎ *04–91–39–33–33* 💶 *€3* ⊗ *Daily 10–6.*

57 With more than 3,000 outfits and accessories, the **Musée de la Mode de Marseille** (Marseille Fashion Museum) has well-displayed and ever-changing exhibitions about fashion, dating from the 1920's to the present. Thematic shows also highlight new and cutting-edge designers like Fred Sathel. ⊠ *11 La Canebière, La Canebière* ☎ *04–96–17–06–00* 💶 *€3* ⊗ *Tues.–Sun. 11–6.*

★ **58** The modern, open-space **Musée d'Histoire de Marseille** (Marseille History Museum) illuminates Massalia's history by mounting its treasure of archaeological finds in didactic displays. There's a real Greek-era wooden boat in a hermetically sealed display case. ⊠ *Centre Bourse, entrance on rue de Bir-Hakeim, Vieux Port* ☎ *04–91–90–42–22* 💶 *€2 includes entry into Jardin des Vestiges* ⊗ *Mon.–Sat. noon–7.*

59 The **Jardin des Vestiges** (Garden of Remains), just behind the Marseille History Museum, stands on the site of Marseille's classical waterfront and includes remains of the Greek fortifications and loading docks. It

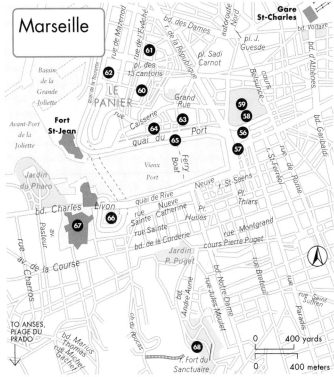

was discovered in 1967 when roadwork was being done next to the Bourse
(Stock Exchange). ✉ *Centre Bourse, Vieux Port* ☏ *04–91–90–42–22*
💶 *€2 includes entry to Museum of History* ☉ *Mon.–Sat. noon–7.*

★ ➌ **Le Panier** is the old heart of Marseille, a maze of high shuttered houses
looming over narrow cobbled streets, *montées* (stone stairways), and
tiny squares. Long decayed and neglected, it is the principal focus of the
city's efforts at urban renewal. Wander this atmospheric neighborhood
at will, making sure to stroll along rue du Panier, the montée des Ac-
coules, rue du Petit-Puits, and rue des Muettes.

★ ➍ At the top of the Panier district, the **Centre de la Vieille Charité** (Center
of the Old Charity) is a superb ensemble of 17th- and 18th-century architecture designed as a hospice for the homeless by Marseillais artist-
architects Pierre and Jean Puget. Even if you don't enter the museums,
walk around the inner court, studying the retreating perspective of
triple arcades and admiring the Baroque chapel with its novel egg-
peaked dome. Of the complex's two museums, the larger is the **Musée
d'Archéologie Méditerranée** (Museum of Mediterranean Archaeology),
with a sizable collection of pottery and statuary from classical Mediterranean civilization, elementally labeled (for example, "pot"). There's also

a display on the mysterious Celt-like Ligurians who first peopled the coast, cryptically presented with emphasis on the digs instead of the finds themselves. The best of the lot is the evocatively mounted Egyptian collection, the second largest in France after the Louvre's. There are mummies, hieroglyphs, and gorgeous sarcophagi in a tomblike setting. Upstairs, the **Musée d'Arts Africains, Océaniens, et Amérindiens** (Museum of African, Oceanic, and American Indian Art) creates a theatrical foil for the works' intrinsic drama: the spectacular masks and sculptures are mounted along a pure black wall, lighted indirectly, with labels across the aisle. ⊠ *2 rue de la Charité, Le Panier* ☎ *04–91–14–58–80* ⊠ *€2 per museum* ⊙ *May–Sept., Tues.–Sun. 11–6; Oct.–Apr., Tues.–Sun. 10–5.*

need a break?

With handsome decor and pale green walls, the pretty 1901 **Café Parisian** (⊠ 1 pl. Sadi Carnot, Le Panier ☎ 04–91–90–05–77) is always buzzing. It's where the club scene comes for breakfast while locals and tourists stop by later in the day. It opens at 4:30 AM and serves until around midnight.

62 A gargantuan, neo-Byzantine 19th-century fantasy, the **Cathédrale de la Nouvelle Major** (⊠ Pl. de la Major, Le Panier) was built under Napoléon III—but not before he'd ordered the partial destruction of the lovely 11th-century original, once a perfect example of the Provençal Romanesque style. You can view the flashy decor—marble and rich red porphyry inlay—in the newer of the two churches; the medieval one is being restored.

63 The **Musée du Vieux Marseille** (Museum of Old Marseille) is set in the 16th-century **Maison Diamantée** (Diamond House)—so named for its diamond-faceted Renaissance facade—and built in 1570 by a rich merchant. Focusing on the history of Marseille, the museum normally features santons, crèches, and furniture, offering a glimpse into 18th-century Marseille life. ⊠ *Rue de la Prison, Vieux Port* ☎ *04–91–55–28–69* ⊠ *€3* ⊙ *June–Sept., Tues.–Sun. 10–7; Oct.–May, Tues.–Sun. 10–5.*

In 1943 Hitler destroyed the neighborhood along the quai du Port—some 2,000 houses—displacing some 20,000 citizens. This act of brutal urban renewal, ironically, laid the ground open for new discoveries. When Marseille began to rebuild in 1947, they dug up remains of a Roman shipping warehouse full of the terra-cotta jars and amphorae that once **64** lay in the bellies of low-slung ships. The **Musée des Docks Romains** (Roman Docks Museum) created around it demonstrates the scale of Massalia's shipping prowess. ⊠ *2 pl. de Vivaux, Vieux Port* ☎ *04–91–91–24–62* ⊠ *€2* ⊙ *Oct.–May, Tues.–Sun. 10–5; June–mid-Sept., Tues.–Sun. 11–6.*

65 Departing from the quai below the Hôtel de Ville, the **Ferry Boat** is a **Fodor's**Choice Marseille treasure. To hear the natives pronounce "fer-ry bo-at" (they've ★ adopted the English) is one of the joys of a visit here. For a pittance you can file onto this little wooden barge and chug across the Vieux Port. ⊠ *Travels between pl. des Huiles on quai de Rive Neuve side and Hôtel de Ville on quai du Port, Vieux Port* ⊠ *€1.*

Founded in the 4th century by St-Cassien, who sailed into Marseille's port full of fresh ideas on monasticism acquired in Palestine and Egypt, ★ ⑥⑥ the **Abbaye St-Victor** grew to formidable proportions. With its severe exterior of crenellated stone and the spare geometry of its Romanesque church, the structure would be as much at home in the Middle East as its founder had been. The Saracens destroyed the first structure, so the abbey was rebuilt in the 11th century and fortified against further onslaught in the 14th. By far the best reason to come is the **crypt,** St-Cassien's original, which lay buried under the medieval church's new structure. In evocative nooks and crannies you'll find the 5th-century sarcophagus that allegedly holds the martyr's remains. Upstairs look for the reliquary containing what's left of St. Victor himself, who was ground to death between millstones, probably by Romans. ⌦ *Crypt entry* €2 ⊙ *Daily 8:30–6:30.*

⑥⑦ The twin structures of **Fort St-Nicolas and Fort St-Jean** flank the entrance to the Vieux Port. In order to keep the feisty, rebellious Marseillais under his thumb, Louis XIV had the fortresses built with the guns pointing *toward* the city. The Marseillais, whose local identity has always been mixed with a healthy dose of irony, are quite proud of this display of the king's (later justified) doubts about their allegiance. To view them, climb up to the Jardin du Pharo.

Towering above the city and visible for miles around, the preposterously ⑥⑧ overscaled neo-Byzantine monument called **Notre-Dame-de-la-Garde** was erected in 1853 by the ever-tasteful Napoléon III. Its interior is a Technicolor bonanza of red-and-beige stripes and glittering mosaics. The gargantuan *Madonna and Child,* on the steeple (almost 30 feet high), is covered in real gold leaf. The boggling panoply of naive ex-votos, mostly thanking the Virgin for death-bed interventions and shipwreck survivals, makes the pilgrimage worth it. ✛ *On foot, climb up cours Pierre Puget, cross Jardin Pierre Puget, cross bridge to rue Vauvenargues, and hike up to pl. Edon. Or catch Bus 60 from cours Jean-Ballard* ☎04–91–13–40–80 ⊙ *May–Sept., daily 7* AM*–8* PM*; Oct.–Apr., daily 7–7.*

off the
beaten
path

★

CHÂTEAU D'IF – François I, in the 16th century, recognized the strategic advantage of an island fortress surveying the mouth of Marseille's vast harbor, so he had one built. Its effect as a deterrent was so successful that it never saw combat, and was eventually converted into a prison. It was here that Alexandre Dumas locked up his most famous character, the Count of Monte Cristo. Though he was fictional, the hole Dumas had him escape through is real enough, and is visible in the cells today. Video monitors playing relevant scenes from dozens of Monte Cristo films bring each tower and cell to life. On the other hand, the real-life Man in the Iron Mask, whose cell is still being shown, was not actually imprisoned here. The boat ride (from the quai des Belges, €10) and the views from the broad terrace alone are worth the trip. ☎ *04–91–59–02–30* ⊕ *www. monuments-france.fr* ⌦ *Château €4.60* ⊙ *Apr.–Sept., daily 9–7; Oct.–Mar., Tues.–Sun. 9–5:30.*

Where to Stay & Eat

$$$$ ✕ **Chez Fonfon.** Tucked into a filmlike setting of the tiny fishing port Vallon des Auffes, this Marseillais landmark has one of the loveliest settings in greater Marseille. A variety of fresh seafood, impeccably grilled, steamed, or roasted in salt crust are served in two pretty dining rooms with picture windows overlooking the fishing boats that supply your dinner. Try classic bouillabaisse served with all the bells and whistles—broth, hot-chili rouille, and flamboyant table-side filleting. ☒ *140 rue du Vallon des Auffes, Vallon des Auffes* ☎ *04–91–52–14–38* ⊕ *www.chezfonfon.com* ⌦ *Reservations essential* ▭ *AE, DC, MC, V* ☺ *Closed Sun. and 1st 2 wks in Jan. No lunch Mon.*

★ **$$$$** ✕ **L'Epuisette.** Artfully placed on a rocky, fingerlike cliff surrounded by the sea, this seafood restaurant offers gorgeous views of crashing surf on one side and the port of Vallon des Auffes on the other. Chef Guillaume Sourrieu has acquired a big reputation (and Michelin stars) for sophisticated cooking—mullet fillets on a bed of peppers and eggplant, sauced with peppery rouille, or sea bass baked in a salt crust, are some top delights—all matched with a superb wine list. Save room for dessert. ☒ *Anse du Vallon des Auffes, Vallon des Auffes* ☎ *04–91–52–17–82* ▭ *AE, DC, MC, V* ☺ *Closed Mon. No lunch Sat. No dinner Sun.*

$$$$ ✕ **Mets de Provence.** Climb the oddly slanted wharf-side stairs and enter a cosseted Provençal world. With boats bobbing out the window and a landlubbing country decor, this romantic restaurant makes the most of Marseille's split personality. Classic Provençal hors d'oeuvres—tapenade, brandade, aioli—lead into seafood (dorade roasted with fennel and licorice) and meats (rack of lamb in herb pastry). The four-course lunch (€38, including wine) is marvelous. ☒ *18 quai de Rive-Neuve, Vieux Port* ☎ *04–91–33–35–38* ▭ *MC, V* ☺ *Closed Sun. No lunch Sat. No dinner Mon.*

$$$$ ✕ **Le Peron.** Chic and stylishly modern with its dark-wood interior and large windows overlooking the sea, this restaurant is the latest magnet for hip, young professionals. The staff are efficient and friendly; meals are well-presented and tasty—try grilled garlic scallops in a puree of purple potatoes or the lobster risotto—and the prix-fixe lunch menu at €43 is worth the splurge. The view is one of the best in the city. ☒ *56 Corniche J.-F.-Kennedy, Endoume* ☎ *04–91–52–15–22* ▭ *AE, DC, MC, V.*

$$–$$$$ ✕ **Les Arcenaulx.** At this book-lined, red-walled haven in the stylish book-and-boutique complex of a renovated arsenal, you can have a sophisticated regional lunch—and read while you're waiting. Look for mussels in saffron with buckwheat crêpes, carpaccio of cod with crushed olives, or rabbit with garlic confit. The terrace (on the Italian-scale cours d'Estienne d'Orves) is as pleasant as the interior. ☒ *25 cours d'Estienne d'Orves, Vieux Port* ☎ *04–91–59–80–30* ▭ *AE, DC, MC, V* ☺ *Closed Sun.*

$$–$$$$ ✕ **Baie des Singes.** On a tiny rock-ringed lagoon as isolated from the nearby city as if it were a desert island, this cinematic corner of paradise was once a customs house under Napoléon III. You can rent a mattress and lounge chair, dive into the turquoise water, and shower off for the only kind of food worthy of such a locale: fresh fish. It's all served at terrace tables overlooking the water. ⊠ *Anse des Croisettes, Les Goudes* ☎ *04–91–73–68–87* ▭ *MC, V* ⊘ *Closed Oct.–Mar.*

¢–$$ ✕ **Au Petit Naples.** With huge portions, a convivial atmosphere, and a small, busy beachfront location, this restaurant is jammed with locals and savvy tourists from every walk of life. Some connoisseurs say that the pizza here is even better than at Marseille's noted Etienne. ⊠ *14 plage de l'Estaque, L'Estaque* ☎ *04–91–46–05–11* ▭ *No credit cards* ⊘ *Closed Sun. No lunch Sat.*

★ ¢–$$ ✕ **Etienne.** This historic Le Panier hole-in-the-wall has more than just good fresh-anchovy pizza from a wood-burning oven. There are also fried squid, eggplant gratin, a slab of rare-grilled beef big enough for two, and the quintessential *pieds et paquets,* Marseille's earthy classic of sheeps' feet and stuffed tripe. Be warned: pizza is considered an appetizer here and main courses are huge. ⊠ *43 rue de la Lorette, Le Panier* ☎ *No phone* ▭ *No credit cards.*

★ $$$$ ✕▭ **Le Petit Nice.** On a rocky promontory overlooking the sea, this fantasy villa was bought from a countess in 1917 and converted to a hotel–restaurant. The Passédat family has been getting it right ever since, with father and son manning the exceptional kitchen (one of the coast's best), creating truffled brandade, sea-anemone beignets, fresh fish roasted whole, and licorice soufflé (the restaurant is closed Sunday and Monday for lunch in summer, and Sunday and Monday for lunch and dinner in winter; prix-fixe menus are €110 and €139). Most rooms are sleek and minimalist, with some art deco–cum–postmodern touches, while outside the fetching pool is illuminated at night by antique gaslight fixtures. ⊠ *Anse de la Maldormé, Corniche J.-F.-Kennedy, Endoume, 13007* ☎ *04–91–59–25–92* ▤ *04–91–59–28–08* ⊕ *www.petitnice-passedat.com* ⇕ *13 rooms, 3 suites* ⚘ *Restaurant, minibars, cable TV, pool, Internet, free parking, some pets allowed (fee)* ▭ *AE, DC, MC, V* ⦿*I MAP.*

★ $$–$$$$ ▭ **Mercure Beauvau Vieux Port.** Chopin has spent the night and George Sand kept a suite in this historic hotel overlooking the Vieux Port. It recently underwent a complete overhaul—even closing for over a year—but its loyal clientele were not disappointed when the doors finally reopened. Public rooms still have real antiques, burnished woodwork, Provençal-style decor, and plush carpets, all comprising a convincing part of this intimate urban hotel's genuine Old World charm. Guest rooms are in the same style but have been updated to include all the modern comforts. Harbor-view rooms, with balconies high over the fish market, more than justify the splurge. ⊠ *4 rue Beauvau, Vieux Port, 13001* ☎ *04–91–54–91–00, 800/637–2873 for U.S. reservations* ▤ *04–91–54–15–76* ⊕ *www.mercure.com* ⇕ *72 rooms* ⚘ *Minibars, cable TV, bar, Internet, some pets allowed (fee)* ▭ *AE, DC, MC, V.*

$ ▭ **Alizé.** On the Vieux Port, its front rooms taking in postcard views, this straightforward lodging has been modernized to include tight double-pane windows, slick modular baths, and a laminate-and-all-weather carpeted look. Public spaces have exposed stone and historic details, and a glass elevator whisks you to your floor. It's an excellent value and location for the price. ⊠ *35 quai des Belges, Vieux Port, 13001* ☎ *04–91–*

33–66–97 ☐ *04–91–54–80–06* ⊕ *www.alize-hotel.com* ➴ *39 rooms* ⎈ *Cable TV, some pets allowed (fee)* ☰ *AE, DC, MC, V.*

Nightlife & the Arts

With a population of more than 800,000, Marseille is a big city by French standards, with all the nightlife that entails. Arm yourself with *Marseille Poche,* a glossy monthly events minimagazine; the monthly *In Situ,* a free guide to music, theater, and galleries; *Sortir,* a weekly about film, art, and concerts in southern Provence; or *TakTik,* a hip weekly on theater and art. They're all in French. Rock, jazz, and reggae concerts are held at the **Espace Julien** (☒ 39 cours Julien, Préfecture ☎ 04–91–24–34–10). **Le Trolleybus** (☒ 24 quai de Rive Neuve, Bompard ☎ 04–91–54–30–45) is the most popular disco in town, with a young, *branché* (hip) crowd. Classical music concerts are given in the **Abbaye St-Victor** (☎ 04–91–05–84–48 for information). Operas and orchestral concerts are held at the **Opéra Municipal** (☒ 2 rue Molière, Vieux Port ☎ 04–91–55–21–24).

Sports & the Outdoors

Marseille's waterfront position makes it easy to swim and sunbathe within the city sprawl. From the Vieux Port, Bus 83 or Bus 19 will take you to the vast green spread of reclaimed land called the **Parc Balnéaire du Prado.** Its waterfront is divided into beaches, all of them public and well equipped. The beach surface varies between sand and gravel. Marseille is a mecca for diving (*plongée*), with several organizations offering *baptêmes* (baptisms, or first dives) to beginners. The coast is lined with rocky inlets, grottos, and ancient shipwrecks, not to mention thronging with aquatic life. For general information contact the **Centre de Loisirs des Goudes** (☒ 2 bd. Alexandre Dumas, Saint-Giniez, 13008 ☎☎ 04–91–25–13–16).

Shopping

Savon de Marseille (Marseille soap) is a household standard in France, often sold as a satisfyingly crude and hefty block in odorless olive-oil green. But its chichi offspring are dainty pastel guest soaps in almond, lemon, vanilla, and other scents.

The locally famous bakery **Four des Navettes** (☒ 136 rue Sainte, Garde Hill ☎ 04–91–33–32–12), up the street from Notre-Dame-de-la-Garde, makes orange-spice, shuttle-shape navettes. These cookies are modeled on the little boat in which Mary Magdalene and Lazarus washed up onto Europe's shores.

Aubagne

69 *16 km (10 mi) east of Marseille, 36 km (22 mi) south of Aix-en-Provence.*

You can spend a delightful morning browsing through Aubagne's Vieille Ville or basking on its broad plane tree–shaded squares. Aubagne claims the title of santon-making capital of Provence. The craft, originally from Marseille, was focused here at the turn of the 20th century, when artisans moved inland to make the most of local clay. The more than a dozen studios in town are set up for you to observe the production process. Make sure you visit Aubagne on a market day, when the sleepy center is transformed into a tableau of Provençal life. The Tuesday market is the biggest.

The town is proud of its native son, the dramatist, filmmaker, and chronicler of all things Provençal, Marcel Pagnol, best known as the author of *Jean de Florette* and *Manon des Sources* (*Manon of the Springs*) and the stories that comprise the Fanny trilogy. You can study miniature dioramas of scenes from Pagnol stories at **Le Petit Monde de Marcel Pagnol** (The Small World of Marcel Pagnol). ⊠ *Esplanade de Gaulle* 🕮 *Free* ☉ *Daily 9–noon and 2–6.*

Even if you haven't read Pagnol's works or seen his films, you can enjoy the **Circuit Pagnol,** a hike in the rough-hewn, arid *garrigues* (scrublands) behind Marseille and Aubagne. Here Pagnol spent his idyllic summers, described in his *Souvenirs d'un Enfance* (*Memories of a Childhood*). When he grew up to be a famous playwright and filmmaker, he shot some of his best work in these hills. After Pagnol's death, Claude Berri came back to find a location for his remake of *Manon des Sources,* but found it so altered by brush fires and power cables that he chose to shoot in the Luberon instead. Although the trail may no longer shelter the pine-shaded olive orchards of its past, it still gives you the chance to walk through primeval Provençal countryside and rewards you with spectacular views of Marseille and the sea. For an accompanied tour with literary commentary, contact the tourist office. ⊠ *To access marked trail by yourself, drive to La Treille, northeast of Aubagne, and follow signs* 🕾 *04–42–03–49–98 tourist office.*

Where to Eat

$–$$$ ✕ **La Farandole.** Cosseted here by rustic Provençal lemon-print cloths, lace curtains, and the region's typical bow-legged chairs, you can enjoy good home cooking with local regulars who claim the same table every day. The inexpensive daily menu may feature crisp green salad with foie gras in a raspberry vinaigrette, garlicky steak and *frites* (fries), or baked goat cheese; wine is included. ⊠ *6 rue Martino, off cours Maréchal, on a narrow street leading into Vieille Ville* 🕾 *04–42–03–26–36* ▭ *MC, V* ☉ *No dinner Sun. and Mon.*

Cassis

⑦ *11 km (7 mi) south of Aubagne, 30 km (19 mi) east of Marseille, 42 km (26 mi) west of Toulon.*

Surrounded by vineyards, flanked by monumental cliffs, guarded by the ruins of a medieval castle, and nestled around a picture-perfect fishing port, Cassis is the prettiest coastal town in Provence. Stylish without being too recherché, it provides shelter to numerous pleasure-boaters, who restock their galleys at its market, replenish their nautical duds in its boutiques, and relax with a bottle of Cassis and a platter of sea urchins in one of its numerous waterfront cafés. Pastel houses set at Cubist angles frame the port, and the mild rash of parking-garage architecture that scars its outer neighborhoods doesn't spoil the general effect, one of pure and unadulterated charm. The **Château de Cassis** has loomed over the harbor since the invasions of the Saracens in the 7th century, evolving over the centuries into a walled enclosure crowned with stout watch-towers. It's private property today and best viewed from a port-side café.

You can't visit Cassis without touring the **calanques,** the fjordlike finger bays that probe the rocky coastline. Either take a sightseeing cruise or hike across the cliff tops, clambering down the steep sides to these barely accessible retreats. Or you can combine the two, going in by boat and hiking back; make arrangements at the port. The calanque closest to Cassis is the least attractive: **Port Miou** was a stone quarry until 1982, when the calanques became protected sites. Now this calanque is an active leisure and fishing port. **Calanque Port Pin** is prettier, with wind-twisted pines growing at angles from the white-rock cliffs. But it's the third calanque

★ that's the showstopper: the **Calanque En Vau** is a castaway's dream, with a tiny beach at its root and jagged cliffs looming overhead. The series of massive cliffs and calanques stretches all the way to Marseille. Note that boats make round-trips several times a day to the Calanques de Cassis from Marseille's Quai des Belges. Here, boat tours to the Calanques are organized by the Groupement des Armateurs Côtiers Marseillais (⊠ 1 quai des Belges ☎ 04–91–55–50–09 ⊕ www.answeb.net/gacm); otherwise, contact the tourism office and they will give the right numbers to call, or they will help organize a tour for the visitor.

Where to Stay & Eat

$–$$$$ ✕ **Monsieur Brun.** One of the most authentic meals you can have in Cassis is a platter of raw shellfish. At this terrace bar-brasserie on the west side of the port, a multitiered tower of shellfish on a bed of kelp is served with nothing but bread, butter, and a finger towelette. Have the nutty little *bleues,* the local oyster, but *oursins* (sea urchins) are a Cassis specialty, and these are brought in daily by the chef's fisherman friend. Omelets and salads are other alternatives. ⊠ *2 quai Calendal* ☎ *04–42–01–82–66* ▤ *No credit cards* ✆ *Closed mid-Nov.–mid-Jan.*

$$–$$$ ✕ **Chez Nino.** This is the best of the many restaurants lining the harbor, with top-notch Provençal food and wine and a spectacular terrace view. The owners, Claudie and Bruno, are extremely hospitable as long as you stick to the menu—don't ask for sauce on the side—and you are as passionate about fish and seafood as they are. The sardines in *escabeche* are textbook perfect, as are the grilled fish and the bouillabaisse. ⊠ *Quai Barthélémy* ☎ *04–42–01–74–32* ▤ *AE, DC, MC, V* ✆ *Closed Mon. and mid-Dec.–mid-Feb. No dinner Sun. off-season.*

★ $$–$$$ ✕▦ **Jardin d'Émile.** Tucked back from the waterfront under quarried cliffs and massive parasol pines, this stylish, cozy inn takes in views of the cape. Rooms are intimate, with rubbed-chalk walls, scrubbed pine, and weathered stone. The restaurant (closed Wednesday) is atmospheric, on a sheltered terrace surrounded by greenery and, by night, the illuminated cliffs. Regional specialties with a cosmopolitan twist—such as snapper filled with goat cheese and wrapped in eggplant—are served on locally made pottery. ⊠ *Plage du Bestouan, 13260* ☎ *04–42–01–80–55* ▦ *04–42–01–80–70* ⊕ *www.lejardindemile.fr* ⇗ *7 rooms* ⚒ *Mini-bars, cable TV* ▤ *AE, DC, MC, V* ✆ *Closed mid-Nov.–mid-Dec.*

$$–$$$$ ▦ **Les Roches Blanches.** First built as a private home in 1887, this cliff-side villa takes in smashing views of the port and the Cap Canaille, both

from the best rooms and from the panoramic dining hall. The beautifully landscaped terrace is shaded by massive pines, and the horizon pool appears to spill into the sea. Yet the aura is far from snooty or deluxe; it's friendly, low-key, and pleasantly mainstream. ⊠ *Rte. des Calanques, 13260* ☎ *04–42–01–09–30* 🖷 *04–42–01–94–23* ⊕ *www.roches-blanches-cassis.com* ⤳ *19 rooms, 5 suites* ⚐ *2 restaurants, pool, bar, some pets allowed (fee); no a/c* ▤ *AE, MC, V* ❙◎❙ *MAP.*

Sports & the Outdoors

To go on a **boat ride** to Les Calanques, get to the port around 10 AM or 2 PM and look for a boat that's loading passengers. Round-trips should include visits to at least three calanques and average €10. To **hike** the calanques, gauge your skills: the GR98 (marked with red-and-white bands) is the most scenic, but requires scrambling to get down the sheer walls of En Vau. The alternative is to follow the green markers and approach En Vau from behind. If you're ambitious, you can hike the length of the GR98 between Marseille and Cassis, following the coastline.

en route   From Cassis head east out of town and cut sharply right up the **route des Crêtes.** This road takes you along a magnificent crest over the water and up to the very top of **Cap Canaille.** Venture out on the vertiginous trails to the edge, where the whole coast stretches below.

Bandol

71 *25 km (16 mi) southeast of Cassis, 15 km (9 mi) west of Toulon.*

Although its name means wine to most of the world, Bandol is also a popular and highly developed seaside resort town. It has seafood snack shacks, generic brasseries, a harbor packed with yachts, and a waterfront promenade. Yet the east end of town conceals lovely old villas framed in mimosas, bougainvillea, and pine. And a port-side stroll up the palm-lined allée Jean-Moulin feels downright Côte d'Azur. But be warned: the sheer concentration of high-summer crowds cannot be exaggerated. If you're not a beach lover, pick up an itinerary from the tourist office and visit a few Bandol vineyards just outside town.

Where to Eat

$$$$ ✕ **Auberge du Port.** This is a fish-first-and-foremost establishment, with a terrace packed night and day—and not because of the splendid view it offers of Ile Bandor. Going off menu for a daily catch special can be costly, but worth it if a memorable fish-dish experience has so far eluded you on the trip. Otherwise, try the excellent *friture* of small fish fried with lemon or the classic fish stew *bourride*. Get here early for something especially fresh and savory. And book ahead. ⊠ *9 allée Jean-Moulin* ☎ *04–94–29–42–63* ⚏ *Reservations essential* ▤ *AE, DC, MC, V.*

Brignoles

72 *86 km (47 mi) northwest of Bandol, 70 km (39 mi) north of Toulon.*

This rambling backcountry hill town, crowned with a medieval château, is the market center for the wines of the Var and the crossroads of this green, ungentrified region—until now, that is. With a Ducasse restaurant now in the region, real estate has rocketed, and le tout Paris whispers that this little corner of nowheresville is *the* next Luberon. The main point of interest in the region is the **Abbaye de La Celle**, a 12th-century Benedictine abbey that served as a convent until the 17th century, when it was closed because its young nuns had begun to run wild and were known less for their chastity than "the color of their petticoats and the name of their lover." There's a refectory and a ruined cloister; the simple Romanesque chapel still serves as the parish church.

Where to Stay & Eat

★ **$$$$** ✕🏨 **Hostellerie de l'Abbaye de La Celle.** Superchef Alain Ducasse put this country inn—buried in the unspoiled backcountry north of Toulon and just south of Brignoles—back on the map a decade ago. Up the road from the town's royal abbey, this beautifully restored 18th-century *bastide* (country house)—a dream in ocher-yellow walls, Arles green shutters, and white stone trim—was once part of the convent where future queens of Provence were raised. Guest rooms mix Louis XVI and regional accents; half are split-level with their own gardens, some with views of vineyards, others of a park thick with chestnut and mulberry tress. Beds are enormous—none more so than those of the Charles de Gaulle suite (where the great man once stayed). Wherever you bed down, the scent of fresh thyme and lemon basil wafts through the windows from the gardens. Today, the formidable kitchen is headed up by Chef Benoît Witz, whose seemingly magical creations find a superb balance between taste and texture: velouté of crawfish gently covering a bruschetta topped with tomatoes and garden herbs, or duck breast with polenta and cherries. ⊠ *Pl. du Général-de-Gaulle, 83170 La Celle* ☎ *04-98-05-14-14* 🖶 *04-98-05-14-15* ⊕ *www.abbaye-celle.com* 🛏 *9 rooms, 1 suite, 3 duplexes* ♿ *Restaurant, minibars, cable TV, pool, Internet, meeting room* ▭ *AE, DC, MC, V.*

Iles d'Hyères

 32 km (20 mi) off the coast south of Hyères. To get to the islands, follow the narrow Giens Peninsula to La Tour-Fondue, at its tip. Boats (leaving every half hour in summer, every 60 or 90 minutes rest of year, for €12 round-trip) make a 20-minute beeline to Porquerolles. For Port-Cros and Levant, you'll depart from Port d'Hyères at Hyères-Plages.

Off the southeastern point of France's star and spanning some 32 km (20 mi), this archipelago of islands could be a set for a pirate movie; in fact, it has been featured in several, thanks to a soothing microclimate and a wild and rocky coastline dotted with palms. And not only film pirates made their appearance: in the 16th century the islands were seeded with convicts to work the land. They soon ran amok and used their adopted base to ambush ships heading into Toulon. A more wholesome population claims the islands today, which are made up of three main areas. **Port-Cros** is a national park, with both its surface and underwater environs protected. **Levant** has been taken over, for the most part, by nudists.

★ **Porquerolles** is the largest and best of the lot—and a popular escape from the modern world. Off-season, it's a castaway delight of pine forests, sandy beaches, and vertiginous cliffs above rocky coastline. Inland, its preserved pine forests and orchards of olives and figs are crisscrossed with dirt roads to be explored on foot or on bikes; except for the occasional jeep or work truck, the island is car-free. In high season (April to October), day-trippers pour off the ferries and surge to the beaches. For information on the islands, contact the tourism office of Hyères.

Where to Stay & Eat

★ **$$$$** ✕🖭 **Mas du Langoustier.** A fabled forgetaway, the Langoustier comes with a lobster-orange building, pink bougainvillea, and a secluded spot at the westernmost point of the Ile de Porquerolles, 3 km (2 mi) from the harbor. Manager Madame Richard—who may pick you up at the port in her Dodge—knows a thing or two about the island: her grandmother was given the island as a wedding gift. Choose between big California-modern rooms and charming old-style Provençal. Chef Joël Guillet creates inspired, spectacular southern French cuisine, to be accompanied by the rare island rosé (note that prices include breakfast and dinner). ✉ *Pointe du Langoustier, 83400 Ile de Porquerolles* ☎ *04–94–58–30–09* 🖷 *04–94–58–36–02* ⊕ *www.langoustier.com* ↪ *50 rooms* ♿ *Restaurant, minibars, cable TV, tennis court, beach, billiards, Internet* ▭ *AE, DC, MC, V* ☉ *Closed Nov.–Apr.* ⑩ *MAP.*

$$$–$$$$ ✕🖭 **Le Manoir.** A mix of southern-coast bourgeois and Provençal decor adds a splash of color to the sunlit airy rooms of this family-owned colonial-style hotel. Private patios overlook a large secluded park bordered by eucalyptus, pink oleanders, and palm trees. Thoughtful service and absolute calm firmly encourage relaxation. After a day of hiking through forests, swimming in the pool, or simply sitting on the flower-filled terrace, you can partake of chef Vincent Cordier's delicious, hearty Provençal fare in the rather plainly decorated restaurant. With a price that includes both your meals and your accommodation, this is a gentle touch of civilization in the isolated wilderness. ✉ *Ile de Port Cros, 83400* ☎ *04–94–05–90–52* 🖷 *04–94–05–90–89* ↪ *23 rooms* ♿ *Restaurant, bar; no a/c in some rooms, no room TVs* ▭ *MC, V* ☉ *Closed end of Oct.–mid-Apr.* ⑩ *MAP.*

$$$ ✕🖭 **Les Glycines.** In soft shades of yellow-ocher and sky-blue, this sleekly modernized little bastide has an idyllic enclosed courtyard. Back rooms look over a jungle of mimosa and eucalyptus. Public salons have Provençal chairs and fabrics. The restaurant, where food is served on the terrace or in the garden, proffers port-fresh tuna and sardines. The inn is just back from the port in the village center. Prices include breakfast and dinner. ✉ *Pl. d'Armes, 83400 Ile de Porquerolles* ☎ *04–94–58–30–36* 🖷 *04–94–58–35–22* ⊕ *www.porquerolles.net* ↪ *8 rooms, 3 suites* ♿ *Restaurant, cable TV, bar, Internet; no a/c* ▭ *AE, MC, V* ⑩ *MAP.*

The Outdoors

You can rent a mountain bike (*velo tout-terrain,* or VTT) for a day to pedal the paths and cliff-top trails of Porquerolles at **Cycle Porquerol** (✉ Rue de la Ferme ☎ 04–94–58–30–32). **L'Indien** (✉ Pl. d'Armes ☎ 04–94–58–30–39) offers a wide variety of bikes. **Locamarine 75** (✉ On port ☎ 04–94–58–35–84) rents motorboats to amateurs with or without license.

PROVENCE A TO Z

To research prices, get advice from other travelers, and book travel arrangements, visit www.fodors.com.

AIR TRAVEL

Marseille is served by frequent flights from Paris and London, and daily flights from Paris arrive at the smaller airport at Nîmes, which serves Arles and the Camargue (the trip takes about an hour). There are direct flights in summer from the United States to Nice, 160 km (100 mi) from Aix-en-Provence.

BIKE & MOPED TRAVEL

Bikes can be rented from the train stations in Aix-en-Provence, Arles, Avignon, Marseille, Nîmes, and Orange at a cost of about €10 per day. Contact the Comité Départemental de Cyclotourisme for a list of scenic bike routes in Provence.

🚲 Bike Maps **Comité Départemental de Cyclotourisme** ⊠ Les Passadoires, 84420 Piolenc ☎ 04-90-29-64-80.

BUS TRAVEL

A moderately good network of bus services—run by a perplexing number of independent bus companies (for best advice on schedules, consult the town tourist office or your hotel concierge)—links places not served, or poorly served, by train. If you plan to explore Provence by bus, Avignon, Marseille, Aix-en-Provence, and Arles are good bases. Avignon is also the starting point for excursion-bus tours and boat trips down the Rhône. In most cases, you can buy bus tickets on the bus itself.

Aix-en-Provence: One block west of La Rotonde, the station (rue Lapierre) is crowded with many bus companies, which offer numerous regional connections, the farthest links being Orange, Nice, Marseille, Avignon, and Arles. **Arles:** The gare routière (av. Paulin Talabot) is adjacent to the train station. Five buses leave daily for Aix-en-Provence and Marseille (only two run on weekends); others travel daily to Avignon and Nîmes. **Avignon:** The bus station is right by the rail station on boulevard St-Roch; lines connect to nearby towns such as Châteauneuf-du-Pape and Fontaine-de-Vaucluse. **Les Baux:** Buses here head for Avignon or Arles. **Nîmes:** The bus station (rue Ste-Félicité) connects with Montpellier, Pont du Gard, and many other places. **Marseille:** The station (3 pl. Victor Hugo) is next to the train station and offers myriad connections to cities and small towns. St-Rémy-de-Provence is 40 minutes from Avignon by bus. **Orange:** The station is on cours Pourtoules, on the eastern edge of the city, and offers links to Avignon, Vaison-la-Romaine, and Marseille. **Pont du Gard:** This is a 40-minute ride from Nîmes; you are dropped off 1 km (½ mi) from the bridge at the Auberge Blanche. **Stes-Maries-de-la-Mer:** As the gateway to the Camargue region (in which there is little or no public transportation), buses head here from Arles, Nîmes, and Aigues-Mortes. For a complete list of bus Web sites for the region, log on to www.provence-jouques.com/fr/venir/venir15.html.

🚌 Bus Information **Les Cars Lieutaud** ☎ 04-90-36-05-22 ⊕ www.cars-lieutaud.fr. **Ceyte Tourisme Méditerranée** ☎ 04-90-93-74-90.

CAR RENTAL

🛈 Local Agencies Avis ✉ 11 bd. Gambetta, Aix ☎ 04-42-21-64-16 ✉ At train station, Avignon ☎ 04-90-27-96-10 ✉ At train station, Marseille ☎ 04-91-64-71-00 ✉ 19 av. Charles de Gaulle, Orange ☎ 04-90-34-11-00.

Budget ✉ Bd. St-Roch, Avignon ☎ 04-90-27-94-95 ✉ 42 bd. Edouard Daladier, Orange ☎ 04-90-34-00-34.

Hertz ✉ 43 av. Victor Hugo, Aix ☎ 04-42-27-91-32 ✉ 2A av. Monclar, Avignon ☎ 04-90-14-26-90 ✉ Train station, Marseille ☎ 04-91-90-14-03.

CAR TRAVEL

A6–A7 (a toll road) from Paris, known as the Autoroute du Soleil—the Highway of the Sun—takes you straight to Provence, where it divides at Orange, 659 km (412 mi) from Paris; the trip can be done in a fast five or so hours.

After route A7 divides at Orange, A9 heads west to Nîmes (723 km [448 mi] from Paris) and continues into the Pyrénées and across the Spanish border. Route A7 continues southeast from Orange to Marseille, on the coast (1,100 km [680 mi] from Paris), while A8 goes to Aix-en-Provence (with a spur to Toulon) and then to the Côte d'Azur and Italy.

LODGING

APARTMENT-VILL
A RENTALS
Properties for rent in Provence are listed by the national house-rental agency, Gîtes de France. Regional offices are in Bouches-du-Rhône, Gard, Var, and Vaucluse. In addition, each of the tourist offices in towns in the region usually publishes lists of independent rentals (*locations meublés*), many of them inspected and classified by the tourist office itself.

🛈 Local Agents Bouches-du-Rhône ✉ Domaine du Vergon, B.P. 26, 13370 Mallemort ☎ 04-90-59-49-40 🖨 04-90-59-16-75. **Gard** ✉ 3 pl. des Arènes, B.P. 59, 30007 Nîmes, Cedex 4 ☎ 04-66-27-94-94 🖨 04-66-27-94-95. **Var** ✉ 1 bd. Maréchal Foch, Draguignan ☎ 04-94-50-93-93 🖨 04-94-50-93-90. **Vaucluse** ✉ Pl. Campana, B.P. 164, Cedex 1, 84008 Avignon ☎ 04-90-85-45-00.

BED &
BREAKFASTS
Gîtes de France, the French national network of vacation lodging, rates participating B&Bs for comfort and lists them in a catalog. For chambres d'hôtes regulated by this national network, contact the local branches, divided by *départements* (administrative regions).

TOURS

PRIVATE GUIDES
Bus tours through the Camargue, departing from Avignon with a passenger pick-up in Arles (behind the tourism office, in front of the Atrium hotel, 9:45 AM) are offered by Self-Voyages Provence for about €45. Ask about the optional riverboat trip down the Rhône. Taxis T.R.A.N. can take you round-trip from Nîmes to the Pont du Gard (ask the taxi to wait while you explore for 30 minutes).

🛈 Self Voyages Provence ✉ 42 bd. Raspail, 84000 Avignon ☎ 04-90-14-70-00 ⊕ www.self-voyages.fr. **Taxis T.R.A.N** ☎ 04-66-29-40-11.

WALKING TOURS
The tourist offices in Arles, Nîmes, Avignon, Aix-en-Provence, and Marseille all organize a full calendar of walking tours (some in summer only).

TRAIN TRAVEL

The high-speed TGV *Méditerranée* line ushered in a new era in Trains à Grande Vitesse travel in France; the route (lengthened last year from the old terminus, Valence, in Haute Provence) means that you can travel from Paris's Gare de Lyon to Avignon in two hours and 40 minutes, with a mere three-hour trip to Nîmes, Aix-en-Provence, and Marseille. Not only is the idea of Provence as a day-trip now possible (though, of course, not advisable), you can even whisk yourself there directly upon arrival at Paris's Charles de Gaulle airport.

After the main line of the TGV divides at Avignon, the westbound link heads to Nîmes and points west; heading east, the line connects with Orange. The southeast-bound link takes in Marseille, Toulon, and the Côte d'Azur. Montpellier is the stop after Nîmes, with other links at Béziers and Narbonne. There is also frequent service by daily local trains to other towns in the region from these main TGV stops. With high-speed service now connecting Nîmes, Avignon, and Marseille, travelers without cars will find a Provence itinerary much easier to pull off. For full information on the TGV *Méditerranée,* log onto the TGV Web site; you can purchase tickets on this Web site or through RailEurope, and you should always buy your TGV tickets in advance.

Aix-en-Provence: The station (pl. Victor Hugo) is a five-minute walk from place du Général-de-Gaulle and offers many connections, with hourly departures to Marseille. **Arles:** The train station (av. Paulin Talabot) has frequent trains to Avignon, Nîmes, Marseille, and other stops. **Avignon:** The Gare d'Avignon (bd. St-Roch) is across from the entrance to the walled city—easy connections here include Arles, Nîmes, Marseille, and Aix-en-Provence. **Marseille:** The station (esplanade St-Charles) serves all regions of France and is at the northern end of center city, a 20-minute walk from the Vieille Ville. Trains run almost hourly to Arles, Aix-en-Provence, Avignon, and Nice. **Nîmes:** Frequent trains connect with Arles, Avignon, Montpellier, and Marseille; to reach the Vieille Ville from the station, walk north on avenue Fauchères. **Orange:** The center city is a 15-minute walk from the train station—walk from avenue Frédéric Mistral to rue de la République, then follow signs.

🚹 Train Information **SNCF** ☎ 08-36-35-35-35 ⊕ www.ter-sncf.com/uk/paca. **TGV** ⊕ www.tgv.com.

TRAVEL AGENCIES

🚹 Local Agent Referrals **Havas** ✉ 4 bd. des Lices, Arles ☎ 04-90-18-31-31 ✉ 35 rue de la République, Avignon ☎ 04-90-80-66-80 ✉ 44 bd. Victor Hugo, Nîmes ☎ 04-66-36-99-99 ✉ 34 rue de la République, Orange ☎ 04-90-11-44-44. **Nouvelle Frontières** ✉ 14 rue Carnot, Avignon ☎ 04-90-82-31-32. **Provence-Camargue Tours** ✉ 1 rue Émile Fassin, Arles ☎ 04-90-49-85-58.

VISITOR INFORMATION

Regional tourist offices prefer written queries only. The mother lode of general information is the Comité Regional du Tourisme de Provence-Alpes-Côte d'Azur. For information specific to one département, contact the following: Comité Départemental du Tourisme des Bouches-du-Rhône, Comité Départemental du Tourisme du Var, Comité

Départemental du Tourisme de Vaucluse. Local tourist offices for major towns covered in this chapter can be phoned, faxed, or addressed by mail.

⚑ Regional Tourist Offices **Comité Regional du Tourisme de Provence-Alpes-Côte d'Azur** ✉ 12 pl. Joliette, 13002 Marseille ☎ 04-91-56-47-00 🖷 04-91-56-47-01 ⊕ www.crt-paca.fr/fre/accueil_flash.jsp. **Comité Départemental du Tourisme des Bouches-du-Rhône** ✉ 13 rue Roux de Brignole, 13006 Marseille ☎ 04-91-13-84-13 🖷 04-91-33-01-82 ⊕ www.visitprovence.com. **Comité Départemental du Tourisme du Var** ✉ 1 bd. Maréchal Foch, 83300 Draguignan ☎ 04-94-50-55-50 🖷 04-94-50-55-51 ⊕ www.tourismevar.com. **Comité Départemental du Tourisme de Vaucluse** ✉ B.P. 147, Cedex 1, 84008 Avignon ☎ 04-90-80-47-00 🖷 04-90-86-86-08.

⚑ Local Tourist Offices **Aigues-Mortes** ✉ pl. St. Louis, 30220 ☎ 04-66-53-73-00 🖷 04-66-53-65-94 ⊕ www.ot-aiguesmortes.fr. **Aix** ✉ 2 pl. du Général-de-Gaulle, B.P. 160, Cedex 1, 13605 ☎ 04-42-16-11-61 🖷 04-42-16-11-62 ⊕ www.aixenprovencetourism.com. **Arles** ✉ 35 pl. de la République, 13200 ☎ 04-90-18-41-21 🖷 04-90-93-17-17 ⊕ www.ville-arles.fr. **Avignon** ✉ 41 cours Jean-Jaurès, 84000 ☎ 04-90-82-65-11 🖷 04-90-82-95-03 ⊕ www.ot-avignon.fr. **Camargue** ✉ 1 pl. Frederic Mistral 13800 St. Gilles du Gard ☎ 04-66-87-33-75 🖷 04-66-87-16-28 ⊕ www.ot-saint-gilles.fr. **Cassis** ✉ Quai des Moulins, 13260 ☎ 04-08-92-25-98-92 🖷 04-92-01-28-31 ⊕ www.cassis.fr. **Fontaine-de-Vaucluse** ✉ Chem de la Fontaine, 84800 ☎ 04-90-20-32-22 🖷 04-90-20-21-37 ⊕ www.oti-delasorgue.fr.

Gordes ✉ Le Chateau, 84220 ☎ 04-90-72-02-75 🖷 04-90-72-02-26 ⊕ www.gorges-village.com. **Hyères** ✉ 3 av. Ambroise Thomas, 83400 ☎ 04-94-01-84-50 🖷 04-94-01-84-51 ⊕ www.ot-hyeres.fr. **L'Isle-sur-la-Sorgue** ✉ Pl. de l'Églisé 84800 ☎ 04-90-38-04-78 🖷 04-90-38-35-43 ⊕ ot-islessurlasorgue.fr. **Le Barroux** ✉ 2 pl. du Général-de-Gaulle, B.P. 160, Cedex 1, 13605 ☎ 04-42-16-11-61 🖷 04-42-16-11-62 ⊕ www.aixenprovencetourism.com. **Les-Baux-de-Provence** ✉ Maison du Roi 13520 ☎ 04-90-54-34-39 🖷 04-90-54-51-15 ⊕ www.lesbauxdeprovence.com. **Marseille** ✉ 4 la Canebière, 13001 ☎ 04-91-13-89-00 🖷 03-91-13-89-20 ⊕ www.destination-marseille.com. **Nîmes** ✉ 6 rue Auguste, 3000 ☎ 04-66-67-29-11 🖷 04-66-21-81-04 ⊕ www.ot-nimes.fr. **Orange** ✉ 5 cours Aristide Briand 84110 ☎ 04-90-34-70-88 🖷 04-42-16-11-62 ⊕ www.ville-orange.fr. **Roussilon** ✉ 2 pl. de la Poste, 84220 ☎ 04-90-05-60-25 🖷 04-90-05-63-31 ⊕ www.roussilon-provence.com. **St-Rémy** ✉ Pl. Jean-Jaurès, 13210 ☎ 04-90-92-05-22 🖷 04-90-92-38-52 ⊕ www.saintremy-de-provence.com. **Stes-Maries-de-la-Mer** ✉ 5 av. Van Gogh 13700 ☎ 04-90-97-82-55 🖷 04-90-97-71-15 ⊕ www.saintesmaries.com. **Tarascon** ✉ 59 rue des Halles ☎ 04-90-91-03-52 🖷 04-90-91-22-96 ⊕ www.tarascon.org. **Vaison la Romaine** ✉ pl. Chanoene Sautel 84110 ☎ 04-90-36-02-11 ⊕ www.vaison-la-romaine.

The Côte d'Azur

WORD OF MOUTH

"The best way to stay on the Riviera is to stay in the small towns. For example, Villefranche-sur-Mer is minutes by train from Nice; Antibes is minutes by train from Cannes. Both towns have darling seaside cafés and restaurants. If you need a more extensive scene, simply hop the frequent, easily accessible trains to the Riviera's big cities."

—Amelia

"Some years back, we would take those fabulous walks along the shore from Beaulieu each day. On one occasion, we fell into step with a really charming chap who said he did that walk every single day from his house. We all stopped in at a café for something to drink and continued talking for a long time. The guy was David Niven."

—Nukesafe

Introduction by
Nancy Coons

Updated by
Sarah Fraser

WITH THE ALPS AND PRE-ALPS PLAYING bodyguard against inland winds and the sultry Mediterranean warming the breezes, the Côte d'Azur is pampered by a nearly tropical climate. This is where the dreamland of azure waters and indigo sky begins, where balustraded white villas edge the blue horizon, the evening air is perfumed with jasmine and mimosa, and parasol pines are silhouetted against sunsets of ripe apricot and gold. As emblematic as the sheet-music cover for a Jazz Age tune, the Côte d'Azur seems to epitomize happiness, a state of being the world pursues with a vengeance.

But the Jazz Age dream confronts modern reality: on the hills that undulate along the blue water, every cliff, cranny, gully, and plain bristles with cubes of hot-pink cement and balconies of ironwork, each skewed to catch a glimpse of the sea and the sun. Like a rosy rash, these crawl and spread, outnumbering the trees and blocking each other's views. Their owners and renters, who arrive on every vacation and at every holiday—Easter, Christmas, Carnival, All Saints' Day—choke the tiered highways with bumper-to-bumper cars, and on just about any day in high summer the traffic to the beach—slow-moving at any time—coagulates and blisters in the hot sun.

There has always been a rush to the Côte d'Azur (or Azure Coast), starting with the ancient Greeks, who were drawn eastward from Marseille to market their goods to the natives. From the 18th-century English aristocrats who claimed it as one vast spa, to the 19th-century Russian nobles who transformed Nice into a tropical St. Petersburg, to the 20th-century American tycoons who cast themselves as romantic sheiks, the beckoning coast became a blank slate for their whims. Like the modern vacationers who followed, they all left their mark—villas, shrines, Moroccan-fantasy castles-in-the-air—temples all to the sensual pleasures of the sun and the sultry sea breezes. Artists, too, made the Côte d'Azur their own, as museum goers who have studied the sunny legacy of Picasso, Renoir, Matisse, and Chagall will attest. Today's admirers can take this all in, along with the Riviera's textbook points of interest: animated St-Tropez; the Belle Époque aura of Cannes; the towns made famous by Picasso—Antibes, Vallauris, Mougins; the urban charms of Nice; and a number of spots where the per-capita population of billionaires must be among the highest on the planet: Cap d'Antibes, Villefranche-sur-Mer, and Monaco. The latter, once a Belle Époque fairyland, has for some time been known as the Hong Kong of the Riviera, a bustling community where the sounds of drills tearing up the ground for new construction has mostly replaced the clip-clop of the horse-drawn fiacres. The ghosts of Grace Kelly and Cary Grant must have long since gone elsewhere.

Veterans of the area know that the beauty of the Côte d'Azur coastline is only skin deep, a thin veneer of coddled glamour that hugs the water and hides a more ascetic region up in the hills. These low-lying mountains and deep gorges are known as the *arriére-pays* (backcountry) for good cause: they are as aloof and isolated as the waterfront resorts are in the swim. Medieval stone villages cap rocky hills and play out scenes of Provençal life—the game of boules, the slowly savored *pastis* (the anise-and-licorice-flavored spirit mixed slowly with water), the farmers' market—as if the ocean were a hundred miles away. Some of them—Èze, St-Paul, Vence—have become virtual Provençal theme parks, catering to busloads of tourists day-tripping from the coast. But just behind them, dozens of hill towns stand virtually untouched, and you can lose yourself in a cobblestone maze.

You could drive from St-Tropez to the border of Italy in three hours and take in the entire Riviera, so small is this renowned stretch of Mediterranean coast. Along the way you'll undoubtedly encounter the downside: jammed beaches, insolent waiters serving frozen seafood, traffic gridlock. But once you dabble your feet off the docks in a picturesque port full of brightly painted boats, or drink a Lillet in a hilltop village high above the coast, or tip your face up to the sun from a boardwalk park bench and doze off to the rhythm of the waves, you—like the artists and nobles who succumbed before you—will very likely be seduced to linger.

Exploring the Côte d'Azur

You can visit any spot between St-Tropez and Menton in a day trip; the hilltop villages and towns on the coastal plateau are just as accessible. Thanks to the efficient raceway, A8, you can whisk at high speeds to the exit nearest your destination up or down the coast; thus, even if you like leisurely exploration, you can zoom back to your home base at day's end. The lay of the land east of Nice is nearly vertical, as the coastline is one great cliff, a corniche terraced by three parallel highways—the **Basse Corniche,** **Moyenne Corniche,** and the **Grande Corniche**—that snake along its graduated crests. The lowest (*basse*) is the slowest, following the coast and crawling through the main streets of resorts—including downtown Monte Carlo, Cap-Martin, Beaulieu, and Villefranche-sur-Mer. The highest (*grande*) is the fastest, but its panoramic views are blocked by villas, and there are few safe overlooks. The middle (*moyenne*) runs from Nice to Menton and offers views down over the shoreline and villages—it passes through a few picturesque towns, most notably Èze. Above the autoroutes, things slow down considerably, but you'll find exploring the winding roads and overlooks between villages an experience in itself.

About the Restaurants & Hotels

Even in tiny villages some haute cuisine places can be as dressy, if not more so, as those in Monaco, but in general, restaurants on the Côte d'Azur are quite relaxed. At lunchtime, a T-shirt and shorts are just fine in all but the fanciest places; bathing suits, however, should be kept for the beach. Nighttime wear is casual, too—but be aware that for after-dinner drinks, many clubs and discos draw the line at running shoes and jeans.

If you've come from other regions in France—even western Provence— you'll notice a sharp hike in hotel prices, costly by any measure, but actually vertiginous in summer. In Cannes and Nice the grand hotels are big on prestige and weak on swimming pools, which are usually just big enough to dip in; their private beaches are on the opposite side of the busy street, and you pay for access, just as nonguests do. It's up in the hills above the coast that you'll find the charm you expect from France, both in sophisticated hotels with gastronomic restaurants and in friendly mom-and-pop

This is the Riviera of Hollywood lore, a land of sunglasses, convertibles, and palm trees lording it over indigo surf. From glamorous St-Tropez and Cannes through picturesque Antibes to sophisticated Nice, this sprawl of pebble beaches and ocher villas has captivated sun lovers and socialites since the days of the Grand Tour. Artists, too: Renoir, Matisse, Picasso, and Cocteau all reveled in its light and adored the golden hill towns of Old Provence: St-Paul, Vence, and Grasse.

Numbers in the text correspond to numbers in the margin and on the Côte d'Azur: St-Tropez to Cannes; the Côte d'Azur: Cannes to Menton; Nice; and Monaco maps.

If you have 3 days

Base yourself for the first two days in **Antibes** 10, exploring the **Cap d'Antibes** 12—one of the few places in the region where the legend lingers; rich and residential, this 3-km-long (2-mi-long) peninsula is studded with private delights (great villas) and public wonders (the Jardin Thuret). Make a day-trip westward to **Cannes** 8, a town that maintains its grand-tour grace and glamour even after the film stars head home from its famous film festival; then stop in Picasso country at **Vallauris** 13; or head inland for **Vence** 16 and **St-Paul-de-Vence** 17, two gorgeous hill towns famous for their modern art treasures (Matisse's Chapelle du Rosaire among them). After your St-Paul overnight, on Day 3 explore the museums and the Vieille Ville of **Nice** 19–36, where buildings are sumptuously adorned with wedding-cake half-domes and cupolas.

If you have 5 days

Spend your first day and night in **St-Tropez** 1, whose fishing-village cachet translates into port-front cafés thick with young gentry affecting nonchalance but peeping furtively over their sunglasses in hope of sighting a film star, then make an excursion up to the hill villages of **Ramatuelle** 2 and **Gassin** 3—the latter has a fetching medieval ambience. The next day cruise (or, in high summer, crawl along) the coastal highway N98, stopping to visit **Fréjus** 5, home to Roman ruins and a fine cathedral. Still on N98, wind around the dramatic Corniche de l'Estérel and make a triumphant entry into **Cannes** 8, straight down La Croisette. Spend your third morning in **Antibes** 10—be sure to visit the famous Château Grimaldi and Picasso museum—then head inland for an afternoon in **Vence** 16 or **St-Paul-de-Vence** 17, both good stopovers (and where hotel dining rooms are often hung with Braque sketches). Day 4 could be spent in dazzling **Nice** 19–36. Then escape for a quiet night in **St-Jean-Cap-Ferrat** 39, a lush peninsula that shelters the lovely gardens of the Musée Ephrussi de Rothschild. On your last day bet your return ticket on the baccarat tables in **Monaco** 42–51.

If you have 8 days

Expand the five-day itinerary with a second night in Cannes so you can make a boat trip to one of the idyllic **Iles de Lérins** 9. Spend two nights in Nice so you can take in the Matisse and Chagall museums and see the Baroque churches in the Vieille Ville. Then spend two nights in **Menton** 53 to visit its heavenly gardens and then make an excursion to **Roquebrune** 52 to see its château and walk the length of the cape.

auberges (inns); the farther north you drive, the lower the prices. Assume all hotel rooms have air-conditioning, TV, telephones, and private bath, unless otherwise noted. Internet, when listed in facilities, means in-room data ports and/or public-area computer provides computer access.

	$$$$	$$$	$$	$	¢
WHAT IT COSTS In euros					
RESTAURANTS	over €30	€23–€30	€17–€23	€11–€17	under €11
HOTELS	over €190	€120–€190	€80–€120	€50–€80	under €50

Restaurant prices are per person for a main course at dinner only, including tax (19.6%) and service; note that if a restaurant offers only prix-fixe (set-price) meals, it has been given the price category that reflects the full prix-fixe price. Hotel prices are for a standard double room in high season, including tax (19.6%) and service charge; higher prices (inquire when booking) prevail for any meal plans. Hotels operate on the European Plan (EP, with no meal provided) unless we note that they use the Breakfast Plan (BP), or also offer such options as Modified American Plan (MAP, with breakfast and dinner daily, known as *demi-pension*), or Full American Plan (FAP, or *pension complète*, with three meals a day). Inquire when booking if these all-inclusive mealplans (which always entail higher rates) are mandatory or optional.

Timing

Unless you enjoy jacked-up prices, traffic jams, and sardine-style beach crowds, avoid the coast like the plague in July and August. Many of the better restaurants simply shut down to avoid the coconut-oil crowd, and the Estérel is closed to hikers during this flash-fire season. Cannes books up early for the film festival in May, so aim for another month (April, June, September, or October). Between Cannes and Menton, the Côte d'Azur's gentle microclimate usually provides moderate winters; it's protected by the Estérel from the mistral wind that razors through places like Fréjus and St-Raphaël.

ST-TROPEZ TO ANTIBES

Flanked at each end by subtropical capes and crowned by the red-rock Estérel, this stretch of the coast has a variety of waterfront landmarks. St-Tropez first blazed into fame when it was discovered by painters like Paul Signac and writers like Colette, and since then it has never looked back. It remains one of the most animated stretches of territory on the Côte d'Azur, getting flooded at high season with people who like to roost at waterfront cafés to take in the passing parade. St-Tropez vies with Cannes for name recognition and glamour, but the more modest resorts—Ste-Maxime, Fréjus, and St-Raphaël—offer a more affordable Riviera experience. Historic Antibes and jazzy Juan-les-Pins straddle the subtropical peninsula of Cap d'Antibes

St-Tropez

▶ ❶ *35 km (22 mi) southwest of Fréjus, 66 km (41 mi) northeast of Toulon.*

At first glance, St-Tropez really doesn't look all that lovely: there's a moderately pretty port full of bobbing boats, a picturesque *Vieille Ville* (Old

12

Relishing the Riviera

The Côte d'Azur is home to such posh villages as Mougins, a medieval township filled with restaurants that showcase the "new Mediterranean cuisine" in all its costly splendor: "scrambled" sea urchins; herb sausages with chopped truffles and lobster; frogs' legs soup with fresh mint; Sisteron lamb with Madeira sauce; and poached sea bass flan with crayfish sauce. Grand names like Alain Ducasse still present such delights at showplaces like Le Louis XV, but there are any number of young stars on the make—Jean-Paul Battaglia at Mougins's Le Feu Follet, to name one. But you can also go the less-than-*haute* route and simply stock up with fixings for a country picnic at any of the village food markets, such as the great one in Valbonne. In between the high and the low, you'll want to get to know the main regional delights. Typical throughout the Côte d' Azur, but especially at home with a slab of fresh coastal fish, the garlicky mayonnaise called aioli is a staple condiment—in many areas of the region this delight is called *la rouille*. Even more pungent is the powerful paste called *anchoiade*, made of strong, salty anchovies. Fresh Mediterranean fish, such as *rouget* (mullet) and *loup* (sea bass), are often served grilled with a crunch of fennel. Niçois specialties include the *pissaladière*, the father of modern pizza, topped with a heap of caramelized onions. Try *socca*, a paste of ground chickpeas smeared on a griddle and scraped up like a gritty pancake; *petits farcis*, a selection of red peppers, zucchini, and eggplant stuffed with spicy sausage paste and roasted; and sardine beignets, fresh, whole sardines fried in a thick puff of spicy batter. Down it all with a glass of one of the great regional rosé wines.

Picasso & Company

Because the Côte d'Azur has long nurtured a relationship among artists, art lovers, and wealthy patrons, this region is blessed with superb art museums. Renoir, Picasso, Matisse, Chagall, Cocteau, Léger, and Dufy all left their mark here; museums devoted to their work are scattered along the coast, most notably the Musée Picasso at Antibes's Château Grimaldi, the smaller Picasso museum in Vallauris, Renoir's house in Cagnes, and the Matisse museum in Nice (not forgetting Matisse's sublime Chapelle de Rosaire in Vence). Formidable collections of modern masters and contemporary works can be seen in the museums of Nice and at the Fondation Maeght above St-Paul, while St-Tropez has a good collection of Impressionist paintings of its port at the Musée de l'Annonciade.

Sunbelievable Beaches

With their worldwide fame as the earth's most glamorous beaches, the real thing often comes as a shock to first-timers: much of the Côte d'Azur is lined with rock and pebble, and the beaches are narrow swaths backed by city streets or roaring highways. Only St-Tropez, Cannes, and isolated bits around Fréjus and Antibes have sandy waterfronts, hence their legendary popularity. Many beaches are privately operated, renting parasols and mattresses to anyone who pays; if you're a guest at one of the local hotels, you'll get a discount. Fees for private beaches average €6–€15 for a dressing room and mattress, between €2 and €4 for a parasol, and between €10 and €25 for a cabana to call your own. Private beaches alternate with open stretches of public frontage.

Town) in candied-almond hues, sandy beaches, and old-fashioned squares with plane trees and *pétanque* (lawn bowling) players. So what made St-Tropez a household name? In two words: Brigitte Bardot. When this *pulpeuse* (voluptuous) teenager showed up in St-Tropez on the arm of the late Roger Vadim in 1956 to film *And God Created Woman,* the world snapped to attention. Neither the gentle descriptions of writer Guy de Maupassant (1850–93) nor the watercolor tones of Impressionist Paul Signac (1863–1935), nor even the stream of painters who followed him (including Matisse and Bonnard) could focus the world's attention on this seaside hamlet as could this one luscious female, in head scarf, Ray-Bans, and capri pants. With the film world following in her steps, St-Tropez became the hot spot it—to some extent—remains. What makes it worthwhile is if you get up early (before the 11 o'clock breakfast rush at Le Gorille Café, and other port-side spots lining quai Suffern and quai Jean-Jaurès), and wander the medieval backstreets and waterfront by yourself, you'll experience what the artists found to love: its soft light, warm pastels, and the scent of the sea wafting in from the waterfront.

Anything associated with the distant past seems almost absurd in St-Tropez. Still, the place has a history that predates the invention of the string bikini, and people have been finding reasons to come here since AD 68, when a Roman soldier from Pisa named Torpes was beheaded for professing his Christian faith in front of Emperor Nero, transforming this spot into a place of pilgrimage. Since then people have come for the sun, the sea, and, more recently, the celebrities. The latter—ever since St-Tropez became "hot" again, there have been Elton, Barbra, Oprah, Jack, and Puffy sightings—stay hidden in villas, so the people you'll see are mere mortals, lots of them, many intent on displaying the best, and often the most, of their youth, beauty, and wealth. Still, if you take an early morning stroll along the harbor or down the narrow medieval streets—the rest of the town will still be sleeping off the Night Before—you'll see just how charming St-Tropez is. There's a weekend's worth of boutiques to explore and many cute cafés where you can sit under colored awnings and watch the spectacle that is St-Trop (*trop* in French means too much) saunter by. Along medieval streets lined with walled gardens and little squares set with dripping fountains you'll be able to discover historic delights like the Chapelle de la Misericorde, topped by its wrought-iron campanile, and Rue Allard, lined with picturesque houses such as the "Maison du Maure." In the evening, everyone moves from the cafés on the quais to the cafés on the squares, particularly place des Lices, where a seat at the Café des Arts allows you to watch the boule players under the glow of hundreds of electric bulbs. Paging Deborah Kerr and David Niven in *Bonjour Tristesse.*

★ Happily, the legacy of the artists who loved St-Tropez has been preserved in the extraordinary **Musée de l'Annonciade** (Annunciation Museum), a 14th-century chapel converted to an art museum that alone merits a visit to St-Tropez. Cutting-edge temporary exhibitions keep visitors on their toes while works by Signac, Matisse, Signard, Braque, Dufy, Vuillard, and Rouault, many of them painted in (and about) St-Tropez, trace the evolution of painting from Impressionism to Expressionism. ✉ *Quai de l'Épi/pl. Georges*

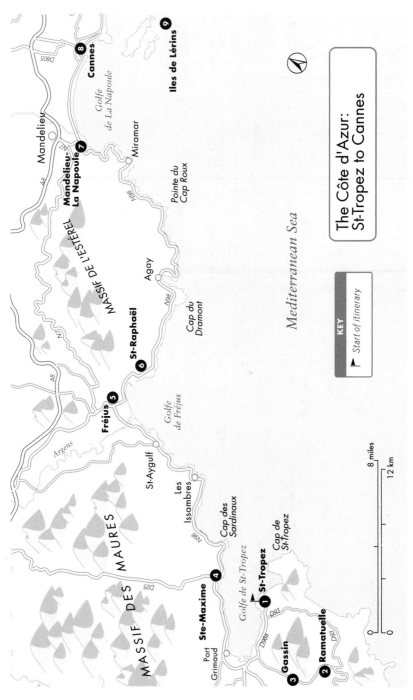

> **585**

The Côte d'Azur:
St-Tropez to Cannes

KEY

▲ Start of itinerary

Mediterranean Sea

Cannes ⑧

Iles de Lérins ⑨

Golfe
de La Napoule

Mandelieu

Mandelieu-
La Napoule ⑦

Miramar

Pointe du
Cap Roux

MASSIF DE L'ESTÉREL

Agay

St-Raphaël ⑥

Cap du
Dramont

Fréjus ⑤

Golfe
de Fréjus

Argens

St-Aygulf

Les
Issambres

Cap des
Sardinaux

MASSIF DES MAURES

Port
Grimaud

Ste-Maxime ④

Golfe de St-Tropez

Cap de
St-Tropez

St-Tropez ①

Gassin ③

Ramatuelle ②

8 miles

12 km

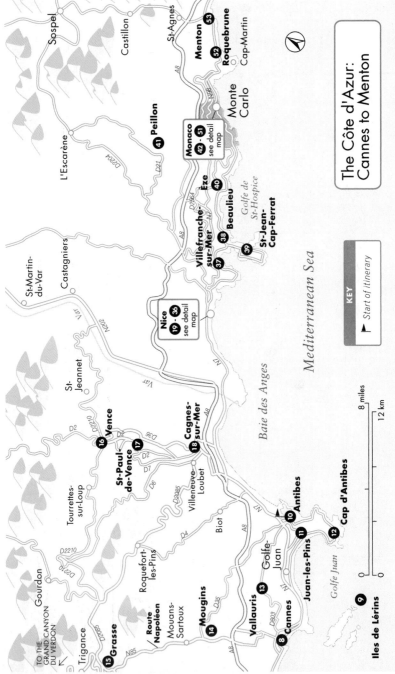

The Côte d'Azur:
Cannes to Menton

KEY

▲ Start of itinerary

Mediterranean Sea

Grammont ☎ *04–94–97–04–01* ✉ *€4.50* ⊙ *June–Sept., Wed.–Mon. 10–1 and 3–7; Oct. and Dec.–May, Wed.–Mon. 10–noon and 2–6.*

From the quai, head up rue Laugier and rue de la Citadelle to the 16th-century **Citadelle,** which stands in a lovely hilltop park; its ramparts offer a fantastic view of the town and the sea. Although hard to imagine St-Tropez as a military outpost amidst today's bikini-clad sun worshipers, inside the Citadelle's donjon, the **Musée Naval** (Naval Museum) displays ship models, cannons, maps, and pictures of St-Tropez from its days as a naval port. Right on the coast is the lovely **Cimetière Marin,** where some notable natives are buried, including film director Roger Vadim. In places, the waves lap up just a few feet from the graves. ⊠ *Rue de la Citadelle* ☎ *04–94–97–06–53* ✉ *€4* ⊙ *Dec.–Easter, Wed.–Mon. 10–12:30 and 1:30–5:30; Easter–Oct., daily 9–12:30 and 1:00–6:30.*

From the citadel head back down and lose yourself in the **Quartier de la Ponche,** the Vieille Ville maze of backstreets and old ramparts daubed in shades of gold, pink, ocher, and sky-blue. Trellised jasmine and wrought-iron birdcages hang from shuttered windows, and many of the tiny streets dead-end at the sea. Wander back across rue Citadelle to the medieval rue Miséricorde, which leads to the 17th-century Chapelle de la Miséricorde, and on to rue Gambetta. Chances are you won't bump into La Bardot—she spends most of her time at her villa, La Madrague, which overlooks the Plage des Canebiers.

Where to Stay & Eat

$$–$$$$ ✗**Lei Mouscardins.** Breton-born chef Laurent Tarridec left the Bistrot des Lices for this spectacular seaside locale offering 180-degree sea views, just on the edge of St-Tropez's Vieille Ville. His cooking, however, maintains the sophisticated tradition of upscale Provençal cuisine: opt for a frothy mullet soup, hearty rabbit stew, escargots with chickpea and lentils, or the tender, long-simmered veal. Fixed-price menus are €58, €98, and €130. ⊠ *Tour du Portalet* ☎ *04–94–97–29–00* ⊕ *www.leimouscardins. com/* ☰ *AE, DC, MC, V* ⊙ *Closed Tues. and mid-Nov.–mid-Dec. and mid-Jan.–mid-Feb.*

$$–$$$$ ✗**La Table du Marché.** With an afternoon tearoom and a summer sushi bar, this charming bistro, masterminded by celebrity chef Christophe Leroy, offers up a mouthwatering spread of regional specialties. For something light, sink into one of the overstuffed armchairs in the upstairs dining room, cozy with warm colors, chic Provençal accents, and antique bookshelves, and try the tomato pistou tart or dive into an €18 or €26 set menu. ⊠ *38 rue Georges Clemenceau* ☎ *04–94–97–85–20* ⊕ *www. christophe-leroy.com* ☰ *AE, MC, V.*

$–$$$ ✗**Le Girelier.** Like his father before him, chef Yves Rouet makes an effort to prepare Mediterranean-only fish for his buffed and bronzed clientele, who enjoy the casual sea-shanty decor and the highly visible Vieux Port–terrace tables. Grilling is the order of the day, with most fish sold by weight, but this is also a stronghold of bouillabaisse. The €33 set menu is one of the best bargains in town. ⊠ *Quai Jean-Jaurès* ☎ *04–94–97–03–87* ⊕ *www.legirelier.com* ☰ *AE, DC, MC, V* ⊙ *Closed Nov.–Mar. and Mon. No lunch July and Aug.*

CloseUp

THE DOGS OF ST-TROPEZ

N AD 68 the **Roman emperor Nero** *had a centurion from Pisa decapitated for his Christian tendencies; to drive the lesson home for witnesses, he had the headless body placed in a boat with a cock and a dog, then set adrift at sea. When the boat washed ashore on St-Tropez's beach, the starving animals still kept their loyal vigil, refusing to touch the holy flesh.*

Perhaps it's because of this heroic act of self-discipline that dogs are held in such high esteem in modern St-Tropez. They are clearly the companion (and accessory) of choice, as prevalent as mobile phones in the Vieux Port cafés.

Whether tucked into handbags, strutted in pairs as beautifully matched as coach horses, dyed to match their mistress's hair, bounding nobly out of yachts, snarling at each other from under café tables, or lapping out of the ice bucket that chilled the champagne, they provide a spectacle almost as intriguing as their owners.

If you want to get the right port-front table at Le Gorille, consider borrowing a dog and accessorizing appropriately. Want to look like your yacht's being swabbed down for that lunch-run to Monte Carlo? A Lhasa Apso to match your ascot. Showing those canvases you daubed in the Alps last winter? Hot pants, hip-length hair, Timberlands, and an Afghan hound.

Your bistro courting the Festival crowd out of Cannes? Green Lacoste sweater, red toupée, red German shepherd. Just drawn up a marriage contract to cover the London flat and Daddy's domain in Burgundy? Matching buckskin jackets, separate phones, and a twinned team of golden retrievers.

$$$$ ✕▨ **Le Byblos.** Arranged like a toy Provençal village, fronted with stunning red, rust, and yellow facades, and complete with ocher-stucco cottagelike suites grouped around courtyards landscaped with palms, olive trees, and lavender, this longtime fave of the glitterati stresses fitness and beauty treatment. Guest rooms are *à la provençale,* but modern in comfort. Chef Georges Pelissier creates artful classics with a Mediterranean touch: sea bass roasted with salsify and garlic chips or rib-sticking beef tournedos with foie gras. Opt for more nouvelle Med fireworks (try the excellent sweet and sour tuna with wok vegetables) on offer at **Spoon Byblos** (⊠ entrance on av. du Maréchal-Foch ☎ 04–94–56–68–20). The latest outpost of superstar chef Alain Ducasse, it boasts a client list that includes the likes of George Clooney, Naomi Campbell, and Jack Nicholson. As evening falls, all head to the hotel's Caves du Roy—a gigantic disco extravaganza where squillionaires have been seen buying champagne by the carton for the crowd. ⊠ *Av. Paul-Signac, 83990* ☎ *04–94–56–68–00* 🖶 *04–94–56–68–01* ⊕ *www. byblos.com* ⊶ *52 rooms, 43 suites* ⚭ *2 restaurants, minibars, cable TV, pool, gym, health club, spa, nightclub, babysitting, Internet, meeting room, free parking, some pets allowed (fee)* ▭ *AE, DC, MC, V* ⊘ *Closed mid-Oct.–Easter.*

\$\$\$\$ ⏍🏨 **La Résidence de la Pinède.** Perhaps the most opulent of St-Tropez's luxe hangouts, this balustraded white villa and its broad annex sprawl elegantly along a private waterfront, wrapped around an isolated courtyard and a pool shaded by parasol pines. Louis XVI bérgères, a beam here and there, gilt frames, indirect spots, and oh-so-comfy beds make for an alluring if somewhat homogenized interior. Pay extra for a seaside room, where you can lean over the balcony and take in broad coastal views and the large seafront restaurant; the chef has a celebrated reputation, and you'll understand why after one taste of his truffled ravioli. Rates including half-board are available. ⊠ *Plage de la Bouillabaisse, 83991* ☎*04-94-55-91-00* 📠*04-94-97-73-64* ⊕*www.residencepinede. com* ↪ *35 rooms, 4 suites* ⚭ *Restaurant, minibars, cable TV, pool, bar, Internet, meeting room, free parking, some pets allowed (fee)* ⊟ *AE, DC, MC, V* ⊗ *Closed mid-Oct.–mid-Apr.* ⏍❘ *MAP.*

\$\$–\$\$\$ 🏨 **Ermitage.** Surrounded by mimosas and lemon trees, this big, old-fashioned, tangerine-hue hotel is on a hill above town and, from its back rooms and garden, commands striking sea views. The fireplace and colonial rattan in the bar; the solid, light-bathed rooms in soft pastels; and owner Annie Bolloreis's friendly welcome make this a real charmer. ⊠*Av. Paul-Signac, 83990* ☎ *04-94-97-52-33* 📠 *04-94-97-10-43* ↪ *27 rooms* ⚭ *Bar, free parking, some pets allowed (fee); no a/c* ⊟ *MC, V.*

★ **\$–\$\$** 🏨 **Lou Cagnard.** Inside an enclosed garden courtyard, this pretty little hotel is owned by an enthusiastic young couple that is fixing it up room by room. Five ground-floor rooms open onto the lovely manicured garden, where breakfast is served in the shade of a fig tree. Freshly decorated rooms have regional tiles and Provençal fabrics. ⊠ *18 av. Paul Roussel, 83900* ☎ *04-94-97-04-24* 📠 *04-94-97-09-44* ⊕ *www. hotel-lou-cagnard.com* ↪ *19 rooms* ⚭ *Some pets allowed (fee); no a/c* ⊟ *MC, V* ⊗ *Closed Nov.–late Dec.*

Nightlife & the Arts

The most elite and sought-after nightspot in St-Tropez is the evergreen **Les Caves du Roy** (⊠ Byblos Hotel, av. Paul-Signac ☎ 04-94-97-16-02). **Le Papagayo** (⊠ Résidence du Port ☎ 04-94-54-88-18 ⊕ www. lepapagayo.com), a vast disco, caters to a crowd of young teens and twentysomethings. The **VIP Room** (⊠ Residence du nouveau Port ☎ 04-94-97-14-70 ⊕ www.viproom.fr) draws a chic mix of young professionals and baby boomers. Every July and August, **classical music concerts** (⊠ Rte. des Salins ☎ 04-94-97-45-21 information) are given in the gardens of the Château de la Moutte. For ticket information inquire at the tourist office.

The Outdoors

The best *plages* (beaches) are scattered along a 5-km (3-mi) stretch reached by the Route des Plages (Beach Road); the most fashionable are **Moorea** and **Club 55**; the most daring is the mostly topless **Tahiti.** Those beaches close to town—**Plage des Greniers** and the **Bouillabaisse**—are accessible on foot, but many prefer the 10-km (6-mi) sandy crescent at **Les Salins** and the long, sandy stretch of the **Plage de Pampelonne,** 4 km (3 mi) from town. Bicycles are an ideal way to get to the beach, and **Espace 83** (⊠ 2 av. Général-Leclerc ☎ 04-94-55-80-00) is a popular place for rentals.

Holiday Bikes (⊠ 14 av. Général-Leclerc ☎ 04–94–97–09–39) offers a wide variety of bikes for hire.

Shopping

Rue Sibilli, behind the quai Suffren, is lined with all kinds of trendy boutiques. The **place des Lices** overflows with produce, regional foods, clothing, and *brocantes* (collectibles) on Tuesday and Saturday mornings. The picturesque little fish market fills up **place aux Herbes** every morning.

Ramatuelle

❷ *12 km (7 mi) southwest of St-Tropez.*

A typical hilltop whorl of red-clay roofs and dense inner streets topped with arches and lined with arcades, this ancient market town was destroyed in the Wars of Religion and rebuilt as a harmonious whole in 1620, complete with venerable archways and vaulted passages. Now its souvenir shops and galleries attract day-trippers out of St-Tropez, who enjoy the pretty drive through the vineyards as much as the village itself. The town cemetery is the final resting place of Gérard Phillipe, an aristocratic heartthrob who died in 1959 after making his mark in such films as *Le Diable au Corps.*

en route From Ramatuelle the lovely ride to the hilltop village of Gassin takes you through vineyards and woods full of twisted cork oaks over the highest point of the peninsula (1,070 feet).

Where to Stay & Eat

$$$$ ✕▣ **Les Moulins.** A satellite of planet St-Tropez, this outpost of showbiz chef Christophe Leroy lures off-duty celebrities and the swank to its lovely perch near Pampelonne beach. Ceiling fans, rattan chairs, and blond-wood accents heighten the pleasure of the scrumptious dishes served here—don't miss out on the vichyssoise with truffles. Upstairs are five cozy, rustic guest rooms. ⊠ *Route des Plages, 83350* ☎ *04-94-97-17-22* 🖷 *04-94-97-11-46* ⊕ *www.christophe-leroy.com* 🛏 *5 rooms* 🖒 *Restaurant, cable TV, some pets allowed* 🖃 *AE, MC, V* ☉ *Closed Nov.–Mar.* ⑩ *MAP.*

$$$$ ✕▣ **Villa Marie.** With its circa-1930's feel, exposed beams, super-chic acid-toned walls and jewel-colored upholstery, this latest hot spot is getting rave reviews. More like a private villa than a hotel, almost all rooms have a secluded terrace. Guests happily relax in the luxurious spa or by the carefully landscaped pool, while the more energetic fuel up with the mod-Med cuisine in the charming restaurant. Try the the delicious homemade fois gras with apricots and sage. ⊠ *Chemin Val Rian, 83350* ☎ *04-94-97-40-22* 🖷 *04-94-97-37-55* ⊕ *www.c-h-m.com* 🛏 *32 rooms* 🖒 *Restaurant, minibars, pool, Internet, spa, some pets allowed (fee)* 🖃 *AE, DC, MC, V.* ☉ *Closed Dec. and Jan.*

$$ ✕▣ **Ferme Ladouceur.** Not far from the talcum-powder beach of Pampelonne and surrounded by vineyards is this *naïf* farmhouse, domain of Constance Ladouceur, whose paintings adorn the hallways and whose restaurant is a draw for budget-minded locals. Quirky, simple, affordable, with breakfast included in the price—little wonder you need to book

here far in advance. ⊠ *Quartier la Rouillère, 83350* 🕾 *04–94–79–24–95* 🖷 *04–94–79–12–14* 🖙 *7 rooms* ⚍ *Restaurant, some pets allowed; no a/c, no room phones, no room TVs* ⊟ *AE, MC, V* ⊘ *Closed Nov.–Mar.* ⊚Ⅼ *BP.*

Gassin

❸ *7 km (4½ mi) north of Ramatuelle.*

Though not as picturesque as Ramatuelle, this hilltop village gives you spectacular views over the surrounding vineyards and St-Tropez's bay. In winter, before the summer haze drifts in and after the mistral has given the sky a good scrub, you may be able to make out a brilliant white chain of Alps looming on the horizon. There's less commerce here to keep you distracted; for shops, head to Ramatuelle.

Where to Stay & Eat

$$$–$$$$ ✕🖾 **Villa Belrose.** Perched on the highest point of the peninsula, this Holleywoodesque palace has unrivaled views of the Gulf of St-Tropez and the kind of decadently rich élan that would make Scott and Zelda feel right at home. Public salons have Louis XVI and Florentine accents, and guest rooms are spacious yet cozy, with marble bathrooms and romantic balconies. Besides the 180-degree views, the restaurant, run by Alain Ducasse disciple Thierry Thiercelin, supplies first-rate Mediterranean cuisine, pleasant service, and a top-drawer wine list. Rates including half-board are available. ⊠ *Bd. des Crètes, 83580* 🕾 *04–94–55–97–97* 🖷 *04–94–55–97–98* ⊕ *www.relaischateaux.fr* 🖙 *35 rooms, 3 suites, 2 apartments* ⚍ *Restaurant, minibars, cable TV, pool, spa, bar, Internet, parking (fee), some pets allowed (fee)* ⊟ *AE, DC, MC, V* ⊘ *Closed Nov.–mid Mar.* ⊚Ⅼ *MAP.*

Ste-Maxime

❹ *8 km (5 mi) east of Port-Grimaud, 33 km (20 mi) east of St-Tropez.*

You may be put off by the heavily built-up waterfront bristling with parking-garage-style apartments and hotels, and its position directly on the waterfront highway, but Ste-Maxime is an affordable family resort with fine sandy beaches. It even has a sliver of car-free Vieille Ville and a stand of majestic plane trees sheltering central place Victor-Hugo. The main beach, north of town, is the wide and sandy La Nartelle.

Fréjus

❺ *19 km (12 mi) northeast of Ste-Maxime, 37 km (23 mi) northeast of St-Tropez.*

After a stroll on the sandy curve along the tacky, overcommercial Fréjus-Plage (Fréjus Beach), turn your back on modern times and head uphill to Fréjus-Centre. Here you'll enter a maze of narrow streets lined with small shops barely touched by the cult of the lavender sachet. The farmers' market (Monday, Wednesday, and Saturday mornings) is as real and lively as any in Provence, and the cafés encircling the fountains and squares nourish an easygoing social scene.

Yet Fréjus has the honor of owning some of the most important historic monuments on the coast. Founded in 49 BC by Julius Caesar himself and named Forum Julii, this quiet town was once a thriving Roman city of 40,000 citizens. Today you can see the remains. Just outside the Vieille Ville is the Roman **Théâtre Antique**; its remaining rows of arches are mostly intact, and much of its stage works is still visible at its center. The **Arènes** (often called the Amphithéâtre) is still used today for concerts and bull-fights. Back down on the coast, a big French naval base occupies the spot where ancient Roman galleys once set out to defeat Cleopatra and Mark Anthony at the Battle of Actium.

★ Set 5 km ([2.5] mi) north of Fréjus on the RN7 is the eccentric **La Chapelle Notre Dame de Jérusalem.** Designed by Jean Cocteau as part of an artists' colony that never happened, it is unusual not only for its oc-tagonal shape, stained glass, and frescos depicting the mythology of the first Crusades, but also because the tongue-in-cheek painting of the apos-tles above the front door boasts the famous faces of Coco Chanel, Jean Marais, and poet Max Jacob. ⊠ *Av. Nicolaï, la Tour de la Mare* ☎ *04–94–53–27–06* 🖼 *Free* ⊙ *Nov.–Mar., daily 2:30–5:30; Apr.–Oct. daily 2–6.*

Fréjus is also graced with one of the most impressive religious monuments in Provence: called the **Groupe Épiscopal**, it's made up of an early Gothic
★ **cathedral,** a 5th-century Roman-style **baptistery,** and an early Gothic **clois-ter,** its gallery painted in sepia and earth tones with a phantasmagoric assortment of animals and biblical characters. Off the entrance and gift shop is a small museum of finds from Roman Fréjus, including a com-plete mosaic and a sculpture of a two-headed Hermès. ⊠ *58 rue de Fleury* ☎ *04–94–51–26–30* 🖼 *Cathedral free; cloister, museum, and baptistery €4.60* ⊙ *Cathedral daily 8:30–noon and 2–6. Cloister, museum, and bap-tistery Apr.–Sept., daily 9–6; Oct.–Mar., Tues.–Sun. 9–noon and 2–5.*

St-Raphaël

❻ *1 km (½ mi) southeast of Fréjus, 41 km (25½ mi) southwest of Cannes.*

Right next door to Fréjus, with almost no division between, is St-Raphaël, a sprawling resort town with a busy downtown anchored by a casino. It's also a major sailing center, has five golf courses nearby, and draws the weary and indulgent to its seawater-based thalassother-apy. It serves as a major rail crossroads, the closest stop to St-Tropez. The port has a rich history: Napoléon landed at St-Raphaël on his tri-umphant return from Egypt in 1799; it was also from here in 1814 that he cast off for Elba in disgrace. And it was here, too, that the Allied forces landed in their August 1944 offensive against the Germans.

Where to Stay & Eat

$$$–$$$$ ✕ **La Bouillabaisse.** Enter through the beaded curtain covering the open doorway to a wood-panel room decked out with starfish and the mounted head of a swordfish: this classic hole-in-the-wall has a brief, straightforward menu inspired by the fish markets. You might have the half lobster with spicy *rouille* (peppers and garlic whipped with olive

oil), the seafood-stuffed paella, or the generous house bouillabaisse. ⊠ *50 pl. Victor-Hugo* ☎ *04–94–95–03–57* ▤ *AE, MC, V* ⊘ *Closed Mon.*

★ $ ▥ **Le Thimothée.** The owners of this bargain lodging are throwing themselves wholeheartedly into improving an already attractive 19th-century villa. They've also restored the garden, with its grand palms and pines shading the walk leading to a pretty little swimming pool. Though it's tucked away in a neighborhood far from the waterfront, top-floor rooms have poster-perfect sea views. ⊠ *375 bd. Christian-Lafon, 83700* ☎ *04–94–40–49–49* 🖷 *04–94–19–41–92* ⊕ *www.thimothee. com* ⇨ *12 rooms* ⌂ *Minibars, cable TV, pool, parking; no a/c in some rooms* ▤ *AE, MC, V.*

| en route | The rugged **Massif de l'Estérel,** between St-Raphaël and Cannes, is a hiker's dream. Made up of rust-red volcanic rocks (porphyry) carved by the sea into dreamlike shapes, the harsh landscape is softened by patches of lavender, scrub pine, and gorse. By car, take N7, the mountain route to the north, and lose yourself in the desert landscape far from the sea. Or keep on N98, the **Corniche de l'Estérel** (the coastal road along the dramatic corniche), and drive past little coves dotted with sunbathers, tiny calanques and sheer rock faces plunging down to the waves. Try to leave early in the morning, as tempers tend to fray when the route gets congested with afternoon traffic. |

Mandelieu–La Napoule

❼ *32 km (20 mi) northeast of St-Raphaël, 8 km (5 mi) southwest of Cannes.*

La Napoule is the small, old-fashioned port village devoured by the big-fish resort town of Mandelieu. You can visit Mandelieu for a golf-and-sailing retreat—the town is replete with many sporting facilities and hosts a bevy of sporting events, including sailing regattas, windsurfing contests, golf championships (there are two major golf courses in Mandelieu right in the center of town by the sea), and, every August, the Kelly Challenge, a rowing regatta named after Grace Kelly's father, a keen oarsman—and La Napoule for a port-side stroll, a meal, or a tour of its peculiar castle.

★   Set on Pointe des Pendus (Hanged Man's Point), the **Château de la Napoule,** looming over the sea and the port, is a bizarre hybrid of Romanesque, Gothic, Moroccan, and Hollywood cooked up by the eccentric American sculptor Henry Clews (1876–1937). Working with his architect-wife, he transformed the 14th-century bastion into something that suited his personal expectations and then filled the place with his own fantastical sculptures. Fond of spouting Nietzsche to his titled dinner guests, surrounding himself with footmen and lackeys, and dedicating his house to Don Quixote (its name is actually "Mancha"), Clews may have had a dubious artistic vision but he certainly enjoyed a vibrant sense of fantasy. The couple resides in their tombs in the tower crypt, its windows left slightly ajar to permit their souls to escape and allow them to "return at eventide as sprites and dance upon the windowsill." Today the château's foundation hosts visiting writers and artists, who set to work surrounded by Clews's gargoyle-ish sculptures. ⊠ *Av. Henry*

Clews ☎ 04–93–49–95–05 ⊕ *www.chateau-lanapoule.com* ✉ €6 ☉ *Guided visits daily at 11:30, 2:30, and 3:30.*

Where to Stay & Eat

$$$$ ✕ **L'Oasis.** This Gothic villa by the sea is home to Stéphane Raimbault, a master of Provençal cuisine and a great connoisseur of Asian techniques and flavorings. The combination creates unexpected delights—Jabugo ham with anise, lobster, and ginger, or Thai-spiced crayfish with squid-ink ravioli—all exceedingly delicious *and* beautifully presented on a garden terrace filled with plants. ✉ *Rue J. H. Carle* ☎ 04–93–49–95–52 ⊕ *www.oasis-raimbault.com* ▤ *AE, MC, V* ☉ *May–Sept., no dinner Sun., no lunch Mon. Closed mid-Jan.–mid-Feb.*

★ **$$$–$$$$** ✕ **Le Boucanier.** The low-ceilinged dining room is upstaged by wraparound plate-glass views of the marina and château at this waterfront favorite. Locals gather here for mountains of oysters and whole fish, grilled simply and served with a drizzle of fruity olive oil, a pinch of rock salt, or a brief flambé in pastis. ✉ *Port de La Napoule* ☎ 04–93–49–80–51 ▤ *AE, DC, MC, V.*

$$$–$$$$ ▥ **Le Domaine d'Olival.** Set back from the coast on its own vast landscaped grounds along the Siagne River, this inn has a Provençal feel that belies its waterfront-resort situation. Bright rooms with country-fresh fabrics have built-in furniture and small kitchenettes. Balconies, ideal for relaxing over breakfast, overlook the semitropical garden. ✉ *778 av. de la Mer, 06210* ☎ 04–93–49–31–00 ▤ 04–92–97–69–28 ↪ *7 rooms, 11 suites* ♨ *Minibars, cable TV, tennis court, pool, Internet, free parking, some pets allowed* ▤ *AE, DC, MC, V* ☉ *Closed Nov.–mid-Jan.*

Sports

The **Golf Club de Cannes-Mandelieu** (✉ Rte. du Golf ☎ 04–92–97–32–00) is one of the most beautiful in the south of France; it is bliss to play on English turf, under Mediterranean pines with mimosa blooming here and there in the spring. The club has two courses—one with 18 holes (par 71) and one with 9 (par 33).

Cannes

❽ *73 km (45 mi) northeast of St-Tropez, 33 km (20 mi) southwest of Nice, 908 km (563 mi) southeast of Paris.*

A tasteful and expensive breeding ground for the upscale (and those who are already "up"), Cannes is a sybaritic heaven for those who believe that life is short and sin has something to do with the absence of a tan. Backed by gentle hills and flanked to the southwest by the Estérel, warmed by dependable sun but kept bearable in summer by the cool Mediterranean breeze, Cannes is pampered with the luxurious climate that has made it one of the most popular and glamorous resorts in Europe. The cynosure of sun worshipers since the 1860s, it has been further glamorized by the modern success of its film festival.

Its bay served as nothing more than a fishing port until 1834, when an English aristocrat, Lord Brougham, fell in love with the site during an emergency stopover with a sick daughter. He had a home built here and returned every winter for a sun cure—a ritual quickly picked up by his peers. With the democratization of modern travel, Cannes has become a tourist and convention town; there are now 20 compact Twingos for every Rolls-Royce. But glamour—and the perception of glamour—is self-perpetuating, and as long as Cannes enjoys its ravishing climate and setting, it will maintain its incomparable panache. If you're a culture-lover into art of the noncelluloid type, however, you should look elsewhere—there are only two museums here: one is devoted to history, the other to a collection of dolls. Still, as his lordship instantly understood, this is a great place to pass the winter.

Pick up a map at the tourist office in the **Palais des Festivals**, the scene of the famous Festival International du Film, otherwise known as the Cannes Film Festival. As you leave the information center, follow the Palais to your right to see the red-carpeted stairs where the stars ascend every year. Set into the surrounding pavement, the **Allée des Etoiles** (Stars' Walk) enshrines some 300 autographed imprints of film stars' hands—of Dépardieu, Streep, and Stallone, among others.

The most delightful thing to do is to head to the famous mile-long waterfront promenade, **La Croisette**, which starts at the western end by the Palais des Festivals, and allow the *esprit de Cannes* to take over. This is precisely the sort of place for which the verb *flâner* (to dawdle, saunter) was invented, so stroll among the palm trees and flowers and crowds of strolling poseurs (fur coats in tropical weather, cell phones on Rollerblades, and sunglasses at night). Head east past the broad expanse of private beaches, glamorous shops, and luxurious hotels (such as the wedding-cake Carlton, famed for its see-and-be-seen terrace-level brasserie). The beaches along here are almost all private, though open for a fee—each beach is marked with from one to four little life buoys, rating their quality and expense.

If you need a culture fix, check out the modern art and photography exhibitions (varying admission prices) held at the **Malmaison**, a 19th-century mansion that was once part of the Grand Hotel. ⊠ *47 La Croisette, La Croisette* ☎ *04–93–06–44–90* ☉ *Sept.–June, Tues.–Sun. 10:30–12:30 and 2–6:30; July and Aug., Tues.–Sun. 10:30–12:30 and 2–7.*

need a break? Head down the Croisette and fight for a spot at **Le 72 Croisette** (⊠ 72 La Croisette ☎ 04–93–94–18–30)—the most feistily French of all the Croisette bars—it offers great ringside seats for watching the rich and famous enter the Martinez hotel next door. It is open 24 hours a day.

Two blocks behind La Croisette lies **rue d'Antibes**, Cannes's main high-end shopping street. At its western end is **rue Meynadier**, packed tight with trendy clothing boutiques and fine food shops. Not far away is the covered **Marché Forville**, the scene of the animated morning food market. Hidden away in this section of town is the tiny, eccentric, and unfortunately easy to miss **Musée de l'Enfance** (Museum of Childhood), where collector Madame Nicod gives an intimate version of 19th-century French history through a display of antique dolls and accessories. ⊠ *2 rue Venizelos, Le Suquet* ☎ *04–93–68–29–28* ⊠ *€5.50* ☉ *By appointment only.*

Climb up rue St-Antoine into the picturesque Vieille Ville neighborhood known as **Le Suquet,** on the site of the original Roman *castrum.* Shops proffer Provençal goods, and the atmospheric theme restaurants give you a chance to catch your breath; the pretty pastel shutters, Gothic stonework, and narrow passageways are lovely distractions. The hill is crowned by the 11th-century château, housing the **Musée de la Castre,** and the imposing four-sided **Tour du Suquet** (Suquet Tower), built in 1385 as a lookout against Saracen-led invasions. ⊠ *Pl. de la Castre, Le Suquet* ☎ *04–93–38–55–26* 🖼 *€3* 🕙 *Apr.–June, Wed.–Mon. 10–noon and 2–6; July–Sept., Wed.–Mon. 10–noon and 2–7; Oct.–Dec. and Feb.–Mar., Wed.–Mon. 10–noon and 2–5.*

Where to Stay & Eat

★ **$$$$** ✕ **La Villa des Lys.** Superstar decorator Jacques Garcia only works for art-collecting billionaires, high-style industrialists, and the most-talked-about restaurants. Into that latter category falls the Villa de Lys, home to the culinary wizard Bruno Oiger, who produces stunning menus that leave discerning palettes craving more. Inspired by the Belle-Époque-meets-the-Parthenon style of the Villa Kerylos (up the coast in Beaulieu), Garcia has garnished these luxe rooms with Homeric chandeliers, Mycenean doorways, egg-and-dart moldings, a retractable ceiling, and fabrics that smolder with ancient terra-cotta hues. No matter: Oiger's creations take center stage. How can they not with such delights as warm duck foie gras with truffle and peanut tapenade in a braised Jerusalem artichoke (€38, yes for an appetizer); or purple urchin soup with crab meat, accompanied by a mincemeat crêpe with coral, or turbot marinèire with lemon breadcrumbs, confit shallots, and creamy arborio risotto, or Breton lobster with black truffles and creamed macaroni? Save room for dessert: the stuffed orange au supréme caramélisé is a little slice of heaven. ⊠ *10 La Croisette, La Croisette* ☎ *04–92–98–77–41* 🥄 *Reservations essential* 🗎 *AE, DC, MC, V* 🕙 *Closed Sun. and Mon.; mid-Nov.–mid-Dec.*

$$–$$$$ ✕ **Astoux et Brun.** Deserving of its reputation for impeccably fresh *fruits de mer,* this restaurant is a beacon to all fish lovers. Well-trained staff negotiate cramped quarters to lay down heaping seafood platters, shrimp casseroles, or piles of oysters shucked to order. Astoux is noisy, cheerful, and always busy, so arrive early to get a table and avoid the line. ⊠ *27 rue Felix Faure, La Croisette* ☎ *04–93–39–21–87* 🗎 *AE, MC, V.*

$–$$$ ✕ **Le Bouchon d'Objectif.** Popular and unpretentious, this tiny bistro serves inexpensive Provençal menus prepared with a sophisticated twist. Watch for terrine of hare with sultanas and Armagnac, stuffed sardines, or a trio of fresh fish with aioli. An ever-changing gallery display of photography adds a hip touch to the simple ocher-and-aqua room. ⊠ *10 rue Constantine, La Croisette* ☎ *04–93–99–21–76* 🗎 *AE, MC, V* 🕙 *Closed Mon. mid-Nov.–mid-Dec.*

$–$$$ ✕ **La Mère Besson.** This long-standing favorite continues to please a largely foreign clientele with its regional specialties such as sweet-and-sour sardines *à l'escabèche* (marinated), monkfish Provençal (with tomatoes, fennel, and onion), and roast lamb with garlic puree. The formality of the damask linens and still-life paintings is moderated by clatter from the open kitchen. Dinner prix-fixe menus are €27 and €32. ⊠ *13 rue* *des Frères-Pradignac, La Croisette* ☎ *04–93–39–59–24* ▭ *AE, DC, MC, V* ⊘ *Closed Sun. Sept.–June. No lunch except during festivals.*

¢–$$$ ✕ **La Pizza.** Sprawling up over two floors and right in front of the old port, this busy Italian restaurant serves steaks, fish, and salads, but go there for what they're famous for: gloriously good right-out-of-the-wood-fire-oven pizza in hungry-man-size portions. ⊠ *3 quai St-Pierre, La Croisette* ☎ *04–93–39–22–56* ▭ *AE, MC, V.*

★ $$$$ ▥ **Carlton Inter-Continental.** As one of the turn-of-the-19th-century pioneers of this resort town, this deliciously pompous Neoclassical landmark quickly staked out the best position: La Croisette seems to radiate symmetrically from its figurehead waterfront site. In an effort to keep up with the Joneses—or in this case with the rival palace hotels—summer 2004 saw seven deluxe suites added to the top floor, each with unsurpassed sea views and every comfort imaginable. Seafront rooms are also snazzy; those at the back compensate for the lack of a sea view with cheery Provençal prints. The restaurant is good, the brasserie swank, and the Bar des Célébrités lives up to its name during the film festival. ⊠ *58 bd. de la Croisette, La Croisette, 06414* ☎ *04–93–06–40–06* 🖷 *04–93–06–40–25* ⊕ *www.interconti.com* ⇝ *338 rooms, 35 suites* ⌂ *3 restaurants, minibars, cable TV, gym, sauna, 2 bars, Internet, meeting rooms, parking (fee), some pets allowed (fee), no-smoking rooms.*

★ $$$$ ▥ **Le Cavendish Boutique Hotel.** Lovingly restored by friendly owners Christine and Guy Welter, this former residence of English Lord Cavendish is a true delight. Rooms—designed by Christopher Tollemar of JoJo Bistro in New York fame—are done in bright swaths of color ("wintergarden" greens, "incensed" reds) that play up both contemporary decor and 19th-century elegance. Beauty, conviviality, even smells—sheets are scented with lavender water and fresh flowers line the entryway—all work together in genuine harmony. The downstairs bar is cozy for a nightcap and the copious breakfast is simply excellent. ⊠ *11 bd. Carnot, St-Nicolas, 06400* ☎ *04–97–06–26–00* 🖷 *04–97–06–26–01* ⊕ *www.cavendish-cannes.com* ⇝ *34 rooms* ⌂ *Minibars, cable TV, bar, parking (fee), some pets allowed (fee)* ▭ *AE, MC, V.*

★ $$$$ ▥ **Martinez.** Built at the end of the Roaring '20s—a time when excess and glamour were key—this hotel has been lovingly preserved by the champagne-making Taittinger family. Perhaps the most casual of the big hotels on the Croisette, the Martinez revels in a history that is unquestionable. However, it has had such a sleek renovation most of its guest rooms are more contempo than authentic Art Deco. No matter—the views out over the sea are delicious. Recent additions have added on new top-level suites in 1930s decor with teak terraces, and a grand Givenchy spa. Don't be surprised to see tuxedo-clad stars at the Palme d'Or restaurant where chef Christian Willer draws lavish praise for his cuisine, served in an extravagantly "moderne" burled-wood and ebony setting. ⊠ *73 bd. de la Croisette, La Croisette, 06400* ☎ *04–92–98–73–00* 🖷 *04–93–39–67–82* ⊕ *www.hotel-martinez.com* ⇝ *369 rooms, 24 apartments* ⌂ *3 restaurants, cable TV, pool, spa, beach, bar, free parking, some pets allowed (fee)* ▭ *AE, DC, MC, V.*

$$–$$$ ▥ **Molière.** Plush, intimate, and low-key, this hotel, a short stroll from the Croisette, has pretty tile baths and small rooms in cool shades of peach,

indigo, and white-waxed oak. Nearly all overlook the vast, enclosed front garden, where palms and cypresses shade terrace tables, and where breakfast, included in the price, is served most of the year. ⊠ *5 rue Molière, La Croisette, 06400* ☎ *04–93–38–16–16* 🖷 *04–93–68–29–57* ⤴ *24 rooms* ⏶ *Cable TV, bar, some pets allowed (fee)* ☰ *AE, MC, V* ☉ *Closed mid-Nov.–late Dec.* ⦺❘ *BP.*

$ ⊞ **Albert Ier.** In a quiet residential area above the Forville market—a 10-minute walk uphill from La Croisette and the beach—this neo-Deco mansion has pretty rooms in pastels, as well as tidy tile baths and an enclosed garden. You can have breakfast on the flowered, shady terrace or in the family-style salon. ⊠ *68 av. de Grasse, Le Suquet, 06400* ☎ *04–93–39–24–04* 🖷 *04–93–38–83–75* ⤴ *11 rooms* ⏶ *Minibars, cable TV, Internet, free parking, some pets allowed; no a/c* ☰ *MC, V.*

Nightlife & the Arts

The Riviera's cultural calendar is splashy and star-studded, and never more so than during the **International Film Festival** in May. The film screenings are not open to the public, so unless you have a pass, your stargazing will be on the streets or in restaurants (though if you hang around in a tux, a stray ticket might come your way).

As befits a glamorous seaside resort, Cannes has two casinos. The famous **Casino Croisette** (⊠ In Palais des Festivals, La Croisette ☎ 04–92–98–78–00) draws more crowds to its slot machines than any other casino in France. The **Palm Beach Casino Club** (⊠ Pl. Franklin-Roosevelt, point de la Croisette, La Croisette ☎ 04–97–06–36–90) manages to retain an exclusive atmosphere even though you can show up in jeans. To make the correct entrance at the popular **Le Cat Corner** (⊠ 22 rue Macé, La Croisette ☎ 04–93–39–31–31), have yourself whisked by limo from the steak house Le Farfalla. At **Jimmy'z** (⊠ Palais des Festivals, La Croisette ☎ 04–93–68–00–07) the cabaret shows are legendary. The stylish and the beautiful flock to **Les Coulisses** (⊠ 29 rue de Commandant André, La Croisette ☎ 04–92–99–17–17). The hip Latin bar **Caliente** (⊠ 84 bd. de la Croisette, La Croisette ☎ 04–93–94–49–59) is jammed in summer until dawn with salsa-dancing regulars.

The Outdoors

Most of the **beaches** along La Croisette are owned by hotels and/or restaurants, though this doesn't necessarily mean the hotels or restaurants front the beach. It does mean they own a patch of beachfront bearing their name, where they rent out chaise longues, mats, and umbrellas to the public and hotel guests (who also have to pay). Public beaches are between the color-coordinated private beach umbrellas and offer simple open showers and basic toilets. Sailboats can be rented at either port or at some of the beachfront hotels.

Iles de Lérins

➒ *15–20 minutes by ferry off the coast of Cannes.*

When you're glutted on glamour, you may want to make a day trip to the peaceful Iles de Lérins (Lérins Islands); boats depart from Cannes's Vieux Port. Allow at least a half day to enjoy either of the islands; you can fit both in only if you get an early start. You have two options: **Horizon/Caribes Company** (⊠ Jetée Edouard, La Croisette ☎ 04–92–98–71–36) or the less comfortable **Estérel Chanteclair** (⊠ Promenade La Pantiéro, La Croisette ☎ 04–93–39–11–82).

It's a 15-minute, €10 round-trip to **Ile Ste-Marguerite**. Its **Fort Royal**, built by Richelieu and improved by Vauban, offers views over the ramparts to the rocky island coast and the open sea.

Behind the prison buildings is the **Musée de la Mer** (Marine Museum), with a Roman boat dating from the 1st century BC and a collection of amphorae and pottery recovered from ancient shipwrecks. ☎ 04–93–43–18–17 ⊠ €3 ⊙ Oct.–Dec., Feb., and Mar., Wed.–Mon. 10:30–12:15 and 2:15–4:30; Apr.–June and Sept., Wed.–Mon. 10:30–12:15 and 2:15–5:30; July and Aug., Wed.–Mon. 10:30–12:15 and 2:15–6:30.

Ile St-Honorat can be reached in 20 minutes (€8 round-trip) from the Vieux Port. Smaller and wilder than Ste-Marguerite, it is home to an active monastery and the ruins of its 11th-century predecessor.

Antibes

▶ ❿ *11 km (7 mi) northeast of Cannes, 15 km (9 mi) southeast of Nice.*

With its broad stone ramparts scalloping in and out over the waves and backed by blunt medieval towers and a skew of tile roofs, Antibes is one of the most romantic old towns on the Mediterranean coast. As gateway to the Cap d'Antibes, Antibes's Port Vauban Harbor has some of the largest yachts in the world tied up at its berths—their millionaire owners won't find a more dramatic spot to anchor, with the tableau of the snowy Alps looming in the distance and the formidable medieval block towers of the Fort Carré guarding entry to the port. Stroll Promenade Amiral-de-Grasse along the crest of Vauban's sea walls, and you'll understand why the views inspired Picasso to paint on a panoramic scale. Yet a few steps inland you'll enter a souklike maze of atmospheric old streets.

To visit Old Antibes, pass through the **Porte Marine,** an arched gateway in the rampart wall. Follow rue Aubernon to **cours Masséna,** where the little sheltered market sells lemons, olives, and hand-stuffed sausages, and the vendors take breaks in the shoebox cafés flanking one side. From cours Masséna head up to the **Église de l'Immaculée-Conception** (⊠ Pl. de la Cathédrale), which served as the region's cathedral until the bishopric was transferred to Grasse in 1244. Its stout medieval watchtower was built in the 11th century with stones "mined" from Roman structures. Inside is a Baroque altarpiece painted by the Niçois artist Louis Bréa in 1515.

FodorśChoice ★ Next door to the cathedral, the medieval **Château Grimaldi** rises high over the water on a Roman foundation. Famed as rulers of Monaco, the Grimaldi family lived here until the Revolution, but this fine old castle was little more than a monument until in 1946 its curator offered use of its vast chambers to Picasso, and at a time when that extraordinary genius was enjoying a period of intense creative energy. The result is now housed in the **Musée Picasso,** a bounty of exhilarating paintings, ceramics, and lithographs inspired by the sea and by Greek mythology—all very

Mediterranean. Even those who are not great Picasso fans should enjoy his vast paintings on wood, canvas, paper, and walls, alive with nymphs, fauns, and centaurs. The museum houses more than 300 works by the artist, as well as pieces by Miró, Calder, and Léger. ⊠ *Pl. du Château* ☎ *04–92–90–54–20* ⊠ *€5* ⊙ *June–Sept., Tues.–Sun. 10–6; Oct.–May, Tues.–Sun. 10–noon and 2–6.*

The Bastion St-André, a squat Vauban fortress, now contains the **Musée Archéologique** (Archaeology Museum). Its collection focuses on Antibes's classical history, displaying amphorae and sculptures found in local digs as well as salvaged from shipwrecks from the harbor. ⊠ *Av. Général-Maizières* ☎ *04–93–34–00–39* ⊠ *€3* ⊙ *Oct.–May, Tues.–Sun. 10–noon and 2–6; June–Sept., Tues.–Sun. 10–6.*

Where to Stay & Eat

★ **$$–$$$$** ✕ **Le Brûlot.** One street back from the market, this bistro remains one of the most popular in Antibes. Burly chef Christian Blancheri hoists anything from pigs to apple pies in and out of his roaring wood oven, and it's all delicious. Watch for the duck and crispy chips, sardines *à l'escabèche* (in a tangy sweet-sour marinade), sizzling lamb chops, or grilled fresh fish. ⊠ *3 rue Frédéric Isnard* ☎ *04–93–34–17–76* ⊟ *MC, V* ⊙ *Closed Sun. No lunch Mon.–Wed.*

$$–$$$$ ✕ **La Jarre.** You can dine under the beams or the ancient fig tree at this lovely little garden hideaway, just off the ramparts and behind the cathedral. It has an ambitious menu of Provençal specialties filtered through an international lens: lobster sushi with butter and basil, roasted sea bass with creamed soya and green asparagus, grilled pepper steak, sweet-and-sour duck breast, and coconut crème brûlée are all headliners here. ⊠ *14 rue St-Esprit* ☎ *04–93–34–50–12* ⊟ *AE, MC, V* ⊙ *Closed Wed.*

$$–$$$ ☷ **Le Mas Djoliba.** Tucked into a residential neighborhood on the crest between Antibes and Juan, this converted Provençal farmhouse is surrounded by greenery and well protected from traffic noise. Rooms decked out in bright colors and floral prints have views of the garden or the sea. Note that in winter prices include breakfast and in summer the restaurant serves half board only. ⊠ *29 av. de Provence, 06600* ☎ *04–93–34–02–48* ☷ *04–93–34–05–81* ⊕ *www.hotel-djoliba.com* ⇥ *13 rooms* ⚭ *Restaurant, minibars, cable TV, pool, Internet; no a/c* ⊟ *AE, DC, MC, V* ⊙ *Closed Nov.–Jan.* ⊠ *BP, MAP.*

$–$$ ☷ **L'Auberge Provençale.** The six rooms in this onetime abbey come complete with exposed beams, canopy beds, and lovely antique furniture. The dining room and the arbored garden are informed with the same impeccable taste; the menu allures with fresh seafood inventions such as rascasse (rock fish) sausage with mint, as well as bouillabaisse and duck grilled over wood coals. The restaurant is closed Monday and for Tuesday lunch. ⊠ *61 pl. Nationale, 06600* ☎ *04–93–34–13–24* ☷ *04–93–34–89–88* ⇥ *7 rooms* ⚭ *Restaurant, cable TV, some pets allowed (fee)* ⊟ *MC, V.*

Nightlife

La Siesta (⊠ Rte. du Bord de Mer, Antibes ☎ 04–93–33–31–31) is an enormous summer entertainment center with seven dance floors (some on the beach), bars, slot machines, and roulette.

The Outdoors

Antibes and Juan together claim 25 km (15½ mi) of coastline and 48 **beaches** (including Cap d'Antibes). In Antibes you can choose between small sandy inlets—such as **La Gravette,** below the port; the central **place de Ponteil;** and **Plage de la Salis,** toward the Cap—rocky escarpments around the Vieille Ville; or the vast stretch of sand above the Fort Carré.

Juan-les-Pins

⓫ *5 km (3 mi) southwest of Antibes.*

If Antibes is the elderly, historic parent, then Juan-les-Pins is the jazzy younger-sister resort town that, with Antibes, bracelets the wrist of the Cap d'Antibes. The scene along Juan's waterfront is something to behold, with thousands of international sunseekers flowing up and down the promenade or lying flank to flank on its endless stretch of sand. The **Plage de Juan-les-Pins** is made up of sand, not pebbles, and ranks among the Riviera's best (rent a beach chair from the nearby hotel concessions, the best of which is Les Belles Rives). Along with these white powder wonders, Juan is famous for the quality—some pundits say quantity—of its nightlife. There are numerous nightclubs where you can do everything but sleep, ranging from casinos to discos to strip clubs. If all this sounds like too much hard work, wait for July's jazz festival—one of Europe's most prestigious—or simply repair to the Juana or Les Belles Rives; if you're lucky enough to be a guest at either hotel, you'll understand why F. Scott Fitzgerald set his *Tender Is the Night* in "Juantibes, " as both places retain the golden glamour of the Riviera of yore. These hotels are surrounded by the last remnants of the pine forests that gave Juan its name. Elsewhere, Juan-les-Pins suffers from a plastic feel and you might get more out of Antibes.

Where to Stay & Eat

★ **$$$$** ✕🏨 **Juana.** The luxuriously renovated Juana is one of the defining monuments of 1930s Côte d'Azur architectural style. Run by the Barrache family since it opened in 1931, the hotel retains a wonderful Gatsby feel, with striped awnings and white balustrades. Pine trees tower over the grounds and the white-marble pool, balconies offer sunset views of the Esterel red-cliff mountains, while rooms are cool and plain-pastel, with marble and acajou accents. And, though two blocks from the waterfront, the Juana has its own private sand beach. Sadly, its famed gastronomic restaurant La Terrasse closed its doors in January 2005, but try a selection of refined seafood at the Juana's new Les Pecheurs, strategically placed on the promenade with a sweeping view of the coast, or settle into the hotel restaurant Le Cap (closed Sept.–June) for dinner—both are very good. ✉ *Av. Georges-Gallice, 06160* ☎ *04–93–61–08–70* 🖶 *04–93–61–76–60* ⊕ *www.hotel-juana.com* 🛏 *45 rooms, 5 suites* 🍴 *2 restaurants, minibars, cable TV, pool, bar, Internet, meeting room, parking (fee)* 🚭 *AE, MC, V.*

★ **$$$–$$$$** ✕🏨 **Les Belles Rives.** If "living well is the best revenge, " then vacationers at this landmark hotel should know. Not far from the one-time villa of Gerald and Sara Murphy—those Roaring Twenties millionaires who devoted their life to proving this maxim—the Belles Rives became the home-away-from-home for literary giant F. Scott Fitzgerald and his wife Zelda (chums of the Murphys). Lovingly restored to 1930's glamour, the public salons and piano bar prove that what's old is new again: France's stylish young set now make this endearingly *neoclassique* place one of their favorites. The restaurant's cuisine is innovative; the fixed menu is good value. Dine on the terrace on a fine summer night, with the sea lapping below and stars twinkling in the velvety Mediterranean sky. There is no pool, but happily the recently renovated private beach is just steps away. ⊠ *Bd. Baudoin, 06160* ☏ *04–93–61–02–79* 🖷 *03–93–67–43–51* ⊕ *www.bellesrives.com* ⇥ *44 rooms* ♨ *2 restaurants, minibars, cable TV, beach, bar, Internet, free parking, some pets allowed (fee)* ⊟ *AE, V.*

$$–$$$ 🏠 **Le Mimosa.** The fabulous setting, in an enclosed hilltop garden studded with tall palms, mimosas, and tropical greenery, makes up for the hike down to the beach. Rooms are small and modestly decorated in Victorian florals, but ask for one with a balcony: many look over the garden and sizable pool. Rates can include half board. ⊠ *Rue Pauline, 06160* ☏ *04–93–61–04–16* 🖷 *04–92–93–06–46* ⇥ *34 rooms* ♨ *Cable TV, pool, free parking, some pets allowed (fee)* ⊟ *AE, MC, V* ⊗ *Closed Oct.–Apr.* ⑂⊙⑂ *MAP.*

Nightlife & the Arts

The glassed-in complex of the **Eden Casino** (⊠ Bd. Baudoin, Juan-les-Pins ☏ 04–92–93–71–71) houses restaurants, bars, dance clubs, and a casino. Every July the **Festival International Jazz à Juan** (☏04–92–90–50–00 information) challenges Montreux for its stellar lineup and romantic venue under ancient pines. This place hosted the European debut performances of such stars as Meels Dah-*vees* (Miles Davis) and Ray Charles. It can only be hoped that by now they've changed the tacky stage decor—a gigantic "rendition" of a Picasso dove.

Cap d'Antibes

⑫   ● *2 km (1 mi) south of Antibes.*

This extravagantly beautiful peninsula, protected from the concrete plague infecting the mainland coast, has been carved up into luxurious estates shaded by thick, tall pines. Since the 19th century its wild greenery and isolation have drawn a glittering guest list of aristocrats, artists, literati, and the merely fabulously wealthy: Guy de Maupassant, Anatole France, Claude Monet, the Duke and Duchess of Windsor, the Greek shipping tycoon Stavros Niarchos, and the cream of the Lost Generation, including Ernest Hemingway, Gertrude Stein, and Scottie and Zelda Fitzgerald. Now the most publicized focal point is the Hotel Eden Roc, rendezvous and weekend getaway of film stars. You can sample a little of what draws famous people to the site by walking up the chemin de Calvaire from the Plage de la Salis in Antibes (about 1 km [½ mi]) and taking in the extraordinary views (spectacular at night) from the hill that supports the old lighthouse, the **Phare de la Garoupe** (Garoupe Lighthouse). Next to the lighthouse, the 16th-century double chapel of **Notre-Dame-de-la-Garoupe** contains ex-votos and statues of the Virgin, all in memory of and for the protection of sailors. ☏ *04–93–67–36–01*

Easter–Sept., daily 9:30–noon and 2:30–7; Oct.–Easter, daily 10–noon and 2:30–5.

Another lovely walk (about 1½ km [1 mi]), along the **Sentier Tirepoil,** begins at the cape's pretty Plage de la Garoupe and winds along dramatic rocky shores, magnificent at sunset. The final destination of the Sentier Tirepoil is the **Villa Eilenroc,** designed by Charles Garnier, who created the Paris Opera—which should give you some idea of its style. It commands the tip of the peninsula from a grand and glamorous garden. You may tour the grounds freely, but, during high season, the house remains closed (unless the owners, on a good day, choose to open the first floor to visitors). But from September to June visitors are allowed to wander through the reception salons, which retain the Louis Seize–Trianon feel of the noble facade. The Winter Salon still has its "1,001 Nights" ceiling mural painted by Jean Dunand, the famed Art Deco designer; display cases are filled with memorabilia donated by Caroline Groult-Flaubert (Antibes resident and goddaughter of the great author); while the boudoir has boiseries from the Marquis de Sévigné's Paris mansion. Today, the estate is maintained by the Mrs. L. D. Beaumont Foundation, which continues to manicure every blade of grass in the gardens to gorgeous effect. Whether or not the estate is haunted by Helene Beaumont, the rich singer who built it, or King Leopold II of Belgium, King Farouk of Egypt, Aristotle Onassis, and Greta Garbo—who all rented here—only you will be able to tell. ⊠ *At peninsula's tip* ☎ *04–93–67–74–33* ⊕ *www. antibes-juanlespins.com* ⊠ *Free* ⊙ *House: mid-Sept.–June, Wed. 9–noon and 1:30–5; Gardens: mid-Sept.–June, Tues. and Wed. 9–5.*

To fully experience the Riviera's heady hothouse exoticism, visit the glorious **Jardin Thuret** (Thuret Garden), established by botanist Gustave Thuret in 1856 as a testing ground for subtropical plants and trees. Thuret was responsible for the introduction of the palm tree, forever changing the profile of the Côte d'Azur. On his death the property was left to the Ministry of Agriculture, which continues to dabble in the introduction of exotic species. From the Port du Croûton head up chemin de l'Aureto, then chemin du Tamisier, and turn right on the boulevard du Cap. ⊠ *62 Bd. du Cap* ☎ *04–93–67–88–66* ⊕ *jardin-thuret.antibes.inra.fr* ⊠ *Free* ⊙ *Weekdays 8:30–5:30.*

At the southwest tip of the peninsula, an ancient battery contains the **Musée Naval et Napoléonien** (Naval and Napoleonic Museum), where you can peruse a collection of watercolors of Antibes, platoons of lead soldiers, and scale models of military ships. ⊠ *Batterie du Grillon, av. Kennedy* ☎ *04–93–61–45–32* ⊠ *€3* ⊙ *Tues.–Sat. 9–12:30 and 2–5:45.*

Where to Stay & Eat

★ $$$$ ✕ **Restaurant de Bacon.** Since 1948, under the careful watch of the Sordello brothers, this has been *the* spot for seafood on the Côte d'Azur. The catch of the day may be minced in lemon ceviche, floating in a top-of-the-line bouillabaisse, or simply grilled with fennel, crisped with hillside herbs. The warm welcome, discreet service, sunny dining room, and dreamy terrace over the Baie des Anges, with views of the Antibes ramparts, justify extravagance. Fixed-menu prices are €50 and €75. ⊠ *Bd.*

de Bacon ☎ *04–93–61–50–02* ⚐ *Reservations essential* ▤ *AE, DC, MC, V* ☿ *Closed Mon. and Nov.–Jan. No lunch Tues.*

$$$$ ✕⊡ **Imperial Garoupe.** This Provençal palace in the Cap is a terra-cotta oasis of Mediterranean comfort and glitz. Fronted by grand gates, surrounded by gardens and spotlit palm trees, and framed by an Andalusian-design patio, the main structure—a recent affair built in traditional style—is lined with balconies and filled with posh Louis XVI and Provençal furnishings. Add in superequipped bathrooms, floor-to-ceiling chintz, thick towels, daily deliveries of fresh fruit, and you have all the fixings for a luxe blow-out stay. Many guests here spend the days relaxing at the adorable private beach or swimming pool, only moving in to L'Anse, the serious restaurant, to dine on soigné offerings such as roasted sea bass with thyme and citrus served with white beans, or rack of lamb slow-basted with mustard and prunes. ⊠ *770 chemin Garoupe, 06160* ☎ *04–92–93–31–61* 🖷 *04–92–93–31–62* ⊕ *www.imperial-garoupe. com* ⤶ *30 rooms, 4 suites* ⚐ *Restaurant, minibars, cable TV, pool, bar, some pets allowed (fee)* ▤ *AE, DC, MC, V* ☿ *Closed Nov.–mid-Apr.*

★ **$$$$** ⊡ **La Baie Dorée.** Clinging to the waterfront and skewed toward the open sea, this elegant little inn provides private sea-view terraces off every room. Guest rooms are plush and subdued, yet even the small standard doubles feel deluxe when you look out the window. The public grounds and terraces are arranged in tiers down to the water, from the shaded restaurant to the private beach on the Baie de la Garoupe. ⊠ *579 bd. de la Garoupe, 06160* ☎*04–93–67–30–67* 🖷*04–92–93–76–39* ⊕*www. baiedoree.com* ⤶ *17 rooms* ⚐ *Restaurant, minibars, cable TV, beach, free parking, some pets allowed (fee)* ▤ *AE, MC, V* ⎮◎⎮ *FAP.*

THE HILL TOWNS: ON THE TRAIL OF PICASSO & MATISSE

The hills that back the Côte d'Azur are often called the *arrière-pays*, or backcountry. This particular wedge of backcountry—behind the coast between Cannes and Antibes—has a character all its own: deeply, unselfconsciously Provençal, with undulating fields of lavender watched over by villages perched on golden stone. Many of these villages look as if they do not belong to the last century—but they do, since they played the muse to some of modern art's most famous exemplars, notably Pablo Picasso and Henri Matisse. A highlight here is the Maeght Foundation, in St-Paul de Vence, one of France's leading museums of modern art. Its neighbor, Vence, has the Chapelle du Rosaire, entirely designed and decorated by Matisse. It's possible to get a small taste of this backcountry on a day trip out of Fréjus, Cannes, or Antibes; even if you're vacationing on the coast, you may want to settle in for a night or two. Of course, you'll soon discover the stooped, stone row houses that are now galleries and boutiques offering everything from neo–Van Gogh sofa art to assembly-line lavender sachets, and everywhere you'll hear the gentle *breet-breet* of mechanical souvenir *cigales* (cicadas). So if you're at all allergic to souvenir shops and middlebrow art galleries, aim to visit off-season or after hours, when the stone-paved alleys are emptied of tourists and the scent of strawberry potpourri is washed away by the natural perfume of bougainvillea and jasmine wafting from terra-cotta jars.

Vallauris

⑬ *6 km (4 mi) northeast of Cannes, 6 km (4 mi) west of Antibes.*

In the low hills over the coast, dominated by a blocky Renaissance château, this ancient village was ravaged by waves of the plague in the 14th century, then rebuilt in the 16th century by 70 Genoese families imported to repopulate the abandoned site. They brought with them a taste for Roman planning—hence the grid format in the Old Town—but, more important in the long run, a knack for pottery making, as well. Their skills and the fine clay of Vallauris proved to be a marriage made in heaven, and the village thrived as a pottery center for hundreds of years. In the 1940s Picasso found inspiration in the malleable soil and settled here in a simple stone house, creating pottery art with a single-minded passion. But he returned to painting in 1952 to create one of his masterworks in the château's Romanesque chapel, the vast multipanel oil-on-wood composition called *La Guerre et la Paix* (*War and Peace*).

★ The chapel is part of the **Musée National Picasso** today, where several of Picasso's ceramic pieces are displayed. There's also a group of paintings by a contemporary of Picasso's, Italian artist Alberto Magnelli. ⊠ *Pl. de la Libération* ☎ *04–93–64–16–05* 🖾 *€3* ⊙ *June–Sept., Wed.–Mon. 10–noon and 2–6; Oct.–May, Wed.–Mon. 10–noon and 2–5.*

Mougins

⑭ *6 km (4 mi) north of Valluris, 8 km (5 mi) north of Cannes, 11 km (7 mi) northwest of Antibes.*

Passing through Mougins, a popular summer-house community convenient to Cannes and Nice and famously home to a group of excellent restaurants, you may perceive little more than suburban sprawl. But in 1961 Picasso found much to admire and settled into a *mas* (farmhouse) that verily became a pilgrimage spot for artists and art lovers; he died here in 1973. You can find Picasso's final home and see why, of all spots in the world, he chose this one, by following D35 2 km (1 mi) south of Mougins to the ancient ecclesiastical site of **Notre-Dame-de-Vie** (⊠ Chemin de la Chapelle). This was the hermitage, or monastic retreat, of the Abbey of Lérins, and its 13th-century bell tower and arcaded chapel form a pretty ensemble. Approached through an allée of ancient cypresses, the house Picasso shared with his wife, Jacqueline, overlooks the broad bowl of the countryside (now blighted with modern construction). Unfortunately, the residence—the former priory—is closed to the public. The chapel is only open during Sunday Mass at 9 AM. Elsewhere in town are a small **Musée Municipal,** set in the 17th-century St-Bernardin Chapel, and a huge **Musée de l'Automobiliste,** with 100 vintage cars, in a modern structure on the aire des Bréguières.

Roger Vergé, mastermind of Provençal sun-kissed cuisine, retired from being a super chef in 2003. He handed over the reins of both his famed Moulin de Mougins (see below) and his **Ecole de Cuisine du Soleil** to Alain

Llorca, whose distinct style has been creating waves in gastromic circles since his first stints at the Negresco in Nice. The cooking school, one of the best on the Côte d'Azur, is in Mougins and offers 2-hour courses daily (in the morning and afternoon) for €56 each. The menu changes for each session and students are encouraged to fully participate, including eating their creations at the end of the course. A booklet of five tickets for five different sessions costs € 255. ⊠ *Pl. du Commandante Lamy* ☎ *04–93–75–35–70* 🖷 *04–93–90–18–55.*

Where to Stay & Eat

$$–$$$$ ✕ **Le Bistrot de Mougins.** Set in an old 15th-century stable with high, curved brick ceilings, this is a restaurant that plays up to its historical past. Rustic chairs and flowered tablecloths offer a real picnic-in-the-country feel. Simple, Provençal-style dishes are hard to beat: escargots in butter and herbs, steak with a green peppercorn sauce, or sea bass grilled with fennel are top choices. ⊠ *Place du Village* ☎ *04–93–75–78–34* 🚍 *AE, MC, V* ☼ *No lunch Wed. and Sat.*

★ **$–$$$$** ✕ **Le Feu Follet.** In a beautiful period-house setting right in the center of the village, reputed chef Jean-Paul Battaglia heads up a battalion of young chefs in an open-plan kitchen. Why so many? Because everything is homemade, from the fois gras to the hand-smoked salmon to mouth-watering basics like roasted scampi with lemon and basil. The best seats are on the enclosed terrace by the quietly tinkling fountain looking out into the mayor's flower garden, but the cozy rooms inside are atmospheric too. The €32-set menu is the best bet in town. Try to save room for dessert—the lavender-infused crème brulée is truly outstanding. ⊠ *Pl. du Commandant Lamy* ☎ *04–93–90–15–78* 🚍 *AE, MC, V* ☼ *Closed Mon. and 1st 3 wks of Dec. No dinner Sun.*

$$$$ ✕🏠 **Le Mas Candille.** Nestled in a huge private park, this 19th-century mas has been cleverly transformed into an ultraluxurious hotel. Rooms— all cool colors and country chic—are very refined: a profusion of pillows, heated towels, and all the hidden electrical hookups you could possibly need. Antique wallpapers, "reissued" vintage furniture, and too many other high-gloss touches make this place *Elle Decor*–worthy, if not really authentic to the locale. The opulent, saffron-hue restaurant is the well-ordered domain of chef Serge Gouloumes whose impressive resume includes stints at Ma Maison in Beverly Hills and the Poisson d'Or in Saint Martin. His succulent menus are causing quite a stir in gastronomic circles; watch for items like wild bass in a rosemary tempura clay crust or fois gras tartin with Armagnac. In addition to the main house and the gourmet restaurant, there's a bastide (villa) and a Shiseido spa. ⊠ *Bd. Clément-Rebuffel, 06250* ☎ *04–92–28–43–43* 🖷 *04–92–28–43–40* ⊕ *www.lemascandille.com* ➟ *39 rooms, 1 suite* ⌂ *2 restaurants, minibars, cable TV, golf course, 2 pools, spa, some pets allowed (fee)* 🚍 *AE, DC, MC, V.*

★ **$$$–$$$$** ✕🏠 **Le Manoir de l'Etang.** In keeping with the charm of a family country home, guests are welcomed here with genuine warmth and friendly, eager-to-please service. The Provençal 19th-century manor house is perched over a lotus pond; inside, guest rooms are *vacance*-stylish, most with a light and airy feel, accented with some striking nouvelle-mod pieces. Il Lago, the superb Italian restaurant specializes in easy-to-eat dishes—

lovely bruschettas, salads, and pastas. Views of the surrounding countryside are also lovely, as is the simple decor, and you simply can't beat the price for this level of luxe. Reserve early. ⊠ *Rte. d'Antibes, allée de Manoir, 06250* ☎ *04–92–28–36–00* 🖷 *04–92–28–36–10* ⊕ *www. manoir-de-letang.com* ↩ *17 rooms, 3 suites* ♺ *Restaurant, minibars, cable TV, pool, some pets allowed (fee)* ▤ *AE, DC, MC, V* ☯ *Closed Nov.–Feb.*

$$$–$$$$ ✕▣ **Le Moulin de Mougins.** Housed in a 16th-century olive mill on a hill above the coastal fray, this sophisticated inn houses one of the most famous restaurants in the region. Culinary wizard Roger Vergé sold it lock, stock and barrel to brilliant young chef Alain Llorca in 2004, and the loyal clientele watched in wary anticipation as the proud new owner initiated a radical face-lift for the much-loved institution. They were not disappointed. Local design guru Jaqueline Morabito achieves marvels in white, pink, and plum tones with remarkable silver and gold Baroque chandeliers. Sculptures by César, Arman, and Folon stand beside the signatures of the restaurant's famous guests—Sharon Stone, Liz Taylor—and the chairs are plush comfort. The menu underwent a full overhaul, too; the result is sun-drenched Mediterranean cuisine that is truly excellent. Try the Italian risotto with fresh garden peas, grated truffles, olive oil, and veal, or the Mediterranean sea bass steamed with seaweed, white coco beans, and shellfish. The chocolate-and-orange cake is a slice of heaven; in summer dine outside under the awnings. Guest rooms are elegant; the apartments small but deluxe. ⊠ *Notre-Dame-de-Vie, 06250* ☎ *04–93–75–78–24* 🖷 *04–93–90–18–55* ⊕ *www.moulin-mougins. com* ↩ *3 rooms, 4 apartments* ♺ *Restaurant, minibars, cable TV, some pets allowed (fee)* ♺ *Reservations essential* ▤ *AE, DC, MC, V* ☯ *Closed mid-Nov.–mid-Jan. Restaurant closed Mon.*

★ $$–$$$ ✕▣ **La Terrasse à Mougins.** Perfectly situated, this friendly little hotel offers a decor that is casual, country, and chic. The dapper yellow, white, and pastel blue walls fade into insignificance before the panoramic views that look out on the edge of the Vieille Ville. Up a hillside staircase is La Villa Lombarde, where guest rooms sparkle in a stripped-down country version of Louis Seize. The service is excellent, the restaurant menu varied, although its decor is nothing to write home about and its windows are plate-glass (we are in rural France, are we not?). In any event, an after-dinner drink on the terrace looking out over the valley should constitute a moment of sheer, unadulterated pleasure. ⊠ *1 Bd. Courteline, 06250* ☎ *04–92–28–36–20* 🖷 *04–92–28–36–21* ⊕ *www. la-terrasse-a-mougins.com* ↩ *2 rooms, 2 suites* ♺ *Restaurant, minibars, cable TV, some pets allowed (fee)* ▤ *AE, DC, MC, V.*

Grasse

⑮ *10 km (6 mi) northwest of Mougins, 17 km (10½ mi) northwest of Cannes, 22 km (14 mi) northwest of Antibes, 42 km (26 mi) southwest of Nice.*

High on a plateau over the coast, this busy, modern town is usually given a wide berth by anyone who isn't interested in its prime tourist industry, the making of perfume. But its unusual art museum featuring works of the 18th-century artist Fragonard and the picturesque backstreets of its very Mediterranean Vieille Ville round out a pleasant day trip from the coast. You can't visit the laboratories where the great blends of Chanel, Dior, and Guerlain are produced, but to accommodate the crowds of tourists who come here wanting to know more, Grasse has three functioning perfume factories that create simple blends and demonstrate production techniques for free. **Fragonard** (⊠ Rte. de Cannes Les 4-Chemins ☎ 04–93–77–94–30 ⊕ www.fragonard.com) operates in a factory built in 1782. **Galimard** (⊠ 73 rte. de Cannes ☎ 04–93–09–20–00 ⊕ www.galimard.com) traces its pedigree back to 1747. **Molinard** (⊠ 60 bd. Victor-Hugo ☎ 04–93–36–01–62 ⊕ www.molinard.com) was established in 1849.

The **Musée International de la Parfumerie** (International Museum of Perfume), not to be confused with the museum in the Fragonard factory, traces the 3,000-year history of perfume-making. ⊠ 8 *pl. du Cours* ☎ *04–93–36–80–20* 🔲 €4 ⊙ *June–Sept., daily 10–7; Oct.–May, Wed.–Sun. 10–12:30 and 2–5:30.*

The **Musée Fragonard** headlines the work of Grasse's most famous son, Jean-Honoré Fragonard (1732–1806), one of the great French artists of his day. The lovely villa contains a collection of drawings, engravings, and paintings by the artist. Other rooms in the mansion display works by Fragonard's son Alexandre-Evariste and his grandson, Théophile. ⊠ *23 bd. Fragonard* ☎ *04–93–36–02–71* 🔲 *€3.50* ⊙ *June–Sept., daily 10–7; Oct.–May, Wed.–Sun. 10–12:30 and 2–5:30.*

The **Musée d'Art et d'Histoire de Provence** (Museum of the Art and History of Provence), just down from the Fragonard perfumery, has a large collection of faïence from the region, including works from Moustiers, Biot, and Vallauris. ⊠ *2 rue Mirabeau* ☎ *04–93–36–01–61* 🔲 *€3* ⊙ *June–Sept., daily 10–7; Oct.–May, Wed.–Sun. 10–12:30 and 2–5:30.*

Continue down rue Mirabeau and lose yourself in the dense labyrinth of the **Vieille Ville** (Old Town), its steep, narrow streets thrown into shadow by shuttered houses five and six stories tall.

Where to Stay & Eat

$$–$$$ ✕ **Arnaud.** Just off place aux Aires, this easygoing corner bistro serves up inventive home cooking under a vaulted ceiling decorated with stenciled grapevines. Choose from an ambitious and sophisticated menu of à la carte specialties—three kinds of fish in garlic sauce, *pieds et paquets* (pigs' feet and tripe), or a hearty *confit de canard* (preserved duck). ⊠ *10 pl. de la Foux* ☎ *04–93–36–44–88* ▭ *AE, DC, MC, V.*

★ **$$$$** ✕▨ **La Bastide Saint-Antoine.** The cicadas live better than most humans at this picture-perfect 18th-century estate overlooking the Estéval and once home of an industrialist who hosted Kennedys and Rolling Stones. Now the domain of celebrated chef Jacques Chibois, it welcomes you with old stone walls, shaded walkways, an enormous pool, and a mouthwatering ocher-hue and blue-shutter mansion draped with red trumpet-flower begonia and purple bougainvillea. The guest rooms glossily mix Louis Seize–style chairs, Provençal embroidered bedspreads, and high-tech delights (massaging showers). Although the restaurant is exceedingly excellent (try the extraordinary truffle, cream and fois gras soup) and expensive (lobster with a black-olive fondue and beet juice will run you €60), lunch here is a bargain €53. ✉ *48 av. Henri-Dunant, 06130* ☎ *04–93–70–94–94* 🖷 *04–93–70–94–95* ⊕ *www.jacques-chibois.com* ⥰ *8 rooms, 3 suites* ⌂ *Restaurant, minibars, cable TV, pool, shop* ⊟ *AE, DC, MC, V.*

Route Napoléon

Extends 176 km (109 mi) from Grasse to Sisteron.

One of the most famous and panoramic roads in France is the Route Napoléon, taken by Napoléon Bonaparte in 1815 after his escape from imprisonment on the Mediterranean island of Elba. Napoléon landed at Golfe-Juan, near Cannes, on March 1 and forged northwest to Grasse, then through dramatic, hilly countryside to Castellane, Digne, and Sisteron. Commemorative plaques bearing the imperial eagle stud the route, inspired by Napoléon's remark, "The eagle will fly from steeple to steeple until it reaches the towers of Notre-Dame." Nowadays there are some lavender-honey stands and souvenir shacks, but they are few and far between. It's the panoramic views as the road winds its way up into the Alps that make this a route worth taking. Roads are curvy but well maintained. The whole route takes about fourteen hours but you can just do part of it and still take in the lovely scenery. In fact, if you like scenic drives, follow the Route Napoléon to Trigance and on to the spectacular gorge called the **Grand Canyon du Verdon.** You can then continue on to the heart of the Var and in a mere 30 minutes be swallowed up in the beauty of the spectacular Gorges Country.

Vence

🔟 *20 km (12 mi) west of Grasse, 4 km (2½ mi) north of St-Paul, 22 km (14 mi) north of Nice.*

Encased behind stone walls inside a thriving modern market town is **la Vieille Ville,** the historic part of Vence, which dates from the 15th century. Though crowded with boutiques and souvenir shops, it's slightly more conscious of its history than St-Paul—plaques guide you through its historic squares and *portes* (gates). Leave your car on place du Grand Jardin and head to the gate to the Vieille Ville, passing place du Frêne, with its ancient ash tree planted in the 16th century, and then through the Portail du Peyra to the place du Peyra, with its fountains. Ahead lies the former cathedral on place Clemenceau, also address to the ocher-color Hôtel de Ville (town hall). A flea market is held on the square on Wednesdays; backstreets and alleys hereabouts have been colonized by craft stores and "art galleries." In the center of the Vieille Ville, the **Cathédrale de la Nativité de la Vierge** (Cathedral of the Birth of the Virgin, on place Godeau) was built on the Romans' military drilling field and traces bits and pieces to Carolingian and even Roman times. It's a hybrid of Romanesque and Baroque styles, expanded and altered over the centuries. Note the rostrum added in 1499—its choir stalls are carved with particularly vibrant and amusing scenes of daily life back when. In the baptistery is a ceramic mosaic of Moses in the bulrushes by Chagall.

★ On the outskirts of "new" Vence, toward St-Jeannet, the **Chapelle du Rosaire** (Chapel of the Rosary) was decorated with beguiling simplicity and clarity by Matisse between 1947 and 1951—the chapel was the artist's gift to nuns who had nursed him through illness. It reflects the reductivist style of the era: walls, floor, and ceiling are gleaming white, and the small stained-glass windows are cool greens and blues. "Despite its imperfections I think it is my masterpiece . . . the result of a lifetime devoted to the search for truth, " wrote Matisse, who designed and dedicated the chapel when he was in his eighties and nearly blind. ⊠ *Av. Henri-Matisse* ☎ *04–93–58–03–26* 💷 *€2.50* ☉ *Tues. and Thurs. 10–11:30 and 2–5:30; Mon., Wed., and Sat. 2–5:30.*

Where to Stay & Eat

★ $$$$ ✕ **Jacques Maximin.** This temperamental legend and superchef has found peace of mind in a gray-stone farmhouse covered with wisteria—his home and his own country restaurant. Here he devotes himself to creative country cooking superbly prepared and unpretentiously priced— salad of artichoke hearts, squid, Parmesan, and penne, Mediterranean fish grilled in rock salt and olive oil, and candied-eggplant sorbet. The yellow dining room is airy and uncluttered; the garden is a palm-shaded delight. Reserve way in advance. ⊠ *689 chemin de la Gaude* ☎ *04–93–58–90–75* ⚁ *Reservations essential* ▭ *AE, MC, V* ☉ *No dinner Sun. No lunch Mon. and Tues. mid-Dec.–May, or Fri. and Sat. Oct.–June; closed mid-Nov.–mid-Dec.*

$$–$$$ ✕ **La Farigoule.** A long, beamed dining room that opens onto a shady terrace casts an easygoing spell and serves as an hors d'oeuvre for some sophisticated Provençal cooking. Watch for tangy pissaladières with sardines marinated in ginger and lemon, salt-cod ravioli, lamb with olive polenta, and a crunchy parfait of honey and hazelnuts. Fixed-menu dinners are €28 and €45. ⊠ *15 rue Henri-Isnard* ☎ *04–93–58–01–27* ▭ *MC, V* ☉ *Closed Tues. and Wed. Oct.–Easter; closed Tues., no lunch Wed. or Sat. June–Sept.*

★ $$$$ ✕▥ **Château du Domaine St. Martin.** Exuding an expensive charm, this famous domain occupies the ancient site of a fortress of the Knights Templars. Sitting on a hilltop perch and surrounded by acres of greenery designed by Jean Mus, the mansion welcomes you with public salons that are light and airy—perhaps too much, as they seem to be overly renovated. All guest rooms are, in fact, junior suites, except for six *bastides* (two- and three-bedroom villas) accented with beautiful antiques. **La Commanderie** restaurant is perhaps the best reason to come here, thanks to its stunning walls adorned with china, chef Philippe Guéin's superb creations, and one of the most panoramic terraces around—the views over Old Vence to the Baie des Anges are eye-popping. ⊠ *Av. des Templiers, 06142* ☎ *04–93–58–02–02* 🖷 *04–93–24–08–91* ⊕ *www.chateau-st-martin.com* ⤵ *38 rooms* ⚘ *2 restaurants, minibars, cable TV, 2 tennis courts, pool, bar, Internet, free parking, some pets allowed (fee)* ▭ *AE, MC, V* ☉ *Closed mid-Oct.–mid-Feb.* ¶◎ *MAP.*

★ $$–$$$ ▥ **Villa Roseraie.** This quiet little inn outside the center is a pet project of the enthusiastic owners, Monsieur and Mme. Martefon, who have scoured antiques shops for regional details and invested in fine local tiles and fabrics. There's a generous breakfast served until 11:30 AM on the terrace by the pool much of the year, and it's a quick walk down to Old Vence. ⊠ *51 av. Henri-Giraud, 06140* ☎ *04–93–58–02–20* 🖷 *04–93–58–99–31* ➘*14 rooms* ♨ *Minibars, cable TV, pool, free parking, some pets allowed (fee); no a/c* ⊟ *AE, MC, V* ⊘ *Closed mid-Nov.–mid-Feb.*

$–$$ ⊡ **L'Auberge des Seigneurs.** Although the entrance is dim and has a certain rustic medieval charm, rooms are surprisingly airy and bright with Provençal fabrics. The small restaurant specializes in roast meats and hearty cheeses and is very convivial. It's also very busy, so be sure to book well in advance. ⊠ *Place du Frêne, 06140* ☎ *04–93–58–04–24* 🖷 *04–93–24–08–01* ➘*6 rooms* ♨ *Restaurant, minibars, cable TV, some pets allowed (fee)* ⊟ *AE, MC, V* ⊘ *Closed mid-Jan.–mid-Feb.*

St-Paul-de-Vence

⑰   *18 km (11 mi) north of Nice, 4 km (2½ mi) south of Vence.*

Fodor's Choice
★
The medieval village of St-Paul-de-Vence can be seen from afar, standing out like its companion, Vence, against the skyline. In the Middle Ages St-Paul was basically a city-state, and it controlled its own political destiny for centuries. But by the early 20th century St-Paul had faded to oblivion, overshadowed by the growth of Vence and Cagnes—until it was rediscovered in the 1920s when a few penniless artists began paying for their drinks at the local auberge with paintings. Those artists turned out to be Signac, Modigliani, and Bonnard, who met at the Auberge de la Colombe d'Or, now a sumptuous inn, where the walls are still covered with their ink sketches and daubs. Nowadays art of a sort still dominates in the myriad tourist traps that take your eyes off the beauty of St-Paul's old stone houses and its rampart views. The most commercially developed of Provence's hilltop villages, St-Paul is nonetheless a magical place when the tourist crowds thin. Artists are still drawn to its light, its pure air, its wraparound views, and its honey-color stone walls, soothingly cool on a hot Provençal afternoon. Film stars continue to love its lazy yet genteel ways, lingering on the garden-bower terrace of the Colombe d'Or and challenging the locals to a game of pétanque under the shade of the plane trees. Even so, you have to work hard to find the timeless aura of St-Paul; get here early in the day to get a jump on the cars and tour buses, which can clog the main D36 highway here by noon, or plan on a stay-over. Either way, do consider a luncheon or dinner beneath the Picassos at the Colombe d'Or, even if the menu prices seem almost as fabulous as the collection.

★   Many people come to St-Paul just to visit the **Fondation Maeght,** founded in 1964 by art dealer Aimé Maeght and set on a wooded cliff top high above the medieval town. It's not just a small modern art museum but an extraordinary marriage of the arc-and-plane architecture of José Sert; the looming sculptures of Miró, Moore, and Giacometti; and a humbling hilltop perch of pines, vines, and flowing planes of water. On display is an intriguing and ever-varying parade of the work of modern masters, including the wise and funny late-life masterwork *La Vie (Life)*, by Chagall. ☎ *04–93–32–81–63* 🗉 *€11* ⊘ *July–Sept., daily 10–7; Oct.–June, daily 10–12:30 and 2:30–6.*

Where to Stay & Eat

★ **$$$$** ✕🏨 **La Colombe d'Or.** The art display here may cause a double-take—are those really Mirós, Bonnards, Picassos, Légers, and Braques hanging on the rustic walls? Yes, they were indeed given in payment by the artists in hungrier days when this auberge was known as the "Café-Restaurant Robinson" and run by the Roux family. It soon became the heart and soul of St-Paul's artistic revival, and the cream of 20th-century France lounged together under its fig trees—Picasso and Chagall, Maeterlinck and Kipling, Yves Montand and Simone Signoret (who met and married here). Today, the inn's *pastorale* history is the lure, not the food, which is unambitious bordering on fine, but high-priced nonetheless. (Note you can enjoy a dinner or drink here without being a hotel guest.) Give in to the green-shaded loveliness of the terrace and the creamy manners of the waitstaff. A dinner table here is lorded over by a ceramic Léger mural, while the pool is an idyllic garden bower, complete with a Calder, and there's even a Braque by the fireplace in the bar. The auberge's stone entry portal is a grand Renaissance set piece, the public salons are most alluring, and the guest rooms possess a certain understated charm, thanks to some Provençal painted borders and murals. This is a guarded star—there are minuses here, but where else can you enjoy your Campari sitting under a Dubuffet? Reserve well in advance for guest rooms. ✉ *Pl. Général-de-Gaulle, 06570* ☎ *04–93–32–80–02* 🖷 *04–93–32–77–78* ⊕ *www.la-colombe-dor.com* ⇱ *16 rooms, 10 suites* ⟂ *Restaurant, minibars, cable TV, pool, bar, Internet, some pets allowed; no a/c in some rooms* ▤ *AE, DC, MC, V* ⊗ *Closed late Oct.–mid-Dec. and 2 wks in Jan.* ⦿ *MAP.*

★ **$$$$** ✕🏨 **Le Saint-Paul.** Right in the center of the labyrinth of stone alleys, with views over the ancient ramparts, this luxurious inn fills a noble 15th-century house with truly splendid comfort and charm. Provençal furniture, golden quarried stone, and lush reproduction fabrics warm the salons; rooms are decked in sleek pastels and botanical prints, and some have balconies looking out over the valley. The restaurant, headed up by chef Frédéric Buzet, serves sophisticated regional specialties like pigeon roasted with Corsican pancetta, or sea bass and lemon cooked in a clay crust, and is fast acquiring a big reputation. And a candlelit meal on the terrace, where flowers spill from every niche, is a romantic's dream. Rates including half or full board are available with a three-night minimum stay. ✉ *86 rue Grande, 06570* ☎ *04–93–32–65–25* 🖷 *04–93–32–52–94* ⊕ *www.lesaintpaul.com* ⇱ *15 rooms, 3 suites* ⟂ *Restaurant, minibars, cable TV, bar, Internet, some pets allowed (fee)* ▤ *AE, DC, MC, V* ⦿ *FAP, MAP.*

$$–$$$ 🏨 **Le Hameau.** Less than 1½ km (1 mi) outside St-Paul, with views of the valley and the village, this lovely little inn is a jumble of terraces, trellises, archways, and honeysuckle vines. The main hotel, built in 1920, has good-size rooms and old Provençal furniture; or you can opt for the 18th-century farmhouse, with smaller, more modern rooms but wonderful views. The friendly owners make for a comfortable welcome and there is a sizable pool. ✉ *528 rte. de La Colle, 06570* ☎ *04–93–32–80–24* 🖷 *04–93–32–55–75* ⊕ *www.le-hameau.com* ⇱ *17 rooms* ⟂ *Minibars, cable TV, pool, Internet, some pets allowed* ▤ *MC, V* ⊗ *Closed mid-Nov.–mid-Dec. and mid-Jan.–mid-Feb.*

¢–$$ 🏠**Hostellerie les Remparts.** With original stone walls, coved ceilings, light-color fabrics, and a warm welcome, this small medieval hotel in the center of town is a real gem. Its restaurant serves good regional specialties, too. ✉ *72 rue Grande, 06570* ☎ *04–93–32–09–88* 📠 *04–93–32–09–88* ⤴ *9 rooms* ♨ *Restaurant, minibars, some pets allowed; no a/c, no room TVs* ⊟ *AE, MC, V.*

Cagnes-sur-Mer

❽ *6 km (4 mi) south of St-Paul-de-Vence, 21 km (13 mi) northeast of Cannes, 10 km (6 mi) north of Antibes, 14 km (9 mi) southwest of Nice.*

Although from N7 you may be tempted to give wide berth to the congested and modern sprawl of Cagnes-sur-Mer, follow the signs inland and up into **Haut Cagnes.** Its steep-cobbled Vieille Ville is crowned by the fat, crenelated **Château de Cagne,** built in 1310 by the Grimaldis and reinforced over the centuries. Within are vaulted medieval chambers, a vast Renaissance fireplace, a splendid 17th-century trompe-l'oeil fresco of the fall of Phaëthon from his sun-chariot, and three small specialized collections dealing with the history of the olive; memorabilia of the cabaret star Suzy Solidor; and a collection of modern Mediterranean artists, including Cocteau and Dufy. ✉ *Pl. Grimaldi* ☎ *04–93–02–47–35* 🎟 *€3, €4.50 joint ticket with Musée Renoir* ⊘ *Oct.–Apr., Wed.–Mon. 10–11:30 and 2–5; May–Sept., Wed.–Mon. 10–11:30 and 2–6.*

After staying up and down the coast, Auguste Renoir (1841–1919) settled in a house in Les Collettes, just east of the Vieille Ville, now the **Musée Renoir.** Here he passed the last 12 years of his life, painting the landscape around him, working in bronze, and rolling his wheelchair through the luxuriant garden, tiered with roses, citrus groves, and some of the most spectacular olive trees along the coast. You can view his home as it has been preserved by his children, as well as 11 of his last paintings. ✉ *Av. des Collettes* ☎ *04–93–20–61–07* 🎟 *€3, €4.50 joint ticket with the Château de Cagne* ⊘ *Oct.–Apr., Wed.–Mon. 10–11:30 and 2–5; May–Sept, Wed.–Mon. 10–11:30 and 2–6. Guided tours in English, Thurs. July and Aug.*

Where to Stay & Eat

★ **$$$–$$$$** ✕🏠 **Le Cagnard.** Housed in a 14th-century residence built on the outer walls of the Grimaldi castle, this lovely hideaway is a modern escape to a medieval world. Faithful to old-world style in antique-abounding decor, the rooms are very elegant but it's the ceiling of the restaurant that is truly remarkable: covered in Renaissance-style murals, it can be retracted to show off the night sky. The lavish menu (no lunch Monday and Tuesday; closed Thursday; reservations essential) lives up to the surrounding splendor with dishes like fois gras cooked with figs, peaches, apricots, and rosemary, or black truffle lasagna. Portions are generous, but try to resist and wait for dessert—the caramelized apple pie is amazing. ✉ *54 rue Sous Barri, Haute Cagnes* ☎ *04–93–20–73–21* 📠 *04–93–22–06–39* ⊕ *www.le-cagnard.com* ⤴ *15 rooms, 11 suites* ♨ *Restaurant, minibars, cable TV, bar, Internet, free parking, some pets allowed (fee)* ⊟ *AE, MC, V* ⊘ *Closed Nov.–mid-Dec.*

NICE

As the fifth-largest city in France, this distended urban tangle is often avoided, but that decision is one to be rued: Nice's waterfront, paralleled by the famous Promenade des Anglais and lined by grand hotels, is one of the noblest in France. It is capped by a dramatic hilltop château, below which the slopes plunge almost into the sea and at whose base a bewitching warren of ancient Mediterranean streets unfold.

It was in this old quarter, now Vieux Nice, that the Greeks established a market-port in the 4th century BC and named it Nikaia. After falling to the Saracen invasions, Nice regained power and developed into an important port in the early Middle Ages. In 1388, under Louis d'Anjou, Nice, along with the hill towns behind, effectively seceded from the county of Provence and allied itself with Savoie as the Comté de Nice (Nice County). It was a relationship that lasted some 500 years and added rich Italian flavor to the city's culture, architecture, and dialect.

Nowadays Nice strikes an engaging balance between historic Provençal grace, port-town exotica, urban energy, whimsy, and high culture. You could easily spend your vacation here, attuned to Nice's quirks, its rhythms, its very multicultural population, and its Mediterranean tides. The high point of the year falls in mid-February when the city hosts one of the most spectacular Carnival celebrations in France (www.nicecarnival.com).

Vieux Nice

Framed by the "château"—really a rocky promontory—and cours Saleya, Nice's Vieille Ville is its strongest drawing point and, should you only be passing through, the best place to capture the city's historic atmosphere. Its grid of narrow streets, darkened by houses five and six stories high with bright splashes of laundry fluttering overhead and jewel-box Baroque churches on every other corner, creates a magic that seems utterly removed from the Côte d'Azur fast lane.

a good walk

First, head for the morning flower market on the **cours Saleya** ⑲ ▶. At the center of cours Saleya is the florid, Baroque **Chapelle de la Miséricorde** ⑳. Thread your way into the Vieille Ville maze to the extravagant **Chapelle de l'Annonciation** ㉑. Continue up Poissonerie to rue de la Place Vieille, then head right to rue Droite; the **Chapelle St-Jacques-Jesu** ㉒ looms large and spare. Turn left on rue Rossetti and cross the square to the **Cathédrale Ste-Réparate** ㉓. Now take a break from the sacred, doubling back up rue Rossetti and continuing left up narrow rue Droite to the magnificent **Palais Lascaris** ㉔. Head next to boulevard Jean-Jaurès, which empties onto the grand, arcaded **place Garibaldi** ㉕; one of its five street spokes points straight to the **Musée d'Art Moderne** ㉖. From place Garibaldi and boulevard Jean-Jaurès, wind your way up to the ruins of the castle, now a park called the **Colline de Château** ㉗.

TIMING   Aim for morning on this walk, so you'll see the market on cours Saleya at its liveliest. If you include a visit to the Palais Lascaris, this could make a full day's outing.

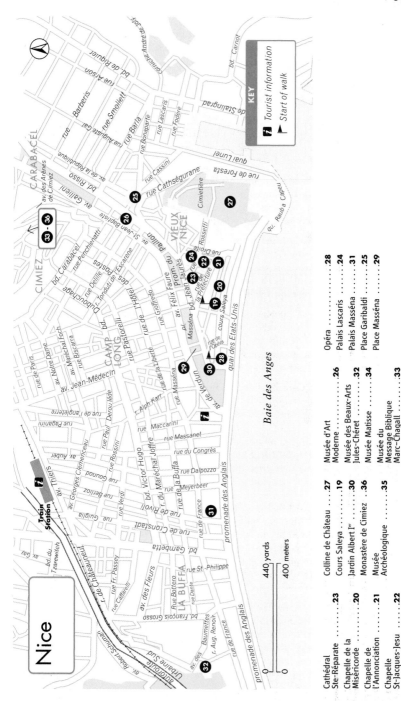

Nice

KEY

🛈 *Tourist information*
▲ *Start of walk*

CARABACEL

CIMIEZ

VIEUX NICE

CAMP LONG

LA BUFFA

Baie des Anges

440 yards
400 meters

Cathédral
Ste-Réparate **23**

Chapelle de la
Miséricorde **20**

Chapelle de
l'Annonciation **21**

Chapelle
St-Jacques-Jesu **22**

Colline de Château **27**

Cours Saleya **19**

Jardin Albert Iᵉʳ **30**

Monastère de Cimiez ..**36**

Musée
Archéologique **35**

Musée d'Art
Moderne **26**

Musée des Beaux-Arts
Jules-Chéret **32**

Musée Matisse **34**

Musée du
Message Biblique
Marc-Chagall **33**

Opéra **28**

Palais Lascaris **24**

Palais Masséna **31**

Place Garibaldi **25**

Place Masséna **29**

Sights to See

㉓ Cathédrale Ste-Réparate. An ensemble of columns, cupolas, and symmetrical ornaments dominates the Vieille Ville, flanked by its own 18th-century bell tower and capped by its glossy ceramic-tile dome. The cathedral's interior, restored to a bright palette of ocher, golds, and rusts, has elaborate plasterwork and decorative frescoes on every surface. ⊠ *Rue Ste-Réparate, Vieux-Nice.*

㉑ Chapelle de l'Annonciation. This 17th-century Carmelite chapel is a classic example of pure Niçoise Baroque, from its sculpted door to its extravagant marble work and the florid symmetry of its arches and cupolas. ⊠ *Rue de la Poissonerie, Vieux-Nice.*

㉒ Chapelle de la Miséricorde. A superbly balanced *pièce-montée* (wedding cake) of half-domes and cupolas, this chapel is decorated within an inch of its life with frescoes, faux marble, gilt, and crystal chandeliers. A magnificent Bréa altarpiece crowns the ensemble. ⊠ *Cours Saleya, Vieux-Nice.*

㉒ Chapelle St-Jacques-Jesu. If the Vieille Ville's other chapels are jewel boxes, this 17th-century chapel is a barn: broad, open, and ringing hollow, this church seems austere by comparison, but that's only because the theatrical decoration is spread over a more expansive surface. ⊠ *Corner of rue Droite and rue Gesu, Vieux-Nice.*

㉗ Colline de Château (Château Hill). Though nothing remains of the once-massive medieval stronghold but a few ruins left after its 1706 dismantling, this park still bears its name. From here take in extraordinary views of the Baie des Anges, the length of the Promenade des Anglais, and the red-ocher roofs of the Vieille Ville. ⊙ *Daily 7–7.*

㉑ Cours Saleya. This street is framed with 18th-century houses and shaded by plane trees. The tall yellow-stone building at the far-east end was home to Henri Matisse from 1921 to 1938.

> **need a break?** Choose from a fantastic array of colorful sorbets, gelati, and ice creams and settle in to do some serious people-watching at one of the patio tables overlooking the fountain at **Fennocchio** (⊠ 2 pl. Rossetti, Vieux-Nice ☎ 04–93–80–72–25).

㉖ Musée d'Art Moderne. The assertive contemporary architecture of the Modern Art Museum makes a bold and emphatic statement regarding Nice's presence in the modern world. The art collection inside focuses intently and thoroughly on contemporary art from the late 1950s onward, but pride of place is given to sculptor Nikki de Saint Phalle's recent donation of over 170 exceptional pieces. ⊠ *Promenade des Arts, Vieux-Nice* ☎ 04–93–62–61–62 ⊕ *www.mamac-nice.org* 🖼 €4 ⊙ *Tues.–Sun. 10–6.*

㉔ Palais Lascaris. The aristocratic Lascaris Palace was built in 1648 for Jean-Baptiste Lascaris-Vintimille, *marechal* to the duke of Savoy. The magnificent vaulted staircase, with its massive stone balustrade and niches filled with classical gods, is surpassed in grandeur only by the Flemish tapestries (after Rubens) and the extraordinary trompe-l'oeil fresco depicting the fall of Phaëthon. The first floor houses faïence displays from the Musée Massséna until the latter's renovations are finally completed in late 2006. ⊠ *15 rue Droite, Vieux-Nice* ☎ *04–93–62–05–54* 🖅 *Free; €3 guided tour, including the Vieille Ville* ⊘ *Wed.–Mon. 10–6.*

㉕ Place Garibaldi. Encircled by grand vaulted arcades stuccoed in rich yellow, the broad pentagon of this square could have been airlifted out of Turin. In the center, the shrinelike fountain sculpture of Garibaldi seems to be surveying you as you stroll under the arcades and lounge in its cafés.

Along the Promenade des Anglais

Nice takes on a completely different character west of cours Saleya, with broad city blocks, vast Neoclassical hotels and apartment houses, and a series of inviting parks dense with palm trees, greenery, and splashing fountains. From the Jardin Albert Ier, once the delta of the Paillon River, the famous promenade des Anglais stretches the length of the city's waterfront. The original promenade was the brainchild of Lewis Way, an English minister in the then-growing community of British refugees drawn to Nice's climate. Nowadays it's a wide multilane boulevard thick with traffic—in fact, it's the last gasp of the N98 coastal highway. Beside it runs its charming parallel, a wide, sun-washed pedestrian walkway with intermittent steps leading down to the smooth-rock beach. A daily parade of *promeneurs,* rollerbladers, joggers, and sun baskers strolls its broad pavement, looking out over the hypnotic blue expanse of the sea. Only in the wee hours is it possible to enjoy the waterfront stroll as the cream of Nice's international society once did, when there was nothing more than hoofbeats to compete with the roar of the waves.

a good walk

From the west end of cours Saleya, walk down rue St-François-de-Paule past the Belle Époque **Opéra** ㉘ ►. Continue up the street, then head right up rue de l'Opéra to **Place Masséna** ㉙, framed in broad arcades and opening onto the vast, green **Jardin Albert 1er** ㉚. Three long blocks past the Casino Ruhl, you'll reach the gates and park of the imposing **Palais Masséna** ㉛. Walk along the waterfront for a few blocks, past busy boulevard Gambetta, then head inland up tiny rue Sauvan. Cross boulevard Grosso and head diagonally up the hill on avenue des Baumettes. In this quiet, once luxurious neighborhood is the **Musée des Beaux-Arts Jules-Chéret** ㉜, built in extravagant Italianate style.

TIMING This walk covers a long stretch of waterfront, so it may take up to an hour to stroll the length of it. Allow a half day if you intend to explore the Palais Massena or the Musée des Beaux Arts.

Sights to See

㉚ Jardin Albert Ier (Albert I Garden). Along the Promenade des Anglais, this luxurious garden stands over the delta of the River Paillon, underground since 1882. Every kind of flower and palm tree grows here, thrown into exotic relief by night illumination.

★ ㉜ Musée des Beaux-Arts Jules-Chéret (Jules-Chéret Fine Arts Museum). While the collection here is impressive, it is the 19th-century Italianate mansion that houses it that remains the showstopper. Originally built for a member of Nice's Old Russian community, the Princess Kotschoubey, this was a Belle Époque wedding cake, replete with one of the grandest staircases on the coast, salons decorated with Neo-Pompiénne frescoes, an English-style garden, and white columns and balustrades by the dozen. After the *richessime* American James Thompson took over and the last glittering ball was held here, the villa was bought by the municipality as a museum in the 1920s. Unfortunately, much of the period decor was sold but, in its place, now hang paintings by Degas, Boudin, Monet, Sisley, Dufy, and Jules Chéret, whose posters of winking *damselles* distill all the *joie* of the Belle Époque. ⊠ *33 av. des Baumettes, Centre-Ville* ☎ *04–92–15–28–28* ⊕ *www.musee-beaux-arts-nice.org* 🖼 €4 ☉ *Tues.–Sun. 10–6.*

㉘ Opéra. A half block west of the cours Saleya stands a flamboyant Italian-style theater designed by Charles Garnier, architect of the Paris Opéra. It's home today to the Opéra de Nice, with a permanent chorus, orchestra, and ballet corps. ⊠ *4 rue St-François-de-Paule, Vieux-Nice/Port* ☎ *04–92–17–40–40.*

㉛ Palais Masséna (Masséna Palace). This handsome Belle Époque building, housing the **Musée d'Art et d'Histoire** (Museum of Art and History), is undergoing a complete renovation and is scheduled to reopen sometime in late 2006. ⊠ *Entrance at 65 rue de France, Centre-Ville* ☎ *04–93–88–11–34.*

㉙ Place Masséna. As cours Saleya is the heart of the Vieille Ville, so this broad square is the heart of the city as a whole. It's framed by an ensemble of Italian-style arcaded buildings first built in 1815, their facades stuccoed in rich red ocher.

Cimiez

Once the site of the powerful Roman settlement Cemenelum, the hilltop neighborhood of Cimiez—4 km (2½ mi) north of cours Saleya—is Nice's most luxurious quarter (use Bus 15 from place Massena or avenue Jean-Médecin to visit its sights).

a good walk

Begin at the **Musée du Message Biblique Marc-Chagall** ㉝, which houses one of the finest collections of Chagall's works based on biblical themes. Then make the pilgrimage to the center of Cimiez and the **Musée Matisse** ㉞, where an important collection of Matisse's life work is amassed in an Italianate villa. Just behind, the **Musée Archéologique** ㉟ displays a wealth of Roman treasures. Slightly east of the museum is the thriving **Monastère de Cimiez** ㊱, a Franciscan monastery.

TIMING Between bus connections and long walks from sight to sight, this walk is a half-day commitment at minimum. Or if you plan to really spend time in the Matisse Museum and the Chagall Museum, it could easily become a day's outing.

Sights to See

㊱ Monastère de Cimiez. This fully functioning monastery is worth the pilgrimage. You'll find a lovely **garden**, replanted along the lines of the original 16th-century layout; the **Musée Franciscain**, a didactic museum tracing the history of the Franciscan order; and a 15th-century **church** containing three works of remarkable power and elegance by Bréa. ⊠ *Pl. du Monastère, Cimiez* ☎ *04–93–81–00–04* ✆ *Free* ☉ *Mon.–Sat. 10–noon and 3–6.*

③⑤ **Musée Archéologique** (Archaeology Museum). This museum, next to the Matisse Museum, has a dense and intriguing collection of objects extracted from the digs around the Roman city of Cemenelum, which flourished from the 1st to 5th centuries. ⊠ *160 av. des Arènes-de-Cimiez, Cimiez* ☎ *04–93–81–59–57* ✆ *€4* ☉ *Wed.–Mon. 10–6.*

③④ **Musée Matisse.** In the '60s the city of Nice bought this lovely, light-bathed

Fodor'sChoice
★ 17th-century villa, surrounded by the ruins of Roman civilization, and restored it to house a large collection of Henri Matisse's works. Matisse settled in Nice in 1917, seeking a sun cure after a bout with pneumonia, and remained here until his death in 1954. During his years on the Côte d'Azur, Matisse maintained intense friendships and artistic liaisons with Renoir, who lived in Cagnes, and with Picasso, who lived in Mougins and Antibes. Settling first along the waterfront, he eventually moved up to the rarified isolation of Cimiez and took an apartment in the Hôtel Regina (now an apartment building), where he lived out the rest of his life. Matisse walked often in the parklands around the Roman remains and was buried in an olive grove outside the Cimiez cemetery. The collection of artworks includes several pieces the artist donated to the city before his death; the rest were donated by his family. In every medium and context—paintings, gouache cutouts, engravings, and book illustrations—it represents the evolution of his art, from Cézanne-like still lifes to exuberant dancing paper dolls. Even the furniture and accessories speak of Matisse, from the Chinese vases to the bold-printed fabrics with which he surrounded himself. A series of black-and-white photographs captures the artist at work, surrounded by personal—and telling—details. ⊠ *164 av. des Arènes-de-Cimiez, Cimiez* ☎ *04–93–81–08–08* ✆ *€4* ☉ *Wed.–Mon. 10–6.*

★ **③③** **Musée du Message Biblique Marc-Chagall** (Marc Chagall Museum of Biblical Themes). This museum has one of the finest permanent collections of Chagall's (1887–1985) late works. Superbly displayed, 17 vast canvases depict biblical themes, each in emphatic, joyous colors. ⊠ *Av. du Dr-Ménard, head up av. Thiers, then take a left onto av. Malaosséna, cross railway tracks, and take first right up av. de l'Olivetto, Cimiez* ☎ *04–93–53–87–20* ✆ *€6.70* ☉ *Wed.–Mon. 10–6.*

Where to Stay & Eat

★ **$$$–$$$$** ✕ **La Mérenda.** The back-to-bistro boom climaxed here when Dominique Le Stanc retired his crown at the Negresco to take over this tiny, unpretentious landmark of Provençal cuisine. Now he and his wife work in the miniature open kitchen, creating the ultimate versions of stuffed sardines, pistou, and slow-simmered *daubes* (beef stews). To reserve entry to the inner sanctum, you must stop by in person (there's no telephone). The dinner menu is €25 to €30. ⊠ *4 rue de la Terrasse, Vieux-Nice* ☎ *No phone* ▭ *No credit cards* ☉ *Closed weekends, last wk July, and 1st 2 wks Aug.*

$$–$$$$ ✕ **Indyana.** Targeting hip twenty- to thirtysomethings, enterprising brothers Christophe and Pascal Ciamos have come up with a stylish, swanky place that fills nightly with an intriguing mix of young entrepreneurs, artsy types, and the fashion-forward. Intimate lighting and an eclectic combination of loft-meets-art-deco-Moroccan decor is matched by a fusion cuisine menu that ranges from sushi to traditional beef platters with potato-zucchini gratin. ✉ *11 rue Gustave Deloye, Vieux-Nice* ☎ *04–93–80–67–69* ⚟ *Reservations essential* ▭ *AE, DC, MC, V* ☾ *Closed Sun.*

★ **$$–$$$$** ✕ **Le Parcours.** Chef Marc Delacourt left the prestigious kitchens of the Château Chevre d'Or hotel to set up this sleek, streamlined restaurant in Falicon, a small perched village on the outskirts of Nice. Decor tends to Zen with a modern twist; there are even TV screens showing what's happening in the kitchen if you can drag your eyes away from the spectacular window views for long enough to watch. Most main courses are delicious, the wine list is short but well thought out, and the €30 lunch menu is a bargain. ✉ *1 pl. Marcel Eusebi, Falicon village: 15 mins outside Nice direction Sospel* ☎ *04–93–84–94–57* ⚟ *Reservations essential* ▭ *MC, V.*

$–$$$ ✕ **Grand Café de Turin.** Whether you squeeze onto a banquette in the dark, low-ceiling bar or win a coveted table under the arcaded porticoes on place Garibaldi, this is *the* place to go for shellfish in Nice: sea snails, clams, plump *fines de claires,* and salty *bleues* oysters, and urchins by the dozen. It's packed noon and night. ✉ *5 pl. Garibaldi, Vieux-Nice* ☎ *04–93–62–29–52* ▭ *AE, DC, MC, V* ☾ *Closed June.*

$–$$$ ✕ **L'Olivier.** In this hole-in-the-wall bistro on place Garibaldi, two brothers have gone back to their roots, and all of Nice has followed. Frank Musso, trained at the Tour d'Argent in Paris, concentrates his sophisticated gifts on simple dishes: tripe simmered in tomatoes, daubes and pork confits, and crêpes with homemade bitter-orange marmalade. His brother Christian provides the cheery welcome. Dinner prix-fixe menus are €25 to €35. ✉ *2 pl. Garibaldi, Vieux-Nice* ☎ *04–93–26–89–09* ⚟ *Reservations essential* ▭ *AE, DC, MC, V* ☾ *Closed Sun. and Aug. No dinner Wed.*

¢ ✕ **Chez René/Socca.** This back-alley landmark is the most popular dive in town for socca, the chickpea-pancake snack food unique to Nice. Rustic olive-wood tables line the street, and curt waiters splash down your drink order. For the food, you get in line at the Socca, choose your €3 plate (or plates), and carry it steaming to the table yourself. It's off place Garibaldi on the edge of the Vieille Ville, across from the *gare routière* (bus station). ✉ *2 rue Miralheti, Vieux-Nice* ☎ *04–93–92–05–73* ▭ *No credit cards* ☾ *Closed Mon.*

$$$–$$$$ ✕▥ **Beau Rivage.** Occupying an imposing late-19th-century town house near cours Saleya, this hotel (guests have included Chekhov, Matisse, and Nietzsche) is just a few steps from the best parts of Old Nice and the beach, though other buildings have long since blocked its sea views. With great hoopla, Jean-Michel Wilmotte—one of France's most cutting-edge designers—redid the interiors, so all is now *Wallpaper*-perfect: beige, minimalist, hard-edge, and just the antidote to all the froufrou found in Nice. What Chekhov would think is another matter, however. ✉ *24 rue St-François-de-Paule, Vieux-Nice, 06000* ☎ *04–92–47–82–82*

🕾 04–92–47–82–83 ⊕ *www.nicebeaurivage.com* ➦ *106 rooms, 12 suites ⚙ Restaurant, minibars, cable TV, beach, bar, some pets allowed, no-smoking rooms* ⊟ *AE, DC, MC, V.*

★ **$$$–$$$$** ✕🖾 **La Perouse.** Just past the Vieille Ville, at the foot of the château, this hotel is a secret treasure cut into the cliff (an elevator takes you up to reception). Some of the best rooms (including Raoul Dufy's favorite) not only have views of the azure sea but also look down into an intimate garden with lemon trees and a cliff-side pool. The restaurant serves meals in the candlelit garden May–September. ⊠ *11 quai Rauba-Capeau, Le Château, 06300* 🕾 *04–93–62–34–63* 🕾 *04–93–62–59–41* ⊕ *www.hroy. com/la-perouse* ➦ *63 rooms ⚙ Restaurant, minibars, cable TV, pool, health club, Internet, meeting room, some pets allowed* ⊟ *AE, DC, MC, V.*

★ **$$–$$$** 🖾 **Windsor.** This is a memorably eccentric hotel with a vision: most of its white-on-white rooms either have frescoes of mythological themes or are works of artists' whimsy. But the real draw of this otherworldly place is its astonishing city-center garden—a tropical oasis of lemon, magnolia, and palm trees. You can breakfast or dine here by candlelight (guests only) and dip into the small, shrubbery-screened pool. ⊠ *11 rue Dalpozzo, Vieux-Nice, 06000* 🕾 *04–93–88–59–35* 🕾 *04–93–88–94–57* ⊕ *www.hotelwindsor.com* ➦ *57 rooms ⚙ Restaurant, minibars, cable TV, pool, gym, Turkish bath, bar, parking (fee); no a/c in some rooms* ⊟ *AE, DC, MC, V* ⦿❙ *MAP.*

¢–$ 🖾 **Felix.** On popular, pedestrian rue Masséna and a block from the beach, this tiny hotel is owned by a hard-working couple (both fluent in English) that make you feel welcome. Rooms are compact but neat and bright, so they don't feel as small, and four have tiny balconies providing a ringside seat over the pedestrian thoroughfare. ⊠ *41 rue Masséna, Vieux-Nice, 06000* 🕾 *04–93–88–67–73* 🕾 *04–93–16–15–78* ➦ *14 rooms ⚙ Minibars, cable TV, Internet* ⊟ *AE, DC, MC, V.*

Nightlife & the Arts

The **Casino Ruhl** (⊠ 1 Promenade des Anglais, Vieux-Nice 🕾 04–93–87–95–87), gleaming neon-bright and modern, is a sophisticated Riviera landmark. With sleek decor, a piano bar, and live bands, the **Dizzy Club** (⊠ 26 quai Lunel, Vieux-Nice 🕾 04–93–26–54–79) is consistently popular. Pretty people throng to the predominantly gay **La Suite du Comptoire** (⊠ 2 rue Bréa, Vieux-Nice 🕾 04–93–92–92–91) to dance to blues and soul music amidst splendid Baroque decor. If you're all dressed up and have just won big, invest in a drink in the intimate walnut-and-velour **Bar Anglais** (⊠ 37 Promenade des Anglais, Vieux-Nice 🕾 04–93–88–39–51), in the landmark Hôtel Negresco.

In July the **Nice Jazz Festival** (🕾 04–92–17–77–77 information) draws performers from around the world. Classical music and ballet performances take place at Nice's convention center, the **Acropolis** (⊠ Palais des Congrès, Esplanade John F. Kennedy, Centre-Ville 🕾 04–93–92–83–00). The season at the **Opéra de Nice** (⊠ 4 rue St-François-de-Paul, Vieux-Nice 🕾 04–92–17–40–40) runs from September to June.

The Outdoors

Nice's **beaches** extend all along the Baie des Anges, backed full-length by the Promenade des Anglais. Public stretches alternate with posh private beaches that have restaurants—and bar service, mattresses and parasols, waterskiing, parasailing, windsurfing, and jet-skiing. One of the handiest private beaches is the **Beau Rivage** (☎ 04–92–47–82–82), set across from the Opera. The sun can also be yours for the basking at **Ruhl** (☎ 04–93–87–09–70), across from the casino.

Shopping

Olive oil by the gallon in cans with colorful, old-fashioned labels is sold at tiny **Alziari** (⊠ 14 rue St-François-de-Paule, Vieux-Nice). A good source for crystallized fruit, a Nice specialty, is the **Confiserie du Vieux Nice** (⊠ 14 quai Papacino, Vieux-Nice), on the west side of the port. The venerable **Henri Auer** (⊠ 7 rue St-François-de-Paule, Vieux-Nice) has sold crystallized fruit since 1820. For fragrances, linens, and pickled-wood furniture, head to **Boutique 3** (⊠ 3 rue Longchamp, Vieux-Nice), run by three Niçoise women of rare talent and taste.

Seafood of all kinds is sold at the **fish market** (⊠ Pl. St-François, Vieux-Nice) every morning except Monday. At the daily **flower market** (⊠ Cours Saleya, Vieux-Nice) you can find all kinds of plants and fruits and vegetables. The **antiques and brocante market** (⊠ Pl. Robilante, Vieux-Nice), by the old port, is held Tuesday through Saturday.

THE EASTERN CÔTE D'AZUR

You may build castles in Spain or picture yourself on a South Sea island, but when it comes to serious speculation about how to spend that first $10 million and slip easily into the life of the idle rich, most people head for France and the stretch of coast that covers the eastern Côte d'Azur. Here, backed by the mistral-proof Alps and coddled by mild Mediterranean breezes, waterfront resorts—Villefranche and Menton—draw energy from the thriving city of Nice, while jutting tropical peninsulas—Cap Ferrat, Cap Martin—frame the tiny principality of Monaco. Here the corniche highways snake above sparkling waters, their pink-and-white villas turning faces toward the sun. Cliffs bristle with palm trees and parasol pines, and a riot of mimosa, bougainvillea, jasmine, and even cactus blooms in the hothouse climate. Crowded with sunseekers, the Riviera still reveals quiet corners with heart-stopping views of sea, sun, and mountains—all within one memorable frame.

Villefranche-sur-Mer

❸ *10 km (6 mi) east of Nice.*

Fodor'sChoice
★

Nestled discreetly along the deep scoop of harbor between Nice and Cap Ferrat, this pretty watercolor of a fishing port seems surreal, flanked as it is by the big city of Nice and the assertive wealth of Monaco. The town is a stage-set of brightly colored houses—the sort of place where Pagnol's

Fanny could have been filmed. Genuine fishermen actually skim up to the docks here in weathered-blue *barques,* and the streets of the Vieille Ville flow directly to the waterfront, much as they did in the 13th century. Some of the prettiest spots in town are around place de la Paix, rue du Poilu, and place du Conseil, which looks out over the water. The deep harbor, in the caldera of a volcano, was once preferred by the likes of Onassis and Niarchos and royals on their yachts (today, unfortunately, these are usually replaced by warships as a result of the presence of a nearby naval base). The character of Villefranche was subtly shaped by the artists and authors who gathered at the Hôtel Welcome—Diaghilev and Stravinsky, taking a break from the Ballet Russe in Monaco; Somerset Maugham and Evelyn Waugh; and, above all, Jean Cocteau, who came here to recover from the excesses of Paris life. Behind towering gates and secluded groves are the private vacation villas of some of the wealthiest people on earth. The most celebrated is La Leopolda, built in the early 20th century by King Leopold of Belgium for his mistress; the villa is private but has a famous garden staircase, immortalized in the film *The Red Shoes,* whose endless stairs may be glimpsed through gates on the road below the villa.

So enamored was Jean Cocteau of this painterly fishing port that he decorated the 14th-century **Chapelle St-Pierre** with images from the life of St. Peter and dedicated it to the village's fishermen. ⊠ *Pl. Pollanais* ☎ *04–93–76–90–70* ▭ *€2* ☉ *Mid-June–mid-Sept., Tues.–Sun. 10–noon and 4–8:30; mid-Sept.–mid-Nov., Tues.–Sun. 9:30–noon and 2–6; end Dec.–Mar., Tues.–Sun. 9:30–noon and 2–5:30; Apr.–mid-June, Tues.–Sun. 9:30–noon and 3–7.*

Running parallel to the waterfront, the extraordinary 13th-century **rue Obscure** (literally, Dark Street) is entirely covered by vaulted arcades; it sheltered the people of Villefranche when the Germans fired their parting shots—an artillery bombardment—near the end of World War II. The stalwart 16th-century **Citadelle St-Elme,** restored to perfect condition, anchors the harbor with its broad, sloping stone walls. Beyond its drawbridge lie the city's administrative offices and a group of minor gallery-museums, with a scattering of works by Picasso and Miró. Whether or not you stop into these private collections of local art (all free of charge), you are welcome to stroll around the inner grounds and to circle the imposing exterior.

Where to Stay & Eat

$ ✕ **La Grignotière.** Tucked down a narrow side street just a few steps away from the marketplace, this small and friendly local restaurant offers up top quality, inexpensive dishes. The homemade lasagna is excellent, as is the spaghetti pistou. ⊠ *3 rue du Poilu* ☎ *04–93–76–79–83* ▭ *MC, V* ☉ *No lunch.*

$–$$ ✕▤ **Hôtel Provençal.** Within walking distance of the port, this inexpensive hotel may not look like much from the outside but is friendly and accommodating. The rooms are large and humbly decorated with deep blue carpets, green velour chairs, and white bedspreads. About half of the rooms have a sea view; the other half look out over colorful rooftops. The Provençal-style restaurant serves up tasty items ranging from freshly

grilled fish to hearty soups on a large terrace overflowing with flowers.
✉ *Av. Maréchal Joffre, 06360* ☎ *04–93–76–53–53* 🖷 *04–93–76–96–00*
⊕ *www.hotelprovencal.com* 🛏 *45 rooms* ⚭ *Restaurant, minibars,*
cable TV, bar, some pets allowed ▤ *MC, V* ⊘ *Closed Nov.–Dec 24.*

★ **$$$** 🖵 **Hôtel Welcome.** When Villefranche harbored a community of artists and writers, this waterfront landmark was their adopted headquarters. Somerset Maugham holed up in one of the tiny crow's-nest rooms at the top, and Jean Cocteau lived here while writing *Orphée.* Elizabeth Taylor and Richard Burton used to tie one on in the bar (now nicely renovated). It's comfortable and modern, with the best rooms brightened with vivid colors and stenciled quotes from Cocteau, and some of the guest rooms have spectacular views. ✉ *Quai Courbet, 06230* ☎ *04–93–76–27–62* 🖷 *04–93–76–27–66* ⊕ *www.welcomehotel.com* 🛏 *36 rooms, 1 apartment* ⚭ *Minibars, cable TV, bar, Internet, some pets allowed (fee)* ▤ *AE, DC, MC, V* ⊘ *Closed mid-Nov.–mid-Dec.*

Beaulieu

❸❽ *4 km (2½ mi) east of Villefranche, 14 km (9 mi) east of Nice.*

With its back pressed hard against the cliffs of the corniche and sheltered between the peninsulas of Cap Ferrat and Cap Roux, this once-grand resort basks in a tropical microclimate that earned its central neighborhood the name *Petite Afrique.* The town was the pet of 19th-century society, and its grand hotels welcomed Empress Eugénie, the Prince of Wales, and Russian nobility. It's still home to some of the poshest hotels and grandest villas (most still private and some still occupied by the British, who particularly favored this town) along the coast.

One manifestation of Beaulieu's Belle Époque excess is the eye-knocking **Villa Kerylos,** a mansion built in 1902 in the style of classical Greece (to be exact, of the villas that existed on the island of Delos in the 2nd century BC). It was the dream house of the amateur archaeologist Théodore Reinach, who originally hailed from a super-rich family from Frankfurt, helped the French in their excavations at Delphi, and became an authority on ancient Greek music. He commissioned an Italian architect from Nice, Emmanuel Pontremoli, to surround him with Grecian delights: cool Carrara marble, rare fruitwoods, and a dining salon where guests reclined to eat *à la Greque.* Don't miss this—it's one of the most unusual houses in the south of France. Not far from the house is the **Promenade Maurice Rouvier,** an enchanting coastal path which leads to St-Jean-Cap-Ferrat. ✉ *Rue Gustave-Eiffel* ☎ *04–93–01–01–44* ⊕ *www.villa-kerylos.com* 🖻 *€7.50, €13.50 to visit both Villa Kerylos and Villa Ephrussi de Rothschild in same wk* ⊘ *Mid-Feb.–June and Sept.–mid-Nov., daily 10–6; July–Aug., daily 10–7; mid-Dec.–mid-Feb., weekdays 2–6, weekends 10–6.*

FodorsChoice appears in the left margin with a ★ symbol.

Where to Stay & Eat

★ **$$$$** ✕🖵 **Métropole.** Affluent travelers have been coming to this palace for more than 100 years, attracted by the heated saltwater pool and beautiful seaside terrace. The Restoration-style furniture and subdued beige and blue-gray tones in the guest rooms offer a welcome change from the Provençal patterns that tyrannize the region. Excellent chef François Blanchet offers up mouthwatering Mediterranean-style cuisine: grilled scallops on balsamic-infused barely, creamed lentil and stuffed ravioli soup, or slow-roasted venison are some best bets. ⊠ *16 bd. Mar. Leclerc, 06160* ☎ *04–93–01–00–08* 🖨 *04–93–01–18–51* ⊕ *www.le-metropole. com* 🛏 *35 rooms, 5 suites* ⚲ *Restaurant, minibars, cable TV, pool, beach, bar, some pets allowed (fee)* ▤ *AE, DC, MC, V* ⊘ *Closed mid-Oct.–mid-Dec.* ¶⊙¶ *FAP, MAP.*

St-Jean-Cap-Ferrat

★ ❸❾ *2 km (1 mi) south of Beaulieu on D25.*

This luxuriously sited pleasure port moors the peninsula of Cap Ferrat; from its port-side walkways and crescent of beach you can look over the sparkling blue harbor to the graceful green bulk of the corniches. Yachts purr in and out of port, and their passengers scuttle into cafés for take-out drinks to enjoy on their private decks.

Fodor'sChoice
★
Between the port and the mainland, the floridly beautiful **Villa Ephrussi de Rothschild** stands as witness to the wealth and worldly flair of the baroness who had it built. Constructed in 1905 in neo-Venetian style (its flamingo-pink facade was thought not to be in the best of taste by the local gentry), the house was baptized "Ile-de-France" in homage to the Baroness Bétrice de Rothschild's favorite ocean liner (her staff used to wear sailing costumes and her ship travel-kit is on view in her bedroom). Precious artworks, tapestries, and furniture adorn the salons—in typical Rothschildian fashion, each room is given over to a different 18th-century "époque." Upstairs are the private apartments of Madame la Baronne, which can only be seen on a guided tour offered around noon. The grounds are landscaped with no fewer than seven theme gardens and topped off with a Temple of Diana (no less); be sure to allow yourself time to wander here, as this is one of the few places on the coast where you'll be allowed to experience the lavish pleasures characteristic of the Belle Époque Côte d'Azur. Tea and light lunches are served in a glassed-in porch overlooking the grounds and spectacular views of the coastline. ⊠ *Av. Ephrussi* ☎ *04–93–01–33–09* 🖲 *Access to ground floor and gardens €8.50, €13.50 joint ticket for Villa Kerylos to be used in same wk, guided tour upstairs €2 extra* ⊘ *Feb.–June and Sept.–Nov., daily 10–6; July and Aug., daily 10–7; Nov.–Jan., weekdays 2–6, weekends 10–6.*

The residents of Cap Ferrat fiercely protect it from curious tourists; its grand old villas are hidden for the most part in the depths of tropical gardens. You can nonetheless walk its entire **coastline promenade** if you strike out from the port; from the restaurant Capitaine Cook, cut right up avenue des Fossés, turn right on avenue Vignon, and follow the chemin de la Carrière. The 11-km (7-mi) walk passes through rich tropical flora and, on the west side, over white cliffs buffeted by waves. When you've traced the full outline of the peninsula, veer up the chemin du Roy past the fabulous gardens of the **Villa des Cèdres,** once owned by King Leopold II of Belgium at the turn of the last century. The king owned several opulent estates along the Côte d'Azur, undoubtedly paid for by his enslavement of the Belgian Congo. His African plunder also stocked the private zoo on his villa grounds, today the town's **Parc Zoologique** (✉ Bd. du Général-de-Gaulle ☎ 04–93–76–04–98). Past the gardens, you'll reach the **Plage de Passable,** from which you cut back across the peninsula's wrist. A shorter loop takes you from town out to the **Pointe de St-Hospice,** much of the walk shaded by wind-twisted pines. From the port climb avenue Jean Mermoz to place Paloma and follow the path closest to the waterfront. At the point are an 18th-century prison tower, a 19th-century chapel, and unobstructed views of Cap Martin.

Where to Stay & Eat

$–$$$ ✕ **Le Sloop.** This sleek port-side restaurant caters to the yachting crowd and sailors who cruise into dock for lunch. The focus is fish, of course: *soupe de poisson* (fish soup), *St-Pierre* (John Dory) steamed with asparagus, roasted whole sea bass. Its outdoor tables surround a tiny "garden" of potted palms. The menu is €26. ✉ *Port de Plaisance* ☎ *04–93–01–48–63* ▤ *MC, V* ◷ *Closed Wed. mid-Sept.–mid-Apr. No lunch Tues. and Wed. mid-Apr.–mid-Sept.*

★ $$$$ ✕▥ **Royal Riviera.** Completely revamped by Parisian designer guru Grace Leo Andrieu, this former *residence hôtelière* for British aristos now invites visitors on an intimate voyage into neo-Hellenic style, complete with an admiring wink at the nearby Villa Kerylos museum. Beyond the jaw-droppingly spectacular reception area, guest rooms are sun-drenched; bleached-wood furniture and shades of lavender, cream and orange sherbet abound. Landscape genius Jean Mus designed the extensive gardens favoring lime-verbena and olive trees, and there's a splendid pool and fitness center. If you can't afford to stay the night, stop for lunch at the poolside restaurant La Pergola—the buffet is worth every euro. ✉ *3 av. Monnet, 06360* ☎ *04–93–76–31–00* 🖷 *04–93–01–23–07* ⊕ *www.royal-riviera.com/history.html* ↝ *70 rooms, 7 suites* ♿ *Restaurant, minibars, cable TV, pool, exercise equipment, beach, bar, free parking, some pets allowed (fee)* ▤ *AE, MC, V.*

★ $$$ ▥ **Brise Marine.** With a glowing Provençal-yellow facade, bright blue shutters, and balustraded sea terrace, this lovely vision fulfills most desires for that perfect, picturesque Cap Ferrat hotel. Pretty pastel guest rooms feel like bedrooms in a private home—many offer window views of the gorgeous peninsula stunningly framed by statuesque palms. ✉ *58 av. Jean Mermoz, 06230* ☎ *04–93–76–04–36* 🖷 *04–93–76–11–49* ⊕ *www. hotel-brisemarine.com* ↝ *18 rooms* ♿ *Minibars, cable TV, bar, parking (fee), some pets allowed* ▤ *AE, DC, MC, V* ◷ *Closed Nov.–Jan.*

$$–$$$ ▥ **Clair Logis.** With soft pastels, antique furniture, and large picture windows, this converted villa is perfectly framed by a sprawling garden park. The main house offers up subtle bourgeois elegance; for the budget-conscious there are other simpler, airy rooms scattered over several small buildings. Most have charming balconies looking out over gently swaying palms. There's no pool, but breakfast on the cobblestone terrace is lovely, and it's a good way to gear up for the 15-minute walk down to the beach. ✉ *12 av. Centrale, point de St-Jean, 06230* ☎ *04–93–76–51–81* 🖷 *04–93–76–51–82* ⊕ *www.hotel-clair-logis.fr* ↝ *18 rooms* ♿ *Minibars, cable TV, free parking, some pets allowed (fee)* ▤ *AE, MC, V.*

Èze

40 *2 km (1 mi) east of Beaulieu, 12 km (7 mi) east of Nice, 7 km (4½ mi)*
Fodor's Choice *west of Monte Carlo.*
★

Towering like an eagle's nest above the coast and crowned with ramparts and the ruins of a medieval château, Èze (pronounced *ehz*) is unfortunately the most accessible of all the perched villages. Consequently, it's by far the most commercialized, surpassing St-Paul-de-Vence for the tackiness of its souvenir shops (some carved out of the rock face) and the indifference of its waiters. It is, nonetheless, the most spectacularly sited; if you can manage to shake the crowds and duck off to a quiet overlook, the village commands splendid views up and down the coast, one of the draws that once lured fabled visitors—lots of crowned heads, Georges Sand, Friedrich Nietzsche—and residents: Consuelo Vanderbilt, when she was tired of being duchess of Marlborough, traded in Blenheim Palace for a custom-built house here.

From the crest-top **Jardin Exotique** (Tropical Garden), full of rare succulents, you can pan your videocam all the way around the hills and waterfront. But if you want a prayer of a chance of enjoying the magnificence of the village's arched passages, stone alleyways, and ancient fountains, come at dawn or after sunset—or (if you have the means) stay the night—but spend the midday elsewhere. The church of **Notre-Dame**, consecrated in 1772, glitters inside with Baroque retables and altarpieces. Èze's tourist office, on place du Général-de-Gaulle, can direct you to the numerous footpaths—the most famous being the **Sentier Friedrich Nietzsche**—that thread Èze with the coast's three corniche highways. Èze extends from hilltop down to the coastal beach; on either side a vast **Grande Corniche Parc** keeps things green and verdant.

Where to Stay & Eat

$$–$$$$ ✕ **Troubadour.** Amid the clutter and clatter, this is a wonderful find: comfortably relaxed, this old family house proffers pleasant service and excellent dishes like roasted scallops with chicken broth and squab with citrus zest and beef broth. Full-course menus range from €28 to €48. ⊠ *4 rue du Brec* ☎ *04–93–41–19–03* ▤ *AE, DC, MC, V* ۞ *Closed Sun. No lunch Mon.*

¢–$ ✕ **Loumiri.** Classic Provençal and regional seafood dishes are tastily prepared and married with decent, inexpensive wines at this cute little bistro near the entrance to the Vieille Ville. The best bet is to order *à l'ardoise*—that is, from the blackboard listing of daily specials. The lunch menu prix-fixe (€15) is the best deal in town. Prix-fixe dinner menus start at €23. ⊠ *Av. Jardin Exotique* ☎ *04–93–41–16–42* ▤ *MC, V* ۞ *Closed Mon. and mid-Dec.–mid-Jan. No dinner Wed.*

★ $$$$ ✕▦ **Château de la Chèvre d'Or.** Though on the main tourist thoroughfare, these weathered stone houses allow you to turn your back on the world and drink in unsurpassed sea views. More than half the creamy white rooms look over the water, and the others compensate with exposed stone, beams, and burnished antiques. The three restaurants all take in the views, too, as does the Louis XIII–style bar. It's the luxurious if occasionally precious main restaurant that draws kudos for its delicate stuffed pastas and near-crunchy risotto, its buttery mullet fillets, and its gingerbread soufflés. The swimming pool alone, clinging like a swallow's nest to the hillside, may justify the investment, as do the liveried footmen who greet you at the village entrance to wave you VIP-style past the cattle-drive of tourists. ☒ *Rue du Barri, 06360* ☎ *04–92–10–66–66* 🖷 *04–93–41–06–72* ⊕ *www.chevredor.com* ➳ *23 rooms, 9 suites* ⚑ *4 restaurants, minibars, cable TV, tennis court, pool, bar, Internet, some pets allowed* ▤ *AE, DC, MC, V* ⊘ *Closed Dec.–Feb.*

$$$$
Fodor'sChoice
★
×🖭 **Château Eza.** Vertiginously perched on the edge of a cliff 3,000 feet above the crouching tiger of St-Jean-Cap-Ferrat, this former residence of Prince William of Sweden is one of the most dramatic, romantic, and expensive inns on the entire Mediterranean coast. Rooms are spread among a cluster of strikingly Romanesque 13th-century buildings on cobblestone streets too narrow for cars. Most have private entrances and all are luxed out to the max: canopy beds, costly objets d'art and antiques, exquisite carpets and tapestries, wood-burning fireplaces and unbelievable views. If you're not staying the night, the views from the panoramic restaurant and outdoor terrace are just as good. The wine list is one of the best on the Côte, though the food has slipped a notch and service can be haughty. Still, for fairy-tale experiences, the surroundings are impossible to beat. ☒ *Rue de la Pise, 06360* ☎ *04–93–41–12–24* 🖷 *04–93–41–16–64* ⊕ *www.chateaueza.com* ➳ *7 rooms, 3 suites* ⚑ *Restaurant, minibars* ▤ *AE, DC, MC, V* ⊘ *Closed Oct.–Mar.*

★ $$
🖭 **La Bastide aux Camelias.** There are only three bedrooms in this lovely B&B, each individually decorated with softly draped fabrics and polished antiques. Close to Èze village, set in the nearby Grande Corniche Park, it offers up the usual run of breathtaking views, but also has inviting, less precipitous ones of garden greenery. Have the complimentary breakfast on the picture-perfect veranda, indulge in a cooling drink by the gorgeous pool, or stretch out on the manicured lawn. There's even a spa, hamman, and Jacuzzi included in the price. It's a gentle hospitality that's much in demand, however, so reserve well in advance. ☒ *Route de l'Adret, 06360* ☎ *04–93–41–13–68* 🖷 *04–93–41–13–68* ⊕ *www.bastide-aux-camelias.fr.st* ➳ *3 rooms* ⚑ *Minibars, cable TV, pool, hot tubs, free parking, some pets allowed (fee)* ⍾❨ *BP.*

Peillon

★ ㊶ *15 km (9 mi) northeast of Nice via D2204 and D21.*

Perhaps because it's difficult to reach and not on the way to or from anything else, this idyllic village has maintained the magical ambience of its medieval origins. You can hear the bell toll here, walk in silence along its weathered cobblestones, and smell the thyme crunching underfoot if you step past its minuscule boundaries onto the unspoiled hillsides. And its streets are utterly and completely commerce-free; the citizens have voted to vaccinate themselves against the plague of boutiques, galleries, and cafés that have afflicted its peers along the coast.

Where to Stay & Eat

★ $$–$$$$ ×🖭 **L'Auberge de la Madone.** With its shaded garden terrace and its impeccable, bright-color rooms, this inn is a charming oasis. A lunch (fixed price menus) of sea bass, pigeon, and goat cheese on the flowery veranda is everything the south of France should be. The inn has a tennis court on the slope above it and, in the village annex Lou Pourtail, six little rooms offering shelter at bargain rates. ⊠ *2 pl. Auguste Arnulf, Peillon Village, 06440* ☎ *04–93–79–91–17* 🖷 *04–93–79–99–36* ⊕ *www.chateauxhotels.com/madone* 🛏 *14 rooms, 3 suites* ⚭ *Restaurant, minibars, tennis court, Internet, no-smoking rooms; no a/c* ▤ *MC, V* ⊗ *Closed late Oct.–Jan.* ⍾ *MAP.*

Monaco

7 km (4½ mi) east of Èze, 21 km (13 mi) east of Nice.

It's positively feudal, the idea that an ancient dynasty of aristocrats could still hold fast to its patch of coastline, the last scrap of a once-vast domain. But that's just what the Grimaldi family did, clinging to a few acres of glory and maintaining their own license plates, their own telephone area code (377—don't forget to dial this when calling Monaco from France or other countries), and their own highly forgiving tax system. Yet the Principality of Monaco covers just 473 acres and would fit comfortably inside New York's Central Park or a family farm in Iowa. And its 5,000 pampered citizens would fill only a small fraction of the seats in Yankee Stadium. The harbor district, known as **La Condamine,** connects the new quarter, officially known as **Monte Carlo,** with the Vieille Ville, officially known as **Monaco-Ville** (or Le Rocher). Have no fear that you'll need to climb countless steps to get to the Vieille Ville, as there are plenty of elevators and escalators climbing the steep cliffs.

Prince Rainier III, the family patriarch who famously wed Grace Kelly and brought Hollywood glamor to his toy kingdom, passed away in April 2005; his son, the imminently responsible Prince Albert, took over as head of the family and principality. Albert traces his ancestry to Otto Canella, who was born in 1070. The Grimaldi dynasty began with Otto's great-great-great-grandson, Francesco Grimaldi, also known as Frank the Rogue. Expelled from Genoa, Frank and his cronies disguised themselves as monks and in 1297 seized the fortified medieval town known today as Le Rocher (the Rock). Except for a short break under Napoléon, the Grimaldis have been here ever since, which makes them the oldest reigning family in Europe (they also seem to be the tackiest, considering all the lurid tabloid coverage of princesses Caroline and Stephanie).

It's the tax system, not the gambling (actually, the latter helps pay for the former), that has made Monaco one of the most sought-after addresses in the world. It bristles with gleaming glass-and-concrete corn-cob-towers 20 and 30 stories high and with vast apartment complexes, their terraces, landscaped like miniature gardens, jutting over the sea. You now have to look hard to find the Belle Époque grace of yesteryear. But if you repair to the town's great 1864 landmark Hôtel de Paris— still a veritable crossroads of the buffed and befurred Euro-gentry—or enjoy a grand bouffe at its famous Louis XV restaurant, or attend the Opéra, or visit the ballrooms of the Casino (avert your eyes at the flashy gambling machines), you may still be able to conjure up Monaco's elegant past and the much-missed spirit of Princess Grace.

★ ❷ Place du Casino is the center of Monte Carlo, and the **Casino** is a must-see, even if you don't bet a sou. Into the gold-leaf splendor of the Casino, the hopeful traipse from tour buses to tempt fate beneath the gilt-edge Rococo ceiling (but do remember the fate of Sarah Bernhardt, who lost her last 100,000 francs here). Jacket and tie are required in the back rooms, which open at 3 PM. Bring your passport (under-21s not admitted). Note that there are special admission fees to get into many of the period gaming rooms—only the Salle des Jeux Americains is free. ✉ Pl. du Casino ☎ 377/92–16–20–00 ⊕ www.sbm.mc ☉ Daily noon–4 AM.

❸ In the true spirit of the town, it seems that the **Opéra de Monte-Carlo** (✉ Pl. du Casino ☎ 377/92–16–22–99), with its 18-ton gilt-bronze chandelier and extravagant frescoes, is part of the Casino complex. The grand theater was designed by Charles Garnier, who also built the Paris Opéra. Its main auditorium, the Salle Garnier, was inaugurated by Sarah Bernhardt in 1879.

❹ Some say the most serious gamblers play at **Sun Casino,** in the Monte Carlo Grand Hotel, by the vast convention center that juts over the water. ✉ 12 av. des Spélugues ☎ 377/92–16–21–23 ☉ Tables open weekdays at 5 PM and weekends at 4 PM; slot machines open daily at 11 AM.

❺ From place des Moulins an elevator descends to the Larvotto Beach complex, artfully created with imported sand, and the **Musée National Automates et Poupées,** housed in a Garnier villa within a rose garden. It has a beguiling collection of 18th- and 19th-century dolls and automatons. ✉ 17 av. Princesse Grace ☎ 377/93–30–91–26 ✑ €6 ☉ Easter–Aug., daily 10–6:30; Sept.–Easter, daily 10–12:15 and 2:30–6:30.

❻ West of Monte Carlo stands the famous Rock, crowned by the **Palais Princier,** where the royal family resides. A 40-minute guided tour (summer only) of this sumptuous chunk of history, first built in the 13th century and expanded and enhanced over the centuries, reveals an extravagance of 16th- and 17th-century frescoes, as well as tapestries, gilt furniture, and paintings on a grand scale. Note that the **Relève de la Garde** (Changing of the Guard) is held outside the front entrance of the palace most days at 11:55 AM. ✉ Pl. du Palais ☎ 377/93–25–18–31 ✑ €6, joint ticket with Musée Napoléon €8 ☉ June–Oct., daily 9:30–5.

❼ One wing of the Palais Princier, open throughout the year, is taken up by the **Musée Napoléon,** filled with Napoleonic souvenirs—including that hat and a tricolor scarf—and genealogical charts. ✉ In Palais Princier ☎ 377/93–25–18–31 ✑ €4, joint ticket with palace apartments €8 ☉ June–mid-Nov., daily 9:30–6:30; Jan.–May, Tues.–Sun. 10:30–12:30 and 2–5.

On the terrasses de Fontvielle are two remarkable sights (opened in 2003):
☾ ❽ the **Collection des Voitures Anciennes** (Collection of Vintage Cars) and
☾ the **Jardin Animalier** (Animal Garden). The former is a collection of Prince Rainier's vintage cars from a De Dion Bouton to a Lambourghini Countach; the latter, a mini-zoo housing the Rainier family's animal collection—an astonishing array of wild beasts including monkeys and exotic

CRASHING THE GRAND PRIX?

In late May, the entire racing world speeds to Monaco to see the best Formula One drivers compete in the Grand Prix. During the event, the streets are roped off, the liquor is iced, the brass is polished, and the superrich alight on rented balconies (some cost €10,000 for the two-day stint). Monaco on the day of the race is one big human sardine can, so buy your train ticket ahead of time. Though reserved bleacher seats start at €520 and are sold months in advance,

tickets for the section along the cliff under the palace, called "Secteur rocher, " cost a mere €110. Come before 10 AM to stake out a place where thousands of people won't block your view. You can buy a ticket at box offices all around town until the race starts at 3:30 PM. Unfortunately, there are no other blocks where you can view the race up close, and police are everywhere to make sure you don't crash the party if you don't have a ticket.

birds. ☒ *Terrasses de Fontvielle* ☎ 377/92–05–28–56 or 377/93–25–18–31 ☜ €6 (Voitures); €4 (Animalier) ⊗ June–Sept., daily 10–6.

㊾ Follow the flow of crowds down the last remaining streets of medieval Monaco to the **Cathédrale de l'Immaculée-Conception** (☒ Av. St-Martin), an uninspired 19th-century version of the Romanesque style. Nonetheless, it harbors a magnificent altarpiece, painted in 1500 by Bréa, and the tomb of Princess Grace.

★ ♨ **㊿** At the prow of the Rock, the grand **Musée Océanographique** (Oceanography Museum) perches dramatically on a cliff. It's a splendid Edwardian structure, built under Prince Albert I to house specimens collected on amateur explorations. Jacques Cousteau (1910–97) led its missions from 1957 to 1988. The main floor displays skeletons and taxidermy of enormous sea creatures; early submarines and diving gear dating from the Middle Ages; and a few interactive science displays. The main draw is the famous **aquarium,** a vast complex of backlighted tanks containing every imaginable species of fish, crab, and eel. ☒ Av. St-Martin ☎ 377/93–15–36–00 ☜ €11 ⊗ July and Aug., daily 9:30–7:30; Sept., May, and June, daily 9:30–7; Oct.–Apr., daily 10–6.

51 Carved out of the rock face and one of Monte Carlo's most stunning escape hatches, the **Jardin Exotique de Monaco** (Monaco Exotic Garden) is studded with thousands of succulents and cacti, all set along promenades, belvederes over the sea, and even framing faux boulders (actually hollow sculptures). There are rare plants from Mexico and Africa, and the hillside plot, threaded with bridges and grottoes, can't be beat for coastal splendor. Thanks go to Prince Albert I, who started it all. Also on the grounds, or actually under them, are the **Grottes de l'Observatoire**—spectacular grottoes and caves a-drip with stalagmites and spotlit with fairy lights. The largest cavern is called "La Grande Salle" and looks like a Romanesque rock cathedral. Traces of Cro-Magnon civilization have been

Fodor's Choice ★

Monaco

KEY

🇮 *Tourist information*

| 0 | 220 yards |
| 0 | 200 meters |

found here so the grottoes now bear the official name of the **Musée d'Anthropologie Préhistorique.** ⊠ *Bd. du Jardin Exotique* ☎ *377/93–30–33–65* 🎫 *€6.70* ⊙ *May–Aug., daily 9–7; Sept.–Apr., daily 9–6.*

Where to Stay & Eat

★ **$$$$** ✕ **Le Louis XV.** This sumptuous neo-Baroque restaurant, in the Hôtel de Paris, stuns with royal pomp that is nonetheless upstaged by its product: the superb cuisine of Alain Ducasse, one of Europe's most celebrated chefs. Ducasse often refers to his deceptively simple style as "country cooking," where caviar and truffles slum happily with stockfish (stewed salt cod) and tripe. In short, it's a panoply of Mediterranean delights. If your wallet is a fat one, this is a must. Menus run from €150 to €180. ⊠ *Hôtel de Paris, pl. du Casino* ☎ *377/92–16–30–01* ⊕ *www.alain-ducasse.com* 🖃 *AE, DC, MC, V* ⊙ *Closed Tues., Wed. (Sept.–mid-June only), and late Nov.–late Dec.*

$$–$$$$ ✕ **Castelroc.** With its tempting pine-shaded terrace just across from the entrance to the palace, this popular local lunch spot serves up specialties of cuisine Monegasque, ranging from anchoiade to stockfish. There are only fixed-price menus: lunch €21, dinner €39. ⊠ *Pl. du Palais* ☎ *377/93–30–36–68* 🖃 *AE, MC, V* ⊙ *Closed weekends and Dec. and Jan.*

$$$ ✕ **Café de Paris.** This landmark Belle Époque brasserie, across from the Casino, offers the usual classics (shellfish, steak tartare, matchstick frites, and fish boned table-side). Supercilious, super-pro waiters fawn gracefully over titled preeners, gentlemen, jet-setters, and tourists alike. Happily, there's good hot food until 2 AM. ⊠ *Pl. du Casino* ☎ *377/92–16–20–20* 🖃 *AE, DC, MC, V.*

$$$$ ⌂ **Hermitage.** A riot of frescoes and plaster flourishes embellished with gleaming brass, this landmark 1900 hotel, set back a block from the Casino scene, nonetheless maintains a relatively low profile. Even if you're not staying, come to see the glass-dome Art Nouveau vestibule and winter garden, designed by Gustav Eiffel. The best rooms face the sea or angle toward the port. ⊠ *Square Beaumarchais, 98005* ☎ *377/92–16–40–00* 🖨 *377/92–16–38–52* ⊕ *www.montecarloresort.com* 🛏 *195 rooms, 14 junior suites, 18 suites* ⌂ *Restaurant, minibars, cable TV, pool, health club, bar, Internet, parking (fee), some pets allowed* 🖃 *AE, DC, MC, V.*

$$$$ ⌂ **Hôtel Columbus.** Situated on the Fontveille harbor, this super-hip, youthful hotel is a refreshing breath of contemporary air—the farthest thing from stuffy or old-world. A lifestyle hotel opened by the owners of the trendy Malmaison chain, its rooms are luxe, decked out in soft beiges, rich browns, and purples, with metal trim and teakwood accents that would do a *Wallpaper* article proud; the bar is a nighttime favorite amongst Formula One drivers and fans, who are no doubt drawn there by part-owner David Coulthard. ⊠ *23 av. des Papalins, 98000* ☎ *377/92–05–90–00* 🖨 *377/92–05–91–67* ⊕ *www.columbushotels.com* 🛏 *153 rooms, 31 suites* ⌂ *Restaurant, minibars, cable TV, bar, Internet, meeting room, parking (fee), some pets allowed (fee)* 🖃 *AE, DC, MC, V* ⍩ *MAP.*

$$$$ ⌂ **Monte Carlo Grand Hotel.** Sprawling long and low along the waterfront at Monte Carlo's base, this ultramodern airport-scale complex is so vast it commands a full-time staff of upholsterers. Bright rooms decked in vivid hues angle onto the open sea. The bars, casino, boutiques, and mall-size lobby easily contain megaconventions, but vacationers will feel at home, too. ✉ *12 av. des Spélugues, 98000* ☎ *377/93–50–65–00* 🖷 *377/93–30–01–57* ⊕ *www.montecarlograndhotel.com* ⇱ *619 rooms, 69 apartments* ☍ *3 restaurants, minibars, cable TV, pool, health club, hot tub, bar, cabaret, casino, Internet, meeting room, parking (fee), some pets allowed (fee)* ⊟ *AE, DC, MC, V* ⑩ *MAP.*

$$$ 🏨 **Alexandra.** The friendly proprietress, Madame Larouquie, makes you feel right at home at this central, comfortable spot just north of the Casino. Though the color schemes clash and the bedrooms are spare, bathrooms are spacious and up-to-date, and insulated windows keep traffic noise out. Breakfast is included in the price. ✉ *35 bd. Princesse-Charlotte, 98000* ☎ *377/93–50–63–13* 🖷 *377/92–16–06–48* ⇱ *56 rooms* ☍ *Minibars, cable TV* ⊟ *AE, DC, MC, V* ⑩ *BP.*

Nightlife & the Arts

There's no need to go to bed before dawn in Monte Carlo when you can go to the **casinos.** Monte Carlo's spring arts festival, **Printemps des Arts,** takes place from early April to mid-May and includes the world's top ballet, operatic, symphonic, and chamber-music performers. Year-round, opera, ballet, and classical music can be enjoyed at the magnificently sumptuous Salle Garnier auditorium of the **Opéra de Monte-Carlo** (✉ Pl. du Casino ☎ 337/92–16–22–99 ⊕ www.opera.mc), the main venue of the Opéra de Monte-Carlo and the Orchestre Philharmonique de Monte-Carlo, both worthy of the magnificent hall.

Sports

Held at the beautiful Monte Carlo Country Club, the **Monte Carlo Open Tennis Masters Series** (⊕ www.masters-series.com/montecarlo) is held during the last two weeks of April every year. When the tennis stops, the auto racing begins: the **Grand Prix de Monaco** (☎ 377/93–15–26–00 for information ⊕ www.monaco.mc/monaco/gprix) takes place in mid-May.

Roquebrune–Cap-Martin

🔢 *5 km (3 mi) east of Monaco.*

In the midst of the frenzy of overbuilding that defines this last gasp of the coast before Italy, two twinned havens have survived, each in its own way: the perched Vieille Ville of Roquebrune, which gives its name to the greater area, and Cap-Martin—luxurious, isolated, exclusive, and the once favored retreat of the Empress Eugénie and Winston Churchill. With its lovely tumble of raked tile roofs and twisting streets, fountains, archways, and quiet squares, Roquebrune retains many of the charms of a hilltop village, although it has become heavily gentrified and commercialized. Rue Moncollet is lined with arcaded passageways and a number of medieval houses. Somerset Maugham—who once memorably described these environs as a "sunny place for shady people"—resided in the town's famous Villa Mauresque (still private) for many years. Roquebrune's main attraction is its **Château Féodal** (Feudal Castle). Around the remains of a 10th-century tower, the Grimaldis erected an impregnable fortress that was state-of-the-art in the 16th century, with crenellation, watchtowers, and a broad moat. 🎫 €4 ⊘ *Oct.–Jan., daily 10–12:30 and 2–5; Feb.–May, daily 10–12:30 and 2–6; June–Sept., daily 10–12:30 and 3–7:30.*

In the **cemetery**, Swiss-French architect Le Corbusier lies buried with his wife in a tomb of his own design. He kept a humble *cabanot* (beach bungalow) on the rocky shore of the Cap-Martin, where he drowned while swimming in 1965. You can see the glorious flora of the cape by walking the **Promenade Le Corbusier.** It leads over chalk cliffs and through dense Mediterranean flora to the famed modernist architect's "Cabanon" bungalow (plans are in the works to open this as a museum—check with local tourist office)—a tiny retreat, as much outdoors as in and designed along the rigorous lines he preferred. Park at the base of the cape on avenue Winston-Churchill and follow the signs.

Menton

⑤ *1 km (½ mi) east of Roquebrune, 9 km (5½ mi) east of Monaco.*

Fodor's Choice

Menton, the most Mediterranean of the French resort towns, rubs shoulders with the Italian border and owes its balmy climate to the protective curve of the Ligurian shore. Its picturesque harbor skyline seems to beg artists to immortalize it, while its Cubist skew of terra-cotta roofs and yellow-ocher houses, Baroque arabesques capping the church facades, and ceramic tiles glistening on their steeples all evoke the villages of the Italian coast. Also worth a visit are the many exotic gardens set in the hills around the town. Menton is the least pretentious of the Côte d'Azur resorts and all the more alluring for its modesty. The **Basilique St-Michel** (⊠ Parvis St-Michel), a majestic Baroque church, dominates the skyline of Menton with its bell tower. Beyond the beautifully proportioned facade—a 19th-century addition—the richly frescoed nave and chapels contain several works by Genovese artists and a splendid 17th-century organ.

Just above the main church, the smaller **Chapelle de l'Immaculée-Conception** answers St-Michel's grand gesture with its own pure Baroque beauty, dating from 1687. Between 3 and 5 you can slip in to see the graceful trompe l'oeil over the altar and the ornate gilt lanterns early penitents carried in processions.

Two blocks below the square, **rue St-Michel** serves as the main commercial artery of the Vieille Ville, lined with shops, cafés, and orange trees. Between the lively pedestrian rue St-Michel and the waterfront, the marvelous **Marché Couvert** (Covered Market) sums up Menton style with its Belle Époque facade decorated in jewel-tone ceramics. Inside, it's just as appealing, with merchants selling chewy bread, mountain cheeses, oils, fruit, and Italian delicacies in Caravaggesque disarray.

On the waterfront opposite the market, a squat medieval bastion crowned with four tiny watchtowers houses the **Musée Jean-Cocteau.** Built in 1636 to defend the port, it was spotted by the artist-poet-filmmaker Jean Cocteau (1889–1963) as the perfect site for a group of his works. There are bright, cartoonish pastels of fishermen and wenches in love, and a fantastical assortment of ceramic animals in the wrought-iron windows he designed. ⊠ *Vieux Port* ☎ *04–93–57–72–30* 🗹 €3 🕑 *Wed.–Mon. 10–noon and 2–6.*

The 19th-century Italianate **Hôtel de Ville** conceals another Cocteau treasure: it was he who decorated the **Salle des Mariages** (Marriage Room), the room in which civil marriages take place, with vibrant allegorical scenes. ✉ *17 av. de la République* 🖼 *€2* ⊙ *Weekdays 8:30–12:30 and 1:30–5.*

At the far west end of town stands the 18th-century **Palais Carnolès** (Carnolès Palace) in vast gardens luxuriant with orange, lemon, and grapefruit trees. It was once the summer retreat of the princes of Monaco; nowadays it contains a sizable collection of European paintings from the Renaissance to the present day. ✉ *3 av. de la Madone* 🕾 *04–93–35–49–71* 🖼 *Free* ⊙ *Wed.–Mon. 10–noon and 2–6.*

The Côte d'Azur was famed for its panoply of grand villas and even grander gardens built by Victorian dukes, Spanish exiles, Belgian royals, and American bluebloods. With its temperate microclimate created by its southeastern and sunny exposure (the Alps were a natural buffer against cold winds), Menton attracted a great share of these wealthy hobbyists, including Major Lawrence Johnston, a gentleman gardener best known for his Cotswolds wonderland, Hidcote Manor. Fair-haired and blue-eyed, this gentle American wound up buying a choice estate in the village of Gorbio—one of the loveliest of all perched seaside villages, set 10 km (6 mi) west of Menton—and spent the 1920s and 1930s making the **Serre** ★ **de la Madone** one of the horticultural masterpieces of the coast. He brought back exotica from his many trips to South Africa, Mexico, and China, and planted them in a series of terraces, accented by little pools, vistas, and stone steps. While most of his creeping plumbago, pink belladonna, and night-flowering cacti are now gone, his garden has been reopened by the municipality. It is best to call for a reservation at the Serre de la Madone; car facilities are very limited but the garden can also be reached from Menton via bus No. 7 (get off at Mers et Monts' stop). Back in Menton, green-thumbers will also want to visit the town's Jardin Botanique, the **Val Rahmeh Botanical Garden** (Av. St-Jacques), planted by Maybud Campbell in the 1910s, much prized by connoisseurs, bursting with rare ornamentals and subtropical plants, and adorned with water-lily pools and fountains. The tourist office can also give you directions to other gardens around Menton, including the Fontana Rosa and the Villa Maria Serena, as well as issue Heritage Passports for select garden visits; log onto www.menton.com. ✉ *74 route de Gorbio* 🕾 *04–93–57–73–90* ⊕ *www.serredelamadone.com/* 🖼 *€8 for Serre, €4 for Val Rehmeh* ⊙ *Mar.–Oct. 31, Tues.–Sun. 10–6; Nov.–Mar. tours only, Tues.–Sun., fax request to 04–93–28–55–42.*

Where to Stay & Eat

★ **$$–$$$** ✕🖼 **Aiglon.** Sweep down the curving stone stair to the terrazzo mosaic lobby of this lovely 1880 garden villa and wander out for a drink or a meal by the pool. Or settle onto your little balcony overlooking the grounds and a tiny wedge of sea. The poolside restaurant, Le Riaumont, serves classic seafood by candlelight; breakfast, included in the price, is served in a shady garden shelter. From here it's a three-minute walk to the beach. ✉ *7 av. de la Madone, 06502* 🕾 *04–93–57–55–55* 🖼 *04–93–35–92–39* ⊕ *www.hotelaiglon.net* ⤴ *28 rooms, 2 apart-*

ments ⚒ *Restaurant, pool, bar, Internet, some pets allowed (fee); no room TVs* 🖃 *AE, DC, MC, V* ⦿〇 *MAP.*

Nightlife & the Arts

In August the **Festival de Musique de Chambre** (Chamber Music Festival) takes place on the stone-paved plaza outside the church of St-Michel. The **Fête du Citron** (Lemon Festival), at the end of February, celebrates the lemon with floats and sculptures like those of the Rose Bowl Parade, all made of real fruit.

THE CÔTE D'AZUR A TO Z

To research prices, get advice from other travelers, and book travel arrangements, visit www.fodors.com.

AIR TRAVEL

There are frequent flights between Paris and Nice on EasyJet, AOM, and Air France, as well as direct flights on Delta Airlines from New York. The flight time between Paris and Nice is about one hour.

AIRPORTS

The Nice–Côte d'Azur Airport sits on a peninsula between Antibes and Nice.

🛂 **Airport Information Nice-Côte d'Azur Airport** ⊠ 7 km (4½ mi) from Nice ☎ 04-93-21-30-30.

BUS TRAVEL

Buses allow you to penetrate deeper into villages and backcountry spots not on the rail line; pick up a schedule for local and commercial excursion buses at the train station, at tourist offices, and at the local *gare routière* (bus station). Phocéens Santa Azur (Voyages) is the best bus service covering the Côte d'Azur region, with buses departing from Nice, Antibes, Cannes, Menton, and Mandelieu and regular minibus service between Nice, Marseille, Toulon, and some towns inland of Nice. Alpes-Maritimes Bus Services—RCA Transport (Rapides Côte d'Azur) covers the coastal area, from Menton to Villeneuve Loubet, and inland, to Peille and Aspremont; routes run between Nice and Cannes, with stops at Cagnes-sur-Mer and Juan-les-Pins and they also service Menton, Villefranche, St-Jean-Cap-Ferrat, Èze, and Monaco (plus a "rapid" airport service from Menton and/or Monaco to Nice International). SAP offers buses serving Vence, St-Paul, La Colle-sur-Loup, St-Laurent-du-Var, and Nice. Compagnie des Autobus de Monaco covers that principality. Rapides Côte d'Azur traffics the routes in and around Cannes, while SODETRAV buses head to and from St-Tropez and St-Raphaël. In addition, the national SNCF service covers more distant locales.

🛂Bus Information **Alpes-Maritimes Bus Services—RCA Transport (Rapides Côte d'Azur)** ⊠ 5 bd. Jean Jaures, Nice ☎ 04-93-85-64-44 ⊕ www.rca.tm.fr. **Compagnie des Autobus de Monaco** ⊠ 2 av. du pdt J. F. Kennedy, Monaco ☎ 377/97-70-22-22 ⊕ www. cam.mc. **Phocéens Santa Azur (Voyages)** ⊠ 4 pl. Massena, Nice ☎ 04-93-13-18-20 ⊠ 5 sq. Mérimée, Cannes ☎ 04-93-39-79-40 ⊠ 8 pl. de Gaul, Antibes ☎ 04-93-34-15-98. **SAP (Société Automobile de Provence)** ☎ 04-93-58-37-60.

SNCF ☎ 08-36-35-35-35 ⊕ www.ter-sncf.com/uk/paca. **SODETRAV (Société départementale de transports du Var)** ☎ 0825/000650 ⊕ www.sodetrav.fr.

CAR RENTAL

Most likely you'll want to rent your car at one of the main rail stops, either St-Raphaël, Nice, Monaco, or Menton, or at the airport in Nice, where all major companies are represented.

🚗 Local Agencies **Avis** ⊠ 2 av. des Phocéens, Nice ☎ 04-93-80-63-52 ⊠ Nice Airport ☎ 04-93-21-42-80 ⊠ 190 pl. Pierre Coullet, St-Raphaël ☎ 04-94-95-60-42. **Budget** ⊠ 23 rue de Belgique, Nice ☎ 04-93-16-24-16 ⊠ Nice Airport ☎ 04-93-21-36-50 ⊠ 40 rue Waldeck-Rousseau, St-Raphaël ☎ 04-94-82-24-44. **Europcar** ⊠ 3 av. Gustave V, Nice ☎ 04-92-14-44-50 ⊠ Nice Airport ☎ 04-93-21-43-54 ⊠ 47 av. de Grande-Bretagne, Monaco ☎ 377/93-50-74-95 ⊠ 54 pl. Pierre Coullet, St-Raphaël ☎ 04-94-95-56-87. **Hertz** ⊠ 1 Promenade des Anglais, Nice ☎ 04-93-87-11-87 ⊠ Nice airport ☎ 04-93-21-36-72 ⊠ 32 rue Waldeck-Rousseau, St-Raphaël ☎ 04-94-95-48-68 ⊠ 27 bd. Albert I, Monaco ☎ 377/93-50-79-60.

CAR TRAVEL

The best way to explore the secondary sights in this region, especially the backcountry hill towns, is by car. It also allows you the freedom to zip along A8 between the coastal resorts and to enjoy the tremendous views from the three corniches that trace the coast from Nice to the Italian border. N98, which connects you to coastal resorts in between, can be extremely slow, though scenic. A8 parallels the coast from above St-Tropez to Nice to the resorts on the Grand Corniche; N98 follows the coast more closely. From Paris the main southbound artery is A6/A7, known as the Autoroute du Soleil; it passes through Provence and joins the eastbound A8 at Aix-en-Provence.

LODGING

APARTMENT & VILLA RENTALS The tourist offices of individual towns often publish lists of *locations meublés* (furnished rentals), sometimes vouched for by the tourist office and rated for comfort. Gîtes de France is a nationwide organization that rents *gîtes ruraux* (rural vacation lodgings) by the week, usually outstanding examples of a region's character. The headquarters for the regions covered in this chapter are listed below. Write or call for a catalog, then make a selection and reservation.

🚗 Local Agents **Gîtes de France Var** ⊠ Rond-Point du 4 Décembre 1974, B.P. 215, 83006 Draguignan Cedex ☎ 04-94-50-93-93 🖷 04-94-50-93-90. **Gîtes de France des Alpes-Maritimes** ⊠ 55 Promenade des Anglais, B.P. 1602, Cedex 01, 06011 Nice ☎ 04-92-15-21-30 🖷 04-93-86-01-06 ⊕ www.crt-riviera.fr/gites06.

SPORTS & THE OUTDOORS

This is golf country, and you can pick up the brochure and map *Les Golfs du Soleil* (*Golf Courses of the Sun*) and *Destination Golf* at local tourist offices to get a complete listing of golf courses and facilities from St-Tropez to Monaco.

TOURS

BUS TOURS Santa Azur organizes all-day or half-day bus excursions to sights near Nice, including Monaco, Cannes, and nearby hill towns, either leaving from its offices or from several stops along the Promenade des Anglais, mainly in front of the big hotels. In Antibes, Phocéens Voyages organizes similar bus explorations of the region.

🚩 Fees & Schedules **Phocéens Voyages** ✉ 8 pl. de Gaulle, Antibes ☎ 04-93-34-15-98. **Santa Azur** ✉ 11 av. Jean-Médecin, Nice ☎ 04-93-85-46-81.

TOUR GUIDES The city of Nice arranges individual guided tours on an à la carte basis according to your needs. For information contact the Bureau d'Accueil and specify your dates and language preferences.

🚩 **Bureau d'Accueil** ☎ 04-93-14-48-00.

TRAIN TOURS A small tourist train goes along the Nice waterfront from in front of the Casino Ruhl, along cours Saleya, and up to the Château.

🚩 Fees & Schedules **Tourist train** ☎ 04-93-92-45-59.

TRAIN TRAVEL

Nice is the major rail crossroads for trains arriving from Paris and other northern cities, as well as from Italy. This coastal line, working eastward from Marseille and west from Ventimiglia, stops at Fréjus, Antibes, Monaco, and Menton. There is no rail access to St-Tropez; St-Raphaël is the nearest stop. To get from Paris to Nice, you can take the TGV, though it only maintains high speeds to Valence before returning to conventional rails and rates.

You can easily move along the coast by train on the Côte d'Azur line, a dramatic and highly tourist-pleasing route that offers panoramic views as it rolls from one famous resort to the next. But train travelers will have difficulty getting up to St-Paul, Vence, Peillon, and other backcountry villages; that you must accomplish by bus or car.

🚩 Train Information **SNCF** ☎ 08-36-35-35-35 ⊕ www.ter-sncf.com/uk/paca.

TRAVEL AGENCIES

🚩 Local Agent Referrals **American Express Voyages** ✉ 11 Promenade des Anglais, Nice ☎ 04-93-16-53-51 ✉ 35 bd. Princess Charlotte, Monte Carlo ☎ 377/93-25-74-45 ✉ 8 rue des Belges, Cannes ☎ 04-93-38-15-87. **Havas Voyages** ✉ 12 av. Félix Faure, Nice ☎ 04-93-62-76-30 ✉ 64 av. Commandant Guilbaud, St-Raphaël ☎ 04-94-19-82-20 ✉ 17 bd. Louis Blanc, St-Tropez ☎ 04-94-56-64-64.

VISITOR INFORMATION

For information on travel within the department of Var (St-Tropez to La Napoule), write to the Comité Départemental du Tourisme du Var. The Comité Régional du Tourisme Riviera Côte d'Azur provides information on tourism throughout the department of Alpes-Maritimes, from Cannes to the Italian border. For information on the Belle Époque splendors of the region, log on to a helpful Comite Régionale Web site www.guideriviera. com/belle-epoque/en. Local tourist offices (*Office du Tourisme*) in major towns discussed in this chapter are listed below by town.

🚩 Tourist Information **Antibes/Juan-les-Pins** ✉ 11 pl. de Gaulle, 06600 Antibes ☎ 04-92-90-53-00 🖥 04-92-90-53-01. **Cannes** ✉ Palais des Festivals, Esplanade G. Pompidou, B.P. 272 06403 ☎ 04-93-39-24-53 🖥 04-92-99-84-23 ⊕ www.cannes-on-line.com. **Comité Départemental du Tourisme du Var** ✉ 1 bd. Maréchal Foch, 83300 Draguignan ☎ 03-94-50-55-50 🖥 04-94-50-55-51 ⊕ www.ville-Draguignan. fr. **Comité Régional du Tourisme Riviera Côte d'Azur** ✉ 55 Promenade des Anglais,

B.P. 1602, Cedex 1, 06011 Nice ☎ 04–93–37–78–78 ⊕ www.crt-riviera.fr. **Éze** ⊠ Pl. du General de Gaulle, 06360 Éze ☎ 04–93–41–26–00 🖨 04–93–41–04–80 ⊕ www.eze-riviera.com. **Fréjus** ⊠ 325 rue Jean-Jaurès, B.P. 8, 83601 ☎ 04–94–51–83–83 🖨 04–94–51–00–26 ⊕ www.ville-frejus.fr. **Grasse** ⊠ Palais des Congrés, 22 Cours Honoré Cresp 06130 ☎ 04–93–36–66–66 🖨 04–93–36–86–36 ⊕ www.grasse-riviera.com. **Menton** ⊠ Palais de l'Europe, av. Boyer, 06500 ☎ 04–92–41–76–76 🖨 04–92–41–76–78 ⊕ www.villedementon.com. **Monaco** ⊠ 2a bd. des Moulins, 98000 Monte Carlo ☎ 377/92–16–61–66 🖨 377/92–16–60–00 ⊕ www.monaco-tourism.com. **Nice** ⊠ 5 Promenade des Anglais, 06000 ☎ 04–92–14–48–00 🖨 04–92–14–48–03 ⊕ www.nicetourism.com or in person at the train station or airport. **St-Jean-Cap-Ferrat** ⊠ 59 av. Denis Semeria, 06230 St-Jean-Cap-Ferrat ☎ 04–93–76–08–90 🖨 04–93–76–16–67 ⊕ www.ville-saint-jean-cap-ferrat.fr/. **St-Paul-de-Vence** ⊠ 2 rue Grande, 06570 ☎ 04–93–32–86–95 🖨 04–93–32–60–27. **St-Raphaël** ⊠ Rue Waldeck-Rousseau, 83700 ☎ 04–94–19–52–52 🖨 04–94–83–85–40 ⊕ www.saint-raphael.com. **St-Tropez** ⊠ Quai Jean-Jaurès, B.P. 183, 83992 ☎ 04–94–97–45–21 🖨 04–94–97–82–66 ⊕ www.ot-saint-tropez.com. **Vence** ⊠ Pl. du Grand Jardin, 06140 ☎ 04–93–58–06–38 🖨 04–93–58–91–81 ⊕ www.ville-vence.fr.

Corsica

13

WORD OF MOUTH

"Ajaccio was a fun town, the birthplace of Napoléon and we visited his birthplace on Bastille Day, then watched the spectacular fireworks from the harborfront that night. Odd though, most of the fireworks were red, white, and green (not blue). I know there is a certain feel for Italy in Corsica, but weren't they getting a little too simpatico with their Bastille Day fireworks?"

—Patrick

"One place I love is the Col de Bavella in the south of the island, with wonderful mountain scenery and close by quaint little villages such as Zonza."

—Jan

Introduction by
George Semler

Updated by
George Semler

"THE BEST WAY TO KNOW CORSICA," according to Napoléon, "is to be born there." Not everyone has had his luck, so chances are you'll be arriving on the overnight ferry from Marseille to discover "the mountain in the sea." This vertical granite world of its own, plopped down in the Mediterranean between Provence and Tuscany, remains France's very own Wild West: a powerful natural setting and, literally, a breath of fresh air. Corsica is where you go to get away from it all, to clear your head, to find your magnetic north; a microcosm of mountains, beaches, fishing ports, wilderness, and the purest strain of proto-Mediterranean culture. Mountain people born and bred, Corsicans have historically distrusted the sea and the cosmopolitan coastal landing points, open to invading forces. The true Corsican is a highland spirit, at home in the dense undergrowth of the *maquis*—the all-sustaining chestnut forest—or the Laricio pines that climb the upper reaches of what Guy de Maupassant christened his "mountain in the sea."

Corsica's gifts of artistic and archaeological treasures, crystalline waters, granite peaks, and pine forests add up to one of France's most unspoiled sanctuaries—a logical crucible for the emergence of a force such as Napoléon Bonaparte. Its strategic location 168 km (105 mi) south of Monaco and 81 km (50 mi) west of Italy made Corsica a prize hotly contested by a succession of Mediterranean powers, notably Genoa, Pisa, and France. Their vestiges remain: the city-state of Genoa ruled Corsica for more than 200 years, leaving impressive citadels, churches, bridges, and nearly 100 medieval watchtowers around the island's coastline. The Italian influence is also apparent in village architecture and in the Corsican language, which is a combination of Italian, Tuscan dialect, and Latin.

Corsica gives an impression of immensity, seeming far larger than its 215 km (133 mi) length and 81 km (50 mi) width, partly because its rugged, mountainous terrain makes for slow traveling and partly because the landscape and the culture vary greatly from one microregion to another. Much of the terrain of Corsica that is not wooded or cultivated is covered with a dense thicket of undergrowth, called the maquis, a variety of wild and aromatic plants including lavender, myrtle, and heather that gave Corsica one of its sobriquets, "the perfumed isle." The maquis, famous for harboring fugitives, became the term used for the French Resistance movement during World War II. In Corsica "going underground" meant taking to the maquis.

Along with the word *maquis,* the term *vendetta* is one of Corsica's contributions to world lexicography. The rough-and-ready legend associated with the island comes from a long tradition of apparent lawlessness and deeply entrenched clannishness. As justice from "the Continent, " whether France or Italy, was usually slow and often unsatisfying, Corsican clans frequently fought each other in blood feuds of honor and revenge.

Although famous as the birthplace of Napoléon Bonaparte (who never returned to the island after beginning his military career), Corsica's real national hero is Pasquale Paoli, who framed the world's first republi-

13

Four days is barely sufficient time to visit Corsica. In five days you can cover most of Haute Corse, and in 10 days it's possible, though not necessarily advisable, to see the whole island. The danger is spending too much time carbound. One approach is to settle in Corte, near the island's center, setting out each day on a quest to see different attractions.

Numbers in the text correspond to numbers in the margin and on the Corsica and Ajaccio maps.

If you have 4 days

Start out in Napoléon's hometown, 🖾 **Ajaccio** ❶ ► – ❽ for a walk through the market, the port and Vieille Ville, and the Musée Fesch. On your second day, head up into the highlands by train or automobile to Corsica's spiritual capital at 🖾 **Corte** ❶. On the third day, drive through the Castagniccia to 🖾 **Piedicroce** ❷ for a night in the chestnut forest. On your final day, find your way out of the Castagniccia to 🖾 **Bastia** ❸ with a stop at **Murato** ❷ for lunch and a look at the San Michele church. From Bastia choose between Livorno, Italy, or Marseille or Nice for a return to the continent.

If you have 10 days

Start in **Ajaccio** ❶ ► – ❽, visiting the market and the Musée Fesch and reaching the megalithic site at **Filitosa** ❿ by midday. Have a look through **Sartène** ⓫ and drive into 🖾 **Bonifacio** ⓮ as the sun sets into the sea. The next day get to the Laricio pine forest, near the **Col de Bavella** ⓯, to see or even walk to the famous granite peaks. Tiny D268 comes out on the east coast at N198, which will take you up to **Aléria** ⓰ and into 🖾 **Corte** ❶ on N200. Make Corte your base: devote day three to Corte and the Restonica Gorge, day four to **Haut-Asco** ㉑, day five to the small villages in **La Castagniccia.** On day six take the **Scala di Santa Regina** drive through the Aitone Forest. Spend the night in 🖾 **Ota** ㉒. Pass through the Scandola Natural Reserve on day seven, reaching the Riviera-like 🖾 **Calvi** ㉔ by evening. Tour its citadel, then dally at the beach in Calvi on day eight for a needed time-out. Check out **Patrimonio** ㉛ and the Orenga de Gaffory vineyards before driving through 🖾 **Nonza** ㉜ and **Centuri** ㉝ to 🖾 **Erbalunga** ㉞ or 🖾 **San Martino di Lota** ㉟ on your ninth day, and check into 🖾 **Bastia** ㊱ for your last and tenth day.

---

can constitution for his independent Corsican nation in 1755. Paoli's ideas significantly influenced the French Revolution, as well as the founding fathers of the United States. Inspiration for generations of literati, from Homer to Mérimée, Boswell, Dumas, and Balzac, Corsica has always been, in Greek, *Kallisté*, "the most beautiful, " a sylvan land and repository for romantic characters from Mérimée's Robin Hood–like *bandit d'honneur* Colomba to comic-book Asterix's pal Aucatarinabellachichix. In the end you'll find Corsica composed of equal parts vendetta, witchcraft, dream hunters, shepherds improvising the rough and haunting Corsican polyphony, megalithic menhirs, chestnuts, free-range livestock, powerful cheeses, and—always—the bittersweet, lemon-pepper fragrance of the maquis, an aroma like no other, described by Dorothy Carrington in her *Granite Island* as "akin to incense," and the only fitting perfume for Balzac's "back of beyond."

Exploring Corsica

Leaving Marseille on the excellent SNCM *Ferryterranée* (which also departs from Toulon and Nice) at sunset and arriving in Ajaccio at sunrise are among the finest moments of any trip to Corsica. Inasmuch as Napoléon claimed he could identify the fragrance of the Corsican maquis from many miles out at sea, approaching the island by some means other than a boat seems like heresy. The northern half of the island (Haute Corse) is generally wilder than the southern half (Corse du Sud), which is hotter and more barren. On the other hand, southern Corsica's archaeological sites at Filitosa and Pianu de Levie, the Col de Bavella and its majestic Laricio pine forest, and the towns of Sartène and Bonifacio all rank indisputably among the island's finest treasures. The least interesting part of the island is the coast road between Porto-Vecchio and Bastia, although one of the prettiest drives is the tour around the northward-pointing finger of Cap Corse. Don't hesitate to drive into the interior highlands, the true Corsica; if you spend too much time at sea level you'll be missing the remote villages and dramatic heights for which the island is famous.

About the Restaurants & Hotels

While entire geopolitical campaigns have been waged over warm-water harborage, this mountain in the Mediterranean has traditionally fled to its highest crags and crannies for defensive reasons, taking its best cooking along with it. The Corsican maquis grows some of Europe's wildest flora and fauna, ranging from free-range pigs to woodcock and pigeon. Chestnuts are a Corsican staple not to miss, whether in pastries, *pulenta,* or beer, while cheeses, especially the characteristic *brocciu* fresh cheese, are omnipresent upland delicacies. Dorothy Carrington accurately described Corsican cuisine as "winter cuisine," better between October and May, when game as well as brocciu are well represented on all menus.

The quantity of construction around Porto-Vecchio in the 1950s was so burdensome to Corsicans that, with some extra unwanted encouragement from separatist bombers, they resolved to avoid excessive, tourist-driven development. Instead, *fermes-auberges* (farmhouse-inns) are being restored at a rapid clip, and tastefully designed hotels are being built. During the peak season (from July to mid-September) prices are higher, and some hotels insist that breakfast and dinner be included as part of the price. The best seaside hotels are priced only marginally lower than on the Riviera, but lodgings in the interior villages remain substantially cheaper. Off-season, good prices can be found all over. Assume all rooms have air-conditioning, TV, telephones, and private bath unless otherwise noted.

13

La Cuisine Sauvage

Authentic Corsican fare is based on free-range livestock, game (especially *sanglier*, or wild boar), herbs, and wild mushrooms best found between October and May in the villages of the mountainous interior. *Civets* (meaty stews) headline menus as do the many versions of the prototypical, hearty Corsican soup (*soupe paysanne, soupe corse,* or *soupe de montagne*) made from herbs and vegetables simmered for hours with a ham bone. Seafood dishes available on the coast include *aziminu,* a rich bouillabaisse. Excellent *charcuterie* (pork products) include *lonzu* (shoulder), *coppa* (fillet), and *figatelli* (liver sausage), along with *prisuttu* (cured ham). Corsica's most emblematic cheese is really not a cheese at all: *brocciu* (pronounced broach), similar to ricotta, is used in omelets, *fiadone* (cheesecake), *fritelli* (chestnut-flour doughnuts), and as stuffing for trout or rabbit. Cheeses from Corsica's microregions include *bastelicaccia,* a soft, creamy sheep cheese, and the harder and sharper *sartenais.* Many of the most powerful cheeses are simply designated as *brebis* (sheep) or *chèvre* (goat). Chestnuts and chestnut flour, major players in Corsican gastronomy, are found in *castagna* (Corsican for chestnut), a cake; *panetta,* a kind of bread; *canistrelli,* dry cookies; beignets (fried dough), often made of chestnut flour; *pulenta,* a doughy chestnut-flour bread; and *Pietra,* chestnut beer. Corsica's best wines include the Arenas, Orenga de Gaffory, and Gentile cellars from the Patrimonio vineyards; Domaine Peraldi, Clos de Capitoro, or Clos Alzeto, from Ajaccio; Fiumicicoli, from Sartène; or Domaine de Torracia, from Porto-Vecchio.

Hiking Heaven

Corsica is really just one big mountain, so coming here without good hiking boots is the highland equivalent of being up a creek without a paddle. From the wild, undeveloped strands of the northern Cap Corse (Cape Corsica) to the Riviera-like tourist beaches near Calvi and Propriano, the island's scenery is astonishingly varied and rugged. In summer, during the *canicule* (literally, dog days), Corsicans take to the rivers, always cooler than the Mediterranean. Others take on the rugged GR 20 (Grande Randonnée 20); considered one of Europe's greatest hiking trails, it requires from 70 to 100 hours to complete and cuts a 160-km (100-mi) path from Calenzana (accessible by bus from Calvi) to Conca, near Porto-Vecchio. Planned in stages from one mountain refuge to another, the well-marked GR 20 is the ultimate way to see Corsica. Reaching altitudes of over 6,000 feet, it remains one of the most difficult hiking trails in Europe, taking 17 days to complete and open from May to October (stormy weather takes over the other months). If you are traveling by car, short probes along the GR 20 are easily feasible. In addition to the GR 20 there are shorter cross-island, coast to coast ("*Tra mare a mare*") hikes with villages and refuges at convenient intervals. If the GR 20 is your idea of hell, you can go for short hikes on some of the other numerous trails in the Parc Naturel Régional de Corse. Pick up area-specific leaflets at most tourist offices. As everywhere, of course, the reward for the blistered feet of all hike-a-holics is Corsica's marvelous scenery. Medieval villages, Genoese towers, live oak trees, megalithic dolmens, menhirs, citadels, and olive groves play counterpoint to rocky cliffs and granite peaks covered with the thick *maquis,* stunted and twisted by the force of the *tramontane,* Corsica's chronic northwest wind. This, after all, was the land that fashioned and tempered Napoléon.

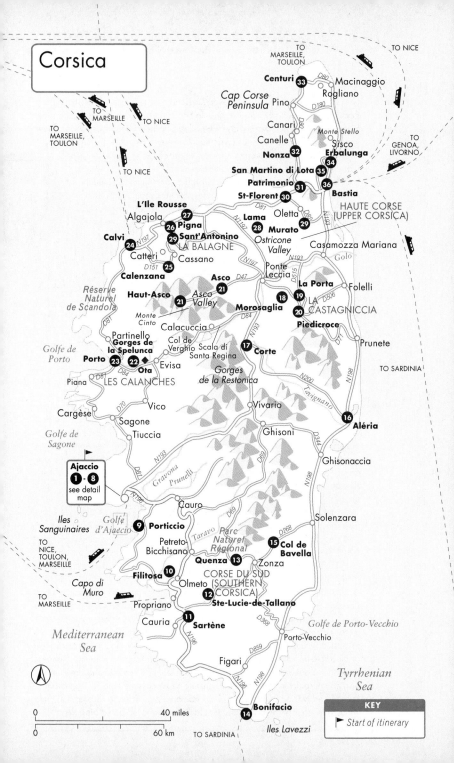

WHAT IT COSTS In euros					
	$$$$	**$$$**	**$$**	**$**	**¢**
RESTAURANTS	over €25	€17–€25	€12–€17	€8–€12	under €8
HOTELS	over €175	€120–€175	€70–€120	€40–€70	under €40

Restaurant prices are per person for a main course only, including tax (19.6%) and service; note that if a restaurant offers only prix-fixe (set-price) meals, it has been given the price category that reflects the full prix-fixe price. Hotel prices are for a standard double room in high season, including tax (19.6%) and service charge. Hotels operate on the European Plan (EP, with no meal provided) unless we note that they use the Breakfast Plan (BP), or also offer such options as Modified American Plan (MAP, with breakfast and dinner daily, known as *demi-pension*), or Full American Plan (FAP, or *pension complète*, with three meals a day). Inquire when booking if these all-inclusive mealplans (which always entail higher rates) are mandatory or optional.

Timing

The best time to visit Corsica is fall or spring, when the weather is cool. Most Corsican culinary specialties are at their best between October and June. Try to avoid July and August, when French and Italian vacationers fill hotels. Prices soar and the Corsican temperament is at its most volatile. In winter the island has the best weather in France, but a majority of the hotels and restaurants are closed.

CORSE DU SUD

Corse du Sud includes the French administrative capital of Ajaccio, the mountainous zones of the Cinarca and Alta Rocca, megalithic treasures at Filitosa and Levie, and the fortresslike towns of Sartène, Bonifacio, and Porto-Vecchio. Perhaps because southern Corsica is on the French side of the island, it seems more Continentalized. Forest fires and the resulting flooding scarred much of the southern part of the island in the mid-'90s, though the irrepressible maquis has quickly rebounded.

Ajaccio

40 mins by plane, 5–10 hrs by ferry from Marseille, Nice, or Toulon.

Ajaccio, Napoléon's birthplace and Corsica's modern capital, is a busy, French-flavored town with a bustling port, beautiful beaches, ancient streets, and, in the Musée Fesch, five centuries of Italian masterpieces. Start at the spectacular **food market** held every morning except Monday in place Campinchi, across the quai from the ferry port, an opportunity to admire an enticing parade of Corsican cheeses, pastries, sausages, and everything from traditional chestnut-flour beignets to prehistoric *rascasse* (red scorpion fish), at the fish market tucked in under the Hôtel de Ville.

 Rows of stately palm trees lead up to a marble statue of Napoléon on **Place Maréchal-Foch**, the city's main square. The **Hôtel de Ville** (town hall) is home to **Le musée Napoléonien**. Here, in an Empire-style grand salon, you'll find portraits of a long line of Bonapartes. Also note the fine bust of Letizia, Napoléon's formidable mother; a bronze death mask of the emperor him-

self; and a frescoed ceiling depicting Napoléon's meteoric rise. ⊠ *Pl. Maréchal-Foch* ☎ *04–95–51–52–62* ⊡ *€2.50* ☉ *Weekdays 9–noon and 2:30–5:30.*

❹ **FodorśChoice** ★ Two short blocks left of the statue of Napoléon on place Maréchal-Foch is the **Maison Bonaparte** (Bonaparte House). Here Napoléon was born on August 15, 1769. Today this large (once middle-class) house contains a museum with portraits of the entire Bonaparte clan. Search out the two family trees woven out of actual human hair. Most of the salons are 20th-century redos and homages to the emperor's favored Empire neoclassical style. Several are distressingly bare, others flaunt antiques created under King Louis-Phillipe (his sworn enemy), while only one—the Chambre à Alcóve—seems to evince the life of the little giant, since legend has it he spent his nights here after his conquest of Egypt. Still, fans of the man—and connoisseurs of *le style empire à la ajacci-enne*—will find this very worthwhile. ⊠ *Rue St-Charles* ☎ *04–95–21–43–89* ⊕ *www.musee-maisonbonaparte.fr* ⊡ *€4* ☉ *Mon. 2–5, Tues.–Sun. 10–noon and 2–5.*

❺ At the corner of rue St-Charles and rue Roi-de-Rome, opposite the tiny church of **St-Jean Baptiste,** are the city's oldest houses. They were built shortly after the town was founded in 1492. For a look at the Citadelle, walk east down rue Roi-de-Rome to boulevard Danielle Casanova. At the corner, the **Musée du Capitellu** traces the history of Ajaccio through the career of a single family. ⊠ *18 bd. Danielle Casanova* ☎ *04–95–21–50–57* ⌑ *€4* ⊙ *Mon.–Sat. 10–noon and 2–6, Sun. 10–noon.*

❻ The 16th-century Baroque **Cathédrale** where Napoléon was baptized is at the end of rue St-Charles. The interior is covered with trompe-l'oeil frescoes, and the high altar, from a church in Lucca, Italy, was donated by Napoléon's sister Eliza after he made her princess of Tuscany. Eugène Delacroix's *Virgin of Sacré Coeur* hangs above the altar. ⊠ *Rue F.-Conti.*

❼ The Renaissance-style **Chapelle Impérial** (Imperial Chapel) was built in 1857 by Napoléon's nephew, Napoléon III, to accommodate the tombs of the Bonaparte family (Napoléon Bonaparte himself is buried in the Hôtel des Invalides in Paris). The Coptic crucifix over the altar was taken from Egypt during the general's 1798 campaign. ⊠ *50 rue Fesch* ⌑ *€1.50* ⊙ *Tues.–Sat. 10–12:30 and 3–7.*

★ ❽ Adjacent to the Chapelle Impérial, the **Musée Fesch** houses a fine collection of Italian masters, ranging from Botticelli and Canaletto to De Tura—part of a massive collection of 30,000 paintings bought at bargain prices by Napoléon's uncle, Cardinal Fesch, archbishop of Lyon, following the French Revolution. Thanks to his nephew's military conquests, the cardinal was able to amass (steal, some would say) many celebrated Old Master paintings, the most famous of which are now in the Louvre. ⊠ *50 rue Fesch* ☎ *04–95–21–48–17* ⊕ *www.musee-fesch. com/* ⌑ *€5.50* ⊙ *Apr., June, Sept., and Oct., Wed.–Mon. 9:30–noon and 3–6:30; July and Aug., Tues.–Sat. 3–9:30, Sun. and Mon. 9:30–noon and 3–6:30; Nov.–Mar., Wed.–Mon. 9:30–noon and 2:30–6.*

Where to Stay & Eat

$$–$$$$ ✕ **Le Floride.** This port restaurant overlooking the docks serves simple but sound combinations of maritime and upland products. Fresh fish and shellfish are the specialty, with spaghetti *au langouste* (with lobster) one of the stars in chef Nicolas Baubé's firmament of seafood creations. ⊠ *Rue Charles Ornano s/n, Port* ☎ *04–95–22–67–48* ⊟ *AE, DC, MC, V* ⊙ *Closed Sun. No lunch Sat.*

$$–$$$ ✕ **A La Funtana.** A fountain greets diners at the door of this noted restaurant, named for a popular Corsican folk song. Fresh flowers and Oriental carpets are the only touches of decoration in the simple white dining room. The house specialty is homemade foie gras; other items worth sampling include *morilles* (morels) in foie gras and homemade sorbets. ⊠ *9 rue Notre-Dame* ☎ *04–95–21–78–04* ⊟ *AE, DC, MC, V* ⊙ *Closed Mon. No dinner Sun.*

$–$$$ ✕ **20123.** This well-loved Ajaccio favorite is known for its traditional cuisine, fresh fish from the nearby market and, in season, game specials such as *civet de sanglier* (wild boar stew) with *trompettes de la mort* (wild mushrooms) served in a bubbling earthenware casserole. ⊠ *2 rue Roi-de-Rome* ☎ *04–95–21–50–05* ⊟ *MC, V* ⊙ *Closed Mon., Tues., and Jan. 15–Feb. 15. No lunch June 15–Sept. 15.*

$$–$$$$ ✕⌸ **La Dolce Vita.** Spread out over flower-filled terraces at the edge of the Golfe d'Ajaccio, this hotel-restaurant is lavishly Italianate. The spectacular swimming pool overlooks the sea, and the restaurant ranks as one of the island's best for stylish interpretations of traditional Corsican dishes. ⊠ *Rte. des Iles Sanguinaires, 8 km (5 mi) from center of town, 20000* ☎ *04–95–52–42–42* 🖷 *04–95–52–07–15* ⇪ *32 rooms* ⚄ *Restaurant, minibars, cable TV, pool, beach, bar, free parking, some pets allowed (fee)* ▤ *AE, DC, MC, V* ⊙ *Closed Nov.–Mar.* ⍟ *MAP.*

★ **$$–$$$** ⌸ **Hôtel San Carlu.** On the edge of the *Vieille Ville* (Old Town), this friendly hotel overlooking the ramparts and the sea makes an ideal base for exploring Ajaccio. Rooms are clean and comfortable; those on the Golfe d'Ajaccio side (east) on the third floor get an abundance of morning sunshine streaming across the beds and into the bathtubs, not a bad way to greet a new day on the Isle de la Beauté. ⊠ *8 bd. Danielle Casanova, 20000* ☎ *04–95–21–13–84* 🖷 *04–95–21–09–99* ✉ *hotel-san-carlu@wanadoo.fr* ⇪ *40 rooms* ⚄ *Minibars; no a/c* ▤ *AE, DC, MC, V* ⊙ *Closed Dec. 20–Feb. 6.*

Nightlife & the Arts

Many of Ajaccio's top nightspots are 4 km (2½ mi) north of town, in the Santa-Lina District along route des Iles Sanguinaires. For in-town action, **Le Pigalle** (⊠ Pl. Charles de Gaulle) is a spot to check. **L'Entre-acte** (⊠ Bd. Lantivy, next to casino) is a popular stop on the night-owl circuit. A continuing success in Ajaccio's night scene is **Le Privilège** (⊠ Rue Macchini, pl. Charles-de-Gaulle). **Le Cohiba** (⊠ Bd. Lantivy, 1 Résidence Diamant) is a vibrant music bar. **La Place** (⊠ Bd. Lantivy) is another well-known boîte and piano bar. On the road to the airport, **Le Duplex** (⊠ Av. Campo dell'Oro) is a brash young addition to the disco scene in the Corsican capital.

The **Fête de la Miséricorde** (Feast of Our Lady of Mercy), on March 18, spotlights the Procession de la Madunnuccia (Procession of the Madonna), Ajaccio's patron saint. In May all Ajaccio celebrates during its festive ★ **Carnival.** A major festival, the **Fêtes Napoléoniennes** (⊕ www.corsica.net/corsica/fr/event/), is held on August 15, Napoléon's birthday.

Sports & the Outdoors

NAVE VA (⊠ 2 rue J. B. Marcaggi ☎ 04–95–21–83–98) operates boating excursions to the Îles Sanguinaires, Reserve Naturelle de Scandola, Girolata, Calanches de Piana, and the chalk cliffs of Bonifacio. **BMS** (⊠ Quai de la Citadelle ☎ 04–95–21–33–75) rents bicycles year-round. **Locacorse** (⊠ 10 av. Bévérini-Vico ☎ 04–95–20–71–20) has bike rentals April–September. **Les Dauphins** (⊠ Rte. des Sanguinaires, Plage de Barbicaja ☎ 04–95–52–07–78) has water-sports gear among other offerings. For information about sailing, contact the **Ligue Corse de Voile** (⊠ Port de la Citadelle ☎ 04–95–21–07–79). A popular spot to rent a sailboat is the **Tahiti Nautic Club d'Ajaccio** (⊠ Plage du Ricanto ☎ 04–95–20–05–95).

Shopping

Much more than just a bookstore specializing in books about Corsica, **Librairie la Marge** (⊠ 7 rue Emmanuelle-Arène) is a hub of Corsican culture, where you can also buy music and attend poetry readings. **Paese Nostru** (⊠ Passage Guinguetta) sells Corsican crafts of all kinds. **U Tilaghju** (⊠ Rue

Forcioli Conti), one of several artisanal shops near the cathedral, has an impressive collection of ceramics.

Porticcio

❾ *17 km (11 mi) south of Ajaccio on N196.*

Across the Prunelli River south of Ajaccio, Porticcio is the capital's upscale suburb and luxurious beach resort town. It's primarily notable for its seawater cures at the **Institut de Thalassothérapie** (Institute of Thalassotherapy), on the Punta di Porticcio, and the *grand luxe* Le Maquis hotel.

Where to Stay & Eat

$$$$ ✗▥ **Le Maquis.** Ranking as one of the island's (and even France's) finest
Fodor'sChoice *hôtels de charme*, this graceful ivy-covered Genoese-style retreat ram-
★ bles down through terraced gardens to a quiet private beach overlooking the Golfe d'Ajaccio. The best rooms have ample views of the sea while some overlook the hills as well. At the candlelit restaurant L'Arbousier, its ancient beams recycled from what was once the Ajaccio prison, a blend of traditional and nouvelle cuisine is served: fish tartare, scrambled eggs with truffles, and fresh tagliatelle. Supreme comfort, taste, service, and discretion are guaranteed at this exquisite hideaway 19 km (11 mi) south of Ajaccio. ✉ *D55, 20166 Porticcio* ☎ *04–95–25–05–55* 🖷 *04–95–25–11–70* ⊕ *www.lemaquis.com* ⇱ *19 rooms, 6 apartments* ♨ *Restaurant, minibars, cable TV, tennis court, pool, beach, bar, meeting rooms, some pets allowed (fee)* ▤ *AE, DC, MC, V* ▯◯▯ *MAP.*

Filitosa

★ **❿** *71 km (43 mi) southeast of Ajaccio off N196.*

Filitosa is the site of Corsica's largest grouping of megalithic menhir statues. Bizarre, life-size stone figures of ancient warriors rise up mysteriously from the undulating terrain, many with human faces whose features have been flattened over time by erosion. A small museum on the site houses archaeological finds, including the menhir known as *Scalsa Murta,* whose delicately carved spine and rib cage are surprisingly contemporary for a work dating from some 5,000 years ago. The guidebook in English (€5) by experts Cesari and Acquaviva is supplemented by information in English at each site. ✉ *Contact Centre Préhistorique Filitosa* ☎ *04–95–74–00–91 for information* ✉ *Guided tours in English €5* ☉ *June–Aug., daily 8–7.*

Sartène

⓫ *27 km (16 mi) southeast of Filitosa on N196.*

Described as the "most Corsican of all Corsican towns" by French novelist Prosper Mérimée, Sartène, first founded in the 16th century, has survived pirate raids and bloody feuding among the town's families. The word "vendetta" is believed to have originated here as the result of a 19th-century family feud so serious that French troops were brought in to serve as a peacekeeping buffer force. Centuries of fighting have left the town with a somewhat eerie and menacing atmosphere. Perhaps adding to this is the annual Good Friday *catenacciu* (enchaining) procession in which an anonymous penitent, dragging ankle chains, lugs a heavy cross through the village streets.

Vieux Sartène (Old Sartène), surrounded by ancient ramparts, begins at place de la Libération, the main square. To one side is the **Hôtel de Ville** (town hall), in the former Genoese governor's palace. Slip into the Middle Ages through the tunnel under the Town Hall to place du Maggiu and the ancient **Santa Anna** quarter, a warren of narrow, cobbled streets lined with granite houses. Scarcely 100 yards from the Hôtel de Ville, down a steep and winding street, is a 12th-century *tour de guet* (watchtower).

Sartène is a key link to Corsica's prehistory, thanks to its proximity to Pianu de Levie's dolmens and megalithic statues. Housed in a magnificently perched stone-castle redoubt, some of the island's best prehistoric relics are at the **Musée Départemental de Préhistoire Corse** (Regional Museum of Corsican Prehistory). In fact, this was the town's former prison, a building as stark and forbidding as the rest of this village. ⊠ *Rue Croce* ☎ *04–95–77–01–09* ⊕ *http://www.toute-la-corse.com/includes/ maquette.php?nav=dmus&=fr* 🖼 *€4* ◷ *Mon.–Sat. 10–noon and 2–6.*

Where to Eat

$$–$$$ ✕ **Auberge de Santa Barbara.** This excellent restaurant is just 1 km (½ mi) north of Sartène. Known as one of the top specialists in authentic Corsican cuisine, chef Giselle Lovighi also serves innovative seafood specialties such as shrimp soufflé and crayfish salad. ⊠ *Rte. de Propriano, Alzone, Sartène* ☎ *04–95–77–09–06* ▭ *MC, V* ◷ *Closed Oct. 15–Mar. 15. No lunch Mon.*

Ste-Lucie-de-Tallano

⑫

Fodor'sChoice
★

15 km (9 mi) northeast of Sartène, 12 km (7 mi) southeast of Levie on D268.

The pretty little village of Ste-Lucie-de-Tallano is in the heart of Mérimée country, the setting for *Colomba,* the tale of a beautiful young Corsican woman caught in an Andromache-like web of love, honor, vendetta, and death. Driving up the Rizzanese Valley, the Spin' a Cavallu (Horse's Back) Bridge, one of the oldest and loveliest Genoese bridges on the island, is the first important sight. The St-François convent and the church of Ste-Lucie are the main religious buildings in town.

Where to Eat

$$ ✕ **Vecchiu Mulinu.** This restored mill serves simple but delicious *cuisine du terroir* (regional country cooking). The local Fiumicicoli red is the perfect match. ⊠ *Bains de Caldanes* ☎ *04–95–77–00–54* ⌲ *Reservations essential* ▭ *MC, V* ◷ *Closed Mon. in Oct.–Easter.*

Quenza

⑬ *8 km (5 mi) west of Zonza on D420.*

Quenza is known for its 10th-century chapel of **Santa Maria.** It's also the headquarters of **I Muntagnoli Corsi** (☎ *04–95–78–64–05*), which organizes guided hikes into the Coscione Forest.

Where to Stay & Eat

★ **$$–$$$** ✕🏠 **Auberge Sole e Monti.** One of southern Corsica's best options for authentic Corsican cooking and a standout as a hotel as well, this place is definitely worth a detour. Rooms are modern and well kept, and the staff is friendly. Try the local version of *soupe corse* (Corsican soup) and, in summer, trout with wild mint and brocciu. Be sure to reserve in advance. ⊠ *1 km (½ mi) east of town on the Zonza road, 20122* 🕾 *04–95–78–62–53* 🖷 *04–95–78–63–88* ⊕ *www.solemonti.com/* 🛏 *20 rooms* ♨ *Restaurant, bar, some pets allowed (fee); no a/c* 🖃 *AE, DC, MC, V* ☾ *Closed Dec.–Mar.* ⍓❙ *MAP.*

Bonifacio

⓮ *52 km (31 mi) southeast of Sartène via N196.*

Fodor's Choice
★

The ancient fortress town of Bonifacio occupies a spectacular cliff-top aerie above a harbor carved from limestone cliffs. It's just 13 km (8 mi) from Sardinia, and the local speech is heavily influenced by the accent and idiom of that nearby Italian island. Established in the 12th century as Genoa's first Corsican stronghold, Bonifacio remained Genoese through centuries of battles and sieges. As you wander the narrow streets of the **Haute Ville** (Upper Village), inside the walls of the citadel, think of Homer's *Odyssey*. It's here, in the harbor, that scholars place the catastrophic encounter (Chapter X) between Ulysses's fleet and the Laestrygonians, who hurled lethal boulders down from the cliffs.

From place d'Armes at the city gate, enter the **Bastion de l'Étendard** (Bastion of the Standard); you can still see the system of weights and levers used to pull up the drawbridge. The former garrison now houses life-size dioramas of Bonifacio's history. 🎫 €2 ☾ *Mid-June–mid-Sept., daily 9–7.*

In the center of the maze of cobbled streets that makes up the citadel is the 12th-century church of **Ste-Marie-Majeure,** with buttresses attaching it to surrounding houses. Inside the church, note the Renaissance baptismal font, carved in bas-relief, and the 3rd-century white-marble Roman sarcophagus. Walk around the back to see the loggia, which is built above a huge cistern that stored water for use in times of siege, as did the circular stone silos seen throughout the town.

★ From Bonifacio you can take a boat trip to the **Dragon Grottoes** (⊠ Boats leave from outside Hôtel La Caravelle 🕾 04–95–75–05–93 for information) and **Venus's Bath** (the trip takes one hour on boats that set out every 15 minutes during July and August) or the **Lavezzi Islands.**

Where to Stay & Eat

$$$ ✕ **La Rascasse.** In prime position to haul the freshest seafood from the boat to your table, this port-side spot is an old favorite in Bonifacio. Try the fish for which the restaurant is named, the prehistorically spiny (and light) rascasse (red scorpion fish). ⊠ *Quai Comparetti* 🕾 04–95–73–01–26 🖃 AE, DC, MC, V ☾ *Closed Nov.–Easter.*

$$ ✕ **Les 4 Vents.** This friendly restaurant near the Sardinia boat terminal is popular with the yachting crowd and family groups. In winter the kitchen serves up such Alsatian specialties as sauerkraut and sausages. In summer the focus is on barbecued fish and meats, as well as typical Corsican dishes. ✉ *29 quai Bando di Ferro* ☎ *04–95–73–07–50* ▭ *MC, V* ⊘ *Closed mid- to late Nov. and Tues. in Nov.–June.*

★ **$-$$** ✕ **Le Voilier.** This popular year-round restaurant in the port serves carefully selected and prepared fish and seafood, along with fine Corsican sausage and traditional cuisine from *soupe corse* to *fiadone* (cheesecake). ✉ *Quai Comparetti* ☎ *04–95–73–07–06* ▭ *AE, DC, MC, V* ⊘ *Closed Mon. No dinner Sun.*

$$$$ ▥ **Hôtel le Genovese.** This small, intimate hotel is built into the ramparts of the upper town's citadel. Peach fabric wallcoverings set the rooms aglow. Upstairs rooms have superb views over the cliffs and out to Sardinia. ✉ *Quartier de Citadelle, Haute Ville, 20169* ☎ *04–95–73–12–34* 🖷 *04–95–73–09–03* ⊕ *www.woda.fr-aa-genovese* ⇆ *15 rooms* ♿ *Minibars, cable TV, pool, bar* ▭ *AE, DC, MC, V* ⊮ *MAP.*

Nightlife & the Arts
Raging until sunrise is the happening **Lollapalooza** (✉ Quai Comparetti ☎ 04–95–73–04–54), open around-the-clock in summer.

Sports & the Outdoors
The area around Bonifacio is ideal for water sports. Contact **Club Atoll** (✉ Rte. de Porto-Vecchio ☎ 04–95–73–02–83). The best golf course on Corsica (and one of the best in the Mediterranean), a 20,106-foot, par-72 gem designed by Robert Trent Jones, is at **Sperone** (✉ Domaine de Sperone ☎ 04–95–73–17–13), just east of Bonifacio.

Col de Bavella

⑮ *50 km (31 mi) northeast of Porto-Vecchio on D368 and D268.*

Fodor'sChoice The granite peaks known as the **Aiguilles de Bavella** (Needles of Bavella) ★ tower some 6,562 feet overhead as you reach the Col de Bavella (Bavella Pass). Hiking trails are well marked. The narrow but mostly well-paved roadway over the pass will take you back to the coast along the Solenzara River.

Where to Stay & Eat
¢ ✕▥ **Auberge du Col.** Near the top of the spectacular drive from Porto-Vecchio to Col de Bavella, this little *gîte d'étape* (hikers' inn) offers Corsican mountain fare and a night in simple but adequate accommodations under immense laricio pines. Each room has six beds. ✉ *Col de Bavella* ☎ *04–95–72–09–87* 🖷 *04–95–72–16–48* ⇆ *4 rooms* ▭ *MC, V* ⊘ *Closed Nov.–Mar.*

Aléria

⑯ *32 km (20 mi) north of Solenzara on N198, 48 km (29 mi) southeast of Corte.*

Just before the village of Aléria are the ruins of the Roman city of the same name. On a pine-studded plateau is the carefully restored 16th-century **Fort de Matra,** which houses the **Musée Jérôme Carcopino.** On display are pottery and tools found on the site, as well as Etruscan, Greek, and Roman artifacts dating from as far back as 500 BC. ⊕ *www.acorsica.com/rpatrimo/musees/musaleri.htm* ▧ €4 ⊙ *Apr.–Oct., daily 8–noon and 2–7; Nov.–Mar., Mon.–Sat. 8–noon and 2–5.*

HAUTE CORSE

Haute Corse (Upper Corsica) is the northeastern end of the island and is, indeed, higher in mean altitude than Corse du Sud, topped by the 8,876-foot Monte Cinto. Most Corsica enthusiasts agree that Haute Corse is the island's finest trove of highland forests, remote villages, hidden cultural gems, vineyards, beaches, alpine lakes and streams. In the center of Haute Corse is the city of Corte, Corsica's historic heart. To the east is the forested region of La Castagniccia, named for its *châtaigniers* (chestnut trees), one of Corsica's treasures, especially in the fall, when fallen leaves and chestnuts blanket the ground. The forest's tiny roadways go through villages with stunning Baroque churches and houses still roofed in traditional blue-gray slate. To the northwest is Calvi, Corsica's Riviera-like beach resort, while farther north the island's finger pointing to the continent is Cap Corse, with the port city of Bastia, Corsica's largest and most Italianate city, at its base.

Corte

⓱
Fodor'sChoice
★

48 km (30 mi) northwest of Aléria on N200, 83 km (51 mi) northeast of Ajaccio, 70 km (43 mi) southwest of Bastia.

Set amid spectacular cliffs and gorges at the confluence of the Tavignano, Restonica, and Orta rivers, Corte is the spiritual heart and soul of Corsica. Capital of Pasquale Paoli's government from 1755 to 1769, it was also where Paoli established the Corsican University in 1765. Closed by the victorious French in 1769, the university, always a symbol of Corsican identity, was reopened in 1981. To reach the upper town and the 15th-century château overlooking the rivers, walk up the cobblestone ramp from place Pasquale-Paoli. Stop in lovely **place Gaffori** at one of the cafés or restaurants. Note the bullet-pocked house where the Corsican hero Gian Pietro Gaffori and his wife, Faustina, held off the Genoese in 1750.

★ The **Citadelle**, a Vauban-style fortress (1769–78), is built around the original 15th-century fortification at the highest point of the cliff, with the river below. It contains the **Musée de la Corse** (Corsica Museum), dedicated to the island's history and ethnography. ☎ *04–95–45–25–45* ⊕ *www.corsica.net/corsica/uk/discov/musees/index.htm* ▧ €5.50 ⊙ *Nov.–Apr., Tues.–Sat. 10–6; May–Oct., daily 10–8.*

The **Palais National** (National Palace), just outside the citadel and above place Gaffori, is the ancient residence of Genoa's representatives in Corsica and was the seat of the Corsican parliament from 1755 to 1769. The building is now part of the Corsican University. ⊠ *Pl. du Poilu* ⊙ *Weekdays 2–6.*

For an unforgettable view of the river junction and the Genoese bridge below and the citadel's tiny watchtower above, walk left along the ★ citadel wall to the **Belvédère.**

Leave the Haute Ville and go through the tiny alleys of the **Quartier de Chiostra.** Follow the cobblestone path (as you look down) to the right from the Belvédère, bearing right and across at the **Chapelle St-Théophile.** Coming into the tiny square on your left, don't miss the open stone staircase on the opposite wall, or the prehistoric fertility goddess carved into the wall to the left. Farther downhill you will rejoin the ramp leading into place Pasquale-Paoli.

Fodor'sChoice The **Gorges de la Restonica** (Restonica Gorges) make a spectacular day hike.
★ At the top of the Restonica Valley, leave your car in the parking area at the end of the road. A two-hour climb will take you to **Lac de Mélo,** a trout-filled mountain lake 6,528 feet above sea level. Another hour up is the usually snow-bordered **Lac de Capitello.** Information on trails is available from the tourist office or the Parc Naturel Régional. Light meals are served in the stone shepherds' huts at the **Bergeries de Grotelle.**

Where to Stay & Eat

$$-$$$ ✕▦ **Hôtel Dominique Colonna.** The modern hotel across from the **Auberge de la Restonica** has sliding doors leading directly out to breakfast nooks by the stream. Owner Dominique "Dumé" Colonna, one of France's (and certainly Corsica's) greatest soccer stars, drops by from time to time. The Auberge serves fine Corsican fare and offers seven more traditional rooms. ⊠ *Vallée de la Restonica, 20250* ☎ *04–95–45–25–65* 🖷 *04–95–61–03–91* ⊕ *www.dominique-colonna.com/* ⇘ *28 rooms* ⚭ *Restaurant, minibars, pool, some pets allowed (fee); no a/c* ⊟ *AE, DC, MC, V* ☽ *Closed Nov. 5–Mar. 14* ▯◎▮ *MAP.*

en route   **Ponte Leccia,** 24 km (15 mi) north of Corte on N193, is the entry point to La Castagniccia: take D71 southeast into the forest. Serving primarily as a rail, road, and river crossing with gas stations and a supermarket, the town has little else to recommend it.

Morosaglia

⑱ *14 km (9 mi) southeast of Ponte Leccia, 9 km (5 mi) east of La Porta.*

The town of Morosaglia is the birthplace of Pasquale Paoli, Corsica's most celebrated national hero and author of the first republican constitution, drafted for Corsica in 1755 (with reverberations extending to the founding fathers of the United States). Letters, portraits, and memorabilia from Paoli's life are on display at the **Maison de Pasquale Paoli** (Pasquale Paoli House). ☎ *04–95–61–04–97* 🖾 *€2* ☽ *Daily 9–5.*

La Porta

⑲ *9 km (5 mi) west of Morosaglia, 14½ km (9 mi) north of Piedicroce on D515.*

As the name of the village suggests, La Porta (the Door) is an entranceway to La Castagniccia. The **St-Jean-Baptiste** church here is widely accepted as the crowning glory of Corsican Baroque art. The bright ocher facade and the five-story bell tower are feasts for the eyes, as are the paintings inside. Look for the *Martyrdom of St. Eulalie of Barcelona* (1848), by Louis Destouches (1819–81), just inside on the left.

Where to Eat

★ **$$** ✕ **L'Ampugnani–Chez Elisabeth.** This excellent restaurant is known throughout Corsica as a treasury of fine local cooking. Specializing in *cuisine du terroir* (local country cooking), it offers such dishes as a superb leg of lamb with herbs and *figatellu* (liver sausage). ⊠ *La Porta* ☎ *04–95–39–22–00* ⌂ *Reservations essential* ▤ *MC, V* ☉ *Closed Mon. Sept. 15–Easter; closed Jan. and Feb.*

Piedicroce

★ **⓴** *14 km (9 mi) south of La Porta on D515, 66 km (40 mi) south of Bastia.*

Piedicroce's panoramic view of La Castagniccia is superb. Be sure to stop in to visit the vividly painted Baroque church of **St-Pierre-et-St-Paul,** one of the finest of its type in the area. The nearby mineral springs of **Orezza** are reputed to have miraculous powers. The **Fium Alto,** running along the road that goes northeast to Folelli, is one of Corsica's best trout streams. To exit La Castagniccia, follow signs for **Folelli** (37 km [22 mi] north) or **Bastia** (66 km [40 mi] north).

Where to Stay & Eat

★ **$** ✕▥ **Le Refuge.** A handy midway point in the labyrinthine La Castagniccia, this hotel-restaurant is a good place for a delicious meal based on the Rafalli family's home-processed charcuterie and a night's sleep in the small but cozy quarters overlooking the Castagniccia and the valley of the Fium Alto. ⊠ *20229 Piedicroce* ☎ *04–95–35–82–65* ▤ *04–95–35–84–42* ⇨ *20 rooms* ⌂ *Restaurant, bar; no a/c, no room TVs* ▤ *MC, V* ☉ *Closed Nov.*

Asco & Haut-Asco

㉑ *22 km (13 mi) west of Ponte Leccia: 2 km (1 mi) north of Ponte Leccia, D147 turns off N197 toward the village of Asco, 16 km (10 mi) away.*

Studded with beehives, the Asco Valley is a honey and cheese haven. The Genoese bridge below Asco is a perfect spot for a swim in the river. Above Asco the granite gorge becomes a cool pine forest for hiking. Follow the road for another 12 km (7 mi) past the village, ending at the top against a wall of mountains. The Asco Valley runs west to an awe-inspiring barrier of mountains crowned by **Monte Cinto,** the highest point in Corsica. As you travel up the valley, the maquis-covered slopes give way to a sheer granite gorge hung with sweet-smelling juniper. Thirteen km (8 mi) above is **Haut Asco,** starting point for the eight- to nine-hour (round-trip) walk up Monte Cinto. From the top, on a clear day, you can see the entire island and even the Apennines on the Italian mainland. Clouds and mist gather after about 10 AM, however, particularly in summer. For this reason a 4 AM start is recommended. Questions can be answered at Le Chalet.

Where to Stay & Eat

¢–$ ✕⬚ **Le Chalet.** This tidy hideaway at the very top of the island has a simple, no-frills restaurant serving Corsican cuisine. Walls are covered with photographs of famous mountaineers. Along with the 22 private rooms there are also a hikers' dormitory, a bar, and a store selling supplies to trekkers, who use the chalet as a way station from the GR 20. ☒ *20276 Haut-Asco* ☏☏ *04–95–47–81–08* ⤺ *22 rooms, plus dormitory without bath* ⟁ *Restaurant, bar, some pets allowed (fee); no a/c, no room TVs* ▭ *MC, V* ☺ *Closed early Nov.–early May.*

Sports & the Outdoors

From at least December to April, Corsica's upper reaches are snowed in, creating options for both alpine and cross-country skiing; consult the **Club Alpin Français** (☏ 04–95–22–73–81) in Ajaccio. For information about hiking up Monte Cinto, in Bastia contact the **Office National des Forêts** (☏ 04–95–32–81–90).

La Scala di Santa Regina

*Fodor's*Choice ★   *9 km (5 mi) south of Ponte Leccia, D84 leaves N193, starts up the Golo River, and turns into La Scala di Santa Regina.*

This road, known as La Scala di Santa Regina (Stairway of the Holy Queen), is one of Corsica's most spectacular, and one of the most difficult to navigate, especially in winter. The route follows the twisty path of the Golo River, which has carved its way through layers of red granite, forming dramatic gorges and waterfalls. Be prepared to stop for herds of animals crossing the road. Follow the road to the **Col de Verghio** (Verghio Pass) for superb views of Tafunatu, the legendary perforated mountain, and Monte Cinto. On the way up you'll pass through the **Valdo Niello Forest,** Corsica's most important woodlands, filled with pines and beeches. The col is considered the border between Haute Corse and Corse du Sud. As you descend from the Verghio Pass through the **Forêt d'Aitone** (Aitone Forest), note how well manicured it is—the pigs, goats, and sheep running rampant through the tall Laricio pines keep it this way. As you pass the village of Evisa, with its orange roofs, look across the impressive **Gorges de Spelunca** (Spelunca Gorge) to see the hill village of Ota. A small road on the right will take you across the gorge, where there's an ancient Genoese-built bridge.

Ota

❷   *16 km (10 mi) northwest of Evisa on La Scala di Santa Regina.*

The tiny village of Ota, overlooking the **Gorges de Spelunca,** has traditional stone houses that seem to be suspended on the mountainside, an amazing view of the surrounding mountains, and a number of trailheads. It's an excellent base for hiking in the area.

Where to Stay & Eat

¢–$ ✕⬚ **Chez Félix.** This homey place serves as dining room, taxi stand, and town hall. Cheerful owner Marinette Ceccaldi cooks up heaping portions of Corsican specialties ranging from wild boar to chestnut-flour beignets. Suites are decorated with curios and antiques, each with a balcony overlooking the gorge. Rooms are comfortable and rustic; some have private bathrooms, others share. The hotel has a van that will transport you out to hiking routes. ⊠ *Pl. de la Fontaine, 20150* 📠 *04–95–26–12–92* ↩ *4 2-bedroom apartments, 36 beds in 4- and 6-bed rooms with shared bath* ♨ *Restaurant, bar, some pets allowed (fee); no a/c, no room TVs* ⊟ *AE, DC, MC, V.*

Porto–Les Calanches

㉓ *5 km (3 mi) west of Ota, 30 km (19 mi) south of Calvi.*

The flashy resort town of Porto doesn't have much character, but its setting on the crystalline **Golfe de Porto** (Gulf of Porto), surrounded by massive pink-granite mountains, is superb. Activity focuses on the small port, where there is a boardwalk with restaurants and hotels. A short hike from the boardwalk will bring you to a 16th-century Genoese tower that overlooks the bay. Boat excursions leave daily for the **Réserve Naturel de Scandola.** Detour south of Porto on D81 to get to **Les Calanches,** jagged outcroppings of red rock considered among the most extraordinary natural sites in France. Look for arches and stelae, standing rock formations shaped like animals and phantasmagoric human faces.

Calvi

㉔ *92 km (58 mi) north of Piana, 159 km (100 mi) north of Ajaccio.*

Calvi, Corsica's slice of the Riviera, has been described by author Dorothy Carrington as "an oasis of pleasure on an otherwise austere island." Calvi grew rich by supplying products to Genoa; its citizens remained loyal supporters of Genoa long after the rest of the island declared independence. Calvi also claims to be the birthplace of Christopher Columbus. During the 18th century the town endured assaults from Corsican nationalists, including celebrated patriot Pasquale Paoli. Today Calvi sees a summertime invasion of tourists, drawn to the 6-km (4-mi) stretch of sandy white beach, the citadel, and the buzzing nightlife.

The Genoese **Citadelle,** perched on a rocky promontory at the tip of the bay, competes with the beach as a major attraction. An inscription above the drawbridge—CIVITAS CALVI SEMPER FIDELIS (The citizens of Calvi always faithful)—reflects the town's unswerving allegiance to Genoa. At the welcome center, just inside the gates, you can see a video on the city's history and arrange to take a guided tour given in English (three times a day) or a self-guided walking tour. ⊠ *Up the hill off av. de l'Uruguay* 📞 *04–95–65–36–74* ⊕ *www.nordsud-calvi.com/visite.htm* 🎫 *Guided tour and video show €9* ⊙ *Tours Easter–early Oct., daily at 10, 4:30, and 6:30.*

Stop in at the 13th-century church of **St-Jean-Baptiste** (⊠ Pl. d'Armes); it contains an interesting Renaissance baptismal font. Look up to see the rows of pews screened by grillwork: the chaste young women of Calvi's upper classes sat here.

Where to Stay & Eat

★ **$$–$$$$** ✕ **Chez Tao.** At Chez Tao, a mandatory stop on almost everyone's itinerary, you can rub elbows with the town's glitterati on the ocher-color 16th-century terraces that look out over the bay. Seafood is what everyone eats, but food plays second fiddle to the atmosphere, which includes Corsican folk singing and a tinkling piano until the wee hours. The charming Tao By, a 60-ish piano bar artist of mixed Russian-Corsican heritage, performs here and on the continent and has recorded numerous successful CDs. ⊠ *Pl. de la Citadelle* ☎ *04–95–65–00–73* ⊕ *www.absolucorse.com/musique/* ▤ *AE, DC, MC, V* ☉ *Closed mid-Sept.–Easter.*

$$–$$$$ ✕ **Emile's.** With panoramic views of the port, this is a lucky place to find a table in summer. Classic French cuisine with *terroir* (local Corsican) touches is available, but fish and seafood hold center stage. ⊠ *Quai Landry* ☎ *04–95–65–09–60* ▤ *AE, DC, MC, V* ☉ *Closed Dec. 1–Jan. 15, Mon. in winter, and Tues. year-round.*

★ **$$$$** ✕▦ **Le Signoria.** This 17th-century country manor (and annex) has homey bedrooms and large bathrooms. From the pool and patio there are panoramic views of the mountains and the bay. The renowned restaurant serves imaginative regional cuisine (it's closed for lunch, except on weekends from July through August). ⊠ *Rte. de la Forêt de Bonifato, 5 km (3 mi) from Calvi, 20260* ☎ *04–95–65–93–00* ☒ *04–95–65–38–77* ⊕ *www.hotel-la-signoria.com* ⇗ *18 rooms* ♿ *Restaurant, pool, Turkish baths, bar, free parking* ▤ *AE, MC, V* ☉ *Closed Nov.–Easter.*

$$–$$$ ✕▦ **Le Magnolia.** Rooms in this cozy 19th-century former mansion between the church and the marketplace are named after French literary figures: the Verlaine overlooks rooftops to the port. Cupids and cherubs perch over beds. The restaurant is in the garden under a giant magnolia tree—thus the name of the hotel. ⊠ *Pl. du Marché, 20260* ☎ *04–95–65–19–16* ☒ *04–95–65–34–52* ⊕ *www.hotel-le-magnolia.com* ⇗ *11 rooms* ♿ *Restaurant, minibars, bar, some pets allowed (fee)* ▤ *AE, DC, MC, V* ☉ *Closed Jan. 15–Mar. 15.*

Nightlife & the Arts

The cabaret-restaurant **Chez Tao** (⊠ Pl. de la Citadelle ☎ 04–95–65–00–73) is the "in" spot in town. **L'Eden Port** (⊠ Quai Landry ☎ 04–95–62–10–32) is one of Calvi's hot piano bars, on Quai Landry next to the port Captaincy. **L'Acapulco** (⊠ On N167) draws a friendly crowd. Note that a free *navette* (shuttle bus) cruises downtown Calvi until dawn collecting and returning club goers.

The **Calvi Jazz Festival** (⊕ www.calvi-jazz-festival.com) is held the last week of June. **Rencontres Polyphoniques,** an international choral festival, is held in mid-September. **Festiventu,** a celebration of wind-powered sports, musical instruments, and scientific artifacts, happens in late October.

Shopping

The major shopping streets are rue Clemenceau and boulevard Wilson. Look for pottery, for which the region is known. Corsican knives are another specialty item, as are regional charcuterie, cheeses, and jams.

Calenzana

㉕ *13 km (8 mi) from Calvi: head east on N197 for 5 km (3 mi), then south on D151.*

Leaving Calvi via the rose-color hill towns of La Balagne—"the garden of Corsica"—will take you through some memorable towns and villages. Calenzana is the jumping-off point for the GR 20, Corsica's challenging 20-day hike over the crest of its mountainous interior. It's also the home of the spectacular wine cellar of the Orsini vineyards, the **Cave du Domaine Orsini** (✉ Clos Rochebelle ☎ 04–95–62–81–01 ⊕ www. domaine-orsini.com/); tours scheduled by appointment. The main house is an impressive porticoed sight; nearby is the Orsini boutique, where a variety of homegrown delights, from vintage wines to "Les Maquisettes" candies can be bought for great gifts back home.

The 11th-century church of **Ste-Restitute,** about 1 km (½ mi) beyond town, has an altar backed by medieval frescoes depicting the life of St. Restitute. Legend has it that the saint was martyred here in the 3rd century, and when the people of the town began building a church on a separate site, the stone blocks were moved here each night by two huge white bulls. Apparently, so the story goes, this happened several times before the townsfolk finally got the divine message and changed building sites.

en route From Calenzana, serpentine D151 winds around hillsides dotted with picturesque villages. The medieval, stone hilltop village of Sant'Antonino, believed to date from the 9th century, is one of the oldest still-inhabited places on the island and home of the polychrome Pisan church of **La Trinité.** The view over La Balagne from Sant'Antonino is superbly panoramic.

Pigna

㉖ *7 km (4 mi) northeast of Sant'Antonino on D151.*

Fodor'sChoice ★ The village of Pigna is dedicated to bringing back traditional Corsican music and crafts. Here you can listen to folk songs in cafés, visit workshops, and buy handmade musical instruments. The Casa Musicale, a concert hall, auberge, and restaurant, is the center of it all; see its Web site for news of upcoming events. Another handy Web site for Corsican music is www.musicorsica.net. The highlight of the year is held during the first half of July, when the Casa hosts a Festivoce (song festival) of vocalists and a cappella groups.

Where to Stay & Eat

$–$$ ✕🏨 **Casa Musicale.** This magnetic spot has traditional local cuisine, music of all kinds—often authentic Corsican polyphonic singing—and a lovely view over La Balagne down to Calvi. Rooms are simple but elegant, with whitewashed walls and rustic furniture; they sleep two, three, or four. ✉ 20220 Pigna ☎ 04–95–61–77–31 🖷 04–95–61–74–28 ⊕ www.casa-musicale.org ⟲ 7 rooms ♿ Restaurant, minibars, bar, some pets allowed (fee); no a/c ☰ MC, V ⊘ Closed Jan. 5–Mar. 5. No dinner Sun. and Mon. except July 14–Aug. 30.

Shopping

The **Casa di l'Artigiani** (☎ 04–95–61–77–29) sells a panoply of local crafts, from jam and honey to musical instruments and hand-knit sweaters.

L'Ile Rousse

27 *10 km (6 mi) northeast of Algajola, 37 km (22 mi) southwest of St-Florent.*

L'Ile Rousse, famous for its market and named for the island of reddish rock now connected to the town by a causeway, is a favorite for vacationers who come to bask in its Riviera-like mise-en-scène. A small two-car train runs along the coast to Calvi, delivering sun-worshipers to beaches not accessible by road.

Where to Stay & Eat

$-$$ ✕▨ **A Pasturella.** This picturesque hotel in Monticello, 5 km (3 mi) southeast of L'Ile Rousse, has simple rooms with modern furnishings and geranium-filled window boxes overlooking the mountains. The widely admired restaurant specializes in seafood and Corsican dishes. ⊠ *5 km (3 mi) outside L'Ile Rousse, 20220 Monticello* ☎ *04–95–60–05–65* 🖷 *04–95–60–21–78* ⇨ *14 rooms* ♻ *Restaurant, bar, some pets allowed (fee)* ▤ *AE, MC, V* ⊘ *Closed Nov. 2–Dec. 1; no dinner Sun. Dec. 15–Mar.* ⦿ *MAP.*

The Outdoors

Two of the best **beaches** in the area are the **Plage d'Ostriconi,** at the mouth of the Ostriconi River (20 km [13 mi] north of town), and the wilder and much-frequented-by-nudists **Plage Saleccia,** used in the 1960s filming of *The Longest Day.*

Lama

28 *15 km (9 mi) southeast of L'Ile Rousse, 57 km (24 mi) north of Corte.*

The charmingly restored medieval village of Lama is only 10 minutes up the Ostriconi Valley. Everyone from the mayor to local children accommodates visitors; people say hello in the streets and seem to know where you are staying. Once a prosperous olive-growing town, the village was nearly deserted after a 1971 fire destroyed 35,000 olive trees in a single afternoon.

Where to Stay & Eat

$-$$ ✕▨ **Auberge de Lama.** Lodgings are scattered throughout the village in small stone cottages that sleep from two to eight. The lively restaurant, open year-round, is the town's informal nerve center. Excellent Corsican specialties are served, such as a mint-and-brocciu omelet or roast kid. ⊠ *20218 Lama* ☎ *04–95–48–22–99* 🖷 *04–95–48–23–77* ⊕ *www.corse-escapades.com* ⇨ *50 cottages* ⦿ *MAP.*

The Outdoors

Riding along the old mule trails on horseback is an excellent way to see the countryside; for this and nearly any other outdoor activity you can imagine, from hang-gliding to canyoning, contact Pierre-Jean Costa at **Corse Escapades** (⊠ Village de Lama, 20218 Lama ☎ 04–95–48–22–99 🖷 04–95–48–23–77 ⊕ www.corse-escapades.com).

Murato

㉙ *15 km (9 mi) west of Lama, 12 km (7 mi) south of Bastia: take N193 to D82 to D305 at Rutalli.*

The village of Murato has two excellent restaurants and a remarkable 12th-century Pisan church, one of Corsica's finest architectural treasures. The polychrome, green-marble, and white-limestone **Église Mosaïque de San Michele de Murato** (Mosaic Church of San Michele of Murato) suggests many interpretations. Look for the relief depicting Eve tempted by a serpent, covering her nakedness with an oversized hand. The site overlooks the Golfe de St-Florent. When the *libecciu* (a powerful and persistent west wind) is blowing full force, the Continent is often visible.

Where to Eat

★ **$$–$$$** ✕ **Le Ferme Campo di Monte.** The Julliard sisters prepare what is widely regarded as Corsica's most authentic cuisine at this lovely 350-year-old stone farmhouse. Especially good are the *storzapreti* (brocciu croquettes). ✉ *D305 Rutali-Murato* ☎ *04–95–37–64–39* ✍ *Reservations essential* ▤ *AE, DC, MC, V* ⊘ *No lunch Mon.–Sat. Closed Mon.–Wed. in Sept.–June.*

★ **$$–$$$** ✕ **U Fragnu.** While this noted spot may be 33 km (20 mi) southwest of Murato, the detour is well worth it. Turn off the N 198 road 22 km (13 mi) south of Bastia and take the drive up to Vescovato and Venzolasca to be rewarded with one of Corsica's finest culinary experiences at U Fragnu. After you've exited La Castagniccia near La Porta, head north to this restaurant for some exquisite local country cooking. Madame Garelli is a specialist in *soupe de berger* (shepherd's soup)—made from a restored original recipe recovered after painstaking research. ✉ *Rte. de Vescovato, Venzolasca, 7 km (4 mi) north of Folelli on N198, then 2 km (1 mi) up D37* ☎ *04–95–36–62–33* ✍ *Reservations essential* ▤ *No credit cards* ⊘ *No lunch Thurs.–Sat. in Nov.–Mar.*

St-Florent

㉚ *28 km (17 mi) northeast of the exit for Lama on D81, 46 km (28 mi) northeast of L'Ile Rousse.*

St-Florent is a postcard-perfect village nestled into the crook of the Golfe de St-Florent between the rich Nebbio Valley and the desert of Agriates. The town has a crumbling citadel and a yacht basin ringed by shops and restaurants. Look for the exceptional Romanesque **Santa Maria Assunta** (✉ Rue Agostino Giustiniani), just outside the village. Standing in isolated splendor among the vineyards, this 12th-century white-limestone church is one of only three Pisan churches remaining on the island. The facade and interior columns are sculpted with human faces, snakes, snails, and mythical animals.

Patrimonio

㉛ *5 km (3 mi) northeast of St-Florent, 18 km (11 mi) west of Bastia.*

Patrimonio lies at the base of the Cap Corse Peninsula, among vineyards that produce most of Corsica's best wines. The most prestigious of the Patrimonio vineyards is the **Orenga de Gaffory** (☎ 04–95–30–11–38 ⊕ www. domaine-orengadegaffory.com) operation, a hard-to-beat combination of wine brewery and art gallery. Tours of the vineyards and of the Orenga de Gaffory gallery can be arranged; they're open weekdays 9–noon and 3–6. **Antoine Arena** (☎ 04–95–37–08–27) is one of the leading young vintners. **Dominique Gentile** (☎ 04–95–37–01–54) is a leading Patrimonio wine maker who combines old techniques and modern technology.

Nightlife & the Arts

The **Nuits de la Guitare** (⊕ www.festival-guitare-patrimonio.com) music festival during the third week of July is one of Corsica's top musical events, featuring blues, jazz, and flamenco guitarists from all over the world.

The Outdoors

One of the most spectacular mountain **hiking** routes in Corsica follows the crest of Cap Corse over the 4,287-foot Monte Stello, from which you can see the hills of Tuscany and Provence. Contact the Parc Naturel Régional de la Corse for details.

Nonza

㉜ *14 km (9 mi) north of Patrimonio, 8 km (5 mi) south of Canelle.*

On your way around Cap Corse, be sure to stop in Nonza. This vertiginous crag seems impossibly high over its famous black beach, the legacy of a former asbestos mine down the coast at Canari. The beach is accessible only by trudging down the 600 steps from Nonza, and no doubt this is the reason why it's usually deserted. The chapel is dedicated to the martyred St. Julie, whose severed breasts, it's said, became the double fountain known as the *Fontaine aux Mamelles* (Fountain of Mammaries) on the way down to the beach. The spectacular gravity-defying tower was constructed by Pasquale Paoli in 1760. Its squared corners made it easier to defend, as famed Captain Casella proved in 1768 when he stood off 1,200 French troops.

Where to Stay & Eat

$ ✕▦ **Auberge Patrizi.** On a shady terrace in the center of town, Marcella Patrizi serves excellent Corsican cuisine in a lively setting. The auberge also has rooms—small and a little too close to the road—with spectacular views. ⊠ *Pl. du Village, 20217* ☎ *04–95–37–82–16* ᐧ *04–95–37–86–40* ⤶ *13 rooms* ⟁ *Restaurant, bar, some pets allowed (fee); no a/c* ☰ *AE, MC, V* ☺ *Closed Nov.–Mar.*

Centuri

㉝ *55 km (34 mi) north of Patrimonio, 41 km (25 mi) north of Nonza.*

Centuri (pronounced *chen*-toori), Cap Corse's top fishing port, is a good place for lunch on your way around the cape. The late afternoon arrival and unloading of the fishing boats is also a major event.

Where to Stay & Eat

★ **$–$$** ✕▦ **Le Vieux Moulin.** Old World charm and authentic Corsican flavor characterize this place. The main house was built in 1870 as a private residence; the eight-room annex is less antique but no less inviting, with bougainvillea cascading from its balconies. The restaurant specializes in Centuri's famous seafood. ⊠ *Rte. de Cap Corse, 20238 Centuri Port* ☎ *04–95–35–60–15* 🖷 *04–95–35–60–24* ⊕ *www.le-vieux-moulin.net/* ⏴ *14 rooms* ⚴ *Restaurant, 2 tennis courts, pool, bar, some pets allowed (fee); no a/c* ⊟ *AE, DC, MC, V* ⊙ *Closed Nov.–Mar.*

Erbalunga

❸❹ *40 km (25 mi) southeast of Centuri, 10 km (6 mi) north of Bastia.*

Erbalunga is one of the most charming villages on Cap Corse's east coast, with stone houses sloping gently down to a Genoese tower built into a rock ledge. Possibly because it was French poet Paul Valéry's ancestral home, a famous colony of artists settled here in the 1920s.

Where to Stay

★ **$$$–$$$$** 🏨 **Castel' Brando.** This 19th-century mansion has dark-green shutters and terra-cotta tiles. The spacious rooms are furnished with country-style antiques. Breakfast is served in the garden next to the swimming pool. ⊠ *Off D80, 20222* 🕮 *B.P. 20* ☎ *04–95–30–10–30* 🖷 *04–95–33–98–18* ⊕ *www.castelbrando.corsica-net.com* ⏴ *27 rooms* ⚴ *Kitchenettes, cable TV, pool, some pets allowed (fee)* ⊟ *AE, MC, V* ⊙ *Closed Nov.–Mar. 15.*

San Martino di Lota

❸❺ *12 km (7 mi) north of Bastia.*

Just 20 minutes from downtown Bastia, the turnoff to the perched village of San Martino di Lota winds through thick vegetation as the flat blue expanse of the Tyrrhenian Sea spreads out below. A hike up to the mountain pass, **Bocca di Santo Lunardo,** above the village, is a perfect way to develop a ravenous appetite: the trek takes between six and eight hours round-trip and provides fantastic views of Cap Corse, the Isle of Elba, and the Tuscan hills of the Italian mainland.

Where to Stay & Eat

$–$$ ✕🏨 **La Corniche.** The Anziani family runs this excellent hotel-restaurant serving innovative Corsican fare that changes with the seasons. The *cabri aux herbes du maquis* (roast kid in maquis herbs) is a winter favorite. Rooms are decorated in light pastels and have panoramic sea views. ⊠ *20200 San Martino di Lota* ☎ *04–95–31–40–98* 🖷 *04–95–32–37–69* ⊕ *www.hotel-lacorniche.com* ⏴ *19 rooms* ⚴ *Restaurant, minibars, pool, bar, some pets allowed (fee); no a/c* ⊟ *AE, DC, MC, V* ⊙ *Closed Dec. and Jan.* ❘◎❘ *MAP.*

Bastia

★ ❸❻ *13 km (7 mi) south of San Martino di Lota, 10 km (6 mi) south of Erbalunga, 23 km (14 mi) east of St-Florent, 93 km (58 mi) northeast of Calvi, 170 km (105 mi) north of Bonifacio, 153 km (95 mi) northeast of Ajaccio.*

Notably more Italianate than the "continental" French capital at Ajaccio, Bastia is, along with Corte, quintessentially Corsican. Despite sprawling suburbs, it has a historic center that retains the timeless, salty flavor of an ancient Mediterranean port, so approaching and departing by sea are particularly dramatic while rounding the Cap Corse peninsula. With its four churches, its ethnographical museum, many picturesque corners, and a number of fine dining options overlooking the comings and goings of boat traffic to the tune of foghorn blasts, Bastia has a full bouquet of sights to savor. Its name is derived from the word bastion, in reference to the fortress the Genoese built here in the 14th century as a stronghold against rebellious islanders and potential invaders. Today the city is Corsica's business center and largest town. The **Terra Vecchia** (Old Town) is best explored on foot. Start at the wide, palm-filled **place St-Nicolas,** bordered on one side by docked ships looming large in the port and on the other by two blocks of popular cafés along boulevard Général-de-Gaulle. From place St-Nicolas head south on boulevard Général-de-Gaulle, which becomes rue Napoléon, for two blocks to the **Église de la Conception** (Church of the Conception; ⊠ Rue Napoléon), occupying a pebble-studded square. Step inside to admire the church's ornate 18th-century interior, although the lighting is poor, requiring a bright day to see much detail. The walls are covered with a riot of wood carvings, gold, and marble, and the ceiling is painted with vibrant frescoes. **Place du Marché,** the market square behind the church, buzzes with activity every morning except Monday. The warren of tiny streets that make up the old fishermen's quarter begins at the far side of the square.

To the south is the picturesque **Vieux Port** (Old Port), along quai des Martyrs de la Libération, dominated by the hilltop citadel. The harbor, lined with excellent seafood restaurants, is berthed by several million-dollar yachts, but you can still find many bright red-and-blue fishing boats and tangles of old nets and lines. A walk around the port takes you to **Terra Nova** (New Town), a maze of not-so-new streets and houses at the base of the 15th-century fortress. Climb the Escalier Romieu steps beside the leafy Jardins Romieu for a sweeping view of the Italian islands of Capraia, Elba, and Montecristo.

Long closed for restoration work but recently reopened in 2005, the vaulted, colonnaded galleries of the **Palais des Nobles Douzes** (also known as the Palais des Gouverneurs Genois, or Genoese Governors' Palace) hold the **Musée d'Ethnographie Corse** (Corsican Ethnographic Museum). Don't miss the *Casablanca,* a French submarine used by the Resistance with swastikas on the turret representing downed Nazi aircraft. ⊠ *Pl. du Donjon* ☎ *04–95–31–09–12.*

A network of cobbled alleyways rambles across the citadel to the 15th-century **Cathédrale Ste-Marie** (⊠ Rue Notre-Dame). Inside, classic Baroque abounds in an explosion of gilt decoration. The 18th-century silver statue of the Assumption is paraded at the head of a religious procession every August 15. The sumptuous Baroque style of the **Chapelle Ste-Croix** (Chapel of the Holy Cross), behind the cathedral, makes it look more like a theater than a church. The chapel owes its name to a blackened oak crucifix, dubbed "Christ of the Miracles, " discovered by fishermen at sea in 1428 and venerated to this day by Bastia's fishing community.

Where to Stay & Eat

$$–$$$ ✕ **La Citadelle.** This rustic and intimate spot, arranged around an ancient oil press, is near the Governor's Palace on the heights of the Terra Nova. Dishes are carefully and elegantly prepared and presented; especially tasty is the rockfish soup, a delicious dark and thick potage. ⊠ *5 rue du Dragon* ☎ *04–95–31–44–70* ▤ *AE, MC, V* ⊘ *Closed Sun. and Dec. 20–Jan. 14. No lunch Sat.*

★ **$–$$** ✕ **A Scaletta.** Enjoy the view of the Vieux Port as you choose from a host of fish and seafood specials at this popular spot. (Lavezzi, next door, has the same view, fine cuisine, and higher prices.) The cuisine in this rollicking little bistro is traditional Corsican with maritime leanings. ⊠ *4 rue St-Jean* ☎ *04–95–32–28–70* ▤ *AE, DC, MC, V* ⊘ *Closed Sun.*

$–$$ ▥ **Posta Vecchia.** The top selling point of this hotel in an old building not far from place St-Nicolas is its quai-side location. The unpretentious rooms have floral wallpaper and wood-beam ceilings; some are quite small. Ask for one in the main house facing the port. ⊠ *Quai des Martyrs-de-la-Libération, 20200* ☎ *04–95–32–32–38* 🖷 *04–95–32–14–05* ⬐ *49 rooms* ♨ *Some pets allowed (fee); no a/c* ▤ *AE, DC, MC, V.*

Nightlife & the Arts

O'Connors (⊠ rue St-Erasme 1 ☎ 04–95–31–13–25) is a popular Irish pub near the Bastia market. Musicians fill the lively patio of the **Pub Chez Assunta** (⊠ Pl. Fontaine Nueve 4 ☎ 04–95–34–11–40) on most summer nights. For straight-up disco, head to **Le Velvet** (⊠ Vieux Port ☎ 04–95–32–63–58) below the Jardin Romieu.

★ One of Corsica's major carnivals, the **Fête du Christ Noir** (Feast of the Black Christ), dedicated to Bastia's most important religious icon, is on May 3. The **Fête de St-Jean,** on Midsummer's Eve (June 23), means concerts in all of Bastia's Baroque spaces. A **Film Festival of Mediterranean Cultures** is held every November. An **International Music Festival** is in early December.

Shopping

Casa di l'Artigiani (⊠ 5 rue des Terrasses) has a wide selection of local crafts. **Mattei Cap Corse** (⊠ 15 Blvd. Général du Gaulle) sells the Mattei family's special Cap Corse liqueur (made from grapes). **U Montagnolu** (⊠ Rue Cesar Campinchi 15) entices with its full range of Corsican sausages, from figatelli to coppa. At the **market** (⊠ Pl. du Marché, behind St-Jean-Baptiste), everything from local cheeses to charcuterie to myrtle liqueur is sold on weekday mornings.

CORSICA A TO Z

To research prices, get advice from other travelers, and book travel arrangements, visit www.fodors.com.

AIR TRAVEL

CARRIERS Air France has daily service connecting Paris and Lyon with Ajaccio, Bastia, and Calvi. Compagnie Corse Méditérranée connects Ajaccio and Bastia to Nice and Marseille, with several flights a day. Delta connects with Air France for flights from the United States to Corsica from May to October. TAT (Transport Aérien Transrégional) flies to Figari from Paris. Air Balagne, ATM (Air Transport Méditérranée), and Kyrnair are airlines with intra-island flights.

🛪 Airlines & Contacts **Air Balagne** ☎04-95-65-02-97. **Air France** ☎04-95-29-45-45 Ajaccio, 01-45-46-90-00 Paris. **ATM** ☎ 04-95-76-04-99. **Compagnie Corse Méditérranée** ☎04-95-29-05-00 Ajaccio. **Delta** ☎800/241-4141. **Kyrnair** ☎04-95-20-52-29. **TAT** ☎ 04-95-71-01-20.

AIRPORTS

Corsica has four major airports: Ajaccio, Bastia, Calvi, and Figari. The airports at Ajaccio and Bastia run regular shuttle-bus services to and from town. At Figari a bus meets all incoming flights and will take passengers as far as Bonifacio and Porto-Vecchio for about €15.38. From Calvi the best way to get into town is to take a taxi for about €15.38.

🛪 Airport Information **Ajaccio–Campo dell'Oro** ☎ 04-95-23-56-56. **Bastia–Poretta** ☎ 04-95-55-96-96. **Calvi–Ste Catherine** ☎ 04-95-65-88-88.

Figari–Sud Corse ☎ 04-95-71-10-10.**BOAT & FERRY TRAVEL**
Regular car ferries run from Marseille, Nice, and Toulon to Ajaccio, Bastia, Calvi, L'Ile Rousse, and Propriano. These crossings take from 5 to 10 hours, with sleeping cabins available. The high-speed ferry from Nice to either Calvi or Bastia takes about three hours. Package deals, which include making the crossing with a car, an onboard cabin, and a hotel in Corsica, are available from SNCM, the Société Nationale Maritime Corse-Méditérranée. Connections from the Italian mainland are run by Corsica Ferries. Moby Lines also runs Italian mainland connections. Sardinia can be reached by ferry from Bastia or Bonifacio on Navarma Lines. Saremar also runs ferries to Sardinia.

🛪 Boat & Ferry Information **CMN** ✉ Compagnie Méridionale de Navigation, Ajaccio ☎04-95-21-20-34 ✉ Bastia ☎ 04-95-31-63-38. **Corsica Ferries** ✉ Bastia ☎ 04-95-32-95-95 ✉ Genoa, Italy ☎ 010-59-33-01. **Moby Lines** ✉ Bastia ☎ 04-95-31-46-29 ✉ Bonifacio ☎04-95-73-00-29 ✉ Genoa, Italy ☎010-20-56-51. **Navarma Lines** ✉4 rue Luce-de-Casablanca, Bastia ☎ 04-95-31-46-29. **Saremar** ✉ Gare Maritime, Bonifacio ☎ 04-95-73-06-75. **SNCM** ✉ Paris ☎ 01-49-24-24-24 ✉ Marseille ☎ 04-91-56-30-30 ✉ Nice ☎ 04-93-13-66-99 ✉ Toulon ☎ 04-94-16-66-66 ✉ Ajaccio ☎04-95-29-66-99 ✉ Bastia ☎04-95-54-66-88 ✉ Calvi ☎04-95-65-01-38 ✉ L'Ile Rousse ☎04-95-60-09-56.

BUS TRAVEL

The local bus network is geared to residents who take it to school and work. At least two buses a day connect all the southern towns with Ajaccio, while northern towns are connected by bus to Bastia.

🛪 Bus Information **Autocars Eurocorse** ☎ 04-95-31-03-79. **Autocars "Les Beaux Voyages"** ☎ 04-95-65-11-35. **Autocars Les Rapides Bleus** ☎ 04-95-31-03-79. **Autocars Santini** ☎ 04-95-37-02-98.

CAR RENTAL

Hertz serves the entire island; its 18 offices are at all airports and harbors and in the major towns. Be sure to reserve at least two weeks in advance in July and August.

🚗 **Local Agencies Avis Ollandini** ⊠ Ajaccio Airport ☎ 04-95-23-25-14. **Europcar** ⊠ 1 rue du Nouveau Port, Bastia ☎ 04-95-31-59-29. **Hertz** ⊠ Ajaccio Airport ☎ 04-95-22-14-84 ⊠ 8 cours Grandval, Ajaccio ☎ 04-95-21-70-94 ⊠ Sq. St-Victor, Bastia ☎ 04-95-31-14-24 ⊠ Quai du Commerce, Bonifacio ☎ 04-95-73-02-47 ⊠ 2 rue Maréchal-Joffre, Calvi ☎ 04-95-65-06-64.

CAR TRAVEL

Though driving is undoubtedly the best way to explore the island's scenic stretches, note that winding, mountainous roads and uneven surfaces can actually double or triple your expected travel time. The Michelin 1/200,000 map No. 90 is essential. Be prepared for spelling anomalies, many of which are Corsican, not French. Drive defensively: you'll find that others on the road tend to move at terrifying speeds.

SPORTS & THE OUTDOORS

Canoeing, kayaking, and rafting are popular pastimes on the mountain rivers; for details write the Association Municipale de Ponte-Leccia.

🚣 **Canoeing, Kayaking & Rafting Association Municipale de Ponte-Leccia** ⊠ 20218 Ponte Leccia.

TOURS

AIRPLANE TOURS ATM and Kyrnair arrange sightseeing tours by plane.

✈ **Fees & Schedules ATM** ☎ 04-95-76-04-99. **Kyrnair** ☎ 04-95-20-52-29.

BOAT TOURS Most of Corsica's spectacular scenery is best viewed from the water. Colombo Line and Promenades en Mer, in Calvi, organize whole-day glass-bottom boat tours of Girolata, the Scandola Nature Reserve, and the Golfe de Porto. The Promenades en Mer, in Ajaccio, organizes daily trips (at 9 and 2) to the Iles Sanguinaires. Vedettes Christina and Vedettes Méditérranée arrange outings from Bonifacio to the Iles Lavezzi, Les Calanches, and Les Grottes.

🚤 **Fees & Schedules Colombo Line** ⊠ Quai Landry, Calvi ☎ 04-95-65-32-10. **Promenades en Mer** ⊠ Port de l'Amirauté, 20000 Ajaccio ☎ 04-95-23-23-38 ⊠ Porto Marine, Calvi ☎ 04-95-26-15-16. **Vedettes Christina** ☎ 04-95-73-14-69. **Vedettes Méditérranée** ☎ 04-95-73-07-71.

BUS TOURS Ollandini arranges whole- and half-day bus tours of the island, leaving from Ajaccio.

🚌 **Fees & Schedules Ollandini** ⊠ 1 rte. d'Alata, Ajaccio ☎ 04-95-21-10-12.

WALKING TOURS Two- and three-day guided hikes through the mountains and lake region are organized by several walking and hiking associations.

🥾 **Fees & Schedules Associu di Muntagnoli Corsi** ⊠ Quartier Pentaniedda, 20122 Quenza ☎ 04-95-78-64-05. **Association Sportive du Niollu** ⊠ Centre Ville, 20224 Calacuccia ☎ 04-95-48-05-22. **La Compagnie Régionale de Guides** ⊠ Centre Ville, 20224 Calacuccia ☎ 04-95-48-10-43. **In Terra Corsa** ⊠ Centre Ville, 20249 Ponte Leccia ☎ 04-95-47-64-48. **Objectif Nature** ⊠ Quartier Terra Vecchia, 20200 Bastia

☎ 04-95-54-20-42. **La Trace** ✉ Quartier Terra Vecchia, 20200 Bastia ☎ 04-95-35-86-37.

TRAIN TRAVEL

The main line of Corsica's simple rail network runs from Ajaccio, in the west, to Corte, in the central valley, then divides at Ponte Leccia. From here one line continues to L'Ile Rousse and Calvi, in the north, and the other to Bastia, in the northeast. Another service runs four times daily between Ajaccio and Bastia. In summer a small train connects Calvi and L'Ile Rousse, stopping at numerous beaches and resorts. Telephone numbers for local train stations are listed below by town.

🚩 **Train Information SNCF Ajaccio** ☎ 04-95-23-11-03. **SNCF Bastia** ☎ 04-95-32-60-06. **SNCF Calvi** ☎ 04-95-65-00-61. **SNCF Ponte Leccia** ☎ 04-95-47-61-29.

TRAVEL AGENCIES

🚩 **Local Agent Referrals Corse Itineraries** ✉ 32 cours Napoléon, Ajaccio ☎ 04-95-51-01-10 🖶 04-45-21-52-30. **Corse Voyages** ✉ Immeuble Les Remparts, bd. Wilson, Calvi ☎ 04-95-65-26-71. **Cyrnea Tourisme** ✉ 9 av. Xavier-Luciani, Corte ☎ 04-95-46-24-62 🖶 04-95-46-11-22. **Kallistour** ✉ 6 av. Maréchal-Sebastiani, Bastia ☎ 04-95-31-71-49 🖶 04-95-32-35-73.

VISITOR INFORMATION

The Agence du Tourisme de la Corse can provide information about the whole island. The Parc Naturel Régional de la Corse, Corsica's wildlife and natural-resource management authority, controlling well over a third of the island, can provide trail maps, booklets, and a wide variety of information. Local tourist offices are listed below by town.

🚩 Tourist Information **Agence du Tourisme de la Corse** ✉ 17 bd. Roi-Jérôme, 20000 Ajaccio ☎ 04-95-51-77-77 🖶 04-95-51-14-40. **Ajaccio** ✉ Hôtel de Ville, pl. Foch ☎ 04-95-51-53-03 ⊕ www.tourisme.fr/ajaccio/. **Bastia** ✉ Pl. St-Nicolas ☎ 04-95-54-20-40 ⊕ www.bastia-tourisme.com/. **Bonifacio** ✉ Rue des Deux Moulins ☎ 04-95-73-11-88 ⊕ www.bonifacio.com. **Calvi** ✉ Port de Plaisance ☎ 04-95-65-16-67 ⊕ www.tourisme.fr/calvi/. **Corte** ✉ La Citadelle ☎ 04-95-46-26-70 ⊕ www.tourisme.fr/corte/. **L'Ile Rousse** ✉ Pl. Paoli ☎ 04-95-60-04-35. **Levie-Alta Rocca** ✉ Rue Sorba ☎ 04-95-78-41-95. **Parc Naturel Régional de la Corse** ✉ Rue du Général-Fiorella ☎ 04-95-21-56-54 ✍ Mailing address: B.P. 417, 20100 Ajaccio. **Piana** ✉ Hôtel de Ville ☎ 04-95-27-84-42. **Piedicroce-Castagniccia** ✉ Piedicroce ☎ 04-95-35-82-54. **Porticcio** ✉ 428 bd. Rive Sud ☎ 04-95-25-01-00. **Porto-Vecchio** ✉ Rue du Député de Rocca Serra ☎ 04-95-70-09-58. **Propriano** ✉ Port de Plaisance ☎ 04-95-76-01-49. **Sartène** ✉ Rue Borgo ☎ 04-95-77-15-40. **Sollacaro-Filitosa** ✉ Filitosa ☎ 04-95-74-07-64. **St-Florent** ☎ 04-95-37-06-04.

The Midi-Pyrénées & the Languedoc-Roussillon

14

WORD OF MOUTH

"Set about 40 km from the Mediterranean, Céret is a truly delightful little town. It was a center of the Fauvist art movement and also the nascent Cubist movement and enjoys an excellent museum of modern art with works by Picasso, Chagall, Dalí, and Matisse. The central square is shaded by stately plane trees and it has a distinctly Catalan air as opposed to French; people still dance the Sardana in this valley and it's not an affectation for tourists but a real part of their cross-border Catalan cultural heritage."

—DrDoGood

"Carcassonne is a medieval marvel. Its Musée Archéologie and the interior of Basilica of St-Nazaire are well worth a visit."

—Cigalechanta

Introduction by
George Semler

Updated by
George Semler

LIKE THE MOST CELEBRATED DISH OF THIS AREA, cassoulet, the southwestern region of France is a feast of diverse ingredients. Just as it would be a gross oversimplification to refer to cassoulet merely as a dish of baked beans, southwestern France is much more than just Toulouse, the peaks of the Pyrénées, and the fairy-tale ramparts of Carcassonne. Rolling, sun-baked plains and rock- and shrub-covered hills dotted with ruins of ancient civilizations parallel the burning coastline; the fortifications and cathedrals of once-great cities like Béziers and Narbonne rise miragelike out of the Mediterranean haze; and Collioure and the famed Côte Vermeille, immortalized by Picasso and Matisse, nestle colorfully just north of the border with Spain. Nevertheless, just as cassoulet *toulousain* (made with goose) is the variety you are most apt to find all over France, so the city of Toulouse tops the tourist "bill of fare" here. Serving as gateway to the region, alive with music, sculpture, and architectural gems, and vibrant with students, Toulouse is all that more famous regional capitals would like to have remained, or to become. Sinuously spread along the romantic banks of the Garonne as it meanders north and west from the Catalan Pyrénées on its way to the Atlantic, "La Ville Rose"—so-called for its redbrick buildings—has a Spanish sensuality unique in all Gaul, a feast for eyes and ears alike. Toulouse was the ancient capital of the province called Languedoc, so christened when it became royal property in 1270, meaning the country where *oc*—instead of the *oïl* or *oui* of northeastern France—meant yes.

Outside Toulouse, the terrain of the Midi-Pyrénées and Languedoc-Roussillon is studded with highlights, like so many raisins sweetening up a spicy stew. Albi, with its Toulouse-Lautrec legacy, is a star attraction, while each outlying town—from Montauban to Moissac to Auch, Mirepoix, or Cordes-sur-Ciel—has artistic and architectural treasures waiting to be uncovered. Besides Albi's Toulouse-Lautrec Museum, other art museums not to miss here are Montauban's Musée Ingres, devoted to France's most accomplished Neoclassical painter, and Céret's Musée d'Art Moderne, which is packed with Picassos, Braques, and Chagalls.

There's also an "open-air museum" prized by artists and poets: the Côte Vermeille, or Vermilion Coast, centered around the fishing village of Collioure, where Matisse, Derain, and the Fauvists committed chromatic mayhem in the early years of the 20th century. The view of the Côte Vermeille from the Alberes mountain range reveals a bright-yellow strand of beach curving north and east toward the Camargue wetlands. From the vineyards above Banyuls-sur-Mer to the hills once traversed by Hannibal and his regiment of elephants, this storied coast has been irresistible to everyone from Pompey to Louis XIV. The Mediterranean smooth and opalescent at dawn; villagers dancing Sardanas to the music of the raucous and ancient woodwind *flavioles* and *tenores*; the flood of golden light so peculiar to the Mediterranean . . . everything about it seems to be asking to be immortalized in oil on canvas. The heart of the region is Collioure, with its narrow, cobbled streets and pink-and-mauve houses. A town of espadrille merchants, anchovy packers, and lateen-rigged fishing boats in the shadow of its 13th-century Château Royal, Collioure, home of the late novelist Patrick O'Brian, is now as much a magnet for tourists as it

14

The Midi-Pyrénées and the Languedoc-Roussillon form the main body of France's traditional southwestern region. Sports- and nature-lovers flock here to enjoy the natural attributes of the area, of which Toulouse—a university town of rosy pink brick—is the cultural star. Here, too, are Albi and its wonderful Toulouse-Lautrec Museum; Moissac and its famous Romanesque cloister; the once-upon-a-timeliness of Carcassonne; the spa towns that enliven the Pyrénées; and the relatively undiscovered city of Montpellier. And when you see picturesque Collioure's stunning Mediterranean setting, you can understand why Fauvist painters Matisse and Derain went color-berserk while there. Getting to know this vast region would take several weeks, or even years. But it's possible to sample its finest offerings in three to seven days, if that's all the time you have.

Numbers in the text correspond to numbers in the margin and on the Midi-Pyrénées & the Languedoc-Roussillon and Toulouse maps.

If you have 3 days

Bask in the rich rose color of ▦ **Toulouse** ❶ ▶ –❷❹ for a day and then head to **Cordes-sur-Ciel** ❷❻, a fortified medieval village. Make Toulouse-Lautrec's home town, ▦ **Albi** ❷❺, your home for the night. On Day 3 explore the medieval citadel at ▦ **Carcassonne** ❸❷.

If you have 7 to 11 days

Spend the first day and a half in ▦ **Toulouse** ❶ ▶ –❷❹; then drive west to ▦ **Auch** ❸❶, the capital of the Gers département. Next, head north to the old Roman town of **Lectoure** ❸❾. Next up is a true high point of the trip: the famous Romanesque sculptures of the abbey church at ▦ **Moissac** ❷❽. On Day 3 study up on the university town of **Montauban** ❷❼ before visiting the medieval age in **Cordes-sur-Ciel** ❷❻. Spend the night in ▦ **Albi** ❷❺. On the fourth day head some 70 mi south to storybook ▦ **Carcassonne** ❸❷ for a day filled with medieval history and glamour. On your fifth day drive into the Pyrénées, passing through **Tarascon-sur-Ariège** ❸❺ to see the Grotte de Niaux, the mountain resorts of **Ax-les-Thermes** ❸❻, and **Font-Romeu** ❸❼. Spend the fifth night in nearby ▦ **Eyne** ❸❽ before continuing east out of the Pyrénées toward the Mediterranean. On your sixth day, pass through the fortified town of **Villefranche-de-Conflent** ❹⓿ and on to the spa town **Vernet-les-Bains** ❹❶, where you'll want to hike up to the amazing Abbaye de St-Martin-de-Canigou. Continue on to ▦ **Prades** ❹❷, famed for its music festival and the Abbaye de St-Michel de Cuxa. After spending your sixth night here, head out to ▦ **Céret** ❹❸, immortalized by Picasso. After your seventh night here, set out on your eighth day to Roussillon's most picturesque coastal town, ▦ **Collioure** ❹❹ and channel the spirits of Matisse and Dufy. Then on the morn of your ninth day, drive north to **Perpignan** ❹❺, the historic hub city of the Roussillon, then head out of the region to discover the sights of ▦ **Narbonne** ❹❼. On your tenth day, make a detour to **Minerve** ❹❾, a sublime medieval hilltop village, then head back northeast past the Languedoc frontier to spend your last night in ▦ **Montpellier** ❺❶ –❺❽; on your eleventh day tour this city's fascinating *Vieille Ville*, steeped in culture, history, and young blood (a famous university is based here).

once was and still is a lure for artists. Although nearby villages are apparently only rich in quaintness, Collioure is surprisingly prosperous, thanks to the cultivation of *primeurs,* early ripe fruit and vegetables, shipped to the markets of northern France.

The abundant mountains, lakes, rivers, wide green valleys, and arid limestone plateaus make many of the areas in this chapter ideal for outdoor activities. The Ariège Valley and the Pyrénées Orientales provide a dramatic route through Cathar country and the Cerdagne Valley on the way to the Mediterranean. For the *sportif,* options run from kayaking and windsurfing to climbing to high Pyrenean lakes and peaks, exploring mountain monasteries such as St-Martin de Canigou, fly-fishing the upper Aude and Ariège rivers, or walking up to the Spanish border at the Gorges de Carança above Thuès-entre-Valls or the Col de Nuria above Eyne. To finish off on a cultural high note, take in the famous Romanesque cloister of St-Guilhem-le-Désert and the nearby student mecca of Montpellier, home to a fine university, museum, and the Ricardo Bofill–designed Quartier Antigone, the old city's nod to the future.

Exploring the Midi-Pyrénées & the Languedoc-Roussillon

France's largest region, Midi-Pyrénées spreads from the Dordogne in the north to the Spanish border along the Pyrénées. Radiating out from Toulouse to the surrounding towns of Albi, Carcassonne, Montauban, and Auch, and up through the Ariège Valley into the Pyrénées Orientales, the central and southern parts of the Midi-Pyrénées are rich in history, natural resources, art, and architecture. Languedoc-Roussillon fits in along the Mediterranean from Collioure north through Perpignan, Narbonne, Beziers, and Montpellier, all once part of Catalonia and the crown of Aragon's medieval Mediterranean empire. Montpellier is at the dead center of the Mediterranean coastline, a five-hour train ride from Paris and Nice, as well as from Barcelona.

This chapter divides the region into three sections. The first covers the lively city of Toulouse. The second encompasses the area to the north and west of Toulouse, including the Gers *département,* Albi, the Lot Valley, Montauban, and verdant Gascony. The third extends southeast into the Languedoc-Roussillon and up the Mediterranean coast to the now-inland crossroads of Narbonne.

About the Restaurants & Hotels

As a rule, the closer you get to the Mediterranean coast, the later you dine and the more you pay for your seafood platter and that bottle of iced rosé. The farther you travel from the coast, the higher the altitude, the more rustic the setting you'll find yourself in, and the more reasonable the prices will be. During the scorching summer months in sleepy mountain villages, lunches are light, interminable, and *bien arrosé* (French for "with lots of wine"). Here you will also find that small personal restaurant where the chickens roasting on spits above the open fire have first names and the cheese comes from the hippie couple down the road who came here in the sixties and love their mountains, their goats, and the universe in general.

14

Cassoulet Cuisine

Dining in the southwest is a rougher, heartier, and more rustic version of classic Mediterranean cooking—the peppers are sliced thick, the garlic and olive oil used with a heavier hand, the herbs crushed or coarsely chopped and served au naturel. Expect *cuisine de marché*, market-based cooking, savory seasonal dishes based on the culinary trinity of the south—garlic, onion, and tomato—straight from the village market. Languedoc is known for powerful and strongly seasoned cooking. Garlic and goose fat are generously used in traditional recipes. Be sure to try some of the renowned *foie gras* (goose or duck liver) and *confit de canard* (preserved duck). The most famous regional dish is *cassoulet*, a succulent white-bean stew with *confit d'oie* (preserved goose). Keep your eyes open for festive *cargolades*—huge communal barbecues starting off with thousands of buttery-garlic snails roasted on open grills and eaten by hand, followed by cured bacon and lamb cutlets and vats (and vats) of local wine. Mountain restaurants and inns serve rugged highland fare—be sure to try a bowl of *ollada,* a thick hearty soup made with sausage and lamb, cabbage and onion, thrown into black cauldrons and left to simmer at least 24 hours. In the Gers *département* (province) finish your meal with a glass of Armagnac, the local brandy distilled throughout the province. In the Pyrénées look for rich, dark *civet d'isard* (stewed mountain goat) or *trinxat,* a Cerdagne Valley specialty of mashed half-frozen cabbage, potato, and bacon. In the Roussillon and along the Mediterranean coast from Collioure up through Perpignan to Narbonne, the prevalent Catalan cuisine features olive oil–based cooking and sauces such as the classic aioli (crushed and emulsified garlic and olive oil). When you're on the coast, it's fish of course, often cooked over wood coals.

Matisse Country

Toulouse, the regional capital, may be nicknamed "La Ville Rose" (the Pink City) because of the color of its brick buildings but head southeast over to the Roussillon—so called for the red color of its earth—and watch the palette get notched up to deep vermilions, breathtaking aquamarines, and shocking magentas (those bougainvilleas). Little wonder, then, that the famous group of painters known as the Fauves were seduced in the early 1900s by La Côte Vermeille and its ochre-color coastal villages. These painters were called Fauves, or "wild beasts," partly because their colors were taken from the savage tones found in Mother Nature, not those of the masters of the Louvre. Where Matisse, Derain, Picasso, Gris, and Braque first vacationed and painted, thousands followed and discovered Collioure and Céret (whose name derives from *cerise,* or "cherry"). Today, Collioure is a living museum, as you can discover by touring its Chemin du Fauvisme, where 20 points along a route through town compare reproductions of noted Fauvist canvases with the actual scenes that were depicted in them (view-finder picture-frames let you see how little has changed in eight decades). After studying some of the paintings created by these masters in Céret's Musée de l'Art Moderne, you can set off through the streets of Collioure's old quarter of Le Mouré to discover numerous studios of contemporary artists. And if their prices are too steep, you can always step outside to the awe-inspiring view from the town beach of Plage Boramar and exult in your own free "3-D" Matisse. If your tastes incline more to Picasso, your place will be Céret, whose rocky landscape is said to have inspired the artist's invention of Cubism.

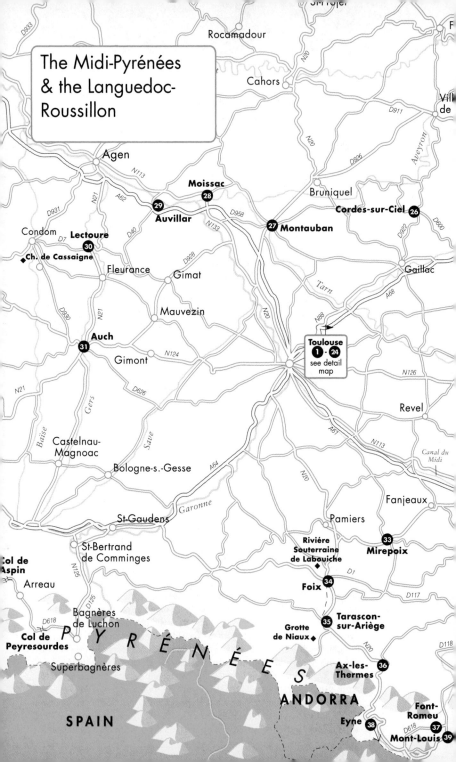

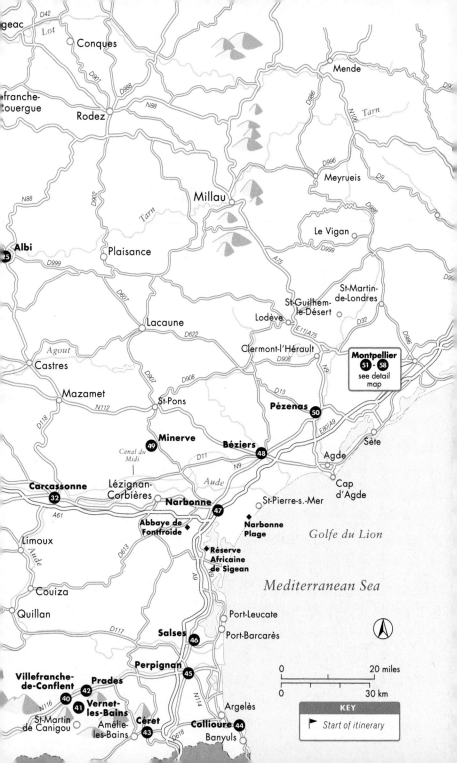

Hotels range from Mediterranean modern to medieval baronial to Pyrenean chalet; most are small and cozy rather than luxurious and sophisticated. Toulouse has the usual range of big-city hotels; make reservations well in advance if you plan to visit in spring or fall. Look for *gîtes d'étape* (hikers' way stations) and table d'hôtes (bed-and-breakfasts), which offer excellent value and a chance to meet local and international travelers and sample life on the farm, as well as the delights of *cuisine du terroir* (country cooking). Assume all hotel rooms have air-conditioning, TV, telephones, and private bath, unless otherwise noted.

WHAT IT COSTS In euros					
	$$$$	**$$$**	**$$**	**$**	**¢**
RESTAURANTS	over €30	€23–€30	€17–€23	€11–€17	under €11
HOTELS	over €190	€120–€190	€80–€120	€50–€80	under €50

Restaurant prices are per person for a main course at dinner, including tax (19.6%) and service; note that if a restaurant offers only prix-fixe (set-price) meals, it has been given the price category that reflects the full prix-fixe price. Hotel prices are for a standard double room in high season, including tax (19.6%) and service charge. Hotels operate on the European Plan (EP, with no meal provided) unless we note that they use the Breakfast Plan (BP), or also offer such options as Modified American Plan (MAP, with breakfast and dinner daily, known as *demi-pension*), or Full American Plan (FAP, or *pension complète*, with three meals a day). Inquire when booking if these all-inclusive mealplans (which always entail higher rates) are mandatory or optional.

Timing
Although spring in this mountainous region is inclined to be rainy, it's also the time when the Pyrenean flowers are at their best. April and May are delightful months on the Côte Vermeille, and June and September are equally good for the inland points. As for "off-season"—if there is such a thing, since chic Parisians often arrive in November in their SUVs with a hunger for the authentic—call ahead and double-check when restaurants and hotels close for their annual hibernation (which usually starts sometime in winter, either before, or right after, the Christmas holidays).

TOULOUSE

The ebullient city of Toulouse is the capital of the Midi-Pyrénées and the fourth-largest city in France. Just 96 km (60 mi) from the border with Spain, Toulouse's flavor is in many ways closer to southern European Spanish than to northern European French. Weathered redbrick buildings line sidewalks, giving the city its nickname, "La Ville Rose" (the Pink City). Downtown, the sidewalks and restaurants pulse late into the night with tourists, workers, college students, and technicians from the giant Airbus aviation complex headquartered outside the city.

Toulouse was founded in the 4th century BC and quickly became an important part of Roman Gaul. In turn, it was made into a Visigothic and Carolingian capital before becoming a separate county in 843. Ruling from this Pyrenean hub that was one of the great artistic and literary capitals of medieval Europe, the counts of Toulouse held sovereignty over nearly all of the Languedoc and maintained a brilliant court known for its fine troubadours and literature. In the early 13th century Toulouse was attacked and plundered by troops representing an alliance between the northern French nobility and the papacy, ostensibly to wipe out the Albigensian heresy (Catharism), but more realistically as an expansionist move against the power of Occitania, the French southwest. The counts toppled, but Toulouse experienced a cultural and economic rebirth thanks to the *woad* (dye) trade; consequently, wealthy merchants' homes constitute a major portion of Toulouse's architectural patrimony.

In 1659 the Roussillon region was officially ceded to France by Spain in the Treaty of the Pyrénées, 17 years after Louis XIII conquered the area from Spain. Toulouse, at the intersection of the Garonne and the Canal du Midi, midway between the Massif Central and the Pyrénées, became an important nexus between Aquitania, Languedoc, and the Roussillon. Today Toulouse is France's second-largest university town after Paris and the center of France's aeronautical industry.

Old Toulouse

The area between the boulevards and the Garonne forms the historic nucleus of Toulouse. Originally part of Roman Gaul and later the capital for the Visigoths and then the Carolingians, by AD 1000 Toulouse was one of the artistic and literary centers of medieval Europe. Despite its 13th-century defeat by the lords of northern France, Toulouse quickly reemerged as a cultural and commercial power and has remained so ever since. Religious and civil structures bear witness to this illustrious past, even as the city's booming student life mirrors a dynamic present. This is the heart of Toulouse, with place du Capitole at its center.

The huge garage beneath place du Capitole is a good place to park, and offers easy walking distance to all the major sites. If you leave your car in another garage, you can take the subway that runs east–west to central Toulouse; it costs €1.20 for one zone, €1.50 for two.

a good walk

Start on **place du Capitole ❶ ▶**, stopping at the donjon (dungeon or tower) next to the **Capitole/Hôtel de Ville ❷**, where there's a tourist office with maps. Rue du Taur, off the square, leads to **Notre-Dame du Taur ❸**. Continue along rue du Taur to the **Ancien Collège de Périgord ❹** to see the oldest part of the medieval university. Toulouse's most emblematic church, **St-Sernin ❺**, is at the end of rue du Taur on place St-Sernin. Next door is the **Musée St-Raymond ❻**, the city's archaeological museum.

Leave place St-Sernin and cut out along rue Bellegarde to the boulevard de Strasbourg, site of the vegetable and produce market. Take the boulevard to rue Victor-Hugo and the **Marché Victor Hugo ❼**, the large market hall. Find your way back to place du Capitole, cross the square, and take rue Gambetta past the colorfully restored Art Nouveau facade on the left to rue Lakanal. To the right is the **Église des Jacobins ❽** with its famous palm vault, one of the city's most important architectural sites.

Back on rue Gambetta is the opulent **Hôtel de Bernuy ❾**. Cut through rue Jean Suau to **place de la Daurade ❿**. **Notre-Dame de la Daurade ⓫** is the nonsteepled and domeless church on your left; the Café des Artistes is to the right. After a pause here, continue up quai de La Daurade past the sculpted goddesses on the facade of the École des Beaux-Arts to the **Pont Neuf** ⑫. Here you can cross the Garonne to the **Château d'Eau** ⑬, the water tower once used to store and pressurize the city's water system, now an excellent photographic gallery-museum. Or you can turn left on rue de Metz to the **Hôtel d'Assézat** ⑭, home of the Fondation Bemberg and its excellent collection of paintings. The nearby **Musée des Augustins** ⑮ has one of the world's finest collections of Romanesque sculpture and is a de rigueur visit, especially on a rainy day.

Take a left on rue des Changes, once part of the Roman road that sliced through Toulouse from north to south; now it's a chic pedestrian-only shopping area. Stop to admire the **Hôtel d'Astorg** ⑯, the **Hôtel d'Arnault Brucelles** ⑰, and the **Hôtel Delpech** ⑱. Continue along rue des Changes to the intersection with rue de Temponières. Note the handsome wood-beam and brick building on the far right corner and the faux granite one at the near left, complete with painted lines between the "stones" and trompe-l'oeil windows (one of the clever ways the good citizens struggled to avoid paying the legendary window tax). The next street to the left, rue Tripière, loops through place du May onto rue du May, which leads to the **Musée du Vieux Toulouse** ⑲, housed in the Hôtel Dumay.

TIMING   This walk covers some 3 km (2 mi) and should take three–four hours, depending on how long you spend at each site. Most sites close punctually at noon, so it's essential that you get an early start. Or better yet, take a long lunch at some lovely spot and continue on again after 1 or 2, when places reopen.

What to See

❹ **Ancien Collège de Périgord** (Old Périgord College). The wooden gallery-like structure on the street side of the courtyard is the oldest remnant of the 14th-century residential college. ⊠ *56–58 rue du Taur.*

❷ **Capitole/Hôtel de Ville** (Capitol/Town Hall). The 18th-century Capitole is home to the Hôtel de Ville and the city's highly regarded opera company. The reception rooms are open to the public when not in use for official functions or weddings. Halfway up the **Grand Escalier** (Grand Staircase) hangs a large painting of the *Jeux Floraux* (*Floral Games*), organized by a literary society created in 1324 to promote the local Occitanian language, Langue d'Oc. The festival continues to this day: poets give public readings here each May, and the best are awarded silver- and gold-plated violets, one of the emblems of Toulouse. At the top of the stairs is the **Salle Gervaise,** a hall used for weddings, over which hangs a series of paintings inspired by the themes of love and marriage. The mural at the far end of the room portrays the Isle of Cythères, where Venus received her lovers, alluding to a French euphemism for getting married: *embarquer pour Cythères* (to embark for Cythères). More giant paintings in the **Salle Henri-Martin,** named for the artist (1860–1943), show the passing seasons set against the eternal Garonne. Look for Jean Jaurès (1859–1914), one of France's greatest socialist martyrs, in *Les Rêveurs* (*The Dreamers*); he's wearing a boater-style hat and a beige coat. At the

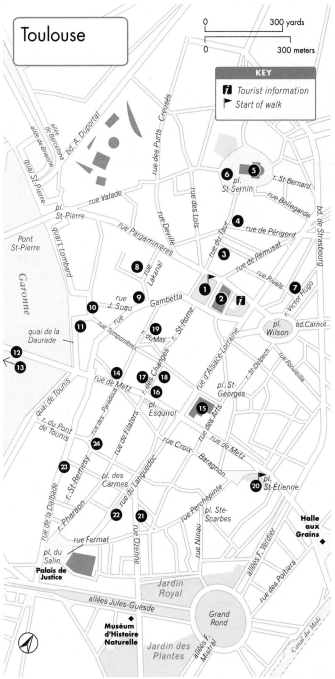

Toulouse

KEY

i Tourist information

▶ Start of walk

far left end of the elegant **Salle des Illustres** (Hall of the Illustrious) is a large painting of a fortress under siege, portraying the women of Toulouse slaying Simon de Montfort, leader of the Albigensian crusade against the Cathars, during the siege of Toulouse in 1218. ✉ *Pl. du Capitole* ☎ *05–61–11–34–12* ✆ *Free* ⊙ *Weekdays 8:30–5, weekends 10–6.*

⑬ **Château d'Eau.** This 19th-century water tower at the far end of the Pont Neuf, once used to store water and build water pressure, is now used for photography exhibits (it was built in 1823, the same year Nicéphore Nièpce created the first permanent photographic images). ✉ *1 pl. Laganne* ☎ *05–61–77–09–40* ✆ *€2.50* ⊙ *Tues.–Sun. 1–7.*

★ ❽ **Église des Jacobins.** An extraordinary structure built in the 1230s for the Dominicans (renamed Jacobins in 1217 for their Parisian base in rue St-Jacques), the church is dominated by a single row of seven columns running the length of the nave. The easternmost column (on the far right) is one of the finest examples of palm-tree vaulting ever erected, the much-celebrated *Palmier des Jacobins,* a major masterpiece of Gothic art. Fanning out overhead, its 22 ribs support the entire apse. The original refectory site is used for temporary art exhibitions. The cloister is one of the city's aesthetic and acoustical gems and in summer hosts piano and early music concerts. ✉ *Rue Lakanal s/n* ☎ *05–61–22–21–92* ✆ *Church free, cloister €2.50* ⊙ *Daily 10–7.*

⑰ **Hôtel d'Arnault Brucelles.** One of the tallest and best of Toulouse's 49 towers can be found at this 16th-century mansion. ✉ *19 rue des Changes.*

⑭ **Hôtel d'Assézat.** Built in 1555 by Toulouse's top Renaissance architect, Nicolas Bachelier, this mansion, considered the city's most elegant, has arcades and ornately carved doorways. It's now home to the **Fondation Bemberg,** an exceptional collection of paintings ranging from Tiepolo to Toulouse-Lautrec, Manet, Monet, and Bonnard. Climb to the top of the tower for splendid views over the city's rooftops. ✉ *Rue de Metz* ☎ *05–61–12–06–89* ✆ *€5* ⊙ *Daily 10–noon and 2–6.*

⑯ **Hôtel d'Astorg.** This 16th-century mansion is notable for its lovely wooden stairways and galleries and for its top-floor *mirande,* a wooden balcony. ✉ *16 rue des Changes.*

❾ **Hôtel de Bernuy.** Now part of a school, this mansion, around the corner from the Église des Jacobins, was built for Jean de Bernuy in the 16th century, the period when Toulouse was at its most prosperous. De Bernuy made his fortune exporting woad, the dark-blue dye that brought unprecedented wealth to 18th-century Toulouse. De Bernuy's success is reflected in the use of stone, a costly material in this region of brick, and by the octagonal stair tower, the highest in the city. You may wander freely around the courtyard. ✉ *Rue Gambetta.*

⑱ **Hôtel Delpech.** Look for the biblical inscriptions carved in Latin in the stone under the windows. ✉ *20 rue des Changes.*

❼ **Marché Victor Hugo** (Victor Hugo Market). This hangarlike indoor market is always a refreshing stop. Consider eating lunch at one of the seven upstairs restaurants. **Chez Attila,** just to the left at the top of the stairs, is the best of them. ⊠ *Pl. Victor-Hugo.*

★ **⓯** **Musée des Augustins** (Augustinian Museum). In this former medieval Augustinian convent, the museum uses the sacristy, chapter house, and cloisters for displaying an outstanding array of Romanesque sculpture and religious paintings. Built in the Mediterranean Gothic style, the architectural complex is vast and holds a collection rich with treasures and discoveries. ⊠ *Rue de Metz* ☏ *05–61–22–21–82* ⊠ *Museum €2.50, museum and exhibit € 4.50; Museum free first Sun. of month* ⊙ *Wed.–Mon. 10–6.*

❻ **Musée St-Raymond.** The city's archaeological museum, next to the basilica of St-Sernin, has an extensive collection of imperial Roman busts, as well as ancient coins, vases, and jewelry. ⊠*Pl. St-Sernin* ☏*05–61–22–21–85* ⊠ *€2.50* ⊙ *Mon. and Wed.–Sat. 8–noon and 2–6, Sun. noon–6.*

⓳ **Musée du Vieux Toulouse** (Museum of Old Toulouse). This museum is worthwhile for the building itself as much as for its collection of Toulouse memorabilia, paintings, sculptures, and documents. Be sure to note the ground-floor fireplace and wooden ceiling. ⊠ *7 rue du May* ☏ *05–62–27–11–50* ⊠ *€2.50* ⊙ *May 15–Oct. 15, Mon.–Sat. 3–6.*

⓫ **Notre-Dame de la Daurade.** Overlooking the Garonne is this 18th-century church. The name *Daurade* comes from *doré* (gilt), referring to the golden reflection given off by the mosaics decorating the 5th-century temple to the Virgin Mary that once stood on this site. ⊠ *Pl. de la Daurade.*

❸ **Notre-Dame du Taur.** Built on the spot where St. Saturnin (or Sernin), the martyred bishop of Toulouse, was dragged to his death in AD 257 by a rampaging bull, this church is famous for its *cloche-mur,* or wall tower. The wall looks like an extension of the facade and has inspired many similar versions throughout the region. ⊠ *Rue du Taur.*

▶ **❶** **Place du Capitole.** This vast, open square in the city center, lined with shops and cafés, is a good spot for getting your bearings or for soaking up some spring or winter sun. A parking lot is conveniently underneath.

⓵ **Place de la Daurade.** On the Garonne, this is one of Toulouse's nicest squares. A stop at the Café des Artistes is almost obligatory. The corner of the quai offers a romantic view of the Garonne, the Hôtel Dieu across the river, and the Pont Neuf.

⓬ **Pont Neuf** (New Bridge). Despite its name, the graceful span of the Pont Neuf opened to traffic in 1632. The remains of the old bridge—one arch and the lighter-color outline on the brick wall of the **Hôtel-Dieu** (hospital)—are visible across the river. The 16th-century hospital was used for pilgrims on their way to Santiago de Compostela. Just over the bridge, on a clear day in winter, the snowcapped peaks of the Pyrénées are often visible in the distance, said to be a sign of imminent rain.

❺ **St-Sernin.** Toulouse's most famous landmark and the world's largest Romanesque church once belonged to a Benedictine abbey, built in the 11th century to house pilgrims on their way to Santiago de Compostela in Spain. Inside, the aesthetic highpoint is the magnificent central apse, begun in 1080, glittering with gilded ceiling frescoes which date from the 19th century. When illuminated at night, St-Sernin's five-tier octagonal tower glows red against the sky. Not all the tiers are the same: The first three, with their rounded windows, are Romanesque; the upper two, with pointed Gothic windows, were added around 1300. ⊠ *Rue du Taur* ☎ *05–61–21–70–18* ✉ *Crypt €2.50* ☉ *Daily 10–11:30 and 2:30–5:30.*

need a break? Just a 10-minute walk from the Basilique St-Sernin, you will find one of the oldest cafés in Toulouse, **Le Concorde** (⊠ 17 rue de la Concorde). This is the perfect place to sip a glass of Banyuls or a *demi* (glass of draft beer) and listen to an evening accordion concert of classic French cabaret.

South of rue de Metz

South of rue de Metz you'll discover the cathedral of St-Étienne, the antiques district along rue Perchepinte, and town houses and palaces along the way on rue Ninau, rue Ozenne, and rue de la Dalbade—all among the top sights in Toulouse.

a good walk From the **Cathédrale St-Étienne** ⑳ ➤ walk down rue Fermat to place Stes-Scarbes and the 17th-century Hôtel du Bourg, at 6 rue Perchepinte, where you'll find the old antiques district, lined with noble 16th- to 18th-century houses all the way down to place du Salin. Take a left on rue Ninau; at No. 15 is the 16th-century Hôtel d'Ulmo, with its graceful tower, front stairs, courtyard, and interior garden; at No. 19 is the 18th-century Hôtel Castagnier. Place Montoulieu opens into rue Vélane, passing brick and timber-frame houses and the narrow 14th-century rue Neuve. At 16 rue Vélane is the 17th-century Hôtel Penautier, with an elegant courtyard, stairway, and garden through the entryway next to the Laure Bandet antiques shop. Rue Vélane emerges back out on rue Perchepinte. Take a left on Perchepinte and a quick right onto rue de la Pléau to get to the **Musée Paul Dupuy** ㉑, a museum of medieval arts. Head right on rue Ozenne to No. 9, the 15th-century Hôtel de Dahus. Go left on rue du Languedoc; at No. 36 is the 15th- and 16th-century mansion **Hôtel du Vieux Raisin** ㉒, crowned by an unusual octagonal tower. Continue back down rue du Languedoc to place du Salin, where farmers sell homemade foie gras on market mornings. Rue de la Dalbade, parallel to the Garonne, leads past one stately facade after another. The finest is No. 25, the **Hôtel de Clary** ㉓, also known as the Hôtel de Pierre (not for Peter but for the stone [*pierre*] used in its construction). Continue up the street to the church of **Notre-Dame de la Dalbade** ㉔. From here cut through rue Pont de Tounis, go past the doorway on the left with the sculpted Gambrinus—legendary Flemish inventor of beer—then over the bridge (which used to span a branch of the Garonne) and out to quai de Tounis. The Pont Neuf is just up to the right.

TIMING This walk will take you about three hours.

Sights to See

▶ ⑳ **Cathédrale St-Étienne.** The cathedral was erected in stages between the 13th and 17th centuries, though the nave and choir languished unfinished because of a lack of funds. A fine collection of 16th- and 17th-century tapestries traces the life of St. Stephen. In front of the cathedral is the city's oldest fountain, dating from the 16th century. ⊠ *Pl. St-Étienne.*

㉓ **Hôtel de Clary.** This mansion, known as the Hôtel de Pierre because of its unusually solid *pierre* (stone) construction—at the time considered a sign of great wealth—is one of the finest 17th- and 18th-century mansions on the street. The ornately sculpted stone facade was built in 1608 by parliamentary president François de Clary. ⊠ *25 rue de la Daurade.*

㉒ **Hôtel du Vieux Raisin.** Officially the Hôtel Maynier, named for the original owner, the house became the Vieux Raisin (Old Grape) after the early name of the street and even earlier inn. Built in 1550, the mansion has an octagonal tower, male and female figures on the facade, and allegorical sculptures of the three stages of life—infancy, maturity, and old age—over the windows to the left. ⊠ *36 rue de Languedoc.*

㉑ **Musée Paul Dupuy.** This museum, dedicated to medieval applied arts, is housed in the Hôtel Pierre Besson, a 16th-century mansion. ⊠ *13 rue de la Pleau* ☎ *05–61–14–65–50* ⌨ *€2.50* ☉ *Wed.–Mon. 10–5.*

㉔ **Notre-Dame de la Dalbade.** Originally Sancta Maria de Ecclesia Alba, in Langue d'Oc (Ste-Marie de l'Église Blanche, in French, or St. Mary of the White Church—*alba* meaning "white"), the name of the church evolved into "de Albata" and later "Dalbade." Ironically, one of its outstanding features today is the colorful 19th-century ceramic tympanum over the Renaissance door. ⊠ *Pl. de la Dalbade.*

Where to Stay & Eat

$$$–$$$$ ✕ **Michel Sarran.** This clean-lined post-nouvelle haven for what is arguably Toulouse's finest dining departs radically from traditional stick-to-your-ribs southwest France cuisine in favor of Mediterranean formulas suited to the rhythms and reasons of modern living. Foie-gras soup with belon oysters, and *loup cuit et cru au chorizo* (sea bass, cooked and raw, with chorizo sausage) are two examples of Michel Sarran's light but flavorful cuisine. ⊠ *21 bd. A. Duportal* ☎ *05–61–12–32–32* ⌨ *Reservations essential* ▤ *AE, DC, MC, V* ☉ *Closed weekends, July 27–Aug. 29, and Dec. 23–31.*

FodorśChoice ★

$$$–$$$$ ✕ **Toulousy–Jardins de l'Opéra.** Dominique Toulousy's elegant restaurant next to the Grand Hôtel de l'Opéra is a perennial favorite. Intimate rooms and a covered terrace around a little pond make for undeniable charm, though some will find the grand flourishes—glass ceilings, *echt* statuary, and mammoth chandeliers—a little too, well, operatic, and might prefer the adjacent brasserie, Grand Café de l'Opéra. The food is an innovative departure from local fare, with seductive nouvelle or Gascon touches such as the ravioli stuffed with foie gras and truffle sauce. ⊠ *1 pl. du Capitole* ☎ *05–61–23–07–76* ⌨ *Reservations essential* ▤ *AE, DC, MC, V* ☉ *Closed Sun. and Mon.*

★ **$–$$$** ✕ **Brasserie Flo "Les Beaux Arts."** Overlooking the Pont Neuf, this elegant brasserie is the place to be at sunset, as painters Ingres and Matisse knew all too well. Watch the colors change over the Garonne from a quayside window or a sidewalk table while enjoying delicious seafood, including a dozen varieties of oysters. The house white wine, a local St-Lannes from the nearby Gers region, is fresh and fruity yet dry, and the service is impeccable. ⊠ *1 quai de la Daurade* ☎ *05–61–21–12–12* ⊟ *AE, DC, MC, V.*

$–$$$ ✕ **Cosi Fan Tutte.** Just steps from Rue Perchepinte and the Musée Paul Dupuy, this Italian specialist might be a welcome change from the webfooted deluge of southwestern French cuisine. *Saint-Jacques poêlés* (scallops) are the cry from mid-January to mid-April, while truffles and wood pigeon also find their way onto a menu that changes constantly with the market. ⊠ *8 rue Mage* ☎ *05–61–53–07–24* ⊟ *AE, DC, MC, V* ☉ *Closed May 20–24, Aug., Dec. 19–Jan. 4, Sun., and Mon.*

★ **$–$$** ✕ **La Corde.** This little hideaway is worth taking the time to find. Built into a lovely 15th-century corner tower hidden in the courtyard of the 16th-century Hôtel Bolé, La Corde claims the distinction of being the oldest restaurant in Toulouse. Try the *effiloché de canard aux pêches* (shredded duck with caramelized peach). ⊠ *4 rue Jules-Chalande* ☎ *05–61–29–09–43* ⊟ *AE, DC, MC, V* ☉ *Closed Sun. No lunch Mon.*

$–$$ ✕ **Le 19.** Centrally placed across the street from the Hôtel des Capitouls and next to the Pont Neuf, this lovely former 16th-century fish market has vaulted ceilings that will take your breath (but not your appetite) away. Sleek contemporary design and international cuisine combine happily and economically here. ⊠ *19 descente de la Halle aux Poissons* ☎ *05–34–31–94–84* ⊟ *AE, DC, MC, V* ☉ *Closed Jan. 1–13, Aug. 13–30, and Sun. No lunch Sat. and Mon.*

¢–$$ ✕ **Au Bon Vivre.** This intimate bistro lined with tables with red-check tablecloths fills up at lunch and dinner every day. Quick, unpretentious, and always good, the house specialties include such dishes as roast monkfish in garlic, venison, and cassoulet. ⊠ *15 pl. Wilson* ☎ *05–61–23–07–17* ⊟ *AE, DC, MC, V.*

¢–$$ ✕ **Chez Paloma.** Go ahead and order the foie gras, the sole *meuniére,* the grilled pigeon, or the delicious duck *à l'orange*—this is the spot for classic cuisine du terroir, but that doesn't mean they don't do a mean vegetable, lushly roasted in garlic, steamed still crisp, or fresh with a side of tangy sauce. Everything is homemade including the bread and the pastries, *and* the prices are delicious, too. ⊠ *54 rue Peyroliers* ☎ *05–61–21–76–50* ⊟ *AE, DC, MC, V* ☉ *Closed weekends.*

★ **$$$–$$$$** ▦ **Grand Hôtel de l'Opéra.** In a former 17th-century convent, this downtown doyen has an Old World feel with 21st-century amenities. Grandeur is the keynote in the lobby, complete with marble columns and Second Empire bergeres and sofas of tasseled velvet. Guest rooms are plush, with rich fabrics and painted headboards in many, while three restaurants range from provincial bistro to international gourmet (⇨ Jardins de l'Opéra, *above*). Even though you're on busy place du Capitole, this hotel is a tranquil oasis. ⊠ *1 pl. du Capitole, 31000* ☎ *05–61–21–82–66* 🖷 *05–61–23–41–04* ⊕ *www.grand-hotel-opera.com* ⇥ *57 rooms* ♿ *3* restaurants, minibars, cable TV, pool, health club, bar, meeting rooms, parking (fee) ☰ AE, DC, MC, V.

$$$ 🏨 **Hôtel Garonne.** In the thick of the most Toulousain part of town, next to the Pont Neuf and the former fish market, this cozy place has small but tasteful rooms; the best suite has a view of the Garonne. The staff is cheery and helpful. ⊠ 22 descente de la Halle aux Poissons, 31000 ☎ 05–34–31–94–80 🖷 05–34–31–94–81 ⊕ www.hotelsdecharmetoulouse.com ⇦ 14 rooms ♨ Minibars, cable TV, parking (fee) ☰ AE, DC, MC, V.

Fodor'sChoice
★

$–$$ 🏨 **Hôtel Albert I.** The building may seem undistinguished and the reception hall is no Versailles, but the rooms are cheerful and spacious (especially the older ones with giant fireplaces and mirrors). The extremely warm and personable owner, Madame Hilaire, is on hand to give suggestions of all kinds. A Continental breakfast is served, and nearby parking can be arranged by the hotel. ⊠ 8 rue Rivals, 31000 ☎ 05–61–21–17–91 🖷 05–61–21–09–64 ⇦ 50 rooms ♨ Cable TV, parking (fee), some pets allowed (fee) ☰ AE, DC, MC, V.

$ 🏨 **Grand Hôtel d'Orléans.** This picturesque former stagecoach relay station was built in 1867 and still retains a certain 19th-century charm. Four floors of wooden balustrades overhung with plants look down over a central patio. Guest rooms are small but cozy. ⊠ 72 rue Bayard, near Matabiau railroad station, 31000 ☎ 05–61–62–98–47 🖷 05–61–62–78–24 ⊕ www.grand-hotel-orleans.fr ⇦ 56 rooms ♨ Restaurant, cable TV, parking (fee), some pets allowed (fee) ☰ AE, DC, MC, V.

Nightlife & the Arts

For a schedule of events, contact the city tourist office. If you want to stay up late—as many do in Toulouse—a complete list of clubs and discos can be found in the weekly *Toulouse Pratique*, available at any newsstand. As for cultural highlights, so many opera singers perform at the **Théâtre du Capitole** and the **Halle aux Grains** that the city is known as the *capitale du bel canto*. The opera season lasts from October until late May, with occasional summer presentations as well. A wide variety of dance companies perform in Toulouse: the **Ballet du Capitole** stages classical ballets; **Ballet-Théâtre Joseph Russilo** and **Compagnie Jean-Marc Matos** put on modern-dance performances. The **Centre National Chorégraphique de Toulouse** welcomes international companies each year in the St-Cyprien quarter.

The most exciting music venue in Toulouse is the auditorium-in-the-round **Halle Aux Grains** (⊠ Pl. Dupuy ☎ 05–61–63–18–65). **Théâtre du Capitole** (⊠ Pl. du Capitole ☎ 05–61–23–21–35) is the orchestra, opera, and ballet specialist. **Théâtre Daniel Sorano** (⊠ 35 allée Jules-Guesde ☎ 05–61–25–66–87) stages dramatic productions and concerts. **Théâtre de la Digue** (⊠ 3 rue de la Digue ☎ 05–61–42–97–79) is a theater and dance venue. **Théâtre du Taur** (⊠ 69 rue du Taur ☎ 05–61–21–77–13) puts on theatrical productions of every stripe and spot.

Begin your night on the town at **Père Louis** (⊠ 45 rue des Tourneurs ☎ 05–61–21–33–45), an old-fashioned winery (and restaurant), with barrels used as tables plus vintage photographs. **Bar Basque** (⊠ 7 pl. St-Pierre

☎ 05–61–21–55–64) is one of the many good watering holes around place St-Pierre. **Brasserie Notre-Dame** (⊠ 5 rue Riguepels ☎ 05–61–25–20–41), near the Cathedral of St-Étienne, is a hot spot for the third-Thursday-in-November Beaujolais Nouveau blowout. Brazilian guitarists perform at **La Bonita** (⊠ 112 Grand-Rue St-Michel ☎ 05–62–26–36–45). For jazz, try **Le Café des Allées** (⊠ 64 allée Charles-de-Fitte ☎ 05–62–27–14–46), a hothouse for local musicians. Be sure to stop by the top jazz spot **Le Mandala** (⊠ 23 rue des Aminodiers ☎ 05–61–21–10–05) for a bit of the bubbly and some of the best jazz in town.

Zoo Punk (⊠ 37 rue de l'Industrie ☎ 05–61–63–17–36) is a trendy restaurant and club with a hip crowd of diners and party animals. **Puerto Habana** (⊠ 12 port St-Étienne ☎ 05–61–54–45–61) is the place for salsa music. **Le Purple** (⊠ 2 rue Castella ☎ 05–62–73–04–67) is a multispace disco that's hot. Outside of town is **La Villa Garden** (⊠ 157 av. de Lespinet ☎ 05–62–52–41–60), which is tricky to find but worth checking out. **La Cinecita** (⊠ 5 rue Labeda ☎ 05–61–22–47–25) is the place for salsa music. **Le Teatro** (⊠ 1 pl. St-Cyprien ☎ 05–61–59–50–00) is frequented by Toulousains looking for everything: food, drink, and action.

If you're looking a pretty terrace for lunch or a late dinner (until 10:30), head for **Les Terrasses de Saint-Rome** (⊠ 39 rue St-Rome ☎ 05–62–27–06–06). Local glitterati and theater stars go to **L'Ubu** (⊠ 16 rue St-Rome ☎ 05–61–23–97–80), the city's top nightspot for 20 years. For a midnight dinner over the Garonne **Brasserie Flo "Les Beaux Arts"** (⊠ 1 quai de la Daurade ☎ 05–61–21–12–12) is the place to be.

Shopping

Toulouse is a chic design outlet for clothing and artifacts of all kinds. **Rue St-Rome, rue Croix Baragnon, rue des Changes,** and **rue d'Alsace-Lorraine** are all good shopping streets.

ALBI & THE GERS

Along the banks of the Tarn to the northeast of Toulouse is Albi, Toulouse's rival in rose colors. West from Albi, along the river, the land opens up to the rural Gers *département*, home of the heady brandy Armagnac and heart of the former dukedom of Gascony. Studded with châteaux—from simple medieval fortresses to ambitious classical residences—and with tiny, isolated villages, the Gers is an easy place to fall in love with, or in.

Albi

★ ㉕ *75 km (47 mi) northeast of Toulouse.*

Toulouse-Lautrec's native Albi is a well-preserved and busy provincial market town. In its heyday, Albi was a major center for the Cathars, members of a dualistic and ascetic religious movement critical of the hierarchical and worldly ways of the Catholic Church. Pick up a copy of the excellent visitor booklet (in English) from the **tourist office** (⊠ Pl. Ste-

Cécile ☎ 05–63–49–48–80 ⊕ www.mairie-albi.fr), and follow the walking tours—of the *Vieille Ville* (Old City), the old ramparts, and the banks of the River Tarn.

Fodor'sChoice One of the most unusual and dazzling churches in France, the huge **Cathédrale Ste-Cécile**, with its intimidating clifflike walls, resembles a cross between a castle and an ocean liner. It was constructed as a symbol of the Church's return to power after the 13th-century crusade that wiped out the Cathars. The interior is an astonishingly ornate contrast to the massive austerity of the outer walls. Maestro Donnelli and a team of 16th-century Italian artists (most of the Emilian school) covered every possible surface with religious scenes and brightly colored patterns—it remains the largest group of Italian Renaissance paintings in a French church. The most striking fresco is a 15th-century depiction of the Last Judgment, on the west wall, just below one of the most splendid organs in the world, built in 1734 and outfitted with 3,500 pipes. ⊠ *Pl. Ste-Cécile* ☎ *05–63–43–23–43* ⊘ *June–Sept., daily 9–6:30; Oct.–May, daily 9–noon and 2–6.*

Fodor'sChoice The **Musée Toulouse-Lautrec** occupies the **Palais de la Berbie** (Berbie Palace), set between the cathedral and the Pont Vieux (Old Bridge) in a garden designed by the famed André Le Nôtre (creator of the famous "green geometries" at Versailles). Built in 1265, the fortress was transformed in 1905 into a museum to honor Albi's most famous son, Belle Époque painter Henri de Toulouse-Lautrec (1864–1901). Toulouse-Lautrec left Albi for Paris in 1882, and soon became famous for his colorful and tumultuous evocations of the lifestyle of bohemian glamour found in and around Montmartre. Son of a wealthy and aristocratic family (Lautrec is a town not far from Toulouse), the young Henri suffered from a genetic bone deficiency and broke both legs as a child, which stunted his growth. The artist's fascination with the decadent side of life led to an early grave at the age of 37 and Hollywood immortalization in the 1954 John Huston film *Moulin Rouge*. With more than 1,000 of the artist's works, the Albi exhibit is the country's largest Toulouse-Lautrec collection. There are other masterworks here, including paintings by Georges de la Tour and Francesco Guardi. ⊠ *Just off pl. Ste-Cécile* ☎ *05–63–49–48–70* 🖾 *€4.50, guided tour €8.50, gardens free* ⊘ *June and Sept., daily 9–noon and 2–6; July and Aug., daily 9–6; Oct.–Mar., daily 10–noon and 2–5; Apr. and May, daily 10–noon and 2–6.*

From the central square and parking area in front of the Palais de la Berbie, walk to the 11th- to 15th-century college and **Cloître de St-Salvy** (⊠ Rue Ste-Cécile). Next, visit Albi's finest restored traditional house, the **Maison du Vieil Albi** (Old Albi House; ⊠ Corner of Rue de la Croix-Blanche and Puech-Bérenguer). If you're a real fan of Toulouse-Lautrec, you might view his birthplace, the **Maison Natale de Toulouse-Lautrec** (⊠ 14 rue Henri de Toulouse-Lautrec), although there are no visits to the house, the Hôtel Bosc, which remains a private residence. Rue de l'Hôtel de Ville, two streets west of the Maison Natale, leads past the Mairie (City Hall), with its hanging globes of flowers, to Albi's main square, **place du Vigan.** Take a break in one of the two main cafés, Le Pontie or Le Vigan.

Where to Stay & Eat

$$$–$$$$ ✕ **Le Moulin de la Mothe.** Set at the foot of Albi Cathedral, this onetime mill on the bank of the Tarn is consequently surrounded by lush vegetation. Chef-owner Michel Pellaprat specializes in inventive cooking *à l'albigeoise*—his hare sausage in beetroot vinaigrette is sublime—based on high-quality products of the Tarn region. ⊠ *Rue de la Mothe* 🕾 *05–63–60–38–15* 🚆 *AE, MC, V* ☉ *Closed Feb. No dinner Sun. (except July and Aug.) or Tues. Sept. 15–Apr. 30.*

$$–$$$$ ✕ **Le Jardin des Quatre Saisons.** A good-value menu and superb fish dishes are the reasons for this restaurant's excellent reputation. Chef-owner Georges Bermond's house specialties include mussels baked with leeks and *suprême de sandre* (a freshwater fish cooked in wine), and change with *les saisons.* ⊠ *19 bd. de Strasbourg* 🕾 *05–63–60–77–76* 🚆 *AE, MC, V* ☉ *Closed Mon. No dinner Sun.*

$$–$$$$ ✕▣ **Hostellerie St-Antoine.** Founded in 1734, this hotel in the center of town is one of the oldest in France. Run by the same family for five generations, this lineage is attested to by the presence of some Toulouse-Lautrec sketches given to the owner's great-grandfather, a friend of the painter. Modern renovations have made it eminently comfortable. Room 30 has a pleasing view of the garden; pristine white furnishings give it a spacious feel. The superb restaurant serves classic Gallic cuisine, such as *foie gras de canard* (duck liver) and saddle of hare with a foie gras–based sauce. ⊠ *15 rue St-Antoine, 81000* 🕾 *05–63–54–04–04* 🖷 *05–63–47–10–47* ⊕*www.saint-antoine-albi.com* ◿*43 rooms* ⌂ *Restaurant, minibars, cable TV, meeting rooms, parking (fee)* 🚆 *AE, DC, MC, V.*

$–$$ ✕▣ **Hôtel Chiffre.** A former stagecoach inn, this centrally located town house has impeccable rooms overlooking a cozy garden. The restaurant serves hearty regional cuisine such as pigeon stuffed with mushrooms or trout with spicy cabbage. ⊠ *50 rue Séré-de-Rivières, 81000* 🕾 *05–63–48–58–48* 🖷 *05–63–47–20–61* ⊕ *www.hotelchiffre.com* ◿ *36 rooms* ⌂ *Restaurant, minibars, cable TV, meeting rooms, parking (fee)* 🚆 *AE, DC, MC, V.*

¢ ▣ **Le George V.** This little in-town B&B is near the cathedral and the train station. Each room is unique, and the garden makes for a pleasant retreat in summer. ⊠ *29 av. Maréchal-Joffre, 81000* 🕾 *05–63–54–24–16* 🖷 *05–63–49–90–78* ◿*9 rooms* ⌂ *Café, some pets allowed (fee); no a/c* 🚆 *AE, DC, MC, V.*

Shopping

Around **place Ste-Cécile** are numerous clothing, book, music, and antiques shops. The finest foie gras in town is found at **Albi Foie Gras** (⊠ 29 rue Mariès 🕾 05–63–38–21–23). **L'Artisan Chocolatier** (⊠ 4 rue Dr-Camboulives, on pl. du Vigan 🕾 05–63–38–95–33) is famous for its chocolate.

Albi has many **produce markets**: one takes place Tuesday through Sunday in the market halls near the cathedral; another is held on Sunday morning on place Ste-Cécile. A Saturday-morning **flea and antiques market** (⊠ Pl. du Castelviel) is held in the Halle du Castelviel.

SEX, DEATH & THE CATHARS

SCORCHED BY THE SOUTHERN HEAT, the dusty ruins perched high atop cliffs in southern Languedoc were once the refuges of the Cathars, the notoriously ascetic religious group persecuted out of existence by the Catholic church in the 12th and 13th centuries. The Cathars inhabited an area ranging from present-day Germany all the way to the Atlantic Ocean. Adherents to this dualistic doctrine of material abnegation and spiritual revelation abstained from fleshly pleasures in all forms—forgoing even procreation and the consumption of animal products. In some cases, they committed suicide by starvation; diminishing the amount of flesh in the world was the ultimate way to foil the forces of evil. However, not thrilled by a religion that did not "go forth and multiply" (and that saw no need to pay taxes to the church), Pope Innocent III launched the Albigensian Crusade (Albi was one of the major Cathar strongholds), and Pope Gregory IX rounded up the stragglers during a period of inquisition starting in 1233. These forces had been given scandalously free reign by the French court, who allowed dukes and counts from northern France to build fortified bastide towns through the area to entrap the peasantry. These counts were more than happy to oblige the pope with a little hounding, an inquisition or two, and some burnings at the stake. Forthwith, entire towns were judged to be guilty of heresy and inhabitants were thrown by the dozens to their deaths from high town walls. The persecuted "pure" soon took refuge in the Pyrénées mountains, where they survived for 100 years. Now that all that remains of this unhappy sect are their former hideouts, with tour groups visiting the vacant stone staircases and roofless chapels of haunted places like Peyrepertuse and Quéribus. For more information (in French), log on to www.cathares.org or go hiking with medievalist Ingrid Sparbier (sp. ingrid@wanadoo.fr).

Cordes-sur-Ciel

26 *25 km (15 mi) northwest of Albi, 80 km (50 mi) northeast of Toulouse.*

Fodor'sChoice ★ A must stop for all travelers, the picture-book hilltop village of Cordes-sur-Ciel, built in 1222 by Count Raymond VII of Toulouse, is one of the most impressively preserved *bastides* (fortified medieval towns built along a strict grid plan) in France. When mists steal up from the Cérou Valley and enshroud the hillside, Cordes appears to hover in midair, hence its nickname, Cordes-sur-Ciel (Cordes-in-the-Sky/Heaven). Many of the restored medieval houses are occupied by artisans and craftspeople; the best crafts shops are found along the main street, Grande-Rue. The village's venerable covered market, supported by 24 octagonal stone pillars, is also noteworthy, as is the nearby well, which is more than 300 feet deep.

Where to Stay & Eat

★ $$$ ✕ **Le Grand Écuyer.** The dramatic hilltop setting of this hotel suits it well—it's a perfectly preserved Gothic mansion. Rooms have period furnishings; the best, Planol, Horizon, and Ciel, have grand views of the rolling countryside. Yves Thuriès is one of the region's best chefs and chocolatiers; sample his salmon and sole twist in vanilla or the guinea fowl supreme in pastry. Menus begin around €38 and culminate in a seven-course gourmet extravaganza that costs more than €72. ☒ *Rue Voltaire, 81170* ☏ *05–63–53–79–50* 🖷 *05–63–53–79–51* ⊕ *www. thuries.fr* ↬ *13 rooms* ⚒ *Restaurant, minibars, cable TV, bar, some pets allowed (fee)* ▭ *AE, DC, MC, V* ⊙ *Closed mid-Oct.–early Apr.* ⦿ *MAP.*

$ ✕🏠 **L'Hostellerie du Vieux Cordes.** This magnificent 13th-century house is built around a lovely courtyard dotted with tiny white tables and shaded by a 200-year-old wisteria. Guest rooms are richly decorated but not nearly as opulent as the vast crimson dining rooms (the restaurant is closed Monday from November to Easter and also the month of January). ☒ *Rue St-Michel, 81170* ☏ *05–63–53–79–20* 🖷 *05–63–56–02–47* ⊕ *www.thuries.fr* ↬ *21 rooms* ⚒ *Restaurant, minibars, cable TV; no a/c* ▭ *AE, DC, MC, V* ⊙ *Closed Jan.*

Montauban

❷❼   *59 km (37 mi) west of Cordes-sur-Ciel, 55 km (33 mi) north of Toulouse.*

Montauban, built in 1144, was one of the first bastides in France. The town is best known as the birthplace of the great painter Jean-Auguste-Dominique Ingres (1780–1867), and is home to a superb collection of

Fodor's Choice   his works. The **Musée Ingres**, overlooking the Tarn River, is housed in
★   what was originally the château of Edward the Black Prince (1330–76), who was briefly ruler of the English principality of Aquitaine. The château was later converted into a bishop's palace in the 17th century. Ingres has the second floor to himself; note the contrast between his love of myth (*Ossian's Dream*) and his deadpan, uncompromising portraiture (*Madame Gonse*). Ingres was the last of the great French Classicists, who favored line over color and used classical antiquity as a source for subject matter. However, Ingres fell out of favor with the strict Neoclassicists of his day as a result of his unusual combination of superb draftsmanship and sensuality. Later, artists such as Degas, Renoir, and Picasso acknowledged their debt to Ingres. Most paintings here are from Ingres's excellent private collection, ranging from his followers (Théodore Chassériau) and precursors (Jacques-Louis David) to Old Masters. ☒ *19 rue de l'Hôtel de Ville* ☏ *05–63–22–12–92* 🎟 *€4* ⊙ *July and Aug., Mon.–Sat. 9:30–noon and 1:30–6, Sun. 1:30–6; Sept.–June, Tues.–Sat. 10–noon and 2–6.*

Beyond the Musée Ingres, there are several other notable sights in town. The 14th-century **Pont Vieux** (Old Bridge), with its seven pointed arches, is another of Montauban's attractions. A chapel dedicated to St. Catherine, protector of mariners (Montauban had some 3,000 river men during the 18th century), used to stand on the fourth piling until it was uprooted and washed away by a flood in 1766. In the 12th-century arcaded and brick-vaulted **place National,** in the center of Montauban, look for the simple wooden cross marking the medieval execution and pillory site (it's in front of the Brasserie des Arts, a good spot for lunch or coffee). Note the sundial on the north side of the square with its carpe diem inscription UNA TIBI ("one for you"—meaning, your hour will come). Markets are held on the square almost every day; Wednesday markets are held across the river on place Lalaque. The **Hôtel Lefranc-de-Pompignon** is a classic 17th- to 18th-century *portail monumentale* (monumental entryway) just north of the Église St-Jacques. One of Montauban's architectural gems, this redbrick portico with its wrought-iron grille announced the residence of M. Lefranc-de-Pompignon (whose unsuccessful tenure at Paris's Royal Academy was once mocked by Voltaire). ✉ *Rue Armand Cambon s/n.*

The mid-13th-century **Église St-Jacques** (✉ Pl. Victor Hugo), with its Toulouse-style steeple, is a dark, single-nave church of austere dignity. The 17th- to 18th-century **Notre-Dame Cathedral** (✉ Pl. Franklin Roosevelt) was built of white stone to contrast with the city's predominant redbrick architecture and to proclaim Catholicism's triumph over Protestantism. On display here is an Ingres masterpiece, *The Vow of Louis XIII,* poorly illuminated.

Where to Stay & Eat

$$–$$$$ ✕ **Les Saveurs d'Ingres.** Cyril Paysserand's *cuisine d'auteur* is some of the best fare in the area, served in a graceful vaulted dining room in midtown Montauban, just a few doors up from the Ingres Museum. Not unlike Ingres himself, Paysserand sticks with the classical canons prepared in novel and sensual ways. If you've maxed out on cassoulet and web-footed fare in general, try the frogs' legs here or the *bécasse* (woodcock) in season for a welcome change of pace. ✉ *13 rue de l'Hôtel de Ville* ☎ *05–63–91–26–42* 🖃 *AE, DC, MC, V* ☾ *Closed Sun. and Mon.*

$$ 🏨 **Hôtel du Midi–Mercure.** The Hôtel du Midi combines old-world elegance with modern comforts. A plaque on the hotel's facade attests that Manuel Azaña, last president of the Spanish Republic, died here in exile in 1940. ✉ *12 rue Notre-Dame, 82000* ☎ *05–63–63–17–23* 🖷 *05–63–66–43–66* ⊕ *www.accorhotels.com* ⬗ *44 rooms* ⚐ *Restaurant, minibars, cable TV, bar, parking (fee), some pets allowed (fee)* 🖃 *AE, DC, MC, V.*

Moissac

28 *29 km (18 mi) west of Montauban, 72 km (45 mi) northwest of Toulouse.*

Moissac has both the region's largest (and most beautiful) Romanesque cloisters and one of its most remarkable abbey churches. The port—at the confluence of the Tarn, Aveyron, and Garonne rivers, and the lateral canal—is a surprising sight so far from the sea. For a spectacular view over this Mississippi-like riverine expanse, France's widest, head to the lookout point at Boudou, 2 km (1 mi) west of Moissac off route N113.

★ Fronted by a magnificent Romanesque sculpted portal that depicts in stone Book 4 of the Apocalypse, the **Abbaye St-Pierre** was founded in the 7th century by Saint Didier, bishop of Cahors, and bears traces of many settlers of the region, Arabs to Normans to Magyars. Little is left of the original abbey, and subsequent religious wars laid waste to its 11th-century replacement. Today's abbey, dating mostly from the 15th century, narrowly escaped demolition early in the 20th century when the Bordeaux-Sète railroad was rerouted within feet of the cloisters. Each of the 76 capitals has a unique pattern of animals, geometric motifs, and religious or historical scenes. Look for the Cain and Abel story on the 19th column to the right of the entry point. The 63rd column (fourth back from the northeast corner) shows St-Sernin being dragged to his death by a bull. On the famed Apocalypse south portal, carved in the 12th century, the representation of a sweetly mournful Jeremiah (author of the Old Testament Book of Lamentations), on the lower part of the door, is especially noteworthy. The **Musée des Arts et Traditions Populaires** (Folk Art Museum), in the abbey, contains regional treasures and a room of local costumes. ⊠ *6 bis rue de l'Abbaye* ☎ *05–63–04–05–73* ⌦ *Cloisters and museum €5* ⊘ *Oct.–Mar., Tues.–Sun. 9–noon and 2–5; Apr.–June and Sept., Tues.–Sun. 9–noon and 2–6; July and Aug., Tues.–Sun. 9–noon and 2–7.*

Where to Stay & Eat

★ ¢–$ ✕⌦ **Le Pont Napoléon.** One of France's rising culinary stars, Michel Dussau, who trained with Alain Ducasse (and others), is a master of refined simplicity and innovative combinations of regional products. Try such dishes as scallops with chestnut-flour pasta or foie gras *pôelé* (sautéed goose liver), and anything made with Moissac's *chasselas* grape (the restaurant is closed Sunday dinner, Monday lunch, and Wednesday). Guest rooms are furnished with elegant, authentic antiques; some have lovely views of the Tarn and the bridge. ⊠ *2 allées Montebello, 82200* ☎ *05–63–04–01–55* 🖷 *05–63–04–34–44* ⊕ *www.le-pont-napoleon. com* ⇆ *12 rooms* ⌂ *Restaurant, cable TV, bar* ⊟ *AE, DC, MC, V* ⊘ *Closed Jan. 5–20.*

Auvillar

★ ㉙ *23 km (14 mi) west of Moissac.*

Officially classified as one of France's most beautiful villages, Auvillar is centered on its gorgeous, covered **Halle aux Grains** (Grain Market), a circular structure built in 1825. Most other buildings in the town are equally lovely, including the stone-and-brick **Tour de l'Horloge** (Clock Tower), now connected to the town's only hotel, in the 18th-century brick-and-beam **Maison des Consuls** (Consuls' House), once the local magistrate's home.

Where to Stay & Eat

¢–$ ✕⌦ **L'Horloge.** Occupying the historic Maison des Consuls, this cozy spot next to (and named for) Auvillar's trademark clock tower is the town's de facto hub and nerve center. The restaurant (no lunch Friday and Saturday, mid-October through mid-April) is a combination brasserie, le Bouchon, and full-scale dining establishment all in one, with menus and *formules* for all tastes and tendencies. The rooms are modest and intimate, and Madame Martigue and her staff are warm and welcoming. ⊠ *Pl. de l'Horloge, 82340* ☎ *05–63–39–91–61* 🖷 *05–63–39–75–20* ⇆ *10 rooms* ⌂ *Restaurant, café, bar; no a/c* ⊘ *Closed Dec. 16–Jan. 19* ⊟ *AE, DC, MC, V* �Ⓞⅼ *MAP.*

Lectoure

㉚ *57 km (35 mi) southwest of Moissac, 94 km (58 mi) northwest of Toulouse.*

Once a Roman city and a fortified Gallic town, Lectoure stands on a promontory above the Gers Valley in the heart of the former dukedom of Gascony. Lectoure was ravaged in 1473 when Louis XI attacked its fortress and established direct royal rule by killing the last count of Armagnac, but there's still plenty to see in its old arched streets. The 13th-century **Fontaine Diane** (Diana Fountain; ⊠ Rue Fontélie) is the town's most interesting monument, as well as a visual feast. The 15th- to 16th-century **Cathédrale St-Gervais et St-Protais** (⊠ Pl. de la Cathédrale) is an enormous structure for a town of this size and an immense trove of art and architecture.

The **Musée Municipal** (Town Museum), near the cathedral, is in the vaulted cellars of the former **Palais Épiscopal** (Bishop's Palace), now the Town Hall. It contains an array of 2,000-year-old Gallo-Roman artifacts ranging from tweezers and hairbrushes to Latin-engraved pre-Christian altars and heads of sacrificial bulls. Ask about the sculpture of Priapus, god of fertility, and what happened to his allegedly heroic virility. ⊠ *Pl. de la Cathédrale, in the Hôtel de Ville* ☎ *05–62–68–70–22* 🖂 *€4* ☉ *Wed.–Mon., 10–noon and 2–6.*

Where to Stay & Eat

★ ¢–$ ✕🖼 **Hôtel de Bastard.** This elegant hotel and restaurant on an 18th-century estate is the creation of chef Jean-Luc Arnaud and his wife, Anne (who speaks excellent English). The rooms, although not spacious, are modern and comfortable and have fine views over the fields. The innovative cuisine is prepared with fresh local produce; try *il était trois foies*, foie gras prepared three ways—raw, steamed, and grilled—all with herbs and vegetables. ⊠ *Rue Lagrange, 32700* ☎ *05–62–68–82–44* 🖶*05–62–68–76–81* ⊕*www.hotel-de-bastard.com* ➘*29 rooms* ⚲*Restaurant, cable TV, pool, bar, some pets allowed (fee); no a/c* ➟ *AE, DC, MC, V* ☉ *Closed Dec. 18–Feb. 1.*

Auch

㉛ *24 km (14 mi) south of Fleurance, 77 km (46 mi) west of Toulouse, 73 km (44 mi) northeast of Tarbes.*

Auch, the capital of the Gers département, is best known for its stunning Gothic **Cathédrale de Ste-Marie.** Most of the stained-glass windows in the choir were done by Arnaud de Moles; vividly colorful, they portray biblical figures and handsome pre-Christian sibyls, or prophetesses. The oak choir stalls are intricately carved with more than 1,500 biblical and mythological figures that took 50 years and three generations of artisans to complete. In June, classical music concerts are held here. ⊠ *Pl. Salinis* 🖂 *€3 (ticket valid for 50% reduction at Musée des Jacobins)* ☉ *Daily 8–noon and 2–6.*

On the first floor of the 15th-century brick and wood-beam Maison Fedel, on the other side of the cathedral, is the **tourist office** (⊠ 1 rue Dessoles), where you can obtain maps and information.

Across place Salinis is a terrace overlooking the Gers River. A monumental flight of 370 steps leads down to the riverbank. Halfway down is the **Statue of D'Artagnan,** the musketeer immortalized by Alexandre Dumas. Although Dumas set the action of his historical novel *The*

Three Musketeers in the 1620s, the true D'Artagnan—Charles de Batz—was born in 1620, probably in Castlemore, near Lupiac, and did not become a musketeer until 1645.

Off place Salinis, in a wood-beam and brick house known as the **Maison d'Henri IV** (✉ 32 rue d'Espagne), the French and Navarran monarch is said to have cavorted with several of his 57 mistresses. A left at the end of rue d'Espagne will take you through one of the *pousterles*, steep and narrow alleys leading up from the river.

The **Musée des Jacobins,** behind the former Archbishop's Palace (now the Préfecture), has a fine collection of Latin American art, pre-Columbian pottery, and Gallo-Roman relics. Look for the white-marble epitaph dedicated by a grief-stricken Roman mistress to her dog Myia, for whose "*douces morcures*" ("sweet love bites") she mourned. ✉ *Rue Daumesnil* ☎ *05–62–05–74–79* 🎟 *€3 (€1.50 with cathedral ticket)* ⊘ *May–Oct., Tues.–Sun. 10–noon and 2–6; Nov.–Apr., Tues.–Sat. 10–noon and 2–5.*

Where to Stay & Eat

★ ¢–$ ✕ **Café Gascon.** This ramshackle and romantic little spot is right over the Halles aux Herbes. The fare is typical country Gascon with innovative personal touches such as the *salade folle* (duck prepared three different ways, with apples, tomatoes, and raspberries on lettuce). Chef, poet, and painter Georges Nosella is likely to come out to your table and serve your *café gascon* (coffee, whipped cream, and flaming Armagnac) with grace and humor. ✉ *5 rue Lamartine* ☎ *05–62–61–88–08* ▭ *MC, V* ⊘ *Closed Sun. Sept.–June, closed Mon. July and Aug.*

★ $–$$$ ✕▭ **Hôtel de France.** Roland Garreau's gourmet restaurant, Le Jardin des Saveurs, is an institution at this classic central Auch hotel; his specialty is the reduction or lighter interpretation of traditional country cooking. The duplex suite behind the circular dormer window on the facade facing the square is worth a look, if not occupied, even if you resist the temptation to spend the €350 it costs to sleep there. Other rooms are cozy, if a bit small and overly fabric-filled. ✉ *Pl. de la Libération, 32000* ☎ *05–62–61–71–71* 🖷 *05–62–61–71–81* ✎ *roland.garreau@wanadoo.fr* ⇆ *29 rooms* ⚘ *Restaurant, cable TV, bar, shop, parking (fee)* ▭ *AE, DC, MC, V* ¶❘ *MAP.*

Shopping

Caves de l'Hôtel de France (✉ Rue d'Étigny) sells a wide selection of Armagnac.

LANGUEDOC-ROUSSILLON

A region immortalized by Matisse and Picasso, Languedoc-Roussillon extends along the southern Mediterranean coast of France to the Pyrénées. Draw a line between Toulouse and Narbonne: the area to the south down to the Pyrénées, long dominated by the House of Aragón, the ruling family of adjacent Catalonia, is known as the Roussillon. Inland, the area, with its dry climate, is virtually one huge vineyard. The Canal du Midi flows through the region to **Le Littoral Languedocien** (the Languedoc Coast). Beaches stretch down the coast to Cerebère at the

Spanish border. This strip is known as the Côte Vermeille (Vermilion Coast) and attracts droves of European sunworshippers even though the beaches are rocky. The farther south you go, the stronger the Spanish influence. Heading northward, the Languedoc region begins around Narbonne and extends to the region's hub, the elegant city of Montpellier. All in all, the Languedoc-Roussillon is one of the most idyllic regions in France. Life here—even in such cities as Béziers or Perpignan, the urban heart of the region—is distinctly relaxed and friendly. You'll probably be taking afternoon *siestes* (naps) before you know it.

Carcassonne

32 *88 km (55 mi) southeast of Toulouse, 105 km (65 mi) south of Albi.*

Fodor'sChoice
★

Set atop a hill overlooking lush green countryside and the Aude River, Carcassonne is a medieval town that looks lifted from the pages of a storybook—literally, perhaps, as its circle of towers and battlements (comprising the longest city walls in Europe) is said to be the setting for Charles Perrault's classic tale *Puss in Boots*. The oldest sections of the walls, built by the Romans in the 1st century AD, were later enlarged, in the 5th century, by the Visigoths. Charlemagne once set siege to the settlement in the 9th century, only to be outdone by one Dame Carcas, a clever woman who boldly fed the last of the city's wheat to a pig in full view of the conqueror; Charlemagne, thinking this indicated endless food supplies, promptly decamped, and the exuberant townsfolk named their city after her. During the 13th century, Louis IX (St. Louis) and his son Philip the Bold strengthened Carcassonne's fortifications—so much so that the town became considered inviolable by marauding armies and was duly nicknamed "the virgin of Languedoc." A town that can never be taken in battle is often abandoned, however, and for centuries thereafter Carcassonne remained under a Sleeping Beauty spell. It was only awakened during the mid-19th-century craze for chivalry and the Gothic style, when, in 1835, the historic-monument inspector (and poet) Prosper Mérimée arrived. He was so appalled by the dilapidated state of the walls he commissioned the painter and historian Viollet-le-Duc (who found his greatest fame restoring Paris's Notre-Dame) to restore the town. Today the 1844 renovation is considered almost as much a work of art as the medieval town itself. No matter if the town is more Viollet than authentic medieval, it still remains one of the most romantic sights in France.

The town is divided by the river into two parts—La Cité, the fortified upper town, and the lower, newer city (the *ville basse*), known simply as Carcassonne. Unless you are staying at a hotel in the upper town, you are not allowed to enter it with your car; you must park in the lot (€2) across the road from the drawbridge. Be aware that the train station is in the lower town, which means either a cab ride, a 45-minute walk up to La Cité, or a ride on the *navette* shuttle bus. Plan on spending at least a couple of hours exploring the walls and peering over the battlements across sun-drenched plains toward the distant Pyrénées. Once inside the walls of the upper town, a florid carousel announces that 21st-century tourism is about to take over. The streets are lined with souvenir shops, crafts boutiques, restaurants, and tiny "museums" (i.e., a

Cathars Museum, a Hat Museum), all out to make a buck and rarely worth that. Staying overnight within the ancient walls lets you savor the timeless atmosphere after the daytime hordes are gone.

The 12th-century **Château Comtal** is the last inner bastion of Carcassonne. It has a drawbridge and a museum, the **Musée Lapidaire,** where stone sculptures found in the area are on display. ☎ 04–68–11–70–77 ≊ €6.10 ☉ *June–Sept., daily 9–6; Oct.–May, daily 9–noon and 2–5.*

The best part about the ville basse, built between the Aude and the Canal du Midi, is the **Musée des Beaux-Arts** (Fine Arts Museum). It houses a nice collection of porcelain, 17th- and 18th-century Flemish paintings, and works by local artists—including some stirring battle scenes by Jacques Gamelin (1738–1803). ⊠ *Rue Verdun* ☎ *04–68–77–73–70* ≊ *Free* ☉ *Nov.–June, Mon.–Sat. 10–noon and 2–6; July and Aug., daily 9–6.*

Where to Stay & Eat

$–$$ ✕ **Le Languedoc.** This restaurant in the ville basse serves up light versions of the region's specialties, from confit to game. In summer the flowery patio is a perfect spot for a long evening dinner. Be sure to try the quail with foie gras, if available. ⊠ *32 allée d'Iéna* ☎ *04–68–25–22–17* ▤ *MC, V* ☉ *Closed mid-Dec.–mid-Jan. and Mon. No dinner Sun. July–Oct.*

$$$$ ✕▨ **Hôtel de la Cité.** Set within the walled upper town, this is *the* spot for celebrities in Carcassonne. This ivy-covered former episcopal palace offers creature comforts the ascetic Cathars would have hated. Afternoon tea is in the library or rotunda lounge with its antique-tile floors, detailed woodwork, and leaded windows (with storybook views). Dining in the sumptuous La Barbacane restaurant—all double-vaulted ceiling, ogival windows, and agate-green walls—is an event. For more casual fare, try the brasserie Chez Saskia or, in summer, the bistro outside on a charmingly cobbled square. A pool, set like a sapphire in the garden, beckons on hot days. ⊠ *Pl. de l'Église, 11000 La Cité de Carcassonne* ☎ *04–68–71–98–71* 🖷 *04–68–71–50–15* ⊕ *www.hoteldelacite.orient-express.com* ⇆ *66 rooms* ♨ *2 restaurants, minibars, cable TV, pool, meeting rooms, parking (fee)* ▤ *AE, DC, MC, V* ☉ *Closed Dec.–mid-Jan.*

★ $$$–$$$$ ✕▨ **Domaine d'Auriac.** This elegant 19th-century manor house southwest of Carcassonne offers an environment of superb grace and comfort. Room prices vary according to size and view; the largest look out onto a magnificent park and vineyards. Next to a terrace planted with mulberry trees, the restaurant, famed as one of the best in the area, offers superlative Languedoc cuisine; enjoy the Provençal-style salon festooned with copper pots while savoring truffled pigeon, John Dory in blueberry wine, and game dishes, in season, accompanied by rare regional vintages. ⊠ *Rte. de St-Hilaire, 4 km (2½ mi) southwest of Carcassonne, 11330 Auriac* ☎ *04–68–25–72–22* 🖷 *04–68–47–35–54* ⊕ *www.relaischateaux.fr* ⇆ *26 rooms* ♨ *Restaurant, golf course, tennis court, pool, bar* ▤ *AE, MC, V* ☉ *Closed Jan., Apr. 27–May 5, Nov. 16–25* ▢▢ *MAP.*

$$$–$$$$ ▨ **Château de Garrevaques.** With a florid Roussillon-ochre facade and set equidistant (50 km [31 mi]) from Toulouse, Carcassonne, and Albi, this retreat makes a particularly apt base camp for exploring the region, the more so since the current châtelaines are the 15th generation to call this home. Marie-Christine and Claude Combes receive guests with a

friendly welcome amid family heirlooms. The only salon in truly baronial style is the main living room graced with a dazzling Zuber suite of
grisaille (grey-and-white) hand-painted wallpaper panels depicting scenes
of the Psyché and Cupid legend. Guest rooms are graced with period accents, stolid antiques, paisley fabrics, and some fetching 19th-century color
schemes. The table d'hôte dinner is a good chance to sample the local
country cooking and meet invariably interesting fellow guests, not to mention Madame and Monsieur Combes. With many acres of parkland to
play with, the Combes have opened a new section (in June 2004) called
the **Pavillon du Château,** occupying the former stables (complete with
heavy wooden beams) with 15 rooms, two restaurants, and a spa. Chocolate massage (yes, massage, this is not dessert) is the house specialty, along
with a hammam and hot-stone treatments. ⊠ *5 km (3 mi) northwest of
Revel, 81700 Garrevaques* ☎ *05–63–75–04–54* 🖷 *05–63–70–26–44*
⊕ *www.garrevaques.com* ⤻ *23 rooms, 1 suite* ⅏ *2 restaurants, cable
TV, tennis court, pool, spa, billiards* ▤ *AE, DC, MC, V* ⏁⏁ *BP.*

$–$$ 🏨 **Hôtel Montségur.** With its ville basse location, this hotel is especially
convenient. Rooms on the first two floors have Louis XV and Louis
XVI furniture, some of it genuine; those above are more romantic, with
gilt-iron bedsteads under sloping oak beams. ⊠ *27 allée d'Iéna, 11000*
☎ *04–68–25–31–41* 🖷 *04–68–47–13–22* ⤻ *21 rooms* ⅏ *Cable TV,
bar, parking (fee), some pets allowed (fee)* ▤ *AE, DC, MC, V* ⊘ *Closed
Dec. 20–Feb. 3.*

The Arts

Carcassonne hosts a major arts festival in July, with dance, theater, classical music, and jazz; for details, contact the **Théâtre Municipal** (⊠ B.P.
236, rue Courtejaire, 11005 ☎ 04–68–25–33–13, 04–68–77–71–26
reservations). The city usually goes medieval in mid-August with **Les
Médiévales,** a festival of troubadour song, rich costumes, and jousting
performances (some years the event isn't held; check with tourist office).
The Bastille Day fireworks over La Cité are spectacular.

Mirepoix

③③ *48 km (29 mi) southwest of Carcassonne, 88 km (53 mi) southeast of
Toulouse, 35 km (22 mi) northeast of Foix.*

The 13th-century walled town of Mirepoix is in the heart of Cathar country. A good time to come here is during Mirepoix's Medieval Festival,
always in July, when a historical procession is held on the third Sunday
of the month. The town is built around the lovely, medieval main square,
place Général-Leclerc, surrounded by 13th- to 15th-century houses with
intricately carved timbers forming arcades or porticoes called *couverts.*

Where to Stay

★ **$$–$$$**   🏨 **La Maison des Consuls.** This extraordinary 14th-century town-house hotel
on the central square is a classified historic site. The 500-year-old carved
timber gargoyles concentrated around the hotel facade make the exquisitely
restored interior even more surprising. Each room is decorated in a different color, most with exposed beams. The Chambre de Dame Louise
and the Chambre du Maréchal, both overlooking the square, are the

best. ⊠ *Pl. des Couverts, 09500* ☎ *05–61–68–81–81* ⊟ *05–61–68–81–15* ⊕ *www.maisondesconsuls.com* ⮌ *7 rooms, 1 suite* ⚐ *Parking (fee), some pets allowed (fee); no a/c* ⊟ *AE, DC, MC, V.*

Foix

34 *16 km (10 mi) north of Tarascon-sur-Ariège, 84 km (52 mi) south of Toulouse, 35 km (22 mi) southwest of Mirepoix, 138 km (86 mi) west of Perpignan.*

Nestled in the Ariège Valley, Foix is the capital of the Ariège départe-ment. Notice the fancy 19th-century administrative buildings south of avenue Fauré, the town's major thoroughfare. Now that you're in the thick of the Midi-Pyrénées, try to do some hiking. East of Foix is one of the best routes, the **Sentier Cathare** (Path of the Cathars)—a tough 182 km (100-mi) trail that takes you through a chain of cliff-side châteaux all the way to the Mediterranean. Pick up maps in Toulouse.

★ One of the leading postcard images of the area, the gigantic 12th-cen-tury **Château de Foix,** sitting impregnably on a promontory above the town and river, has three enormous towers reaching skyward like sentinels. The castle **museum** features archaeological finds and regional history, in-cluding the castle's earliest history as a Benedictine monastery, its later starring role in the Cathar wars, and its function as a redoubt for figures ranging from Saint Augustine to the blond and bold Count of Foix, Gas-ton Phoebus. Tours in French are offered on the hour, while there is one English tour scheduled daily at 1. ⊠ *Rue Mercadal* ☎ *05–34–09–83–83* ☜ *€4.20* ☉ *July and Aug. daily 9:45–6:30; June and Sept. 9:45–noon and 2–6; Oct.–May Wed.–Sun. 10:30–noon and 2–5:30.*

A 5-km (3-mi) drive northwest from Foix along D1 leads to the **Rivière Souterraine de Labouiche** (Labouiche Subterranean River), a mysterious underground stream whose waters have tunneled a 5-km (3-mi) gallery through the limestone. The 75-minute boat trip covers a 1½-km (1-mi) stretch, past weirdly shaped, subtly lighted stalactites and stalagmites, ending at a subterranean waterfall. Dry land is 230 feet overhead. ☎ *05–61–65–04–11* ☜ *€7.80* ☉ *Apr.–mid-June and mid-Sept.–mid-Nov., daily 2–5; mid-June–mid-Sept., daily 10–noon and 2–5.*

Where to Stay & Eat

¢–$$ ✕ **Le Phoebus.** The views across the Ariège and over the Château de Foix, which once belonged to the illustrious Gaston Phoebus himself, the most famous of the counts of Foix, are superb. The Phoebus is known for game specialties in season and cuisine du terroir, such as *foie de canard mi-cuit* (half-cooked duck liver) and *rable de lièvre au poivrade* (hare in pepper sauce). ⊠ *3 cours Irénée Cros* ☎ *05–61–65–10–42* ⊟ *AE, DC, MC, V* ☉ *Closed Mon. and mid-Feb.–mid-Mar. No lunch Sat.*

$ ✕☷ **Lons.** This former post house in the town center has comfortable, modernized rooms that vary in size. The restaurant is reasonably priced and overlooks the Ariège; it's closed Saturday in winter. ⊠ *6 pl. Georges-Dutilh, 09000* ☎ *05–61–65–52–44* ⊟ *05–61–02–68–18* ⮌ *39 rooms, 37 with bath or shower* ⚐ *Restaurant, parking (fee)* ⊟ *AE, DC, MC, V* ☉ *Closed Dec. 20–Jan. 4; restaurant closed Dec. 20–Jan. 20* ❑ *MAP.*

Tarascon-sur-Ariège

㉟ *16 km (10 mi) south of Foix.*

★ Tarascon is best known for its superb grotto and its collection of prehistoric art second only to that of Lascaux. As you enter Tarascon, veer left along D8 to the **Grotte de Niaux**, which contains scores of red-and-black Magdalenian rock paintings done in charcoal and iron oxide. Stylized horses, goats, deer, and bison, dating from about 20,000 BC, gallop around a naturally circular underground gallery (known as the Salon Noir, or Black Room) 1 km (½ mi) inside the entrance. Now that the famous caves at Lascaux in the Dordogne can be seen only in reproduction, this is the finest assembly of prehistoric art open to the public anywhere in France. Guided tours only; call ahead for reservations and to check schedule. ☎ 05–61–05–88–37 ⊡ €10 ⊙ *July–Sept., tours daily every 45 mins 8:30–11:30 and 1:30–5:15; Oct.–June, tours daily at 11, 3, and 4:30.*

Ax-les-Thermes

㊱ *26 km (15 mi) southeast of Tarascon-sur-Ariège, 104 km (64 mi) southwest of Carcassonne.*

A summer and winter resort town, Ax-les-Thermes has more than 80 mineral springs—at one, in the middle of town, you can often see local merchants on a coffee break or lunch hour reading the newspaper with trousers rolled to the knees and legs immersed. There are ski stations in Ax-Bonascre and Ascou-Pailhères, 5 km (3 mi) from town, and crosscountry skiing is available at the Plateau de Beille and Domaine de Chioula, 10 km (6 mi) from town; for complete information, contact the **tourist office** (☎ 05–61–64–60–60). After a day of skiing, come back to Ax for a thermal hot bath—an unbeatable winter combination. Crisscrossing the surrounding heights are 400 km (248 mi) of hiking trails.

Font-Romeu

㊲ *75 km (45 mi) southeast of Ax-les-Thermes, 87 km (54 mi) southeast of Tarascon-sur-Ariège, 88 km (55 mi) southwest of Perpignan.*

In this high-altitude vacation spot, French Olympians trained for the Mexico City games of 1968. The views over the Cerdagne Valley from the balcony across from the tourist office should not be missed. Sports facilities include various ski lifts (one operates from the center of town), an ice rink, a riding school, a swimming pool, tennis courts, and a 9-hole golf course. As it is known for the sunniest slopes and best snowmaking machines in the area, the skiing can get very crowded during peak Christmas and Easter vacation weekends. The **École de Ski Français** (☎ 04–68–30–03–74) is a local resource for sport fans.

Where to Stay & Eat

¢–$$ ✕⊡ **Pyrénées.** This modern hotel perched above the Cerdagne Valley offers stunning views over the sunniest and widest highland space in the Pyrénées. A five-minute walk from the gondola ski lift up to the snow (or to hiking trails in summer), rooms are small but command unforgettable panoramas, and the hotel pool seems all but suspended over the valley. ⊠*Pl. des Pyrénées, 66120* ☎*04–68–30–01–49* 🖷*04–68–30–35–98* ↩*37 rooms* ⚬ *Restaurant, pool, sauna, bar; no a/c* ☐ *AE, DC, MC, V* ☉ *Closed Apr. 20–June 1 and Oct. 19–Dec. 1* ⭕*MAP.*

Sports & the Outdoors

For general advice and ski equipment in Font-Romeu, look for the knowledgeable and English-speaking Roy van der Groen at **Sport 2000** (⊠102 av. Emmanuel Brousse ☎04–68–30–15–99 🖷04–68–30–09–34). For fly-fishing, contact **Marc Ribot** (⊠ 6 impasse des Lutins ☎ 04–68–30–30–93 🖷 04–68–30–06–75), who can arrange for guides, equipment, and fly-fishing courses.

Eyne

❸❽ *12 km (7 mi) southeast of Font-Romeu, 5 km (3 mi) southwest of Mont-Louis.*

Eyne Village, with a grand total of zero in-town commercial establishments—not even a café or a bakery—is one of the purest and best-preserved villages remaining in the broad, bi-national (France and Spain) Pyrenean Cerdagne valley. There are archaeological walks to megalithic menhirs and dolmens, a ski station uphill (2 km [1 mi] away), and hiking trails to neighboring villages and thermal springs. Set below a nationally classified botanical park, the **Réserve Naturelle d'Eyne,** the town has been famous since the 17th century as the point where Atlantic and Mediterranean weather systems and vegetation converge. Information about the park can be obtained at the park headquarters and museum in Eyne Village. ☎ *04–68–04–08–05.*

Where to Stay & Eat

★ **$–$$** ✕🖫 **Cal Pai.** In a lovely old farmhouse filled with heavy wooden beams and massive granite pillars, this *gîte d'étape* (way station for hikers and skiers) has a variety of accommodations (doubles, dormitory-style beds, with bathrooms and without) and table d'hôte (communal prix-fixe dinners) of uncommon quality—note that the room rate includes breakfast and dinner (confirm when booking, as rate schedule may change). Manager and chef Françoise Massot knows every wild mushroom and raspberry in the valley and puts them to delicious use in memorable breakfasts and dinners. ⊠ *Eyne Village* ☎ *04–68–04–06–96* 🖷 *04–68–04–10–60* ✉ *calpai@libertysurf.fr* ↩*9 rooms, 5 with bath* ⚬ *Dining room; no a/c, no room TVs* ☐ *No credit cards* ⭕*MAP.*

Mont-Louis

❸❾ *30 km (18 mi) west of Villefranche-de-Conflent, 5 km (3 mi) east of Eyne, 118 km (73 mi) south of Carcassonne.*

This fortified village, at 5,200 feet France's highest, was set up as a border stronghold by Vauban in 1679, and commands views over the Cerdagne Valley to the west, the Capcir to the north, and the Conflent to the east. The ramparts and the citadel, never attacked, are perfectly preserved. A solar oven—over the bridge and inside the portal in the town—is the only one in France in commercial use and is a key attraction.

Where to Stay & Eat

¢–$ ✕🏠**Lou Rouballou.** Famed as the best value and top cuisine in Mont-Louis, mother and daughter Christiane and Christine Bigorre's tiny flower-covered hideaway is the place to go (closed for lunch). Rooms are simple, small, and cozy. The cuisine is rich in sauces based on Pyrenean herbs, wild mushrooms, and game; try the *chartreuse de perdreaux* (partridge with winter cabbage) or the *ouillade* (a soup of potatoes, pork, and cabbage). ⊠ *Rue des Écoles Laïques, 66210* 🕾 *04–68–04–23–26* 🖷*04–68–04–14–09* 🖎 *Reservations essential* 🛏*7 rooms* 🖧 *Restaurant; no a/c* ⊟ *AE, DC, MC, V* ☉ *Closed May and Nov.*

Villefranche-de-Conflent

❹ ❶ *6 km (4 mi) west of Prades, 30 km (18 mi) east of Mont-Louis, 49 km (30 mi) southwest of Perpignan.*

If you spent your childhood poring over *Quentin Durward* and *The Three Musketeers*, you'll delight over the ramparts and donjons of the villages in this region. Named for its location at the confluence of the Têt and Cady rivers, Villefranche-de-Conflent has remnants of an 11th-century fortress, with Vauban improvements from the 17th century. Cross the tiny St-Pierre Bridge over the Têt and use the pink-marble "stairway of a thousand steps" to climb up to Fort Liberia for views of the village, the Canigou, and the valleys east to Prades. A guided tour of the ramparts and the town can be arranged in advance by calling the **Villefranche tourist office** (🕾 04–68–96–22–96).

Le petit train jaune ("Little Yellow Train") is a fun way to see some of the most spectacular countryside in the Pyrénées. This life-size toy train makes the 63-km (40-mi) three-hour trip from Villefranche to La Tour de Carol about five times a day. When the weather is nice, ride in one of the open-air cars. For information about hours and prices, contact the Villefranche tourist office or the SNCF Web site (⊕ www.ter-sncf.com/languedoc).

Where to Eat

$$–$$$ ✕**Auberge Saint-Paul.** One of the best-known tables in the area, this warm stone-surrounded refuge is known for its fine Catalan and Roussillon cuisine, such as *truite à la llosa* (trout on slate slabs) and *civet d'isard* (stewed mountain goat). It also has one of the best wine selections in the area—opt for one of the delicious local wines from Collioure. Dining al fresco is recommended in summer, but bring along a light jacket—it gets chilly at night. ⊠ *7 pl. de l'Église* 🕾 *04–68–96–30–95* 🖎 *Reservations essential* ⊟ *MC, V* ☉ *Closed June 16–20, Nov. 24–Dec. 2, Jan. 5–28. Closed Mon. No dinner Sun.*

Vernet-les-Bains

❹ ❶ *12 km (7 mi) southwest of Prades, 55 km (34 mi) west of Perpignan.*

English writer Rudyard Kipling came to take the waters in Vernet-les-Bains, a long-established spa town that is dwarfed by imposing Mont Canigou. The celebrated medieval abbey, **Abbaye St-Martin du Canigou,** is a steep 30-minute climb up from the parking area in Casteil, 2 km (1

Fodor's Choice ★

mi) south of Vernet-les-Bains. One of the most photographed abbeys in Europe thanks to its sky-kissing perch atop a triangular promontory at an altitude of nearly 3,600 feet, it was constructed in 1007 by Count Guifré of Cerdagne in expiation for murdering his son. Damaged by earthquake in 1428 and abandoned in 1783, the abbey was (perhaps too) diligently restored by the bishop of Perpignan early in the 20th century. Parts of the cloisters, along with the higher (and larger) of the two churches, date from the 11th century. The lower church, dedicated to Notre-Dame-sous-Terre, is even older. Rising above is a stocky, fortified bell tower. Although the hours vary, masses are sung daily; call ahead to confirm. Easter Mass here is especially joyous and moving. Note the abbey is closed January and also on Tuesday from October to Easter. ☎ 04–68–05–50–03 ⌦ €4 ☉ *Mid-June–mid-Sept., tours daily at 10, noon, 2, 3, 4, and 5; mid-Sept.–mid-June, Mon.–Sat. at 10, 12:30, 2:30, 3:30, and 4:30, Sun. 11 and 12:30.*

Prades

❷ *6 km (4 mi) east of Villefranche-de-Conflent, 43 km (27 mi) west of Perpignan.*

Once home to Catalan cellist Pablo Casals, the market town of Prades is famous for its annual summer music festival (from late July to mid-August), the **Festival Pablo Casals.** Founded by Casals in 1950, the music ★ festival is primarily held at the medieval **Abbaye de St-Michel de Cuxa** (⌂ 3 km [2 mi] on D7 south of Prades and Codalet ☎ 04–68–96–15–35 ⊕ www.prades-festival-casals.com ⌦ €3 ☉ Daily 9:30–11:30 and 2–5). One of the gems of the Pyrénées, the abbey's sturdy, crenellated four-story bell tower is visible from afar. If the remains of the cloisters here seem familiar, it may be because you have seen the missing pieces in New York City's Cloisters Museum. The 10th-century pre-Romanesque church is a superb aesthetic and acoustical venue for the summer cello concerts. The six-voice Gregorian vespers service held (somewhat sporadically—call to confirm) at 7 PM in the monastery next door is hauntingly simple and medieval in tone and texture.

Where to Stay & Eat

★ ¢ ✕ **Le Jardin d'Aymeric.** Locals swear by this semisecret gem, a charming little place that serves excellent cuisine du terroir in a relaxed and rustic setting. The menu changes seasonally and the market rules supreme. On the walls you'll find a changing show by local artists, as only befits this slightly bohemian refuge. ⌂ 3 av. Géneral de Gaulle ☎ 04–68–96–53–38 ⊟ MC, V ☉ Closed June 25–July 8, Feb., and Mon. No dinner Wed. 15 Oct. 15–Apr. 15 and Sun.

¢ 🏨 **Les Glycines.** This flower-covered, traditional hotel in the middle of Prades offers small but charming rooms of impeccable cleanliness and simplicity. A healthy hike from St-Michel-de-Cuxa, this cozy spot has a rambling restaurant of its own as well, serving up fine home cooking and plenty of friendly good cheer. ⌂ 129 av. Gén de Gaulle, 66500 ☎ 04–68–96–51–65 🖶 04–68–96–45–57 ⊕ www.lesglycines.fr ⇱ 19 rooms ⌕ Restaurant, cable TV, parking (fee); no a/c ⊟ MC, V.

Céret

43   *68 km (41 mi) southeast of Prades, 35 km (21 mi) west of Collioure,*
Fodor'sChoice   *31 km (19 mi) southwest of Perpignan.*
★

"The "Barbizon of Cubism," Céret achieved immortality when leading artists found this small Pyrenean town irresistible at the beginning of the 20th century. Here in this medieval enclave set on the banks of the Tech River, Picasso and Gris developed a vigorous new way of seeing that would result in the fragmented forms of Cubism, a thousand years removed from the Romanesque sculptures of the Roussillon chapels and cloisters. Adorned by cherry orchards—the town famously grows the first and finest crop in France—the town landscapes have been captured in paintings by Picasso, Gris, Dufy, Braque, Chagall, Kisling, and others.

★   Some of these are on view in the fine collection of the **Musée d'Art Moderne** (Modern Art Museum). ⊠ *8 bis Maréchal-Joffre* ☎ *04–68–87–27–76* ⊕ *www.musee-ceret.com* 🎫 *€7* ☺ *May–Sept., Wed.–Mon. 10–6.*

The heart of town is, not surprisingly, the place Pablo Picasso. Like the Spanish roots of this artist, Céret is proud of its Catalan heritage and it often hosts sardana dances. Be sure to stroll through pretty **Vieux Céret** (Old Céret) : find your way through **place des Neufs Jets** (Nine Fountains Square), around the church, and out to the lovely fortified **Porte de France** gateway. Then walk over the single-arched **Vieux Pont** (Old Bridge).

Where to Stay & Eat

★ **$$–$$$**   ✕🍴 **Les Feuillants.** One of the top restaurants in the area (closed Monday; no dinner Sunday), this elegant address offers refined Mediterranean and international cuisine, a good wine list, traditional-contemporary design, and paintings by Michel Becker. Dishes, such as panfried cuttlefish, are showpieces of the region and often come with flowers, herbs, cherries (the town emblem), and a hint of Catalonian *cuisine d'auteur* thrown in. Touches of creativity—seared foie gras with cherry and raisin chutney, a violet artichoke heart cooked tempura style—are often in evidence. Guest rooms, though few, are gems. ⊠ *1 bd. La Fayette, 66400* ☎ *04–68–87–37–88* 🖨 *04–68–87–44–68* ⊕ *www.feuillants.com* 🛏 *3 rooms, 3 apartments* ☖ *Restaurant, cable TV* 🖃 *AE, DC, MC, V* ☺ *Closed 2 wks in Feb. and 2 wks in Nov.* ⅋ *MAP.*

★ **¢–$**   🍴 **Les Arcades.** This comfortable spot in mid-Céret looks, smells, and feels exactly the way an inn ensconced in the heart of a provincial French town should. That the world-class collection of paintings of the Musée d'Art Moderne and the top-rated Les Feuillants restaurant (⇨ *above*) are both just across the street puts it over the top. ⊠ *1 pl. Picasso, 66400* ☎ *04–68–87–12–30* 🖨 *04–68–87–49–44* ⊕ *www.hotel-arcades-ceret. com* 🛏 *30 rooms* ☖ *Cable TV, parking (fee); no a/c* 🖃 *MC, V.*

Collioure

44   *35 km (21 mi) east of Céret, 27 km (17 mi) southeast of Perpignan.*
Fodor'sChoice
★   The heart of Matisse Country, this pretty seaside fishing village with a sheltered natural harbor has become a summer magnet for tourists (be-

ware the crowds in July and August). Painters such as Henri Matisse, André Derain, Henri Martin, and Georges Braque—who were dubbed Fauves for their "savage" (*fauve* means "wild animal") approach to color and form—were among the early discoverers of Collioure. The view they admired remains largely unchanged today: to the north, the rocky Îlot St-Vincent juts out into the sea, a modern lighthouse at its tip, whereas inland the Albères mountain range rises to connect the Pyrénées with the Mediterranean. The town harbor is a painting unto itself, framed by a 12th-century royal castle and a 17th-century church fortified with a tower. Collioure continues to play the muse to the entire Côte Vermeille—after all, it gave rise to the name of the Vermilion Coast because Matisse daringly painted Collioure's yellow-sand beach using a bright red terra-cotta hue. Matisse set up shop in the summer of 1905 and was greatly inspired by the colors of the town's terra-cotta roofs. The town's information center, behind the Plage Boramar, has an excellent map that points out the main locales once favored by the Fauve painters. In the streets behind the Vieux Port you'll see former fishermen's stores now occupied by smart boutiques and restaurants. To find tomorrow's Matisses and Derains, head to the streets behind the place du 18-Juin and to the old quarter of Le Mouré, set under Fort Miradou, to find studios filled with contemporary artists at work. Today, the most prized locales are the café-terraces overlooking the main beach where you can feast on Collioure's tender, practically boneless anchovies and the fine Rivesaltes and other local wines from the impeccably cultivated vineyards surrounding the town.

Near the old Quartier du Mouré is the 17th-century church of **Notre-Dame-des-Anges** (⌧ Pl. de l'Église). It has exuberantly carved, gilded Churrigueresque altarpieces by celebrated Catalan master Josep Sunyer and a pink-dome bell tower that doubled as the original lighthouse.

A slender jetty divides the Boramar Beach, beneath the church, from the small landing area at the foot of the **Château Royal**, a 13th-century castle, once the summer residence of the kings of Majorca (from 1276 to 1344), remodeled by Vauban 500 years later. ☎ *04–68–82–06–43* 🔖 *€3* ☾ *Mar.–Oct., daily 10–noon and 2–5.*

If you're around the first Sunday of September, the **Concours de Sardanes** (⌧ Place du 18-Juin ☎ 04–68–82–15–47) is a festival of Catalan dance and music. Contact the town tourist office for full information. Throughout the region, in neighboring towns like Céret, other Sardane events are also held during this time of year.

Where to Stay & Eat

$$–$$$$ ✕🏨 **Relais des Trois Mas.** The vistas are priceless, but are they worth the very pricey room rates? Overlooking the harbor from the cliffs south of town, this hotel enjoys a perfect perch. Inside are small but interestingly furnished rooms—headboards, for example, are made from antique Spanish doors. Rooms are named for painters whose work appears on the bathroom tiles. Below is a pebbled beach, though you may prefer the small pool (hewn from rock) or the huge Jacuzzi. Dine at the restaurant, La Balette, on the terrace or in one of the two small dining rooms looking over the harbor. ⊠ *Rte. de Port-Vendres, 66190* ☎ *04–68–82–05–07* 🖷 *04–68–82–38–08* ⇗ *19 rooms, 4 suites* ⚬ *Restaurant, 2 dining rooms, minibars, cable TV, pool, gym, hot tub, beach* ═ *MC, V* ☉ *Closed Jan.* ⚏ *FAP.*

★ $ ✕⚏ **Les Templiers.** Universally considered the "soul" of Collioure, this place merits a visit on every itinerary. Way back when, Matisse, Maillol, Dalí, Picasso, and Dufy used to hang out here (occasionally paying for a meal or room with a watercolor). Today, owner Jojo Pous, son of the force behind Collioure's art colony, is proud to show off the more than 2,500 original works hanging from every nook and cranny (including the ceiling and stairs)—one of the most glorious sights in Languedoc-Roussillon. The bar itself is a work of art, curved like the hull of a skiff and ending with a wood sculpture of a mermaid suckling an infant sailor. Collioure is Catalan in all senses but cartographically, so the food here is mostly Catalan and usually excellent; be sure to try dishes that feature the town's fabled anchovies. The rooms overlooking the château are cozy, but be sure yours is not in the annex. ⊠ *Quai de l'Amirauté, 66190* ☎ *04–68–98–31–10* 🖷 *04–68–98–01–24* ⊕ *www.hotel-templiers. com* ⇗ *43 rooms* ⚬ *Restaurant, café, cable TV, bar; no a/c* ═ *AE, DC, MC, V* ☉ *Closed Jan.* ⚏ *FAP.*

$–$$$ ⚏ **Casa Pairal.** An idyllic, palm-shaded 19th-century town house surrounded by a leafy garden, this small oasis is a handy address in often tumultuous (for all its idyllic reputation) Collioure. The main house is more charming than the annex but all rooms are comfortable and tastefully appointed. A two-minute walk to the water's edge, the hotel is comfortingly traditional, while the alluring courtyard, garden, and pool are relaxing and intimate. ⊠ *Impasse des Palmiers, 66190* ☎ *04–68–82–05–81* 🖷 *04–68–82–52–10* ⊕ *www.hotel-casa-pairal. com* ⇗ *28 rooms* ⚬ *Cable TV, pool, parking (fee)* ═ *AE, DC, MC, V.*

Perpignan

④⑤ *27 km (17 mi) northwest of Collioure, 64 km (40 mi) south of Narbonne, 204 km (126 mi) southeast of Toulouse.*

Salvador Dalí once called Perpignan's train station "the center of the world." That may not be true but the city is certainly the capital hub of the Roussillon. Although it's big, the few squares of the *centre ville*, grouped near the quays of the Basse River, are the places to be for evening concerts and casual tapas sessions—you might even succumb to the "cosmological ecstasy" Dalí said he experienced here. In medieval times Perpignan was the second city of Catalonia (after Barcelona), before falling to Louis XIII's French army in 1642. The Spanish influence is evident in Perpignan's leading monument, the fortified **Palais des Rois de Majorque** (Kings of Majorca Palace), begun in the 14th century by James II of Majorca. Highlights here are the majestic **cour d'Honneur** (Courtyard of Honor), the two-tier Flamboyant Gothic chapel of **Ste-Croix,** and the **Grande Salle** (Great Hall) with its monumental fireplaces. ⊠ *Rue des Archers* ☎ *04–68–34–48–29* ⬛ *€4* ☉ *Daily 9–5.*

Perpignan's centre ville is sweet and alluring, lined in blooming rosemary bushes and landmarked by a medieval monument, the 14th-century

Le Castillet, with its tall, crenellated twin towers. Originally this hulking brick building was the main gate to the city; later it was used as a prison. Now the **Casa Pairal,** a museum devoted to Catalan art and traditions, is housed here. ⊠ *Pl. de Verdun* ☎ *04–68–35–42–05* 🎫 €4 ⊘ *Wed.–Mon. 9–noon and 2–6.*

The **Promenade des Plantanes,** across boulevard Wilson from Le Castillet, is a cheerful place to stroll among flowers, plane trees, and fountains. To see other interesting medieval buildings, walk along the streets—the **Petite Rue des Fabriques d'En Nabot** is the best—near Le Castillet and the adjacent place de la Loge, the town's nerve center. Note the frilly wrought-iron campanile and dramatic medieval crucifix on the **Cathédrale St-Jean** (⊠ Pl. Gambetta).

Where to Stay & Eat

★ **$–$$** ✕ **Les Antiquaires.** With traditional Rousillon cooking served up in a rustic setting in a corner of old Perpignan, this friendly spot lives up to its title as a refuge for things antique. Duck à l'orange, a house favorite, has been on the menu here for 32 years, by popular demand. Foie gras in a Banyuls sauce is another staple in this pretty spot known for unpretentious yet refined cuisine. ⊠ *Pl. Després* ☎ *04–68–34–06–58* 🖃 *AE, DC, MC, V* ⊘ *Closed Mon. and July 1–23. No dinner Sun.*

$–$$ ✕ **Le France.** In the center of Perpignan in a 15th-century former stock market with exposed beams and arcades, this café-restaurant is perfect for a light meal or a glass of iced champagne under the parasols as you watch the world go by. The menu changes every three months, but try the light appetizers such as scallops marinated in orange, two different types of oysters, or a Nordic salad with smoked fish and steamed potatoes. Grilled duck breast with prunes, salmon fillet with fresh vegetable spaghetti, or the *tagine de lotte* (monkfish stew) are also found here in season. ⊠ *1 pl. de la Loge* ☎ *04–68–51–61–71* 🖃 *MC, V* ⊘ *No dinner Sun.*

$$–$$$ ✕🏨 **La Villa Duflot.** In a large park filled with olive and cypress trees, this hotel–restaurant complex serves some of the best meals in one of the calmest, prettiest settings in the city. Request a room with a view over the park—they're airy and comfortable with warm creamy colors—the rooms with the view of the patio aren't nearly as nice although they are a bit more economical. The ambience here is relaxed, all the finesse is saved for the food and the food is *good.* The gastronomic restaurant popular with haute Perpignan serves light Mediterranean specialties around the pool—try the *parillade,* an assortment of the freshest catch of the day grilled to perfection and served with tangy aioli. ⊠ *Rond Point Albert Donnezan 66000* ☎ *04–68–56–67–67* 🖶 *04–68–56–54–05* 🛏 *32 rooms* ⚿ *Restaurant, minibars, cable TV, bar, some pets allowed* 🖃 *AE, DC, MC, V.*

Shopping

Rue des Marchands, near Le Castillet, is thick with chic shops. **Maison Quinta** (⊠ Rue Louis Blanc) is a top design and architectural artifacts store. Excellent local ceramics can be found at the picturesque **Sant Vicens Crafts Center** (⊠ Rue Sant Vicens, off D22 east of town center).

Salses

46 *16 km (10 mi) north of Perpignan, 48 km (30 mi) south of Narbonne.*

Salses has a history of sieges. History relates that Hannibal stormed through the town with his elephants on his way to the Alps in 218 BC, though no trace of his passage remains. The colossal and well-preserved **Fort de Salses,** built by Ferdinand of Aragon in 1497 and equipped for 300 horses and 1,000 soldiers, fell to the French under Cardinal Richelieu in 1642 after a three-year siege. Bulky round towers ring the rectangular inner fort, and the five-story keep, with its narrow corridors and small-scale drawbridges, was designed to keep the fort's governor safe to the last. ☎ 04–68–38–60–13 ⌑ €6.50 ☉ *July and Aug., daily 9–6; Sept. and Oct. and Easter–June, daily 9:30–11:30 and 2–5:30; Nov.–Easter, 9:30–11:30 and 2–4.*

Narbonne

47 *64 km (40 mi) north of Perpignan, 60 km (37 mi) east of Carcassonne, 94 km (58 mi) south of Montpellier.*

In Roman times, bustling, industrial Narbonne was the second-largest town in Gaul (after Lyon) and an important port, though today little remains of its Roman past. Until the sea receded during the Middle Ages, Narbonne prospered. The town's former wealth is evinced by the 14th-century **Cathédral St-Just-et-St-Pasteur** (⌗ Rue Armand-Gauthier); its vaults rise 133 feet from the floor, making it the tallest cathedral in southern France. Only Beauvais and Amiens, in Picardy, are taller, and as at Beauvais, the nave at Narbonne was never built. The "Creation" tapestry is the cathedral's finest treasure.

Richly sculpted cloisters link the cathedral to the former **Palais des Archevêques** (Archbishops' Palace), now home to **museums** of archaeology, art, and history. Note the enormous palace kitchen and the late-13th-century keep, the Donjon Gilles-Aycelin; climb the 180 steps to the top for a view of the region and the town. ⌗ *Palais des Archevêques* ☎ 04–68–90–30–30 ⌑ €8, includes all town museums ☉ *May–Sept., daily 9–noon and 2–6; Oct.–Apr., Tues.–Sun. 10–noon and 2–5:30.*

On the south side of the Canal de la Robine is the **Musée Lapidaire** (Sculpture Museum), in the handsome 13th-century former church of **Notre-Dame de la Mourguié.** Classical busts, ancient sarcophagi, lintels, and Gallo-Roman inscriptions await you. ⌗ *Pl. Lamourguier* ☎ 04–68–65–53–58 ⌑ €8, includes all town museums ☉ *May–Sept., daily 9–noon and 2–6; Oct.–Apr., Tues.–Sun. 10–noon and 2–5:30.*

Where to Stay & Eat

$$$ ✕⊞ **Le Relais du Val d'Orbieu.** This pretty spot 14 km (8 mi) west of town is a viable solution to Narbonne's scarcity of good hotels. Owner Jean-Pierre Gonsalvez speaks English and is extremely helpful. Grouped around a courtyard, most rooms are reached through covered arcades. The better ones are pleasantly simple, with bare tile floors and large French doors leading onto terraces; the standard ones are slightly smaller and do not have terraces or views. The prix-fixe menu restaurant (no luncheon served November–March) lacks intimacy, but is more than serviceable. ⊠ *14 km (8 mi) west of Narbonne, D24, 11200 Ornaisons* ☎ *04–68–27–10–27* 🖶 *04–68–27–52–44* ⊕ *www.relaisduvaldorbieu. com/anglais/suite.htm* ⤵ *13 rooms, 7 apartments* ⚭ *Restaurant, minibars, cable TV, tennis court, pool; no a/c* ⊟ *AE, DC, MC, V* ⊙ *Closed Nov. 5–Feb. 5* ⦿ *MAP.*

$–$$ 🏨 **Résidence.** One block from the Canal de la Robine and another single block from the Place Salengro and the cathedral, this traditional favorite has housed France's artistic crème de la crème from Georges Brassens to Michel Serrault. The 19th-century building is charming, while rooms combine old-fashioned charm with modern comforts. ⊠ *Rue 1 Mai, 11100* ☎ *04–68–32–19–41* 🖶 *04–68–65–51–82* ⤵ *25 rooms* ⚭ *Parking (fee); no a/c* ⊟ *AE, DC, MC, V* ⊙ *Closed Jan. 15–Feb. 15.*

Béziers

48 *20 km (12 mi) northeast of Narbonne, 54 km (33 mi) southwest of Montpellier.*

The Languedoc's *capital du vin* (wine capital)—crowds head here for *dégustation* tastings during the October wine harvest festival—and centerpiece of the Canal du Midi, Béziers owes its reputation to the genius of native son and royal salt-tax collector Pierre-Paul Riquet (that's his statue presiding over the allées Paul Riquet). He was a visionary at a time when roads were in deplorable shape and grain was transported on the backs of mules. Yet he died a pauper in 1680, a year before the canal's completion (it was begun by the ancient Romans) and the revolutionizing of commerce in the south of France. Few would have predicted much of a future for Béziers in July of 1209, after Simon de Montfort, leader of the crusade against the Cathars, scored his first major victory here, massacring 20,000. Today the Canal du Midi hosts mainly pleasure cruisers, and Béziers sits serenely on its perch overlooking the distant Mediterranean and the foothills of the Cévennes Mountains. Early August sees the four-day *féria*—a festival with roots in Spain and replete with gory bullfighting (you've been warned).

The heavily restored **Église de la Madeleine** (⊠ Off rue de la République), with its distinctive octagonal tower, was the site of the beginning of the 1209 massacre. About 7,000 townspeople who had sought refuge from Simon de Montfort in the church were burned alive before he turned his attention to sacking the town; the event is known as "*le grand mazel*" ("the great bonfire"). Restoration work means that you may only be able to admire the crenellations, gargoyles, floral frieze, and crooked arches of the late 11th-century pentagonal apse.

Béziers's late-19th-century **Halles** (Market Hall) was done in the style of the architect Baltard, who built the original Les Halles in Paris. This is a particularly beautiful example, with large stone cabbages gracing the entrance like urns. ⊠ *Entrances on rue Paul Riquet, pl. Pierre Sémard* ⊙ *Daily 6:30–12:30.*

The **Ancienne Cathédrale St-Nazaire** (⊠ Pl. des Albigeois) was rebuilt over several centuries after the sack of Béziers. Note the medieval wall along rue de Juiverie, which formed the limit between the cathedral precincts and the Jewish quarter of town. The western facade resembles a fortress for good reason: it served as a warning to would-be invaders. Look for the magnificent 17th-century walnut organ and the frescoes about the lives of St. Stephen and others.

Adjoining the cathedral are a 14th-century cloister and the **Jardin des Evêques** (Bishops' Garden), conceived of as a terraced garden descending to the banks of the Orb. The views from here, which take in Béziers's five bridges, are magnificent. ⊠ *Pl. des Albigeois* ۞ *Oct.–Apr., daily 10–noon and 2–5:30; May–Sept., daily 10–7.*

Where to Stay & Eat

$$–$$$ ✕🏨 **Château de Lignan.** Set in its own park, this elegant estate northwest of Béziers has four slender roof-tiled towers, lending a vaguely Italianate feel to go with the austere stucco facade. Pity that rooms have little to distinguish them from standard chain hotels except their size and louvered windows, but the restaurant is exceptional. The octagonal sprawl of the skylit dining room is cheery and welcoming. Simple, streamlined fare such as strongly flavored *loup en papillote* (sea bass cooked in foil) makes a perfect prelude to the vanilla ice cream–filled baked pears. ⊠ *Pl. de l'Église, 6 km (4 mi) northwest of Béziers, 34490 Lignan-sur-Orb* ☎ *04–67–37–91–47* 🖷 *04–67–37–99–25* ⊕ *www. chateauxhotels.com* 🛏 *50 rooms* ♿ *Restaurant, minibars, cable TV, pool* ⊟ *AE, DC, MC, V* ¶◯¶ *MAP.*

The Outdoors

Daylong excursions on the Canal du Midi include passage over the canal bridge spanning the Orb and through the nine locks. Some companies working the Canal de Midi have extensive routes, some as far as the Mediterranean resort town of Agde, 21 km (14 mi) away. **Les Bâteaux du Soleil** (⊠ 6 rue Chassefière, 34300 Agde ☎ 04–67–94–08–79 🖷 04–67–21–28–38) includes some wide-ranging excursions.

Minerve

❹❾ *40 km (25 mi) west of Béziers, 30 km (19 mi) northwest of Narbonne.*

Fodor's Choice
★

Surrounded by the meandering, juniper-covered limestone gorges of the Vallée de la Cesse, Minerve is the quintessential medieval hilltop village. The town sheltered a large number of heretics at the start of the Albigensian Crusade. But its defensive position was no match for Simon de Montfort's army in July 1210, when after a seven-week siege the dehydrated citizens capitulated and 180 Cathar *Perfecti* (elite Cathari) were burned. De Montfort's army had blocked the village well with the aid of a catapult called La Malvoisine (the Evil Neighbor), which has been reconstructed on its original strategic site. Stroll around the remaining fortifications and try to imagine the assault. Around Minerve are a number of geological and archaeological curiosities, including *ponts naturels* (natural bridges), enormous tunnels in the rock cut by the path of the Cesse River, prehistoric grottoes, and dolmens.

Maps and information are available from the somewhat hidden **Syndicat d'Initiative** (⊠ 9 rue des Martyrs ☎ 04–68–91–81–43), the tourist office in the center of the village. You can also get addresses of local winemakers who produce the classed wine Minervois (a rough, fruity red) from grapes grown in arid, pebbly soil.

The austere, Romanesque **Église St-Etienne** has one of the oldest altar tables in Europe, dating from AD 456. Next to the church is a carving of a dove, a monument to the village's resistance during the Crusades. The château was destroyed by Simon de Montfort. Only the curious, candlelike **Tour du Guet** (Watchtower) remains on a ledge at the far end of the village.

The **Musée Hurepel** re-creates the events of the Albigensian Crusade in a series of figurine-populated dioramas and does a good job of explaining how villagers would have interacted with the Cathars they sheltered. ⊠ *5 rue des Martyrs* ☎ *04–68–91–12–26* 💳 *€4* ☉ *Daily 10:30–12:30 and 2–6:30; Closed mid-Nov.–Mar.*

Where to Stay & Eat

¢–$ ✗🏨 **Le Relais Chantovent.** Overlooking the gorges of the Brian River, this oak-beamed, terra-cotta-tile restaurant and inn is decorated with exceptional paintings by local artists. Rooms are basic but quaint, with old lamps, framed prints, and wooden furniture. Owners Maïté and Loulou Evenou serve up elegantly garnished local fare, including strong, salty *jambon de la Montagne Noire* (Black Mountain ham) and trout in a cream and red-pepper sauce. The restaurant (prix-fixe menu only) is closed Monday, and there is no dinner Sunday. ⊠ *17 Grande-Rue, 34210* ☎ *04–68–91–14–18* 🖶 *04–68–91–81–99* 📲 *10 rooms* 🍴 *Restaurant; no a/c, no room TVs* ▭ *MC, V* ☉ *Closed mid-Dec.–mid-Mar.* ¶◉¶ *MAP.*

★ $$–$$$ 🏨 **Les Aliberts.** Ensconced among the vine- and asphodel-covered hills outside Minerve, with stunning views of the Pyrénées and the Montagne Noire, this *gîte* (hiker's way-station) is in a restored and renovated set of 12th- to 17th-century farm buildings. Cosmopolitan owners Pascal and Monique Bourgogne treat guests like friends. The majestic main farmhouse has common rooms with an enormous fireplace, library, and piano. The five cozy houses (€540 to €1,950 per week, with accommodations for from 4 to 10 persons), range in style from Scandinavian to Asian to French contemporary; all have full kitchens and fireplaces. Meals and breakfasts can be ordered in advance. ⊠ *Les Aliberts, off D10 south toward Olonzac, 34210* ☎ *04–68–91–81–72* 🖶 *04–68–91–22–95* 🌐 *www.gite.com/aliberts* 📲 *5 houses, with 13 rooms total* 🍴 *Pool, library, laundry facilities, Internet; no room TVs* ▭ *No credit cards* ¶◉¶ *FAP.*

Pézenas

🔟 *23 km (14 mi) northeast of Béziers, 52 km (32 mi) southwest of Montpellier.*

Pézenas retains the courtly appearance and feel it acquired in the 16th century, when the Estates General of the Languedoc, the regional administrative body, governed from here. The town made its fortune with

16th- to 18th-century textile fairs, at which denim was sold. Hence you have Pézenas's architectural richness: around every picturesque corner is another *hôtel particulier* (town-house mansion)—and because of architectural competition among the wealthy, they are all unique. Some notable streets are rue Triperie Vieille; rue de la Foire, where you'll find the Maison Carrion de Nizas and the Hôtel de Wicque; cour Jean-Jaurès, famous for its Maison Émile Mâzuc, at No. 10; place du 14 Juillet and its outstanding Hôtel des Barons de Lacoste; and rue Émile Zola, home to the Maison de Jacques Coeur. At the end of rue Émile Zola is a rounded archway leading into the rue Juiverie, also called La Carriera, which in the Occitan language denotes a Jewish ghetto.

The tourist office, which organizes a variety of tours of Pézenas, is in the **Maison du Barbier Gély** (⊠ 1 pl. Gambetta), once home to Molière's barber and friend, Monsieur Gély. Pézenas's most impressive hôtel particulier is the **Hôtel d'Alfonce,** with its twisted Baroque columns, three-tiered balustraded loggia overlooking the garden, and vinelike corner staircase. This was the residence of the Prince de Conti, who sponsored visits by Molière and his acting troupe in 1650, 1653, and 1655. *Le Médecin Volant (The Flying Doctor)* may have premiered here shortly before Conti, mad from syphilis, purged his illustrious court. The owners, Monsieur Aubert and his daughter, give private tours of their family home and rent out two double rooms with bath. (€100 with breakfast). ⊠ *32 rue Conti* ☎ *04–67–90–71–89* ✆ *€2* ☉ *June–Sept., Mon.–Sat. 10–noon and 2–6.*

Nightlife & the Arts

As part of **La Mirondela Del Arts** festival in July and August, Molière's spirit comes alive with performances by comedy troupes; there are also Occitan-language music and poetry events. In February the town's medieval mascot, **Le Poulain** (a giant horse made out of chestnut and cloth), gets toted around in honor of Carnival.

Montpellier

40 km (25 mi) southeast of St-Guilhem-le-Désert, 42 km (26 mi) southwest of Nîmes.

Vibrant Montpellier (pronounced monh-pell-*yay*), capital of the Languedoc-Roussillon region, has been a center of commerce and learning since the Middle Ages, when it was a crossroads for pilgrims on their way to Santiago de Compostela, in Spain, and an active shipping center trading in spices from the East. With its cargo of exotic luxuries, it also imported Renaissance learning, and its university—founded in the 14th century—has nurtured a steady influx of ideas through the centuries. Though the port silted up by the 16th century, Montpellier never became a backwater, and as a center of commerce and conferences it keeps its focus on the future. An imaginative urban planning program has streamlined the 17th-century Vieille Ville, and monumental perspectives dwarf passersby on the 17th-century Promenade du Peyrou. An even more utopian venture in urban planning is the Antigone district: a vast, harmonious 100-acre complex designed in 1984 by Barcelona architect Ricardo Bofill. A student population of some 65,000 keeps things lively, especially on the place de la Comédie, the city's social nerve center. The Old Town is a pedestrian paradise; you can travel around the entire city on the excellent bus system (the gare routière station is by the train terminal on rue Jules Ferry).

★ ⑤ Montpellier's grandest avenue is the **Promenade du Peyrou,** built at the end of the 17th century and dedicated to Louis XIV. The Peyrou's cen-
⑤ terpiece is the enormous **Arc de Triomphe,** designed by d'Aviler in 1689 and finished by Giral in 1776; it looms majestically over the peripheral highway that loops around the city center. Together, the noble scale of these harmonious stone constructions and the sweeping perspectives they frame make for an inspiring stroll through this posh stretch of town. At the end of the park is the **Château d'Eau,** a Corinthian temple and the terminal for **les Arceaux,** an 18th-century aqueduct; on a clear day the view from here is spectacular, taking in the Cévennes Mountains, the sea, and an ocean of red-tile roofs (it's worth it to come back here at night to see the entire promenade lit up).

Boulevard Henri IV runs north from the Promenade du Peyrou to
⑤ France's oldest botanical garden, the **Jardin des Plantes,** planted on order of Henri IV in 1593. An exceptional range of plants, flowers, and trees grows here. ◲ *Free* ☉ *Gardens Mon.–Sat. 9–noon and 2–5. Greenhouses weekdays 9–noon and 2–5, Sat. 9–noon.*

After taking in the broad vistas of the Promenade de Peyrou, cross over into the Vieille Ville and wander its maze of narrow streets full of pretty shops and intimate restaurants. At the northern edge of the Vieille Ville,
⑤ visit the imposing **Cathédrale St-Pierre** (⊠ Pl. St-Pierre), its fantastical and unique 14th-century entry porch alone worth the detour: two cone-topped towers—some five stories high—flank the main portal and support a groin-vaulted shelter. The interior, despite 18th-century reconstruction, maintains the formal simplicity of its 14th-century origins.

⑤ Next door to the cathedral, peek into the noble **Faculté de Médecine,** on rue de l'École de Médecine, one of France's most respected medical schools, founded in the 14th century and infused with generations of international learning—especially Arab and Jewish scholarship.

From the medical school follow rue Foch, which slices straight east. The number of bistros and brasseries increases as you leave the Vieille Ville to cross place des Martyrs; veering right down rue de la Loge, you spill
⑤ out onto the festive gathering spot known as **Place de la Comédie.** Anchored by the Neoclassical 19th-century **Opéra-Comédie,** this broad square is a beehive of leisurely activity, a cross between Barcelona's Ramblas and a Roman *passagiata* (afternoon stroll, en masse). Brasseries, bistros, fast-food joints, and cinemas draw crowds, but the pleasure is getting there and seeing who came before, in which shoes, and with whom.

From place de la Comédie, boulevard Sarrail leads north past the shady
★ ⑤ esplanade Charles de Gaulle to the **Musée Fabre.** Closed for renovations until an as yet unspecified date in 2006, the museum is a mixed bag of

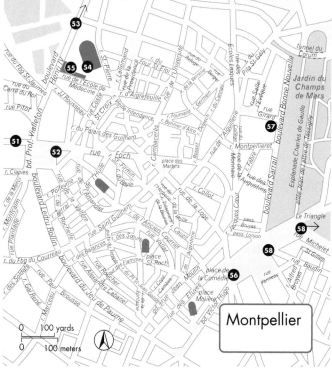

Montpellier

architectural styles (a 17th-century *hôtel,* a vast Victorian wing with superb natural light, and a remnant of a Baroque Jesuit college). This rich art museum has a surprisingly big collection, thanks to its namesake. François-Xavier Fabre, a native of Montpellier, was a student of the great 18th-century French artist David, who established roots in Italy and acquired a formidable collection of masterworks—which he then donated to his hometown, supervising the development of this fine museum. Among his gifts were the *Mariage Mystique de Sainte Catherine,* by Veronese, and Poussin's coquettish *Venus et Adonis.* Later contributions include a superb group of 17th-century Flemish works (Rubens, Steen), a collection of 19th-century French canvases (Géricault, Delacroix, Corot, Millet) that inspired Gauguin and Van Gogh, and a growing group of 20th-century acquisitions that buttress a legacy of paintings by early-Impressionist Frédéric Bazille. ⊠ *3 bd. Bonne Nouvelle* ☎ *04–67–14–83–00* ⊠ €6 ⊙ *Tues.–Fri. 9–5:30, weekends 9:30–5.*

**need a
break?**

Enjoy a 15-minute stroll from the Musée Fabre to the very chic café-bar **Les Planches** (⊠ 5 pl. Jean Jaurès ☎ 04–67–66–43–60). Pop in for an aperitif, a look at the ever-changing exhibit of local artists and trendy Montpellierains nibbling olives.

At the far-east end of the city loop, Montpellier seems to transform itself into a futuristic ideal city, all in one smooth, low-slung postmodern style. This is the **Antigone** district, the result of city planners' efforts (and local industries' commitment) to pull Montpellier up out of its economic doldrums. It worked. This ideal neighborhood, designed by the Catalan architect Ricardo Bofill, covers 100-plus acres with plazas, esplanades, shops, restaurants, and low-income housing, all constructed out of stone-color, prestressed concrete. Be sure to visit place du Nombre d'Or—symmetrically composed of curves—and the 1-km-long (½-mi-long) vista that stretches down a mall of cypress trees to the glass-fronted **Hôtel de Region** (⊠ Av. du Pirée).

Where to Stay & Eat

$$$–$$$$ ✕ **Le Jardin des Sens.** Blink and look again: twins Laurent and Jacques
FodorśChoice Pourcel, trained under separate masters, combine forces here to achieve
★ a quiet, almost cerebral cuisine based on southern French traditions. At every turn are happy surprises: foie gras crisps, dried-fruit risotto, and lamb sweetbreads with *gambas* (prawns). A modest lunch menu (in the $$ category) lets you indulge on a budget. Decor is minimal stylish, with steel beams and tables on three tiers. Truth is, this is in a rather *delabré* working-class neighborhood and from the outside looks like an anonymous warehouse. Rooms are spacious, impeccably equipped and comfortable, and, best of all, not far from the table. ⊠ *11 av. St-Lazare* ☎ *04–99–58–38–38* 🖷 *04–99–58–38–39* ⊕ *www.jardindessens.com* ▭ *AE, DC, MC, V* ⊘ *Closed Jan. and Sun. No lunch Mon.*

$$–$$$$ ✕ **Le Chandelier.** On the sixth and seventh floors of a building in the Antigone district, this restaurant has dramatic views, impeccable service, and bold blue-and-yellow Mediterranean decor. Chef Gilbert Furlan's inventive cuisine takes Provençal ingredients to sophisticated levels: sample his squid sautéed in fresh thyme, dried mullet eggs with brandade mousse, and pigeon roasted with cinnamon and nutmeg, all with a good range of Languedoc wines. ⊠ *39 pl. Zeus* ☎ *04–67–15–34–38* ▭ *AE, DC, MC, V* ⊘ *Closed Sun. No lunch Mon.*

★ **$–$$$** ✕ **Le Petit Jardin.** On a quiet Vieille Ville backstreet, this simple restaurant lives up to its name: you dine looking over (or seated in) a lovely, deep-shaded garden with views of the cathedral. A simple omelet with pepper sauce, spicy bourride, or hearty osso buco (veal shanks in saffron-tomato sauce) mirrors the welcome, which is warm and unpretentious. ⊠ *20 rue Jean-Jacques Rousseau* ☎ *04–67–60–78–78* ▭ *AE, DC, MC, V* ⊘ *Closed Jan. and Mon.*

$ ✕ **Chez Mémé.** This ever-popular restaurant is the perfect spot for a traditional dinner reminiscent of *cuisine de Mémé* (Grandma's cooking), serving grilled trout with almonds, ratatouille, and warm apple tart with a dollop of cream. The portions are ample, the atmosphere is fast, fun, and friendly with local musicians playing for their soup, *and* it's ever so light on the pocket. *Yippee!* ⊠ *18 rue Ecoles Laïques* ☎ *04–67–02–43–26* ▭ *MC, V* ⊘ *Closed Sun. No lunch.*

★ **$$–$$$** 🏩 **Le Guilhem.** On the same quiet backstreet as the restaurant Le Petit Jardin, this jewel of a *hôtel de charme* is actually a series of 16th-century houses. Rebuilt from ruins to include an elevator and state-of-the-art white-tile baths, it nonetheless retains original casement windows (many overlooking the extraordinary old garden), slanting floors, and views toward the cathedral. Soft yellows and powder blues add to its gentle, *temps perdu* atmosphere. Tiny garret-style rooms at the top are great if you're traveling alone; if not, ask for the largest available. ✉ *18 rue Jean-Jacques-Rousseau, 34000* ☎ *04–67–52–90–90* 🖷 *04–67–60–67–67* ⊕ *www.leguilhem.com* ⬧ *36 rooms* ♿ *Cable TV, parking (fee)* ▤ *AE, DC, MC, V.*

Nightlife & the Arts

Concerts are performed in the 19th-century **Théâtre des Treize Vents** (✉ 11 bd. Victor Hugo ☎ 04–67–60–05–45). The **Orchestre National de Montpellier** (☎ 04–67–61–66–16) is a young and energetic group of some reputation, performing regularly in the Opéra Berlioz in the Corum conference complex. The resident **Opera Comédie de Montpellier** (☎ 04–67–60–19–99) performs in the very imposing Opéra-Comédie on place de la Comédie. For rousing student hangouts, head to **place Jean-Jaurès**.

THE MIDI-PYRÉNÉES & THE LANGUEDOC-ROUSSILLON A TO Z

To research prices, get advice from other travelers, and book travel arrangements, visit www.fodors.com.

AIR TRAVEL

CARRIERS Air France has regular flights between Paris and Toulouse; Montpellier is served by frequent flights from Paris and London. Be sure to check out Ryanair, EasyJet, and Buzz, who offer surprisingly cheap flights to Perpignan, Montpellier, or Toulouse—often as low as €30 one way.
🛈 **Airlines & Contacts Air France** ☎ 08-20-82-08-20 ⊕ www.airfrance.com. **Buzz** ☎ 01-55-17-42-42. **Easy Jet** ☎ 08-25-08-25-08 ⊕ www.easyjet.com. **Ryanair** ☎ 08-92-55-56-66 ⊕ www.ryanair.com.

AIRPORTS

All international flights for Toulouse arrive at Blagnac Airport, a 20-minute drive from the center of the city. Airport shuttles run regularly (every half hour between 8:15 AM and 8:45 PM) from the airport to the bus station in Toulouse (at the train station; fare €4) and also at 9:20 PM, 10 PM, and 10:45 PM. From the Toulouse bus station to the airport, buses leave every half hour 5:30 AM–8:30 PM.
🛈 **Airport Information Airport Montpellier-Méditerranée** ☎ 04-67-20-85-00. **Airport Perpignan-Rivesaltes** ☎ 04-68-52-60-70. **Airport Béziers-Vias** ☎ 04-67-90-99-10. **Blagnac Airport** ☎ 05-61-42-44-00.

BUS TRAVEL

As in most rural regions in France, there's an array of bus companies (in addition to SNCF buses, Intercars, Semvat, Courriers du Midi, Salt Autocars, among others) threading the Midi-Pyrénées countryside; be sure to stop in the bigger tourist offices on your route to inquire in advance for detailed bus schedules and advice on which bus routes to use for your sightseeing itinerary. Toulouse's bus links include Albi, Auch, Castres, Foix, and Montauban; Albi connects with Cordes-sur-Ciel (summer only) and Montauban; Montauban with Moissac and Auch; Montpellier with Béziers. For Courriers Catalans and Car Inter 66 buses to the Côte Vermeille, Collioure, Céret, and Prades, depart from Perpignan. Everyone says you should take the train to Carcassonne, although buses do head there.

🚍 Bus Information Montpellier Gare Routière ☎ 04-67-92-01-43. Toulouse Gare Routière ☎ 05-61-61-67-67.

CAR RENTAL

🚍 Local Agencies Avis ✉ 13 bd. Conflent, Perpignan ☎ 04-68-34-26-71 ✉ Blagnac Airport, Toulouse ☎ 05-61-30-04-94. **Budget** ✉ Montpellier train station ☎ 04-67-92-69-00. **Hertz** ✉ Pl. Lagarrasic, Auch ☎ 05-62-05-26-26 ✉ 5 av. Chamier, Montauban ☎ 05-63-20-29-00 ✉ 18 rue Jules Ferry, Montpellier ☎ 04-67-58-65-18.

CAR TRAVEL

The fastest route from Paris to Toulouse (700 km [435 mi] southwest) is via Bordeaux on A10, then A62; the journey time is about nine hours. If you choose to head south over the Pyrénées to Barcelona, the Tunnel du Puymorens saves half an hour of switchbacks between Hospitalet and Porta, but in good weather and with time to spare the drive over the Puymorens Pass is spectacular. Plan on taking three hours between Toulouse and Font-Romeu and another three to Barcelona. The fastest route from Toulouse to Barcelona is the four-hour, 421-km (253-mi) drive via Carcassonne and Perpignan on A61 and A9, which becomes AP7 at Le Perthus.

A62/A61 slices through the region on its way through Carcassonne to the coast at Narbonne, where A9 heads south to Perpignan. At Toulouse, where A62 becomes A61, various highways fan out in all directions: N124 to Auch; N117/E80 to St-Gaudens, Tarbes, and Pau; A62/N20 to Montauban and Cahors; N20 south to Foix and the Ariège Valley; N88 to Albi and Rodez. A9 (La Languedocienne) is the main highway artery that connects Montpellier with Beziers to the south and Nîmes to the north.

MUSIC FESTIVALS

Fifty music festivals a year take place in the smaller towns throughout the region; the Comité Régional du Tourisme (CRT) and larger tourist offices can provide a list of dates and addresses. For complete musical information contact the Délégation Musicale Régionale.

🎵 Délégation Musicale Régionale ✉ 56 rue du Taur, 31080 Toulouse ☎ 05-61-29-21-00.

SPORTS & THE OUTDOORS

For information on canoeing or kayaking, contact the Ligue de Canoë-Kayak. For information on hiking or horseback riding, contact the Comité de Randonnées Midi-Pyrénées. Local tourist offices also have detailed maps of more than 3,220 km (2,000 mi) of marked trails. The Comité Regional du Tourisme du Languedoc-Roussillon publishes a brochure on golf courses in the area and sells a pass honored at 14 courses.

🚣 Canoeing, Kayaking & Rafting Canoë-Kayak Toulousain ✉ Ile du Ramier, 18 Chemin des Loges, 31000 Toulouse ☎ 05-61-55-30-80.

🪧 **Hiking** Comité de Randonnées Midi-Pyrénées (CORAMIP) ✉ 4 rue Berry, 31000 Toulouse ☎ 05-61-40-81-59. For hiking and tours of the Cathar country with an expert medievalist, contact **Ingrid Sparbier** ✉ La Fermette, 09500 Rieucross (near Mirepoix) ☎ 05-61-68-29-14.

TOURS

Contact the Toulouse tourist office for information about walking tours and bus tours in and around Toulouse. Ask for the English-speaking, encyclopedic, and superbly entertaining Gilbert Casagrande for a non-pareil tour of Toulouse. The Comité Régional du Tourisme has a brochure, "1,001 Escapes in the Midi-Pyrénées," with descriptions of weekends and short organized package vacations.

In addition to publishing map itineraries that you can follow yourself, the **Montpellier tourist office** (☎ 04-67-60-60-60) provides guided walking tours of the city's neighborhoods and monuments daily in summer and on Wednesday and Saturday during the school year (roughly, September–June). They leave from the place de la Comédie. There are also **horse-drawn carriage tours** (☎ 04-67-60-60-60 information) between the square and the Esplanade Charles de Gaulle; you can go for 15 minutes up to an hour and a half. A small **tourist train** (☎ 04-67-60-60-60 information) with broadcast commentary leaves from the Esplanade between 2 and 9, Monday through Saturday.

🪧 **Comité Régional du Tourisme (CRT)** ✉ 54 bd. de l'Embouchure, 31200 Toulouse ☎ 05-61-13-55-55. **Montpellier** ✉ 30 allée Jean de Lattre de Tassigny, Esplanade Comédie ☎ 04-67-60-60-60. **Toulouse tourist office** ✉ Donjon du Capitole ☎ 05-61-11-02-22 ⊕ www.ot-toulouse.fr.

TRAIN TRAVEL

The regional French rail network in the southwest provides regular service to many towns, though not all. Béziers is linked by train to Carcassonne, Perpignan, Narbonne, and Montpellier, as well as Paris (but via slow trains that take hours, not via TGVs). There's no train service to Pézenas, Minerve, and St-Guilhem. Most trains for the southwest leave from Paris's Gare d'Austerlitz. There are direct trains to Toulouse, Carcassonne, and Montauban. For Rodez, change in Brive, and for Auch, in Toulouse. Seven trains leave Paris (Gare de Lyon) daily for Narbonne and Perpignan; a change at Montpellier is often necessary. Most of these trips take between six or seven hours. Note that at least three high-speed TGV (Trains à Grande Vitesse) per day leave Paris (Gare Montparnasse) for Toulouse; the journey time is five hours. A TGV line also serves Montpellier.

Within the Midi-Pyrénées region, Toulouse is the biggest hub, with a major line linking Carcassonne, Béziers, Narbonne (change here for Perpignan), and Montpellier; trains also link up with Albi and Montauban; the latter connects with Moissac. Montpellier connects with Carcassonne, Perpignan, Narbonne, Béziers, and other towns.

🪧 **Train Information** SNCF ☎ 08-36-35-35-35 ⊕ www.ter-sncf.com/languedoc/default_uk.asp.

TRAVEL AGENCIES

⚑ Local Agent Referrals Havas ✉ 2 pl. de la Comédie, Montpellier ☏ 04-67-91-31-70 ✉ 73 rue d'Alsace-Lorraine, Toulouse ☏ 05-61-23-16-35. **Carlson Wagonlit** ✉ Voyages Dépêche, 42 bis rue d'Alsace-Lorraine, Toulouse ☏ 05-62-15-42-70.

VISITOR INFORMATION

The regional tourist office for the Midi-Pyrénées is the Comité Régional du Tourisme. For Pyrénées-Roussillon information, contact the Comité Départemental de Tourisme. For the Languedoc-Roussillon contact the Comité Régional du Tourisme du Languedoc-Roussillon. Local tourist offices are listed by town below. Other handy Web sites for the regions in this chapter include www.audetourisme.com and www.tourisme-tarn.com.

⚑ Tourist Information Comité Régional du Tourisme (CRT) ✉ 54 bd. de l'Embouchure, 31200 Toulouse ☏ 05-61-13-55-55. **Comité Départemental de Tourisme** ✉ Quai de Lattre de Tassigny, B.P. 540, 66005 Perpignan ☏ 04-68-34-29-94. **Comité Régional du Tourisme du Languedoc-Roussillon** ✉ 20 rue de la République, 34000 Montpellier ☏ 04-67-22-81-00 🖷 04-67-58-06-10 ⊕ www.cr-languedocroussillon.fr/tourisme. **Albi** ✉ Pl. Ste-Cécile ☏ 05-63-49-48-80 ⊕ www.mairie-albi.fr. **Auch** ✉ 1 rue Dessoles ☏ 05-62-05-22-89. **Béziers** ✉ Palais des Congrès, 29 av. St-Saëns ☏ 04-67-76-47-00. **Carcassonne** ✉ 15 bd. Camille-Pelletan ☏ 04-68-25-07-04 ⊕ www.carcassonne.org. **Céret** ✉ 1 bd. Clemenceau ☏ 04-68-87-00-53 ⊕ www.ot-ceret.fr. **Collioure** ✉ Pl. 18-juin ☏ 04-68-82-15-47 ⊕ www.collioure.com. **Cordes-sur-Ciel** ✉ Maison Fonpeyrouse ☏ 05-63-56-00-52. **Eyne** ✉ Eyne Station ☏ 04-68-04-08-01. **Fleurance** ✉ 2 pl. de la République ☏ 05-62-64-00-00. **Foix** ✉ 45 Cours G.-Fauré ☏ 05-61-65-12-12. **Font-Romeu** ✉ Av. E. Brousse ☏ 05-68-30-68-30. **Larressingle** ✉ Syndicat D'Initiative ☏ 05-62-28-37-02. **Lectoure** ✉ Pl. de l'Église ☏ 05-62-68-76-98. **Minerve** ✉ Pl. du Monument aux Morts ☏ 04-68-91-81-43. **Mirepoix** ✉ Pl. Mar.-Leclerc ☏ 05-61-68-83-76. **Montauban** ⊕ Ancien College, B.P. 201 ☏ 05-63-63-60-60 ⊕ www.montauban.com/. **Moissac** ✉ 6 pl. Durand de Bredon ☏ 05-63-04-01-85. **Mont-Louis** ✉ Rue Vauban ☏ 04-68-04-21-97. **Montpellier** ✉ 30 allée Jean de Lattre de Tassigny, Esplanade Comédie ☏ 04-67-60-60-60 ⊕ www.ot-montpellier.fr. **Narbonne** ✉ Pl. Roger-Salengro ☏ 04-68-65-15-60. **Perpignan** ✉ Quai de Lattre de Tassigny ☏ 04-68-66-30-30. **Pézenas** ✉ 1 pl. Gambetta ☏ 04-67-98-36-40 ⊕ www.perpignantourisme.com. **Prades** ✉ 4 rue Victor-Hugo ☏ 04-68-05-41-02. **St-Guilhem-le-Désert** ✉ 2 rue de la Font du Portal ☏ 04-67-57-44-33. **Toulouse** ✉ Donjon du Capitole ☏ 05-61-11-02-22 ⊕ www.ot-toulouse.fr. **Villefranche-de-Conflent** ✉ Pl. de l'Eglise ☏ 05-62-64-00-00.

The Basque Country, Gascony & Hautes-Pyrénées

15

WORD OF MOUTH

"St-Jean-de-Luz in the extreme southwest corner is lovely, and the Basque countryside is as well. Further east is Pau, a less-touristy city with nice restaurants and a château worthy of a visit (the birthplace of Henry IV). Any of the roads into the mountain passes of the Pyrénées is worth a trip for the gorgeous mountain scenery."

—Bob

"We drove from Lourdes to the fabulous little village of Gavarnie in just over an hour. It was a beautiful drive. There are some lovely little inns there, perfect for a mountain holiday. Do walk up to the Cirque de Gavarnie, an awesome circle of waterfalls."

—Keldar

Introduction by
George Semler

Updated by
George Semler

A PELOTA-PLAYING MAYOR IN THE PROVINCE OF SOULE recently welcomed a group of travelers with the following announcements: that the Basque Country is the most beautiful place in the world; that the Basque people were very likely direct descendants of Adam and Eve via the lost city of Atlantis; that his own ancestors fought in the Crusades; and that Christopher Columbus was almost certainly a Basque. There, in brief, was a composite picture of the pride, dignity, and humor of the Basques. And if Columbus was not a Basque (a claim very much in doubt), at least historians know that whalers from the regional village of St-Jean-de-Luz sailed as far as America in their three-masted ships and that Juan Sebastián Elkano, from the Spanish Basque village of Guetaria, was one of those intrepid adventurers who accompanied Magellan on his voyage around the world.

The distinctive culture—from berets and pelota matches to Basque cooking—of this little "country" straddling the French and Spanish Pyrénées has cast its spell over the corners of the earth. And continues to do so—just witness the best-seller status of Mark Kurlansky's *The Basque History of the World* several years ago. Today travelers bruised by the crowding and commerce of more frequented parts of France are increasingly heading to this southwest region to enjoy its relatively undiscovered panoply of rich cultures and landscapes. In an easy stretch, a midsummer's day begun surfing in Biarritz could end at sunset glacier skiing at the Brèche de Roland above Gavarnie. The ocher sands along the Bay of Biscay and the bright reds and blues of the St-Jean-de-Luz fishing fleet are less than an hour from the emerald hills of St-Jean-Pied-de-Port in the Basque Pyrénées. Atlantic salmon and native Pyrenean trout still thrive in the River Nive, while puffball sheep tumble about in the moist highland pastures.

Center stage is held by the three Pays Basque provinces—Labourd, Soule, and Basse Navarre—which share with their four cousin Basque provinces in Spain a singular culture including: jai alai, whaleboat regattas, stone lifting, world-famous cuisine, as well as a mysterious and ancient non-Indo-European language. The origins of this culture remain obscure. The purported resemblance of the Basque evening (or war) call, the *irrinzina,* to that of the Upper Amazon Indians only adds to the mystery, as does the common use by both the Basques and the ancient Mayans of base 20 to reckon math. Some trace Basque origins back to the Berbers of North Africa, though the most tenable theory is that they are descended from aboriginal Iberian peoples who successfully defended their unique language and cultural identity from the influences of Roman and Moorish domination felt elsewhere on the peninsula.

At the eastern edge of the Basque Country, the ski and spelunking town of Pierre-St-Martin marks the start of the Béarn, with its splendid capital city of Pau and the pristine valleys of Aspe, Ossau, and Barétous descending from the Pyrénées. Sauveterre-de-Béarn's medieval drawbridge, Navarrenx and its *bastide* over the rushing Gave d'Oloron, and the Romanesque and Mudejar Ste-Croix church at Oloron-Ste-Marie provide stepping-stones into the limestone heights surrounding the 8,263-foot Pic d'Anie, the highest point in the Béarn.

15

The Basque Country boasts some of France's most dramatic natural extremes: from Atlantic beaches and lush, green pre-Pyrenean hills to the Béarn's rolling meadows and rushing trout and salmon streams, to the lofty heights of the Hautes-Pyrénées and their greatest marvel—the sheer granite walls of La Cirque de Gavarnie. Whether you head for Bay of Biscay resorts like Biarritz, picturesque villages like St-Jean-de-Luz, or the towering peaks of the central Pyrenean cordillera, you will discover some of France's most fascinating man-made and natural wonders in these parts. Consider Dax and Eugénie-les-Bains as excellent side trips to the basic itinerary outlined here. Begin in Bayonne, exploring the Basque coast, and then head east into the Atlantic Pyrénées.

Numbers in the text correspond to numbers in the margin and on the Basque Country & the Hautes-Pyrénées maps.

If you have 3 days

There is nothing leisurely about this three-day tour, nor is there time to do much walking, which is why it is recommended only if your time is limited and your curiosity unlimited. Begin in **Bayonne** ❶ �, spending a morning exploring the town. See the cathedral and the Bonnat Museum before hitting **Biarritz** ❷— still redolent with Belle Époque *parfum*—in time for afternoon tea. Spend the night in 🏨 **St-Jean-de-Luz** ❸, famed for its picturesque fishing port. On Day 2 drive through **Sare** ❹, studded with Basque architecture, and relentlessly pretty **Ainhoa** ❺ and past **Pas de Roland** ❻ on the way up the Nive River to the fortified town of **St-Jean-Pied-de-Port** ❼ for lunch. Explore the Haute Soule during the afternoon: drive through the Irati Forest to the hiker's paradise of **Larrau** ❽ and **Ste-Engrâce** ❿, noted for its Basque-style church, on the way through **Oloron-Ste-Marie** ⓬ to the Béarn's capital, 🏨 **Pau** ⓯, where you should overnight. On Day 3 have a look around Pau, see the great shrine-church of **Lourdes** ⓲ at midday, and get up to 🏨 **Gavarnie** ⓴ in time to see the sun set from the legendary Hôtel du Cirque et de la Cascade.

If you have 8 days

Begin in 🏨 **Bayonne** ❶ �, spending a morning exploring the town. See the cathedral and the Bonnat Museum. The second day head back to the coast at soigné **Biarritz** ❷ for some time at the beach. Spend the night in the fetching harbor town of 🏨 **St-Jean-de-Luz** ❸. On Day 3 climb La Rhune (or take the little train to the top) for a stunning view over the entire Basque coast. Drive through **Sare** ❹ and **Ainhoa** ❺ and past **Pas de Roland** ❻ on the way up the Nive River to spend the night at 🏨 **St-Jean-Pied-de-Port** ❼. Explore the town and the Haute Soule on your fourth morning: drive through the Irati Forest to 🏨 **Larrau** ❽ and do the Holçarté Gorges walk to 🏨 **Ste-Engrâce** ❿ if there is time; return to Larrau if not. On Day 5 explore the lower Soule, **Oloron-Ste-Marie** ⓬, and 🏨 **Pau** ⓯. On Day 6 walk around Pau, tour the château, then head up to 🏨 **Eugénie-les-Bains** ⓰ and the fabulous domains created by superstar restaurateur-hotelier Michel Guéard. After a day and night of blissful *luxe, calme, et volupté*, it will be time, on the seventh day, to check out your more spiritual side in **Lourdes** ⓲. Then make the ascent to 🏨 **Gavarnie** ⓴ in time to see the sun set from the Hôtel du Cirque et de la Cascade. On Day 8 explore the area around Gavarnie.

East through the Aubisque Pass, at the Béarn's eastern limit, is the heart of the Hautes-Pyrénées, where France's highest Pyrenean peaks—Vignemale (10,820 feet) and Balaïtous (10,321 feet)—compete with other legendary natural treasures. The Cirque de Gavarnie, the world's most spectacular cirque (or natural amphitheater), is centered around a 1,400-foot waterfall. The nearby Brèche de Roland is a dramatic breach, or cleft, in the rock wall between France and Spain, while to the east, the Cirque de Troumouse is the largest of its kind in all the Pyrénées. When you get your fill of mountaintop vistas and Basque peaks, you can head to the regional spa towns and coastal cities, whose tony refinements once lured the crowned heads of Europe. It was Empress Eugénie who gave Biarritz its coming-out party, transforming it, in the era of Napoléon III, from a simple bourgeois town into an international favorite. Today, after a round of sightseeing, you can still enjoy the Second Empire trimmings from a perch at the roulette table in the town's casino.

Exploring the Basque Country, Gascony & Hautes-Pyrénées

From the lazy, sandy sea level around Bayonne, Biarritz, and St. Jean-de-Luz, this southwest tag end of the Pyrénées hops suddenly up to La Rhune (3,000 feet) and from there it's ever higher, through lush green hills of the inland Basque and Béarn countries past the 6,617-foot Pic d'Orhy to the 6,700-foot Vignemale peak just west of Gavarnie and its historically famous Cirque. Bayonne and Pau are the urban and cultural centers anchoring and connecting these lofty highlands to the rest of France, while the Basque, Béarn, Gascon, and Bigorre cultures offer linguistic as well as culinary variety as you meander eastward and upward from the Basque coast. Gascony is the realm bordered by the Bay of Biscay to the west, the Pyrénées to the south, and the Garonne River to the north and east—pretty Pau is the main city in the region, which sweeps south past Lourdes to Cauterets. Whether you approach from the Atlantic or the Mediterranean, you won't want to miss these beauty spots: Gavarnie, Ste-Engrâce, St-Jean-Pied-de-Port, Sauveterre-de-Béarn, Ainhoa, or St-Jean-de-Luz. Trans-Pyrenean hikers (and drivers) generally prefer moving from west to east for a number of reasons, especially the excellent light prevailing in the late afternoon and evening during the prime months of May to October.

About the Restaurants & Hotels

As with expensive bottles of wine, the point of diminishing returns in Basque dining arrives in a hurry, the local cuisine nearly always more satisfying in simple environments where the fare always seems better than it has any right to be. Once described as "essentially the art of cooking fish," the Basque coast's traditional fresh seafood is unsurpassable every day of the week except Monday, the fleet having stayed in port on Sunday. The inland Basque country and upland Béarn is famous for game in fall and winter and lambs in spring. In the Hautes-Pyrénées, the higher altitude makes power dining attractive and thick bean soups and wild boar stews come into their own.

15

Attention Hike-a-holics

Supping on the hearty regional cuisine makes perfect sense after a day of hiking along the gorges and into the mountains of the Pyrénées, which are best explored on foot. The lengthy GR (Grande Randonnée) 10, a trail signed by discreet red-and-white paint markings, runs all the way from the Atlantic at Hendaye to Banyuls-sur-Mer on the Mediterranean, through villages and up and down mountains. Placed along the way are mountain refuges. The HRP (Haute Randonnée Pyrénéenne, or High Pyrenean Hike) stays closer to the border crest, following the terrain of both France and Spain irrespective of national borders. Local trails are also well indicated, usually with blue or yellow markings. Some of the classic walks in the Basque Pyrénées include the Iparla Ridge walk between Bidarrai and St-Étienne-de-Baïgorry, the Santiago de Compostela Trail's dramatic St-Jean-Pied-de-Port to Roncesvalles walk over the Pyrénées, and the Holçarté Gorge walk between Larrau and Ste-Engrâce. Trail maps are available from local tourist offices.

Gonzo over Games

Perhaps the best-known and most spectacular of Basque sports is the ancestral ball game of pelota, a descendant of the medieval *jeux de paume* (literally, palm games), a fundamental element of rural Basque culture. A Basque village without a fronton (backboard and pelota court) is as unimaginable as an American town lacking a baseball diamond. There are many versions and variations on this graceful, fast-paced sport, played with the bare hand, with wooden bats, or with curved basketlike gloves; a real wicker *chistera*—the wicker bat used in the game—is an interesting souvenir to buy (and makes a very pretty fruit basket, but let no Basque hear that bit of heresy). Other rural Basque sports include scything, wood-chopping and -sawing, sack hauling, stone lifting, long-distance racing, tug-of-war, competitive whaleboat rowing, and, for those who really want to take the weight of the world on their shoulders, *orga yoko*, or cart lifting—hefting and moving a 346-kilo (761-pound) hay wagon (you read it here).

La Cuisine de Pays Basque

Dining in the regions of the Basque country is invariably a feast, whether it's on seafood or upland dishes ranging from beef to lamb to game birds such as the famous migratory *palombes* (wood pigeons). Dishes to keep in mind include *ttoro* (hake stew), *pipérade* (tomatoes and green peppers cooked in olive oil, and often scrambled eggs), *bakalao al pil-pil* (cod cooked in oil "*al pil-pil*"—the bubbling sound the fish makes as it creates its own sauce), *marmitako* (tuna and potato stew), and *zikiro* (roast lamb). Home of the famous *sauce béarnaise*, Béarn is famous for its *garbure*, thick vegetable soup with *confit de canard* (preserved duck) and *fèves* (broad beans). *Civets* (stews) made with *isard* (wild goat) or wild boar are other specialties. La Bigorre and the Hautes-Pyrénées are equally dedicated to garbure, though they may call their version *soupe paysanne bigourdane* (Bigorran peasant soup) to distinguish it from that of their neighbors.

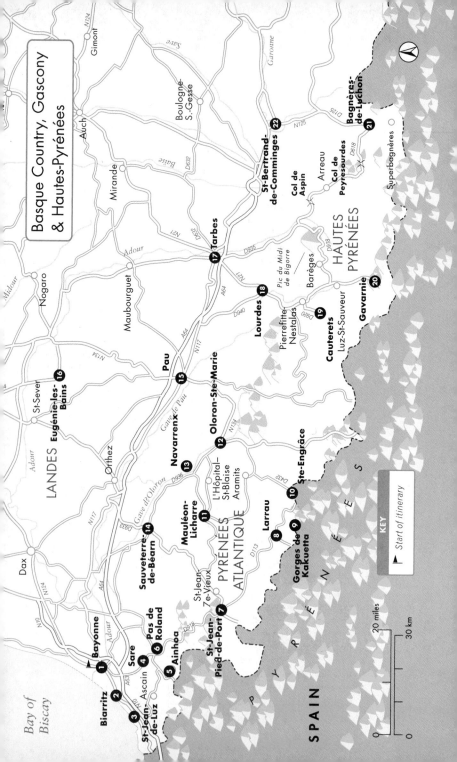

Basque Country, Gascony & Hautes-Pyrénées

Bay of Biscay

LANDES

PYRÉNÉES ATLANTIQUE

HAUTES PYRÉNÉES

SPAIN

KEY

▲ *Start of itinerary*

20 miles

30 km

Gimont
Auch
Mirande
Nogaro
St-Sever
Dax
Orthez
Maubourguet
Pau
Tarbes
Boulogne-S.-Gesse
St-Bertrand-de-Comminges
Arreau
Col d'Aspin
Col de Peyresourdes
Bagnères-de-Luchon
Superbagnères
Pic du Midi de Bigorre
Barèges
Luz-St-Sauveur
Gavarnie
Cauterets
Pierrefitte-Nestalas
Lourdes
Oloron-Ste-Marie
Navarrenx
L'Hôpital-St-Blaise
Aramits
Mauléon-Licharre
Sauveterre-de-Béarn
St-Jean-le-Vieux
St-Jean-Pied-de-Port
Larrau
Ste-Engrâce
Gorges de Kakuetta
Pas de Roland
Ainhoa
Sare
St-Jean-de-Luz
Ascain
Biarritz
Bayonne
Eugénie-les-Bains

① Bayonne
② Biarritz
③ St-Jean-de-Luz
④ Sare
⑤ Ainhoa
⑥ Pas de Roland
⑦ St-Jean-Pied-de-Port
⑧
⑨ Gorges de Kakuetta
⑩ Ste-Engrâce
⑪ Mauléon-Licharre
⑫ Oloron-Ste-Marie
⑬
⑭ Sauveterre-de-Béarn
⑮ Pau
⑯ Eugénie-les-Bains
⑰ Tarbes
⑱ Lourdes
⑲ Cauterets
⑳ Gavarnie
㉑ Bagnères-de-Luchon
㉒ St-Bertrand-de-Comminges

From palatial beachside splendor in Biarritz to simple mountain auberges in the Basque Country to Pyrenean refuges in the Hautes-Pyrénées, the gamut of lodging in southwest France is conveniently broad. For top value and camaraderie, look for *gîtes* or *tables d'hôtes* (rustic bed-and-breakfasts and way stations for hikers and skiers), where all guests dine together. Be sure to book summertime lodging on the Basque coast well in advance, particularly for August. In the Hautes-Pyrénées only Gavarnie during its third-week-of-July music festival presents a potential booking problem. An even better approach is to make it up as you go: the surprises that come along are usually very pleasant. Assume all hotel rooms have air-conditioning, TV, telephones, and private bath, unless otherwise noted.

WHAT IT COSTS In euros					
	$$$$	**$$$**	**$$**	**$**	**¢**
RESTAURANTS	over €25	€17–€25	€12–€17	€8–€12	under €8
HOTELS	over €175	€120–€175	€70–€120	€40–€70	under €40

Restaurant prices are per person for a main course at dinner, including tax (19.6%) and service; note that if a restaurant offers only prix-fixe (set-price) meals, it has been given the price category that reflects the full prix-fixe price. Hotel prices are for a standard double room in high season, including tax (19.6%) and service charge. Hotels operate on the European Plan (EP, with no meal provided) unless we note that they use the Breakfast Plan (BP), or also offer such options as Modified American Plan (MAP, with breakfast and dinner daily, known as *demi-pension*), or Full American Plan (FAP, or *pension complète*, with three meals a day). Inquire when booking if these all-inclusive mealplans (which always entail higher rates) are mandatory or optional.

Timing

From early May through late October is the best time to explore this region. June and September are the height of the season. July is the only month you can be nearly 100% sure of being to able to, say, walk safely over the glacier to the Brèche de Roland. In winter, beach life is over and the Pyrénées are snowed in; many hotels and restaurants close. Only for skiing and the pleasure of the nearly total absence of tourists is the winter season recommended.

THE BASQUE COAST

La Côte Basque—a world unto itself with its own language, sports, and folklore—occupies France's southwesternmost corner along the Spanish border. Inland, the area is laced with rivers: the Bidasoa River border with Spain marks the southern edge of the region, and the Adour River, on its northern edge, separates the Basque country from the neighboring Les Landes. The Nive River flows through the heart of the verdant Basque littoral to join the Adour at Bayonne, and the smaller Nivelle River flows into the Bay of Biscay at St-Jean-de-Luz. Bayonne, Biarritz, and St-Jean-de-Luz are the main towns along the coast, all less than 40 km (25 mi) from the first peak of the Pyrénées.

Bayonne

1 *48 km (30 mi) southwest of Dax, 184 km (114 mi) south of Bordeaux, 295 km (183 mi) west of Toulouse.*

At the confluence of the Adour and Nive rivers, Bayonne, France's most indelibly Basque city, was in the 4th century a Roman fort, or *castrum,* and for 300 years (1151–1451) a British colony. Source of the name of the bayonet blade (from the French *baïonnette*), invented here in the 17th century, today's Bayonne is more famous for its ham (*jambon de Bayonne*) and for the annual Basque pelota world championships held in September. Even though the port is spread out along the Adour estuary some 5 km (3 mi) from the sea, the two rivers and five bridges lend this small gem of a city a definite maritime feel. The houses fronting the quai, the intimate place Pasteur, the Château-Vieux, the elegant 18th-century homes along rue des Prébendés, the 17th-century ramparts, and the cathedral are some of the town's not-to-be-missed sights. The Les Halles market in the Place des Halles on the left bank of the Nive is also a must visit. The **Cathédrale** (called both Ste-Marie and Notre-Dame) was built mainly in the 13th century, and is one of France's southernmost examples of Gothic architecture. Its 13th- to 14th-century cloisters are among its best features. The airy, modernized **Musée Bonnat,** in itself reason enough to visit Bayonne, has a notable treasury of 19th-century paintings collected by French portraitist and historical painter Léon Bonnat (1833–1922). ✉ *5 rue Jacques-Lafitte* ☎ *05–59–59–08–52* 🌐 *www.musee-bonnat.com* *€5.50* ⏲ *May–Oct., Wed.–Mon. 10–6; Nov.–Apr., Wed.–Mon. 10–12:30 and 2–6.*

The handsomely designed and appointed **Musée Basque** on the right bank of the Nive offers an ethnographic history of the Basque country and culture. ✉ *37 quai des Corsaires* ☎ *05–59–46–61–90* *€5.50* ⏲ *Tues.–Sun. 10–12:30 and 2–6 (ticket window closes 1 hr before closing time).*

Where to Stay & Eat

★ $$$–$$$$ ✕ **L'Auberge du Cheval Blanc.** This innovative Basque establishment in the Petit Bayonne quarter near the Musée Bonnat serves a combination of *cuisine du terroir* (home-style regional cooking) and original concoctions in contemporary surroundings. Jean-Claude Tellechea showcases fresh fish as well as upland specialties from the Basque hills, sometimes joining the two in groundbreaking dishes such as the *merlu rôti aux oignons et jus de volaille* (hake roasted in onions with essence of poultry). The local Irouléguy wines offer the best value on the wine list. ✉ *68 rue Bourgneuf* ☎ *05–59–59–01–33* ▭ *MC, V* ⏲ *Closed Mon. (except Aug.), June 25–July 2, and Feb. 10–Mar. 8. No dinner Sun.*

$$–$$$ ✕ **Le Grand Hôtel.** Just down the street from the Château-Vieux, this central spot has pleasant, comfortable rooms with an old-world feel. The restaurant, Les Carmes, built in a former Carmelite convent, is excellent. ✉ *21 rue Thiers, 64100* ☎ *05–59–59–62–00* 🖷 *05–59–59–62–01* 🌐 *www.bw-legrandhotel.com* *54 rooms* *Restaurant, minibars, cable TV, bar, parking (fee), some pets allowed (fee)* ▭ *AE, DC, MC, V* *MAP.*

Biarritz

②

8 km (5 mi) south of Bayonne, 190 km (118 mi) southwest of Bordeaux, 50 km (31 mi) north of San Sebastián, 115 km (69 mi) west of Pau.

Once a favorite resort of Charlie Chaplin, Coco Chanel, and exiled Russian royals, Biarritz first rose to prominence when rich and royal Carlist exiles from Spain set up shop here in 1838. Unable to visit San Sebastián just across the border on the Basque coast, they sought a summer watering spot as close as possible to their old stomping ground. Among the exiles was Eugénie de Montijo, soon destined to become empress of France. As a child, she vacationed here with her family, fell in love with the place, and then set about building her own palace once she married Napoléon III. During the 14 summers she spent here, half the crowned heads of Europe—including Queen Victoria and Edward VII—were her guests in Eugénie's villa, a gigantic wedding-cake edifice, now the **Hôtel du Palais,** set on the main sea promenade of town, the **quai de la Grande Plage,** where the fashionable set used to stroll in Worth gowns and picture hats. Whether you consider Napoléon III's bombastic architectural legacies an eyesore or an eyeful, they at least have the courage of their convictions. Biarritz may no longer lay claim to the title "the resort of kings and the king of resorts," however, today, there is no shortage of deluxe hotel rooms or bow-tie gamblers ambling over to the casino. Unfortunately, the old, down-to-earth charm of the former fishing village has been thoroughly trumped by Biarritz's glitzy Second Empire aura, although you won't find the bathing beauties and high-rollers here complaining.

Far from as drop-dead stylish as it once was, the town is making a comeback as a swank surfing capital with its new casino and convention center. But if you are here to explore yesteryear Biarritz, start by exploring the narrow streets around the cozy 16th-century church of **St-Martin.** Adjacent to the Grand Plage are the set-pieces of the Hôtel du Palais and the **Eglise Orthodoxe Russe,** a Byzantine-style church built by the White Russian community that considered Biarritz their 19th-century Yalta-by-the-Atlantic. The duchesses often repaired to the terraced restaurants of the festive **place Ste-Eugénie,** still considered the social center of town. A lorgnette view away is the harbor of the **Port des Pêcheurs** (Fishing Port), which provides a tantalizing glimpse of the Biarritz of old. Leading off the port is the plateau de l'Atalaye, where you can head through a tunnel to a Gustave Eiffel–designed footbridge and the **Rocher de la Vierge** (Rock of the Virgin). Her sculpted figure has blessed sailors in the Bay of Biscay since 1865. Enjoy the spectacular vista of the coast from the Rocher, then return to town. Biarritz's beaches attract crowds—particularly the fine, sandy beaches of **La Grande Plage** and the neighboring **Plage Miramar,** both set amid craggy natural beauty. A walk along the beach promenades gives a view of the foaming breakers that beat constantly upon the sands, giving the name Côte d'Argent (Silver Coast) to the length of this part of the French Basque coast.

★ If you wish to pay your respects to the Empress Eugénie, visit **La Chapelle Impérriale,** which she had built in 1864 to venerate a figure of a Mexican Black Virgin from Guadelupe (and perhaps to expiate her sins for furthering her husband's tragic folly of putting Emperor Maximilian and Empress Carlotta on the "throne" of Mexico). The style is a charming hybrid of Roman-Byzantine and Hispano-Mauresque. ⊠ *Rue Pellot* ☉ *Apr. 15–July 15, Sept. 16–Oct. 15, Mon., Tues., Sat. 3–7; July 16–Sept. 15, Mon.–Sat. 3–5; Oct. 15–Dec. 31, Sat. 3–5.*

Where to Stay & Eat

$–$$$$ ✗ **Chez Albert.** In summer it's nearly impossible to find a place on the terrace of this easygoing and popular seafood restaurant. Views of the fishing port and the salty harborside aromas of things maritime make the hearty fish and seafood offerings all the more irresistible here. ⊠ *Port des Pêcheurs s/n* ☎ *05–59–24–43–84* ▭ *AE, DC, MC, V* ☉ *Closed Dec. 1–15, Jan. 5–10, Feb., and Wed. except July and Aug.*

★ **$$$$** ✗▥ **Château de Brindos.** Take Jazz Age glamour, Spanish Gothic and Renaissance stonework, and the luxest of guest rooms and you have this Pays Basque Xanadu—a large, rambling, white-stone manor topped with a Spanish belvedere tower set 4 km (2½ mi) east of Biarritz in Anglet. This was originally the home of Sir Reginald Wright, whose great soirées held here in the 1920s and '30s are conjured up in the saloon, now presided over by that premier mixologist, barman Marc Pony. In recent years, interiors have been lovingly restored by Serge Blanco, who has managed to honor the mansion's history while installing state-of-the-art technology and comfort. Tapestries, wrought-iron Spanish wall sconces, Louis Quatorze–style armchairs, and dramatic stone fireplaces all dazzle the eye, as do views of the estate's private lake from guest rooms rife with quilted fabrics, overstuffed chaise-longues, and a general air of Baudelairean *luxe, calme, et volupté.* In summer dine out under the willows at the edge of the water at the grand restaurant. Chef Antoine Antunès has trained with the best, from Guerard to Arrambide, and offers a guarantee of creative dining. ⊠ *1 allée du Château, 64600* ☎ *05–59–23–89–80* ▤ *05–59–23–89–81* ⊕ *www.chateaudebrindos.com* ↪ *24 rooms, 5 suites* ⧄ *Restaurant, minibars, cable TV, pool, bar, meeting rooms, parking (fee), some pets allowed (fee)* ▭ *AE, DC, MC, V* ☉ *Closed 2 wks in winter, dates vary.*

★ **$$$$** ✗▥ **Hôtel du Palais.** Set on the beach, this majestic, colonnaded redbrick hotel with an immense driveway, lawns, and a grand semicircular dining room, still exudes an opulent, aristocratic air, no doubt imparted by Empress Eugénie when she built it in 1855 as her Biarritz palace. Napoleonic frippery is everywhere in the public areas, but don't go looking for it in the more standard guest rooms, none of which have sea views. Still, the lobby alone may be worth the price of admission. The three restaurants—Hippocampe (where lunch is served beside the curved pool above the Atlantic), the regal dinner spot Villa Eugénie, and the La Rotonde (with its spectacular soaring columns, gilt trim, and sea views)—are all creatively directed by star chef Jean-Marie Gautier. Don't miss out on his lobster gazpacho. ⊠ *1 av. de l'Impératrice, 64200* ☎ *05–59–41–64–00* ▤ *05–59–41–67–99* ⊕ *www.hotel-du-palais.com* ↪ *134 rooms, 22 suites* ⧄ *3 restaurants, minibars, cable TV, pool, bar, parking (fee), some pets allowed (fee)* ▭ *AE, DC, MC, V* ☉ *Closed 2 wks in winter, dates vary* ▯◎▯ *MAP.*

$$–$$$ ✕⊡ **Windsor.** This hotel, built in the 1920s, is close to the casino and the beach. Rooms are modern and cozy; those with sea views cost about twice as much as the ones facing the inner courtyard and street. The restaurant serves up a fine terrine de foie gras with Armagnac, and ravioli stuffed with crab. ⊠ *19 bd. du Général-de-Gaulle, 64200* ☎ *05–59–24–08–52* 🖷 *05–59–24–98–90* ⊕ *www.hotelwindsorbiarritz.com* 📞 *48 rooms* ♣ *Restaurant, bar, parking (fee), some pets allowed (fee); no a/c* ⊟ *AE, MC, V* ⊙ *Closed Jan.–mid-Mar.*

$–$$ ⊡ **Hôtel La Romance.** This tiny, early-19th-century villa on a quiet alley near the Hippodrome des Fleurs race track is an intimate refuge, and just a 10-minute walk from downtown Biarritz. Madame Subra takes patient care of everyone here, while the minuscule garden becomes a dappled oasis of serenity during the midsummer Biarritz maelstrom. Quarters are tight but homey. ⊠ *6 allée des Acacias, 64200* ☎ *05–59–41–25–65* 🖷 *05–59–41–25–65* ⊕ *www.touradour.com/hotels/fr/hotels-biarritz. asp* 📞 *10 rooms* ♣ *No a/c* ⊟ *AE, MC, V* ⊙ *Closed mid-Jan.–Mar.*

¢–$ ⊡ **Hôtel Palym.** This excellent budget choice is stationed over a restaurant with a terrace five minutes from the Plage du Port-Vieux. Rooms range from low-end without bath to slightly more expensive with complete in-room bath facilities. The restaurant serves all-you-can-eat paellas in summer, as well as acceptable prix-fixe menus and à la carte selections. ⊠ *7 rue du Port-Vieux, 64200* ☎ *05–59–24–16–56* 🖷 *05–59–24–96–12* ⊕ *www.le-palmarium.com* 📞 *28 rooms, 16 without bath* ♣ *Restaurant, cable TV, bar, some pets allowed (fee); no a/c* ⊟ *AE, MC, V* ⊙ *Closed Dec. 1–15 and Jan. 15–30.*

Nightlife & the Arts

During September, the three-week **Le Temps d'Aimer** festival presents dance performances, from classical to hip-hop, in a range of venues throughout the city. They are often at the Théâtre Gare du Midi, a renovated railway station. Troupes such as the Ballets Biarritz, Les Ballets de Monte-Carlo, and leading etoiles from other companies take to the stage in an ambitious schedule of events. At the **Casino de Biarritz** (⊠ 1 av. Edouard-VII ☎ 05–59–22–77–77) you can play the slots or blackjack, or go dancing at the Flamingo. **Le Queen's Bar** (⊠ 25 pl. Clemenceau ☎ 05–59–24–70–65) is a comfortable hangout both day and night. **Le Caveau** (⊠ 4 rue Gambetta ☎ 05–59–24–16–17) is a mythical Biarritz dance club with guaranteed action every night.

Sports & the Outdoors

France's Atlantic Coast has become one of the hottest surfing destinations in the world. The "Endless Summer" arrives in Biarritz every year in late July for a **Biarritz Surf Festival. Désertours Aventure** (⊠ 65 av. Maréchal-Juin ☎ 05–59–41–22–02) organizes rafting trips on the Nive River and four-wheel-drive-vehicle tours through the Atlantic Pyrénées. **Golf de Biarritz** (⊠ 2 av. Edith-Cavell ☎ 05–59–03–71–80) has an 18-hole, par-69 course. **Pelote Basque: Biarritz Athletic-club** (⊠ Parc des Sports d'Aguilera ☎ 05–59–23–91–09) offers instruction in every type of Basque pelota including *main nue* (bare-handed), *pala* (paddle), *chistera* (with a basketlike racquet) and *cesta punta* (another game played with the same curved basket). On Wednesday and Saturday at 9 PM in

July, August, and September, you can watch pelota games at the **Parc des Sports d'Aguilera** (☎ 05–59–23–91–09).

St-Jean-de-Luz

❸
Fodor'sChoice
★
23 km (16 mi) southwest of Bayonne, 24 km (18 mi) northeast of San Sebastián, 54 km (32 mi) west of St-Jean-Pied-de-Port, 128 km (77 mi) west of Pau.

Back in 1660, Louis XIV chose this tiny fishing village as the place to marry the Infanta Maria Teresa of Spain. Ever since, travelers have journeyed here to enjoy the unique coastal charms of St-Jean. Situated along the coast between Biarritz and the Spanish border, it remains memorable for its colorful harbor, old streets, curious church, and elegant beach. Its iconic port shares a harbor with its sister town Ciboure, on the other side of the Nivelle River. The glorious days of whaling and cod fishing are long gone, but some historic multihue houses around the docks are evocative enough. The tree-lined **place Louis-XIV,** alongside the Hôtel de Ville (Town Hall), with its narrow courtyard and dainty statue of Louis XIV on horseback, is the hub of the town. In summer, concerts are offered on the square, as well as the famous "Toro de fuego" festival, which honors the bull with a parade and a papier-mâché beast. Take a tour of the twin-towered **Maison Louis-XIV.** Built as the Château Lohobiague, it housed the French king during his nuptials and is austerely decorated in 17th-century Basque fashion. ⊠ *Pl. Louis XIV* ☎ *05–59–26–01–56* ☑ *€6* ☉ *July and Aug., daily 10–10; Apr.–June, Sept., and Oct., daily 10:30–noon and 2–6:30; Nov.–Mar., by appointment.*

The marriage of the Sun King and the Infanta took place in 1660 in the church of **St-Jean-Baptiste** (⊠ Pl. des Corsaires). The marriage tied the knot, so to speak, on the Pyrénées Treaty signed by Mazarin on November 7, 1659, ending Spanish hegemony in Europe. Note the church's unusual wooden galleries lining the walls, creating a theaterlike effect. Fittingly, St-Jean-Baptiste hosts a "Musique en Côte Basque" festival of early and Baroque music during the first two weeks of September. The church is open daily from 9 to 6, with a three hour closure for lunch.

Of particular note is the Louis XIII–style **Maison de l'Infante** (Princess's House), between the harbor and the bay, where Maria Teresa of Spain, accompanied by her mother, Queen Anne of Austria and a healthy entourage of courtiers, stayed prior to her marriage to Louis XIV. ⊠ *Quai de l'Infante.*

Where to Stay & Eat

$$–$$$$ ✕ **Chez Pablo.** The catch of the day determines the daily offering here. Long tables covered with red-and-white tablecloths, benches, and plaster walls give off a casual vibe but the dishes are often excellent. ⊠ *Rue Mme. Etxeto* ☎ *05–56–26–37–81* ▭ *No credit cards* ☉ *Closed Sun.*

$$–$$$ ✕ **Chez Dominique.** A walk around the picturesque fishing port to the Ciboure side of the harbor will take you past the house where Maurice Ravel was born (No. 27) to this rustic maritime eatery. The simple, home-style menu here is based on what the fishing fleet caught that morning; try the *marmitako* (tuna stew). The views over the harbor are unbeatable. ✉ *15 quai M. Ravel* ☎ *05–59–47–29–16* 🖃 *AE, DC, MC, V* ⊘ *Closed Mon. (except mid-June–Aug.) and mid-Feb.–mid-Mar. No dinner Sun.*

$$–$$$ ✕ **La Taverne Basque.** This well-known midtown standard is one of the old-faithful local dining emporiums, specializing in Basque cuisine with a pronounced maritime emphasis. Try the *ttoro* (a rich fish, crustacean, potato, and vegetable soup). ✉ *5 rue République* ☎ *05–59–26–01–26* 🖃 *AE, DC, MC, V* ⊘ *Closed Mon. and Tues. (except July and Aug.) and Mar.*

$$–$$$ ✕ **Txalupa.** The name is Basque for "skiff" or "small boat," and you'll feel like you're in one when you're this close to the bay—yachts and fishing vessels go about their business just a few yards away. This well-known haunt with a terrace over the port serves the famous *jambon de Bayonne* (Bayonne ham) in vinegar and garlic sauce, as well as fresh fish and natural produce such as wild mushrooms. ✉ *Pl. Louis-XIV* ☎ *05–59–51–85–52* 🖃 *AE, DC, MC, V.*

$$$$ ✕🏨 **Le Grand Hôtel.** Deservedly famed as St-Jean-de-Luz's premier hotel, this elegant spot with panoramic ocean views offers intimacy and a sense of being where the action is. Rooms are decorated in colorful pastels, wood, and marble, and the unbeatable location at the northern end of the St-Jean-de-Luz beach will make you feel like the Sun King himself. ✉ *43 bd. Thiers, 64500* ☎ *05–59–26–35–36* 🖷 *05–59–51–99–84* ⊕ *www.luzgrandhotel.fr* ➦ *50 rooms* ⚭ *Restaurant, minibars, cable TV, pool, bar, some pets allowed (fee)* 🖃 *AE, DC, MC, V* ⊘ *Closed Dec.–early Apr.*

THE ATLANTIC PYRÉNÉES

The Atlantic Pyrénées extend eastward from the Atlantic to the Col du Pourtalet, and encompass Béarn and the mountainous part of the Basque Country. Watching the Pyrénées grow from rolling green foothills in the west to jagged limestone peaks to glacier-studded granite massifs in the Hautes-Pyrénées makes for an exciting experience. The Atlantic Pyrénées' first major height is at La Rhune (2,969 feet), known as the Balcon du Côte Basque (Balcony of the Basque Coast). The highest Basque peak is at Orhi (6,617 feet); the Béarn's highest is Pic d'Anie (8,510 feet). Not until Balaïtous (10,381 feet) and Vignemale (10,820 feet), in the Hautes-Pyrénées, does the altitude surpass the 10,000-foot mark. Starting east from St-Jean-de-Luz up the Nivelle River, a series of picturesque villages that includes Ascain, Sare, Ainhoa, and Bidarrai leads up to St-Jean-Pied-de-Port and the Pyrénées.

This journey ends in Pau, far from the Pays Basque and set in the Béarn, akin in temperament to the larger region of which it is an enclave, Gascony. Gascony may be purse-poor, but is certainly rich in scenery and lore. Its proud and touchy temperament is typified in literature by the character d'Artagnan in Dumas's *Three Musketeers* and in history by the lords of the château of Pau. An inscription over its entrance, TOUCHEZ-Y, SI TU L'OSES—"Touch this if you dare"—was that of Gaston Phoebus, a golden-haired and volatile count of Foix. For an arts lover, he had a nasty temper, which led him to murder his own brother and his only son.

Sare

❹ *14 km (8 mi) southeast of St-Jean-de-Luz, 9 km (5½ mi) southwest of Ainhoa on D118: take the first left.*

The gemlike village of Sare is built around a large fronton, or backboard, where a permanent pelota game rages around the clock. Not surprisingly, the Hôtel de Ville (town hall) offers a permanent exhibition on Pelote Basque (open July and August, daily 9–1 and 2–6:30; September–June, daily 3–6). Sare was a busy smuggling hub throughout the 19th century. Its chief attractions are colorful wood-beam and white-washed Basque architecture, the 16th-century late-Romanesque church with its lovely triple-decker interior, and the **Ospitale Zaharra** pilgrim's hospice behind the church. More than a dozen tiny chapels sprinkled around Sare were built as ex-votos by seamen who survived Atlantic storms. Up the Sare Valley are the panoramic Col de Lizarrieta and the **Grottes de Sare,** where you can study up on Basque culture and history at a **Musée Ethnographique** (Ethnographical Museum) and take a guided tour (in five languages) for 1 km (½ mi) underground and see a son-et-lumière (sound and light) show. ☎ *05–59–54–21–88* 🖃 *€6* ⊘ *Feb.–Dec., Tues.–Sun. 11–7.*

⚓ West of Sare on D4, at the Col de St-Ignace, take the **Petit Train de la Rhune,** a tiny wood-panel cogwheel train that reaches the less-than-dizzying speed of 5 mph while climbing up La Rhune peak. The views of the Bay of Biscay, the Pyrénées, and the grassy hills of the Basque farmland are wonderful. ☎ *05–59–54–20–26* 🖃 *€12* ⊘ *Round-trip (1 hr): Easter vacation and May and June, daily 10 and 3; July–Sept., daily every 35 mins.*

FodorśChoice ★

Where to Stay & Eat

★ $ ✕▥ **Baratxartea.** This little inn 1 km (½ mi) from the center of Sare in one of the town's prettiest and most ancient *quartiers* is a find. Monsieur Fagoaga's family-run hotel and restaurant occupy a 16th-century town house complete with *colombiers* (pigeon roosts), and are surrounded by some of the finest rural Basque architecture in Labourd. ✉ *Quartier Ihalar, 64310* ☎ *05–59–54–20–48* 🖷 *05–59–47–50–84* 🖃 *22 rooms* ♨ *Restaurant, cable TV, some pets allowed (fee); no a/c* ▤ *AE, DC, MC, V* ⊘ *Closed Jan.–mid-Mar.*

Ainhoa

❺ *9 km (5½ mi) east of Sare, 23 km (14 mi) southeast of St-Jean-de-Luz, 31 km (19 mi) northwest of St-Jean-Pied-de-Port.*

FodorśChoice ★

The Basque village of Ainhoa is officially registered among the villages selected by the national tourist ministry as the prettiest in France. A town that best represents the Labourd region, it was established in the 13th century by Juan Perex de Bastan. Today, the streets are lined with lovely 16th- to 18th-century houses graced with whitewashed walls, flower-filled balconies, brightly painted shutters, and carved master beams. The Romanesque church of **Notre-Dame de l'Assomption** has a traditional Basque three-tier wooden interior with carved railings and ancient oak stairs. Explore Ainhoa's little streets, dotted with artisanal

PARLEZ-VOUS EUSKERA?

ALTHOUGH THE BASQUE PEOPLE speak French on their side of the Spanish border, they consider Euskera their first language and identify themselves as the "Euskaldunak" (the "Basque speakers"), not French. Euskera remains one of the great enigmas of linguistic scholarship. A bewildering range of theories connects it with everything from Sanskrit to Japanese to Finnish, even to the language of the mythical island of Atlantis or the language spoken by Adam and Eve. What is certain is where Euskera did not come from, namely the Indo-European family of languages that includes the Germanic, Italic, and Hellenic language groups. Attempts to link the Basque language to Iberian, Berber, and Etruscan languages have also proved inconclusive, though philologist Ramón Menéndez Pidal's En torno a la lengua Vasca (On the Basque Language) makes a convincing case, based on toponyms, that the language was spoken by aboriginals from the Iberian Peninsula, especially across the Pyrénées, and only endured in corners farthest from the reach of Roman and Moorish colonization. Presently spoken by about a million people in northern Spain and southwestern France, Euskera sounds like a consonant-ridden version of Spanish, with its five pure vowels, rolled "r" and palatal "n" and "l." Uniquely, Euskera uses suffixes to denote case and number and to form new words. Despite numerous Latinate loanwords, Basque has survived two millennia of cultural and political pressure and is the only remaining language of those spoken in southwestern Europe before the Roman conquest. Since the 10th century, Euskera has gradually been supplanted by Castilian Spanish, but under the present constitutional monarchy, Euskera has flourished through normalized academic instruction, radio and television broadcasts, newspapers, and literary publications.

ateliers and art galleries. Unfortunately, you'll need your own wheels to get to Ainhoa.

Where to Stay & Eat

★ $$$ ✕🏨 **Ithurria.** This is a registered historic monument, once a staging post on the fabled medieval pilgrims' route to Santiago de Compostela. If you are doing a modern version of the pilgrims' journey or just need a stopover on the way deeper into the mountains, the Ithurria—set in a 17th-century building in the prevailing Basque style and surrounded by a garden—will give you a fine atmospheric night. The rustic dining room is the gemstone here, with fare to match, combining inland game and fresh seafood from the Basque coast in creative ways. Guest rooms are modern, comfortable, and tastefully decorated. ✉ *Rue Principale, 64250* ☎ *05-59-29-92-11* 🖷 *05-59-29-81-28* ⊕ *www.ithurria.com/* ⬎ *27 rooms* ♨ *Restaurant, minibars, pool, gym, bar, some pets allowed (fee); no a/c* ▤ *AE, DC, MC, V* ⊘ *Closed Nov.–Apr. 1 and Wed. (except in July and Aug.).*

$ ✕🏨 **Oppoca.** This 17th-century *relais,* or stagecoach relay station, on Ainhoa's main square and pelota court remains one of the loveliest Basque houses in town. Rooms are small but adequate and the owners are a jolly group, always ready to share their knowledge about the locals and the locale. The restaurant serves creditable upland Basque specialties. ⊠ *Pl. du Fronton s/n, 64250* ☎ *05–59–29–90–72* 🖷 *05–59–29–81–03* 🛏 *12 rooms* ⚘ *Restaurant, minibars, bar, some pets allowed (fee); no a/c* ⊟ *AE, DC, MC, V* ⊘ *Closed mid-Nov.–mid-Dec.* ¹⊚¹ *MP.*

Pas de Roland

❻ *15 km (9 mi) east of Ainhoa, 30 km (18 mi) northwest of St-Jean-Pied-de-Port; follow signs for Itxassou and proceed past the town up to the pass.*

Legend has it that the Pas de Roland (Roland's Footprint) was where the legendary medieval French hero Roland enabled Charlemagne's troops to move forward by cutting a passageway through an impeding boulder with his magic sword, Durandal. In the process he purportedly left his footprint in the rock, where the "evidence" may be seen to this day. The drive along this bend in the Nive River is a scenic detour off the D918 road up to St-Jean-Pied-de-Port.

Where to Stay & Eat

⊄ ✕🏨 **Hôtel du Pas du Roland.** Just upstream from the Pas de Roland, this rustic little inn is a good place for a meal or a night. Native trout is available from the nearby Nive River, if you're skillful enough to capture one; otherwise, try the *pipérade basquaise au jambon* (an egg dish with tomatoes, green peppers, onions, and ham). Rooms are simple but clean and cozy. ⊠ *Laxia, 64250 Itxassou* ☎ *05–59–29–75–23* 🖷 *05–59–29–85–86* 🛏 *8 rooms with showers and sinks, toilet in hall* ⚘ *Restaurant, cable TV, bar, some pets allowed (fee); no a/c* ⊟ *AE, DC, MC, V* ⊘ *Restaurant closed Wed. Between Dec.–Mar. call to confirm whether hotel and restaurant are open* ¹⊚¹ *MAP.*

St-Jean-Pied-de-Port

❼ *54 km (33 mi) east of Biarritz, 46 km (28 mi) west of Larrau.*

St-Jean-Pied-de-Port, a fortified town on the Nive River, got its name from its position at the foot (*pied*) of the mountain pass (*port*) of Roncevaux (Roncesvalles). The pass was the setting for *La Chanson de Roland* (*The Song of Roland*), the 11th-century epic poem considered the true beginning of French literature. The bustling town center, a major stop for pilgrims en route to Santiago de Compostela, seems, after a tour through the Soule, like a frenzied metropolitan center—even in winter. In summer, especially around the time of Pamplona's San Fermin blowout (the running of the bulls, July 7–14), the place is filled to the gills and is somewhere between exciting and unbearable.

Walk into the old section through the Porte de France, just behind and to the left of the tourist office, climb the steps on the left up to the walkway circling the ramparts, and walk around to the stone stairway down to the rue de l'Église. The church of **Notre-Dame-du-Bout-du-Pont** (Our Lady of the End of the Bridge), known for its magnificent doorway, is at the bottom of this cobbled street. The church is a characteristically Basque three-tier structure, designed for women to sit on the ground floor, men to be in the first balcony, and the choir in the loft above. From the **Pont Notre-Dame** (Notre-Dame Bridge) you can watch the wild trout in the Nive (also an Atlantic salmon stream) as they pluck mayflies off the surface. Note that fishing is *défendu* (forbidden) in town. Upstream, along the left bank, is another wooden bridge. Cross it and then walk around and back through town, crossing back to the left bank on the main road.

The **Relais de la Nive** bar and café—hanging over the river at the north end of the bridge in the center of town—is the perfect spot to have a coffee while admiring the reflection of the pont de Notre-Dame upstream and watching the trout working in the current.

On **rue de la Citadelle** are a number of sights of interest: the **Maison Arcanzola** (Arcanzola House), at No. 32 (1510); the **Maison des Évêques** (Bishops' House), at No. 39; and the famous **Prison des Évêques** (Bishops' Prison), next door to it. Continue up along rue de la Citadelle to get to the **Citadelle,** a classic Vauban fortress, now occupied by a school. The views from the Citadelle, complete with maps identifying the surrounding heights and valleys, are panoramic.

Where to Stay & Eat

$$–$$$ ✕ **Chez Arbillaga.** Tucked inside the citadel ramparts, this lively bistro is a sound choice for lunch or dinner. The food represents what the Basques do best: simple cooking of excellent quality, such as *agneau de lait à la broche* (roast lamb), in winter, or *coquilles St-Jacques au lard fumé* (scallops with bacon), in summer. ⊠ *8 rue de l'Église* ☎ *05–59–37–06–44* ▭ *MC, V* ☉ *Closed 1st 2 wks of June and Oct. and Wed. Jan.–May.*

$$–$$$$ ✕▦ **Les Pyrénées.** This inn boasts the best restaurant (closed Tuesday
Fodor'sChoice from late September to end of June; no dinner Monday November to
★ March) in the Pyrénées, directed by renowned master chef Firmin Arrambide. Specializing in contemporary *cuisine d'auteur* and offering dishes such as ravioli and prawns with caviar sauce and hot wild-mushroom terrine, Arrambide, from his highland perch, has created a culinary school of thought all his own. Rooms are modern and vary in size; four have balconies. ⊠ *19 pl. Charles de Gaulle, 64220* ☎ *05–59–37–01–01* ▤ *05–59–37–18–97* ⊕ *www.relais-chateaux.com/pyrenees* ↝ *18 rooms, 2 apartments* ⏦ *Restaurant, minibars, cable TV, pool, bar, some pets allowed (fee)* ▭ *AE, DC, MC, V* ☉ *Closed last 3 wks Jan. and late Nov.–late Dec.* ¶⊙¶ *MAP.*

$–$$ ✕▦ **Central Hôtel.** Get the best quality for price in town at this family-run hotel and restaurant over the Nive, where trout could be literally (though illegally) caught from certain rooms. The wonderfully musical 200-year-old oak staircase is another memorable detail. The owners speak Basque, Spanish, French, English, and some German, so communicating is rarely a problem. The cuisine is superb, especially the lamb and *magret de canard* (duck breast). ⊠ *1 pl. Charles de Gaulle, 64220* ☎ *05–59–37–00–22* ▤ *05–59–37–27–79* ↝ *14 rooms* ⏦ *Restaurant, cable TV; no a/c* ▭ *AE, DC, MC, V* ☉ *Closed mid-Dec.–early Mar.* ¶⊙¶ *MAP.*

Larrau

8 *46 km (28 mi) east of St-Jean-Pied-de-Port, 20 km (12 mi) west of Ste-Engrâce, 42 km (26 mi) southwest of Oloron-Ste-Marie.*

Larrau is a cozy way station on the road over the pass into Spain. The town has several hotels of distinction and a number of extraordinarily ancient, rustic mountain houses. Once known for its 19th-century forges, Larrau is now a winter base camp for hunters and a summer center for hikers. It's a good departure point for the **Holçarté Gorges walk.** This classic trek is a 90-minute round-trip hike, including a spectacular bridge that hangs 561 feet above the rocky stream bed. The full tour looping back around to the Logibar is a four-hour walk, although the hike over to Ste-Engrâce is a seven-hour trip each way, a good two-day project over and back. The well-marked trail begins at the Logibar Inn, 3 km (2 mi) east of Larrau.

Where to Stay & Eat

★ **$** ✕🛏 **Hôtel Etxemaïté.** This sophisticated country inn has spectacular views and is one of the area's top dining spots (closed Monday and no dinner Sunday from November to June 1). The dining room seems suspended over the garden and often fills up in summer. The inn is well furnished with Basque antiques, including several unusual *susulia* chair-and-table combinations. The Basque cooking is excellent: terrine *de poule au foie gras* (hen with duck liver) is just one good choice. Rooms are done in light woods and cheery colors. ☒ *Rte. D26, 64560* ☎ *05–59–28–61–45* 🖷 *05–59–28–72–71* ⊕ *www.hotel-etchemaite.fr/* ⤵ *16 rooms* ⚲ *Restaurant, cable TV, bar; no a/c* ⊟ *AE, DC, MC, V* ⊘ *Closed Nov. 29–Dec. 7 and Jan. 4–Feb. 7* ⏀ *MAP.*

¢ ✕🛏 **Logibar.** This simple inn with a *gîte d'étape* (way station) for hikers serves nonpareil garbure and an even better *omelette aux cèpes* (wild mushroom omelet). Rooms are tiny but cozy, and the Quihilliry family, in its fourth generation running this well-known spot, has a knack for making you feel at home. ☒ *Rte. D26, 64560* ☎ *05–59–28–61–14* 🖷 *05–59–28–61–14* ⊕ *www.aubergelogibar.fr.st* ⤵ *2 doubles, 4 rooms for 4, 1 room for 8, dormitory for 10* ⚲ *Restaurant, bar; no a/c, no room TVs* ⊟ *MC, V* ⊘ *Closed early Dec.–early Mar.*

Gorges de Kakuetta

9 *13 km (8 mi) east of Larrau, 3 km (2 mi) west of Ste-Engrâce.*

Fodor'sChoice
★ A right turn onto D113 at the confluence of the Uhaitxa and Larrau rivers will take you toward Ste-Engrâce and past one of the area's great natural phenomena, the Gorges de Kakuetta (the Basque spelling). A famous canyon cut through the limestone cliffs by the Uhaitxa River, the gorge is at times as narrow as 12 feet across while reaching depths of more than 1,155 feet. Stairways are cut into the rock, and hanging bridges span the watercourse. A waterfall and a grotto mark the end of the climb, a two-hour walk round-trip. This hike is recommended only during low-water conditions, normally between June and October. Good hiking shoes are indispensable. ☎ *05–59–28–73–44* ✉ *€4* ⊘ *Mid-Mar.–mid-Nov., daily 8 AM–dark.*

Ste-Engrâce

10 *66 km (40 mi) east of St-Jean-Pied-de-Port, 37 km (23 mi) southwest of Oloron-Ste-Marie, 100 km (62 mi) southwest of Pau.*

Ste-Engrâce is at the eastern edge of the Basque Country in the Haute Soule (Upper Soule). Soule is the smallest of the three French Basque provinces. Nearly all the inhabitants speak Euskera (Basque), a non-Indo-European language of uncertain (though probably native Pyrenean and Iberian) origins.

Medieval pilgrims on the way to Santiago de Compostela in northwest Spain once flocked to the village's lovely 11th-century church of **Ste-Engrâce** to venerate the arm of Sancta Gracia, a young Portuguese noblewoman martyred around the year 300. When pillaging Calvinists removed the cherished relic in 1569, a ring finger was sent from the scene of her martyrdom in Zaragoza to replace the stolen arm. The church has an asymmetrical, slanting roof, typical of the *maison Basque* (Basque house) design. Its gray stone contrasts eerily with the green hills and fields behind. The ornate interior is a surprising contrast to the church's stark exterior. The town remains a key crossroads for pilgrims traveling to Santiago and trans-Pyrenean trekkers going east across the "dragon's back," as generations of Pyreneists have respectfully dubbed the mountain range's jagged profile.

Where to Stay

$ **Auberge Elichalt.** This cozy gîte d'étape (hikers' way station) and table d'hôte (B&B) has 50 beds in varying situations. There are double rooms, dormitory beds, and an apartment for rent, all in the shadow of the church. Monsieur and Madame Burguburu (Euskera for "head of town") can recommend hikes into the mountains. ⊠ *64560 Ste-Engrâce* ☎ *05–59–28–61–63* 🖷 *05–59–28–75–54* ⊕ *www.gites64.com* ⤢ *5 double rooms, 1 apartment for 5, 40 dormitory beds without bath* ⊟ *No credit cards* ⏍ *MAP.*

Sports & the Outdoors

The nearby ski station, 10 km (6 mi) away in **Pierre-St-Martin,** has Alpine and Nordic skiing. If you're interested in fly-fishing, the **Gave d'Oloron** (*gave* is the word for river in the language of the Béarn), flowing through Sauveterre-de-Béarn, is a trout and Atlantic salmon fishery. On D919 between Aramits and Oloron-Ste-Marie, look for the Vert River and the nearby town of **Féas.** The gently flowing Vert is well populated with trout.

en route — The **Basse Soule** (Lower Soule), also known as the Barétous region, is a transition zone between the Basque Country and Béarn characterized by rolling green hills and cornfields. To explore the Basse Soule, take D132 from Pierre-St-Martin down to Arette. Drive the loop beginning west toward the hometown of the legendary Aramis of *The Three Musketeers* at **Aramits,** continuing through **Lannes, Trois-Villes, and Gotein,** with its characteristic *clocher-calvaire,* a three-peak bell tower designed as an evocation of Calvary. Just short of Mauléon-Licharre on D918 is the rustic 11th-century **Chapelle St-Jean-de-Berraute,** built by the Order of Malta for pilgrims heading to Santiago de Compostela.

Mauléon-Licharre

⑪ *16 km (10 mi) southwest of Navarrenx, 40 km (24 mi) northeast of St-Jean-Pied-de-Port.*

Mauléon-Licharre, capital of the Soule, is the upland Basque Country's only industrial city, manufacturing rope-soled espadrilles. Spread along the banks of the Saison River, the 16th-century **Hôtel de Maytie** (also known as the Château d'Andurain), the 17th-century **Hôtel de Montréal,** and the remains of the 12th-century **château fort** fortress are the main spots to seek out.

Where to Stay & Eat

$ ✕🏠 **Bidegain.** This classic 18th-century Basque town house is filled with heavy oak beams and creaky wooden stairs and floorboards. Just off the trout-filled Gave du Saison, this onetime stagecoach and pony-express relay station serves excellent Basque country cooking in a four-course, prix-fixe *formule* with a choice of four desserts. The shady garden out back is a cool and quiet summer retreat. ⊠ *13 rue de Navarre, 64560* ☎ *05–59–28–16–05* 🖨 *05–59–19–10–26* ✍ *bidegain-hotel@wanadoo.fr* ➷ *20 rooms* ♻ *Restaurant, cable TV; no a/c* ▭ *AE, DC, MC, V* ❖❶ *MAP.*

Oloron-Ste-Marie

⑫ *33 km (20½ mi) southwest of Pau on N134.*

Oloron-Ste-Marie straddles the confluence of two rivers, the Gave d'Aspe and the Gave d'Ossau. Trout and even the occasional Atlantic salmon can (with luck) be spotted when the sun is out. Originally an Iberian and later a Roman military outpost, the town was made a stronghold by the viscounts of Béarn in the 11th century. The **Quartier Ste-Croix** occupies the once fortified point between the two rivers and is the most interesting part of town. The fortresslike church of **Ste-Croix,** with its Moorish-influenced cupola inspired by the mosque at Cordoba; the two Renaissance buildings nearby; and the 14th-century **Tour Grède** (Grède Tower) are the main attractions. A walk around the **Promenade Bellevue** along the ramparts below the west side of the church will give you a view down the Aspe Valley and into the mountains behind. The 12th- and 13th-century **Église Ste-Marie,** in the **bourg de Ste-Marie** across the river on the left bank of the Gave d'Aspe, is famous for its surprisingly well-preserved Romanesque doorway of Pyrenean marble.

Where to Stay & Eat

$–$$ ✕ **Le Biscondau.** Come here to sample some of the finest garbure, the hearty peasant vegetable soup, in Oloron. The view over the Gave d'Ossau is at its best from the terrace in summer. ⊠ *7 rue de la Filature* ☎ *05–59–39–06–15* ▭ *DC, MC, V* ◔ *Closed Mon.*

$$ ✕🏠 **Alysson.** This modern building in the middle of town is a safe-and-sound, if charmless, place to spend a night in Oloron-Ste-Marie. The rooms are small but newly furnished and equipped. The restaurant serves excellent garbures (mountain soups with beans, vegetables, and duck confit) and *piperades* (red peppers, tomatoes, and eggs sautéed in

goose fat and served with fatback or bacon). ⊠ *Bd. Pyrénées, 64400*
☎ *05–59–39–70–70* 🖷 *05–59–39–24–47* 🖅 *34 rooms* ⚹ *Restaurant,
cable TV, pool, some pets allowed (fee); no a/c* ☰ *AE, DC, MC, V.*

¢–$ 🏠 **Chambre d'Hôtes Paris.** This B&B in Féas, run by Christian and
Marie-France Paris, is a great deal, especially if you like fly-fishing. Christian, a registered guide, knows every trout in the Barétous by name. ⊠ *7½
km (5 mi) past Oloron-Ste-Marie, 64570 Féas* ☎ *05–59–39–01–10*
🖅 *3 rooms* ⚹ *No a/c* ☰ *No credit cards* ⊘ *Closed late Dec.–early Jan.*
🍴 *MAP.*

Navarrenx

⑬ *19 km (11 mi) northwest of Oloron-Ste-Marie.*

Perched over the Gave d'Oloron, Navarrenx was built in 1316 as a *bastide*
(fortified town) at an important crossroads on the Santiago de Compostela pilgrimage route. Henri d'Albret, king of Navarre, constructed
the present ramparts in 1540. The bastion of Porte St-Antoine, with its
miniature turret, is one of the Soule's best-known sights. The town
motto, *Si You Ti Baou* (Béarnais for "If I should see you"), refers to the
cannon guarding the approach to the town across the bridge. The Gave
d'Oloron is an excellent trout and salmon river. Salmon angling is an
important part of Navarrenx tradition: every year a salmon-fishing
championship takes place, during which spectators line the banks of the
legendary salmon pool about 300 yards upstream from the bridge.

Where to Stay & Eat

$ ✕🏠 **Hôtel du Commerce.** As the best restaurant and most traditional lodg-
ing in Navarrenx, the Commerce is an easy choice. Rooms are old-fashioned and cozy and have renovated, spacious bathrooms. The exquisite
menu spotlights such items as *pigeonneau au style bécasse* (woodcock-
style squab served up in a fragrant Madeira sauce), or *foie gras frais au
myrtille* (fresh duck liver in a berry sauce). ⊠ *Pl. des Casernes, 64190*
☎ *05–59–66–50–16* 🖷 *05–59–66–52–67* ⊕ *www.hotel-commerce.fr*
🖅 *28 rooms* ⚹ *Restaurant, cable TV, bar, some pets allowed (fee); no
a/c* ☰ *AE, DC, MC, V* 🍴 *MAP.*

Sauveterre-de-Béarn

⑭ *19 km (11 mi) northwest of Navarrenx, 39 km (23 mi) northwest of*
Fodor'sChoice *Oloron-Ste-Marie, 39 km (23 mi) northeast of St-Jean-Pied-de-Port.*
★
Make your first stop the terrace next to the church: the view from here
takes in the Gave d'Oloron, the fortified 12th-century drawbridge, the
lovely Montréal Tower, and the Pyrénées rising in the distance, and is among
the finest in the region. The bridge, known both as the **Vieux Pont** (Old
Bridge) and the Pont de la Légende (Bridge of the Legend), was named
after the legend of Sancie, widow of Gaston V de Béarn. Accused of murdering a child after her husband's death in 1170, Sancie was subjected to
the "Judgment of God" and thrown, bound hand and foot, from the bridge
by order of her brother, the king of Navarre. When the river carried her
safely to the bank, she was deemed exonerated of all charges.

Where to Stay

★ $–$$ ⊡ **Hôtel de la Reine Sancie.** Enjoying a picture-perfect spot, this medieval manor house is built into the town's fortified 12th-century drawbridge, the Pont de la Légende, and sits atop the old foundations of the medieval Maison du Sénéchal. The views over the river and up to the ramparts of Sauveterre are superb. Rooms range from cozy and comfortable to grand and baronial (ask for the one in the corner, which has two views of the river and an immense bathroom). ⊠ *Rue du Pont de la Légende, 64390* 🕾 *05–59–38–95–11* 🖨 *05–59–38–99–10* 🛏 *6 rooms* ♦ *Restaurant, bar, some pets allowed (fee); no a/c* ═ *AE, DC, MC, V* ۞ *Closed mid-Dec.–mid-Apr.* ﴾◎﴿ *MAP.*

Pau

🔟 *106 km (63 mi) east of Bayonne and Biarritz.*

The stunning views, mild climate, and elegance of Pau—the historic capital of Béarn, a state annexed to France in 1620—make it a lovely place to visit and a convenient gateway to the Pyrénées. The birthplace of King Henri IV, Pau was "discovered" in 1815 by British officers returning from the Peninsular War in Spain, and it soon became a prominent winter resort town. Fifty years later English-speaking inhabitants made up one-third of Pau's population, many believing in the medicinal benefits of mountain air (later shifting their loyalties to Biarritz for the sea air). They started the Pont-Long Steeplechase, still one of the most challenging in Europe, in 1841; created France's first golf course here in 1856; introduced fox hunting to the region; and founded a famous British tea shop where students now smoke strong cigarettes while drinking black coffee.

Fodor'sChoice
★ Pau's regal past is commemorated at its **Musée National du Château de Pau,** begun in the 14th century by Gaston Phoebus, the flamboyant count of Béarn. The building was transformed into a Renaissance palace in the 16th century by Marguerite d'Angoulême, sister of François I. A woman of diverse gifts, her pastorales were performed in the château's sumptuous gardens. Her bawdy *Heptameron*—written at age 60—furnishes as much sly merriment today as it did when read by her doting kingly brother. Marguerite's grandson, the future king of France Henri IV, was born in the château in 1553. Exhibits connected to Henri's life and times are displayed regularly, along with portraits of the most significant of his alleged 57 lovers and mistresses. His cradle, a giant turtle shell, is on exhibit in his bedroom, one of the sumptuous, tapestry-lined royal apartments. ⊠*Rue du Château* 🕾*05–59–82–38–00* ⊕*www.musee-chateau-pau.fr/* 🎟 *€5, free 1st Sun. of month* ۞ *Apr.–Oct., daily 9:30–11:30 and 2–5:45; Nov.–Mar., daily 9:30–11:30 and 2–4:30.*

To continue on your royal path, follow the **Sentiers du Roy** (King's Paths), a marked trail just below the Boulevard des Pyrénées. When you reach the top, walk along until the sights line up with the mountain peaks you see. For some man-made splendors instead, head to the **Musée des Beaux-Arts** and feast on works by El Greco, Degas, and Rodin. ⊠ *Rue Mathieu-Lalanne* 🕾 *05–59–27–33–02* ⊕ *musee.ville-pau.fr* 🎟 *€2.50* ۞ *Tues.–Sun. 10–noon and 2–6.*

While in Pau, enjoy some of life's sweetest pleasures with a visit to the **Confiserie Francis Miot** (⊠48 rue Joffre ☎05–59–27–69–51 ⊕www.feerie-gourmande.com) and enjoy his signature delicacies, "Les Coucougnettes du Vert Galant"—small, red, tender bonbons made from almond paste. Their name is echoic of the Occitanian argot for testicles (in Spanish, *cojones*) and why not? Henri IV—a.k.a. le Vert Galant ("the dirty old man" or "the swordsman")—was famed for his 57 lovers. At the gates of Pau, in the village of Uzos, Miot has his own **Musée des Arts Sucré.**

Where to Stay & Eat

$–$$$ ✕ **Gousse d'Ail.** In the Hédas district, the deep mid-city canyon in the oldest part of Pau, this lovely hideaway is tucked under the stairway at the end of the street. Traditional Béarn cooking and international cuisine are served; try the magret de canard cooked over coals. ⊠ *12 rue du Hédas* ☎ *05–59–27–31–55* 🖶 *05–59–06–10–53* ▭ *AE, DC, MC, V* ⊘ *Closed Sun. No lunch Sat.*

$–$$ ▥ **Hôtel de Gramont.** Five minutes from the château, the Gramont is a cozy and convenient base for exploring Pau. Ask for one of the *chambres mansardées* (dormered bedrooms) under the eaves overlooking the Hédas. ⊠ *3 pl. de Gramont, 64000* ☎ *05–59–27–84–04* 🖶 *05–59–27–62–23* ⤶ *36 rooms* ⌂ *Cable TV; no a/c* ▭ *AE, DC, MC, V.*

Nightlife & the Arts

During the music and arts **Festival de Pau,** theatrical and musical events take place almost every evening from mid-July to late-August, nearly all of them gratis. Nightlife in Pau revolves around the Hédas district, where bars and restaurants line the alleys heading down into this onetime river gorge. The streets around Pau's imposing château are sprinkled with cozy pubs and dining spots, although the **casino** (⊠ Parc Beaumont ☎ 05–59–27–06–92) offers racier entertainment.

Eugénie-les-Bains

⑯ *56 km (34 mi) north of Pau, 140 km (87 mi) south of Bordeaux.*

Empress Eugénie popularized Eugénie-les-Bains at the end of the 19th century, and in return the villagers renamed the town after her. Michel and Christine Guérard brought the village back to life in 1973 by putting together one of France's most fashionable thermal retreats, which became the birthplace of nouvelle cuisine, thanks to the great talents of chef Michel. Their little kingdom now includes two restaurants, two hotels, a cooking school, and a spa. The 13 therapeutic treatments address everything from weight loss to rheumatism. Two springs are certified by the French Ministry of Health: L'Impératrice and Christine-Marie, whose 39°C (102°F) waters come from nearly 1,300 feet below the surface.

Where to Stay & Eat

★ **$$$$** ✕▥ **La Ferme aux Grives.** With four superb rooms for the lucky first-comers, Michel Guérard's delightfully re-created old coaching inn, set at one end of their Prés d'Eugénie fiefdom, is meant to be a more rustic alternative to their main flagship restaurant. Nature's bounty is the theme: a banquet table is laid out with vegetables and breads, darkened beams cast romantic shadows, and hunting paintings cover the walls.

Grandmother's food is given a nouvelle spin, and nearly everything is *authentique*: even the suckling pig turns on a spit in the fireplace. ✉ *40320 Eugénie-les-Bains* ☎ *05–58–05–05–06* 🖨 *05–58–51–10–10* 🛏 *4 rooms* ⚭ *Restaurant, minibars, cable TV, bar, some pets allowed (fee); no a/c* ▤ *AE, DC, MC, V* ⊘ *Closed Jan. 4–Feb. 12* ⦿ *MAP.*

$$$$
Fodor'sChoice
★

✕⫿ **Les Prés d'Eugénie.** Ever since Michel Guérard's eponymous restaurant fied the first shots of the nouvelle revolution of the late 1970s, the excellence of this suave culinary landmark has been a given (so much so that the breakfast here outdoes dinner at most other places). Thanks to Guérard's signature flair, *cuisine minceur*—the slimmer's dream—collides with the lusty fare of the Landes region (langoustines garnished with foie gras and mesclun greens, lobster with confetti-ed calf's head). In the lovely Second Empire–style hotel, set in a fine garden, grandeur prevails and rooms are formal. However, those in the "annex"—the former 18th-century **Couvent des Herbes**—have an understated luxe and look out over the herb garden. To top it all off, the complex includes an excellent spa, dance studio, two pools, and a 9-hole golf course, and "theme" weeks are devoted to cooking, perfumes, wines, or gardening. ✉ *40320 Eugénie-les-Bains* ☎ *05–58–05–06–07, 05–58–05–05–05 restaurant reservations* 🖨 *05–58–51–10–10* ⦿ *www.michelguerard. com* 🛏 *22 rooms, 6 apartments* ⚭ *Restaurant, minibars, cable TV, golf course, 2 tennis courts, 2 pools (1 indoor), gym, bar, some pets allowed (fee); no a/c* ▤ *AE, DC, MC, V* ⦿ *MAP.*

★ **$$$–$$$$**
✕⫿ **La Maison Rose.** A low-cost, low-calorie alternative to Les Prés d'Eugénie, Michel and Christine Guérard's newest hotel beckons with a sybaritically simple spa approach. Set in a renovated, super-stylish 18th-century farmhouse adorned with old paintings hung with ribbons, rustic antiques, and Pays Basque handicrafts, this is a retreat that would have delighted the sober Madame de Maintenon—if she had wanted to lose weight, that is. This is a serious spa, complete with slimming cures and the most stylish relaxation room in France (oh, those Provençal-style chaises longues). No room service—everyone eats in the main dining room, a two-story, beam-ceiling delight. The kitchen's touch remains an inventive benediction to local produce. ✉ *40320 Eugénie-les-Bains* ☎ *05–58–05–06–07* 🖨 *05–58–51–10–10* ⦿ *www. michelguerard.com* 🛏 *26 rooms, 5 studios* ⚭ *Restaurant, kitchenette, minibars, cable TV, pool, gym, some pets allowed (fee); no a/c* ▤ *AE, DC, MC, V* ⦿ *MAP.*

THE HAUTES-PYRÉNÉES

The Hautes-Pyrénées include the highest and most spectacular natural wonders in the cordillera. Although mountain peaks soar in this region, there are also centers of more civilized charms—notably, the towns of Cauterets and Bagnères-de-Luchon, set in a spa region that once attracted such formidable luminaries as Montaigne, Madame de Maintenon, Henri IV, and the composer Rossini. Traditionally known as La Bigorre, the border with the Béarn is at the Col d'Aubisque southeast of Oloron-Ste-Marie, and the eastern border with the Haute Garonne is at the Col de Peyresourde just west of Bagnères-de-Luchon. The legendary Cirque de Gavarnie (natural mountain amphitheater), the Vignemale peak (10,817 feet) and glacier, the Balaïtous peak (10,312 feet), the Brèche de Roland, and the Cirque de Troumouse are the star attractions in the Hautes-Pyrénées.

Tarbes

⑰ *40 km (24 mi) east of Pau, 152 km (94 mi) southwest of Toulouse, 214 km (133 mi) southeast of Bordeaux.*

Tarbes is the commercial and administrative center of the Bigorre region and the Hautes-Pyrénées Département. If Tarbes is your point of entry into the Hautes-Pyrénées, stop by the **tourist office** (✉ 3 cours Gambetta ☎ 05–62–51–30–31) for information, brochures, and maps of the region. The **Halle Marcadieu** is the commercial center. The Thursday market offers a chance to check out widely acclaimed local products ranging from the *choux-fleurs* (cauliflower) of Arros to the carrots of Asté, from the onions of Trébons to the famed *haricot tarbais*, a delicate-skinned kidney bean essential in any authentic garbure.

Tarbes was the **birthplace of Maréchal Ferdinand Foch** (✉ 2 rue de la Victoire ☎ 05–62–93–19–02), the general most responsible for the 1918 Allied victory. The town is also home to the **Haras National** (✉ 70 av. du Régiment-de-Bigorre ☎ 05–62–34–44–59), a stud farm and dressage academy. A nice place for a walk on a warm day is the **Jardin Massey** (Massey Garden), a luxuriant park that is home to ducks and an abundance of flowers in summer.

Where to Stay & Eat

$$$ ✕ **L'Ambroisie.** Properly named for "the food of the gods," this 19th-century vicarage with squeaky wooden floorboards serves the finest cuisine in Tarbes. Choices vary seasonally but the wood pigeon, duck liver, and (from late August to late October) famous local *coco tarbais,* or white beans from Tarbes, are difficult to surpass, especially when they are accompanied by the Madiran wines of the region. ✉ *48 rue Abbé Torné* ☎ *05–62–93–09–34* ▤ *AE, DC, MC, V* ☉ *Closed Sun.–Mon. and May 2–10, Aug. 29–Sept. 6, Dec. 24–29.*

$–$$ ▥ **Henri IV.** This comfortable spot in midtown Tarbes, near the Massey Garden and three blocks from the train station, is a safe if unspectacular choice for a night in town. The staff will direct you to the gastronomical star of Tarbes, L'Ambroisie, just two blocks toward the cathedral. ✉ *7 av. B. Barère, 65000* ☎ *05–62–34–01–68* ▤ *05–62–93–71–32* ⤳ *22 rooms* ⌂ *Cable TV, some pets allowed (fee); no a/c* ▤ *AE, DC, MC, V.*

Lourdes

⑱ *41 km (27 mi) southeast of Pau, 19 km (12 mi) southwest of Tarbes.*

Five million pilgrims flock to Lourdes annually, many in quest of a miraculous cure for sickness or disability. A religious pilgrimage is one thing, but a sightseeing expedition has other requirements. The famous churches and grotto and the area around them are woefully lacking in beauty. Off-season, acres of empty parking lots echo. Shops are shuttered, restaurants closed. In season a mob jostles to see the grotto behind a forest of votive candles. Some pundits might say that Lourdes ingeniously combines the worst of both worlds.

It all started in February 1858 when Bernadette Soubirous, a 14-year-old miller's daughter, claimed she saw the Virgin Mary in the **Grotte de Massabielle,** near the Gave de Pau (in all, she had 18 visions). Bernadette dug in the grotto, releasing a gush of water from a spot where no spring had flowed before. From then on, pilgrims thronged the Massabielle rock for the water's supposed healing powers, though church authorities reacted skeptically. It took four years for the miracle to be authenticated by Rome and a sanctuary erected over the grotto. In 1864 the first organized procession was held. Today there are six official annual pilgrimages between Easter and All Saints' Day, the most important on August 15.

Lourdes celebrated the centenary of Bernadette Soubirous's visions by building the world's largest underground church, the **Basilique Souterraine St-Pie X,** with space for 20,000 people—more than the town's permanent population. Above St-Pie X stands the unprepossessing neo-Byzantine **Basilique du Rosaire** (1889). The **Basilique Supérieure** (1871), tall and white, hulks nearby.

The **Pavillon Notre-Dame,** across from St-Pie X, houses the **Musée Bernadette** (Museum of Stained-Glass Mosaic Religious Art), with mementos of Bernadette's life and an illustrated history of the pilgrimages. In the basement is the **Musée d'Art Sacré du Gemmail.** ☒ *72 rue de la Grotte* ☏ *05–62–94–13–15* ☎ *Free* ☉ *July–Nov., daily 9:30–11:45 and 2:30–6:15; Dec.–June, Wed.–Mon. 9:30–11:45 and 2:30–5:45.*

Across the river is the **Moulin de Boly** (Boly Mill), where Bernadette was born on January 7, 1844. ☒ *12 rue Bernadette-Soubirous* ☎ *Free* ☉ *Easter–mid-Oct., daily 9:30–11:45 and 2:30–5:45.*

The **cachot,** a tiny room where, in extreme poverty, Bernadette and her family took refuge in 1856, can also be visited. ☒ *15 rue des Petits-Fossés* ☏ *05–62–94–51–30* ☎ *Free* ☉ *Easter–mid-Oct., daily 9:30–11:45 and 2:30–5:30; mid-Oct.–Easter, daily 2:30–5:30.*

The **château** on the hill above town can be reached by escalator, by 131 steps, or by the ramp up from rue du Bourg (from which a small Basque cemetery with ancient discoidal stones can be seen). Once a prison, the castle now contains the **Musée Pyrénéen,** one of France's best provincial museums, devoted to the popular customs, arts, and history of the Pyrénées. ☒ *25 rue du Fort* ☏ *05–62–94–02–04* ☎ *€5* ☉ *Easter–mid-Oct., daily 9–noon and 2–7, last admission at 6; mid-Oct.–Easter, Wed.–Mon. 9–noon and 2–7, last admission at 6.*

FodorśChoice
★

Where to Stay & Eat

$ ✕▥ **Hôtel Albret/La Taverne de Bigorre.** The Moreau family's popular establishment serves traditional French mountain cooking such as hearty garbure. Rooms are clean and comfortable, with a personal touch that is very welcome in Lourdes. ☒ *21 pl. du Champ Commun, 65100*

☎ 05–62–94–75–00 🖷 05–62–94–78–45 ➥ *27 rooms* ⚃ *Restaurant, bar, parking (fee); no a/c* ▤ *AE, DC, MC, V* ⊘ *Closed Jan.*

Cauterets

⓳ *30 km (19 mi) south of Lourdes, 49 km (30 mi) south of Tarbes.*

Cauterets (which derives from the word for hot springs in the local *bigourdan* dialect) is a spa and resort town (for long-term treatments) high in the Pyrénées. It has been revered since Roman times for thermal baths thought to cure maladies ranging from back pain to female sterility. Novelist Victor Hugo (1802–85) womanized here; Lady Aurore Dudevant—better known as the writer George Sand (1804–76)—is said to have discovered her feminism here. Other famous visitors include Gastón Fébus, Chateaubriand, Sarah Bernhardt, King Edward VII of England, and Spain's King Alfonso XIII.

en route | Two kilometers (1 mi) south of Cauterets is the parking lot for the thermal baths, where the red-and-white-marked GR10 **Sentier des Cascades** (Path of the Waterfalls) departs for Pont d'Espagne. This famous walk (three hours round-trip) features stunning views of the waterfalls and abundant *marmottes* (Pyrenean groundhogs). From **Pont d'Espagne,** to which you can also drive, continue on foot or by chairlift to the plateau and a view over the bright blue **Lac de Gaube,** fed by the river of the same name. Above is **Le Vignemale** (10,817 feet), France's highest Pyrenean peak. Return via Cauterets to Pierrefitte-Nestalas and turn right on D921 up Luz-St-Saveur and Gavarnie.

Gavarnie

⓴ *30 km (19 mi) south of Cauterets on D921, 50 km (31 mi) south of Lourdes.*

FodorśChoice
★

The village of Gavarnie is a good base for exploring the mountains in the region. For starters, it's at the foot of **Le Cirque de Gavarnie,** one of the world's most remarkable examples of glacial erosion and a daunting challenge to mountaineers. Horses and donkeys, rented in the village, are the traditional way to reach the head of the valley (though walking is preferable), where the Hôtel du Cirque has hosted six generations of visitors. When the upper snows melt, numerous streams tumble down from the cliffs to form spectacular waterfalls; the greatest of them, Europe's largest, is the **Grande Cascade,** dropping nearly 1,400 feet.

Another dramatic sight is 12 km (7 mi) west of the village of Gavarnie. Take D921 up to the Col de Boucharo, where you can park and walk five hours up to the **Brèche de Roland** glacier (you cross it during the last two hours of the hike). For a taste of mountain life, have lunch high up at the Club Alpin Français's **Refuge de Sarradets ou de la Brèche.** This is a serious climb, only feasible from mid-June to mid-September, for which you need (at least) good hiking shoes and sound physical conditioning. Crampons and ice axes are available for rent in Gavarnie; check with the Gavarnie tourist office for weather reports and for information about guided tours.

Where to Stay & Eat

★ $-$$$ ✕ **Hôtel du Cirque.** With its legendary views of the Cirque de Gavarnie, this spot is magical at sunset. Despite its name it's just a restaurant, but not just any old eating establishment: the garbure here is as delicious as the sunset is grand. Seventh-generation owner Pierre Vergez claims his recipe using water from the Cirque and *cocos de Tarbes*, or *haricots tarbais* (Tarbes broad beans) is unique. ⊠ *1-hr walk above the village of Gavarnie* ☎ *05–62–92–48–02* ☰ *MC, V* ☉ *Closed mid-Sept.–mid-June.*

$ ✕⌂ **Hôtel Marboré.** This multigabled house over a rushing mountain brook offers all the history and tradition of Gavarnie along with delightful creature comforts. Rooms are bright and pleasant and look out onto lush hillside meadows. The kind and lively owner-manager Roselyne Fillastre attends to all with great warmth and vivacity. The restaurant, too, is excellent: look forward to fine cuisine prepared with the freshest ingredients. ⊠ *Village de Gavarnie, 65120* ☎ *05–62–92–40–40* 🖶 *05–62–92–40–30* ⊕ *www.lemarbore.com* ➷ *24 rooms* ⌂ *Restaurant, cable TV, bar; no a/c* ☰ *MC, V* ☉ *Closed Nov.–Dec. 20* ⊙⌿ *MAP.*

Nightlife & the Arts

Every July Gavarnie holds an outdoor ballet and music performance, **La Fête des Pyrénées** (☎ 05–62–92–49–10 information), using the Cirque de Gavarnie as a backdrop; show time is at sunset. For information contact the tourist office.

en route | The dramatic mountain scenery is impressive all along D921 between Gavarnie and **Luz-St-Sauveur.** Continuing east from Luz-St-Sauveur along D918 toward Arreau, the road passes through the lively little spa town of **Barèges** and under the brow of the mighty **Pic du Midi de Bigorre,** a mountain peak towering nearly 10,000 feet above the Col du Tourmalet pass. The finest views—and the sharpest curves—are found toward the Col d'Aspin pass. Another spectacular road is D618 from Arreau over the **Col de Peyresourde** to Bagnères de Luchon.

Bagnères-de-Luchon

㉑ *150 km (93 mi) east of Gavarnie.*

The largest and most fashionable Pyrenean spa is Bagnères de Luchon (generally known simply as Luchon), at the head of a lush valley. Dubbed the "Reine des Pyrénées" (Queen of the Pyrénées), Luchon was considered by the Romans to rank second as a spa only to Naples. Thermal waters here cater to the vocal cords: opera singers, lawyers, and politicians hoarse from spurious electoral promises all pile in to breathe the healing vapors. The **Parc des Quinconces** is a pretty stroll in summer. Look for the beautiful Couteillas sculpture *Le Baiser à la Source* (*The Kiss at the Spring*), hidden under a pine tree.

On display at the **Musée du Pays de Luchon** (⊠ 18 allée d'Étigny ☎ 05–61–79–29–87 ⌨ €2 ⊙ daily 9–noon and 2–6) are exhibits about Pyrenean history and lore and artifacts such as a curious sculpture portraying a woman and a serpent.

Where to Stay & Eat

$$–$$$ ✕⊡ **Hôtel Corneille.** This elegant spot with a lovely terrace and park has all the comforts you could want and then some. Most of the furnishings are original Napoléon III. The staff is very helpful and pleasant. ⊠ *5 av. A. Dumas, 31110* ☎ *05–61–79–36–22* ⊟ *05–61–79–81–11* ⏎ *54 rooms* ♿ *Restaurant, bar, meeting rooms, some pets allowed (fee); no a/c* ⊟ *AE, DC, MC, V* ⊙ *Closed late Nov.–mid-Dec.* ⏀ *MAP.*

$ ✕⊡ **L'Esquerade.** This little inn and restaurant, 6 km (4 mi) west of Bagnères, offers elegance, friendly service, intimacy, and excellent value. Rooms are comfortable, if small, and the cuisine has won deserved local fame for its classic Pyrenean fare. ⊠ *Rte. D618, 31110 Castillon-de-Larboust* ☎ *05–61–79–19–64* ⊟ *05–61–79–26–29* ⊕ *www.esquerade. com* ⏎ *12 rooms* ♿ *Restaurant, some pets allowed (fee); no a/c* ⊟ *AE, DC, MC, V* ⊙ *Closed mid-Nov.–mid-Dec.* ⏀ *MAP.*

St-Bertrand-de-Comminges

㉒
32 km (20 mi) north of Bagnères-de-Luchon, 57 km (35 mi) southeast of Tarbes, 107 km (66 mi) southwest of Toulouse.

A Roman road once led directly from Luchon to St-Bertrand-de-Comminges (then a huge town of 60,000). This delightful village, whose inhabitants today number just over 200, is dwarfed beneath the imposing (mostly) 12th-century **Cathédrale Ste-Marie-de-Comminges** (⊠Rue des Gouverneurs); don't miss the cloisters and the intricately and playfully carved wood choir stalls. Described as a land-bound Mont-St-Michel, St-Bertrand numbers old houses, sloping alleyways, and crafts shops that add to its charm. The summer music festival held here and in neighboring villages in July and August is excellent.

Where to Stay & Eat

$ ✕⊡ **Moulin d'Aveux.** Four kilometers (2½ mi) west of St-Bertrand, this onetime cereal mill next to the trout-infested Ourse river is a restored barn. Specialties range from garbure to fresh trout. Rooms are cheery and rustic. ⊠ *Rte. D925, 65370 Aveux* ☎ *05–62–99–20–68* ⊟ *05–62–99–22–27* ⏎ *10 rooms* ♿ *Restaurant, some pets allowed (fee); no a/c* ⊟ *AE, DC, MC, V* ⊙ *Closed Oct. 8–17, Jan. 1–13; Mon. and Tues. Oct.–May* ⏀ *MAP.*

$ ⊡ **Comminges.** This pretty spot overlooking the magnificent cathedral partly occupies a former convent. Rooms are equipped with traditional French country furniture and decorated in somber though rich hues and tones in old world elegance. The awning-covered terrace downstairs across from the cathedral is a memorable refuge. ⊠ *Place de la Cathédrale s/n, 31510* ☎ *05–61–88–31–43* ⊟ *05–61–94–98–22* ⏎ *14 rooms* ♿ *No a/c* ⊟ *AE, DC, MC, V* ⊙ *Closed Nov.–Mar.*

THE BASQUE COUNTRY, GASCONY & HAUTES-PYRÉNÉES A TO Z

To research prices, get advice from other travelers, and book travel arrangements, visit www.fodors.com.

AIR TRAVEL

CARRIERS Air France flies to Pau, Bayonne, and Biarritz from Paris and from other major European destinations. Air Littoral flies between Biarritz, Pau, Toulouse, Nice, and Marseille.

🛪 Airlines & Contacts **Air France** ☎ 05-59-33-34-35. **Air Littoral** ☎ 05-59-33-26-64.

AIRPORTS

Biarritz-Parme Airport serves Bayonne and Biarritz and has several daily flights to and from Paris and several weekly to London, Marseille, Geneva, Lyon, Nice, and Pau. Pau-Pyrénées International Airport has 10 flights daily to and from Paris as well as flights to Nantes, Lyon, Marseille, Nice, Biarritz, Madrid, Rome, Venice, Milan, and Geneva.

🛪 Airport Information **Biarritz-Parme Airport** ☎ 05-59-43-83-20. **Pau-Pyrénées International Airport** ☎ 05-59-33-33-00.

BUS TRAVEL

Various private bus concerns—STAB (serving the Bayonne–Anglet–Biarritz metropolitan areas) and ATCRB (up and down the coast and inland to many Basque towns)—service the region. Where they don't, the trusty SNCF national bus lines can occasionally come to the rescue. Beware of peak-hour traffic on roads in the summer, which can mean both delays in transport time and few seats on buses. Check in with the local tourist office for handy schedules or ask your hotel concierge for the best advice.

🚌 Bus Information **STAB-Biarritz** ✉ Rue Louis Barthou, Biarritz ☎ 05-59-24-26-53. **ATCRB** ☎ 05-59-26-06-99.

CAR RENTAL

🚗 Local Agencies **Avis** ✉ Biarritz-Parme Airport, Biarritz ☎ 05-59-23-67-92 ✉ 107 bd. Général-de-Gaulle, Hendaye ☎ 05-59-20-79-04 ✉ Pau-Pyrénées International Airport, Pau ☎ 05-59-33-27-13 ✉ Train station, St-Jean-de-Luz ☎ 05-59-26-76-66. **Budget** ✉ Biarritz-Parme Airport, Biarritz ☎ 05-59-23-58-62 ✉ Pau-Pyrénées International Airport, Pau ☎ 05-59-33-77-45. **Eurodollar** ✉ Biarritz-Parme Airport, Biarritz ☎ 05-59-41-21-12. **Europcar** ✉ Train station, Bayonne ☎ 05-59-55-38-20 ✉ Biarritz-Parme Airport, Biarritz ☎ 05-59-23-90-68 ✉ Pau-Pyrénées International Airport, Pau ☎ 05-59-33-24-31. **Hertz** ✉ Biarritz-Parme Airport, Biarritz ☎ 05-59-43-92-92 ✉ Pau-Pyrénées International Airport, Pau ☎ 05-59-33-16-38.

CAR TRAVEL

A64 connects Pau and Bayonne in less than an hour, and A63 runs up and down the Atlantic coast. N117 connects Hendaye with Toulouse via Pau and Tarbes. N134 connects Bordeaux, Pau, Oloron-Ste-Marie, and Spain via the Col de Somport and Jaca. The D918 from Bayonne through Cambo and along the Nive river to St-Jean-Pied-de-Port is a pretty drive, continuing on (as D919 and D920) through the Béarn country to Oloron-Ste-Marie and Pau.

ROAD CONDITIONS
Roads are occasionally slow and tortuous in the more mountainous areas, but valley and riverside roads are generally quite smooth and fast. D132, which goes between Arette and Pierre-St-Martin, can be snowed in between mid-November and mid-May, as can N134 through the Valley d'Aspe and the Col de Somport into Spain.

TOURS

In Biarritz, Aitzin organizes tours of Bayonne, Biarritz, the Basque coast, and the Basque Pyrénées. The Association des Guides, in Pau, arranges tours with guides of the city, the Pyrénées, and Béarn and Basque Country. The Bayonne tourist office gives guided tours of the city. La Guild du Tourisme des Pyrénées-Atlantiques offers information on and organizes visits and tours of the Basque Country and the Pyrénées. Guides Culturels Pyrénéens, in Tarbes, arranges many tours, including explorations on such themes as cave painting, art and architecture, Basque sports, hiking, and horseback riding.

🏴 **Aitzin** ☎ 05-59-24-36-05. **Association des Guides** ☎ 05-59-30-44-01. **Bayonne tourist office** ☎ 05-59-46-01-46. **Guides Culturels Pyrénéens** ☎ 05-62-44-15-44. **La Guild du Tourisme des Pyrénées-Atlantiques** ☎ 05-59-46-37-05.

TRAIN TRAVEL

High-speed trains (TGVs, Trains à Grande Vitesse) cover the 800 km (500 mi) from Paris to Bayonne in 4½ hours. To get to Pau, take the TGV to Bordeaux (three hours) and connect to Pau (two hours). Bayonne and Toulouse are connected by local SNCF trains via Pau, Tarbes, Lourdes, Lannemezan, and St-Gaudens. A local train runs along the Nive from Bayonne to St-Jean-Pied-de-Port. Local trains go between Bayonne and Biarritz and from Bayonne into the Atlantic Pyrénées, a slow but picturesque trip. Hendaye is connected to Bayonne and to San Sebastián via the famous *topo* (mole) train, so-called for the number of tunnels it passes through.

🏴 **Train Information** SNCF ☎ 08-36-35-35-35 ⊕ www.ter-sncf.com/uk/aquitaine/default.htm.

TRAVEL AGENCIES

Note that the American Express agencies receive mail, but don't do any banking transactions.

🏴 **Local Agent Referrals** **Adour Voyages** ✉ 3 rue Gardères, Biarritz ☎ 05-59-24-14-25. **Agence Garrouste** ✉ 10 rue Thiers, Bayonne ☎ 05-59-59-02-35. **American Express** ✉ 14 Chausée du Bourg, Lourdes ☎ 05-62-94-40-84. **Havas Voyages** ✉ 5 rue Lormand, Bayonne ☎ 05-59-46-29-26. **L'Accueil Pyrénéen** ✉ 26 av. Maransin, Lourdes ☎ 05-62-94-15-62. **Maison du Pélerin** ✉ 12 av. Maransin, Lourdes ☎ 05-62-94-70-05. **Saga Tours** ✉ 4 av. du Maréchal-Foch, Biarritz ☎ 05-59-24-39-39.

VISITOR INFORMATION

🏴 **Tourist Information** **Ainhoa** ✉ Mairie ☎ 05-59-29-92-60. **Bagnères-de-Luchon** ✉ 18 allée d'Etigny ☎ 05-61-79-21-21. **Bayonne** ✉ Pl. des Basques ☎ 05-59-46-01-46 ⊕ www.ville-bayonne.fr/. **Biarritz** ✉ 1 sq. Ixelles ☎ 05-59-22-37-10 ⊕ www.biarritz.

fr/. **Cauterets** ✉ 15 Cauterets ☎ 05-62-92-50-27. **Gavarnie** ✉ In center of village ☎ 05-62-92-49-10 ⊕ www.gavarnie.com/. **Hendaye** ✉ 12 rue des Aubépines ☎ 05-59-20-00-34 ⊕ www.hendaye.com/. **Lourdes** ✉ Pl. Beyramalu ☎ 05-62-42-77-40 ⊕ www.lourdes-france.com/. **Navarrenx** ✉ Mairie ☎ 05-59-66-10-22. **Oloron-Ste-Marie** ✉ Pl. de la Résistance ☎ 05-59-39-98-00 ⊕ www.oloron-ste-marie.fr/. **Pau** ✉ Pl. Royale ☎ 05-59-27-27-08 ⊕ www.ville-pau.fr/. **St-Bertrand-de-Comminges** ✉ Mairie ☎ 05-61-88-33-12. **St-Jean-de-Luz** ✉ Pl. Foch ☎ 05-59-26-03-16 ⊕ www.saint-jean-de-luz.com/. **St-Jean-Pied-de-Port** ✉ 14 pl. Charles-de-Gaulle ☎ 05-59-37-03-57. **Sare** ✉ Mairie ☎ 05-59-54-20-14. **Sauveterre-de-Béarn** ✉ Mairie ☎ 05-59-38-50-17 ⊕ www.tourisme.fr/office-de-tourisme/sauveterre-de-bearn.htm.

Bordeaux, Dordogne & Poitou-Charentes

16

WORD OF MOUTH

"In the Dordogne, I would visit the medieval market town of Sarlat-la-Canéda. The buildings are all of golden stone, which are gas lamp–illuminated at night. The town is a warren of alleys and narrow streets—the type of place filled with nooks and crannies that kids love."

—LEVernon

"It was amazing to hear that Lascaux's prehistoric cave dwellers are considered artists as they used the natural curves of the walls to create the most realistic depictions of muscles possible. Guides use laser pointers to outline objects for you and, at one point, they turn off the lights and light a candle—it gives you goosebumps to see the paintings come to life when the flame flickers."

—Wendy

Introduction by
Nancy Coons

Updated by
Thomas
Cussans

IF YOU'RE LOOKING FOR THE GOOD LIFE, your search may be ended. No other region of France packs such a concentration of fine wine, extraordinary spirits, and gustatory delights ranging from exquisite cuisine to the most rib-sticking of country cooking. It's almost too much to ask that it be lovely, too—but it is. Viewed by generations of British as the quintessential French escape and now enjoying a new vogue with American travelers, Dordogne is a picture-postcard fantasy of green countryside, stone cottages, and cliff-top châteaux, crowned by the enchanting medieval wine town of St-Émilion. The Atlantic coast north of Bordeaux offers elite enclaves of white-sand beach. The vineyards of Médoc extend their lush green rows to the south. And beyond the fertile outreaches of Charente, the canal-laced Marais Poitevin—France's "Green Venice"—is a luxuriant, watery bower.

It's no wonder the English fought for it so determinedly throughout the Hundred Years' War. This coveted corner of France was home to Eleanor of Aquitaine, and when she left her first husband, France's Louis VII, to marry Henry II of England, both she and the land came under English rule. Henry Plantagenet was, after all, a great-grandson of William the Conqueror, and the Franco-English ambiguity of the age exploded in a war that defined much of modern France and changed its face forever. Southwestern France was the stage upon which much of the war was conducted. Hence the region's defensive châteaux-forts; hence no end of sturdy churches dedicated to the noble families' cause; and hence the steady flow of Bordeaux wines to England, where it is still dubbed "claret," after *clairet,* a light red version from earlier days.

What they sought, the world still seeks. The wines of Bordeaux set the standard against which other wines are measured, especially the burgeoning worldwide parade of Cabernets. From the grandest *premiers grands crus*—the Lafite-Rothschilds, the Margaux—to the modest *supérieur* in your picnic basket, the rigorously controlled Bordeaux commands respect. Fans and oenophiles come from around the world to pay homage; to gaze at the noble symmetries of estate châteaux, whose rows of green-and-black vineyards radiate in every direction; to lower a nose deep into a well-swirled glass to inhale the heady vapors of oak and almond and leather; and, finally, to reverently pack a few bloodline labels into a trunk or a suitcase for home.

The rest you will drink on site, from the mouthful of golden Graves that eases the oysters down to the syrupy sip of Sauternes that civilizes the smooth gaminess of the foie gras to the last glass of Médoc paired with the salt-marsh lamb that leads to pulling the cork on a Pauillac—because there is, still to come, the cheese tray. . . .

But brace yourself: you've barely scratched the culinary surface. Take a deep breath and head inland, following the winding sprawl of the Dordogne River into duck country. This is the land of the *gavée* goose, force-fed extravagantly to plump its liver into one of the world's most renowned delicacies. Duck or goose fat glistens on potatoes, on salty confits, on *rillettes d'oie,* a spread of potted duck that melts on the tongue as no mere butter ever could. Wild mushrooms and truffles weave their

From the grand châteaux of Bordeaux country to the stone-cottage pastorale of Dordogne, from the broad, sandy beaches of Royan to the watery bower of the Marais Poitevin, this region offers a wondrous mix of high culture and elemental nature. And in the land of foie gras and cognac you'll eat (and quaff) like the kings (and queens) who once disputed this coveted south-west corner, staking it out with châteaux-forts and blessing it with Romanesque churches. But to try to see all of the region in one trip would be overambitious, so you need to be selective. If you love the beach and the outdoors, head to the Royan Peninsula or the islands of Ré and Oléron. If you're a gourmand, go straight to Dordogne; if wine is your passion, use Bordeaux as your base. For nature, seek out the Marais-Poitevin. Following are two suggested itineraries.

16

Numbers in the text correspond to numbers in the margin and on the Bordeaux, Dordogne & Poitou-Charentes map.

If you have
3 days

Have a morning tour and lunch in vibrant **Bordeaux** ❶ ▶ –❾ before heading on to medieval ⊠ **St-Émilion** ⓬, showplace of the Bordeaux wine region, during the afternoon. On the second day head east to the heart of the storybook Dordogne region, ⊠ **Sarlat-la-Canéda** ㉓ and enjoy its golden-stone houses, narrow, twisty streets, and lovely Renaissance ambience. If you are up for France's second most visited tourist site, keep heading east to ⊠ **Rocamadour**⓳, whose medieval Cité Réligieuse famously clusters its way up a towering rock bluff. If, on the other hand, maddening crowds are not for you, spend a day touring fairy-tale sights in the Dordogne, such as the hilltop castle at **Beynac** ㉒, the enchanting cliffside village of **La Roque-Gageac** ㉑, and the château at **Biron** ⓰, before heading back east to Bordeaux and dinner.

If you have
7 days

Finish off your morning tour with lunch in **Bordeaux** ❶ ▶ –❾ before whizzing back to the Middle Ages in ⊠ **St-Émilion** ⓬ during the afternoon. On the second day visit the fortified medieval village of **Monpazier** ⓯ and the mighty château in **Biron** ⓰, before veering north to overnight at ⊠ **La Roque-Gageac** ㉑, huddled beneath a towering cliff. On Day 3 head along the Dordogne River to the castle at **Beynac** ㉒, lunch on foie gras and truffles in the medieval market town of ⊠ **Sarlat-la-Canéda** ㉓, then check out the cave paintings at the **Lascaux II** ㉕ or the archaeological finds at the Musée Nationale de Préhistoire in **Les Eyzies-de-Tayac** ㉔. Rest up near ⊠ **Hautefort** ㉖. On Day 4 leave Dordogne via quaint **Brantôme** ㉘ en route to hilltop **Angoulême** ㉙. Try to get to **Cognac** ㉚ by afternoon to pay a call on a *chai,* then continue along the Charente Valley before spending the night in ⊠ **Saintes** ㉛. On Day 5 drive up to the lovely ⊠ **Ile de Ré** ㉝. After an overnight, head to ⊠ **La Rochelle** ㉜ where you can explore the Vieille Ville and picturesque harbor, then enjoy your last overnight. On your final day head east to the Marais Poitevin, lunching in the pretty village of **Coulon** ㉞, and continuing to **Poitiers** ㉟ to end your tour.

musky perfume through dense game pâtés. The wines, such as Bergerac and Cahors, are coarser here, as if to stand up to such an onslaught of earthy textures and flavors. And a snifter of amber cognac is de rigueur for the digestion.

Dining thus, in a vine-covered stone *ferme auberge* deep in the green wilds of Dordogne, the day's parade of châteaux and chapel tours blurring pleasantly into a reverie of picturesque history, you'll begin to understand what the Plantagenets were fighting for.

Exploring Bordeaux, Dordogne & Poitou-Charentes

For three centuries during the Middle Ages, this region was a battlefield in the wars between the French and the English. Of the castles and châteaux dotting the area, those at Biron, Hautefort, and Beynac are among the most spectacular. Robust Romanesque architecture is more characteristically found in this area than the airy Gothic style in view elsewhere in France: Poitiers showcases the best examples, notably Notre-Dame-la-Grande, with its richly worked facade. The Romanesque style can also be admired in Angoulême and Périgueux, and in countless village churches.

If there is a formula for enjoying this region, it would include cultural highlights, relaxing by the sea, tasting wine, and indulging in oysters, truffles, and foie gras. Swaths of sandy beaches line the Atlantic coast: well-heeled resorts like Royan and Arcachon are packed with glistening bodies baking in the sun. The world-famous vineyards of Médoc, Sauternes, Graves, Entre-Deux-Mers, Pomerol, and St-Émilion surround the elegant 18th-century city of Bordeaux, set on the southwest edge of the region near the foot of the Gironde Estuary.

If you prefer solitude, you won't have any trouble finding it in the vast, underpopulated spaces stretching inland and eastward in the rolling countryside of Dordogne, chock-full of storybook villages, riverside châteaux, medieval chapels, and prehistoric sites. To the north, the rural region of Poitou-Charentes reaches from Angoulême through Cognac country to the Atlantic coast, and back inland through the canals around Niort to Poitiers. Between La Rochelle and Poitiers lies the Marais Poitevin, a marshy area known as "Green Venice" for its network of crisscrossing waterways.

About the Restaurants & Hotels

Apart from cosmopolitan Bordeaux and the university towns of Poitiers and La Rochelle, this region of southwest France can seem pretty sleepy outside the summer months. You'll never have too much trouble finding a good place to eat in the larger coastal resorts like Royan and Arcachon, but if you're traveling in the Dordogne or the Marais Poitevin between October and March it's essential to call ahead to avoid disappointment. Closing times, too, can be variable.

Vacationers flock to the coast and islands, and for miles around hotels are booked solid for months in advance. Farther inland—except for the Dordogne Valley—the situation eases up, but there aren't as many places

Grape Expectations

Everyone in Bordeaux is celebrating because the 2000 vintage was acclaimed as the "crop of the century, " a vintage that comes along once in a lifetime. But bringing everything down to earth are the increasingly loud whispers that Bordeaux may be "over." Some critics feel the world has moved away from pricey, rich, red wines and more people are opting for lighter choices from other lands. Be that as it may, if you have any aspirations to being a wine connoisseur, Bordeaux will always remain the top of the pyramid. It has been considered so ever since the credentials of Bordeaux wines were traditionally es- tablished in 1787. That year, Thomas Jefferson went down to the region from Paris and splurged on bottles of 1784 Château d'Yquem and Château Margaux, for prices that were, he reported, "indeed dear." Jefferson knew his wines: In 1855, both Yquem and Margaux were offi- cially classified among Bordeaux's top five. And two centuries later, some of his very bottles fetched upward of $50,000 when offered in a high-flying auc- tion in New York City. His Margaux—of which Jefferson boasted "there can- not be a better bottle of Bordeaux" (in fact, it was a half-bottle) was sold in the late 1980s for $30,000. As it turns out, Bordeaux's reputation dates from the Middle Ages. From 1152 to 1453, along with much of what is now western France, Bordeaux belonged to England. The light red wine then produced was known as *clairet,* the origin of our word "claret."

Today no other part of France has such a concentrated wealth of top-class vine- yards. The versatile Bordeaux region yields sweet and dry whites and fruity or full-bodied reds from a huge domain extending on either side of the Gironde (Blaye and Bourg to the north, Médoc and Graves to the south) and inland along the Garonne (Sauternes) and Dordogne (St-Émilion, Fronsac, Pomerol) or in between these two rivers (Entre-Deux-Mers). Farther north, the verdant hills of Cognac pro- duce the world's finest brandy. Less familiar appellations are also worth seeking out, including Bergerac, Pécharmant, and Monbazillac, along the Dordogne River, and the lighter whites and reds of the Fiefs Vendéens, north of La Rochelle.

At the top of the government-supervised scale—which ranks, from highest to lowest, as Appelation d'Origine Contrôlée (often abbreviated AOC); Vin Délim- ité de Qualité Supérieur (VDQS—a level that represents about 10 percent of French wines); Vins de Pays, and Vin de Table—are the fabled vintages of Bor- deaux, leading off with Margaux. The vineyards of Margaux are among the ugliest in France, lost amid the flat, dusty plains of Médoc. Bordeaux is better represented at historic St-Émilion, with its cascading cobbled streets, or at Sauternes, where the noble rot (a fungus that sucks water from the grapes, leaving them sweeter) steals up the riverbanks as autumn mists vanish in the summer skies. At this time, the harvests, or *vendanges,* begin in September and can last into December. In Sauternes, at Château d'Yquem, up to seven successive manual harvests may be required, with each grape inspected individually and picked only after achieving the right degree of maturity. It is one of the miracles of Bordeaux that these grapes—which often look like foul, shriveled messes—are transformed into one of the most sublime wines in the world.

16

Of course, sour grapes remain. In this world of nouvelle cuisine and uncellared wines, the heavy, expensive vintages of Bordeaux are increasingly *démodé* and lack "relevance." Nevertheless, Bordeaux will always remain one of the bedrocks of French viticulture. It's just too bad that many vineyards, especially those of the Médoc, have nothing to show except bottles of their product, and dusty hillsides covered with vines. Many are inaccessible without a car or bike. This is why a tour group might be best—the Bordeaux tourist office arranges such trips. If you're determined to go it alone, the Maison du Vin can tell you how to get to many of the vineyards by bus.

Along the Shore

Although the region's two main islands, Ile de Ré and Ile d'Oléron, are linked to the mainland by bridges, boats still ply the Atlantic waters south of La Rochelle, visiting Fort Boyard and docking at Ile d'Aix. Explore the oyster beds of the Baie de Seudre or make an excursion across the Gironde to the Cordouan Lighthouse, stranded on a sandbank in mid-estuary. Ferries ply the Gironde from Royan and Blaye; punts, steered with long poles, glide peacefully along the canals of the Marais Poitevin; and the Dordogne River is a favorite with canoers. French families concentrate on resort towns like Royan, but there are plenty of other spacious beaches where you can escape the crowds: along the forest-girdled Côte Sauvage (Wild Coast) north of Royan; along the shores of the islands of Ré, Aix, and Oléron; and beneath the huge dunes south of Arcachon.

On the Menu

Truffles, foie gras, walnuts, plums, trout, eel, oysters, and myriad species of mushrooms jostle for attention on restaurant menus. The hearty food of Dordogne, the rich dairy bounty of Poitou-Charentes, and shoals of succulent seafood from the Atlantic make for diversified table fare. The versatile wines of Bordeaux make fine accompaniments to most regional dishes. Cognac is de rigueur at the end of a meal; sweet, tangy *pineau des Charentes*—made from cognac and unfermented grape juice—at the beginning.

---

to choose from. Advance booking is particularly desirable in Bordeaux, at any time, and in Dordogne, where hotels fill up quickly, in midsummer. Many country or small-town hotels expect you to have at least one dinner with them, and if you have two meals a day with your lodging and stay several nights, you will save money. Prices off-season (October–May) often drop as much as 20%. Assume all hotel rooms have air-conditioning, TV, telephones, and private bath, unless otherwise noted.

WHAT IT COSTS In euros					
	$$$$	**$$$**	**$$**	**$**	**¢**
RESTAURANTS	over €30	€23–€30	€17–€23	€11–€17	under €11
HOTELS	over €180	€120–€180	€80–€120	€50–€80	under €50

Restaurant prices are per person for a main course at dinner, including tax (19.6%) and service; note that if a restaurant offers only prix-fixe (set-price) meals, it has been given the price category that reflects the full prix-fixe price. Hotel prices are for a standard double room in high season, including tax (19.6%) and service charge. Hotels operate on the European Plan (EP, with no meal provided) unless we note that they use the Breakfast Plan (BP), or also offer such options as Modified American Plan (MAP, with breakfast and dinner daily, known as *demi-pension*), or Full American Plan (FAP, or *pension complète*, with three meals a day). Inquire when booking if these all-inclusive mealplans (which always entail higher rates) are mandatory or optional.

Timing

Spring and fall are the best times to visit—there aren't as many tourists around, and the weather is still pleasant. The *vendanges* (grape harvests) usually begin about mid-September in the Bordeaux region (though you can't visit the wineries at this time), and two weeks later in the Cognac region, to the north. A number of hotels are closed from the end of October through March.

THE BORDEAUX REGION

As the capital of the Gironde *département* (province), Bordeaux is both the commercial and cultural center of southwest France and an important transportation hub for the entire region. And if you're a wine connoisseur, it is still the doorway to paradise: pretty Sauternes and Graves lie to the south; Pomerol and St-Émilion to the east; the flat and dusty Médoc peninsula to the northwest, looking across the Gironde Estuary at the vineyards of Bourg and Blaye.

Bordeaux

Fodor's Choice ★ *580 km (360 mi) southwest of Paris, 240 km (150 mi) northwest of Toulouse, 190 km (118 mi) north of Biarritz.*

Bordeaux as a whole, rather than any particular points within it, is what you'll want to visit in order to understand why Victor Hugo described it as Versailles plus Antwerp, and why, when he was exiled from his native Spain, the painter Francisco de Goya chose it as his last home (he died here in 1828). The capital of southwest France and the region's largest city, Bordeaux remains synonymous with the wine trade: wine shippers have long maintained their headquarters along the banks of the Garonne, while buyers from around the world arrive for the huge biannual Vinexpo show. An aura of 18th-century elegance permeates downtown Bordeaux, where fine shops invite exploration. To the south of the city center are the old docklands undergoing gradual renewal—one train station has now been transformed into a big multiplex cinema—but the area is still a bit shady. As a whole, Bordeaux is a less exuberant city than many others in France. That noted, lively and stylish elements are making a dent in the city's conservative veneer, and the cleaned-up riverfront is said by some, after a bottle or two, to exude an elegance redolent of St. Petersburg. Some of that ambience, however, is currently under assault by the city's construction of a multibillion-euro tramway system, though at least the worst of the work, scheduled for completion in 2007, is now over. To get a feel for the historic port of Bordeaux, take the 90-minute boat trip that leaves quai Louis-XVIII every weekday afternoon, or the regular passenger ferry that plies the Garonne between Quai Richelieu and the Pont d'Aquitaine.

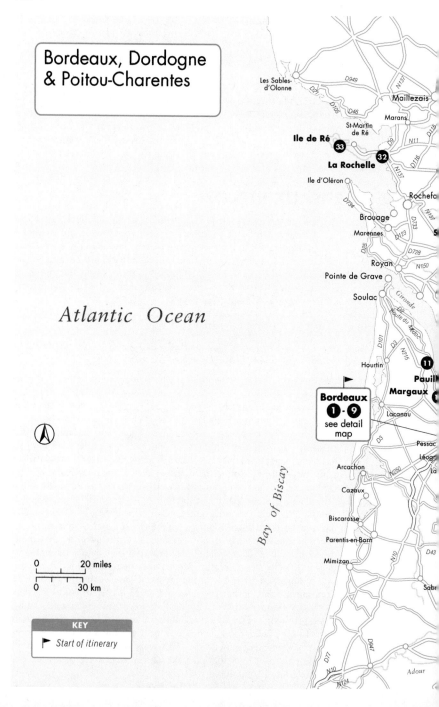

Bordeaux, Dordogne & Poitou-Charentes

Atlantic Ocean

Les Sables-d'Olonne

Maillezais

Marans

St-Martin de Ré

Ile de Ré ③③

La Rochelle ③②

Ile d'Oléron

Rochefo

Brouage

Marennes

S

Royan

Pointe de Grave

Soulac

Gironde

Hourtin

⑪

Pauill

Margaux

Bordeaux ❶ - ❾ see detail map

Lacanau

Pessac

Léog

Arcachon

La

Cazaux

Biscarosse

Parentis-en-Born

Mimizan

Sabr

Bay of Biscay

D77

N10

Adour

| 0 | | 20 miles |
| 0 | | 30 km |

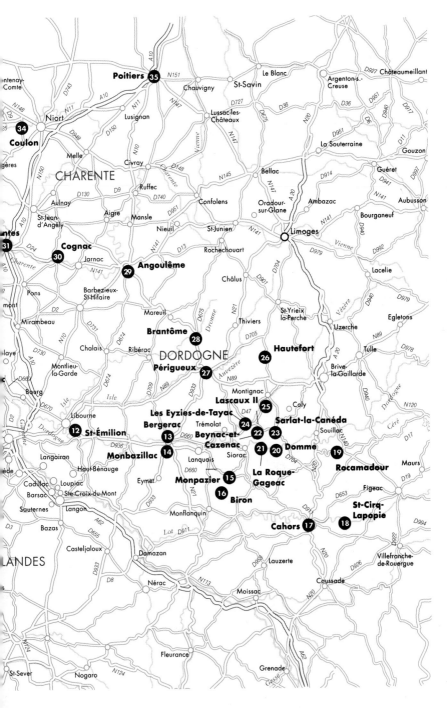

► ❶ For a view of the picturesque quayside, stroll across the Garonne on the **Pont de Pierre,** built on the orders of Napoléon between 1810 and 1822 and until 1965 the only bridge across the river; in calm weather you'll see a tethered balloon that allows sightseers to soar 500 yards overhead, ❷ moored to the left (€10). Return to the left bank and head north to **Place de la Bourse,** an open square (built 1730–55) ringed with large-windowed buildings designed by the era's most esteemed architect, Jacques-Ange Gabriel, who later worked for Marie-Antoinette at Versailles. A few blocks to the southeast of the place de la Bourse is the **place du Parlement,** also ringed by elegant 18th-century structures and packed with lively outdoor cafés. Just north of the Esplanade des Quinconces, a sprawling ❸ square, is the two-story **Musée d'Art Contemporain** (Contemporary Art Center), imaginatively housed in a converted 19th-century spice warehouse, the Entrepôt Lainé. Many shows here showcase cutting-edge artists who invariably festoon the huge expanse of the place with hanging ropes, ladders, and large video screens. ⊠ *7 rue Ferrère* ☎ *05–56–00–81–50* 🔲 *€5 (free the first Sun. each month)* ⊙ *Tues.–Sun. 11–6.*

> **need a break?** The trendy **museum café,** next to the art library on the top floor of Musée d'Art Contemporain, offers a good choice of beverages and snacks, and fine views over the Bordeaux skyline. It's open Tuesday through Sunday, noon until six. ⊠ *7 rue Ferrère.*

❹ Close by along the quayside is the **Musée des Chartrons,** in an 18th-century vintner's house, retracing the history of the wine trade through a fine collection of old barrels and antique bottles. ⊠ *41 rue Borie* ☎ *05–57–87–50–60* 🔲 *€5.10* ⊙ *Tues.–Sat. 10:30–2:30 and 2–5; 1st Sun. each month 11–5.*

★ ❺ Turn back along the Garonne and cross Esplanade des Quinconces to tree-lined cours du XXX-Juillet and the **Maison du Vin,** run by the CIVB (Conseil Interprofessionnel des Vins de Bordeaux), the headquarters of the Bordeaux wine trade. Before you set out to explore the regional wine country, stop here to gain clues from the staff (some are English-speaking) on the art of *dégustation* and pointers for where to go; their publication *Vineyards and Wine Cellars in the Bordeaux Area* is helpful. More important, tasting a red (like Pauillac or St-Émilion), a dry white (like an Entre-Deux-Mers or Côtes de Blaye), and a sweet white (like Sauternes or Loupiac) will help you decide which of the seven wine regions to explore. Remember: Before visiting any country château vineyard, always call ahead to see if the tasting is free and whether you need an appointment—the staff here can help with these questions. You can also make purchases at the **Vinothèque** opposite. ⊠ *8 cours du XXX-Juillet* ☎ *05–56–52–32–05* ⊕ *www.la-vinotheque.com* 🔲 *Free* ⊙ *Mon. 2–7:30, Tues.–Sat. 10–7:30.*

❻ One block south is the city's leading 18th-century monument: the **Grand Théâtre,** designed by Victor Louis and built between 1773 and 1780. It's the pride of the city, with an elegant exterior ringed by graceful Corinthian columns and a dazzling foyer with a two-winged staircase and a cupola. The theater hall has a frescoed ceiling with a shimmering chan-

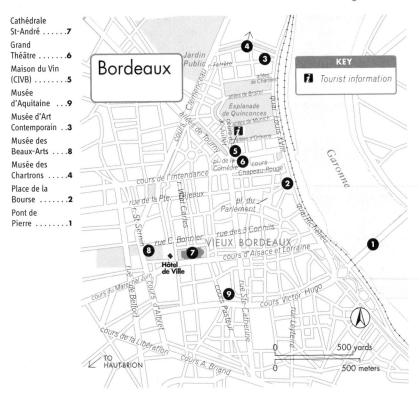

delier composed of 14,000 Bohemian crystals. ⊠ *Pl. de la Comédie* ☏ *05–56–00–66–00* ⊕ *www.opera-bordeaux.com* ☞ *€5* ☞ *Contact tourist office for guided tours.*

➐ Continue south on rue Ste-Catherine, then turn right on cours d'Alsace et Lorraine to reach the **Cathédrale St-André** (⊠ Pl. Pey-Berland). This hefty edifice isn't one of France's finer Gothic cathedrals, but the intricate 14th-century chancel makes an interesting contrast with the earlier nave. Excellent stone carvings adorn the facade. You can climb the 15th-century, 160-foot **Tour Pey-Berland** for a stunning view of the city; cost is €4.60, and it's open Tuesday–Sunday 10–12:30 and 2–5.

➑ The nearby **Musée des Beaux-Arts,** across tidy gardens behind the ornate Hôtel de Ville (town hall), has a collection of works spanning the 15th–20th centuries, with important paintings by Paolo Veronese (*Apostle's Head*), Camille Corot (*Bath of Diana*), and Odilon Redon (*Apollo's Chariot*), and sculptures by Auguste Rodin. ⊠ *20 cours d'Albret* ☏ *05–56–10–20–56* ☞ *€5.50 (free 1st Sun. each month)* ☉ *Wed.–Mon. 11–6.*

➒ Two blocks south of the Cathédrale St-André is the **Musée d'Aquitaine,** an excellent museum that takes you on a trip through Bordeaux's history, with emphases on Roman, medieval, Renaissance, port-harbor, colonial, and 20th-century daily life. The detailed prehistoric section almost saves you a trip to Lascaux II, which is reproduced here in part. ⊠ *20 cours Pasteur* ☎ *05–56–01–51–00* ⊡ *€5.50* ⊙ *Tues.–Sun. 11–6.*

One of the region's most famous wine-producing châteaux is actually within the city limits: follow N250 southwest from central Bordeaux for 3 km (2 mi) to the district of Pessac, home to **Haut-Brion,** producer of the only non-Médoc wine to be ranked a *premier cru* (the most elite wine classification). It is claimed the very buildings surrounding the vineyards create their own microclimate, protecting the precious grapes and allowing them to ripen earlier. The white château looks out over the celebrated pebbly soil. The wines produced at **La Mission–Haut Brion,** across the road, are almost as sought-after. ⊠ *133 av. Jean-Jaurès, Pessac* ☎ *05–56–00–29–31* ⊕ *www.chateau-haut-brion.tm.fr* ⊡ *Free 1-hr visits by appointment, weekdays only, with tasting* ⊙ *Closed mid-July–mid-Aug.*

Where to Stay & Eat

Old Bordeaux has many small restaurants, particularly around the 18th-century place du Parlement, like bustling L'Ombrière (No. 14), with fairly priced steaks, and pricey Chez Philippe (No. 1), one of the city's top fish restaurants. What is lacking are charming hotels. You may want to consider staying outside Bordeaux: at Château Lamothe in St-Sulpice & Cameyrac, 20 km (12 mi) east of the city, for instance.

$$$$ ✕ **Le Chapon-Fin.** With all the laurels and stars thrown at Thierry Marx,
Fodor'sChoice the culinary wizard ensconced at Pauillac's Château Cordeillan-Bages,
★ it was just a matter of time before he would swoop in and give Bordeaux's own landmark restaurant an all-out reenergizing shot in the arm. It needed one: Founded in 1825, favored by such V.I.P.s as Sarah Bernhardt, Toulouse-Lautrec, and Edward VII, and graced with an extraordinary decor (half winter-garden, half rococo-grotto), the Chapon-Fin had hardened with age. Marx has now stepped aside for one of his protegés, Nicolas Frion. Together, they have fashioned a face-lift that includes such nouvelle delights as foie gras on a bed of candied peaches with a sauce of reduced Port; lobster with sweet chestnuts and wild mushrooms; and Pauillac lamb grilled in a Bordeaux sauce. You haven't really been to Bordeaux until you've been here—so book now. ⊠ *5 rue Montesquieu* ☎ *05–56–79–10–10* 🖷 *05–56–79–09–10* ⊕ *www.chapon-fin.com* ⌂ *Reservations essential* ⊟ *AE, MC, V* ⊙ *Closed Sun. and Mon.*

★ **$$–$$$$** ✕ **La Tupina.** With much glory stolen by its noble cellars, Bordeaux has struggled mightily against its reputation as a culinary backwater. Happily, fine new chefs are arriving all the time and one of the best is Stéphane Gabrielly, whose earthy spins on *cuisine de terroir* are served up at this lovely restaurant set on one of Bordeaux's oldest streets. Inside, dried herbs hang from the ceiling, a Provençal grandfather clock ticks off the minutes, and an antique fireplace sports a grill bearing sizzling morsels of duck and chicken. Both the decor and the menu aspire to the *"nostalgie des anciennes menus"* and both succeed. On the same street (No. 34) is the owner's Bar-Cave, a cheaper bistro, with another fetching ambience. ⊠ *6 rue Porte de la Monnaie* ☎ *05–56–91–56–37* ⊕ *www.latupina.com* ⌂ *Reservations essential* ⊟ *AE, MC, V.*

★ **$$–$$$** ✗ **Chez Philippe.** Something of an institution in Bordeaux, Chez Philippe, right in the city center, offers spectacular seafood: its *fruits de mer* are gleaming mounds of oysters, shrimp, langoustine, and lobster that carry with them the authentic tang of the sea. ✉ *1 pl. du Parlement* ☎ *05–56–81–83–15* 🟰 *AE, DC, MC, V* 🕙 *Closed Sun., Mon. and Aug.*

$$ ✗ **L'Estacade.** *Le tout Bordeaux* now congregates at this fashionable spot, spectacularly set in a pierlike structure right on the Garonne River. Enormous bay windows allow you to drink in a beautiful panorama of the 18th-century place de la Bourse on the opposite bank. The cuisine is creative (prawn risotto, mullet with trout roe); the wine list has few selections to offer other than young Bordeaux, but that seems only fitting. ✉ *Quai des Queyries* ☎ *05–57–54–02–50* 📠 *05–57–54–02–51* 🌐 *www.lestacade.com* 🟰 *MC, V.*

$–$$ ✗ **Le Café Français.** For more than 30 years, Mme. Jouhanneau has presided over this venerable bistrot in the heart of the Vieille Ville hard by the Cathédrale St-Andre. The decor, with large mirrors and plush curtains, is sober, the mood busy. But it's the food, solidly based on regional specialties, that counts, and, for solid sustenance at reasonable prices, it's hard to beat. Try for a table on the terrace: the view over place Pey-Berland is never less than diverting. ✉ *5 pl. Pey-Berland* ☎ *05–56–52–96–69* 📠 *05–56–01–16–79* 🟰 *AE, DC, MC, V.*

$$$–$$$$ ✗🏨 **Burdigala.** Of the three luxury hotels in Bordeaux, Burdigala (Latin for "Bordeaux") is the only one within walking distance of the center of town. Although the modern exterior is unappealing, the inside is comfortable. The soundproof rooms are smart and neat; No. 416 is especially quiet and sunny. Deluxe rooms have marble bathrooms with whirlpool baths. The Jardin du Burdigala restaurant serves nouvelle cuisine. ✉ *115 rue Georges Bonnac, 33000* ☎ *05–56–90–16–16* 📠 *05–56–93–15–06* 🌐 *www.burdigala.com* 🛏 *68 rooms, 15 suites* 🍴 *Restaurant, minibars, cable TV, Internet, some pets allowed (fee)* 🟰 *AE, DC, MC, V* 🍽 *MAP.*

$$–$$$ 🏨 **Quality Hotel Sainte-Catherine.** This fully modernized hotel is in an 18th-century building in the old part of town. Service is limited, but the reception staff is helpful. The compact, pastel-tone rooms are decorated with light floral fabrics. ✉ *27 rue du Parlement-Ste-Catherine, 33000* ☎ *05–56–81–95–12* 📠 *05–56–44–50–51* 🌐 *www.quality-hotel-sainte-catherine-bordeaux.federal-hotel.com/* 🛏 *82 rooms* 🍴 *Minibars, cable TV, bar, some pets allowed (fee)* 🟰 *AE, DC, MC, V* 🍽 *BP.*

$–$$ 🏨 **Des Quatre Soeurs.** In an elegant 1840 town house near the Grand Théâtre, this hotel has sober, well-kept rooms of varying sizes, all with air-conditioning. It's changed a bit since Richard Wagner stayed here. ✉ *6 cours du XXX-Juillet, 33000* ☎ *05–57–81–19–20* 📠 *05–56–01–04–28* 🌐 *http://4soeurs.online.fr/anglais/* 🛏 *29 rooms, 5 suites* 🍴 *Cable TV, Internet, some pets allowed (fee)* 🟰 *AE, MC, V* 🍽 *MAP.*

Nightlife & the Arts

A respected and long-established Bordeaux hangout, **Les Argentiers** (✉ 33 rue des Argentiers) is the place for jazz. **L'Aztécal** (✉ 61 rue du Pas-St-Georges) is a comfortable spot for a drink. **Sénéchal** (✉ 57 bis quai de Paludate), near the station, is the place to dance the night away.

The **Grand Théâtre** (✉ Pl. de la Comédie ☎ 05–56–00–85–95 ⊕ www. opera-bordeaux.com) puts on performances of French plays and occasionally operas. Bordeaux's four-day **Fête du Vin** (Wine Festival; ⊕ www.bordeaux-tourisme.com) at the end of June sees glass-clinking merriment along the banks of the Garonne. The tourist office Web site has the details.

Shopping

Between the cathedral and the Grand Théâtre are numerous pedestrian streets where stylish shops and clothing boutiques abound—Bordeaux may favor understatement but there's no lack of elegance. For an exceptional selection of cheeses, go to **Jean d'Alos** (✉ 4 rue Montesquieu). The **Vinothèque** (✉ 8 cours du Juillet) sells top-ranked Bordeaux wines. **La Maison des Millesimes** (✉ 37 rue Esprit des Lois) has a wide range of great wines and will deliver to anywhere in the world.

Route du Médoc

North of Bordeaux, the Route du Médoc wine road (D2)—sometimes called the Route des Châteaux—winds through the dusty Médoc Peninsula, past the townships of Margaux, St.-Julien, Pauillac, and St-Estèphe.

❿ Even the vines in Médoc look dusty, and so does the ugly town of **Margaux,** the area's unofficial capital, 27 km (17 mi) northwest of Bordeaux. Yet **Château Margaux** (☎ 05–57–88–83–83), housed in a magnificent Neoclassical building from 1802, is recognized as a producer of premiers crus, whose wine qualifies with Graves's Haut-Brion as one of Bordeaux's top five reds. As with all the top Bordeaux châteaux, visits to Château Margaux are restricted to the wine chai on weekends, made through appointment only. The well-informed, English-speaking staff at the **Margaux Maison du Vin** (☎ 05–57–88–70–82 or 05–57–88–38–27) can direct you to other châteaux such as **Lascombes** and **Palmer,** which have beautiful grounds, reasonably priced wines, and are open without reservations. In nearby Cussac, visit the winery and carriage museum at **Château Lanessan.**

★ ⓫ Some 90 km (56 mi) north of Bordeaux on highway D2 is **Pauillac,** home to the three wineries—Lafite-Rothschild, Latour, and Mouton-★ Rothschild—that produce Médoc's other top reds. Renowned **Château Latour** (☎ 05–56–73–19–80) sometimes requires reservations a month in advance for its wine-tastings (available for groups up to 8). If the posh prices of these fabled *grands crus* are not for you, rent a bike at the La Verrerie **tourist office** (☎ 05–56–59–03–08), and visit any of the slightly less-expensive nearby wineries. Of all the towns and villages in the Médoc, Pauillac is the prettiest; you may want to stroll along the riverfront and stop for refreshments at one of its restaurants. A train line connects Pauillac to Bordeaux, running several times in the summer.

★ **Lafite-Rothschild** is among the most resonant names of the wine world. Even by the giddy standards of the Médoc, Lafite—owned by the Rothschild family since 1868 (but first recorded as making wine as early as 1234)—is a high temple of wine making at its most memorable. Prices may be sky high but no one fortunate enough to sample one of the château's classic vintages will forget the experience in a hurry. Too bad you can't visit the family château on the grounds—its rooms are the defining examples of *le style Rothschild,* one of the most opulent styles of 19th-century interior decoration. ✉ *33250 Pauillac* ☎ *05–56–59–26–83* ⊕ *www.lafite.com* ⊠ *Free* ⊗ *By appointment only, reservations to be made at least two weeks in advance; closed Aug.–Oct.*

Most of the great vineyards in this area are strictly private (the owners, however, are usually receptive to inquiries about visits from bona fide wine connoisseurs). One vineyard, however, has long boasted a welcoming ★ visitor center: **Mouton-Rothschild,** whose eponymous wine was brought to perfection in the 1930s by that flamboyant figure Baron Philippe de Rothschild, whose American-born wife, Pauline, was a great style-maker of the 1950s. The baron's daughter, Philippine, continues to lavish money and love on this growth, so wine lovers should flock here for either the one-hour visit, which includes a tour of the cellars, *chai* (brandy warehouse), and museum, or the slightly longer visit that tops off the tour with a tasting. ✉ *Le Pouyalet, 33250 Pauillac* ☎ *05–56–73–21–29* ⊕ *www.bpdr.com* ⊠ *€5; with tasting, €12.50* ⊗ *Mon.–Thurs. 9–12:30 and 2–6, Fri. 9–12:30 and 2–5.*

At the tip of the Gironde peninsula, near a memorial commemorating the landing of U.S. troops in 1917, is the **Pointe de Grave,** where you can take the *bac* (ferry) across the Gironde to Royan; it runs at least six times daily and costs €20.50 per car and €3 per passenger. During the 20-minute crossing, keep an eye out for the **Phare de Cordouan** on your left, a lighthouse that looks as if it's emerging from the sea (at low tide, its base is revealed to rest on a sandbank).

Where to Stay & Eat

★ **$$$–$$$$** ✗🏨 **Château Cordeillan-Bages.** This marble-face, single-story 17th-century "chartreuse" just outside Pauillac is surrounded by the vines that produce its own *cru bourgeois.* Paris-trained Thierry Marx, whose takeover of the Le Chapon-Fin restaurant in Bordeaux itself has won plaudits verging on the ecstatic, is considered the highest-rated chef in the region, no mean accolade in a part of France where food can take second place to wine. His fortes range from local salt-meadow lamb and spit-roasted kid with shallots to smoked eel with apple and crisp potato slices layered with ox-tail and truffles. Of course, who will be able to resist the accompaniment of one of the 1,000-plus Bordeauxs from the cellars? (The restaurant is closed Monday other than for guests in the hotel, and Tuesday and Saturday lunch.) The dining room decor is cookie-cutter-château, but the guest rooms are cozy, comfortable, and Relais-&-Châteaux stylish. ✉ *Rte. des Châteaux, 1½ km (1 mi) south of town, 33250 Pauillac* ☎ *05–56–59–24–24* 🖶 *05–56–59–01–89* ⊕ *www.cordeillanbages.com* ⇋ *25 rooms* ⚐ *Restaurant, minibars, cable TV, bar; no a/c in some rooms* ▭ *AE, DC, MC, V* ⊗ *Closed mid-Dec.–mid-Feb.* ⊚ *MAP.*

$ 🏨 **France & Angleterre.** A convenient choice for those who wish to explore Pauillac's winding streets, this low-key spot offers some doubles overlooking the quaint waterfront. The restaurant is closed weekends late fall to early spring. ✉ *3 quai Albert-Pichon, 33250 Pauillac* ☎ *05–56–59–01–20* 🖶 *05–56–59–02–31* ⇋ *29 rooms* ⚐ *Restaurant; no a/c* ▭ *AE, DC, MC, V* ⊗ *Closed mid-Dec.–mid-Jan.* ⊚ *MAP.*

St-Émilion

⑫   *128 km (80 mi) southeast of Royan, 35 km (23 mi) east of Bordeaux.*

Fodor'sChoice
★

Suddenly the sun-fired flatlands of Pomerol break into hills and send you tumbling into St-Émilion. This jewel of a town has old buildings of golden stone, ruined town walls, well-kept ramparts offering magical views, and a church hewn into a cliff. Sloping vineyards invade from all sides, and thousands of tourists invade down the middle, many thirsting for the red wine and macaroons that bear the town's name. The medieval streets, delightfully cobblestoned (though often very steep), are filled with wine stores (St-Émilion reaches maturity earlier than other Bordeaux reds and often offers better value for the money than Médoc or Graves), crafts shops, bakeries, cafés, and restaurants.

The **Office de Tourisme** (Tourist Office; ☒ Pl. des Créneaux ☎ 05–57–55–28–28 ⊕ www.saint-emilion-tourisme.com) hires out bikes (€14 per day) and organizes tours of the pretty local vineyards—the fabled **Château Pétrus** and **Cheval Blanc,** among others—including wine tastings and train rides through the vineyards. Note that it is best to hit the road on a weekday, when more châteaux are open.

A stroll along the 13th-century ramparts takes you to the **Château du Roi** (King's Castle), built by the English during the reign of Henry III (1216–72). From the castle ramparts, cobbled steps lead down to **Place du Marché,** a leafy square where cafés remain open late into the balmy summer night. Beware of the inflated prices charged at the café tables.

The **Église Monolithe** (Monolithic Church) is one of France's largest underground churches, hewn out of the rock face between the 9th and 12th centuries. The church was built by monks faithful to the memory of St-Émilion, an 8th-century hermit and miracle worker. Its spire-topped *clocher* (bell tower) rises out of the bedrock, dominating the center of town. ☒ *Pl. du Marché* ☒ *€5.50* ☉ *Tours leave from tourist office, daily from 10–12 and 2–5.*

Just south of the town walls is **Château Ausone,** an estate that is ranked with Cheval Blanc as a producer of St-Émilion's finest wines.

Where to Stay & Eat

¢–$ ✕ **Chez Germaine.** Family cooking and regional dishes are the focus at this central St-Émilion eatery. The candlelit upstairs dining room and the terrace are both pleasant places to enjoy the reasonably priced set menus. Grilled meats and fish are house specialties; for dessert, go for the almond macaroons. ☒ *13 pl. du Clocher* ☎ 05–57–74–49–34 ▭ *MC, V* ☉ *Closed Dec.–Feb.*

$$$–$$$$ ✕▣ **Grand Barrail.** This turn-of-the-20th-century luxury hotel just outside St-Émilion, flanked by a lake and vineyards, may seem a little stiff and heavy, but rooms are unusually large and smartly furnished; about half are in the transformed former stables. Talented chef Fabrice Giraud serves pumpkin soup, and calamari and goat-cheese risotto, in the Belle Époque dining room (no dinner Sunday, no lunch Tuesday, closed Monday January and February). St-Émilions constitute at least 60% of the impressive wine list. ⊠ *5 rue Marzelle, 4 km (2½ mi) northwest of St-Émilion on D243, 33330* ☎ *05–57–55–37–00* 🖶 *05–57–55–37–49* ⊕ *www.grand-barrail.com* 🛏 *33 rooms, 9 suites ⚒ Restaurant, minibars, cable TV, pool, bar, Internet, some pets allowed (fee)* ⊟ AE, DC, MC, V ⊗ *Closed 3 wks Feb., late Nov.–mid-Dec.* ⎮◯⎮ *MAP.*

★ **$$$–$$$$** ✕⛫ **L'Hostellerie de Plaisance.** Part of the Relais & Château group, this sumptuous hotel has long been considered the top address in St.-Émilion. Set next to the tourist office in the upper part of town and housed in a stunningly elegant limestone mansion, it's just across the way from the town's famous stone Église Monolithe. Rooms are warm and appealing and many come with terraces overlooking the tile roofs of the town; some, like the Descault Room, have excellent views of the vineyards. Dinner is often accompanied by St-Émilion wines; you need to pick and choose from the menu selections, but the crab stuffed with cabbage, pork with mango chutney, or the truffled bananas are all winners. ⊠ *3 pl. du Clocher, 33330* ☎ *05–57–55–07–55* 🖶 *05–57–74–41–11* ⊕ *www.hostellerie-plaisance.com* 🛏 *18 rooms ⚒ Restaurant, some minibars, cable TV, some pets allowed (fee); no a/c in some rooms* ⊟ AE, DC, MC, V ⊗ *Closed Jan.–mid-Feb.* ⎮◯⎮ *MAP.*

$$$$ ⛫ **Château Lamothe.** Many of St-Émilion's hotels are in-and-out tourist stops, while those in Bordeaux can lack charm. For something much more authentic, try this manor house located halfway between the two. The spacious guest rooms have large four-poster beds with soft cotton sheets; you may find them a little too frilly, but they are very comfortable. Owner Jacques Bastide speaks English and is extremely helpful with suggestions. ⊠ *6 rte. du Stade, 25 km (16 mi) west of St-Émilion, 20 km (12 mi) northeast of Bordeaux, 33450 St-Sulpice & Cameyrac* ☎ *05–56–30–82–16* 🖶 *05–56–30–88–33* 🛏 *5 suites ⚒ Pool, fishing, Internet; no a/c* ⊟ MC, V ⊗ *Closed Nov.–Mar.* ⎮◯⎮ *BP.*

$–$$ ⛫ **Commanderie.** Close to the ramparts, this 19th-century two-story hotel has a garden and a view of the vineyards. Rooms are small but clean and individually decorated with colorful prints; some have exposed stonework. Try for rooms 2, 3, 7, or 8, as they overlook the small garden. ⊠ *Rue des Cordeliers, 33300* ☎ *05–57–24–70–19* 🖶 *05–57–74–44–53* ⊕ *www. aubergedelacommanderie.com* 🛏 *26 rooms ⚒ Cable TV, bar, Internet; no a/c in some rooms* ⊟ MC, V ⊗ *Closed mid-Jan.–mid-Feb.*

DORDOGNE

What's not to love? Fairy-tale castles, geese flocks, storybook villages, prehistoric wonders, and medieval alleyways—little wonder the Dordogne has become one of the hottest destinations in France. Formerly one of those off-the-beaten-path regions, it's in danger of getting four-starred, boutiqued, and postcarded to death. Indeed, one sometimes has the sensation that visitors outnumber locals. But scratch the surface and you'll find one of the most authentic and appealing areas of rural France. What's more, and unlike the Loire Valley, for example, where attractions are often 35 km (18 mi) apart, you can discover romantic riverside château after château with each kilometer traveled. The département centers on Sarlat, whose impeccably restored medieval buildings make it a

THE GRAPE ESCAPE

BARON PHILIPPE DE ROTHSCHILD, legendary owner of Bordeaux's famed Mouton-Rothschild vineyard, was known for his custom of drinking vin ordinaire at most lunches and dinners. Indeed, any French person knows you can't enjoy fine vintages at every meal. Still, if you're traveling to Bordeaux, you're going to want to enjoy some of the region's celebrated liquid fare. To find the best vineyards, just head in any direction from the city of Bordeaux. The city is at the hub of a patchwork of vineyards: the Médoc peninsula to the northwest; Bourg and Blaye across the estuary; St-Émilion inland to the east; then, as you wheel around clockwise, Entre-Deux-Mers, Sauternes, and Graves.

The nearest vineyard to Bordeaux itself is, ironically, one of the best: Haut-Brion, on the western outskirts of the city, and one of the five châteaux to be officially recognized as a premier cru or first growth. There are only five premiers crus in all, and Haut-Brion is the only one not in the Médoc (Château Mouton-Rothschild, Château Margaux, Château Latour, and Château Lafite-Rothschild complete the list). The Médoc is subdivided into various appellations, wine-growing districts with their own specific characteristics and taste. Pauillac and Margaux host premiers crus; St-Julien and St-Estèphe possess many domaines of almost equal quality, followed by Listrac and Moulis; wines not quite so good are classed as Haut-Médoc or, as you move farther north, Médoc, pure and simple. Wines from the Médoc are made predominantly from the cabernet sauvignon grape, and can taste dry, even austere, when young. The better ones often need 15 to 25 years before "opening up" to reveal their full spectrum of complex flavors. When considering lighter reds for earlier consumption,

serious connoisseurs prefer to head southeast beyond Libourne to the stunning Vieille Ville of St-Émilion. The surrounding vineyards see the fruity merlot grape in control, and wines here often have more immediate appeal than those of the Médoc. There are several small appellations apart from St-Émilion itself, the most famous being Pomerol, whose Château Pétrus is the world's most expensive wine.

South of St-Émilion is the region known as Entre-Deux-Mers ("between two seas"— actually two rivers, the Dordogne and Garonne), whose dry white wine is particularly flavorsome if made from the vineyards near the ruined castle of Haut-Benauge. The picturesque villages of Loupiac and Sainte-Croix du Mont are sandwiched between the Garonne River and hillside vineyards producing sweet, not dry, white wine. But the best sweet wine produced hereabouts—some would say in the world—comes from across the Garonne and is made at Barsac and Sauternes. Nothing in the grubby village of Sauternes would suggest that mind-boggling wealth lurks amid the picturesque vine-laden slopes and hollows. The village has a wine shop where bottles gather dust on rickety shelves, next to handwritten price tags demanding small fortunes. Making Sauternes is a tricky business. Autumn mists steal up the valleys to promote Botrytis cinerea, a fungus known as pourriture noble or noble rot, which sucks moisture out of the grapes, leaving a high proportion of sugar. Heading back north toward Bordeaux you encounter the vineyards of the Graves region, so called because of its gravelly soil. Santé!

great place to use as a base while exploring the region. Stretching along the Dordogne, Isle, Dronne, and Auvezère rivers, the Dordogne's wooded hills and valleys are packed with small villages. It's also one of the premier "prehistoric" areas in Europe, dotted with noted sites, including the incomparable Lascaux cavern paintings (today, in reality, the not-so-incomparable Lascaux II). These sites are centered in the region known as Les Eyzies. You may want to spend a week exploring the small country roads and picnicking on riverbanks, but hurry. Ever since the British discovered this area two decades ago and made it among their favored vacation spots in France, the buzz has grown and grown.

The 10-km (6-mi) stretch of the Dordogne river from Montfort to Beynac is easily accessible by car, bike, canoe, or on foot, and shouldn't be missed. Fields of sunflowers line the banks in season, and medieval châteaux perch high above the river. Another 30 km (19 mi) west, toward Bergerac, the land is dedicated to viticulture. All these attractions don't go unnoticed; in July and August even the smallest village is often packed with sightseers.

Bergerac

⑬ *57 km (36 mi) east of St-Émilion via D936, 88 km (55 mi) east of Bordeaux.*

Cyrano never lived here, but no matter—the town still claims the long-nosed swashbuckler as a local son (his family had roots here but he was actually a Parisian playwright who lived from 1619 to 1655). Bergerac is a lively town with ancient half-timber houses, narrow alleys, and colorful Wednesday and Saturday (the larger of the two) markets. It's also a fine railway hub, with trains often arriving from Bordeaux, Sarlat, and St-Émilion. Guided walking tours of the Vieille Ville (1 hr, €4) leave from the **tourist office** (⊠ 97 rue Neuve d'Argenson ☎ 05–53–57–03–11 ⊕ www.bergerac-tourisme.com). There are also hour-long cruises along the Dordogne (€6.50) in old wooden sailboats with **Périgord Gabarres** (☎ 05–53–24–58–80). Details available from the tourist office.

The **Cloître des Récollets**, a former convent, is in the wine business. The convent's stone-and-brick buildings range in date from the 12th to the 17th centuries and include galleries, a large vaulted cellar, and a cloister where the **Maison des Vins** (Wine Center) provides information on, and samples of, local vintages of sweet whites and fruity young reds. ⊠ *Quai Salvette* ☎ *05–53–63–57–55* ⊠ *Free* ☉ *Sept.–Dec. and Feb.–May, daily 10:30–12:30 and 2–6; June–Aug., daily 10–7.*

You can learn about another local industry—tobacco growing—from its pre-Columbian origins to its spread worldwide, at the **Musée du Tabac** (National Tobacco Museum). It's housed in the 17th-century Maison Peyrarède, near the quayside. ⊠ *Pl. du Feu* ☎ *05–53–63–04–13* ⊠ *€3.50* ☉ *Tues.–Fri. 10–noon and 2–6, Sat. 10–noon and 2–5, Sun. 2:30–6:30.*

Where to Stay & Eat

$ ✕⌂ **Bordeaux.** One of the better hotels in town, the family-owned Bordeaux has contemporary furnishings and neat rooms. Request one on the garden courtyard or No. 22, which is slightly more spacious. Though you're not obliged to eat at the restaurant, Le Terroir (closed Friday–Saturday in November–March), it's difficult to refuse the marinated salmon in anisette and lime or the panfried *escalope de foie gras* (sautéed foie gras). The owner, Monsieur Maury, speaks fluent English. ☒ *38 pl. Gambetta, 24100* ☏ *05–53–57–12–83* 🖶 *05–53–57–72–14* ⊕ *www.hotel-bordeaux-bergerac.com* 📮 *40 rooms* ♨ *Restaurant, cable TV, pool, some pets allowed (fee); no a/c* ▤ *AE, DC, MC, V* ⦿ *FAP.*

Monbazillac

⑭ *6 km (4 mi) south of Bergerac via D13.*

From the hilltop village of Monbazillac are spectacular views of the sweet wine–producing vineyards tumbling toward the Dordogne. The storybook corner towers of the beautifully proportioned 16th-century graystone **Château de Monbazillac** pay tribute to the fortress tradition of the Middle Ages, but the large windows and sloping roofs reveal a Renaissance influence. Regional furniture and an ornate early-17th-century bedchamber enliven the interior. A wine tasting is included to tempt you into buying a case or two of the famous but expensive bottles. The restaurant on the grounds serves expensive meals. ☏ *05–53–63–65–00 weekdays, 05–53–61–52–52 weekends* ⊕ *www.chateau-monbazillac.com* 🎟 *€5.80* ☽ *June–Sept., daily 10–7:30; mid-Feb.–May and Oct.–Dec., Tues.–Sun. 10–noon and 2–6.*

Monpazier

⑮ *43 km (27 mi) southeast of Monbazillac via D14/D104.*

Fodor'sChoice
★
Monpazier, on the tiny Drot River, is one of France's best-preserved and most photographed bastide towns. It was built in ocher-color stone by English king Edward I in 1284 to protect the southern flank of his French possessions. The bastide has three stone gateways (of an original six), a large central square, and the church of **St-Dominique,** housing 35 carved-wood choir stalls and a would-be relic of the True Cross. Opposite the church is the finest medieval building in town, the **Maison du Chapître** (Chapter House), once used as a barn for storing grain. Its woodbeam roof is constructed of chestnut to repel insects.

Where to Stay & Eat

¢ ✕🏠 **France.** Once an outbuilding on the estates of the Château de Biron, the Hôtel de France has never capitalized on its 13th-century heritage or its 15th-century staircase. Instead, it has remained a small, modest family-run hotel that caters less to tourists than to locals at its bar and restaurant, serving rich regional food. Rooms are a clutter of old furniture (with a plastic-cabinet shower and toilet squeezed into the corner); some are quite large. ☒ *21 rue St-Jacques, 24540* ☏ *05–53–22–60–06* 🖶 *05–53–22–07–27* 📮 *10 rooms* ♨ *Restaurant, bar; no a/c, no room TVs* ▤ *MC, V* ⦿ *MAP.*

Biron

🔟 *8 km (5 mi) south of Monpazier via D2/D53.*

★ Stop in Biron to see its massive hilltop castle, the **Château de Biron.** Highlights of the château, which with its keep, square tower, and chapel dates from the Middle Ages, include monumental staircases, Renaissance-era apartments, the kitchen with its huge stone-slab floor, and a gigantic dungeon, replete with a collection of scarifying torture instruments. The classical buildings were completed in 1730. English Romantic poet Lord Byron (1788–1824) is claimed as a distant descendant of the Gontaut-Biron family, which lived here for 14 generations. ✉ *221 bis rte. d'Angoulême* ☎ *05–53–35–50–40* 🎫 *€5.50* ⏱ *Apr.–June, Sept., and Oct., Tues.–Sun. 10–12:30 and 2–6; July and Aug., daily 10–7.*

Cahors

🔟 *60 km (38 mi) southeast of Monpazier via D660.*

Less touristy and populated than the neighboring Dordogne, the Lot Valley has a subtler charm. The cluster of towns along the Lot River and the smaller rivers that cut through the dry, vineyard-covered plateau have a magical, abandoned feel. Just an hour north of southwestern France's main city, Toulouse, Cahors remains the Lot area's largest town and its information center and makes a fine base from which to explore the Lot River valley, a 50-km (31-mi) gorge punctuated by medieval villages. Here and on other routes—notably the GR46, which spans the interior of the Lot region, with breathtaking views of the limestone plateaus and quiet valleys between Rocamadour and St-Cirq-Lapopie—*cyclotourisme* (biking) rules supreme.

Modern Cahors encircles its *ville antique* (Old Town), which dates from 1 BC. Once an opulent Gallo-Roman town, Cahors, sitting snugly within a loop of the Lot River, is famous for its vin de Cahors, a tannic red wine known to the Romans as "black wine." Many of the small estates in the area offer tastings and the town tourist office on the place Mitterrand can point you in the direction of some of the more notable vineyards of the area, including the Domaine de Lagrezette (in Caillac) and the Domaine de St-Didier (in Parnac). The town's finest sight is the 14th-century **Pont Valentré,** a bridge with three elegant towers that constitutes a spellbinding feat of medieval engineering. Also look for the fortresslike **Cathédrale St-Étienne** (✉ Off rue du Maréchal-Joffre), with its cupolas and cloisters connecting to the courtyard of the archdeaconry, which is awash with Renaissance decoration and thronged with townsfolk who come for art exhibits.

FodorśChoice
★

The hour-long bike ride between Rocamadour and the Gouffre de Padirac might just be one of your most memorable experiences in France, as will day-long bike trips through the neighboring Célé valley and the 35-km (22-mi) trip to the **Grotte du Pech-Merle,** one of the finest caves with prehistoric drawings and carvings, located outside the town of Cabrerets. Happily, Cahors has plenty of places for bike rentals and picnic fixings (head for the town's covered and outdoor markets).

Where to Stay & Eat

$$$–$$$$ ✕📷 **Château de Mercuès.** The former home of the count-bishops of Cahors, on a rocky spur just outside town, has older rooms in baronial splendor (ask for one of these), as well as unappealing modern ones (which tend to attract midges). One of the best is "Tour," with a clever ceiling that slides back to expose the turret. Duck, lamb, and truffles reign in the restaurant, but the high prices lead you to expect more creativity from chef Philippe Combet than is delivered. The restaurant is closed Monday, and there's no lunch Tuesday–Thursday. ✉ *8 km (5 mi) northwest of Cahors on road to Villeneuve-sur-Lot, 46090 Mercuès* ☎ *05–65–20–00–01* 📠 *05–65–20–05–72* ⊕ *www.chateaudemercues. com* 🛏 *24 rooms, 8 suites* ⚒ *Restaurant, minibars, cable TV, 2 tennis courts, pool, Internet, some pets allowed (fee); no a/c* ▭ *AE, DC, MC, V* ⊗ *Closed Nov.–Easter* ⦿ *MAP.*

St-Cirq-Lapopie

⑱ *32 km (20 mi) east of Cahors via D653, D662, and D40.*

Fodor'sChoice
★

The beautiful 13th-century village of St-Cirq (pronounced san-*sare*) is on a rocky spur 250 feet up, with nothing but a vertical drop to the Lot River below. Filled with artisans' workshops and not yet renovated à la Disney, the town has so many dramatic views you may end up spending several hours here. Traversing steep paths and alleyways among flower-filled balconies, you'll realize it deserves its description as one of the most beautiful villages in France. A mostly ruined château can be reached by a stiff walk along the path that starts near the Hôtel de Ville. Stop by the tourist office in the center of town for information on other points of interest in town and morning hikes in the misty gorges in the valley.

Where to Stay

$–$$ 📷 **Hôtel de la Pélissaria.** This intimate 16th-century hotel is small and simple but chock-full of atmosphere. The best rooms look out across the village or the valley and river; some rooms in the garden have less grand views (Nos. 3 and 4 are very small). The lounge is a snug place to relax in front of the fire in the evening. ✉ *46330 St-Cirq-Lapopie* ☎ *05–65–31–25–14* 📠 *05–65–30–25–52* ✉ *lapelissariahotel@minitel.net* 🛏 *10 rooms* ⚒ *Pool, bar, some pets allowed (fee); no a/c* ▭ *MC, V* ⊗ *Closed Nov.–Mar.* ⦿ *MAP.*

Rocamadour

⑲ *72 km (45 mi) north of St-Cirq via Labastide-Murat.*

Rocamadour is a medieval village that seems to defy the laws of gravity; it surges out of a cliff 1,500 feet above the Alzou River gorge—an awe-inspiring sight that makes this one of the most-visited tourist spots in France. The town got its name after the discovery in 1166 of the 1,000-year-old body of St. Amadour "quite whole." The body was moved to the cathedral, where it began to work miracles. Legend has it that the saint was actually a publican named Zacheus, who, after the honor of entertaining Jesus in his home, came to Gaul after the crucifixion and, under the name of Amadour, established a private chapel in the cliff here.

Pilgrims have long flocked to the site, climbing the 216 steps to the church on their knees, especially around August 15 (Assumption Day) and during the week of September 8 (the Virgin Mary's birthday). Making the climb on foot is sufficient reminder of the medieval penchant for agonizing penance; today an elevator lifts weary souls. Unfortunately, the summer influx of a million tourists has brought its own blight, judging by the dozens of tacky souvenir shops. Cars are not allowed; park in the lot below the town.

The town is split into three levels joined by steep stairs. The lowest level is occupied by the village of Rocamadour itself, and mainly accessed through the centuries-old Porte du Figuier (Fig Tree Gate). Past this portal, the **Cité Médiévale,** or the **Basse Ville,** though in parts grotesquely touristy, is full of beautifully restored structures, such as the 15th-century **Hôtel de Ville,** near the Porte Salmon, which houses the **tourist office** and an excellent collection of tapestries. ▨ *Free* ☉ *Mon.–Sat. 10–noon and 3–8.*

The Basse Ville's Rue Piétonne, the main pedestrian street, is lined with crêperies, tea salons, and hundreds of tourists, many of whom are heading heavenward by taking the **Grand Escalier** staircase or elevator (fee) from place de la Carreta up to the **Cité Religieuse,** set halfway up the cliff. If you walk, pause at the landing 141 steps up to admire the fort. Once up, you'll see tiny place St-Amadour and its seven sanctuaries: the basilica of **St-Sauveur** opposite the staircase; the **St-Amadour crypt** beneath the basilica; the chapel of **Notre-Dame** to the left; the chapels of **John the Baptist, St-Blaise,** and **Ste-Anne** to the right; and the Romanesque chapel of **St-Michel** built into an overhanging cliff. St-Michel's two 12th-century frescoes—depicting the Annunciation and the Visitation—have survived in superb condition. On the Parvis du Sanctuaire, the **Musée d'Art Sacré** has gilded reliquaries and chalices on view for a separate admission fee. ▨ *Centre d'Accueil Notre-Dame* ▨ *Tips at visitors' discretion* ☉ *Guided tours Mon.–Sat. 9–5* ☞ *English-speaking guide available.*

FodorsChoice
★

On the uppermost plateau stands the **Château de Rocamadour,** a private residence of the church fathers. Open to the public for an admission fee are its ramparts, which have spectacular views of the gorge (however, you can enjoy the same views for free just by walking the **Chemin de la Croix** up to the castle).

Where to Stay & Eat

$$$$ ✕▦ **Château de la Treyne.** Certainly the most spectacular château-hotel
FodorsChoice in the Dordogne (and one of the most gorgeous and expensive in all France),
★ this Xanadu sits in a picture-perfect perch on a cliff overlooking the Dordogne River. Part of the Relais & Châteaux group, set in Lacave, 6 km (3½ mi) northwest of Rocamadour, La Treyne has guarded the region since the 14th century. From the luxe and stylish rooms here, you would never know that the castle's history was a tumultuous one: Nearly destroyed in the 16th-century Wars of Religion between Huguenot and Catholic forces, it was happily reconstructed under the reign of Louis XIII. Today, the Great Lounge restaurant is a symphony of chandeliers,

delicate embroideries, oak panels, and Louis Treize chairs—but who can resist dining on the storybook terrace set with tables overlooking the river (restaurant closed for lunch Tuesday to Friday)? Here you can feast on Fried Scallops on Chestnut Gallettes with a Cappuccino of Mushrooms, just one of the dishes featured in the hotel's special Menu St. Jacques de Compostelle, which pays homage to the castle's history as a stopping-off point for pilgrims on the ancient Compostela route to Spain. Or repair to the adjacent Music Lounge, with its gigantic fireplace and Old Master paintings or enjoy your after-dinner cognac with a stroll through the enchantingly Baroque formal gardens. Best of all are the astonishingly stylish guest rooms, ranging from the Louis XIII apartment (pink brocade, oak four-poster, parquet floors) to the Prison Doreé, or "Golden Prison" (set atop the castle tower, replete with centuries-old stone walls and panoramic views), or the most charming of all, the "Soleil Levant" (the former chapel, now glowing in historic limes and yellow). Apart from these showstoppers, there are numerous other rooms, all impressive essays in elegant style. The smallest, such as the Vendages, do come up short for their high price (rooms here range from €360 to €660 *but* include breakfast and dinner). There's also modern luxe to be had, as most rooms come complete with an array of facilities from Jacuzzis to minibars. For taste in every sense of the word (ooh, those scallops), La Treyne is tops. ✉ *La Treyne, 21 km (13 mi) northwest of Rocamadour, 46200 Lacave* ☎ *05–65–27–60–60* 🖷 *05–65–27–60–70* ⊕ *www.relaischateaux. com/treyne* 🛏 *14 rooms, 2 suites* ⟡ *Restaurant, minibars, tennis court, pool, sauna, Internet, some pets allowed (fee)* ▭ *AE, DC, MC, V* ⊗ *Closed mid-Nov.–Christmas, Jan.–Apr.* ⦿ *MAP.*

$–$$ ✕▥ **Grand Hôtel Beau Site.** This is the best of the few Vieille Ville hotels in Rocamadour. The charm of the ancient beams, exposed stone, and open hearth in the foyer ends, however, as you climb the stairs; rooms are modern and functional. The modern, large-window Jehan de Valon restaurant overlooks the canyon, serving foie gras, local lamb, and walnut gateau. Best of all, you can park inside Rocamadour if you stay here. ✉ *Cité Médiévale, 46500* ☎ *05–65–33–63–08* 🖷 *05–65–33–65–23* ⊕ *www. bw-beausite.com* 🛏 *40 rooms, 3 suites* ⟡ *Restaurant, cable TV, bar, Internet, some pets allowed (fee)* ▭ *AE, DC, MC, V* ⊗ *Closed mid-Nov.–mid-Feb.* ⦿ *MAP.*

$ ▥ **Lion d'Or.** In the center of Rocamadour, this gently priced hotel conveniently has a restaurant on the premises. ✉ *Cité Médiévale, 46500* ☎ *05–65–33–62–04* 🖷 *05–65–33–72–54* ⊕ *www.liondor-rocamadour. com* 🛏 *35 rooms* ⟡ *Restaurant; no a/c* ▭ *MC, V* ⊗ *Closed Nov.–Easter.*

Domme

❷⓪ *50 km (31 mi) west of Rocamadour via Payrac.*

The historic cliff-top village of Domme is famous for its **grottoes,** where prehistoric bison and rhinoceros bones have been discovered. You can visit the 500-yard-long illuminated galleries, which are lined with stalactites. ✉ *Pl. de la Halle* 🎟 *€6* ⊗ *Apr.–Sept., daily 10–noon and 2–6; Mar. and Oct., daily 2–6.*

La Roque-Gageac

㉑ *5 km (3 mi) northwest of Domme via D46/D703.*

Across the Dordogne from Domme, in the direction of Beynac, romantically huddled beneath a cliff, is strikingly attractive La Roque-Gageac, one of the best-restored villages in the valley. Crafts shops line its narrow streets, dominated by the outlines of the 19th-century mock-medieval Château de Malartrie and the Manoir de Tarde, with its cylindrical turret. If you leave the main road and climb one of the steep cobblestone paths, you can check out the medieval houses on their natural perches and even hike up the mountain for a view down to the village.

Where to Stay & Eat

$ ✕🏠 **La Plume d'Oie.** This small inn overlooks the river and the limestone cliffs. Rooms, in light fabrics and wicker furniture, vary in size and price. La Plume d'Oie's major raison d'être, however, is the stone-walled restaurant, at which you are expected to have at least one meal. Chef–owner Marc-Pierre Walker prepares classic regional cuisine, such as fillet of beef cooked in red wine, and ragout of foie gras (the restaurant is closed Monday and does not serve lunch Tuesday). ✉ *24250 La Roque-Gageac* ☎ *05–53–29–57–05* 🖨 *05–53–31–04–81* 🛏 *4 rooms* ⛄ *Restaurant; no a/c* ▤ *MC, V* ⊗ *Closed Christmas–Feb.*

Beynac-et-Cazenac

㉒ *11 km (7 mi) west of La Roque-Gageac via D703.*

Fodor's Choice
★ One of the most enchanting sights in the Dordogne is the medieval castle that sits atop the wonderfully restored town of Beynac. Perched atop a sheer cliff face beside an abrupt bend in the Dordogne river, the muscular 13th-century **Château de Beynac** has unforgettable views from its battlements. During the Hundred Years' War this castle often faced off with forces massed directly across the way at the fort of Castenaud. Star of many films, Beynac was last featured in Luc Besson's 1999 life of Joan of Arc, *The Messenger.* Tours of the castle are in English as well as French. ☎ *05–53–29–50–40* 🎫 €7 ⊗ *May–Sept., daily 10–6:30; Oct.–Apr., daily 10–6.*

With a fabulous mountaintop setting, the now-ruined castle of **Castlenaud,** containing a large collection of medieval arms, is just upstream from Beynac across the Dordogne; it's open May–October, daily 10–7, and admission is €6. Five kilometers (3 mi) from Castlenaud is the turreted **Château des Milandes** (☎ *05–53–59–31–21* ⊕ www.milandes.com), open April to November, daily 9:30–7 (€7.50). Built around 1489 in Renaissance style, it has lovely terraces and gardens and was once owned by the American-born cabaret star of Roaring '20s Paris, Josephine Baker. Here she housed her "rainbow family," a large group of adopted children from many nationalities. Today, there's a museum devoted to her memory and, in summer, falconry displays. From here D53 (via Belvès) leads southwest to Monpazier.

One of the most regal yet picturesque sights in the Perigord Noir is the garden of the **Château de Marqueyssac**, set in Vézac, about 4 km (2 mi) south of Beynac-et-Cazenac. The park was founded in 1682 and its design, including an enchanting parterre of cut topiaries, was greatly influenced by the designs of André le Nôtre, the "green geometer" of Versailles. Shaded paths boarded by 150,000 hand-pruned boxwoods are graced with breathtaking viewpoints, rock gardens, waterfalls, and verdant glades. From the belvedere 400 feet above the river, there is an exceptional viewpoint of the Dordogne Valley, with its castles and beautiful villages such as Beynac, Fayrac, Castelnaud, Roque-Gageac, and Domme. A tea salon is open from May to September and is just the place to drink in the panoramic views from the parterre terrace. ⊠ *Belvédère de la Dordogne, Vézac, 9 km (5 mi) southwest of Sarlat* ☎ *05–53–31–36–36* ✍ *€6.60* ☯ *July and Aug., daily 9–8 Sept.–June, daily 2–8.*

Where to Eat & Stay

¢–$$ ✕▦ **Hôtel Pontet.** Set just a few blocks from the Dordogne river and within the shadow of cliff-top Château de Beynac, this is one of the hotel mainstays of the adorably Dordognesque town of Beynac. Guest rooms are sweet and simple, and a short hike down to the river will bring you to the hotel's Hostellerie Maleville, a big riverside restaurant, where you'll want to forgo a table in the modern, wood-beamed dining room for a blissfully magical perch on the river bank itself. Here, umbrellas and willow trees shade diners eating away happily on goose neck stuffed with truffles with Beynacoises potatoes. ⊠ *24220 Beynac-et-Cazenac* ☎ *05–53–29–50–06* 🖶 *05–53–28–28–52* ⟋ *12 rooms* ⟐ *Restaurant; no a/c* ▭ *No credit cards.*

$$–$$$ ▦ **Abbaye.** Named for the abbey of Augustinian friars that once stood on the spot, this historic hotel dating from the 18th century overlooks the pretty medieval village of St-Cyprien, midway between Sarlat and Les Eyzies. Most rooms have reproduction furniture, stone walls, and beamed ceilings. Trees shade the small swimming pool, attractively sited with the village church visible in the distance. ⊠ *Rue de l'Abbaye des Augustins, 10 km (6 mi) west of Beynac on D703, 24220 St-Cyprien* ☎ *05–53–29–20–48* 🖶 *05–53–29–15–85* ⊕ *www.abbaye-dordogne.com* ⟋ *23 rooms* ⟐ *Restaurant, cable TV, pool, some pets allowed; no a/c* ▭ *AE, DC, MC, V* ☯ *Closed mid-Oct.–mid-Apr.*

Sarlat-la-Canéda

㉓ *10 km (6 mi) northeast of Beynac via D57, 74 km (46 mi) east of Bergerac.*

Tucked among hills adorned with corn and wheat, Sarlat (as it is usually known) is a beautiful, well-preserved medieval town that, despite attracting huge numbers of visitors, has managed to retain some of its true character. With its storybook streets, Sarlat is filled most days with tour groups, and is especially hectic on Saturday, market day: all the geese on sale are proof of the local addiction to foie gras. To do justice to the town's golden-stone splendor, wander through its medieval streets in the later afternoon or early evening, aided by the tourist office's walking map. The tourist office also organizes walking tours, which for €4 give you an in-depth look at the town's medieval buildings. There are trains to Sarlat from Bordeaux about five times a day.

Of particular note is rue de la Liberté, which leads to **place du Peyrou,** anchored on one corner by the steep-gable Renaissance house where writer-orator Étienne de la Boétie (1530–63) was born. The elaborate turreted tower of the **Cathédrale St-Sacerdos** (⊠ Pl. du Peyrou), begun in the 12th century, is the oldest part of the building and, along with the choir, all that remains of the original Romanesque structure. The sloping garden behind the cathedral, the **cour de l'Évêché** (Bishop's Courtyard), contains a strange, conical tower known as the Lanterne des Morts (Lantern of the Dead), which was occasionally used as a funeral chapel. Rue d'Albusse, adjoining the garden behind the cathedral, and rue de la Salamandre are narrow, twisty streets that head to place de la Liberté and the 17th-century **Hôtel de Ville.** Opposite the town hall is the rickety former church of **Ste-Marie,** overlooking place des Oies. Ste-Marie points the way to Sarlat's most interesting street, **rue des Consuls.** Among its medieval buildings are the Hôtel Plamon, with broad windows that resemble those of a Gothic church, and, opposite, the 15th-century Hôtel de Vassal. Another winner is **rue Montaigne,** where the great 16th-century philosopher, Michel de Montaigne, once lived— some of the half-timbered houses that line this street define enchantment.

Where to Stay & Eat

★ ¢-$ ✕⌧ **St-Albert & Montaigne.** The Garrigou family has two hotels on this delightful square in the center of town. The Montaigne is in a rather elegant stone hôtel particulier that seems air-lifted in from Paris; most rooms have been spiffed up in a modern, traditional style, but ask for lovely Room 33 to get a chamber with exposed beams. The St-Albert has simply furnished rooms of varying size. Hearty regional fare is served by chef René Fontaine in the restaurant (closed Sunday and Monday). Over dinner, discuss your next day's itinerary with Monsieur Garrigou: he not only knows the region well but is also the town's backroom politician. ⊠ 10 pl. Pasteur, 24200 ☎ 05–53–31–55–55 🖷 05–53–59–19–99 ⊕ www.hotelmontaigne.fr/ ⧖ 53 rooms ⌂ Restaurant, bar, Internet, some pets allowed (fee); no a/c in some rooms ▭ AE, MC, V ⦿ MAP.

Les Eyzies-de-Tayac

❷❹ 21 km (13 mi) northwest of Sarlat via D47.

Sitting comfortably under a limestone cliff, Les Eyzies is the doorway to the prehistoric capital of France. Many signs of Cro-Magnon man have been discovered in this vicinity; a number of excavated caves and grottoes, some with wall paintings, are open for public viewing, including the Font de Gaume, just south of the town, with very faint drawings to be seen on a tour, and the Grotte de Combarelles. Stop by the town tourist office for the lowdown on all the caves in the area—the office also sells tickets for most sites and you should reserve here because a surprising number of tours sell out in advance (sometimes there are only six people allowed at any one time in a cave). Amid the dimness of the **Grotte du Grand-Roc,** you can view weirdly shaped crystalline stalactites and stalagmites—not for the claustrophobic. ✉ *48 av. de la Préhistoire* ☎ *05–53–06–92–70* ⊕ *www.grandroc.com* ✉ *€5.50* ⊗ *Feb.–mid-Nov., daily 10–6.*

The **Musée National de Préhistoire** (National Museum of Prehistory), in a Renaissance château, attracts large crowds to its renowned collection of prehistoric artifacts, including primitive sculpture, furniture, and tools. You can also get ideas at the museum about excavation sites to visit in the region. ✉ *Le Bourg* ☎ *05–53–06–45–45* ✉ *€4.50* ⊗ *Apr.–Oct., Wed.–Mon. 9:30–noon and 2–6; Nov.–Mar., Wed.–Mon. 9:30–noon and 2–5.*

As you head north from Les Eyzies-de-Tayac toward Lascaux, stop off 7 km (4 mi) north of Les Eyzies near the village of Tursac to discover the enchanting troglodyte "lost village" of **La Madeleine,** found hidden in the Valley of Vézère at the foot of a ruined castle and overlooking the Vézère river. Human settlement here dates back to 15,000 BC, but what is most eye-catching now is its picturesque cliff-face chapel—seemingly half Cro-Magnon, half Gothic, it was constructed during the Middle Ages. The "Brigadoon" of the Dordogne, La Madeleine was abandoned once more in the 1920s. Guided visits tour the site (call ahead, English available). ✉ *Tursac, 7 km (4 mi) north of Les Eyzies-de-Tayac* ☎ *05–53–06–92–49* ✉ *€5.50* ⊗ *July and Aug. daily 10–8, Sept.–June daily 10–6.*

FodorsChoice
★

Where to Stay & Eat

$$$–$$$$ ✕🏨 **La Centenaire.** Though it's also a stylish, modern Relais & Châteaux hotel, Le Centenaire is known foremost as a restaurant. Chef Roland Mazère adds flair to the preparation of local delights: risotto with truffles or snails with ravioli and gazpacho. The dining room's golden stone and wood beams retain local character (on Thursday and on weekends, the restaurant serves lunch only; a jacket is required). ✉ *24620 Les Eyzies-de-Tayac* ☎ *05–53–06–68–68* 🖷 *05–53–06–92–41* ⊕ *www. hotelducentenaire.fr* 🛏 *19 rooms* ⎙ *Restaurant, minibars, cable TV, pool, health club, sauna, some pets allowed (fee)* ▤ *AE, DC, MC, V* ⊗ *Closed Nov.–Apr.* ⏁ *MAP.*

★ **$$$–$$$$** ✕🏨 **Le Vieux Logis.** Built around the most gorgeous dining room in the Dordogne, this vine-clad manor house on the edge of Trémolat remains one of the best hotels of the region. The warm guest rooms vary in size; most face the well-tended garden and a rushing brook. One favorite, No. 22, has a terra-cotta tile floor, exposed beams, stone walls, and a suitelike bathroom. Be sure to enjoy a meal in the restaurant, a stunning vision in half-timbering and pink and red *paisleys à la indiennes* fabrics. For dinner, the five-course Menu Vieux Logis (€45) might include the chef's forte, pigeon terrine (the restaurant is closed January and February; there's no lunch weekdays September–June). ✉ *24 km (15 mi) west of Les Eyzies, 24510 Trémolat* ☎ *05–53–22–80–06* 🖷 *05–53–22–84–89* ⊕ *www.vieux-logis.com* 🛏 *19 rooms, 5 suites* ⎙ *Restaurant, minibars, cable TV, pool, Internet, some pets allowed (fee); no a/c* ▤ *AE, DC, MC, V* ⏁ *MAP.*

Lascaux

㉕ *27 km (17 mi) northeast of Les Eyzies via D706.*

Fodor'sChoice
★
The famous **Grotte de Lascaux** (Lascaux Caves), just outside Montignac, contain hundreds of prehistoric wall paintings—thought to be at least 20,000 years old. The undulating horses, cow, black bulls, and unicorn on their walls were discovered by chance in 1940. Although the caves have been sealed off to prevent damage, two of the galleries and many of the paintings have been reproduced in vivid detail in the Lascaux II exhibition center nearby. The copy is almost as awe-inspiring as the original. Unlike caves marked with authentic prehistoric art, Lascaux II is completely geared toward visitors, and you can watch a fancy presentation about cave art or take a tour in the language of your choice. Purchase tickets at the tourist office in Montignac before setting off. ⊠ *Rte. de la Grotte* ☎ *05–53–51–95–03* 🖷 *€8* ☉ *Mid-Feb., Mar., Oct., Nov., and Dec., Tues.–Sun. 10–12:30 and 2–5:30; Apr., May, June, and Sept., daily 9:30–6:30; July–Aug., daily 9–8.*

Where to Stay & Eat

$$–$$$$ ✕🏠 **Manoir d'Hautegente.** This old, ivy-covered manor (originally a forge) enjoys a pastoral nook by the Vézère River. Inside, the modernized rooms have beige-fabric wall coverings, and the colorful curtains match the bedspreads. Chef Bernard Villain's specialties include crayfish in Pernod, duck with truffles, and chestnut mousse. The restaurant is closed Monday through Wednesday and there's no lunch Thursday. ⊠ *Haute Gente, 12 km (7 mi) east of Lascaux, 24120 Coly* ☎ *05–53–51–68–03* 🖷 *05–53–50–38–52* ⊕ *www.manoir-hautegente. com* 🛏 *15 rooms* ♨ *Restaurant, minibars, cable TV, pool, Internet; no a/c in some rooms* ▤ *DC, MC, V* ☉ *Closed Nov.–Easter.*

Hautefort

㉖ *32 km (20 mi) north of Lascaux via D704.*

★ The reason to come to Hautefort is to see its castle, which presents a disarmingly arrogant face to the world. The silhouette of the **Château de Hautefort** bristles with high roofs, domes, chimneys, and cupolas. The square-lined Renaissance left wing clashes with the muscular, round towers of the right wing, as the only surviving section of the original medieval castle—the gateway and drawbridge—plays referee in the middle. Adorning the inside are 17th-century furniture and tapestries. ⊠ *Le Bourg* ☎ *05–53–50–51–23* 🖷 *€7* ☉ *Apr.–June, daily 10–noon and 2–6; July–Aug., daily 9:30–7; Sept.–Mar., daily 2–6.*

Périgueux

㉗ *46 km (27 mi) west of Hautefort via D5, 120 km (75 mi) northeast of Bordeaux.*

Périgueux is best known for its weird-looking cathedral. Finished in 1173 and restored in the 19th century, the **Cathédrale St-Front** looks like it might be on loan from Istanbul, given its shallow-scale domes and elongated conical cupolas sprouting from the roof like baby minarets. You may be struck by similarities with the Byzantine-style Sacré-Coeur in Paris; that's no coincidence—architect Paul Abadie (1812–84) had a hand in the design of both. Duty visit to the cathedral over, make for the cluster of tiny pedestrian-only streets that run through the heart of Périgeux. Stylish and sophisticated, they are the best reason for visiting this thriving town. Specialty food shops proliferate, as do dimly lit cafés and elegant fashion haunts. For anyone tired of the bucolic delights of the Perigord, even a short visit here may prove a welcome reimmersion in classy urban ways, the whole in a stage-set setting. ⊠ *Pl. de la Clarté.*

Brantôme

②③ FodorśChoice ★

27 km (17 mi) north of Périgueux via D939.

When the reclusive monks of the abbey of Brantôme decided the inhabitants of the village were getting too nosy, they dug a canal between themselves and the villagers, setting the *brantômois* adrift on an island in the middle of the river Dronne. How happy for them, or at least for us. Brantôme has been unable to outgrow its small-town status and remains one of the prettiest villages in France. Today it touts itself as the "Venice of Périgord." Enjoy a walk along the river or through the old, narrow streets. The meandering river follows you wherever you stroll. Cafés and small shops abound. At night the **Abbaye Benedictine** is romantically floodlighted. Possibly founded by Charlemagne in the 8th century, it has none of its original buildings left, but its bell tower has been hanging on since the 11th century (the secret of its success is that it is attached to the cliff rather than the abbey, and so withstood waves of invaders). Fifth-century Christians carved out much of the abbey and some rooms have sculpted reliefs of the Last Judgment. Also here is a small museum devoted to the 19th-century painter Fernand-Desmoulin. ☎*05–53–05–80–63* ⊠ *€3* ⊗ *July–Sept. 15, daily 10–7; Sept. 15–Oct. and Apr.–June, Wed.–Mon. 10–12:30 and 2–6; Nov.–Mar., Wed.–Mon. 10–noon and 2–5.*

Where to Stay

$$$$ FodorśChoice ★

⊞ **Moulin de l'Abbaye.** Storybook-perfect and set in the heart of Brantôme, this ivy-covered, blue-shuttered stone building looks directly over the placid waters of the Dronne, making this the ideal place to sample the watery charms of this little town. All the lovely and stylish rooms—named after wine châteaux—are individually decorated. Both Château Montrose and Château Cheval-Blanc have four-poster beds. The restaurant, presided over by chef Bernard Villain, has eight magnificent arched windows with views of the river—a truly memorable setting for delights such as white and green asparagus in morel sauce, sautéed *maigret de canard,* and chocolate "velvet" with toasted sesame nougatine and orange-anise. The food is so good, you'll probably want to splurge on the half-board rates (which raises the tab here considerably), but set some time aside for feasts at the nearby fishermen's bistro, Au Fil de l'Eau, which has an exquisite riverside terrace. For even more luxe and prettier guest rooms, explore the owner's other Brantôme hostelries, set nearby—the riverbank Maison de l'Abbé and the cliffside Maison du Meunier, which has an eye-dazzling, two-story drawing room. ⊠ *1 rte.*

des Bourdeilles, 24310 ☎ *05–53–05–80–22* 🖷 *05–53–05–75–27*
⊕ *www.moulin-abbaye.com/* ⟿ *19 rooms* ♨ *Some pets allowed* ▤ *AE,*
DC, MC, V ⊘ *Closed Nov.–Apr* ¶⊙¶ *BP.*

POITOU-CHARENTES

Poitou-Charentes occupies the northern part of the region covered in this chapter. Rural, rolling Poitou is named for the ancient town of Poitiers. Charentes refers to the two *départements* linked by the Charente River: Charente-Maritime, with its islands and sandy Atlantic beaches; and, inland, Charente. Highlights of Poitou-Charentes include the "Green Venice" of the Marais Poitevin and the town of Cognac, famed for its brandy, though almost wherever you go in the *deux* (two) Charentes you will find the ample vineyards that produce cognac grapes.

Angoulême

㉙ *59 km (37 mi) northwest of Brantôme via D939, 120 km (75 mi) northeast of Bordeaux.*

Angoulême is divided, like many other French towns, between an old, picturesque section around a hilltop cathedral and a modern, industrial area sprawling along the valley and railroad below. The 19th-century novelist Honoré de Balzac is one of the town's adopted sons; he described Angoulême in his meaty novel *Lost Illusions*. The Ville Haute (Upper Town), known as *Le Plateau,* has a warren of quaint old streets around the Hôtel de Ville (Town Hall) and stunning views from the ramparts. The 12th-century **Cathédrale St-Pierre** (⊠ Pl. St-Pierre) bears little resemblance to the majority of its French counterparts because of the cupolas topping each of its three bays. The cathedral was partly destroyed by Calvinists in 1562, then restored in a heavy-handed manner in 1634 and 1866. Its main attraction is its magnificent Romanesque facade, whose layers of rounded arches bear 70 stone statues and bas-reliefs illustrating the *Last Judgment.*

Where to Stay & Eat

$ ✕ **La Tour des Valois.** Diagonally across from the market, this rustic 15th-century restaurant offers substantial regional food. Sample one of Gérard André's veal dishes—the one using the local mustard from Jarnac is particularly good—and the locally made foie gras, served warm with plum and apple. ⊠ *7 rue Massillon* ☎ *05–45–95–23–64* ▤ *AE, MC, V* ⊘ *Closed part of Feb., mid-Aug.–early Sept., and Mon. No dinner Sun.* ¶⊙¶ *MAP.*

$$$–$$$$ ✕▥ **Château de Nieuil.** If high-class bucolic bliss is to your taste rather than a hotel in Angoulême itself, this is the place to stay. It's an easy 35 km (20 mi) drive northeast from the city (follow the signs for La Rochefoucauld-Limoges, N141). An avenue of trees opening onto a circular lawn leads to this former hunting lodge—a huge Renaissance château with towers. Rooms vary: some have traditional furnishings and pastel blue fabric; others have a *petit salon* (small sitting area) or a garden view. If the reception area is small, the formidable dining room (no dinner Sunday; September to June closed Monday) has a large stone fireplace with sculpted family crests and a multifaceted chandelier. Enjoy Pascal Pres-

sac's superb lamb (a regional specialty) or scallop of milk-fed veal with grapes. ✉ *Château de Nieuil, 16270 Nieuil* ☎ *05–45–71–36–38* 🖨 *05–45–71–46–45* ⊕ *www.chateaunieuilhotel.com* ➬ *11 rooms, 3 suites* ⌂ *Restaurant, minibars, cable TV, tennis court, pool, bar, babysitting, Internet, some pets allowed (fee)* ▤ *AE, DC, MC, V* ⊘ *Closed Nov.–Apr.* ⦿I *MAP.*

$$ ✕🖽 **Mercure France.** On the edge of the Ville Haute, across from the covered market, this hotel has a traditional air. From the garden there are fine views of the city. Rooms lull in shades of pale blue with striped curtains and bedspreads. The staff is professional and accustomed to speaking English. The Jardins des Arceaux restaurant (closed for lunch on weekends) serves solid regional cuisine. ✉ *1 pl. des Halles-Centrales, 16000* ☎ *05–45–95–47–95, 0181/741–3100 in U.K., 800/637–2873 in U.S.* 🖨 *05–45–92–02–70* ➬ *89 rooms* ⌂ *Restaurant, bar, Internet, some pets allowed (fee)* ▤ *AE, DC, MC, V* ⦿I *BP.*

Cognac

➌⓪ *42 km (28 mi) west of Angoulême via N141.*

The black-walled town of Cognac seems an unlikely home for one of the world's most celebrated drinks. You may be disappointed initially by the town's unpretentious appearance but, like the drink, it tends to grow on you. Cognac owed its early development to the transport of salt and wine along the Charente River. When 16th-century Dutch merchants discovered that the local wine was both tastier and easier to transport if distilled, the town became the heart of the brandy industry. Most cognac houses organize visits of their premises and *chais,* the local name for cognac warehouses. Wherever you decide to go, you will literally be inhaling the atmosphere of cognac: 3% of the precious cask-bound liquid evaporates every year. It's known as *la part des anges,* the angels' share. This has two consequences: each chai smells delicious, and a small black fungus, which feeds on cognac's alcoholic fumes, forms on walls throughout the town.

The leading monument in Cognac is the former **Château François-I**er, now the premises of **Otard Cognac.** Volatile Renaissance monarch François I was born here in 1494. The remaining buildings are something of a hodgepodge, though the chunky towers recall the site's fortified origins. The tour of Otard Cognac combines slick propaganda with historical comment on the drink itself. At the end you get to sample free cognac, and you can buy some at reduced prices. ✉ *127 bd. Denfert-Rochereau* ☎ *05–45–35–72–68* ⊕ *www.otard.com* 🖾 *€4* ⊘ *Apr.–June, Sept. and Oct. daily 10–noon and 2–6, July and Aug. 10–noon and 1:30–7, Nov. and Dec. tours at 11, 2:30, 3:45, and 5.*

Hennessy, along the banks of the Charente and easily recognized by the company's mercenary emblem—an ax-wielding arm carved in stone—includes in its tour a cheerful jaunt across the Charente in old-fashioned barges. You begin at an historic warehouse, then boat over to a new Hennessy exhibition center designed by Jean-Michel Wilmotte. ✉ *Quai Richard-Hennessy* ☎ *05–45–35–72–68* ⊕ *www.hennessy-cognac.com* 🖾 *€6* ⊘ *June–Sept., daily 10–6; Oct.–Dec. and Mar.–May, daily 10–5.*

Among the Cognac houses, **Martell** gives the most polished guided tour and its chais are perhaps more picturesque than Hennessy's. ⊠ *7 pl. Édouard-Martell* ☏ *05–45–36–33–33* ⊕ *www.martell.com* ⊠ *€5* ⊗ *June–Sept., weekdays 9:30–5, weekends 11–5; Oct. and Mar.–May, weekdays 9:30–noon and 2–5.*

Rue Saulnier, alongside the Hennessy premises, is the most atmospheric of the somber, sloping cobbled streets that compose the core of Cognac, dominated by the tower of **St-Léger** (⊠ Pl. d'Armes), a church with a notably large Flamboyant Gothic rose window.

Busy boulevard Denfert-Rochereau twines around the Vieille Ville, passing the town hall and the neighboring **Musée de Cognac** (Town Museum) with its collection of cognac posters, glasses, and other marketing artifacts. ⊠ *48 bd. Denfert-Rochereau* ☏ *05–45–32–07–25* ⊕ *www.ville-cognac.fr* ⊠ *€2.50* ⊗ *June–Sept., Wed.–Mon. 10–noon and 2–6; Oct.–May, Wed.–Mon. 2–5:30.*

Where to Stay & Eat

★ **$$–$$$** ✕⊡ **Château de l'Yeuse.** For some, style and comfort may be reasons enough to stay in this lushly appointed hotel on Cognac's southern outskirts but, for most, it's the knock-out view of the Charente valley that is the real attraction. Built up around a 19th-century château—picturesquely done up in red-and-white-stone stripes—this hotel has long been a regional lure (celebrities, from Alain Delon to Brian de Palma, love this place). Everyone agrees there are few more appealing places to sit and sip a cognac aperitif—"le long drink," to the French—on a summer evening. Alternatively, in winter, make yourself snug in the gloriously warm and wood-paneled Cognac Club. The mirror-lined, spaciously elegant restaurant is just the place to treat yourself to the "Havana" dessert, a crunchy confection made with cognac-flavor custard. Upstairs, guest rooms are flocked in designer fabrics and adorned with pretty accent pieces. ⊠ *65 rue de Bellevue, F-16100 Châteaubernard* ☏ *05–45–36–82–60* 🖷 *05–45–35–06–32* ⊕ *www.yeuse.fr* 🛏 *21 rooms, 3 suites* ♿ *Restaurant, pool, health club, bar; no a/c* ☰ *AE, DC, MC, V* ⏀ *FAP.*

Shopping

A bottle of old cognac makes a fine souvenir; try **La Cognathèque** (⊠ 8 pl. Jean-Monnet), in Cognac itself, though you can usually find the same item infinitely cheaper at a local producer or in most regional supermarkets (even if the choice will be more limited).

Saintes

❸❶ *27 km (17 mi) northwest of Cognac via D24.*

On the banks of the Charente River, Saintes, littered with religious edifices and Roman ruins dating from the 1st century, exudes stately serenity. The town owes its development to the salt marshes that first attracted the Romans to the area some 2,000 years ago. The Romans left their mark with the impressive **Arènes** (Amphitheater; ⊠ Rue Lacurie ⊠ €1 ⊗ Apr.–Oct., daily 9–7; Nov.–Mar., Tues.–Sun. 10–12:30 and 2–4:30). There are several better-preserved examples in France, but few as old—

CloseUp

TAKEN TO CASK

To the world, Cognac is not a place but a drink. That's cool with the locals of Cognac, who are perfectly content to take a back seat to the liquor that is lovingly aged in their cellar casks, sweetens their air, blackens their houses, and pumps their economy. The secret of cognac was supposedly discovered by the knight of La Croix Maron, a fan of the local eau-de-vie (wine distilled by a high alcohol content) who thought something wasn't quite right with the drink. Maybe he imbibed too heavily one night, because he had this dream about the devil, hellfire, and saving the "soul" of the eau-de-vie, which, in his interpretation, meant distilling the wine a second time to capture its essence. After his death, local monks inherited his twice-distilled eau-de-vie in oak casks, but didn't bother opening it for 15 years. When they did, they found the liquid had not only turned a rich amber color, but that it also went down a hell of a lot smoother.

it dates from AD 40 and could hold 15,000. You'll find it to the west of the town center, close to the church of St-Eutrope with its mighty spire. On the bank of the Charente stands a grand Roman triumphal arch, the **Arc de Germanicus** (☎ 05–46–74–23–82 information), dedicated to Emperor Tiberius and built in AD 19 as the entry to Saintes on the old Roman road from Lyon (the arch was moved to its present site in the 19th century). Boats leave alongside for river trips in summer.

Climbing above the red roofs of the Vieille Ville is the **Cathédrale St-Pierre** (⊠ Pl. du Synode), which seems to stagger beneath the weight of its stocky tower. Engineering caution foiled plans for the traditional pointed spire, so the tower was given a shallow dome—incongruous, perhaps, but distinctive. The austere 16th-century interior is lined with fat round pillars. The narrow pedestrian-only streets clustered around the cathedral contrast with the broad boulevards that sweep through the town and over the river.

Saintes's ecclesiastical pride and joy is the **Abbaye aux Dames** (Ladies' Abbey), consecrated in 1047. The abbey church is fronted by an exquisite, intricately carved, arcaded facade. Although the Romanesque choir remains largely in its original form, the rest of the interior is less harmonious, as the abbey fell on hard times after the death of the last abbess—the 30th—in 1792. It became a prison, then a barracks, and is now a cultural center. British visitors hankering for marmite, baked beans, and HP sauce can stock up at La Perfide Albion, at 11 rue Arc de Triomphe. Its English owner, a grandson of novelist Evelyn Waugh, is a font of local knowledge. ⊠ 7 pl. de l'Abbaye ☎ 05–46–97–48–48 ▨ €3 ⊙ Apr.–Sept., daily 10–12:30 and 2–7; Oct.–Mar., Sat. 10–12:30 and 2–7, Sun.–Tues., Thurs., and Fri. 2–6.

La Rochelle

★ ㉜ *72 km (45 mi) northwest of Saintes via A610/ N137.*

La Rochelle is a vibrant, appealing town, with ancient streets and a pic-ture-postcard harbor, the Vieux Port, which has become one of the lead-ing yachting centers in France—which is to say in Europe. Vast numbers of gleamingly expensive boats are based here and anyone with salt in their veins will relish a stroll around their serried ranks. Standing sentinel on either side of the harbor are two fortresslike 14th-century **towers**, the **Tour St-Nicolas** (to the left) and the **Tour de la Chaîne** (right); a third tower, the 15th-century **Tour de la Lanterne**, emerges a little farther along the quayside. You can climb to the top of any of them for a view of the bay toward Ile d'Aix. ☒ *Each tower €4.60 ⊘ Mid-May–mid-June and 1st 2 wks Sept., daily 10–12:30 and 2–6:30; July and Aug., daily 10–7; mid-Sept.–mid-May, Tues.–Sun. 10–12:30 and 2–5:30.*

Porte de la Grosse Horloge (Gate of the Giant Clock) is a massive stone gate marking the entrance to the narrow, bustling streets of the Vieille Ville. From Porte de la Grosse Horloge head down rue du Palais and onto rue Gargoulleau: halfway down on the left is the 18th-century Bishop's Palace, now the **Musée des Beaux-Arts** (Museum of Fine Arts). ☒ *28 rue Gargoulleau* ☎ *05–46–41–64–65* ☒ *€3.50, joint ticket for all town museums €6.60 ⊘ Apr.–Sept., Mon. and Wed.–Sat. 2–6, Sun. 2:30–6; Oct.–Mar., Mon. and Wed.–Fri. 1:30–5, weekends 2:30–6.*

At the **Musée du Nouveau-Monde** (New World Museum), in an 18th-cen-tury building, old maps, engravings, watercolors, and even wallpaper evoke the commercial links between La Rochelle and the New World. ☒ *10 rue Fleuriau* ☎ *05–46–41–46–50* ☒ *€3.50, joint ticket for all town museums €6.60 ⊘ Apr.–Sept., Mon. and Wed.–Sat. 10–12:30 and 2–6, Sun. 2:30–6; Oct.–Mar., Mon and Wed.–Fri. 9:30–12:30 and 1:30–5, weekends 2:30–6.*

The **Aquarium** is an elegant glass and wood building close to the Vieux Port. The highlight is a huge tank in which sharks, turtles, manta rays, and other denizens of the deep glide in alarming abandon. ☒ *Bassins des Grands Yachts* ☎ *05–46–34–79–49* ⊕ *www.aquarium-larochelle. com/* ☒ *€12 ⊘ July and Aug., daily 9 AM–11 PM; Apr.–June and Sept., daily 9 AM–8 PM; Oct.–Mar., daily 10 AM–8 PM.*

In summer, boats operated by **Inter-Iles** leave La Rochelle harbor daily for cruises to **Ile de Ré, Ile d'Oléron, Ile d'Aix,** and **Fort Boyard.** ☒ *14 bis Cours de Dames* ☎ *05–46–50–55–54* ⊕ *www.inter-iles.com.*

Where to Stay & Eat

★ **$$$–$$$$** ✕ **Maryse et Richard Coutanceau.** Widely acknowledged as the region's premier chef, Richard Coutanceau presides over something of a culinary dynasty in La Rochelle. With his children, he owns no less than five restau-rants in the town. This was his first, however, opened in 1980 and still setting standards. Seafood dominates, with eel, bass with basil, and spi-der crab with asparagus among his specialties. ☒ *Plage de la Concur-*

rence ☎ *05–46–41–48–19* ⊕ *www.coutanceauonline.com* ▤ *AE, DC, MC, V* ⊗ *Closed Sun.*

$–$$ ✕ **Bar André.** The salty decor may be a bit excessive—with fishing nets fluttering from the ceiling—but the Bar André, in business since 1947, is a veritable La Rochelle institution. Food and service have such gusto that you'll be hard put to resist, especially if you order the monumental seafood platter and wash it down with a bottle of white Charentes wine. *Mouclade Charentaise* (mussels in a creamy Pineau sauce) is a perennial winner. A variety of fixed-price menus keep meal costs within all budgets. ⊠ *7 rue St-Jean-du-Pérot* ☎ *05–46–41–28–24* ⊕ *www.bar-andre.com* ▤ *AE, DC, MC, V.*

$–$$ ▦ **Monnaie.** This 17th-century house by the Vieux Port has a wonderful lobby and cobblestone courtyard. Rooms are less inspiring; the quietest overlook the courtyard. Free parking is adjacent to the hotel, a definite plus as it's only a few minutes' walk from the harbor and town. ⊠ *3 rue de la Monnaie, 17000* ☎ *05–46–50–65–65* ⊟ *05–46–50–63–19* ⊕ *www.hotel-monnaie.com* ⤳ *31 rooms, 4 suites* ⚲ *Cable TV, Internet, free parking, some pets allowed (fee)* ▤ *AE, DC, MC, V* ⎪⊙⎪ *BP.*

¢–$ ▦ **Tour de Nesle.** This 19th-century hotel is well situated near the Vieux Port. Rooms are a bit cramped but up-to-date—ask for one overlooking the port or the church of St-Sauveur across the canal. Solid value all round. ⊠ *2 quai Louis-Durand, 17000* ☎ *05–46–41–05–86* ⊟ *05–46–41–95–17* ⊕ *www.hotel-la-tour-de-nesle.com* ⤳ *28 rooms* ⚲ *Some pets allowed (fee); no a/c* ▤ *AE, DC, MC, V.*

Ile de Ré

㉝ *11 km (7 mi) west of La Rochelle via Pont-Viaduc.*

L'Ile de Ré used to be a hush-hush, keep-it-quiet alternative to the Riviera. The few in the know enjoyed 30 mi of beaches with golden sand, an ornithological reserve, a citadel, a lighthouse, and great seafood, all baked by a sun that seems brighter here than anywhere else in France. But the secret is out and today the whole place smells more and more like burning money, with huge yachts in the old port towns, intellectuals splitting hairs in cafés, and Rolex watches jingling on the dance floors. A toll bridge curves across just north of La Rochelle to this cheerful island just 26 km (16 mi) long and never more than 6 km (4 mi) wide. Vineyards sweep over the eastern part of the island; oyster beds straddle the shallow waters to the west. The first village on the north coast reached from the mainland is **La Flotte.** The rectangular harbor hiding tiny fishing boats is surrounded by sturdy houses ready to stand against Atlantic gales. Ten kilometers (6 mi) farther on is the largest village on the island, **St-Martin de Ré** (population 3,000). It has a lively harbor and a citadel built by ace military architect Sébastien de Vauban in 1681. Many of its streets also date from the 17th century, and the villagers' low, white houses are typical of that period. **Ars**, a smaller village 10 km (6 mi) farther west, has a black-and-white church spire, a fine street market, and a cute harbor. If you go all the way to the northwestern end of Ile de Ré, be sure to climb up the **Phare de la Baleine** (Whale Lighthouse) for sweeping views of the Atlantic. At its foot is the **Café du Phare,** which has a surprising Art Deco setting full of artsy '30s lamps and serves a good *poutargue,* a local specialty made from smoked cod roe accompanied by shallots and sour cream.

Where to Stay & Eat

$$$$ ✗⊡ **L'Océan.** It may not be fancy, but for stripped-down elegance with a nautical note—model ships abound, ship pictures stud the walls—this is the place. Levels of comfort are solidly high while the restaurant (closed Wednesday) is never less than reliable, especially the fine fish stew. ⊠ *172 rue de St-Martin, 17580 Le Bois-Plage-en-Ré* ☎ *05–46–09–23–07* 📠 *05–46–09–05–40* 🛏 *29 rooms* ⅄ *Restaurant, pool* ▤ *AE, DC, MC, V* ☉ *Closed Jan.* ⎮⊙⎮ *MAP.*

en route	Head inland from La Rochelle along D9 and D20 northeast toward Marans, once a thriving seaport but now linked to the sea only by canal. The landscape is flat, barren, almost eerie: this is the **Marais Desséché** (Dry Marsh), and your first encounter with the Marais Poitevin. The verdant, tree-lined waterways that form the more scenic **Marais Mouillé** (Wet Marsh) gradually take over as you continue east. Take D114 from Marans, then a left on D116 just before Courçon and head north to Maillezais and its ruined abbey. Return south on D15 and turn left to Damvix, continuing along the pretty, canal-like Sèvre Niortaise to Arçais and Coulon.

Coulon

㉞ *60 km (38 mi) northeast of La Rochelle.*

The photogenic village of Coulon is the best base for exploring the Marais Poitevin. The ideal way to explore the Marais is by rowboat—or, more typically, on a *pigouille* (a flat, narrow boat maneuvered with a long pole). You can rent them in Coulon. They cost about €15 per hour per boat, maximum six persons, or you can hire a boat with a guide (for 45 minutes at €20) and get an earful of local lore as well. The town also has a lovely medieval church and a regional folk museum, the **Maison du Marais Mouillés.** ⊠ *Pl. de la Coutume* ☎ *05–49–35–81–04* ⊕ *www. parc-marais-poitevin.fr* 🎟 *€5* ☉ *May, June, and Sept, weekdays 10–noon and 2–7, weekends 10–1 and 2–7; July and Aug., daily 10–8; Oct. and Dec.–Apr., Tues.–Sun. 10–noon and 2–7; Nov., daily 2–7.*

One of the best ways to explore the area is by bicycle (a detailed map is advisable). You can rent them at **La Libellule** (⊠ *94 quai Louis-Tardy* ☎ *05–49–35–83–42).*

Where to Stay & Eat

¢–$$$ ✗⊡ **Le Central.** Just opposite the church on the town square, this hotel has a fine restaurant (closed Sunday evening and all day Monday) much favored by the local bourgeoisie, who enjoy an obsequious welcome from the blue-blazered owner. The fine choice of regional fare includes succulent lamb, eel fricassee, and warm oysters cooked with nettle leaves. Rooms are small and functional—good for an overnight stop, perhaps, but no longer. ⊠ *4 rue d'Autremont, 79510* ☎ *05–49–35–90–20*

🏠 *05–49–35–81–07* 🍴 *5 rooms* △ *Restaurant; no a/c, no room TVs* 🔲 *AE, MC, V* ☺ *Closed part of Oct. and Jan.* 🍽 *MAP.*

Poitiers

★ ㉟ *88 km (55 mi) northeast of Coulon via Niort/A10, 340 km (212 mi) southwest of Paris.*

Thanks to its majestic hilltop perch above the Clain River and its position halfway along the Bordeaux–Paris trade route, Poitiers became an important commercial, religious, and university town in the Middle Ages. Life quieted down after the 17th century, but tranquillity has resulted in excellent architectural preservation. For a taste of old Poitiers, explore the narrow streets of the Vieille Ville, most lined with weathered half-timbered buildings: Rue de la Chaîne, Rue des Veilles Boucheries, Rue du Marcheæ, and Grand'Rue. The church of **Notre-Dame-la-Grande** (✉ Pl. Charles-de-Gaulle), in the town center, is an impressive example of the Romanesque architecture so common in southwestern France. Its 12th-century facade, framed by rounded arches and decorated with a multitude of bas-reliefs and sculptures, comes alive during a 15-minute light show that highlights the details in color every evening at 10:30 from mid-June through September.

The **Cathédrale St-Pierre** (✉ Pl. de la Cathédrale), a few hundred yards beyond Notre-Dame-la-Grande, was built between the 12th and the 14th centuries. With a huge portal showing plump gargoyles without and tremendous open space and luminosity within, the largest church in Poitiers has a distinctive facade marked by two asymmetrical towers. The imposing interior is noted for its late-18th-century organ, stained glass, and 13th-century wooden choir stalls, claimed as the oldest in France.

The **Musée Ste-Croix** houses archaeological discoveries, traditional regional crafts, and European paintings from the 15th to the 19th centuries. The **Musée Rupert-de-Chièvres** (✉ 9 rue Victor-Hugo ☎ 05–49–41–42–21) displays Renaissance furniture, ceramics, and Old Master paintings.

★ ☺ **Futuroscope,** just north of Poitiers, is a smorgasbord of cinema thrills that has attracted more than 20 million visitors since it opened in 1987, making it western France's leading tourist attraction. Choose between half-dome screens (L'Omnimax); high-resolution screens (Cinéma Haute Résolution); theaters with mechanical seat effects (Cinémas Dynamiques); the Cinéma 360°, where you stand in mid-theater as nine images, shot in a circle, re-create a surf-pounding trimaran ocean race; the Magic Carpet, where a huge front screen is synchronized with another below your feet; Destination Cosmos, featuring the giant Hubble telescope; or Solido, where a pair of stereoscopic shades send you on a virtual swim. ✉ Exit 28 off A10, 86130 La Flotte-en-Ré Jaunay-Clan ☎ 05–49–49–11–12 ⊕ www.futuroscope.com/ 💶 1 day: adults €31, children €23. 2 days: adults €58, children €41. ☺ Feb.–Dec., daily 10–nightfall (typically 10 in summer, 6 in winter, but call for latest information).

Where to Stay & Eat

$$ ✕ **Maxime.** Reasonable prix-fixe menus and chef Christian Rougier's cooking have made Maxime a stylish crowd pleaser. Enjoy foie gras and duck salad in the pastel dining room lined with '30s-style frescoes. ✉ *4 rue St-Nicolas* ☎ *05–49–41–27–37* ⚷ *Reservations essential* ▭ *AE, DC, MC, V* ⊗ *Closed weekends and mid-July–mid-Aug.* ⍒ *MAP.*

$ ▦ **Europe.** An early-19th-century building with a modern extension houses this unpretentious hotel in the middle of town. Because it's off the main street and has a forecourt, rooms are quiet. It also has a pleasant garden in the back for an afternoon tea or an evening aperitif. ✉ *39 rue Carnot, 86000* ☎ *05–49–88–12–00* ⎙ *05–49–88–97–30* ⇨ *88 rooms* ⚷ *Cable TV, Internet, some pets allowed; no a/c* ▭ *AE, DC, MC, V.*

BORDEAUX, DORDOGNE & POITOU-CHARENTES A TO Z

To research prices, get advice from other travelers, and book travel arrangements, visit www.fodors.com.

AIR TRAVEL
🛈 Airlines & Contacts **Air France** ☎ 08-02-80-28-02.

AIRPORTS
Frequent daily flights on Air France link Bordeaux and the domestic airport at Limoges with Paris.
🛈 Airport Information **Aéroport de Bordeaux-Mérignac** ☎ 05-56-34-50-50 ⊕ www.bordeaux.aeroport.fr.

BUS TRAVEL
The regional bus operator is CITRAM; the main Gare Routière (bus terminal) in Bordeaux is on Allées de Chartres (by Esplanade des Quinconces), near the Garonne River. CITRAM buses cover towns in the wine country and beach areas not well served by rail (for instance, one or two buses run daily to St-Émilion and Pauillac). The Dordogne region is serviced by Trans-Périgord and CFTA; the region around La Rochelle by Océcars. Sarlat is a main bus hub, with connections to Les Eyzies, Périgueux, and Bordeaux. The Sarlat–Périgueux line has a stop at Montignac for the Lascaux Caves. CITRAM buses from Cognac end up in Angoulême. Coulon in the Marais Poitevin is serviced by Casa Buses. Bus service in and around Poitiers is offered by Société des Transports Poitevins.
🛈 Bus Information **Casa** ✉ 13 chemin Fief-Binard, 79000 Niort ☎ 05-49-24-93-47. **CFTA** ✉ Gare Routière, pl. Francheville, 24000 Périgueux ☎ 05-53-08-43-13. **CITRAM** ✉ 8 rue de Corneille, 33000 Bordeaux ☎ 05-56-43-68-43. **Océcars** ✉ 31 rue des Rameaux, 17000 La Rochelle ☎ 05-46-00-95-15. **Société des Transports Poitevins** ✉ 9 rue de Northampton, 86000 Poitiers ☎ 05-49-44-77-00. **Trans-Périgord** ✉ Cabarnat, 24250 Veyrines-de-Domme ☎ 05-53-28-52-20.

CAR RENTAL
🛈 Local Agencies **Avis** ✉ Gare St-Jean, Bordeaux ☎ 05-56-91-65-50 ✉ 133 bd. du Grand-Cerf, Poitiers ☎ 05-49-58-13-00 ✉ 166 bd. Joffre, La Rochelle ☎ 05-46-41-13-55.

Hertz ✉ Pl. de la Gare, Bergerac ☎ 05-53-57-19-27 ✉ 105 bd. du Grand-Cerf, Poitiers ☎ 05-49-58-24-24.

CAR TRAVEL

As the capital of southwest France, Bordeaux has superb transport links with Paris, Spain, and even the Mediterranean (A62 expressway via Toulouse). The A10, the Paris–Bordeaux expressway, passes close to Poitiers, Niort (exit 33 for La Rochelle), and Saintes before continuing toward Spain as A63. The generally fast N137 connects La Rochelle with Saintes via Rochefort; Angoulême is linked to Bordeaux and Poitiers by N10; and D936 runs along the Dordogne Valley to Bergerac. N89 links Bordeaux to Périgueux.

EMERGENCIES

🚑 **Ambulance** ☎ 15. **Hôpital St-André** ✉ 1 rue Jean-Burguet, 33800 Bordeaux ☎ 05-56-79-56-79.

TOURS

The Office de Tourisme in Bordeaux organizes four-hour coach tours of the surrounding vineyards every Wednesday and Saturday afternoon. The office has information on other wine tours and tastings, and on local and regional sights; a round-the-clock phone service in English is available.
🏛 **Fees & Schedules Bordeaux Office de Tourisme** ✉ 12 cours du XXX-Juillet, cedex, 33080 Bordeaux ☎ 05-56-00-66-00.

TRAIN TRAVEL

The superfast TGV (Train à Grande Vitesse) Atlantique service links Paris (Gare Montparnasse) to Bordeaux—585 km (365 mi) in three hours—with stops at Poitiers and Angoulême (change for Cognac, and Saintes); and to La Rochelle—465 km (290 mi) in three hours—with a stop in Niort. Trains link Bordeaux to Lyon (8–9 hours) and Nice (eight hours) via Toulouse. Six trains daily make the 3½-hour, 400-km (250-mi) trip from Paris to Limoges.

Bordeaux is the region's major train hub. Trains run regularly from Bordeaux to Bergerac (80 minutes), with occasional stops at St-Émilion, and three times daily to Sarlat (nearly three hours). At least six trains daily make the 90-minute journey from Bordeaux to Périgueux, and four continue to Limoges (2 hours, 20 minutes). Poitiers is the connecting point for Niort, La Rochelle, and Rochefort; Angoulême is the connecting point for Jarnac, Cognac, and Saintes.
🚆 **Train Information SNCF** ☎ 08-36-35-35-35 ⊕ www.ter-sncf.com/uk/poitou-charentes.

TRAVEL AGENCIES

🏛 **Local Agent Referrals American Express** ✉ 14 cours de l'Intendance, Bordeaux ☎ 05-56-00-63-33. **Carlson-Wagons-lit** ✉ 43 rue de la Porte-Dijeaux, Bordeaux ☎ 05-56-52-92-70.

VISITOR INFORMATION

🏛 **Tourist Information Angoulême** ✉ 7 bis rue du Chat ☎ 05-45-95-16-84 ⊕ www.tourisme.fr/office-de-tourisme/angouleme.htm. **Bergerac** ✉ 97 rue Neuve d'Argenson ☎ 05-53-57-03-11 ⊕ www.bergerac-tourisme.com. **Bordeaux** ✉ 12 cours du

XXX-Juillet ☎ 05-56-00-66-00 ⊕ www.bordeaux-tourisme.com. **Cognac** ✉ 16 rue du XIV-Juillet ☎ 05-45-82-10-71 ⊕ www.tourism-cognac.com. **La Rochelle** ✉ Pl. de la Petite-Sirène ☎ 05-46-41-14-68 ⊕ www.larochelle-tourisme.com. **Pauillac** ✉ La Verrerie ☎ 05-56-59-03-08 ⊕ www.pauillac-Medoc.com. **Périgueux** ✉ 25 rue du Président-Wilson ☎ 05-53-35-50-24. **Poitiers** ✉ 8 rue des Grandes-Écoles ☎ 05-49-41-21-24 ⊕ www.ot-poitiers.fr. **Royan** ✉ Rond-Point de la Poste ☎ 05-46-05-04-71 ⊕ www.royan-tourisme.com. **St-Émilion** ✉ 15 rue du Clocher ☎ 05-57-55-28-28 ⊕ www.saint-emilion-tourisme.com. **Saintes** ✉ 62 cours National ☎ 05-46-74-23-82 ⊕ www.ot-saintes.fr. **Sarlat** ✉ Pl. de la Liberté ☎ 05-53-31-45-45 ⊕ www.sarlat-en-perigord.com.

UNDERSTANDING FRANCE

À LA FRANÇAISE

THERE IS AN OLD FAMILIAR SAYING: "Everyone has two countries, his or her own—and France." For France is the Land of Cockaigne, where every man and woman does what he or she pleases, where you can allow your personal idiosyncracies full play and apologize for them with complete acceptability by the simple remark, *Je suis comme ça.* I am like that. It's all that need be said. In France everyone has a right to be like him or herself. One needn't conform to the model of another.

It is this freedom that, millennia ago, made France the cultural—and hoopla—capital of the world; and it is this freedom that has given us Notre-Dame, Chartres, Versailles, and the Tour Eiffel; writers like Molière, Hugo, Balzac, and Proust; composers like Berlioz and Debussy; and painters like Georges de la Tour, Fragonard, Monet, Cézanne, and Matisse. Only when Picasso came to Paris from Spain did he become Picasso; only when Van Gogh traveled to Provence from Holland did he become Van Gogh. Clearly there are few other countries that can contribute so much to the spiritual development of the individual. If environment can add to a person's stature, the environment of France can be counted on to do it by virtue of the influence she brings to bear on everyone sensitive to beauty, measure, and intellectual stimulation. In addition to the roll-call listed above, the best witnesses to that are the many American and British expatriates who came to admire, and remained to praise.

For the expats, France is neither too hot nor too cold, neither too wet nor too dry, neither too flat nor too crammed with inconvenient mountains. At any rate, that is what the French say. They will go on to tell you that countries should be hexagonal in shape and about 600 mi across. Spain is too square, Norway is frayed at the edges, l'Angleterre (which is what the French usually call Great Britain) is awkwardly surrounded by cold water, Switzerland is landlocked and too small, and the United States is too large.

Appropriately for les Français, France sits squarely in the middle of Western Europe; according to Francophiles, it might just as well be the center of the universe. The country has been the locus of European intellectual life ever since the founding of the Sorbonne in Paris in the 13th century. During the next few centuries the entire Western world began to adopt the French language and aspects of French culture. Then, with the French Revolution of 1789 and Napoléon's frolic over the European continent, France established itself as a world political, as well as cultural, power—a fact the proud French have not forgotten, and are always eager to remind you about.

In more recent years, the tables have turned, and foreign cultures have been invading France. And here "foreign" means American. For decades now, young French people have emulated Americans in the way they dress, the music they listen to, and even in their manner of speaking. Levi's go for $80 a pair and can be seen gracing the legs of any slick twentysomething, buskers sing Bob Dylan tunes in the streets, and teenagers hang out in the local MacDo (MacDonald's to the French), not in the corner café. And though they curse American movies to the death, the French love-hate relationship with Yankee films has let Hollywood win over the big screen.

But the French also fear the movement toward what they call *mondialisation* (globalization), which to many is a synonym for Americanization. The older generation in particular sees the infiltration of American fads and the country's integration into the European Union (EU) as eroding traditional French ways of life. Many grumble about the universality of the English language, which is commandeering worldwide chat rooms across the Internet and is the common parlance in international business deals. The Académie Française, tireless preserver of French culture, even set about to strike English words (like "le weekend" and "le parking") from the French vocabulary and establish 66% French-music quotas for radio stations. The proposed changes stuck like wet Velcro when a cultural minister accidentally slipped an English word into his announcement speech. But even with the trend toward mondialisation, French culture remains, well, distinctly French. Paris is still the world center of the ultrastylish, and its cafés continue to be the breeding ground for smoking, coffee-drinking, armchair intellectuals. And in the French provinces, with their pastoral landscapes, stunning architecture, and delicious cuisine, there remains a determination to keep old-world charm uncompromised.

It's also important to remember, however, that there is not just one France: the country's geography is as diverse as the people who inhabit it. The Riviera attracts an international jet-set crowd to its famous strips of sand. In the south you can find an influx of recent immigrants and myriad cultures to match, a phenomenon that has met hostility from the steadily expanding Front National, France's ultraright party. In Provence the soil yields many gifts, and sunny pride blends with Spanish influence and Roman history to create an intriguing culture. In the southwest, along the Spanish border, the Basque people struggle to preserve their culture and their unique language, Euskera, in the face of trends toward centralization. Alsace-Lorraine, on the eastern edge of France, is almost as German as it is French. And in Brittany, one of the last regions to be incorporated into France, people still oc-

casionally speak Breton and celebrate their Celtic heritage.

An essay such as this has to contain rash generalizations. Is there an average French person? Obviously not. There are the rich and the poor, for example. The poor in France like champagne, oysters, and foie gras, but they get them less often than do the rich. The same is true of other aspects of life. The gulf between one class and another is not one of tastes and aspirations; rich and poor are in broad agreement on what constitutes a pleasant life. The poor are simply further away from it than are the rich. The surge of prosperity in the '60s brought improvements to French life, with some drawbacks, but basic traditions die hard. The young ape foreign fashions, with a fast-food/motorcycle/mid-Atlantic pop noise/comic-strip culture, but they grow out of it. Official morality has changed. Contraception used to be forbidden; Paris was famed for its elegant brothels, but women had to go to London for diaphragms and to Switzerland for abortions. All that has gone. In 1988 the rise of AIDS caused a quickly smothered quarrel among bishops about the sinfulness of condoms, which are now readily available. *Le topless* is seen on most beaches, and total nakedness on some. But the family remains a powerful, cohesive unit.

In the end, there are those who love France and those who don't. It's a matter of taste and character. The former find it easy to slip into the French way of life for a week or a month or permanently. The latter are better off in Paris or on the Riviera. But really, the French are canny operators when it comes to enjoying *la douceur de vivre,* the sweetness of life. If you follow their example while in France, you can't go far wrong. (One way to go wrong would be to quote almost any paragraph from this essay to them; at any rate, it will start a vigorously French argument.)

FURTHER READING

Books on Paris alone can fill several libraries. Two titles that have recently hit the best-seller lists are *A Year in the Merde*, by Stephen Clarke, and *Paris to the Moon*, by Adam Gopnik—the distinguished Paris-based correspondent of the *New Yorker*. For a look at American expatriates in Paris between the wars, read *Sylvia Beach and the Lost Generation*, by Noel R. Fitch, or *A Moveable Feast*, by Ernest Hemingway. George Orwell's *Down and Out in Paris and London* gives an account of life on a shoestring in these two European capitals. More essays about Paris are excerpted in *A Place in the World Called Paris*. Yet another anthology of essays on Paris is the *Travelers' Tales Guides: Paris*. For a visual feast, delight in John Russell's *Paris*—a compendium of city scenes painted by great masters accompanied by an illuminating text.

Three memoirs by Americans who have lived in Paris are Art Buchwald's *I'll Always Have Paris*, Edmund White's *The Flâneur*, and Stanley Karnow's *Paris in the Fifties*. *Paris Notebooks*, by Mavis Gallant, is her observations on Paris life. *A Corner in the Marais: Memoir of a Paris Neighborhood* is Alex Karmel's history of the neighborhood. Edmund White and Hubert Sorin have also weighed in with *Our Paris: Sketches with Memory*.

The best introduction to modern France is John Ardagh's *France Today*. A witty but less complete survey of the country and its people is Theodore Zeldin's *The French*. Another entry on the list is Richard Bernstein's *Fragile Glory*. An immensely popular, if slightly satiric, introduction to French country life is provided by Peter Mayle's two autobiographical books on Provence, *A Year in Provence* and *Toujours Provence*, as well as his novel *Chasing Cézanne*.

Nancy Mitford's readable *The Sun King* covers the regal grandeur of the 17th century, while Alfred Cobban's workmanlike *History of Modern France* describes trends and events from the death of Louis XIV up to 1962. Another readable and fascinating book about French history is Barbara Tuchman's *A Distant Mirror*. Dorothy Carrington's classic work on Corsica, *Granite Island: A Portrait of Corsica*, is available at the library. For modern French history, particularly the Vichy era, a good bet is Robert Paxton's *Vichy France and the Jews*. For a scholarly study of Romanesque and Gothic architecture, read Henri Focillon's thoughtfully illustrated *The Art of the West*, available at the library.

Charles Dickens's *A Tale of Two Cities*, Flaubert's *Sentimental Education*, Henry James's *The Ambassadors*, Colette's *The Complete Claudine*, F. Scott Fitzgerald's *Tender Is the Night*, Hemingway's *The Sun Also Rises*, and Émile Zola's *La Curée*, *L'Assommoir*, *Nana*, and *La Débâcle* are just a handful of the classic novels set in France.

As for books about French wine and cuisine, Patricia Wells's *The Food Lover's Guide to Paris* and *The Food Lover's Guide to France* provide a good beginning. Waverly Root's *The Food of France* is a great accompaniment to any trip. Alexis Lichine's *Guide to Wines and Vineyards of France* is still the classic wine guide, though it's now only available from the library. For more books about French wine, try Robert M. Parker's *Bordeaux: A Comprehensive Guide to the Wines Produced from 1961–1997* and *Wines of the Rhône Valley*. A. J. Liebling's *Between Meals* provides a more literary look at the fine art of eating in France.

CHRONOLOGY

Here's a minihistory of France—an *aide mémoire* to monarchs and moments.

58–51 BC Julius Caesar conquers Gaul; writes up the war in *De Bello Gallico*.

52 BC Lutetia, later to become Paris, is built by the Gallo-Romans.

46 BC Roman amphitheater built at Arles.

14 BC Pont du Gard aqueduct at Nîmes is erected.

The Merovingian Dynasty

486–511 Clovis, king of the Franks (481–511), defeats the Roman governor of Gaul and founds the Merovingian dynasty. Great monasteries, such as those at Tours, Limoges, and Chartres, become centers of culture.

497 Franks convert to Christianity.

The Carolingian Dynasty

768–78 Charlemagne (768–814) becomes king of the Franks (768), conquers northern Italy (774), and is defeated by the Moors at Roncesvalles, Spain, after which he consolidates the Pyrénées border (778).

800 The pope crowns Charlemagne Holy Roman Emperor in Rome. Charlemagne expands the French kingdom far beyond its present borders and establishes a center for learning at his capital, Aix-la-Chapelle (Aachen, in present-day Germany).

The Capetian Dynasty

987 Hugh Capet (987–996) is made king of France and establishes the principle of hereditary rule for his descendants. Settled conditions and the increased power of the Church see the flowering of Romanesque architecture in the cathedrals of Autun and Angoulême.

1066 Norman conquest of England by William the Conqueror (1028–87).

ca. 1100 First universities in Europe include one in Paris. Development of European vernacular verse: *Chanson de Roland*.

1140 The Gothic style of architecture first appears at St-Denis and later becomes fully developed at the cathedrals of Chartres, Reims, Amiens, and Paris's Notre-Dame.

ca. 1150 Struggle between the Anglo-Norman kings (Angevin empire) and the French; when Eleanor of Aquitaine switches husbands (from Louis VII of France to Henry II of England), her extensive lands pass to English rule.

The Valois Dynasty

1337–1453 Hundred Years' War between France and England: fighting for control of those areas of France gained by the English crown following the marriage of Eleanor of Aquitaine and Henry II.

1428–31   Joan of Arc (1412–31), the Maid of Orléans, sparks the revival of French fortunes in the Hundred Years' War but is captured by the English and burned at the stake at Rouen.

1434   Johannes Gutenberg invents the printing press in Strasbourg, Alsace.

1453   France finally defeats England, terminating the Hundred Years' War and English claims to the French throne.

1475   Burgundy is at the height of its power under Charles the Bald.

1494   Italian wars: beginning of Franco-Habsburg struggle for hegemony in Europe.

1515–47   Reign of François I, who imports Italian artists, including Leonardo da Vinci (1452–1519), and brings the Renaissance to France. The château of Fontainebleau is begun (1528).

1562–98   Wars of Religion: Catholics versus Huguenots (French Protestants).

The Bourbon Dynasty

1589   The first Bourbon king, Henri IV (1589–1610), is a Protestant who converts to Catholicism and achieves peace in France. He signs the Edict of Nantes, giving limited freedom of worship to Protestants. The development of Renaissance Paris begins.

1643–1715   Reign of Louis XIV, the Sun King, a monarch who builds the Baroque power base of Versailles and presents Europe with a glorious view of France. With his first minister, Colbert, Louis makes France, by force of arms, the most powerful nation-state in Europe.

1660   Classical period of French culture: dramatists Pierre Corneille (1606–84), Molière (1622–73), and Jean Racine (1639–99), and painter Nicolas Poussin (1594–1665).

ca. 1715   Rococo art and decoration develop in Parisian boudoirs and salons, typified by the painter Antoine Watteau (1684–1721) and, later, François Boucher (1703–70) and Jean-Honoré Fragonard (1732–1806).

1700–onward   Writer and pedagogue Voltaire (1694–1778) is a central figure in the French Enlightenment, along with Jean-Jacques Rousseau (1712–78) and Denis Diderot (1713–84), who in 1751 compiles the first modern encyclopedia. The ideals of the Enlightenment—for reason and scientific method and against social and political injustices—pave the way for the French Revolution.

The French Revolution

1789–1804   The Bastille is stormed on July 14, 1789. Following upon early-republican ideals comes the Reign of Terror and the administration of the Directory under Robespierre. There are widespread political executions—Louis XVI and Marie-Antoinette are guillotined in 1793. Reaction sets in, and the instigators of the Terror are themselves executed (1794). Napoléon Bonaparte enters as Champion of the

Directory (1795–99) and is installed as First Consul during the Consulate (1799–1804).

The First Empire

1804   Napoléon crowns himself emperor of France at Notre-Dame in the presence of the pope.

1805–12   Napoléon conquers most of Europe. The Napoleonic Age is marked by a Neoclassical artistic style called Empire as well as by the rise of Romanticism—characterized author Marie-Henri Stendhal (1783–1842) and painters Eugène Delacroix (1798–1863).

1812–14   Winter cold and Russian determination defeat Napoléon outside Moscow. The emperor abdicates and is transported to Elba.

Restoration of the Bourbons

1814–15   Louis XVIII, brother of the executed Louis XVI, regains the throne after the Congress of Vienna settles peace terms.

1815   The Hundred Days: Napoléon returns from Elba and musters an army on his march to the capital but lacks national support. He is defeated at Waterloo (June 18) and exiled to the island of St-Helena, in the south Atlantic.

1830   Bourbon king Charles X, locked into a pre-Revolutionary state of mind, abdicates. A brief upheaval (called Three Glorious Days) brings Louis-Philippe, the Citizen King, to the throne.

1846–48   Severe industrial and farming depression contributes to Louis-Philippe's abdication (1848).

Second Republic & Second Empire

1848–52   Louis-Napoléon (nephew and step-grandson of Napoléon I) is elected president of the short-lived Second Republic. He is declared emperor of France, taking the title Napoléon III.

ca. 1850   The ensuing period is characterized in the arts by the emergence of realist painters, such as Jean-François Millet (1814–75) and Gustave Courbet (1819–77), and late-Romantic writers, among them Honoré de Balzac (1799–1850) and Charles Baudelaire (1821–87).

1863   Napoléon III inaugurates the Salon des Refusés in response to critical opinion. It includes work by Édouard Manet (1832–83), Claude Monet (1840–1926), and Paul Cézanne (1839–1906), and is commonly regarded as the birthplace of Impressionism and of modern art in general.

The Third Republic

1870–71   The Franco-Prussian War sees Paris besieged by and then fall to the Germans. Napoléon III takes refuge in England.

1871–1914   Before World War I, France builds vast colonial empires in North Africa and Southeast Asia. Sculptor Auguste Rodin (1840–1917), composer Claude Debussy (1862–1918), and poets such as Stéphane Mallarmé (1842–98) and Paul Verlaine (1844–96) set the stage for modernism.

1889   The Eiffel Tower is built for the Paris World Exhibition.

1918–39   Between the wars, Paris attracts artists and writers, including Americans Ernest Hemingway (1899–1961) and Gertrude Stein (1874–1946). France nourishes major artistic and philosophical movements: Constructivism, Dadaism, Surrealism, and Existentialism.

1939–45   At the beginning of World War II, France sides with the Allies until invaded and defeated by Germany in 1940. The French government, under Marshal Philippe Pétain (1856–1951), moves to Vichy and cooperates with the Nazis.

1944   D-Day, June 6: The Allies land on the beaches of Normandy and successfully invade France. Additional Allied forces land in Provence. Paris is liberated in August 1944, and France declares full allegiance to the Allies.

The Fourth Republic

1946   France adopts a new constitution; French women gain the right to vote.

1954–62   The Algerian War leads to Algeria's independence from France. Other French African colonies gain independence.

The Fifth Republic

1958–69   De Gaulle is the first president under a new constitution; he resigns in 1969, a year after widespread disturbances begun by student riots in Paris.

1994   The Channel Tunnel (or Chunnel) opens; trains link London to Paris in three hours.

1995   Jacques Chirac, mayor of Paris, is elected president.

2002   Throughout France, the widespread introduction of euro bills and coins goes off without a hitch.

2005   The popular vote in France seeks to preserve national identity by rejecting adoption of a European constitution.

FRENCH VOCABULARY

One of the trickiest French sounds to pronounce is the nasal final *n* sound (whether or not the *n* is actually the last letter of the word). You should try to pronounce it as a sort of nasal grunt—as in "huh." The vowel that precedes the *n* will govern the vowel sound of the word, and in this list we precede the final *n* with an *h* to remind you to be nasal.

Another problem sound is the ubiquitous but untransliterable *eu,* as in *bleu* (blue) or *deux* (two), and the very similar sound in *je* (I), *ce* (this), and *de* (of). The closest equivalent might be the vowel sound in "put," but rounded.

Words and Phrases

English	French	Pronunciation

Basics

English	French	Pronunciation
Yes/no	Oui/non	wee/nohn
Please	S'il vous plaît	seel voo **play**
Thank you	Merci	mair-**see**
You're welcome	De rien	deh ree-**ehn**
That's all right	Il n'y a pas de quoi	eel nee ah pah de **kwah**
Excuse me, sorry	Pardon	pahr-**dohn**
Sorry!	Désolé(e)	day-zoh-**lay**
Good morning/afternoon	Bonjour	bohn-**zhoor**
Good evening	Bonsoir	bohn-**swahr**
Goodbye	Au revoir	o ruh-**vwahr**
Mr. (Sir)	Monsieur	muh-**syuh**
Mrs. (Ma'am)	Madame	ma-**dam**
Miss	Mademoiselle	mad-mwa-**zel**
Pleased to meet you	Enchanté(e)	ohn-shahn-**tay**
How are you?	Comment ça va?	kuh-mahn-sa-**va**
Very well, thanks	Très bien, merci	tray bee-ehn, mair-**see**
And you?	Et vous?	ay **voo**?

Numbers

English	French	Pronunciation
one	un	uhn
two	deux	deuh
three	trois	twah
four	quatre	**kaht**-ruh

five	cinq	sank
six	six	seess
seven	sept	set
eight	huit	wheat
nine	neuf	nuff
ten	dix	deess
eleven	onze	ohnz
twelve	douze	dooz
thirteen	treize	trehz
fourteen	quatorze	kah-**torz**
fifteen	quinze	kanz
sixteen	seize	sez
seventeen	dix-sept	deez-**set**
eighteen	dix-huit	deez-**wheat**
nineteen	dix-neuf	deez-**nuff**
twenty	vingt	vehn
twenty-one	vingt-et-un	vehnt-ay-**uhn**
thirty	trente	trahnt
forty	quarante	ka-**rahnt**
fifty	cinquante	sang-**kahnt**
sixty	soixante	swa-**sahnt**
seventy	soixante-dix	swa-sahnt-**deess**
eighty	quatre-vingts	kaht-ruh-**vehn**
ninety	quatre-vingt-dix	kaht-ruh-vehn-**deess**
one-hundred	cent	sahn
one-thousand	mille	meel

Colors

black	noir	nwahr
blue	bleu	bleuh
brown	brun/marron	bruhn/mar-**rohn**
green	vert	vair
orange	orange	o-**rahnj**
pink	rose	rose
red	rouge	rooje
violet	violette	vee-o-**let**
white	blanc	blahnk
yellow	jaune	zhone

Days of the Week

Sunday	dimanche	**dee**-mahnsh
Monday	lundi	**luhn**-dee
Tuesday	mardi	**mahr**-dee
Wednesday	mercredi	**mair**-kruh-dee
Thursday	jeudi	**zhuh**-dee
Friday	vendredi	**vawn**-druh-dee
Saturday	samedi	**sahm**-dee

Months

January	janvier	**zhahn**-vee-ay
February	février	**feh**-vree-ay
March	mars	marce
April	avril	a-**vreel**
May	mai	meh
June	juin	zhwehn
July	juillet	**zhwee**-ay
August	août	oot
September	septembre	sep-**tahm**-bruh
October	octobre	awk-**to**-bruh
November	novembre	no-**vahm**-bruh
December	décembre	day-**sahm**-bruh

Useful Phrases

Do you speak . . . English?	Parlez-vous . . . anglais?	par-lay **voo ahn**-glay
I don't speak . . . French	Je ne parle pas . . . français	zhuh nuh parl **pah** frahn-**say**
I don't understand	Je ne comprends pas	zhuh nuh kohm-prahn **pah**
I understand	Je comprends	zhuh kohm-**prahn**
I don't know	Je ne sais pas	zhuh nuh say **pah**
I'm American/ British	Je suis américain/ anglais	zhuh sweez a-may-ree-**kehn**/ahn-**glay**
What's your name?	Comment vous appelez-vous?	ko-mahn voo za-pell-ay-**voo**
My name is . . .	Je m'appelle . . .	zhuh ma-**pell** . . .
What time is it?	Quelle heure est-il?	kel air eh-**teel**
How?	Comment?	ko-**mahn**

When?	Quand?	kahn
Yesterday	Hier	yair
Today	Aujourd'hui	o-zhoor-**dwee**
Tomorrow	Demain	duh-**mehn**
This morning/ afternoon	Ce matin/cet après-midi	suh ma-**tehn**/set ah-pray-mee-**dee**
Tonight	Ce soir	suh **swahr**
What?	Quoi?	kwah
What is it?	Qu'est-ce que c'est?	kess-kuh-**say**
Why?	Pourquoi?	**poor**-kwa
Who?	Qui?	kee
Where is . . .	Où se trouve . . .	oo suh **troov**
the train station?	la gare?	la gar
the subway?	la station de?	la sta-**syon** duh
station?	métro?	may-**tro**
the bus stop?	l'arrêt de bus?	la-**ray** duh **booss**
the airport?	l'aérogare?	lay-ro-**gar**
the post office?	la poste?	la post
the bank?	la banque?	la bahnk
the hotel?	l'hôtel?	lo-**tel**
the store?	le magasin?	luh ma-ga-**zehn**
the cashier?	la caisse?	la **kess**
the museum?	le musée?	luh mew-**zay**
the hospital?	l'hôpital?	lo-pee-**tahl**
the elevator?	l'ascenseur?	la-sahn-**seuhr**
the telephone?	le téléphone?	luh tay-lay-**phone**
Where are the rest rooms?	Où sont les toilettes?	oo sohn lay twah-**let**
Here/there	Ici/là	ee-**see**/la
Left/right	A gauche/à droite	a goash/a drwaht
Straight ahead	Tout droit	too drwah
Is it near/far?	C'est près/loin?	say pray/lwehn
I'd like . . .	Je voudrais . . .	zhuh voo-**dray**
a room	une chambre	ewn **shahm**-bruh
the key	la clé	la clay
a newspaper	un journal	uhn zhoor-**nahl**
a stamp	un timbre	uhn **tam**-bruh
I'd like to buy . . .	Je voudrais acheter . . .	zhuh voo-**dray** **ahsh**-tay
a cigar	un cigare	uhn see-**gar**
cigarettes	des cigarettes	day see-ga-**ret**
matches	des allumettes	days a-loo-**met**

dictionary	un dictionnaire	uhn deek-see-oh-**nare**
soap	du savon	dew sah-**vohn**
city map	un plan de ville	uhn plahn de **veel**
road map	une carte routière	ewn cart roo-tee-**air**
magazine	une revue	ewn reh-**vu**
envelopes	des enveloppes	dayz ahn-veh-**lope**
writing paper	du papier à lettres	dew pa-pee-**ay** a **let**-ruh
airmail writing paper	du papier avion	dew pa-pee-**ay** a-vee-**ohn**
postcard	une carte postale	ewn cart pos-**tal**
How much is it?	C'est combien?	say comb-bee-**ehn**
It's expensive/cheap	C'est cher/pas cher	say share/pa share
A little/a lot	Un peu/beaucoup	uhn peuh/bo-**koo**
More/less	Plus/moins	plu/mwehn
Enough/too (much)	Assez/trop	a-say/tro
I am ill/sick	Je suis malade	zhuh swee ma-**lahd**
Call a . . . doctor	Appelez un . . . médecin	a-play uhn mayd-**sehn**
Help!	Au secours!	o suh-**koor**
Stop!	Arrêtez!	a-reh-**tay**
Fire!	Au feu!	o fuh
Caution!/Look out!	Attention!	a-tahn-see-**ohn**

Dining Out

A bottle of . . .	une bouteille de . . .	ewn boo-**tay** duh
A cup of . . .	une tasse de . . .	ewn **tass** duh
A glass of . . .	un verre de . . .	uhn **vair** duh
Ashtray	un cendrier	uhn sahn-dree-**ay**
Bill/check	l'addition	la-dee-see-**ohn**
Bread	du pain	dew pan
Breakfast	le petit-déjeuner	luh puh-**tee** day-zhuh-**nay**
Butter	du beurre	dew burr
Cheers!	A votre santé!	ah vo-truh sahn-**tay**
Cocktail/aperitif	un apéritif	uhn ah-pay-ree-**teef**
Dinner	le dîner	luh dee-**nay**
Special of the day	le plat du jour	luh plah dew **zhoor**
Enjoy!	Bon appétit!	bohn a-pay-**tee**

Fixed-price menu	le menu	luh may-**new**
Fork	une fourchette	ewn four-**shet**
I am diabetic	Je suis diabétique	zhuh swee dee-ah-bay-**teek**
I am on a diet	Je suis au régime	zhuh sweez oray-**jeem**
I am vegetarian	Je suis végé-tarien(ne)	zhuh swee vay-zhay-ta-ree-**en**
I cannot eat . . .	Je ne peux pas manger de . . .	zhuh nuh **puh** pah mahn-**jay** deh
I'd like to order	Je voudrais commander	zhuh voo-**dray** ko-mahn-**day**
I'm hungry/thirsty	J'ai faim/soif	zhay fahm/swahf
Is service/the tip included?	Le service est-il compris?	luh sair-**veess** ay-teel com-**pree**
It's good/bad	C'est bon/mauvais	say bohn/mo-**vay**
It's hot/cold	C'est chaud/froid	say sho/frwah
Knife	un couteau	uhn koo-**toe**
Lunch	le déjeuner	luh day-zhuh-**nay**
Menu	la carte	la cart
Napkin	une serviette	ewn sair-vee-**et**
Pepper	du poivre	dew **pwah**-vruh
Plate	une assiette	ewn a-see-**et**
Please give me . . .	Merci de me donner . . .	Mair-**see** deh meh doe-**nay**
Salt	du sel	dew sell
Spoon	une cuillère	ewn kwee-**air**
Sugar	du sucre	dew **sook**-ruh
Waiter!/Waitress!	Monsieur!/Mademoiselle!	muh-**syuh**/mad-mwa-**zel**
Wine list	la carte des vins	la **cart** day van

MENU GUIDE

French	English

General Dining

French	English
Entrée	Appetizer/Starter
Garniture au choix	Choice of vegetable side
Selon arrivage	When available
Supplément/En sus	Extra charge
Sur commande	Made to order

Appetizers/Starters

French	English
Anchois	Anchovies
Andouille(tte)	Chitterling sausage
Assiette de charcuterie	Assorted pork products
Crudités	Mixed raw vegetable salad
Escargots	Snails
Jambon	Ham
Jambonneau	Cured pig's knuckle
Pâté	Liver puree blended with meat
Quenelles	Light dumplings
Saucisson	Dried sausage
Terrine	Pâté in an earthenware pot

Soups

French	English
Bisque	Shellfish soup
Bouillabaisse	Fish and seafood stew
Julienne	Vegetable soup
Potage/Soupe	Soup
Potage parmentier	Thick potato soup
Pot-au-feu	Stew of meat and vegetables
Soupe du jour	Soup of the day
Soupe à l'oignon gratinée	French onion soup
Soupe au pistou	Provençal vegetable soup
Velouté de . . .	Cream of . . .
Vichyssoise	Cold leek and potato cream soup

Fish and Seafood

French	English
Bar	Bass
Bourride	Fish stew from Marseilles
Brandade de morue	Creamed salt cod
Brochet	Pike
Cabillaud/Morue	Fresh cod
Calmar	Squid
Coquilles St-Jacques	Scallops

Crabe	Crab
Crevettes	Shrimp
Daurade	Sea bream
Écrevisses	Prawns/crayfish
Harengs	Herring
Homard	Lobster
Huîtres	Oysters
Langouste	Spiny lobster
Langoustine	Prawn/lobster
Lotte	Monkfish
Moules	Mussels
Palourdes	Clams
Rouget	Red mullet
Saumon	Salmon
Thon	Tuna
Truite	Trout

Meat

Agneau	Lamb
Ballotine	Boned, stuffed, and rolled
Blanquette de veau	Veal stew with a white-sauce base
Boeuf	Beef
Boeuf à la Bourguignonne	Beef stew
Boudin blanc	Sausage made with white meat
Boudin noir	Sausage made with pig's blood
Boulettes de viande	Meatballs
Brochette	Kabob
Cassoulet	Casserole of white beans, meat
Cervelle	Brains
Châteaubriand	Double fillet steak
Côtelettes	Chops
Choucroute garnie	Sausages and cured pork served with sauerkraut
Côte de boeuf	T-bone steak
Côte	Rib
Cuisses de grenouilles	Frogs' legs
Entrecôte	Rib or rib-eye steak
Épaule	Shoulder
Escalope	Cutlet
Foie	Liver
Gigot	Leg
Langue	Tongue
Médaillon	Tenderloin steak
Pavé	Thick slice of boned beef
Pieds de cochon	Pig's feet
Porc	Pork

Ragoût	Stew
Ris de veau	Veal sweetbreads
Rognons	Kidneys
Saucisses	Sausages
Selle	Saddle
Tournedos	Tenderloin of T-bone steak
Veau	Veal
Viande	Meat

Methods of Preparation

À point	Medium
À l'étouffée	Stewed
Au four	Baked
Bien cuit	Well-done
Bleu	Very rare
Bouilli	Boiled
Braisé	Braised
Frit	Fried
Grillé	Grilled
Rôti	Roast
Saignant	Rare
Sauté/poêlée	Sautéed

Game and Poultry

Blanc de volaille	Chicken breast
Caille	Quail
Canard/Caneton	Duck/duckling
Cerf/Chevreuil	Venison
Coq au vin	Chicken stewed in red wine
Dinde/Dindonneau	Turkey/Young turkey
Faisan	Pheasant
Lapin	Rabbit
Lièvre	Wild hare
Oie	Goose
Pigeon/Pigeonneau	Pigeon/Squab
Pintade/Pintadeau	Guinea fowl/Young guinea fowl
Poularde	Fattened pullet
Poulet/Poussin	Chicken/Spring chicken
Sanglier/Marcassin	Wild boar/Young wild boar
Volaille	Fowl

Vegetables

Artichaut	Artichoke
Asperge	Asparagus
Aubergine	Eggplant

Carottes	Carrots
Champignons	Mushrooms
Chou-fleur	Cauliflower
Chou (rouge)	Cabbage (red)
Choux de Bruxelles	Brussels sprouts
Courgette	Zucchini
Cresson	Watercress
Épinard	Spinach
Haricots blancs/verts	White kidney/green beans
Laitue	Lettuce
Lentilles	Lentils
Maïs	Corn
Oignons	Onions
Petits pois	Peas
Poireaux	Leeks
Poivrons	Peppers
Pomme de terre	Potato
Pommes frites	French fries
Tomates	Tomatoes

Desserts

Coupe (glacée)	Sundae
Crêpe	Thin pancake
Crème brûlée	Custard with caramelized topping
Crème caramel	Caramel-coated custard
Crème Chantilly	Whipped cream
Gâteau au chocolat	Chocolate cake
Glace	Ice cream
Mousse au chocolat	Chocolate mousse
Sabayon	Egg-and-wine-based custard
Tarte aux pommes	Apple pie
Tarte tatin	Caramelized apple tart
Tourte	Layer cake

Alcoholic Drinks

À l'eau	With water
Avec des glaçons	On the rocks
Kir	Chilled white wine mixed with black-currant syrup
Bière	Beer
blonde/brune	*light/dark*
Calvados	Apple brandy from Normandy
Eau-de-vie	Brandy
Liqueur	Cordial
Poire William	Pear brandy
Porto	Port

Vin	Wine
sec	*dry/neat*
brut	*very dry*
léger	*light*
doux	*sweet*
rouge	*red*
rosé	*rosé*
mousseux	*sparkling*
blanc	*white*

Nonalcoholic Drinks

Café	Coffee
noir	*black*
crème	*with steamed milk/cream*
au lait	*with steamed milk*
décaféiné	*caffeine-free*
Express	Espresso
Chocolat chaud	Hot chocolate
Eau minérale	Mineral water
gazeuse/non gazeuse	*carbonated/still*
Jus de . . .	. . . juice
Lait	Milk
Limonade	Lemonade
Thé	Tea
au lait/au citron	*with milk/lemon*
glacé	*Iced tea*
Tisane	Herb tea

INDEX

ABOUT THE AUTHORS

Author of Fodor's *Provence and the Côte d'Azur*, **Nancy Coons** has become adept at describing the golden light of Arles from under the iron-gray clouds back home in Lorraine from her 300-year-old farmhouse.

Four years ago, Bordeaux updater **Thomas Cussans** finally found a way to escape the drudgery of desk-bound life in London for the bucolic idyll of the Charente-Maritime. He writes regularly for the London *Times*.

Paris shopping updater **Jennifer Ditsler-Ladonne** decamped her longtime home of Manhattan for Paris and its fabulous boutiques. If you're looking to find either rare medieval arcana or Paris's wild edible mushrooms, she's the person to call.

With an avid interest in French history and the cold of her native Canada promting frequent escapes to anywhere hot, Provence and Cote d'Azur updater **Sarah Fraser** went in search of the perfect tapendade in the South of France. An area resident, she also contributes to *Fodor's Provence and the Cote d'Azur.*

Heather Stimmler-Hall came to Paris as a university student in 1995 and has since made a career out of reading between the lines of glossy hotel brochures. She writes for the London *Times*, *ELLE*, and her own monthly e-newsletter, www.secretsofparis.com., and has updated our Smart Travel Tips chapter and Paris lodging and nightlife sections.

Simon Hewitt headed to Paris straight from studying French and art history at Oxford. It was a return to base; his grandmother was French, as is his daughter Anaïs. He is a Paris correspondent for *Art & Auction*. His main hobby is cricket and he is now national coach. He has updated our Ile de France, Loire Valley, North, Brittany, Burgundy, and Massif Central chapters.

Paris food critic **Rosa Jackson**'s love affair with French pastries began at age four, when she spent her first year in Paris before returning to the Canadian north. Early experiments with éclairs and croissants led her to enroll in the Paris Cordon Bleu, where she learned that even great chefs make mistakes. A Parisian since 1995, Rosa has eaten in hundreds of Paris restaurants—and always has room for dessert.

Brittany and Alsace-Lorraine updater, **Christopher Mooney** originally came to Paris to study French philosophy, smoke Gîtanes cigarettes, and hang out in cafés. Fourteen years later he's still there, now ensconced as coeditor of the *Paris Ritz Magazine* and the *Paris-Athéné Magazine*; his articles have appeared in *Elle* and *Condé Nast Traveler.*

As a travel writer, Paris Exploring updater **Lisa Pasold** has been thrown off a train in Belarus and has mushed huskies in the Yukon, but her favorite place to explore remains the fabulous tangle of streets around her Paris home. She writes for the *Chicago Tribune* and *The Globe and Mail.*

Paris Exploring updater **Mathew Schwartz** followed his wife to Paris, where he is a freelance freelance writer for such publications as the London *Times* and *Wired News.*

George Semler lives over the border in Spain, but he has skied, hiked, fly-fished, and explored every side of the Pyrénées. For this edition, he updated our chapters on Lyon and the Alps, Basque Country, the Midi-Pyrénées, and Corsica. He also writes for a variety of magazines, including *Saveur.*

Robert I. C. Fisher, editor of *Fodor's France 2006*, succeeded in getting one foot in the caviar when he was sent to Paris to write up the noted Ile St-Louis residence of Baron and Baroness Guy de Rothschild for *Town & Country*. Any last recommendations? "Don't forget to take a pre-dawn hike through the streets of Montmartre to the steps of Sacre-Coeur to watch the sun come up over Paris."